International Handbook of Violence Research

VOLUME 1

T0379362

International Handbook of Violence Research

Edited by

Wilhelm Heitmeyer

and

John Hagan

KLUWER ACADEMIC PUBLISHERS
DORDRECHT / BOSTON / LONDON

iv

A C.I.P. Catalogue record for this book is available from the Library of Congress.

ISBN 1-4020-3980-8

Published by Kluwer Academic Publishers,
P.O. Box 17, 3300 AA Dordrecht, The Netherlands.

Sold and distributed in North, Central and South America
by Kluwer Academic Publishers,
101 Philip Drive, Norwell, MA 02061, U.S.A.

In all other countries, sold and distributed
by Kluwer Academic Publishers,
P.O. Box 322, 3300 AH Dordrecht, The Netherlands.

Printed on acid-free paper

Preface

An international manual is like a world cruise: a once-in-a-lifetime experience.

All the more reason to consider carefully whether it is necessary. This can hardly be the case if previous research in the selected field has already been the subject of an earlier review—or even several competing surveys. On the other hand, more thorough study is necessary if the intensity and scope of research are increasing without comprehensive assessments. That was the situation in Western societies when work began on this project in the summer of 1998. It was then, too, that the challenges emerged: any manual, especially an international one, is a very special type of text, which is anything but routine. It calls for a special effort: the "state of the art" has to be documented for selected subject areas, and its presentation made as compelling as possible. The editors were delighted, therefore, by the cooperation and commitment shown by the eighty-one contributors from ten countries who were recruited to write on the sixty-two different topics, by the constructive way in which any requests for changes were dealt with, and by the patient response to our many queries.

This volume is the result of a long process. It began with the first drafts outlining the structure of the work, which were submitted to various distinguished colleagues. Friedhelm Neidhardt of Berlin, Gertrud Nunner-Winkler of Munich, and Roland Eckert of Trier, to name only a few, supplied valuable comments at this stage.

A working group set up by the Interdisciplinary Institute for Conflict and Violence Research developed the draft into a form that was discussed in the spring of 1999 by Wilhelm Heitmeyer and John Hagan (who was then still working in Toronto). Invitations to contributors were then sent out—successfully, as this compilation demonstrates.

The complexity of this project was further increased by the fact that we had planned from the outset to publish as nearly simultaneously as possible in German and in English. This meant that, even while the chapters were still being written and revised, they also had to be translated, into German or English as the case might be. We recruited Ina Goertz of Tradukas, Berlin, as our translation coordinator: she and her team including Adelheid Baker did excellent work, and our working relationship was an exceptionally friendly one. But for her, this manual could never have arrived at its present form.

We received equally fruitful assistance when we found ourselves working outside the boundaries of the skills available to the Institute's editorial team and urgently needed additional expertise. In this context, we must especially mention Harald A. Euler of Kassel University, who provided invaluable assistance on, for example, the texts and problems relating to the evolutionary psychology of violence.

Editors can never achieve much without the support of a highly committed, enthusiastic team, able to draw upon a wide range of very different skills—academic, editorial, linguistic, organizational, communicative, and technical. That applies to the core editorial team: Heiner Bielefeldt and Johannes Vossen, in particular, were invaluable, and they were well supported at different times by other members of the Institute's staff, including some of the contributors to this manual.

For a long period, until she left the team to work in a different project, Julia Tölke was an outstanding coordinator, taking charge of communication with contributors and the technical revision of the text. She was replaced by Peter Sitzer, who worked closely with Stefanie Müller to maintain the same standards in this important task. Our secretaries, Mrs. Ward and Mrs. Passon, were persistent and efficient in dealing with our numerous and sometimes hectic communications needs and the collating of the translations. Finally— as was only to be expected—Monika Näther brought a perfectionist's dedication to the complex technical preparation of the print copy for the German version.

Last but not least, without financial support such project can not be brought to fruition—especially if it is to be published in two languages, with all the time and cost-intensive translation work involved. We are therefore deeply grateful to Dr. Wolf Jenkner of the Ministry of Science of the Land of North Rhine-Westphalia, without whose backing this project would never have been launched.

WILHELM HEITMEYER AND JOHN HAGAN
BIELEFELD AND CHICAGO

Contents

2.   Groups and Collectivities: Political and Ideological Violence

3.   Violent Individuals: Perpetrators and Motives

4.   Victims of Violence: Individuals and Groups

5. Social Opportunity Structures: Institutions and Social Spaces

6. Violence Discourses: Ideologies and Justifications

7.   Processes and Dynamics: Escalation and De-Escalation

III.   THEORETICAL AND METHODOLOGICAL ISSUES IN RESEARCH ON VIOLENCE

PART I

THE FRAMEWORK OF THE HANDBOOK

Violence: The Difficulties of a Systematic International Review

WILHELM HEITMEYER AND JOHN HAGAN

I. THE OBJECTIVES OF VIOLENCE RESEARCH

Ambitious academic studies generally serve their purpose when they provide accurate definitions of problems, clear descriptions, considered explanations, as well as convincing assessments, and encourage long-term work in the field. The whole process must be a reflexive one, allowing room for expressions of doubt and maintaining a critical detachment from the subject. This means that an international manual of violence research has to meet certain standards and fulfill certain expectations. The first question to be answered by a manual of this kind, dealing with one of the most enigmatic and, at the same time, most serious social phenomena, concerns the possible forms, types, and characteristics of violence. In answering that question, the manual must carefully distinguish between the many different phenomena, ranging from the individual act to the organized actions of groups or states. Explanations of violence are to be found in quite different academic disciplines and therefore have to be considered across the spectrum from psychological to sociostructural approaches. The standards applied and the normative foundations of assessments need to be clearly stated in each case. Finally, the study must highlight differentiated ways of dealing with violence, from individual therapy to changes in the structure of society. Even taken alone, these reasons are enough to make publishing a manual of violence research a rather audacious venture.

Almost all relatively detailed studies make it clear that violence takes extremely varied forms and may possess many different qualities; not only is there a very substantial range of (current) definitions, but there are also many disagreements about the authority of definitions of what violence is, or is said to be. Consequently, theories of violence not only vary in their validity and significance but also address different subjects and involve con-

W. Heitmeyer and J. Hagan (eds.), *International Handbook of Violence Research*, 3–11.
© 2003 Kluwer Academic Publishers. Printed in the Netherlands.

troversial assessments of the efficacy of possible strategies for addressing the problem. Moreover, what seems the clear condemnation of violence is significantly challenged in many social and political situations, so that it is highly advisable to approach violence, and its different areas and contexts, on a basis of clear distinctions.

II.   THE AMBIGUOUS CONTENT OF VIOLENCE

One of the central problems confronting a manual on violence is the *ambiguity* of violence itself, which is apparent in the characterization and framing of its phenomena, the logic of its occurrence and possible escalation, supposed causal explanations, and its evaluation. As a result, it frequently happens that clear divisions between levels of analysis and escalation dynamics become blurred, with the result that analyses cease to do justice to the complexity of violence.

The problems of violence research begin at the outset, with the attempt to determine exactly what should be classified as violence. There is, admittedly, a broad consensus that violence causes injury and sometimes death and results in many different forms of destruction, so that there are always victims. But at that point, if not before, the consensus certainly ends. It is not even clear precisely who or what has been injured, or how serious that injury is. Can cases of mental devastation be classified as violence, or—because they cannot be objectively recorded—are they merely subjectively nuanced injuries, where the victims themselves may even come under suspicion? Should the definition of violence include structural forms, which need no direct perpetrators but undeniably produce their victims, or is the use of the label "structural violence" merely denunciatory? This manual offers no solutions to these hitherto unresolved problems, which easily give rise to disputes over definitions and boundaries.

Any attempt to determine definitively what constitutes violence is a high-risk undertaking in various ways. The basic principle that constantly becomes apparent is the *overstepping of boundaries*, which—in an age when moral, sexual, educational, and legal standards and values are being abandoned, or at least widely relaxed—almost defies the drawing of clear, traditional dividing lines. Lawyers, for example, may arrive at narrow definitions in order to identify situations within the reach of the criminal law, but in a context of social reality the phenomenon of violence is always more multifaceted. New boundaries are being drawn around acts of violence, for example, because of increased sensitivity (marital rape) or changed models of perception (the sit-in as violence). It is precisely because the problematic of violence is a particularly unclear one that it needs to be addressed with greater sensitivity and reflexivity.

Another of these gray areas is that we have little soundly based or prognostic knowledge of the *logic governing outbreaks* of violence, and do not know whether violence will develop *regularly* or *irregularly*. Sequences of violent events are dependent on numerous alternative options for action, because violence represents a resource that is available for use by anyone at any time. If, for example, expressive forms of violence arise, where the act of violence itself or the intoxication of violent action is all that matters, the victims are random and are afforded little protection by "early warning systems." If the violence is more instrumental in nature, it often seems predictable or calculable. Ultimately, violence can be perpetuated, reinforced, or prevented not only by action but also by inaction. Thus our attention is directed to motives, but also, at the same time, to unmotivated acts. Violence, then, either has rationally comprehensible causes or is shifted into the context of the inexplicable.

Violence also involves quite different types of victim. It matters little who is responsible for the violence—the police, as the executive arm of the state monopoly on violence, or the individual youthful perpetrator, or the plundering, pillaging, murderous mob: for those against whom violence is directed, violence is always violence. Here again, however, the degree and severity of injury suffered, the nature and type of the violence, and its extent and duration determine the physical aftereffects, the mental stresses, and the apparent or concealed traumas that the victims have to endure. The particular historical, contemporary, political, and cultural interpretations of perpetrators, victims, and bystanders appear to be central in the process of coping with experienced violence.

The diversity of social situations and political conflicts that are classified as violence thus makes it impossible even to begin to describe all its variations, especially as there seem to be no limits to the brutal ingenuity of individuals, groups, and government agencies when it comes to harming other human beings, individually or collectively. The events of September 11, 2001, provided particularly tragic confirmation of this, and those acts of violence against cultural symbols of the world of Western capitalism have opened up new dimensions of fear. But the consensus that that terrible day can clearly be classified as an instance of violence does not mean that its assessment is equally unambiguous: some see it as a barbarous violent assault, others as a reaction to the United States' own policy of violence. This again suggests that the prospects of certainty—as a solid moral base when academic and political approaches to violence have so few points in common—are slight. For that reason, a manual such as this is well advised to concentrate its analyses on Western industrial societies and to justify its selection of contributions.

III. THE FIELD OF STUDY: VIOLENCE IN MODERN WESTERN INDUSTRIALIZED SOCIETIES

The twentieth century witnessed a devastating level of violence by individuals, groups, and states. This applies both in comparison to earlier periods, and in contrast with the desire of the individual to preserve his or her integrity, the social and political utopian dreams of a world at peace, and the duty of states to protect human life and preserve social order.

In Western societies, the dream of a nonviolent modern age clashes with a reality that is massively overshadowed, if not totally plunged into darkness, by overt acts of violence and the potential for destruction. The founding fathers of sociological analysis of contemporary history and society—Karl Marx, Max Weber, and Emile Durkheim—predicted the price that modern society would have to pay for its processes of modernization in terms of inhumanity and destruction. Defying all the optimistic hopes of progress, the modern age is specifically not an age of nonviolence, even if the state monopoly on violence provides a mechanism for dealing with inherently violent tensions. Even a modern state can act barbarically. But different societies deal with the potentiality for violence in quite different ways, for example, by striking a balance between traditional and modern universalistic group identities, in order, for example, to prevent the disintegration of whole sectors of the population and so also defuse the ethnicized potential for violence. In other cases there may be a binding canon of values providing for a graduated scale of punishments for violations. Often, however, violence is also seen as a phenomenon that decreases over the course of modern development, and as one that is securely encapsulated by the state monopoly on violence; in other words, as a phenomenon that is no longer a significant component of modern societies. Nevertheless, the basic question—the paradox, as it were—of the modern age remains: whether it repeatedly devours its own postulates of reason and cultural achievements (in the form of processes of recognition, for example), and so constantly releases further violence that manifests itself in many different individual, collective, and state variants.

This reflects a basic pattern of Western industrialized societies, which can be described as *self-deception that circumvents enlightenment* and in which insufficient account is taken of the ambivalence of the modern age. Among the regions of the world and their cultural and sociopolitical systems there are hardly any substantive differences in the modes of violence, although differences do exist in the ways in which violence is handled or dealt with. For example, in the former communist world there was a *taboo on enlightenment* that *suppressed* consideration of violence within society and between states, and similar problems are caused by the still apparently *enlightenment-resistant self-evident truths* such as are manifest in forms of violence in the "Third World," some of which are cast in the form of traditions and preserved by solid constellations of power.

At the same time, an air of civilized superiority is unjustified in view of the discrepancy between self-image and reality in Western industrialized societies. It is appropriate, therefore, to direct the focus of this manual primarily—self-reflexively, so to speak—toward this type of society, as a way of making a differentiated contribution to self-enlightenment. No violence comes without a price to be paid—not even in societies that perceive themselves as democratic republics with liberal constitutions.

IV. THE PROBLEM OF AMBIVALENT CONSEQUENCES

The ambivalence of the modern age is reflected in the ambivalence of violence. This is true even if the prevalent opinion is that violence is *always* destructive and is based on the *devaluation of life* and the *exaltation of power*.

Violence is an ambivalent phenomenon, because the same acts can have different consequences in different social contexts and political systems. Under totalitarian political systems or demeaning private conditions of power, violence may open the way to restructuring or to less violent power relationships. In libertarian and democratic systems, violence is generally associated with restrictions on spaces or life that are free from fear. Violence is negative where it involves the destruction of human beings and humanity; it may be positive where the focus is on the preservation or restoration of humanity. Both the destruction of order and the creation of order can involve violence.

The central precondition in both cases is the opportunity to wield power. This may be either an end in itself—offering the oppressed or disadvantaged the opportunity to use violence to obtain their "fair" share of the benefits offered by society—or violence may serve as a means to destroy the power of a dictator. Whichever perspective is adopted, the ambivalence remains, constantly raising the question of how to distinguish between the legitimate and the illegitimate, the lawful and the unlawful. This leads us into the area of transition between academic analysis and social and political commitment, i.e., the need to evaluate violence or to set up a counter-definition. One way of doing this is by demanding integrity, freedom from harm, because it is not for nothing that the modern history of human rights is considered to begin with the Habeas Corpus Act (1679), which set out to safeguard that right to human integrity.

V. CONTENTIOUS INTERPRETATIONS OF EMPIRICAL LINES OF DEVELOPMENT

Both the ambivalence of the modern age and the ambivalence of violence cause consider-able problems with interpreting the lines along which violence develops. This becomes apparent in many cases of long-term studies of violence, although there have been consid-erable advances in the availability of empirical data on various forms of violence. The fundamental problems with the appraisal of violence are also contained in the assessment of lines of development, and are reflected by academic and political disputes over inter-pretation, which also overlie intensive research into long-term causative complexes, inter-vening factors, and evident consequences. Thus, in cases of individual violence, it still remains to be seen whether the number recorded, which fell in Western democracies for many years before rising again from the late 1960s, represents a reversal of the trend or is no more than a temporary development. As far as collective violence is concerned, there is no clearly apparent downward trend, while cases of state violence are even on the in-crease.

For the time being, various interpretations of the increase or decrease of violence are almost impossible to verify. Thus, conjectures to the effect that violence is inevitable in the biological sense are as nonsensical as the expectation of a nonviolent society is uto-pian. All that ever seems to happen in the sphere of human coexistence is that levels of violence rise or fall.

The hope of so many theoreticians of culture and civilization that the human race is involved in a permanent civilizing process, the provisional end result of which will be a nonviolent modern age, has proven an illusion. The notion that violence was more wide-spread in premodern societies, is encountered much more frequently in foreign societies, and is only an exceptional phenomenon in modern societies seems to be a myth involving significant misconceptions.

However, the alternative reading of history as a disaster, which sees the civilizing modern age as fundamentally barbaric, is highly one-sided, despite the apocalyptic erup-tions of violence and extraordinary destructiveness of the twentieth century. It is one-sided because it takes the excessively linear view of ascribing to modern civilization a rationality that is exclusively instrumental, and a power to determine the course of history, without at the same time taking sufficient account of appropriate conditions for the un-leashing of violence.

Authors who adopt a more anthropological line of argument have drawn the conclu-sion from these irreconcilable positions that there are no links at all between modern civi-lization and violence: First, because there has been no civilizing process at all, in the sense of a development of human standards of conduct and emotional and motivational struc-tures toward a reduced propensity to violence. And secondly because earlier societies had already found ways and means of containing violence, so that there can be no question at all of the human species in the modern age having a better, let alone superior, moral equip-ment. This view assumes that the exercise of violence has always been contingent and historically variable and must to a certain degree be accepted as a specific form of human inventiveness.

A worrying pattern clearly emerges, however. The evolution of democratic institu-tions for the processing of conflicts, thus improving the prospects of avoiding or effec-tively containing open violence, individual or collective, has gone hand in hand with the perfecting of the technology for the exercising of violence. This is happening against a background of developments in which the integration mechanisms and qualities of modern societies, in the form of means of access and recognition for many members and groups, are also proving precarious, meaning that the risk of their disintegration is increasing, so that violence, too, can become more significant as an effective resource, available at any time, for defense against individual and group-focused disdain.

VI. THE APPROACH TO VIOLENCE: THEMATIZATION TRAPS

Both the ambivalent meaning of violence and the lack of clarity regarding lines of development call for a cautious approach to the phenomenon under discussion here. This is particularly true because violence emotionalizes, creates fear, and can be politically exploited.

Risky approaches to violence become apparent when the attitude adopted to one's own or others' points of view and spoken or unspoken assumptions is not sufficiently self-reflexive. There is the danger of falling into the "thematization traps" of the violence discussion, to six of which particular attention must be drawn.

The *"re-interpretation trap"* arises when violence is exclusively personalized, generally pathologized, or even biologized, because in such cases all socially causative relationships are disregarded. As a result, those in power might take this as a pretext for moral self-exculpation, on the one hand, and repressive administrative measures, on the other. The *"scandalization trap"* takes effect when a dramatic vocabulary of violence is employed, in a climate dominated by the mass media, as a more effective or quicker way of obtaining a hearing. The *"inflation trap"* comprises expanding the discourse of violence in everyday affairs, creating the impression that there are virtually no remaining areas where violence is insignificant or absent, since it is lurking everywhere. The *"moralization trap"* arises on the basis of discourses of concern, with their simplistic perpetrator/victim structure and a morality that clearly identifies good and evil. The *"normality trap"* perceives and interprets the violence of particular groups as a "normal" transient stage of development, or even as "natural," thus involving the danger of trivializing violence. The *"reduction trap"* involves a withdrawal from the great complexity of the phenomenon of violence into simple explanatory analyses or the attribution of violence to the personal characteristics of individuals.

The multidimensional conception of this international manual is intended to help ensure that the academic, general, media, and political approaches to violence do not lead to the "thematization traps" that do nothing to further the aims of reducing violence.

VII. THE CONCEPTION OF THE MANUAL

The intensity of violence research in modern Western societies has increased in recent years. Possible reasons for this include new sensitivities and, in some cases, partial or intermittent increases in certain variants of violence, but also the resurgence of older forms of violence in different areas of society.

As a consequence, the concern felt by society and politicians has resulted in the publication of major surveys, such as the German federal government's 1990 report on violence, or regular reports, such as those that appear in the United States. Even so, it is noteworthy that there is no international manual of violence research in either German or English. The only works of this kind to have appeared previously are manuals dealing with specific aspects of the problem, such as domestic violence, or encyclopedic approaches that pursue other aims.

The *development* of violence and the absence of a broad *overview of research* on the theme of violence justify the concept behind this manual of violence research, of bringing together the international experts as authors. The fact that violence is a complex phenomenon makes it logical to involve numerous different disciplines. However, the very idea of a manual means that certain decisions have to be made. In this manual, the central focus is on sociology, because it offers a wide range of empirical studies from which *phenomena* and *concepts* have been formulated, and whose *theoretical approaches* form the framework of reference. That framework encompasses contributions from eight other disciplines—philosophy, cultural studies, law, criminology, political science, psychology, history, and sociobiology—to broaden the perspectives.

Any presentation of the current state of research that does justice to the problem must adopt a suitable logic for grouping the relevant elements (cf. Fig. I-1.1).

The starting point is the assumption that violence is the *result of social processes* and not a mere means to an end. This not only leads to consideration of a logic of interaction, but also to investigation of *social structures and institutions*, the *social conditions* to be found there, and the *state actors* (see section II.1). The focus then moves on to *collectives and groups*, to examine the *politically and ideologically motivated violence* of these actors (see section II.2). The ways in which *individual violence* is learned and the social and evolutionary conditions under which individuals become *perpetrators of violence* form the subject of the chapters in section II.3.

Within this design, the frequently neglected *victims of violence* are given due consideration as both *individuals* and *groups* (see section II.4). This is necessary, because

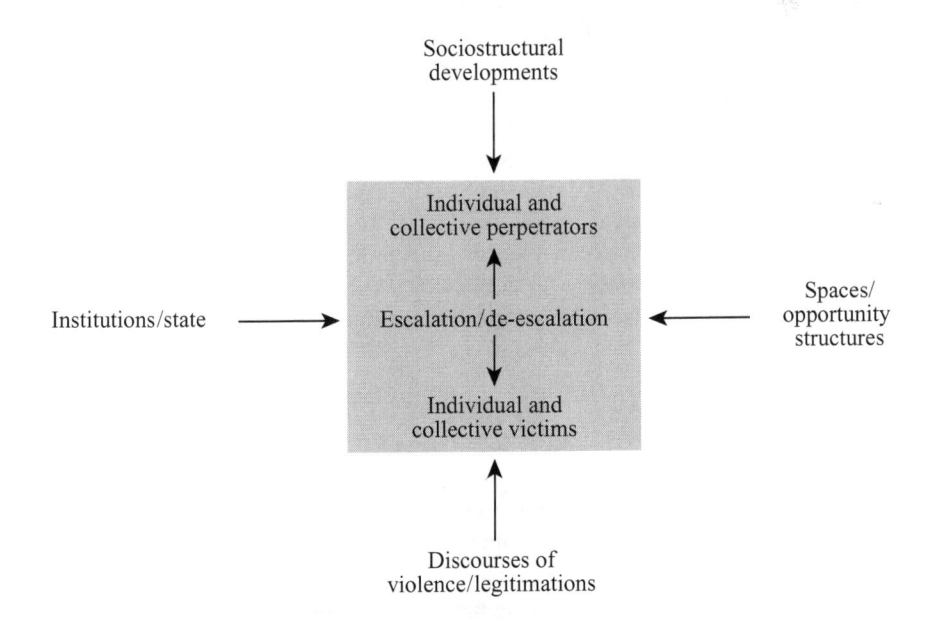

FIGURE I-1.1. Central structural categories of the handbook.

they are generally not given adequate attention either in violence research or in society in general, not to mention the lack of sensitive long-term social and psychological care for traumatized victims. Adequate consideration of both perpetrators and victims not only calls for an analysis of those actors who practice violence in the name of the state, but also requires that attention be directed to *social opportunity structures* with their *institutions* and public and private *spaces* (see section II.5).

If violence is considered as a *destructive form of conduct*, generally arising in *conflicts* caused by a configuration of individual and collective *actors, institutional conditions*, public or private *opportunity structures* in association with *structures of meaning* (including political philosophies), as well as special *group affiliations*, then an appropriate analysis must also address the processes of interaction and *discourses of violence* (see section II.6), which generate specific *political cultures, ideologies and justifications*, partly in order to lower the thresholds of violence. These discourses are important elements of the *processes and dynamics of violence* (see section II.7) which make it possible to understand and explain *escalation* or *de-escalation of violence*.

If this kind of *"interaction model"* is taken as the underlying logic for grouping the chapters, this not only makes due allowance for the multilayered nature of the phenomenon of violence, but also avoids an inappropriate concentration on any one "explanatory model." This is particularly important in the case of a manual that is not designed to favor one explanatory approach but aims to present the widest possible spectrum of existing knowledge, taking into account contradictory findings and gaps in research.

Of course, a manual also involves its own specific limitations, and cannot cover everything. Certain important areas, although they have not been forgotten, are *not* explicitly treated here because of the conceptual concentration on phenomena of violence within Western societies. These omissions include examples of genocide outside Europe. Similarly, *war*, as violence between states, is not a central subject here. Another equally tragic perspective, *violence in the "Third World,"* could not be adequately covered here. In particular, only certain specific aspects of tribal violence, in Africa for example, are considered in this manual—those where ethnicity plays a central role. Forms of endemic violence, such as *clan warfare* and *political guerrilla activities* in South America are absent, as are typical variants of violence in South Asia which, in extreme cases, take the form of the killing of female children at birth. Another important aspect not covered here is *state violence* in the former communist sphere, with its countless victims and diverse forms of repression: an adequate treatment of its extent, and the specific features of the system of dominance and apparatus of power, would require more space than was available here.

This brief list is in itself sufficient to show that this manual does not adopt an encyclopedic approach, but rather follows a deliberately limited design which nevertheless emphasizes the international nature of perspective on violence.

VIII. THE FUTURE OF VIOLENCE AND VIOLENCE RESEARCH

The question is whether the field of violence research is adequately prepared for the study of violence in the twenty-first century. Some forms and variations are likely to remain constant, while others are likely to change in their quality and quantitative dimensions. If violence is conceived as a social phenomenon, in the sense that it generally takes place in an interactive field, in which the actors and victims learn and suffer over and over again, it is also logical to expect qualitative changes, which are normally not analyzed by academic research until the violence has taken place. Nevertheless, it is the task of researchers to move closer to the events and not to allow themselves to be misled by incorrect or hasty generalizations or seduced by "political correctness," which is attractive because of its low conflict potential. When we look to the future, violence appears particularly threatening in connection with the following constellations:

There is the return of violence to Europe in the form of ethnic violence. Phenomena such as civil wars in the Balkans, riots in British cities, and massive xenophobic violence in Germany were no longer anticipated in the social scientists' theories on the development of modern societies, with their assumptions of differentiation and civilization.

Secondly, 'September 11' seems to have brought about new qualities and quantities of violence. Was this terrorist attack the bursting of a dam, which will lead to new analyses and views of international, religiously motivated terrorism, which in turn may assist the development of new political strategies to counter the "next generation" of terrorism—or should we already be adjusting to completely new scenarios of violence, following an increasingly apparent logic of escalation?

Thirdly, we still have to look ahead to the time when conflicts over scarce ecological resources, especially water, will flare and become endemic. This violence will presumably not become virulent within modern Western societies, but it may return in the form of terrorism and the long-range effects in these societies may further undermine the already precarious peaceful treatment of minorities.

Fourthly, we have to consider the changing nature of war. The conventional idea of conflict between states is becoming overshadowed by civil wars and so-called low intensity wars within societies, where forms of violence with high death tolls become long-term phenomena.

Fifthly, greater sensitivity will also be required in the future in order to enable us appropriately to identify forms of violence that may only now be germinating and to analyze their severity and consequences. A particular danger could be cyberviolence, which can be seen as representing "mediated violence" in electronic space, the originators of which may in future become impossible to track down, and whose destructive consequences are unforeseeable.

If, in the light of the above, we consider the controversies highlighted in the chapters of this manual and the empirical and theoretical desiderata, the state of social sciences violence *research* must also come under scrutiny. Although there is now a broad differentiation in various disciplines and methods, and although an international body of knowledge in violence research can be documented, there is as yet no such thing as *international violence research*. Too much research still takes place in *national* contexts. The academic *areas of discourse* are in some cases partitioned by language barriers and mired down in national traditions of research. Reciprocal theoretical *adoptions of perspectives* play little part in the current repertoire, and it is still unusual to permit disruption of *established patterns of interpretation*.

This situation poses the question of whether it might not be reasonable to set up an *"international agency for violence research,"* which would help to process the desiderata that have only briefly been indicated here, and to present new initiatives. In pursuing those activities, it would be possible to draw upon the body of knowledge documented in this international manual of violence research.

The Concept of Violence

PETER IMBUSCH

I. INTRODUCTION

Violence is one of the most elusive and most difficult concepts in the social sciences. Since the late 1960s there has been a considerable increase in violence in Western industrialized countries, counter to the long-term trend, and consequently the issue of violence has become the subject of much consideration, reflected in countless articles, essays and books. Yet the controversial questions remain unresolved, concerning an appropriate definition, substantive differentiation, sociopolitical assessment, and moral evaluation of violence. Even popular encyclopedias present a multitude of controversial interpretations of the phenomenon, and divergent meanings of the concept, and not least present the concept of violence in a range of collocations and compounds (Gewaltverhältnisse—relations of violence; Gewaltordnung—system based on violence; Gewaltmonopol—monopoly of violence; Gewaltenteilung—separation of powers, etc.). Violence is clearly an extremely complex phenomenon involving major ambiguity between the destruction and the creation of order. The hope that violence might prove a more precise concept at least in everyday language, because everyone knows essentially what it means, and that its analytical useful contours were only lost through its use in the social sciences, has been in vain. Public opinion polls reveal that the concept of violence is extremely diffuse (Kaase & Neidhardt, 1990), extending from physical and psychological injury, particular forms of crime and uncouth behavior on the roads and in sports, to sociopolitical discrimination. We are thus left with a notion which is at best purely phenomenological, is highly selective due to the omission of significant aspects of violence, and is strongly molded by the processes of media interest.

Not only has the question what is violence remained the subject of constant debate, but also the issue of the origins of violence. There are two diametrically opposed views here, as violence is both ascribed to human nature, which is considered immutable, and also to social conditions. There is also continuous debate on appropriate strategies for

W. Heitmeyer and J. Hagan (eds.), *International Handbook of Violence Research*, 13–39.
© 2003 Kluwer Academic Publishers. Printed in the Netherlands.

dealing with violence, where the spectrum of possible answers ranges from simple repression and the threat of more severe punishment to various forms of upbringing and education. John Lawrence thus wrote: "Violence ... evolves diverse questions and conflicting answers. Is violence an outrage or a necessity? An enemy of freedom and social order or their indispensable foundation? A rational means or a self-frustrating instrument? Is it the outcome of perverted learning or a normal, instinctual need? Is violence a pathological form of behavior or a voluntary one for which agents bear full responsibility? Can societies prevent its occurrence or must they resign themselves to an order including it? The need for philosophical clarity is evident not only in the controversial answers to these typical questions, but also in the manner in which the very questions are stated" (Lawrence, 1970:31). It is the "protean richness of form" and "chameleon-like colorations" (Narr, 1978:158) of the social phenomenon of violence that produce the diversity of competing attempts to explanation, with their totally different range and often inconclusive evidence, thus impeding agreement and revealing the differences between the many concepts of violence.

Finally, precise use of the concept of violence is hampered by connotations that partially overlap with semantically-related concepts (force, aggression, conflict, power, etc.) that are however not identical with violence. A precise terminology is also confounded by substantialist applications of the concept or precipitate reifications (violence as war, as murder, etc.). The latter may still be indispensable for substantiating justiciable elements of a violence criminal offense—police criminal statistics concentrate on murder, manslaughter, mercy killing, infanticide, rape and sexual coercion, robbery, bodily harm that may or may not result in death, extortionary kidnapping, hostage-taking, acts of violence against air traffic, and damage to property—but otherwise it narrows the field of vision more than aiding the necessary differentiation (Albrecht, Backes, & Kühnel 2001).

These are the difficulties faced by research into violence in the social sciences (see Imbusch 2000b). Violence itself is omnipresent, a largely contingent phenomenon, and its ubiquity is independent of the particular cultural area (Rauchfleisch, 1992; Brednich & Hartinger, 1994). We encounter violence everywhere, in matters large and small, at national and international level. It occurs as apolitical violence in immediate social environments (e.g., in the family, at school, in streets and public spaces, against children and women), as violent crime (with all its different facets, from murder and manslaughter to organized crime), and extends as far as politically motivated violence (terrorism and assassinations, persecution and torture). Acts of brutality and sadism are always being committed somewhere in the world, there are expulsions and persecution, open violence and wars. No society, no region of the world, no culture is free of violence: the peaceful savage of earlier civilizations turned out to be a myth just like the expectations of a violence-free modern age (Keeley, 1996; Joas, 1994). Although no peoples are known that ever fully relinquished violence, there are considerable differences from case to case in the forms of violence and their degrees of intensity (with corresponding gradation). The twentieth century with its world wars, dictatorships and revolutions may have seen far more than its share of violence (Imbusch 2000a), but there was a considerable degree of violence in all previous centuries too. "Violence is intriguing. It is universally condemned yet to be found everywhere. Most of us are both fascinated and horrified by it. It is a fundamental ingredient of how we entertain ourselves (children's stories, world literature, the movie industry) and an essential feature of many of our social institutions. In most parts of the world it is notoriously common in family life, religious affairs, and political history" (Litke, 1992:173).

Since the word violence is used for phenomena of very different kind and quality, can be used in a purely descriptive way, or more analytically, or polemically, and can also be used for very different purposes and fulfill various functions, this chapter will first discuss the etymological origins and changes in the meaning of the concept of violence (section II), before typologically dissecting the word violence itself (section III). After the necessary differentiation of individual, collective, and state violence (section IV), attention is given to the various manifestations of violence (section V), and different applications of the concept of violence are presented (section VI), before a brief summary is given in conclusion (section VII).

II.   ETYMOLOGY AND DELINEATION:
THE ORIGINS OF THE CONCEPT OF VIOLENCE
AND CHANGES IN ITS MEANING

Friedhelm Neidhardt (1986: 114) pointed out that the complications of the concept of violence in German begin with its polysemy—it is used with distinctly divergent meanings in different contexts. One meaning is purely descriptive and value-free and is used to designate a social relationship; another is loaded with judgments and indicates an assessment of a matter. Moreover, the semantics of the concept of violence have changed over time and the concept overlaps to a lesser or greater extent with a whole range of similar or related concepts. The ambiguity of violence and its use as a "competence concept" and "action concept" can be derived from the etymology of the word "violence" and the incongruity of Germanic and Roman legal systems with their different conceptual and terminological traditions. Historically the concept of violence has been used to refer to a wide range of political and social affairs for which there were always various parallel Latin terms. Inversely, the Latin concepts were often expressed by several German terms (Grimmsches Wörterbuch, 1911).

Verifying the basic etymological meaning of the word "violence" is also of significance, however, because the German word *Gewalt*, in contrast to Anglo-Saxon, francophone or Ibero-American usage, is of limited linguistic precision, since it did not make the distinction between direct personal violence (violentia) and legitimate institutional violence (potestas), which otherwise gained general acceptance through the centuries. Only in the German-speaking countries does the word *Gewalt* stand both for physical assault and for the authority of the state and its institutions. This particular ambiguity is avoided in the other cases mentioned by recognizing *violence/violence/violencia* and *power/pouvoir/poder* as two distinct concepts and making the distinction crystal clear. Here we see clearly that the concept of *Gewalt* reflects the two Latin roots vis/violentia and potentia/potestas. Although there is a clear distinction between these concepts, their proximity explains the connection commonly made between power and violence.

1.   The Origins of the Word *Gewalt*

The origins of the word *Gewalt* in German go back even further and are derived from the Indo-European root "val" (Latin: "valere") that was originally a verb ("giwaltan," "waldan") meaning to possess the ability to dispose of something and to wield power. But it was also used in a broader sense meaning to have strength, to have power, to have something at one's disposal, to control something (Faber, Ilting, & Maier, 1982; Röttgers and Saner,

1978). In the Germanic sphere, however, *Gewalt* was not used to denote a legal term as it was in Roman usage, but rather an area of freedom not covered by the law. Gothic had two original concepts of *Gewalt*, "vulbus" (reputation, honor) and "valdufni" (synonymous with the Latin "potestas"). On the other hand *Macht* (power), from Old High German and Middle High German "maht," comes from the Germanic word "mahti" and is an abstraction from the Gothic "magan" (to be able or capable). Although it was conceptually related to *Gewalt* and partly even used as a synonym right from the beginning, it expresses more strongly a physical or psychological strength or corresponding ability (which "vis," "facultas," "potentia," or "virtus" stood for in Latin).

In the ancient world the clearest and most far-reaching distinctions were made by the Romans, who placed *Gewalt* in the same general semantic group as rule, government and power. This differentiation ran through the entire Middle Ages and up into modern times in the Romance-speaking world and later also in the Anglo-Saxon areas: At an early stage *Gewalt* came into use here as "violentia" (violence, impetuosity), a noun which was used in compound expressions parallel to concepts in Latin, the language of state. Among these were "potestas" (primarily power of disposal, authority), "potentia" (power in the general sense of the word—ability, strength, also excessive power and instruments of power), "auctoritas" (weight and significance of the opinion of an individual or body, translated into influence), "imperium," "dominatus," and "maiestas" (territorial sovereignty, power over a territory), "vis" (strength, power, but also force and violence) and "facultas" (legitimate possibility of exercising power). Here there are obvious similarities and semantic links to power, strength, power of attorney, and not least injustice. Later there are some uses of *Gewalt* to mean reputation, splendor and magnificence ("dignitas"—prestige and reputation that one gains by virtue of rank and position) and various objectifications and personifications of the concept. "Potestas" (meaning authority and rule) and "potentia" (power) denoted states of affairs or conditions and were used to describe the supposed personal attributes of leading political or institutional figures.

Seen against this background, German usage is a special case. Significant differentiation in the understanding of violence did not arise here until toward the late Middle Ages and in the transitional period to the modern age, so that finally four variants of the concept can be distinguished: Firstly, *Gewalt* was used to denote the power of public institutions connected to a legal system; secondly, *Gewalt* gave a value-free description of the territorial authorities, the authority of the state, or their concrete representatives; thirdly, *Gewalt* expressed relations of disposal or actual ownership; fourthly and finally, the noun *Gewalt* and the adjective *gewaltig* served to characterize the use of physical violence and compulsion in the political realm but also to describe individual violent actions in the sense of "vis" and "violentia" (Faber et al., 1982:866ff.). Although *Macht* and *Gewalt* long remained interchangeable concepts in German, *Macht* ultimately came to denote the potential or real physical and psychological powers of a person or thing, whereas *Gewalt* was aimed at overcoming resistance and thus developed into compulsion. Violence in the sense of "violentia" was first codified in the late sixteenth century in Austrian municipal law ("Allgemeines Österreichisches Landrecht") where it was defined as existing in every legally unjustified violation of another person's body and possessions (see Faber et al., 1982:842). From then on corresponding additions had to be used for characterizing state authorities (such as *höchste Gewalt*—supreme authority; *Civil-Gewalt*—civil state; *weltliche Gewalt*—secular power; or Staatsgewalt—state authority) in order to make them contrast with "common violence," a term which denoted that such violence was illegal or illegitimate.

It was not until the rise of the absolute state that violence in the sense of physical compulsion was successively concentrated, monopolized and exploited in the hands of persons and institutions specifically intended for this purpose, and the use of violence outside this framework was punished. This allowed a parallel development, a progressive bridling of impulsiveness (Elias, 1976), and in people's everyday consciousness the concept of violence gradually lost its former meaning of "potestas" and shifted completely to that of "violentia." The state as a "coercive institution" was still based on violence, but in view of its regulatory function it was now only perceived as a threat in exceptional situations. Max Weber was later to see the essence of the modern state in the concentration and monopolization of the means of physical coercion through a political institution specially legitimized for the purpose, whose violent origins have fallen into oblivion (Breuer, 1998).

The bridling of violence by means of establishing a civilized state was preceded by prolonged struggles of elimination, revolutions, and civil wars, as expressed in the political upheavals and accelerated social change since the French Revolution. Power thus became a laden word in the philosophy of history and also an ideologically exploitable keyword, increasingly developing from an ability linked to persons or institutions to a basic condition of human existence. Thus it not only finds its legitimization in itself, but also develops ever stronger links to particular rational purposes. In addition to becoming brute force—massive coercion—violence now also becomes a resource able to be legitimized "from below," a force able to be actively applied and capable of determining the course of history. It is well known that Robespierre coined the concept of "progressive violence" in the French Revolution explicitly toward the achievement of particular political goals (Papcke, 1973; Claussen, 1982).

Finally, in the twentieth century, power and violence as scientific expressions and instrumental terms in politics have come to cover a wide semantic spectrum which partly overlaps with other concepts. A typological analysis of its fundamental meanings is provided in the following section. Thus the history of the concept of violence in the German-speaking countries has developed from a relatively restricted, concrete term for authorities, whose legitimacy is unquestioned, to a broad and relatively indistinct meaning of the term exhibiting considerable variance and also conveying various different normative and descriptive components.

2. Proximity and Distance to Related Concepts

The existence of numerous related concepts has repeatedly necessitated definitional demarcation and internal differentiation of the concept of violence in order to sharpen its contours, on the one hand, and on the other hand to avoid its unconsidered equation with related concepts. A brief sketch of related concepts—power, which has already been treated, and also conflict, aggression, war, and compulsion—would therefore seem meaningful and necessary, since the lack of clarity surrounding the concept of violence results to a considerable extent from precipitate objectifications or reifications. If one first regards violence restrictively and essentially as physical violence and takes it to mean physical injury or use of other force against people by various means, one can follow Heinrich Popitz's definition (1992:48) that violence is an act of power "leading to intentional physical injury of another, regardless of whether its purpose for the agent is actually in carrying it out (purely to demonstrate power) or whether the action is intended to be translated into threats and lead to lasting subjugation (as binding power)." So defined, violence could easily by distinguished from the other mentioned concepts.

As we have seen, it is the concept of power that overlaps to the greatest extent with the concept of violence, at least historically. If one regards power first in purely objective terms as a "possibility," as "skill and ability" and emphasizes its proximity to the concepts of "strength" and "energy," it can be defined as a sociologically amorphous concept. As Max Weber wrote: "Power means every chance of getting one's way within a social relationship, including against resistance, no matter what this chance is based upon." Weber did not neglect to add: "All a person's conceivable qualities and all conceivable combinations of factors can put someone in a position to get their own way in a given situation" (Weber, 1976: 28ff.). Violence is by no means the only way of getting one's will, but it is one way. Violence as calculated force is a way of exercising power, and it is a very effective instrument of power because it enforces obedience directly and overcomes resistance. Conversely, one will obviously have to concede that not all power is of violent character. However, one should not separate the two categories quite as neatly as did Hannah Arendt (1970), whose communicative concept of power led her to see power and violence as phenomena without any gradations. She saw sharp contrasts because for her power ended where violence began (see Arendt, 1970; Reemtsma, 2000; on further differentiation of the concept of power see also Imbusch, 2002).

On the other hand, the close connection postulated between conflict and violence is essentially due to misperceptions conveyed by the media, or to reduced perception, because the two concepts are not of the same order. If one defines conflicts as social facts which involve at least two parties and are based on differences in the social position and/ or interests of the parties involved (Bonacker & Imbusch, 1999:75), one avoids mixing up descriptive and normative elements and intentional ascriptions to the agents. In this way one also avoids taking recourse to causes, contexts, and methods of conflict resolution, which also do not belong to a general definition of conflict. Violence itself is not a conflict, but it can be the indication of one. In this sense violence can be either a characteristic of a conflict or a form of conflict resolution, though it should be noted that most conflicts by far are resolved without resorting to violence.

Moreover, everyday consciousness tends to see certain violent phenomena as the essence of violence. This can be the case with wars, murder, manslaughter, bodily harm, and other criminal offenses. This is problematic insofar as such association limits the concept of violence, reducing it to just one particular form. Such association basically reifies the concept, i.e., it considers one form of violence to constitute the entire phenomenon and is thus an inappropriate definitional objectification, describing one possible concrete form of the phenomenon violence but otherwise inappropriately restricting the concept (on war see Geyer, 1995; Matthies, 1994).

Social coercion, by comparison, is aimed at social control of people by people and is therefore identical with a form of exercising power, but not necessarily with violence. Coercion in the strict sense is understood to mean the threat of physical assault or a particular means of enforcing compliance, so this is more a preliminary stage of violence where perceived threat or pressure suffices to achieve particular behavior, and actual violence is not required. However, suppression and coercion in a broader sense also become forms of social compulsion, which Galtung and others have termed structural violence.

Aggression, on the other hand, is a concept originally derived from psychology which in the strict sense of aggressive behavior is used to describe a manifest action aimed at causing physical or psychological injury or harm to another, but in the broader sense of aggressiveness it can denote a latent potential or disposition to such an action or such behavior. In the first case there is some overlapping with violence (compulsion is thus at least one of the ways of exercising power), whereas in the latter aggression constitutes a preliminary stage of violence and must be distinguished from it when the concept is defined (Bierhoff & Wagner, 1998). Erich Fromm (1977) systematically distinguished malicious aggression (in the sense of cruelty and destructiveness) from benign aggression (when it is defensive), and it seems that he only considered the first definitely to represent violence. Whether an action or behavior is considered aggression, or is perceived as such, would seem to depend not least on context-specific variables.

By comparison the use of the terms "violence" and "power" outside the German-speaking countries has always been more precise: There the term "power" is above all a neutral means of denoting the ability to do something, to achieve an effect or exercise influence, whereas "violence" is considered the problematic exercise of physical strength with the goal of harming or injuring a person or thing. There are also the concepts of "force," "coercion," and "aggression," which are along the same semantic lines but obviously arouse different associations than "violence." The term "force" suggests primarily strength, power, energy, pressure, and compulsion, and only then power, influence and violence. "Coercion" essentially means compulsion and repression, and thus denotes the power to make someone submit to one's wishes; only then comes the meaning of violence. It seems only to be the term "aggression" where usage in German, English and the Romance languages largely coincides. In all cases the word is used either for concrete aggressive or vicious behavior ("disposed to attack") or for a latent disposition, and in all cases the delimitation from the concept of violence is clear enough despite there being some concrete points of reference. Moreover, this overview of the semantics of the concept of violence has given grounds to support the idea that the counterconcept of violence is nonviolence or freedom from violence (in the sense of freedom from physical and psychological harm), but not peace or freedom from conflict. Peaceful ways of life are not at all free of conflict, but are characterized by having peaceful and civilized models of conflict resolution (Senghaas, 1995).

III. CONCEPTS AND UNDERSTANDINGS OF VIOLENCE

At the end of the above discussion of the etymology of the concept of violence the ambiguity and complexity of the concept of violence in the twentieth century was noted, which make it difficult to reach an appropriate and uncontested understanding of violence. Precisely for this reason it is not enough to merely confirm the indistinct and contradictory meaning and character of violence. Rather, the task is to typologically classify this ambiguity and its different connections and thus gain a certain overview of the different applications of the concept of violence. It then becomes clear that individual understanding of the concept may relate to very different forms of violence, so that the diversity of the concept of violence can today be considered to a good extent to be the diversification of different ways of understanding violence which previously did not exist as such. Types and forms, dimensions and structures of meaning, dynamics and contexts must thus be distinguished in order to do justice to the ambiguity of violence. The differentiation mentioned is itself ultimately the result of a long historical process of democratization and civilization, which has taught us to distinguish between legitimate and illegitimate forms of violence and has brought about a greater sensitivity to phenomena of violence than ever before.

1.   The Concept of Violence and its Strands of Meaning

If one proceeds from a narrow concept of violence which relates to the core area of violence, violence can essentially be deduced through seven questions, which at the same time refer to different strands of meaning of the concept:

- *Who* exercises violence? This is above all the question as to the perpetrators, the initiators of an act of violence, the subjects of an action classified as violence. The perpetrators themselves can be subtly differentiated according to the type and structure of their involvement: They can be isolated individuals, groups or other bodies, but institutions or organizations can also be agents. Violence of this kind is aimed at the one-sided enforcement of claims and expectations by means of physical coercion in direct physical confrontation with an opponent. Collective violence is considered to be the more or less planned clash of groups or social movements. If institutions or organizations are the vehicles of violence, the resulting forms of violence can take on very different qualities. But violence can also relate in an abstract way to particular structures which produce violence or make it possible, and these structures must then be examined individually as to their violence potential.
- *What* happens when violence is exercised? This is first of all the question as to the facts of an action understood as violence and as to the particular sequence of events in violence. Here we are dealing with a phenomenology of violence. This question is therefore also concerned with the effects of violence, with what has been achieved—violence as a quintessence of sensory experience is aimed primarily at the body of another, which is why the physicality of the experience of violence has particular significance. The spread and scale of violence and its intensity are thus of interest here. This shows that violence always exists in a particular space and time and as a rule occurs in graduated form because it is not capable of unlimited growth (von Trotha, 1997).
- *How* is violence exercised? This is the question as to the ways in which violence is exercised and the means used. The course of an act of violence as well as its spread and scale vary considerably depending on these means. It is clear from the outset that a lone individual with his or her fists can spread less fear than an armed group, whose area of activity is broader, and that the violence of such a group is in turn markedly inferior to the significant technological means employed by states in wars. Culture and civilization have greatly increased the potential for violence, their artifacts and institutions make violence more effective and they provide reasons and justifications for their use. "Technological progress consequently also means an increase in the efficiency of the technical means of violence. No examples are needed. Suffice to say that an 'increase in efficiency' here also means increased productivity in the actual acts of violence. The effort (measured in people or time) to kill a particular number of people has constantly decreased" (Popitz, 1992:178ff.). But at least equally as important in this context

is the question as to third parties, the bystanders, who as people or institutions are present in every perpetrator-victim relationship either directly or indirectly, hindering violence or abetting it, as supporters or sympathizers. This is ultimately the question as to how the society and its institutions, the elites or other circles exercising a decisive influence on public opinion, relate to violence.

- *Who* is the violence directed at? This is the question as to the human victims of violence, those who suffer or endure violence, who it is inflicted upon in different contexts and various ways. They are the objects of an act of violence or violent behavior. When we speak of violence we must not pass over the victims. "The aim of violence is not resistance, but overcoming it: the pain that forces submission. Violence aims to overpower. The victory of one is the suffering, the death of the other" (Sofsky, 1997:104; see Scarry, 1992). Analyses of violence which restrict themselves to the actions of perpetrators, processes of interaction, and the course of conflicts, are one-sided, because they do not face the adversities of violence but only take account of particular aspects of the complex figuration of violence.

- *Why* is violence exercised [reasons]? On the one hand, this is the abstract question as to the general causes of violence, which up until today has been reflected in a considerable range of different expert explanations. On the other hand, it asks as to the particular reasons for an act of violence. As a rule different degrees of expedience are assumed, or the explanations advance predominantly instrumental motives. However, violence can also be exercised without there being a particular reason—it can be an end in itself or can be completely irrational, occurring without any purpose.

- *Why* is violence exercised [objectives]? This is the question as to the goals and possible motives of violence, which examines intentions and purposes in search of an explanation. Violence can only be exercised purposefully if it is based on particular intentions. These can be to harm, injure, or kill another person. The expedience of violence can be set out along different lines. Firstly, violence can arise in a concrete situation in the heat of the moment. Such situational violence can be explained on the basis of the escalation of particular conflict situations which are each unique and cannot be repeated. Secondly, violence can be exercised rationally. It can be used instrumentally insofar as it is a means to an end. Here violence is channeled by the purpose, it is given a particular direction, a beginning and an end. It provides justifications for its use, but also limits its use and extent. Violence is rational from the point of view of the theory of action but also in terms of the power relations involved. Thirdly and finally, purposive violence also has an expressive and communicative dimension. It finds its meaning in the preconventional enjoyment of the bloody-minded squabble and the symbolically conveyed gratification through violence (as in sadomasochistic rituals). In order to explain violence, three typical sets of factors therefore have to be differentiated: a) interests—reference to interests almost always gives violence a purposive character and provides manifest justification for its use; b) possibilities—these open up chances and options to use violence, without yet telling us anything about the appropriateness of using violence; c) contingencies—structures of coincidence relate to processes of indistinct, less purposive exercise of violence, which involve risk and danger potentials which are difficult to calculate.

TABLE I-2.1. The concept of violence and its strands of meaning

Category	Relevant dimensions	Definition criteria	Elements of definition
Who?	Subjects	Perpetrators as agents	Individuals, groups, institutions, structures
What?	Phenomenology of violence	Injury, harm, other effects	People, objects
How?	Ways in which violence is exercised	Means, circumstances	Physical, psychological, symbolic, communicative
Whom?	Objects of violence	Victims	People, objects
Why? (Reasons)	Causes and reasons	Interests, possibilities, contingencies	Forms of justification
Why? (Objectives)	Goals and motives	Degrees of expedience	Intentions
Why? (Justifications)	Models of justification	Deviating from or corresponding to norms	Legal/illegal Legitimate/illegitimate

- *Why* is violence exercised [justifications]? This is the question as to the models of justification and legitimization strategies of violence. Different justifications for acts of violence can be advanced depending on the sort and type of violence we are dealing with. The legitimacy of each justification is related to the prevailing norms of the given society. It is the higher norms and values of this kind that determine whether the exercise of violence is considered legal or illegal, legitimate or illegitimate.

Even these brief explanations point to the fact that violence is always a complex figuration whose perpetrator-victim relationships need to be complemented by taking into account the situations of third parties. It is a process with both an action and a structural component. Traditional ways of understanding violence, which aimed to get to the core of the phenomenon using simple causal models such as a direct cause-and-effect relationship of one or just a few key variables, have now been superceded by more adequate process models. These include both the objective conditions and subjective interpretations of a conflict situation and take account of the different degrees of freedom for individual or collective violent behavior which result from the restrictions and pertaining conditions. This went hand in hand with new fields of research into violence in the social sciences, which were now more interested in the "what" and "how" questions and in the dynamics of violence generally, than in the "why" question as to the causes, grounds, and contexts of the emergence of violence (Nedelmann, 1997).

2.   The Dimensions and Ways of Understanding Violence

Since so far violence has been looked at according to the concept's individual elements of meaning, now in a second step it shall be differentiated according to individual levels of application. Proceeding in this way allows us to elicit different ways of understanding violence and their correlations and thus also to deal with further distinctions—the elements of definition mentioned in Table I-2.1. Distinguishing direct physical violence, institutional violence, structural violence, and cultural or symbolic violence is in many respects fundamental for differentiating the semantics and various meanings of the concept. Violence also occurs in a figurative sense in a multitude of metaphorical senses and ritualized forms.

Metaphorical concepts involving violence should first be distinguished from the core area of violence. Here we are not dealing with the real exercise of violence, but rather with the graphic description of a phenomenon, state of affairs, or impression, which suggests particular power, strength or superiority. In this sense we are talking of the forces of nature (*Naturgewalten*), notable events (*gewaltige Ereignisse*) or impressive buildings (*gewaltige Bauwerke*), the violence of passion (*Gewalt der Leidenschaft*), or overpowering impressions (*überwältigende Eindrücke*).

However, *direct physical violence*—aimed at harming, injuring, or killing other people—indubitably stands at the center of the whole issue of violence. This form of violence is always exercised in a manifest manner and is mostly intentional. Heinrich Popitz (1992:48ff.) considered people's relative freedom from instinctual behavior, which brings a far-reaching release from social factors enforcing or inhibiting action, to be the anthropological basis of this kind of violence. The fact that people need not exercise violence, but may always have the choice to do so, is what makes violence so disturbing: violence is a behavioral option that can be used at any time. It does not require lasting superiority in instruments of power because its power stems from the elemental vulnerability of the human body. The use of physical violence thus produces effects by itself, it has no cultural preconditions, is universally effective, and does not first have to be understood. "Violence is a universal language—assuming we mean physical violence ... It is crucial for this distinctive feature that its application produce effects with greater reliability, thoroughness and general applicability than other means of coercion and that when used as a last resort it is superior to all other tools of control and instruments of political power" (Neidhardt, 1986:134).

Here we can also mark out the difference to *psychological violence* which is aimed at the mind, the soul, the psyche of a person. Although it remains tied to the physicality of human existence, it is not only far harder to detect but can also be considerably more inhumane than physical violence. Psychological violence is based on words, gestures, pictures, symbols, or deprivation of the necessities of life, so as to force others into subjugation through intimidation and fear, or specific "rewards." Psychological violence certainly includes some forms of psychological cruelty and particular kinds of torture. Whereas physical violence involves a strong connection between cause and effect and its results are to a great extent predictable, the effects of psychological violence cannot be predicted in the same way, since they can be eluded by the victim through a range of defense mechanisms, by taking refuge, or by suppression. Physical violence always causes open, visible harm or injuries, whereas psychological violence works undetected, it is not outwardly visible. Frequently the full extent of it is only revealed after a certain time and is then manifested in serious traumas. Thus the effects of psychological violence are diverse, and control by the perpetrator is less direct, although the consequences are by no means less serious for the victim.

Institutional violence goes beyond direct personal violence insofar as it not only describes a specific modality of social behavior, but is also directed toward lasting relations of dependence and submission. A first definition of it would be as "power of disposition over subjects and dependents granted to holders of positions within a hierarchy and supported by physical sanctions ... The prototype of institutional violence in modern times is the state's claim to sovereignty and the obedience it demands from individuals in its dealings with them" (Waldmann, 1995:431). We are thus dealing here with violence's regulatory function, as exercised by state security services (police, secret services) or state organizations (e.g., the military). Their physical, coercive interventions must be regarded as violence, even if in principle the police enjoy a bonus of legitimacy over their opponents when they employ violence in the constitutional-democratic context. It is the criteria of legality/illegality and legitimacy/illegitimacy which make institutional violence appear either as relatively unproblematic or as injustice—though very contradictory and unclear combinations are possible. This immediately becomes apparent when we look at the limits of the state monopoly of violence, which may seem to be clear-cut, but are quite blurred in concrete instances—in the form of police attacks, implementation of the death penalty, particular types of warfare, or various forms of combating insurgency and terrorism. The limits of legitimate and legally exercised violence were far exceeded by the forms of state terror endemic in the twentieth century. Here those in power used the entire arsenal of brute force and coercion to achieve their political-ideological goals, though outwardly they still tried to maintain a semblance of legality. Institutional violence can thus be of widely differing quality depending which forms it assumes and which organizations employ it.

The concept of *structural violence* was originally formulated by Johan Galtung (1975). He introduced it to complement his concept of direct violence and to encompass all those kinds of violence which result from systemic structures and are reflected in the various forms of anonymous mass impoverishment and the death of huge numbers of people world-wide due to basic inequality of opportunity. There is definitely human responsibility involved here, but the blame can no longer be individually apportioned. For Galtung these problems ultimately result from the violent structures of global society themselves. Galtung considers that structural violence is always present when there is no direct perpetrator but a permanent state of violence. Violence must therefore be inherent in the social structures of a society or system. Accordingly, Galtung considers that violence always exists "when people are influenced in such a way that their current somatic and mental fulfillment is less than their potential fulfillment" (Galtung, 1975:9). Violence has thus become a cause for the difference between the Real and the Possible, between what is and what could have been at a particular level of social development. The criteria which Galtung cites to define this gap are firstly global wealth and the corresponding level of available knowledge, and then the uneven distribution of resources, unequal power conditions, and the different opportunities which this gives rise to. Galtung's description of structural violence, where poverty, oppression and alienation are structural elements of the definition, is at the same time a far-reaching delimitation of distinctions within the concept of violence: "So as not to overtax the word violence, now and again we will refer to the condition of structural violence as *social injustice*" (Galtung, 1971:62). Although one can criticize the vagueness or even indeterminability of the concept of structural violence—the way it allows forms and conditions of violence to be stretched ad infinitum such that ultimately everything appears to be violence as long as it is conceivable that normatively it could be better—it is nonetheless not clear why violence should be restricted to its direct and institutional forms, since dealing with less tangible forms of violence need not lead to an inflationary use of the concept of violence. Neither Niklas Luhmann nor Jürgen Habermas were afraid to use the concept of structural violence for the forms of marginalization, multiple exclusion from various social subsystems, or the new forms of segmentation and lasting *underclass* underprivilege resulting from globalized conditions of reproduction (Schroer, 2000; Habermas, 1990; Luhmann, 1995).

The concept of *cultural violence* or *symbolic violence* has different elements of meaning. The introduction of the concept of cultural violence by Johan Galtung (1990) was of central significance for the issue to be discussed here; earlier Pierre Bourdieu had put forward a similar concept of symbolic violence. Galtung defined cultural violence by extending his concept of structural violence to include those aspects of culture which can be used for justifying or legitimizing direct, illegitimate institutional (or structural) violence. Cultural violence is aimed at making other forms of violence appear just—or at least not unjust—and thus making them acceptable for society. Cultural violence functions by switching the moral connotations of an action from wrong to right—or at least acceptable or unobjectionable—and is successful to the extent that it succeeds in obscuring society's perception of actions or facts as violence (Galtung, 1998:341ff.). Religion, ideology, language, art, and science are media particularly suited to this task. The real or potential legitimation of violence is thus the sign by which cultural violence can be recognized. By comparison, Pierre Bourdieu saw symbolic violence as being the violence embodied in concepts, language, and systems of symbols aimed at obscuring, veiling and glossing over unspoken conditions of rule. Conditions of power and government and the structures of violence they embody, he wrote, become unrecognizable to the extent that they seem no longer able to be challenged and are thus overlooked, but at the same time are accepted. Discrimination and deception are thus already attendant in the very symbol, or systems of symbols, and therefore anyone who is fond of a particular system of symbols, or uses it, is inevitably exercising symbolic violence, at times unwittingly (Bourdieu, 1993; Bourdieu & Passeron, 1973).

In addition there is another understanding of symbolic violence that lays special emphasis on the symbolism of exercising violence and comprehends violence as language or cultural expressiveness (Erzgräber & Hirsch, 2001). Symbolic violence as linguistically conveyed violence means such mental acts of violence and spoken words, for example, that consist in shouting, abusing, offending, slandering, libeling, discrediting, belittling, disparaging, debasing, ignoring, or making a fool of someone, including humiliation and character assassination. It is built into language and communication in the form of hate speech—words with a racist or sexist background aimed at injuring the personal, ethnic, or sexual integrity of a person (Butler, 1998). Verbal violence, which can also be found in propaganda and the media, is aimed at intimidating and belittling others. Although it is termed symbolic, its mode of effect actually makes it more a variant of psychological violence.

Ritualized forms of violence must also, like metaphorical descriptions, be distinguished from the central concept and semantics of violence. Ritualized violence here does not mean public burnings at the stake in the Middle Ages or prescribed routines of torture, but those forms of communicative (social) violence which, if they can be categorized at all, tend more toward manifest physical violence because they do not constitute a use of force against another person with the aim of overcoming their resistance or causing them harm or injury—which would make them acts of power as defined by Popitz. Rather, such violence is embedded in an action or interactive scenario and directed toward a different goal. This violence is overwhelmingly theatrical and functions without malicious intent to injure—either through conveying the domination and subordination processes of violent acts of power with their clearly recognizable victim and perpetrator roles in purely sym-

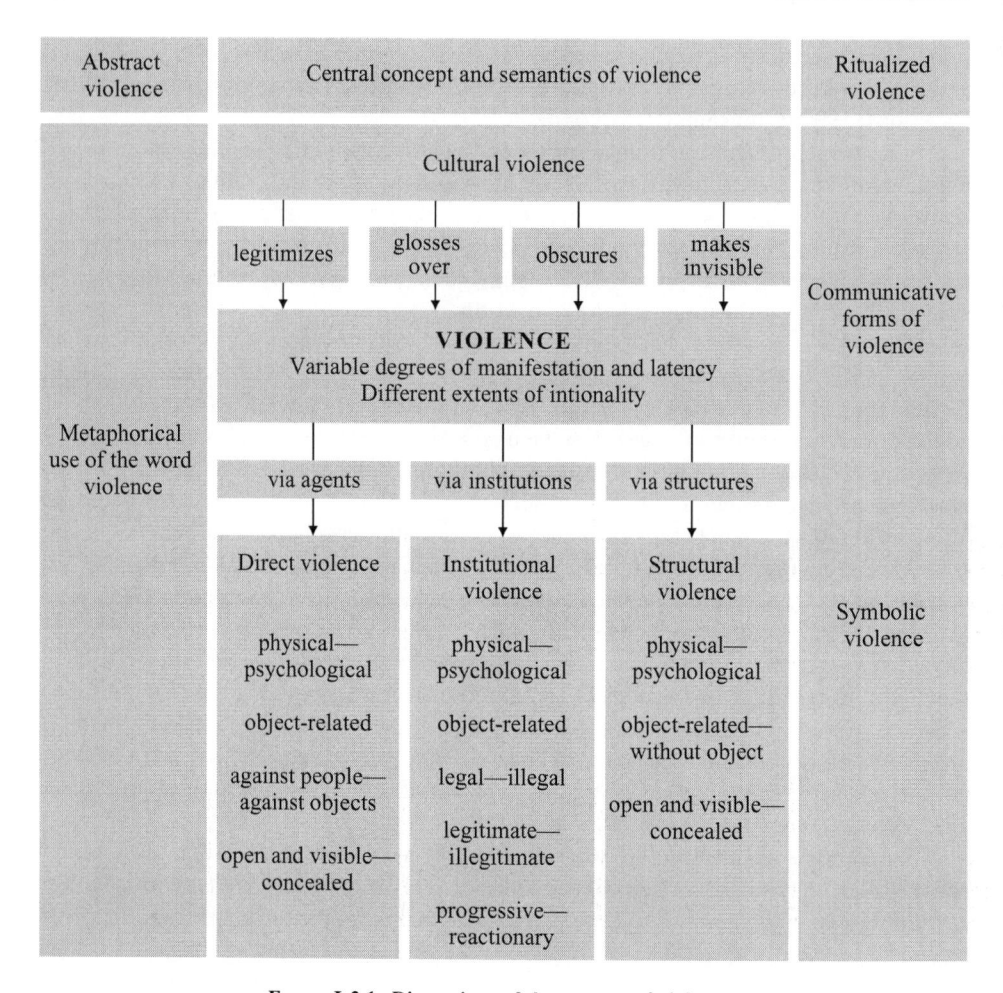

FIGURE I-2.1. Dimensions of the concept of violence.

bolic ways, or by doing without them at all. Such staged "violence" is based on the voluntariness and equality of the participants. These forms of violence, which are frequently found in specific subcultures, help to build the community through their characteristically playful-ritual form and are not destructive, not least because they are standardized and regimented in a particular way. These forms of ritualized-playful violence can be observed at various types of hardcore concerts (Inhetveen, 1997) and also in particular sexual practices such as sadomasochism (Wetzstein, Steinmetz, Reis, & Eckert, 1993; Hitzler, 1995): A particular measure of 'violence' is part of the fun, and in the case of sadomasochistic practices it is even fundamental to the pleasure. It is also an essential ingredient of particular sports where violence is part of the contest—the games are intended to be violent, and this is what gives them their appeal (Elias & Dunning, 1983).

Figure I-2.1 helps to clarify the various dimensions of the concept of violence by systematically summarizing the individual concepts and giving an overview of the central concept and semantics, their links, and related aspects.

IV. DISTINGUISHING MICROVIOLENCE AND MACROVIOLENCE

In addition to the historical changes in the meaning of the concept of violence and the fundamental typologization of violence, every serious examination of the phenomenon of violence will also have to consider the differences between individual, collective and nonlegitimate state violence. This is because collective and nonlegitimate state violence cannot simply be considered the sum of individual acts of violence, and also follow completely different structural principles that cannot be derived from the behavior of individuals. Collective violence and illegitimate state violence exhibit a qualitatively different character. Although in this case the person exercising violence is ultimately always an individual, their behavior cannot be seen as an isolated act or event (as with individual perpetrators), but only in the context of collective action or organization (group violence, state or parastate organizations). The individual act can only be understood by taking account of the entire social conflict it is based on. It is fundamentally conformist, nondeviant behavior because it takes place in accordance with the behavioral norms of a relevant higher collective and in this respect is tied to particular norms and roles (unlike deviant individual perpetrators who have a low attachment to norms) (Jäger, 1982, 1989).

The goals of individual perpetrators must include at least some kind of personal motive in relation to a victim, who to them is otherwise an individual without particular characteristics—in principle anyone can fall victim of this kind of violence!—and the perpetrator aims to injure, do harm, or enforce a change of behavior. In the case of collective violence, however, there is usually a predominance of superindividual motives for causing injury and harm to designated groups: people are ascribed particular characteristics or are identified as belonging to a group, and are then made victims. Since macroviolence cannot really be explained convincingly on the basis of individual behavioral dispositions, and considering that all collective violence nevertheless has an individual dimension, we are faced with a particularly pertinent question: How is intended collective violence translated into individual dispositions to violence such that real acts of violence are carried out? Inversely, what brings individuals to participate in collective violence? Micro-violence and macroviolence differ considerably, even at the purely phenomenological level.

The violence used by individuals tends to be intentional in nature, and since it is basically always limited to the immediate social environment, it is overwhelmingly nonpolitical. Collective and institutional violence, by comparison, is exercised more functionally and in most cases has a strong political component. The context and course of the different forms of violence contrast sharply. As a rule the individual perpetrator does not act in public (third parties are unwelcome at the action), the violence he or she exercises is not necessarily bound to any conditions, nor are there always particular preconditions. Collective violence and illegitimate state violence, by comparison, are public or semi-public because of their scale alone, and the injuring and killing is itself dependent on particular conditions and circumstances. Such violence is bound up with many preconditions because it is subject to collective norms, carried out in dependence on a group, or legitimized by the state. With such violence there are always onlookers, accessories, and accomplices (Hilberg, 1996).

These situations have an effect on the perpetrators' sense of justice and possible feelings of guilt since a different source of legitimization is at hand for some types of violence: Whereas individual perpetrators are more likely to realize the wrongfulness of their behavior and later cite rationalizations of particular acts in an attempt to legitimate them, in the case of collective or illegitimate state violence the perpetrators frequently have a poorly-developed sense of right and wrong, or none at all, because the act has been prepared for ideologically, committed "with a clean conscience," or has been carried out in accordance with recognized norms and roles. Apart from a handful of legally condoned exceptions (self-defense, the right to resist), individual violence is distinguished in many cases by subsequent justifications, and guilt can be attributed more clearly because the individual perpetrator bears full criminal responsibility for his or her acts. In the case of macroviolence, by comparison, the legitimization and justification of acts from higher up in the hierarchy make it difficult to clearly attribute responsibility, so a good measure of doubt is appropriate (e.g., when an individual claims to have acted under binding orders). However, it has recently been proved that perpetrators of macroviolence also have considerable room for maneuver (Browning, 1993; Goldhagen, 1996), and the relationship between the sense of responsibility and irresponsible behavior can by no means be regarded as a dichotomy. Rather, with personal guilt there is a continuum of levels of responsibility, and individual perpetrators can also be prosecuted in cases of collective violence. Last but not least, there are also varied adiaphorization strategies connected with the circumstances under which violence is exercised: Whereas individual perpetrators always seek individual justifications for their violence and complete aimlessness is rare among the personal calculations of benefit, in the case of collective or illegitimate state violence there need be no personal legitimization of the act through a previous change in basic moral values. Instead, the act is rationalized in a specific way as social necessity, as following the path of duty, acting under binding orders, group pressure, or the pressure to conform. In the case of collective violence and illegitimate state violence there are also a range of neutralization mechanisms (changes in collective moral values, dehumanization of the victim, desensitization processes regarding the use of violence, exoneration from responsibility, and actual a priori decriminalization of the acts) which contribute to the attenuation, relativization, or erasure of taboos on violence and killing and can go as far as moral anesthesia.

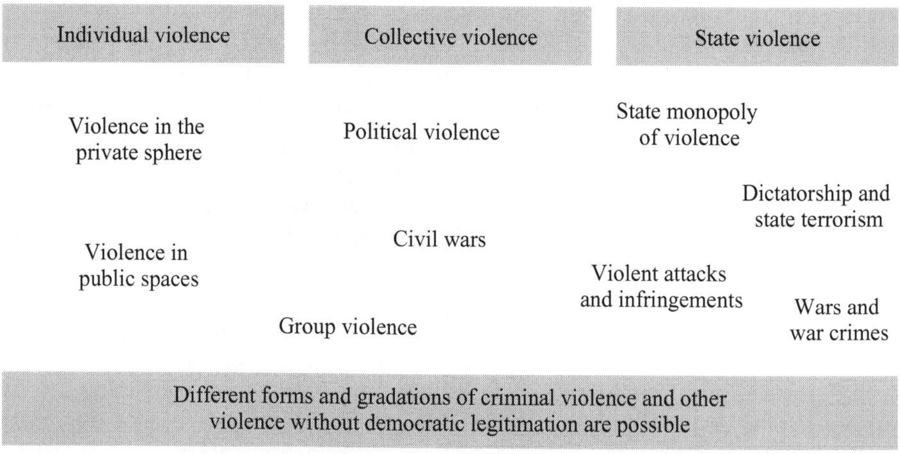

Individual violence	Collective violence	State violence
Violence in the private sphere	Political violence	State monopoly of violence
		Dictatorship and state terrorism
Violence in public spaces	Civil wars	
		Violent attacks and infringements
	Group violence	Wars and war crimes

Different forms and gradations of criminal violence and other violence without democratic legitimation are possible

FIGURE I-2.2. Typology of violent phenomena.

V. MANIFESTATIONS OF VIOLENCE

In the introduction to this chapter it was pointed out that the ambiguities and uncertainties of the concept of violence are not least the result of the diverse forms and types of violence themselves, which cannot be reduced to a common denominator, let alone be clearly evaluated. It is therefore helpful to systematize the diverse manifestations of violence so as to bring out the specific characteristics of all the central categories. This list does not claim to be exhaustive and is to an extent arbitrary, not only because further categories could easily be added, but also because the categorizations are not always clear-cut and partly overlap. It is more of use for classifying and illustrating the diverse manifestations of violence rather than laying claim to taxonomic precision. This even applies when violence is differentiated according to the type and number of agents involved, their degree of organization, or their legitimacy.

1. Individual Violence

One general manifestation of violence, which we have already spoken about in the scope of direct physical violence, is *individual violence*. This is exercised by individual perpetrators (or by individuals in *peer groups*) against strangers in the street, in public spaces or public institutions, and also exercised in the private sphere against friends and relatives, etc. There can—but need not—be a social relationship between perpetrator and victim. Individual violence can be directed not only against people but also against objects and take the form of vandalism or damage to property (Demandt, 1997). It can also take the form of theft and robbery and constitute offenses against property.

If, by comparison, violence is exercised in one's immediate social environment such as in communities with only a limited number of members (family, relatives, friends, co-workers, etc.), one speaks more of *private violence* (Godenzi, 1994; see also the corresponding contributions in Kurtz, 1999). This violence is private insofar as it takes place "behind the scenes," away from the public eye. Here aggressions and violence can arise from the compulsive character of communal life (family relations) and the necessity of communicating and getting along with one another within the family. The family is also a focus of violence with regard to the relationship between the sexes (O'Toole & Schiffman, 1997). Here we see the dark side of the family not only in implicit or explicit threats, surveillance of the activities of the partner, pathological jealousy and verbal humiliation, which can go as far as psychological maltreatment, but also in very manifest forms of violence against women, children, and older people. Blows and beatings by their husbands are everyday experiences of women; rape in (and outside of) marriage and sexual coercion are forms of sexual violence; child abuse and the various degrees of child neglect should be qualified as violence in exactly the same way; incest and other forms of sexual abuse of children constitute sexual violence against children. At this point one should also mention the whole repertoire of physical and psychological disrespect for the will of older, sick and vulnerable people, or those in need of help. For a long time these forms of domestic violence were effectively kept private and withdrawn from public intervention through the protection of privacy. Only recently have they attracted the attention of a broader public, allowing the full extent of the problem to be realized (Rauchfleisch, 1992:62ff.).

2. Forms of Collective Violence

Collective violence represents the opposite of individual violence, and its public character also makes it the opposite of private violence. The term collective violence is used in particular to designate those forms of violence which to a certain degree are under the control of a leadership—however legitimized—and for which a particular degree of organization and a public challenge are constitutive elements. Group size is of crucial importance for this definition and must exceed a particular number of people, since otherwise we are merely dealing with simple group delinquency or gang violence (street gangs, hooligans, etc.). Typical examples of collective violence are rebellions and pogroms, along with social revolts and violent mass protests. However, the latter represent a gray zone which verges on political violence, which includes principally terrorism, guerilla movements, rebellions, revolutions, civil wars, and coups d'état (Waldmann, 1977, 1998).

Unlike collective violence, whose irregular and irrational variants must by no means always be political, the central delimiting criterion of *political violence* is not so much group size as the intentions of the agents and the reactions of the state. Political violence is characterized by the goal which is to be achieved through violence—winning political power or changing established conditions of government. In this respect it is primarily directed against the state or a political regime and its representatives who the violent actions are aimed at, but it can also be against particular stigmatized groups or foreigners. Political violence can thus be considered an act of destruction, of causing injury or harm, and its goals, targets (objects or human victims), circumstances, explanations, and intended effects possess political significance. This kind of violence with an ideological background is aimed at changing the behavior of other people or institutions or, if possible, replacing a political, social, or economic system. Political violence thus aims to change the functional principles of a political system or collective entity (see Tilly, 1986; Waldmann, 1977; Zimmermann, 1977, 1999).

3. The Heterogeneity of State Violence

The last form of violence, albeit one which is extremely heterogeneous in itself, is *state violence* (Narr, 1973, 1980; Giddens, 1985). The applications of the concept of violence in connection with the political structure of the state are diverse and in each case denote highly differing types and forms of violence, to which serious analyses of violence should give careful consideration, since they also display various qualities of violence. These extend from the legitimate state monopoly of violence to forms of state terrorism and war. If today in the leading Western industrialized countries state violence is sometimes no longer perceived as such, or only in exceptional cases, this is above all because the democratic state essentially employs its legitimate monopoly of violence for maintaining order. This can by no means be taken for granted, as history shows—for long periods it was more the exception than the rule. This also becomes clear from a glance at the many Second and Third World countries where the state possesses only a very patchy monopoly of violence, and has frequently become an agent of violence itself as a power-wielding institution.

The first variant of state violence is thus the legal violence of the state which occurs in constitutional democracies in the form of the state monopoly of violence and is considered legitimate. Max Weber was one of the first to realize that every state is a coercive institution founded on violence and that specific means of physical violence are characteristic of the modern state by definition. In this sense Weber viewed the state as a relationship of rule of people over people based on means of legitimate violence (Weber, 1976:822). With regard to legal state violence, a distinction must be made, at least, between a repressive function and one that is based on regulating law and order. Each function is accompanied by both manifest and latent forms of state violence. The manifest forms take effect above all in the state's repressive function. Here we are dealing with the action of state agencies against criminals, i.e., applying sanctions to deviant behavior or suppressing violent political protest movements or political rebels. By comparison, the various warning, deterrence and definition processes of violence, as well as the procedural, decision-making and isolation methods which the state uses to counter acts of direct violence "from below," must be considered to belong to the latent forms of state violence which the state uses more in its function as the guarantor of order (see Waldmann, 1977:78ff.).

The observation that the modern state is based on violence is also correct in a much more direct sense, considering that the development of the state as a form of government and the successful enforcement of its monopoly of violence in Western Europe was not only a historically unique process, but resulted only after lengthy and exceedingly violent and costly clashes—the ultimate monopolization of violence was by no means a clear and foregone conclusion. Both in Europe and the United States, nations were born and states built through bloody civil strife, revolutions and wars, which frequently caused chaos and almost always plunged the population into misery (Tilly, 1975, 1985; Moore 1974) This was what prompted Charles Tilly to write: "War made the state, and the state made war" (Tilly, 1975:42; see Krippendorff, 1985; Parker, 1990; Porter, 1994). Some of the violent founding mythologies of modern states can also be understood in this context (Girard, 1992).

A third variant of state violence are the violent attacks of particular state agencies in combating crime and illegal violence. These are often overreactions, and the level of force and repression is at issue. Here we are dealing with disproportionate operational strategies at demonstrations and in raids, gray areas in combating terrorism, belligerent police deployments which cause tense situations to escalate, and the use of ever more effective weapons. Excessively tightened laws, states of emergency and security legislation can be out of proportion to the situation and also be constitutionally dubious in the way they seriously undermine liberal constitutional rights. It is characteristic of these forms of state violence that the limits of legality and legitimacy become blurred, and the legality and legitimacy of state action can drift apart. For example, a particular police operation can be legal, but this does not mean it will be considered legitimate. Conversely, rebels and insurgent movements can exercise violence which formally is illegal but which in view of state repression or illegitimate government can be legitimized by a majority of the population.

Dictatorships are a further variant of state violence. The despotic violence exercised by dictatorships is based not only on the state's monopoly of violence but also on other state organizations and institutions (such as the domestic use of the armed forces) and turns their potential violence against the population. The threat of violence and the actual exercise of violence can fluctuate so that it is possible to distinguish "soft" dictatorships (which rule by tightened surveillance, pressure, repression, and repealing democratic rights) from "hard" dictatorships (which use direct violence, severe repression, persecution, and torture as means of keeping down and intimidating the population or particular sections of it). The possible number of victims and the consequences of the violence are also correspondingly different, and this in turn has consequences for the ways in which a society may attempt to come to terms with its dictatorial past. Dictatorships are particular forms of rule which nonetheless still depend on a level of legitimacy and as a rule advance political justifications for the way they exercise power. Their power basis itself is variable: Beyond the ruling circle there are always backers, supporters, profiteers, and third parties, without whom dictatorial power could not be exercised. Not least, dictatorships can serve quite different purposes and follow various goals related to establishing and maintaining order (Linz, 1975).

A distinction should be made between simple dictatorships and forms of state terrorism in which violence is used systematically as a general political tool. State terrorism does not restrict itself to the persecution and murder of opponents of the regime or other defined enemy groups, but aims to intimidate, frighten, terrorize, and unsettle people by means of abduction, "disappearing" people, cruel torture, and injury. The terrorist element of this violence consists in it being largely arbitrary and unpredictable, not in it being randomly spread. Nonetheless state terror always needs an irrational excess (in the sense of a random choice of victims and a contingent point in time for the use of violence) for its violence exercised by state or parastate institutions to function properly. Modern state terrorism also requires justifications, ranging from the necessary struggle against domestic "subversion" to the establishment of a new and supposedly more progressive model of society (Tobler & Waldmann, 1991; Ternon, 1996).

War, finally, is a form of violence arranged and specially authorized by the state. Its central element is mass slaughter organized by states and carried out by people (Knöbl & Schmidt, 2000; Joas, 2000). War is "organized and calculated killing designed to break the will of the opponent" (Geyer, 1995:144) which in modern conditions and with the use of advanced technology (as in World War One and Two, or with the atomic bomb) takes on features of total violence, leading to mass extermination and wholesale destruction. Wars can take the classical form of international wars between different societies or can be inner-societal phenomena such as civil wars (van Creveld, 1998). Wars are thus violently conducted mass conflicts whose battles involve the regular armed forces of a government on at least one side, where there is at least a minimum of centralized organization of the combatants on both sides, and their armed operations are carried out with a certain degree of continuity (Kende, 1982). A distinction should be made, moreover, between the "normal" run of war, even in the intense and escalated form of modern high-technology warfare, and war crimes which show particular disregard for the international law of war (Wette & Ueberschär, 2001).

In view of the many different forms of state violence, any positive prejudice toward the violence embodied in the state, as can be found in conservative notions of the state, appears one-sided. The state monopoly of legitimate violence has not abolished violence, but only redistributed it, and in the twentieth century it was precisely the nation states which repeatedly used extensive illegitimate violence against their own citizens and those of other states. The "death" toll of state violence in the twentieth century exceeds the figures for individual and collective violence in society many times over. This suggests that the state is an instrument of social coercion which has become independent of society's control. It must be placed under democratic control and submit to principles of constitutional law which are to govern its actions.

4. Distinguishing between Legitimate and Legal Violence

One typology of violent phenomena, which is in many respects fundamental, is the dual distinction between legality/illegality and legitimacy/illegitimacy. This, however, cuts across all the previous distinctions because it is not about "differences in scale" of violence, but rather about the infringement of norms and the evaluation of these. Distinguishing between legal and illegal violence allows us to typologize a first pair of categories—democratically legitimized violence as opposed to *criminal violence*. The basis for characterizing an act of violence as criminal is its previous official labeling as illegitimate and its successive establishment as illegal in criminal law. Criminal violence can be a part of almost all the forms of violence treated above, extending from damage to property, robbery, injury, and killing to organized crime and mafia-type structures. Criminal violence occurs in two forms and takes on a different quality in each case. As instrumental violence it is in a strict sense always a means for achieving a particular end. Expressive violence, on the other hand, is essentially about working off violence, so the victim or the particular object affected is only a kind of substitute or pretext for the violent perpetrator. The criminalization of particular actions defined as violent is subject to historical change—it depends on sensitivity to violence and the sociopolitical perceptions of it (Lindenberger & Lüdtke, 1995; Foucault, 1994; Albrecht et al., 2001).

VI. APPLICATIONS OF THE CONCEPT OF VIOLENCE

The heterogeneity of the phenomenon of violence, and the different facets of violence, are probably responsible to a good extent for the many different ways in which the concept of violence is applied and the ease with which it is ideologized. Thomas Platt pointed out that "the happy combination of relatively vague descriptive content, coupled with a negative moral and emotional connotation, makes the word violence ideal for use in polemic discourse" (Platt, 1992:187ff.). For the moment it is less significant that various scientific disciplines all have their own focuses on violence and display a different sensitivity to violent phenomena, and that their analyses all involve specialist objectives of their own and present explanatory approaches that can be either very broad or rather more narrow. More significant is that particular applications of violence fulfil contradictory functions at the same time. This shows that violence is not only a social practice, but is also always manufactured through discourse and is thus part of a social construction of reality. In this sense violence is more a label than a clear description, it is a "summary symbol" and functions as an intensifier (Cremer-Schäfer, 1992:24).

Firstly we should note that what is considered violence at a particular point in time is not laid down as such unequivocally or immutably. Certain forms of violence, for example, disappeared completely during the processes of civilization—at some stage they were considered antiquated or were correspondingly sanctioned—while others were at least shifted "behind the scenes" and thus withdrawn from public view. On the other hand, reference must be made to an extension of the understanding of violence which accompanies the process of civilization and occurs at a higher level of development. After particular taboos have become established, new sensitivities to particular forms of human behavior appear, which in contrast to former times are now also classified as violence. Just as direct physical assault has long been banned, so today it is joined by forms of psychological cruelty and violence in marriage which in former times were given little attention. Caning by teachers at school, which in the past was often considered "normal," has largely disappeared in the Western democracies today. Here, therefore, on the strength of processes of sensitization, emancipation, and equality, the taboo on violence has been extended in a thoroughly positive way to include offenses which previously were not considered to constitute violence (Elias, 1976; Sieferle & Breuninger, 1998; Lindenberger & Lüdtke, 1995; Hugger & Stadler, 1995; Calließ, 1983). Overall, this kind of extension and sensitization of the perceptions of violence should be interpreted as a further advance in the process of civilization.

At the same time, however, there is a form of conceptual maneuvering that follows various political-ideological imperatives, since strategies to extend or narrow the concept of violence are also part of social conflicts. There has been an ongoing debate in the scholarly and political public in the last few decades about what one should understand violence to mean and how it should be distinguished from nonviolence. The tangible consequences of such attempts at definition show clearly that this is more than just a dispute about words. In the social protest movements, for example, attempts were made to politicize the concept of violence and push it toward structural violence, thus allowing a wide range of social ills and problems to be labeled, discredited, and set upon. At the same time the attempt was made at militant demonstrations to define the concept of violence as narrowly as possible, so that forms of civil disobedience, resistance to state authority, and damage to property did not figure as violence at all. State agencies, on the other hand, endeavored to label merely the violence of the opposing side as violence, so as to avoid being put under pressure to justify the coercive measures of the police and be able to present their own actions as a legitimate reaction to violent challenges. State authorities are ultimately able to use their special power of interpretation to criminalize particular actions that were previously considered peaceful forms of protest or nonviolent resistance, and thus establish new criminal offenses labeled as violent (e.g., "intellectual complicity" in the context of the terrorism debates, or sit-ins). Political-ideological conceptual maneuvering of this sort is hotly disputed because a commitment of any kind has considerable influence on the distribution of chances in conflict situations. If something which hitherto bore a relatively harmless label is now termed violence, this allows someone to kick up a row which will not only discredit their opponents, but will possibly also deliver a justification for counterviolence. Achieving recognition of a particular act as violence depends to a significant extent on the overall balance of power in society (Neidhardt, 1986).

This already suggests a third problematical application of the concept of violence—the general suitability of the word violence for kicking up rows and dramatizing particular acts or situations so as to achieve publicity and urge the resolution of political problems (Cremer-Schäfer & Stehr, 1990). In this sense violence has an indicative and denunciatory component whose validity cannot be denied a priori or in general—its purpose is denunciation or accusation of particular things and moralization about guilt. But it thus all too frequently loses sight of the actual facts of violence and their extent. Characterizing a massive crime against humanity as genocide, for example, will certainly achieve more media attention than talking about a series of supposedly unrelated individual crimes. It will also mobilize state reactions because the use of the word genocide goes beyond breached norms and moralization and sets in motion a cycle of redefinitions and threats, thus forcing the state to take determined action. The media's high level of interest in violence or its corresponding treatment of crimes can also lead to an overestimation of the extent and range of violence. The subjective perception and objective development of violence then differ widely. Conversely, the danger of an inflationary use of the word violence is that its ominous contents could lose their effect. Violence could appear virtually normal and result in desensitization toward violent phenomena or a delegitimization of the taboo on violence. This would undermine the feeling that violence is wrong, and the violence threshold would drop.

Given all the problematical applications of the concept of violence mentioned here, there is finally the danger of becoming ensnared in the discussion of violence. This can lead to reinterpreting the inner meaning of violence, using simplistic perpetrator-victim dichotomies that lead to a discourse based on—forced—emotional shock reactions and reduce the complex causes of violence to individual characteristics (Heitmeyer et al., 1995:425ff.). More than anything else, the different applications point out that assessments of the forms, functions, and severity of violence are subject to historical change, and that when evaluating violence it is necessary to take account of its full, complex meaning and quality.

VII. SUMMARY

Violence is an exceedingly complex concept which should not be subject to hurried evaluations. This is particularly true because the effects of violence, depending on the context, cannot always be clearly classified as positive or negative. The long-term perspective is also difficult to determine since there is very little certain knowledge about the empirical trends of violence (Chesnais, 1981; Eisner, 2001). Interpretative disputes and semantic shifts in the meaning of violence have frequently hindered a more exact diachronic and synchronic survey of acts of violence and thus complicated reliable historical longitudinal studies. This has been due in part to imprecise quantification and qualification criteria and diverse intermittent variables influencing judgment, and, not least, has also been affected by the contradictory and shifting assessment of what violence is all about. Zygmunt Bauman wrote: "It is not possible to say with any claim to objectivity whether modern history is a history of increasing or decreasing violence—because it is impossible to 'objectively' measure the total amount of violence ... All previous estimates of the historical trends of violence have had no chance of lasting recognition—due to the nature of the issue they are no less controversial and disputed than the legitimacy of coercive measures or the classification of these as violence (depending on the question of legitimacy)" (Bauman, 2000:32ff.). Although human behavior has always had the option of violence, every society has also found means and ways of stemming violence and preventing it from becoming endemic, at least in the long term. Not least, this points to the self-domestication of people as cultural beings, which began during processes of civilization. However intermittent this development may have been, people have learned to reflect on and adjust their behavior while withstanding aggressive impulses and the allure of violence—this is a core of their sociality (Elias, 1976).

   This insight suggests that we should be open to a sophisticated survey of the cultural progress of humanity while at the same time taking account of the considerable scale of violence (Sofsky, 1996; Duerr, 1988–1997). The modern age with its democratic-rational institutions has created better chances for the realization of humanity, nonviolence, and peacefulness, but at the same time it has vastly increased the potential for violence through new technologies, the greater degree of social distance between members of society, and the molding and repression of human nature (Miller & Soeffner, 1996). The concrete level of violence in any particular society would thus seem to depend on a complex parallelogram of forces: "Ultimately, the level of violence is affected by the interaction of motivational and cognitive, 'psychological', forces, societal bonds, structures and procedures, and the technologies available to the violent. Hence there is no isolated, basic treatment of violence ... Only a just and cohesive society, responsive to new demands, satisfying old ones, providing a meaningful life to its members, would sharply reduce violence, and even such a society would not eliminate it" (Etzioni, 1971:741).

Translated by Tradukas

REFERENCES

Albrecht, Günter, Otto Backes, & Wolfgang Kühnel (Eds.) (2001). *Gewaltkriminalität zwischen Mythos und Realität*. Frankfurt a. M.: Suhrkamp.

Apter, David, (Ed.) (1997). *The Legitimization of Violence*. Houndsmill: MacMillan.

Arendt, Hannah. (1970). *Macht und Gewalt*. München: Piper.

Bauman, Zygmunt. (1992). *Dialektik der Ordnung. Die Moderne und der Holocaust*. Hamburg: Europäische Verlagsanstalt.

Bauman, Zygmunt. (1995). *Moderne und Ambivalenz. Das Ende der Eindeutigkeit*. Frankfurt a. M.: Fischer.

Bauman, Zygmunt. (2000). Alte und neue Gewalt. *Journal für Konflikt- und Gewaltforschung, 1*, 28–42.

Bierhoff, Hans Werner, & Ulrich Wagner (Eds.) (1998). *Aggression und Gewalt. Phänomene, Ursachen und Interventionen*. Stuttgart et al.: Kohlhammer.

Bonacker, Thorsten, & Peter Imbusch. (1999). Begriffe der Friedens- und Konfliktforschung. Konflikt, Gewalt, Krieg, Frieden. In Peter Imbusch & Ralf Zoll (Eds.), *Friedens- und Konfliktforschung. Eine Einführung* (pp. 73–116). Opladen: Leske & Budrich.

Bourdieu, Pierre. (1993). *Sozialer Sinn*. Frankfurt a. M.: Suhrkamp.

Bourdieu, Pierre, & Jean-Claude Passeron. (1973). *Grundlagen einer Theorie der symbolischen Gewalt*. Frankfurt a. M.: Suhrkamp.

Brednich, Rolf W., & Walter Hartinger (Eds.) (1994). *Gewalt in der Kultur. 2 Bände*. Passau: Universitätsverlag.

Breuer, Stefan. (1998). *Der Staat. Entstehung, Typen, Organisationsstadien*. Reinbek: Rowohlt.

Browning, Christopher. (1993). *Ganz normale Männer. Das Reserve-Polizeibataillon 101 und die 'Endlösung' in Polen*. Reinbek: Rowohlt.

Butler, Judith. (1998). *Haß spricht. Zur Politik des Performativen*. Berlin: Berlin-Verlag.

Calließ, Jörg. (1983). *Gewalt in der Geschichte. Beiträge zur Gewaltaufklärung im Dienste des Friedens*. Düsseldorf: Schwann.

Chesnais, Jean-Claude. (1981). *Histoire de la violence en Occident de 1800 à nos Jours*. Paris: Editions Robert Laffont.

Chesnais, Jean-Claude. (1992). The History of Violence. Homicide and Suicide Through the Ages. *International Social Science Journal, 132*, 217–234.

Claussen, Detlev. (1982). *List der Gewalt. Soziale Revolutionen und ihre Theorien*. Frankfurt a. M.: Campus.

Cremer-Schäfer, Helga. (1992). Skandalisierungsfallen. Einige Anmerkungen dazu, welche Folgen es hat, wenn wir das Vokabular 'der Gewalt' benutzen, um auf gesellschaftliche Probleme und Konflikte aufmerksam zu machen. *Kriminologisches Journal, 24*, 23–36.

Cremer-Schäfer, Helga, & Johannes Stehr. (1990). Das Moralisieren und Skandalisieren von Problemen. Anmerkungen zur Geschichte von 'Gewalt' als Dramatisierungskonzept und Verdichtungssymbol. *Kriminalsoziologische Bibliographie, 17*(68), 21–42.

Creveld, Martin van. (1998). *Die Zukunft des Krieges*. München: Gerling Akademie Verlag.

Dabag, Mihran, Antje Kapust, & Bernhard Waldenfels (Eds.) (2000). *Gewalt. Strukturen, Formen, Repräsentationen*. München: Fink.

Demandt, Alexander. (1997). *Vandalismus. Gewalt gegen Kultur*. Berlin: Siedler.

Duerr, Hans Peter. (1988–1997). *Der Mythos vom Zivilisationsprozeß. 4 Bände*. Frankfurt a. M.: Suhrkamp.

Eisner, Manuel. (2001). Individuelle Gewalt und Modernisierung in Europa 1200–2000. In Günter Albrecht, Otto Backes & Wolfgang Kühnel (Eds.), *Gewaltkriminalität zwischen Mythos und Realität* (pp. 71–100). Frankfurt a. M.: Suhrkamp.

Elias, Norbert. (1976). *Über den Prozeß der Zivilisation. Soziogenetische und psychogenetische Untersuchungen. 2 Bände*. Frankfurt a. M.: Suhrkamp.

Elias, Norbert, & Eric Dunning. (1983). *Sport im Zivilisationsprozeß*. Münster: Lit.

Erzgräber, Ursula, & Alfred Hirsch (Eds.) (2001). *Sprache und Gewalt*. Berlin: Berlin-Verlag.

Etzioni, Amitai. (1971). Violence. In Robert K. Merton & Robert Nisbet (Eds.), *Contemporary Social Problems* (pp. 709–741). New York: Harcourt Brace Jovanovich Inc.

Faber, Karl-Georg, Karl-Heinz Ilting, & Christian Meier. (1982). Macht, Gewalt. In Otto Brunner, Werner Conze & Reinhard Koselleck (Eds.), *Geschichtliche Grundbegriffe, Band 3* (pp. 817–935). Stuttgart.

Foucault, Michel. (1994). *Überwachen und Strafen.* Frankfurt a. M.: Suhrkamp.

Fromm, Erich. (1977). *Anatomie der menschlichen Destruktivität.* Reinbek: Rowohlt.

Galtung, Johan. (1971). Gewalt, Frieden, Friedensforschung. In Dieter Senghaas (Ed.), *Kritische Friedensforschung* (pp. 55–104). Frankfurt a. M.: Suhrkamp.

Galtung, Johan. (1975). *Strukturelle Gewalt.* Reinbek: Rowohlt.

Galtung, Johan. (1990). Cultural Violence. *Journal of Peace Research, 3,* 291–305.

Galtung, Johan. (1998). *Frieden mit friedlichen Mitteln. Friede und Konflikt, Entwicklung und Kultur.* Opladen: Leske & Budrich.

Geyer, Michael. (1995). Eine Kriegsgeschichte, die vom Tode spricht. In Thomas Lindenberger & Alf Lüdtke (Eds.), *Physische Gewalt* (pp. 136–161). Frankfurt a. M.: Suhrkamp.

Giddens, Anthony. (1985). *The Nation State and Violence.* Cambridge: Polity Press.

Girard, René. (1992). *Das Heilige und die Gewalt.* Frankfurt a. M.: Fischer.

Godenzi, Alberto. (1994). *Gewalt im sozialen Nahraum.* Basel, Frankfurt a. M.: Helbing und Lichtenhalm.

Goldhagen, Daniel Jonah. (1996). *Hitlers willige Vollstrecker. Ganz gewöhnliche Deutsche und der Holocaust.* Berlin: Siedler.

Grimmsches Wörterbuch. (1911). *Gewalt* (pp. 4910–5094). Leipzig: Verlag von S. Hirzel.

Habermas, Jürgen. (1990). Gewaltmonopol, Rechtsbewußtsein und demokratischer Prozeß. In Jürgen Habermas, *Die nachholende Revolution* (pp. 167–175). Frankfurt a. M.: Suhrkamp.

Heitmeyer, Wilhelm, Birgit Collmann, Jutta Conrads, Ingo Matuschek, Dietmar Kraul, Wolfgang Kühnel, Renate Möller, & Matthias Ulbrich-Herrmann. (1995). *Gewalt. Schattenseiten der Individualisierung bei Jugendlichen aus unterschiedlichen Milieus.* Weinheim, München: Juventa.

Hilberg, Raul. (1996). *Täter, Opfer, Zuschauer. Die Vernichtung der Juden 1933–1945.* Frankfurt a. M.: Fischer.

Hitzler, Ronald. (1995). Sadomasochistische Rollenspiele. *Soziale Welt, 46,* 138–153.

Hugger, Paul, & Ulrich Stadler (Eds.) (1995). *Gewalt. Kulturelle Formen in Geschichte und Gegenwart.* Zürich: Unionsverlag.

Imbusch, Peter. (2000a). *Zivilisation und Gewalt.* Habilitationsschrift, Institut für Soziologie der Philipps-Universität Marburg.

Imbusch, Peter. (2000b). Gewalt – Stochern in unübersichtlichem Gelände. *Mittelweg, 36*(2), 24–40.

Imbusch, Peter. (2002). Macht und Herrschaft. In Hermann Korte & Bernhard Schäfers (Eds.), *Einführung in die Hauptbegriffe der Soziologie. 6. Aufl* (pp. 161–181). Opladen: Leske & Budrich.

Imbusch, Peter, & Ralf Zoll (Eds.) (1999). *Friedens- und Konfliktforschung. Eine Einführung.* Opladen: Leske & Budrich.

Inhetveen, Katharina. (1997). Gesellige Gewalt. Ritual, Spiel und Vergemeinschaftung bei Hardcorekonzerten. In Trutz von Trotha (Ed.), *Soziologie der Gewalt* (pp. 235–260). Opladen, Wiesbaden: Westdeutscher Verlag.

Jäger, Herbert. (1982). *Verbrechen unter totalitärer Herrschaft.* Frankfurt a. M.: Suhrkamp.

Jäger, Herbert. (1989). *Makrokriminalität. Studien zur Kriminologie kollektiver Gewalt.* Frankfurt a. M.: Suhrkamp.

Joas, Hans. (1994). Der Traum von der gewaltfreien Moderne. *Sinn und Form, 46*(2), 309–318.

Joas, Hans. (2000). *Kriege und Werte. Studien zur Gewaltgeschichte des 20. Jahrhunderts.* Weilerswist: Velbrück.

Kaase, Max, & Friedhelm Neidhardt. (1990). Politische Gewalt und Repression. Ergebnisse von Bevölkerungsumfragen. In Hans-Dieter Schwind, Jürgen Baumann, Friedrich Lösel, Helmut Remschmidt, Roland Eckert, Hans-Jürgen Kerner, Alfred Stümper, Rudolf Wassermann, Harro Otto & Walter Rudolf (Eds.), *Ursachen, Prävention und Kontrolle von Gewalt. Band IV* (pp. 7–71). Berlin: Duncker und Humblot.

Keeley, Lawrence. (1996). *War before Civilization. The Myth of the Peaceful Savage.* New York: Oxford University Press.

Kende, Istvan. (1982). *Kriege nach 1945. Eine empirische Untersuchung.* Frankfurt a. M.: Haag und Herchen.

Knöbl, Wolfgang, & Gunnar Schmidt. (2000). *Die Gegenwart des Krieges. Staatliche Gewalt in der Moderne.* Reinbek: Rowohlt.

Kurtz, Lester (Ed.) (1999). *Encyclopedia of Violence, Peace, Conflict. 3 Vols.* New York u. a.: Academic Press.

Lawrence, John. (1970). Violence. *Social Theory and Practice, 1*(2), 31–49.

Lindenberger, Thomas, & Alf Lüdtke (Eds.) (1995). *Physische Gewalt. Studien zur Geschichte der Neuzeit.* Frankfurt a. M.: Suhrkamp.

Linz, Juan J. (1975). Totalitarian and Authoritarian Regimes. In F.I. Greenstein & N.W Polsby (Eds.), *Handbook of Political Science, 3*, 175–411.

Litke, Robert F. (1992). Violence and Power. *International Social Science Journal, 132*, 173–183.

Luhmann, Niklas. (1995). Inklusion—Exklusion. In Niklas Luhmann, *Soziologische Aufklärung. Band 6: Die Soziologie und der Mensch* (pp. 237–264). Opladen: Westdeutscher Verlag.

Matthies, Volker. (1994). *Immer wieder Krieg?* Opladen: Leske & Budrich.

Miller, Max, & Hans-Georg Soeffner (Eds.) (1996). *Modernität und Barbarei. Soziologische Zeitdiagnose am Ende des 20. Jahrhunderts*. Frankfurt a. M.: Suhrkamp.

Moore, Barrington. (1974). *Soziale Ursprünge von Diktatur und Demokratie*. Frankfurt a. M.: Suhrkamp.

Narr, Wolf-Dieter. (1973). Gewalt und Legitimität. *Leviathan, 1*, 7–42.

Narr, Wolf-Dieter. (1978). Gewalt. In Ekkehard Lippert & Günther Wachtler (Eds.), *Frieden. Ein Handwörterbuch* (pp. 158–173). Opladen: Westdeutscher Verlag.

Narr, Wolf-Dieter. (1980). Physische Gewaltsamkeit, ihre Eigentümlichkeit und das Monopol des Staates. *Leviathan, 8*(4), 541–573.

Nedelmann, Birgitta. (1997). Gewaltsoziologie am Scheideweg. Die Auseinandersetzungen in der gegenwärtigen und Wege der künftigen Gewaltforschung. In Trutz von Trotha (Ed.), *Soziologie der Gewalt* (pp. 59–85). Opladen, Wiesbaden: Westdeutscher Verlag.

Neidhardt, Friedhelm. (1986). Gewalt. Soziale Bedeutungen und sozialwissenschaftliche Bestimmungen eines Begriffs. In Bundeskriminalamt (Ed.), *Was ist Gewalt? Auseinandersetzungen mit einem Begriff. Band 1: Strafrechtliche und sozialwissenschaftliche Darlegungen* (pp. 109–147). Wiesbaden: BKA.

O'Toole, Laura L., & Jessica Schiffman (Eds.) (1997). *Gender Violence. Interdisciplinary Perspectives*. New York: New York University Press.

Papcke, Sven. (1973). *Progressive Gewalt. Studien zum sozialen Widerstandsrecht*. Frankfurt a. M.: Fischer.

Parker, Geoffrey. (1990). *Die militärische Revolution. Die Kriegskunst und der Aufstieg des Westens 1500–1800*. Frankfurt a. M.: Fischer.

Platt, Thomas. (1992). The Concept of Violence as Descriptive and Polemic. *International Social Science Journal, 132*, 185–191.

Popitz, Heinrich. (1992). *Phänomene der Macht*. Tübingen: J.C.B. Mohr (Paul Siebeck).

Porter, Bruce. (1994). *War and the Rise of the State. The Military Foundations of Modern Politics*. New York.

Rauchfleisch, Udo. (1992). *Allgegenwart von Gewalt*. Göttingen: Vandenhoeck und Ruprecht.

Reemtsma, Jan Philipp. (2000). Die Gewalt spricht nicht. Zum Verhältnis von Macht und Gewalt. *Mittelweg, 36*(2), 4–23.

Reiss, Albert J., & Jeffrey A. Roth (Eds.) (1993ff). *Understanding and Preventing Violence*. 4 Vols. Washington DC: National Academic Press.

Röttgers, Kurt, & Heinz Sahner (Eds.) (1978). *Gewalt. Grundlagenprobleme in der Diskussion der Gewaltphänomene*. Basel, Stuttgart: Schwabe.

Scarry, Elaine. (1992). *Der Körper im Schmerz. Die Chiffren der Verletzlichkeit und die Erfindung der Kultur*. Frankfurt a. M.: Fischer.

Schroer, Markus. (2000). Gewalt ohne Gesicht. Zur Notwendigkeit einer umfassenden Gewaltanalyse. *Leviathan, 4*, 434–451.

Senghaas, Dieter. (1995). Frieden als Zivilisierungsprojekt. In Dieter Senghaas (Ed.), *Den Frieden denken* (pp. 196–223). Frankfurt a. M.: Suhrkamp.

Sieferle, Rolf Peter, & Helga Breuninger (Eds.) (1998). *Kulturen der Gewalt. Ritualisierung und Symbolisierung von Gewalt in der Geschichte*. Frankfurt a. M.: Campus.

Sofsky, Wolfgang. (1996). *Traktat über die Gewalt*. Frankfurt a. M.: Fischer.

Sofsky, Wolfgang. (1997). Gewaltzeit. In Trutz von Trotha (Ed.), *Soziologie der Gewalt* (pp. 102–121). Opladen, Wiesbaden: Westdeutscher Verlag.

Ternon, Yves. (1996). *Der verbrecherische Staat. Völkermord im 20. Jahrhundert*. Hamburg: Hamburger Edition.

Tilly, Charles. (1975). *The Formation of National States in Western Europe*. Princeton: Princeton University Press.

Tilly, Charles. (1985). War Making and State Making as Organized Crime." In Peter B. Evans, Dietrich Rueschemeyer & Theda Skocpol (Eds.), *Bringing the State Back in* (pp. 169–191). Cambridge et al.: Cambridge University Press.

Tilly, Charles. (1986). European Violence and Collective Action Since 1700. *Social Research, 53*(1), 159–184.

Tobler, Hans Werner, & Peter Waldmann (Eds.) (1991). *Staatliche und parastaatliche Gewalt in Lateinamerika*. Frankfurt a. M.: Vervuert.

Trotha, Trutz von (1997). Zur Soziologie der Gewalt. In Trutz von Trotha (Ed.), *Soziologie der Gewalt* (pp. 9–56). Opladen, Wiesbaden: Westdeutscher Verlag.

Waldmann, Peter. (1977). *Strategien politischer Gewalt*. Stuttgart et al.: Kohlhammer.

Waldmann, Peter. (1998). *Terrorismus. Provokation der Macht*. München: Gerling Akademie Verlag.

Waldmann, Peter. (1995). Politik und Gewalt. In Dieter Nohlen & Rainer-Olaf Schultze (Eds.), *Politische Theorien. Band 1 des Lexikon der Politik* (pp. 430–435). München: C.H. Beck.

Weber, Max. (1976). *Wirtschaft und Gesellschaft. Grundriss der verstehenden Soziologie*. Tübingen: J.C.B. Mohr (Paul Siebeck).

Wette, Wolfram, & Gerd R. Ueberschär (Eds.) (2001). *Kriegsverbrechen im 20. Jahrhundert*. Darmstadt: WBG.

Wetzstein, Thomas, Linda Steinmetz, Christa Reis, & Roland Eckert. (1993). *Sadomasochismus. Szenen und Rituale*. Reinbek: Rowohlt.

Zimmermann, Ekkart. (1977). *Soziologie der politischen Gewalt. Darstellung und Kritik vergleichender Aggregatdatenanalysen aus den USA*. Stuttgart: Ferdinand Enke.

Zimmermann, Ekkart. (1999). Politische Gewalt. Rebellion, Revolution, Krieg. In Günter Albrecht, Axel Groenemeyer, & Friedrich W. Stallberg (Eds.), *Handbuch soziale Probleme* (pp. 556–574). Opladen, Wiesbaden: Westdeutscher Verlag.

The Long-Term Development of Violence: Empirical Findings and Theoretical Approaches to Interpretation

Manuel Eisner

I. INTRODUCTION

Since the great theories of evolution in the nineteenth century, sociology has been interested in the question as to whether modernity should be interpreted as a process of civilization which, if it does not actually nip violence and barbarism in the bud, then at least limits their extent. The issue is dealt with within the parameters of two extremes: the optimistic narrative of progress, which sees civilization as the principle of modernization, and the pessimistic interpretation, which emphasizes the murderous potential of dynamics of coercion and discipline (Miller & Soeffner, 1996).

Thus, in the early 1980s, when Ted Robert Gurr (1981, 1989) first attempted a statistical overview of the development of murder and manslaughter from the Middle Ages to the present, he was driving right at the core of sociological interpretations of modernity. Gurr's analysis was based above all on evidence from England, where studies on the history of crime had produced statistics on the frequency of murder and manslaughter for several historical epochs. Gurr created a graph showing around twenty estimated values between 1200 and 1800 and added his own statistics on more recent developments. He produced an elegant curve, which begins with approximately twenty homicides per 100,000 inhabitants in the High and Late Middle Ages, and ends after a long gradual decline with around one case per 100,000 in the twentieth century. Gurr interpreted this trend as evidence for a long-term decrease in interpersonal violence, as "a manifestation of cultural

W. Heitmeyer and J. Hagan (eds.), *International Handbook of Violence Research*, 41–59.
© 2003 Kluwer Academic Publishers. Printed in the Netherlands.

change in Western society, especially the growing sensitization to violence and the development of increased internal and external control on aggressive behavior" (Gurr, 1981:258).

Since then crime historians have been involved in an increasingly intense debate centered on the old question as to the relationship between modernization and individual violence (see for example Johnson and Monkkonen, 1996; Pihlajamäki, 1991; Rousseaux, 1996). This debate is stoked by an increasing number of studies on the history of crime, which paint an ever richer and more varied picture of the historical manifestations of individual violence and now include far more regions of Europe than Gurr was able to consider twenty years ago. This broader range of findings now makes it possible to formulate the empirical questions in a more discriminating manner than was possible twenty years ago. For the secular development of individual violence, these questions might be as follows: How general is the long-term decline in murder and manslaughter? When did the decline take place? In which regions of Europe did the fall in homicide frequency first begin? Can any contrary trends be empirically proven? In the following I will consider three crucial issues which are at the center of this debate: What kind of data do we actually possess for long periods of time, and can these data be compared across time? Which long-term developments can we identify? And which theoretical approaches can explain the observed trends?

II. EMPIRICAL DEVELOPMENTS ON HOMICIDE

1. Sources and Data

For an investigation of secular trends in the development of violence the first question to be asked is: For which kinds of individual violence do we possess data which allow an evaluation of developments over time? Is it possible to make statistical observations on the frequency of bodily harm, rape, or robbery over several centuries? Today most crime historians would probably agree that it is not. Shifts in the intensity of prosecution, in crime reporting behavior, in the legal framework, and in the kind of sources and statistics available all make any conclusions concerning "real" trends behind the existing data at best hazardous. If there is any form of individual violence at all for which we can draw conclusions about historical shifts in frequency, then this is murder and manslaughter (see Chesnais, 1992; Österberg, 1996a; Sharpe, 1996). There are several reasons for this. First, since the High Middle Ages at the latest murder as a crimen capitale attracted great interest from all institutions of power and was normally dealt with in the high courts, whose activities were recorded from an early date (Rousseaux, 1999). Second, notwithstanding historical changes in the legal system, the significance of murder and manslaughter probably retained a relatively stable core over time. Certainly a study of medieval or early modern detailed descriptions allows the conclusion that the vast majority of cases would still be seen today as culpable homicides and not, for example, as accidents or cases of involuntary manslaughter (see for example Muchembled, 1984). Third, homicide is the only offence on which we have information other than court proceedings, thus allowing for comparison between different sources. Spierenburg (1996), for example, uses the autopsy reports made over several centuries by the city physicians of Amsterdam to compile estimates on the frequency of homicides. Similar information is provided by coroner's rolls from fourteenth-century England investigated by Hanawalt (1979), where royal coroners meticulously listed all the known cases of unusual deaths (murders, suicides, and accidents).

The advent of the statistical age, in most Western states between the late eighteenth and mid-nineteenth century, marks the most important caesura for the quantity and quality of historical statistical information on homicides. All quantitative information for the prestatistical age is based on laborious historiographic investigations of archive sources. The criminal proceedings files which are so important here were instigated in the thirteenth century as a consequence of refinements to and formalization of criminal law in the High Middle Ages (Rousseaux & Lévy, 1997). But, as a result of the fragmented legal systems in premodern Europe, the fact that sources are preserved by chance in a particular town or region, and the particular theoretical and empirical interests of researchers, we are dealing here with a patchwork of localized and temporally limited studies. Today, the boom in historical crime research over the last 20 years means that we nonetheless possess hundreds of studies of quantitative aspects of crime in medieval and early modern Europe (for overviews of research see Österberg, 1996a; Rousseaux, 1999; Schüssler, 1996; Sharpe, 1988; Ylikangas et al., 2000). As far as homicides are concerned, England, Scandinavia, and Belgium and the Netherlands are by far the best-documented regions. These studies present a remarkably rich picture, which is by no means limited to number counts for offenses and the kinds of sentence pronounced. Some studies, for example, provide an insight into the relationship between victims and perpetrators (Cockburn, 1991), profession and social status of the alleged offenders (Given, 1977; Muchembled, 1984), the weapons used, and situational conditions relating to the offense (Schüssler, 1991), or the age and gender of the victims (Spierenburg, 1996).

Statistics on cause of death are highly significant for analyses of long-term trends in the frequency of homicide since the nineteenth century. They are based on standardized classifications of the medically confirmed cause of death, and usually they contain at least statistical information on the age and gender of the victims. The earliest statistics on cause of death were introduced in Sweden and Finland (which belonged to Sweden at the time) in 1751 (von Hofer, 1991). By contrast, cause of death statistics are not found in most other Western European states until the second half of the nineteenth century. In some countries, other types of statistical data may be used to analyze long-term trends. England and Wales, and also Italy, for example, have kept police crime statistics which contain homicides registered with the police since the second half of the nineteenth century. In other countries such as France detailed court or sentencing statistics can provide information on trends.

Although homicides are probably the only form of violence for which meaningful observations on long-term developments can be made at all, the significant limitations of the available data must be noted (for critical discussions see Rousseaux, 1993, 1999; Sharpe, 1984; Stone, 1983). The incomplete nature of archives, changes in legal definitions, shifts in age structure and in medical capabilities, and also inaccuracies in population estimates all limit the comparability of homicide rates over long periods of time. Many of these problems, however, can at least partly be solved. Spierenburg (1996) and Monkkonen (1999, 2000), for example, use information on the time elapsed between the violent act and the actual death to estimate how many murder victims in earlier epochs might have been saved by today's medicine. Monkkonen was also the first to examine over a long period of time the extent to which changes in age structure distort overall homicide rates. In cases where data from various sources are available, it is also possible to use capture-recapture methods to test whether the same population statistics are found at different archive levels.

The closer an investigation gets to the present day, the easier it is to cross-validate statistics. The analyses show a very high degree of agreement for comparisons of sets of

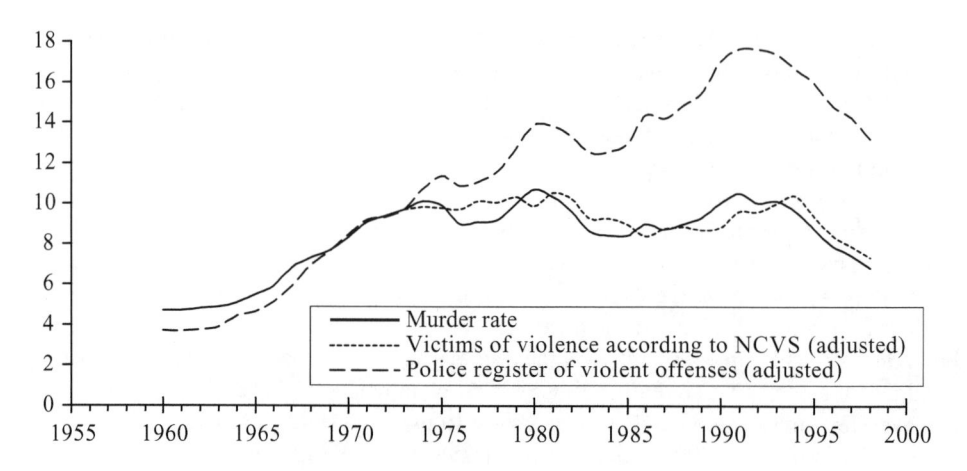

FIGURE I-3.1. **Homicide rate, police register of violent offenses, and victims of violence according to NCVS in comparison.** *Note*: Police data and data on victims adjusted to the year 1973. *Source*: U.S. Department of Justice, Bureau of Justice Statistics (http://www.ojp.usdoj.gov/bjs).

data on homicides committed (police statistics, cause of death statistics, sentencing statistics) (Cantor & Cohen, 1980; von Hofer, 1985). The picture is different, however, when homicide statistics and indicators for other forms of violence are compared. One impressive example of this is the clear discrepancy between the development of homicide rates and of police statistics on nonlethal violence since the 1950s. In most Western states the frequency of homicides increased two or threefold between the late 1950s and the early 1990s. Police statistics show, however, a five to twenty fold increase in cases of assault up to the present day. Research on this problem has now revealed that the massive increase of cases of assault in police statistics is mainly caused by a greater intensity of reporting and recording (for youth crime see for example Estrada, 1999). American statistics illustrate this best. Since 1973 the "National Crime Victim Survey" has included widely verified estimates for rates for victims of violence, independent of police activities. Figure I-3.1 compares these data with the data on police registered violent offenses and with the corresponding homicide rates. It reveals a massive discrepancy between the trends in police registered violent offenses ("aggravated assault," "robbery," and "rape") and the development of homicide rates. Yet there is near perfect agreement between the murder rate and the rate for victims of violent offenses in surveys of victims, although the reported experiences of violence are approximately five hundred times more frequent than homicides. Findings such as these support the thesis that homicides do represent a good general indication of levels of individual violence—even over long periods of time.

2. The Long-term Trend: Homicides from 1200–2000

In view of the great diversity of the sources, the inaccuracy of population counts, and historical shifts in legal concepts, some historians are skeptical about the usefulness of calculating homicide rates for medieval and early modern society (Schuster, 2000; Stone, 1983). Other crime historians such as Spierenburg (1991), or Johnson and Monkkonen

(1996), on the other hand, are of the view that the increasing number of well-founded studies will make it possible to assess the quality of available data, to compare local estimated values, and to put together a sound empirical picture which, whilst certainly remaining incomplete, will nonetheless permit broad trends to be assessed. In concurrence with this view, Eisner (2001) has drawn together all available quantitative analyses on the frequency and structure of homicides in premodern Europe in a systematic database. This task was made considerably easier by a number of recent overviews of research, including Spierenburg (1996) for the Netherlands, Österberg (1996a) for Sweden, Ylikangas (1998) and Ylikangas et al. (2000) for Finland, Eibach (1996) for Germany, and Rousseaux (1999) and Schüssler (1996) for various European regions.

Using around eighty primary publications to date, the database systematically codes all the available information on the numbers of recorded homicides, the regions and epochs investigated, the kind of sources used, maximum and minimum estimates for the relevant population size, and assessment of the quality of the primary data. If the information is available, details of the gender and age of victims and perpetrators, and details on the relationship between victims and perpetrators are also included. At the present time, the data set contains approximately 290 estimated values for homicide rates in the prestatistical age. On average, each estimate is based on an investigated period of about twenty years and about 100,000 inhabitants.

As a result of the geographical focus of the research used, five large regions can be identified in which existing studies allow a meaningful examination of secular trends. England is by far the best-documented region. Scandinavia is relatively well documented

TABLE I-3.1. Homicide rates in five European regions, 1200–2000

Period	England	Netherlands, Belgium	Scandinavia	Germany, Switzerland	Italy	All regions
13th and 14th c.	22	(83)	—	43	48	28
15th c.	—	38	32	(11)	32	28
16th c.	5.4	16	21	(8)	(50)	20
17th c., 1st half	5.9	5.0	33	—	—	14
17th c., 2nd half	3.5	4.3	10	(1.7)	—	4
18th c., 1st half	2.1	5.5	3.0	4.2	21	4
18th c., 2nd half	1.5	2.8	0.7	3.9	8.1	2.4
1800–24	1.2	1.5	1.0	2.6	11.0	3.4
1825–49	1.7	—	1.4	—	—	1.6
1850–74	1.6	0.9	1.2	2.1	—	1.5
1875–99	1.3	1.5	0.9	2.2	5.5	2.3
1900–1924	0.8	1.7	0.8	2.0	3.9	1.8
1925–49	0.8	1.3	0.6	1.4	2.6	1.3
1950–74	0.7	0.6	0.6	0.9	1.3	0.8
1975–94	1.2	1.2	1.2	1.2	1.7	1.3

Note: the numbers show the simple arithmetic mean of all estimates for the relevant period. Numbers given in parentheses are particularly dubious, since they are based on less than five individual estimates. Entries in italics are based on the relevant national statistics.

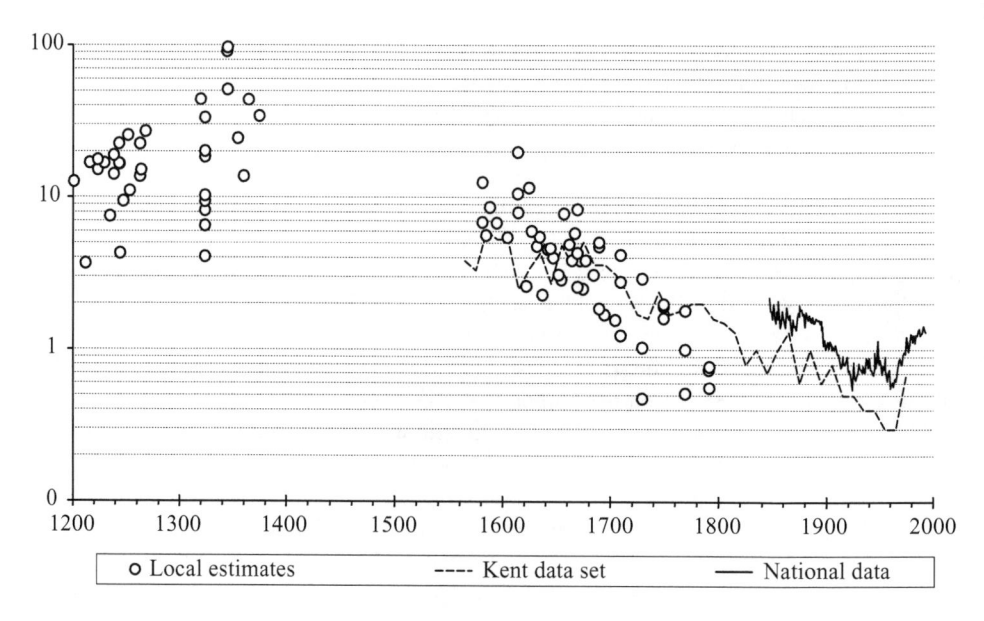

FIGURE I-3.2. Homicide rates in England.

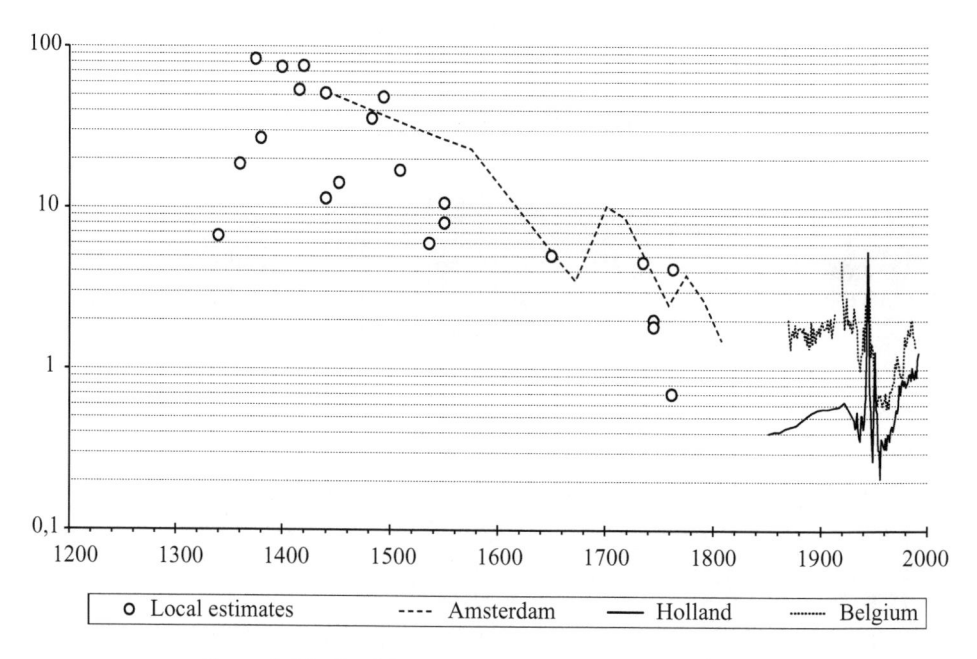

FIGURE I-3.3. Homicide rates in the Netherlands and Belgium.

for long periods of time, as is the region which today makes up Belgium and the Nether-lands. There are large temporal and regional gaps, however, for Italy and the German-speaking region, where southern Germany and Switzerland are best documented. The results of the meta-analyses can be summarized in terms of five fundamental findings (see Table I-3.1 and Figures I-3.2–6) (for a detailed discussion of the findings see Eisner, 2001).

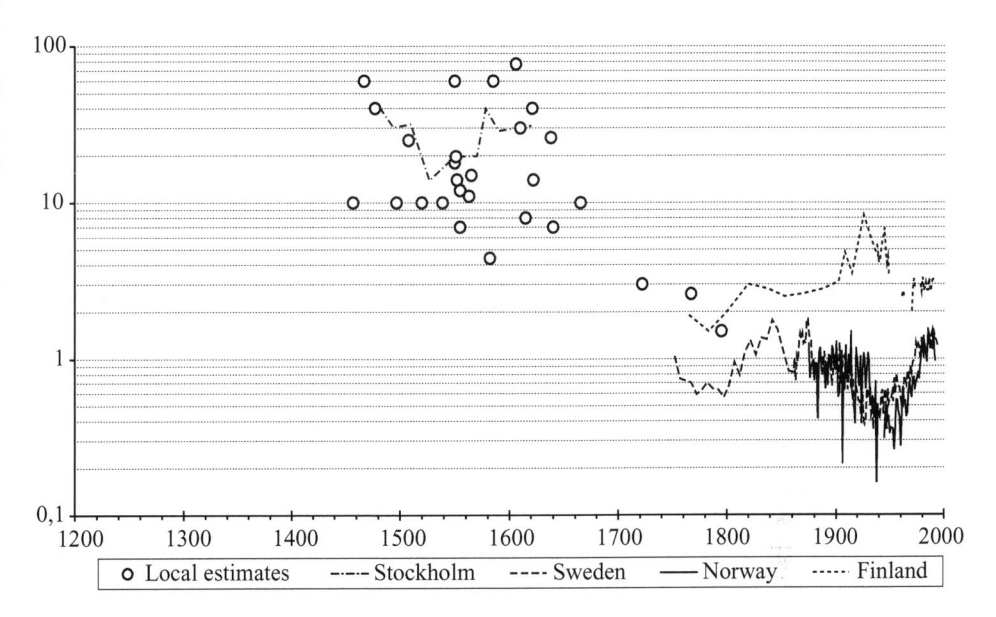

FIGURE I-3.4. Homicide rates in Scandinavia.

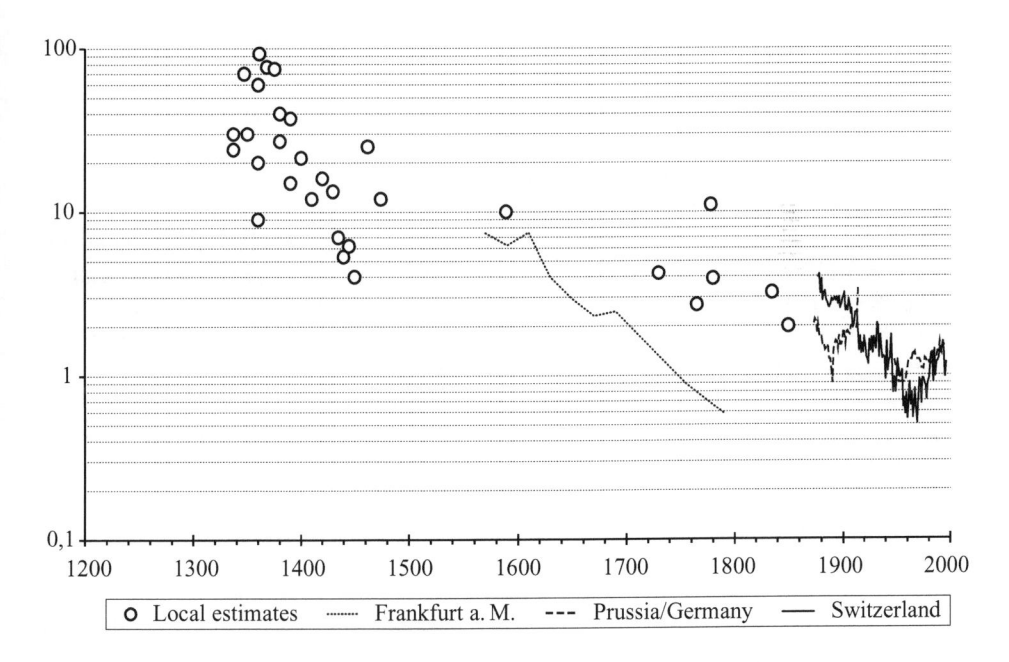

FIGURE I-3.5. Homicide rates in Germany and Switzerland.

These statistics confirm, firstly, the assumption of a long-term decrease in homicide rates over many centuries. Figures I-3.2–6 show this development for Scandinavia, England, the Netherlands and Belgium, the German-speaking region, and Italy. These regions are now relatively well documented by a comparatively large number of studies. Until the middle of the sixteenth century, homicide rates as derived from archive sources typically

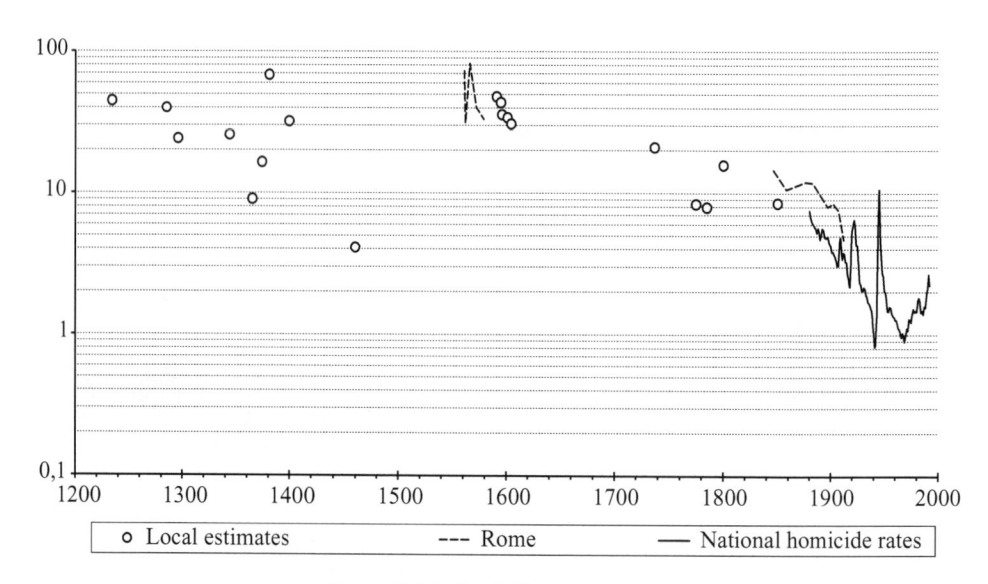

FIGURE I-3.6. Homicide rates in Italy.

averaged twenty-five to thirty offenses per 100,000 inhabitants. From the sixteenth century to the advent of national statistics there is a remarkably strong decline in homicide rates. And at the end of the eighteenth century typical local estimates for Sweden, the Netherlands, and England were as low as 0.5–1.5 offenses per 100,000 inhabitants. This difference between the centuries is so large that there can hardly be any further doubt that the process of European modernization saw a secular decline in the individual use of violence.

Secondly, the above values allow at least a rough estimate as to when the dynamics of declining homicide rates set in. Both the analysis of the data and assessments by experts on the history of crime permit the conclusion that the late sixteenth century can be seen as the turning point, after which European homicide rates assume a clear downward trend. The averages do indicate a small decrease in homicide rates from perhaps thirty to twenty capital offenses per 100,000 inhabitants for the period from the fourteenth to the sixteenth centuries, but the low reliability of data makes it impossible to draw any definite conclusions here. In contrast, the documented data clearly show that homicide rates declined by a factor of about five to ten between the sixteenth and the eighteenth centuries. After that the rate of decline slows and for the whole of the twentieth century the average for seven European states is 1.3 capital offenses per 100,000 inhabitants.

Thirdly, the statistics indicate that the transformation from a society marked by high homicide rates to a society with low homicide rates involved considerable regional differences. It seems to be the case that by the late sixteenth century English homicide rates were already notably lower than in the Late Middle Ages, and that they generally declined according to a log-linear trend over several centuries. Available estimates suggest that the secular trend in the Netherlands and Belgium was very similar. In Sweden, however, the phase of declining homicide rates clearly begins later, around the middle of the seventeenth century. For Italy, all available data suggest that individual violent offenses remained very frequent into the early nineteenth century and probably only began a downward trend in the middle of the nineteenth century, which then was particularly steep. As far as the German-speaking region is concerned, it can at least be noted that homicide rates in the towns in the High and Late Middle Ages conform with the findings for other regions, and that by the second half of the eighteenth century, at the latest, the frequency of homicide was much lower. The incomplete nature of the data means that it is not even possible to speculate about the development in the intermediate period.

These regional differences can be imagined as the gradual emergence of a kind of "violence dip," which originates with the pioneers of the modernization process, England and Holland, in the sixteenth century and gradually reaches further regions in secular dynamics. This image certainly concurs with the statistically well-documented observation that the regional distribution of homicide rates in Europe in the nineteenth and early twentieth centuries had the shape of a central lowland plain surrounded by higher ground. For the late nineteenth century, Durkheim (1983:416) had already identified a circle of high murder rates, which led from Ireland, through Spain, the south of France, Italy, Austria and Hungary, and surrounded a zone of lower homicide frequency. In addition, a cartographic presentation by Chesnais (1981) confirms the findings for the 1920s, that there were low homicide rates in all the countries of north-west and western Europe, around which there was a belt of high homicide rates stretching from Portugal, the south of France, the south of Italy, through the eastern European states, and up to Finland.

Finally, the data reveal a number of counter movements to the long-term trend. Before the twentieth century these medium-term increases probably reflect regional peculiarities, which may be linked to phases of accelerated social change and political unrest. Such phases have been observed for England around 1620 (Sharpe, 1984:60f.), for example, in Amsterdam around 1700 (Spierenburg, 1996:83), and in Sweden and England in the early decades of the nineteenth century (Emsley, 1996; von Hofer, 1991). An increase in homicide rates over the past forty years, however, can be observed in all European states (with the exception of Finland). This increase by no means represents a return to the premodern frequency of homicide, but it is true that improved medical capabilities and changes in age structure—a lower share of younger age cohorts—tend to mean that the increase is underestimated. In my view, this development thus represents a significant shift, which requires interpretation in the light of the secular trends (see Eisner, 1995, 1997).

3. Contextual Changes: Age, Gender, and Social Relationship

Today there are a number of studies which tabulate and interpret homicide rate estimates over several centuries (for example Gurr, 1981; Österberg, 1996a; Rousseaux, 1996). There have been very few attempts, however, at systematic analysis of other features of homicides in a secular perspective. This is certainly surprising since many studies compile information about the gender of perpetrators and victims, and some investigations also provide data on the relationship between perpetrators and victims, their age, the situational context of the offense, or the weapons used. It seems to be the case, for example, that in medieval and early modern Europe social and territorial outsiders had a higher than average involvement in homicides (Schüssler, 1991), that taverns and other public meeting places were a typical violent context (Hammer, 1978), and that disputes of honor between young men regularly escalated into violence (Spierenburg, 1998b). I will demonstrate the potential for systematic analysis of this type of information using three examples.

Many sources include information about the gender of the perpetrators, going as far back as archive data from the Middle Ages (for an overview see Jütte, 1991). Where this

TABLE I-3.2. Percentage of female offenders, selected time periods and geographical regions

Region	Time period	Female offenders as % of total	Source
England	13th c.	9 %	Given, 1977:169
Norfolk	1300–1348	7 %	Hanawalt, 1976:268
Nuremberg	1285–1400	2 %	Schüssler, 1991:178
Utrecht	15th c.	4 %	Berents, 1985:140
Essex	1620–80	16 %	Sharpe, 1983:124
Surrey	1663–1802	13 %	Beattie, 1975:90
France	1830s	12 %	Perrot and Robert, 1989:27
German Reich	1890s	8 %	Johnson, 1995:189
United States	1990s	11 %	Sourcebook of Criminal Justice Statistics 1994–1998 (ed. U. S. Department of Justice)
Switzerland	1990s	10 %	Police Criminal Statistics 1990–1999 (ed. Bundesamt für Kriminalwesen)

information has been investigated, it reveals a remarkably constant picture. Table I-3.2 shows selected findings on the proportion of female homicide offenders. From the thirteenth century to the present day, the proportion of women among all recorded perpetrators seems never to have been more than 20 percent. Typically the proportion remained at 5–12 percent over eight centuries. This very broad stability of the female proportion across large geographical regions, and long periods of history, and within very large differences in the frequency of violence, is exceptionally remarkable, and has not received sufficient theoretical attention to date.

The situation is different for the proportion of female victims. Where estimates for medieval and early modern Europe are available, they show a consistently and remarkably

TABLE I-3.3. Percentage of female victims of homicide, selected time periods and geographical regions

Region	Time period	Female victims as % of total	Source
Oxford	1340s	0 %	Hammer, 1977
Nuremberg	1285–1400	9 %	Schüssler, 1996:178
England	14th/15th c.	4–10 %	Hanawalt, 1976:306
Amsterdam	1667–1816	21 %	Spierenburg, 1996:85
Prussia	1887–1907	30 %	Johnson, 1995:224
Switzerland	1876–1899	31 %	Bundesamt für Statistik, Cause of death satistics, unpublished tables
Switzerland	1900–1949	40 %	Ibid.
Switzerland	1950–1994	51 %	Ibid.
Switzerland	1990s	45 %	Ibid.

low proportion of female victims. Most studies on this period indicate a proportion of female victims of less than 10 percent. It is not until the seventeenth and eighteenth centuries that the share of female victims gradually begins to rise—with the general homicide rate now much lower. In today's societies women generally make up 30–50 percent of victims of homicides. One argument here could be that the lower proportion of female victims in earlier periods is a result of the low rate of registration and prosecution of violent offenses in the family. There are probably more arguments in favor of Verkko's (1967) old thesis, however, that societies with a high homicide frequency normally also have a high proportion of male victims.

A third dimension, which would in principle provide important insight for an understanding of long-term trends, is information on the personal relationships between victims and perpetrators. This kind of information can already be found relatively frequently in early modern sources, but to date there have been no attempts to examine the data as a whole. Existing studies on isolated aspects of the issue certainly present remarkable findings. Foremost among these is Cockburn's (1991) study of homicides which were brought before the assize courts in the county of Kent between 1560 and 1959. One of Cockburn's conclusions is that for all known cases the proportion of offenses against children, servants, and apprentices follows a long-term downward trend. Here Cockburn emphasizes that, as far as the early figures are concerned, there will have been a very high number of unreported cases of infanticide. In contrast, the proportion of homicides of adult members of the family shows a clear increase from approximately 11 percent in the late sixteenth century to 28 percent in the first half of the twentieth century. Spierenburg (1996:91) has noted similar findings for Amsterdam. Whilst overall homicide rates fell sharply between the late seventeenth and the late eighteenth centuries, the relative share of offenses against members of the family (intimates) increased during this period from 11 percent to 47 percent. At the same time the share of homicides of strangers decreased from 47 percent to 15 percent. Insofar as these findings reflect real trends, they add a significant dimension to our understanding of the long-term development. They show that the secular decline of homicide rates in Europe up to the middle of the twentieth century was probably accompanied by an above average decline in fatal encounters between men—neighbors or strangers—coming into conflict with one another in public spaces (on the history of the role of honor in violent offenses see Burghartz, 1990; Simon-Muscheid, 1991; Spierenburg, 1998b).

III. THEORETICAL APPROACHES

Notwithstanding the great increase in research, many details relating to the long-term development of homicides are still unclear, but it can be said that there is now a broad consensus on the general trend patterns. Most scholars also share the view that the secular history of murder and manslaughter can only be understood in the context of a broad perspective, in which it is necessary to consider changes of social structures of power, legal developments, questions of mentality, and cultural and economic conditions. In the following I will discuss the most important approaches to interpretation and a number of unresolved questions.

An obvious theoretical starting point, which has been frequently used in research, is Norbert Elias's theory of civilization (1976, 1983). As is well known, this is based on a bold combination of societal macroprocesses, changes in internal or psychological structures, and the resulting transformation of typical patterns of individual behavior. Elias's thesis is that over a gradual process lasting several centuries a dominant personality type emerges, which is characterized by a high degree of regulation of the emotions, a reduction in their intensity, and a planned, rational approach to life. All of this amounts to an increased level of self-control. Elias sees two interlinked processes as central causes of this process of psychological transformation. On the one hand, there is the process of the formation of nation states and the assertion of the state monopoly of violence leading to pacified social spaces, in which social status is achieved less as a result of the physical potential for violence than through education, good manners, and economic success. On the other hand, Elias argues that in the course of modernity the growth of markets and transport facilities extends chains of interdependence, and that planning and self-control thereby gain greater significance.

This series of arguments is sometimes taken up with near total agreement in current debate on the history of crime—as by Spierenburg (1996). Frequently it is critically modified (see for example Stone, 1983) and sometimes refuted as being completely insufficient (Schuster, 2000). It should at least be noted that, beyond the secular decline expected by Elias, a civilization theory framework is able to accommodate various empirical regularities. Among these is the observation made by several researchers, that the decline between the Late Middle Ages and the early modern period was evidently accompanied by a decrease in the involvement of members of the upper classes in homicides (see for example Österberg, 1996b:55; Sharpe, 1988:129), and the fact that in the European context phases of particularly fast decline in rates of homicide frequently coincide with phases of expansion and internal stabilization of the state, as the examples of seventeenth-century Sweden or post-unification Italy show.

Of all the more recent analyses of long-term developments in criminal violence, Spierenburg most strongly adheres to the civilization theory of Norbert Elias (Spierenburg, 1991). He argues that the secular decline in individual violence in European history should be interpreted as an aspect of a shift in mentality, with identification with the other and empathy for the suffering of the other at its core. In this context Spierenburg sees the decline of torture, public executions, and corporal punishment, and the decline in individual violence as equally fundamental manifestations of the general process toward higher levels of civilization. In more recent studies Spierenburg has linked the civilization theory approach to the secular decline in violence with thoughts on the function of concepts of masculinity in historical change (Spierenburg, 1998a). He argues that in pre-industrial Europe the concept of male honor was strongly linked to the ability and willingness to gain respect and power, if necessary through the use of physical force (Spierenburg, 1998a:6). With the spread of the market economy in the early modern European centers, an ideal of masculinity linking male honor more strongly to economic success became established. In addition the institution of the duel ritualized and domesticated the settling of conflicts.

1. The Formation of Institutions and Disciplining

One central weakness of the theory of the civilization process for explaining long-term trends in homicide frequency concerns the question of how to conceive in detail the link between very general concepts such as "the formation of monopolies," or "the extension of chains of interdependence," and historical changes in real lifestyle, the actual setting of violence. Elias's evolution theory can only offer an incomplete theoretical framework for investigating the influence of legal ideas and practices of sanction on the perception of violence, or the connection between forms of everyday social conflict and modes of deal-ing with conflict. A number of historians of crime have therefore attempted to find more historically discriminating concepts.

Here the concept of "social disciplining," developed by the social historian Gerhard Oestreich and based on Max Weber, seems to be particularly useful (Breuer, 1986; Oestreich, 1968; Schulze, 1987). In comparison to Elias, this approach produces more precise hy-potheses on the onset of declining frequencies of violence and the social processes which contributed to this. Oestreich argues that between the mid-sixteenth and mid-seventeenth century there was a massive intensification of forms of penetrating and systemized social control which took place in all the various models of statehood. On the political and ad-ministrative level, these forms of control include the creation of central administrative and judicial organizations, which increasingly placed social conflicts within a legal context. In addition there is the consolidation of bureaucratic control of everyday life, for the purpose of raising taxes for example, and also the instigation and expansion of state armies (Tilly, 1992). In this context Oestreich particularly emphasizes a number of regulating and disci-plining encroaches into everyday life, which derive from an ever tighter net of regulations from above on such matters as clothing, the consumption of alcohol, or the attendance of religious services (Frank, 1995). In a similar way, van Dülmen (1993, 1996) investigates European cultural history of the early modern period and argues that social disciplining should be understood as the result of a complex interaction of various social forces. Along-side intensifying state power, the increase in denominationalism at the time of the Refor-mation and Counter-Reformation, the expansion of the school system, and the early capitalist organization of labor should all be seen as independent causes of the process of the disci-plining of everyday life in the early modern period.

Using a similar framework of interpretation, Rousseaux has examined the shifts in legal ideas and penal practices relating to homicides (Rousseaux, 1999). He shows that particularly in the period between the second half of the sixteenth century and the early seventeenth century homicides were subjected to a wave of control and repression across broad regions of Europe. Tolerance of forms of manslaughter which had been seen as excusable cases of killing in the Middle Ages dwindles, private means of dealing with violent events are eradicated, penal measures are intensified, and state involvement is extended. It is precisely at this period that the steep and irreversible decline in homicide in northern Europe sets in. In the light of these findings, it would seem sensible to consider the effect of the religious reform movements since the middle of the sixteenth century in any interpretation of processes of social and self-disciplining, and the corresponding ways of dealing with violence. This approach would then lead to an interpretation of secular homicide rates in terms of a theory of modernization and would involve a stronger link to Max Weber than has been the case in research to date. As is well known, Weber saw Protestantism, with its emphasis on values such as the fulfillment of duty, sobriety, and a methodical approach to life, as an all-encompassing project in disciplining, with methodi-cal and systematic self-control in all areas of life at its core (Weber, 1920).

2. From Collectivism to Individualism

A further obvious problem in Elias's civilization theory is that the medieval individual is seen as a childlike personality, deficient in terms of civilization. This individual is pre-sented as a being driven by instinct, and lacking shame or reason, with unbridled aggression manifested in spontaneous outbreaks of violence. Much of this is reminiscent of Hobbes's notion of the original struggle of each against the other, which is neutralized by the power of the Leviathan in the form of the modern state.

Most crime historians today believe that this view neither does justice to medieval society, nor to the process of modernization (Muchembled, 1984; Schuster, 2000; Stone, 1983). Yet to this day, the search for alternative theoretical approaches has not made much progress. One remarkable approach to explaining secular trends in a new theoretical light was recently presented by Thome (Thome, 1995; for a similar approach Eisner, 2001). Thome looks at the possibility of using the theory of anomie derived from Emile Durkheim to interpret the long-term development of violence. Forty years before Elias, Durkheim had postulated that the number of murders would decrease with the progress of civilization (Durkheim, 1991:161). In work which to date has been largely neglected by crime historians, Durkheim developed a theoretical structure which can be read as a counterthesis to Elias's civilization theory. In particular, Durkheim strongly rejects the thesis—popular long before Elias—that a high frequency of violence could be interpreted as an expression of an instinctual primal condition which is then contained by cultural institutions. Rather, individual violence should always be interpreted as a product of a particular moral culture, a component of the cultural context (Durkheim, 1991). Secondly, Durkheim does not view the decline in capital offenses as the consequence of the coercive and disciplining potential of the state, as is central to Elias's theory, but as the result of the liberation of the individual from collective responsibilities (on this see in particular Thome, 2000). Thus, for Durkheim, high frequencies of violence are an expression of the intensity of passionate "collective emotions," which bind the individual "to groups or objects which are symbolic for these groups," and Durkheim points in particular to the tradition of blood feuds in this context (Durkheim, 1991). Violence declines in proportion to the degree to which the individual is freed from a sacred responsibility to the collective and an individualistic culture facilitates both a higher level of subjective reflection and higher emotional indifference in conflict situations.

This approach will probably open up promising new and better ways of understanding the causes and processes relating to the secular decline in homicide. Far more than Elias's model, Durkheim's approach offers a theoretical framework for analyzing the manifold ways in which violence was culturally constituent to medieval society, in particular the significance of violations of honor in inciting conflict which has been frequently noted in research (Burghartz, 1990; Muchembled, 1984; Schuster, 2000; Schwerhoff, 1991). This is characteristic of a society, in which "honor" is an essential social value for the (male) individual as a representative of the group, and in which the use of avenging violence to preserve honor at all costs amounts to a culturally sanctioned requirement (see Schmidt, 1994).

An approach based on Durkheim also opens up a more plausible view of the transformations of the image of the individual and shifts in sensibility since the early modern period. For example, theoretical considerations may benefit considerably from Charles Taylor's study of the making of modern identity (Taylor, 1989). There Taylor describes the cultural diffusion of a specifically modern, individualized ideal of the self, whose key features he sees to be "disengagement" and "inwardness." This involves a methodically guided, reflective distance from the given external and internal world, and an orientation on ideals such as autonomy, responsibility, and authenticity. This development does follow a cultural and intellectual logic of its own, but it is linked with mutually reinforcing religious, political, economic, and artistic practices (Taylor, 1989:206). In this context Taylor refers, for example, to the permanent self-examination in the religious reform movements, the increasing definition of an independent private sphere, the emergence of a market shored up by contracts, and artistic production along the lines of individual originality. Social disciplining is thus certainly a central feature of early modernity, but the age of the sixteenth and early seventeenth centuries equally represents the emergence of the specifically modern individual which Durkheim assumes is responsible for the decline in individual violence (van Dülmen, 1997; Junge, 1996; Taylor, 1989). This would mean that the secular decline in violence took place especially in those regions where institutional structures and educational practices supported the stabilization and spread of that type of individualized identity that is designed for the requirements of the lifestyle of the modern age.

3. Fluctuations

A final problem I would like to raise has direct implications for contemporary debate. It concerns the issue of fluctuations and deviations from the model sketched out above. For the prestatistical period, it is not possible to go beyond isolated cases of speculation on this issue. Some crime historians have noticed, for example, that both in England and in the German-speaking region (the only two geographical regions for which there is a larger number of studies on the High Middle Ages) estimated homicide rates for the period after the great plagues of 1348 were considerably higher than in the preceding periods (Hanawalt, 1995). Whether this is really the case, will probably never be known with certainty. For the statistical age, however, it is possible to identify several phases when homicide frequencies rose conspicuously over several decades. This was the case, for example, in Sweden from the late seventeenth to the mid-eighteenth century, when homicide rates nearly trebled. In a similar way national statistics from France, Belgium, and Prussia suggest an increase in numbers of killings in the years before World War I (Chesnais, 1981; Johnson, 1995; Thome, 1992). And we find an almost universal increase in homicide rates from the late 1950s to the early 1990s. But there exist more deviations. In particular, the trends sketched out above represent an adequate description of experience in various regions of western Europe. However, in spite of considerable reductions in the last ten years, many American cities still display homicide rates which are reminiscent of conditions in early modern Europe. In addition, the long-term trend in the United States fails to comply with the picture of secular decline. Monkkonen (1999), for example, has investigated the development in New York between 1830 and 1990. His data do not show so much a long-term trend, but rather a sequence of cycles with phases of higher homicide frequency in the 1860s and the 1930s, and an explosion in homicide rates between 1970 and 1990. There is a similar problem for the less well-known case of Finland, where homicide rates showed a steep increase up to around 1910, and notwithstanding some decline still remain at levels which are atypically high for Europe.

Observers who look at these phenomena from the point of view of civilization theory tend to interpret them rather helplessly as deviations from the general trend (see for example Franke, 1994; Gurr, 1981; Spierenburg, 1996). In this case, however, there must be a theoretically substantiated hypothesis as to which modernization processes cause these deviations from the general pattern. One possibility, suggested by Thome (1995, 2001), understands the dynamics of modernization as a conflictual relationship between anomic forces engendering violence on the one hand, and civilizing forces on the other. According to this view, temporary increases in homicide frequency would occur when the anomic and disintegrative forces of social change are dominant. In a similar way Heitmeyer (1994) and Eisner (1997), for example, support the thesis that since the 1960s the interplay of economic polarization and cultural and social individualization has produced a society in which the risk of outsider situations and social disintegration as a potential for violence has considerably increased. From this perspective follows the difficult task, however, of empirically proving this interplay and then testing whether it really can explain any "deviations" from the basic pattern.

IV. CONCLUSION

Theoretical reflection begins wherever differences are observed. As the number of structured differences that can be observed increases, discriminating theoretical arguments become more meaningful. Over the last thirty years, research into crime history has made enormous progress in painting an increasingly detailed picture of long-term developments in violent crime in Europe. Today it is possible to sketch in broad terms the development of murder and manslaughter frequencies over eight centuries, to present at least an approximate description of the decisive turning points, and to do more than just speculate about broad differences. But that is not all. As I have attempted to show, a systematic reanalysis of existing studies would probably make it possible to draw relatively well-founded conclusions over longer periods of time on such questions as the gender of perpetrators and victims, the nature of relationships and motives at different historical periods, and the participation of various social classes in this fundamental form of individual violence. This information will then represent a contribution to the ongoing debate among crime historians on the connection between social modernization and individual violence, and it will help to decide between alternative approaches to interpretation. Furthermore, knowledge of the frequency and structure of individual violence in earlier historical phases represents an increasingly significant test case for theories on violence in the present day and the question as to how far these can be generalized.

Translated by Tradukas

REFERENCES

Beattie, J. M. (1975). The Criminality of Women in 18th Century England. *Journal of Social History, 8*, 80–116.

Berents, Dirk Arend. (1985). *Het werk van de vor. Samenleving an criminaliteit in de late middeleeuwen.* Zutphen: Walburg Press.

Breuer, Stefan. (1986). Sozialdisziplinierung. Probleme und Problemverlagerungen eines Konzeptes bei Max Weber, Gerhard Oestreich und Michel Foucault. In Christoph Sachße & Florian Tennstedt (Eds.), *Soziale Sicherheit und soziale Disziplinierung. Beiträge zu einer historischen Theorie der Sozialpolitik* (pp. 45–69). Frankfurt a. M.: Suhrkamp.

Burghartz, Susanna. (1990). *Leib, Ehre und Gut. Delinquenz in Zürich Ende des 14. Jahrhunderts.* Zürich: Chronos.

Cantor, David, & Lawrence E. Cohen. (1980). Comparing Measures of Homicide Trends: Methodological and Substantive Differences in the Vital Statistics and Uniform Crime Report Time Series. *Social Science Research, 9*, 121–145.

Chesnais, Jean-Claude. (1981). *Histoire de la Violence en Occident de 1800 à nos jours.* Paris: Robert Laffont.

Chesnais, Jean-Claude. (1992). The History of Violence and Suicide through the Ages. *International Social Science Journal, 44*(2), 217–234.

Cockburn, J. S. (1991). Patterns of Violence in English Society: Homicide in Kent, 1560–1985. *Past and Present, 130*, 70–106.

Dülmen, Richard van. (1993). *Gesellschaft der frühen Neuzeit: kulturelles Handeln und sozialer Prozess. Beiträge zur historischen Kulturforschung.* Wien: Böhlau.

Dülmen, Richard van. (1996). Norbert Elias und der Prozess der Zivilisation. Die Zivilisationstheorie im Lichte der historischen Forschung. In Karl-Siegbert Rehberg (Eds.), *Norbert Elias und die Menschenwissenschaften. Studien zur Entstehung und Wirkungsgeschichte seines Werkes* (pp. 264–274). Frankfurt a. M.: Suhrkamp.

Dülmen, Richard van. (1997). Die Entdeckung des Individuums, 1500–1800. Frankfurt a. M.: Fischer.

Durkheim, Emile. (1983). *Der Selbstmord.* Frankfurt a. M.: Suhrkamp.

Durkheim, Emile. (1991). *Physik der Sitten und des Rechts. Vorlesungen zur Soziologie der Moral.* Frankfurt a. M.: Suhrkamp.

Eibach, Joachim. (1996). Kriminalitätsgeschichte zwischen Sozialgeschichte und historischer Kulturforschung. *Historische Zeitschrift, 263*(3), 681–715.

Eisner, Manuel. (1995). The Effects of Economic Structures and Phases of Development on Crime. In Council of Europe (Ed.), *Crime and Economy. Criminological Research, Vol. 32* (pp. 13–52). Strasbourg: Council of Europe.

Eisner, Manuel. (1997). *Das Ende der zivilisierten Stadt? Die Auswirkungen von Individualisierung und urbaner Krise auf Gewaltdelinquenz.* Frankfurt a. M.: Campus.

Eisner, Manuel. (2001). Modernization, Self-control and Lethal Violence; the Long-Term Dynamics of European Homicide Rates in Theoretical Perspective. *British Journal of Criminology, 41*, 618–638.

Elias, Norbert. (1976). *Über den Prozess der Zivilisation. Soziogenetische und psychogenetische Untersuchungen.* Frankfurt a. M.: Suhrkamp.

Elias, Norbert. (1983). *Die höfische Gesellschaft. Untersuchungen zu einer Soziologie des Königtums und der höfischen Aristokratie.* Frankfurt a. M.: Suhrkamp.

Emsley, Clice. (1996). *Crime and Society in England, 1750–1900.* Harlow: Longman.

Estrada, Felipe. (1999). Juvenile Crime Trends in Postwar Europe. *European Journal of Criminal Policy and Research, 7*(1), 23–42.

Frank, Michael. (1995). *Dörfliche Gesellschaft und Kriminalität. Das Fallbeispiel Lippe 1650–1800.* Paderborn: Ferdinand Schöningh.

Franke, Herman. (1994). Violent Crime in the Netherlands. A Historical-Sociological Analysis. *Crime, Law, and Social Change, 20*(1), 73–100.

Given, James B. (1977). *Society and Homicide in Thirteenth-century England.* Stanford: Stanford University Press.

Gurr, Ted Robert. (1981). Historical Trends in Violent Crime: A Critical Review of the Evidence. *Crime and Justice. An Annual Review of Research, 3*, 295–350.

Gurr, Ted Robert. (1989). Historical Trends in Violent Crime: Europe and the United States. In Ted Robert Gurr (Ed.), *Violence in America, Vol. 1: The History of Crime* (pp. 21–54). Newbury Park: Sage.

Hammer, Carl I., Jr. (1978). Patterns of Homicide in a Medieval University Town: Fourteenth-Century Oxford. *Past and Present, 78*, 3–23.

Hanawalt, Barbara A. (1976). Violent Death in Fourteenth and Early Fifteenth-Century England. *Comparative Studies in Society and History, 18*, 297–320.

Hanawalt, Barbara A. (1979). *Crime and Conflict in English Communities, 1300–1348.* Cambridge: Cambridge University Press.

Hanawalt, Barbara A. (1995). Obverse of the Civilizing Process in Medieval England. *International Association for the History of Crime and Criminal Justice Bulletin, 20*, 49–59.

Heitmeyer, Wilhelm. (1994). Entsicherungen. Desintegrationsprozesse und Gewalt. In Ulrich Beck & Elisabeth Beck-Gernsheim (Eds.), *Riskante Freiheiten* (pp. 376–401). Frankfurt a. M.: Suhrkamp.

Hofer, Hanns von. (1985). *Brott och straff i Sverige. Historisk kriminalstatistik 1750–1984.* Stockholm: Urval.

Hofer, Hanns von. (1991). Homicide in Swedish Statistics 1750–1988. In Annika Snare (Ed.), *Criminal Violence in Scandinavia: Selected Topics* (pp. 30–45). Oslo: Norwegian University Press.

Johnson, Eric A. (1995). *Urbanization and Crime. Germany 1871–1914.* Cambridge: Cambridge University Press.

Johnson, Eric A., & Eric H. Monkkonen (Eds.) (1996). *Violent Crime in Town and Country Since the Middle Ages.* Illinois: University of Illinois Press.

Junge, Matthias. (1996). Individualisierungsprozesse und der Wandel von Institutionen: ein Beitrag zur Theorie reflexiver Modernisierung. *Kölner Zeitschrift für Soziologie und Sozialpsychologie, 48*(4), 728–747.

Jütte, Robert. (1991). Geschlechtsspezifische Kriminalität im Späten Mittelalter und in der frühen Neuzeit. *Zeitschrift der Savigny-Stiftung für Rechtsgeschichte, Germanistische Abteilung, 108*, 86–103.

Miller, Max, & Hans-Georg Soeffner (Eds.) (1996). *Modernität und Barbarei. Soziologische Zeitdiagnose am Ende des 20. Jahrhunderts.* Frankfurt a. M.: Suhrkamp.

Monkkonen, Eric. (1999). New York City Offender Ages. How Variable Over Time? *Homicide Studies, 3*(3), 256–269.

Monkkonen, Eric. (2000). American Homicide Rates: New Estimates. Paper presented at the European Social Science History Conference, 12–15 April 2000, Amsterdam.

Muchembled, Robert. (1984). Crime et Société Urbaine: Arras au Temps de Charles Quint (1528–1549). In Pierre Goubert, *La France d'Ancien Régime. Etudes Réunies en l'honneur de Pierre Goubert* (pp. 481–490). Toulouse: Ed. Privat.

Oestreich, Gerhard. (1968). Strukturprobleme des europäischen Absolutismus. *Vierteljahreszeitschrift für Sozial- und Wirtschaftsgeschichte, 55,* 329–347.

Österberg, Eva. (1996a). Criminality, Social Control, and the Early Modern State: Evidence and Interpretations in Scandinavian Historiography. In Eric A. Johnson & Eric H. Monkkonen (Eds.), *The Civilization of Crime. Violence in Town and Country Since the Middle Ages* (pp. 35–62). Urbana: Illinois University Press.

Österberg, Eva. (1996b). Gender, Class, and the Courts: Scandinavia. In Clive Emsley & Louis A. Knafla (Eds.), *Crime History and Histories of Crime. Studies in the Historiography of Crime and Criminal Justice in Modern History* (pp. 47–66). Westport: Greenwood Press.

Perrot, Michelle, & Philippe Robert (Eds.) (1989). *Compte Général de l'administration de la Justice Criminelle en France Pendant l'année 1880 et Raport Relatif aux Années 1826 a 1880* (publié par le Ministère de la Justice et des Cultes, Paris 1882). Genève: Slatkine.

Pihlajamäki, Heikki (Ed.) (1991). *Theatres of Power, Social Control and Criminality in Historical Perspective.* Helsinki: Matthias Calonius Society.

Rousseaux, Xavier. (1993). Civilisation des moeurs et/ou déplacement de l'insécurité? La violence à l'épreuve du temps. *Déviance et Société, 17*(3), 291–297.

Rousseaux, Xavier. (1996). From Medieval Cities to National States, 1350–1850: The Historiography of Crime and Criminal Justice in Europe. In Clive Emsley & Louis A. Knafla (Eds.), *Crime History and Histories of Crime; Studies in the Historiography of Crime and Criminal Justice in Modern History* (pp. 3–32). Westport: Greenwood Press.

Rousseaux, Xavier. (1999). From Case to Crime: Homicide Regulation in Medieval and Modern Europe. In Dietmar Willoweit (Ed.), *Die Entstehung des öffentlichen Strafrechts. Bestandsaufnahme eines europäischen Forschungsproblems* (pp. 143–175). Köln: Böhlau Verlag.

Rousseaux, Xavier, & René Lévy (Eds.) (1997). *Le Pénal dans tous ses Etats. Justice, Etats et Sociétés en Europe.* Bruxelles: Publications des Facultés universitaires Saint-Louis.

Schmidt, Axel. (1994). 'Wo die Männer sind, gibt es Streit'. Ehre und Ehrgefühl im ländlichen Sardinien. In Ludgera Vogt & Arnold, Zingerle (Eds.), *Ehre. Archaische Momente in der Moderne* (pp. 193–211). Frankfurt a. M.: Suhrkamp.

Schulze, Winfried. (1987). Gerhard Oestreichs Begriff 'Sozialdisziplinierung in der frühen Neuzeit'. *Zeitschrift für historische Forschung, 14,* 265–302.

Schüssler, Martin. (1991). Statistische Untersuchung des Verbrechens in Nürnberg im Zeitraum von 1285 bis 1400. *Zeitschrift der Savigny-Stiftung für Rechtsgeschichte, Germanistische Abteilung, 108,* 117–191.

Schüssler, Martin. (1996). Quantifizierung, Impressionismus und Rechtstheorie. Ein Bericht zur Geschichte und zum heutigen Stand der Forschung über Kriminalität im Europa des Spätmittelalters und der frühen Neuzeit. *Zeitschrift für Rechtsgeschichte, 113,* 247–278.

Schuster, Peter. (2000). *Eine Stadt vor Gericht: Recht und Alltag im spätmittelalterlichen Konstanz.* Paderborn: Schöningh.

Schwerhoff, Gerd. (1991). *Köln im Kreuzverhör: Kriminalität, Herrschaft und Gesellschaft in einer frühneuzeitlichen Stadt.* Bonn: Bouvier.

Sharpe, James A. (1983). *Crime in Seventeenth-Century England. A County Study.* Cambridge: Cambridge University Press.

Sharpe, James A. (1984). *Crime in Early Modern England, 1550–1750.* London: Longman.

Sharpe, James A. (1988). The History of Crime in England c. 1300–1914. *British Journal of Criminology, 28*(2), 254–267.

Sharpe, James A. (1996). Crime in England: Long-term Trends and the Problem of Modernization. In Eric A. Johnson & Eric H. Monkkonen (Eds.), *The Civilization of Crime. Violence in Town and Country Since the Middle Ages* (pp. 17–34). Urbana: University of Illinois Press.

Simon-Muscheid, Katharina. (1991). Gewalt und Ehre im spätmittelalterlichen Handwerk am Beispiel Basels. *Zeitschrift für historische Forschung, 18*(1), 1–31.

Spierenburg, Pieter. (1991). *The Broken Spell—A Cultural and Anthropological History of Pre-Industrial Europe (1250–1850)*. Basingstoke: Macmillan.

Spierenburg, Pieter. (1996). Long-term Trends in Homicide: Theoretical Reflections and Dutch Evidence, Fifteenth to Twentieth Centuries. In Eric A. Johnson & Eric H. Monkkonen (Eds.), *The Civilization of Crime: Violent in Town and Country since the Middle Ages* (pp. 63–108). Urbana: University of Illinois Press.

Spierenburg, Pieter. (1998a). Masculinity, Violence, and Honor: An Introduction. In Pieter Spierenburg (Ed.), *Men and Violence. Gender, Honor, and Rituals in Modern Europe and America* (pp. 1–37). Columbus: Ohio State University Press.

Spierenburg, Pieter (Ed.) (1998b). *Men and Violence. Gender, Honor, and Rituals in Modern Europe and America*. Columbus: Ohio State University Press.

Stone, Lawrence. (1983). Interpersonal Violence in English Society, 1300–1980. *Past and Present, 101*, 22–33.

Taylor, Charles. (1989). *Sources of the Self. The Making of Modern Identity*. Cambridge: Cambridge University Press.

Thome, Helmut. (1992). Gesellschaftliche Modernisierung und Kriminalität. Zum Stand der sozialhistorischen Kriminalitätsforschung. *Zeitschrift für Soziologie, 21*(3), 212–228.

Thome, Helmut. (1995). Modernization and Crime: What is the Explanation? *IAHCCJ Bulletin, 20*, 31–47.

Thome, Helmut. (2000). *Explaining Long Term Trends in Violent Crime*. Paper presented at the European Social Science History Conference in Amsterdam, 12–15 April 2000.

Thome, Helmut. (2003). Theoretische Ansätze zur Erklärung langfristiger Gewaltkriminalität seit Beginn der Neuzeit. In Wilhelm Heitmeyer & Georg Soeffner (Eds.), *Paradigmen und Analyseprobleme der Gewaltforschung* (forthcoming). Frankfurt am Main: Suhrkamp.

Tilly, Charles. (1992). *Coercion, Capital, and European States, AD 1990–1992*. Cambridge: Blackwell.

Verkko, Veli. (1967). Static and Dynamic 'Laws' of Sex and Homicide. In Marvin Wolfgang (Ed.), *Studies in Homicide* (pp.36–44). New York: Harper and Row.

Weber, Max. (1920). Die protestantische Ethik und der 'Geist' des Kapitalismus. In Max Weber (Ed.), *Gesammelte Aufsätze zur Religionssoziologie, Vol. 1* (pp. 17–206). Tübingen: Mohr.

Ylikangas, Heikki. (1998). *What Happened to Violence? An Analysis of the Development of Violence from Medieval Times to the Early Modern Era Based on Finnish Source Material*. Helsinki: Suomen Akatemia.

Ylikangas, Heikki, Petri Karonen, & Marrti Lehti. (2000). *Five Centuries of Violence in Finland and the Baltic Area*. Columbus: Ohio State University Press.

RESEARCH ON VIOLENCE: AN INTERDISCIPLINARY APPROACH WITH A FOCUS ON SOCIAL SCIENCES

SOCIETAL STRUCTURES AND INSTITUTIONS: SOCIAL CONDITIONS AND STATE AGENTS

PART II-1-1

SOCIAL STRUCTURES AND INEQUALITIES

Poverty and Violence

ROBERT D. CRUTCHFIELD AND TIM WADSWORTH

I. INTRODUCTION

Poverty is widely believed to cause violence. The general public treats this notion as a truism, and most academics also accept it as such. Debates among the latter tend to be over which social mechanisms cause poverty to affect violence. But there are other positions to be sure. Poverty has been linked to violence in a number of ways. Most scholars as well as lay persons believe that those who live in poverty more frequently engage in acts of violence as a consequence of conditions that they are subjected to. There is, however, disagreement among scholars about which conditions are important and how and why they lead to violence. These conditions may include poor housing (Stark, 1987), distressed neighborhood (Krivo & Peterson, 1996), and disrupted families (Sampson & Groves, 1989). Living conditions of this sort are ordinarily defined as social structural consequences of poverty. While this structural approach has usually viewed poverty as the independent variable and violence as the dependent, some scholars have also argued that violence can cause poverty at the aggregate level by creating an unstable or dangerous environment which is not conducive to economic development or growth (Staley, 1992). It may also be that those who are financially better off will move out of areas with high rates of violence leaving only those who are economically unable to relocate (Wilson, 1996).

Cultural conditions have also been linked to high levels of violence among the poor. In particular, cultures of poverty are said to include norms which promote violence (Banfield, 1970). It has also been argued that welfare dependence by the poor creates lifestyles conducive to social pathology, including violence (Murray, 1984). Broader views of the link between poverty and violence have also been suggested. Poverty is seen by some as a cause of revolutionary violence (Gurr & Ruttenburg, 1967). The poor, tiring of their subordinated position, use political violence to seek redress. Or the poor are subjected to violence by political elites seeking to maintain the status quo (Spitzer, 1975). Still other scholars have written about the link between poverty and violence, not in causal

W. Heitmeyer and J. Hagan (eds.), *International Handbook of Violence Research*, 67–82.
© 2003 Kluwer Academic Publishers. Printed in the Netherlands.

terms, but rather as a correlation that is produced by a common source, such as political or economic arrangements. We will briefly describe the arguments of scholars focusing on these latter types of relationships between poverty and violence, but we will primarily focus on the theories and research that describe conditions that purportedly lead the poor to engage in higher levels of interpersonal violence than do others.

Violence in reaction to political or economic oppression can take the form of organized, purposive action—e.g., the activities of the African National Congress during South Africa's apartheid years; or less organized, less clearly politically purposive action—e.g., robbery by inner-city African Americans (Sullivan, 1989); or even rape, according to Eldridge Cleaver (1968). As Marx predicted, a rising up of the downtrodden in violent revolution against the capitalist elite has occurred in many countries in the twentieth century. More often than not the intelligentsia mobilized the poor, convincing them to take up arms by pointing to the society's economic inequality and their poverty.

Conflict theorists also argue that the observed correlation between poverty and violence is spurious. Both poverty and violence are caused by the exercise of power by elites in the cause of perpetuating their privileged position. To some extent the southern subculture of poverty thesis also treats the correlation between poverty and violence as spurious. Gastil (1971) defines the South's regional history of slavery and persecution, and consequent lack of economic development (until recent decades) as common causes of both the region's poverty and high violence rates.

Violence here shall be defined as physical rather than emotional or developmental damage. There is no doubt that physical violence and victimization can exact substantial emotional tolls. For example, children subjected to abuse frequently suffer accompanying damage to personality development, and many rape victims and some victims of other forms of assault are now thought to suffer from post-traumatic stress syndrome. However, in this paper, we will limit consideration to the research literature that deals specifically with acts such as homicide, assault, and rape, and not with work that examines additional costs and consequences of violence. We also will not write here about "violence" perpetrated by corporations via acts such as the selling of faulty products or abusive marketing or distribution strategies, or illegal dumping. We will not discuss the literature that asserts that government policy towards people such as the homeless, the mentally ill, or prisoners, is violence. By defining corporate and government behavior outside of the scope of this article, we are not denying the damage of this behavior, or even that it constitutes violence. Our intention is only to limit the focus of the present discussion to a manageable scope.

We will also confine this discussion to acts of serious violence. An important debate which began in the mid-1970s illustrates the importance of this definitional choice. Tittle, Villimez and Smith (Tittle & Villimez (1977); Tittle, Villimez, & Smith (1978)) concluded after a review of the literature that socioeconomic status was not significantly related to crime. A number of scholars disagreed (e.g., Braithwaite, 1981). Hindelang, Hirschi, and Weis (1979, 1981) offered a solution to the debate, arguing that there appeared to be a class/crime correlation for serious crimes, especially violent crime. We will discuss this debate more fully below, but for the purpose of defining the scope of this paper, we will not discuss widespread forms of less serious violence typified by schoolyard spats. We are, however, concerned when what may have formerly been settled on the schoolyard with fists escalates to stabbings or drive-by shootings.

Defining poverty would seem to be more straightforward, but here too we should be clear. The U.S. government defines its official poverty level as an income below the amount necessary to sustain a family of four. Other Western countries have similar designations. While this type of definition is useful when studying poverty within a single economic system, its major faults are illustrated when one compares the impoverished in Western industrialized nations with the poor in the developing world. A related problem is illustrated by comparing the urban poor of New York or Chicago with those of Appalachia or the American Deep South. The social reality of what it is like to live on $13,000 per year will be very different in each of these locations. The faults of officially designated poverty levels spawned another important criminological debate. Blau and Blau (1982) asserted that absolute poverty, measured as the percent of the population living below the official U.S. government poverty level, was not the cause of violence (homicide in their analyses) but rather relative income inequality. Others (Messner, 1982; Williams, 1984) responded that indeed poverty rates are more important determinants of criminal homicide than relative deprivation and that the important question focuses on which mechanisms link poverty to violence. It is safe to say that the debate over whether absolute poverty or relative poverty is the most important cause of violence is not fully resolved among social scientist. Measures of income inequality and absolute poverty both appear in the extant literature. For our purpose, we will define the poor as those who live at the bottom of systems of economic stratification.

II.   THEORETICAL APPROACHES AND EMPIRICAL RESULTS

Much of the best research on poverty and violence has focused on urban areas. This is clearly a weakness in the existing literature, but application of some of the theories that have been developed need not be so limited. While some of them have been applied to rural areas (subculture of poverty), others such as those that describe an isolated underclass might help us to understand the relationship between poverty and violence in nonurban areas. Another weakness in the present body of literature is that much of the research has focused on Western industrialized nations. A challenge to scholars is to use what we have learned to gain a better understanding of processes that link poverty and violence in the less developed word.

1. The Relationship between Poverty and Violence

Economic factors have been a major focus of attempts to understand and explain violence since the birth of the social sciences. From the empirical work of Guerry and Quetelet in nineteenth century France (Vold, Bernard, & Snipes, 1998) to Durkheim's writings on anomie at the turn of the century (1897), through the Chicago School in the first half of the twentieth century, and on up to contemporary theories of the organization of employment (Colvin & Pauly, 1983; Crutchfield, 1989; Wilson, 1996), economic and employment stratification have played key roles in causal explanations of crime and delinquency. Despite a vast body of theory and research, there is little consensus or definitive conclusion concerning the relationship between economic factors, including poverty and violence.

For many decades the idea that delinquency and crime, both violent and nonviolent, are inversely correlated to social class was widely accepted in criminological theory. While exactly how social class and violence are related has varied across different perspectives, most of the contemporary classical and positivist theories suggest an inverse relationship between the two variables (Sutherland, 1947; Merton, 1949; Cohen, 1955; Hirschi, 1969).

Merton's anomie theory (1949) assumed that frustration among lower-class youth as a result of blocked opportunities to culturally defined goals would be the catalyst of delinquent behavior. Cloward and Ohlin (1960) extended Merton's theory in saying that the type of subcultural development (stable criminal, violent/conflict oriented, or retreatist), and the resulting level of violence that was manifested, would be determined by the availability of *illegitimate* opportunity structures that would provide an alternative means to alleviating poverty. Hirschi's (1969) social control theory claimed that lower-class youth would hold fewer stakes in conformity and therefore would have weaker bonds inhibiting delinquent behavior. The findings from macro-level research conducted in the first half of the twentieth century (e.g., Shaw & McKay, 1942) were offered as support of the class/crime relationship.

In the 1978 watershed article discussed above, Tittle and his collaborators attacked this belief by demonstrating in a meta-analysis of 363 studies that there is only a slight negative relationship between class and criminality, that this relationship is decreasing over time, and that this association is lower in self-report than official data. The authors not only claimed that the empirical support for the class/crime relationship was extremely limited, but also suggested that the little support that did exist for a relationship may be based, not on variance by class in individual involvement in criminal behavior, but in the bias of the criminal justice process. Tittle, Villimez, and Smith argued that the only true relationship between class and criminality may be that actors in the criminal justice system are more likely to arrest, prosecute, and convict individuals of lower socioeconomic status. The authors concluded that we must move away from many of our theories that rest on the false premise of a relationship between class and crime.

Braithwaite (1981) responded to Tittle et al. with findings from a larger meta-analysis (which included many of the same studies) that suggested qualified support for the relationship between class and delinquency. In addition to questioning Tittle et al.'s bias in study selection, Braithwaite claimed that the relationship is more apt to exist for serious interpersonal crimes which are often omitted from self-report studies due to extremely low variance. Stark had suggested this problem in his 1987 discussion of the ecology of crime when, in expressing concern about the shift to a social science dominated by the self-report survey, he wrote,

> social scientists lost touch with significant aspects of crime and delinquency. Poor neighborhoods disappeared to be replaced by individual kids with varying levels of family income, but no detectable environment at all. Moreover, the phenomena themselves became bloodless, sterile and almost harmless, for questionnaire studies cannot tap homicide, rape, assault, armed robbery, or even significant burglary or fraud—too few people are involved in these activities to turn up in significant numbers in feasible samples. So delinquency, which once meant offenses serious enough for court referrals, soon meant taking $2 out of mom's purse... This transformation soon led repeatedly to the "discovery" that poverty is unrelated to delinquency. (Stark, 1987:894)

Elliot, Huizinga and Ageton (1985), in an analysis of The National Youth Survey, discovered further support for Braithwaite and Stark's claim that the class/delinquency relationship is more prominent in analyses concerning serious offenses. The authors found that there was a significant relationship between class and juvenile crime when looking at both the prevalence and incidence rates of serious offenses. When nonserious offenses were under consideration, class position had an inverse relationship with incidence, but no significant relationship with prevalence. However, even the relationship between socio-economic status and serious violent offenses has not been consistently found in individual level analyses using self-report data. In their *Measuring Delinquency*, Hindelang, Hirschi and Weis (1981) found no support for a relationship between nonserious or serious delinquency among their sample of Seattle youths.

While the seriousness of the dependent variables and the official vs. self-report issues have remained central to the controversy, a few other issues have also been identified as important. Brownfield (1987), Hindelang, Hirschi, and Weis (1981), and Hagan (1992) have all suggested that the most delinquent adolescents are also the least likely to be included in self-report studies due to a lack of involvement with schools or other institutions through which survey respondents are usually contacted. These same adolescents are also the most likely to be poor. Underreporting by African-Americans, who tend to come from lower SES backgrounds, has also been identified as a problematic issue in class/delinquency research (Hindelang, Hirschi, & Weis, 1981). These concerns about underreporting by African-Americans and an exclusion of the poorer and more violent from our samples suggest another problem. While the relationship between economic standing and violence may be more evident when we are considering serious violence, it may also be more evident when we are considering extremes in socioeconomic status, or in this case, poverty. As Stark had pointed out, the move to self-report data shifted much of the focus of research away from an examination of seriously disadvantaged neighborhoods and towards measures of different socioeconomic statuses. In representative survey samples we may not be including sufficient numbers of severely disadvantaged individuals, or important information concerning the economic status of the geographic area in which the respondent is living.

So, while the late 1970s brought a heated debate between social scientists over the empirical validity (and the theoretical utility) of the relationship between economic status and criminal behavior, the years since have demonstrated a continued, and perhaps renewed interest in the role of social class as a determinant of crime and violence. The lessons from the past have been taken to heart and much of the contemporary theoretical and empirical work focuses on the influence that poverty and serious economic disadvantage have on serious interpersonal criminal behavior. Much of the empirical work in this area takes a macro-level approach because it is primarily by using aggregate level data that we are able to have enough variation in both our independent and dependent variables (poverty and serious violence) in representative samples.

This discussion of current trends in research and theory emphasizes what the authors see as the critical questions within the arena of poverty and violence. We mention them here and discuss each of them in more detail below. The first issue, which was mentioned briefly above, is the question whether it is the relative or absolute poverty of an area that encourages higher rates of criminal behavior (Blau & Blau, 1982; Messner, 1982; Williams, 1984; Martinez, 1996). The second question central to the discussion of poverty and violence developed out of a renewed focus on the extremely disadvantaged members of society, a population that has come to be known as the underclass (Wilson, 1987, 1996; Anderson, 1999). The primary focus of this debate concerns the relative influence of structure and culture in the development of violent patterns of behavior within poor urban communities. Most scholars agree that an oppositional culture, with norms and values at variance with those of the dominant culture, may be more accepting of violence. The degree to which such a culture is carried by residents of poor communities, as well as whether the culture can persist without its structural antecedents, is hotly contested.

2. Income Inequality or Poverty

The inequality vs. poverty issue arose in 1982 when Blau and Blau, working within the theoretical framework of Merton's structural strain theory, examined the effect of relative poverty on the violent crime rates in 125 of the largest cities in the U.S. While many studies using aggregate level data had offered evidence for a relationship between poverty and violence (Loftin & Hill, 1974; Parker & Smith, 1979), Blau and Blau (1982) were interested in testing whether income inequality within cities was a better predictor of violence than the percentage of cities' populations living below the U.S. government established poverty level. They claimed that it was not objective poverty that encouraged violence, but relative deprivation. Their reasoning was that the poor living in proximity to others who were considerably better off would become frustrated because of their comparative disadvantage. This frustration would lead to hostility. To be sure, they did not suggest purposive political aggression, but a more reactive striking out. Of course, those most likely to be caught in the resulting violence would be other poor people living in the same area. The results of their analysis offered support to the relative deprivation argument and indicated that income inequality was especially good at explaining variation in homicide rates across metropolitan areas when it was racially based. That is, those urban areas where there was the greatest difference between white and black incomes also tended to have the highest homicide rates.

In the same year, Messner (1982), in a study including 204 U.S. metropolitan areas, found little support for the inequality/crime relationship after controlling for poverty, but found a significant *negative* relationship between poverty and violent crime. In a response to the findings of both Blau and Blau (1982) and Messner (1982), Williams (1984) challenged the conclusion that there was not a positive relationship between poverty and crime, or that the relationship was really due to economic inequality. He asserted that by using predictive models involving nonlinear equations, which he argued were more theoretically justified, poverty levels were superior to overall income inequality in predicting violence, as indicated by homicide rates. Williams' nonlinear equations involved the use of a quadratic poverty term, which means that rather than expressing the relationship between poverty and homicide in a linear fashion, the relationships is nonlinear, that is, its slope increases. The effect of poverty on homicide occurs principally in those cities where there is an extremely large impoverished population. In support of the Blaus, Williams also found that interracial income inequality had a significant positive relationship with homicide rates.

The evidence for the relationships between inequality and crime, and poverty and crime continues to be mixed. Harer and Steffensmeier (1992) suggested the need to both disaggregate crime by race and focus on different types of inequality (total inequality, within-race inequality, and interracial inequality) in order to test the theoretical assumptions underlying the relative deprivation thesis. The authors claimed that if interracial inequality was, in fact, encouraging violent crime, we should see an increase in the crime rate of blacks. Surprisingly, they found that both total inequality and intra-racial inequality was related to high rates of violent crime for whites, but neither interracial or intra-racial inequality had any effect on the violent crime rates for blacks. While somewhat puzzled, Harer and Steffensmeier suggested that whites may hold more egalitarian views concerning upward mobility and therefore respond differently when opportunities are blocked, whereas blacks may be less optimistic about the equity of income distribution. In applying the relative deprivation thesis to Latinos in the United States, Martinez (1996) found that intra-race inequality was a strong predictor of lethal violence among Latinos, while over-all inequality had less of an effect. He explained this finding by pointing out that members in tight-knit ethnic communities are more likely to use other group members rather than outsiders as reference points. By this process, Latinos would more likely experience frustration, resulting in aggression, by experiencing inequality within the Latino community. Because the Latino community is more likely than the larger society to experience concentrations of extreme disadvantage, this finding offers further support to Williams' (1984) claim that we must model the equations in a manner that captures large impoverished populations.

While scholars disagree about which particular method of measuring poverty is appropriate, and what the best analytic form of the predictive model is, they do agree that there is an important relationship between the presence of the extremely disadvantaged in a population and the level of violence where they live. When this issue is viewed in the light of the class/crime debate between Tittle et al. and their critics, more support for Stark's concerns emerges. It may be that, while there is no relationship between social class and crime, except the most serious crime, the relationship may also be dependent on focusing on serious disadvantage. In other words, both the independent and dependent variables must be modeled in a nonlinear fashion for a relationship to be present. It is the very disadvantaged who are more likely to commit violent behavior, and it is only serious violent offenses that they are more likely to commit. The traditional relationships that have been proposed between social class and crime at the individual level, and poverty and violence at the aggregate level look like Figures II-1-1-1.1 and II-1-1-1.2.

The best evidence offers little support for the relationship suggested by Figure II-1-1-1.1, and moderate support for the relationship in Figure II-1-1-1.2. However, if these relationships are modeled differently, and are not assumed to take a linear form, the findings do offer some support to the relationship between class and crime at the individual level, and consistent support for the relationship between poverty and violence at

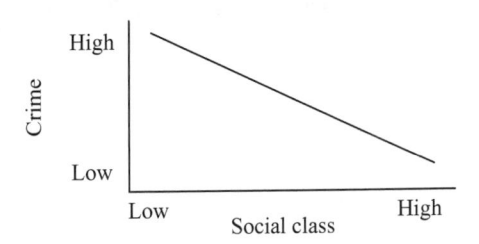

Figure II-1-1-1.1. Individuals' social class and crime.

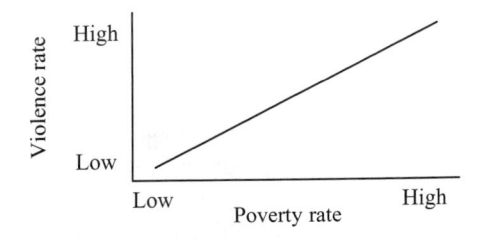

Figure II-1-1-1.2. Aggregate poverty rates and violence rates.

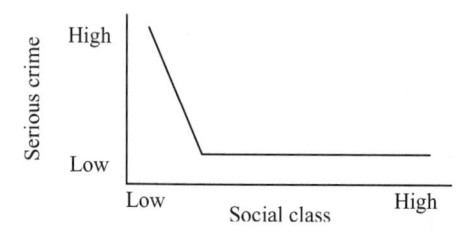

Figure II-1-1-1.3. Individuals' social class and crime.

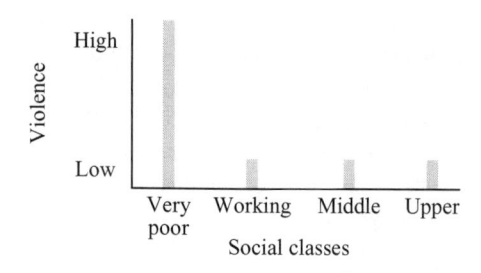

Figure II-1-1-1.4. Aggregate poverty rates and violence rates.

the aggregate level. Better specified models suggest relationships that look like Figure II-1-1-1.3 at the individual level, and Figure II-1-1-1.4 at the aggregate level.

Having established these relationships, we are left with three very important questions. Are the poor actually more likely to engage in violence? Or do they simply reside in dangerous places? And if the poor are more likely to engage in violence, why?

We suggest that the answer to the first two questions is yes. The research indicates that the poor are more likely to engage in violent behavior, but they are by no means the only participants. Research has indicated that there is no significant difference between the levels of serious violence between the upper class, middle class, and working class. There is not, to our knowledge, credible research establishing a significant difference in violence between these groups. But what about the very poor? In particular, what about that group which Wilson (1987) called the "underclass"? Figures II-1-1-1.3 and II-1-1-1.4 illustrate what the relationship between poverty and violence would look like if the very poor engaged in more violence and other social class categories had comparable rates of violence.

Our interpretation of the research literature leads us to believe that the poor do engage in more violence (Williams, 1984), but they also live in more dangerous places (Krivo & Peterson, 1996; Wilson, 1987, 1996; Anderson, 1999), and not simply because they live among other poor people. Research has suggested that communities with high levels of poverty tend to have a harder time maintaining informal social controls which deter violent and criminal behavior amongst both community members and outsiders (Sampson & Groves, 1989; Stark, 1987). This work, which draws on the ideas of social disorganization theory (which is discussed in more detail below) suggests that these informal institutions of social control, such as community organizations, religious institutions and friendship and kin networks, are less stable in areas which have lower rates of employment (Crutchfield, 1989), home ownership (Stark, 1987), and stable families (Sampson, 1995), and higher rates of mobility (Crutchfield, Geerken, & Gove, 1982). Thus, the disorganized nature of poor communities makes them better locations for crime enterprises to operate. Disorganized poor communities are less capable of regulating the behavior associated with such things as drug markets or street prostitution. These activities, and competition for territory and markets, generate violence (Staley, 1992). In areas that are characterized by such violence, residents may adopt defensive behavior stances which result in the regular use of violence for conflict resolution (Krivo & Peterson, 1996). It has also been argued (Stark, 1987) that law enforcement is less diligent about maintaining order in areas characterized by this type of "disorganization." This leniency results in the further development of illicit markets and an increased presence of outsiders going to these areas to participate in illicit or violent activities. Staley (1992) has suggested a multidirectional relationship in which poverty breeds illegal markets, violence, and community instability. These factors discourage economic development by private interests which allows the cycle of unemployment, poverty, and violence to continue. Concerning the last question of why the poor engage in more violence, there are a number of competing theoretical explanations.

3. Competing Explanations

The research literature on poverty and violence is built around a series of debates about how poverty causes violence. There are structural arguments, which can be divided between those from a consensus tradition such as strain or disorganization theory, and conflict arguments, e.g., Marxist theory. These approaches focus on the political and economic structures and opportunities from which stratification and inequality emerge. There are also cultural arguments, such as the culture of poverty thesis, which look to the values and attitudes of a community to explain violence among the poor. Others combine structural and cultural explanations of violence, believing that normative, cultural, and behavioral adaptations to structural deprivation explain how living in poverty leads to higher levels of violence. The difference between this latter approach and other "cultural" perspectives may seem slight, and at times even nonexistent, but there are important differences in the weight they place on structural conditions in the perpetuation of normative systems that produce violent behavior.

     Social disorganization theory, which was developed by University of Chicago sociologists (Park, 1925; Shaw & McKay, 1942), building on the writings of European scholars (Durkheim, 1951), has seen a resurgence in recent years (Sampson & Groves, 1989; Bursik & Grasmick, 1992). Disorganization theorists have shown that breakdowns in community organization can allow crime, including violence, to increase. Poor neighborhoods are not by definition disorganized. However, mobile populations, disrupted families, and weak institutions (i.e., schools, churches, community organizations), which are often the result of inadequate economic resources, increase levels of disorganization. This lack of resources occurs, in part, because with institutionalized power the larger community frequently does not adequately support institutions in poor neighborhoods. The high crime in poor neighborhoods itself may also lead to further deterioration of the relationships and institutional structures which characterize organized neighborhoods. That is, the poor live in communities where they are subjected to a vicious cycle where disorganization leads to higher levels of violence which in turn contributes to continuing and maybe even deepening disorganization. Disorganization encourages violence among the poor residents because of accompanying breakdowns in behavioral norms and social control. Sutherland's (1947) differential association suggested that poor youths would have a higher frequency of association with definitions favorable to delinquency and violent behavior because they are more likely to be living in socially disorganized areas, where exposure to these associations will be more common.

Strain theories, which include Merton's anomie theory briefly described above, are consistent with popular beliefs that the poor engage in aggression as a by-product of frustration (Blau & Blau, 1982), or because of utilitarian involvement in crime. Blocked legitimate opportunity leads to pecuniary crime such as drug dealing and prostitution, exposing participants to situations conducive to violence (Staley, 1992).

Cohen (1955) and Miller's (1966) subcultural theories proposed that structural inequality created a culture of poverty and violence which was passed on from one generation to the next, whether or not the structural conditions from which it originally arose remained. This subculture held pro-violence and crime norms that opposed those of the larger society. While this opposition was originally a rebellious adaptation to a stratified opportunity structure, the authors claimed that the adaptation would remain despite shifts in opportunity.

In the past three decades, a new debate that focuses on the causes of poverty has emerged which intensified after the mid-1980s. On one side are writers such as Banfield (1970) and Murray (1984) who explain the persistence of poverty, and accompanying maladies including violence and crime, as a consequence of persistent subcultures of poverty. The other side represented by, among others, Wilson (1987, 1996) and Massey and Denton (1993), relate poverty to the persistence of structural inequalities. These structural explanations argue that historical, economic, political, and social arrangements of the society cause poverty, the oppositional cultural norms and values that some poor people carry, and social pathologies, such as violence. Wilson eschews making sweeping statements about the poor and focuses on a subgroup, which he called the "underclass." He traces the present plight of the urban underclass to historical patterns of racial stratification and to changes in the economy and job markets. Massey and Denton focus on the importance of racial residential segregation as the underlying cause of many of the problems associated with severe urban poverty.

The first group's position, which can be labeled "the subculture of poverty" thesis, argues that the norms and values of those in this subculture heighten the likelihood that they will engage in violence. Banfield's (1967) position is that the inability to defer gratification is both a sign that people are carriers of the subculture of poverty and a cause of much of their own problems. This inability to defer gratification means that they have neither the temperament nor the inclination to avoid violence if it is either a short cut to fulfillment of desires or an expression of frustration. Murray (1984) believes that poverty as we know it today is a by-product of the modern welfare state. The poor's reliance on welfare systems has undercut their pride and feelings of self-worth, as well as their motivation, and led to a number of social pathologies, including violence. While both Banfield and Murray minimally acknowledge that the social structural position of the poor is important, central to both of their arguments are the norms and values that they believe to be key elements of the subculture of poverty.

The structural causes of poverty and attendant social pathologies are central in the explanations of Wilson (1987, 1996) and Massey and Denton (1993). Wilson, who focuses on a subset of mostly minority individuals who are living in isolated urban ghettos characterized by concentrated poverty, argues that this underclass is a consequence of changes in the international economy that led to change in American industrial composition. The disappearance of many low-skilled jobs left many inner-city residents without work and without hope. The resulting changes in the communities where these people live led to increased strain, disorganization, and violence. Massey and Denton (1993) have focused on how racial residential segregation has been a powerful force which concentrates the effect of negative social change, such as economic and employment shifts, and social problems, such as drug use and crime, onto poor blacks. Both of these structural arguments acknowledge the importance of historic social arrangements. They also both recognize that once social and economic structures cause poverty, oppositional cultures that can encourage violence *may* emerge.

Perhaps the simplest way to differentiate these structural arguments from the sub-culture of poverty positions is that the latter appears to believe that if the norms and values of the poor were changed, problematic behavior such as violence would change. The former argues that in order to change the poverty, the oppositional culture, and the violence, the structural arrangements causing them must be altered.

These perspectives are alike in that neither of them clearly elaborates the mechanisms by which poverty causes violence. Subcultural explanations argue that values peculiar to the poor encourage violence, but proponents do not explain how these values emerge or why the majority of the poor do not behave violently. In other words, they overpredict the amount of violence that occurs in poor neighborhoods. The structural explanations have implied a "frustration aggression" mechanism, but have not clearly specified the mechanisms by which living in poverty causes individuals to act more violently. These structural explanations have also drawn on social disorganization and differential association theory, which have been somewhat more successful in identifying mechanisms and explaining why some individuals in disadvantaged neighborhoods may be more likely than others in their same neighborhood to engage in violent or criminal behavior. An example of this is Sampson and Wilson's (1995) development of a theoretical model that incorporates structural and cultural arguments relating race, crime, and inequality in urban areas in the U.S. Their basic approach is that inequality based on residential segregation encourages social isolation and ecological concentrations of severely disadvantaged populations. These patterns lead to structural barriers and cultural adaptations that encourage the breakdown of social organization and the ability to control crime.

A literature is currently emerging that is elaborating and testing models that will help us to better understand the mechanisms that translate poverty into violent behavior. Anderson (1999) describes a "code of the street," which is a by-product of the helplessness of urban poverty. Young men adapt to their circumstances by adopting exaggerated conceptions of honor and respect. They do this in a circumstance where they are not afforded opportunity to normal pathways to respect such as jobs, careers, and a capacity to be self-determining. According to Anderson, violence occurs when these poor young men perceive their honor to be besmirched, or when they are disrespected, or "dissed." Central to Anderson's position is the notion that this oppositional culture is a product of structural arrangements that perpetuate a race/class-based stratification system. The effects of this stratification system are exacerbated by racial residential segregation. Those living in impoverished neighborhoods were condemned to remain there and the neighborhoods did not improve, as did some neighboring communities, because residents in the former lacked economic and political power.

Krivo and Peterson (1996) found that extreme economic disadvantage creates unusually high violent crime rates, but not property crime. They argue that an important reaction to poverty is the adoption of a defensive stance in order to protect oneself (i.e., carrying weapons, being hypersensitive to insults, etc.); this, in conjunction with the routine activities of the poor, make the occurrence of violent events more likely.

Research on segmented labor markets explains how systems of stratification perpetuate poverty and marginality (Kalleberg & Sorenson, 1979; Kasarda, 1990). In the last decade, a literature has emerged that indicates that this same stratification of labor helps to explain variability in violence (Crutchfield, 1989). These arguments suggest that both poverty and violence may be products of a common cause. In segmented labor markets, which characterize many industrial nations, a portion of the population is consistently employed in low status, low-paying, marginal jobs. The poor, when they are employed, work in sectors of the economy composed of these types of jobs. When they are not employed, the poor constitute the reserve pool of labor that allows employers to pay those working in this sector low wages with few benefits. Evidence suggest that the distribution of labor within segmented labor markets partially explains both the distribution of poverty and violence (Crutchfield, 1989; Allen & Steffensmeir, 1989). The unemployed, those with marginal employment, and their children are thought to have weakened bonds to conventional behavior (Crutchfield & Pitchford, 1997; Wadsworth, 2000). These loosened bonds theoretically lead to less regulated, less controlled lifestyles that make crime, including violence, more likely.

These explanations are but the beginning of explorations of the mechanisms which may actually cause those living in poverty to engage in violent behavior more frequently than others. Further development of these or other theoretical elaborations of the mechanisms linking poverty to violent behavior is an important agenda for future research.

III.   DESIDERATA

One of the two major controversies of the last several decades seems to have withered. Few scholars are arguing over whether absolute poverty or income inequality is the better predictor of violence. It appears that scholars use variables measuring one or both concepts. The controversy over the primacy of structure or culture, which is more important when interpreting the correlation between poverty and violence, seems to be abating among scholars, but it rages outside of the academy. Recent research is beginning the process of specifying how structural patterns influence culture, which in turn influences violence (Bellair, Roscigno, & Velez, 1999). Those doing research on poverty and violence are likely to define structure and culture as influences on each other, both effecting levels of violence in poor communities (Anderson, 1999).

Outside of the academy, however, there remains a popular tendency to attribute violence in poor communities—or even nations—to culture, without recognizing the importance of social, economic, and political structures. For example, high violent crime rates in South Africa are attributed to the invasion of people from Central Africa rather than high levels of income inequality and joblessness. Ethnic violence elsewhere in sub-Saharan Africa and in Eastern Europe is a consequence of historic tribal warfare rather than economic stratification that has accompanied the political disenfranchisement of some. Hip-hop music is viewed as an important cause of American inner-city violence, rather than the continuing economic marginalization of people who live there. These cultural explanations are comfortable for many because they "blame the victims" of structured inequality for the violence in which the poor are the most likely victims. Structural theories, or even those explanations that combine the two types of explanations, threaten status quo social arrangements. So in spite of growing agreement among scholars who study poverty and violence, it is unlikely that popular and political debate will soon follow the same path.

We expect that in the near future studies of poverty and violence will continue to elaborate how features of social life influence violent behavior. Two especially interesting approaches along these lines focus on racial residential segregation (Peterson & Krivo, 1999; Liska & Bellair, 1995) and labor markets (Crutchfield, Glusker, & Bridges, 1999; Uggen, 1999), and how these social forces mediate the relationship between poverty and violence. Research along these lines will assist us in understanding the mechanisms by which the experience of poverty influences violence.

Another clear research need is studies that are comparative. Comparative studies have been stymied by a lack of comparable data for both poverty and violence. Yet, if we are to disentangle the relationship between poverty and violence from the peculiarities of history and political systems, comparative research is imperative. For instance, the theoretical and empirical work in the area of poverty and violence by North American scholars must be viewed within the particular context of race relations in countries that experienced chattel slavery, black/white racial antagonism, and genocide against native populations. While scholars are increasingly interested in and capable of parceling out these influences, our understanding of the poverty/violence relationship will be enhanced with increased research using nations with different histories of racial and ethnic relations.

IV. APPROACHES OF PREVENTION

There are three approaches to preventing violence related to poverty. Fix the problem people (the poor), fix the causes of poverty, or fix the situations of those who have already violated the law. The first two approaches are primary prevention strategies. The latter attempts to reduce crime and violence by former prison inmates, by making it less likely that they will return to a life of limited opportunity and poverty.

The most prominent example of an attempt to "fix poor people" is the U.S. Government's welfare reform policies. Underlying changes in federal welfare policies is the position espoused by Charles Murray in *Losing Ground* (1984). Murray contends, as we described above, that the American welfare state led to the erosion of morals and values among the dependent, which in turn produced pathologies such as violence. Proponents of policies that have forced people off welfare point to declines in the number of poor in the U.S., and declining crime and violence rates, as evidence that the reforms are having positive effects. The problem with drawing this conclusion is obvious. The U.S. economy has experienced its longest sustained growth since World War II during this same period. It is very likely that the declines in poverty rates are a consequence of the strong economy. Declines in violence rates have been explained by a host of other factors as well, including the economy, an aging population, and changes in law enforcement. A real test of the Murray approach to prevention will occur with economic downturn.

Preventing violence by addressing the structural causes of poverty is a tricky proposition. In the early 1960s, Lyndon Johnson's administration seized on the work of criminologists Richard Cloward and Lloyd Ohlin and integrated arguments from their *Delinquency and Opportunity* (1960) into plans for the War on Poverty (Lemann, 1991). The Administration believed that reducing poverty would reduce delinquency, crime, and violence. Poverty did decline, but unfortunately crime and violence increased. Also unfortunately, increased crime has been cited as evidence that the War on Poverty was a failure. One cannot reasonably draw that conclusion. Violence rates may well have grown considerably higher without the programs that constituted the War on Poverty.

Recent decreases in poverty at the same time that violence levels have fallen are consistent with Wilson's positions (1987, 1996). Reductions in joblessness, he argues, should decrease both. It may be that it takes periods of sustained economic growth before joblessness among the underclass is appreciably affected. And it would take an even longer period of healthy economic growth before the culture produced by earlier periods of deep poverty is changed.

The residential segregation and ghettoization of minority populations is a structural feature that exacerbates the effects of poverty causing inordinately high levels of crime in these communities (Massey & Denton, 1993; Peterson & Krivo, 1999). It is easy to see how meaningful prevention could be achieved by reducing segregation. It is considerably harder to actually reduce residential segregation, especially when the social distance between groups is great.

The policies and practices described above can be thought of as primary violence prevention strategies. Secondary prevention strategies are more directly aimed at those who have already violated norms or who have been exposed to violence. Examples of these are programs to mitigate the effect of living in proximity to violence on poor children or those that seek to employ or train ex-felons.

Criminal justice practitioners have long believed that finding employment for those released from prison reduces recidivism. The reasons for this position are obvious. Work gives ex-convicts something to do, but perhaps more importantly it reduces the chances of falling into poverty. Programs to employ them can be thought of as secondary violence prevention efforts. The evidence for the efficacy of these programs has been mixed, but recently several have been demonstrated to have desired effects (Uggen, 1999).

Green (1993) found that it is possible to construct intervention programs that can mitigate the negative consequences—more violence, fear, mental health problems, etc.—(Dubrow & Garbarino, 1989; McKendrick & Senoamadi, 1993) that poor children experience as a consequence of being exposed to violence. By mobilizing community centers and schools, engaging in "street outreach," and by providing family intervention programs, it may be possible to dampen the effects of exposure to violence.

The difficulty in developing effective strategies for preventing violence by the poor is that until we build better understanding of the specific mechanisms that translate poverty into violence, it is difficult to know how to address the problem. The prevention question thus harkens back to the research question, what mechanisms cause poverty to increase violence?

REFERENCES

Allen, Emilie Anderson, & Darrel J. Steffensmeier. (1989). Underemployment, and Property Crime: Differential Effects of Job Availability and Job Quality on Juvenile and Young Adult Arrest Rates. *American Sociological Review, 54*(1), 107–123.

Anderson, Elija. (1999). *Code of the Street: Decency, Violence, and the Moral Life of the Inner City.* New York: W. W. Norton.

Banfield, Edward C. (1970). *The Unheavenly City.* Boston: Little Brown & Company.

Bellair, Paul E., Vincent J. Roscigno, & Maia B. Velez. (1999). *Local Labor Market Opportunity, Subcultural Formation, and Adolescent Violence.* Presented at the 1999 Meetings of the American Society of Criminology.

Blau, Judith, & Peter Blau. (1982). The Cost of Inequality: Metropolitan Structure and Violent Crime. *American Sociological Review, 47,* 114–128.

Braithwaite, John. (1981). The Myth of Social Class and Criminality Reconsidered. *American Sociological Review, 46*(1), 36–57.

Brownfield, David-H. (1987). A reassessment of Cultural Deviance Theory: The Use of Underclass Measures. *Deviant Behavior, 8*(4), 343–359.

Bursik, Robert J., Jr., & Harold G. Grasmick. (1992). Longitudinal Neighborhood Profiles in Delinquency: The Decomposition of Change. *Journal of Quantitative Criminology, 8*(3), 247–263.

Cleaver, Eldridge. (1968). *Soul on Ice.* New York: Dell.

Cloward, Richard A., & Lloyd E. Ohlin. (1960). *Delinquency and Opportunity.* New York: The Free Press.

Cohen, Albert K. (1955). *Delinquent Boys: The Culture of the Gang.* Glenncoe: Free Press.

Colvin, Mark, & John A. Pauly. (1983). Critique of Criminology: Toward an Integrated Structural-Marxist Theory of Delinquency Production. *American Journal of Sociology, 89*(3), 513–551.

Crutchfield, Robert D. (1989). Labor Stratification and Violent Crime. *Social Forces, 68*(2), 489–512.

Crutchfield, Robert D., Anne Glusker, & George S. Bridges. (1999). A Tale of Three Cities: Labor Markets and Homicide. *Sociological Focus, 32*(1), 65–83.

Crutchfield, Robert D., & Susan R. Pitchford. (1997). Work and Crime: The Effects of Labor Stratification. *Social Forces, 76*, 93–118.

Crutchfield, Robert D., Michael R. Geerken, & Walter R. Gove. (1982). Crime Rate and Social Integration: The Impact of Metropolitan Mobility. *Criminology, 20*(3–4), 467–478.

Dubrow, Nancy F., & James Garbarino. (1989). Living in the War Zone: Mothers and Young Children in a Public Housing Development. *Child-Welfare, 68*(1), 3–20.

Durkheim, Emile. (1951). *Suicide.* Translated by John A. Spaulding & George Simpson. New York: The Free Press.

Elliot, Delbert S., David Huizinga, & Suzanne S. Ageton. (1985). *Explaining Delinquency and Drug Use.* Beverly Hills: Sage Publications.

Gastil, Raymond D. (1971). Homicide and a Regional Culture of Violence. *American Sociological Review, 36*(3), 412–427.

Green, Michael B. (1993). Chronic Exposure to Violence and Poverty: Interventions that Work for Youth. *Crime and Delinquency, 39*(1), 106–124.

Gurr, Ted Robert, & Charles Ruttenberg. (1967). *The Conditions of Civil Violence; First Tests of a Causal Model.* Princeton: Center for International Studies.

Hagan, John. (1992). The Poverty of a Classless Criminology. The American Society of Criminology 1991 Presidential Address. *Criminology, 30*(1), 1–19.

Harer, Miles D., & Darrell Steffensmeier. (1992). The Differing Effects of Economic Inequality on Black and White Rates of Violence. *Social Forces, 70*(4), 1035–1054.

Hindelang, Michael J., Travis Hirschi, & Joseph G. Weis. (1979). Correlates of Delinquency: The Illusion of Discrepancy between Self-Report and Official Measures. *American Sociological Review, 44*(6), 995–1014.

Hindelang, Michael J., Travis Hirschi, & Joseph G. Weis. (1981). *Measuring Delinquency.* Beverly Hills: Sage Publications.

Hirschi, Travis. (1969). *Causes of Delinquency.* Berkeley: University of California Press.

Kalleberg, Arne L., & Aage B. Sorensen. (1979). The Sociology of Labor Markets. *Annual Review of Sociology, 5*, 351–379.

Kasarda, John D. (1990). Structural Factors Affecting the Location and Timing of Urban Underclass Growth. *Urban Geography, 11*, 234–264.

Krivo, Lauren J., & Ruth D. Peterson. (1996). Extremely Disadvantaged Neighborhoods and Urban Crime. *Social Forces, 75*(2), 619–648.

Lemann, Nicholas. (1991). *The Promised Land: The Great Black Migration and How it Changed America.* New York: Vintage Books.

Liska, Allen E., & Paul E. Bellair. (1995). Violent-Crime Rates and Racial Composition: Convergence over Time. *American Journal of Sociology, 101*(3), 578–610.

Loftin, Colin, & Robert H. Hill. (1974). Regional Subculture and Homicide: An Examination of the Gastil–Hackney Thesis. *American Sociological Review, 39*(5), 714–724.

Martinez, Ramiero, Jr. (1996). Latinos and Lethal Violence: The Impact of Poverty and Inequality. *Social Problems, 43*(2), 131–146.

Massey, Douglas S., & Nancy A. Denton. (1993). *American Apartheid: Segregation and the Making of the Underclass.* Cambridge: Harvard University Press.

McKendrick, B. W., & W. Senoamadi. (1993). Some Effects of Violence on Squatter Camp Families and their Children. *Maatskaplike Werk/ Social Work, 29*(3), 213–221.

Merton, Robert K. (1949). *Social Theory and Social Structure: Toward the Codification of Theory and Research*. New York: The Free Press.

Messner, Steven F. (1982). Poverty, Inequality, and the Urban Homicide Rate. *Criminology, 20*(1), 103–114.

Miller, Walter B. (1966). Violent Crimes in City Gangs. *Annals of the American Academy of Political and Social Science, 364*, 96–112.

Murray, Charles. (1984). *Losing Ground: American Social Policy 1950–1980*. New York: Basic Books.

Park, Robert Ezra. (1925). *The City*. Chicago: The University of Chicago Press.

Parker, Robert Nash, & Dwayne M. Smith. (1979). Deterrence, Poverty, and Type of Homicide. *American Journal of Sociology, 85*(3), 614–624.

Peterson, Ruth D., & Lauren J. Krivo. (1999). Racial Segregation, the Concentration of Disadvantage, and Black and White Homicide Victimization. *Sociological Forum, 14*(3), 465–493.

Sampson, Robert J. (1995). Unemployment and Imbalanced Sex Ratios: Race-Specific Consequences for Family Structure and Crime. In Belinda Tucker M. & Claudia Mitchell Kernan (Eds.), *The Decline in Marriage among African Americans: Causes, Consequences and Policy Implications* (pp. 229–254). New York: Russell Sage Foundation.

Sampson, Robert J., & William Julius Wilson. (1995). Toward a Theory of Race, Crime, and Urban Inequality. In John Hagan & Ruth D. Peterson (Eds.), *Crime and Inequality* (pp. 37–54). Stanford: Stanford U Press.

Sampson, Robert J., & Byron W. Groves. (1989). Community Structure and Crime: Testing social-disorganization theory. *American Journal of Sociology, 94*(4), 774–802.

Shaw, Clifford R., & Henry McKay. (1942). *Juvenile Delinquency and Urban Areas*. Chicago: The University of Chicago Press.

Spitzer, Steven. (1975). Punishment and Social Organization. *Law and Society Review, 9*, 613–637.

Staley, Sam. (1992). *Drug Policy and the Decline of American Cities*. New Brunswick: Transaction Publishers.

Stark, Rodney. (1987). Deviant Places: A Theory of the Ecology of Crime. *Criminology, 25*(4), 893–909.

Sullivan, Mercer L. (1989). *Getting Paid: Youth Crime and Work in the Inner City*. Ithaca: Cornell University Press.

Sutherland, Edwin H. (1947). *Principles of Criminology, 4th Edition*. Philadelphia: Lippincott.

Tittle, Charles R., & Wayne J. Villemez. (1977). Social Class and Criminality. *Social Forces, 56*(2), 474–502.

Tittle, Charles R., Wayne J. Villemez, & Douglas A. Smith. (1978). The Myth of Social Class and Criminality: An Empirical Assessment of the Empirical Evidence. *American Sociological Review, 43*(5), 643–656.

Uggen, Christopher. (1999). Ex-offenders and the Conformist Alternative: A Job Quality Model of Work and Crime. *Social Problems, 46*(1), 127–151.

Vold, George B., Thomas J. Bernard, & Jeffrey B. Snipes. (1998). *Theoretical Criminology, 4th Edition*. New York: Oxford University Press.

Wadsworth, Tim. (2000). Labor Markets, Delinquency and Social Control Theory: An Empirical Assessment of the Mediating Process. *Social Forces, 78*(3), 1041–1066.

Williams, Kirk. (1984). Economic Sources of Homicide. *American Sociological Review, 49*(2), 283–289.

Wilson, William Julius. (1987). *The Truly Disadvantaged: The Inner City, the Underclass, and Public Policy*. Chicago: University of Chicago Press.

Wilson, William Julius. (1996). *When Work Disappears: The World of the Urban Poor*. New York: Alfred A. Knopf.

Ethnic Segregation and Violence

James F. Short, Jr.*

> No European city has experienced the level of concentrated poverty and racial and ethnic segregation that is typical of American metropolises.
>
> *William Julius Wilson*, 1996

> It is a fundamental law of sociology and anthropology that social separation produces cultural differentiation.
>
> *Daniel Glaser*, 1971

I. INTRODUCTION

It is impossible to understand how race and ethnicity are related to violence without taking into consideration poverty, segregation, migration, and cultural and historical experiences. Indeed, given the paucity of systematic studies focussing specifically on segregation and violence, the nature of relationships among all of these influences is of critical importance for understanding violence.

Modernization theories once predicted, or implied, that status relations among individuals and groups would in the future be based less on ascriptive criteria, such as ethnicity and race, than on universally applied criteria, such as rational exchange and competence (see Armer & Katsillis, 1992). Similarly, as industrialization and urbanization increased worldwide, and populations became more highly educated and influenced by media of mass communication, ethnic traditions and loyalties were predicted to give way as the basis for interpersonal and institutional relationships. Convergence would, in other words, change institutions, values, modes of living, and the ways individuals relate to each other.

No one would deny that institutions, values, and modes of living have changed, or that convergence has occurred as institutions have adapted to the driving forces of social

*I am grateful for the assistance in preparing this article to Scott Akins, Annabel Cook, Viktor Gecas, Janet Lauritsen, Jeffrey Morenoff, Richard Rosenfeld, and Charles Tittle.

W. Heitmeyer and J. Hagan (eds.), *International Handbook of Violence Research*, 83–96.

change identified by modernization theorists; indeed, technological and global development and exchange have continued to accelerate even as the popularity of modernization theories has faded. Political and economic relationships are increasingly dominated by global change. Yet, at the turn of the twenty-first century, violence associated with ethnic conflict has become endemic throughout much of the globe. Indeed, rather than convergence, violence appears to have become "ethnicized," in the words of two recent observers (Brubaker & Laitin, 1998).

Critics of modernization theory, and those who advanced competing theories of social change (e.g., conflict, dependency, and world systems theorists), noted the circularity in modernization arguments that sometimes identified "*indicators* of social, political, and cultural development" (e.g., urbanization, literacy rates, political democracy, capitalism, secularization) as "'conditions' for development" (Armer & Katsillis, 1992:1303), and they were unduly influenced by Western models of development and capitalist economies. Their evolutionary perspective assumed replication of the stages through which advanced societies in the West had developed. More importantly, in the context of this essay, they failed to appreciate the depth and strength of ethnic loyalties, and how these would be affected by forces of change during the last half of the twentieth century (Chirot, 1981; Brubaker & Laitin, 1998).

For the most part, competing theories addressed ethnic violence only indirectly. Modernization theory underestimated, or could not foresee, other changes that later proved to be harbingers of ethnic violence, e.g., the extent and the dynamics of international migration and the effects that it would have within nations, especially those associated with segregation, subcultural formation, and conflict. Moreover, it did not fully appreciate the implications for ethnic and nationalist tensions that resulted from the breakup of the Soviet empire, or of the rapid diffusion of rationalist and democratic thinking that occurred following the Second World War, even though the latter was predicted by modernization theories. Perhaps most importantly, despite its centrality to their theories, the impact of the revolution in communication technologies on ethnic, racial, and religious identities *and on organized opposition to them*, could not have been fully anticipated. As Inglehart and Baker (2000:48) note, "protracted economic collapse" (such as has occurred in several countries where ethnic conflicts have occurred) "can reverse the effects of modernization ..." The resulting return to traditional values may, in addition, create new ethnic tensions or exacerbate old tensions. Modernization creates both winners and losers and often results in increasing both social and economic distance between them. New technologies enhance both promotional and oppositional interests, making possible more rapid communication, cooperation, emulation, and organization. Scholarly research suggests that opposition to racial and ethnic mixing (through marriage, friendship, business relationships, etc.) has in some cases overcome nationalistic and xenophobic interests within nations; that is, concerns over racial and ethnic "purity" sometimes cut across national boundaries (Kaplan & Bjørgo, 1998).

The impact of these developments has varied enormously in different settings of time and place. All theories failed fully to take into consideration local events: the historical and traditional contexts that shape relationships among ethnic groups (Chirot, 1981; Evans, 1992). The spread of democratic thinking led to peaceful movements toward devolution in countries such as the United Kingdom and in some previously European colonies, but to conflict in others and in the Balkan countries and Indonesia. Discrimination against, and segregation of, ethnic, racial, and economically deprived populations has been accompanied by violence in many parts of the world. The conduct of international relations changed dramatically toward the end of the twentieth century, as international intervention in the internal affairs of nations occurred repeatedly against such extreme forms of ethnic violence as "ethnic cleansing."

The vast bulk of ethnic and racial violence stops far short of ethnic cleansing, of course, and it is regarded as internal to nations. Regrettably, systematic data relating ethnic segregation and violence of any degree of seriousness are rare, and systematic analyses are rarer still. The nine Western countries selected by Michael Tonry for study of patterns of offending, victimization, and experience in justice systems of ethnic populations, for example, were chosen on the basis of "empirical research traditions that have generated research findings or well-maintained official statistics on which credible assertions can be based." (Tonry, 1997:3) Had selection been restricted to countries for which systematic data concerning segregation and violence were available, the United States would stand virtually alone. For this reason, following a brief note on definitions of ethnicity and race, I begin with U.S. studies, followed by studies in other countries. Emerging theoretical perspectives are then discussed, followed by ethnographic studies that inform the topic. The chapter closes with a crude theoretical paradigm and provocative speculations regarding possible futures of ethnic relations and violence.

The relevance of categories of poverty, socioeconomic status (SES), race, and ethnicity to understanding the causes of violent crime is problematic for several reasons: 1) Such categories are social constructions. Classification of persons by SES, race or ethnic category is based not on rigorous scientific criteria, but on often arbitrary social criteria; persons so identified often identify themselves in very different terms (see Short, 1997; Tonry, 1997). 2) In every nation for which data are available—and for states and communities within nations—these relationships change, often dramatically, over time. 3) They exhibit great variation among nations, and within them. 4) Rates of violent behavior, insofar as they can be determined, typically exhibit greater variation *within* socioeconomic status (SES), racial and ethnic categories than *between* them. 5) SES, racial, and ethnic categories mask variation in the *circumstances of living* of persons so classified. 6) SES, ethnic, and race-specific data on violent offending and victimization and on explanatory variables and processes often are lacking or are of poor quality. 7) Theory is poorly developed, rendering interpretation difficult and often ambiguous. This being said, data for the United States are, in general, less arbitrary and research more rigorous than is the case for other nations.

II.   SEGREGATION AND ETHNIC VIOLENCE IN THE UNITED STATES: QUANTITATIVE ANALYSES

The vast majority of U.S. studies focus on African-Americans in large cities. America's "dilemma" (Myrdal, 1944) remains of critical importance to understanding crime and violence. Even here, many questions remain unanswered—and unanswerable, without more adequate theory and relevant data. Studies of segregation and violence have focused on a variety of units of analysis, time periods, and measures of segregation; findings are not clear cut. Virtually all studies struggle with problems of disentangling the complex relationships between discrimination against African-Americans, segregation, and poverty (both absolute and relative) as they are related to violent crime (see Blau & Blau, 1982). Most studies utilize an index of dissimilarity as a measure of segregation, reflecting the proportion of the black population that would have to be relocated into white areas in order to achieve racial balance (Lieberson, 1981).

A few studies focus on robbery. National victimization surveys do not inquire about homicide in U.S. households, and robbery is an especially feared crime that is believed to be associated with "white flight," and thus to contribute to segregation and isolation of the most disadvantaged segments of society. Messner and South (1986) found that the *percentage black of a city's population* increased both interracial and intraracial robbery when blacks were the offenders, but decreased both interracial and intraracial robbery when whites were the offenders. *Racial segregation* increased the rate of blacks reporting robbery victimization by black offenders, but decreased the rate of white victims' reports that they had been robbed by blacks (racial segregation had a lower positive relationship with white/white robbery, and a lower negative relationship with black/black robbery). Messner and South interpret these findings as evidence that increases in the percentage black (about 12% of the U.S. population in the late twentieth century) increased opportunities for interracial contact, while racial segregation decreased such opportunities.[1]

William Julius Wilson (1987, 1996) has been the most persistent and influential scholar of economic, racial, and ethnic relationships in the United States. Wilson's thesis is that a permanent underclass emerged in some U.S. cities during the 1970s and 1980s, in large part as the result of industrial restructuring and the loss of jobs. Wilson theorizes that segregation of the underclass, which occurred disproportionately among blacks, resulted increasingly in their isolation from mainstream social, economic, and political life. Although the underclass thesis is race neutral, to the extent that all ethnicities and races are affected by the same forces, African-Americans are especially vulnerable, and it is the concentrated poverty and social isolation of black underclass neighborhoods that fuels black violence. Most studies of violence have focused on homicide, the most reliable and valid measure of violence.

Ruth Peterson and Lauren Krivo (1993) related the dissimilarity index and a measure of racial concentration to four black homicide victimization rates (homicides involving family members, acquaintances, and strangers, and total rates) for the years, 1979–1981 (computed from Federal Bureau of Investigation data for central cities with a population of at least 100,000 and a black population of at least 5,000). Both measures of segregation were positively and significantly related to acquaintance and stranger homicides, but not to homicides involving family members. Neither poverty nor income inequality were significantly related to homicide, leading Peterson and Krivo to speculate that the generally high level of economic and other forms of deprivation among African-Americans makes poverty and income inequality, across communities, less meaningful for blacks than for whites. They argue that their findings support Wilson's theory.

Edward Shihadeh and Nicole Flynn (1996) employed a measure of segregation designed specifically to reflect the social isolation of blacks in U.S. large city census tracts. Their analysis suggests that social isolation is a better predictor than dissimilarity of both black homicide and robbery; indeed, that social isolation may account for the relationship between the index of dissimilarity and black urban violence.

Industrial restructuring also has drawn the attention of Shihadeh and Graham Ousey (1998), who focus on entry-level jobs, economic deprivation, and homicide in large U.S. cities for 1970 and 1990. Racial segregation was modestly correlated with both black and white economic deprivation (.31 and .16, respectively), but no statistically significant direct or indirect relationship was found between segregation and the homicide rate for either race. Segregation was positively related to economic deprivation for both blacks

[1] South and Richard Felson (1990) also found racial segregation to be negatively related to interracial rape.

and whites in both years, and changes in the availability of low-skill jobs were negatively related to economic deprivation and, indirectly, to homicide for both races. The findings suggest that industrial restructuring of cities—the loss of manufacturing jobs, especially low-level entry jobs—led to increases in economic deprivation for both blacks and whites, which is positively related to both black and white homicide rates.

Scott Akins (2000), attempting to resolve inconclusive city-level findings regarding serious crimes of violence—and to add serious property crime data—finds that correlations between segregation and six crimes reported by Uniform Crime Report under "violent crimes" in U.S. cities with populations of 25,000 and over were robust and positive for both 1980 and 1990. Correlations for homicide were .43 and .44 in 1980 and 1990, respectively. For a combined violent crime index they were higher in 1990 than in 1980 (.43 and .35). Standardized regression coefficients for segregation and crime, controlling for variables with previously established relationships with crime (median age of residents, region of the country, percent nonwhite, size of place) as well as the percentage of female-based households, a measure of education among adult residents, and the number of manufacturing employees (as indicators of social control and industrial restructuring) were statistically significant, ranging from .18 for homicide to .27 for robbery in 1990.[2]

Although these studies are informative, they lack precision concerning the nature of operative causal processes. For this purpose, *within-city* studies are more appropriate. Krivo and Peterson (1996) focus on extreme disadvantage, local structural disadvantage, and the FBI index of violent (homicide, forcible rape, robbery, and aggravated assault) and property crimes in Columbus, Ohio, 1990. Although no measure of segregation is included in the analysis, Krivo and Peterson note that Columbus is a highly segregated city, and they perform separate analyses for census tracts that are at least 70% black or white, respectively. The study's most striking finding is that "race effects tend to be smaller than the effects of disadvantage," and that the effects of extreme disadvantage (e.g., Wilson's "truly disadvantaged") are pronounced only for violent crime. They also note that extremely disadvantaged black neighborhoods are situated in closer proximity to one another, in a classic "black belt" pattern, than are extremely disadvantaged white communities, which tend to be more dispersed throughout the city. This pattern, and the conclusion "that racial residential segregation means that urban blacks and whites live in different neighborhoods that tend to have divergent levels of social status and disadvantage" (p. 640), are of special relevance theoretically as they bear on isolation as an explanatory mechanism.[3]

Douglas Massey and his colleagues, building on earlier research on processes of residential succession, classified Philadelphia census tracts as white, black entry (the earliest stage of blacks moving into previously all-white tracts), transition, established black, and black declining (the latter "a residual category of predominantly white tracts that are losing both racial groups ... probably closest to transition tracts" in that "the loss of whites is greater than the loss of blacks") (Massey et al., 1987:33). Rates of homicide, rape, assault, and robbery, and a combination of violent and accidental death rates, were all lowest for white tracts, followed by entry, transition, and established black tracts. Rates for the residual black declining tracts were in all cases lower than those for established black tracts, but higher than transition tract rates.

---

[2] Correlations for robbery and rape, and for burglary and car theft were also positive and significant. Among all crimes studied, only the beta coefficient for auto theft (1980) was not statistically significant.

[3] Peterson et al. (2000) also report that rates of violence are negatively related to the presence of recreation centers, but positively related to the presence of bars, adding an institutional dimension to the picture.

Massey et al.'s major point—that racial segregation creates unique barriers to social and spatial mobility for blacks, with distinct disadvantages for those who seek to improve the conditions in which they live—is strongly supported by their data. Another implication, however, supports Wilson's thesis that neighborhoods in transition, though they may be socially disadvantaged (compared to white and black entry neighborhoods) nevertheless have the advantage of the presence of more stable and affluent residents, and more effective institutions, than do established black neighborhoods. As the latter are abandoned by middle class blacks, only the "truly disadvantaged" remain, isolated and with few resources for social control (Wilson, 1987, 1996). Ethnographic studies likewise find that, when stable (and highly visible to young people) "old heads" in black ghettos leave or lose status to less stable residents (who are often younger and engaged in criminal pursuits such as the drug trade), a major consequence is that "decent" residents, compared to those with "street" orientations, lose control over their communities, especially in their ability to influence the young who are most at risk for violent and other criminal behavior (Anderson, 1990, 1999). Paradoxically, the difficulties experienced by middle class blacks in improving their spatial (residential) position enhance the social control capacities of many black communities. These benefits are lost when economically stable and upwardly mobile blacks, as well as whites, leave communities that then become overwhelmingly black and poor.[4]

1. Theory Development

Theory in this sprawling area often has been characterized by speculation concerning both general areas of agreement and what seem to be anomalous findings.

John Hagan and colleagues build upon subcultural theory to suggest that today's increasingly global and market-oriented economy gives rise to a highly individualized "culture of competition" that encourages the acceptance of inequality, repudiation of social outgroups, and a subterranean tradition of hierarchic self-interest that fosters amorality and group delinquency (see Hagan et al., 1998; also Messner & Rosenfeld, 1994). Measures employed in their study of German youth emphasized rejection of "foreigners." Three of the four types of delinquency comprising the group delinquency measure involved fighting or property damage. The study is an ambitious effort to relate global economic processes to individual and group values and behaviors that increasingly characterize ethnic relations in many countries.

Focusing on social capital and spatial dynamics, Robert Sampson and colleagues advance a theory at the local community level (Sampson et al., 1997, 1999). A large sample of Chicago residents were studied to inform the ability of neighborhoods to exert effective control over violence. Child-centered social capital, measured by responses to questions concerning intergenerational closure, reciprocal exchange among local residents, and expectations regarding mutual aid, was significantly lower in highly segregated, disadvantaged, residentially unstable, and high-density areas (Sampson et al., 1999; see, also,

[4]Logan and Messner (1987) found that for the years 1970 and 1980 segregation in *suburban* regions of large U.S. cities was positively related to robbery, aggravated assault, and the Uniform Crime Report violent crime index, but not to homicide or forcible rape. Race and violent crime were reciprocally related in suburbs for the years 1970, 1980, and 1990 (Liska et al. 1998), as well as in central cities (Liska and Bellair 1995). Robbery is the crime that most affects racial composition.

Taylor et al., 1984). Concentrated disadvantage was associated with low shared expectations for public action regarding children, while concentrated affluence was linked to mechanisms that activated networks of intergenerational closure and reciprocated exchange. Significantly, *proximity* of poor and more affluent communities was advantageous to the former with respect to collective efficacy. Collective efficacy (social cohesion among neighbors and willingness to intervene on behalf of the common good) were, in turn, linked to reduced violence in those communities (Sampson et al., 1997).

Spatial proximity with affluent areas may have a spill-over effect that encourages residents in disadvantaged areas to take a more active role in child supervision and intergenerational exchange. Sampson et al. compared two neighborhoods: A, which has low shared expectations for child social control, adjoins neighborhoods in which expectations are much higher; B, which has high expectations for child control, is located near neighborhoods in which there is considerably less willingness to intervene on behalf of children. Reflecting the effects of segregation, neighborhood A is 90% white; B is 99% black. The finding that residential stability, as well as concentrated affluence, is important to collective efficacy, and that the advantage of these relationships characterizes white neighborhoods to a greater extent than black neighborhoods, confirms spatial concentration ("black belt") effects documented by Krivo and Peterson (1996), Massey et al. (1987) in Columbus and Philadelphia, as well as by Wilson, and others (Morenoff & Tienda, 1997; Morenoff & Sampson, 1997) in Chicago. Ecological analyses over time suggest that Chicago's neighborhoods are increasingly characterized by spatial polarization, racially, ethnically, and in terms of concentrated affluence and poverty.

A large body of research documents that poverty exacerbates the vicissitudes of daily living and increases the *motivation* for crime and violence as means of solving problems (Agnew, 1999). Communities characterized by concentrated poverty select and retain individuals who are experiencing extraordinary economic, status, interpersonal, and familial strains, as well as strains in their relationships with institutions such as schools, police and the juvenile and criminal justice systems, welfare agencies, insurance and other businesses (see Valentine, 1978; Anderson, 1990, 1999; Hannerz, 1969; Harris & Curtis, 1998; Sampson & Bartusch, 1998; Wilson, 1987, 1996). When combined, as they often are in highly segregated and deprived communities, such strains have cumulative and amplifying effects (Lauritsen & Sampson, 1998). General strain theory seeks to explain how such adverse macrolevel conditions influence individual motivations and decision-making with the frequent result of violence and other types of criminal behavior. Crime and criminal victimization are, of course, major sources of strain on individuals, families, and communities.

2.   Ethnographic Research, Subcultural Theory, and Social Identity

Concentration effects of poverty, family disruption, and residential instability are fundamental to "*cultural social isolation*," as well as to the disruption of institutional and interpersonal networks that make social control possible (Sampson & Wilson, 1995:44). Ethnographic research confirms the mediating influences of community social organization and collective processes in producing violence among the truly disadvantaged. Elijah Anderson identifies interpersonal violence and aggression as the most pressing of problems besetting the poor inner-city black community. Violence is an adaptive response that "springs from the circumstances of life among the ghetto poor—the lack of jobs that pay a living wage, limited basic public services (police response in emergencies, building maintenance, trash pickup, lighting, and other services that middle-class neighborhoods take for granted), the stigma of race, the fallout from rampant drug use and drug trafficking, and the resulting alienation and absence of hope for the future" (Anderson, 1999:32). At the heart of "street culture" is the "code of the streets," which often demands adherence for survival and competes with "decency" as a guide to behavior. Young people, especially, must negotiate relationships that are fraught with tension and potential conflict, in "staging areas" where individuals and groups vie for status—and where trivial matters can turn into matters of "respect" that must be settled on the spot. Youth culture, ubiquitous in much of the world, poses special problems for those who cannot afford the artifacts that are so skillfully marketed to youth (Sullivan, 1989). Gang culture often adds to this volatile mix, raising the stakes in contests for status and respect.

Although decency remains the norm among the vast majority of the truly disadvantaged, for some, wider cultural values lack viability in the struggle to survive (Valentine, 1978; Anderson, 1990, 1999; Sampson & Bartusch, 1998). Social and personal *identities* may shift in response to intergroup relationships and situational contingencies (Turner & Onorato, 1999). Group processes, as well as processes of socialization contribute to the adaptations that people make to the physical circumstances of their lives.

3. Ethnicity, Immigration, and Violence in Canada, England and Wales, Western Europe, and Australia

Immigration effects on segregation and violence depend heavily on the relative power of host and immigrant populations. In the United States, Canada, and Australia, native peoples were subjugated by immigrants, yet data concerning crime among indigenous peoples are relatively undeveloped.[5]

Canadian criminologists have devoted more attention to crime among aboriginal peoples, much less to other racial and ethnic categories. Crime rates are generally higher among aboriginals than among nonaboriginals, although the lumping together of all persons so classified masks enormous racial and ethnic variations in both categories. Severe economic deprivation and other social ills characterize aboriginals, both on and off "reserves," but little is known specifically about segregation effects, as Canadian researchers continue to search for baseline data that would permit such study (Roberts & Doob, 1997). Until 1941, a non-European, nonaboriginal origin category of "racial origins" referred to "Negro or Mongolian (Chinese or Japanese) as the case may be" (Roberts & Doob, 1997:473). Mosher (1998), however, documents the "the racialization of crime" in Canada focusing increasingly on blacks.

Ethnic populations vary greatly across Canada, with most blacks immigrating from the United States prior to the 1960s, when increasing numbers of black immigrants arrived from Africa and the West Indies. Mosher's analysis suggests that this change triggered increased prejudice and discrimination against blacks and a tendency among law enforcement officials to attribute crime problems, especially violent crime, to blacks. Factors contributing to higher rates of violent crime in the United States, compared to Canada, are higher rates of residential segregation of the poor, the greater availability of firearms, and a more urbanized population (Ouimet, 1999; Hagan & Foster, 2000).

---

[5]Only recently has the United States begun to devote systematic attention to crime among American Indians (see Greenfeld and Smith 1999), and has yet to study crime in relation to patterns of residence.

Systematic study of crime among Australian Aborigines is recent and limited. Aborigines are less urban, and higher proportions of them live in rural and remote areas. Rates of violent crimes and victimization are higher among Aborigines and are associated with many of the same problems as are found among blacks and the United States and Canada. Beyond these similarities striking differences are found. Aboriginal females are "substantially more at risk" of violence than are males, for example, and "the differential risks (the ratio of Aborigine/non-Aborigine) tend to *increase* with age" (Broadhurst, 1997:420; emphasis added). Compared to non-Aborigines, homicide victimization rates among Aborigines are even higher than total violence victimization rates. Broadhurst (1997:456–457) invokes conflict and subcultural theory, and the "frontier" character of life in more remote areas of Australia to explain high rates of violence and imprisonment among Aborigines—"vast areas remain 'wilderness' and settlers or immigrants and the surviving indigenous people contest the social, economic, and moral domains, especially at the geographic and cross-cultural margins ... social order and solidarity is conditional and constantly redefined to meet evolving circumstances."

4. Europe, England and Wales

When two populations that are already separated by culture come into contact in societies dominated by one of those cultures—particularly when the dominant culture is ethnically relatively homogeneous—the basis is laid for conflict. Problems are exacerbated when multiple "foreign" populations enter an established society. This is what has happened since World War II in much of the West, especially the United States and Canada, Britain and several Western European countries. Tonry's "Ethnicity, Crime, and Immigration" (1997) makes few explicit references to segregation; nor do contributors to "Urban Housing Segregation of Minorities in Western Europe and the United States" (Huttman et al., 1991) discuss violence or crime. It is clear, however, that both immigrant and indigenous, but minority populations are located in less desirable housing, overcrowded dwellings, and communities with high rates of social problems; and that they suffer from a variety of types of discrimination. The macrolevel forces vary a great deal: among established native peoples, as in Australia, Canada, and the United States, international migration as guest-workers or refugees in many countries. Systematic data on specific immigrant streams and violence are virtually nonexistent, however. In Germany, reaction to the Nazi regime's treatment of minorities resulted in the elimination of all references to race and ethnicity in official information systems (Albrecht, 1997). In Sweden, even to inquire about a person's race in a survey or for purposes of an official record is considered discriminatory (Martens, 1997). However, a careful study of Stockholm reports that the "ethnic dimension" of co-offending youth networks is "governed . . . not by the ethnic background of the actors themselves, but rather by the type of residential segregation" in the city (Sarnecki, 2000:167).[6] Delinquent networks often are formed in suburban locations *outside* large cities where a variety of relatively small ethnic populations settle. The networks typically consist of youth from these varied populations, together with Swedes living in these suburbs—many of whom are from underclass families.

Relevant findings from the Tonry volume are: 1) Offense rates for some minorities exceed those for majority populations in all countries studied, but the higher rates often

---

[6]The page number for this quotation refers to Sarnecki's unpublished manuscript.

are for relatively minor property crimes. 2) Differences in offending, rather than bias appear to be the primary basis for higher rates of incarceration of minorities; however, disadvantages experienced at earlier stages of justice system processing have cumulative effects on later stages. 3) Minorities "characterized by high crime and imprisonment rates are also characterized by various indicators of social and economic disadvantage." (Tonry, 1997:13) 4) Behaviors and stereotypes of minority populations often contribute to their disadvantages in justice systems and elsewhere in host societies.

Racial and ethnic peoples differ a great deal in their adaptations to minority status. David J. Smith contrasts the "outgoing survival strategy adopted by black people in Britain" with "the culturally enclosed strategy of South Asians":

> White people were just as much inclined to discriminate against South Asians as against black people, but black people were far more likely to encounter discrimination because they were more likely, for example, to apply for a job cold, whereas the South Asian would be more likely to seek out opportunities through relatives and friends. One consequence of these different approaches to surviving in Britain may be that white people have formed very different notions of the black and South Asian communities. They are more likely to feel the need to control the behavior of black than that of South Asian people, because the behavior of South Asians tends to be hidden from them. (Smith, 1997:174)

These observations suggest both social capital and subcultural explanations. South Asians have an advantage in the relationships and contacts (social capital) that facilitate employment. Applying for a job "cold" suggests that blacks lack this type of social capital. Correspondingly, differences in survival strategies may relate to greater structural deprivation and cultural adaptations among blacks.

5. Segregation and Youth Group Violence

Although most of their behavior is neither violent nor otherwise criminal, youth gangs and other collectivities have long been associated with violence. And although media reports tend to exaggerate their occasionally violent behavior, gang membership clearly facilitates and amplifies such behavior.

The race and ethnicity of youth groups that are classified as gangs in the United States has a varied and changing history. Until mid-twentieth century, most members of such groups were boys and young men from the many white ethnic groups that comprised the ethnic patchwork of local communities in large U.S. cities (Thrasher, 1927; Short, 1997). Although gangs of white youth continue to exist, especially in small cities and rural counties, many—perhaps most—gangs in the United States are black or Hispanic, and racially and ethnically unmixed. Asian gangs are also an increasing presence in the United States. These patterns are to a large extent a direct result of immigration and of racial and ethnic segregation. Recent (1998) data suggest that the ethnic composition of U.S. youth gangs may be changing in two important respects: as many as one-third of youth gangs are composed of a significant mixture of two or more racial/ethnic groups, and the age distribution of gang members appears to be increasing.[7] The latter trend is especially pronounced in large cities, the result, in large part, of two developments: 1) The loss of jobs in the inner city areas where many gangs are located. 2) The return from prison of gang members to local communities.

[7]Data supplied by the National Youth Gang Center (U.S. Department of Justice 1999; National Youth Gang Center 2000).

Economic dislocations are also associated with violence among gangs in the United Kingdom and in Europe. However, the structure of such groups, their behavior and ethnicity, and their ecological distribution differ from gangs in the United States. In Europe, as in the United States, popular depictions of gangs as highly cohesive and tightly organized and violent are misleading. It is clear, however, that European gangs tend to be less criminal and less violent than are many gangs in the United States, and there are fewer of them. European cities lack the strong gang traditions that exist in some large U.S. cities; hence their gangs tend to be less territorial—a characteristic associated also with the ecological structure of European cities, many of which have constructed low income housing in outlying areas rather than in inner cities, as has been the case in the United States.

Youth gangs in Europe often are comprised of the children of guest-workers and refugees from many countries, with no one ethnic population dominating; hence, the mixed ethnic composition of many youth groups. Much violence is perpetrated against ethnic minorities by majority youth groups. On balance, scholars conclude that many European cities have street gangs, and that gang members tend to form among youth who have been marginalized by virtue of ethnicity or economic circumstances. Law enforcement attention to gangs clearly has increased in Europe, in the United Kingdom, and in some of the former Soviet Union countries in recent years.[8]

III. CONCLUSION: COMPETING FUTURE SCENARIOS

Massey (1996), noting that the industrial revolution radically changed both the amount and the distribution of wealth, sketches a future of an increasingly urbanized world characterized by extreme concentration of affluence and poverty. Citing population trends and the ecological distribution of crime in U.S. cities, Massey argues that the affluent and the poor are likely to be increasingly segregated spatially and separated socially. The resulting cultural differentiation, he argues, will lead to higher rates of crime and violence among the poor that, in turn, will result in further withdrawal of the affluent and greater isolation of the poor, and thus contribute to an accelerating cycle of social class alienation.

This bleak scenario rests on several assumptions: continuation of world trends toward urbanization, increased segregation of the affluent from the poor, continued and increasing crime and violence in poor communities, leading to further protective measures by the affluent (such as gated communities), leaving poor communities with diminished resources to cope with disorder. The first of these assumptions seems quite likely, but the remainder are at least problematic. The association of urbanization with crime is well established in some countries, but it is historically controversial (Gillis, 1996), and proximity of poor and more affluent neighborhoods may be advantageous to the former, as we have seen. The spill over effects of residential proximity of the affluent and the disadvantaged clearly would be limited, however, should the more affluent seal themselves off from the poor, with gated communities and other security measures.

---

[8] Weitekamp (2000) provides an excellent summary of gangs in Europe, based on papers presented at two "Eurogang Workshops," held in Schmitten, Germany, in 1998, and in Oslo, Norway, in 1999. Other papers presented at the Oslo workshop questioned the appellation "gangs" as applied to all but a few of youth groups in their countries.

IV.   DESIDERATA

Future interethnic, interracial, and social class relationships—and their relationship to violence—remain quite uncertain. Global urbanization and its impacts are likely to vary greatly along many dimensions, including levels of technological development among nations and cities, access to global markets, the character of political regimes, the activities of racist and antiminority organizations, institutional, structural and cultural traditions—each of which will influence crime and its control. No single theoretical framework as yet encompasses the richness of the economic, institutional, and interest group contexts within which ethnic violence occurs.

Modernization enthusiasts were not the only theorists who failed to anticipate the ethnicization of violence. Without "disaggregation" of ethnic violence, neither world system theory, dependency theory, nor conflict theory can explain the causal heterogeneity of the behaviors that are so loosely grouped under the rubric of ethnic violence (Brubaker and Laitin, 1998:446; see also Evans, 1992). Clearly this is the case with respect to crime. More is required than better record keeping. Better official records would help, but there is need also for in-depth case studies, and better classification schemes, theoretical perspectives, and documentation of the mechanisms that characterize ethnic violence. There is, finally, a need for "a community of researchers and policy makers in many countries who will attempt to establish what is known, what is knowable, and how current knowledge might be advanced through comparative inquiry" (Tonry, 1997:26).

REFERENCES

Agnew, Robert. (1999). A General Strain Theory of Community Differences in Crime Rates. *Journal of Research in Crime and Delinquency, 36*, 123–155.

Akins, Scott. (2000). *A Longitudinal Examination of Segregation and Crime*. Unpublished paper, Department of Sociology, Washington State University.

Albrecht, Hans-Jörg. (1997). Ethnic Minorities, Crime, and Criminal Justice in Germany. In Michael H. Tonry (Ed.), *Ethnicity, Crime, and Immigration: Comparative and Cross-National Perspectives. Crime and Justice: A Review of Research, 21* (pp. 31–99). Chicago: University of Chicago Press.

Anderson, Elijah. (1990). *Streetwise: Race, Class and Change in an Urban Community*. Chicago: University of Chicago Press.

Anderson, Elijah. (1999). *Code of the Street: Decency, Violence, and the Moral Life of the Inner City*. New York: W. W. Norton.

Armer, J. Michael, & John Katsillis. (1992). Modernization Theory. In Edgar Borgatta & Marie L. Borgatta (Eds.), *Encyclopedia of Sociology, 3* (pp. 1299–1304). New York: Macmillan.

Blau, Judith R., & Peter M. Blau. (1982). The Cost of Inequality: Metropolitan Structure and Violent Crime. *American Sociological Review, 47*, 114–129.

Broadhurst, Roderic. (1997). Aborigines and Crime in Australia. In Michael H. Tonry (Ed.), *Ethnicity, Crime, and Immigration: Comparative and Cross-National Perspectives. Crime and Justice: A Review of Research, 21* (pp. 407–468). Chicago: University of Chicago Press.

Brubaker, Rogers, & David D. Laitin. (1998). Ethnic and Nationalist Violence. *Annual Review of Sociology, 24*, 423–452.

Chirot, Daniel. (1981). Changing Fashions in the Study of the Social Causes of Economic and Political Change. In James F. Short Jr. (Ed.), *The State of Sociology: Problems and Prospects* (pp. 259–282). Beverly Hills: Sage.

Evans, Peter B. (1992). Global Systems Analysis. In Edgar Borgatta & Marie L. Borgatta (Eds.), *Encyclopedia of Sociology, 2* (pp. 772–778). New York: Macmillan.

Gillis, A. R. (1996). Urbanization, Sociohistorical Context, and Crime. In John Hagan, A. R. Gillis & David Brownfield (Eds.), *Criminological Controversies: A Methodological Primer* (pp. 47–74). Boulder: Westview.

Glaser, Daniel. (1971). *Social Deviance*. Chicago: Markham.

Greenfeld, Lawrence A., & Steven K. Smith. (1999). *American Indians and Crime*. Washington: Bureau of Justice Statistics, U.S. Department of Justice.

Hagan, John, Gerd Hefler, Gabriele Classen, Klaus Boehnke, & Hans Merkens. (1998). Subterranean Sources of Subcultural Delinquency beyond the American Dream. *Criminology*, 36, 309–341.

Hagan, John, & Holly Foster. (2000). Making Corporate and Criminal America Less Violent: Public Norms and Structural Reforms. *Contemporary Sociology*, 29(1), 44–53.

Hannerz, Ulf. (1969). *Soulside: Inquiries into Ghetto Culture and Community*. New York: Columbia University Press.

Harris, Fred R., & Lynn A. Curtis (Eds.) (1998). *Locked in the Poorhouse: Cities, Race, and Poverty in the United States: A Milton S. Eisenhower Foundation Update of the Kerner Commission Report*. Lanham: Rowman & Littlefield.

Huttman, Elizabeth D., Wim Blauw, & Juliet Saltman (Eds.) (1991). *Urban Housing Segregation of Minorities in Western Europe and the United States*. Durham: Duke University Press.

Inglehart, Ronald, & Wayne E. Baker. (2000). Modernization, Cultural Change, and the Persistence of Traditional Values. *American Sociological Review*, 65, 19–51.

Kaplan, Jeffrey, & Tore Bjørgo (Eds.) (1998). *Nation and Race: The Developing Euro-American Racist Subculture*. Boston: Northeastern University Press.

Krivo, Lauren J., & Ruth D. Peterson. (1996). Extremely Disadvantaged Neighborhoods and Urban Crime. *Social Forces*, 75, 619–650.

Lauritsen, Janet, & Robert J. Sampson. (1998). Minorities, Crime, and Criminal Justice. In Michael H. Tonry (Ed.), *Handbook of Crime and Punishment* (pp. 58–84). New York: Oxford University Press.

Lieberson, Stanley. (1981). An Asymmetrical Approach to Segregation. In Ceri Peach, Vaughan Robinson & Susan Smith (Eds.), *Ethnic Segregation in Cities* (pp. 61–82). Athens: University of Georgia Press.

Liska, Allen E., & Paul E. Bellair. (1995). Violent Crime Rates and Racial Composition: Convergence Over Time. *American Journal of Sociology*, 101, 578–610.

Liska, Allen E., John R. Logan, & Paul E. Bellair. (1998). Race and Violent Crime in the Suburbs. *American Sociological Review*, 63, 27–38.

Logan, John R., & Steven F. Messner. (1987). Racial Residential Segregation and Suburban Violent Crime. *Social Forces*, 68, 510–527.

Martens, Peter L. (1997). Immigrants, Crime, and Criminal Justice in Sweden. In Michael H. Tonry (Ed.), *Ethnicity, Crime, and Immigration: Comparative and Cross-National Perspectives. Crime and Justice: A Review of Research, 21* (pp. 183–256). Chicago: University of Chicago Press.

Massey, Douglas S., Gretchen A. Condran, & Nancy A. Denton. (1987). The Effect of Residential Segregation on Black Social and Economic Well-being. *Social Forces*, 66, 29–56.

Massey, Douglas S. (1996). The Age of Extremes: Concentrated Affluence and Poverty in the Twenty-first Century. *Demography*, 33(4), 395–412.

Messner, Steven, & Scott J. South. (1986). Economic Deprivation, Opportunity Structure, and Robbery Victimization: Intra- and Interracial Patterns. *Social Forces*, 64, 975–991.

Messner, Steven, & Richard Rosenfeld. (1994). *Crime and the American Dream*. New York: Wadsworth.

Morenoff, Jeffrey D., & Robert J. Sampson. (1997). Violent Crime and the Spatial Dynamics of Neighborhood Transition: Chicago, 1970–1990. *Social Forces*, 76, 31–64.

Morenoff, Jeffrey D., & Marta Tienda. (1997). Underclass Neighborhoods in Temporal and Ecological Perspective. *The Annals of the American Academy of Political and Social Science, 551*, 59–72.

Mosher, Clayton James. (1998). *Discrimination and Denial: Systemic Racism in Ontario's Legal and Criminal Justice Systems, 1892–1961*. Toronto: University of Toronto Press.

Myrdal, Gunnar, with the assistance of Richard Sterner and Arnold Rose. (1944). *An American Dilemma: The Negro Problem and Modern Democracy*. New York: Harper.

National Youth Gang Center. (2000). *1998 National Youth Gang Survey*, unpublished report. Tallahassee.

Ouimet, Marc. (1999). Crime in Canada and in the United States: A Comparative Analysis. *Canadian Review of Sociology and Anthropology/La Revue Canadienne de Sociologie et D'Antropologie, 36*(3), 389–408.

Peterson, Ruth D., & Lauren J. Krivo. (1993). Racial Segregation and Black Urban Homicide. *Social Forces*, 75, 1001–1026.

Peterson, Ruth D., Lauren J. Krivo, & Mark A. Harris. (2000). Disadvantage and Neighborhood Violent Crime: Do Institutions Matter? *Journal of Research in Crime and Delinquency*, 37, 31–63.

Roberts, Julian V., & Anthony N. Doob. (1997). Race, Ethnicity, and Criminal Justice in Canada. In Michael H.

Tonry (Ed.), *Ethnicity, Crime, and Immigration: Comparative and Cross-National Perspectives. Crime and Justice: A Review of Research, 21* (pp. 469–522). Chicago: University of Chicago Press.

Sampson, Robert J., & William Julius Wilson. (1995). Toward a Theory of Race, Crime, and Urban Inequality. In John Hagan & Ruth D. Peterson (Eds.), *Crime and Inequality* (pp. 37–54). Stanford: Stanford University Press.

Sampson, Robert J., Stephen Raudenbush, & Felton Earls. (1997). Neighborhoods and Violent Crime: A Multilevel Study of Collective Efficacy. *Science, 277*, 918–924.

Sampson, Robert J., & Dawn Jeglum Bartusch. (1998). Legal Cynicism and (Subcultural?) Tolerance of Deviance: The Neighborhood Context of Racial Differences. *Law & Society Review, 32*, 777–804.

Sampson, Robert J., Jeffrey D. Morenoff, & Felton Earls. (1999). Spatial Dynamics of Collective Efficacy for Children. *American Sociological Review, 64*, 633–660.

Sarnecki, Jerzy. (2000). *Delinquent Links. Network Analysis of Youth Co-Offending*. Cambridge: Cambridge University Press.

Shihadeh, Edward H., & Nicole Flynn. (1996). Segregation and Crime: The Effect of Black Social Isolation on the Rates of Black Urban Violence. *Social Forces, 74*, 1325–1352.

Shihadeh, Edward H., & Graham Ousey. (1998). Industrial Restructuring and Violence: The Link between Entry-Level Jobs, Economic Deprivation, and Black and White Homicide. *Social Forces, 77*, 185–206.

Short, James F. Jr. (1997). *Poverty, Ethnicity, and Violent Crime*. Boulder: Westview.

Smith, David J. (1997). Ethnic Origins, Crime, and Criminal Justice in England and Wales. In Michael H. Tonry (Ed.), *Ethnicity, Crime, and Immigration: Comparative and Cross-National Perspectives. Crime and Justice: A Review of Research, 21* (pp. 101–182). Chicago: University of Chicago Press.

South, Scott J., & Richard B. Felson. (1990). The Racial Patterning of Rape. *Social Forces, 69*(1), 71–93.

Sullivan, Mercer. (1989). *Getting Paid: Youth Crime and Work in the Inner City*. Ithaca: Cornell University Press.

Taylor, Ralph, Stephen Gottfredson, & Sidney Brower. (1984). Block Crime and Fear: Defensible Space, Local Social Ties, and Territorial Functioning. *Journal of Research in Crime and Delinquency, 21*, 303–331.

Thrasher, Frederic M. (1927). *The Gang: A Study of 1,313 Gangs in Chicago*. Chicago: University of Chicago Press.

Tonry, Michael H. (Ed.) (1997). *Ethnicity, Crime, and Immigration: Comparative and Cross-National Perspectives. Crime and Justice: A Review of Research, 21*. Chicago: University of Chicago Press.

Turner, John C., & Rina S. Onorato. (1999). Social Identity, Personality, and the Self-Concept: A Self-categorization Perspective. In Tom R. Tyler, Roderick M. Kramer & Oliver P. John (Eds.), *The Psychology of the Social Self* (pp. 11–46). London: Lawrence Erlbaum Associates.

U.S. Department of Justice. (1999). *1996 National Youth Gang Survey*. Washington: Office of Juvenile Justice and Delinquency Prevention.

Valentine, Bettlou. (1978). *Hustling and Other Hard Work: Life Styles in the Ghetto*. New York: Free Press.

Weitekamp, Elmar G. M. (2000). Gangs in Europe: Assessments at the Millennium. In Malcolm W. Klein, Hans-Jürgen Kerner, Cheryl Maxson, & Elmar G. M. Weitekamp (Eds.), *The Eurogang Paradox: Street Gangs and Youth Groups in the U.S. and Europe* (pp. 309–322). New York: Kluwer/Plenum.

Wilson, William Julius. (1987). *The Truly Disadvantaged: The Inner City, the Underclass, and Public Policy*. Chicago: University of Chicago Press.

Wilson, William Julius. (1996). *When Work Disappears: The World of the New Urban Poor*. New York: Knopf.

A Comparative Examination of Gender Perspectives on Violence

CAROL HAGEMANN-WHITE

I. INTRODUCTION

1. Violence as a Gender Issue

When violence is perceived and named as such, this raises implicit and explicit questions about the social order and power relationships. During the 1970s, naming gender-related violence was itself a violation of the social order, even in the social sciences. In family sociology William Goode (1971/1975) had written about violence in the family and explained it in terms of resource theory, but he did so using assumptions about men's rights to power over wife and children, based on the premise of unquestionable order in gender relations, in a way that is difficult to imagine today. The feminist movement, with its slogan "the personal is political," completely rejected this approach. Violence in heterosexual relationships and marriage was seen to expose the structure of relationships between women and men as a system for regulating power relationships that should no longer be tolerated.

The political challenge was followed by a broad change of consciousness that had a specific influence not only on practice, but also on research into violence. That is the subject of this chapter. The introductory section delineates the areas of research chosen for comparison and aims to clarify some concepts. In the second section various analytical and theoretical approaches to the subject of violence are examined and compared, whereby the internationally better-known American contributions are presented in less detail. Differences are identified between the developments of feminist analyses of violence, the origins of the knowledge base on gender-related violence, the theoretical traditions, and the nature of the relationship between research and politics. The third section presents

W. Heitmeyer and J. Hagan (eds.), *International Handbook of Violence Research*, 97–117.
© 2003 Kluwer Academic Publishers. Printed in the Netherlands.

selected empirical data on the types, extent, and context of two main forms of violence. The aim here is to show how in each discourse, certain findings are possible and others are absent. Results of studies evaluating intervention and assistance are not dealt with in detail, and attitude research can only be mentioned briefly. The article ends with consideration of desiderata for research.

2. Aims and Topics for a Comparative Perspective

Although women's movements grew out of local conditions and motives, their central issues—including violence against women—took shape in a process of international discussion. In Europe the "International Tribunal on Crimes Against Women" in 1976 in Brussels sparked off activities that soon resulted in the successful founding of women's shelters in West Germany. In the following period, too, the translation of "movement literature," especially from the United States and Great Britain, often initiated the "career" of a new topic; its further development grew with reports of local experience, as well as following an independent discussion within each country. The ease with which issues and practical approaches spread around the world indicated that globalization already existed in real terms, contributing to a sustained scandalization of both gender-specific violence, now made visible, and the respective local legal and social conditions, wherever these allowed male violence to go unpunished, or even encouraged it.

Thus the gender perspective on violence has included both comprehensive international and local, "home-grown" dimensions. The present chapter explores the tensions between the global and the local by means of a comparison. To this end, the scope of the topic has been limited and two contrasting discourses chosen: post-1976 German-language[1] research (publications in [West] Germany, Austria, and Switzerland referred continuously to each other) on the one hand, and English-language literature, especially the post-1970 discussion in the United States, on the other. Both of the issues selected are the subject of global political discussion: violence in marriage, and rape and sexual coercion.

Linguistic regions do not always represent the boundaries of a discourse. In the case of gender-based violence, however, language divides the discourse in a specific fashion, as can be seen very clearly in Europe. In proximity to social movements and to practice, as well as to politics, discussion and publications take place in the national language and are rarely translated, while the international literature in English is read and used extremely selectively. In the United States, by contrast, the national language is also the dominant global language of science, and foreign-language research from other countries is practically ignored. For feminist research in Great Britain and for oppositional positions in the United States it is particularly difficult to swim against the social science mainstream, while German, French, and Swedish researchers, for example, always had the option of referring to local traditions and ignoring American perspectives or treating them as curiosities. This has also meant, however, that avowedly feminist voices in the American discourse looked to Great Britain for support. Thus the British literature cannot be completely excluded here, because it has an important, if often indirect influence on the flow of the American discussion. The German-language discussion is taken as exemplary for a continental European perspective that has increasingly entered into an internal research dialogue since the mid-1990s, gaining impetus from initiatives of the Council of Europe and later the European Union.

[1] The discussion in the Netherlands was also closely related to that in Germany, so it is also referred to in places.

For a successful comparison it is necessary to select themes. This overview is restricted to physical violence in marriage and marriage-like relationships (in the following: domestic violence) and rape and sexual coercion or assaults (sexual violence). These two fields have generated by far the most research: they have become an issue in all countries where a gender perspective on violence has taken on clear contours; and it is often assumed that statements on these issues have almost global validity. Their outstanding significance also springs from the seriousness of injury involved and from their distribution throughout society, suggesting that women from all social situations are affected. These fields are also particularly suitable for international comparison. The women's movements in Western industrialized countries differed in whether they made sexual violence or domestic violence their primary public issue (Hanmer 1996; Hagemann-White 2000); the discourses in the United States and the European Union also differ as to whether these forms of violence (in particular domestic violence) are to be regarded as gender-related. These two fields thus can illuminate different contours of a gender perspective.

3.   Central Concepts and Social Context

Gender perspectives on violence were molded by a feminist analysis[2], whose core—across all local discourses—is the location of violence in gender relations. The discovery of the frequency with which acts of sexual or physical violence were committed by men against women formed only one point of reference. Of equal importance were the recognition that this occurred largely in the context of relationships or against women who were known personally, and the fact that the deeds overwhelmingly encountered no sanctions and remained without consequences for the perpetrator, while the perpetrators themselves assumed and indeed asserted that they were exercising legitimate rights. The interaction of these three aspects—empirical frequency, relationship context, and societal tolerance of assaults—resulted in the thesis that violence against women is characteristic of patriarchy: the unequal economic and social power of the sexes is linked to systematic disregard for the sexual self-determination and the physical and psychological integrity of women (cf. e.g., Dobash & Dobash 1979). This analysis does not see only women and girls as victims; it includes the possibility that men can also be victims of gender-based violence if they fail to meet the standards of hegemonic masculinity or pose a threat to it. In general, feminist approaches assess interpersonal violence by its role in maintaining the normative underpinnings of gender inequality, while conversely the existing gender relations are judged by the extent to which violence is associated with masculinity and belongs to normality.

   This internationally developed basic position is significantly differentiated according to the concrete social environment. The rapidly growing awareness of "violence against women" brought with it a loss of context: empirical findings, analyses, explanations, and recommendations for practice were discussed as if they were universal facts. Furthermore, knowledge of violence creates per se a pressure to act, and because politicians tend to

---

[2]These are not identical. A gender perspective is not necessarily feminist, especially in the United States where the term "gender" has largely replaced "sex" as the preferred designation for male/female. Conversely, however, a feminist analysis always relates to gender as a relationship of social inequality; in the European context, use of the English term "gender" points to such a relationship.

react to statistics, research was not immune to premature generalizations. To this day, both in feminist literature and in social science research (and then also in the growing interface between the two) there is a strong tendency to cite empirical findings from North America as if they were automatically valid for other countries. Today, it is important to restore context to arrive at more complex knowledge.

Loss of context is particularly problematic where the subject is violence. Even the deed itself—the violent character of an act—cannot be identified beyond doubt without reference to sociocultural and subjective dimensions. Even Heinrich Popitz's limited definition of violence as "an action of power leading to intentional physical injury to another" (Popitz 1992:48), requires an interpretation of each specific situation in order to identify the power to act and the requisite intention. The context is explicitly integrated in the broad concept of abuse or battering that emerged from the experience of the first shelter, covering "any assault on the physical and psychological integrity of a person using a preexisting societal position of relative power" (Hagemann-White et al. 1981:24).

While physical overpowerment with consequential physical injury remains emblematic for both fields of violence—domestic abuse and rape each represent the whole spectrum—taken-for-granted local understandings shape the practical application of the definition of violence, determining what is understood as violence in the concrete social context of the research.

This becomes clear in the case of sexual violation as soon as it is incriminated on its own account rather than solely for the additionally applied violence (for example to overcome resistance). The fact of bodily contact cannot serve to distinguish between violation and intimacy, so questions of will and cultural norms become unavoidable. Researchers often ask about sexual acts that the interviewee "did not want" (Krahé, Scheinberger-Olwig, & Waizenhöfer 1999; cf. Muehlenhard et al. 1992b). Hans-Christian Harten objects that especially with young adults this covers too broad a spectrum of conflicts and misunderstandings and calls for a narrower definition of sexual violence that can distinguish "between advances that a woman can reject and the enforcement of own sexual goals against the will of the woman" (Harten 1995:33). However, this narrowing only underlines that violence cannot be delineated without consideration of the sociocultural rules.

The American ritual of "dating" defines the possibilities for rejection and their presence or absence differently from the German "*Miteinander gehen*"[3]. In the case of harassment at work, German labor law and worker participation rules form a very different framework than in the United States.[4] Differences between country and milieu are even greater with respect to those factors that are often linked with violence. For example, living together as a couple without marrying has a different sociocultural meaning in the United States than in Germany or Scandinavia, and the same applies to claiming state welfare benefits after a separation, the availability of health insurance, and the legal options for protection from and compensation for physical violence. Thus it makes sense to relate the research to the country or region and the culture. In the process, different nuances become apparent even in the meaning of concepts.

---

[3] Often-repeated American studies show that many young people there believe sexual coercion to be justified if the man regularly dated the woman according to the rules of dating and paid the costs, cf. Koss et al. 1994.

[4] Although this says nothing about which system better allows a woman to escape from unwanted advances. Depending on the "atmosphere," the ease with which American companies can dismiss "problem cases" without notice can either silence the woman or offer her fast protection.

II. CONTRASTING TRENDS IN RESEARCH IN GERMANY AND THE UNITED STATES

The most important areas of empirical research in German-speaking countries to date have been: documenting the various forms of violence against women and their relationships to one another; evaluating services and measures; analyzing the experience of violence and how it is overcome in the context of women's lives; and investigating attitudes, stereotypes, and strategies for change. Research in the United States is more broadly spread, and there are different views on the relevance of gender. Phenomena that the European discussion automatically treats as gender-related violence can in American research be regarded through a positivist lens, where gender is only one of many variables. With respect to sexual violence, criminological models compete with those that locate the problem in gender relations (cf. Muehlenhard, Harney, & Jones 1992).

Because of the common language, specifically American trends and controversies have more influence on British research (cf. Kelly 1988; Dobash & Dobash 1992) than is the case on the continent. Nonetheless, avowedly feminist research on violence is significantly better established and developed in Great Britain than in the United States, due among other reasons to close cooperation with politics on the one hand and with locally based practice on the other. The British literature, in turn, has had a lasting effect on the formation of feminist positions in the American discourse[5], for example with several contributions in the influential anthology by Ylló and Bograd (1988), which opened the American dialogue between the feminist and family sociology research approaches.

Other important problems that are relatively well documented in the German as well as in the U.S. literature but for which little theory has emerged were excluded from this overview. They include trafficking in women and sex tourism (cf. Heine-Wiedenmann & Ackermann 1992; Leidholdt 1996); violence experienced by women in vulnerable situations, e.g., in prostitution (Leopold & Steffan 1997; O'Neill 1996) or in psychiatric care (Enders-Dragässer & Sellach 1998); and sexual harassment at work (MacKinnon 1979; Koss et al. 1994; Holzbecher et al. 1990; Kuhlmann 1996). In terms of methodology, the overview focuses on characterizing the German research and describing and contrasting the corresponding American discussion.

1. Identifying and Analyzing the Problem

In Germany, Austria, and Switzerland, as well as in other countries such as the Netherlands and Scandinavia, the issue of violence against women was first raised by the women's movement. The state was the main adversary in the political conflicts and the main addressee for demands for legal reforms and financing of feminist projects to support women. Feminist studies identified themselves as serving this movement, while the mainstream of social research largely ignored the subject and the problem well into the 1990s. In the mid-1980s, attention to the effects of sexual violence began to awaken within psychotherapy and psychosomatic medicine, leading to a body of clinical literature on rape and on the consequences of early abuse, based on research primarily using case study methods. Overall, the feminist perspective not only played a pathbreaking role in opening

---

[5] Rebecca and Russel Dobash, Jalna Hanmer, Jeff Hearn, Marianne Hester, Liz Kelly, Jill Radford, and Elisabeth Stanko, for example, are regularly quoted in the American periodicals.

up the debate, but it also laid out the coordinates for all further research on the subject. Domestic and sexual violence are both regarded as gender-related issues that cannot be adequately investigated or understood without reference to gender. The problem is defined, in the general consensus, as violence against women.

The "Versuch über Sexualität und Aggression" (Essay on Sexuality and Aggression) by sexologist Eberhard Schorsch (1989) can serve as evidence of this successful definition of the agenda. Schorsch sought an approach to sexualized violence that was *not* gender-polarizing. He wrote that he had been astonished to discover how gender-blind the classics of aggression theory such as Erich Fromm had been. "Some epistemological turning points are irreversible. Pointing out that sexual violence is gender-related is such a turning point. Once it has been said it is self-evident and banal, but this was plainly not always the case." (Schorsch 1989:16) Even for a critic of feminist theory like Schorsch, who questions the "informative value of collective gender biographies," thinking about sexuality and aggression means thinking about gender relations.

Developments in the United States were different. There the public discussion of violence in marriage and the family arose from two competing discourses. In the American women's movement rape was taken as paradigmatic for conditions of patriarchal violence, and the first rape crisis centers were set up in 1970 (cf. Koss & Harvey 1991). At the same time family sociologists were turning their attention to the problem of physical violence within the family (cf. Steinmetz & Straus 1974). When the feminist discussion started paying more attention to the issue of violence against women in marriage, sociology already had an established research concept that gave only secondary significance to gender, while its primary concern was the transmission of acceptance of violence within the family over the generations.

A contributing factor was that, compared to Germany, the American feminist projects of women's advocacy, counseling, and help were much more strongly tied to the local community, and often to cooperation between colleges and the community. Much more often than in Germany, institutions of academic training were the addressees of feminist demands for active support for women. By contrast, the idea that the state bore a responsibility for supporting women who had suffered violence (almost axiomatic in northern Europe) was either weak or nonexistent in the United States. In the American context, state and national responsibility with respect to violence was seen as a matter for the legislature, where numerous experiments and innovations were in fact tried out. In Germany, by contrast, legal changes normally had very long preparatory periods and were often made only after innovative practice had first been tested and evaluated.[6]

Against this backdrop we can understand why by the 1970s American researchers were already embroiled in often bitter controversies concerning the definition of the object of research, the determination of adequate research methods, and theoretical interpretation of data and results (cf. Yllö & Bograd 1988; Gelles & Loseke 1993). British authors were also involved in these debates (Kelly 1988; Dobash & Dobash 1992), and a weak echo can be found in the introductions to some German publications. In continental Europe, however, these controversies have remained largely insignificant. The "epistemological turning point," that sexualized and domestic violence have to do with gender (even when they occur between men or between women) can also be found in more recent crimi-

---

[6]For example, the law on rape had been under discussion since 1977 but was not reformed to expand the range of acts covered and make rape within marriage a criminal offence until 1997, after prosecution and jurisdiction had already changed markedly in practice.

nological research, in social science research, in psychiatry and psychotraumatology, and in the feminist literature itself. It is also reflected in political declarations by the European Union and the Council of Europe, where violence against women is treated as a symptom of the failure to achieve full gender equality.

2.   Emerging Knowledge Bases on Violence against Women

On the international level, it is frequently regretted that there is a great deal of research into violence in society, but little scientific evaluation of intervention and assistance. This state of affairs is reversed in Germany. In Germany the empirical base of knowledge on gender-related violence stems overwhelmingly from research accompanying woman-centered practice. Since the mid-1970s almost all new approaches for intervention and assistance in the area of violence against women were introduced as pilot projects that were publicly funded and evaluated. The basic body of empirical research on violence against women arose because politics took up the issue and because the state's adoption of responsibility was associated with funding for related research. In this period—from 1976 (when the first shelter was opened in Berlin as a pilot project) until the 1990s—research into violence against women in (West) Germany was either commissioned by women's affairs ministries and departments at the national, state, or local level, or it was independent research, usually by former staff members of projects offering practical support, without additional resources and often in the interests of gaining an academic qualification[7]. A few studies have an intermediate character between state commission and institute-based research (Baurmann 1983; Honig 1986). Classical pure research, however, is not found at all before the 1990s and is still rare.

The wealth of scientific evaluation studies in (West) Germany is a consequence of federalism. Since political responsibility in these areas belongs to the states, national funding of intervention activities is restricted in duration and subject to scientific assessment designed to reflect the innovative character of the model and investigate both its success and the possibilities of transfer to other states and local authorities. However in practice, because funding for the model amounts to political recognition of the significance of the problem and of the state's responsibility, the funding agency and the project team share a common interest that the research findings should confirm the success of the project. This shared interest poses a danger to scientific integrity, to which researchers have responded by developing and refining the concept of formative process evaluation (cf. Helfferich et al. 1997; Kavemann et al. 2000), where the project receives intermediate feedback on possible undesirable developments in time to allow for correction. Evaluation becomes an instrument of quality control, while at the same time collecting and analyzing data with the best methods possible in order to enlighten the wider public on the needs and problems of the target group of this project.

In the United States, on the other hand, research was largely fed by sources in social science and psychology that are often remote from practice. At the practical level, a much wider range of different measures have been applied, often growing from pragmatic local initiatives. Most of the facilities for battered women operate as short-term crisis assistance[8],

---

[7] In Germany this can involve a very casual relationship with the university. Sometimes the finished work is simply submitted for assessment.

[8] Most shelters in the United States restrict the woman's stay to about two weeks.

followed by psychotherapeutic support; evaluation frequently uses psychological tests (cf. Dziegielewski, Resnick, & Krause 1996). Scientific evaluation has been directed in particular at politically mandated measures such as mandatory arrest policies for domestic violence, or compulsory participation in treatment programs for perpetrators (cf. Hamberger & Hastings 1993; Edleson & Eisikovits 1996; Gondolf 1997). Evaluation of such programs usually aims to measure outcomes, for which simple indicators are defined, e.g., whether the man is charged with another violent offense (although evaluation of interinstitutional projects sometimes functions differently, and more like the German model, cf. Shepard 1999). More complex investigations, too, often follow the positivist model; in the ideal case different forms of intervention are applied at random in various samples to compare the effects. This type of evaluation plays no role in intervention against violence in Germany, where it would be regarded as scientifically and ethically questionable, since the principle of informed consent is almost impossible to apply, and also because the total population of violent men and women with experience of violence cannot be determined, since many victims do not speak about their injuries until they are in safety or have found reliable support.

Many issues in project evaluation in Germany, e.g., the question of the support needed to cope successfully with violent experiences, appear in the United States primarily in the psychological literature, based on clinical therapeutic experience. Psychotherapy is much better established in American society and provides a broad, flexible everyday framework for dealing with personal problems—problems that in Germany would more likely be assigned to the fields of social work or self-help. However, this is not always the case. For example, Lee Ann Hoff (1990) investigated the process of separation and overcoming an abusive relationship in the context of social network analysis. The shared ground of the distinct country-specific discourses comes to light when a psychotherapeutic work that integrates feminist social criticism is translated into German and widely read, as occurred in the case of Judith Herman (1992). Such impulses are more likely to flow into project assessment (Helfferich et al. 1997) or social science research (Heynen 2000) than into psychology.

German research's strong ties to questions arising in conjunction with projects has left certain gaps. There is little research on the effectiveness of different forms of intervention. Studies comparable with the work of, for example, Lee Bowker (1983), who interviewed American women who had managed to overcome or leave an abusive situation without help from specialized institutions, have not yet been carried out in Germany. This means that German researchers have almost nothing to say about the need for different forms of assistance and help among women who do not (want to) contact the emergency services or a shelter.

3.   Theoretical Traditions and Their Impact on Research

In German-speaking countries the development of research generally followed a theoretical discussion that took the feminist analysis of gender-related violence as its starting point. Soon, however, the interpretation purely in terms of power theory receded into the background, where it is definitely still present: one often finds token recognition of the idea that men's collective interests in domination profit from violence against women and that this violence restricts and impairs the lives of all women (e.g., in Brückner 1983, 1987; Hanetseder 1992; Godenzi 1989, 1996; Schröttle 1999, and in almost all project evaluation research). Furthermore, this thesis is often debated by critics of "radical" feminism (e.g., in Honig 1986; Harten 1995; Kersten 1997; Bohner 1998). Generally, however, the paradigm that male violence serves primarily to secure power, argued persistently and combatively in the British literature (cf. Hester, Kelly, & Radford 1996; Hanmer & Itzin 2000), has long ceased to govern German feminist research. Even where the power dimension remains central, it is reinterpreted in terms of socialization theory. Violence by men is explained as a result of the excessive demands made by normative expectations of dominance, which boys and later men cannot live up to in real life (Heiliger & Engelfried 1995). For the most part, more complex theoretical questions take precedence, however. These originate from independent theoretical traditions, each of which generates different specific questions for empirical consideration.

a) The tradition of critical theory or the "Frankfurt School" suggested exploiting the potential of psychoanalysis for social theory. This approach was adopted, for example, by Margrit Brückner (1983, 1987) with her analysis of the collective fantasies of femininity and masculinity that shed light on the behavior of women in abusive relationships as well as on problematic aspects of the work of committed feminist helpers. Using this approach, she also explained the difficulties abused women face in applying their—unquestionably existing—strengths to defending themselves against violence and dissolving such relationships. Eberhard Schorsch (1989) developed an alternative approach to sexual violence based on psychoanalysis, looking at the psychodynamic amalgamation of sexuality and aggression in both sexes.

A similar approach to Brückner's analysis is the American study of the "collective representations" of woman-battering and of the battered woman, which Donileen Loseke (1992) used to illuminate contradictions in shelter work. Loseke, however, draws on a purely sociological theoretical tradition of the social construction of reality and her method was ethnographic. In the American discussion, psychoanalytical categories tend to be restricted to a therapeutic context.

b) The Berlin school of "critical psychology" developed further the Marxist tradition as a materialist approach for explaining the formation of individual behavior. This is the point of departure for the concept of feminine socialization, which was taken up, among others, by Roswitha Burgard (1985) to interpret the entanglement of battered women in abusive relationships and the process of getting free. The concepts of advocacy and involvement cited by Burgard also derives from a Marxist theoretical tradition (cf. Kavemann in: Hagemann-White, Kavemann, & Ohl 1997); they were formulated as a critique of capitalism by Maria Mies (1988) and—in analogy with action research—presented as a way for women to become aware of violence as a collective experience. However, the analogy between gender and class was soon dropped; differentiating violence by socioeconomic position appeared to be irreconcilable with its distribution through all social strata.

There is also a Marxist strand to the American discussion, although more in the sense of historical materialism. Julia and Herman Schwendinger (1983) explained sexual violence economically, using cross-cultural comparison as well, in terms of the contradictions of the respective mode of production; this is also a topic in feminist ethnology. The continued presence of this approach in American feminist analysis of violence can be seen in the theoretical section of Laura O'Toole and Jessica Schiffman's work (1997). In their wide-ranging empirical research in the health services, Evan Stark and Ann Flitcraft (1996) interpret battering as an expression of the contradiction between a patriarchal family structure and a capitalist market that pushes women into paid labor. Such theoretical models tend to have a rather loose relationship to empirical evidence.

c) Johan Galtung's concept of structural violence points to the interrelationship of macro- and microstructures, thus integrating the political and structural dimension in explaining how interpersonal violence arises and is maintained. This concept, which found great resonance in the 1980s as a framework for analyzing violence, has been developed for empirical work by Monika Schröttle (1999) and explicitly related to physical violence. She inquired which sociopolitical factors influence the dynamics and maintenance of gender-specific violence in heterosexual couple relationships, in particular in comparison between East and West Germany before and after reunification.

d) Bram van Stolk and Cas Wouters (1987) of the Netherlands applied the process sociology of Norbert Elias in interviews and participatory observation in a crisis shelter, arriving at the formulation "from misfortune to injustice" to summarize the changes in the interpretation of violence within marriage. They explain why many women who leave a violent man with radical plans to separate nonetheless return to him by the conflict between a figurative ideal of harmonious inequality and the real power shifts between the sexes since the 1960s.

e) Biographical research emphasizes the interaction between individual and social structuring of biographies, as well as respect for the heterogeneous. This approach was taken by Christa Hanetseder (1992) and Monika Büttner (1997) to analyze the significance of violence in couple relationships and the end of violence after a stay in a shelter. For Hanetseder the biographical approach offers the possibility to evaluate both the shelter project and the significance of experience there for women in reconstructing and reassessing this period of their lives. Susanne Weissmann (1994) also adopts the approach of narrative interviews and the documentary method of data analysis (she follows Straub 1989) to interpret the biographies of sexually abused women.

Extensive life histories of women who endured violence are often found in American research, but primarily for illustrative purposes, whether to demonstrate a syndrome or to describe coping strategies. Systematic interpretation is rare; one notable exception is Hoff's (1990) study of separation and coping processes in formerly battered women.

f) German reception of American psychological research also influences empirical studies. For example, Erika Steinert and Ute Straub (1988) applied Carol Gilligan's theory of women's moral development to the processes of change following a stay in a shelter. Their study shows that women in a marriage characterized by male dominance and violence (have to) remain at a stage of conventional morality. Interaction with the expectation in the shelter that they take responsibility for themselves can induce a moral maturing process that increases the chance of staying out of such relationships.

g) Investigation of the effects of violence, and trauma theory in particular, have been highly significant in American feminist research. Judith Herman (1992/1994) merged clinical insights and research on rape and domestic violence with a broader context of research findings on war trauma, terror, imprisonment, and torture. In Germany her analysis is often integrated with coping theories. In this way Maren Licht (1991), Harald Feldmann (1992), Ulrike Kretschmann (1993), and Susanne Heynen (2000), for example, have investigated the effects of rape and the professional help and/or personal resources required. To date in Germany, recent knowledge about traumatization has been applied only to sexual violence, in particular to understand the long-term effects of childhood sexual abuse (cf. Reddemann 2001). Application to battered women has not yet been discussed.

h) Theories from cognitive social psychology are very influential in American research. In Germany they tend to be included in a supplementary form, as when Heynen explores the influence of subjective theories on the coping process. In an analysis of court rulings and their justifications, Henriette Abel (1988) demonstrated the prevalence of rape myths in the West German judiciary. Gerd Bohner (1998) experimentally studied how the acceptance of different cognitive representations is associated with assignment of responsibility, inclination to exercise sexual violence, feeling threatened by rape, self-esteem, and self-categorization by gender. Overall, however, there is little emulation of the experimental research on violence that is widespread in the United States.

i) In the wide-ranging American research one cannot easily speak of "dominant" or especially well-established theoretical currents, because younger researchers are often encouraged first to learn to collect and prepare (quantitative) data, whereas in Germany a theoretical foundation is required. Pragmatic empiricism is very widespread. The result is a different interaction between research and politics. Relative freedom from binding theoretical traditions allows American researchers to deploy a wide range of research questions and empirical designs. Quantitative studies dominate, with statistical analysis of the results usually being used to substantiate one of several theories introduced at the outset. A great proportion of the research is characterized by a plurality of theories that are compared by means of quantitative findings, and there is a tendency to identify a single "main cause" for each event. This model clearly has consequences. In smaller studies, and in the commonly practiced reduction of complex interrelationships to indicators, data from a single survey is rarely sufficient to test a theory. This creates a pressure to replicate, or to adopt successfully established instruments and designs in the expectation that cumulative results will give definitive answers to questions concerning causal relationships.

The dominance of the quantitatively substantiated causal model is closely associated with ideas about social intervention, whereby violence is seen as a plague to be eradicated: The important thing is to identify the virus. Feminist positions (cf. Koss & Harvey 1991, who draw an explicit analogy with public health for preventing sexual violence) and proponents of the "family violence" diagnosis (cf. e.g., Straus 1991b, who views the experience of violence between parents as the cause of later deviance and criminality of the children) are united in arguing along the lines of such models. This sets up a potentially endless controversy—*either* gender *or* family. The discussion in Germany, by contrast, has tended to take quantitative data (most of it from the United States) to confirm the existence of a problem, but concentrated on qualitative results when assessing what is helpful in terms of intervention.

The open competition between positions in the United States has plainly stimulated research, and allowed the issue to become broadly accepted in the academic landscape at an early stage (cf. e.g., Finkelhor et al. 1983; Koss et al. 1996), while research on gender-related violence is still a marginal field in academic institutions in German-speaking countries. It takes place primarily outside the academic system through the sustained interest of politics and society in intervention and prevention. In the American approach, problems have been described in many aspects and classified methodically; American research now provides a vast body of data. Theoretical interests and questions in research often subsequently draw on this wealth of data, as was already clear in the anthology by Yllö and Bograd (1988).

With the exception of trauma theory, the theories accepted from abroad have had less influence on the German scientific, social policy and practical discussion than contributions based on a conceptual framework that was already well established in Germany. However, in discussion of the prevalence of particular forms of violence and the harmful nature of the consequences, English-language research as such is seen as more authoritative and functions as a source for facts, correlations, and factor models.

III. EMPIRICAL STUDIES: TYPES AND EXTENT
OF VIOLENCE AGAINST WOMEN

1. Data from Evaluation Research

During the 1970s, while public awareness was being created, most practice-oriented research prioritized description, asking which forms of violence women and girls experienced, under what conditions and with which consequences; from what backgrounds they
come and what support and help they need if they are to escape from violence and successfully overcome the effects. Linking qualitative and quantitative methods in cooperation
with innovative institutions was an obvious step. Although this only included the help-
seeking clientele, it did so in great detail and often with impressive thoroughness. Although the findings belong to the empirical basis for feminist theory, they received little
attention in German social science discourse.

a) DOMESTIC VIOLENCE.   In 1978/79 demographic data were recorded from 1,090 women
seeking safety in the first shelter in Berlin, and 300 women completed a longer questionnaire
about their experience of abuse, previous attempts to find help, and the situation of their
children (Hagemann-White et al. 1981)[9]. At the same time Mildred Pagelow (1981) carried
out a comparable investigation involving 350 women in California and Florida. Both the
sociodemographic data and the information on the course of the relationship and previous
attempts to cope or separation attempts were astonishingly similar. However, while Pagelow
found that many women had a higher level of formal education than the man (and similar
American findings have generated hypotheses that men turn to physical violence when their
wife or partner is verbally superior), three quarters of the Berlin women in the survey had no
equivalent of the American high school diploma, while most of the men at least had a formal
vocational qualification. In fact, this reflects the differing gender patterns of participation in
education in the two countries and points to the necessity of comparative research.

     In both studies most of the women had been suffering repeated unpredictable as-
saults for a year or longer (in Berlin 37 percent for more than six years). The Berlin evaluation study also contacted former residents from the first two years and provided the first
empirical evidence of widespread stalking after separation. Cross-sectional comparison of
the Berlin data did not confirm that violence in a marriage increases over time; there was
no correlation between the length of the relationship and the frequency of assaults. Interviews, however, did indicate an increase in both the frequency and intensity of violence,
reflecting the dynamics experienced by the individual woman within the relationship; a
relative increase in intensity was often a reason to seek out a place of safety.

     The previous living situation was characterized by economic dependency only up to
a point: two fifths of the women in Berlin had earned their own living. (In Pagelow's
study, which posed slightly different questions, the proportion was more than half.) However, the man normally took charge of the money and the woman received only a meager
amount for housekeeping. Unlike the United States, the German state guarantees basic

---

[9] Of the 548 residents who stayed longer than three days in the shelter, almost half filled out the longer questionnaire (N=246); 18 percent of the longer questionnaires were filled out by women who stayed three days or
less. Altogether 35.8 percent of all women seeking help stayed just one day or one night, often at the weekend,
in an acute crisis situation. In the second model project, a shelter in a rural area (Bergdoll and Namgalies-
Treichler 1987), fifty women were interviewed using similar questions.

assistance to those who have no other income, and this was granted to women who left a violent man. As long as the children are still small, the mother is not expected to seek employment. The security provided by welfare benefits allows women to stay longer in the shelter, and a stay of six weeks or longer correlated with successful separation. As a result, counseling acquired in-depth knowledge of the life histories and of the dynamics of bonding and separation in violent relationships; comparable American research is only found in the field of psychotherapy.

Today shelters and other institutions report changes that have, however, not yet been confirmed by research. According to these reports the proportion of women from long-term abusive relationships has decreased since the problem became publicly known. Women stay in shelters for shorter periods, more women go to counseling centers or are able to use other support options. The number of immigrants is also growing, because they have least access to other options.

It was recognized at an early stage that domestic violence is by no means restricted to the lower social strata. Using in-depth interviews, Cheryl Benard and Edit Schlaffer investigated the phenomenon of violence in the middle classes, which is characterized above all by the preferred choice of means. "The men of the middle and upper middle classes apply a broader spectrum of means of violence, including financial, social, and psychological pressure" (Benard et al. 1991:5). The authors describe financial violence, social sadism, and social violence as particular manifestations. They found purely physical violence to be less common, but it still occurred in almost all cases. Sexual violence appears regularly in all social strata. Very conspicuous in the case studies are the variety, imaginativeness, and sometimes subtlety of the means of securing male dominance, which leave the woman living in fear of sanctions for her "failure." The socially privileged situation of the men[10] plainly gave them abundant means of power that a worker would not normally have, but it did not follow that punching and kicking were missing from their repertoire.

b) Sexual Violence.   The data from evaluation of projects on sexual violence is very much less substantial, because it proved difficult to contact raped women during the time immediately after the crime. The rape hotline and counseling project in Mainz that was evaluated as a German pilot project in 1981–82 (Teubner, Becker, & Steinhage 1983) was rarely contacted directly after the event, as might be expected from a "crisis line." In a second pilot project ten years later (Helfferich et al. 1997), almost one third of the women came within twenty-four hours after the crime, but the majority came much later for therapy or support. The largest group sought therapy more than five years afterward (cf. also Kretschmann 1993). For this reason, findings on the effects of rape and the process of overcoming the effects are influenced by American empirical and clinical research, while independent German research only began much later.

The data on the circumstances of the crime was the most important factor for the public discussion. At least two thirds of the perpetrators are known to the victim, and the most common scene of the crime is indoors (the home of the woman or of another person). While in the first pilot project more than 40 percent of the rapists were only casual acquaintances, the data from the second project shows not only a category of "well known" men, but also a significant proportion of relatives and in particular partners and ex-partners (the latter category with a share of almost 14 percent). The emerging public aware-

---

[10] The men in the case studies are, for example, doctor, judge, architect, university professor, manager, businessman.

ness during the 1990s that rape is a crime evidently allowed more women than ten years previously to define sexual coercion by the husband or partner as rape.

2. Prevalence Surveys

Survey research represents one of the great differences between American and German research. The political debate in the United States also places more importance on such surveys.

a) DOMESTIC VIOLENCE. American research was strongly influenced by the early development of a tradition of surveys using standardized questionnaires to measure the frequency of violence within families in the general population. In theoretical terms physical violence was understood as a way of dealing with conflict. The standardized instrument, which became known as the "conflict tactics scale", was first tested in 1971 and has since been developed and validated. Initially in regional and smaller-scale studies, and later with representative national samples, it was primarily used to find out how often particular physical assaults—summarized as "minor" and "severe" violence according to the presumed potential to cause injury—occur within marriage (Straus 1990; Schwartz 1987; Smith 1987). Research into violence using the conflict tactics scale thus "occupied" the field at an early stage. Results of major studies in 1975 and 1985 raised doubts as to the gender basis of violence within families (Straus & Gelles 1990). This was certainly one reason for the intensity of the debate over the usefulness of the survey instrument (Straus 1991a; Dobash et al. 1992; Schwartz 2000; Gordon 2000). Later studies have drawn on the findings of qualitative research into domestic violence to develop their survey instruments (Johnson 1996; Tjaden & Thoennes 2000; DeKeseredy 1999). In this way a wide variety of forms of gender-related violence were successively investigated in the United States. The effects of violence in marriage on children (Jaffe, Wolfe, & Wilson 1990) and violence in lesbian relationships (Renzetti 1992), for example, were brought to public attention significantly earlier than in Europe.

For a long time there was little German research into the existence or perception of the problem in the population as a whole, and only isolated attempts at survey research among those who experienced violence but did not seek out a pilot project. Only in the course of an explicit European policy—that has declared active measures to reduce violence against women to be a consensus in the European Union since about 1998—has the collection of reliable prevalence data in the individual EU member states been understood as a (public) responsibility (cf. Hagemann-White 2001). A representative German survey aimed at collecting data that will be comparable at the European level was commissioned in 2002.

In Vienna Cheryl Benard and her colleagues carried out a survey in doctors' waiting rooms and other public places; 820 questionnaires were returned. On the basis of the results they estimated that at least one in every five Austrian women had experienced violence in a relationship with a man (Benard et al. 1991:105). A representative survey in Switzerland interviewing women currently or until recently living with a man as a couple found a (lifetime) prevalence of physical violence in relationships of 12.6 percent (Gillioz, Puy, & Ducret 1997). By comparison, a postal survey in Finland with a return rate of more than 70 percent found that 22 percent of the women who were living with a man said that he had hit her or threatened to hit her at least once (Heiskanen & Piispa 1998).

Renée Römkens (1992, 1997) integrated qualitative and quantitative methods for her representative study in the Netherlands. More than a quarter of the women interviewed (26.2 percent) had experienced acts of physical aggression by a man with whom they were living. For a small group this was mutual combat, which rarely or never led to injury. Unilateral violence on the part of the man, where the woman rarely or never struck back, was described by 20.8 percent of the respondents. For about 9 percent, however, this was infrequent and only rarely caused injury. However, 11.1 percent of all the women questioned reported repeated abuse of medium or severe intensity, originating unilaterally from the man, and often resulting in injury.

One fundamental problem in this research is the operationalization of the concept of violence (cf. DeKeseredy 2000, Gordon 2000, Hagemann-White 2000). Since the major representative survey by Statistics Canada (Johnson and Sacco 1995; Johnson 1996), it has become established procedure to ask about specific acts that represent a physical assault, which are then evaluated by the researcher as more or less serious violence. Respondents are generally not asked how far they themselves experience the incidents as violence or perhaps only as a "normal" expression of aggressivity (but cf. Mirrlees-Black 1999), and there is only very limited inquiry into reciprocal aggression of this type.

Most differentiated prevalence surveys in Europe have, like the Canadian survey, only interviewed women. The fact that the government expresses concern for the security and well-being of women and is collecting data to that end appears to elicit broad acceptance. In general, however, it appears to be more difficult to recruit respondents when it is made clear from the outset that the survey will inquire into the private sphere. In both the Netherlands and Switzerland the quota of interviews actually carried out represented about one third of the original random sample of women living in a couple relationship. On the other hand, prior information seems to awaken willingness to reveal information among those who do respond.

Since the late 1990s European prevalence research has entered into a process of mutual interchange, in which the definition of the research goals, the development of survey instruments, and the analysis and presentation of the results are slowly converging. Although this process avoids giving preference to any one model, interesting perspectives for comparative analysis are nonetheless emerging. At the beginning, when documentation of the problem in its practical relevance was at the fore, the similarity of the data from shelters appeared to suggest great uniformity across countries, but now more attention is being paid to the differences (cf. Hagemann-White 2000). This could result in strong stimuli for more differentiated research.

b) SEXUAL VIOLENCE.   Surveys on the prevalence of rape were not carried out in the United States until the 1980s (cf. Muehlenhard, Harney, & Jones 1992; Muehlenhard et al. 1992). The legal definition—at that time narrow—was applied initially, partly in order to assess the numbers of crimes not recorded in police statistics. Later more sophisticated instruments were developed to discover the range of forms of sexual violence and sexual acts committed against the will of the victim (Koss & Harvey 1991; Bachman 2000). The different definitions have, however, left room for vehement controversy. While in the case of physical violence it is generally considered correct methodology to ask about specific acts and avoid emotionally charged words like "violence," this approach is disputed in the case of sexual violence, with the argument that women must know if they have really been raped (cf. Muehlenhard et al. 1992). American surveys that specifically asked about the use of physical violence to force sexual intercourse have found a lifetime prevalence for adult women of about 20 percent.

In Germany there have been local surveys in various milieus (recruitment in public places or questionnaires distributed to students) that were methodologically modeled on American surveys and thus tended to work with a relatively broad definition of sexual violence. From a series of surveys each with an overall population of about 100 people, Gerd Bohner reports proportions between 14 and 23.5 percent of female respondents who had actually been forced by a man to commit sexual acts against their will at least once, while between 18 and 27.5 percent had experienced attempted rape or sexual coercion (cf. Bohner 1998:63–65; Krahé et al. 1999 also report similarly high figures for young women).

The representative survey carried out in 1992 by the Criminological Research Institute of Lower Saxony provided the first data on rape within close relationships. Combining data from different parts of the investigation showed that 8.6 percent of women had experienced rape or attempted rape when aged 18 or over. About 2 percent of all women said that they had been raped by their husband or partner during the past five years (Wetzels & Pfeiffer 1995).

Overall, the research results to date give the impression that gender-related violence is more sexualized in the United States. Women in Germany less often report rape in the narrow sense, but the use of alcohol and drugs to make women sexually compliant appears to be similarly widespread, especially among adolescents and young adults.

IV. RESEARCH DEFICITS AND OPEN QUESTIONS

German research on violence against women is empirically and theoretically rich and exhibits independent lines of development. Empirically, however, it is striking that some areas are unexplored. In American research, gaps are bridged more quickly. Lively competition for prestige between different research approaches is both a strength and a weakness; a side effect is that important results of single studies sometimes receive insufficient recognition and are not followed up.

One notable deficit in German research and practice is the field of health (cf. Schornstein 1997; Stark & Flitcraft 1996). Although it has become standard practice to include chapters on violence against women in the women's health reports called for by the WHO, there has been almost no research into the health effects of experiencing violence (cf. Verbundprojekt 2001). It is symptomatic for the predominant practical responses to the problem that in German-speaking countries legal research has progressed a good deal further than medical and public health research.

Although interactions between research and practical attempts to bring about change are quite common in the United States, these are each usually confined to a specific and narrow segment of the issue of violence. Studies that integrate experience of violence in the life history and living conditions, rather than viewing it in isolation, are rarely followed up by other researchers; instead this perspective often draws on British research (e.g., Kelly 1988; Fawcett et al. 1996; Hanmer & Itzin 2000).

The wealth of biographical exploration notwithstanding, research concerning the needs and resources of women who have suffered violence (and even more concerning victimized men) is inadequate with respect to questions of how violence can be restricted, ended, and overcome. American work on this is predominantly psychotherapeutically orientated. The unbroken succession of project evaluation studies in Germany has resulted in a certain focus on the perceptions and experiences of the committed professionals, but their views are not necessarily identical with the perspectives of women facing violence in their lives. There has been too little integration between evaluative research on measures and services and qualitative research on women's experience.

German-language research tells us almost nothing about the men who perpetrate this violence. Alberto Godenzi's small study (1989) in Switzerland on perpetrators not registered by any sanctioning authority has not been replicated. Programs for violent men were introduced in the United States in 1975, now exist in large numbers, and are estimated to receive 80 percent of their clients through court orders. This has facilitated research on perpetrators, which is now quite extensive (cf. Stordeur & Stille as early as 1989), although there is controversy over whether research should identify violence-prone perpetrator types, or whether norms of masculinity are decisive (cf. Bowker 1998). The small number of working counseling services in German-speaking countries (cf. Kavemann et al. 2000) is embroiled in controversy over whether it is true that perpetrators have no sense of wrong-doing and suffer no internal pressure to change, or whether to the contrary every man who batters or rapes actually suffers himself and wishes to receive assistance. The European continent has produced no empirical data on this question.

Very cautiously, a discussion is now beginning about men as victims of violence (Lenz 2000), which might contribute to creating a more complex image of men in this field of research. The material available to date indicates that adult men suffer physical and sexual violence largely at the hands of other men. During childhood both men and women can exercise sexual violence on boys, but in this area as well, the majority of perpetrators are men, especially outside the family (cf. Meuser 1999). There are not yet any reports or empirical data on husbands being beaten by their wives.

Psychological violence, which is exercised by both sexes, is generally given more weight in European research, as a result of the tradition of qualitative studies. Women appear to tolerate humiliation and insults often out of fear of physical abuse that has occurred at least once, as well as due to their conviction of the man's physical superiority in case of open conflict. It is not known what factors might lead men to remain in a relationship despite psychologically hurtful attacks. There is reason to believe that a culture where men are not allowed to appear as victims increases their tendency to become perpetrators. To that extent, paying more serious attention to men's victimization would also further the feminist approach.

German research as a whole has managed to avoid fragmentation of the perception of the problem and to maintain an understanding of how various forms and circumstances of violence relate to a broader context (cf. Hagemann-White et al. 1997). The dialogue between women and men in this area, however, appears to be blocked from both sides in Germany, or to progress only very slowly. Literature concentrating on women often treats the threatening or violent man as an alien being deliberately satisfying his own needs at the expense of others. The gradually growing body of literature from men's perspective rarely discusses the German feminist findings and explanatory models, often preferring to discuss American approaches, and sometimes to critique early feminist popular books. The discourse is divided. An internally relatively integrated discussion of violence against women has successfully developed, but at the price of implicitly relying on the "gendering of thought" (Schorsch 1989). More exact differentiation of the local discourses and more attention to the links between women's studies research on violence and broader theoretical currents might improve the conditions for dialogue.

Translated by Tradukas

REFERENCES

Abel, Maria Henriette. (1988). *Vergewaltigung. Stereotypen in der Rechtsprechung und empirische Befunde.* Weinheim, Munich: Juventa.

Bachman, Ronet. (2000). A Comparison of Annual Incidence Rates and Contextual Characteristics of Intimate-Partner Violence against Women from the National Crime Victimization Survey (NCVS) and the National Violence Against Women Survey (NVAWS). *Violence Against Women, 6*(8), 839–867.

Baurmann, Michael C. (1983). *Sexualität, Gewalt und psychische Folgen. Eine Längsschnittuntersuchung bei Opfern sexueller Gewalt und sexueller Normverletzungen anhand angezeigter Sexualkontakte.* Wiesbaden: Bundeskriminalamt Forschungsreihe.

Benard, Cheryl, Edit Schlaffer, Britta Mühlbach, & Gabriele Sapik. (1991). *Gewalt in der Familie: Teil I: Gewalt gegen Frauen.* Vienna: Bundesministerium für Umwelt, Jugend und Familie.

Bergdoll, Karin, & Christel Namgalies-Treichler. (1987). *Frauenhaus im ländlichen Raum.* Stuttgart: Kohlhammer.

Bohner, Gerd. (1998). *Vergewaltigungsmythen. Sozialpsychologische Untersuchungen über täterentlastende und opferfeindliche Überzeugungen im Bereich sexueller Gewalt.* Landau: Verl. Empirische Pädagogik.

Bowker, Lee H. (1983). *Beating Wife-Beating.* Lexington, MA: Lexington Books.

Bowker, Lee H. (Ed.) (1998). *Masculinities and Violence.* Thousand Oaks et al.: Sage.

Brückner, Margrit. (1983). *Die Liebe der Frauen. Über Weiblichkeit und Misshandlung.* Frankfurt am Main: Verlag Neue Kritik.

Brückner, Margrit. (1987). *Die janusköpfige Frau. Lebensstärken und Beziehungsschwächen.* Frankfurt am Main: Verlag Neue Kritik.

Burgard, Roswitha. (1985). *Misshandelte Frauen – Verstrickung und Befreiung.* Weinheim: Beltz.

Büttner, Monika. (1997). *Weibliche Biographie und Gewalterfahrungen in Paarbeziehungen. Integrationschancen subjektiver Bewältigungs- und Präventionsstrategien.* Frankfurt am Main: dipa.

DeKeseredy, Walter S. (1999). Tactics of the Antifeminist Backlash against Canadian National Women Abuse Surveys. *Violence Against Women, 5*(1), 258–1276.

DeKeseredy, Walter S. (2000). Current Controversies on Defining Nonlethal Violence against Women in Intimate Heterosexual Relationships. Empirical Implications. *Violence against Women, 6,* 728–746.

Dobash, Rebecca E., & Russell P. Dobash. (1979). *Violence against Wives: A Case against the Patriarchy.* New York: Free Press.

Dobash, Rebecca E., & Russell P. Dobash. (1992). *Women, Violence and Social Change.* London: Routledge.

Dobash, Russell P., Rebecca E. Dobash, Margo Wilson, & Martin Daly. (1992). The Myth of Sexual Symmetry in Marital Violence. *Social Problems, 39*(1), 71–91.

Dziegielewski, Sophia F., Cheryl Resnick, & Nora B. Krause. (1996). Shelter-Based Crisis Intervention with Battered Women. In Albert R. Roberts (Ed.), *Helping Battered Women. New Perspectives and Remedies* (pp. 159–187). Oxford et al.: Oxford University Press.

Edleson, Jeffrey L., & Zvi C. Eisikovits. (Eds.) (1996). *Future Interventions with Battered Women and their Families.* Thousand Oaks: Sage

Enders-Dragässer, Ute, & Brigitte Sellach. (Eds.) (1998). *Frauen in der stationären Psychiatrie. Ein interdisziplinärer Bericht.* Lage: Jacobs.

Fawcett, Barbara, Brid Featherstone, Jeff Hearn, & Toft, Christine. (Eds.) (1996). *Violence and Gender Relations. Theories and Interventions.* London: Sage.

Feldmann, Harald. (1992). *Vergewaltigung und ihre psychischen Folgen. Ein Beitrag zur posttraumatischen Belastungsreaktion.* Stuttgart: Enke.

Finkelhor, David, Richard J. Gelles, Gerald T. Hotaling, & Murray A. Straus. (Eds.) (1983). *The Dark Side of Families. Current Family Violence Research.* Beverly Hills et al.: Sage

Gelles, Richard. J., & Donileen R. Loseke. (Eds.) (1993). *Current Controversies on Family Violence.* London et al.: Sage.

Gillioz, Lucienne, Jacqueline de Puy, & Véronique Ducret. (1997). *Domination et violence envers la femme dans le couple.* Lausanne: Editions Payot.

Godenzi, Alberto. (1989). *Bieder, brutal: Frauen und Männer sprechen über sexuelle Gewalt.* Zürich: Unionsverlag.

Godenzi, Alberto. (1996). *Gewalt im sozialen Nahraum.* Basel: Helbing & Lichtenhahn.

Gondolf, Edward W. (1997). Expanding Batterer Program Evaluation. In Glenda K. Kantor & J. L. Jasinski (Eds.), *Out of Darkness. Contemporary Perspectives on Family Violence.* Thousand Oaks, et al.: Sage, pp. 208–218

Goode, William J. (1971/1975). Gewalt und Gewalttätigkeit in der Familie. In Heinrich Bast, Angela Bernecker, Ingrid Kastien, Gerd Schmitt, & Reinhart Wolff (Eds.), *Gewalt gegen Kinder. Kindesmisshandlungen und ihre Ursachen* (pp. 131–155). Reinbek bei Hamburg: Rowohlt.

Gordon, Malcolm. (2000). Definitional Issues in Violence against Women. Surveillance and Research from a Violence Research Perspective. *Violence against Women, 6*(7), 747–783

Hagemann-White, Carol. (2000). Male Violence and Control. Constructing a Comparative European Perspective. In Simon S. Duncan & Birgit Pfau-Effinger (Eds.), *Gender, Work and Culture in the EU* (pp. 171–207). London: UCL/Routledge.

Hagemann-White, Carol. (2001). European Research on the Prevalence of Violence against Women. *Violence against Women, 7*(7), 731–759.

Hagemann-White, Carol, Barbara Kavemann, Johanna Kootz, Ute Weinmann, Carola Wildt, Roswitha Burgard, & Ursula Scheu. (1981). *Hilfen für misshandelte Frauen. Abschlussbericht der wissenschaftlichen Begleitung des Modellprojekts Frauenhaus Berlin.* Stuttgart: Kohlhammer.

Hagemann-White, Carol, Barbara Kavemann, & Dagmar Ohl. (1997). *Parteilichkeit und Solidarität. Praxiserfahrungen und Streitfragen zur Gewalt im Geschlechterverhältnis.* Bielefeld: Kleine.

Hamberger, L. Kevin, & James E. Hastings. (1993). Court Mandated Treatment of Men who Assault Their Partner. In N. Zoe Hilton (Ed.), *Legal Responses to Wife Assault. Current Trends and Evaluation* (pp. 188–229). Newbury Park, et al.: Sage.

Hanetseder, Christa. (1992). *Frauenhaus: Sprungbrett zur Freiheit? Eine Analyse der Erwartungen und Erfahrungen von Benutzerinnen: Beitrag zur Evaluation eines feministischen Projekts.* Bern: Haupt.

Hanmer, Jalner. (1996). The Common Market of Violence. In R. Amy Elman (Ed.), *Sexual Politics and the European Union. The New Feminist Challenge* (pp. 131–146). Providence, RI: Berghahn Books.

Hanmer, Jalna, & Catherine Itzin. (Eds.) (2000). *Home Truths about Domestic Violence.* London: Routledge.

Harten, Hans Christian. (1995). *Sexualität, Missbrauch, Gewalt. Das Geschlechterverhältnis und die Sexualisierung von Aggression.* Opladen: Westdeutscher Verlag.

Heiliger, Anita, & Constance Engelfried. (1995). *Sexuelle Gewalt: Männliche Sozialisation und potentielle Täterschaft.* Frankfurt am Main: Campus.

Heine-Wiedenmann, Dagmar, & Lea Ackermann. (1992). *Umfeld und Ausmaß des Menschenhandels mit ausländischen Mädchen und Frauen.* Stuttgart: Kohlhammer.

Heiskanen, Markku, & Minna Piispa. (1998). *Faith, Hope, Battering: A Survey of Men's Violence against Women in Finland.* Helsinki: Statistics Finland.

Helfferich, Cornelia, Anneliese Hendel-Kramer, Eva Tov, & Jürgen von Troschke. (1997). *Anlaufstelle für vergewaltigte Frauen. Abschlussbericht der wissenschaftlichen Begleitforschung.* Stuttgart: Kohlhammer.

Herman, Judith L. (1992). *Trauma and Recovery.* New York: Basic Books. (German 1994: *Die Narben der Gewalt. Traumatische Erfahrungen verstehen und überwinden.* Munich: Kindler)

Hester, Marianne, Liz Kelly, & Jill Radford. (Eds.) (1996). *Women, Violence and Male Power.* Buckingham: Open University.

Heynen, Susanne. (2000). *Vergewaltigt.* Weinheim, Munich: Juventa.

Hoff, Lee Ann. (1990). *Battered Women as Survivors.* London: Routledge.

Holzbecher, Monika, Anne Braszeit, Ursula Müller, & Sibylle Plogstedt. (1990). *Sexuelle Belästigung am Arbeitsplatz.* Stuttgart: Kohlhammer.

Honig, Michael-Sebastian. (1986). *Verhäuslichte Gewalt. Soziale Konflikte, wissenschaftliche Konstrukte, Alltagswissen, Handlungsstrategien. Eine Explorativstudie über Gewalthandeln in Familien.* Frankfurt am Main: Suhrkamp.

Jaffe, Peter G., David A. Wolfe, & Susan Kaye Wilson. (1990). *Children of Battered Women.* Newbury Park, et al.: Sage.

Johnson, Holly, & Vincent F. Sacco. (1995). Researching Violence against Women: Statistics Canada's National Survey. *Canadian Journal of Criminology, 37*, 281–304.

Johnson, Holly. (1996). *Dangerous Domains: Violence against Women in Canada.* Scarborough: Nelson Canada.

Kavemann, Barbara, Beate Leopold, Gesa Schirrmacher, & Carol Hagemann-White. (2000). *Modelle der Kooperation gegen häusliche Gewalt.* Stuttgart: Kohlhammer.

Kelly, Liz. (1988). *Surviving Sexual Violence.* Minneapolis: University of Minnesota.

Kersten, Joachim. (1997). *Gut und (Ge)schlecht. Männlichkeit, Kultur und Kriminalität.* Berlin: de Gruyter.

Koss, Mary P., & Mary R. Harvey. (1991). *The Rape Victim: Clinical and Community Interventions, 2nd Edition.* Newbury Park: Sage.

Koss, Mary P., Lisa A. Goodman, Angela Browne, Louise F. Fitzgerald, Gwendolyn P. Keita, & Nancy Felipe

Russo. (1994). *No Safe Haven. Male Violence against Women at Home, at Work, and in the Community.* Washington DC: American Psychological Association.

Krahé, Barbara, Renate Scheinberger-Olwig, & Eva Waizenhöfer. (1999). Sexuelle Aggression zwischen Jugendlichen: Eine Prävalenzerhebung mit Ost-West-Vergleich. *Zeitschrift für Sozialpsychologie, 30*(2/3), 165–178.

Kretschmann, Ulrike. (1993). *Das Vergewaltigungstrauma: Krisenintervention und Therapie mit vergewaltigten Frauen.* Münster: Westfälisches Dampfboot.

Kuhlmann, Ellen. (1996). *Gegen die sexuelle Belästigung am Arbeitsplatz. Juristische Praxis und Handlungsperspektiven.* Pfaffenweiler: Centaurus.

Leidholdt, Dorchen. (1996). Sexual Trafficking in Women in Europe. In R. Amy Elman, *Sexual Politics and the European Union. The New Feminist Challenge* (pp. 83–95). Providence RI, Oxford: Berghahn.

Lenz, Hans-Joachim, Hrsg. (2000). *Männliche Opfererfahrungen. Problemlagen und Hilfeansätze in der Männerberatung.* Weinheim, Munich: Juventa.

Leopold, Beate, & Elfriede Steffan. (1997). *Dokumentation zur rechtlichen und sozialen Situation von Prostituierten in der Bundesrepublik Deutschland.* Stuttgart: Kohlhammer.

Licht, Maren. (1991). *Vergewaltigungsopfer. Psychosoziale Folgen und Verarbeitungsprozesse: empirische Untersuchung.* Pfaffenweiler: Centaurus.

Loseke, Donileen R. (1992). *The Battered Woman and Shelters. The Social Construction of Wife Abuse.* Albany, NY: SUNY.

MacKinnon, Catherine A. (1979). *Sexual Harassment of Working Women.* New Haven CT: Yale University Press.

Meuser, Michael. (1999). Gewalt, hegemoniale Männlichkeit und doing masculinity. In Löschper, Gabi & Gerlinde Smaus (Eds.), Das Patriarchat und die Kriminologie. *Kriminologisches Journal, 7* (Beiheft) 49–65).

Mies, Maria. (1988). *Patriarchat und Kapital. Frauen in der internationalen Arbeitsteilung.* Zürich: Rotpunktverlag.

Mirrlees-Black, Catriona. (1999). *Domestic Violence: Findings from a New British Crime Survey Self-Completion Questionnaire.* London: Home Office.

Muehlenhard, Charlene L., Patricia A. Harney, & Jayme W. Jones. (1992a). From "Victim-Precipitated Rape" to "Date Rape": How far have we come? *Annual Review of Sex Research, 3,* 219–253.

Muehlenhard, Charlene L., Irene G. Powch, Joi L.Phelps, & Laura M. Giusti. (1992b). Definitions of Rape. Scientific and Political Implications. *Journal of Social Science, 18*(1), 23–44.

O'Neill, Maggie. (1996). Researching Prostitution and Violence: Towards a Feminist Praxis. In Marianne Hester, Liz Kelly & Jill Radford (Eds.), *Women, Violence and Male Power. Feminist Activism, Research and Practice* (pp. 130–147). Buckingham: Open University.

O'Toole, Laura L., & Jessica R. Schiffman. (Eds.) (1997). *Gender Violence. Interdisciplinary Perspectives.* New York, London: New York University.

Pagelow, Mildred D. (1981). *Woman-Battering. Victims and Their Experiences.* Beverly Hills, et al.: Sage.

Popitz, Heinrich. (1992). *Phänomene der Macht. 2.* Greatly enlarged edition. Tübingen: Mohr Siebeck.

Reddemann, Luise. (2001). *Imagination als heilsame Kraft. Zur Behandlung von Traumafolgen mit ressourcenorientierten Verfahren.* Stuttgart: Pfeiffer bei Klett-Cotta.

Renzetti, Claire M. (1992). *Violent Betrayal: Partner Abuse in Lesbian Relationships.* Newbury Park, et al.: Sage.

Römkens, Renée. (1992). *Gewoon geweld? Omvang, aard, gevolgen en achtergronden van gewald tegen vrouwen in heteroseksueelle relaties.* Amsterdam: Swets & Zeitlinger.

Römkens, Renée. (1997). Prevalence of Wife Abuse in the Netherlands. Combining Quantitative and Qualitative Methods in Survey Research. *Journal of Interpersonal Violence, 12,* 99–125.

Schorsch, Eberhard. (1989). Versuch über Sexualität und Aggression. *Zeitschrift für Sexualforschung, 2*(1), 14–28.

Schröttle, Monika. (1999). *Politik und Gewalt im Geschlechterverhältnis. Eine empirische Untersuchung über Ausmaß, Ursachen und Hintergründe von Gewalt gegen Frauen in ostdeutschen Paarbeziehungen vor und nach der deutsch-deutschen Vereinigung.* Bielefeld: Kleine.

Schornstein, Sherri L. (1997). *Domestic Violence and Health Care. What Every Professional Needs to Know.* Thousand Oaks: Sage.

Schwartz, Martin D. (1987). *Gender and Injury in Spousal Assault. Sociological Focus, 20*(1), 61–75.

Schwartz, Martin D. (2000). Methodological Issues in the Use of Survey Data for Measuring and Characterizing Violence against Women. *Violence against Women, 6*(8), 815–838.

Schwendinger, Julia R., & Herman Schwendinger. (1983). *Rape and Inequality*. Beverly Hills et al.: Sage.

Shepard, Melanie F. (1999). Evaluating a Coordinated Community Response. In M. F. Shepard & E. L. Pence (Eds.), *Coordinating Community Responses to Domestic Violence. Lessons from Duluth and beyond* (pp. 169–191). Thousand Oaks, et al.: Sage.

Smith, Michael D. (1987). The Incidence and Prevalence of Woman Abuse in Toronto. *Violence and Victims*, 2(3), 173–187.

Stark, Evan, & Ann Flitcraft. (1996). *Women at Risk: Domestic Violence and Women's Health*. Thousand Oaks, et al.: Sage.

Steinert, Erika, & Ute Straub. (1988). *Interaktionsort Frauenhaus. Möglichkeiten und Grenzen eines feministischen Projektes*. Heidelberg: Wunderhorn.

Steinmetz, Suzanne, & Murray Straus. (Eds.) (1974). *Violence in the Family*. New York: Harper & Row.

Stordeur, Richard A., & Richard Stille. (1989). *Ending Men's Violence against their Partners. One Road to Peace*. Newbury Park, et al.: Sage.

Straub, Jürgen. (1989). *Historisch-psychologische Biographieforschung. Theoretische, methodologische und methodische Argumentationen in systematischer Absicht*. Heidelberg: Asanger.

Straus, Murray A. (1990). Injury and Frequency of Assault and the "Representative Sample Fallacy" in Measuring Wife Beating and Child Abuse. In Murray A. Straus & Richard J. Gelles (Eds.), *Physical Violence in American Families: Risk Factors and Adaptation to Violence in 8,145 Families* (pp. 75–91). New Brunswick: Transaction.

Straus, Murray A. (1991a). New Theory and Old Canards About Family Violence Research. *Social Problems*, 38(2), 180–197.

Straus, Murray A. (1991b). Discipline and Deviance: Physical Punishment of Children and Violence and Other Crime in Adulthood. *Social Problems*, 38(2), 153–134.

Straus, Murray A., & Richard J. Gelles. (Eds.) (1990). *Physical Violence in American Families: Risk Factors and Adaptation to Violence in 8,145 Families*. New Brunswick: Transaction.

Teubner, Ulrike, Ingrid Becker, & Rosemarie Steinhage. (1983). *Untersuchung "Vergewaltigung als soziales Problem – Notruf und Beratung für vergewaltigte Frauen*. Stuttgart: Kohlhammer.

Tjaden, Patricia, & Nancy Thoennes. (2000). Prevalence and Consequences of Male-to-Female and Female-to-Male Intimate Partner Violence as Measured by the National Violence Against Women Survey. *Violence against Women*, 6(2), 142–161.

van Stolk, Bram, & Cas Wouters. (1987). *Frauen im Zwiespalt. Beziehungsprobleme im Wohlfahrtsstaat. Eine Modellstudie*. Frankfurt am Main: Suhrkamp.

Verbundprojekt Frauengesundheit in Deutschland. (2001). *Bericht zur gesundheitlichen Lage von Frauen in Deutschland. Eine Bestandsaufnahme unter Berücksichtigung der unterschiedlichen Entwicklung in West- und Ostdeutschland*. Stuttgart: Kohlhammer.

Weissman, Susanne. (1994). *Überlebenskünstlerinnen. Lebenswege sexuell missbrauchter Frauen*. Pfaffenweiler: Centaurus.

Wetzels, Peter, & Christian Pfeiffer. (1995). *Sexuelle Gewalt gegen Frauen im öffentlichen und im privaten Raum. Ergebnisse einer KFN-Opferbefragung 1992*. Hannover: KFN Forschungsbericht.

Yllö, Kersti, & Michele Bograd. (Eds.) (1988). *Feminist Perspectives on Wife Abuse*. Newbury Park, et al.: Sage

PART II-1-2

VIOLENCE IN AND BY STATE INSTITUTIONS

CHAPTER II-1-2.1

Violence and the Rise of the State

Michael Hanagan

I. THE FORMS OF VIOLENCE

Let us define "violence" as the infliction of physical damage on persons or property. The "forms of violence" refer to the relationship between a violent actor or actors and at least one other actor who may or may not engage in violence; collectively these forms describe how violence is used in a given society. The four principal forms of violence are public violence, symbolic violence, everyday violence, and private violence. Public violence occurs in public places, involves coordinated action, and some kind of claim-making; the two most important types of public violence are warmaking and collective protest. "Public violence" is part of a public "dialogue." When Carl von Clausewitz asserted that "war is a true political instrument, a continuation of political intercourse, carried on with other means," as when Charles Tilly (1994) insists that intrastate violence arises out of routine actions between states and claim-making groups, they both locate violence within larger processes of social negotiation, bargaining and political exchange. In times of "civil war" the two major forms of public violence come together. Violence can speak volumes! When Zapotec warriors beheaded a rival town's political leaders for refusing to send tribute and displayed their heads in a rack, they communicated powerfully with a public, just as when Czarist troops fired on peaceful demonstrators.

"Symbolic violence" involves actual violence and often occurs in public but, in contrast with public violence, it carefully follows a well-defined script and is sponsored or approved by public authorities. Symbolic violence is a "monologue;" authority addresses a public and only a choreographed assent is expected. Symbolic violence includes out-of-the-ordinary violence, often tied to holy days, celebrations or commemorations, as well as state-mandated legal punishment. Roman gladiatorial games, American criminal executions, and Aztec ritual sacrifices validate the established order and assert the rulers' power over the contingent and chaotic.

W. Heitmeyer and J. Hagan (eds.), *International Handbook of Violence Research*, 121–137.
© 2003 Kluwer Academic Publishers. Printed in the Netherlands.

"Everyday violence" refers to the routine violence of social life. It uses direct means to accomplish immediate ends and does not assert public claims, a soliloquy that speaks for itself to itself. An angry London crowd destroying a brothel to protest the restoration of the Stuarts is an example of public violence, a Saturday-night fight among clients of a brothel is everyday violence. Much criminal conduct belongs to this category where perpetrators include: petty street criminals, cattle rustlers, and Viking raiders. Much anticrime violence also belongs to this category. In pre-industrial cities, states generally tolerated the definition and enforcement of public order by violent nonauthorized groups, such as local toughs, bounty hunters, bands of neighbors, or elite-sponsored gangs, and their actions are included in our category of "everyday violence" which also includes routine police activity. The borderline between everyday and public violence is sometimes difficult to draw. Authorities often label contentious claim-makers as "criminals" and use routine police tactics against them to emphasize their rejection of protestors' demands. When are cattle-raiding clansmen stealing, when are they attempting to take tribute, and when are they asserting claims over land confiscated from their forefathers? To understand such violence, context is crucial but a characteristic feature of everyday violence is its taken-for-granted character—taken for granted, to be sure, by society, not necessarily by victims and their friends.

"Private violence" occurs in social space outside the public purview. Where public violence may be classified as a dialogue, ritual violence as a monologue, and everyday violence as a soliloquy, private violence is silent. Like everyday violence, it is often taken for granted; its distinctive feature is that, while not intrinsically private, it is construed as private by society. In late nineteenth-century East London, although thin tenement walls hid few secrets, wife beating went unreported so long as it did not result in serious injury. Private violence denotes internal violence within a unit variably defined as the "family" or "household," including the violence of adult males against women, children, and dependent household members but also the violence of powerful kin against less powerful.

The forms of violence change in regard to frequency, repertoire, and boundary. Repertoire refers to the way people act together in pursuit of shared interests. Between 1848 and 1851, in the heat of revolutionary events, the repertoire of French rural protest changed abruptly. Charivaris and grain riots turned to demonstrations and rallies as peasants directed their discontent away from local elites and toward a centralized power that suddenly looked tractable. The boundaries between forms of violence also change. Modern America does not treat the murder of a servant by a master as a private matter as it did in the slave South a century and a half ago.

Each of the forms of violence identified here marks a distinctive relationship among actors, including the perpetrators and the targets of violence. Although the relationships are distinctive, they can overlap. In the midst of intense conflict, embattled public contenders, trying to enlarge their vocabulary and reach a wider audience, may draw on understandings generated within other forms of violence. In the French Revolution, the slaying of public officials and the display of their severed heads was modeled on the practice of royal justice for executing traitors.

While insisting that the forms of violence vary historically, it is necessary to reject traditional arguments that require violence to follow a unilinear or even dialectical trajectory, usually culminating in the abolition of violence itself. Such interpretations take many forms. Auguste Comte (1975) saw history as beginning in an age of offensive war, giving way to an age of defensive war, and finally climaxing in the age of industry (which he believed Europe was then entering). In the age of industry, human cooperation and the scientific spirit would end the reign of violence. In contrast, Karl Marx argued that the growth of capitalism led to the intensification of both internal class struggle and international war but these cataclysms would lead to proletarian revolution and the end of collective violence. Even the rhythmic ebb and flow of violence as portrayed by Ibn Khaldun, Vilfredo Pareto and Oswald Spengler is inadequate to faithfully analyze changing forms of violence. Pareto's contrast of rising ruling classes, devoted to an ideal and willing to use brute force, and declining ruling classes, holding power through manipulation and surreptitious violence, is exemplary. But in Pareto's Italy, fascist violence required the support of the entrenched ruling classes and the actual fascist use of violence fluctuated wildly.

Abandoning efforts to uncover processes that undergird all human history and that follow invariant patterns, our analysis portrays violence as a form of communication and, drawing on the tradition of J.-J. Rousseau (Rousseau & Herder 1966) and Mikhail Bakhtin (1981), argues that violence like language is based on shared understandings. The processes of state formation and the organization of society were different in the valley of the Oaxaca, in southern Mesopotamia, and in the Yellow River valley and the varying forms of violence that predominate in each region cast light on these social, economic and cultural differences. Rousseau depicted forms of communication, including violent forms of communication, as changing in response to the spread of individualism and the expansion of northern peoples. Bakhtin insisted that language expresses a relationship between speaker and communicate. Our approach focuses on the communicative, relational aspects of violence. However reprehensible or arbitrary, no violent act is completely sense*less* because it embodies both established social values and the possibility of their rejection. Changes in the forms of violence help as much in the analysis of the mainstream as of the marginal.

Significant changes in the frequency, repertoire, or the boundaries of the forms of violence, are usually associated with important shifts within the political and economic order. Our claim is that the forms of violence are socially-constituted relationships that order the realm of collective action and that great changes in the political and economic organization of society inevitably result in their reconfiguration. In particular, state transformation, alterations in the character of the state or in its relations to other states, result in the redefining of the "public," "private," "symbolic," and "everyday." No claim is made that state transformation is associated with determinate and similar forms of violence across continents and eras. The processes of state transformation and the forms of violence were different in the valley of the Oaxaca, in southern Mesopotamia, and in the Yellow River valley. No single path of state transformation nor even the appearance of the state itself is inevitable. Sub-Saharan African societies successfully devised non-state ways of cooperation using associations, chiefdoms, and fictive kinship systems.

To analyze variations in the forms of violence, this essay looks at different contexts of state transformation and shows how the forms of violence respond to changed contexts. Four kinds of state transformation are examined: the rise of the state, the transformation of city-state into empire, the evolution of empire into a state system and the appearance of the consolidated state. Contemporary forms of violence are then placed in their historical context.

II.   VARIATIONS IN THE FORMS OF VIOLENCE

1.   Violence and the Rise of the State

To get an idea of some ways in which the forms of violence might change as non-state societies of hunters and gatherers gave way to agriculture-based states, let us look at the Oaxaca Valley in modern day Mexico as analyzed by Joyce Marcus and Kent V. Flannery (1996). As social hierarchy, political organization, and agriculture developed in the Oaxaca valley, so did warmaking and symbolic violence. Although comparable research has not been done in the Oaxaca Valley, in some areas of Mesoamerica evidence suggests that the spread of agriculture also led to increases in private violence.

Beginning 10,000 years ago when humans were already present in the Chihuahuan steppe, the main division of labor was along gender lines and a rough egalitarianism was the rule. Lacking evidence of collective violence, archaeologists and anthropologists generally conclude that it was limited to personal rivalries, shaming procedures by which the village maintained social equality, and the occasional violence of men against their wives and children. Most inhabitants were gatherers and foragers moving seasonally between oak-covered uplands, piedmont thorn-forest and valley-floor thickets of mesquite. In times of scarcity, the dwellers dispersed in family groups, but in times of abundance everyone assembled in campsites where rituals were performed at a common area in the camp.

About 5,000 years ago public violence, warmaking, arose in Oaxaca as community members defended their encampment sites and the productive terrain they had created from other migrating groups. Such defenses were necessary because a long process of sedentarization was already well under way. Instead of following animals or plants, the length of time spent in encampments grew while "task groups" brought plants and animals to the camp. More time was devoted to shaping the environment near the camp sites, encouraging the growth of squash, beans and *teosinte* (the ancestor of maize) and discouraging mesquite. The campsite became a valuable resource and their role in increasing its fertility gave its inhabitants incentive to assert their claim to possession.

Starting a process with great impact on violence, somewhere between 3,000 and 4,000 years ago, more prestigious males began to band together and gender differences were formally institutionalized, with inequality between men and women increasing. Some men grew more maize than others did and, able to pay the dowries, acquired multiple wives. "Blood relatives" asserting common mythological ancestors appeared and developed into fraternal orders including the most respected men in the community. Village rituals were divided along gender lines with men gathering in the Men's House while women practiced their rituals at home.

About 3,200 years ago, social and economic hierarchy became ever more pervasive leading to endemic warmaking and ritual violence. Social differentiation became not only widespread but also hereditary. Villagers abandoned religious explanations that attributed individual accomplishment to the will of the gods or an individual's success in obtaining the gods' favors. They adopted new beliefs that some men and women were descended from the gods. Distinctions attributed to a successful war leader or a highly-skilled individual did not die out with the person but were transferred to offspring. Accumulating power from generation to generation, hereditary leaders increased their control over farmers, craftsmen and warriors and sought to increase them still more. In pursuit of this goal, they built Men's Houses to attract followers, formed alliances with lineage groups in other villages—and made relentless war. The ritual execution of captured enemies demonstrated publicly the fate of those who refused to acknowledge the leader's supremacy.

About 2,500 years ago, internecine village warfare yielded its ultimate product—territorial concentration of power by an enduring ruling establishment—the appearance of the state. Power was permanently centered in a Zapotec territorial capital in the hands of hereditary leaders and aristocracy with skilled craftsmen and its dependent peasantry living in the city and in the large network of villages and tributary cities. The absence of wheeled vehicles and draft animals made long distance transportation difficult in Mesoamerica where narrow roads slowed the movement of armies while seasonal demand for agricultural labor restricted the length of the warmaking period. Transportation difficulties and seasonal warfare made it difficult to rule at a distance and encouraged empires based on tribute taking rather than direct administration. Public sacrifices of captured prisoners before representatives from potentially rebellious communities used terror to overcome distance.

While we know little about changes in private violence in the Oaxaca valley, elsewhere in Mesoamerica recent research has shown that in some cases the shift toward agriculture led to domestic violence. Recent work such as that of Debra L. Martin (1997)in the southwest United States has suggested that increases in social differentiation among some groups of pre-contact Amerindians promoted violence against women and children. A thousand years ago Pueblo Indians lived along the La Plata River Valley which lies between modern day New Mexico and Arizona and also in the Black Mesa in northeastern Arizona. Permanently watered, with plentiful wild game and turkey, and a productive agriculture, La Plata was a desirable place to live, with some similarities to the Oaxaca valley, and an analysis of skeleton remains shows a generally healthy population. In comparison, Black Mesa was a marginal and isolated environment with insecure water supply, dependent on maize, nondomesticated plants and small game. Morbidity was high with many inhabitants suffering from anemia and infections. Yet, analyses of skeletal remains reveal systematic violence toward women and small children in La Plata and comparatively little violence in Black Mesa.

To understand this difference, archaeologists have emphasized the stress placed on women in the shift from hunting, to gathering, to agriculture. Women carried a disproportionate part of the burden in agriculture and the settled life that it entailed; they ground corn, prepared food, gathered wood, built and mended houses, made pottery and clothing while men were responsible for farming, occasional hunting, and religious and ceremonial activities. Prosperity in La Plata also led to higher fertility and increased migration. Higher fertility meant that women were pregnant over a longer proportion of their married life and this may have increased tension at a time when the spread of agriculture increased women's workload. In turn, increased demand for female labor is associated with the presence of an underclass of immigrant women who were routinely battered, their young children killed. Thus, the private realm provided the nurturing environment for the early development of oppressive social relations.

In the Oaxaca valley, the rise of the state showed dramatic changes in the forms of violence. As people settled down and a social hierarchy arose, systematic organization for war grew ever more important and, with war, the spread of new and terrifying rituals of violence. Although lacking Mexican evidence, a look at very recent work in the American southwest suggests that the development of agriculture in situations similar to that of Oaxaca could certainly lead to domestic violence against women although whether or not it did there must remain unknown.

2. City States to Empires

Leaving Mesoamerica with the foundation of the city-state, let us turn to the Yellow River Valley of China for an example of how city-states effectively ruled by warrior aristocrats were incorporated into an empire effectually ruled by bureaucrats. Recent studies by Mark E. Lewis (1990) and Robin D. S. Yates (1999) have shown that, although the symbolic violence characteristic of aristocratic militarism gave way to less bloodthirsty rituals, aristocratic defeat was achieved by the formation of large peasant armies. The elevation of knowledge and education as essential values of Chinese society coincided with a tremendous escalation in the scale of warfare. Moreover, emperors and imperial bureaucracies created new forms of everyday violence to replace lineage-based systems of policing, with implications for private violence.

Between the seventh and sixth centuries B.C.E., while the Shang and Zhou dynasties proclaimed their domination over most of northeastern China, effective political administration was concentrated in small walled cities and statelets that acknowledged the supremacy of the emperors but possessed considerable religious and military autonomy. Warrior aristocrats sorted into lineages organized warmaking and symbolic violence; initially senior lineages had dominated but gradually junior lineages established themselves and the feeling spread that all aristocrat lineages shared a common equality. In stark contrast to later eras, the great aristocratic families regarded the emperor as first among equals and criticized him publicly. Chariot-equipped warrior aristocrats controlled much of the land and, in return, levied their own military contingents and brought them into battle when summoned by the emperor.

Aristocrats monopolized rituals including human sacrifice, probably the sacrifice of prisoners captured in warfare and executed to accompany a deceased ruler or to consecrate an ancestral temple. During recurrent periods of great unrest, the central religious rituals were "blood covenants." Only agreements among equals could suspend the endless warfare caused by an aristocratic code of honor that made all lineage members responsible for the crimes of any. Lineage self-policing itself was a form of violence designed to prevent inter-elite conflict by encouraging senior lineage members to restrain their kinsmen. The invisibility covering family relationships enabled senior family members to exert pressure on juniors that would have been viewed as intolerable affronts in the public world. Yet once a bloody exchange had occurred between two lineages the aristocratic code of vengeance led easily and rapidly to an uncontrolled escalation of violence.

Aristocratic domination hinged on their control over the land and monopoly of the means of violence. In the period of the Warring States (403–221 B.C.E.) the power of centralized states asserted itself as the spread of new technologies permitted arming peasants and forming an effective infantry. At the same time, greater control over water resources brought new land into cultivation, and rulers were able to use these new lands to tie peasant soldiers directly to central power. The major benefactors of the collapse of aristocratic lineages were rulers, bureaucratic administrators, and male household heads. Major social and political transformation had dramatic ramifications for all forms of violence. Rulers rid themselves of aristocratic pretensions of equality and an educated administrative elite triumphed over men of the sword. Military prowess was redefined not, as formerly, as a matter of personal courage but as a form of knowledge to be mastered by a literate elite. The stress on the centrality of book learning to warfare effectively undercut the major justification of the aristocracy's warrior ethos. The blood sacrifice rituals among equals lost their centrality, displaced by oath-taking rituals binding inferiors to superiors. Literate officeholders increasingly condemned human sacrifice as barbaric.

A change in the form of everyday violence was also introduced, one with a long future in Chinese history. The aristocratic code of lineage responsibility was universalized; while most private vengeance was outlawed, all families were made responsible for the behavior of close kin—with the state itself pledged to punish family members who failed to report their criminal activity. Knowledge of criminal activity by close family members and failing to report it was punishable by death.

The worlds of the public and private was reconfigured and with it the role of violence. The spread of independent landholdings, the mobilization of troops from family units, and the new system of family-based law enforcement made the father a pivotal force in allocating family resources. With the decline of the lineage-based aristocracy, private violence was no longer necessary to enforce discipline within the lineage and became confined to the realm of the household. The centrality of the male household head was reflected in the exaltation of this relationship as a model for all others hierarchical relationships. Abandoning the earlier emphasis on a common code of honor shared by a military elite, relationships between rulers and elites were defined in the language of gender. Ministers and generals portrayed their relationship to the monarch as analogous to the subordinate relationship between men and women.

The transition from a decentralized era dominated by warrior aristocrats to a more centralized era presided over by powerful bureaucrats witnessed dramatic changes in all forms of violence; from chariot armies in which military aristocrats played the leading role to mass peasant armies; from an era of human sacrifice and blood rites to an era of peaceful oathtaking; from a violent autonomous code of personal aristocratic ethics to a state-imposed universal system of surveillance; and from a system of family control within lineages to one based on the male household head. The decline of lineage-based aristocracies fundamentally redefined the relationship between public and private; this transition certainly decreased violence within the lineage and probably increased violence within the household.

3. Empire to State System

While city-states have played an important role in political history, the central players have usually been composite states like the Chinese empire, units cobbled together from a variety of preexisting political units by aggressive rulers. Inside these ramshackle states, all were subjects but not all were equally subject. Not only did laws demarcate elites from commoners and the unfree, but also they marked off members of established religions from others, and often privileged urban dwellers over rural. Distinctive features of early modern Europe were the failure and breakup of empires, the creation of a state system designed to prevent the rise of a single hegemon, and perpetual violence. The new system originated in the breakup of the Habsburg kingdom of Charles V, the great composite empire stretching westward from Vienna to Manila. To understand the relationship between this state system and changes in the forms of violence, let us look at Europe between 1500 and 1700, as it was shaken by revolts heralding the appearance of capitalism.

Warfare within the divided European state system created opportunities for popular groups to exert independent influence at a time when rulers' power was stretched to the very limit. A diverse political order emerged as Bohemian princes took up arms to resist Habsburg power, as Catalan burghers rose to protest the imposition of taxes to carry on war, as Dutch provinces mobilized their citizens in the streets to increase their autonomy, and as German peasant villagers marched out with pitchforks to strike for freedom. United by their fear of menacing overlords, communities possessing disparate collections of rights allied together. Associations played an essential role throughout the early modern period and, within these associations, popular mobilization often played a powerful role in sustaining resistance. A confederation of Castilian cities was the heart of the Comunero rebellion: peasant rebels also joined together in rural Germany and France. The French Catholic League, Irish Confederates and German Schmalkalden League were only a few of the diverse groups that waged war against centralizing rulers. Protestant rebels led the resistance to Habsburg power. Religious differences complicated the struggle against imperial rule and accusations of heresy made it more brutal, increasing the use of symbolic violence including the burning of heretics and judicial torture.

A whole spectrum of political outcomes emerged from the era of continuous warfare. The collapse of composite states created new sovereignties that often retained the particularities and gradated citizenship that marked their origins in polities whose rulers had conceded particular sets of rights to towns, religious groups, and all kinds of intermediate assemblies. Holland and Switzerland were founded as confederate provinces that mobilized their citizens and prevailed against composite overlords; the different political, religious, and legal arrangements in the separate provinces that constituted independent Holland and Switzerland greatly complicated later efforts at unified political action. Where princes had managed to consolidate their hold over cities and contiguous territories more direct forms of rule emerged, as in England, France and Sweden. Between these two poles lay all sorts of complicated layers of sovereignties in which free cities, estates, and provinces reforged new relations with rulers in the wake of imperial collapse. The German Empire was the major site of such complicated arrangements although Spain and the southern Spanish Netherlands (roughly modern Belgium) were also examples. In strategic locations throughout Europe, violent popular intervention also affected religious outcomes. In the German Empire, where urban populations demanded reform and met with support from local authorities or were able to overcome their resistance, Protestantism spread. Where popular pressure was weak and/or where resolute local authorities stood by the Church, Catholicism endured; in the seventeenth century, the Counter-Reformation mustered Catholic popular support.

Ironically, European intrastate warfare was the condition for the rise of a capitalism that periodically attested its love of peace and free markets. The true enemy of capitalism was not war but pacific empire. With peace consolidated, emperors in China, India, Japan and Rome seized the property of great merchants; vulgar moneymaking had enabled these merchants to emulate the lifestyles of courtiers, and high level officials felt this as an intolerable usurpation of status. Besides, seizing great merchants' property was an easy way to enlarge state coffers. But in Europe nearly continuous war and the perpetual threat of war strengthened capitalists' role as underwriters of war and made them irreplaceable— at least in the urban areas of Europe where they constructed and controlled financial networks that permitted large-scale capital accumulation.

However, the urbanized areas of Western and Central Europe were not only centers of capitalist power but also sites of popular struggle. Recent work by scholars such as Peter Blickle (1992) and Wayne Te Brake (1998) have shown that common people participated in all the struggles of the period and their intervention was often significant. The forms of everyday violence bore importantly on whether popular emotions could be channeled into public protest that was sometimes violent. Let us take the case of late seventeenth-century London policing as studied by Tim Harris (1987). Like other monarchs, the Stuarts did not devote large expenditures for policing. As in so many other European cities, the ability of the London crowd to intervene in life and death political was rooted in the practice of imposing police obligations upon unpaid, part-time officials who rotated in office. Much of the burden of law enforcement fell on neighbors and passersby who were legally responsible for responding to cries of alarm and assisting beadles, watchmen and constables. If things got out of control, these officials called on militia regiments recruited within and stationed around London, but the militia's reliability was not unquestioned; in 1673 several regiments had seemed to support striking weavers. The ultimate alternative was the regular army, but here all sides hesitated for this meant large-scale bloodshed.

In moments of political crisis, such systems of voluntary policing were extremely susceptible to community pressure. In theory, all householders were supposed to participate in local police institutions but many wealthier householders hired replacements giving policing a very popular character. Yet, small masters and laborers involved in policing were still subject to the influence of the political views of powerful local patrons. Consequently, when crowds assembled to express popular sentiments or demands supported by influential local residents, those charged with policing the crowd often faded into the crowd.

The character of policing explains the often violent crowds mobilized by both friends and enemies of the royal family. Between 1679 and 1681, several unsuccessful attempts were made to exclude the duke of York, the future James II, from the succession because of his Catholicism. To rally crowds in areas of London where they exerted influence, such as Westminster, Whig politicians drew on anti-Catholic sentiments and organized parades in which effigies of the Pope were burned along with ecclesiastical vestments. However, Whig attacks on Catholicism were often interpreted by Church of England clergymen and Tories as covert attacks on themselves. Mobilizing their own crowds, Tories drew on a long-standing hostility to nonconformists and their war on popular culture and recreational life and organized meetings in which effigies of Oliver Cromwell or "Jack Presbyter" were burned along with the exclusion bill and the king's health was drunk. Against the Whigs, the Stuarts' supporters were successful in rallying crowd opinion; only when Charles II's advocacy of Catholic toleration turned the Tory Anglican clergy against him did the monarchy lose the battle for London opinion.

In territorial monarchies where princes enhanced their control over the church, the relationship between state and family life was redefined. Formerly, the Church had controlled the right to decide the legitimacy of marriages. Wealthy families seeking to arrange profitable marriages for their children feared penniless suitors and found the Church unwilling to annul marriages that had been carried out with the proper rituals and duly consummated. However, following Sarah Hanley (1987), even in Catholic France, state organizations began to insist on controlling marriage law to invalidate too hasty marriages and to threaten the disobedient with capital punishment for rape and kidnapping. The key role in the redefinition of power over families was played by a Parlement, composed of representatives of the wealthiest French families, that in 1634 issued a decree assuming judicial competence over marriages. By redefining marriage as a civil rather than a religious act the Parlement gave parents much greater control over their children's marriage and threatened with death those who failed to receive parental consent.

A look at Europe between 1500 and 1700 shows how the collapse of empire led to the emergence of a new state system with enormous changes in the forms of violence. The major character was the construction of a new state system in which war was routinely used to maintain a balance of power among rival nations. Battles between monarchs and those resisting royal powers presented unprecedented opportunities for popular intervention. Administrative centralization also led to greater state control over families with important repercussions for family violence.

4. The Rise of the Consolidated State

The greatest state transformation of the modern period was wrought by the French Revolution and it also marked a similarly unprecedented change in the forms of violence. In 1789, on the eve of the revolution, divided into provinces that included vast Languedoc and tiny Foix, France retained many of the marks of its origins as a composite empire. The south of France was largely subject to Roman law while customary law ruled the north. Sixteen areas of France retained their own separate estates possessing a variety of rights and privileges, and tax barriers slowed trade at the very center of the country.

The revolution created a new "consolidated state"—centralized, differentiated, and coercion monopolizing—that concentrated enormous power over everyday life in its own hands. The creation of a new kind of state altered dramatically both political claim making and warmaking and thus changed the character of public violence. Such a concentration of power forced ordinary men and women to turn their attention to this new political unit. Demanding far more from its population than any previous state, the new French government compensated for its exactions by extending citizenship to a large proportion of the country's male population and granting them participation in political decision-making. Increased popular involvement in the politics of a great established power created new opportunities for the rise of sometimes violent mass movements and new calls for violent repression; within a year of the passage of the Constitution of 1791, armed members of popular political clubs overthrew the monarchy. Possessing the speed and efficiency required by an age of mass politics, the guillotine became the new symbol of democratic violence, replacing class-specific methods, the axe for nobles, the rope for commoners.

As demonstrated so conclusively by Isser Woloch's work (1994), the French Revolution involved the state in the life of ordinary men and women in unparalleled fashion. Revolutionaries abolished the intermediary institutions of the old order, the parlements, tax farmers, semi-independent charitable establishments, and provincial estates. France was departmentalized, districted and communalized. The powerful new government asserted claims on the civilian population exceeding those of the most thoroughgoing European absolutisms.

The expansion of popular citizenship was linked to warmaking. Compulsory male military participation was a mainstay of its gendered concept of citizenship. Conscription was considered partly as a tribute paid by localities to the government but also as an expression of membership in the polity. In 1791, repudiating the monarchy's reliance on mercenaries, the Constituent Assembly forbade foreigners to enlist in the French army and prohibited the entry of bodies of foreign soldiers into France without legislative consent. The revolution enormously simplified the legal status of subjects of the French state, dividing them into "active" and "passive" citizens. At its widest, in the constitution of 1793, written during the highpoint of revolutionary military mobilization, active citizenship belonged to most adult males. Excluded from the military, women's membership in the polity was mediated by their relationship to men.

The state's ability to levy unprecedented numbers of troops from a male population that identified with the national cause was an essential aspect of a new kind of "total war" introduced by the French Revolution. Unlike the runaways and vagabonds incorporated into *ancien régime* armies, many of the new French recruits identified with their national cause. French armies traveled fast because, in contrast to the harshly-disciplined common soldiers in the counterrevolutionary armies, they were not afraid of mass desertion if they marched at night or through rugged terrain or urban areas. Solving a problem that had defeated Frederick the Great, revolutionary generals sent skirmishers and sharpshooters out in front of their columns relying on the men's loyalty and commitment to fight on their own initiative.

The French strategy of "total war" not only motivated the troops and conscripted the general male population but it mobilized the civilian population. Dissatisfied with the inability of the French private arms industry to produce sufficient muskets, revolutionary engineers carried out a daring and by-and-large successful reorganization of the French arms industry, introducing the manufacture of interchangeable parts. Still, the engineers' attempts to impose a new discipline on small masters and artisans met with considerable resistance, a portent perhaps of the workers' wartime resistance to military mobilization that was such a powerful force in the twentieth century.

As the revolution polarized France, peasants learned that grain riots and rural insurrections made national legislators sit up and take notice. With counterrevolutionaries allied with foreign nations, legislators realized that the support of the rural population was essential. Even passive citizens were accorded some basic rights, and the revolution's conception of basic right grew as it radicalized and relied more heavily on popular support. In 1789, the Declaration of the Rights of Man recognized the rights to a fair trial, religious toleration, and freedom of the press. Seigniorial obligations with their connotation of personal dependence were converted into allodial freeholding. Legally-privileged social statuses disappeared entirely. A law of June 1793 pledged pensions to aged and sick indigents and to impoverished families and widows. A law of November 1794 required the establishment of a primary school and the presence of a teacher in every commune of one thousand or more. As the republic mobilized all its resources for war, however, the promises of government social provision for the needy and popular schooling were deferred and eventually revoked. Nonetheless, the designation of schooling and social welfare as fundamental human rights constituted an institutional agenda to be pursued later by citizens. Between 1804 and 1811 a standardized legal system, tailored to the needs of a market society, was imposed on the entire country.

The benefits received from the revolution and participation in the political process produced a new sense of popular consciousness that reshaped the identity of violent actors over the next two centuries. The importance of popular identification with a shared body of law and a common legislature, a political project that was not linguistic, racial, or cultural, was the major message of the many public ceremonies that revolutionary propagandists used to educate the people. In the eyes of some patriots, establishing the popular will required the teaching of French to the six million French people whom they estimated did not speak any French at all. However, revolutionary assemblies avoided this issue and refused to compel instruction in French.

The revolution also altered the character of everyday violence; revolutionaries sought to monopolize the police power and some went so far as to incorporate webs of patriotic informers into the state apparatus. At their high point during the Terror, revolutionaries attempted to create a system of total policing that abolished all intermediary institutions between state and citizen. A good example of the goal toward which the revolution was moving is shown in Colin Lucas's study (1973) of the institutions created by the *représentant en mission*, Claude Javogues, in the Loire in 1793–1794. Solely responsible to the central government, Javogues established local surveillance committees composed of resident patriots and run in close cooperation with patriotic clubs. In village and small towns, patriotic committees issued certificates attesting individuals' patriotism, denounced and arrested suspicious individuals, and searched for evidence of Sunday gatherings (possibly Catholic masses). The penetration of state surveillance and control into intimate aspects of community life revealed the nightmare possibilities of the new consolidated state.

In the baggage of French armies, the model of the consolidated state with its rights and responsibilities was brought to central and southern Europe in the revolutionary and Napoleonic eras. The consolidated state remained after Napoleon's defeat. Retaining the new duties of citizenship without its rights, the reestablished monarchies were bound to provoke unrest, discontent, and a resurgent revolutionary spirit.

Developments in central, eastern and southern Europe were to have great influence on the character of future violence. In these regions, the problem confronting patriots after 1815 was not simply one of demanding the restoration of rights but of establishing coherent territorial units or of re-establishing coherent national units that had been temporarily created by the revolution or Napoleon. In these areas, a new kind of nationalism arose which was both derived from French examples but contained decisively new elements. In Germany, intellectuals and politicians, influenced by the writings of Fichte and Herder, reformulated the French concept of nationalism; in place of the French focus on nationalism as a shared political identity, they championed nationalism as a shared ethnic or cultural identity. Such ideas emerged inevitably in places such as Germany, Italy, or Poland where peoples with ancient traditions of historical unity and similar languages found themselves partitioned across several states.

The rise of the consolidated states witnessed a dramatic change in the forms of violence. The military revolution brought about by universal conscription and military reorganization required every potential military power to reorganize. Ordinary men and women began to demand relief and assistance from central states, sometimes violently. The politicization of masses of people was caused not simply by the expansion of political participation but by the entry of the state into everyday political life on an unequaled scale. The new consolidated state inevitably transformed policing by bringing state power front and center into the world of everyday violence. The notion that consolidated states should share a common culture and language gradually amalgamated with the French Revolution's emphasis on a common political participation and spread widely in the first half of the nineteenth century. This new nationalist amalgam would have great impact on the character of public violence.

III.   FORMS OF VIOLENCE IN THE CONTEMPORARY WORLD

Over the last two hundred years, much political violence has been variations within the basic transformation brought about by the consolidated states. Even at a time when Western and Central Europeans and, to a much lesser extent, North Americans, are creating transnational state structures such as the European Union and the North American Free

Trade Zone, much of the violence that appears in our newspapers follows the forms established by the French revolution and its twentieth-century heritors. The continuing unraveling of the legacy of colonial rule, with their gerrymandered colonial states, and the collapse of the Soviet bloc have kept the formation of consolidated states and the violence associated with it in our headlines.

From the French Revolution descends directly the modern idea of total war—the mobilization of the entire national population to achieve complete victory. The technologies have advanced considerably but universal male conscription and the mobilization for war industries in World Wars I and II were drawn from the French Revolution. The major innovation in this direction has been that twentieth-century warfare not only involves the populace in the war effort but can also take a huge toll of civilian lives. One of the goals of American military doctrine in the Vietnam era, according to George Herring (1994), was to develop a strategy of "limited war" that would allow policymakers to carry on a sustained violent military engagement without involving the entire nation in the war effort. Military men sought an alternative to total war because they recognized that democracies did not make such military commitments easily and that once a popular audience was fully committed to war, it was difficult to settle for anything less than total victory. The failure of the Vietnam policy convinced many military men that democracies are ill-suited to fight limited wars and that serious military commitments demand broad popular support and firm government commitments. Quick battles involving overwhelming military force are one way around this problem but, in the case of longer engagements, the American military still has no alternative to total war.

If warmaking remains in the thrall of the French Revolution so does much political claim making. At the end of the twentieth century as at its beginning, the central political claims that mobilize masses and thus often lead to violence, either the violence of protestors or of repressors, concern rights and citizenship. In Brazil as in South Africa, large mass movements demanding equal citizenship have successfully challenged governments that have resisted guerilla movements and attempts at violent insurrection. The centrality of citizenship demands stems from the continued construction of consolidated states on a worldwide scale.

Do consolidated states serve as the model toward which post-World War II new nations aspire and does the construction of consolidated states inevitably entail the language of rights and citizenship? The verdict remains out. Scholars such as R. Bin Wong (1998) have suggested, for example, that in China the government has traditionally undertaken to guarantee its subjects protection against catastrophe and to promote a broad economic equality and that this constitutes a language of government obligation that is an alternative to the Western rights tradition. Although the rights and citizenship tradition profoundly influenced Sun-Yat-Sen, Wong may have a point; still, the goddess of liberty so prominent in the Tiananmen Square protest in 1989 bears a striking resemblance to the statue of liberty.

Even in Europe and America, demands for rights and citizenship continue to impel political movements that profoundly affect the character of violence. Woman's suffrage and the second wave of feminist mobilization in the 1970s proved powerful forces in reordering the private world of the family. Women's rights movements have organized and fought to publicize violent acts committed within families. New legislation as well as the enforcement of existing laws has substantially redefined the character of family life and imposed new limits on family violence. Recent efforts to champion children's rights may promise even more changes.

If demands for citizenship and rights remind us of the liberating power of state transformation, accelerating waves of ethnic cleansing and genocide recall its dark and murderous side. These fearful acts too result from the legacy of the French Revolution and the transformation of its ideals in the post-Revolutionary period. The dynamic force behind the French consolidated state was the identification of the people with a national community—although in the revolution itself such identification was mainly based on participation in politics, not on culture or language. Within a few decades, however, even radical French republicans followed German and Italian nationalists in agreeing that cultural and ethnic identification were a prerequisite of national identity. Confronted with disparities between cultural identity and territorial claims, nineteenth-century nationalists generally responded by seeking to assimilate, often forcefully, these groups into the national culture. Where assimilationism brought little advantage to leaders of ethnic groups, they responded by asserting their own nationalist identity.

World War I was a watershed in the nationalist turn toward murderous violence. For ethnic nationalists, the embrace of the principle of "self-determination" by political leaders as diverse as Woodrow Wilson and Vladimir Lenin was an object lesson; significant concentrations of minorities were the nucleus of new nations and must be avoided. For minority groups, the widespread adoption of self-determination was an enormous political opportunity. In Eastern Europe, in the aftermath of World War I, new solution to the problem of ethnic minorities were attempted; instead of moving borders to reflect population composition or forcing the assimilation of recalcitrant minorities, nationalists moved the populations to reflect the borders or killed minorities outright. The newly-created Polish state adopted a policy of intimidation toward Germans. Turks and Greeks carried out significant population exchanges as well as killing obdurate minorities. In the case of the Armenians, the Turks were the first to turn to genocide as a way of avoiding a difficult and unpopular partition. During World War II, terror and forced resettlement were used wholesale by Hitler in the east and then again, in the aftermath of World War II, the methods that the Germans had first employed in Eastern Europe were used against them by restored Eastern nations.

Although the new nationalism built on old ethnic prejudices, the mass killings and forced migration of the twentieth century differ dramatically from those in the pre-1789 period. In *ancien régime* Europe, minorities such as Jews and Muslims in Christian Europe and Jews and Orthodox Christians in Muslim Europe, possessed distinctive rights protected by rulers. In return for protection they owed financial contributions to rulers and were sometimes allowed special privileges such as the monopoly of trade with particular foreigners, the right to enforce laws within their communities, or the right to lend money. In both Christian and Muslim Europe, as David Nirenberg (1996) maintains, attacks on minorities often occurred within the context of struggles against central rulers, with angry crowds demanding the more thorough subordination of minority groups. Subjects of composite states perpetrated their own bloody deeds but the goal of a culturally or ethnically homogenous state, the goal of modern ethnic cleansing, would have been utterly incomprehensible.

In the twentieth century, much mass bloodshed has been supported by government officials and has come because of the fear that minorities will refuse to assimilate. In the first decade of the twentieth century, some Polish nationalists were infuriated by the refusal of many Jews and Ukrainians to identify themselves as Poles. The justification of much contemporary violence is the acceptance of the premise that grew up during the French Revolution and in the wake of the Revolutions of 1848 that nations must be culturally unified communities. Nazi racism drew on these doctrines although it refused membership to a racially-defined category of Jews, including even those who were masters of German culture. Although often inconsistent and shifting, Nazi policies toward Jews and Slavs blended the worst aspects of the post-French Revolutionary world of consolidated states with the savage practices of the older world of composite empires. The core of the Reich would be culturally unified and racially purified; in the eastern lands controlled by the Reich, rigid ethnic and racial hierarchy would prevail with Germans at the top and Slavs below. Jews were to be eliminated everywhere.

Contemporary globalization does not necessarily entail the end of the modern era of nationalist violence. Despite the rise of new transnational organizations and prophecies of a new global order, so far international organizations may have on balance promoted ethnic cleansing rather than prevented it. There is no paradox here, for the basic unit of all our international organizations is the consolidated state. Even if contemporary political leaders no longer believe in a sacred "right to self-determination," they often see ethnic partition as a pragmatic measure to ensure peace. Mary Kaldor (1999) persuasively argues that expectations that the United Nations, NATO or other supranational bodies will intervene to settle civil disputes by ethnic partition have lowered the threshold for ethnic mobilization and increased its potential rewards. Where small groups of self-proclaimed nationalists, often young men, sometimes teenagers or boys, can obtain access to scarce resources such as diamond mines or oil deposits, they can sustain movements with only a minimum of local support. In some cases, nationalist movements sustain their efforts by extorting contributions from their own ethnic group. Unconcerned with mobilizing popular support, their hope is that enduing chaos will lead to international intervention and, as the only mobilized forces within territorial regions, their movements will serve as makers of claims to sovereignty. The popular weakness of such movements however means that they are no longer likely to be successful in bringing peace. In such cases, the legacy of the French Revolution is clearly wearing thin and new types of state organization are beginning to emerge.

If the legacy of the French Revolution can be seen in Sierra Leone or Tajikistan, it has not swept every field. Our concept of "everyday violence" has been transformed by the French Revolution but, in this area, the transformation has been very partial; two hundred years after the American and French revolutions, equal citizenship remains an unachieved goal. Modern students of protest have sometimes followed scholars such as Michel Foucault (1977) and exaggerated the extent of police power, seeing realities in what are only statist dreams. If the state has seized a firm hold on the police power, it has seldom established the all powerful surveillance apparatus desired by the firebrands of the French Revolution such as Claude Javogues. Only a few states such as Stalinist Russia, Hitlerian Germany and Maoist China have really made the effort and no state has been able to sustain such policing for long.

The reasons for the absence of the Surveillance State in the modern world are the same as those that led Stuart monarchs to leave policing in the hands of unpaid householders. Policing is expensive and total policing demands the incorporation of informed local supporters into a police hierarchy. Winning informed local support often involves significant concessions. Moreover, it is politically dangerous to scrutinize the wealthy too carefully and there are far cheaper ways to discipline the poor. While state leaders exert enormous power, total policing demands policies of political alliance deemed too costly and politically objectionable by established systems of power.

Not total policing but class, immigrant, and race biased policing tend to be the predominant strategies in much modern policing. Some evidence suggests that the greater the division between rich and poor, the more policing practices toleration toward upper class felons and brutal repression and intimidation toward whole sections of the lower classes. In South America some police forces openly boast of killing not only criminals but also marginal people who *might* turn to crime. In 1991 in the metropolitan area of São Paulo Brazil, according to Paul Chevigny (1995), the police carried out about fifteen percent of all homicides. Off-duty policemen carried out seventy percent of the police homicides and many were of unarmed suspects. Faced with soaring crime, some political commentators cheered the police, but one of the factors in the collapse of the Brazilian military dictatorship was that it extended the violent and murderous police practices of its elite strike force, the *Rota*, to middle-class political opponents.

In modern policing of the poor, everyday violence and symbolic violence come together. Police brutality is really a form of exemplary punishment that substitutes for reliable information and the ability to distinguish between criminals and honest citizens. While police brutality is formally illegal and it is not carried out publicly, it is accepted by political authorities. In both Los Angeles and New York, for example, cities routinely pays large sums of money to settle cases of police violence or to pay sums awarded by juries, yet multimillion dollar awards do not routinely damage the careers of the police officers whose illegal violence is the source of the awards. Politicians are willing to pay a rather large price to maintain a system of police brutality toward the poor. Modern police forces possess very substantial leeway in defining and enforcing crime and are often encouraged to use their discretion to reinforce existing social and economic divisions in society.

IV.   CONCLUSIONS

Forms of violence are strongly influenced by historical context and political traditions. Although warrior societies typically have violent rituals, these may vary from Aztec human religious sacrifice to Roman gladiatorial combats. The major forms of violence, public, symbolic, everyday, and private, are deeply rooted in social life because they are rooted in state structures and cultural and economic relations. At the same time, however, violent means are often used to reshape societies and even to create new social and political orders. There is a great deal of interaction between the forms of violence and the character of societies. Whenever and by whatever means economic and political structures change, they inevitably entail changes in the forms of violence. The greatest changes in economic and political life produce the greatest changes in the forms of violence.

REFERENCES

Bakhtin, Mikhail Mikhailovich. (1981). *The Dialogic Imagination*. Austin: University of Texas Press.
Blickle, Peter. (1992). *Communal Reformation: the Quest for Salvation in Sixteenth Century Germany*. Atlantic Highlands: Humanities Press.
Chevigny, Paul. (1995). *Edge of the Knife: Police Violence in the Americas*. New York: The New Press.
Comte, Auguste. (1975). *Auguste Comte and Positivism: The Essential Writings*. Chicago: University of Chicago Press.
Foucault, Michel. (1977). *Discipline and Punish: The Birth of the Prison*. New York: Pantheon.
Hanley, Sarah. (1987). Family and State in Early Modern France: The Marriage Pact. In Marilyn J. Boxer & Jean H. Quataert (Eds.), *Connecting Spheres: Women in the Western World, 1500 to the Present* (pp. 53–63). Oxford: Oxford University Press.

Harris, Tim. (1987). *London Crowds in the Reign of Charles II: Propaganda and Politics from the Restoration until the Exclusion Crisis*. Cambridge: Cambridge University Press.

Herring, George C. (1994). *LBJ and Vietnam: A Different Kind of War*. Austin: University of Texas Press.

Kaldor, Mary. (1999). *New and Old Wars: Organized Violence in a Global Era*. Stanford: Stanford University Press.

Lewis, Mark Edward. (1990). *Sanctioned Violence in Early China*. Albany: State University of New York Press.

Lucas, Colin. (1973). *The Structure of the Terror: The Example of Javogues in the Loire*. Oxford: Oxford University Press.

Marcus, Joyce, & Kent V. Flannery. (1996). *Zapotec Civilization: How Urban Society Evolved in Mexico's Oaxaca Valley*. London: Thames and Hudson.

Martin, Debra L. (1997). Violence in La Plata River Valley (A. D. 1000–1300). In Debra L. Martin & David W. Frayer (Eds.), *Troubled Times: Violence and Warfare in the Past* (pp. 45–76). Amsterdam: Gordon and Breach.

Nirenberg, David. (1996). *Communities of Violence: Persecution of Minorities in the Middle Ages*. Princeton: Princeton University Press.

Rousseau, Jean-Jacques, & Johann Gottfried Herder. (1966). *On the Origin of Language: Two Essays*. Chicago: University of Chicago Press.

Te Brake, Wayne. (1998). *Shaping History: Ordinary People in European Politics, 1500–1700*. Berkeley: University of California Press.

Tilly, Charles. (1994). Entanglements of European Cities and States. In Charles Tilly & Wim Blockmans (Eds.), *Cities and the Rise of States in Europe A. D. 1000–1800* (pp. 1–43). Boulder: Westview Press.

Woloch, Isser. (1994). *The New Regime: Transformations of the New Civic Order, 1789–1820's*. New York: Norton.

Wong, R. Bin. (1998). *China Transformed: The Limits of the Western Experience*. Ithaca: Cornell University Press.

Yates, Robin D. S. (1999). Early China. In Kurt Raaflaub & Nathan Rosenstein (Eds.), *War and Society in the Ancient and Medieval Worlds* (pp. 7–45). Cambridge: Harvard.

Holocaust

PETER LONGERICH

I. INTRODUCTION

The Word "Holocaust"

Words influence and direct our perception of a historical phenomenon; this is particularly so when a word is chosen to describe a complex, barely imaginable event.

Literally, the Greek word "holocaust" means "something that is entirely consumed by fire." It is particularly used to refer to a burnt offering, in which the sacrificed animal is entirely burned; in this sense it can be found as early as Xenophon, but especially in the Greek translation of the Bible. Over and above its original biblical meaning, the word was also used in a secular context in various European languages during the nineteenth century, especially to refer to a disaster, in the sense of an all-consuming fire (on the history of the word, see Petrie, 2000; Wyrwa, 1999).

In the English language, the word "holocaust" has also been occasionally used since the 1940s to refer to the murder of the Jews by the Nazi regime. However, it is only since the early 1960s that the term has also come to be widely used in this sense in the United States, and indeed with an increasing tendency for the word "Holocaust" (now capitalized) to be used only to refer to this specific historical event. In German usage, the term "Holocaust" was virtually unknown until the broadcasting of the American television series in 1978, but has since been increasingly used to refer to the murder of European Jewry.

Although the term has become internationally established, it is not used consistently. In many cases it covers the entire history of the persecution of the Jews by the Nazi regime from 1933 (or 1938) onwards; a minority of authors believe it should also be extended to include the racist persecution of non-Jewish groups by that regime. In addition, there are signs of a tendency to use the term in a generic sense, over and above the historical case of the Jewish genocide, to describe the total annihilation of members of an ethnic group (Bauer, 1987).

W. Heitmeyer and J. Hagan (eds.), *International Handbook of Violence Research*, 139–169.
© 2003 Kluwer Academic Publishers. Printed in the Netherlands.

The prevalent practice of using the term "Holocaust" exclusively to refer to the murder of Europe's Jews is often associated with the idea that this was a unique historical event for which it is was necessary to have one specific term. The concept, then, is linked to a basic issue of interpretation: is the Holocaust simply one chapter in a long sequence of genocides, extending throughout human history, or does it differ significantly from other massacres so that it should also be distinguished by a specific name of its own?

Many distinguished historians and authors in other fields argue in favor of the uniqueness of the Holocaust. Some of these academics regard the murder of Europe's Jews as such an extraordinary event that it cannot be captured by conventional descriptive language—indeed, that it is basically inconceivable. Examples of those who take this view include the literature specialist George Steiner (1988) and the historian Isaac Deutscher (1968).

Among historians, the Israeli Saul Friedländer is one who believes that there is no historical classification that can come to terms with the gigantic extent of this event; the Holocaust, he says, is an exceptional historical phenomenon, from which there may be no lessons to be learned for the future of modern industrialized society (Friedländer, 1991). This viewpoint can be summarized by saying that Auschwitz as a hiatus in civilization simply cannot be portrayed by historiographic means, because historiography itself, after all, is an expression of the civilization that was so shatteringly called into question by that event.

This view, however, is by no means shared by all proponents of the "uniqueness" thesis. Yehuda Bauer, for example, makes the point that the Holocaust, being an act committed by human beings, is in principle possible to describe and even possible to explain. Bauer understands "Holocaust" as meaning the total physical annihilation of an ethnic or religious group, and in that sense considers the term fully applicable only to the murder of the Jews by the Nazi regime. The event most nearly comparable to the murder of the Jews, he says, is the genocide perpetrated against the Armenians, which he sees as a "Holocaust-related event" but one that does not fully satisfy the Holocaust criteria. What matters to Bauer is the "pseudo-religious" motivation of National Socialist anti-Semitism, which formed part of the ideological core of National Socialism and behind which lay the desire to remove all trace of the Jews from the face of the earth (Bauer, 1990, 1991).

Like Bauer, the German historian Eberhard Jäckel emphasizes that "the murder of Jews by the National Socialists was unique because never before had a state, backed by the authority of its appointed leader, decided and announced that it would do everything it could to kill an entire group of human beings, including the old, women, children, and babies, and then used all the available resources of the state to put that decision into practice" (Jäckel, 1986). Christopher Browning, too, regards "the totality and scope of intent" and "the means employed" as the critical elements "that both define the singularity of the Holocaust" (Browning, 2000:32).

Probably the most ambitious attempt to demonstrate the uniqueness of the Holocaust by empirical methods is the three-volume work planned by Steven Katz (Katz, 1994, only the first volume has so far been published). Like Bauer and Jäckel, Katz regards the Holocaust as unique because there is no other example in history of a state setting itself the objective of total extermination of the members of a large group. This intent of total destruction is, for Katz, the decisive defining criterion.

The philosopher Barel Lang points out that the concept of genocide was only coined in the aftermath of the murder of the Jews; that historic event served as a paradigm for the definition of the term. The Holocaust, in turn, was "as yet [the] most explicit and fully determined occurrence" of genocide (Lang, 1990:7f.).

The majority of those who endorse the thesis of the uniqueness of the Holocaust not only prefer to distinguish it from other cases of genocide but, in particular, also try to draw a clear dividing line between the National Socialist murder of the Jews and the murders by the Nazi regime of members of other groups defined in racist terms, such as the Gypsies, the mentally ill, the Slav "subhumans," and others. Thus, for example, Bauer and Jäckel adhere to the view that the murder of the Gypsies cannot be included within the term "Holocaust," because the Nazi regime never conceived the same intent of total destruction of this group as it did in the case of the Jews (Bauer, 1987; Jäckel, 2000). Recent results of empirical research can be cited in support of these arguments (Lewy, 2000).

An important contribution to the objectification of the debate about the "uniqueness" of the Holocaust is Barel Lang's suggestion that the term "unique" be used in the sense of "unexampled" or "unprecedented." In this way, the argument that the Holocaust is unique would be a historically verifiable one and could be kept free of the metaphysical speculation inevitably associated with the concept of "uniqueness" (Lang, 1990). It must of course be borne in mind here that Lang is using the term historically: a historical event can be described as "unprecedented" only at the time at which it occurs; from that point on, that event itself provides us with a precedent that can be studied with the resources of historiography and may occur again in a similar form. Anyone who challenges the principle of this possibility of repetition is moving the debate outside historical parameters.

The first obvious argument that can be put forward against the assertion that the Holocaust was unprecedented is that this is a methodologically banal statement. Any historical event is ultimately unique and, as such, unrepeatable. That argument, of course, is intellectually unsatisfactory. If the assertion that the murder of the Jews was historically unprecedented is to make any sense, systematic historical comparisons are needed to show that essential elements of that event cannot in fact be found to exist in any other known instance of genocide. "Defying comparison" is basically alien to the terminology of historiography. But this leaves open the question of what we are supposed to be comparing. The debate is made more difficult by the fact that there is no generally accepted definition of genocide. The definition contained in the 1948 UN Convention, which represents the result of a political compromise, is fairly general and therefore difficult to apply (Lang, 1990). We also need to consider how far back in history the comparison is to go: for example, should we take it back to the days of antiquity or consider only "modern" genocides, meaning, perhaps, those committed during the last 200 years or during the twentieth century alone?

Critics and proponents of the theory of the uniqueness of the Holocaust have now begun to substantiate their arguments with empirical findings and comparisons. Comparative genocide research has been a booming specialist field for the last few years. Whatever results these comparisons may bring, they are likely, if anything, to reinforce a general trend toward the historicization and contextualization of the Holocaust. If these research projects are successful in demonstrating what makes the Holocaust historically unique, fears that the murder of the European Jews may be subsumed within a general debate on violence and genocide until it becomes unrecognizable will prove unfounded (Fackenheim, 1982).

Even the most cursory glance at other great massacres of the modern age makes it clear that the argument that the Holocaust was unique cannot be justified on the basis of the numbers of people murdered. Nor is there any meaningful sense of uniqueness in the argument that the Jewish victims had played a special role in European history or that it was a particularly significant phenomenon that the atrocity was carried out by members of a "civilized nation." Any attempt to create a hierarchy of victims or perpetrators runs counter to an unprejudiced comparative approach. The argument that the Holocaust was unique can probably only be sustained if emphasis is laid on the persecutors' intent to kill the entire Jewish population and, at the same time, on the systematic nature of the persecutions and mass murders, to the point where actual factories of death came into being. If these definition criteria are applied, there are arguments in favor of saying that the Holocaust is indeed unexampled, and the Armenian genocide can be seen to be the historical case that most closely resembles the murder of the Jews in terms of these two criteria (intention and systematic character).

There is no overlooking the fact that the argument of uniqueness must be seen in the context of political debate. Especially in the German debate, the singularity of the event is employed as a weapon to argue against attempts to "normalize" and trivialize the Holocaust—this was a particular feature of the German *Historikerstreit*, a public dispute between historians during the late 1980s. By contrast, the American debate can be seen to be founded on a kind of competition between various ethnic groups to determine which has the most traumatic history; while in the Israeli case, the self-assertion of the Jewish state plays a critical role. Such political implications cannot be dismissed as "exploitation," but reflect different approaches to drawing conclusions from such a gigantic tragedy—approaches that remain legitimate as long as their justification is open to argument.

II.   OVERVIEW OF RESEARCH

1.   Phase I: From the Beginnings until the Early 1960s

The first attempts to highlight the systematic annihilation of European Jews by the Nazi regime appeared while World War II was still in progress, one example being the "Black Book" of Polish Jewry by Jacob Apenszlak, written in New York as early as 1943 and containing, among other things, descriptions of the extermination camps of Chelmno and Treblinka (Apenszlak, 1943).

In the Soviet Union, a fairly large number of publications dealing with the fate of the Jews appeared between 1941 and 1946. This situation changed radically in 1946, when the "Black Book" published by Grossmann and Ehrenburg was banned (Grossmann & Ehrenburg [1946] 1994). In Hungary, too, a substantial number of largely documentary studies on the Holocaust appeared between 1945 and 1949, including, for example, the "Black Book" on the fate of the Hungarian Jews (Levai, 1948; summarized in Katzburg, 1988). Yugoslav historians also began to describe the Holocaust in their own country only a few years after the war ended (Jelinek, 1988).

The early 1950s saw the first general accounts of the killing of the European Jews, most of them in fact based on the copious documentation produced in the course of the Nuremberg trials. Particular mention should be made here of the works of Poliakov and Wulf (1955), Reitlinger (1953) and Tenenbaum (1956); a precursor is the annotated collection of documents published as early as 1947 by the American Jewish Congress (Krieger, 1947).

This first series of studies culminated in the comprehensive account given by Raul Hilberg in a dissertation completed in 1955, and not published in book form until six years later. Hilberg concentrated on the fateful role and the process of annihilation, the individual stages of which he traced in minute detail: definition—expropriation—concentration—murder (Hilberg, 1961). Less interest was aroused by another general account of the National Socialist persecution of the Jews, also published in 1961, by the Polish historian Artur Eisenbach, only part of which was published in English (Eisenbach, 1961, 1962).

Ever since the early 1940s, and increasingly since the 1950s, a number of institutions have concentrated on collecting and evaluating Holocaust documents, most notably Yad Vashem (Israel's national Holocaust remembrance authority), the Wiener Library in London, the Yidisher Visnshaftlekher Institut [Jewish Institute for Scientific Research] in New York, the Centre de Documentation Juive Contemporaine [Contemporary Jewish Documentation Center] in Paris, and the Zydowski Instytut Historyczny [Jewish Historical Institute] in Warsaw. A periodical devoted to the history of the Holocaust, *Yad Vashem Studies*, has been published since 1957.

In Germany, established research paid little attention to the persecution of the Jews until the end of the 1950s. Exceptions were a number of editions of sources, mostly emanating from the *Institut für Zeitgeschichte* [Institute for Contemporary History], such as the edition of the Gerstein Report (eye-witness reports, 1953), the publication of a number of documents on the Reich Kommissar for Byelorussia, Kube (Heiber, 1956), and an edition of the memoirs of Rudolf Höss (Broszat, 1958). Other research studies published in German mainly originated from academic outsiders, private researchers who in many cases were themselves emigrants or Holocaust survivors, such as the numerous documentary records by Joseph Wulf (1958, 1961, 1962), the first study of the special law applicable to Jews under Nazism by Bruno Blau (1952), and the pioneering studies by Hans-Günther Adler (1955, 1958, 1974).

2. Phase II: From the Early 1960s to the Late 1970s

The silence of German researchers persisted until the early 1960s. There then began a phase of more intensive preoccupation with the persecution of the Jews, which lasted roughly until the second half of the 1970s. A critical factor here was the readiness of government departments in the Federal Republic, ten years after its foundation, to face up to the challenge represented by the legacy of the National Socialist regime. In particular, the beginning of the prosecutions of Nazi war criminals in the late 1950s led to a number of basic studies of the persecution of the Jews and the history of the SS and of the concentration camp system. The *Institut für Zeitgeschichte* demonstrated its leading position in this field of research, especially by publishing expert witness testimony given during the war crimes trials (Buchheim et al., 1964; Institut für Zeitgeschichte, 1958).

A further stimulus to research was produced by the state's efforts in the field of political education, which sponsored a number of publications (for example Wulf, 1958, 1962; Kolb, 1962; Scheffler, 1960). The pattern for later efforts by regional and local archive administrators to document the fate of the Jews was set by a six-volume documentary study produced by the Baden–Württemberg government archive (Archivdirektion Stuttgart, 1969; Hundsnurscher & Taddey, 1968; Sauer, 1966a, 1966b, 1969) and a collection of documents on the history of Frankfurt's Jews, produced at the initiative of a group who had emigrated to London (Andernacht, 1963).

Since the mid-1960s, when the Allies returned the Nazi archives to German institutions, researchers have had an opportunity for a systematic study of the persecution of the Jews. The starting point here was Helmut Genschel's study of how the Jews were driven out of German business (1966) and, in particular, the dissertation by Uwe Adam (1972), author of the first complete account of the persecution of the Jews based on a thorough analysis of the files of the ministerial bureaucracy.

As a whole, however, researchers made only inadequate use of the greatly improved availability of sources. Instead, all aspects of research into National Socialism were over-shadowed by disputes between the proponents of various overriding interpretative concepts. From the late 1960s onward, the debate focused especially on "totalitarianism" and "fascism," and on the question of whether the Nazi system should be regarded primarily as Hitler's creation or whether it should be considered a "polycracy." The persecution and murder of the Jews were not central to these various concepts.

Thus, it is hardly surprising that although the first comprehensive German accounts of the Nazi period did provide specific chapters or sections giving a more or less detailed account of the persecution of the Jews, nevertheless the authors evidently found it difficult to integrate this aspect of Nazi rule into an overall interpretation (Bracher, 1969; Broszat, 1969; Hildebrand, 1979).

In the same period, between the early 1960s and late 1970s, a number of important studies of the Holocaust appeared outside Germany, in particular the standard work by Isaac Trunk (1972) on the role of the *Judenräte* (the Jewish councils set up in the ghettos by the German occupation authorities) and the comprehensive survey by Reuben Ainsztein (1974) of Jewish resistance in German-occupied Eastern Europe.

Mention should also be made of the study by Kurt Schleunes on the persecution of the Jews prior to 1939, highlighting the lack of purpose demonstrated by German policy toward the Jews in that period (Schleunes, 1972), and the two extensive accounts by Nathan Eck (1976) and Dov Kulka (1975), which have hitherto only been published in Hebrew. General studies in the English language were produced by Nora Levin (1968) and Lucy Dawidowicz (1975). It seems to be a feature of this phase that these works—some of them monumental—took the form of individual research projects rather than forming part of a mainstream current of research.

In the extensive Soviet literature on World War II published between the 20th Party Congress in 1956 and the late 1960s, virtually no mention was made of the Jews. This line became even harder in the late 1960s, and critics have seen an early precursor of the Western phenomenon of Holocaust denial here (Arad, 1988). In Madajczyk's standard Polish work on National Socialist occupation policy, published in 1970, the murder of the Jews was described, but was depicted rather as a marginal phenomenon (Madajczyk, 1988).

3. Phase III: Research from the Late 1970s to the Late 1980s

A revival of research in Germany became apparent from 1977 onward. However, it is typical of the state of research into the subject as it then stood that it took the absurd argument of a David Irving to give new impetus to the debate: in a book published in 1977, Irving asserted that Hitler not only had not ordered the "final solution" but had known nothing about the systematic murders until the fall of 1943. This prompted Martin Broszat, one of the more radical proponents of the "polycratic" or "functionalist" school, to propose an interpretation of the decision process on the "final solution" which, although it left no doubt as to Hitler's responsibility for the genocide perpetrated against the European Jews, nevertheless particularly emphasized the part played by the processes and structures typical of the Nazi system in bringing about the decision to murder the Jews (Broszat, 1977). This "functionalist theory" was then put more strongly by Hans Mommsen (1983), and its proponents had to defend it against the "intentionalists" at a 1984 Stuttgart conference (Jäckel & Rohwer, 1987). Overall, this debate was notable for various statements of general principles based on a relatively narrow selection of sources.

From the end of the 1970s, however, a number of important works published in Germany considerably broadened existing knowledge of the "final solution." They include, in particular, the documentation assembled by Kogon and others on the use of poison gas in Nazi extermination camps (Kogon & Langbein, 1983), the volume on the extermination camps published by Albert Rückerl, director of the Ludwigsburg Central Office for the Prosecution of National Socialist Crimes (Rückerl, 1977), and the standard work by Krausnick and Wilhelm on the *Einsatzgruppen* or "special duties" squads (Krausnick & Wilhelm, 1981). The collection of essays published by Wolfgang Benz (1991) is not only an important contribution to the debate on the number of victims of the National Socialist genocide but also a significant step toward reconstructing the entire chain of events.

German researchers now also began to extend their studies to include non-Jewish groups who had been victims of racist persecution. This trend brought important works by Alfred Streim and Christian Streit on the murder of Soviet prisoners of war (Streim, 1981; Streit, 1978), numerous studies of the killing of institutionalized patients (for example, Klee, 1985; Schmuhl, 1987), Ulrich Herbert's study of the fate of the foreign workers (1985), and the work by Diemut Majer (1981) on legal discrimination against the various *fremdvölkisch* (alien) groups in the Third Reich. These works are to some extent the result of critical introspection which had become apparent in the course of one generation within those academic disciplines that had made their respective contributions to the marginalization, persecution, and murder of Jews and other groups under the Third Reich, especially medicine, psychiatry, and jurisprudence. These self-critical approaches have now produced what has become an overwhelming mass of local, regional, and special studies.

Outside Germany, the main driving force behind research since the late 1970s has been the pioneering work of Christopher Browning. Beginning with his study of the involvement of the German *Auswärtiges Amt* (the Nazi equivalent of the State Department) in the final solution, Browning spent the years that followed writing numerous important essays in which, in particular, he reconstructed the decision process, always endeavoring to adopt an even-handed and constructive position (Browning, 1985, 1992b).

As early as the 1960s, and increasingly from the 1970s onward, extensive studies on the persecution of the Jews appeared in countries occupied by or allied with Germany, in particular Denmark (Yahil, 1969), the Netherlands (Presser, 1968), France (Marrus & Paxton, 1981), Italy (Michaelis, 1978; Zuccotti, 1987), Bulgaria (Chary, 1972), and Hungary (Braham, 1981). Helen Fein (1979) made an initial attempt to produce a systematic comparative study of the persecution of the Jews in different countries.

The much more intensive research since the late 1970s has been reflected in a number of important summaries, especially the general account by the Israeli historian Leni Yahil (1990), who produced an exemplary magnum opus combining the perspectives of perpetrators and victims, in the volume by Michael Marrus (1987) that proved extremely stimulating for further research, and in the *Encyclopedia of the Holocaust* produced under the auspices of Yad Vashem (Gutman, 1989).

Most importantly of all, however, research during the 1980s gave rise to a subdiscipline: "Holocaust Studies," with its own professorial chairs, research institutes, and periodicals. In particular, the American Holocaust Memorial Museum, founded in 1980, has a research department of its own and publishes its own journal, *Holocaust and Genocide Studies*.

4. Phase IV: Research since 1990

Today, at the start of the new millennium, Holocaust research is going through a fourth phase, which began with the opening of the Eastern European archives during the early 1990s. On the international scale, the subdiscipline of Holocaust studies has been institutionalized, with increasing interdisciplinary links and closer ties between researchers, not least as a result of the use of the Internet (H-net Holocaust; nizkor.org).

Particularly noteworthy here are regional research, which has persisted beyond the turn of the millennium, and the great interest in the other groups that were victims of racist persecution by the National Socialists. There is also a high degree of thematic diversification. Interesting developments include the rise of a new German school of Holocaust research, generally led by younger researchers outside the academic establishment. This new wave of research is particularly notable for its extensive use of primary sources. Not only have the more recently accessible Eastern European archives been used, but sources that have actually been available to researchers for many years have now been more fully studied, including in particular the files of the German criminal prosecution authorities.

One of the main trends of this empirical research, regionalization, meaning a meticulous reconstruction of the Holocaust as it was manifested in the individual territories under German rule, based on detailed analysis of regional sources, began with an important essay by the British historian Ian Kershaw (1992) on the persecution of the Jews in the Warthegau, an administrative district of German-occupied Poland. Kershaw's study was followed by others by Dieter Pohl (1997b) and Thomas Sandkühler (1996) on eastern Galicia, Andrew Ezergailis (1996) on Latvia, Dieter Pohl (1993) and Bogdan Musial (1999) on the Lublin district of the *Generalgouvernement* (German-occupied central Poland), by Christian Gerlach on Byelorussia (1999), by Ralf Ogorreck (1996) on the *Einsatzgruppen* in the Soviet Union, and by Sybille Steinbacher (2000) on eastern Upper Silesia.

The second main trend of research, pronounced thematic diversification, can also be traced back to the early 1980s. Götz Aly and Susanne Heim, studying the plans of German social scientists in the Nazi period, were able to demonstrate empirically the widespread existence of ideas that resulted in the "decimation" of the population in occupied Eastern Europe and, in some cases, the "disappearance" of the Jews. However, they were not able to show the causal relationship thus suggested with the decision to murder the Jews (Aly & Heim, 1991). This "rational" approach to an explanation was taken up again by Götz Aly (1995) a few years later: Aly now established a link between the failure of the megalomaniac plans for the demographic restructuring of the occupied territories and the beginning of the systematic murder of the Jews. These attempts at a "rational" explanation are also in evidence in the work of Christian Gerlach, who tries to demonstrate a connection between a general policy of starvation pursued by the German occupying power and the commencement, spread, and acceleration of the murder of Jews in the occupied Polish and Soviet territories (Gerlach, 1998, 1999).

Another aspect of broader thematic diversification is the great interest taken in the factor of Jewish forced labor in the context of persecution and extermination (Gruner, 1997; Maier, 1994; Wagner, 2000; various articles in Frei, Steinbacher, & Wagner, 2000). It becomes increasingly clear in this case that forced labor by the Jews cannot be measured against the yardstick of the most effective use possible of available Jewish labor. The use of Jewish forced workers, which began with the drafting of Jews to perform degrading and physically exhausting forced labor in 1939 and ended in the concept of "annihilation through work," pursued from 1941/42 onward, was always primarily a supplementary factor to the progressively advancing policy of persecution and annihilation.

A number of authors have emphasized the role of the Wehrmacht as the motive force and executive organ of the war of racist destruction (cf. in particular the articles in Heer & Naumann, 1995). Other works have highlighted the part played in the process of the systematic annihilation of the Jews by the various parts of the bureaucratic machine, such as the local authorities (Gruner, 1999), the labor administration (Maier, 1994), and the financial bureaucracy (Kenkmann & Rusinek, 1999). The pioneering study by Robert Jan van Pelt and Debórah Dwork (1996) on Auschwitz has made it clear that the architectural history of the extermination camps is of great importance in reconstructing the decision to proceed with the "final solution." Further important studies have been added to the large numbers of works on concentration camps (Herbert, Orth, & Dieckmann, 1998; Orth, 1999; Orth, 2000). David Bankier has again posed the question of the attitude of the German population to the persecution of the Jews (Bankier, 1992), while the studies by Browning (1992a) and Goldhagen (1996) have triggered a renewed debate on the perpetrators and their motives. In addition, further attention has been paid to the old problem of whether one particular point in time can be identified at which the leaders of the Nazi state took the decision to murder the Jews (Browning, 1996, 2000; Gerlach, 1997; Longerich, 1998).

III. THE PRACTICE OF VIOLENCE: THE PERPETRATORS

The practice of violence by states is intended to bring about or consolidate a position of power. It ends, as a rule, when the purpose of the violence has been achieved, in other words, for example, when another country has been defeated in war or when opposition movements or uprisings within the government's own territory have been put down or the efforts of minorities to gain autonomy have been successfully suppressed. If these terms are applied to the Holocaust, it must be said that the unprecedented extent to which the Nazi regime practiced violence against the Jewish minority in Europe was driven by an absolute urge for power over that group that could not have been more extreme: the intent to bring about the complete and systematic physical annihilation of all people of Jewish descent in Europe.

In the context of the Holocaust, then, violence cannot be functionally interpreted as an instrument used in a calculated manner to achieve particular political aims or desires for power; in this case, violence became the essential expression of government policy. Research on the use or application of violence in the Holocaust can be seen to follow two main approaches.

In earlier accounts, especially, the dominant attitude is to portray the Holocaust as a calculated administrative murder, and the perpetrators as deskbound killers. More recent studies have radically revised this view; they tend to describe the Holocaust as a series of massacres and huge murderous operations and to spread the net of responsibility for the events more widely.

The theory of coldly organized administrative murder left its mark on both the two main lines of traditional perpetrator-oriented history, the "intentionalist" and "functionalist" schools. They describe the Holocaust from a safe distance, from the global perspective of the murder headquarters and bureaucratic executioners, without looking too closely at the fate of the victims. Whereas the intentionalists looked for an explanation in the radical anti-Semitic ideology and agenda of Hitler and the National Socialist leadership (Jäckel, 1969; Hillgruber, 1972), the functionalists take it as their starting point that the Holocaust was the result of a "cumulative process of radicalization" (Hans Mommsen) within the machinery of the Nazi dominion, a competition between institutions that ran out of control, where forces inherent in the system arranged for a "selection of the negative worldview elements" (Broszat, 1970).

Despite the heated debate over whether the principal author of the genocide was the dictator or the self-autonomizing structures, both lines of research did agree that the actual responsibility for events could be laid at the door of a relatively small group of criminals, while the others involved in the crimes were seen as mere tools.

As research has progressed over the last twenty years, this model has reached its limit in terms of providing possible explanations. The more research is dominated by thematic cross sections, regionally based studies, and microstudies, the clearer it becomes that the murder of the European Jews was a gigantic massacre of millions of people, carried out by over a hundred thousand perpetrators and helpers in full view of an unimaginably large number of contemporaries who became passive witnesses to crime.

At institutional level, the almost seamless interaction between the various participating organizations is becoming more and more apparent. The independent initiative of leaders at high, middle, and low levels in the hierarchy is emphasized, as is Hitler's leading role in the "Jewish question" and his personal intervention to attend to details of the process of the annihilation. These two views are clearly not mutually contradictory. Institutional rivalries and squabbles over jurisdiction did nothing to limit the murderous efficiency of the killing process. The genesis and execution of the murder of the European Jews obviously cannot be adequately described in terms of the history of institutions and the interactions between them: events become explicable only if a relatively broad consensus to eliminate the Jews of Europe in one way or another can be assumed to have existed within the leadership strata of the regime.

As a result of the expansion of research during the 1990s a large number of new archives kept by specialized administrative departments were brought to light, and with these their "arguments" as to why the Jews had to be "removed" from their area. This applies especially to the plans laid by economists and demographers described by Aly and Heim (1991), the activities of the resettlement authorities portrayed by Aly (1995), and the detailed study by Gerlach of the food and housing policies pursued by the occupation authorities in the east (1998, 1999). These various studies may be very useful in giving us a comprehensive picture of the institutions involved in the policy of annihilation, but a danger nevertheless remains: the quest for a "rational" explanation may result in the "material constraint," cited by the perpetrators as the justification for the further radicalization of the persecution, being removed from its historical context and interpreted as an absolute. The fundamental objection to this "utilitarian" line of research is that it underestimates the actual driving force behind the persecution of the Jews—the anti-Semitic policy of the regime—and plays down the great extent to which that policy influenced the "material decisions" in the various political arenas (Schneider, 1991; Longerich, 1998).

On the other hand, especially recently, researchers have tried to find answers in biographies or group biographies to questions relating to the motivation and conduct of responsible decision makers. This focuses the debate on the role of ideology and the special position of the elites and their "world view" within National Socialism.

In addition to the studies by Peter Black on Kaltenbrunner (1984), Ruth-Bettina Birn on the senior SS and police leadership (1986), and Richard Breitman on Himmler's role in the "final solution" (1991), particular attention should be paid to the study by Ulrich Herbert of the SS official Werner Best, who, as the organizational head of the Gestapo and the Reich Central Security Office (RSHA), was one of the architects of the machine that carried out the "final solution" from 1941 onward (Herbert, 1996).

Herbert describes Best as the prototype of the active, ideologically driven middle-ranking Nazi official. He points out that for individuals of this type there was no conflict between action motivated by expediency and commitment to a world view. As an adherent of the *völkisch* ideology, Best saw the German nation as his "highest purpose in life"; for him, the vital interests of his own *Volk* took absolute precedence, becoming a value in themselves and subject to no higher laws. On the basis of this fundamental conviction, derived "from life itself," Best evolved the belief that any means were legitimate in the almost inevitable struggle between *Völker*. Herbert portrays Best as a typical representative of the bourgeois *Kriegsjugend* ("war youth") generation, meaning those born in the first decade of the twentieth century who had already lived through and been aware of World War I but had been too young for military service; for this generation, the reversal of fortune of 1918 became the catastrophe that shaped their lives. To come to terms with the effects of that catastrophe, young, intellectual right-wing radicals like Best evolved a "generational style" that is described by Herbert with the key phrases of cold objectivity, hardness, and consistency; armor plating that was to protect them from emotion and from bourgeois or humanitarian traditions. Herbert has probably succeeded in capturing the real-life archetype of the SS official whom Himmler thanked in his speech at Posen (Poznan) in October 1943 for his "decency" when confronted by mountains of corpses.

The main results of Herbert's study have been confirmed by other works on the leading figures in the *Sicherheitspolizei* (security police) (Hachmeister, 1998; Paul & Mallmann, 1995). The study of the *Sicherheitspolizei* leaders by Banach (1996) makes it clear that Best was indeed a typical member of this group. About half of those who made up the leadership of the *Sicherheitspolizei* were university graduates, and about 60 percent of those had studied law. The great majority were of middle-class origin, and the relatively large number who were sons of civil servants (over one third) is notable. Almost half belonged to the *Kriegsjugend* generation, and fewer than 20 percent were born before 1900.

However, the study of Heinrich Müller, head of the Gestapo, by Andreas Seeger (1996) presents a completely different picture: an anti-intellectual, shaped by the mentality of the former minor civil servant; an enforcer not primarily driven by ideology but capable of anything. In other words, we should not make too much of the homogeneity of the leaders of the *Sicherheitspolizei*.

What do we know today about the average SS member or policeman—the men who carried out their orders to murder? Much of our knowledge derives from the book entitled *Verbrechen unter totalitärer Herrschaft* by the criminologist Herbert Jäger, published as long ago as 1967, which provided a classification of the criminals. On the basis of German files compiled during war crimes investigations in the years 1958 to 1963, Jäger concluded that about 20 percent of those who participated in Nazi crimes of violence were "criminals of excess," meaning that they killed without orders or exceeded the orders given them. A further 20 percent he describes as "initiative criminals," meaning that their killings were within the limits of the orders given them but took place on their own initiative—thus including, for example, those who volunteered for shootings. Jäger does, however, concede that the files he assessed mainly related to particularly serious cases, so that these first two groups may have been overrepresented in his material. Jäger classifies 60 percent of perpetrators as "criminals by order," but makes it clear that only some of these former SS members and policemen acted automatically, and that while many were convinced of the rightness of the orders given them, there were also many who acted out of opportunism, peer-group pressure to conform, or simply secondary criminal motives. Jäger notes that only about 1 in 3 or 4 of the "criminals to order," or 15–20 percent of the total, had problems with the orders they were given. On the basis of these data alone, Jäger rules out the theory that their crimes resulted primarily from compulsion and terror: "Pressure to obey can be said to have existed only in a relatively small proportion of cases."

Jäger undertook detailed studies of 103 cases in which members of the SS or police resisted orders to kill, or refused to carry them out. All the cases studied show that there was no instance in which participants risked physical harm by resisting orders. None of the disciplinary measures available to the superior officers of those who refused to obey (trial and sentence by an SS and police court, court martial, internment in a concentration camp, etc.) was applicable to those who refused to participate in mass shootings. If any adverse consequences at all were apparent, they were relatively minor: men could be posted away, to the front or elsewhere, have black marks on their records, or be subjected to everyday harassment. Jäger also points out that even under the so-called code of honor of the SS, refusal to participate in such shootings was regarded only as a failure, not as a crime.

In his much-admired book *Ordinary Men*, Christopher Browning (1992a) examined the conduct of the German policemen who made up Police Reserve Battalion 101, referring primarily to the records of German trials. The members of the battalion, most of them middle-aged fathers of ordinary Hamburg families, shot at least 38,000 Jews in occupied Poland during 1942 and 1943.

Only a very small minority of the battalion's members—about a dozen men out of 500, according to Browning's findings—accepted the offer of the battalion commander and declined to participate in shootings. Browning estimates that a total of some 10–20 percent of them subsequently endeavored to find ways of escaping from taking part in shootings.

In trying to answer the question of why "ordinary men," average family men, could become murderers, Browning considers numerous possible factors. As there are no indications that the members of the battalion were selected for their particularly fanatical National Socialist beliefs, Browning emphasizes the significance of situation rather than disposition: the dehumanization of the "enemy" in the context of the war, indoctrination, the prospect of career advantages, peer-group conformity, and the habit of obeying authority (although no compulsion to obey orders).

The most controversial study of Nazi perpetrators produced in recent years is Daniel Goldhagen's *Hitler's Willing Executioners* (Goldhagen, 1996), which attracted great public attention although the verdict of professional critics was very largely negative. Goldhagen's book combines three microstudies of aspects of the Holocaust to which little attention has hitherto been paid: a study of police battalions, in which Goldhagen uses the same documents on Battalion 101 as Browning did, but reaches different conclusions; the conditions in the forced labor camps in Poland; and the "death marches," forced upon the concentration camp prisoners when the camps were cleared at the end of the war and in which hundreds of thousands of people died.

The central focus of the book is the argument that previous researchers have overlooked the particular cruelty of the criminals to their Jewish victims and underestimated the radical anti-Semitism that found expression in those crimes. But, runs Goldhagen's argument, if the criminals were average Germans, their behavior suggests conclusions about the radically anti-Semitic attitude of the German population as a whole. To substantiate this thesis further, Goldhagen integrates his case studies into an analysis of German anti-Semitism stretching back into the Middle Ages and claims to be able to discern an almost continuous climate of "exterminatory" anti-Semitism.

Criticism (see especially Birn, 1997; Pohl, 1997a; and Browning, 1998) is directed first against Goldhagen's selective use of the source material. It remains an open question how representative his accounts are. For example, the fact that Goldhagen rejects all self-exculpatory statements by the criminals as fundamentally unbelievable is extremely problematical. Goldhagen is also accused of overlooking the special conditions existing in a paramilitary unit under wartime conditions. The behavior of the units, say the critics, was conditioned less by the mentality of the ordinary policeman than by the leading part played by the officers and NCOs of the units. The latter, however, were professional police officers, specially selected to lead paramilitary police units under a terrorist dictatorship, or volunteers hoping to be transferred to the ordinary police force—in other words, hardly a sample of "normal" Germans. This understatement of the part played by the unit's leaders can, incidentally, also be criticized in Browning's work.

Furthermore, Goldhagen's claim that the simple *Ordnungspolizei* (Order Police) reservists were average Germans is demonstrably wrong; in fact, there was some degree of selection procedure involved here, which included questions about their political reliability (Longerich, 1998). Comparisons show that the criminals behaved with equal cruelty when murdering non-Jews; and there are numerous examples to show that non-German members of the SS and police machine (such as police auxiliaries from the Baltic states or the Ukraine) were guilty of similar cruelty. Moreover, ethnic Germans who had grown up in Eastern Europe were disproportionately overrepresented in the SS and police, as were Austrians.

The labor camps in Poland selected by Goldhagen for a case study were an SS domain; the argument that average Germans were "willing executioners" is not applicable here. Nor can anti-Semitism be shown to be a central motive for the many murders committed during the death marches: Jews and non-Jews alike were victims here. The model of "exterminatory" anti-Semitism is rejected by critics as being excessively indiscriminate; not all sections of German society were equally anti-Semitic, and anti-Semitism took various forms. The emancipation of the Jews in the nineteenth century and their rise in society during that period contradicts this argument.

Despite these serious shortcomings, Goldhagen's study does to some extent mark a turning point in the portrayal of the Holocaust, because he drew attention to the cruelty of events at local level which had not been adequately explained by earlier research fixated on the "functionalist image of the criminals" (the term used by Jäger in a 1997 review).

IV. THE SUFFERING OF VIOLENCE: THE VICTIMS

In the field of Holocaust studies, much attention focuses on descriptions of the victims' sufferings and their reaction to the process of extermination. First, researchers have concentrated mainly on the reaction of the Jewish elites to the German extermination policy. In dealing with the reaction by Jewish populations in Europe as a whole, researchers have focused primarily on the aspect of resistance, in whatever form it took place. By contrast, other reactions to the genocide by the mass of the Jewish population—apathy, submission, self-deception—have received much less attention. Recently, researchers have taken an increasing interest in the fate and reaction of Jewish women (Ofer & Weitzmann, 1998) and children (Dwork, 1991), and have studied the roles of gender within the situation of persecution (Kaplan, 1998; Baumel, 1998).

The primary concern of studies of the Jewish resistance, which first became widespread in the mid-1960s, is to dispel the popular belief that Europe's Jews put up no resistance to the National Socialist policy of extermination but were led "like lambs to the slaughter." This belief was put forward in the early 1960s in much-discussed publications by two leading Jewish scholars, and gave rise to widespread protest.

First, Raul Hilberg, in his comprehensive account of the National Socialist murder of the Jews, stated as a generalization that there had been little Jewish resistance. Among the Jewish elites, the primary attitude, he said, had been that the orders given by the Germans should be obeyed. This attitude Hilberg describes as the result of two thousand years of conditioning. The Jewish leaders had realized too late that the National Socialist policy of total physical annihilation differed fundamentally from the pogroms of earlier ages. Hilberg has maintained this fundamental criticism in further editions of his book (Hilberg, 1961:662ff; Hilberg, 1985:1030ff.):

Hannah Arendt, too, in her greatly respected book *Eichmann in Jerusalem*, takes a critical attitude to what she sees as the largely passive or affirmative conduct of the Jewish elites in wartime Europe, and concludes that the attitude of the Jewish Councils, in particular, facilitated the implementation of the National Socialist murder policy (Arendt, 1963:103ff.).

Researchers who in subsequent years frequently took critical exception to these arguments and began to examine the subject of Jewish resistance were faced by a number of fundamental problems. Even the historical documentation of Jewish resistance, whose authors had in many cases not survived, confronted researchers with particular challenges because, after all, the persecutors had made every effort to destroy all traces of the whole process of extermination. Any attempt to generalize about the Jewish resistance comes up against the problem that it took as many different forms, in the various countries under German rule, as did the living conditions of the Jewish minorities concerned and their relationship to the majority among the population. In principle, however, it can be said that the initial conditions for Jewish resistance were as bad as they could conceivably be. The Jewish minorities were not organized on a unified basis but were fragmented and disunited; they lacked the necessary resources to put up resistance; they were in most cases isolated from the remainder of the local population; and the threat posed by the policy of total extermination was something far beyond the limits of the victims' experience, a point that should be borne in mind in the *ex post facto* criticism of inappropriate behavior by Jewish leaders.

Resistance research endeavors to distinguish between particular motives for specific Jewish resistance and the more general (political, patriotic, or universal) motives of Jewish resistance fighters; to distinguish, in other words, between Jews in the resistance and Jewish resistance. On the other hand, however, it is clear that the achievements of Jewish resistance can only be properly assessed if set in the context of generalized resistance in Europe. This kind of historical classification is also helpful when it comes to creating a typology of Jewish resistance activity and defining the concept of resistance as such.

If these fundamental problems are taken into account, the most important results of resistance research can be summarized as follows (important surveys and research reports include Steinberg, 1970; Ainsztein, 1974; Lustiger, 1994; Marrus, 1996). The armed struggle can be defined as the core of the Jewish resistance; the reconstruction and portrayal of that struggle are central to Jewish resistance research. (In this context, a fact that should not go unmentioned is that an estimated 1.5 million Jewish soldiers fought in the Allied armies (Paucker, 1989)). It is one of the sobering conclusions of resistance research that the Jewish resistance was in no position to stop the process of extermination as a whole, and that most participants in armed Jewish resistance were aware of that fact. Thus the individual motives for participation in the armed struggle were of a different kind. For many Jews, armed struggle represented the only chance of survival; in addition, revenge and belief in the need to send out a signal of the collective desire for self-assertion played a part as well.

The question of how far resistance offered by Jews can also be regarded as specifically Jewish resistance has been intensively discussed with reference to the example of the "Baum Group." This group existed in Berlin from 1937 to 1942; its resistance activities culminated in 1942 in an arson attack against an anti-Soviet exhibition organized by the Ministry of Propaganda, in the aftermath of which almost all members of the group were arrested and murdered.

The young Jews that made up this group were for the most part communists and members of the Jewish youth movement, many of them left-leaning Zionists motivated by solidarity with the communist struggle. The formation of the group corresponded to the communist tactic of organizing Jews in groups of their own so as to minimize the additional threat to the organization as a whole. The Baum Group were outsiders within the communist underground, and were acting outside the context of the Jewish community. They can be seen both as a part of the communist resistance and as an example of youthful rebellion against the Nazi regime; be that as it may, however, one factor in the particular history of this group is the fact that the young people belonging to it were Jews and thus had to suffer particular persecution by the Nazi regime, and that this influenced their behavior (Kwiet & Eschwege, 1984; Paucker & Steinberg, 1971).

In German-occupied Western Europe, the participation of Jews in the general armed resistance to the Nazi regime is more extensively documented. Most of these Jewish resistance fighters did not form part of the Jewish establishment but were foreigners, Zionists, and communists. In addressing the issue of integration of Jewish resistance fighters into general resistance, researchers are again trying to answer the question of the extent to which a particular Jewish motivation for resistance can be distinguished from other motives. This question is easier to answer in the context of the purely Jewish resistance organizations, which existed in Western Europe in limited numbers and mainly toward the end of the war. Consequently, resistance research has concentrated especially on these groups, such as the French *Armée Juive* ("Jewish army") (Latour, 1970; Lazare, 1987; Poznanski, 1989).

In Eastern Europe, the initial conditions for Jewish resistance were different again. In the former Soviet territories, there were initially substantial obstacles to the acceptance of large numbers of Jews into the partisan groups: the general caution of such groups about recruiting new members who were unknown to them, reluctance to accept unarmed members of partisan bands, but anti-Semitic motives as well. A resistance group that accepted Jews—people who were persecuted simply for existing—thus exposed itself to an additional risk that many were not prepared to take.

This policy did not change until September 1942, when the partisans, responding to an order by Stalin, began to accept members from all sectors of the population including, especially, the Jews and other persecuted minorities. The functions of the partisans were now shifting increasingly toward the protection of the civilian population, which was particularly beneficial to the surviving Jews. About 10–15,000 Jews survived in "family camps"—hiding places created in the forests—on Soviet territory. Among the approximately 500,000 Soviet partisans there were between 20,000 and 30,000 Jews, who also formed a number of all-Jewish partisan units (Levin, 1985; Arad, 1988; Arad, 1989a; Tec, 1993; Slepyan, 2000).

In Poland, a limited number of Jewish resistance groups can be traced from 1942 onward. However, these groups did not cooperate extensively with the relatively well organized Polish underground, which did not regard the assisting and rescuing of Jews as a priority. The great majority of those Jews who fled from the ghettos into the forests— estimates put the number at approximately 25,000—did not survive the end of the war. The reasons for this failure of the Polish resistance to help the Jews are hotly disputed between Polish and Jewish historians. While the former particularly stress the different strategies pursued by the Polish resistance and its Jewish counterpart, the latter lay the main emphasis on the anti-Semitism of the Polish population (Krakowski & Gutman, 1986).

The largest armed resistance organization in Poland, the *Armia Krajowa* ("national army"), was preparing for an uprising planned to take place at a point immediately prior to the withdrawal of the German occupying force; it therefore had no interest in exposing itself prematurely by conducting campaigns to rescue Jews. The *Armia Krajowa* was also reluctant to accept Jews in its ranks. Right-wing underground groups persecuted and even killed Jews who had escaped into the forest. Only the communist-oriented *Armia Ludowa* ("people's army") welcomed Jewish fighters into its ranks, though this only played a major part from 1943 onward, when the process of annihilation was already virtually complete. All in all, the number of Jewish resistance fighters in Poland is estimated at about 5,000 (Krakowski, 1984).

More favorable conditions for Jewish resistance prevailed in the eastern Polish territories that had been occupied by the Soviet Union between 1939 and 1941. In these areas, Jewish resistance fighters were accepted in large numbers into both Soviet and Polish partisan groups, where they were also able to form independent subunits.

We now have details of those attempted uprisings whose purpose was to stop the murder process by violent action in the extermination camps themselves. Although the risings in Treblinka (August 1943), Sobibor (October 1943), and Auschwitz-Birkenau (October 1944) were swiftly put down, a number of members of the camp staff were killed in all three cases. In Birkenau, the prisoners succeeded in destroying a crematorium, while at Sobibor and Treblinka a relatively large group of prisoners in each case was able to escape (Arad, 1989b; Kulka, 1989). Additional uprisings and escapes have also been documented for other camps (Ainsztein, 1974; Lustiger, 1994).

Researchers have now succeeded in documenting a broad picture of revolts and mass escapes in many Eastern European ghettos. Here again, the leading role of the Zionist youth movement has been established. Relations with the official Jewish authority, the *Judenrat*, varied greatly. As a rule, however, preparations for such acts of resistance only began when the Germans started killing the inhabitants of the ghetto. In other words, resistance was an act of despair: only under the most favorable circumstances might it achieve the modest success of allowing a small group of fighters to escape from the ghetto, the more normal result being the death of all the insurgents (Ainsztein, 1974; Arad, 1996).

Public protests were another form of resistance to the policy of annihilation. One of the best-known protest campaigns was mounted by non-Jewish women who, in February

1943, demanded the release of their husbands who had been arrested in February in the course of the massive drive to arrest Berlin's Jews; they demonstrated outside the Gestapo-occupied building of the Jewish community authority on Rosenstrasse (Stoltzfus, 1996). Although it has now been established that this demonstration did not prevent the deportation to Auschwitz of these Jews living in "mixed marriages"—there were no plans to deport this group at that time—nevertheless the events on Rosenstrasse showed that opportunities for civil resistance did exist even in Berlin, the city where the headquarters of the systematic mass murder machine was located (Gruner, 1997).

The systematic collection and dissemination of information on the policy of extermination can be regarded as another form of resistance. Researchers have succeeded in establishing the existence of extensive contemporary records and archives, in which the ghetto populations tried to document the stages of the persecution and the reality of life in the ghetto (for Lodz: Dobroszycki, 1984; Adelson & Lapides, 1989; for Warsaw's *Oneg Shabbat* [Sabbath Gathering] archive: Kermish, 1986; Sakowska, 1993). Furthermore, it has been pointed out that an extensive Jewish underground press existed in various countries (Gutman, 1982; Rayksi, 1998; Kwiet & Eschwege, 1984:239ff.). In addition, researchers have succeeded in reconstructing a number of the channels of communication by which information on the process of extermination was smuggled out of the German-occupied territories (Laqueur, 1980).

Other forms of resistance were organized escape and rescue work and the setting-up of networks to protect and assist Jews living underground (Gutman & Zuroff, 1978). In France, for example, between 7,000 and 9,000 Jewish children were rescued largely by the activities of the Jewish resistance (Poznanski, 1989:479).

Researchers into Jewish resistance—and, indeed, into resistance in general—display a strong tendency to extend the concept of resistance. In view of the extremely unfavorable initial conditions for any form of Jewish resistance, as described above, there is an obvious inclination on the part of researchers to set a low standard for the use of the term in order to be able to record all manifestations of revolt against extermination. Many historians argue that self-assertion and continued adherence to cultural, educational, and religious activities (Michman, 1993), the organization of assistance facilities in the ghettos, and even the actual will to survive should be regarded as essential parts of resistance (Bauer, 1979). On the other hand, Konrad Kwiet has pointed out that even suicide can be regarded as a form of resistance, representing as it does the most radical attempt possible to escape the process of extermination (Kwiet, 1979). Other historians, however, prefer a narrower definition of resistance in which the significant issue is whether an act was performed out of a conscious desire to resist (in whatever way) the process of extermination. This generally involves the act of resistance having a political dimension (Marrus, 1996).

Closely linked to the debate on the possibilities, forms, and historical significance of Jewish resistance is a second controversy regarding the role of the Jewish Councils within the German policy of annihilation.

The first Jewish Councils were set up in Poland in 1939 on the orders of the German occupiers. For the most part, these councils consisted of leading members of the Jewish communities, and their function was to ensure that German orders were obeyed. In particular, they were to make labor available from the Jewish population, were responsible for surrendering articles of value, had to provide detailed statistical information on the population of the ghetto, and eventually were forced to take the necessary administrative steps to prepare for the deportations. To carry out these duties, they generally had a "civil service" of their own. At the same time, they were responsible for providing accommodation and care for Jews under totally inadequate conditions. Later, local Jewish Councils were also compulsorily set up in the other occupied countries, such as the occupied Soviet territories and Hungary.

In addition to the local Jewish Councils, the Germans established centrally organized, enforced communities of Jews in various occupied territories, such as the *Union Générale des Israélites de France* (General Union of French Jews) or the *Joodse Rat* (Jewish Council) in the Netherlands. The *Reichsvereinigung der Juden in Deutschland* (Reich Association of Jews in Germany), a compulsory organization formed in 1939 which replaced the *Reichsvertretung der deutschen Juden* (Reich Agency for German Jews), based on voluntary membership, may be regarded as a predecessor of the Jewish Councils.

A lively debate on the evaluation of the Jewish Councils has sprung up, prompted in part by the criticisms advanced by Hilberg and Arendt. The detailed studies resulting from this dispute give a more subtle image of these institutions (Trunk, 1972; Ainsztein, 1974; Weiss, 1974; Gutman & Haft, 1979). In the course of the debate, the terrible dilemma faced by the Jewish Councils has become clear: in doing what the Germans wanted, they were trying to make life more tolerable for those living in the ghettos; but at the same time, ultimately, they were playing into the hands of the German policy of total destruction. Two questions that have particularly interested researchers are when the Jewish Councils first understood the ultimate objective of the German policy and whether, and if so how, they adjusted their actions to that new understanding.

A classification of the Jewish Councils includes the following behavior patterns: total refusal to cooperate with the Germans; partial compliance with German orders but refusal to hand over people; resigned acceptance of the murder of some of the Jewish community in the hope of saving other people as a result; or total submission to German orders in the hope of securing personal advantages. The important thing is that these different attitudes cannot be associated with any particular political, ideological, or religious leanings within the Jewish minorities; the overall picture of behavior patterns is, indeed, extremely diverse (Weiss, 1989; Bauer, 1989). Many members of Jewish Councils believed that obedience to German orders to provide labor would enable them to save at least part of the ghetto population. They spread the slogan of "salvation through work," reflecting their belief that the conduct of the German overlords would ultimately be determined by their rational interest in Jewish labor.

In that context, the attitude of the Jewish Councils to Jewish resistance in the ghettos is particularly interesting. Many Jewish Councils regarded the resistance groups—which for the most part were relatively small—primarily as a threat to the mass of ghetto residents, since any act of resistance brought massive retaliatory measures from the Germans. In practice, the attitude of the Jewish Councils to the resistance circles was highly diverse, ranging from total rejection through tolerance and support to active participation by council members in underground activities.

Trunk's study demonstrates, through example, that only a rejection of blanket condemnation of the Jewish Councils makes it possible to work toward a fuller understanding of what they actually did, and of living conditions in the ghettos. A careful reconstruction of social conditions and everyday events in the ghettos (as already initiated by the contemporary ghetto chroniclers mentioned earlier) is an essential condition for understanding the initial conditions for Jewish resistance and other forms of reaction to the persecution (examples of such studies: Roland, 1992; Beinfeld, 1998; programmatic outline: Ofer, 1995).

V. COEXISTING WITH VIOLENCE: THE BYSTANDERS

A third major area of Holocaust studies deals with the role of the bystanders—those who witnessed the events as contemporaries without themselves being either perpetrators or victims. The main concern of this line of research is to reconstruct what the bystanders knew of the Holocaust and how they reacted to it.

In the most comprehensive study to date of the German population's knowledge of the Holocaust, David Bankier reached the conclusion that large numbers of those living in Germany, Jews and non-Jews alike, knew or at least suspected what was happening in the occupied Eastern European territories (Bankier, 1992). The fact that the official reports on public opinion were largely silent on the subject of the "Jewish question" did not reflect the true situation as far as the exchange of information within the population was concerned. In actual fact, as Bankier shows, various sources of information on the fate of the Jews were available to the population, such as reports by soldiers and foreign workers, and Allied propaganda. This information was the subject of widespread rumor. Although any attempt to reconstruct the actual level of information among the German population from such disparate sources must remain no more than an impression, the following points can be regarded as certain in the light of Bankier's researches: While the deportations of the German Jews generally took place in full public view and in some case were the main subject of the day's conversation, the mass shootings were known to much of the population from the reports of soldiers who had been eyewitnesses to such executions. Rumors of mass murder with the aid of poison gas were current, though they were frequently nebulous and confused. Despite systematic secrecy, information on the existence of death camps did filter through, even though impressions of what took place there remained vague.

Bankier also emphasizes that the German public obviously had great difficulty in grasping and accepting the reality of the mass murders. The rejection and suppression of information because of feelings of guilt clearly did play a major part and helped to create the impression that the Germans were largely indifferent to the genocide. That indifference, identified some time ago in the studies by Ian Kershaw and interpreted as "passive complicity" by Dov Kulka and Aron Rodrigue (Kershaw, 1981, 1986; Kulka & Rodrigue, 1984), seems however to have been very largely no more than a façade. In the great crises of the second half of the war, when the imminence of military defeat became apparent, fear of vengeance began to spread among the German public, especially because of the crimes committed against the Jews.

In this connection, the attitude of the only major social institutions not completely forced into alignment by the National Socialists—the churches—is of particular interest. Research by German historians has shown how deeply anti-Semitism had penetrated into the Protestant Church. While the organized National Socialist German Christians within the Protestant Church fully supported the official persecution of the Jews, the majority of official representatives of the church were indifferent to the fate of the Jews; only the dissident "Confessional Church" whose adherents were by no means free of anti-Semitic prejudices, raised a modest protest. Only a small minority of Protestant Christians openly rejected the persecution of the Jews. The weak resistance to the National Socialist persecution of the Jews was particularly apparent in the relative failure to assist Christians of Jewish descent, who, irrespective of their religious beliefs, were fully subjected to the persecutions (Gerlach, 1987; Büttner, 1997).

Despite many interventions to help Jews and, especially, "non-Aryan" Christians, and repeated intercessions on their behalf, Germany's Catholic bishops were unable to find the resolution to protest publicly against the persecution and murder of the Jews. The most critical opinion is to be found in a pastoral letter of September 1943, protesting against the killing of the sick, prisoners of war, and "people of foreign race and descent" (Nellessen, 1992).

It has been established by various studies published in the 1970s and 1980s, and based on contemporary documents, that the Allies, although they became aware during 1942 of the systematic killing of Europe's Jews, did not regard the rescuing of Jewish people as one of their principal war aims. Indeed, in case of doubt, the priorities they selected often worked to the disadvantage of European Jews. In his analysis of British and American secret service sources Richard Breitman has emphasized that the Allies were well informed about many details of the murder of the Jews—in particular through eavesdropping on German police radio. In the fall of 1941, for example, they were already aware of mass shootings of Jews in the occupied eastern territories. Breitman contrasts this information with the widespread inactivity of the machinery of government (Breitman, 1998). The debate on the Allies' failings, possible alternative courses of action, and the motives of those involved is still far from over.

"There is little to celebrate in this account of British policy towards the Jews of Europe between 1939 and 1945" (Wasserstein, 1979:345). This general summary, representing Wasserstein's conclusion drawn over twenty years ago from his study of British policy toward the Nazi persecution of the Jews, has been confirmed by research to date. In particular, despite the availability from mid-1942 of credible information on the annihilation of the Jews, no significant efforts were made to rescue Jews (for example, from countries not yet affected by the Holocaust that were allied with Germany).

In contrast to Wasserstein, who lays the blame for this attitude primarily on bureaucratic indifference and the Allies' strategic priorities, Kushner (1994) reaches a different conclusion in an in-depth analysis of British policy. In his view, an unconditional adherence to liberal values, closely linked to an "exclusive nationalism" and a strong emphasis on "Englishness," made it impossible for the British government to regard the Jews as a separate group, let alone as a nation; the government's standard response was that they were to be treated in exactly the same way as any other people of alien nationality. A highly developed "liberal imagination" and strong "monocultural liberalism" restricted the British government's ability to understand and act.

Following the 1970 study by Henry L. Feingold, an early critic of the Roosevelt administration's failure to adopt an effective policy of rescue, David S. Wyman (1984) listed in his study a catalog of American failings; the War Refugee Board (WRB), a government body dedicated to the rescue of German refugees which came into existence early in 1944, should have been set up much earlier. The United States should have exerted greater pressure on Hitler and his allies to discontinue the deportations to the death camps. Germany's allies should have been pressurized to do all they could to open up possible escape routes for the Jews. Simultaneous appeals by neutral states, the International Red Cross, and the Vatican should have been supported, or indeed initiated in the first place. Opportunities for escape would have been improved if neutral states had been encouraged to declare their willingness to accept Jews and to set up suitable camps in North Africa, the United States itself, or elsewhere. Emergency supplies for camps and ghettos could have been organized on a large scale. The murder process itself could have halted by the bombing of railroad tracks and death camps. A wide-ranging campaign should have been mounted to ensure that everyone was aware of the existence of the "final solution," thus sending a warning to Jews who had not yet been caught up in the machinery of annihilation and deterring supporters of the National Socialists.

William D. Rubinstein (1997), by contrast, is at pains to show that such alleged alternative courses of action are no more than wishful thinking. All the operations listed, he says, would either have been impracticable or would have been beyond the scope of the historical actors involved. This point of view has been largely rejected by specialists (Breitman, 1998).

If we attempt to evaluate these conflicting standpoints, we necessarily find ourselves arguing against the facts and so moving into the realms of speculation. It is true that the effects of a deliberate policy of rescue are difficult to assess. After all, even if we were to conclude that individual rescue operations might have saved the lives of hundreds or thousands of people, the fundamental and necessarily speculative question still remains: would such actions really have slowed the process of annihilation or been more likely to accelerate it? All discussions regarding the practicability of rescue activities must necessarily take account of the question of the Nazi regime's priorities: Would not more determined rescue attempts have been seen by the National Socialists as confirmation of their view that they were fighting against a "Jewish world conspiracy," and would they not indeed have stepped up their campaign against the alleged members of that conspiracy? Is not the fact that the Nazi regime continued systematically murdering Jews until the end of the war partly explicable as an attempt to make governments still allied to Germany accomplices in an unprecedented crime and so bind them completely and utterly to the dominant German power, to the bitter end? And if we assume that intention, would not a more determined intercession by the Allies on behalf of the European Jews have been precisely the attitude for which the Nazi regime was hoping?

A skeptical view must also be taken of the prospects of halting the mass murder, or obtaining the release of significant numbers of Jews, by direct negotiation with the Nazi regime (Bauer, 1994). Such negotiations did take place on occasion during the second half of the war, after Hitler had authorized Himmler in late 1942 to release Jews—by way of an exception to the rule—in exchange for payment, preferably in foreign currency. In 1943/ 44, the Germans negotiated—ultimately without success—to exchange Jewish children for Germans held by the Allies; one of the demands made was that the deal should be publicized in the form of a statement made to the British House of Commons. In 1944, the SS tried to negotiate with the Allies, using two Jewish intermediaries from Hungary, to exchange Hungarian Jews for trucks and merchandise and at the same time to establish political contacts with the Allies. Finally, in 1944, Himmler allowed some 1,700 Jews from Hungary to travel to Switzerland. A closer study of these negotiations does show that the National Socialists probably had only a very limited willingness to use Jews to obtain foreign currency or other considerations; it is clear that it was always the primary objective of the SS to use such operations for propaganda purposes (specifically, portraying the rescue of the Jews as an Allied war aim), or to enter into discussions on a separate peace and so bring disunity into the Allied camp.

The comparison between the United States and Britain leads Kushner to an interesting observation in his analysis of the Allied rescue attempts. While the general inactivity of the British government was at odds with the British public's widespread sympathy for rescue operations, the rescue operations mounted by the American WRB, with its admittedly limited successes, took place against a background of significantly increasing popular anti-Semitism. There thus seems to be no direct, linear correlation between anti-Semitism and a passive attitude on the part of governments.

In studies on the attitudes of neutral states to the systematic murder of European Jews, we again find the view expressed that the attempts made to save human beings from the machinery of destruction fell far short of what might possibly have been done, as demonstrated, for example, by studies of the situation in Sweden (Koblik, 1988) or Switzerland (Haas, 1997).

The study by Jean-Claude Favez, first published in French in 1988, takes a critical look at the question of whether the International Committee of the Red Cross might not have done more to rescue the European Jews. Admittedly, even Favez reaches the basic conclusion that the Committee's scope for action was restricted, since the organization concerned—an association of Swiss citizens—could not claim any kind of general responsibility for political prisoners or for the treatment of the civilian population in occupied countries. Moreover, opportunities to intercede with the German government on behalf of Jewish deportees were extremely limited, as the German Red Cross, under National Socialist control, refused to cooperate. Even so, the IRC did send aid packages to the concentration camps and sounded out Germany's allies about the possibility of stopping the deportations; but it was only in the final phase of the war that these efforts had any success.

In October 1942, the IRC drafted a general appeal for better treatment of civilians by the belligerents, though ultimately it was unable to reach a decision on a public declaration. The IRC also said nothing about the discrimination against Jewish prisoners of war by the German Reich, the crucial issue here being the fear that any such protest might jeopardize the IRC's work with prisoners of war as a whole.

Most researchers have also taken a critical view of the Vatican's attitude to the Jewish genocide. Even in the light of more recent research, one must still agree with Morley's summary, emphasizing that "Vatican diplomacy failed the Jews during the Holocaust by not doing all that it was possible for it to do on their behalf. It also failed itself because in neglecting the needs of the Jews, and pursuing a goal of reserve rather than humanitarian concern, it betrayed the ideas that it had set for itself. The nuncios, the secretary of state, and, most of all, the Pope share the responsibility for this dual failure" (Morley, 1980:209; see also Lewy, 1964; while the latest study by Cornwell (1999) adopts an even more critical position without contributing anything much new to the debate).

An especially critical view is taken of the public silence of Pope Pius XIII on the subject of the Jewish genocide. The fate of the Jews was never the subject of any of the Vatican's encyclicals, even though the Holy See was informed with very little delay about the progress of the policy of annihilation in the various countries under German occupation. The Pope was unable to make up his mind to make any direct reference to the fate of the Jews in one of his addresses; in his Christmas address of 1942 he made only a highly qualified reference to the murder of the Jews. The Vatican was even silent on the subject of the arrest and deportation of more than 1,000 Roman Jews in October 1943.

Various explanations have been offered for this attitude on the part of Pius XIII, including the Pope's sympathy for Germany and the Vatican's very pronounced anti-Bolshevism. But the most likely reason for the Pope's silence was the Vatican's efforts to maintain diplomatic ties with all belligerent states and to safeguard the continued existence and cohesion of the Catholic Church in all circumstances. The neutrality of the Vatican was the principal precondition for this, and it was precisely that attitude that prevented the Vatican from making any clear statement. Nor should we underestimate the Pope's fear that the belligerents might incapacitate the headquarters of the Catholic world by occupation or bombing.

On the other hand, it has been pointed out that the Pope refrained from any powerful protest because he would not have expected such a step to produce any positive effects for the Jews. Instead, proponents of this view emphasize the personal role played by Pius XIII in the Vatican's diplomatic efforts directed at the leadership of countries allied with Germany, and also that the Vatican supported the rescue operations undertaken by the Catholic Church in Italy and elsewhere by which tens of thousands of Jews were hidden and rescued from their persecutors. Thus, for example, during the German round-up of October 1943, up to 4,000 Jews were hidden in monasteries and ecclesiastical buildings in Rome. Critical authors object, however, that even the Catholic Church's rescue activities could have been far more effective if they had been more resolutely backed by the moral authority and material resources of the Vatican (Phayer, 2000; for a more sympathetic view of the Vatican's stance, see, for example, Falconi, 1970; and Rhodes, 1973). Overall, justifiable doubts remain as to whether the Vatican, especially in view of its exceptional moral authority, did indeed do everything in its power to try to prevent the murder of the Jews.

The Yishuv, the community of Jews living in the British mandated territory of Palestine, which had declared its support for the struggle against Hitler immediately after war broke out, was kept informed of the persecution of the Jews in German-occupied Europe by a relatively continuous flow of news. From September 1942, the Yishuv began to receive reports to the effect that the Nazi regime had begun to murder all the Jews in Europe. It was only gradually, however, that the true dimensions of this crime, far exceeding any previous concepts of persecution, became apparent.

This may help to explain the curiously passive reaction of the Yishuv to the murders in Europe. When Palestine's Jewish press published the first reports on the European massacres in 1942, it did not devote exceptional coverage to them. The Jewish Agency, the leadership of the Yishuv, did make an official declaration on the genocide of Europe's Jews in November 1942, but during 1943 and 1944, as the murders rapidly spread to cover the whole of Europe, it did not treat them as a top priority. Reports of events in Europe had only a marginal influence on the world of the Yishuv: life, in general, simply went on. Consequently, even rescue operations, organized by the Joint Rescue Committee set up in January 1943, were not pursued with the utmost energy; no striking successes were achieved, and only a few thousand people were saved from the gas chambers in minor rescue operations.

The behavior of the Yishuv leadership is not uncontroversial in Israeli literature. The majority of authors, such as Dina Porat (1986), take the view that the moderate success achieved by the rescue activities was primarily attributable to the impotence of the Yishuv; if the utmost efforts had been made, according to Porat's estimate, 10,000 or 20,000 people might have been saved in minor operations involving such activities as the forging of papers, the influencing of neutral states, the issuing of additional visas, bribery, the development of escape routes, etc. However, Tom Segev (1993) also believes that Zionist ideology was an essential reason why no appropriate rescue policy was evolved: the Yishuv leadership, he says, had become totally fixated by the future foundation of the Jewish state; it had perceived the deaths of millions of Jews in Europe as primarily a threat to its future plans, based as they were on mass immigration from Europe, and therefore had not pursued with sufficient energy the rescuing of small groups of individuals while it was still possible.

The extensive literature on contemporary understanding and actual or failed opportunities for rescue, affecting so many different countries, organizations, and cultures, does nevertheless seem to reflect one common, fundamental problem: the evident inability of contemporaries to recognize the totally new dimension of the persecution of the Jews by the Nazi system, let alone react to it appropriately. This applies equally to the German population, the Allies, the neutral countries, the Catholic Church, the International Red Cross, and Jewish organizations, but most of all to the direct victims. This completely new dimension of violence was also, probably, an essential reason why it took historical researchers decades before they were able to describe the whole course of events at all.

This completely new dimension of violence, described at the beginning of this chapter as "unique" or "unprecedented," is thus not only significant in the context of an academic debate on the historical classification of the murder of the Jews by the Nazi regime. The fact that the murder of the European Jews, at the time it occurred, defied comparison with any act of violence known over the course of history is in itself a clue to understanding the helpless reaction of the victims and their contemporaries to this unprecedented event.

Translated by Richard Sharp

REFERENCES

Adam, Uwe Dietrich. (1972). *Judenpolitik im Dritten Reich*. Düsseldorf: Droste.

Adelson, Alan, & Robert Lapides. (1989). *Lodz Ghetto. Inside a Community Under Siege*. New York: Viking.

Adler, Hans Günter. (1955). *Theresienstadt. Das Antlitz einer Zwangsgemeinschaft*. Tübingen: Mohr.

Adler, Hans Günter. (Eds.) (1958). *Die verheimlichte Wahrheit. Theresienstädter Dokumente*. Tübingen: Mohr.

Adler, Hans Günter. (1974). *Der Verwaltete Mensch. Studien zur Deportation der Juden aus Deutschland*. Tübingen: Mohr.

Ainsztein, Reuben. (1974). *Jewish Resistance in Nazi-Occupied Eastern Europe with a Historical Survey of the Jew as Fighter and Soldier in the Diaspora*. London: Elek.

Aly, Götz. (1995). *'Endlösung'. Völkerverschiebung und der Mord an den europäischen Juden*. Frankfurt a. M.: Fischer. [English: Aly, Götz. (1999). *Final Solution. Nazi Population Policy and the Murder of the European Jews*. London: Arnold.]

Aly, Götz, & Susanne Heim. (1991) *Vordenker der Vernichtung. Auschwitz und die deutschen Pläne für eine neue europäische Ordnung*. Hamburg: Hoffmann und Campe.

Andernacht, Dietrich. (Eds.) (1963). *Dokumente zur Geschichte der Frankfurter Juden 1933–1945*. Frankfurt a. M.: Kramer.

Apenszlak, Jakob. (Ed.) (1943). *The Black Book of Polish Jewry*. New York: American Federation of Polish Jewry.

Arad, Yitzhak. (1988). The Holocaust in Soviet Historiography. In Yisrael Gutman & Gideon Greif (Eds.), *The Historiography of the Holocaust Period. Proceedings of the Fifth Yad Vashem International Historical Conference* (pp. 187–216). Jerusalem: Yad Vashem.

Arad, Yitzhak. (1989a). Jewish Family Camps in the Forests—An Original Means of Rescue. In Michael Marrus (Ed.), *The Nazi Holocaust. Historical Articles on the Destruction of European Jews. Vol. 7* (pp. 219–239). London: Meckler.

Arad, Yitzhak. (1989b). Jewish Prisoner Uprisings in the Treblinka and Sobibor Extermination Camps. In Michael Marrus (Ed.), *The Nazi Holocaust. Historical Articles on the Destruction of European Jews. Vol. 7* (pp. 240–283). London: Meckler.

Arad, Yitzhak. (1996). The Jewish Fighting Underground in the Ghettos of Eastern Europe—Ideology and Reality. In Yisrael Gutman (Ed.), *Major Changes within the Jewish People in the Wake of the Holocaust. Proceedings of the Ninth Yad Vashem International Historical Conference* (pp. 337–357). Jerusalem: Yad Vashem.

Archivdirektion Stuttgart. (Eds.) (1969). *Die Opfer der nationalsozialistischen Judenverfolgung in Baden-Württemberg 1933–1945. Ein Gedenkbuch*. Stuttgart: Kohlhammer.

Arendt, Hanna. (1963). *Eichmann in Jerusalem. A Report on the Banality of Evil*. New York: Viking.

Augenzeugenberichte. (1953). Augenzeugenberichte zu den Massenvergasungen. *Vierteljahreshefte für Zeitgeschichte, 1*, 177–194.

Bankier, David. (1992). *The Germans and the Final Solution*. Cambridge: Blackwell.

Banach, Jens. (1996). *Heydrichs Elite. Das Führerkorps der Sicherheitspolizei und des SD 1936–1945*. Paderborn: Schöningh.

Bauer, Yehuda. (1979). Forms of Jewish Resistance. In Yehuda Bauer, *The Jewish Emergence from Powerlessness* (pp. 26–40). Toronto University Press.

Bauer, Yehuda. (1987). On the Place of the Holocaust in History. In Honour of Franklin H. Little. *Holocaust and Genocide Studies, 2*(2), 209–220.

Bauer, Yehuda. (1989). The Judenräte—Some Conclusions. In Michael Marrus (Ed.), *The Nazi Holocaust. Historical Articles on the Destruction of European Jews. Vol. 6* (pp. 165–175). London: Meckler.

Bauer, Yehuda. (1990). Is the Holocaust Explicable? *Holocaust and Genocide Studies, 5*, 145–155.

Bauer, Yehuda. (1991). Holocaust and Genocide: Some Comparisons. In Peter Hayes (Ed.), *Lessons and Legacies. The Meaning of the Holocaust in a Changing World* (pp. 36–46). Northwestern University Press.

Bauer, Yehuda. (1994). *Jews for Sale? Nazi–Jewish Negotiations, 1933–1945*. New Haven, London: Yale.

Baumel, Yehudit Tydor. (1998). *Double Jeopardy. Gender and the Holocaust*. London: Vallentine Mitchell.

Beinfeld, Solon. (1998). Health Care in the Vilna Ghetto. *Holocaust and Genocide Studies, 12*, 66–98.

Benz, Wolfgang. (Ed.) (1991). *Dimension des Völkermords. Die Zahl der jüdischen Opfer des Nationalsozialismus*. München: Oldenbourg.

Birn, Ruth Bettina. (1986). *Die Höheren SS- und Polizeiführer. Himmlers Vertreter im Reich und in den besetzten Gebieten*. Düsseldorf: Droste.

Birn, Ruth Bettina. (1997). Revising the Holocaust. *Historical Journal, 40*, 195–215.

Black, Peter. (1984). *Ernst Kaltenbrunner: Ideological Soldier of the Third Reich*. Princeton University Press.

Blau, Bruno. (1952). *Das Ausnahmerecht für die Juden in den europäischen Ländern, Teil I: Deutschland*. New York: Selbstverlag.

Bracher, Karl Dietrich. (1969). *Die deutsche Diktatur. Entstehung, Struktur, Folgen des Nationalsozialismus*. Köln: Kiepenheuer & Witsch. [English: Bracher, Karl Dietrich. (1970). *The German Dictatorship. The Origin, Structure and Effects of National Socialism*. New York: Praeger.]

Braham, Randolph L. (1981). *The Politics of Genocide: The Holocaust in Hungary. 2 Vols*. New York: Columbia Press.

Breitman, Richard. (1991). *The Architect of Genocide Himmler and the Final Solution*. New York: Knopf.

Breitman, Richard. (1998). *Official Secrets. What the Nazis Planned, What the British and Americans Knew*. New York: Hill and Wang.

Broszat, Martin. (Eds.) (1958). *Rudolf Höss. Kommandant in Auschwitz. Autobiographische Aufzeichnungen*. Stuttgart: Deutsche Verlags Anstalt.

Broszat, Martin. (1969). *Der Staat Hitlers. Grundlegung und Entwicklung seiner inneren Verfassung*. München: Deutscher Taschenbuchverlag.

Broszat, Martin. (1970). Soziale Motivation und Führer-Bindung des Nationalsozialismus. *Vierteljahrshefte für Zeitgeschichte, 18*, 302–409.

Broszat, Martin. (1977). Hitler und die Genesis der 'Endlösung'. Aus Anlass der Thesen David Irvings. *Vierteljahrshefte für Zeitgeschichte, 25*, 739–775. [English: Broszat, Martin. (1979). Hitler and the Genesis of the 'Final Solution': An Assessment of David Irving's Theses. *Yad Vashem Studies, 13*, 73–125.]

Browning, Christopher R. (1985). *Fateful Months. Essays on the Emergence of the Final Solution*. New York, London: Holmes & Meier.

Browning, Christopher R. (1992a). *Ordinary Men: Reserve Police Battalion 101 and the Final Solution in Poland*. New York: Harper Collins.

Browning, Christopher R. (1992b). *The Path to Genocide. Essays on Launching the Final Solution*. Cambridge: Cambridge University Press.

Browning, Christopher R. (1996). A Final Decision for the 'Final Solution'? The Riegner-Telegram Reconsidered. *Holocaust and Genocide Studies, 10*, 3–10.

Browning, Christopher R. (1998). Ordinary Germans or Ordinary Men? A Reply to the Critics. In Michael Berenbaum & Abraham J. Peck (Eds.), *The Holocaust and History: The Known, the Unknown, the Disputed, and the Reexamined* (pp. 251–265). Bloomington: Indiana University Press.

Browning Christopher R. (2000). *Nazi Policy, Jewish Workers, German Killers*. Cambridge: Cambridge University Press.

Buchheim, Hans, Martin Broszat, Hans-Adolf Jacobsen, & Helmut Krausnick. (1964). *Anatomie des SS-Staates. 2 Vols*. Olten, Freiburg i.Br.: Walter Verlag.

Büttner, Ursula. (1997). 'Die Judenfrage wird zur Christenfrage.' Die deutsche evangelische Kirche und die Judenverfolgung im Dritten Reich. *Zeitschrift für Geschichtswissenschaft, 45*, 581–596.

Chary, Frederick Barry. (1972). *Bulgaria and the Jews: 'The Final Solution', 1940 to 1944*. Pittsburgh: University of Pittsburgh.

Cornwell, John. (1999). *Hitler's Pope The Secret History of Pius XII*. London: Penguin.

Dawidowicz, Lucy S. (1975). *The War Against the Jews, 1933–1945*. London: Penguin.

Deutscher, Isaac. (1968). *The Non-Jewish Jew and Other Essays*. London: Oxford University Press.

Dobroszycki, Lucjan. (Ed.) (1984). *The Chronicle of the Lodz Ghetto, 1941–1944*. New York: Yale University Press.

Dwork, Debórah. (1991). *Children with a Star: Jewish Youth in Nazi Europe*. New Haven: Yale University Press.

Eck, Nathan. (1976). *The Holocaust of the Jews in Europe* [Hebrew]. Tel Aviv: Hakibbutz Hameuchad.

Eisenbach, Artur. (1961). *Hitlerowska polityka zaglady Zydów*. Warszawa: Zydowski Instytut Historyczny.

Eisenbach, Artur. (1962). Operation Reinhard. Mass Extermination of the Jewish Population in Poland. *Polish Western Affairs, 3*, 80–124.

Ezergailis, Andrew. (1996). *The Holocaust in Latvia, 1941–1944. The Missing Center*. Riga, Washington: Historical Institute of Latvia.

Fackenheim, Emil L. (1982). *To Mend the World. Foundations of Future Jewish Thought*. New York: Schocken.

Falconi, Carlo. (1970). *The Silence of Pius XII*. Boston: Little Brown.

Favez, Claude. (1988). *Une mission impossible?* Lausanne: Editions Payot. [English: Favez, Claude. (1999). *The Red Cross and the Holocaust*. Cambridge: Cambridge University Press.]

Fein, Helen. (1979). *Accounting for Genocide. National Response and Jewish Victimization During the Holocaust*. New York, London: The Free Press.

Feingold, Henry L. (1970). *The Politics of Rescue. The Roosevelt Administration and the Holocaust, 1938–1945*. New Brunswick: Rutgers University Press.

Frei, Norbert, Sybille Steinbacher, & Bernd C. Wagner. (Eds.) (2000). *Ausbeutung, Vernichtung, Öffentlichkeit. Neue Studien zur nationalsozialistischen Lagerpolitik*. München: K. G. Saur.

Friedländer, Saul. (1991). The 'Final Solution'. On the Unease in Historical Interpretation. In Peter Hayes (Ed.), *Lessons and Legacies. The Meaning of the Holocaust in a Changing World* (pp. 23–35). Evanston: Northwestern University Press.

Genschel, Helmut. (1966). *Die Verdrängung der Juden aus der Wirtschaft im Dritten Reich*. Göttingen: Musterschmidt.

Gerlach, Christian. (1997). Die Wannsee-Konferenz, das Schicksal der deutschen Juden und Hitlers politische Grundsatzentscheidung, alle Juden Europas zu ermorden. *Werkstattgeschichte, 19*, 7–44.

Gerlach, Christian. (1998). *Krieg, Ernährung, Völkermord. Forschungen zur deutschen Vernichtungspolitik im Zweiten Weltkrieg*. Hamburg: Hamburger Edition.

Gerlach, Christian. (1999). *Kalkulierte Morde. Die deutsche Wirtschafts- und Vernichtungspolitik in Weißrussland, 1941 bis 1944*. Hamburg: Hamburger Edition.

Gerlach, Wolfgang. (1987). *Als die Zeugen schwiegen. Bekennende Kirche und die Juden*. Berlin: Kirche und Judentum.

Goldhagen, Daniel Jonah. (1996). *Hitler's Willing Executioners. Ordinary Germans and the Holocaust*. London: Little Brown & Co.

Goldhagen, Daniel Jonah. (1996). *Hitlers willige Vollstrecker. Ganz gewöhnliche Deutsche und der Holocaust*. Berlin: Siedler Verlag.

Grossmann, Wassili, & Ehrenburg, Ilja. (1994). *Das Schwarzbuch. Der Genozid an den sowjetischen Juden*. Reinbek b. Hamburg: Rowohlt. [First Russian (1946).]

Gruner, Wolf. (1997). *Der geschlossene Arbeitseinsatz deutscher Juden. Zur Zwangsarbeit als Element der Verfolgung, 1938–1943*. Berlin: Metropol.

Gruner, Wolf. (1999). The German Council of Municipalities: Deutscher Gemeindetag and the Coordination of Anti-Jewish Local Politics in the Nazi State. *Holocaust and Genocide Studies, 13*(2), 171–199.

Gutman, Yisrael. (1982). *The Jews of Warsaw, 1939–1943. Ghetto, Underground, Revolt*. Brighton: Harvester Press.

Gutman, Israel. (Ed.) (1989). *Encyclopedia of the Holocaust*. New York: Macmillan.

Gutman, Yisrael, & Cynthia J. Haft. (1979). *Patterns of Jewish Leadership in Nazi Europe 1933–1945*. Jerusalem: Yad Vashem.

Gutman, Yisrael, & Efraim Zuroff. (1978). *Rescue Attempts during the Holocaust: Proceedings of the Second Yad Vashem International Historical Conference, Jerusalen, 8–11 April, 1974*. New York: Ktav Publishing House.

Haas, Gaston. (1997). *'Wenn man gewusst hätte, was sich drüben im Reich abspielte...' 1941–1943. Was man in der Schweiz von der Judenvernichtung wusste. 2nd edition*. Basel, Frankfurt a. M.: Helbing & Lichtenhahn.

Hachmeister, Lutz. (1998). *Der Gegnerforscher. Die Karriere des SS-Führers Alfred Six*. München: C. H. Beck.

Heer, Hannes, & Klaus Naumann. (Eds.) (1995). *Vernichtungskrieg. Verbrechen der Wehrmacht 1941–1944*. Hamburg: Hamburger Edition. [English: Heer, Hannes & Klaus Naumann (Eds.) (2000). *War of Extermination: The German Military in World War II, 1941–44*. New York, Oxford: Berghahn Books.]

Heiber, Helmut. (1956). Aus den Akten des Gauleiters Kube. *Vierteljahrshefte für Zeitgeschichte, 4*, 67–95.

Herbert, Ulrich. (1985). *Fremdarbeiter: Politik und Praxis des 'Ausländer-Einsatzes' in der Kriegswirtschaft des Dritten Reiches*. Berlin, Bonn: Dietz. [English: Herbert, Ulrich. (1997). *Foreign Labor in Germany under the Third Reich*. Cambridge: Cambridge University Press.]

Herbert, Ulrich. (1996). *Best: biographische Studien über Radikalismus, Weltanschauung und Vernunft, 1903–1989*. Bonn: Dietz.

Herbert, Ulrich, Karin Orth, & Christoph Dieckmann. (Eds.) (1998). *Die nationalsozialistischen Konzentrationslager. Entwicklung und Struktur. 2 Vols*. Göttingen: Wallstein.

Hilberg, Raul. (1961). *The Destruction of the European Jews*. Chicago: Quadrangle Books.

Hilberg, Raul. (1985). *The Destruction of the European Jews. Revised new edition*. New York: Holmes & Meier.

Hildebrand, Klaus. (1979). *Das Dritte Reich*. München, Wien: Oldenburg. [English: Hildebrand, Klaus. (1984). *The Third Reich*. London, New York: Routledge.]

Hillgruber, Andreas. (1972). Die 'Endlösung' und das deutsche Ostimperium als Kernstück des rassenideologischen Programms des Nationalsozialismus. *Vierteljahrshefte für Zeitgeschichte, 20*, 133–153.

Hundsnurscher, Franz, & Gerhard Taddey. (1968). *Die jüdischen Gemeinden in Baden. Denkmale, Geschichte, Schicksale*. Stuttgart: Kohlhammer.

Institut für Zeitgeschichte. (1958). *Gutachten des Instituts für Zeitgeschichte. 2 Vols*. München: Institut für Zeitgeschichte.

Jäckel, Eberhard. (1969). *Hitlers Weltanschauung. Entwurf einer Herrschaft*. Tübingen: Wunderlich. [English: Jäckel, Eberhard. (1981). *Hitler's World View. A Blueprint for Power*. Cambridge, London: Harvard University Press.]

Jäckel, Eberhard. (1986). Die elende Praxis der Untersteller. Das Einmalige der nationalsozialistischen Verbrechen lässt sich nicht leugnen. In *Die Zeit*, 12.9.86, [reprinted in: Augstein, Rudolf et al. (1987). *'Historikerstreit'. Die Dokumentation der Kontroverse um die Einzigartigkeit der nationalsozialistischen Judenvernichtung* (pp. 115–122). München, Zürich.]

Jäckel, Eberhard. (2000). *Wider zwei Legenden über den Holocaust Plädoyer für Einzigartigkeit des Genozids, den die Nazis an den Juden verübten*. Frankfurter Allgemeine Zeitung, 30.6.2000.

Jäckel, Eberhard, & Jürgen Rohwer. (Eds.) (1987). *Der Mord an den europäischen Juden. Entschlussbildung und Verwirklichung*. Frankfurt a. M.: Fischer.

Jäger, Herbert. (1967). *Verbrechen unter totalitärer Herrschaft. Studien zur nationalsozialistischen Gewaltkriminalität*. Olten, Freiburg: Walter. [New Expanded Edition: Jäger, Herbert. (1982). *Verbrechen unter totalitärer Herrschaft. Studien zur nationalsozialistischen Gewaltkriminalität*. Frankfurt a. M.: Suhrkamp.]

Jäger, Herbert. (1997). Die Widerlegung des funktionalistischen Täterbildes. Daniel Goldhagens Beitrag zur Kriminologie des Völkermords. *Mittelweg, 36*(1), 73–85.

Jelinek, Yeshayahu. (1988). The Holocaust of Slovakian an Croatian Jewry from the Historiographical Viewpoint—A Comparative Analysis. In Yisrael Gutman & Gideon Greif (Eds.), *The Historiography of the Holocaust Period. Proceedings of the Fifth Yad Vashem International Historical Conference* (pp. 343–368). Jerusalem: Yad Vashem.

Kaplan, Marion A. (1998). *Between Dignity and Despair, Jewish Life in Nazi Germany*. New York: Oxford University Press.

Katz, Steven T. (1994). *The Holocaust in Historical Context*. New York, Oxford: Oxford University Press.

Katzburg, Nathaniel. (1988). The Destruction of Hungarian Jewry in Hungarian Historiography. In Yisrael Gutman & Gideon Greif (Eds.), *The Historiography of the Holocaust Period. Proceedings of the Fifth Yad Vashem International Historical Conference* (pp. 369–387). Jerusalem: Yad Vashem.

Kermisch, Joseph. (Ed.) (1986). *To Live with Honor and Die with Honor: Selected Documents from the Warsaw Underground Archive 'O. S.'*. Jerusalem: Yad Vashem.

Kershaw, Ian. (1981). The Persecution of the Jews and German Popular Opinion in the Third Reich. *Leo Baeck Institute Year Book, 26*, 261–289.

Kershaw, Ian. (1986). German Popular Opinion and the 'Jewish Question' 1939–1945: Some Further Reflections. In Arnold Paucker (Ed.), *Die Juden im nationalsozialistischen Deutschland* (pp. 365–385). Tübingen: Mohr.

Kershaw, Ian. (1992). Improvised Genocide? The Emergence of the 'Final Solution' in the 'Warthegau'. *Transactions of the Royal Historical Society, 6*(2), 51–78.

Klee, Ernst. (1985). *'Euthanasie' im NS-Staat. Die 'Vernichtung lebensunwerten Lebens'*. Frankfurt a. M.: Fischer.

Kenkmann, Alfons, & Bernd A. Rusinek (Eds.) (1999). *Verfolgung und Verwaltung. Die wirtschaftliche Ausplünderung der Juden und die westfälischen Finanzbehörden*. Münster: Villa ten Hompel.

Koblik, Steven. (1988). *The Stones Cry Out. Sweden's response to persecution of the Jews 1933–1945*. New York: Holocaust Library.

Kogon, Eugen, & Hermann Langbein et al. (Eds.) (1983). *Nationalsozialistische Massentötungen durch Giftgas. Eine Dokumentation*. Frankfurt a. M.: Fischer.

Kolb, Eberhard. (1962). *Bergen-Belsen*. Hannover: Verlag für Literatur und Zeitgeschehen.

Krakowski, Shmuel. (1984). *The War of the Doomed. Jewish Armed Resistance in Poland 1942–1944*. New York: Holmes & Meier.

Krakowski, Shmuel, & Yisrael Gutman. (1986). *Unequal victims. Poles and Jews During World War II*. New York: Holocaust Library.

Krausnick, Helmut, & Hans Heinrich Wilhelm. (1981). *Die Einsatzgruppen der Sicherheitspolizei und des SD 1938–1942*. Stuttgart: Deutsche Verlags Anstalt.

Krieger, Seymour. (Ed.) (1947). *Nazi Germany's War against the Jews*. New York: American Jewish Conference.

Kulka, Erich. (1989). Escapes of Jewish Prisoners from Auschwitz-Birkenau and Their Attempts to Stop the Mass Extermination. In Michael Marrus (Ed.), *The Nazi Holocaust. Historical Articles on the Destruction of European Jews* (pp. 316–331). London: Meckler.

Kulka, Otto Dov. (1975). *The 'Jewish Question' in the Third Reich; Its Significance in National Socialist Ideology and Politics and its Role in Determining the Status and Activities of The Jews* [Hebrew]. Jerusalem: Self Publishing Company.

Kulka, Otto Dov, & Aron Rodrigue. (Eds.) (1984). The German Population and the Jews in the Third Reich: Recent Publications and Trends in Research on German Society and the 'Jewish Question'. *Yad Vashem Studies, 16*, 421–35.

Kushner, Tony. (1994). *The Holocaust and the Liberal Imagination. A Social and Cultural History*. Oxford, Cambridge: Blackwell.

Kwiet, Konrad. (1979). Problems of Jewish Resistance Historiography. *Leo Baeck Institute Yearbook, 24*, 37–60.

Kwiet, Konrad, & Helmut Eschwege. (1984). *Selbstbehauptung und Widerstand. Deutsche Juden im Kampf um Existenz und Menschenwürde, 1933–1945*. Hamburg: Christians.

Lang, Barel. (1990). *Act and Idea in the Nazi Genocide*. Chicago, London: Chicago University Press.

Laqueur, Walter. (1980). *The Terrible Secret: Suppression of the Truth about Hitler's 'Final Solution'*. London: Weidenfeld & Nicolson.

Latour, Anny. (1970). *La Résistance juive en France*. Paris: Stock. [English: Latour, Anny. (1981). *The Jewish Resistance in France, 1940–1944*. New York: Holocaust Library.]

Lazare, Lucien. (1987). *La Résistance en France, 1940–1944*. Paris: Stock.

Levai, Eugene. (1948). *Black Book on the Martyrdom of Hungarian Jewry*. Zürich: Central European Times Publication.

Levin, Don. (1985). *Fighting Back: Lithuanian Jewry's Armed Resistance to the Nazis, 1941–1945*. New York: Holmes and Meier.

Levin, Nora. (1968). *The Holocaust. The destruction of European Jewry 1933–1945*. New York: Thomas Y. Crowell.

Lewy, Guenter. (1964). *The Catholic Church and Nazi Germany*. New York: McGraw-Hill & Co.

Lewy, Guenter. (2000). *The Nazi Persecution of the Gypsies*. Oxford University Press.

Longerich, Peter. (1998). *Politik der Vernichtung. Eine Gesamtdarstellung der nationalsozialistischen Judenverfolgung*. München: Piper.

Lustiger, Arno. (1994). *Zum Kampf auf Leben und Tod! Das Buch vom Widerstand der Juden, 1933–1945*. Köln: Kiepenheuer & Witsch.

Madajczyk, Czeslaw. (1988). *Die Okkupationspolitik Nazideutschlands in Polen 1939–1945*. Köln: Pahl-Rugenstein. [First Polish (1970).]

Maier, Dieter. (1994). *Arbeitseinsatz und Deportation. Die Mitwirkung der Arbeitsverwaltung bei der nationalsozialistischen Judenverfolgung in den Jahren 1938–1945*. Berlin: Hentrich.

Majer, Diemut. (1981). *Fremdvölkische im Dritten Reich*. Boppard a. Rhein: Boldt.

Marrus, Michael. (1987). *The Holocaust in History*. Hanover, London: University Press of New England.

Marrus, Michael. (1996). Varieties of Jewish Resistance. Some Categories and Comparisons. In Yisrael Gutman (Ed.), *Major Changes within the Jewish People in the Wake of the Holocaust. Proceedings of the Ninth Yad Vashem International Historical Conference* (pp. 269–293). Jerusalem: Yad Vashem.

Marrus, Michael, & Robert O. Paxton. (1981). *Vichy-France and the Jews*. New York: Basic Books.

Michaelis, Meir. (1978). *Mussolini and the Jews: German–Italian Relations and the Jewish Question in Italy, 1922–1945*. Oxford: Clarendon Press.

Michman, Dan. (1993). Jewish religious Life under Nazi Domination: Nazi Attitudes and Jewish Problems. *Studies in Religion*, 22, 147–165.

Mommsen, Hans. (1983). Die Realisierung des Utopischen: Die 'Endlösung der Judenfrage' im Dritten Reich. *Geschichte und Gesellschaft*, 9, 381–420. [English: Mommsen, Hans. (1989). The Realization of the Unthinkable: The Final Solution of the Jewish Question in the Third Reich. In Michael Marrus (Ed.), *The Nazi Holocaust. Historical Articles on the Destruction of European Jews. Vol. 3* (pp. 217–264). London: Meckler.]

Morley, John F. (1980). *Vatican Diplomacy and the Jews during the Holocaust 1939–1943*. New York: KTAV Publishing House.

Musial, Bogdan. (1999). *Deutsche Zivilverwaltung und Judenverfolgung im Generalgouvernement. Eine Fallstudie zum Distrikt Lublin, 1939–1944*. Wiesbaden: Harrassowitz.

Nellessen, Bernd. (1992). Die schweigende Kirche. Katholiken und Judenverfolgung. In Ursula Büttner (Ed.), *Die Deutschen und die Judenverfolgung im Dritten Reich* (pp. 259–271). Hamburg: Christians.

Ofer, Dalia. (1995). Everyday Life of Jews Under Nazi Occupation. Methodological Issues. *Holocaust and Genocide Studies*, 9, 42–69.

Ofer, Dalia, & Leonore L. Weitzmann (Eds.) (1998). *Women in the Holocaust*. New Haven: Yale University Press.

Ogorreck, Ralf. (1996). *Die Einsatzgruppen und die 'Genesis der Endlösung'*. Berlin: Metropol.

Orth, Karin. (1999). *Das System der nationalsozialistischen Konzentrationslager. Eine politische Organisationsgeschichte*. Hamburg: Hamburger Edition.

Orth, Karin. (2000). *Die Konzentrationslager-SS. Sozialstrukturelle Analysen und biographische Studien*. Göttingen: Wallstein.

Paucker, Arno. (1989). *Jüdischer Widerstand in Deutschland*. Berlin: Gedenkstätte deutscher Widerstand. [English: Paucker, Arno. (1991). *Jewish Resistance in Germany. The Facts and the Problems*. Berlin: Gedenkstätte deutscher Widerstand.]

Paucker, Arnold, & Lucien Steinberg. (1971). Notes on Jewish Resistance. *Leo Baeck Institute Yearbook*, 16, 239–248.

Paul, Gerhard, & Michael Mallmann. (Eds.) (1995). *Die Gestapo. Mythos und Realität*. Darmstadt: Wissenschaftliche Buchgesellschaft.

Pelt, Robert-Jan van, & Debórah Dwork. (1996). *Auschwitz. 1270 to the Present*. New York, London: Norton & Company.

Petrie, Jon. (2000). The Secular Word Holocaust: Scholarly Myths, History, and 20th Century Meanings. *Journal of Genocide Research*, 2, 31–64.

Phayer, Michael. (2000). *The Catholic Church and the Holocaust, 1930–1965*. Bloomington, Indianapolis: Indiana University Press.

Pohl, Dieter. (1993). *Von der 'Judenpolitik' zum 'Judenmord'. Der Distrikt Lublin des Generalgouvernements 1939–1944*. Frankfurt a. M.: Lang.

Pohl, Dieter. (1997a). Die Holocaust-Forschung und Goldhagens Thesen. *Vierteljahreshefte für Zeitgeschichte*, 45, 1–48.

Pohl, Dieter. (1997b). *Nationalsozialistische Judenverfolgung in Ostgalizien, 1941–1944. Organisation und Durchführung eines staatlichen Massenverbrechens*. München: Oldenbourg.

Poliakov, Léon, & Josef Wulf. (1955). *Das Dritte Reich und die Juden*. Berlin: Arani. [First French: Poliakov, Léon. (1951). *Bréviaire de la Haine. Le IIIe Reich et les Juifs*. Paris: Calman-Levy.]

Porat, Dina. (1990). *The Blue and the Yellow Stars of David. The Zionist Leadership in Palestine and the Holocaust, 1939–1945*. Cambridge: Harvard University Press. [First Hebrew (1986).]

Poznanski, Renée. (1989). A Methodological Approach to the Study of Jewish Resistance in France. In Michael Marrus (Ed.), *The Nazi Holocaust. Historical Articles on the Destruction of European Jews. Vol. 7* (pp. 443–481). London: Meckler.

Presser, Jacob. (1965). *Ondergang. De verfolging en verdelging van het Nederlands Jodendom, 1940–1945*. 2 Vols. 's-Gravenhage: Nijhoff. [English: Presser, Jacob. (1968). *Ashes in the Wind. The Destruction of the Dutch Jewry*. London: Souvenir Press.]

Rayksi, Adam. (1998). The Jewish Underground Press in France and the Struggle to Expose the Nazi Secret of the Final Solution. In Michael Berenbaum & Abraham J. Peck (Eds.), *The Holocaust and History: The Known, the Unknown, the Disputed, and the Reexamined* (pp. 616–626). Bloomington: Indiana University Press.

Reitlinger, Gerald. (1953). *The Final Solution. The Attempt to Exterminate The Jews of Europe 1939–1945*. London: Valentine, Mitchell & Co.

Rhodes, Anthony. (1973). *The Vatican in the Age of the Dictators, 1922–1945*. New York: Holt, Rinehart and Winston.

Roland, Charles G. (1992). *Courage under Siege. Starvation, Disease, and Death in the Warsaw Ghetto*. New York: Oxford University Press.

Rubinstein, William D. (1997). *The Myth of Rescue. Why the Democracies Could not Have Saved more Jews from the Nazis*. London, New York: Routledge.

Rückerl, Adalbert. (Ed.) (1977). *Nationalsozialistische Vernichtungslager im Spiegel deutscher Strafprozesse. Belzec, Sobibor, Treblinka, Chelmno*. München: Deutscher Taschenbuchverlag.

Sakowska, Ruta. (1993). *Die zweite Etappe ist der Tod. NS-Ausrottungspolitik gegen die polnischen Juden, gesehen mit den Augen der Opfer. Ein historischer Essay und ausgewählte Dokumente aus dem Ringelblum-Archiv 1941–1943*. Berlin: Edition Hentrich. [First Polish, Wroclaw (1986).]

Sandkühler, Thomas. (1996). *'Endlösung' in Galizien. Der Judenmord in Ostpolen und die Rettungsinitiative von Berthold Beitz, 1941–1944*. Bonn: Dietz.

Sauer, Paul. (Ed.) (1966a) *Dokumente über die Verfolgung der jüdischen Bürger in Baden-Württemberg durch das nationalsozialistische Regime, 1933–1945*. 2 Vols. Stuttgart: Kohlhammer.

Sauer, Paul. (1966b). *Die jüdischen Gemeinden in Württemberg und Hohenzollern. Denkmale, Geschichte, Schicksale*. Stuttgart: Kohlhammer.

Sauer, Paul. (Ed.) (1969). *Die Schicksale der jüdischen Bürger Baden-Württembergs während der nationalsozialistischen Verfolgungszeit, 1933–1945. Statistische Ergebnisse der Erhebungen der Dokumentationsstelle bei der Archivdirektion Stuttgart und zusammenfassende Darstellung*. Stuttgart: Kohlhammer.

Scheffler, Wolfgang. (1960). *Judenverfolgung im Dritten Reich*. Berlin: Colloquium.

Schleunes, Karl A. (1972). *The Twisted Road to Auschwitz. Nazi Policy Toward German Jews, 1933–39*. London: Deutsch.

Schmuhl, Hans-Walter. (1987). *Rassenhygiene, Nationalsozialismus, Euthanasie. Von der Verhütung zur Vernichtung 'lebensunwerten Lebens', 1890–1945*. Göttingen: Vandenhoeck & Ruprecht.

Schneider, Wolfgang. (Ed.) (1991). *'Vernichtungspolitik'. Eine Debatte über den Zusammenhang von Sozialpolitik und Genozid im nationalsozialistischen Deutschland*. Hamburg: Junius.

Seeger, Andreas. (1996). *'Gestapo Müller'. Die Karriere eines Schreibtischtäters*. Berlin: Metropol.

Segev, Tom. (1993). *The Seventh Million. The Israelis and the Holocaust*. New York: Hill and Wang. [First Hebrew (1991).]

Slepyan, Kenneth. (2000). The Soviet Partisan Movement and the Holocaust. *Holocaust and Genocide Studies, 14*, 1–27.

Steinbacher, Sybille. (2000). *'Musterstadt' Auschwitz. Germanisierungspolitik und Judenmord in Oberschlesien*. München: K. G. Saur.

Steinberg, Lucien. (1970). *La Révolte des Justes. Les Juifs contre Hitler, 1933–1945*. Paris: Fayard.

Steiner, George. (1988). The Long Life of a Metaphor: An Approach to the 'shoah'. In Berel Lang (Ed.), *Writing and the Holocaust* (pp. 154–173). Bloomington: Indiana University Press.

Stoltzfus, Nathan. (1996). *Resistance of the Heart. Intermarriage and the Rosenstrasse Protest in Nazi Germany*. New York: Norton.

Streim, Alfred. (1981). *Die Behandlung sowjetischer Kriegsgefangenen im 'Fall Barbarossa'*. Heidelberg, Karlsruhe: C. F. Müller.

Streit, Christian. (1978). *Keine Kameraden Die Wehrmacht und die sowjetischen Kriegsgefangenen 1941–1945*. Stuttgart: Deutsche Verlags-Anstalt. [Revised Edition, Bonn: Dietz (1997).]

Tec, Nechama. (1993). *Defiance. The Bielsik Partisans*. Oxford: Oxford University Press.

Tenenbaum, Joseph. (1956). *Race and Reich. The Story of an Epoch*. New York: Twayne.

Trunk, Isaac. (1972). *Judenrat. The Jewish Councils in Eastern Europe under Nazi Occupation*. Lincoln: University of Nebraska Press.

Wagner, Bernd C. (2000). *IG Auschwitz. Zwangsarbeit und Vernichtung von Häftlingen des Lagers Monowitz, 1941–1945*. München: Saur.

Wasserstein, Bernhard. (1979). *Britain and the Jews of Europe, 1939–1945*. London, Oxford: Clarendon Press.

Weiss, Aharon. (1974). Leadership in Occupied Poland. *Yad Vashem Studies, 10*, 277–294.

Weiss, Aharon. (1989). Artikel 'Judenrat'. In Israel Gutman (Ed.), *Encyclopedia of the Holocaust. 4 Vols.* New York: Macmillan.

Wulf, Josef. (1958). *Vom Leben, Kampf und Tod im Ghetto Warschau.* Bonn: Bundeszentrale für Heimatdienst.

Wulf, Josef. (1961). *Das Dritte Reich und seine Vollstrecker. Die Liquidation von 500.000 Juden im Ghetto Warschau.* Berlin: Arani.

Wulf, Josef. (1962). *Lodz: Das letzte Ghetto auf polnischem Boden.* Bonn: Bundeszentrale für Heimatdienst.

Wyman, David S. (1984). *The Abandonment of the Jews. America and the Holocaust 1941–1945.* New York: The New Press.

Wyrwa, Ulrich. (1999). Holocaust. Notizen zur Begriffsgeschichte. *Jahrbuch für Antisemitismusforschung, 8,* 300–311.

Yahil, Leni. (1969). *The Rescue of the Danish Jewry. Test of a Democracy.* Philadelphia: Jewish Publication Society.

Yahil, Leni. (1990). *The Holocaust. The Fate of European Jewry, 1932–1945.* Oxford Univesity Press.

Zuccotti, Susan. (1987). *The Italians and the Holocaust. Persecution, Rescue and Survival.* London: Halban.

Violence within the Military

GERHARD KÜMMEL AND PAUL KLEIN

I. INTRODUCTION

The actual or threatened use of violence is one of the essential characteristics of the military. More precisely, the military is a "social organization for the achievement of political aims through the threatened and actual use of armed force" (Wachtler, 1988:268). The armed forces, in the words of Carl von Clausewitz, are an instrument of the modern state. They are recruited, paid and deployed in the interests of the security of an individual state, the term "security" here referring primarily to the external security of one state against threats from other states. Traditionally, the functions of the armed forces are defined in two different ways. While the deterrent and defensive capability can be regarded as a defensive role, the ability to launch an attack on another state, in order to assert national interests and claims of political domination, can be seen as an offensive role. This aspect, however, has gradually lost its legitimacy over the course of the twentieth century, as witness the prohibition of violence enshrined in international law.

In the global political climate after the end of the Cold War, these two traditional functions have ceased to be politically relevant in some macroregions of the world. Hopes of global peace have gained fresh impetus, and there are widespread calls for disarmament, arms control, and a reduction in the strength of the armed forces. Nevertheless, the armed conflicts that still continue in many parts of the world have a spill-over potential which threatens to spread to the existing islands of prosperity and peace. This might be called the dark side of globalization: no effective barriers can be erected around regions of conflict. For this reason, the planning staffs of many countries devise strategies for humanitarian intervention and pacifying and peace-keeping missions, generally comprising both civilian and military aspects. These missions have added a third, nontraditional role to the traditional functions of the military. They introduce the idea of a diversification of military deployments (cf. Bredow & Kümmel, 1999). At the same time, this means that the military as an institution, and its potential for violence and destruction, will remain indispensable for the foreseeable future.

W. Heitmeyer and J. Hagan (eds.), *International Handbook of Violence Research*, 171–187.
© 2003 Kluwer Academic Publishers. Printed in the Netherlands.

It follows that the *modus operandi* of the military is subject to contextual changes, the reasons for which may lie in individual societies or in the overall international picture. We can identify an important, though not continuous, trend here over the course of time: democratization. Democratization means more rights for the individual, tighter control by society over the military, and the increased subjection of military action to international standards and international law. As a result, the military is losing its sense of inviolability and secrecy; the membrane of the interface between society, the public and the military is becoming more permeable, so that a more critical eye is now directed at violations of rules by and in the military. It is these violations, this violence, with which we are concerned here. Hitherto, there has been no study that has addressed this subject comprehensively and systematically. One reason for this may be that the academic discipline that deals with the military and its relationship to society—military sociology (cf. Kümmel, 2000)—often suffers "from the oppressive dominance of the field with which it is concerned," a dominance reflected in an excess of research issues concerned with day-to-day politics (Lippert, 1989:140). Secondly, there are various obstacles to be overcome before soldiers who commit such violations or become victims or witnesses of them report these occurrences to the competent authorities or release information to the public. Finally, at a time when the acceptance and legitimacy of the armed forces in society is crumbling, they have an understandable interest in ensuring that such violations do not take place or, if they do, are not publicized. Academic access to this area of research, therefore, may well not always be easy. But the control of the military institution over information is crumbling as well, especially in democratic societies, so that knowledge of breaches of rules cannot be suppressed *ad infinitum*. Not only that, but there are signs of a process—admittedly not an uninterrupted one—by which the military is increasingly developing into a self-reflexive institution, recognizing that knowledge of this and other problem areas may be important to its functional capabilities.

It follows from this that violence within the military is a terrain that is not easily mapped. The paths that we are now going to try to clear through the thicket of this subject thus represent something of a voyage of exploration. The problem begins at the outset: in identifying the subject matter. Violence, in this handbook, is understood as a social phenomenon, a destructive activity that occurs in cases of conflict as a result of a fabric of individual or collective actors, institutional conditions, and public or private opportunity structures in association with conceptual structures and particular allegiances, that allows room for different dynamics. But the actual and threatened use of violence are the *raison d'être* of the military. So where does violence within the military become a problem?

We are concerned here with violations of standards and rules, so that the legitimate use of violence by troops, sanctioned by national and international legislation, does not fall within our scope. Our interest, then, is focused on forms of unlawful violence practiced by the armed forces. The victims of that violence, however, are to be found in a variety of areas. Because a soldier's profession brings him into contact with members of the armed forces—those to which he himself belongs or those with which formal or informal ties are established in the context of international bilateral and multilateral military cooperation—the victims are to be found (1) among the narrower or broader circle of his colleagues. Because he also has dealings with members of a society to which he himself belongs, they are also to be found (2) in his narrower (family) or broader social environment. And because he can be deployed on military operations beyond his own national frontiers, they can be found (3) among the enemy troops and the population of the enemy country.

II.   EMPIRICAL RESULTS AND THEORETICAL APPROACHES

1.   Violence Among Comrades

"Your negligence has caused the deaths of our sons—the soldiers and sailors, the sergeants and petty officers—or their mutilation and moral degeneration. Your refusal to control the generals, your wretched agents enmeshed in a web of corruption and war crimes, makes you the murderer of our children. We ... as parents ... say that it is impossible for us to send our sons to serve in this bandit army" (Internationale Gemeinschaft für Menschenrechte (IGFM) 1991:12). These words are to be found in a letter dated September 9, 1990, from the First All-Union Congress of Soldiers' Parents to the President of the Soviet Union, Mikhail S. Gorbachev. The letter forms part of a collection assembled by the German section of the International Society for Human Rights (ISHR) on the public activities of the Committee of Soviet (later Russian) Soldiers' Mothers, which was awarded the alternative Nobel Prize in 1996. The letter reports on the notorious and dreaded practice of *dedovshina* (hazing), a system combining drill, violence, torture and rape, under which young recruits, the "greenhorns," were subjected to virtually unlimited, organized cruelty by the longer-serving elder comrades. Humiliation, mental torture, oral and anal rape and other forms of physical abuse, resulting in broken bones, organ damage, head injuries, physical and mental disability, and unexplained deaths each year running into four-figures and officially recorded as accident or suicide—these all formed part of the daily routine in the Soviet armed forces. Evidently, non-Russian recruits such as those from the Baltic States were frequent victims of *dedovshina*, so that the system also contained elements of victimization based on ethnicity or nationality. Soldiers regarded as intellectuals were also singled out. Furthermore, there were isolated reported cases of the victims resorting to retaliatory violence.

Dedovshina is by no means a thing of the past, as one might assume in view of the breakup of the USSR. In the 1990s, for example, reports on the practice in the Russian army appeared in the press. The system owes some of its durability to widespread ignorance, tacit acceptance, and occasional active support by NCOs and officers. Clearly, the common soldier is still regarded by sections of the officer corps as "the dirt beneath their feet" (Siegl, 2000:13). In addition, the system is probably assisted by the general political, economic, and social situation, where anomie is widespread, undermining the military ethos and military discipline. Evidence of this can be found in reports on the sale of Russian weaponry, the cannibalizing of missiles and heavy military hardware to sell the noble metals they contain, and dubious dealings with buildings at times when Russian troops were being paid irregularly, if at all. These incidents often involved officers, even generals, and there were reports that even elite units were participating.

The example of the Soviet/Russian military is certainly not an isolated one. The collapse of military discipline and the softening of the military code of honor, resulting in serious offenses by soldiers against their own comrades, are not confined to the armed forces of authoritarian or totalitarian political systems or to periods of sweeping social change, crisis, and anomie. Armed forces all over the world have been the subject of similar reports. For example, the picture of crime in the West German army during the late 1970s was very similar to that in society as a whole. In the years 1978–80, between 13,700 and 15,500 soldiers, most of them (nearly 80%) conscripts and NCOs (nearly 20%) were convicted of offenses, of which 16–17% were classified as actual bodily harm, often under the influence of alcohol (Klinge-Wipfelder, 1984). In the early 1960s, the German public was shaken by the "Nagold case." In a paratroop training company at Nagold, a candidate NCO ordered troops to do push-ups over an open clasp knife. Even today, the German army sees isolated cases of degrading treatment and abuse of subordinates by superiors, brawls among the troops, and violent assaults on NCOs or officers, as witness, for example, the annual reports of the commissioner for the armed forces.

Acts of violence by soldiers against their comrades in arms are encountered in the armed forces of other democratic societies, too. In early 1995, for example, the Canadian public was shocked by the disclosure of a video showing humiliating and degrading rites of initiation in a paratroop unit. Sexual molestation and violence is also an important problem area, and likely to become more so as the number of female soldiers in the armed forces of many countries increases. This is clear from the American example, where this phenomenon has already been under investigation for some considerable time as a result of various high-profile incidents such as the Tailhook scandal of 1991. The likelihood of being a victim of sexual harassment in the American armed forces is much greater—three or four times greater, according to some estimates—than in the population at large. In a survey of more than 3,600 American female veterans, 55% had experienced sexual harassment and 23% sexual violence during their service (Skinner et al., 2000). By contrast, a study undertaken by the American Department of Defense in 1995 found that 4% of all female troops in the United States Army had been victims of actual or attempted rape and 61% had experienced various forms of sexual molestation (High, 1997:4).

The likelihood of becoming a victim of sexual violence seems to be significantly higher in the army than in the air force or navy. By comparison with women who have experienced neither sexual harassment nor sexual violence in the military, those who have have suffered from aftereffects that adversely affect the efficiency and effectiveness of the service. They report unfit for duty more frequently, have lower job satisfaction, encounter more problems in finding employment after leaving the service, and suffer from more frequent feelings of anxiety, more serious problems with alcohol and drugs, more frequent bouts of depression, and more intensive feelings of anger and hatred (Skinner et al., 2000).

Sexual harassment and violence have also been studied in the context of military operations. In a study of 160 American women soldiers in the Gulf War, 13 of the 160 questioned reported incidents of sexual violence; 52 reported physical and 105 verbal sexual harassment (Wolfe et al., 1998). Although these figures are comparable with those produced by studies of American female students, they are higher than those for the population at large. These results, then, suggest "that military settings may be prone to increased sexual aggression toward women" (Wolfe et al., 1998:51).

Although sexual harassment and violence have for some time been generally understood as problems that mainly affect women, male soldiers may also suffer. As long ago as 1988, the American Defense Department conducted a survey of 20,000 female and male soldiers. In total, over 40% of those questioned reported experiencing sexual harassment, women doing so much more often than men (70.1% against 36.9%). In both cases, the perpetrators were generally their fellow soldiers (men 47.7%, women 43.2%). Women were much more likely than men to be harassed by their direct military superiors (21.9% against 11.8%) or other higher-ranking military personnel (men 8.6%, women 18.7%). By contrast, men were more often harassed by subordinates (men 20.3%, women 11.3%). In the case of women, the perpetrators had been almost exclusively male: 76.0% were men acting alone while 21.1% of cases involved sexual harassment by two or more men. Among the male victims, however, the picture was much more diverse: 25.7% of offenders were men acting alone, under 8% two or more men, 47% women acting alone, about 10% two or more women, and in nearly 7% of cases both men and women were involved. Furthermore, it was also possible to form a link—stronger in the case of women than that of men—between harassment and rank: the lower a person's rank, the greater the probability of becoming a victim of sexual harassment (Firestone & Harris, 1994). Overall, the Firestone and Harris findings also cast light on the problem of sexual harassment with men as victims, though it also becomes clear that women are far more likely to be affected than men. Firestone and Harris (1994:34) referred to "a pervasive pattern of sexual harassment of women that spans rank and work site locations."

It should be borne in mind here that the data quoted give only an incomplete picture of the extent of the problem of sexual harassment, and of sexual violence; the true figures are probably even higher. Some of the features of military life are identified as being structurally favorable to such conduct: the environment is traditionally a male-dominated one, in which male troops are far more numerous than female, so that women, too, usually serve under male superiors; in this kind of setting, which in any case exists against a patriarchal sociocultural and social background, traditional concepts of relationships between the sexes, misogynistic attitudes, and the identification of the military with masculinity and the acceptance of interpersonal violence are relatively widespread (cf. Firestone & Harris, 1994; Polaschek, Ward, & Hudson, 1997:121; Wolfe et al., 1998:51; Seifert, 1996).

In addition, it is argued that the specific military culture makes it more difficult to deal with sexual violence and, in particular, to report it, so that there are indications of significant differences between sexual violence in a military and in a nonmilitary context (Skinner et al., 2000:305). Some authorities, however, imply the opposite opinion, maintaining that the structures are such as to provide women with a positive incentive to make accusations—not all of them justified—of sexual molestation and violence (DeYoung, 2000).

2. Violence in Soldiers' Families

When considering the subject of violence in soldiers' families, a distinction can be drawn between violence against the spouse or partner (usually the wife) and violence against children, though the two may take place concurrently in many families. Studies of violence in military families have hitherto been undertaken especially in the North American armed forces, and against a background of widespread domestic violence in society as a whole (Straus & Gelles, 1990). According to 1982 figures provided by American police forces, violence against the spouse/partner takes place in 28% of all families (Wasileski, Callaghan-Chaffee, & Chaffee, 1982), and in a 1985 study, physical violence is said to be a problem in one out of six American couples (Hotaling et al., 1988). In the same year, of every 1,000 American children 619 were reportedly exposed to minor levels of violence and 110 to serious violence, a picture that is largely consistent with the situation in 1975 (Wolfner & Gelles, 1993). In Canada during the 1990s, 10% of women were assaulted by their husbands/partners; 25% of girls and 10% of boys experienced sexual abuse (Truscott & Wait, 1996:24ff.). In the light of this general data, it is hardly surprising that such events are also to be encountered in military families.

However, analysis of violence in soldiers' families to date provides only an incomplete picture for both Canada and the United States. Even so, there are important findings for some areas. For example, the records of the central registry of the United States Air Force for 1986 show 6,229 cases of child abuse, of which nearly 50% were substantiated.

TABLE II-1-2-3.1. Types of abuses in absolute numbers based on central register of U.S. Air Force

		Physical abuse	Sexual abuse	Emotional abuse	Neglect	Number of cases
1988	of children	1,306	562	175	1,131	3,174
	of spouse	2,333	13	116	14	2,476
1989	of children	1,345	512	277	1,195	3,329
	of spouse	3,094	17	276	10	3,397

Source: Mollerstrom, Patchner, & Milner, 1992:371.

In the same year, there were 2,929 reported cases of spousal abuse. Of these, nearly 84% were substantiated. The figures for 1989 were in some cases significantly higher: of 6,670 cases of child abuse, nearly 49% were validated. The spousal abuse figures rose even more sharply, by about one third to nearly 4,000 cases. Of these, about 82% were confirmed. The forms of abuse and their relative frequency are shown in Table II-1-2-3.1, where it should be noted that two or more forms of abuse may occur in a single instance.

For the United States Air Force, a further study by the same group of authors on child abuse in the years 1987–92 produced the results shown in Table II-1-2-3.2.

A comparable study of substantiated cases of child abuse in the families of the American military also exists for the army, though the period considered is much longer, covering the years 1975–97. The study distinguishes between similar categories of abuse but also establishes two categories of physical abuse, depending on severity. The results for the more serious forms of abuse are shown in Table II-1-2-3.3.

For the Canadian armed forces, data is available from the military police, the Directorate of Personnel Career Administration, the Directorate of Health Treatment Services and the Military Family Resource Centres. However, as the results differ little from the figures given for the American military, there is no need to examine them more closely here (but cf. Truscott & Wait, 1996).

TABLE II-1-2-3.2. Child abuse in the period of 1987–1992 based on central register of U.S. Air Force

	1987	1988	1989	1990	1991	1992
Reported cases	6,172	6,463	6,501	6,877	6,988	7,177
Substantiated cases	2,998	3,275	3,314	3,565	3,617	3,872
thereof:						
Physical abuse	1,348	1,236	1,215	1,360	1,388	1,306
Neglect	1,019	1,039	1,150	1,117	1,306	1,113
Sexual abuse	521	460	488	487	409	497
Emotional abuse	199	373	275	323	255	385
Multiple abuse	87	80	59	25	13	4

Source: Mollerstrom, Patchner, & Milner, 1995:327.

TABLE II-1-2-3.3. Serious physical and sexual abuses in the period of 1975–1997 in families of American soldiers

Year	Serious physical abuse %	Sexual abuse %	Number of cases
1975	—	—	9
1976	0.8	1.6	125
1977	3.2	2.3	309
1978	1.2	2.8	431
1979	1.4	3.7	654
1980	0.9	3.5	911
1981	1.2	5.2	1,252
1982	1.0	5.9	1,669
1983	5.7	5.7	2,156
1984	13.9	8.2	2,722
1985	11.2	8.6	2,800
1986	11.6	11.1	3,336
1987	5.6	12.1	4,236
1988	3.2	11.6	4,327
1989	3.5	11.1	4,653
1990	3.9	12.7	4,797
1991	2.7	12.3	4,907
1992	3.4	16.0	4,303
1993	3.6	17.3	4,351
1994	3.8	14.7	4,109
1995	3.4	12.4	3,607
1996	3.4	13.6	3,643
1997	4.6	12.5	3,334

Source: McCarroll et al., 1999:858.

The data produced by these studies show, depending on category, slightly or significantly lower rates of abuse than among the civilian population, but these can only be regarded as approximations. For one thing, the population data on which the abuse rates are based are themselves based on estimates. For another, these data are affected by "underreporting" (Truscott & Wait, 1996:V), in other words based on information provided by persons in care or cases officially reported to the military authorities, which therefore do not reflect the true, higher extent. The fact is that a reported case of family violence can adversely affect the husband's professional career and therefore the financial security of the family as a whole. For this reason, battered wives sometimes protect their husbands against disciplinary activities and military justice by failing to report occurrences or electing not to undergo medical treatment. It is also assumed that the military, as an institution, is more likely to record cases where the socioeconomic status and educational level of those involved is lower, so that domestic violence in officers' families tends to be largely ignored, one consequence of which is that there generally seems to be a correlation between the abuse rate and military rank (Cronin, 1995; Mollerstrom, Patchner, & Milner, 1995; Raiha & Soma, 1997). On the other hand, there are factors which argue in favor of a lower overall rate of abuse in the military context—though not as much lower as has been cited. In particular, the figures for neglect—a less serious category of abuse—actually appear to be substantially lower than in the civilian population. The explanation suggested here is that military families enjoy a relatively high level of financial security, because at least one of the two spouses is in permanent employment. Educational levels are relatively high, at least as far as the servicemen themselves are concerned, and their training and everyday routine involve a program in which they learn self-control and a soldierly code of conduct. This, however, is evidently effective only up to a certain level, since the fact that the figures for the other forms of abuse are only slightly lower and hence relatively similar indicates "that factors influencing physical, emotional, and sexual abuse may not differ markedly between military and civilian families" (Raiha & Soma, 1997:765).

It can thus be assumed, initially, that the factors which studies of the civilian population have found to play a part in the abuse of spouses and children are similar in the military context. The use of violence in the domestic setting may be a form of behavior that is learned and handed down from one generation to the next by a process of imitation and modeling (Wasileski, Callaghan-Chaffee, & Chaffee, 1982). It may be encouraged by the abuse of alcohol and drugs, low socioeconomic status, low self-esteem, social isolation, personality disorders, certain characteristics in the victim, social and structural stress, and related environmental conditions. In cases of violence in military families, the widespread culture of machismo, the hierarchical and authoritarian nature of the military, based on the principle of obedience to orders, the training in the use of violence, the social and geographical isolation resulting from numerous moves and periods of absence on active service, constantly recurring to disrupt the equilibrium within the family system, and the soldier's potentially and actually life-threatening employment may act as stressors that encourage violence. There are, however, some factors that tend to produce the opposite effect, such as the social-psychological screening before induction into the armed forces and before active service deployment, career reviews, military discipline, the soldierly ethos, and the extensive system of social support within the organization, although recourse to this network of social support does involve the risk that private matters may become public property within the institution (cf. Truscott & Wait, 1996:12–20; De Jongh & Bassett-Scarfe, 1987; De Jongh, Bassett-Scarfe, & Malpas, 1988).

The basic question of whether the military context encourages domestic violence, and whether or not it produces a greater susceptibility to domestic violence, is answered in different ways by researchers, depending on how these influencing factors are evaluated. Truscott and Wait (1996) are undecided, regarding the risk factors as approximately the same in both military and civilian environments. Whereas the studies referred to above indicate a lower level of susceptibility to domestic violence, other authors argue that the risk to military families is greater, referring to the legitimization of the use of violence in the military and to stressors genuinely associated with the military profession (Martin, 1976; Dubanovski & McIntosh, 1984). This interpretation seems to be supported by a study of American students at the University of Maryland in the mid-1990s. All of their parents were stationed in Europe, and all of them worked in the American armed forces, though some were civilian and others military personnel. The children of parents involved in military duties reported a significantly higher incidence of domestic violence (spousal abuse, in this case) than the children of civilian parents. These differences applied irrespective of ethnic origin or military rank (Cronin, 1995). Cronin's study, however, cannot unambiguously determine "whether the military environment contributes to increased spousal violence or whether individuals prone to abusive behavior are more likely to join the military" (Cronin, 1995:121).

3. Violence in the Enemy's Country

As regards the real use of armed force in war, certain ground rules developed during the nineteenth and twentieth centuries. In broad outline, they can be summarized as follows: only other soldiers are to be regarded as enemies, they must be armed, no atrocities must be committed in combat, and enemy troops who have surrendered must be spared. The civilian population (especially women and children) are not to be regarded as enemies. In the armed forces of many countries, especially Western ones, soldiers have been and are required to abide by these rules, which are codified in international military law, are intended to reduce violence, and form a list of standards that represent an "ethical minimum" (Dau, 1985:299). However, past and present examples of violations of this code are legion—even in today's humanitarian military actions and peace missions. And, being classified as excessive use of force, they can be identified as violations of the rules (van Doorn & Hendrix, 1975).

If we confine ourselves to the period of World War II and afterwards, it is an established historical fact that German atrocities against the civilian population and cases of mass murder were not confined to members of the SS or the *Einsatzgruppen* (special service units). Members of the German army collaborated in such activities from time to time or even engaged in them on their own account (cf. Krausnick, 1985). In Poland in 1941, police battalions, most of them made up of reservists, literally declared open season on Jews, thousands of people being shot dead or taken to concentration camps (cf. Browning, 1997). When the Red Army advanced into Germany, its progress was accompanied by mass rapes. In the Pacific theater, Japanese troops were notorious for the cruelties practiced on prisoners of war and the civilian population (Daws, 1994) and, especially, for the mass sexual enslavement of Korean "comfort women." American troops, too, took no prisoners in this theater. The commander of the submarine USS *Wahoo*, for example, turned his machine guns on Japanese soldiers struggling in the sea, in violation of international military law, which did not prevent his being awarded the Navy Cross and the Army Distinguished Service Cross (Dower, 1986:330). Similar offenses such as the torture and murder of prisoners of war and assaults on the civilian population were committed by the Dutch army in Indonesia (van Doorn & Hendrix, 1975) and by French troops in the Algerian war (on the treatment of POWs see, for example, Sutker et al., 1991; Margalit, Ezion and Rabinowitz, 1993). And as late as the beginning of the 1970s, 15 officers and NCOs of the penal battalion of the French Foreign Legion on Corsica maltreated the legionaries imprisoned there, some of whom died while others were driven mad (cf. Alainmat, 1976). During the Vietnam war, whole villages such as My Lai and Son My were virtually wiped off the map, none of the troops involved doing anything to prevent it. And in the war in the Balkans, the mass rape of women was employed as an instrument and element of warfare (cf. Stiglmayer, 1993).

In the very recent past, acts of violence have been committed even during humanitarian deployments and UN peace missions. In mid-March 1993, Canadian paratroops in Somalia tortured the 16-year-old Shidane Arone to death. Similar accusations were made against Belgian and Italian troops in Somalia, though so far the military court proceedings in Brussels have resulted only in acquittals for lack of evidence—despite the existence of incriminating photographs—while inquiries in Italy have produced no concrete results at all. In the former Yugoslavia, too, UN soldiers were guilty of attacks on the civilian population, including rape and other crimes of violence. For example, Canadian UN troops stationed at Bacovici (Bosnia-Herzegovina) made headlines with massive violations of discipline, including such offenses as alcohol abuse, sexual misconduct, physical violence, insubordination and black marketeering (cf. Omaar & de Waal, 1993; Haas and Kernic, 1998; Winslow, 1997, 1998).

Several attempts have been made, on different levels, to explain such misconduct by the armed forces and the violence to which it leads. It is notable, for example, that those involved in many of these acts of violence were very often professional soldiers—elite units such as the *Waffen-SS*, the U.S. marines or the paratroops. This, then, raises the suspicion that service in such units appeals to a particular type of person, whose characteristics include a taste for adventure, ruthlessness, toughness, aggression, and a degree of social rootlessness. He is attracted by a "(distorted) image of archaic, martial activity" (Vogt, 1993:117), focusing on the glorification of violence and the idealization of male superiority. If such soldiers find themselves in an environment where, because of existing cultural differences or reasons of racial ideology, they perceive themselves as superior to certain sections of the population, this sense of power may seduce them into exercising their prejudices and ruthlessly breaking down any resistance to them. Often, too, an exaggerated display of subservience results in a sense of omnipotence among the strong. One reason for joining an elite unit or volunteering for special duties may also be that the person concerned suffers from low self-esteem and seeks to compensate for his inferiority by membership of a particularly "tough" community. Such efforts to prove to himself and others that he is a full member of the group can easily lead to overreactions that spill over into violence.

John Steiner (1980), in a study of men who volunteered for the SS, reached the conclusion that there was a process of self-selection for duties involving brutality. His hypothesis, based on Adorno's (1950) concept of the authoritarian personality, was that individuals with a tendency to violence seek opportunities for it. Ultimately, too, there are two types that constantly recur among soldiers, described in Eysenck's typology (1970) as the neurotic and the psychopath. The first type, the neurotic, needs a leader in whom he can trust and a group that accepts him. Real problems occur only when this is not the case. Even if unusual or unexpected events occur in his work or at home, he shows a high degree of sensitivity and a low tolerance threshold for frustration. If this kind of soldier has no ability or opportunity to discuss his problems, or if those problems are not understood or accepted, the uncontrolled use of violence is never far away. Problems are encountered more often with the other type—the soldier with psychopathic tendencies. They result from nonintegration into the group or lack of recognition from a superior. If a soldier of this kind is below or above average intelligence, he may call attention to himself by acts of violence. In the case of the less intelligent soldier, his potential for aggression can easily run out of control, resulting in a tendency to be quarrelsome and unpredictably aggressive. The intelligent soldier, by contrast, is liable to question the acts of his superiors and seek to become the unofficial leader of the group. Often, he is intelligent enough to make sure he never oversteps the limit and commits a breach of discipline, but this is not always the case. If not, his aggression may be directed inwards—against his fellow soldiers—or outwards, against innocent bystanders (cf. Kernic, 1996).

However, reducing the phenomenon of violence to certain character traits and to self-selection is not an adequate explanation of brutality. After all, there have been notable cases of violence by military units which could certainly not be described as volunteers and had not been subjected to any selection process of any kind. For example, Reserve Police Battalion 101 was not a collection of "Rambo" types but made up of some 500 "totally normal" men who were too old for the German army. Their orders were to hunt down Jews in Poland, single out men who were still fit for work to serve in work details, and shoot the others (the old and sick, women and children). Before their first mission, the battalion commander offered to reassign to other duties any of his troops who lacked the stomach for this task. Only 12 men out of 500 stepped forward (Browning, 1997). The determining factor here seems to have been not so much personality traits as situative forces, as described for example in Haney, Banks and Zimbardo (1983) in their prison experiment and Milgram (1985) in his classical experiments. The members of Police Battalion 101 obeyed their murderous instructions just as the majority of the students randomly selected as "prison warders" in the simulated prison situation rapidly resorted to brutality, degradation and humiliation, and many of Milgram's subjects dealt out "lethal" electric shocks when instructed to do so by an authority.

Another explanation for the use of violence against civilians or captured/disarmed soldiers is that those who commit such acts hope to be rewarded for them, or at least have no reason to fear sanction, because they can assume that their superiors approve of their actions or will at least tolerate them. Indeed, brutality and even law-breaking was more of a recommendation in the SS than a stain on a man's record. The best example of this is the career of Oskar Dirlewanger: his 36th SS Infantry Division was composed mainly of professional criminals, who butchered the civilian population with the utmost brutality (Artzt, 1987:106). Hans Loritz, one of the commandants of Sachsenhausen concentration camp, may be cited as another example (Segev, 1992:199). Even misconduct and brutality on the part of UN troops is rarely punished. If any penalties are imposed at all, they are usually innocuous. In most cases, the worst that can happen to a UN soldier is for him to be sent home (cf. Kernic, 1996). Far more frequently, attempts are made to play down or conceal the criminal acts—assuming they become known in the first place. In the case of the Canadian UN troops, for example, a parliamentary commission of inquiry concluded that senior officers had persistently tried to obstruct them in their work (Winslow, 1997). Even the UN itself has often tried to hush up the dark side of its peacekeeping operations: the UN special envoy for Bosnia, Yasushi Akashi, reacted to charges that UN soldiers had been guilty of violence and misconduct by telling the press, "It is important that UNPROFOR as an international force should be above criticism" (quoted in Haas & Kernic, 1998:171).

In addition, abnormal behavior and violence against the population are quite often a way in which a soldier reacts to a situation with which he feels unable to cope. In World War II—and also in Vietnam and Algeria, and in the recent UN and NATO deployments in, for example, Somalia and the former Yugoslavia—the soldiers have quite often been confronted by irregular troops, guerrillas and terrorists whose actions flouted the conventions of international military law, combining deviousness and cruelty. They committed atrocities and then, quite often, disappeared anonymously among the civilian population. The regulars were often helpless to deal with such conduct. But they saw its results—women and children massacred or mutilated, and in some cases their own comrades as well—and sometimes exacted "an eye for an eye." When this occurred, they frequently failed to distinguish between guilty and innocent, regarding any member of the indigenous population as a covert enemy who was liable to attack unless he himself was attacked first. Any qualms of conscience are particularly likely to be suppressed if such acts of violence receive institutional approval (cf. van Doorn & Hendrix, 1975).

Soldiers on active service can also become a problem if their psychological disposition makes them unsuited to endure unusual conditions: separation from their families, constant alertness, boredom, lack of privacy, homesickness, or celibacy. The first signs of this are behavioral changes: for example, excessive anxiety, shirking, or seeking refuge in hypochondria or simulated illness. More serious manifestations are also possible, however, such as outbreaks of rage, arguing or fighting with comrades or anyone else who gets in the way, such as local people drafted in to do auxiliary tasks, or quite simply the population in general. Recourse to alcohol and/or drugs is not unusual and encourages or exacerbates these forms of behavior (cf. Kernic, 1996).

Bullying of the population or prisoners, brutality, torture, murder, and rape are quite often group phenomena, sometimes reinforced by excessive use of alcohol and drugs. On the one hand, this can easily become self-perpetuating, with each individual trying to prove to the others that he can be even tougher, more brutal, and more insensitive, or at least that he is not to be regarded as a coward or weakling. On the other hand, nonparticipation in acts of violence can all too easily be regarded by others as an antisocial act, so that the prevailing attitude—especially on service abroad—can become one of exaggerated loyalty and automatic solidarity with the group, which is seen as the extended family. Group cohesion, then, is an ambivalent phenomenon (cf. Bryant, 1974, 1979; Browning, 1997; Winslow, 1997, 1998).

Informal or formal leaders can also play an important part in violent behavior. If they are accepted as authorities, the other group members follow their instructions and wishes even when they are clearly unlawful. The behavior of troops responsible for guarding prisoners of war or concentration camp inmates provides dreadful confirmation of the extent to which people's actions are influenced by (supposed) authorities and their environment. Contrary to what is often claimed, virtually no one in the concentration camps was forced to commit atrocities, and in the course of the postwar trials in Germany not a single case came to light where it was proven that a soldier who refused to take part in the shooting of prisoners suffered any serious consequences for doing so (Jäger, 1982:95–122). Even so, the great majority of camp staff fitted in with the prevailing climate and in some cases practiced almost inconceivable cruelties (Artzt, 1987:107). In addition to excessive trust in authority and reflex military discipline, a reduced sense of personal responsibility and involvement in such acts of violence can also be prompted by blind obedience (Bryant, 1974; Walkin, 1979; Osiel, 1999), encouraged for example by the drill in barracks and cadet schools described by Theweleit—in volume two of *Male Fantasies*, which makes the soldier into a "stereometric figure" (Elias Canetti). In this instance, the nature of the military as a "total institution," in the words of Erving Goffman (1962), seems to play a supporting part. Barracks life and relative social isolation, the sense of being physically cut off from society, is a feature of the military; it has its own particular greeting rituals, dress code and standardized habits of speech, generating a quite heavy pressure to conform. A specific feature of socialization in the military, then, is the encouragement of the "us and them" mindset, which makes it more difficult to develop empathy with the other side.

Both from Somalia and from Yugoslavia, there were reports of UN troops allegedly participating in rape. Opinions differ as to why such acts form part of the routine of war. Kernic (1996) argues, for example with reference to UN deployment, that soldiers build up sexual expectations before such a mission, which are generally disappointed. More typical of the reality of active service are constant confinement to barracks, lack of contact with the population, and an absence of opportunities for leisure activities. A state of tension builds up between the increasingly powerful sexual desire and the inability to do anything to relieve it, eventually resulting either in sexual violence or in other forms of deviant behavior such as increased consumption of alcohol or drugs. It must not be overlooked here, though, that troops can obtain sexual satisfaction in brothels, which very rapidly sprout out of the ground around UN camps. Ruth Seifert (1993) sees rape during and after hostilities not as an aggressive expression of sexuality but as a sexual expression of aggression. Rape is a demonstration of masculine power, a display of the ability to subjugate others and take possession of them. Its objective is not to satisfy lust but to humiliate. It is aimed not only against the women who are the immediate victims but, primarily, against their menfolk, who are in no position to protect their women, so that their masculinity is undermined as a result.

Finally, with regard to peacekeeping operations and humanitarian missions, it has been assumed that their psychological challenges, especially the need for restraint in dangerous situations, are particularly difficult for troops to handle, especially for those with combat experience. This pressure can result in violence against fellow soldiers, the raping of female members of the civilian population, and even domestic violence after the troops return home (cf. Litz et al., 1997b). This leads to the assumption that "peacekeeping operations under perilous conditions may represent a unique class of potentially traumatizing experiences not sufficiently captured by traditional descriptors of war zone exposure ... [T]he effects of war zone stress in a peacekeeping context may represent the prototype of a new paradigm in military operations" (Litz, Orsillo, & Friedman, 1997a:183).

III.   APPROACHES TO PREVENTION

The subject of violence within the military, three aspects of which have been dealt with in this article, would dissolve into nothingness if either one of its constituent parts—violence and the military—ceased to exist. The former would require the creation of a new human race and a new social existence, and is therefore unlikely. The latter seems to be almost equally improbable, because mankind has always lived, and will live for the foreseeable future, in dangerous contexts that make it necessary to use violent means as a specific way of containing violence. The only realistic objective, then, can be to reduce the forms of unlawful violence described in this article by taking precautions to rule out its use from the outset. This, of course, cannot be completely achieved, though any reduction would be welcomed and is the responsibility of both the military and society in general. As far as domestic violence in the American armed forces is concerned, each military unit has for some time had its "family advocacy program," and the Canadian forces are now also following a similar line. Programs like these, which exist at least in embryo in the armed forces of other countries as well, amount almost to an extension—admittedly, one still in need of improvement—of the social welfare network within the institution. The same applies to training, educational, and antistress programs which, in the area of unlawful violence among fellow soldiers, aim to increase awareness and prevent sexual harassment and sexual violence in the armed forces. In this context, the aspects of discipline, military justice, and criminal law must also not be overlooked. The aim here must be to ensure that the precise facts of the case are covered by the appropriate legislation, and to institute the necessary proceedings immediately in the event of violations. The threat and institution of disciplinary and legal proceedings in the appropriate situations is also a necessary part of preventing the unlawful use of violence in enemy territory. This preventive work must also form part of training and conflict preparation programs for active service abroad, as indeed it already does in many armed forces. The responsibility of superiors to act in a way that performs a special role model function, and so creates a climate that is hostile to misconduct, must constantly be emphasized. This, in any case, is also the duty of each individual soldier among his comrades and also the responsibility of the broader society of which the armed forces form a part.

Considered all in all, this is certainly no easy undertaking, since it requires the military as an institution to improve its levels of transparency, reflexivity, participation, and what we may call internal democracy. It also requires the armed forces to be prepared to collect data and information on the three identified areas of violence within the military and to permit and encourage academic studies of these problem areas—studies which may also perhaps reveal areas of interference and interpenetration between the three fields of violence. There are convincing indications that such effects exist. For example, the phenomenon of posttraumatic stress syndrome (PTSD) has been studied with particular reference to the example of America's Vietnam veterans (Deering et al., 1996; Southwick, Morgan, & Charney, 1997; King et al., 1998; Shay, 1998; Taft et al., 1999; King et al., 1999; Schnurr et al., 1999). This is a form of depression that can arise as a result of "normal" combat activities, involvement in violations of international military law, and captivity. The traumatic events experienced both by victims of violence and by its perpetrators can clearly pave the way for aggression and violent behavior after the troops return home: the violence rate is significantly higher among PTSD patients than among veterans who have not suffered from it (cf. Kulka et al., 1990; Sutker et al., 1991; Chemtob et al., 1997; Monahan & Steadman, 1994; Zatzick et al., 1997; Engdahl et al., 1997). In addition, there may be a connection between domestic violence and sexual harassment/violence in the military. Broader studies of this kind might possibly provide answers to the central questions involved in this subject area. How does the military context influence violent behavior in the three areas discussed? Does it have no effect on that behavior? Or does it promote it by reinforcing an existing predisposition? Or does it even generate it via socialization in the military? As these questions show, the scope for research is extensive.

Translated by Richard Sharp

REFERENCES

Adorno, Theodor W., Else Frenkel-Brunswik, Daniel J. Levinson, & R. Nevitt Sanford. (1950). *The Authoritarian Personality*. New York: Harper.

Alainmat, Henry. (1976). *L'épreuve. Le 'bagne' de la Légion*. Paris.

Artzt, Heinz. (1987). *Mörder in Uniform*. Reinbek: Rowohlt.

Bredow, Wilfried von, & Gerhard Kümmel. (1999). *Das Militär und die Herausforderung globaler Sicherheit. Der Spagat zwischen traditionalen und nicht-traditionalen Rollen. SOWI-Arbeitspapier Nr. 119.* Strausberg: SOWI.

Browning, Christopher R. (1997). *Ganz normale Männer. Das Reserve-Polizeibataillon 101 und die Endlösung in Polen*. Reinbek: Rowohlt.

Bryant, Clifton D. (1974). Socialization for Khaki-Collar Crime: Military Training as Criminalization Process. In Clifton D. Bryant (Ed.), *Deviant Behavior. Occupational and Organizational Bases*. Chicago: Rand McNally, pp. 239–251.

Bryant, Clifton D. (1979). *Khaki-Collar Crime. Deviant Behavior in the Military Context.* New York: Free Press.

Chemtob, Claude M., Raymond W. Novaco, Roger S. Hamada, & Douglas M. Gross. (1997). Cognitive-Behavioral Treatment for Severe Anger in Posttraumatic Stress Disorder. *Journal of Consulting and Clinical Psychology, 65*(1), 184–189.

Cronin, Christopher. (1995). Adolescent Reports of Parental Spousal Violence in Military and Civilian Families. *Journal of Interpersonal Violence, 10*(1), 117–122.

Dau, Klaus. (1985). Die Verantwortung des Offiziers im Umgang mit dem Recht. In Evangelisches Kirchenamt für die Bundeswehr (Eds.), *De officio. Zu den ethischen Herausforderung des Offizierberufs* (pp. 296–299). Hannover: Lutherisches Verlagshaus.

Daws, Gavan. (1994). *Prisoners of the Japanese. POWs of World War II in the Pacific.* New York: Morrow.

De Jongh, John, & Lynn Bassett-Scarfe. (1987). Child Abuse in Military Families. *Defence Force Journal, 67,* 23–29.

De Jongh, John, Lynn Bassett-Scarfe, & Joan Malpas. (1988). The Protection of Children in Military Families: Implications of the Hamilton Report. *Defence Force Journal, 73,* 11–15.

Deering, Catherine G., Susan G. Glover, David Ready, H. Clay Eddleman, & Renato D. Alarcon. (1996). Unique Patterns of Commorbidity in Posttraumatic Stress Disorder from Different Sources of Trauma. *Comprehensive Psychiatry, 37*(5), 336–346.

DeYoung, Marie E. (2000). *This Woman's Army. The Dynamics of Sex and Violence in the Military.* Central Point: Hellgate.

Doorn, Jacques van, & William J. Hendrix. (1975). Use of Violence in Counter Insurgency: The Indonesian Scene 1945–49. In Doorn, Jacques van, *The Soldier and Social Change. Comparative Studies in the History and Sociology of the Military* (pp. 133–177). Beverly Hills, London: Sage.

Dower, John W. (1986). *War without Mercy: Race and Power in the Pacific War.* New York: Pantheon Books.

Dubanovski, Richard A., & S. R. McIntosh. (1984). Child Abuse and Neglect in Military and Civilian Families. *Child Abuse and Neglect, 8*(1), 55–67.

Engdahl, Brian, Thomas N. Dikel, Raina Eberly, & Arthur Jr. Blank. (1997). Posttraumatic Stress Disorder in a Community Group of Former Prisoners of War: A Normative Response to Severe Trauma. *American Journal of Psychiatry, 154*(11), 1576–1581.

Eysenck, Hans Jürgen. (1970). *The Structure of Human Personality. 3rd ed.* New York: Methuen.

Firestone, Juanita M., & Richard J. Harris. (1994). Sexual Harassment in the U.S. Military: Individualized and Environmental Contexts. *Armed Forces and Society, 21*(1), 25–43.

Goffman, Erving. (1962). *Asylums: Essays on the Social Situation of Mental Patients and Other Inmates.* Chicago: Aldine.

Haas, Harald, & Franz Kernic. (1998). *Zur Soziologie von UN-Peacekeeping-Einsätzen.* Baden-Baden: Nomos.

Haney, Craig, Curtis Banks, & Philip Zimbardo. (1983). Interpersonal Dynamics in a Simulated Prison. *International Journal of Criminology and Penology, 1,* 69–97.

High, Gil. (1997). Combating Sexual Harassment. *Soldiers, 52*(2), 4–5.

Hotaling, Gerald T., David Finkelhor, John T. Kirkpatrick, & Kenneth M. Straus. (1988). *Family Abuse and Its Consequences. New Directions in Research.* Newbury Park: Sage.

Internationale Gesellschaft für Menschenrechte/IGFM, Deutsche Sektion e.V. (1991). *Schule des Hasses und der Gewalt. Die Sowjetische Armee tötet Tausende ihrer Soldaten mitten im Frieden. Informationssammlung der IGFM.* Frankfurt: IGFM.

Jäger, Herbert. (1982). *Verbrechen unter totalitärer Herrschaft.* Frankfurt: Fischer.

Kernic, Franz. (1996). Friedensengel ohne Heiligenschein. Soziologische Anmerkungen über die Schattenseiten und sozio-politischen Problemfelder von UN-Einsätzen. In Georg-Maria Meyer (Ed.), *Friedensengel im Kampfanzug* (pp. 207–239). Opladen: Westdeutscher Verlag.

King, Daniel W., Lynda A. King, David W. Foy, Terence M. Keane, & John A. Fairbank. (1999). Posttraumatic Stress Disorder in a National Sample of Female and Male Vietnam Veterans: Risk Factors, War-Zone Stressors, and Resilience-Recovery Variables. *Journal of Abnormal Psychology, 108*(1), 164–170.

King, Lynda A., Daniel W. King, John A. Fairbank, Terence M. Keane, & Gary A. Adams. (1998). Resilience-Recovery Factors in Post-Traumatic Stress Disorder among Female and Male Vietnam Veterans: Hardiness, Postwar Social Support, and Additional Stressful Life Events. *Journal of Personality and Social Psychology, 74*(2), 420–434.

Klinge-Wipfelder, Stephanie. (1984). *Die Kriminalität Wehrpflichtiger in der Bundeswehr. Erscheinungsformen und Ursachen.* Koblenz: Bernard & Graefe.

Krausnick, Helmut. (1985). *Hitlers Einsatzgruppen. Die Truppe des Weltanschauungskrieges 1938–1942.* Frankfurt: Fischer.

Kulka, Richard A., John A. Fairbank, B. Kathleen Jordan, Dani Weiss, & Alan Cranston. (1990). *Trauma and the Vietnam War Generation*. New York: Brunner Mazel.

Kümmel, Gerhard (Ed.) (2000). *Military Sociology: The Richness of a Discipline*. Baden-Baden: Nomos.

Lippert, Ekkehard. (1989). Gewalt im Sozialisationsfeld der Bundeswehr. In Wilhelm Heitmeyer, Kurt Möller & Heinz Sünker (Eds.), *Jugend—Staat—Gewalt. Politische Sozialisation von Jugendlichen, Jugendpolitik und politische Bildung* (pp. 137–147). Weinheim, Munich: Juventa.

Litz, Brett T., Susan M. Orsillo, & Matthew J. Friedman. (1997a). Posttraumatic Stress Disorder Associated with Peacekeeping Duty in Somalia for U.S. Military Personnel. *American Journal of Psychiatry, 154*(2), 178–184.

Litz, Brett T., Lynda A. King, Daniel W. King, Susan M. Orsillo, & Matthew J. Friedman. (1997b). Warriors as Peacekeepers: Features of the Somalia Experience and PTSD. *Journal of Consulting and Clinical Psychology, 65*(6), 1001–1010.

Margalit, Chaim, Talia Ezion, & Stanley Rabinowitz. (1993). Israel Defence Forces Experiences with Treatment of POWs and Families: An Innovative Multifaceted Treatment Model. *Military Medicine, 158*(6), 376–378.

Martin, Del. (1976). *Battered Wives*. New York: Praeger.

McCarroll, James E., John H. Newby, Laurie E. Thayer, Robert J. Ursano, Ann E. Norwood, & Carol S. Fullerton. (1999). Trends in Child Maltreatment in the U.S. Army, 1975–1997. *Child Abuse and Neglect, 23*(9), 855–861.

Merrill, Lex L., Carol E. Newell, Cynthia J. Thomsen, Steven R. Gold, Joel S. Milner, Mary P. Koss, & Sandra G. Rosswork. (1999). Childhood Abuse and Sexual Revictimization in a Female Navy Recruit Sample. *Journal of Traumatic Stress, 12*(2), 211–225.

Milgram, Stanley. (1985). *Das Milgram-Experiment. Zur Gehorsamsbereitschaft gegenüber Autorität*. Reinbek: Rowohlt.

Mollerstrom, Willard W., Michael A. Patchner, & Joel S. Milner. (1992). Family Violence in the Air Force: A Look at Offenders and the Role of the Family Advocacy Program. *Military Medicine, 157*(7), 371–374.

Mollerstrom, Willard W., Michael A. Patchner, & Joel S. Milner. (1995). Child Maltreatment: The United States Air Force's Response. *Child Abuse and Neglect, 19*(3), 325–334.

Monahan, John, & Henry J. Steadman. (Eds.) (1994). *Violence and Mental Disorder. Developments in Risk Assessment*. Chicago: University of Chicago Press.

Omaar, Rakiya, & Alex de Waal. (1993). *Somalia. Human Rights Abuses by the United Nations Forces*. London: Africa Rights.

Osiel, Mark J. (1999). *Obeying Orders. Atrocity, Military Discipline and the Law of War*. New Brunswick/London: Transaction.

Polaschek, Devon L. L., Tony Ward, & Stephen M. Hudson. (1997). Rape and Rapists: Theory and Treatment. *Clinical Psychology Review, 17*(2), 117–144.

Raiha, Nancy K., & David J. Soma. (1997). Victims of Child Abuse and Neglect in the U.S. Army. *Child Abuse and Neglect, 21*(8), 759–768.

Rosen, Leora N., & Lee Martin. (1996). Impact of Childhood Abuse History on Psychological Symptoms among Male and Female Soldiers in the U.S. Army. *Child Abuse and Neglect, 20*(12), 1149–1160.

Schnurr, Paula P., & Matthew J. Friedman. (1999). The National Center for PTSD: The Past 10 Years. *PTSD Research Quarterly, 10*(4), 1–2.

Segev, Tom. (1992). *Die Soldaten des Bösen. Zur Geschichte der KZ-Kommandanten*. Reinbek: Rowohlt.

Seifert, Ruth. (1993). *Krieg und Vergewaltigung. SOWI-Arbeitspapier Nr.76*. Munich: SOWI.

Seifert, Ruth. (1996). *Militär—Kultur—Identität. Individualisierung, Geschlechterverhältnisse und die soziale Konstruktion des Soldaten*. Bremen: Edition Temmen.

Shay, Jonathan. (1998). *Achill in Vietnam. Kampftrauma und Persönlichkeitsverlust*. Hamburg: Hamburger Edition.

Siegl, Elfie. (2000). Ein Soldat, das ist Dreck unter den Stiefeln. *Frankfurter Allgemeine Zeitung, 14,* März 2000, 13.

Skinner, Katherine M., Nancy Kressin, Susan Frayne, Tara J. Tripp, Cheryl S. Hankin, Donald R. Miller, & Lisa M. Sullivan. (2000). The Prevalence of Military Sexual Assault among Female Veterans' Administration Outpatients. *Journal of Interpersonal Violence, 15*(3), 291–310.

Southwick, Steven M., C. Andrew III Morgan, & Dennis S. Charney. (1997). Consistency of Memory for Combat-Related Traumatic Events in Veterans of Operation Desert Storm. *American Journal of Psychiatry, 154*(2), 173–177.

Steiner, John M. (1980). The SS Yesterday and Today: A Sociopsychological View. In Joel E. Dimsdale (Ed.),

Survivors, Victims and Perpetrators. Essays on the Nazi-Holocaust (pp. 431–445). Washington: Hemisphere.

Stiglmayer, Alexandra (Ed.) (1993). *Massenvergewaltigung. Krieg gegen die Frauen.* Freiburg i.Br.: Kore.

Straus, Murray A., & Richard J. Gelles. (Eds.) (1990). *Physical Violence in American Families. Risk Factors and Adaptations to Violence in 8,145 Families.* New Brunswick: Transaction.

Sutker, Patricia B., Daniel K. Winstead, Z. Harry Galina, & Albert N. Allain. (1991). Cognitive Deficits and Psychopathology among Former Prisoners of War and Combat Veterans of the Korean Conflict. *American Journal of Psychiatry, 148*(1), 67–72.

Taft, Casey T., Amy S. Stern, Lynda A. King, & Daniel W. King. (1999). Modeling Physical Health and Functional Health Status: The Role of Combat Exposure, Posttraumatic Stress Disorder, and Personal Resource Attributes. *Journal of Traumatic Stress, 12*(1), 3–22.

Theweleit, Klaus. (1986). *Männerphantasien, 2 Bde.* Basel, Frankfurt: Stroemfeld/Roter Stern. [English: *Male Fantasies 1987/89, 2 vols.* Minnesota: Minnesota University Press]

Truscott, Susan, & Tracey Wait. (1996). *Military Family Violence and Violence against Women: Causes and Incidence. ORD Report 9602.* Ottawa: Department of National Defence, Operational Research Division.

Vogt, Wolfgang R. (1993). Berufsbilder des Offiziers im Widerstreit. In Paul Klein, Jürgen Kuhlmann & Horst Rohde (Eds.), *Soldat—Ein Berufsbild im Wandel. Bd. 2: Offiziere* (pp. 107–122). Bonn/Dortmund.

Wachtler, Günther. (1988). Stichwort: Militär. In Ekkehard Lippert & Günther Wachtler (Eds.), *Frieden. Ein Handwörterbuch* (pp. 266–277). Opladen: Westdeutscher Verlag.

Walkin, Malhalm M. (Ed.) (1979). *War, Morality and the Military Profession.* Boulder: Westview.

Wasileski, Maryann, Martha E. Callaghan-Chaffee, & R. Blake Chaffee. (1982). Spousal Violence in Military Homes: An Initial Survey. *Military Medicine, 147*, September, 761–765.

Winslow, Donna. (1997). *The Canadian Airborne in Somalia: A Socio-Cultural Inquiry.* Ottawa: Ministry of Public Works and Government Services.

Winslow, Donna. (1998). The Role of Culture in the Breakdown of Discipline During Peace Operations. *Canadian Review of Sociology and Anthropology, Special Issue: Organizational Crisis, 35*(3), 345–368.

Wolfe, Jessica, Erica J. Sharkansky, Jennifer P. Read, Ree Dawson, James A. Martin, & Paige-Crosby Ouimette. (1998). Sexual Harassment and Assault as Predictors of PTSD Symptomatology among U.S. Female Persian Gulf War Military Personnel. *Journal of Interpersonal Violence, 13*(1), 40–57.

Wolfner, Glenn D., & Richard J. Gelles. (1993). A Profile of Violence toward Children: A National Study. *Child Abuse and Neglect, 17*(2), 197–212.

Zatzick, Douglas F., Charles R. Marmar, Daniel S. Weiss, Warren S. Browner, Thomas J. Metzler, Jacqueline M. Golding, Anita Stewart, William E. Schlenger, & Kenneth B. Wells. (1997). Posttraumatic Stress Disorder and Functioning and Quality of Life Outcomes in a Nationally Representative Sample of Male Vietnam Veterans. *American Journal of Psychiatry, 154*(12), 1690–1695.

Violence in Prisons/Torture

Ronald D. Crelinsten

I. INTRODUCTION

The UN Convention Against Torture and Other Cruel, Inhuman or Degrading Treatment or Punishment defines torture as:

> any act by which severe pain or suffering, whether physical or mental, is intentionally inflicted on a person for such purposes as obtaining from him or a third person information or a confession, punishing him for an act he or a third person has committed or is suspected of having committed, or intimidating or coercing him or a third person, or for any reason based on discrimination of any kind, when such pain or suffering is inflicted by or at the instigation of or with the consent or acquiescence of a public official or other person acting in an official capacity. It does not include pain or suffering arising only from, inherent in or incidental to lawful sanctions.

This definition highlights those concepts central to the legal conception of torture: severe pain or suffering, including both physical and mental forms, intentional infliction by a public official who has custody or exerts control over the victim, and a variety of purposes ranging from forced confessions to punishment, coercion, or intimidation.

The degree and form of pain and suffering are complex issues, as reflected in the combination of the word "torture" with the phrase "other cruel, inhuman or degrading treatment or punishment" (hereafter referred to as "ill-treatment"). Unlike torture, ill-treatment is never explicitly defined. This is in part related to the problem of lawful sanctions, which in some countries include corporal punishment. Rodley (1999:77–78) describes "a scale of criteria [that] has to be climbed" if torture is to be said to occur. "First, the behaviour must be degrading treatment; second, it must be inhuman treatment; and third, it must be an aggravated form of inhuman treatment, inflicted for certain purposes." There is clearly a grey area between the lower part of the scale—degrading—and the upper part—severe and purposive. Should medical experimentation, as in the Nazi case, or sensory deprivation, such as in the Ulster hooded technique in Northern Ireland, or severe shaking,

W. Heitmeyer and J. Hagan (eds.), *International Handbook of Violence Research*, 189–205.

as in Israel, be included? And what about conditions of imprisonment or corporal punishment? If political prisoners are placed in cells with tuberculosis- or AIDS-infected common prisoners, does this constitute inhuman treatment or even torture? Does flogging or stoning constitute inhuman punishment, or does it merely reflect cultural differences in public attitudes towards violence and punishment?

In the UN Body of Principles for the Protection of All Persons under Any Form of Detention or Imprisonment, Principle 6 uses the classic two-part phrase, "torture or cruel, inhuman or degrading treatment or punishment." Yet a footnote states that the second term "should be interpreted so as to extend the widest possible protection against abuses, whether physical or mental, including the holding of a ... person in conditions which deprive him, temporarily or permanently, of the use of any of his natural senses, such as sight or hearing, or of his awareness of place and the passing of time." This comment clearly refers to sensory deprivation and solitary confinement. Article 7 of the International Covenant on Civil and Political Rights follows the familiar injunction against torture and ill-treatment with one against subjection to "medical or scientific experimentation."

As for which public officials are intended by the definition of torture, in the context of violence in prisons these officials would most often include guards or correctional officers, but could also involve a variety of other state actors, including medical doctors, psychiatrists, police interrogators, military personnel, or even other inmates working in cooperation with prison officials. This is because there are a number of different uses of confinement: detention before trial, deportation or expulsion, incommunicado detention such as within the context of counterinsurgency or state terror, imprisonment of individuals convicted of crimes, solitary confinement, or other harsh detention regimes as disciplinary punishment of already imprisoned persons. This contribution will therefore not restrict itself to convicted and imprisoned persons or those on remand pending trial, but will consider "any persons who are so positioned as to be unable to remove themselves from the ambit of official action and abuse" (Rodley, 1999:5–6). Such persons could include refugees, illegal immigrants, asylum-seekers, common criminals, political prisoners, convicted terrorists, criminal suspects, suspected subversives, or completely innocent people who are targeted by the state for purposes of intimidation and repression. As such, the victims of torture can be much more diverse than implied by a prison context.

With regard to the purposive nature of torture, the list of purposes in the legal definition is not meant to be comprehensive, but includes the most common ones. The emphasis on intention does, however, raise the problem of whether certain forms of negligence can amount to torture or ill-treatment. This is particularly true for conditions of imprisonment or detention. If appalling conditions are the result of a deliberate policy of neglect, they would probably constitute ill-treatment, if not torture. If they are the result of negligence, however, it is unclear whether they would. From a social science perspective, these grey areas may not be as important as they are from a legal perspective. Torture and ill-treatment often occur in conjunction with other gross human rights violations, such as extrajudicial murder, disappearances, sanctioned massacres, or even genocide. To understand these phenomena and how they might be prevented, definitional clarity is not always as important as clearly delineating the social contexts and conditions that are most conducive to their development. However, such grey areas can pose ethical and methodological problems, some of which will be discussed below.

Finally, the term "violence in prisons" is much broader than the term "torture" and could include riots, hostage-taking, or interpersonal violence between prisoners. While these forms of violence will not be considered, it should be noted that riots and hostage-taking could occur as reactions to persistent patterns of torture and ill-treatment. Conversely, torture and ill-treatment could be part of the official response to riots or other inmate behavior perceived by authorities as disruptive. Clearly, the prison environment and the behavior of those within it can be an important variable in studying the genesis and prevention of torture in the prison context.

II. THEORETICAL APPROACHES AND EMPIRICAL RESULTS

Amnesty International (2000) reports that three quarters of the world's governments have used torture between 1997 and mid-2000. They report the use of torture and ill-treatment by state agents in over 150 countries since 1997, with widespread use in more than 70 countries, and its use resulting in death in more than 80 countries. Given its prevalence in today's world, there is surprisingly little theoretical work done on torture, per se, whether in the prison context or elsewhere. The study of torture is closely intertwined with the study of punishment, prison and imprisonment, human rights, and the exercise of state power, and theory has usually focused on torture only as an element in some wider formulation (Schmid, 1989). The torture literature has been dominated by the legal and medical sciences: the former in the areas of human rights standard-setting, prevention, legal responsibility and accountability; the latter in the areas of effects, treatment, and the role of medical professionals in torture. There are significant studies done in other disciplines as well, especially history and social and political psychology, and many studies that do not focus specifically on torture, most notably those on political policing, counterinsurgency and the national security state. The subject of torture is a highly complex one and no single discipline can provide a comprehensive picture of its place in modern society.

1. Legal Approaches

UN Special Rapporteur on Torture, Nigel Rodley, has written a classic text (Rodley, 1999) that provides a comprehensive survey of developments in international law regarding the treatment of prisoners. His range of topics attests to the conceptual links between torture and other forms of state violence: torture and other ill-treatment, extralegal executions, the death penalty, disappearances, conditions of imprisonment or detention, corporal punishment and arbitrary arrest and detention. Rodley provides a history of international efforts to set legal standards for the treatment of persons detained by the state and the appendices provide the full texts of the major international declarations and conventions. His work makes it clear that torture is universally condemned in international law and that the prohibition is absolute. In particular, he demonstrates how the utilitarian argument that torture or ill-treatment are justifiable if it serves a greater good (the classic argument is the "ticking bomb" case where a suspected terrorist is the only one who knows where a bomb set to detonate in a crowded public place is located) has been thoroughly rejected by case law (Rodley, 1999:80–84).

While Rodley demonstrates that definitional clarity is sufficient to determine which kinds of treatment are acceptable and which are not, he does identify cases where the lesser form of ill-treatment was found instead of the greater one of torture. He attributes this to a desire by the courts to operate by consensus and to avoid dissenting opinions (Rodley, 1999:292). A work that substantiates much of Rodley's research is the personal narrative by Antonio Cassese, who from 1989 to 1993 headed a group of international inspectors mandated under the European Convention for the Prevention of Torture to inspect places of detention in contracting states (Cassese, 1996). His narrative also highlights some of the methodological problems inherent in monitoring a practice that is characterized by secrecy, dissimulation, and often blatant obstruction. Interviews with prisoners, detainees, guards, prison directors, and ministers of justice provide valuable information on practices of torture and ill-treatment, as well as the institutional and bureaucratic parameters of their support structure, including the methods used by officials to hide the existence of such practices.

2. Methodological Challenges

The social scientist is faced with the same inventory of problems encountered by the international monitor of human rights. These problems affect the collection, reliability, generalizability, analysis and interpretation of data. Research on human rights monitoring has revealed the differences and interrelations between scholarly, activist, and policy approaches to human rights violations in general, including the kinds of data collected and the kinds of questions asked (Schmid & Jongman, 1992). These concerns are particularly relevant to the study of torture. Yet the very limitations imposed by the nature of the torturer's closed world also provide opportunities for applying techniques of discourse and textual analysis that can capture the constructed and hidden meanings of documents and narratives produced by torture regimes and their practitioners (see, e.g., Graziano, 1992). Stanley Cohen (2001) has analyzed the kinds of discourse, mechanisms of denial, and cognitive techniques of neutralization that officials and other groups in society use to justify torture while simultaneously denying its existence. Thus, at the level of the individual, the institution, and society at large, research on torture can produce fruitful results despite the problematic nature of the object of study.

3. History of Torture

Historical studies have pointed to two distinct transition periods in the history of torture: its disappearance from Europe during the eighteenth and early twentieth centuries and its reemergence in the late nineteenth and early twentieth centuries. Edward Peters has written the definitive text on this history:

> The history of torture in western Europe may be traced from the Greeks, through the Romans, through the Middle Ages, down to the legal reforms of the eighteenth century and the abolition of torture in criminal legal procedure virtually throughout western Europe by the first quarter of the nineteenth century. Removed from ordinary criminal law, however, torture was re-instituted in many parts of Europe and in its colonial empires from the late nineteenth century on, and its course was greatly accelerated by changing concepts of political crime during the twentieth century (Peters, 1996:5).

The history of torture is to a large extent a legal one. It includes historical and political analysis of the changing modes of punishment over time (Foucault, 1975 is the definitive work here), as well as the rise of the modern state (Peters, 1996:ch. 4). It is this latter aspect of torture's history that shows how definitions of political crime and national security play a role in facilitating torture. The most commonly studied cases include the totalitarian regimes of Nazi Germany and Stalinist Russia, Algeria in the 1950s (Maran, 1989), the anticommunist, national security states of the Greek junta (1967–1974), the military dictatorships in Brazil (1964) and the Southern Cone (1970s) (Guest, 1990; Weschler, 1990), and apartheid South Africa (Foster & Davis, 1987). Broader works that do not focus explicitly on torture have elucidated the structural, political, and interstate variables that create an international climate in which torture is supported or tolerated (Huggins, 1998; McClintock, 1992).

While some have attributed the reemergence of torture in part to barbaric cultural values, the current consensus is that modern torture is not the province of one particular culture or political regime.

> It is easy—and initially tempting—to correlate torture with a temper of brutality attributed to another race, culture, ideology, or particular regime. It is more reliable to observe the anthropology of particular cases than to make broad and unverifiable assumptions about the character of particular races or regimes. Historically, torture has proved to be adaptable to too many different cultures for it to be attributed exclusively to one or two especially feral ones (Peters, 1996:186).

This last sentence has been amply demonstrated by a case study of torture in Iran (Rejali, 1994), which traces the history of torture in that country from 1850 to 1990. The analysis covers four distinct periods and regimes: the nineteenth century Qajar dynasty, the Constitutional Revolution (1905–1925), the Pahlavi dynasty and the Islamic Republic beginning in 1979. While the first regime practiced "classical" or "ceremonial" torture, this kind of torture was replaced by "modern" or "disciplinary" torture near the end of the nineteenth century—a transition coinciding with Peters' primarily European history. It also coincides with Michel Foucault's analysis of the history of prisons, whereby public, sanguinary punishments that involved extreme forms of physical torture disappeared when prisons emerged and the infliction of punishment moved from the public sphere to the confines of the prison system. Rejali makes explicit use of Foucault's analysis in his own work, yet he rejects Foucault's thesis that the rise of the prison obviated the need for torture. Instead, Rejali shows how torture changed in form and purpose to conform to the new disciplinary regime that Foucault rightly saw emerging in many social institutions, from the prison, to the hospital, to the juvenile reformatory, and the school. Torture, as a social institution in and of itself, simply underwent the same transformation as other social institutions. In this way, the supposed paradox identified by Foucault disappears and the persistence of torture after the rise of "disciplinary society" is no longer a mystery.

Peters (1996:106) identifies two causes of the reemergence of torture identified by earlier historians that he considers important: the rise of the totalitarian state and the urgent need for military political intelligence resulting in the creation of special services and techniques of interrogation. Developing this idea further, Peters examines police practices, military intelligence services and espionage, and the emergence of a new doctrine of political crime that considered the political criminal "more dangerous—and more repulsive—than the ordinary criminal" (Peters, 1996:120). The rise of political police who had special duties not answerable to the judiciary, but to political authority, "offered considerable latitude for the re-emergence of torture, even in some states with a strong and independent judiciary and statutory prohibition of torture" (Peters, 1996:114). The increasing need for military intelligence and the rise of anarchist terrorism in the late nineteenth century created "a second area [the military] relatively uncontrolled by the judiciary and hence ultimately unanswerable to the rules of civilian jurisprudence" (Peters, 1996:116). Related changes in conceptions of political crime, triggered in particular by "the experience of intensified internal political dissent and intensified external opposition, whether from rival powers or revolutionary movements" (Peters, 1996:121), led to a tendency to equate internal and external political crime. The rise of the revolutionary state, which identified itself with a people or *Volk*, facilitated the distinction between insider and outsider and the identification of enemies of the state, whether internal or external. In time, the extrajudicial nature of modern torture gradually transformed as torture was once again incorporated into the legal systems of these revolutionary states as a means of dealing with those threats deemed to be the most serious, deserving of special forms of interrogation, treatment and punishment. Peters summarizes the transition this way:

> Infinitely more wealthy and powerful, moved by ideologies that excited more and more of its citizens, possessed of organs and intelligence that could dispense with traditional divisions of authority, the coercive revolutionary state of the twentieth century could reintroduce torture into any or all of its procedures, for it had developed not only new powers, but a new anthropology. In place of the rights of man and citizen, there was substituted the exclusive right of the *Volk* or Revolution. (Peters, 1996:130–131)

4. Penal Philosophy, Science, Medicine

These transformations parallel the transition from punishing the crime to punishing the criminal that marked the evolution from a classical model of punishment to a more "scientific" model based on criminal types. The proactive nature of policing these criminal types, defined as criminal because of who they are, not what they have done, necessitates a science of identification and classification that will help identify criminal classes and types regardless of whether or not individual members of these classes have broken any laws. A similar transition has occurred in contemporary Europe in the context of counterterrorism policy, increasing the likelihood of abuses during arrest or detention, particularly of immigrants, refugees, and asylum-seekers (Crelinsten & Özkut, 2000). Similar considerations arise in studies of the new penology that emphasizes management and containment rather than treatment and rehabilitation, especially in the supermaximum penitentiaries that have developed in the U.S. (Miller, 1996; Feeley & Simon, 1994). The penal philosophy underlying such an approach is seen by critics as increasing the likelihood of human rights abuses, often with racial undercurrents.

Just as the role of science in criminal justice was enhanced by the need to classify criminals, so the role of science, and particularly medical science, was enhanced in the reemergence of torture in the context of political policing, military intelligence, and revolutionary justice. The move from public, ceremonial, sanguinary torture to secret, more sophisticated, psychological, disciplinary punishment entailed the increasing involvement of doctors, psychiatrists, and other practitioners of pain in the torture process. Robert Lifton's classic study of the Nazi doctors (Lifton, 1986) and the British Medical Association's report on doctors and torture (1992) examine this issue further.

Rodley (1999:297–300) examines the issue of medical and scientific experimentation and its prohibition both by the Geneva Conventions, which deal with armed conflict and the protection of prisoners of war and civilians in time of war, and by article 7 of the International Covenant on Civil and Political Rights, which deals with the prohibition of torture and ill-treatment. While the Conventions rely on the concept of medical necessity, the Covenant requires only the "free consent" of the individual before any experimentation can proceed. Rodley considers the issue of free consent problematic for those under any form of detention or imprisonment, since the very nature of captivity undermines the concept of consent. In particular, Rodley mentions behavior modification and enforced rehabilitation as areas "especially open to abuse, even where prisoners do consent" (Rodley, 1999:299).

This issue highlights a crucial problem underlying any social scientific endeavor to research the effects of particular treatments in a carceral setting. The prison is not a laboratory, but a social institution with an administrative structure that divides the watcher from the watched and the cooperative prisoner from the disruptive one. This structure and the relationships that underpin it will always constitute a contaminating variable in any study of treatment in the context of imprisonment, detention, and punishment. For example, the use of solitary confinement as a means to control difficult prisoners—in a sense, the *raison d'être* of the supermaximum prison—is considered a form of therapy or treatment by its practitioners, to help difficult prisoners adapt, but as ill-treatment or even torture by its critics, who see the intention more in terms of forcing prisoners to adapt. This ambiguity surrounding intention poses distinct problems for theorizing about motivational and cognitive factors in torture, as well as assessing whether intention to torture or ill-treat was present in cases involving "management" of prisoners, detainees, or deportees.

A similar controversy arose in the 1970s over the issue of sensory deprivation, solitary confinement, and the Northern Ireland case involving five techniques of interrogation: wall-standing; hooding; subjection to noise; sleep deprivation; and deprivation of food and drink (Rodley, 1999:90–95; Kennedy, 1990). While the European Commission of Human Rights unanimously found these techniques to constitute torture, arguing the intensity of the stress caused and the purpose to which the techniques were put, the European Court of Human Rights surprisingly found that the techniques did not constitute torture, but only inhuman and degrading treatment. The majority's argument against torture focused on the intensity of suffering inflicted, contending that it was not sufficient to be called torture. Rodley (1999:92) disagrees with this opinion, as did many others at the time, including Amnesty International. One critic suggested that the Court's decision reflected a cultural bias against developing countries who use less sophisticated techniques than developed countries. This raises an important issue that touches on cultural imperialism and the spread of psychological techniques of torture to replace physical ones. Legal decisions that are seen to favor those states that use refined methods and single out for censure only those that use crude, barbaric ones can only send the message that adopting more "scientific" techniques will spare the offending state the opprobrium of the international community.

Ironically, interviews with torturers—who often call themselves doctors when torturing their victims—argue that they are helping their victims by making it easier for them to confess. This corruption of the normal conception of the patient–doctor relationship is often an integral part of the torture process. What might appear to be therapeutic in a laboratory or a clinical setting may inevitably become an integral part of the coercive, punitive apparatus of a prison setting, particularly in the context of controlling "disruptive" prisoners who are perceived by authorities as threatening the efficient functioning of the system. This raises important methodological and ethical questions for the study of what constitutes torture or ill-treatment in the context of imprisonment or detention, even in democratic states.

5. Psychological Approaches

When we turn from the broader level of analysis that legal, historical, and political approaches provide to the level of the individual, it is the disciplines of social and political psychology that provide the most heuristic concepts (Suedfeld, 1990). Because torture and ill-treatment usually involve the commission of violent acts within a group context and because the violence is usually justified as a means to an end rather than as an end in itself, those theories that look at violence as a socially mediated behavior where cognitive and attitudinal factors play an important part lend themselves most readily to understanding torture. Theories that look at violence as an instinctual or internally driven behavior where sadism, intrapsychic conflict, or defective psychic functioning play an important part are less relevant. Torture regimes tend to screen out sadistic individuals as too likely to kill their victims before the torture has achieved its goal. Sometimes death of the victim is counterproductive, as in cases where individuals broken by torture are deliberately released so as to serve as deterrents to others. Those theories that stress the importance of situational factors leading to violence in a group setting and recognize the importance of an individual's definition of the situation, of his own role in that situation and the significance of the victim in that particular context, are most fruitful in explaining specific findings in the case study literature.

The following concepts help to explain how normal individuals, in interaction with others in a particular situation or context, can change their attitudes and beliefs to the point where the commission of violent acts against persons becomes routine, normal or, at the very least, expedient: *role orientation* (Kelman & Hamilton, 1989), whereby an individual behaves according to role expectations rather than consequences of his deeds; the *agentic state* (Milgram, 1974), whereby normal individuals commit violent acts in situations of authority in which they perform according to an overarching ideology that supersedes his or her moral conscience; *groupthink* (Janis, 1983), whereby individuals censor their own doubts about a particular course of action rather than challenge or threaten the developing consensus within the group; *coercive persuasion* (Schein, 1971) that emphasizes the importance of peer influence in a context where alternatives are not available; and, generally, *group influence* and *peer pressure to conform*.

Once people cross the violence threshold, a whole new dynamic begins, whereby commitment to the group, its ideology, and to violence, deepens as the practice of violence continues. The following concepts help explain how, once a violent course of action is taken, an individual's very identity can become a central element in the maintenance of that course of action: *schismogenesis* (Bateson, 1958), whereby symmetrical or complementary behaviors by two parties (be they individuals, as in a victimizer/victim dyad, or groups, such as the torture regime vs. opposition groups) lead to progressive polarization; the *looking-glass self* (Mead, 1934), whereby a person's self-image is constructed via an interpretative process of defining the self in the context of interaction with others; and the consistent finding that *group solidarity and loyalty* to one's "buddies" is the prime reason why men in combat continue to fight (Dyer, 1985).

This change over time involves a dynamic progression in self-image, other-image and definition of the situation, and the role an individual plays in that situation. This can help to explain how torture becomes more severe, violence escalates into atrocities, targeting becomes more indiscriminate, and exit from the group becomes increasingly difficult. Given that most torturers operate in whole or in part in secret and that many refuse to discuss their activities with family and friends, the self-contained, impermeable worldview of the group, the overarching ideology and its self-sealing premises, the group dynamics and the role orientation of individual members all serve to accentuate the progressive polarization between the group and the outside world and to deepen the commitment to the group regardless of the efficacy of the violence or the success of individual cases.

6. Torture Training

The reasons individuals become involved in torture can differ from those for which they continue. Individual pathways to torture can vary, as can the particular situations and contexts in which individuals find themselves inducted into torture. This is why case studies of perpetrators, how they were recruited and trained, and how their training enabled them to do their work are so important in this field (Crelinsten & Schmid, 1995). Ronald Crelinsten (1995:36) summarizes the central elements of the torturer's work:

> First, the torturer is doing a *job*, he is "doing torture"; second, he is supposed to do it well, "mastering torture"; third, he is supposed to achieve certain results ("make them talk"), i.e., obtaining confessions, breaking the enemy's will; fourth, the central method used to achieve these results is inflicting pain ("make them hurt"); fifth, the people upon whom this pain is inflicted are defined as "enemies". The information, the confessions, and, ultimately, the broken people, are the end products of the torturer's work. It is these end products by which he is judged as skilled or unskilled, deserving of promotion or dismissal, considered indispensable or expendable. It is this *judgment* or *assessment* of the torturer's work that leads us to the final feature of the torturer's world: the torturer is working in an institutional context, within a hierarchy in which others, his superiors and their superiors and their superiors, decide who is an enemy, what needs to be known, and what must be done to know it.

Torture training usually includes techniques designed to supplant normal moral restraints about harming (innocent) others with cognitive and ideological constructs that justify torture and victimization and neutralize any factors that might lead to pangs of conscience or disobedience to authority. As such, it amounts to a kind of reality construction that involves the deconstruction of "objective" reality, as reflected in conventional morality, and its replacement with a new reality that is defined by the ideological dictates of a particular regime that holds power, be it secular or religious. In order to maintain this reality, the torture regime must endeavor to ensure that it is reflected in all sectors of society and all aspects of social and political life. Everything must be reshaped according to the new template: laws rewritten or, at the very least, reinterpreted, new language and vocabulary devised, social relations redefined, and all these processes of transformation channeled through and amplified by the mass media. As such, the techniques used to train prospective torturers are but a reflection of a much wider process: the transformation of society. The torture system itself is but a microcosm of this larger phenomenon. To enable torture to be practiced systematically and routinely, not only do torturers have to be trained and prepared, but wider elements of society must also be prepared and, in a sense, trained to accept that such things go on. As such, it is not only the perpetrators of torture that participate in this reality construction, but also bystanders (Staub, 1989), who are not directly involved as either perpetrator or victim, and, in a cruelly ironic sense, the victims themselves.

A central feature of this reality construction is the creation of a powerful and dangerous enemy that threatens the social fabric, a process similar to what Peters describes for political crime at the end of the nineteenth century. Laws are directed against this enemy, labels to describe this enemy are promulgated and disseminated via the mass media, people are divided into us and them, for us or against us. To imbue this purported enemy with sufficient substance to render the presumed threat credible, the police or the military target groups most likely to be perceived by the general population as enemies, such as ethnic or religious minorities or political dissidents. If such groups happen to include violent insurgents, so much the better, since the threat will be more easily depicted as real. But this is not always necessary: mere change is violence to the status quo and so, in the eyes of the power holders, peaceful advocacy and nonviolent dissent can be perceived as subversion or violence. In the Dirty War in Argentina, for example, the net of subversion was drawn so wide as to include Marxism, Zionism, Freemasonry, and Progressive Catholicism, along with human rights, women's rights, and peace groups, all the way to "indirect aggression," which consisted of everything from drug and alcohol abuse, political and economic liberalism, lay education and trade union corruption, to social and sexual deviance, the media, and the creative arts (Donnelly, 1998:41).

Herbert Kelman (1995) identifies three processes which, together, facilitate the institutionalization of torture: authorization, routinization, and dehumanization. The first operates at the level of the authority structure and involves the ideological and epistemological definition of a situation so as to legitimize torture. The second operates at the level of the institution within which torture is conducted and involves the creation of a professional torturer operating within a system of incentives, rewards, and punishments. The third operates at the level of victimization, whereby the object of torture is stripped of his or her humanity and dignity, demonized, and reified into The Enemy. The training process is a progressive one that goes through discrete stages from basic to specialized. Crelinsten (1995:46) speaks of "the *gradual* movement from one world view (human, civilian, empathic, caring) to another (inhuman, torturer, cruel, detached). The subject (the conscript/recruit/torturer-to-be) is progressively desensitized while the object (the subversive/Communist/terrorist/victim-to-be) is progressively dehumanized, objectivized, stripped of any identity except the demonizing labels of the dangerous enemy who will take your life if you do not protect yourself." In a simulated prison context, Philip Zimbardo's classic 1971 Stanford prison experiment, in which college students set up a mock prison and played the roles of prisoners and guards, demonstrated these dynamics in an experimental setting. The experiment had to be discontinued because the behavior of prisoners and guards became so polarized that sadistic behavior by guards finally emerged. This finding underscores the fact that sadism is not unknown in the torture context, but that it generally represents a late stage in the progressive dynamics of torturer–victim interaction.

Mika Haritos-Fatouros (1995, 1991) has done the most comprehensive work on interviewing known torturers and analyzing their training and development. She interviewed ex-military policemen who had served under the Greek military dictatorship and made use of testimonies of army police servicemen at the first torturers' trial in 1975. She examined the selection and training procedures used by the military in order to understand how new recruits ended up becoming torturers. The training procedures emphasized blind obedience to authority, insensitivity to degradation and pain, role modeling and a system of rewards and punishments. Haritos-Fatouros concludes that a learning model rather than a disposition towards sadism best explains obedience to an authority of violence. She is currently working on a book, *The Psychological Origins of Institutionalized Torture*, which promises to be the definitive work in the area.

7. Victims of Torture

Research on victims of torture has also contributed to a greater understanding of the torture process. The literature is huge and diverse, covering physical, psychological, psychiatric, social, and cultural effects (Rasmussen, 1990; Başoðlu, 1992; Peltzer, 1996; Eliass, 1997; Jaranson & Poplin, 1998). Special topics include the tortured refugee or exile, the effects on women and children, and intergenerational effects (Bar-On, 1989; Danieli, 1998), suggesting that the impact of torture goes far beyond the direct victims. Amnesty International (2000) claims that the most frequent victims of torture by state agents today are common criminals and criminal suspects (more than 130 countries), followed by political prisoners (more than 70 countries), and by nonviolent demonstrators (more than 60 countries). The most common form of torture is beating, while most torturers are police officers.

What these studies show is that torture can have many purposes and many rationalities.

> Torture can be exercised by different sorts of administration characterized by specific forms of rationality. The torturer may act on the tortured as a priest seeking a conversion, a surgeon operating on a patient, a psychiatrist transforming a subject. He may explain what he does in the same terms as a detective, a publicist, or a counterinsurgency expert. Each of these ways of acting describes a distinctive mode of government and casts an entirely different light on how torture operates in a society (Rejali, 1994:164).

Victims have reported that they were tortured even though they had no useful information to provide. Sometimes the torturer was clearly after a confession, but sometimes the torture was aimed at destabilizing the victim's personality or rendering them incapable of political activity when released. The use of victim testimony, as well as that of perpetrators, helps to identify the way torture actual works in different contexts and situations. Such data is invaluable for developing theory (Schmid, 1989).

8. Four Theoretical Approaches

Darius Rejali (1994:160–176) identifies four theoretical approaches to torture: humanist, developmentalist, state terrorist, and Nietzschean. The first he identifies primarily with Hannah Arendt and her concept of the banality of evil or the bureaucratic torturer. This is consistent with the routinization and professionalization of torture described above. Its limitation is that it restricts the explanation of torture to one kind of rationality and ignores others, such as what Rejali (1994:83–132) characterizes as "tutelary torture," whereby the victim of torture, far from being objectified or dehumanized, is a subject to be reformed. The suggestion that torture can function to reform individuals as well as to break or destroy them highlights once again the problem surrounding intention discussed above. For Rejali, the strength of the humanist approach is its recognition that modern torture is not an aberration, but part of modern political systems, with the same kind of rationality characterized by bureaucratic systems.

The second approach is identified with modernization theorists such as Samuel Huntington, Lucian Pye, and Mancur Olson, who relate torture to the practice of counterinsurgency and thus are able to describe specific military, police, and bureaucratic conventions employed by practitioners of torture. For these theorists, torture is an aberration or dysfunction stemming from a lack of political development. They argue that the incidence of torture is proportional to the extent of civil opposition and as such is primarily reactive. This thesis flies in the face of the proactive nature of much political policing, discussed above, as well as the fact that torture often continues long after civil opposition is successfully suppressed (Rejali, 1994:164–167).

The third approach is identified with the work of Noam Chomsky and Edward Herman who identify torture with a complex mode of governance with global links to arms suppliers, foreign aid and training, and transfer of torture technology. They relate this to the international economic system and the creation of national security states in developing countries designed to "crush class protests while maintaining economic growth on behalf of multinational interests" (Rejali, 1994:168). While this approach can easily explain why government violence is proactive and why it is out of proportion to the incidence of civil opposition, Rejali argues that it does not explain why states use torture instead of other forms of repression.

The fourth approach stems from Nietzsche's concept of self-regulation through memory of punishment, which Rejali relates to the thesis that torture declined in Europe due to the rise of disciplinary society. The strength of this approach is its recognition of the sociological processes that shape punishment. Rejali's critique, referred to above when discussing Foucault, is that this thesis cannot explain why torture reemerged and how it functions as a tool of modern governance. Foucault assumes that torture is wasteful, as opposed to discipline, which is efficient. Rejali rejects this equation between torture and an economy of waste, arguing that utility is a matter of interpretation. What is wasteful and what is useful can vary according to how torture is used and rationalized. Analyzing how torture works in detail can identify what does and does not count as waste and for whom.

For Rejali, all four approaches fail to explain modern torture adequately: "The causes they identify are too general to account for the details of torture complexes" (Rejali, 1994:175). To develop satisfactory explanations of torture, research must focus on the minutiae of how torture works in specific contexts. Rejali (1994:176) also argues that "we need to be careful about how the use of increasingly specialized ways of talking can serve to mislead us about what is actually happening when torture occurs." The most productive methodological approaches appear to be detailed case studies and discourse and linguistic analysis of how torturers and their masters talk about what they do (see Cohen, 2001; Crelinsten & Schmid, 1995).

III. DESIDERATA

1. The Scientific Study of Torture

There are difficult moral and ethical problems that arise when scientists attempt to study torture. This is in part related to the different roles that scientists play in the area of human rights and in part related to notions of scientific objectivity. Academics and intellectuals, and quite often social scientists in particular, can become victims of torture precisely because of the kinds of analysis they make of torture regimes. Even if "objective" in the ideal sense, these researchers are seen to be enemies of those whose power is maintained by the torture regime. In the case of activists who take a stand against torture on moral or ethical grounds, or professionals who do so in conformity to standards that proscribe involvement in torture, the likelihood of victimization is even greater. On the other hand, scientists can use the cloak of objectivity to turn a blind eye from the excesses of the state and, in doing so, end up lending passive support to the regime in their capacity as "neutral" bystander. Studying the causes of torture can also lead to a feeling of impotence, frustration, or apathy when increased understanding of how torture complexes work leads to a sense that nothing can be done to stop them. It is important to realize that torture regimes will always be able to find people to do their dirty work for them, given the empirical findings outlined above. While the common wisdom is that anyone can become a torturer, this is probably not true, however, and more research should be done on those who refuse to torture, try and escape their torture role, or are screened out as unsuitable by their masters and trainers. Similarly, research should be done on how professionals involved in rehabilitation or therapy in the prison setting justify the use of techniques that fit the legal definition of torture or ill-treatment. If one rationale of torture is to reform the person tortured, then how do we distinguish this form of torture from rehabilitation or treatment?

2. Definitional Scope

Edward Peters (1996:153) argues that the term "torture" is overused and as a result "it becomes simply picturesque, its legal definition is gutted and in its place is substituted a vague idea of moral sentiment." Among the formulations he specifically rejects is "the 'torture' of a battered wife by a brutal husband" (Peters, 1996:154–155).

Peters has been criticized for his narrow, legal approach. Rhonda Copelon (1994:139) argues that "Peter's [sic] approach illustrates the way the public/private dichotomy privileges the political and renders trivial the private." Taking the central elements of the legal definition of torture, she examines how each one applies to domestic violence against women. The result of her analysis suggests that the social scientific study of torture, as traditionally defined, could well benefit from studies of other contexts, such as domestic violence against women, where many of the structural and situational factors are more comparable than might at first be imagined. As one example, Copelon shows how the concept of detention or imprisonment can be applied to domestic violence, since many batterers encourage dependency in their victims and isolate them in an attempt to destroy their sense of autonomy and dignity, often imprisoning them in their own homes and the narrow confines of their domestic lives. Studies of child abuse have also shown how abusers create a kind of closed world, impervious to outside influences and conventional morality, that is quite comparable to the closed world of the torturer. The dynamics of violence in the domestic context and that of official violence in institutional contexts such as the prison or the concentration camp probably have more commonalities than suggested by their segregation in different specializations. Speaking of the experience of captivity and dehumanization, Copelon (1994:139) cites Primo Levi from his poignant account of his experiences in Auschwitz: "take care not to suffer in your own homes what is inflicted on us here." Future work in this area could benefit from the kind of transdisciplinary collaboration characterized by certain international societies or comprehensive publications. The International Society for Stress and Trauma Studies comes to mind, as do some recent volumes on the many contexts of stress, trauma, and coping (Danieli, 1998; Eliass, 1997; van der Kolk et al., 1996).

3. Treatment Models

There is a tension in the treatment literature about therapeutic approaches that treat the problems of torture survivors as purely medical, despite the political context in which much torture occurs. Anti-psychiatry sentiments, as well as antipathy to Western science in general, have contributed to this tension: "Torture is viewed by some as primarily, or even solely, a political issue and medical, psychiatric or psychological approaches to the problem are regarded as reductionist 'medicalizing'. There are also concerns that the study of torture would amount to a new discipline, 'torturology', the very existence of which might imply a passive acceptance of the practice of torture. These views have generated considerable resistance in the field to scientific approaches to the problem" (Başoðlu, 1992:5). Part of the problem is whether torture survivors should be considered "sick" or "abnormal," or whether they exhibit "normal responses to abnormal situations." It is now generally accepted that the aftereffects of torture vary so widely across contexts, situations, and victims that a common "torture syndrome" does not exist. However, some practitioners feel that the most common effects do resemble the basket of symptoms called "post-traumatic stress disorder" (PTSD). There is disagreement as to whether the two are the same and further research could help clarify this issue. Başoðlu (1992:8) argues that "the alternative to a purely political approach to torture is an integrated model which gives due weight to all relevant aspects of the problem." Recognizing torture as "a complex phenomenon with interacting social, cultural, political, medical, psychological, and biological dimensions," he expresses the hope that such an integrated approach might achieve some synthesis between widely divergent views in the field. Future research should endeavor to find innovative ways to further advance this approach.

The same need for integration surrounds the study of ill-treatment, particularly conditions of imprisonment and detention. Much research on torture focuses on political prisoners or prisoners of conscience. However, common prisoners around the world suffer from terrible conditions of detention and ill-treatment. The ideological, cognitive, and attitudinal underpinnings of such treatment are often less obvious or visible than in the political context. As such, they are more difficult to tease out and identify. One of the greatest challenges to research in this area is to integrate theories and empirical findings that critique and deconstruct traditional criminal justice and penological goals with those that do the same for gross human rights violations, state crime, and politically-motivated torture and ill-treatment.

IV.   APPROACHES OF PREVENTION

There are two sets of conditions under which torture is likely to occur (Cohen & Golan, 1991:110). The first is a set of social and political conditions that reflect much of the research on national security states, counterinsurgency and crimes of obedience and authority:

- A national emergency or other perceived threat to security;
- the need to process large numbers of suspects;
- the dehumanization of an outgroup (national, religious, or ethnic);
- a high level of authorization to violate normal moral principles;
- the presence of a "sacred mission" which justifies anything.

The second is a set of legal conditions:

- a long period in incommunicado detention, particularly without access to a lawyer;
- the inability to identify interrogators;
- trials under military law or other similar procedure;
- the absence of independent checks on the detainees' medical condition;
- rules of evidence which do not automatically rule out confessions obtained under torture;
- some degree of immunity enjoyed by interrogators from legal prosecution.

The traditional approach to the first set is exemplified by Amnesty International's emblem, the torch shining through barbed wire. By shedding light on the activities of torture complexes, through detailed reports on techniques used, effects suffered by victims, statistics on incidence and prevalence around the world, Amnesty International (2001, 2000; Duncan, 1996) and human rights watchdog groups like it have succeeded in cataloguing and publicizing the extent and diversity of torture in today's world. Because of this strategy of mobilization of shame, governments rarely admit that they commit or condone torture. The work of the Danish Rehabilitation and Research Centre for Torture Victims and its International Rehabilitation Council for Torture Victims (IRCT) has played a major role in researching and publicizing the effects of torture and developing a global network of rehabilitation centers in countries around the world (IRCT, 1998). Their quarterly journal *Torture* is an indispensable source in the field. Professional groups have promoted research on torture that can be applicable to prevention and treatment efforts (Randall & Lutz, 1991). Early warning and monitoring serve to identify situations where torture is more likely to occur, while public education campaigns help to inoculate a society against torture-facilitating ideologies.

Site visits to prisons and places of detention are the best way to address the legal set of conditions (IRCT, 1997). Such visits can counter both opportunity to commit torture and impunity for doing it. The elimination of incommunicado detention and the enforcement of existing international law to bring torturers to justice can reduce the incidence of torture. Research on the impact of site visits, enforcement of professional codes of conduct, legal restrictions on the use of confessions and lengthy incommunicado detention, and the prosecution of those responsible for creating and implementing regimes of torture can address the legal conditions that are conducive to torture.

Research has also shown that many torturers experience psychological and other problems because of their activities. Research on perpetrators could contribute to information campaigns in countries where torture still occurs, aimed at sensitizing potential recruits to the torture apparatus that their participation can have serious personal consequences. Human rights education for those who exercise the state's monopoly on violence can also help to prevent torture. Trade in equipment and expertise that can be used for torture or ill-treatment should be prohibited, while the use of nonlethal police and security equipment that has unknown medical effects or is open to abuse should be carefully controlled and monitored (Amnesty International, 2001).

REFERENCES

Amnesty International. (2000). *Take a Step to Stamp out Torture*. London: Amnesty International Publications.
Amnesty International. (2001). *Stopping the Torture Trade*. London: Amnesty International Publications.

Bar-On, Dan. (1989). *Legacy of Silence: Encounters with Children of the Third Reich.* Cambridge: Harvard University Press.

Başoðlu, Metin (Ed.) (1992). *Torture and Its Consequences: Current Treatment Approaches.* Cambridge: Cambridge University Press.

Bateson, Gregory. (1958). *Naven. 2nd Edition.* Stanford: Stanford University Press.

British Medical Association. (1992). *Medicine Betrayed: The Participation of Doctors in Human Rights Abuses.* London: Zed Books.

Cassese, Antonio. (1996). *Inhuman States: Imprisonment, Detention and Torture in Europe Today.* Cambridge: Polity Press.

Cohen, Stanley. (2001). *States of Denial: Knowing about Atrocities and Suffering.* London: Polity Press.

Cohen, Stanley, & Daphna Golan. (1991). *The Interrogation of Palestinians During the Intifada: Ill-treatment, 'Moderate Physical Pressure' or Torture?* Jerusalem: The Israeli Information Center for Human Rights in the Occupied Territories.

Copelon, Rhonda. (1994). Intimate Terror: Understanding Domestic Violence as Torture. In Rebecca J. Cook (Ed.), *Human Rights of Women: National and International Perspectives* (pp. 116–152). Philadelphia: University of Pennsylvania Press.

Crelinsten, Ronald D. (1995). In Their Own Words: The World of the Torturer. In Ronald D. Crelinsten & Alex P. Schmid (Eds.), *The Politics of Pain: Torturers and Their Masters* (pp. 35–64). Boulder: Westview Press.

Crelinsten, Ronald D., & Iffet Özkut. (2000). Counterterrorism Policy in Fortress Europe: Implications for Human Rights. In Fernando Reinares (Ed.), *European Democracies Against Terrorism: Governmental Policies and Intergovernmental Cooperation* (pp. 245–270). Hampshire: Ashgate.

Crelinsten, Ronald D., & Alex P. Schmid (Eds.) (1995). *The Politics of Pain: Torturers and Their Masters.* Boulder: Westview Press.

Danieli, Yael (Ed.) (1998). *International Handbook of Multi-Generational Legacies of Trauma.* New York: Plenum Press.

Donnelly, Jack. (1998). *International Human Rights. 2nd Edition.* Boulder: Westview Press.

Duncan, Forrest (Ed.) (1996). *A Glimpse of Hell: Reports on Torture Worldwide.* London: Amnesty International.

Dyer, Gwyn. (1985). *War.* New York: Crown.

Eliass, Peter. (1997). *Treating Victims of Torture and Violence: Theoretical, Cross-Cultural, and Clinical Implications.* New York: New York University Press.

Feeley, Malcolm, & Jonathan Simon. (1994). Actuarial Justice: The Emerging New Criminal Law. In David Nelken (Ed.), *The Futures of Criminology* (pp. 173–201). London: Sage.

Foster, Don, & Dennis Davis. (1987). *Detention and Torture in South Africa: Psychological, Legal and Historical Studies.* New York: St. Martin's Press.

Foucault, Michel. (1975). *Surveiller et Punir, Naissance de la Prison.* Paris: Gallimard.

Graziano, Frank. (1992). *Divine Violence: Spectacle, Psychosexuality, and Radical Christianity in the Argentine 'Dirty War'.* Boulder: Westview Press.

Guest, Iain. (1990). *Behind the Disappearances: Argentina's Dirty War Against Human Rights and the United Nations.* Philadelphia: University of Pennsylvania Press.

Haritos-Fatouros, Mika. (1991). Die Ausbildung des Folterers. In Jan Philipp Reemtsma (Ed.), *Folter: Zur Analyse eines Herrschaftsmittels* (pp. 73–91). Hamburg: Junius.

Haritos-Fatouros, Mika. (1995). The Official Torturer: A Learning Model for Obedience to the Authority of Violence. In Ronald D. Crelinsten & Alex P. Schmid (Eds.), *The Politics of Pain: Torturers and Their Masters* (pp. 129–146). Boulder: Westview Press.

Huggins, Martha K. (1998). *Political Policing: The United States and Latin America.* Durham: Duke University Press.

IRCT. (1997). *Conditions in Prisons: Prison Visits, Medical Legality. Torture. Supplementum No. 1.* Copenhagen: International Rehabilitation Council for Torture Victims.

IRCT. (1998). *Organization of Torture Survivor Rehabilitation. Torture. Supplementum No. 1.* Copenhagen: International Rehabilitation Council for Torture Victims.

Janis, Irving L. (1983). *Groupthink. 2nd Edition, Revised.* Boston: Houghton Mifflin.

Jaranson, James M., & Michael K. Poplin (Eds.) (1998). *Caring for Victims of Torture.* Washington: American Psychiatric Press.

Kelman, Herbert C. (1995). The Social Context of Torture: Policy Process and Authority Structure. In Ronald D. Crelinsten & Alex P. Schmid (Eds.), *The Politics of Pain: Torturers and Their Masters* (pp. 19–34). Boulder: Westview Press.

Kelman, Herbert C., & V. Lee Hamilton. (1989). *Crimes of Obedience: Toward a Social Psychology of Authority and Responsibility*. New Haven: Yale University Press.

Kennedy, Steven B. (1990). 'Hooded Men': Victims of Psychological Research? In Peter Suedfeld (Ed.), *Psychology and Torture* (pp. 117–128). New York: Hemisphere.

Lifton, Robert J. (1986). *The Nazi Doctors: Medical Killing and the Psychology of Genocide*. New York: Basic Books.

Maran, Rita. (1989). *Torture and the Role of Ideology: The French-Algerian War*. New York: Praeger.

McClintock, Michael. (1992). *Instruments of Statecraft: U. S. Guerrilla Warfare, Counter-Insurgency, Counter-Terrorism, 1940–1990*. New York: Pantheon.

Mead, George Herbert. (1934). *Mind, Self and Society*. Chicago: University of Chicago Press.

Milgram, Stanley. (1974). *Obedience to Authority: An Experimental View*. New York: Harper & Row.

Miller, Jerome G. (1996). *Search and Destroy: African-American Males in the Criminal Justice System*. New York: Cambridge University Press.

Peltzer, Karl. (1996). *Counselling and Psychotherapy of Victims of Organised Violence in Sociocultural Context*. Frankfurt: IKO-Verlag für Interkulturelle Kommunikation.

Peters, Edward. (1996). *Torture. Expanded Edition*. Philadelphia: University of Pennsylvania Press.

Randall, Glenn R., & Ellen L. Lutz. (1991). *Serving Survivors of Torture: A Practical Manual for Health Professionals and Other Service Providers*. Washington: American Association for the Advancement of Science.

Rasmussen, Ole Vedel. (1990). Medical Aspects of Torture. *Danish Medical Bulletin, 37* (Suppl. 1), 1–88.

Rejali, Darius M. (1994). *Torture and Modernity: Self, Society, and State in Modern Iran*. Boulder: Westview Press.

Rodley, Nigel S. (1999). *The Treatment of Prisoners Under International Law. 2nd Edition*. Oxford: Clarendon Press.

Schein, Edgar H. (1971). *Coercive Persuasion*. New York: W. W. Norton.

Schmid, Alex P. (1989). *Research on Gross Human Rights Violations: A Programme. 2nd Enlarged Edition*. Leiden: C. O. M. T.

Schmid, Alex P., & Albert J. Jongman (Eds.) (1992). *Monitoring Human Rights Violations*. Leiden: C.O.M.T.

Staub, Ervin. (1989). *The Roots of Evil: The Origins of Genocide and Other Group Violence*. New York: Cambridge University Press.

Suedfeld, Peter (Ed.) (1990). *Psychology and Torture*. New York: Hemisphere Publishing.

Van der Kolk, Bessel A., Alexander C. McFarlane, & Lars Weisaeth (Eds.) (1996). *Traumatic Stress: The Effects of Overwhelming Experience on Mind, Body, and Society*. New York: Guilford Press.

Weschler, Lawrence. (1990). *A Miracle, a Universe: Settling Accounts with Torturers*. New York: Pantheon.

Violence and the Police

JEAN-PAUL BRODEUR

I. INTRODUCTION

Egon Bittner defines the role of the police as "a mechanism for the distribution of non-negotiably coercive force employed in accordance with the dictates of an intuitive grasp of situational exigencies" (Bittner, 1970/1990:131).[1] This definition should be read in conjunction with Max Weber's dictum that the State is defined by its monopoly on the use of legitimate force (Weber, 1946) and Norbert Elias' work on the domestication of violence within Western societies (Elias, [1989], 1996). With slight variations, it stands as the customary definition of the role of police in the scientific literature of different countries (Bayley, 1983; Monjardet, 1996; Funk, 1986; Schneider, 1987; Lofthouse, 1996; Waddington, 1999). The use of force is then viewed as the core of policing. Hence, far from being inherently problematic, the relationship between violence and policing is viewed as fundamentally unquestionable.

The word "police" refers here to *public* policing organizations, as opposed to private security agencies. Although private security personnel may covertly resort to physical coercion (e.g., bouncers in bars and clubs), private security agencies allegedly operate by assent, often extorted by threat, and they are granted few powers by the legislation of the various countries where they are based. Opinions differ significantly in the literature as to the meaning of the growth of private policing. Some authors believe that it threatens the monopoly on the use of force enjoyed by the public police (Johnston, 1992) and others think, on the contrary, that the legal power to use force in any situation where it is justified

---

[1] All of Bittner's papers on policing were collected in Bittner (1990). When quoting the number of a page, the article refers to Bittner (1990), which is then preceded by the original date of the paper's publication (e.g., Bittner, 1970/1990:131). In May 1999, I spent two days in Berkeley with Professor Bittner, discussing his work with him. My interpretation of his thought is based on a reading of his papers and on our discussions, which were taped. I thank him warmly for spending time with me. Unfortunately, verbal discussion offers no guarantee against misinterpretation and I take all responsibility for any mistake in interpreting his thought.

W. Heitmeyer and J. Hagan (eds.), *International Handbook of Violence Research*, 207–224.

still is the criterion that separates public policing from private security (Jones & Newburn, 1998). For the last ten years, public policing was closely associated with the community policing reform. Community policing was initially viewed as a means to bring the police and the community, particularly ethnic communities, closer. Thus, the emphasis on the role of force in defining the police function receded into the background, and it was for a time superseded by the notion of policing by consent. However, the holistic "broken windows" approach initially advocated by Wilson and Kelling (1982) has been progressively stripped down to an aggressive zero tolerance style of policing that seriously backfired in highly mediatized incidents involving the use of excessive force. In consequence, police violence is now again at the forefront of public attention and policy makers are eagerly sponsoring research into the field.

Two very different questions are asked in relation to the use of force by the police. A first question raises the *factual* issue of the police use of force outside a normative framework. What is at stake here is the extent and the descriptive features of the use of force and not its propriety under a particular set of values and circumstances. A second question precisely raises the issue of propriety that is eschewed by the factual question; its formulation is then explicitly *normative*. Whether facts and norms can be dichotomized with respect to a concept such as force is open to debate. What, however, is clear enough is that research is presently conducted on the basis of that dichotomy (Adams, 1999a, 1999b).

Two further clarifications must be given in relation to the factual issue. To begin with, the research literature on policing uses the word "force" instead of the term "violence" (this is not only true of the research published in English but also in other languages). However, this usage does not imply that there is a crucial distinction between force and violence, the first notion referring to a legitimate use of physical coercion and the second to an illegitimate one. For instance, the French penal legislation does not shy from using the word "*violence*" when it refers to police powers. Furthermore, in languages such as German "violence" (*Gewalt*) does not have a pejorative normative connotation. Hence, for the purposes of this article, "force" and "violence" are treated as synonyms. The semantic differences between force and violence lie at the level of what Wittgenstein calls "deep grammar," which is outside the scope of this article. For instance, there is no semantic oddity in speaking of "excessive force." However, the expression "excessive violence" strikes us a somewhat pleonastic, violence being associated in itself with excess.

The next clarification goes beyond semantics: In policing research, force is essentially conceived as being spread across a *continuum*. The elements of this continuum may vary slightly among authors, but they usually follow a similar ranking: (1) *physical presence*, with its various levels of threatening appearance; (2) *verbalization*, up to command voice; (3) *neutralizing agents* not targeting individuals, such as gas; (4) *physical contact*—firm grip, takedown, pain compliance; (5) *impact techniques*—water cannon, police car, intermediate weapons (chemical spray, electrical weapons for stunning, rubber and plastic bullets); (6) *deadly force*—choke holds, firearms. The police continuum of force *ends where the military one begins*, that is, with lethal force involving a growing number of casualties (automatic rifle, cannon, tanks... up to mass destruction weapons). This is in part why the growing militarization of the police is such a threatening development.

The greatest obstacle to addressing the normative question in relation to the use of force is that we do not possess a shared criterion for evaluating whether an occurrence of police use of force is condemnable or not. Therefore, developing a *count* of police misuse of force that is beyond all dispute is not presently an achievable task (Adams, 1999a:10). There is a miscellany of words that are used to refer to the misuse of force by police, such as police brutality, improper, abusive, illegitimate or, finally, illegal use of force, for which we have no standard of application. For instance, the distinction between what is illegitimate and what is illegal is deeply contentious, many persons claiming that illegitimacy should coincide with illegality, when we are dealing with police misuse of force. Within this article, it is the notion of *excessive force* that will be preferred over those enumerated above. Excessive force is the designation of choice because it leads into a distinction between two issues that should be treated separately, although they are closely related. The first of these issues refers to the application of a quantum of force disproportionate to the problem which it is intended to solve, and it is discussed at the level of a case by case assessment. The second issue concerns excessive frequency in the use of force, and it is more of a systemic issue, certain police organizations being prone to seek a violent solution to a greater number of incidents than others.

Both the factual and the normative questions will be addressed. With respect to the factual question, most reported findings draw on research conducted in Anglo-Saxon countries, particularly in the United States and in the United Kingdom. Because of a special awareness of the violence involved in U.S. policing, research into this question is more elaborate in this country than in any other. This is at the same time a blessing for and a limitation of research.

II. THEORETICAL APPROACHES

Although there are growing intimations of change, police research is still presently conducted within a Weberian paradigm. Max Weber insisted upon defining the State by its specific means—violence—rather than by its ends, which he viewed as indefinite and therefore as unspecific. He also claimed that the State was endowed with a monopoly on the legitimate use of violence. Weber's position on the State monopoly of violence consists in postulates which he considered to be historically self-evident and which he did not attempt to demonstrate. For instance, in his 1919 conference on politics as a vocation, he relies on the authority of Leon Trotsky to support his point that the State's specific instrument is violence.

Weber spoke more of the State than of the police. However, since the police are, with the military, the embodiment of his theory of the State, it was natural to apply to the police what he said of the State. In the U.S., William Ker Muir developed a theory of the police based on Max Weber's characterization of politics as a vocation (Muir, 1977). It is, however, Egon Bittner who articulated the most detailed argument for viewing the capacity to use force as the core of the police role. Bittner's insights were further developed by Klockars (1985), and they illuminate the approach taken within the Anglo-Saxon common law tradition to the police use of force. Not only does Bittner's work shed light on the main tenets of this productive tradition but, more importantly, it did set in great part the research agenda on policing in the English speaking world. Bittner's argument is complex and brings together several assertions which, taken as a whole, present an integrated perspective on public policing. The main elements of this paradigm, to the development of which other authors also contributed, are the following:

1. The Police and the Civilizing Process

As recounted by Bittner, the foundation of the police in nineteenth century England should be understood within the context of a general movement to limit as much as it was possible the resort to violence (Bittner, 1970/1990:102–108). Concentrating the legitimate use of physical coercion into the hands of a public institution accountable to an elected parliament was a momentous step in the process of social pacification. The account given by Bittner of the foundation of the British police is remarkably consonant with the work of Norbert Elias ([1939] 1994; [1989] 1996). In his description of the civilizing process, Elias pays more attention to the transformation of warriors into courtiers than he does to the creation of the French *Lieutenance de Police* by Louis XIV at the end of the seventeenth century. However, following the logic of his work, Elias would not have averted from accounting for the foundation of the French police as a moment in the civilizing process. The upshot of these remarks is to stress how much one misunderstands Bittner's position in taking it as a tough-minded ideology stressing the aggressive nature of police work. For this school of thought, the invention of modern public policing takes place within the context of a movement towards the *minimization* of the use of force within society. In a classic paper, where he contrasts the role of the police as pursuers of such notorious criminals as Willie Sutton, on the one hand, and as emulators of Florence Nightingale, the founder of trained nursing as a profession for women, on the other, Bittner wrote:

> Believing that the real ground for his existence is the perennial pursuit of the likes of Willie Sutton—for which he lacks both opportunity and resources—the policeman feels compelled to minimize the significance of those instances of his performance in which he seems to follow the footsteps of Florence Nightingale. Fearing the role of the nurse or, worse yet, the role of the social worker, the policeman combines resentment against what he has to do day in, day out with the necessity of doing it. And in the course of it he misses his true vocation. (Bittner, 1974/ 1990:263)

Those lines provide context for the claim that the capacity to use force is at the heart of the police function.

2. Situational vs. Instrumental Force

This is one of the crucial divides in the theory of policing. Reflecting upon his theory, Bittner declared:

> (...)I am *not* saying the police work consists of using force to solve problems, but only that police work consists of coping with problems in which force *may have to be used.* This is a distinction of extraordinary importance.(Bittner, 1974/1990:256, emphasis in text)

"Situationalists" like Bittner do not assume that force *will be used as a rule* to solve the problems for which police are called upon. Whether force will be used or not depends on the features of a situation as they are perceived by the intervening police officer. Situationalists and instrumentalists differ in two basic respects. First, although the former conceive the use of force as the core of the police role, they do not reduce policing to its hard core and view the police as forming a diverse organization geared to the solving of miscellaneous problems. The latter tend to reduce the police to a compact instrument, largely uniform in its nature, such as for instance a hammer, to use Monjardet's metaphor

(Monjardet, 1996:15). Second, the features of the situation mobilizing the intervention of the police, on the one hand, and the expectations of the public, on the other, are for the situationalists the prime determinants of police action. Instrumentalists tend to stress the demands of the governing political authorities as the main influence on police operations (Monjardet, 1996:16).

However varied may be the circumstances in which the police are summoned, they share one common trait which is summarized by Bittner as involving *something-that-ought-not-to-be-happening-and-about-which-someone-had-better-do-something-now* (Bittner, 1974/1990:249). Noting the difficulty of defining contemporary police mainly in terms of their function, police sociologists have recently sought in the *emergency* nature of the situations which trigger a demand for police intervention the basic feature of policing (Reiner, 1997:1007). Indeed, the use of force is in a significant number of instances consequent upon the emergency character of a situation. Emergency crises are precisely the type of situations where there is no time for anything else than nonnegotiable forceful action, and where resistance to the attempted solution must be overpowered in order to prevent the crisis from reaching its undesirable outcome.

3. The Fundamentality of Force

For Bittner and like-minded thinkers, the police are then nothing else than a mechanism for the distribution of situationally justified force in society (Bittner, 1970/1990:123). The emphasis given to the justification provided by the context of intervention leads Bittner to declare that the question "What are policemen supposed to do?" is almost tantamount to the question "What kinds of situations require remedies that are non-negotiably coercible?" (Bittner, 1970/1990:125). The stress that situationalists put on the force-inducing circumstances that surround police action may generate an important misunderstanding. The features of a situation requiring the police to intervene may explain why they *actually* resort to force. It would, however, be a mistake to further conclude that beneath emergency there is a primordial or an idealtypical situation providing the ground for endowing the police with their unique *capacity* to use force when need arises. Such being the cultural connection between policing and crime control, the most common form of this mistake would be to believe that the police are granted powers of physical coercion *because* they are required to enforce the criminal law. This conception of the police role puts things upside down:

> It is *not* that policemen are entitled to use force because they must deal with nasty criminals. Instead, the duty of handling nasty criminals devolves on them *because* they have the more general authority to use force *as needed* to bring about desired objectives (Bittner, 1974/1990:257, emphasis in text).

Bittner underlines the precedence of force over crime control by making a perspicuous remark: police actually show little interest in offenders against whom force may not have to be used in bringing them to justice. The truth of this remark is ever more obvious today, when the scope of economic, environmental, and cyber crime is better known. According to a survey of police executives conducted by the Canadian Association of Chiefs of Police, 73 percent of the respondents admitted that they would not give a high priority to the fight against white-collar crime, although 83 percent of them admitted that the social and economic costs of this type of crime were among the greatest (KPMG Canada,

1995). The same thing can be said of law enforcement: police show limited interest for enforcing laws that conceivably need little coercion to be implemented (e.g., offenses against justice such as perjury or bribery, traffic regulations, municipal bylaws, and so forth). These remarks raise, however, an arduous question. If police coercive powers do not spring from any unique ground situation that the police have to manage nor from the duty to enforce the law, including the criminal law, whence do they derive? Saying that they originate from all the previous taken together is not providing any specific answer. Within the Weber–Bittner paradigm, force appears to underlie all else so that it ultimately defies to be ascribed an origin.

4. Competence and Performance

One of the constitutive distinctions in the social sciences was first formulated in linguistics, which was at one time a pilot discipline for the humanities. Whether it distinguishes between language and speech (Saussure), system and process (Hjelmslev), or competence and performance (Chomsky), linguistics makes a crucial distinction between the general capacity for language and its actualization in various speech acts (Searle). Likewise, Bittner differentiates between the police capacity to use force (Bittner, 1970/1990:120), which is more precisely called the specific *competence* of the police in later work (Bittner, 1974/1990:255), and its actualization. With due caution, a comparison between linguistics and police sociology may provide important keys for probing deeper into the theory of policing.

First, competence and performance are wholly distinct. Persons may take vows of silence for various purposes without ever loosing their competence for speech. In the same way, Bittner stresses that "the actual use of physical coercion and restraint is *rare* for all policemen and that many policemen are *virtually never in the position of having to resort to it*" (Bittner, 1970/1990:125, emphasis not in text). He even envisages a brave new world where police would no more resort to force, but where there would still be a need to maintain their specific competence to do so (Bittner, 1970/1990:187). This being said on a general level, there is an important difference between competence and performance as conceived in linguistics and in police sociology. Speaking persons not only exercise their linguistic competence on a very regular basis, but it is expected from them to do so. In contradistinction, not only do police rarely apply their competence to use force, as far as we know, but more importantly they are *not* expected to (in the kind of democratic society that Bittner is talking about).

Second, linguistics stumbled upon the question of finding the root of human competence to perform speech, this competence being boldly stated by Chomsky to be innate, in his *Cartesian Linguistics*. The source of the police mandate to resort to force is likewise problematic. Bittner adamantly stresses that their mandate cannot be interpreted as resting on the substantive authorizations contained in the penal codes or any other codes (Bittner, 1974/1990:263). This position is actually supported by an examination of various countries' legislation. For instance, the law in Belgium only provides for three cases in which the police can resort to physical coercion: self-defense, the protection of persons, places and property under the care of the *Gendarmerie* or the *Police communale* and the dispersion of crowds (Valkeneer, 1991:90–91). These legal authorizations being too narrow to account for the general mandate of the Belgian police (or any other) to use force, de Valkeneer indirectly derives this mandate from the legal prohibition for the police to use force without legitimate reason (*sans motif légitime*). The reasoning seems to be the following: since legislation explicitly forbids police to have recourse to force without a legitimate ground, it must therefore also authorize force in all legitimate cases. Notwithstanding the fact that this reasoning is largely tautologous, the police mandate thus construed largely extrapolates the letter of the law. Bittner's claim that the use of force not involving firearms is almost entirely uncharted is in essence vindicated (Bittner, 1970/1990:188). With the exception of the U.S. Supreme Court ruling in *Tennessee v. Garner* (105 S.Ct. 1694 (1985)), which held that the use of deadly force to stop a fleeing suspect is not reasonable unless the officer has a probable cause to believe that this individual poses a danger either to the police or the community, the police continuum of force is a legal *terra incognita* in its other parts. Although *Tennessee v. Garner* does not legally apply elsewhere, it was influential in all Anglo-Saxon common law countries.[2]

5. The Specific Character of the Police Competence to Use Force

Of all features of the Weber–Bittner paradigm there is one which was particularly assailed by critics. Both Weber and Bittner grant to the public police a *monopoly* on the use of force. There are actually an important number of professions that do legally exercise a great deal of force, among which the medical profession is prominent. Surgeons, for instance, are legally licensed by the Canadian Criminal Code (C.C.C., section 45) to inflict grievous injuries (surgical cuts) on persons for the alleged sake of their health, this claim being now successfully challenged in court with increasing frequency when operations are needlessly performed. Psychiatric institutions may be even more violent than prisons, with their paraphernalia of electrical and chemical treatments. In addition to the medical profession, prison guards and private security readily come to mind in addition to the vestigial authority vested in ship captains (C.C.C., s. 44), parents, and teachers. With respect to parents and teachers, there is in the Anglo-Saxon tradition a punitive streak against children, who were in the nineteenth century submitted to whipping and caning by their parents and teachers, as the novels of the British writer A. C. Swinburne eloquently testify to. Parents and teachers are still endowed by the C.C.C. with correctional powers—within reasonable limits—in relation to their wards (C.C.C., s. 43). The authority of parents to use physical violence against their children was questioned in 2000 by the Canadian courts. The debate revolved around the issue of abolishing this parental power or to spell out more explicitly its limitations. It was decided not to modify the C.C.C. and leave section 43 in its present obsolete form. The difference between police powers and all others becomes salient when police are compared to prison guards. The authority of prison guards to use

---

[2]Editor's note: The police legislation in some of the States in the Federal Republic of Germany entails explicit regulation concerning the use of firearms which is allowed only

- · to defend oneself against imminent danger of life or physical integrity,
- · to prevent an imminent crime which itself includes the use of firearms or explosives,
- · to arrest persons suspected of the aforementioned crimes,
- · to prevent the flight of persons who are (or are earmarked to be) in official arrest, under certain circumstances defined by law.

Besides these regulations, the police use of firearms can be justified also in accordance with general provisions for situations of self-defense or assistance in a case of emergency. In these cases, a careful scrutiny is required as to whether the use of firearms was necessary or whether alternative (i.e., "milder") means were available.

force is limited to the inmates of a particular institution over which they rule by virtue of a specific legal command (Bittner, 1970/1990:122–123). Limitations also apply to all alleged competitors of the police: private security is limited to a sliver of private space, teachers only ruled over their own students, and parents over their own children. Not so with the police, who are endowed, within their territorial jurisdiction, with the general capacity to use force against anyone therein and under all circumstances in which they exercise their considerable discretion.

The encompassing nature of their power to use force is what sets the police apart from all other individuals and professions. It is also why this power cannot be explicitly spelled out in law. Bittner already acknowledged that the creation of an elite police organization monopolizing the use of force magnifies the danger of tyranny (Bittner, 1970/1990:207). Formally embedding in law the *all-embracing* power to use force that the police exercise in practice, albeit on a limited scale in democratic societies, would run the risk of facilitating the advent of an authoritarian State (or worse).

6. Collective Violence

Bittner's work is as much exemplary in what it skips than in what it says. Based on what he witnessed in the U.S., he believes that the police are grossly inadequate in handling civil disorder, and he suggests that the policing of political protest should be left to a military peacekeeping force such as the U.S. National Guard (Bittner, 1970/1990:191). The important implication is that this position spares him the need to discuss in any detail the whole issue of the maintenance of order in the case of mass demonstrations and of collective violence.

There may be various reasons for this blank, one of them being his relentless criticism of militarism within police organizations (Bittner, 1970/1990:136 and f.). The true explanation may, however, lie outside Bittner's theoretical commitments and rest on features of U.S. society and Anglo-Saxon policing. There was, beginning from the great rallies against racial segregation in the mid-fifties until the end of the war in Vietnam in 1975, a great wave of political protest in the U.S. However, the tradition of mass demonstrations never gained in North America and perhaps more generally in Anglo-Saxon countries as strong a foothold as in Continental Europe, because, among other reasons, labor conflicts are not politicized as much. Large police organizations specializing in the control of crowds such as the French *Compagnie républicaines de sécurité* (CRS) or, in the various German *Länder*, the *Bereitschaftspolizei* were not created in Anglo-Saxon countries, with the exception of rather small police units using shock tactics. Notwithstanding the events in Northern Ireland, which are by themselves a separate field of research, violent demonstrations during the Thatcher years and the rise of football hooliganism raised increasingly the issue of police militarization in the U.K. However, this debate is fairly recent (Jefferson, 1990; Waddington et al., 1989; Waddington, 1993) and has generated only a fraction of the research devoted to policing individual offenders.

The consequences of this conjuncture is that Bittner's research agenda was largely followed and that research on the policing of collective behavior is in a state of underdevelopment in the English-speaking world. In a telling illustration, a recently published treatise on police ethics defines *order maintenance* as "the peacekeeping role of police, in which police intervene in disputes between *two people* or between *a citizen* and a neighborhood." (Crank and Caldero, 2000:262, emphasis not in text). This relative incapacity to go beyond the policing of individuals is to be regretted for at least two important reasons. First, the policing of collective behavior is itself achieved through collective or group policing. Once it is decreed that collective behavior in most of its manifestations falls outside the regular police mandate, the greater part of policing in groups is also barred by the same token from the research agenda. Second, since the policing of collective behavior takes place in public and also on television, it therefore provides the most perceptible examples of police use of excessive force. Consequently, by focussing on the policing of individual delinquents by police individuals, the research agenda on the use of violence fails to provide explanations and remedies for the highest profile abuses, with the exception of sensationalized instances of the most excessive brutality against individuals (e.g., the beating of Rodney King in Los Angeles and the Abner Louima incident in New York) and of police shootings of innocent persons (e.g., the killing of Amadou Diallo, which also occurred in New York; in France, police killings of ethnic youths have sparked devastating riots).

III.   EMPIRICAL RESEARCH

One of the difficulties particular to the study of force is that methods and findings are so intertwined that they are at risk of becoming involved in a vicious circle. There are two statements that one finds repeatedly in the research literature: the first one is that police use force infrequently (Adams, 1999a:3), and the second is that the study of infrequent events is methodologically daunting (Adams, 1999a:5). However, it may be that it is the other way around: the study of incidents involving force, most specially its excessive use, raises nearly insuperable problems, and we declare the phenomenon to be infrequent because it is difficult to observe. A recent and important report by the Office of Justice Programs of the U.S. Department of Justice provides a striking illustration of this circularity. In one of the report's chapters entitled "What we know about police use of force," Kenneth Adams writes approvingly:

> As Bayley and Garofalo observed, police-citizen encounters that involve use of force and injury are "quite rare" (Adams, 1999a:3).

Yet in the closing chapter of the same report, Adams also writes:

> Observational methods are highly inefficient at capturing use-of-force incidents not only because these are infrequent events but also because a researcher can observe only one or two officers on assignment at a time. Bayley and Garofalo had six observers spend a total of 2,000 hours observing police officers in the field. These observations identified 37 use-of-force incidents by police, the majority of which involved relatively low levels of force. (Adams, 1999b:68)

The first of these two quotes imply that police use of force is *in fact* infrequent. The second implies that this infrequency may be the result of inefficient observation methods. The problem is that both statements refer to the same research, Bayley and Garofalo's.

As Reiner rightly noticed, the pioneering study of policing in the U.K.—Banton (1964)—initiated the dominant research strategy for most subsequent work in this field, that is, detailed participant observation (Reiner, 1997:1001). The pathbreaking research of Westley ([1951], 1970), Bittner (1970), and Manning (1977), which stressed the role of force in policing, also used qualitative methods (participant observation and intensive interviewing). More recent research is now increasingly using quantitative methods based on the statistical analysis of police official records, use of force reports, civilian injury and hospital records, death certificates, court records, and various forms of surveys. In the U.S., several important surveys were conducted in the last few years. The Police Foundation undertook a mailing survey using an extensive 18-page questionnaire that was answered by a total of 1,111 law enforcement agencies (Pate, Fridell, & Hamiston, 1993). The Bureau of Justice Statistics (BJS) supplemented in 1996 the National Crime Victimization Study with a pilot test of its Police–Public Contact Study (PPCS). The 1996 pilot test involved interviews with 6,421 persons; the 1999 PPCS questionnaire will survey a much larger sample. The BJS is also cofunding with the International Association of Chiefs of Police (IACP) a national use-of-force database to which 110 police agencies have already supplied information on police use of physical, chemical, electronic, impact, and lethal force since 1995, on a voluntary and anonymous basis. As seen before, researchers who develop large databases tend to regard observational methods as being "highly inefficient" at capturing use-of-force incidents (Adams, 1999b:68). They are also critical of what they view as overgeneralizations based on the simple accumulation by human rights militants of alleged incidents involving excessive use of force in various sites (see the comments of Adams, 1999a:2, 13; note 3 on Human Rights Watch, 1998:1–28). Not unexpectedly, human rights organizations are themselves suspicious of U.S. federal data collection of police use of violence (Human Rights Watch, 1998:106–111).

Following Adams (1999a, 1999b), the findings are presented according to what is known about the police use of force, what is reasonably suspected, and what is not known.

1.   What Is Known: The Rareness of Force

This statement first means that *police use force infrequently*. This is a consistent finding of all research that attempted to develop a count of force (see the review of prior literature by Pate et al., 1993:149). Using observational methods, Bayley and Garofalo coded 467 potentially violent police mobilizations out of some 1,500 events that were observed in three New York precincts selected for their high levels of activity; the police used force against citizens in 37 cases, that is 2.5 percent of all the events observed (Bayley and Garofalo, 1989:5–7). Extrapolating from interviews conducted with 6,421 persons in the PPCS 1996 pilot test, it was estimated that one in five U.S. residents age 12 or older (44.6 million persons) had face-to-face contact with the police, many of these contacts being in connection with traffic stops; approximately 1 percent or 500,000 of these persons were subjected to use of force or threat of force (Greenfeld, Langan, & Smith, 1997). This figure is reduced to 0.0419 percent—four hundredths of 1 percent, that is, 25 times lower—in the preliminary findings based on the IACP database, which may be subject to reporting biases. Interestingly, it is the observational research, alleged to be the most inefficient, which captured the highest rate of police use of force (2.5 percent).

Rareness of violence primarily means that when police resort to force they resort to the lesser forms of violence in the continuum of police coercion (physical contacts). In the Police Foundation extensive survey of police agencies, it was found that the use of the upper range of the spectrum of police violence was indeed infrequent, but that relatively high rates were reported for the use of bodily force and of handcuffs, and for the unholstering of weapons (Pate et al., 1993:153). Interestingly enough, firearms are infrequently *used,* but they are the most frequent weapon *displayed* (Garner & Maxwell, 1999:31).

Arrest, particularly when the suspect is resisting or caught in hot pursuit, is the most typical context where force is used. Garner and Maxwell (1999:33) found that out of 7,712 arrests performed by officers from six different police departments 1,184 cases (15.8 percent) involved the use of at least one weaponless physical violence tactic. This is far more than the 1 percent of use of force that was found in all face-to-face police–citizen encounters in the PPCS pilot test. Jobard makes the important point that there may be a *concentrated* and therefore much more frequent use of force against persons that the police consider their own "property" (drug addicts, prostitutes, habitual criminals; Jobard, 1999:100; for the notion of "police property," see Lee, 1981). Nevertheless, 84 percent of all arrests involved no violence, and the ones that did involved mostly grabbing. The significance of these figures is enhanced when they are compared to the use of lethal force in a country like Brazil. Blumberg (1986, 1997) estimated that between 300 and 700 persons were killed yearly by the police in the U.S., 450 persons being the most often given figure. Official figures for the one State of Sao Paulo in Brazil reveal that 1,074 and 1,470 civilians were respectively killed by the military police in 1991 and 1992—898 civilians were killed in 1991 in the Metropolitan Area of Sao Paulo alone (Chevigny, 1995:148). Against the Brazilian data, it does appear that the use of force by the police is a relatively rare occurrence in the U.S. This is all the more significant in view of the fact that the U.S. police are more violent than their counterparts in other Western-style democracies.

In summary, what is known is essentially relevant for answering the *descriptive* questions about the use of force, considered in its extent and factual character. It contrasts strongly with what is reported in the media and believed by public opinion, as it is shaped by the media. Both tend to overstate the extent of police violence, particularly with regard to deadly force. The findings are also at odds with police culture, where the mystique of energy with its cluster of themes (power, action, urgency, risk, force, machismo) plays an overwhelming role (Crank, 1998:c. 5). Lastly, the findings on the infrequency of the use of force by police are mostly negative in their nature. Reflecting upon their extensive survey, Pate et. al. (1993:165) declared that "one of the most important lessons of this study is the finding that so little is known about such a critical topic—the extent, nature, causes, and methods of dealing with police use of force."

2. What Is Suspected: The Selective Use of Force

It was learned that persons resisting arrest are more likely to have force used against them. We also know that persons under the influence of alcohol or drugs, or who are mentally impaired, are more likely to use body language instead of speech and to be or be perceived by the police as more confrontational. To this extent, there is a higher probability that these persons would receive force by an arresting officer. There are numerous findings that support this hypothesis (Adams, 1999a:7–8). Other findings are ambiguous. Alpert and Dunham (1999:51) report that impaired suspects were no more likely to be physically coerced than nonimpaired suspects; however, they also found that impaired suspects are more than twice as likely than sober suspects to use a gun to resist the police (thereby leaving the police with little choice other than using force against them). Bittner, who investigated thoroughly the apprehension of mentally ill persons by police, noted that their emergency apprehension involved the use of physical violence in only a very few instances (Bittner, 1967/1990:68). Nevertheless, some of the most grievous incidents of lethal police brutality in Canada have involved mentally ill persons who were in a crisis.

The situation is even more controversial with regard to the use of force against ethnic minorities. From the pioneering work of Westley ([1951], 1970), Banton (1964), and

Bittner (1974/1990:259) to the most recent reports (Human Rights Watch, 1998), the evidence is internationally overwhelming and accepted: racial and ethnic minorities are the object of a disproportionate amount of police force. However, the part allowed to racial and ethnic *discrimination* in the explanation of this disparate treatment is the focus of bitter and persistent controversy. Two quotes from the work of the British sociologist Robert Reiner epitomize the present conundrum in this respect. Reiner wrote in 1989 that despite methodological caveats, "the quantity and quality of evidence is such as to render any doubts about discrimination fanciful" (Reiner, 1989:8). He also added in 1992 that is was "inconceivable that the (statistical) approach could ever conclusively establish racial discrimination" (Reiner, 1992:5). Therein lies the substantial paradox. On the one hand, the evidence for disparity in treatment is so shattering that it seemingly does not allow of explanations other than racial and ethnic prejudice. On the other hand, most statistical attempts to demonstrate the presence of police discrimination are inconclusive, when all variables are rigorously controlled for.

The most telling illustration of the above predicament are the results of Fyfe's classic study of the 2,926 police shootings in New York City between 1971 and 1975 (Fyfe, 1981:370). Fyfe came to the following conclusions:

- black and Hispanic officers shot and wounded citizens approximately twice as often as white officers (rates per 1,000 officers = 49.8, 46.3, and 25.4, respectively);
- black and Hispanic officers engaged in fatal shootings with significantly greater frequency than whites (rates per 1,000 officers = 29.4, 21.6, and 15.3, respectively);
- black and Hispanic officer rates of involvement in fatal interracial shootings (black versus black fatal shooting rate per 1,000 officers = 19.6; Hispanic versus Hispanic rate = 9.9) are more than twice as high as the white officer rates versus members of those minority groups (8.2 and 3.6, respectively);
- black officers engaged in off-duty shootings five times as frequently as white officers and Hispanics nearly four times as often (rates per 1,000 officers, black = 59.7, Hispanic = 39.4, and white = 10.1).

These figures are explained in great part by the fact that black and Hispanic officers are deployed among their own respective people in ghettos where the level of violence is much higher than in other parts of New York. They also live in these violent communities, which accounts at least partially for the fact that their rate of off-duty shootings is much higher than their white colleagues. Whatever may be the interpretation of these findings, they cannot be seen as confirming that white racial or ethnic prejudice is the source of the disproportionate use of deadly force against minorities. Many other studies can be quoted that lead to similar conclusions.

3.   What Is Not or Little Known: Excessive Force and Group Policing

Taking into account academic research and the reports published by various commissions of inquiry and by agencies devoted to the protection of human rights, there is a fairly extensive literature on police deviance (for a review of this literature, see Kappeler, Sluder, & Alpert, 1998). This literature addresses several topics, and excessive force is only one of them. The research devoted to this specific issue is much more narrow. It suffers from three limitations. First, since no common criterion for counting occurrences of excessive force has been so far developed, its extent cannot be objectively measured. More generally speaking, the systematic methods of quantitative research find little application in this field. Consequently, issues such as modeling the enfolding of situations, which are conducive to the use of excessive force, and issues such as measuring the impact of the various remedies brought against the use of disproportionate violence are not comprehensively addressed. Second, excessive force being a form of deviance, it tends to hide behind a wall of secrecy. The data which are presently used are mostly collected by specially appointed commissions of inquiry, police complaints committees and civilian review boards, and police internal affairs units (who rarely disclose their statistics); researchers can also review civil law suits against police, criminal prosecutions, and press reports. With the exception of the legal proceedings, these sources of data record externally provided information, and their reliability is as limited as other reactive recording mechanisms by underreporting and reporting biases. Finally, it is very difficult to approach normative issues without a normative commitment, which may appear to harbor research biases. The result of all these limitations is that research on excessive force is embroiled in controversy and that it often generates acute antagonism between the policing and the legal establishments, the advocates of human rights being singled out for caricature as being the criminal's boon and the policeman's scourge.

This is not to say that a state of complete ignorance prevails in respect to the normative issue. A U.S. commission of inquiry into the police use of excessive force—the 1991 Christopher Commission who investigated the beating of Rodney King by officers of the Los Angeles Police Department—found that less than one half on 1 percent of the department's sworn officers accounted for more than 15 percent of allegations of excessive force or improper tactics. This finding of a disproportionate involvement of a small proportion of officers in the use of excessive force echoes similar findings about career criminals. It needs, however, to be replicated in other police departments to be considered as confirmed.

As is eloquently shown by P. A. J. Waddington (1993: Methodological Appendix), the policing of mass demonstrations lends itself to observational methods, since it does take place in public. Despite this advantage for research, both the descriptive and the normative issues have largely been overlooked with respect to the policing of collective behavior, with the recent exceptions of France (Favre, 1992; Wieviorka et al., 1999) and the U.K. (Waddington et al., 1989; Waddington, 1992; Critcher & Waddington, 1996). In both France and the U.K., the research does not focus exclusively on police operations but on mass demonstrations and riots in all of their aspects. D. Waddington and his colleagues have developed the "flashpoints model" which stresses the role of the police in triggering riots either through provocation or a breach of negotiated agreements with demonstrators (Waddington, 1992:26–27). In a newly published collection of essays on the policing of protest in seven different Western countries, the various authors have emphasized that the police has been using less confrontational tactics in recent years, but that there were indications of an impending hardening of their strategy (della Porta and Reiter, 1998). Wieviorka balances both approaches towards the role of the police in mass demonstrations. In his general analysis, he stresses that the police apparatus may contribute to generate the mass violence which it has a mandate to contain, particularly through its increasing militarization and loss of legitimacy (Wieviorka et al., 1999:57–61). In the more detailed analyses, however, his colleagues show that the individual police officers (*îlotiers*) who are stationed in the ethnic suburbs where most of the violence is taking place have a deeper understanding of the local youth population involved in the riots than their colleagues aggressively practicing crime control (*Brigades Anti-Criminalité*—BAC), and the military police who are dispatched in mass to counter public disorders (Wieviorka et al., 1999:260–262).

IV.   FUTURE DEVELOPMENTS

When the British invented modern policing in 1829, they insisted that all police be in uniform; plainclothes investigators were allowed to operate only in 1841 after strong debate. The theory of public policing which has been developed so far is traditional in the sense that its primary, if not its only object is the activity of patrolmen in uniform (Bittner, 1974/1990:241). There are relatively few books on criminal investigation. This focus of research on the uniformed rank and file has several consequences, the first one being that this research looks rather to the past of policing than to its future.

1.   Epistemology

The defining character of patrolmen in uniform is their visibility. Police visibility plays a cardinal role in police strategy, particularly in the case of community policing. This emphasis on the deterrent effect of police visibility results in the fact that the perceived physical *presence* of police is integrated into the continuum of police *force*, thus conflating capacity with actuality. This conflation indicates a deep-seated problem within the Weber–Bittner paradigm: whether it is open to empirical falsification is questionable. If, for the police, just *being* there is tantamount to *acting* there, it becomes nearly impossible to refute (or to validate) empirically the claim that the police are defined by their capacity to use force. They exercise this capacity merely by being present in the context of situation.

However, when the main finding of empirical research is said to be that the police use force infrequently, what is thereby meant by force is much more tangible than their mere physical presence (if not more than that was meant, then the police could *always* be said to be using force). There is a pressing need to seek a closer fit between the meaning of the capacity to use force, which defines the role of the police in theory, and the meaning of the actual use of force, when use-of-force incidents are the object of a count in the context of empirical research. The back-and-forth movement from theory to practice implies constantly switching from an equation between policing and force to a dichotomy between the two notions. One way of reaching a closer fit between theory and practice would be to develop what Merton called middle-range theories that would fill the gap between the construction of paradigms and the multiplication of narrow empirical monographs on a particular use of violence, such as deadly force (Pate et al., 1993:149; Geller & Scott, 1992).

2.   Research Agenda

It may be that force is defined too broadly in relation to policing as it is performed by patrolmen in uniform. To the contrary, it may also be that the continuum of force, as it is presently constructed, is actually *too narrow* to encompass the whole of policing.

There is a significant amount of force which is used by police *investigators*, particularly when they are trying to obtain a confession from a suspect. Police force in obtaining confessions also ranges over its own spectrum, which extends from psychological pressure to various forms of physical violence (sleep deprivation, beatings, and torture). Not only is there little research into police interrogation, but the whole issue of the specific kind of coercion which is used by police investigators is sidestepped. Needless to say, this kind of violence is exceedingly difficult to research because it is surrounded by the deepest secrecy.

One of the most striking evolutions in the field of policing is the development of technical surveillance (Ericson & Haggerty, 1997) and of undercover policing (Marx, 1988). This development raises a difficult question: to what extent does covert surveillance, which is exercised over individuals and groups without their consent, fit into the category of force? Should it be conceived as a form of *violence* since it undoubtedly is a *violation* of a person's privacy? Monjardet (1996:21) has coined the term "non contractual operational means" (*moyens d'action non contractuels*) in order to refer to police tactics targeting individuals without their consent, and he classifies all of them under the heading of the use of force. The problem with this answer is that covert surveillance is not only exercised without its target's consent but also without his or her *awareness*. There is something counterintuitive in identifying as violence an action which is taken against a person without his or her knowledge. Elucidating the various relationships between the notions of force and of nonconsensual surveillance is of primary importance for the future and might open a whole new field of research.

Brodeur (2000) proposes a typology of the various organizations using force. This typology is the result of cross-tabulating two pairs of traits, that is, on the one hand, the police ethos of minimum force as opposed to the military ethos of destructive force and, on the other hand, the police firepower as opposed to the military firepower. In short, ethos may be viewed as *contextual ethics* and may thereby strongly conflict from one institutional context to another; it should not be confused with general morality as conceived by Kant. For instance, Clausewitz who is probably the foremost influence on the shaping of the military ethos asserts that the aim of war is the destruction (*Vernichtung*) of the enemy's military power, and that maximum or utmost violence (*Äusserste Anwendung der Gewalt*) should be used to achieve this end (Clausewitz [1932–1934] 1972:c. II, p. 215 and c. I, section 3, p. 192; for thoughtful comments, see Aron, 1976:123, 183). With regard to the traits related to firepower, it must emphasized that compared to the military, the firepower of the police is negligible. A two-by-two combination of these features results in four types of organization: (1) *police*: police ethos combined with police firepower; (2) *military*: military ethos with military firepower; (3) *military police*: military ethos with police firepower; (4) *international peacekeeping forces*: police ethos with military firepower.

Traditional public police organizations are already studied, and the military fall outside the proper scope of a theory of policing. The two interesting cases are the hybrid ones (3 and 4) because both point to emerging trends in policing. In terms of firepower, the military police are still much closer to policing than to military organizations. However, compared to traditional police agencies, their firepower is significantly greater. Military police have begun to be studied in the U.K. (Jefferson, 1990; Waddington, 1993), and it is to be hoped that there will be an increasing volume of research on this crucial topic.

The challenging element in the study of peacekeeping is that it brings out how much the idea of a monopoly of legitimate force rests on the notion of a national State. In the international context where States clashes against each others, the idea of a monopoly on legitimate force is vacuous. All externally imposed force is perceived as oppression by at least one party to a conflict. There is an imposing body of literature on peacekeeping, but almost nothing in it addresses the issue of peacekeeping from a policing perspective (Brodeur, 1997).

V. THE PREVENTION OF THE USE OF EXCESSIVE FORCE

The prevention of the use of excessive violence by the police is a frustrating subject. There is basically no agreement on the scope of the problem, and consequently no agreement on the amount of effort that should be devoted to its solution. There is not even accord on whether there is a problem or not, for public opinion swings wildly between cycles where policing is claimed to be a bigger threat than crime itself, and cycles where moral panics precipitate a demand for more police power.

The mechanisms for the prevention of the use of excessive force are well known and have little varied since the 1960s. They include selective recruitment, training (which is increasingly encompassing the teaching of ethics—Crank and Caldero, 2000), supervision in the field, and a variety of controls enhancing accountability. Among the latter, one finds internal administrative and investigative controls, external controls such as civilian complaint boards, judicial control (exclusion of evidence), legal controls (criminal prosecutions, civil lawsuits), and ministerial political control. Although there is no profession which is under as much scrutiny as the police, there is a dearth of assessment of the impact of these various forms of control. Every major police department is periodically embroiled in a huge scandal involving the use of excessive force, which generates the impression that the police are under no control. The most important thing to stress in respect to these prevention and control mechanisms is that there is not one of them that will singly provide the answer to the use of excessive force. It is only through an approach where various elements are interlocking that abusive police violence will be contained. The greatest illusion of all is believing that criminal prosecutions of police abusers of force will remedy the problem (Pate et al., 1993:157).

There is a growing movement to place policing under the aegis of human rights (Cranshaw et al., 1998; Patten, 1999; Waddington, 1999; Institut für Bürgerrechte und Öffentliche Sicherheit: CILIP, 1981ff). With respect to policing, human rights may be divided into three categories: fundamental rights (e.g., freedom, life, and security), derivative rights, which are often expressed in the negative (e.g., the right not to be arbitrarily arrested or incarcerated, which derives from the fundamental right to be free), and procedural rights, such as the right to the assistance of a lawyer when arrested by the police. Those who advocate placing policing under the scope of human rights have a tendency to stress the significance of derivative and procedural rights at the expense of fundamental rights. Thereby, they put the emphasis on the limiting or, as viewed by the police, the negative aspects of human rights in respect to their "most noble cause," crime control. Police might be more receptive to the message of human rights defenders if the latter laid more stress on the police's own particular role in protecting fundamental rights such as life and security.

REFERENCES

Adams, Kenneth. (1999a). What We Know about Police Use of Force. In Kenneth Adams, Geoffrey Alpert, Roger Dunham, Joel Garner, Lawrence Greenfeld, Mark Henriquez, Patrick Langan, Christopher Maxwell & Steven Smith (Eds.), *Use of Force by Police. Overview of National and Local Data* (pp. 1–14). Washington: National Institute of Justice, Research Report, Jointly Published with the Bureau of Justice Statistics.

Adams, Kenneth. (1999b). A Research Agenda on Police Use of Force. In Kenneth Adams, Geoffrey Alpert, Roger Dunham, Joel Garner, Lawrence Greenfeld, Mark Henriquez, Patrick Langan, Christopher Maxwell & Steven Smith (Eds.), *Use of Force by Police. Overview of National and Local Data* (pp. 61–74). Washington: National Institute of Justice, Research Report, Jointly Published with the Bureau of Justice Statistics.

Alpert, Geoffrey P., & Roger G. Dunham. (1999). The Force Factor: Measuring and Assessing Police Use of Force and Suspect Resistance. In Kenneth Adams, Geoffrey Alpert, Roger Dunham, Joel Garner, Lawrence Greenfeld, Mark Henriquez, Patrick Langan, Christopher Maxwell & Steven Smith (Eds.), *Use of Force by Police. Overview of National and Local Data* (pp. 45–60). Washington: National Institute of Justice, Research Report, Jointly Published with the Bureau of Justice Statistics.

Aron, Raymond. (1976). *Penser la guerre, Clausewitz. I: L'âge européen. Vol. 1.* Paris: Gallimard.

Banton, Michael. (1964). *The Policeman in the Community.* London: Tavistock.

Bayley, David. (1983). Police: History. In Sanford H. Kadish (Ed.), *Encyclopedia of Crime and Justice* (pp. 1120–1131). New York: The Free Press.

Bayley, David H., & James Garofalo. (1989). The Management of Violence by Police Patrol Officers. *Criminology, 40*(1), 1–23.

Bittner, Egon. (1967). Police Discretion in Apprehension of Mentally Ill Persons. *Social Problems, 14*(3), 278–292.

Bittner, Egon. (1970). *The Function of the Police.* Rockville: Center for Studies of Crime and Delinquency, National Institute of Mental Health, Crime and Delinquency Issues Series.

Bittner, Egon. (1974). Florence Nightingale in Pursuit of Willie Sutton: A Theory of the Police. In Herbert Jacob (Ed.), *The Potential for Reform of Criminal Justice, Sage Criminal Justice System Annuals* (pp. 17–44). Beverly Hills: Sage Publications.

Bittner, Egon. (1990). *Aspects of Police Work.* Boston: Northeastern University Press.

Blumberg, Mark. (1986). Issues and Controversies with Respect of the Use of Deadly Force by Police. In Thomas Barker & David L. Carter (Eds.), *Police Deviance* (pp. 222–241). Cincinnati: Pilgrimage.

Blumberg, Mark. (1997). Controlling Police Use of Deadly Force: Assessing Two Decades of Progress. In Roger G. Dunham & Geoffrey P. Alpert (Eds.), *Critical Issues in Policing. Contemporary Readings. 3rd edition* (pp. 506–530). Prospect Heights: Waveland Press.

Brodeur, Jean-Paul. (1997). *Violence and Racial Prejudice in the Context of Peacekeeping.* Ottawa: Minister of Pubic Works and Government Services Canada.

Brodeur, Jean-Paul. (2000). Force policière et force militaire. *Éthique publique, 2*(1), 157–166.

Chevigny, Paul. (1995). *Edge of the Knife. Police Violence in the Americas.* New York: The New York Press.

Clausewitz, Carl von. (1972). *Vom Kriege [1932–1934].* Bonn: Ferd. Dümmlers Verlag.

Crank, John P. (1998). *Understanding Police Culture.* Cincinnati: Anderson Pub.

Crank, John P., & Michael A. Caldero. (2000). *Police Ethics. The Corruption of the Noble Cause.* Cincinnati: Anderson.

Cranshaw, Ralph, Barry Devlin, & Tom Williamson. (1998). *Human Rights and Policing. Standards for Good Behaviour and a Strategy for Change.* The Hague, London, Boston: Kluwer Law International.

Critcher, Chas, & David Waddington. (1996). *Policing Public Order: Theoretical and Practical Issues.* Aldershot UK, Brookfield USA: Avebury.

Della Porta, Donatella, & Herbert Reiter. (1998). *Policing Protest. The Control of Mass Demonstrations in Western Democracies.* Minneapolis, London: University of Minnesota Press.

Elias, Norbert. (1994). *The Civilizing Process.* Oxford: Blackwell. [First Published in German in 1939.]

Elias, Norbert. (1996). Civilization and Violence. On the State Monopoly of Violence and its transgression. In Norbert Elias, *The Germans. Power Struggles and the Development of Habitus in the Nineteenth and Twentieth Centuries* (pp. 171–203). New York: Columbia University Press. [First Published in German in 1989.]

Ericson, Richard V., & Kevin D. Haggerty. (1997). *Policing the Risk Society.* Toronto, Buffalo: Toronto University Press.

Favre, Pierre (Dir.). (1992). *La manifestation.* Paris: Presses de la Fondation Nationale des Sciences Politiques.

Funk, Albrecht. (1986). *Polizei und Rechtsstaat.* Frankfurt: Campus Verlag.

Fyfe, James. (1981). Who Shoots? A Look at Officer Race and Police Shootings. *Journal of Police Science and Administration, 9*(4), 367–382.

Garner, Joel H., & Christopher D. Maxwell. (1999). Measuring the Amount of Force Used By and Against the Police in Six Jurisdictions. In Kenneth Adams, Geoffrey Alpert, Roger Dunham, Joel Garner, Lawrence Greenfeld, Mark Henriquez, Patrick Langan, Christopher Maxwell & Steven Smith (Eds.), *Use of Force by Police. Overview of National and Local Data* (pp. 25–44). Washington: National Institute of Justice, Research Report, Jointly Published with the Bureau of Justice Statistics.

Geller, William, & Scott James. (1992). *Deadly Force. What We Know.* Washington: Police Executive Forum.

Greenfeld, Lawrence A., Patrick A. Langan, & Steven K. Smith. (1997). *Police Use of Force: Collection of National Data.* Washington: U.S. Department of Justice, Bureau of Justice Statistics and National Institute of Justice, November 1997, NCJ 165040.

Human Rights Watch. (1998). *Shielded from Justice. Police Brutality and Accountability in the United States.* New York, Washington, London, Brussels: Human Rights Watch.

Institut für Bürgerrechte und Öffentliche Sicherheit e. V. (1981ff). *Bürgerrechte und Polizei: CILIP.* Berlin: Verlag CILIP.

Jobard, Fabien. (1999). L'habilitation à l'usage de la force policière. *Revue de la Gendarmerie Nationale. Gendarmerie et citoyenneté, 192–193,* 100–102.

Jefferson, Tony. (1990). *The Case Against Paramilitary Policing.* Milton Keynes: Open University Press.

Jones Trevor, & Tim Newburn. (1998). *Private Security and Public Policing.* Oxford: Clarendon Press.

Johnston, Les. (1992). *The Rebirth of Private Policing.* New York: Routledge.

Kappeler, Victor E., Richard D. Sluder, & Geoffrey P. Alpert. (1998). *Forces of Deviance. Understanding the Dark Side of Policing. 2nd edition.* Prospect Heights: Waveland Press.

Klockars, Carl. (1985). *The Idea of Police.* Beverly Hills: Sage Pub.

KPMG Canada. (1995). *1995 Police Chiefs Surveys.* Toronto: Peat Marwick Thorne—KPMG Investigation and Security Inc. [URL: http://www.kpmg.ca/isi/vl/pcsur95e.htm or ftp://ftp.kpmg.ca/pub/isi/pcsur95e.pdf]

Lee, John Alan. (1981). Some Structural Aspects of Police Deviance in Relation with Minority Groups. In Clifford D. Shearing (Ed.), *Organizational Police Deviance* (pp. 49–82). Toronto: Butterworths.

Lofthouse, Michael. (1996). The Core Mandate of the Police. In Chas Critcher & David Waddington (Eds.), *Policing Public Order: Theoretical and Practical Issues* (pp. 39–51). Aldershot: Avebury.

Manning, Peter K. (1977). *Police Work: The Social Organization of Policing.* Cambridge: MIT Press.

Marx, Gary. (1988). *Undercover: Police Surveillance in America.* Berkeley: University of California Press.

Monjardet, Dominique. (1996). *Ce que fait la police. Sociologie de la force publique.* Paris: Éditions La Découverte.

Muir, William Ker, Jr. (1977). *Police, Street Corner Politicians.* Chicago: The University of Chicago Press.

Pate, Anthony M., Lorie A. Fridell, & Edwin E. Hamiston. (1993). *Police Use of Force: Official Reports, Citizen Complaints and Legal Consequences.* Washington: Police Foundation.

Patten, Christopher. (1999). *A New Beginning: Policing in Northern Ireland. The Report of the Independent Commission on Policing for Northern Ireland.* Belfast: Stationery Office.

Reiner, Robert. (1989). Race and Criminal Justice. *New Community, 16,* 5–21.

Reiner, Robert. (1992). *The Politics of the Police.* Toronto: University of Toronto Press.

Reiner, Robert. (1997). Policing and the Police. In Mike Maguire, Rod Morgan & Robert Reiner (Eds.), *The Oxford Handbook of Criminology. 2nd edition* (pp. 997–1049). Oxford: Oxford University Press.

Schneider, Hans Joachim. (1987). *Kriminologie.* Berlin, New York: Walter de Gruyter.

Valkeneer, Christian de. (1991). *Le droit de la police.* Bruxelles: De Boeck-Wesmael.

Waddington, David. (1992). *Contemporary Issues in Public Disorder. A Comparative and Historical Approach.* London, New York: Routledge.

Waddington, Peter A. J. (1993). The Case Against Paramilitarism Policing Considered. *British Journal of Criminology, 33*(3), 353–373.

Waddington, Peter A. J. (1999). *Policing Citizens: Authority and Rights.* London, Philadelphia: University College London, Taylor & Francis Group.

Waddington, David, Karen Jones, & Chas Critcher. (1989). *Flashpoints: Studies in Public Disorder.* London: Routledge.

Weber, Max. (1946). Politics as a Vocation. In Hans Gerth & Charles Wright Mills (Eds.), *From Max Weber: Essays in Sociology* (pp. 77–128). Oxford, New York: Oxford University Press.

Westley, William. (1970). *Violence and Police. A Sociological Study of Law, Custom and Morality.* Cambridge: MIT. [First Presented as a Ph.D. Dissertation in 1951.]

Wieviorka, Michel, Philippe Bataille, Karine Clément, Olivier Cousin, Farhad Khosrokhavar, Séverine Labat, Éric Macé, Paola Rebughini, & Nikola Tietze. (1999). *Violence en France.* Paris: Éditions du Seuil.

Wilson, James Q., & George Kelling. (1982). Broken Windows. *The Atlantic Monthly, 249*(3), 29–38.

GROUPS AND COLLECTIVITIES: POLITICAL AND IDEOLOGICAL VIOLENCE

Ethnopolitical Conflict and Separatist Violence

TED ROBERT GURR AND ANNE PITSCH

I. INTRODUCTION

The pursuit of political autonomy was the central issue of a great many of the world's most intense and protracted conflicts during the 1980s and 1990s. The protagonists in these conflicts were, on the one side, politically organized ethnic groups seeking greater autonomy or independence, and on the other, governments seeking to maintain their states' central authority and territorial integrity. Some of these conflicts have had appalling human costs, for example two million civilian deaths in Sudan between 1983 and 1999 and more than 140,000 in Bosnia.[1] Every heterogenous state with regionally concentrated minorities is at risk of separatist conflicts. The conflicts are not inherently violent, however. Many culturally distinct groups pursue separatist objectives by nonviolent political means, for example the Tatars of the Russian Federation and the First Nations of Canada. The 16 successor states of the USSR gained independence with virtually no violence, similarly the Czech and Slovak republics divorced peacefully in 1993. Even when organized violence has occurred in separatist conflicts, they are susceptible to negotiated settlement, as has happened in the Palestinian–Israeli conflict and the 20-year war between the Chakma peoples of the Chittagong Hills and the government of Bangladesh.

This chapter has three objectives. The first is to review some conceptual and theoretical issues in social science explanations of separatist conflicts. Second, it examines the

---

[1] Millard Burr (1993) estimates that 1.3 million southern Sudanese died of war-related causes between May 1983 and May 1993. An update of his report (Burr, 1999) says that renewed war, including fighting among contending southern factions, brought the death toll by early 1999 to two million. The U.N. has estimated that by the end of 1993, the Yugoslav war resulted in between 140,000–250,000 killed or missing and over four million displaced (Daadler, 1996:54).

W. Heitmeyer and J. Hagan (eds.), *International Handbook of Violence Research*, 227–245.

strategies used by 154 separatist groups in the 1990s and assesses the effects of three general factors on whether those groups chose violent or nonviolent strategies: discriminatory treatment, state repression, and the impact of democratization. Finally, it looks at evidence on the prospects for peaceful settlement of separatist conflicts. The conclusion identifies issues for further research.

II.   CONCEPTUAL AND EMPIRICAL DISTINCTIONS

Several distinctions about ethnicity and separatism are essential to defining the subject of this chapter. Most separatist movements are initiated by or on behalf of people who claim common ethnic or national interests. *Ethnic groups* or *ethnies* are peoples who share a distinctive and enduring collective identity based on a belief in common descent, shared experiences, and cultural traits. Their sense of shared identity may be ancient or recent, latent or active. *Ethnopolitical groups* is our term for ethnies whose ethnicity has political consequences, resulting either in differential treatment of group members or in political action on behalf of group interests, or both. The principal test of whether an identity group is "ethnopolitical" is whether (some of) its members articulate collective interests and objectives that are pursued in the political arena. Table II-2-1.1 provides estimates of numbers of ethnopolitical groups in the 1990s whose political objectives include separate political status, based on the Minorities at Risk study's global survey (see note 4, below). They are of three types:

- *Ethnonationalists* (40 groups) are regionally concentrated peoples with a history of organized political autonomy with their own state or states, traditional rulers, or regional government who have supported political movements for autonomy at some time since 1945. Examples are Scots, Kashmiris, and Kurds.
- *National minorities* (46 groups) are segments of a trans-state people with a history of organized political autonomy whose kindred control an adjacent state but who now constitute a minority in the state in which they reside. Examples are Albanians in Serbia and Macedonia, Russians in the Soviet successor states, and some of the Chinese communities in Southeast Asian countries.

Table II-2-1.1.   Number of ethnopolitical groups in the 1990s by group type and region

Region	Ethno-nationalist	Indigenous	National minority	Other minorities	Total
Western democracies and Japan	8	6	3	13	30
Eastern Europe and newly independent states	9	8	34	10	61
East, Southeast and South Asia	10	20	6	23	59
North Africa and the Middle East	8	4	3	13	28
Africa South of the Sahara	5	10	0	52	67
Latin America and the Caribbean	0	20	0	12	32
Global	40	68	46	123	277

Note: These data are compiled from the Minorities at Risk project, described in footnote 4. "Other minorities" include ethnoclasses, communal contenders, and religious sects (see Gurr, 2000:chap. 2).

- *Indigenous peoples* (68 groups) are conquered descendants of earlier inhabitants of a region who live mainly in conformity with traditional social, economic, and cultural customs that are sharply distinct from those of dominant groups. Indigenous peoples who had durable states of their own before conquest, like Tibetans, or who have given sustained support to modern movements aimed at establishing their own state, like the Kurds, are counted as ethnonationalists, not indigenous peoples.

Next we distinguish among different manifestations of separatism. The essential separatist demand is that the group gain greater political control over its own resources and destiny. This objective is usually defined in territorial terms but not necessarily in terms of independent statehood. Ethnonationalists often seek, or are prepared to settle for, substate autonomy in which they gain limited sovereignty within the state rather than internationally-recognized independence. National minorities usually pursue regional autonomy and cultural rights, but sometimes want to be reunified with their external kindred. Most indigenous peoples phrase their demands in terms of self-governance and control of their traditional lands within the framework of existing states. Moreover, separatists who are prepared to remain within existing states usually seek, in addition to territorial autonomy, access to central decision making, a greater share of state resources, and official recognition and protection of their culture and their separate status.

III.   THEORETICAL ISSUES IN THE STUDY OF SEPARATISM

Probably the most basic theoretical debate in studies of ethnicity and ethnonational movements centers on alternative assumptions about the nature of group identities. The *primordial* view is that ethnic movements are a manifestation of collective identity among people who share a common descent, history, and culture. Communal identities are analogous to family identities (see Horowitz, 1985:ch. 2). They are more essential and transcendent than associational identities, therefore political movements based on them are likely to be especially intense and persistent (see Geertz, 1963; Stack, 1986; van den Berghe, 1981). In this view, ethnonationalism "is a form of identity politics in which individuals seek statehood as an expression of their uniqueness" (Roeder, 2000:4; also see Connor, 1994; Greenfeld, 1992). Anthony D. Smith, for example, contends that historical ethnic identities provide the underpinnings of contemporary nationalist movements (Smith, 1986, 1998).

Critics of primordial assumptions argue that ethnicity is one among many alternative bases of identity. Ethnic identities gain significance when invoked by leaders with *instrumental* objectives, such as maintaining boundaries among groups, mobilizing a mass following, and seeking redress for discriminatory treatment. According to Paul Brass (1991), the transition from ethnic identity to nationalism is the result of elite competition for power, material gain, and status in modernizing societies. This parallels Michael Hechter's interpretation of separatist movements in Europe in the 1960s and 1970s as a strategic response of local politicians to their region's peripheral or "colonial" status vis-à-vis the state (Hechter, 1975; see also Tiryakian & Rogowski, 1985).

Similar to the instrumental view is the *constructivist* argument that ethnic identities are mutable social constructions. From this perspective, group identities are much more variable and more subject to manipulation than is implied by the primordial view (see

Brass, 1991; Laitin, 1998). Ernest Gellner has proposed a widely cited constructivist interpretation of European nationalisms, showing that they are the creation of intellectuals who revived, or in some instances created, the traditions, symbols, and language of national peoples (Gellner, 1983).

Efforts have been made to bridge the differences among these approaches (see McKay, 1982; Scott, 1990). Virginia Tilley recognizes that ethnic identities are based on shared social experiences and norms that are "adaptive and contingent" but "not entirely malleable" (Tilley, 1998:5). In Roeder's perspective, ethnic identities may be mutable in the longer run, but in the shorter run they are "primordial-like" constraints on the strategies followed by ethnopoliticians; his empirical analysis supports this view (Roeder, 2000). We suggest the following general formulation to link the primordial, instrumental, and constructivist perspectives: Ethnonational identities are likely to be persistent because they are rooted in shared culture and experiences, but their specific content, expression, and importance for a group vary in response to changes in the group's social and political environment and the strategies chosen by group leaders for responding to threats and opportunities in that environment.

A second issue of theoretical debate is specification of the social and structural conditions that give rise to ethnonational movements. One general approach emphasizes inequalities among peoples in heterogenous societies. Horowitz, in a wide-ranging study of separatist movements in postcolonial societies, observes that the great majority of secessionists live in economically backward regions of new states. Backward peoples in such regions are "early seceders" who act from fear of economic competition and political dominance by groups at the center. Advanced groups in backward regions are late and uncommon seceders but will attempt to do so when targeted by "reverse discrimination" and ethnic violence (Horowitz, 1985:ch. 6). Hechter, cited above, attributes regional separatism in West European societies essentially to uneven development. The Scots, Walloons, Bretons, and others spawned separatist movements based on resentment that they did not share in the prosperity generated by economic growth at the center. The next section outlines a general framework for explaining contemporary ethnonational movements that attempts to synthesize a wide range of such theories.

IV. AN ANALYTIC FRAMEWORK FOR EXPLAINING CONTEMPORARY SEPARATIST MOVEMENTS

Ethnically based movements for independence and autonomy increased sharply in the 1980s and 1990s. They were especially prominent in late and post-communist societies, where journalists and policy commentators often attributed them to the emergence of "repressed national identities" and "ancient hatreds." Such explanations reflect primordialist assumptions. Academics and others offered alternative instrumental and constructivist interpretations, suggesting the movements were the creation of opportunistic political leaders willing to play the "ethnic card" to build mass support. The "ancient hatreds" explanation for the Balkans' ethnic wars of the 1990s begs the question why the Balkan peoples were not at one another's throats from the 1950s to the 1980s. The same principle also "predicts" that American southerners should have resumed the Civil War and that black South Africans should be waging a race war against whites who once oppressed them. The "opportunistic leaders" explanation begs two other kinds of questions. It does not explain whether and why large numbers of people respond to some kinds of symbols and leaders but not others. And it does not explain why ethnonational leaders like Franjo Tudjman in Croatia and Slobodan Milosevic in Serbia led their people into war and ethnic cleansing campaigns, while others like Tatarstan's Mintimer Shaimiev and South Africa's Nelson Mandela led their peoples peacefully to self-determination.[2] Ancient grievances and the stratagems of leaders are misleadingly incomplete as explanations of separatist movements. Four general factors must be assessed to understand when and why such movements arise.[3] First is *the salience of a national people's identity* for its members, second is *the extent of their collective incentives* for political action. The salience of a national people's identity and their incentives for action both depend on their situation. If people are treated differently by others because of their ethnicity or nationality, and especially when they are targets of discrimination and repression, group identity becomes more important—indeed it may crowd out any and all other identities. Discrimination and repression also establish strong incentives for the group to act collectively to protect themselves and to improve their situation. Ancient hatreds, such as those generated by a history of conquest and repression, often contribute to incentives, but for most people their present situation is more important than historical traumas. Leadership also is important to remind people of their shared identity and interests, and to organize them for action, but it is not sufficient. National peoples need some prior sense of identity, and active awareness of grievances about unjust treatment, if they are to respond enthusiastically to leaders who advocate autonomy or independence. In short, explanations that give priority to ancient hatreds focus too far back in the chain of causality. Explanations which say leadership is most important do not look back far enough.

The other two key factors for explaining separatist movements are a group's *capacity for collective action* and *the balance of threat and opportunity* in its political environment. A national people's capacity is high to the extent that its members have shared identity and interests (in other words, capacity builds on salience and incentives), are linked by networks of authority and communication, and have authentic leaders—that is, leaders whose legitimacy is accepted by most members of the group. A group's geographic dispersion is another dimension of capacity: a territorial base makes it easier to build a coherent organization and is a necessary condition for groups seeking independence or substate autonomy (for empirical evidence, see Fearon & Laitin, 1999).

If a national people's security is threatened by rival groups or the state, its capacity for coercion becomes very important. Collective survival often depends on whether it has a liberation army or militia or *peshmergas* trained and equipped to fight. External patrons often help build group capacity. During the Cold War, the superpowers and their client states often provided the sanctuaries, training, and equipment that enhanced fighting capacity. The end of the Cold War has increased the visibility and commonality of other external sources of support, among them regional rivalries (e.g., Pakistan's military support for Kashmiri rebels), kindred groups in adjacent countries (such as Serbia's support for Serbian national minorities in the Yugoslav successor states), and politically organized diasporas (material support from Kurds in Europe for PKK rebels in Turkey, and from Sikhs in Canada for their kindred in Punjab). A recent comparative survey shows that, during the 1990s, virtually all

---

[2] President Shaimiev and other Tatar leaders declared Tatarstan's sovereignty in 1990 but worked throughout the early 1990s to negotiate a regional power-sharing arrangement with the Russian Federation that was signed in February 1994. See Kaplan (1998) and Tishkov (1997).

[3] This discussion is derived from a theoretical framework developed in Gurr (2000:ch. 3).

ethnonational groups and about half of politically active indigenous peoples enumerated in Table II-2-1.1 received some form of external support (Khosla, 1999).

A national people may be well-organized, amply supplied and encouraged by foreign patrons, and have respected leaders who can plan strategies for gaining self-determination. *Threats and opportunities* account for the onset of separatist campaigns, the strategies they follow, and—in part—their outcomes. The ethnonational conflicts that accompanied the deconstruction of the USSR and the Yugoslav federation are recent examples. The unpredictability of nationalist politics in post-communist states created a threatening security dilemma for a number of minorities (Posen, 1993; Fearon, 1998). They feared, often with good reason, that dominant groups would exclude them from political participation, undermine their local governments and institutions, and disrespect their culture and language. The fragility of new states' institutions also provided domestic opportunities for their leaders to pursue ethnonational objectives. The question was whether leaders should try to protect group interests in new and untried institutions that were only nominally democratic, or mobilize to fight for group rights and autonomy while there was still time to do so. Some chose to trust the new institutions, like the leaders of Magyar communities in Romania and Slovakia and of Russians in Ukraine. Others, including Serbs in Bosnia and Croatia, Abkhaz and South Ossetians in Georgia, and Armenians in Nagorno-Karabakh, chose to fight. The role of both threat and opportunity factors is evident in these examples. The threat was posed by blustering nationalists, whereas the collapse of the old system of governance provided opportunities for action—during the brief interlude while nationalists were building and taking control of new political institutions, armies, and police.

In other parts of the world, the mix of threats and opportunities that have prompted contemporary ethnonational and indigenous movements usually are more localized. The transition to democracy that began in Indonesia in 1998 provided an opening for renewed separatist rebellions by the Aceh of northern Sumatra and native Papuans in Irian Jaya. It also provoked increased international pressure that led the weakened new government to agree to an independence referendum in East Timor—and subsequent violence by anti-independence forces. Transitions toward democracy also provided the context, and in some cases the provocation, for separatist movements elsewhere. South Africa's transition to nonracial democracy, in the mid-1990s, posed a serious threat to the autonomy of KwaZulu state, controlled by Zulu chief Buthelezi. The Zulu-based Inkatha movement was the instrument of communal violence against Nelson Mandela's African National Congress, violence that persisted until political and constitutional agreements were reached that preserved Zulu regional autonomy and Buthelezi's authority.

In Latin America, a combination of global activism and democratic transitions helped empower indigenous peoples. The global indigenous rights movement had profound effects during the 1970s and 1980s on the aspirations and political skills of indigenous peoples throughout the Americas. Activists propounded doctrines of indigenous rights—control of traditional lands and resources, promotion of indigenous cultures—the effect of which, in theoretical terms, was to increase the salience of group identity. The portrayal of indigenous successes elsewhere, especially in the United States, increased local incentives for political action and provided positive examples of strategies and tactics (see Wilmer, 1993; Brysk, 1994). Democratization in countries like Nicaragua, Panama, Chile, Ecuador, and Bolivia provided opportunities for indigenous groups to pursue their objectives in the political arena. In Ecuador and Bolivia, where indigenous peoples are a numerical majority, they sought and achieved substantial representation and influence in central governments. In the other countries named, they framed their objectives in terms of local autonomy and, with a few exceptions, pursued them by nonviolent means.

Chiapas state in quasi-democratic Mexico is the venue of a recent violent struggle for indigenous rights in the Americas, motivated by desires for local autonomy and an end to government corruption. In this case, symbolic and political support from a great many international actors has been instrumental in dissuading the Mexican government from violent suppression of the rebellion, but has not persuaded the government to negotiate a settlement. The Chiapas conflict shows how the international environment, in combination with domestic factors, helps shape the opportunities and outcomes of self-determination conflicts (see Escobar & Alvarez, 1992; Brysk, 1994).

V.   A SURVEY OF VIOLENT AND NONVIOLENT SEPARATIST MOVEMENTS IN THE 1990S

The theoretical framework outlined above helps explain the emergence of separatist movements based on ethnic identities but does not directly explain the intensity of violence that accompanies such conflicts, nor does it explain how conflicts engendered by separatist demands can be resolved. Relevant evidence is provided by the Minorities at Risk project's comparative evidence on ethnopolitical conflicts in the 1990s.[4] We use the evidence to address two research questions about the strategies and outcomes of these conflicts: Under what circumstances do the protagonists in separatist conflicts choose to rely on coercive strategies, that is, the use and threat of violence? And what policies and courses of action are most likely to avoid or contain violence? Before proceeding, two assumptions should be made explicit. First, we think of violence as part of a coercive strategy that can be initiated by either party to a separatist conflict. When one side does choose to use violent tactics the alternatives are narrowed for the other party, usually setting in motion tit-for-tat or escalating sequences of violent actions and reactions. Second, we also regard the management of separatist conflict as a result of interacting decisions by the principals and by external actors. Separatist conflicts are not usually settled by unilateral actions but through political discourse, reciprocated acts of cooperation, and mutual concessions.

The analysis that follows uses a four-way distinction among the political strategies followed by ethnonationalists, indigenous peoples, and national minorities. Table II-2-1.2 shows the highest level of political action observed for these groups at any time during the 1990s, counting each group only once based on the most disruptive strategy used. About one third of these groups, 53 of 154 identified in the Minorities at Risk study, were involved in guerrilla and civil wars. Another 31 employed terrorism or organized local rebellions. By contrast, 70 groups relied on nonviolent techniques of political action. Of these 42, used the tactics of mass protest and 28 groups used more limited political strategies of symbolic protest. This latter category includes eight groups who were politically

[4]The Minorities at Risk (MAR) project is an ongoing global study of the status, grievances, and conflicts of politically active ethnic groups that as of 2000 includes detailed information on some 300 groups. The Minorities at Risk (MAR) project was begun by the author in 1986 and since 1988 has been based at the University of Maryland's Center for International Development and Conflict Management. Funding for work summarized in this chapter has been provided by the United States Institute of Peace, the National Science Foundation, and the Hewlitt Foundation. For detailed reports on findings, see Ted Robert Gurr (1993, 2000). For documentation on all groups in the study, see the project's web site at www:http://www.bsos.umd.edu/cidcm/mar.

Table II-2-1.2. Political strategies of separatist groups in the 1990s, classified by type

Group type	Limited political action	Mass political action	Small-scale rebellion	Large-scale rebellion	Totals
Ethnonationalists	2	8	9	21	40
Indigenous peoples	12	20	13	23	68
National minorities	14	14	9	9	46
Totals	28	42	31	53	154

Note: Groups are categorized according to the highest level of open conflict with governments reported at any time from 1990–1998. Conflict with other groups is not taken into account in this tabulation.
- Limited political action = verbal opposition or symbolic resistance; groups with no reported political activity in the 1990s are also counted here;
- Mass political action = demonstrations, rallies, strikes, or riots;
- Small-scale rebellion = terrorism or local rebellions;
- Large-scale rebellion = guerrilla activity and civil wars.

inactive throughout the 1990s, according to our evidence. The appendix to this chapter identifies 48 groups whose rebellions persisted for five years or more during the 1990s and summarizes the status of their conflicts in mid-2000.

This four-way classification of groups gives us one basis for addressing our first question: What characteristics of national peoples, and states, help explain why some separatist conflicts are violent and some are not? The data suggest that a group's situation and objectives help determine its strategies. Ethnonationalists' pursuit of independence usually can be attained only through force and usually is met by force, therefore 30 of the 40 ethnonationalist groups were involved in organized violence in the 1990s. Indigenous peoples typically pursue more limited objectives of regional and cultural autonomy, and therefore are somewhat more likely than ethnonationalists to rely on nonviolent political action. Nonetheless more than half—36 of 68—indigenous groups were in open rebellion in the 1990s. Among them were the upland tribal peoples of South and Southeast Asia, the Tuareg of Mali and Niger, and, in Latin America, the Mayas of Chiapas and the Miskitos in Nicaragua. Least likely to rebel are national minorities, a type of group heavily concentrated in East Central Europe, most of whom—28 of 46—pursued limited objectives using conventional political strategies and nonviolent mass action.

Another part of the explanation is that rebellion is rarely used as a strategy of first resort by groups with grievances against their governments. Groups typically try other political strategies, including protests and demonstrations, civil disobedience, and applying to international patrons, to get their grievances addressed before resorting to armed rebellion. These strategies may be pursued for years before rebellion is adopted as the main strategy of political action, and the trigger for the onset of rebellion very often is the government's decision to use coercion against activists and demonstrators. In evidence, we examined the antecedents of protracted rebellions, those that persisted for at least five years during 1990–1998. Two thirds of the groups in protracted rebellion had used nonviolent political strategies prior to the outbreak of rebellion and another nine used nonviolent political strategies in conjunction with rebellion. National minorities, the majority of whom are in the post-communist states, were the type most likely to engage in rebellion after a very brief attempt, or no attempt at all, to resolve their grievances through conventional political strategies.

1. Effects of Group Discrimination

The theoretical argument is that collective disadvantages are one of the root causes of ethnopolitical action. Discriminatory treatment helps define group boundaries and enhances the salience of group identity. Redress of grievances about invidious treatment and the desire to gain advantages are principal sources of group incentives for action. Two kinds of discrimination are examined for their effects on separatist violence: economic and political. The Minorities at Risk project provides coded biennial data on group political discrimination for the 1990s using these general categories;[5] similar categories are used for economic discrimination: None

- Substantial underrepresentation in political office holding or participation or both, due to historical neglect, or restrictions. Explicit public policies are designed to protect or improve the group's political status.
- Substantial underrepresentation due to historical neglect or restrictions. No social practice of deliberate exclusion. No formal exclusion. No evidence of protective or remedial public policies.
- Substantial underrepresentation due to prevailing social practice by dominant groups. Formal public policies toward the group are neutral or, if positive, inadequate to offset discriminatory practices.
- Public policies (formal exclusion or recurring repression or both) substantially restrict the group's political participation in comparison with other groups.

Analysis shows that groups using large-scale rebellion in the 1990s were much more likely to be the victims of both economic and political discrimination resulting from social exclusion and public policies, the two highest scale categories, than groups that used only limited political action or strategies of protest and demonstrations. Table II-2-1.3 compares the percentages of each group experiencing no versus high levels of economic and political discrimination during 1990–1998. Over half of groups using large-scale rebellion experienced active political discrimination (the two highest categories listed above) throughout the decade. Moreover, 45–50% of them experienced active economic discrimination as well. In contrast, about a third of groups using conventional strategies experienced political discrimination, while only 10–14% experienced economic discrimination. We observe little difference between the groups using the two intermediate strategies of political action, that is small-scale rebellion and mass political action. What does differentiate groups using these intermediate strategies is the severity of economic discrimination: between 40 and 60% of those in small-scale rebellion experienced serious economic discrimination, twice the frequency of economic discrimination against groups using mass political action.

Another way to look at the relationship between political and economic discrimination and political violence by separatist groups is to examine peoples who were in rebellion for at least five years in the 1990s versus all others. Differences between these two categories of groups (not shown because of space limitations) are even more striking than the differences in Table II-2-1.3. Of those in protracted rebellion during the 1990s, 69% experienced serious political discrimination at the beginning of the decade while only 11% experienced none. The comparable figures for economic discrimination are 56% for groups in protracted rebellions and 31% for others.

---

[5]Data also were coded on specific types of political and cultural restrictions, available on the project's web site (note 4). Other analyses of the discrimination data are reported in Gurr (1993:ch. 2); Dudley and Miller (1998); Gurr and Moore (1997); and Gurr (2000:ch. 4).

Table II-2-1.3.   Political and economic discrimination among separatist groups using different strategies

Group strategy and level of discrimination	Political discrimination (%)			Economic discrimination (%)		
	1990	1994	1998	1990	1994	1998
Large-scale rebellion						
No discrimination	7.5	18.9	22.6	13.2	18.9	13.2
Active discrimination	67.9	60.4	50.9	52.4	54.7	45.3
Small-scale rebellion						
No discrimination	25.8	29.0	25.8	30.0	30.0	26.7
Active discrimination	48.4	38.7	45.2	60.0	60.0	40.0
Mass political action						
No discrimination	28.6	35.7	40.5	38.1	35.7	31.0
Active discrimination	50.0	40.5	35.7	28.5	30.9	23.8
Limited political action						
No discrimination	35.7	35.7	32.1	42.9	46.4	39.3
Active discrimination	35.7	35.7	35.7	14.3	14.3	10.7

Note: Active discrimination includes groups at the two highest levels of discrimination described in the text, that is, discrimination due to current social practices and government policies. Groups at lower levels of discrimination are not included in this table.

In summary, groups that experience high levels of discrimination are also those more likely to engage in violent political actions in order to advance their claims against the state. Some groups that use more conventional political strategies such as protest and mass mobilization also are subject to active discrimination but in diminished numbers by comparison with those using armed violence as their main political strategy. Across types of discrimination and across time, groups in large-scale and protracted rebellion experienced much more serious discrimination than those who use limited, conventional political action.

2.   The Impact of State Repression

Here we examine how repressive state actions varied across the three different types of separatist groups in the late 1990s. All groups in the Minorities at Risk study were profiled on 23 categories of state repression, examples of which are "political arrests against group leaders," "torture used to intimidate or interrogate," "ethnic cleansing," and "military massacres of suspected rebel supporters."[6] An index, ranging from 0 to 23, was created by

[6]The categories are as follows: a few group members arrested; many group members arrested; leaders arrested, disappeared or detained; show trials of group members or leaders; torture used to intimidate or interrogate; members executed by authorities; reprisal killings of civilians; systematic killings by paramilitaries; property confiscated or destroyed; restrictions on movement; forced resettlement; interdiction of food supplies; ethnic cleansing; systematic domestic spying; states of emergency; saturation tactics by police or military; limited use of force against protesters; unrestrained force again protesters; military campaigns against armed rebels; military targets and destroys rebel areas; military massacres of suspected rebel supporters; other repression. The data are included in the Minorities at Risk dataset; this is their first published analysis. For macro indicators of state repression and their effect on ethnopolitical conflict, see Gurr and Moore (1997).

summing the presence or absence of repression against a group on each of the 23 categories. No group experienced more than 13 of the 23 types of repression in any given year.
Therefore, scores of one to three on the composite index are considered low-level state
repression and scores of four to eight are medium level, while scores of nine or greater are
considered high-level state repression.

Though we have repression data for only 1996–98, some interesting patterns are
evident. Ethnonationalists were most likely to suffer from high levels of repression. Of the
40 ethnonationalist groups 17% suffered from high levels of repression compared to
less than 3% of the 68 indigenous peoples and none of the 46 national minorities. At the
lower end of the scale, 70% of national minorities experienced no repression compared
to half of indigenous peoples and 40% of ethnonationalists. Recall that half of
ethnonationalists used large-scale rebellion during the 1990s while only one third of
indigenous peoples and about one fifth of national minorities used the same strategy for
making demands on the state. Of groups using large-scale rebellion in the 1990s, nearly
15% experienced high levels of repression in 1998 while among groups using conventional political strategies only low or medium levels of repression were experienced.
Less than one quarter of groups that had used large-scale rebellion experienced no repression in 1998—mostly groups whose rebellions had ended by that year. Among groups
using conventional political strategies, three quarters experienced no state repression of
any kind during 1996–98.

As with political and economic discrimination, variations in levels of state repression are connected to the strategies separatists use to pursue their objectives. We cannot
assume simple one-way causality by which discrimination and repression lead to rebellion, nor that rebellion provokes government to ratchet up discrimination and repression.
Rather, these conditions and actions reinforce one another. The political and economic
environment of separatist peoples help determine their incentives for collective action
and, in a repressive and discriminatory environment, group identity becomes more important along with the motivation for action. At the same time, leaders must judge that the
timing for collective action is right. Specific threats and opportunities account for the
onset of political action, and the specific strategies followed.

The interplay between state action and group action often locks each party into coercive strategies in which rebellion by the group reinforces repressive and discriminatory
action by the state, policies that help sustain rebellion. Frequently, it takes external engagement, for example by regional and international bodies, or media and human rights
campaigns, to prompt a shift to greater cooperation and accommodation (see Zartman,
1989; Carment & James, 1998; Wallensteen, 1998; Crocker, Hampson, & Aall, 1999;
Jentleson, 2000). For example, the NATO bombing campaign in Serbia in spring 1999
eventually resulted in the end of the government's repression against the Kosovo Albanians. At the same time, however, resentment between the Kosovars and the Serbs remains,
and the peace is threatened by retaliatory intercommunal violence. In the Chittagong Hill
Tracts of Bangladesh, two decades of small-scale rebellion by the indigenous Chakma
peoples and short-sighted policies by governments of the 1970s and 1980s led to a situation in which neither government nor rebels could achieve decisive victory. War-weari-
ness, improved relations with India, and the promise of development assistance from abroad
eventually led both sides to the negotiating table.

3. The Effects of Democracy and Democratization

Democracy has well-documented effects on the character of political conflict in general and ethnopolitical conflict specifically. Three general patterns are summarized here. First, ethnopolitical groups in democratically governed states are more likely to use strategies of protest, whereas similar groups in autocratic states rely more on rebellion.[7] Specifically, empirical evidence of the Minorities project shows that both old and new democracies between 1985 and 1998 had fewer ethnic wars and lower magnitudes of rebellion than transitional and autocratic regimes. But ethnic protest also is relatively common in nondemocratic societies, where we observe that about one ethnopolitical group in five organized major protest campaigns during the fourteen-year period under review, compared with one group in three in democratic societies. This implies that the institutions and policies of autocratic regimes do not effectively suppress ethnic protest. Rather, they make protest less attractive than rebellion as a strategy for political action. Second, the process of democratization is associated with short-term increases in protest but usually leads to a decline in rebellion. We did before-and-after comparisons of the magnitudes of ethnopolitical protest and rebellion in all countries that made transitions toward democracy, successful or not, complete or partial, between 1985 and 1995. Such transitions tended to be followed by increases in ethnopolitical protest. In the countries of the global South—Latin America, Asia, and Africa—democratization also was typically followed by declines in ethnic rebellion. Ethnic rebellion declined most, however, not in new full democracies but in quasi-democracies and failed democracies. We suspect that, in the Third World, regimes with a mix of democratic and autocratic features are somewhat better able to contain violent ethnopolitical conflict than new Western model democracies.

The post-communist states show a different pattern. Transitions to full or partial democracy almost inevitably were followed by increases in both ethnopolitical protest and rebellion, especially separatist rebellions (see also Roeder, 1999). This anomaly is open to different theoretical interpretations. One kind of explanation emphasizes incentives and threats: democratization provided incentives for ethnopolitical entrepreneurs, encouraged outbidding among rival politicians, and posed a security dilemma for minority peoples. A complementary explanation emphasizes opportunities: when central authority weakened in Moscow and Belgrade, it became possible for peoples to act on long-suppressed ethnic identities and hostilities. A third explanation emphasizes capacities: the USSR and Yugoslavia both gave ethnicity a political and territorial basis, so that when central control was relaxed, titular nationalities had administrative and party structures through which to pursue their own interests. A fourth kind of explanation points to the crucial role of state formation. Ethnic warfare in the post-communist states was specific to new states: it erupted in Croatia and Georgia, Moldova and Azerbaijan, but not in Romania or Czechoslovakia. Seen from a distance, the pattern of ethnopolitical action in the territorially intact post-communist states resembles that of new and transitional democracies in Latin America, Asia, and Africa, where protest usually increased after democratic transitions but rebellion ordinarily did not. The supposition, therefore, is that the incentives, opportunities, and capacities for ethnonational warfare in periods of democratic transition are greatest in *new* states.

---

[7]The evidence summarized here and below is based on detailed analysis of the MAR data as reported in Gurr (2000:ch. 5).

VI. TOWARD PREVENTION OF VIOLENT ETHNONATIONALISM

Armed conflicts within states increased during much of the Cold War and reached a peak in the early 1990s, but thereafter began to decline.[8] The majority of these conflicts are ethnonational wars. For example the State Failure project, established by the Clinton Administration, has plotted the incidence of ethnic wars and of genocides and politicides (political mass murder) from 1955 through 1998. The percentage of countries with ethnic wars more than doubled from 10% in the mid-1960s to over 20% in 1993 but has since declined to about 15%. The trend in episodes of massive human rights violations is just as relevant because most are targeted at ethnic and religious groups, including—in the case of politicides—separatist rebels like Tibetans and southerners in Sudan. The proportion of countries with continuing episodes reached a maximum of 8% in the late 1980s but has since declined sharply. The last new geno/politicide occurred in Rwanda in 1994, and as of early 2000 the only ongoing case is in southern Sudan[9]. The Minorities at Risk project provides more detailed evidence. Figure II-2-1.1 documents a gradual shift in the political strategies of 154 separatist peoples during the 1990s. The percentage of groups in large-scale rebellion fell from a high of 24% in 1992 to half that by 1998. Small-scale rebellions show a less pronounced decline—in part because they include some de-escalating large-scale rebellions. Mass political action also declined after 1994, whereas limited political action increased. In brief, there was a significant shift during the decade away from violent strategies and toward conventional politics.

Another analysis focuses on the onset and outcome of separatist rebellions, 54 of which we have tracked from the mid-1950s to the present. As shown in Figure II-2-1.2, from the late 1960s through the end of the 1980s the number of new wars in each five-year period substantially outnumbered those contained or settled. During the 1990s the number of wars contained or settled increased sharply: three were contained and eight were settled in the first four years of the 1990s, then between 1995 and 1999 the balance shifted even more decisively: eight ethnonational wars were contained and twelve were settled, whereas only two escalated, in southern Thailand and Kosovo. By the beginning of 2000 only eighteen ethnonational wars were being fought—the lowest number since the early 1970s.

The next question is what conditions are associated with these trends. We showed above that separatist groups that experience active political and economic discrimination are the most likely to engage in large-scale rebellion. Did discrimination against ethnopolitical groups decline in the 1990s, paralleling the decline in armed conflicts? We did a series of comparative analyses to provide some general answers to this question (see Gurr, 2000:chs. 4 and 5). The Minorities at Risk project has coded data on levels of discrimination and restrictions for each ethnopolitical group from 1990–91 through 1998. Analysis of the MAR data on levels of discrimination and restrictions showed an improving trend in the status of all 275 groups in the study during the 1990s. Political discrimination declined the most. About 30% of groups restricted by political discrimination in

---

[8] Researchers who have documented a global decline in serious internal conflicts during the 1990s, with some evidence of an upturn in 1998–99, include Wallensteen and Sollenberg (1999), Ayres (2000), and Marshall (2001).

[9] For graphic summaries, see Esty et al. (1999:52–53). The comparative data on genocides and politicides are from Harff (1992), updated for the Task Force. Details of cases are available at www.bsos.umd.edu/cidcm/statefail.

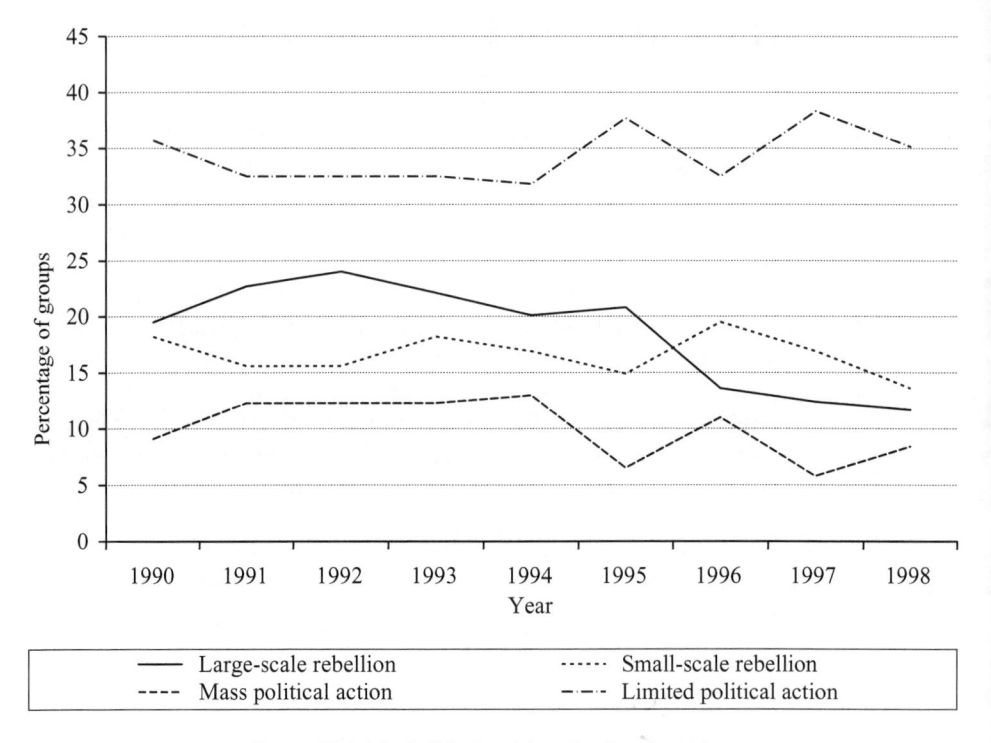

Figure II-2-1.1. Political activity of national peoples.

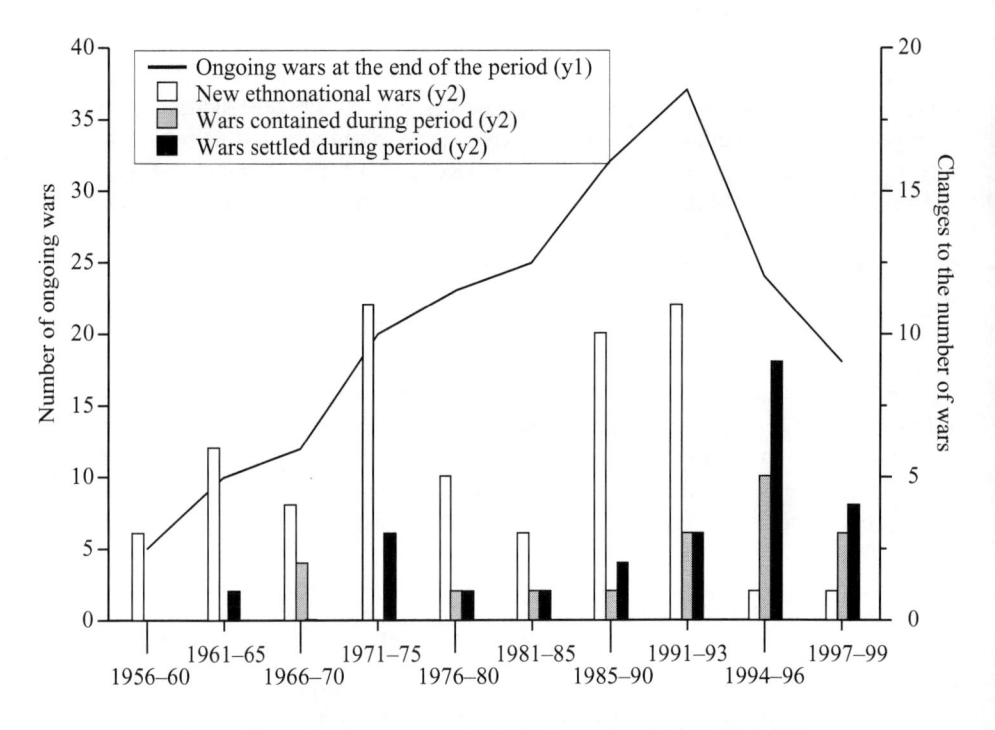

Figure II-2-1.2. Trends in outcomes of ethnonational wars, 1956–1999.

1990–91 had greater political rights and access by 1998, gains that were only partly offset by increased political discrimination imposed on a few of them. One in three groups that experienced cultural restrictions in 1990–91 had greater cultural rights by 1998. Economic discrimination changed least, but the trend was an improving one. Overall, more than one third of the 277 groups in the Minorities survey were better off in 1998 than at the beginning of the decade.

When the 154 separatist groups are examined separately, the data in Table II-2-1.3 (above) show a decline in both kinds of discrimination. Active political discrimination, for example, diminished across the decade for groups using three of the four strategies of political action, parallel to the decline in separatist rebellions shown in Figure II-2-1.1. Only those using limited tactics showed a low and steady level of serious discrimination. This may indicate that the strategies of rebellious groups were successful, i.e., that large-scale armed conflict induced some governments to negotiate, decrease active discrimination, and seek accommodation. Alternatively, years of active discrimination and repression may have dissuaded some groups from using strategies of violence, which in turn prompted government to ease restrictive politics. We also see that levels of economic discrimination changed little during the decade. This probably is so because it is easier for most governments to redress political discrimination, for example by opening up their political systems to participation by all groups, than to redress economic inequalities. The latter usually requires redistribution of scarce economic resources and opportunities, policies that may be beyond the capacity of governments, especially in the global south.

We documented above that transitions to democracy, which were especially numerous in the late 1980s and 1990s, generally led to a shift away from ethnorebellion and toward protest. The Russian Federation's negotiation of an autonomy agreement with Tatarstan, cited above, illustrates the general disposition of authorities in democratic Russia for peaceful accommodation of regional interests. After the Tatarstan agreement Moscow negotiated substate autonomy agreements with Bashkiria and some 40 other regions in the Federation (see Herd, 1999; Treisman, 1999). To test whether democratization helped account for the global decline in ethnonational rebellions, we examined the political circumstances in which wholly or partly successful negotiated settlements were reached in 26 separatist wars between 1956 and 1998. The settled wars were only slightly more likely to have begun under autocratic regimes than in democracies, by a ratio of 14 to 12. But by a ratio of 19 to 7 the settlements were negotiated by democratic or partly democratic governments. Democratic regimes also have a good record of negotiating settlements with rebels whose wars began in democracies—India is a leading example. Equally important, democratic transitions increase the prospects for settling or de-escalating separatist wars that began during autocratic rule. Spain is one example, where the Basque rebellion that began against the Franco regime in 1959 was largely settled when the new democratic government granted regional autonomy in 1980. Bangladesh is another, where the rebellion of the Chittagong Hill people began in 1975, during a period of military rule, and was ended in 1997–99 when a democratic government negotiated a regional autonomy pact with the rebels.

Major changes in the international system are a third factor that has made it easier to avoid new separatist conflicts and to settle old ones. During the early 1990s, Western advocates of human rights shifted their emphasis from individual rights to the collective rights of national peoples and minorities. The Organization for Security and Cooperation in Europe (OSCE) and the Council of Europe have been especially active in promoting and defending group rights in Europe. Membership in the Council of Europe and provision of economic aid are among the incentives used to induce East and Central European countries to moderate their policies toward minorities. Elsewhere, especially in Africa, regional organizations have sought to play a similar role by engaging in preventive diplomacy and in encouraging negotiated settlements of ethnic and other disputes within states. Since the end of the Cold War, the United Nations, the European powers, and the United States have actively promoted the principles of minority rights and negotiated settlements of ethnopolitical wars and supported peacekeeping and peacemaking operations. Nongovernmental organizations have become much more active in publicizing violations of group rights, working for changes in government policy, and urging international action. The net effect of these principles and practices is that the international balance has tipped away from policies that encouraged and sustained violent separatist movements, such as the promotion of proxy wars, toward policies aimed at containing them (see Carnegie Commission on Preventing Deadly Conflict, 1997; Peck, 1998; Hopmann, 1999). Even the international trade in light arms, the last major international factor that sustains violent separatist movements, is subject to increased scrutiny and criticism (Wood & Peleman, 1999).

VII. QUESTIONS FOR FURTHER RESEARCH ON VIOLENT SEPARATISM

The evidence summarized in this chapter raises a number of general questions about the preconditions and containment of violent separatist conflict that should be examined in future comparative research.

First are questions about the relative importance of different preconditions. For instance, we showed that groups targeted by high levels of discrimination and repression are especially likely to engage in armed rebellion. What is uncertain is whether changes in discrimination and repression lead or lag armed rebellion—under some circumstances they may be causes, in other instances consequences. A second issue, not directly raised by evidence cited here, is the importance of incentives, such as the desire to end discrimination and gain security from repression, relative to changes in groups' capabilities to act and the opening of opportunities in their political environment. It is easy to make the theoretical claim that incentives, capabilities, and opportunities all are important. What is difficult is to design comparative studies that show the ways in which they are sequenced and their relative importance in different circumstances.

The role of democracy vs. democratization in checking separatist violence also needs further study. It is clear that separatist violence is limited in most of the established democracies because separatists use other political means to pursue their objectives. On the other hand, the process of democratization often is associated with increasing ethnic contention and rebellion. Not enough is known about the circumstances in which democratization as process leads toward or away from violent separatist conflict.

International factors are of vital importance in understanding the origins of violent separatist conflict and the means for containing it. Separatist movements have spillover effects on neighboring states and peoples by providing potentially powerful signals or models that inspire peoples elsewhere, and prompt threatened regimes to take preventive action. More detailed understanding of these processes is needed, along with assessments of how influential external assistance is in determining a group's strategies at a given point in time (on these issues, see Carment & James, 1997; Walter & Snyder, 1999). For example, we should understand better the importance of regional concentrations of ethnic kin in bordering states. The transboundary dispersion of ethnonationalists seems likely to facilitate rebellion, whereas the transboundary dispersion of indigenous peoples is associated with the spread of nonviolent mass movements. Why? And in another example, in some circumstances governments with transboundary minorities cooperate to contain ethnonationalism, whereas in other circumstances they promote rebellions to destabilize a neighboring state. What circumstances lead to such divergent policies?

Another set of questions concerns the effects of international action in controlling separatist conflicts, either before they reach the level of armed conflict or after an extended period of warfare. A great deal of attention is being given by scholars and policy makers to preventive diplomacy and other forms of international engagement as ways of deflecting and transforming ethnopolitical conflict. Also numerous are studies of international mediation, negotiation, and peacekeeping as strategies for containing and, sometimes, settling separatist rebellions. But some rebellions persist despite intense international engagement, and others are settled with little or no outside participation. There are few systematic comparative studies of preventive diplomacy and even fewer efforts to generalize about the optimum strategies and the mix and match of international and domestic policies most likely to be effective in ending ethnonational wars (exceptions include Jentleson, 2000; Walter & Snyder, 1999; Kelley, 2000).

A final question concerns the potential for future separatist conflicts. We have shown that there are mitigating tendencies in the international system in the 1990s, including declining political discrimination against national peoples and a complementary tendency to settle separatist conflicts through negotiations that usually concede political autonomy. There are two underlying questions that determine whether these trends are likely to continue. How many other culturally distinct, territorially based groups might claim the right to independence or autonomy, and be prepared to use violent means to those ends? While most of the groups now at risk of separatist rebellion are included in the 154 groups analyzed in the Minorities at Risk project, others will undoubtedly emerge, especially in the global south and in weak, repressive states. The second underlying question concerns the effects of the big dynamics that are driving the global system: population growth, increased consumption of and competition for scarce resources, the widening gap between the global haves and have-nots, and the emergence of new disease vectors. The concentration of malign conditions such as overpopulation, scarcity, inequality, and disease may lead to devastating local wars among contending peoples that combine the worst features of communal warfare, separatist rebellions against collapsing states, and genocidal retaliation. Research needs to be done that identifies the places and peoples at risk of such human disasters; and international actors, once forewarned, should focus their political, material, and diplomatic resources on these crisis zones.

REFERENCES

Ayres, R. William. (2000). A World Flying Apart? Violent Nationalist Conflict and the End of the Cold War. *Journal of Peace Research, 37*(1), 105–117.

Brass, Paul. (1991). *Ethnicity and Nationalism.* Newbury Park: Sage Publications.

Brysk, Alison. (1994). Acting Globally: Indian Rights and International Politics in Latin America. In Donna Lee Van Cott (Ed.), *Indigenous Peoples and Democracy in Latin America.* Basingstoke: Macmillan.

Burr, Millard. (1993). *Quantifying Genocide in the Southern Sudan 1983–1993.* Washington: U.S. Committee for Refugees Issue Paper.

Burr, Millard. (1999). *Quantifying Genocide in the Southern Sudan 1983–1998*. Washington: U.S. Committee for Refugees Issue Paper.

Carment, David, & Patrick James. (1997). *Wars in the Midst of Peace: The International Politics of Ethnic Conflicts*. Pittsburgh: University of Pittsburgh Press.

Carment, David, & Patrick James (Eds.) (1998). *Peace in the Midst of Wars: Preventing and Managing International Ethnic Conflicts*. Columbia: University of South Carolina Press.

Carnegie Commission on Preventing Deadly Conflict. (1997). *Preventing Deadly Conflict: Final Report*. Washington: Carnegie Commission on Preventing Deadly Conflict.

Connor, Walker. (1994). *Ethno-Nationalism: The Quest for Understanding*. Princeton: Princeton University Press.

Crocker, Chester, Fen Olser Hampson, & Pamela Aall (Eds.) (1999). *Herding Cats: Multiparty Mediation in a Complex World*. Washington: United States Institute of Peace Press.

Daalder, Ivo. (1996). Fear and Loathing in the Former Yugoslavia. In Michael E. Brown (Ed.), *The International Dimensions of Ethnic Conflict* (pp. 35–67). Cambridge/London: The MIT Press.

Dudley, Ryan, & Ross A. Miller. (1998). Group Rebellion in the 1980s. *Journal of Conflict Resolution, 42*, 77–96.

Escobar, Arturo, & Sonia E. Alvarez (Eds.) (1992). *The Making of Social Movements in Latin America*. Boulder: Westview Press.

Esty, Daniel C., Jack A. Goldstone, Ted Robert Gurr, Barbara Harff, Marc Levy, Geoffrey D. Dabelko, Pamela T. Surko, & Alan N. Unger. (1999). State Failure Task Force Report: Phase II Findings. *Environmental Change and Security Project Report, 5*, 49–72.

Fearon, James D. (1998). Commitment Problems and the Spread of Ethnic Conflict. In David A. Lake & Donald Rothchild (Eds.), *The International Spread of Ethnic Conflict: Fear, Diffusion, and Escalation* (pp. 107–126). Princeton: Princeton University Press.

Fearon, James D., & David D. Laitin. (1999). *Weak States, Rough Terrain, and Large-scale Ethnic Violence since 1945*. Paper presented at the Annual Meeting of the American Political Science Association, Atlanta.

Geertz, Clifford. ed. (1963). *Old Societies and New States*. New York: Free Press.

Gellner, Ernest. (1983). *Nations and Nationalism*. Oxford: Oxford University Press.

Greenfeld, Liah. (1992). *Nationalism: Five Roads to Modernity*. Cambridge: Harvard University Press.

Gurr, Ted Robert. (1993). *Minorities at Risk: A Global View of Ethnopolitical Conflicts*. Washington: United States Institute of Peace Press.

Gurr, Ted Robert. (2000). *Peoples versus States: Minorities at Risk in the New Century*. Washington: United States Institute of Peace Press.

Gurr, Ted Robert, & Will H. Moore. (1997). Ethnopolitical Rebellion: A Cross-Sectional Analysis of the 1980s with Risk Assessments for the 1990s. *American Journal of Political Science, 41*(4), 1079–1103.

Harff, Barbara. (1992). Recognizing Genocides and Politicides. In Helen Fein (Ed.), *Genocide Watch* (pp. 27–41). New Haven: Yale University Press.

Hechter, Michael. (1975). *Internal Colonialism: The Celtic Fringe in British National Development, 1536–1966*. Berkeley: University of California Press.

Herd, Graeme P. (1999). Russia: Systemic Transformation or Federal Collapse? *Journal of Peace Research, 36*, 259–269.

Hopmann, Philip Terrence. (1999). *Building Security in Post-Cold War Eurasia: The OSCE and U.S. Foreign Policy*. Washington: United States Institute of Peace Press.

Horowitz, Donald L. (1985). *Ethnic Groups in Conflict*. Berkeley: University of California Press.

Jentleson, Bruce W. (Ed.) (2000). *Opportunities Missed, Opportunities Seized*. Lanham: Rowman and Littlefield.

Kaplan, Cynthia S. (1998). Ethnicity and Sovereignty: Insights from Russian Negotiations with Estonia and Tatarstan. In David A. Lake & Donald Rothchild (Eds.), *The International Spread of Ethnic Conflict: Fear, Diffusion and Escalation* (pp. 251–274). Princeton: Princeton University Press.

Kelley, Judith. (2000). *When Can International Institutions Change State Behavior? The Case of European Integration and Ethnic Politics in Latvia and Estonia*. Paper presented to the Annual Meeting of the International Studies Association, Los Angeles.

Khosla, Deepa. (1999). Third World States as Intervenors in Ethnic Conflicts: Implications for Regional and International Security. *Third World Quarterly, 20*(6), 1143–1156.

Laitin, David D. (1998). *Identity in Formation: The Russian-Speaking Populations in the Near Abroad*. Ithaca: Cornell University Press.

Marshall, Monty G. (2001). Assessing the Impact of Societal and Systematic Warfare. In David Malone & Fan Osler Hampson (Eds.), *From Reaction to Prevention: Opportunities for the UN System in the New Millennium*. Boulder: Lynne Rienner.

McKay, James. (1982). An Exploratory Synthesis of Primordial and Mobilizationist Approaches to Ethnic Phenomena. *Ethnic and Racial Studies*, *5*, 395–420.

Peck, Connie. (1998). *Sustainable Peace: The Role of the UN and Regional Organizations in Preventing Conflict*. Lanham: Rowman and Littlefield.

Posen, Barry R. (1993). The Security Dilemma and Ethnic Conflict. *Survival*, *35*(1), 27–47.

Roeder, Philip G. (1999). Peoples and States after 1989: The Political Costs of Incomplete National Revolutions. *Slavic Review*, *58*(4), 854–882.

Roeder, Philip G. (2000). *When Ethnopoliticians Become Nationalists: Primordial Constraints on Instrumental Choices*. University of California, San Diego. Prepublication paper.

Scott, George M., Jr. (1990). A Resynthesis of the Primordial and Circumstantial Approaches to Ethnic Group Solidarity: Towards an Explanatory Model. *Ethnic and Racial Studies*, *13*, 147–171.

Smith, Anthony D. (1986). *The Ethnic Origins of Nations*. Cambridge, UK: Blackwell.

Smith, Anthony D. (1998). *Nationalism and Modernism: A Critical Survey of Recent Theories of Nations and Nationalism*. New York: Routledge.

Stack, John F., Jr. (Ed.) (1986). *The Primordial Challenge: Ethnicity in the Contemporary World*. New York: Greenwood Press.

Tilley, Virginia Q. (1998). *State Identity Politics and the Domestic Political Arena*. Paper presented at the Annual Meeting of the International Studies Association, Minneapolis.

Tiryakian, Edward A., & Ronald Rogowski. (1985). *New Nationalisms of the Developed West: Toward Explanation*. Boston: Allen and Unwin.

Tishkov, Valery. (1997). *Ethnicity, Nationalism, and Conflict in and after the Soviet Union: The Mind Aflame*. London: Sage Publications for the International Peace Research Institute, Oslo.

Treisman, Daniel S. (1999). *After the Deluge: Regional Crises and Political Consolidation in Russia*. Ann Arbor: University of Michigan Press.

Van den Berghe, Pierre L. (1981). *The Ethnic Phenomenon*. New York: Elsevier North Holland.

Wallensteen, Peter (Ed.) (1998). *Preventing Violent Conflicts: Past Record and Future Challenges*. Stockholm: Elanders Gotab for the Department of Peace and Conflict Research, Uppsala University.

Wallensteen, Peter, & Margareta Sollenberg. (1999). Armed Conflict, 1989–98. *Journal of Peace Research*, *36*(5), 593–606.

Walter, Barbara F., & Jack Snyder (Eds.) (1999). *Civil Wars, Insecurity, and Intervention*. New York: Columbia University Press.

Wilmer, Franke. (1993). *The Indigenous Voice in World Politics: Since Time Immemorial*. Newbury Park: Sage.

Wood, Brian, & Johan Peleman. (1999). *The Arms Fixers: Controlling the Brokers and Shipping Agents*. Oslo: International Peace Research Institute, Basic Research Report 99.3.

Zartman, William. (1989). *Ripe for Resolution: Conflict and Intervention in Africa*. New York: Oxford University Press.

Ethnic Violence

ANDREAS WIMMER AND CONRAD SCHETTER

I. INTRODUCTION

Western public opinion finds ethnic violence a particularly repellant and illegitimate form of violence. 'Ethnic cleansing' in the form of mass shootings, systematic rape or massacres on a genocidal scale is considered the quintessence of terror and a prime symbol of the 'new world disorder'. The systematic use of violence against the noncombatant civilian population is particularly repulsive, as too is the random selection of candidates for liquidation based solely on the logic of categorical ascription, knowing that once thinking along ethnic lines has become firmly established, a murder victim will always be seen as a Catholic or Protestant, Serb or Croat, Tamil or Singhalese.

Researchers agree that there has been a significant quantitative increase in ethnic violence since the fall of the Berlin Wall and that since then it has been the proportionally most significant category of violent political conflict (see Gurr, 1993a:101, 1994:369–374; Scherrer, 1994:74). However, interpretations of these trends are highly divergent. Some see ethnically motivated violence and in particular ethnic cleansing as an intermediate stage on the path toward a culturally homogeneous state capable of modernization (e.g., Gellner, 1991; Nairn, 1993). Others explain the currency of ethnic violence in terms of the delegitimation of class-struggle based models of conflict interpretation and their replacement with ascribed identity-political characteristics which have gained respectability globally since the fall of the Wall (see Brubaker & Laitin, 1998). Others again (e.g., Wimmer, 1997) are of the opinion that the spread of ethnic-national conflicts in the Balkans, along the southern rim of the former Soviet empire, in the southeast Asian archipelago, and in West Africa can be attributed to a new wave of nation-state formation and democratization.

It would certainly make sense to give an overview of these different explanations of the currency of ethnic violence. Perhaps it would be even more convincing to review the literature along the lines of paradigmatic classifications, for example by contrasting the

W. Heitmeyer and J. Hagan (eds.), *International Handbook of Violence Research*, 247–260.

work done in a rational-choice perspective with that informed by structural functionalism or symbolic discourse theory—as in the comprehensive overview by Brubaker and Laitin (1998). We decided to take a different path and to integrate the diverse perspectives and approaches into a composite view of our own. We proceed from the idea—epistemologically naive but useful for our purpose—that different paradigms deal with different aspects of reality using their own terminological and theoretical tools and that an encompassing approach may integrate these different aspects. Therefore our discourse will be cumulative, not falsifying.

We first want to outline the phenomenon of ethnic violence in greater detail and to clarify to what extent we are dealing with a particular type of violence with a logic of its own. The second section will address the macropolitical changes which form the background conditions for the emergence of ethnic violence. Our third task is to inquire into the more specific institutional and political conditions which make violence a feasible option in ethnic conflicts. Finally, we will present an anatomy of the violent escalation of such conflict. We thus progress from the general to the specific, from macrostructural prerequisites to microanalysis, from structural conditions to the processual logic of violence.

II.   THE SPECIFICITY OF ETHNIC VIOLENCE

Ethnic violence can be defined as actions aimed at physically harming persons on the basis of their ethnic background (see Popitz, 1992; von Trotha, 1997). Pogroms, riots, and massacres are forms of collective violence which occur frequently in the context of ethnic conflicts but can also be observed in conflict constellations which are not ethnically tainted. Ethnic cleansing, ethnocide, and the extreme case of the Holocaust, however, represent specific forms of ethnic violence. Since various authors in this volume deal with individual aspects of ethnic violence (Bergmann with pogroms, Longerich with the Holocaust), this essay discusses the specificity of ethnic violence without looking at the differences between its various manifestations.

At the individual psychological level ethnic violence has the effect of projecting (repressed) aggressive desires and fears onto an outgroup. The ego identity is thus freed from ambivalence and its identificatory alignment stabilized in the ethnic dimension (Volkan, 1988). On a large scale this mechanism leads to the reinforcement of ethnic boundaries. The ethnic group is now perceived as a community sharing a common fate and the boundaries between ethnic groups become increasingly rigid (Conversi, 1999:568–570).

Whereas such group differentiation can also be observed with other forms of violence, the specificity of ethnic violence arises from the way groups are defined. In Weber's view (1980:238) an ethnic group is conceived as a large, extended family. Common origins and shared cultural traditions shape the focus of this form of self-identification (Wimmer, 1995:468).

When violence spreads, this belief in community can intensify and become a purity fetish which is often further strengthened by the 'racialization' of the notion of descent: one's own community is now formed through the purity of blood and must not be polluted by the blood of 'others'. The body of one's group is to be purged of the otherness (Chasseguet-Smirgel, 1996; Appadurai, 1998; Volkan, 1999).[1] This purity fetishism can

---

[1] The most obvious example of the significance attached to the belief in blood ties in ethnic-nationalist concepts is the linking of nationality to *jus sanguinis*, which is embodied in law in many countries.

lead to the exclusion or even the extermination of people of dubious or hybrid ethnic classification so as to allow clear borders to be drawn (Hayden, 1996; Herzfeld, 1993, 1997). In extreme cases this obsession with racial purity becomes pathological hatred and prepares the ground for the systematic extermination of the ethnic outgroup (Anderson, 1983).

Against this background women gain extraordinary significance as guarantors of the continuation and reproduction of the group. They symbolize its purity and represent its most vulnerable and precious possession. Rape, an expression of aggression and the will to power and domination which accompanies every war (Seifert, 1993), can thus gain additional symbolic and strategic significance in ethnic conflicts (Calic, 1996:140; Nagengast, 1994:121). Rape means not only the humiliation and dishonoring of the enemy, who has thus proven incapable of protecting 'his women', but is also intended to weaken his reproductive capacity (see Kora, 1994:502; Mac Kinnon, 1994). In the Bosnian conflict Serbian propaganda revived a perverted model of the 'devshirme' or 'child-tribute'. In accordance with patrilineal modes of thought, Muslim women were now to bear Serbian children, thus increasing the number of Serbs while demographically decimating the Muslims (see Allen, 1996; Volkan, 1999:95–97).

A second specific feature of ethnic violence is ethnic cleansing. It too is closely related to the idea of ethnic descent and purity and can be interpreted as an "almost sacral act of purification" (Waldmann, 1995:351). The spectrum extends from policies of enforced assimilation with threats of violence (Stavenhagen, 1990:91; Hayden, 1996:784) to the expulsion of ethnic aliens from the territory claimed as one's 'own', and culminates in ethnocide as practiced in Rwanda (Prunier, 1995), Bosnia-Herzegovina (Calic, 1996) or Armenia (Dadrian, 1995). All of these acts of violence are not only an assault on the life and limb of those classified as ethnic enemies, but also on the symbols of their history and identity, for example memorials, places of worship, and graves.

Ethnic violence is often described as being particularly brutal. There is a widespread opinion among journalists (e.g., Kaplan, 1993) and politicians (e.g., Eagleburger cited in Holbrooke, 1998:23) that 'deep-seated, ancient feelings of hatred' handed down from generation to generation are responsible for this particular intensity (Bowen, 1996). There are arguments which speak against this theory. Members of different ethnic groups often lived in harmony and only became enemies in the course of an ethnicization of political conflicts (Harvey, 2000:43; Rajasingham, 1997). Many ethnic groups were constituted in the recent past or only attained political significance in the course of recent developments, as we will show in the following chapter (see Elwert, 1989). A prominent example is the ethnic difference between Hutu and Tutsi which became politically salient only by the (post-)colonial practice of divide and rule (Lemarchand, 1994; Malkki, 1995). The argument that ethnic hatred is handed down from one generation to the next often corresponds to the hostile parties' own perception, but not always to the actual historical development. This is not to contest the fact that the memory of past violence and atrocities can be of great significance for current conflicts, as is shown by the events in the former Yugoslavia, in particular the mobilization of the Serbian population (Denich, 1994).

However, even among researchers there is widespread support for the opinion that ethnic disputes are especially violent forms of conflict. With reference to Bourdieu (1983), Esser (1996) attributes this to the fact that ethnic conflicts revolve around the defense of 'specific capital'. This specific capital (e.g., a language, cultural traditions) is only of value within one's own ethnic group. Ethnic conflicts are thus a race to declare one's own specific capital the valid currency in a society and the constitution of a state. For this particular reason ethnic conflicts often develop into zero-sum conflicts which only allow a winner and a loser. As soon as it is a matter of 'all or nothing', conflicts are fought out with particular ferocity (Senghaas, 1994:87).

A further argument is that people can more easily fall victim to violence in ethnic conflicts because they do not need to be of any particular ideological persuasion, but can be singled out on the basis of their belonging to an ethnic group. In many cases the opponents can be identified by clearly perceptible attributes (Malkki, 1995:88)—language (e.g., in Sri Lanka, in the Kurdish conflict), physical features (e.g., in Afghanistan) or an entry on one's ID card (e.g., in Rwanda) represent simple distinguishing criteria which enable mass violence. Large-scale massacres in which thousands of people are murdered are only practicable when the victims' ethnic identity can be easily determined and the danger of accidentally murdering 'one's own people' is kept to a minimum (Schetter, 1999:104).

There are examples of similar dimensions of violence in ideological conflicts, however, and this speaks against the view that ethnic violence is particularly excessive (see Mann, 1999b). The events in Cambodia, in the Soviet Union under Stalin, or in Peru in the 1980s and 1990s show that mass murder can also be carried out without a predominant ethnic ideology. It must also be taken into account that ethnic attributes are not as unambiguous as some researchers have it: individuals can avoid clear categorization by passing and code switching (Lyman & Douglass, 1973:349–355), and anthropological attributes (e.g., skin color, height) often allow only the broadest of distinctions (Appadurai, 1998:232). The struggle for the validity of specific capital is also present in ideological conflicts ('socialism or barbarism'). As an interim finding we can note that the specificity of ethnic violence is expressed in particular forms of violence such as ethnic cleansing and ethnocide. It seems to us, however, that in terms of its extent or intensity ethnic violence cannot be distinguished from other conflict constellations.

III.   POLITICAL MODERNIZATION

In the following we try to locate ethnic violence in contextual and macrohistorical terms. Typical techniques for expelling ethnic-cultural others from one's own area—mass shootings, rape, pillage, and plunder—first arose toward the end of the *reconquista* in the fifteenth century with the expulsion of the Moors and Jews from the Iberian peninsula. The Peace of Westphalia (1648), with its principle of *cuius regio, eius religio*, then institutionalized the ideal of the congruence of political unit and ethnic-religious community which was to become one of the central legitimation models of the impending world order of nation-states (Schilling, 1992; Calhoun, 1997:ch. 4; see also Hastings, 1997). Equals in ethnic, cultural and religious terms were now to rule over their like, and 'foreign rule' changed from being the normal state of affairs in dynastically ruled Europe to the expression of political injustice *par excellence*. The exiling of the Huguenots beginning with the St. Bartholomew's Day massacre (August 24, 1572) and the expulsion and pogrom-like hate campaign against the gypsies under Henry VIII (1491–1547) are further examples in a chain of early-modern outbreaks of ethnic-religious violence which followed the strategic goal of cleansing one's 'own' territory of 'foreign bodies' and thus forcibly bringing about religious-national homogenization.

Ethnic violence acquired an almost systematic dimension as the various waves of nation-state formation rolled through the Western world and then went on to engulf the rest of the globe (on the following issues see Wimmer, 2002). Cultural homogeneity was now the standard and it was linked up structurally to the basic political principles of the modern age, i.e., to the development of democratic procedures of legitimizing power and to the legal enforcement of equality, codified in the institution of citizenship. Political modernization thus meant the transformation of the mechanisms of integration and exclusion, more precisely the dissolution of the hierarchical, potentially global mechanisms of inclusion characteristic of premodern empires, and their replacement by egalitarian and at the same time territorially defined mechanisms such as operate in modern national states. Political modernization and ethnic-national modes of integration and exclusion are interlinked by three mechanisms. Firstly, hierarchically structured society with its culturally defined stratification—which often overlap with ethnic categories—is reconceived as an egalitarian community of equals. The external borders of this community are defined in ethnic-cultural terms: only those who are the same can be equal. The people in the sense of the community of citizens with equal rights and duties toward the state is identified with the people as a cultural community. Secondly, the democratic principle of popular rule—institutionalized in the possibility of the citizens effecting a change of government through an expression of their will and in the political participation of the entire population in this process—is interwoven with a discourse on ethnic homogeneity. Since the sovereign and the source of legitimate power is no longer the prince by the grace of God but instead the national community, the rulers and the ruled now have to be alike in ethnic-cultural terms, i.e., they have to speak the same language, be of the same religious denomination, and adhere to the same everyday practices which constitute their ethnic distinctiveness. Thirdly and finally, this isomorphism of a people as citizenry, sovereign, and nation leads to the coincidence of the three corresponding territorial delineations and thus to the intensification of a process which had begun when absolutist states emerged: the external borders of the state were no longer vaguely defined zones of transition between the spheres of influence of distant political centers as they had been in premodern empires, but were now sharply drawn and guarded lines separating the homogeneous inside from the heterogeneous and hostile beyond (see Giddens, 1984; Guenée, 1986; Nordman, 1996).

These three mechanisms cause an ethnicization and territorialization of the principles of inclusion and exclusion and thus lead to the development of various 'minorities': citizens of other states ('foreigners') who live on one's 'own' territory; ethnic minorities whose 'own' state is somewhere else; religious or ethnic diasporas without their 'own' state who live side by side with the dominant ethnic group. Because legal and political inclusion is linked to the principle of nationality, the relationship to these 'minorities' becomes structurally problematic: since only those who belong 'to us' in cultural-ethnic terms can legitimately be included in the community of equals before the law, and since only those who belong to the 'right' nation can be part of the electorate and be voted into political office, minorities are more often than not denied their full right to equality and the assumption of loyalty. They are perceived as a political problem, a fifth column of foreign powers on own territory, a thorn in the flesh of the nation.

The past two centuries have seen myriad examples of ethnic violence: the wars of extermination against the Indian 'minorities' of the United States and Argentina and the Yaqui in Mexico, the Western European 'wars of national liberation and unification' in the second half of the nineteenth century, the two Balkan Wars (1912–1913) and the outbursts of violence in the course of the transformation of the Ottoman and Austro-Hungarian empires into a series of nation-states at the end of World War I, the wave of nationalist-motivated cleansing and expulsion at the end of World War II, the bloodshed accompanying many a declaration of independence and the ensuing ethnic conflicts—for instance the foundation of India and Pakistan in 1948—and the wave of violence in the course of the foundation of nation-states after the fall of the Wall (Bell-Fialkoff, 1996; Jackson Preece, 1998). All these manifestations of ethnic violence were driven by the endeavor to realize the same ideal—one people, one state, one territory—in a world which de facto is characterized by ethnic-cultural intermixture, overlapping, and ambiguity.

In terms of the scale and the systematic nature of the politics of extermination involved, the Holocaust represents the culmination of modern terror. Mann (1999a) correctly emphasizes that reference to 'the people', in whose name violence against members of the outgroup is practiced, represents a perversion of the idea of democratic inclusion and lends the appearance of modern legitimacy to even the most monstrous acts of extermination.

The claim that there is a correlation between the establishment of popular rule and ethnic violence seems however to contradict the findings of Gurr's statistical study (1993b:183ff.) according to which a greater degree of democratization is accompanied by peaceful forms of ethnic conflict resolution. However, Gurr's sample also includes many Western democracies which are more readily able to resolve conflicts through redistribution and decentralization on the basis of their strong resources. If one looks closely at Gurr's study, the examples given (Gurr, 1993b:184ff., 187) show that between 1975 and 1986 *democratization* in developing countries had the effect of tending to exacerbate conflicts which often ended in renewed authoritarianism (Gurr, 1993b:184ff.).[2] In a recently published study Snyder (2000) gives a range of mainly European examples taken from two centuries to show that democratic inclusion and exclusion on the basis of ethnic-nationalist ascriptions are historically and systematically interlinked and frequently lead to violent conflict constellations. This theory is not exactly popular with the political advisors and politicians since it contradicts the idea that democratization, as it were, leads all by itself to the civilizing of society and the dissolution of ethnic-national patterns of conflict.

As late as in the first half of the twentieth century practices of ethnic cleansing were still legitimized in some cases by international treaties and were played down with euphemistic terms such as 'exchange of population', as in the Treaty of Sèvres (1920) between Greece and Turkey. Today different political conditions prevail and the weight has shifted in favor of those normative components of the modern age which allow the protection of human life and the right of existence of minorities to be held up against the unitary impetus of the national idea. From this perspective—simultaneity of the nonsimultaneous—the episodes successfully repressed from the historical memory of the formation of one's own state are projected in the present on to the others and transmuted into an expression of their perceived primitiveness (as in the case of Rwanda and Burundi) or fundamentally violent character (as in the case of the Balkans).

One structural precondition for the occurrence of ethnic violence is thus political modernity which first gave legitimacy to ethno-nationally definitions of friend and enemy and corresponding strategies of violence. Premodern violence, however, sought its objects with a different logic whose constitutive elements were the dichotomies loyal-rebellious (violence of the imperial centers against rebellious peripheries), conformist-nonconformist (institutionalized violence against delinquents or witches), believer-unbeliever (campaigns against heretics, anti-Jewish pogroms) (Moore, 1987). It is interesting to note that none of these forms of violence explicitly intended the extermination of its victims; rather, they were to be reintegrated into the hierarchical structure of society. It would seem, as

---

[2]On the possibility of genocidal excesses in democracies in general see Mann (1999a).

Bauman (1992) has established, that programs of extermination spring from the genuinely modern incapability to tolerate ambivalence.

The context of political modernization reinforces the special feature of ethnic violence that we derived from the structure of ethnic categorization in the preceding section. In the framework of the logic of the nation-state, according to which every territorialized national group should have its own state, the strategy of ethnic-cultural 'cleansing' of territories and their unambiguous allocation to a single state pays off. All attempts at de-escalation through external mediation are correspondingly difficult. The experiences of the past decade (in Chechnya, Bosnia, Liberia, or also in the great lakes region of east-central Africa) show that efforts to bring about 'win-win' situations at the negotiating table often end in failure (see Sisk, 1996): the logic of ethnic-territorial classification ordains that a particular village or region must always belong to one or the other project of nation-state formation.

IV. POLITICAL-INSTITUTIONAL CONFLICT CONSTELLATIONS

However, examples such as Switzerland, Belgium, or Cameroon show the limits to the explanatory power of the model delineated above. Evidently, democracy and a civic ethos can be introduced and linked to the national idea without this necessarily leading to the outbreak of ethnic violence. Political modernization represents a necessary but not a sufficient condition for ethnic violence—a structural prerequisite and not a cause with uniform effect. All in all, ethnic violence is relatively rare when seen in proportion to the possibility of its occurrence (Brubaker & Laitin, 1998:424).

Whether or not this potential for ethnic conflict is activated depends on the structure of the political institutions and processes. In keeping with the cumulative logic of our argumentation, we must therefore also enter the field of political science research, in which a large number of studies on the phenomenon of ethnic violence have recently been published. Two fundamental remarks should be made at the outset: Firstly, ethnic violence occurs in all types of modern political systems, both in multi-party democracies and in one-party regimes, in consociational democracies and in military dictatorships (see Wimmer, 1997)—contrary to the liberal conviction that all good things in life go together and that democracy as the best of all forms of government also rules out ethnic violence. Secondly—and contrary to the equally popular theory of violence as a pressure valve—violence does not represent the final stage of a build up of pressure in a situation of pervasive conflict. Rather, violence can also be consciously employed as an escalation strategy and create the very conflicts which seem to be the cause of the phenomenon of violence (Brubaker & Laitin, 1998:426; Eckert, 2000). In the following we distinguish between four paths of escalation that depend on the institutional structure of the state and the constellation of actors involved.

In the first path of escalation, radicalized political groups, which according to Waldmann (1989) originate mainly in proletarian-peasant social milieus, employ a strategy of violence as a means of attaining goals which they cannot reach in any other way—for example through the ballot-box or through the political mobilization of large sections of the population. Examples of this are the terrorist activities of ETA, the Quebecois separatists or the Shivsena in India. Sometimes it is the violent action which first leaves an ethnic mark on a particular political constellation and forces the established actors to take a stand on the issue of the ethnic character of a state and to respond to the ethnicizing discourse of the groups with a propensity for violence.

The holding of elections in an environment of politicized ethnicity can also lead to violence (see Horowitz, 1985:319–332). In constellations of this kind, the parties have already redefined themselves along ethnic lines so that the general perception of party A is that it stands for ethnic group X and party B for ethnic group Y. Under these circumstances an election becomes a census establishing the size of each group, and the democratic principle of majority rule determines and cements the ethnic balance of power. For radicalized party militias it is thus a conceivable and possibly even worthwhile strategy to use violence and intimidation to keep the other party—or rather its voters—from participating in the elections.

The third, most widely discussed path to violence evolves by itself, as it were, from the very logic of the democratic process: in an ethnicized party system the political positions frequently radicalize (Rabushka & Shepsle, 1972; Horowitz, 1985:ch. 7). In non-ethnicized party systems politicians have to try above all to gain the support of floating voters in the middle of the political spectrum: thus they exercise moderation. An ethnic party, on the other hand, competes for votes only *within* a clearly demarcated segment of the population, because in a climate of tension the affiliation of individuals to a particular group is beyond doubt. For the leaders of ethnic parties it therefore makes sense to adopt radical positions and in this way beat their rivals in representing the 'true' interests of the group; in ethnically divided electorates they can be assured of receiving the support of moderate voters. After all, where there are clear demographic majority conditions and open political competition, the political subordination of minorities is cemented, and a change can only be brought about through violence. However, the question as to whether this dynamics of escalation is inevitable, or whether the majority ethnic group can—or must—split into several moderate parties, so that in the end trans-ethnic coalition governments can be formed, is still a controversial issue (see van Amersfoort & van der Wusten, 1981; Rothschild, 1981; Horowitz, 1985:ch. 8; Brass, 1991:ch. 9; Kaufman, 1996).

The fourth and final path to violence is taken by state authorities themselves when they organize state terror or even extermination campaigns against individual ethnic groups (van den Berghe, 1990; Harff & Gurr, 1989; Mann, 1999b). It would perhaps make sense to distinguish between cases in which the state apparatus is controlled by an ethnic minority (see Horowitz, 1985:486–501) and those where the demographic majority ethnic group controls the state. Under modern political conditions—where the ethnic-cultural representativeness of the government is a central legitimizing principle—the status and position of minority elites are particularly precarious; for this reason they tend to a drastic use of violence at any sign of protest against their ethnocracy. The events in Burundi in 1972, 1988, and 1993 were exemplary: no sooner had educated Hutu dared to question the dominance of the Tutsi than they were massacred in pogroms throughout the country (Lemarchand, 1994). A different logic would seem to apply in cases where violence is used by a state elite belonging to the majority ethnic group to preempt or neutralize irredentist aspirations—for example the case of the Armenian genocide in the course of the foundation of the Turkish state (Dadrian, 1995). Such policies are also typically connected with the foundation of new nation-states upon the ruins of empires, for example after the collapse of the Soviet empire in the 1990s—national polarization within the state and the accompanying mobilization of the population at the very moment when the issue of the republics' borders was on the political agenda led to a spiral of violence (Beissinger, 1998).

These four paths of escalation can lead to similar or different forms of ethnic violence, to phenomena characteristic of ethnic violence such as ethnocide or general ones such as terrorist acts against individual members of an enemy group. Irrespective of the institutional-political context discussed above, the very logic of ethnic-national category-formation implies certain dynamics of violence and counterviolence, a specific dramaturgy of terror.

V. THE ANATOMY OF ETHNIC VIOLENCE

Contrary to the image frequently encountered in the media, recent research has shown that this dramaturgy of terror follows certain rules (e.g., Brass, 1996; Esser, 1996, 1999; Tambiah, 1996; Waldmann, 1999, Horowitz, 2001). Let us first address the spiral of political radicalization, which immediately precedes the outbreak of violence. The propensity to violence grows with increasing fear and deepening mistrust toward the political representatives of other groups, and toward the state as the holder of the monopoly on the legitimate use of force and protector from arbitrary violence.

Various authors (e.g., Tambiah, 1996; Gallagher, 1997; Schetter, 1999) stress that groups with a propensity to violence play an outstanding role in the production of this kind of climate. To do this they must depict ethnicity as the unquestioned principle of group formation in times of crisis and ethnic violence as a legitimate means of defending collective interests (ethnic framing in the terminology of Esser, 1996). Various authors (see Chrétien, 1991; Tambiah, 1996; Neubert, 1999) emphasize that access to the media facilitates this framing. Calls to violence on radio or television accompanied the riots in Southeast Asia, for example, as well as the massacres in Rwanda and the ethnic cleansing in Yugoslavia. The spreading of rumors is also a widely practiced technique of ethnic framing (Tambiah, 1996:236–239).

Fear and mistrust give credibility to rumors and in turn are increased by credible rumors (Horowitz, 1985:175–184). Lake and Rothchild (1996) investigated this process in detail. The misinterpretation of information causes the loss of credibility of the other ethnic group, which can ultimately lead to a security dilemma: each group feels that the enemy is capable of the worst (Posen, 1993). The thinner the network of relations between the groups, the more likely misinterpretation of information becomes (see Kuper, 1977; Varshney, 1997). The greater the mistrust and fear, the sooner relations will be broken off and the greater is the likelihood of misinterpretation. In this way fear and misinterpretation can culminate in the conviction that discrimination, repression, or even destruction can only be avoided by taking recourse to armed offensives before the enemy does so (Waldmann, 1995:350; Elwert, 1999:92).

The radicalization of ethnic stereotypes and the reinforcement of symbolic hierarchies fuels the expectation of and propensity to violence. One's own culture is stylized as the only acceptable form of human existence, and the past is idealized in terms of a history of the oppression or grandeur of one's own group (Malkki, 1995; Schetter, 1999). The more comprehensive such a "shared social frame of reference" has become, the more readily a propensity to violence can be brought about by the propaganda of radicalized groups (Esser, 1999:247). The opposing group is demonized (Gallagher, 1997) and viewed disparagingly as a horde of faceless creatures deprived of all individuality (Rösel, 1997:168). As shown by the defamation of the Tutsi as 'cockroaches' by the Hutu propagandists or of the Hazaras as 'mules' by Tajik and Pashtun leaders, the disparagement of the enemy can go so far as to be condensed into one single pejorative word. The use of violence against groups denigrated and dehumanized in this way thus appears legitimate and even desirable.

When the fear of a demonized and dehumanized enemy spreads, every new event which fits into the ethnic friend-enemy scheme reinforces the validity of the scheme and the ethnicized interpretation of the situation. Even attacks on individuals in no way directly connected with the conflict can be interpreted as attacks on the ethnic group as a whole. Groups with a propensity to violence can use this mechanism to trigger off dynamics of escalating violence through selective assassinations and thus keep a conflict alive. In this context Wright (1988:11) speaks of the representativeness of (ethnic) violence. The victims are not 'selected' by reason of their personal characteristics but purely on the basis of their group membership. In this way all members of the entire group become potential victims, and the actual victim represents them all. Interpreting violence as 'ethnic' paves the way for further violence (Lemarchand, 1994:19) and can escalate into ethnic riots or even wars.

Riots and civil wars differ in their intensity and scale. Riots can mark the beginning of civil wars, while in some cases wars are directly initiated by militias or armies without the involvement of civilians. Ethnic civil war therefore does not necessarily represent an intensified form of ethnic riots, as implied by the popular idea that ethnic wars are an expression of increasing hatred between opposed ethnic groups. Rather, ethnic conflicts are usually characterized by an oscillation of violence such as in Sri Lanka, the Basque Country, or Northern Ireland, and less by linear dynamics of escalation (Elwert, Feuchtwang, & Neubert, 1999:10ff.).

In contrast to their appearance as spontaneous, unbridled, and uncontrolled manifestations of hatred, riots and pogroms show some regularities and structures. Firstly, instigators, organizers and manipulators play a major role (Tambiah, 1996:266). Often pogroms have been triggered off by public or concealed calls to violence by prominent politicians; the attackers thus thought themselves safe from criminal prosecution and their acts of violence appeared legitimate, or even desirable. Servaes (1996:166ff.) points out that the massacres of Tutsi in Burundi were even initiated and partly carried out by government institutions. Bergmann (1998) even sees a structural feature of pogroms in the passivity or tacit sympathy of government executive bodies with the attackers.

Secondly, the cyclical occurrence of such riots can lead to a routinization and ritualization of ethnic violence. Brass (1996:12) speaks in this context of "institutionalized riot systems." Often ethnic identity is celebrated symbolically in specific locations (memorials, holy places, churches, etc.) and on particular holidays or days of mourning. These occasions often become the trigger and focal point of ethnic violence (Tambiah, 1996:239–243). This is because localized festivals and processions offer an appropriate occasion for riots, or provoke the opposing group to commit acts of violence (for example on the occasion of the Orange Order procession). Attacks and pogroms clearly show that regardless of how an individual defines him or herself, it is ethnic classification that decides life and death (Rösel, 1997:169). The representativeness of ethnic violence makes everyone a 'prisoner' of the groups with a propensity to violence. Anyone who rejects or even simply fails to actively support their 'own' protectors, is branded a traitor or informer and runs the risk of being left completely at the mercy of the enemy. The survival of the individual then depends very much on the power relations between ethnic groups (Bowman, 1994:143). In ritualized 'riot systems' of this kind there is therefore an increasing tendency toward formation of ethnic ghettos within which protection from the enemy is more readily afforded. Communication is limited to members of one's 'own' ethnic group since those on the 'other side' are no longer to be trusted (Waldmann, 1989:209). This lack of communication, in turn, fuels mutual mistrust.

Such 'riot systems' can stabilise and have a life of their own, often in a localized context without direct repercussions on the macropolitical constellations. In other cases attacks of this kind trigger off—or provide the welcome occasion for—large-scale violence which challenge the basic structures of the political system. In an 'ethnicized climate' in which all political decisions are judged and justified from the angle of ethnic stereotypes, ethnic violence presents itself as an instrument for attaining long-term political objectives. The exact motives and violence strategies vary with the political-institutional constellations, which we described in the preceding section above. However, all the actors in such ethnic civil wars remain tied to the logic of the nation-state—the idea that power can be justified by reference to an ethnically defined people, and that every people is entitled to a state which then merits recognition.

Ethnic civil war frequently begins with the occupation or conquest of territories which are considered strategically significant for the security of one's 'own' ethnic group. The territorialization and ethnicization of concepts of belonging, characteristic for politics in the age of nation-states, also determines the further course of ethnic civil wars: the tendency toward expulsion or destruction of ethnic others from the territory of one's 'own' future state, the use of expellees of one's own ethnic group for the colonization of such 'cleansed' areas, the wanton destruction of remaining niches of interethnic coexistence, the particular brutality unleashed upon everything mixed and hybrid, the destructive frenzy toward everyday signs of the existence of 'foreign' groups: blowing up houses, filling in wells with concrete, the destruction of arable land, razing temples, churches, statues, etc., which could serve as a memory of those who once 'owned' the territory. Members of the enemy group—demonized and dehumanized—fall victim to the violent practices of marauding bands of young fighters: they are shot as an example to terrorize the survivors and make them flee, or they are herded together in camps or 'resettled', or—as the ultimate form of ethnic violence—they are murdered en masse as in Rwanda or in Bosnia in minutely planned operations.

Translated by Tradukas

REFERENCES

Allen, Beverly. (1996). *Rape Warfare: The Hidden Genocide in Bosnia-Herzegovina and Croatia*. Minneapolis: University of Minnesota Press.

Anderson, Benedict. (1983). *Imagined Communities: Reflections on the Origin and Spread of Nationalism*. London: Verso.

Appadurai, Arjun. (1998). Dead Certainty: Ethnic Violence in the Era of Globalization. *Public Culture, 10*(2), 225–247.

Bauman, Zygmunt. (1991). *Moderne und Ambivalenz*. Hamburg: Junius.

Beissinger, Mark R. (1998). Nationalist Violence and the State: Political Authority and Contentious Repertoires in the Former USSR. *Comparative Politics, 30*(4), 401–422.

Bell-Fialkoff, Andrew. (1996). *Ethnic Cleansing*. New York: Griffin.

Bergmann, Werner. (1998). Pogrome: Eine spezifische Form kollektiver Gewalt. *Kölner Zeitschrift für Soziologie und Sozialpsychologie, 50*(4), 644–665.

Bourdieu, Pierre. (1983). Ökonomisches Kapital, kulturelles Kapital, soziales Kapital. In Reinhard Kreckel (Ed.), *Soziale Ungleichheiten* (pp. 185–187). Göttingen: Schwartz.

Bowen, John R. (1996). The Myth of Global Ethnic Conflict. *Journal of Democracy, 7*(4), 3–14.

Bowman, Glenn. (1994). Ethnic Violence and the Phantasy of the Antagonist: The Mobilisation of National Identity in Former Yugoslavia. *Polish Sociological Review*, 2, 133–153.

Brass, Paul R. (1991). *Ethnicity and Nationalism. Theory and Comparison*. New Delhi: Sage Publications.

Brass, Paul R. (1996). Introduction: Discourses of Ethnicity, Communalism, and Violence. In Paul R. Brass (Ed.), *Riots and Pogroms* (pp. 1–55). New York: New York University Press.

Brubaker, Rogers, & David D. Laitin. (1998). Ethnic and Nationalist Violence. *Annual Review of Sociology*, 24, 423–452.

Calhoun, Craig. (1997). *Nationalism*. Buckingham: Open University Press.

Calic, Marie-Janine. (1996). *Krieg und Frieden in Bosnien-Herzegowina*. Frankfurt: Suhrkamp.

Chasseguet-Smirgel, Janine. (1996). Blood and Nation. *Mind and Human Action*, 7, 31–33.

Chrétien, Jean-Pierre. (1991). 'Presse Libre' et propagande raciste au Rwanda. Kangura et 'les 10 commandements du Hutu.' *Politique Africaine*, 42(6), 109–120.

Conversi, Daniele. (1999). Nationalism, Boundaries, and Violence. Millennium. *Journal of International Studies*, 28(3), 553–684.

Dadrian, Vahakn N. (1995). *The History of the Armenian Genocide*. Providence: Berghahn Books.

Denich, Bette. (1994). Dismembering Yugoslavia: Nationalist Ideologies and the Symbolic Revival of Genocide. *American Ethnologist*, 21(2), 367–390.

Eckert, Julia. (2000). *The Politics of Violent Action. Towards a Sociology of Anti-Democratic Movements*. Unpublished Manuscript.

Elwert, Georg. (1989). *Ethnizität und Nationalismus. Über die Bildung von Wir-Gruppen (Ethnizität und Gesellschaft. Occasional Papers 22)*. Berlin: Arabisches Buch.

Elwert, Georg. (1999). Gewaltmärkte. Beobachtungen zur Zweckrationalität der Gewalt. In Georg Elwert, Stephan Feuchtwang & Dieter Neubert (Eds.), *Dynamics of Violence. Processes of Escalation and De-Escalation in Violent Group Conflicts (Supplements to Sociologus 1)* (pp. 86–101). Berlin: Duncker und Humblot.

Elwert, Georg, Stephan Feuchtwang, & Dieter Neubert. (1999). The Dynamics of Collective Violence – An Introduction. In Georg Elwert, Stephan Feuchtwang & Dieter Neubert (Eds.), *Dynamics of Violence. Processes of Escalation and De-Escalation in Violent Group Conflicts (Supplements to Sociologus 1)* (pp. 9–31). Berlin: Duncker und Humblot.

Esser, Hartmut. (1996). Ethnische Konflikte als Auseinandersetzung um den Wert von kulturellem Kapital. In Wilhelm Heitmeyer & Rainer Dollase (Eds.), *Die bedrängte Toleranz. Ethnisch-kulturelle Konflikte, religiöse Differenzen und die Gefahren politisierter Gewalt* (pp. 64–99). Frankfurt: Suhrkamp.

Esser, Hartmut. (1999). Die Situationslogik ethnischer Konflikte. *Zeitschrift für Soziologie*, 28(4), 245–262.

Gallagher, Tom. (1997). My Neighbour, My Enemy: The Manipulation of Ethnic Identity and the Origins and Conduct of War in Yugoslavia. In David Turton (Ed.), *War and Ethnicity. Global Connections and Local Violence* (pp. 47–75). San Marino: University of Rochester Press.

Gellner, Ernest. (1991). Nationalism and Politics in Eastern Europe. *New Left Review*, 189, 127–43.

Giddens, Anthony. (1984). *The Nation-State and Violence*. Berkeley: University of California Press.

Gueneé, Bernard. (1986). Des limites féodales aux frontières politiques. In Pierre Nora (Ed.), *Les lieux de mémoire. La nation. Vol. 2* (pp. 11–61). Paris: Gallimard.

Gurr, Ted Robert. (1993a). *Minorities at Risk: A Global View of Ethnopolitical Conflict*. Washington: United States Institute of Peace Press.

Gurr, Ted Robert. (1993b). Why Minorities Rebel: A Global Analysis of Communal Mobilization and Conflict Since 1945. *International Political Science Review*, 14, 161–201.

Gurr, Ted Robert. (1994). Peoples against the State: Ethnopolitical Conflict in the Changing World System. *International Studies Quarterly*, 38, 347–377.

Harff, Barbara, & Ted R. Gurr. (1989). Victims of the State: Genocide, Politicide and Group Repression Since 1945. *International Review of Victimology*, 1(1), 23–41.

Harvey, Frank P. (2000). Primordialism, Evolutionary Theory and Ethnic Violence in the Balkans: Opportunities and Constraints for Theory and Policy. *Canadian Journal of Political Science*, 33(1), 37–65.

Hastings, Adrian. (1997). *The Construction of Nationhood. Ethnicity, Religion and Nationalism*. Cambridge: Cambridge University Press.

Hayden, Robert. (1996). Imagined Communities and Real Victims: Self-Determination and Ethnic Cleansing in Yugoslavia. *American Anthropologist*, 23(4), 783–801.

Herzfeld, Michael. (1993). *The Social Production of Indifference: Exploring the Symbolic Roots in Western Bureaucracy*. Chicago: Chicago University Press.

Herzfeld, Michael. (1997). *Cultural Intimacy: Social Poetics in the Nation-State*. New York: Routledge.

Holbrooke, Richard. (1998). *To End a War*. New York: Random House.

Horowitz, Donald. (1985). *Ethnic Groups in Conflict*. Berkeley: University of California Press.

Horowitz, Donald. (2001). *The Deadly Ethnic Riot*. Berkeley: University of California Press.

Jackson Preece, Jennifer. (1998). Ethnic Cleansing as an Instrument of Nation-State Creation: Changing State Practices and Evolving Legal Norms. *Human Rights Quarterly, 29*, 817–842.

Kaplan, Robert. (1993). *Balkan Ghosts: A Journey through History*. New York: Vintage Books.

Kaufman, Stuart J. (1996). Spiraling to Ethnic War: Elites, Masses, and Moscow in Moldova's Civil War. *International Security, 21*(2), 108–138.

Kora, Maja. (1994). Representation of Mass Rape in Ethnic Conflicts in what Was Yugoslavia. *Sociology, 36*(4), 495–514.

Kuper, Leo. (1977). *The Pitty of it All: Polarization of Racial and Ethnic Relations*. Minneapolis: University of Minnesota Press.

Lake, David A., & Donald Rothchild. (1996). Containing Fear. The Origins and Management of Ethnic Conflict. *International Security, 21*(2), 41–75.

Lemarchand, René. (1994). *Burundi. Ethnocide as Discourse and Practice*. Cambridge: Cambridge University Press.

Lyman, Stanford M., & William A. Douglass. (1973). Ethnicity: Strategies of Collective and Individual Impression Management. *Social Research, 40*, 344–365.

Mac Kinnon, Catharine A. (1994). Rape, Genocide and Women's Human Rights. In Alexandra Stigmayer (Ed.), *Mass Rape: The War against Women in Bosnia-Herzegovina* (pp. 183–196). Lincoln and London: University of Nebraska Press.

Malkki, Liisa H. (1995). *Purity and Exile: Transformations in Historical-National Consciousness among Hutu Refugees in Tanzania*. Chicago: Chicago University Press.

Mann, Michael. (1999a. *Explaining Murderous Ethnic Cleansing: The Macro-Level*. Unpublished Manuscript.

Mann, Michael. (1999b. The Dark Side of Democracy: The Modern Tradition of Ethnic and Political Cleansing. *New Left Review, 235*, 18–45.

Moore, Richard I. (1987). *The Formation of a Persecuting Society: Power and Deviance in Western Europe, 950–1250*. Oxford: Blackwell.

Nagengast, Carole. (1994). Violence, Terror, and the Crisis of the State. *Annual Review of Anthropology, 23*, 109–136.

Nairn, Tim. (1993). All Bosnians now? *Dissent, Fall*, pp. 403–410.

Neubert, Dieter. (1999). Dynamics of Escalating Violence. The Genocide in Rwanda. In Georg Elwert, Stephan Feuchtwang & Dieter Neubert (Eds.), *Dynamics of Violence. Processes of Escalation and De-Escalation in Violent Group Conflicts (Supplements to Sociologus 1)* (pp. 153–174). Berlin: Duncker und Humblot.

Nordman, Daniel. (1996). Des limites d'etat aux frontières nationales. In Pierre Nora (Ed.), *Realms of Memory: Rethinking the French Past* (pp. 1125–1146). New York: Columbia University Press.

Popitz, Heinrich. (1992). *Phänomene der Macht*. Tübingen: J.C.B. Mohr.

Posen, Barry R. (1993). The Security Dilemma and Ethnic Conflict. *Survival, 35*(1), 27–47.

Prunier, Gérard. (1995). *The Rwanda Crisis. History of a Genocide*. London: C. Hurst & Co.

Rabushka, Alvin, & Kenneth Shepsle. (1972). *Politics in Plural Societies: A Theory of Democratic Instability*. New York: Charles E. Merrill.

Rajasingham, Darini. (1997). The Unmixing of Peoples. Topographies of Displacement in Sri Lanka. In Tapan K. Bose & Rita Manchanda (Eds.), *States, Citizens and Outsiders* (pp. 291–315). Katmandu: South Asia Forum for Human Rights.

Rösel, Jakob. (1997). Vom ethnischen Antagonismus zum ethnischen Bürgerkrieg. Antagonismus, Erinnerung und Gewalt in ethnischen Konflikten. In Trutz von Trotha (Ed.) *Soziologie der Gewalt (Kölner Zeitschrift für Soziologie und Sozialpsychologie, Sonderheft 37)* (pp. 162–182). Opladen: Westdeutscher Verlag.

Rothschild, Jonathan. (1981). *Ethnopolitics. A Conceptual Framework*. New York: Columbia University Press.

Scherrer, Christian. (1994). *Ethno-Nationalismus als globales Phänomen. Zur Krise der Staaten in der Dritten Welt und der früheren UdSSR*. INEF (Institut für Entwicklung und Frieden der Universität-GH-Duisburg), Report 6.

Schetter, Conrad. (1999). Ethnizität als Ressource der Kriegführung. In Conrad Schetter & Almut Wieland-Karimi (Eds.), *Afghanistan in Geschichte und Gegenwart. Beiträge zur Afghanistanforschung (Schriftenreihe der Mediothek für Afghanistan 1)* (pp. 91–108). Frankfurt: IKO-Verlag.

Schilling, Heinz. (1992). *Religion, Political Culture, and the Emergence of Early Modern Society: Essays in German and Dutch History*. Leiden: Brill.

Seifert, Ruth. (1993). Die zweite Front. Zur Logik sexueller Gewalt in Kriegen. Sicherheit und Frieden. *Vierteljahresschrift für Sicherheit und Frieden, 11*, 66–71.

Senghaas, Dieter. (1994). *Wohin driftet die Welt? Über die Zukunft friedlicher Koexistenz*. Frankfurt: Suhrkamp.

Servaes, Sylvia. (1996). Gewalt so nötig wie Wasser? In Erwin Orywal, Aparna Rao & Michael Bollig (Eds.), *Krieg und Kampf. Die Gewalt in unseren Köpfen* (pp. 157–170). Berlin: Dietrich Reimer Verlag.

Sisk, Timothy D. (1996). *Power Sharing and International Mediation in Ethnic Conflicts*. Washington: United States Institute of Peace.

Snyder, Jack. (2000). *From Voting to Violence. Democratization and Nationalist Conflict*. New York: Norton.

Stavenhagen, Rudolfo. (1990). *The Ethnic Question: Conflict, Development and Human Rights*. Tokyo: United Nations University Press.

Tambiah, Stanley J. (1996). *Leveling Crowds. Ethnonationalist Conflicts and Collective Violence in South Asia*. Berkeley: University of California Press.

Trotha, Trutz von. (1997). Zur Soziologie der Gewalt. In Trutz von Trotha (Ed.), *Soziologie der Gewalt (Kölner Zeitschrift für Soziologie und Sozialpsychologie. Sonderheft 37)* (pp. 9–56). Opladen: Westdeutscher Verlag.

van Amersfoort, Hans, & Herman van der Wusten. (1981). Democratic Stability and Ethnic Parties. *Ethnic and Racial Studies, 4*(4), 476–485.

van den Berghe, Pierre (Ed.) (1990). *State Violence and Ethnicity*. Niwot: University Press of Colorado.

Varshney, Ashutosh. (1997). Postmodernism, Civic Engagement, and Ethnic Conflict. A Passage to India. *Comparative Politics, 30*(1), 1–20.

Volkan, Vamik D. (1988). *The Need to Have Enemies and Allies: From Clinical Practice to International Relationship*. Northvale: Jason Aronson.

Volkan, Vamik D. (1999). *Das Versagen der Diplomatie. Zur Psychoanalyse nationaler, ethnischer und religiöser Konflikte*. Giessen: Psychosozial-Verlag.

Waldmann, Peter. (1989). *Ethnischer Radikalismus. Ursachen und Folgen gewaltsamer Minderheitenkonflikte am Beispiel des Baskenlandes, Nordirlands und Quebecs*. Opladen: Westdeutscher Verlag.

Waldmann, Peter. (1995). Gesellschaften im Bürgerkrieg. Zur Eigendynamik entfesselter Gewalt. *Zeitschrift für Politik, 42*(4), 343–368.

Waldmann, Peter. (1999). Societies in Civil War. In Georg Elwert, Stephan Feuchtwang & Dieter Neubert (Eds.), *Dynamics of Violence. Processes of Escalation and De-Escalation in Violent Group Conflicts (Supplements to Sociologus 1)* (pp. 61–83). Berlin: Duncker und Humblot.

Weber, Max. (1980 [1921]. *Wirtschaft und Gesellschaft*. Tübingen: J.C.B. Mohr.

Wimmer, Andreas. (1995). Interethnische Konflikte: Ein Beitrag zur Integration aktueller Forschungsansätze. *Kölner Zeitschrift für Soziologie und Sozialpsychologie, 47*(3), 464–493.

Wimmer, Andreas. (1997). Who Owns the State? Understanding Ethnic Conflict in Post-Colonial Societies. *Nations and Nationalism, 3*(4), 631–665.

Wimmer, Andreas. (2002). *Nationalist Exclusion and Ethnic Conflict: Shadows of Modernity*. Cambridge: Cambridge University Press.

Wright, Frank. (1988). *Northern Ireland. A Comparative Analysis*. Dublin: Gill and Macmillan.

CHAPTER II-2.3

The Socio-Anthropological Interpretation of Violence

GEORG ELWERT

I. INTRODUCTION

Research on violence is dominated by two major options: the etiological approach, or search for causes, which attributes violence to particular (overt or latent) individual failings and conflicts; and the analysis of the system of violence as a part of the social system. This latter approach investigates specific forms of the embedding of violence and institutions that regulate conflicts. Increasingly, comparative social research by social anthropologists and ethnologists is uniting behind the latter standpoint (cf. Abbink, 1994a, 1994b; Bollig, 1991; Elwert, Feuchtwang, & Neubert, 1999; Halbmayer, 2000; Orywal, 1996; Schlee, 2000; Schmidt & Schroeder, 2001).

This chapter, based on social anthropological and ethnological findings, argues in favor of a link between two standpoints: the systematic differentiation of façades of violence and violent actions on the one hand, and the analysis of conflict patterns on the other. The effect is to highlight the "normalcy" of conflict. In this context, violence appears to be a "default option."[1]

---

[1] This term can be illustrated with reference to a metaphor. Any well-written computer program has default options that still function if other sections of the program have crashed. Human society can be described as an action program. Violence is one of the default options of purposeful action.

II.   A HISTORY OF VIOLENCE AS A SUBJECT OF ETHNOLOGICAL RESEARCH[2]

1.   Disappointments and Results of Comparative Studies

In the history of social anthropology/ethnology, the subject of violence has prompted a number of comparisons. Frequently, however, these studies have merely endeavored to confirm certain normative evaluations based on the authors' own societies. For example, the stereotype of violent and therefore uncivilized "savage" society has been cited as a justification for the violence of the slave trade and colonialism. As early as the Enlightenment, the stereotype of the "noble savage" was postulated as a countermodel. Studies such as that by Georg Forster ([1789] 1967, 1985:72–92), who described the social mores of the rules of encounter and confrontation in the South Seas, were too subtly differentiated to serve any simple political purpose. Little attention was subsequently paid to his researches.

It was not until the 1940s that this discipline first began the systematic formulation of theories on the subject of violence. It would be a long time yet—not until the 1990s—before the key words "conflict" and "violence" made an appearance in ethnological works of reference. In the history of research, major disappointments predominated, with only a handful of general studies to set against the massive preoccupation with empirical material that is typical of social anthropology.

As late as 1949, White was still asserting that organized violence was largely absent from relatively noncomplex societies that resemble neolithic societies. Otterbein, in a comparative study dating from 1970, was finally able to dispel this notion. We find both individual and organized violence in every type of society (though individual violence rarely became the subject of social anthropological theorization). Among the many types of society, there are individual societies where the incidence of violence is relatively high, just as there are those where it is relatively low. To that extent, social anthropology had cut the ground from under Hobbes's thesis ([1651] 1965) that society is founded on violence and the expectation of violence. Civilization always presupposes adherence to rules and hence a restriction of the arbitrary, in just the same way as it necessarily includes violations of rules, noncommunication, withdrawal of cooperation and hence violence.[3] Adherence to rules as a precondition of communication and cooperation is as indispensable as the possibility of breaking the rules as a precondition for the assertion of interests and innovation.

This systematic duality of society, however, is frequently neglected and ignored—even by researchers. On the basis of individual examples and general assumptions about human nature, Lorenz believed in 1966 that he could analyze an inherent "instinct of violence" as such. Montagu was able to oppose these and similar theories in 1968 with an impressive breadth of ethnological material that emphasized the idea of the social framework of the use of violence. The most influential text on this subject was written by Gluckman in 1952 (1963). Citing South African examples, he highlighted the institutional order behind organized violence, which, in the case of the Swazi, he interpreted as rituals of rebellion. In 1964 Voget suggested that war, in particular, can only be interpreted as a product of institutional rules—the earliest form of institutionalization, in his opinion. In

---

[2] I am indebted to many of my colleagues for their advice and criticism. I may well have promptly internalized some of their ideas and forgotten their authors. The development of my work can be seen in a longer working-paper version (Sozialanthropologische Arbeitspapiere, Berlin).

[3] The fact that Hobbes (in the Dedication to *De Cive*) had already addressed the subject of this bilateralism was subsequently overlooked by those who cited him.

the German-speaking countries, Mühlmann (1940)[4] had already formulated the paradoxical-sounding theory of "regulated war." What seemed to him specifically typical of premodern societies was what we today describe as the social embedding of violence. Violence follows predetermined paths and its exercise is limited by rules (Abbink, 1994a, 1994b). This insight applies to both pre-industrial and industrial societies.

It was recognized at an early stage that the motives for violence were in each case specific to particular cultures. In his study of the Kapauku of New Guinea, Pospisil (1958) also highlighted the diversity of motives from the internal view of the societies concerned (on the theme of diversity of motives even within one society, cf. Otterbein, 1970). Understanding and describing the internal view, the logic that applied within a group, and the perception and contextualization of the motivation and legitimation of violence within a social group are the particular contributions made by social anthropology.

The motive of prestige was long undervalued. It was touched upon only in descriptions of blood-feud systems (cf. Black-Michaud, 1975; Schwandner-Sievers, 1999). Evans-Pritchard (1940a, 1957) showed that without that motive it would be impossible to explain the institutionalized military campaigns of the Nuer and Azande. In 1973, Erdheim expanded the study of the prestige motive to form a theory that also encompassed ritual and individual violence. In 1961, Vayda emphasized the subject of material resources. He proposed an equilibrium model of resource utilization and resource competition. Helbling (1999) sensibly demonstrated that the cases described by Vayda, and by Chagnon (1967) who followed him, cannot be generalized in that way—population density must be incorporated as a variable. The frequency or rarity of feuds, raids, and wars increases within a certain type of society as population density increases. The fact that economically motivated violence may, under particular historical conditions, become the central basis for the reproduction of a political system was demonstrated by Elwert in 1973 in his study of the slave-raid production system. The organized abduction and sale of slaves in precolonial West Africa provided the economic basis of several kingdoms along the coast and in the hinterland (Danxome, for example).

Particularly by absolutizing economic motives and rape as features of the reproduction of political power, Vayda (1968) had formulated a functionalistic explanation of war, which he interpreted as a necessary means for the reconstitution of certain properties of the system. Hallpike demonstrated the inconsistency of this theoretical construct in 1973. It is problematic to interpret a particular form of society as an optimum adaptation to its natural geographical and social environment. There are several possible forms of adaptation to any combination of environmental conditions. It is impossible, therefore, to explain certain forms of social violence simply as adaptation defined by the economics of survival. Under identical conditions, not only are there different social forms of dealing with violence but there are even different forms of institutionalized violence within a society.

It was long hoped that it might be possible to formulate more general rules, at least for certain types of social organization. Thus, for example, Sahlins (1961), in a highly regarded article on the Tiv of Nigeria, formulated the theory that genealogical proximity in societies organized in accordance with the principle of kinship—"lineage societies"—reduced the occurrence of violence. In the lines of kinship he described, where expansion took place through pillage, individual groups banded together in accordance with their ge-

---

[4] Radically conservative evaluations are unmistakable in the formulation of his 1940 theory. An adjustment to the prevalent ideology can be assumed. In the later versions of his theory (1972, cf. also his important studies of arms technology 1962:219–251) the only remaining trace of those evaluations is a distantly skeptical stance toward peace policy.

nealogical proximity, as a way of establishing superiority over less closely related groups. Of course, this generalization (perhaps not so intended by the author) overlooked important studies by Evans-Pritchard (1940b) and Barth (1959a, 1959b), which demonstrated that lineage societies (the Anuak of the Sudan or the Pashtun of Pakistan) could form enmities and alliances based on quite different patterns: in each case, a group would seek an alliance with another that was in conflict with the first group's direct competitors (for a current example in Somalia, see Schlee, 2000).

For some time, it appeared that the theory of crosscutting ties evolved by Max Gluckman (1956) might explain phenomena of the suppression of violence. It seemed logical to assume that if the enemies of a group were simultaneously in alliance with allies of the group concerned, this third group would press for an ending to the conflict. Of course, such rules cannot be generalized, as Hallpike demonstrated (cf., in the case of East Africa, Schlee, 2000). Crosscutting lines of alliance could in some cases even increase the frequency of violence (Hallpike, 1977). The cost/benefit calculations of direct—often neighboring—parties to a conflict clearly outweighed any possible joint interests in the conflict genesis phase. Alliances that had only recently been formalized took second place to expectations of plunder and the lure of honor. However, these third parties could play an important part in resolving the consequences of conflict; they were called upon when the agreement of peace terms became an issue.

However, there are two observations that are constantly confirmed throughout this history of research: the ethnocentrism thesis and the cohesion thesis. As early as 1911, Sumner had coined the term "ethnocentrism" for the practice of defining a group and associating that group with positive values. Ethnocentrism can occur in all types of society. Sumner had also pointed out that the drawing of boundaries is a precondition for organized violence. That, of course, need not be interpreted as a chain of causation, as if the violence resulted from the boundaries. Leach dryly pointed out in 1965 that the killing of people has a classifying effect on the group memberships of survivors. Reviewing also ethnographic material, Coser (1956) developed his major sociological conflict theory that was able to show that conflict strengthens the cohesion of groups (cf. also Young, 1965). (Violent) conflict entails the creation or revival of rules. To that extent, conflict always plays a formative role in society.

The theory that poverty causes violence can be seen as a variation on the idea of the savagery of pre-industrial societies. The poverty thesis was unable to make any headway in the formation of anthropological theories, because it was obvious that both relatively rich and relatively poor societies could display a tendency to violence. Egalitarian societies can demonstrate a high incidence (frequent occurrence) of violence no less than societies with rich/poor divides.

2. The Thesis of Ethnic Heterogeneity

The theory that heterogeneity generates violence was more plausible,[5] and even generated a demand for ethnological contributions to the theory of violence, as a result of which it also found its protagonists within the field. Many ethnic conflicts seem to support the

---

[5] Particularly in political science, which seeks out close contacts with fashions of political rhetoric, heterogeneity is assumed to be a cause of conflict (Connor, 1972), though this begs the question of whether perceiving differentness and treating it as a problem may not be an expression of political strategy or of a weakness of the institutions which regulate conflicts.

theory. However, the "natural" consequence of differentness is certainly not violence but, more probably, avoidance of contact or curiosity. Every human society has institutions for dealing with strangers, other societies, and new ideas. These contact institutions for establishing relations with "the other" serve for the exchange of goods, the adoption of strangers, and the acceptance of new ideas. Every human society has to confront a variety of options for action; that is normality. Human society without internal heterogeneity is inconceivable. The institutionally regulated use of diversity forms part of the necessary inventory of human societies. They differ, of course, in the form this takes. In societies that are forced or have been forced to reproduce themselves under conditions of latent violence (such as slave raids), these institutions are in most cases somewhat weakly developed. Although exchange is not prevented, it is seen as high-risk. Modern societies, by contrast, in principle possess an inventory of rules and institutions to convert foreignness into internal diversity. The system, and the sanctions that form part of it, intercept potentially harmful individual behavior that follows alien rules. If it serves particular interests, of course, violence can also be directed against individuals defined as "foreign," because foreignness is always ambivalent. In such cases, however, it is those interests and not the foreignness that determine the origin of the conflict. Violence may generate foreignness.[6]

Forms of deprivation, specifically "suppression" and assaults on "ethnic identity" or "national dignity," have been held by political theorists (for example Gurr, 1994) to be responsible for violence. Certainly, in the nineteenth and twentieth centuries, these words have frequently been chosen by elites for purposes of mobilization and legitimation. Deprivation theories have dealt, especially, with the conflicts in the disintegrating Soviet Union. Valery Tishkov (1997) systematically studied these assumptions and was unable to verify them. Instead, he found that violence was specifically initiated not by marginalized groups but by well-established "titular nations" organized by the state and/or by their elites.

In the way they portray themselves, societies for the most part tend not to portray organized diversity but to homogenize (make uniform). Against that background, foreignness can then become an argument for mobilization and collective attacks. The differences of form between societies are reified. This even finds expression in one definition—a less common one today—of ethnicity: the essentialist view. According to this, ethnic groups are groups that share a common essence created by a common language or religion and (everyday) culture. However, Mühlmann had already shown (1962, drawing upon Martius, 1867) that many groups that are understood by themselves and others as ethnic are clearly heterogeneous and indeed consciously express that fact *(colluvies gentium)*. "Colluvial tribes are formed, for example, by refugees banding together for self-defense in areas where they have found asylum. Insofar as they incorporate the management of heterogeneity into their organizational principles, they may become particularly resistant to attacks from outside or even display expansionist tendencies.

The fact that all ethnic groups have something "formal" in common—the social organization that draws the boundaries—is essential to the formalist definition of ethnicity, which takes the self-definition of groups as its starting point (Barth, 1969). Such definitions may occur with explicit reference to the recognition of a particular system (legal or defense institutions), as in the case of colluvial ethnic groups, or on the basis of language,

---

[6]The experience of violence must, of course, include another interpretation, which draws boundaries as a result of internal distinctions and so excludes the other from the regulated internal community. Such instances of marginalization and stereotyping are specifically not based on experience—except experience of violence—but on *topoi* of literature, as convincingly demonstrated by Mayer and Münkler (1998) in the case of Italian humanism.

religion, or custom. Ethnic groups differ from other self-defining groups in that they incorporate families. Membership—even membership acquired through conversion—is inherited (at least as an option). The formalistic theories of ethnicity may also explain phenomena[7] that the essentialism approach recognizes, if at all, only as exceptions (and then immediately marginalizes them): multiple attribution (plural "identity") and switching between different memberships (Canfield, 1973; Nagata, 1974). People react to fluctuating economic prospects, to violence, and to exclusion from access to law, by changing or switching their self-classification (Elwert, 2002). A stock of latent multiple affiliations facilitates these processes. Thus, ethnic boundaries do not necessarily entail a potential for violence.[8]

3. Definitions

Social anthropology/ethnology always has to consider two simultaneous definitions of violence: the culturally immanent (emic) definition and the abstractly general definition that aims at comparison.[9] In contrast to emic concepts of ethnicity, which describe constructs based on collective recognition, we have in the case of violence a not flexibly constructed concept but a paradigmatic core: physical harm and intentional action.[10] This core is added to by other forms of conduct which are to be identified as undesirable, and which differ from society to society.

Most ethnologists, like sociologists, define violence narrowly (cf. Riches, 1991; Halbmayer, 2000). We understand *violence* as "*goal-oriented and undesirable physical harm caused to others.*"

Because it is goal-oriented, violence is one of the forms of power action. The reference to the intentions of both parties ("deliberate" and "undesirable") distinguishes violence from other serious forms of harm (such as disasters caused by negligence and ritual operations) and invites comparison with these precisely because of this differentiation. The definition given above does not exclude the possibility that the two parties to a confrontation may not agree on what was desirable and what the aim of an act was. As social anthropology is not a theology, which forms judgments from an absolute standpoint, this cannot be ruled out by definition. Consequently, such differences of perspective are among

---

[7] Particularly more recent studies such as Wimmer (1995) and Lentz (1998) demonstrate that political history should not be written without analysis of the ethnic dynamic—and that it cannot be written with recourse to a static view of ethnic tradition.

[8] The fact that violence does not derive from ethnic difference is convincingly demonstrated by the authors of the volume edited by Scheffler (1991) with specific reference to the countries of Africa and Asia, which, because of current conflicts, are frequently cited as a basis for such a simplistic interpretation.

[9] Abstract general concepts aiming at comparison are described by Kenneth Pike (1967) as "etic."

[10] Searle (1997:130–137) refers to causal properties in connection with such terms which are not merely constructs transcending social conventions but refer to a physical element of reality beyond our communication (in this case, contacts with and changes to bodies). His linguistic analysis of the steps from "crude" to "institutional facts" is important to social anthropology/ethnology insofar as it distinguishes the analysis of socially construed institutional facts from the general suspicion of constructivism. To demonstrate that, for example, the concept of "ethnic groups" has no inherent natural essence is something different from simply attaching a suspicion to every linguistic category, "deconstructing" it. Humans associate facts which are already outside their control, and which they would like to process functionally, with facts that are the product of human institutionalization. To separate the two again in analysis and neither interpret all events as natural nor present everything as a social construct is the art of the social sciences.

the most important matters for analysis. This is not purely academic. In 1961, when the vaccinator and his team began mass vaccination against smallpox among the Holli, in the east of what was then Dahomey (now Benin), the necessary small incisions in the skin of the upper arm were interpreted by the Holli as violence. They seized their weapons, injured several of their "attackers," and killed one medical orderly.

Attempts are frequently made, however, to broaden the definition of violence. If the starting point is causing harm to the individual, there are two obvious ways of doing this. First, anything that causes lasting physical harm could be described as violence. Pain caused for ritual reasons or with a view to treating the body medically or embellishing it (as by cutting, tattooing, or deformations of the skull or feet) would then also qualify as "violence." The mutilating ritual of excision has therefore been classified as violence because it does lifelong physical harm. A more accurate analysis, however, suggests that where this practice is customary the victims themselves take the mutilation for granted or approve of it in retrospect. The intention is not harm but a rite of passage (Peller, 2000; and on initiations in general Young, 1965).[11] The problem with these uses of the term, then, is that the intentions of perpetrators and victims would have to be disregarded, so that this concept of violence is hardly suitable for the formation of a social scientific theory.

Secondly, violence could be used to describe everything against which an individual tries to defend himself. That definition would then cover any form of harm that can cause anxiety or fear. Galtung, for example, coined the term "structural violence" (1969, 1978),[12] which laid the blame upon politically determined poverty. The broadening of the emotionally charged term "violence" undoubtedly achieved a mobilizing effect. The problem with such coining of terms, of course, is that the subjective approach varies to an extraordinary extent beyond what is clearly physical harm, so that the theory always involves a very high degree of arbitrary positioning on the part of observers. If the concept of violence is broadened, or even used in a sense that has only metaphorical associations with the strict concept of violence, the term loses focus and becomes useless for analytical purposes.

In addition, both of these extensions of the term prevent one necessary component in the formation of a theory: comparison. In order to make a comparison, we consider similar forms of human behavior that differ in one parameter. The study of ritual bodily harm or medical treatment that causes injury, in comparison to culturally established forms of violence intended to harm, may be notably enlightening for our understanding of the latter, as James demonstrated in 1995 and Allen in 1998. The definition of what is an acceptable—injurious—therapy influences forms of violence. Historical anthropological studies of torture have shown highly significant differences in the application of physical and "mental" violence (cf. Marx, 2000). It is only this comparison that makes us aware of the destructive potential of mental torture.

[11] This distinction makes it possible to compare the conditions and effects of enforced excision (which is violence) with those of an "automatic" excision (a damaging ritual).

[12] Galtung (1990:291–305) now also writes of "cultural violence," which he describes as "any aspect of a culture that can be used to legitimize violence in its direct or structural form," but this must be seen merely as a literary repetition of his terminology, rather than the strategic creation of new terminology. From mother-love through the beauty of home-bred cattle or inherited houses and aversion to dirt or bizarre marriage rules to the hatred of blasphemers—there is absolutely nothing that cannot be used as a cultural justification for violence. In other words, since the term includes everything and no longer excludes anything, it becomes meaningless.

III.   RESULTS AND CONTROVERSIES

1.   Façades and Staging of Violence

Why do people resort to violence on an organized and lasting basis, even though the risks are unforeseeable? In attempting to answer that question, it would be disastrous to consider declared intentions only: one would become a participant in a process of staging, where what is actually required is phenomenological distance. In order for the staging of suddenness to take effect and the build-up of counterviolence to be crippled, violence needs a distinction between façade and structure. Camouflage is not only a military tactic. Violence must veil its social architecture—system and planning. Sometimes it takes the form of staged spontaneity, sometimes it is routine that one would like to suppress, sometimes it appears as an act created by emotional inspiration, sometimes it is glorified as conquest or revenge. Surprise—the careful staging of spontaneity—facilitates its success. In order to be effective, it is necessary to pursue at least one of two strategies that dissociate one's own actions from opponents' perceptions: the adversary's early warning period must be shorter than is necessary for the planning of countermeasures or the act must be staged in such a way as to spread crippling terror.

a) TERROR.   When a report of past or future violence is intended to be so overwhelming that countermeasures are prevented, we call this terror. Terror was a particularly important weapon in slave raiding. The intention was that the potential slaves should be unable either to run or to fight. A battle produces corpses and casualties, but not many satisfactory slaves. The empire of Danxome in precolonial West Africa had perfected the slave raid. Human sacrifices, to which numerous spectators were invited, pictures and songs of cruelty, and the paradox of a particularly brutal elite troop consisting exclusively of women carried the message of terror effectively to the victims (Elwert, 1973).

b) LACK OF INFORMATION AND STRATEGIES OF CAUTION.   Façades created by disinformation may lull suspicion and prevent resistance; but they may also generate a climate of alarm. If little specific information is received regarding a perceived threat of violence, but at the same time a real experience of violence or virtual information make a high level of risk obvious, this produces a specific type of reaction that appears irrational to the outsider. The insufficiently informed adopt a defensive posture and react to the first indications—or what they interpret as indications—by fleeing or attacking. Witch hunts or attacks intended as defensive measures can arise in this way. What may appear to the outsider as panic seems to the insider to be a reasonable reaction in terms of the information available.

c) "ERUPTIONS".   In descriptions of violent ethnic conflicts, clichés of eruptions of emotionalism are often forced upon us. The social anthropological study of the prehistory of conflicts is at odds with this. Before confrontations can take effect, configurations first have to be constructed or trivialized as social procedures. Enduring or repetitive violence is a social process. It presupposes rules and penalties, roles and channels of communication, plans and calculations—it cannot be based on emotions alone. The fact that violence seems unplanned and transrational—"eruption of popular fury," "deep-seated xenophobia"—is deliberate. Stylized in this way, it reduces the need for legitimacy.

d) STRATEGISTS AND WARRIORS. In all forms of social cooperation, a more or less pronounced division of labor may arise between those who give orders and those who carry them out. In the case of acts of violence, this divide is particularly common and particularly deep. Myths and paintings show us the strategists amid the heat of the actual hostilities. That is the exception. The strategists seek remoteness, in order to be able to make their plans without endangering themselves and without worrying too much about the deaths of others. Sustained, strategically deployed violence calls for logistics and cool-headed planning. Strategists must be able to mobilize the emotions of others—fear or pugnacity—at selected moments in order to convert fear into bravery.

The point is illustrated by the 1994 massacre in Rwanda. This is often cited as an example of a supposed "outbreak." In fact it was not a sudden explosion at all but an interplay of systematically planned and ideologically prepared violence, with a process of escalation that developed dynamics of its own (Neubert, 1999). It all became possible because a set of conflicts existed previously but the institutions for resolving them worked only inefficiently (Neubert & Brandstetter, 1996). Those conflicts were not the cause of the genocide but a necessary condition for the process of escalation and the deployment of planned violence.

Interpretations which postulate "deep historical roots" are encouraged by the ideology-creating protagonists of the ethnonational movements and their imaginative interpretations of the past (for a critical view here, see Hobsbawm & Ranger, 1973 and, specifically on the Balkans, Colovic, 1994).

e) FAÇADES AND THE HOMOGENIZATION OF GROUPS. In order for a violent conflict between groups to arise in the first place, becoming something more than a mere duel of words between would-be leaders, two things have to happen. First, the risks of engaging in the conflict must be played down (or the aims must seem worthwhile, which amounts to the same thing), and secondly the respective groups themselves must be virtually homogenized (made apparently uniform) and coordinated. Elements of playing down the risk include emphasizing one's own strength and mitigating the fear of losing one's own life by the promise of honor (on Afghanistan, see Orywal, 1986). Virtual homogenization means combining, in the individual perception of individual people, the many individual interests and the many features that divide them to form common motives ("interests") and common characteristics (a common "culture") (Scheffler, 1995). A diversity of motives can bring together differing interests and thereby promote conflicts. One aspect of homogenization may be coordination of the action through compulsion; the fighters are compelled to fight. In the precolonial African empire of Danxome, the main fighting was done by vassals armed only with swords, spears, and bows, while behind them stood soldiers with firearms who fired on them if they gave ground (Elwert, 1973).

2. Social Embedding

a) ROUTINE VIOLENCE AND RIGID ORDER. Early ethnographers were slow to realize that violence springs from order. Since it appears logical, amid the routine of one's own society, to ascribe startling conduct to emotions, that interpretation was also projected onto alien societies. Societies with a notable propensity to violence were called "savage," seeming closer to the state of nature, and expressing their emotions in an uncontrolled manner. The fact that such enduring violence occurred in the vicinity of militarily powerful empires, areas open to violence, and situations where there was unusual competition for resources—in other words, that it certainly served a purpose—was overlooked. Researchers who consider the social system in its entirety find such societies remarkable less for their violence than for an unusually rigid social order (for example, Schlee, 1979 on the Rendille). Ceremonials grow up around the status of warrior. Only after certain rituals have been observed can anyone become a warrior. Among the Kayan of Borneo, future warriors had first to drum upon a freshly taken skull (Heine-Geldern, 1923:899). Success is expressed by the right to wear special clothing. The leading fighters on Solor, in the Sunda Islands, were so decorated as to appear like moving works of art (Müller, 1839–1844). The ritual preparation and order of the combat itself guarantee that certain emotional states—for example, extreme bravery without inhibition of aggression—occur only in particular forms and on particular occasions. Among the Baseda of West Africa, a special drum is beaten to summon fighters to battle, and the warriors (including women, in rare cases) fall into a trance (or simulate one) (Elwert, 2001a). The first sound of the drum strikes fear into adversaries who know about this arrangement. In some societies, a schematic age system specializes young men of a particular age in the role of warriors. These societies organized by age and generation classes, which are to be found primarily in areas open to violence, are particularly notable for the rigidity of their systems.

b) RATIONALITY IN VIOLENCE. Anyone who were to see violence only as the release of tensions would overlook its most common form: the planned, rationally targeted deployment of violence as a means for resolving conflicts. We use the term "rationally targeted" here as an opposite of "traditionally motivated" and "emotionally motivated." In contrast to a commonplace use of the term "rationality," however, we are not implying that the conduct in question is calculated in every individual case. We regard conduct as rationally motivated if it can be seen to be optimized under evolutive conditions. "Evolutive" here means that not all conduct of this kind is successful, but it is subject to systematic selection, which creates a variable probability that the various different forms of action will fail. This includes the possibility that optimum behavioral strategies may be hit upon "by chance."

Few other forms of interaction are so greatly affected by selection as violence. Those who practice uncontrolled violence die young as victims of violence, or are banished.[13] The situation is similar with belligerents driven primarily by their emotions; they are rapidly defeated and destroyed, or they adapt and rationalize their use of violence (Elwert, 1997). This implies a process of selection in favor of rational violence. The emotional effect evidently present in the practice of violence is a phenomenon which, although exploited, is not a structural factor in repetitive patterns of violence. Where violence escalates, however, we are dealing with self-reinforcing dynamics which, as a result of emotions and consequent compulsions, breaks the link between action and a rationally motivated assessment of the consequences and may result in self-destruction (Elwert et al., 1999; Waldmann, 1999).

c) EMBEDDING. The emphasis on the rationally motivated deployment of violence brings us to the second basic assumption of the more recent social anthropology of violence: violence is primarily *socially embedded*. Since violence is a commonplace way of assert-

---

[14] This standpoint is clearly adopted, for example, by works of the Balandier school (Bazin & Terray, 1982; Terray, 1987).

ing the will, the ways in which it is channeled, synchronized, and classified into strategic associations require explanation. Violence is always channeled. Particular aims, victims, weapons, battlefields, and even time periods can be defined. To this extent, violence is also—in every society—always inhibited.

This limitation of violence is illustrated by a frequent form of violence in pre-industrial societies: the feud. In this clearly channeled form of violence, the weapons, the potential victims, the place of the conflict (in New Guinea, even a special battlefield), and often the time are determined in advance. In particular, the rules for ending the conflict are also established even before it begins. The study of these limitations of violence, the "inhibitors," is a task of present-day research. The social anthropological question of the influence of violence-promoting values on the outbreak of armed conflicts is directed toward the same complex (Orywal, 1996), because the inhibitors are never eliminated but only circumvented by situations.

As a rule, violence is channeled by penalties or by moral disapproval of certain excesses. The sanctions may be physical or may consist merely of dishonor. In most cases, the transgressor loses status, which not only damages his reputation but also restricts his physical—economic, for example—scope of activity. A violation of the rules by one section of a warring party may also result in the adversary's violence breaking free of its constraints. The indication of legitimate aims of violence also has an integrating effect. This kind of definition results in prioritization. Violence that pursues other aims than, for example, the attacking of "enemies" would be a waste of strength and resources. A person who attacks anyone other than the "enemy" may even be regarded as usurping a right of definition that is vested only in the leaders. One prediction that can be inferred from this aspect of the embedding theory is that an increase in internal violence may follow an armistice or peace treaty, because the violence has ceased to be embedded as a result of a predetermined objective. South Africa during the 1990s provides an example of this.

The embedding of violence can be understood by using the metaphor of the riverbed. The river may burst its banks. It would be unrealistic to expect complete control of violence. On the contrary, particularly in the case of violence, we should expect a clear difference between convention (rules) and performance (actual behavior). In addition, a society's standards need not be shared equally by all members of that society; in the course of a lifetime, the same individual may adopt different positions (Strecker, 1999:235–236). Every social system includes deviation from the system. But since these deviations are not random, we must concentrate in the following sections mainly on the different forms of embedding.

3. Motives and Conflict System

a) Conflict as a Universal. The fact that human conduct is controlled only to a relatively small extent by a natural program means that it potentially involves a high degree of randomness. It follows from this that human activity constantly and ubiquitously generates conflict. The possibility of conflict is a precondition for the expression of interests and a condition for social change (Dahrendorf, 1954). In other words, conflict is part of the system by which society operates. Violence is a ubiquitous option as the last resort of power to impose the will. The perspective of the normality of violence also includes the thematization of the equally ubiquitous inhibitors, the individual and social restrictions on the use of violence. Violence may break the rules or serve to enforce the rules; it may also lie in between: regular violence may result in the creation of new rules.

The approach outlined above, which places the emphasis on the contingency of action and the inevitable but never total institutional embedding of violence, is that of conflict theory (Gluckman, 1956; Koch, 1976). By contrast, structuralism, the antithesis of this current of opinion (Lévi-Strauss, 1971; for a critical view, Balandier, 1956) excludes conflict and violence from its systematic portrayal of society. Violence is treated in the ethnographic report merely as deviant behavior and is interpreted—with a great deal of effort—in myth as symbolic. The fact that violence is part of a social order and motivates institutions will be demonstrated below.[14]

b) Motives. The contingency of human behavior is perceived on two levels: that of motive and that of procedure. Individual violence is often erratic and is only embellished, "motivated," and justified retrospectively by interpretations and by being embedded in a history. Repeated or collective violence, by contrast, is a systemic event—part of a system.[15]

c) Types of Motives and Parameters for Evaluating Success. In various cultures, distinctions can be made between different motives: "reputation," "power," material "profit," and "fear."[16] Of course, not every society differentiates between the first three of these four terms or associates them with violence, though the majority do so. This distinction obviously becomes clearly apparent if a society is given to reflecting on its own activities. Prestige, power, and profit are each independent pay-off arrangements, independent systems of parameters, for determining a winner.[17] Fear as a motive for action is rather different and is rarely considered by researchers. It is an emotionally determined motive for defensive action which alone cannot develop into extended chains of action. In interaction with other motives, however, it may generate a highly mobilizing effect. Without investigating motives inherent in cultures—emic motives, as social anthropologists call these inner perspectives—we cannot model violent activity.[18]

The different parameters for evaluating success in each case have effects on the organization of violence. What distinguishes the victor? There are various possibilities here. (1) The gaining of prestige or honor. A killer, too, can achieve these: in such cases he becomes a "hero" or "martyr." If "martyr" designates the highest point on the prestige

---

[13] Here I thank Kristóf Gosztonyi for insights based on his observations in Bosnia.

[15] It is not common for motives to be expressed within a society in cases of repetitive, "oscillating" violence. Escalating violence, by contrast, virtually cries its motives aloud (Elwert, Feuchtwang, & Neubert, 1999).

[16] Although social activity is fragmented by division of labor, it is also always summarized in comprehensible form by concentration on accumulating parameters. In order to achieve an interpersonal understanding, they have to be abstract in nature. The properties of power, prestige, and goods meet this requirement. The parallelism and fundamental equivalence of these properties have been objections to a market-fixed sociology advanced by social anthropologists since the discipline was first created. Significantly, although not aiming at conceptual clarity, they are also the subject of Bourdieu's terms such as "social capital," etc. (see, for example, Bourdieu, 1982, 1989).

[17] Pay-off system is a term borrowed from game theory. Jürg Helbling (1999) has shown how fruitfully a game theory perspective can be applied to stable or fluctuating forms of violence even in pre-industrial societies. Game theory is rejected by some researchers because its form of presentation necessarily enforces simplifications. Its strength, however, is linked to the same formulative character: it compels clarity of thought. In this case, this is apparent from the pay-off parameters that necessarily arise in the model. There can be no speculation on what constitutes a "pay-off."

[18] This inclusion of emic motives, which first have to be filtered out as systematic motives from numerous—and in some cases obscure or contradictory—individual declarations is also the basis of game theory models (cf. Helbling, 1999).

scale, the willingness of fighters to take risks increases. (2) The gaining of power, in the sense of control over others. A single attack is insufficient for this: the violence must be retained in latent form—as the latent compulsion behind the power.[19] (3) The gaining of wealth. This is compatible with the loss of people or control over them, provided that the fighting resources are sufficient to repeat the plundering. Anyone whose primary aim is to cause fear, however, does not strive for victory. Restraining those in fear from further violence calls for changed patterns of cognition.

Unambiguous conflict situations are admittedly rare. For researchers, however, they are particularly important because they can be used as a basis for the development of models.

d) REPUTATION. There is a reason—not an obvious one—for referring to "reputation" instead of the more ordinary terms of "honor" and "prestige." Openly acknowledged motives for action that we frequently encounter in existing research include such attractive ones as the word "honor" or references to a desirable social status (such as that of an officer) that carries prestige. Both can also be described as "reputation." But there is another—usually unadmitted—motive for action: fear of disgrace or shame. Disgrace, too, is reputation—negative reputation.

The unambiguous motive situations may include blood-feud systems.[20] Schwandner-Sievers (1996, 1999), in her analysis of blood-feud systems in the northern Balkans, was able to show that "honor" is particularly cited as a motive there. The reference to honor and disgrace represents the determining rhetorical reference system.[21] Killing may create social status, which then improves or restores prospects of marriage. Social status created or re-established in this way is important, either directly or indirectly, by way of strategic marriages, for the obtaining of land. In the analysis, it also becomes clear that this prestige system is concerned not only with honor but also with negative reputation or dishonor. An unavenged death dishonors the person whose obligation it was to avenge it. The failure to exact retribution for a murder destroys a positive reputation; a revenge murder restores "honor."

e) GOODS. When it comes to the motive of appropriating property, again, we must distinguish between façade and demonstrably effective motives for action. The objective of appropriating property and material resources appears to the layman to be a plausible motive for violence, yet arises less often than is assumed, because the supply of goods, in human societies, is the subject of a complex organization based upon cooperation.

However, the appropriation of property can be a demonstrable and dominant motive for action. If groups are to be mobilized against one another, important issues often (though

---

[19] The violence must be capable of being experienced in order to give the power credible stability. But at the moment when violence is exercised, no power exists, there is no "control over the actions of others" (Luhmann, 1974:118). Therefore violence aimed at the acquisition of power must always keep a surplus of potential violence in reserve.

[20] However, blood-feud systems may also be a façade to conceal a different set of motives; see Koehler, 2000.

[21] It seems to me more appropriate here to refer to prestige or reputation rather than cultural or social capital (Bourdieu, 1982). The word "capital" suggests a possibility of quantification that simply cannot exist so clearly. When terms are no longer used in the context of a precise empirical study (in Bourdieu's case of social ascendancy in France during the twentieth century), adjectives such as "social" and "cultural" refer to a broad, almost unlimited field. The link to the emic terms "honor" and "disgrace" associated with prestige and reputation (cf. Peristiany, 1966) seems to me more precise.

by no means always) include the long-term utilization of resources. Natural resources, agricultural land, the right to live in particular areas, and access to particularly lucrative occupations are among the subjects of typical resource conflicts. The boundary between this kind of violent conflict and robbery is not always easy to draw. If the exercise of violence is more unilateral and the emphasis is on the consumption or resale of the property acquired by violence, the word used tends to be "robbery." From the standpoint of the participants in the violence, it is an ordered and regulated form of conduct. In cases where this violent appropriation—robbery—is a long-term institution, this arises not from want as a motive but represents a trade, that of the ("honorable") robber, that is reproductive in itself.

In areas with a market economy, or with access to external markets, robbery may be undertaken by specific practitioners of violence, the warlords. In this case, robbery is typical not of the poor but of the rich. Among the warlords, in addition to the numerous overt motives, which vary in accordance with the context of those discussing them (these entrepreneurs prefer to portray themselves as freedom fighters or leaders of civil war factions), we find one motive that is central to the maintenance of the system of war and robbery: the acquisition of material goods. This economic motive is achieved irrespective of whether the means are peaceful or unpeaceful. For the warlords, almost the entire spectrum of economic activity, from robbery through hostage-taking, blackmail, and "duties" and "taxes" to smuggling, legitimate trade, and the acquisition of donations for ideological aims are subjectively legitimate ways of doing business. Whether they are aware of the entrepreneurial nature of their activities or not (for example, because they feel a commitment to an ideal) has no influence on the conditions of their reproduction. Anyone who intends to survive as a warlord needs arms and mercenaries (even though the latter may be called "volunteers"). The proceeds have to cover the cost of the violence and show a profit. These are the decisive criteria by which a warlord must be guided if he is not to fail. In other words, warlords have to show sufficient profits to guarantee the reproduction of labor, troops, and the resources of violence—arms and infrastructural investment (Elwert, 1999). Markets based on violence cannot form everywhere: an essential condition is an area open to violence—such as on the fringes of weakened major empires or in collapsing states (see also, on civil wars, Waldmann, 1999). There is no monopoly on violence. If, of course, a legitimate monopoly on violence is re-established (Weber, 1922), markets based on violence cannot survive.

f) POWER.   The use of violence to acquire power may be intended to enable the attackers to replace those who currently hold power, to change the rules and the system based upon them, or to strengthen the attackers' own capabilities. This third purpose is served by killings, interpreted as sacrifices, based on assumptions of supernatural ("magic") relationships of cause and effect (Jensen, 1948; Tornay, 1986). When a state exercises legitimate force in the form of physical sanctions, this too is violence with (the acquisition of) power as its motive.

Violence may also be the expression of a striving for power in the sense of the ability to shape events. Anyone who intends to change something, wants to be a protagonist in events, and sees no other possible way of doing so will find violence the obvious means provided that its course is clearly signposted. When that is not the case, depression or drug-induced delusions are a more likely solution. We can identify this violence for the purpose of achieving the power to influence events in the feuds and raids indulged in by the age sets of young warriors. And it is precisely here, too, that we can recognize that there are alternatives to this violence. When "young warriors" in West Africa had the opportunity to accumulate money at a very early age as migrant workers, this attractive objective replaced the violence of the feuds. On the other hand, where there are no other opportunities to shape events, young males invent their own violent rituals and feuds, even in the absence of specific historical models, in order to experience the power of action.

g) FEAR. Fear can motivate violence. Violence is a necessary part of self-defense, too. Fear is not a sufficient sole or dominant motive for long-term mobilization. However, fear can be mobilized effectively. It is precisely when fear clouds the thinking of the potential victims or indirect participants that others can exercise their energies for their own purposes. In Bosnia, as in Rwanda, warlords mobilized people against their own neighbors by broadcasting warnings on television or radio of invaders who were secretly supported by their own neighbors (Bringa, 1993,, 1995; Brandstetter & Neubert, 1996; Macek, 2001). Massacres motivated by fear saved the warlords the expense of paying and deploying their own troops.

While fear is more likely to be a deterrent from violence, except in situations perceived as immediately threatening, it may stabilize the propensity to violence when working in conjunction with other motivations. In the Balkans, for example, mythologies of sacrifice played a significant role. A person who had once been a victim of violence might suffer the same fate again. The myth promises that history repeats itself. An attack actually intended by strategists as an expansion of power or economic enrichment is justified as a preventive, defensive strike.

h) CONSEQUENCES. Clear motivational situations enable us to recognize that every conflict situation has its own specific consequential dynamics of reaction to violence. In each case, there are specific ways in which the conflict can and cannot be ended. They may differ considerably if the ending of the conflict is not brought about by the destruction of an adversary. In blood-feud systems, the honor of the participants must be defended or increased, otherwise the peace will not last. In markets based on violence, the warlords must be threatened by economic loss, or an alternative economic activity must offer greater profits, in order for the violence to be abandoned and peace concluded. Where power is the aim, either one side's potential for violence must be suppressed or both sides' opportunities to determine events must increase as a result of the peace. The consequential dynamics of violence motivated by fear seems paradoxical: A defeat confirms that the fear was justified. However, victory without the destruction of the other side leads—assuming reciprocal motivation—to fear of an act of revenge. Fear can be dispelled only if changes in the organization and embedding of violence on the part of the potential adversary and the perception of those changes coincide.

i) CHANGES OF MOTIVE. Configurations of violence are typified by characteristic processes of self-organization that change motivational situations. Violence itself also creates motives. This does not make things any easier for researchers. Most participants are able to formulate a motive for action after the event, even if the action itself was erratic. Stable patterns of violence, however, promote, through retroactive self-reinforcement, those types of violence that are based on organized (and hence more easily identifiable) chains of events (see Waldmann, 1999 on the motives generated by the violence of civil war).

Motives are subject to a change in values—especially during the escalation phase of the war. The image of the adversary is dehumanized, and he thus becomes, for cognitive purposes, an "other," a subhuman or nonhuman. Values and rules are constructed that justify the exercise of violence against him and treat it as necessary. Then the newly constructed values and rules are further consolidated in the war itself (cf. on Sierra Leone, Peters & Richards, 1998). These processes can be interpreted as socialization; people are being molded into a new value system.[22] A static understanding of "culture" is meaningless when confronted with this socialization of violence.[23] Within a few months, apparently basic values can be radically altered. "Violent values" are less often a cause of conflicts than their consequence. Subsequently, when war has already broken out, such values make a substantial contribution to the perpetuation of the violence.

An example of how violent conflict creates a new system of prestige is provided by the conflicts among and between the indigenous communities in Chiapas from the 1970s onwards and, in particular, the massive formation of paramilitary groups in the villages from the mid-1990s on. Those groups are made up primarily of young people with no possessions, jobs or land. Having no possessions, they (and/or their parents) usually also lack the resources to pay the dowry necessary to marry in accordance with local convention. They are in no position to meet the established role expectations or to provide for a wife and children. This, ultimately, prevents them from making the transition to the status of an adult and a full member of society. For many of these young people confronted by a largely hopeless situation, joining a paramilitary group opens up new opportunities to obtain income (through war taxes and the plundering of stock, harvests, household equipment, and trucks) and, not least, gaining respect. Even the possession of a modern firearm (in contrast to a hunting rifle) brings prestige (Gabbert, 2001).

j) COMPLEX MOTIVES. Simple motivational situations can provide a clear answer to the question of who has won, but these situations are rare. We can hypothesize one reason for this: if the continuation of a conflict offers benefits for at least one side—for example, leading figures within one of the parties to the conflict—then it serves their purpose to combine several motivational situations, to prolong the conflict. If the aims of the conflict and hence the criteria for success are unambiguous, victory or defeat would result in the unambiguous end of the conflict and exclude a contamination. The combination of different motives for conflict is particularly useful for (potential) elites if the internal social structure in the conflict situation is different from the peacetime structure. Those who gain power as a result of the conflict may have an interest in maintaining the tension. Those elected to power only for the duration of the conflict—perceived as a limited one—such as the Roman *dictator* or the Germanic *herzog* would retain power if the conflict continues. Increasing the complexity of the conflict enables it to be extended and power retained.

---

[22] Wolfgang Gabbert referred me to Kelman (1973), who in this context stresses the importance of the routinization of violence and reduction of the responsibility for decisions in a hierarchical system.

[23] This criticism of a static understanding of culture in connection with the theme of changing values might be misunderstood. "Postmodern" relativism which calls for understanding and tolerance of violent regimes cite the indisputable fact that societies and their normative patterns change (e.g., Zizek, 2001). But anyone who pursues just one of the three objectives, "accumulation of social knowledge," "expression of individuality," and "capacity for social innovation," cannot go along with this form of relativization of values. He or she must prefer less violent forms of society, which at the same time institutionalize the conflict.

k) ENDOSTRATEGIC CONFLICTS AND MOBILIZATION. Conflicts can arise not only from real divergences in interests between groups but also from the construction of such external differences for the purposes of a strategy within the group. In most conflicts, there is something of both. It is relatively unusual, however, for the aims portrayed as the interests of the group actually to represent the interests of the majority of the members. That conflict strengthens the divide between groups and the external world and makes them more uniform internally[24]—"welds them together"—while at the same time bringing new leaders to the fore is almost the general rule.

The fact that an external conflict is constructed in order to further an internal aim of the group can be described as "endostrategic mobilization" (Eckert et al., 1999). This stirring of a conflict is intended to homogenize the group, to establish new rules or leadership structures, and to emphasize the dividing lines between the group and "the others."

Anyone who analyzes conflicts between ethnic groups or nations would be well advised not only to inquire into their diverging interests but also to study who, *within* the various groups, gains power, influence, or resources as a result of the conflict. Individuals who were previously marginalized but are organized as a strategic group may in some circumstances seize the leadership within their self-defined group if, citing the external enemy, they enforce certain rules and processes of decision-making—beneficial to them—and stigmatize others (not necessarily their competitors) as internal enemies. When the alarm sounds, individuals who were previously considered as outsiders because they appeared impetuous, paranoid, or brutal may become leaders.

In a situation of threat, other political structures may become plausible alternatives. A person who has always preached separation from "the others" seems more credible in a situation of tension. An imagined "enemy" or actually threatening adversary (who often only becomes threatening as a result of provocation) enables such strategic groups (Evers & Schiel, 1988) to attain dominance within their self-defined group. Thus, within the group, people may be labeled as "strangers" and marginalized in order for violence to be used against them (Zitelmann, 1998). If the argument of competition for material resources is insufficient to mobilize the self-defined group, it is common to resort to resource that is entirely a social construct: prestige. In other words, the conflict is exaggerated as a conflict for the honor of the participating groups.

l) POPULAR THEORIES. Anyone who writes about motives for violence has to confront the widespread hope that violence has roots and that those roots can be weeded out. If violent systems are seen to be part of the social system, it makes no sense to identify specific roots of violence.[25] Such popular theories—emic theories—on the "roots of (undesirable) violence" may themselves, however, become an important subject of research. They project counterworlds of evil. The presence of "strangers," the secret activities of "unbelievers," genetic inheritance, drugs, lack of education, wealth, unemployment, or loss of identity are regarded as causing the occurrence of violence. Admittedly, some of these can indeed act as transmitters, stabilizing certain elements of a system of violence. But a social anthropological theory of violence must deal with all forms of possible human

---

[24] This kind of standardization of the group as part of the events of the conflict is described by Gabbert (1999a) in the case of the nineteenth-century caste war in Yucatan.

[25] Ferguson and Whitehead's collection of essays (1992) is still largely devoted to this kind of "quest for causes." The number of identifiable causes becomes infinite. Using the same subject matter—nongovernmental societies on the margins of governmental control—Abbink (1994a) clearly shows the value of analyzing a violent system (in this case: "culture of violence").

existence. It must withstand testing against the most diverse societies. Popular theories fail to do this. They do, however, provide us with important indications regarding a society's self-perception. They reveal information about the objectives which individual factions[26] in society would like to adopt. Based on the counterworlds referred to above, the marginalization of others, common sense, a modest lifestyle, general employment, regulated education, and clear systems of membership emerge as implicit models.

4. Resources of Violence

The popular view, nourished by tales of robbers, is that violence is concerned mainly with the appropriation of resources. This makes it easy to overlook the fact that violence needs resources—especially social resources—in order to take place. It is clear that, other things being equal, different degrees of access to one resource, weapons, in other words the ability to lay hands on dangerous weapons, significantly influences the frequency of severely harmful physical violence. Dramatically cut-price weapons are today important conditions for the perpetuation of violence in large parts of Africa, Central Asia, New Guinea, and the Andes. In the cases of New Guinea and northeast Africa, it has been clearly shown that an increased availability of weapons (and considerably lower prices) made violence a more viable option (Strathern, 1992; Bollig, 1991; Abbink, 1994a).[27]

For the social sciences, however, the main requirement is to refer to the social resources of violence, and the way in which embedding and organization promote violence. The place taken by male youth in the system of violence and—for the establishment of new collective actors—the internal potential for sanctions must therefore be addressed.

a) MALE YOUTH. The place that the social system accords to male youth, and the effect of the embedding of violence on this group within a society, are further-reaching than the effects of the same mechanisms on other members of society. It is no matter of chance that in most states male youths and young men are overrepresented among perpetrators of murders and unlawful killings. The differences between the age-groups and the sexes are never natural or given. They are highly molded, leveled out, or accentuated by the social system. But the differences also remain—though never exclusively—the expression of natural (genetically programmed) dispositions, which find various forms of expression as a function of the environment and of the aging and maturing processes. How the interaction of genetic program and social form takes effect is still largely a matter for (informed) speculation. From the social anthropological—comparative—standpoint, we can establish some specifics for this age-group (including women): an intensive pursuit of self-created social ties (which facilitates the development of autonomous groups, where this is permitted), and a need to define and experience the self through individual acts and achievements. Age-specific mental and physical powers (power of association, creativity, speed

---

[26] I deliberately write of the objectives which individual factions in society would like to adopt, rather than "objectives of society." Especially in the area with which we are concerned, it is important to appreciate that any society is divided into different factions, in each of which different objectives are regarded as acceptable or desirable.

[27] Gabbert confirms this in a letter in the light of his examination of the literature on and personal experience of Central America. At present, the disintegration of guerilla movements is resulting in cheaper availability of weapons and contributing to the rising frequency of violence.

of reaction, muscular strength) open up specific opportunities here. Ambition and a different relative risk assessment seem to be even more marked among young men than among young women. They also seem particularly prone to perceiving boredom as an (almost) physical stress.[28] The "kick" of an exciting experience, the quest for an "adrenaline surge," seems to be even more important for this age-group than for others. This does not necessarily mean that these potentials have to be utilized through specialization in violence. A society may also allocate special tasks to its youth that are constructive and creative. The phenomenon of the young warriors is not unavoidable. But if a society defines the role of men of this particular age-group through violence, or if violence is the escape option when other avenues are closed, this has very significant consequences for the society itself or its neighbors.

b) THE INTERNAL POTENTIAL FOR SANCTIONS.   One necessary condition of organized violence is almost always overlooked, although its observation would offer a fair means of forecasting: the potential for internal sanctions. As soon as a self-defined group or a clientelist network has the opportunity to impose internal sanctions for deviation from the self-imposed rules, an internal ethic can develop. If the capacity for sanctions is greater than the power of the state to protect these persons, then the group is "ready for civil war." The construction of such an internal capacity for sanctions is one of the most important indicators of the threat of an outbreak of violence. This capacity for sanctions is a condition for the creation of command structures. Command always requires communication and a latent sanction. The communication of command—the "chain" in military parlance— is easier to create if social networks with reciprocal obligations existed before the outbreak of violence. This means that clientelism of every form (in other words, not only religious or ethnic but also purely economic, based for example on the marketing of illegal goods) is a very effective means of creating structures that produce violence.

Violence always involves risks. This presupposes the establishment of particular values—in other words, propaganda. The function of propaganda is to reduce the perception of the risks, to play down moral reservations, and to downgrade the relevance of the social inhibitors. We encounter not a complete reversal of values but merely a change in their relative positions as a result of a particular framework placed around events (Gosztonyi, 1999). A specific framework that presents the current situation as one of impending loss is more likely to create an acceptance of violence than a framework that portrays it as an opportunity for profit. The fear of a threatened loss of standing can create a more lasting acceptance of violence than the mere hope of acquiring property.

5.   Avenues and Institutions for Conflict Management and Conflict Resolution

In common parlance, conflict is often associated with the violent course of a conflict. This is not necessarily so, although violence is often a factor in group conflicts. Conflicts can be avoided by sidestepping them (the "exit option," Hirschman, 1970) or can be resolved by procedural means. Where peaceful institutions fail, violence may be selected as a regular default option.

---

[28] Any exciting experience, not merely violence, can relieve this stress of boredom. Drugs, too, can at least prevent the physical suffering caused by boredom.

Table II-2-3.1.   Forms of conflict

		Measure of the intensity of violence	
		Low violence	Intensive violence
Extent of conrol	Strongly controlled	*Procedures* (legal procedure, competition, disposing oracle)	*Struggle* (struggle between protagonists, feud, regulated war)
	Weakly controlled	*Avoidance* (flight, contact taboos)	*Destruction* (genocide)

In open conflict, each side denies the other the achievement of an objective. In a conflict of rules, the actions of one person or group violate a rule and provoke a social reaction. We will now deal first, and in more detail, with open conflict.

The time at which violence occurs is partly dependent on the various forms of conflict. The sequences or avenues of conflict can be classified within a four-pole field, depending on the degree of control through embedding and the degree of violence.[29] The term "poles" is used because there are transitions between the various types. In every society, several forms of dealing with violence exist in parallel. In each case, the violent events take different forms. In view of the transitions and diversity, any systematic presentation—such as the one given here—is a crude simplification. But, precisely because of its simplicity, this kind of breakdown does say something about differences in the embedding of violence.

a) AVOIDANCE.   The particular feature of this classification is that "avoidance" defines a zero point. It is important to define this zero point because avoidance is an institutional configuration that is not itself directly conducive to violence but refers to violence. In some societies, the prevalent rule in the face of impending confrontation is not merely to step aside but actually to divide the community in two (Elwert, 2001a). Radcliffe-Brown (1952:108ff, 135ff.) pointed out that avoidance is one of the dominant behavior patterns in a great many pre-industrial societies. However, we should not imagine those societies to be eternally peaceful. When avoidance is abandoned, the most obvious next step is not a low-violence procedure but destruction. Societies where avoidance dominates may seem peaceful and therefore productive; but their major problem is dealing with new events (processing innovation). Even to discuss potentially different systems is a conflict that must be avoided. Adapting and changing production becomes a problem.

b. DESTRUCTION.   Destruction, or on a larger scale genocide, aims at the complete elimination of the other party.[30] The question of how reciprocal relationships might be estab-

---

[29] For more extensive distinctions, see Otterbein, 1973; Orywal, Rao, & Bollig, 1996; von Trotha, 1999; Elwert, Feuchtwang, & Neubert, 1999.

[30] There is no space here to consider the extensive literature on genocide. The subject is addressed elsewhere in this manual. It is striking, however, that social anthropology/ethnology addressed the subject only belatedly and hesitantly. An eyewitness report was supplied by the French ethnologist Germaine Tillon (1946). The first systematic study of the destruction of the North American Indians was supplied by an outsider in *Bury My Heart at Wounded Knee* (Brown, 1971). An up-to-date discussion of the literature, including social anthropological literature, is supplied by Chalk and Jonassohn (1990). A quantitative overview with critical commentary on sources was supplied by Rummel (1994).

lished again after the violence ends forms no part of the planning of destruction—in contrast to warring. Nevertheless, even destruction has its rules: some forms of behavior are checked as being inappropriate or immoral, or excluded by being punished by fellow fighters. For example, only particular weapons are considered appropriate (cf. Tishkov, 1997:154). This appears inconsistent at first glance, in a case where, after all, the objective is to kill the other party. But societies introduce rules on violence partly for their own protection: uncontrolled outbreaks of violence are feared.

c) WARRING. The category of warring includes feuds as well as warfare. In feuds, as noted above, violence is significantly limited. In warfare, too, the rules of war determine the weapons that may not be used, the times at which an attack may not be launched, and the individuals or districts that must be spared any violence. Contraventions of these rules are regarded as war crimes. Conflict may take its course in the form of a competition between the respective sides' champions or representatives—in tournaments, a mere two. Even this marks a transition to procedural ways of resolving conflict.

In many societies, legitimate violence and the acquisition of prestige are incorporated into an age-group system, which makes warring the specialty of a particular male age-group. This is particularly apparent in societies organized by age and generation classes (Tornay, 1984; Bernardi, 1985; Schlee, 1990; Zitelmann, 1990). In such societies, there is an age set of young warriors (for example among the Oromo and Masai of East Africa, where they are known as *moran*). Within this age set, the young men gain "honor" by stealing cattle, taking human trophies (heads, for example), or similar violent activities. The young warriors organize their own groups and adopt their own internal order. Their violent sorties are undertaken on their own initiative.

d) PROCEDURES. Procedures are a low-violence or nonviolent form of conflict resolution. For that very reason, we need to treat them in detail here. They include elections, judicial proceedings, and competitions. It cannot be said a priori whether what society emically calls a procedure is also regarded in that light by the empirical social sciences. Here social anthropology must depart from the automatic principle of presupposing a particular practice, as advocated by Luhmann (1969). If we define the term "procedure" operationally, the definition criteria have to include sequential organization, autonomy of time, the constraint of power, an uncertain outcome, conclusiveness, and consequences in action. Procedures differ from everyday activities by having an ordered sequence of events, that order being defined, which ensures recognition. To that extent, procedure corresponds to ritual. For the duration of the procedure, the potentials of the conflicting parties for power and violence are wholly or partially neutralized (Luhmann, 1969). For example, the possibility of the physically stronger person injuring the weaker can be ruled out.

The outcome of the procedure is always open. This is particularly clear in the case of oracles with a disposing effect, such as trials by ordeal or the drawing of lots. A procedure, in the sense of conflict anthropology, is notable for the fact that a result is determined. It is conclusive. A specific procedural power is also created: the decisions that take place at the outcome of the procedure have consequences for action. The decisions must be enforced. This distinguishes the procedure as such (conclusive procedure) from the "pending procedure,"[31]

---

[31] The term, in this definition, originates with Hans-Rudolf Wicker (1993). Bierschenk (1999) provides illustrative examples from conflicts over land rights in the West African city of Paraku, where a single conflict ranged to and fro for years between subprefects, court, gendarmerie, and "traditional authorities," without ever being resolved.

which has no consequences in terms of action. The pending procedure is more in the nature of a feud, because it can create enduring irritation and depletion of forces (annoyance potential).

The enforcement of the results (conclusions) of the procedure requires sanctions. These sanctions may take very different forms, some of them violent. A form that is particularly prevalent in non-state societies is the sanction of reputation. This means that the person who fails to abide by the decision is punished by disgrace and devaluation of his social status. This degradation has social and economic consequences in terms of the possibility of finding allies or marriage partners. Reputation sanctions are particularly effective where there are judges or arbitrators, who can themselves contribute a substantial "capital of reputation."

Competitions are closely related in form to warring—sporting competitions being an example. If competitions are procedurally organized and success is measured against abstract parameters such as speed or money, then they allow almost continuous conflicts without violence. The procedural resolution of a conflict without any violence other than the enforcement of the agreed effects constitutes the core of many economically significant institutions of conflict resolution. For example, they may regulate access to land and water—as land registries, surveyors acting under oath, and civil courts.

Procedures create their own time. The period of the procedures takes priority over the acts that may follow the procedures. This is one of the preconditions for eliminating differences in the potential for force and violence. To this extent, expeditive (extremely accelerated) "procedures," such as lynching, are not procedures in the strict sense. The notion that lynching is typical of "primitive" societies is unjustified. All human societies—including pre-industrial ones—are familiar with procedures.[32] Lynching is no more and no less than a particularly impressive and yet relatively ineffective form of sanction, which offers particularly good chances of concealing the identity of the perpetrator.

The fact that procedures generate their own time can also, however, cancel out their effect in damping down conflict. This is particularly true when the timeframe for decisions is very long or, in the case of pending procedures, completely unlimited. This situation makes a particular form of policy and mobilization plausible: actionism, as is also typical of many fascist movements. The political leaders promise rapid action in place of protracted "bureaucratic" procedures. In this context, the political will for action is perfectly represented by violence (Eckert, 1999).

e) TRANSITIONS. We can study transitions between forms of conflict, and in particular we have the opportunity to illustrate, within different societies, examples of the more or less pronounced occurrence of the individual forms of violence. We can see, as stated earlier, that the transition from avoidance to the procedural form of conflict resolution is very rare, but that a switch from avoidance to destruction is far more common. The various forms of conflict differ in their ability to stabilize particular motivational situations. In the case of war, the use of violence is confined within more or less narrow limits. In the case of procedure, it is actually suspended altogether for a certain period. The transition from warring to destruction is, admittedly, not outwardly apparent because the same technology of violence is employed; but as far as society is concerned it represents the overflowing of violence. Where feuds and the highly organized form of the blood feud are dominant, the transition to destruction seems less likely, according to Koehler (2000).

---

[32] On council decisions with procedural form, see Kuper & Richards, 1971.

Different milieus give priority to different motives and try to develop their own institutional orders. If honor is a dominant motive, the limitation of violence can be relatively easily stabilized through rules of war. But honor is also an attribute that is very difficult to deal with in procedural forms. In the historical process, the difference in the systems of violence represents a reversal of the motives for violence. The transition to forms of society in which conflicts are regulated primarily by procedures is incompatible with the dominance of honor over economic motives or the desire to acquire power.

In different ways and with differing intensity, every society has developed ways of acquiring resources which open up access to scarce resources for mutual benefit and/or through compromise. Institutions for the development of compromises are particularly useful to the aim of suppressing violence. They include markets, courts of justice, and parliaments. Their particular property is that they can convert an alternative conflict (Hirschman, 1994; either/or antithesis) into an incremental conflict (more/less antithesis). Where procedures for achieving compromises are underdeveloped, however, the probability of violent conflict increases.

Whether the procedural form creates legitimacy, as Luhmann (1969) believes, or a particular distribution model which is subject to the normative procedures, as Engels (1878) suggests, cannot be clearly determined. What is certain is that a deficient procedural practice may result in people turning away from the rules on which the procedure is based. The distributional order, which underlies the compromises to the extent that they cannot deviate significantly from it, may appear unjust against the background of an alternative order (for example as "class rule" in Marx and Engels).

Rules by which institutions are stabilized create areas of predictability (forecast areas). If the rules become unclear or offer too little certainty, predictability collapses and the default option of violence becomes more probable.

The absence of institutions for the achievement of compromises, and of the procedures they support, can also become apparent in countries where, in formal terms, a state with a legal apparatus exists. If the preparedness for peace is based on the intervention of outsiders, who are not available because of the collapse of the old form of state power, violence becomes more probable because of the absence of local compromise institutions. This statement can be applied in general terms to broad areas of the former Soviet empire (Tishkov, 1997).

Where social institutions for conflict resolution are unreliable or underdeveloped, or indeed absent altogether, clientelism offers itself as an organizational model that is not very demanding in institutional terms. In clientelism, a scarce resource such as agricultural land, secure jobs, or protection against violence is administered by a "gatekeeper" or patron (Boissevain, 1974). He dispenses this asset as a favor or gift (or, in borderline cases, sells it for corrupt payments) and expects reciprocal services (allegiance) and contributions in return. Clientelist networks are hierarchically organized. Their material objective is often ideologically exaggerated. If material aims appear "low," emotional connotations such as "homeland" or prestige constructs such as "family honor" may become the focus of attention. A particularly effective device is the camouflaging of clientelist networks as self-defined we-groups. Competition between clientelist networks is thus reinterpreted as ethnic, politico-ideological, or religious conflict, as described by Gabbert (1999b) in the case of Chiapas in Mexico. Instead of fighting for land or appointments, people fight—or perceive themselves as fighting—for the ideological aim. The patrons of the clientelist networks act as arbitrators, negotiate compromises between themselves, or order their entourage to go to war. The personality of the patrons has to achieve what institutions achieve in other forms of society. In postcolonial Africa, a type of virtuoso politician arose who built up networks, played them off against one another, and in so doing created an image of traditional power in the mediation of conflicts and the illegal appropriation of resources (Bayart, 1989). When the competence of such a patron vanishes, violence becomes more frequent, as demonstrated by the case of Mobutu in Congo/Zaire.

Economic growth can promote clientelism and violence. For example, if land becomes more valuable as a result of market economy reforms or if increasing state revenues mean that activities close to government become more profitable, but at the same time the institutions for regulating conflicts remain unchanged, then they are no longer able to meet the growing need for regulation. The weaker social institutions for conflict resolution are, in comparison with the requirements, the more likely people are to take refuge in the patronage of ethnic or religious clientelist networks. If the patrons fail as mediators or expect an advantage as a result of violence that they cause to be practiced by others, violence becomes more probable. If the monopoly on violence is fragile, they may be likely to become warlords.

6. Regulatory Conflicts

In this classification of conflicts, we have previously considered only conflicts between actors, not regulatory conflicts in the sense of the breaking of rules by people subject to those rules. That violence occurs here also has been noted above (cf. III.3). Not every society has an executive body responsible for enforcing the rules. Enforcement could also be entrusted to paid service providers. In parts of West Africa, this function was performed by "secret societies," who were commissioned with the punishment of a wrongdoer by those who saw themselves as injured by his action. In Yemen, Sharia courts may give judgment in favor of a litigant, but he then has to hire armed men to enforce it (Würth, 2000). In acephalous societies (societies without a state), we find self-help in addition to the enforcement of law by service providers. Anyone who wishes to enforce a legitimately recognized right or penalty must himself resort to violence; in such circumstances, feuds may be seen as a form of legal self-help (Spittler, 1980). Along with a central governmental authority for enforcing rights, service providers, and self-help, there is a fourth way of dealing with regulatory conflict: denial. In order not to show weakness, one acts as if the rule had not been broken (Sommer, 2000).

In societies with state constitutions, too, the other forms of dealing with regulatory conflicts exist. In some cases, they are tolerated by the state. Some of them are illegal practices used to enforce illegal rules. Anyone who carries on an illegal business needs service providers—known as mafias—to enforce his rights (Krauthausen, 1997). If, in a society with a state constitution, the alternative forms of dealing with regulatory conflicts become more important, rules can be changed by the exercise of violence within that framework. The embedding of violence becomes less effective; the level of violence increases.

It might be helpful to explain the individual application of violence with the terminology of collective violence. In fact, even in industrial societies, we find that the motives expressed by murderers cover the whole spectrum of what we know as socially organized violence: an act of violence may be justified as legitimate appropriation (in the case of robbery), as the punishment of another person (perhaps because he refused to obey an order given or a rule laid down by the perpetrator), or a reflection of a feud. If this overriding regulatory system is shared by others in the perpetrator's environment, or if the act, as a collective action, even affirms the "validity" of these imagined and desired patterns and rules of violence, the step toward violence becomes easier to take. In this way, the feud may be described by perpetrators as a trial of strength, a sporting competition, based on their own rules. Thus membership of groups or milieus which develop their own subcultural rules and targets for success becomes an essential level of explanation of violence as a breach of rules. From the perpetrators' standpoint, criminal violence then appears to be conduct guided by internal rules.

Luhmann (1974) sees the distinction between rule-breaking and rule-enforcing violence as an obvious starting point. Social anthropology can accept this distinction as universal only in the sense that violence everywhere—emically—can be distinguished in this manner. As a result of the occurrence of violence, however, the perception of who is subject to a rule or what the rule is may also change.

In research on violence in industrialized societies, the study of illegitimate—rule-breaking—violence is seen to be crucial. Even the enforcement of conduct that complies with the rules ultimately takes physical effect on those persons who resist, and thus applies violence. This rule-enforcing violence also creates models for other acts of violence. How violently or nonviolently conflicts between protagonists are resolved is not unaffected by what is observed day by day in the ways in which the state enforces the rules. As demonstrated by the relatively high murder rates in countries which use the death penalty, rule-breakers, too, are influenced in their conduct by the model of the rule-enforcing state authority. In societies with state constitutions, the personnel of the enforcement executive (Weber, 1922), meaning policemen, soldiers, bailiffs, etc., frequently, though not always, act in accordance with statutory rules when they perform enforcement. Where the servants of the state systematically contravene the rules that regulate the enforcing power, and where the monopoly of violence no longer acts legitimately (in other words, in compliance with the law), the exercise of violence in accordance with other rules becomes legitimate. Autonomous violence arises. The history of modern Africa provides examples of how, after the collapse of the legitimate monopoly on violence as a result of unlawful violence by the servants of the state, counterviolence comes into being and may trigger civil wars (Wirz, 1982).

IV. SUMMARY

The "roots" or "causes of violence" vary from society to society, from one historical period to the next, and between political milieus. This diversity cannot therefore form the starting point of a society-based comparative theory of violence. What these emic "root theories" do offer, however, is an interesting reference to counterimages of the good society that are inherent within society, which would itself have merited closer scrutiny in research. Instead of seeking individual causes for the supposed breakdown of the social order in these images of society, social anthropological/ethnological researchers are increasingly coming to accept a view of the "normalcy of violence," establishing the theory of a "violence order."

Conflicts are an inevitable part of social life. Without conflicts, there can be no expression of individual interests and no social change. Conflicts do not necessarily imply violence. Certain institutional configurations—especially procedures—may so minimize conflicts that they are resolved nonviolently. From this angle, violence is the default option of purposeful action. Where it occurs regularly, it is directed toward a purpose.

Violence is an action option inbuilt into social structures. Every society has a violence order, within which violence has predictable—lawful and unlawful—locations. This leads to the methodological requirement that violence must be analyzed in the context of the institutions that monitor and perpetuate it. Violence is embedded—and thus both channeled in its directions and limited—by rules, sanctions (including the reputation system), objectives, and control of access to the means of violence. This allows forecasts to be made: if the embedding becomes less stringent, for example as a result of the disappearance of the adversary, unreliability of the sanctions system, or unrestricted access to arms, then the level of violence rises.

A society may marginalize the legitimate use of violence as a "sport" or "duel" by definition, or transpose it to self-defined limits as violence against "enemies." Violence thus assumes the appearance of unlawfulness in principle. However, there are also two legitimate types of conflict in which the use of violence can be expected: as a sanction in the event of a regulatory conflict and as a means to victory in the (collective) conflict between protagonists. In both cases, violence has to be regarded as a means to power. The emic view resulting from this transfer of violence to the border or threshold, this "eliminalization," holding that violence lies outside the structure of society, is one that comparative social science cannot share. Society consists of sequences of discontinuous processes, of which violence must be regarded as a systemic part.

Assuming that the embedding of violence undergoes no change of form, the following can be forecast: violence will increase (1) if institutions fail or (2) if the requirements to be met by the institutions increase and the latter fail to change. In other words, social anthropology can formulate a moderately optimistic conclusion: if the requirements to be met by the institutions fall or if the institutions deal more effectively with conflicts, the probability of violence may recede.

REFERENCES

Abbink, Jon. (1994a). Changing Patterns of 'Ethnic' Violence: Peasant–Pastoralist Confrontation in Southern Ethiopia and its Implications for a Theory of Violence. *Sociologus*, *43*(1), 66–78.

Abbink, Jon. (1994b). Tribal Violence, Peacemaking and Ethnology. A Comment. In Bahru Zewde, Richard Pankhurst & Taddese Beyene (Eds.), *Proceedings of the XIth International Conference of Ethiopian Studies II* (pp. 1–7). Addis Ababa: Institute of Ethiopian Studies.

Allen, Tim. (1998). The Violence of Healing. *Sociologus*, *47*(2), 101–128.

Balandier, Georges. (1956). Grandeur et Servitude de l'Ethnologue. *Cahiers du Sud*, *337*, 450–456.

Barth, Fredrik. (1959a). *Political Leadership among the Swath Pathans*. London: Athlone.

Barth, Fredrik. (1959b). Segmentary Opposition and the Theory of Games. A Study of Pathan Organization. *Journal of the Royal Anthropological Institute*, *89*(1), 5–21.

Barth, Frederik. (1969). Preface. In Frederik Barth (Ed.), *Ethnic Groups and Boundaries* (pp. 9–38). Bergen: Universitets Forlaget.

Bayart, Jean-François. (1989). *L'État en Afrique*. La Politique du Ventre. Paris: Fayard.

Bazin, Jean, & Emmanuel Terray. (1982). *Guerres de Lignages et Guerres d'États en Afrique*. Paris: Edition des Archives Contemporaines.

Bernardi, Bernardo. (1985). *Age Class Systems*. Cambridge: Cambridge University Press.

Bierschenk, Thomas. (1999). Herrschaft, Verhandlung und Gewalt in einer afrikanischen Mittelstadt (Parakou, Rép. du Bénin). *Afrika-Spectrum*, *34*(3), 321–348.

Black-Michaud, Jacob. (1975). *Cohesive Force: Feud in the Mediterranean and the Middle East*. Oxford: Blackwell.

Boissevain, Jeremy. (1974). *Friends of Friends: Networks, Manipulators, and Coalitions*. Oxford, Blackwell.

Bollig, Michael. (1991). Intra- und interethnisches Konfliktmanagement in Nordwestkenia. In Thomas Scheffler (Ed.), *Etnizität und Gewalt* (pp. 33–66). Hamburg: Deutsches Orient-Institut.

Bourdieu, Pierre. (1982). *Die feinen Unterschiede. Kritik der gesellschaftlichen Urteilskraft*. Frankfurt a. M.: Suhrkamp. [Orig.: Bourdieu, Pierre. (1979). *La Distinction. Critique du Jugement Social*. Paris: Les Éd. de Minuit.]

Bourdieu, Pierre. (1989). Social Space and Symbolic Power. *Sociological Theory*, 7, 14–25.

Brandstetter, Anna-Maria, & Dieter Neubert. (1996). Regionale und internationale Konfliktlinien in Ruanda. In Peter Meyns (Ed.), *Staat und Gesellschaft in Afrika. Erosions- und Reformprozesse* (pp. 462–471). Hamburg, Münster: Lit. Verlag.

Bringa, Tone. (1993). *We Are All Neighbours*. Film. Granada TV.

Bringa, Tone. (1995). *Being Muslim the Bosnian Way: Identity and Community in a Central Bosnian Village*. Princeton, New Jersey: Princeton University Press.

Brown, Dee. (1971). *Bury My Heart at Wounded Knee. An Indian History of the American West*. New York: Holt, Rinehart & Winston.

Canfield, Robert Leroy. (1973). *Faction and Conversion in a Plural Society. Religious Alignments in the Hindu Kush. Anthropological Paper No. 50*. Ann Arbor: University of Michigan.

Chagnon, Napoleon. (1967). Yanomamö—the Fierce People. *Natural History*, 76, 22–31.

Chalk, Frank, & Kurt Jonassohn. (1990). *The History and Sociology of Genocide*. New Haven: Yale University Press.

Colovic, Ivan. (1994). *Bordell der Krieger. Folklore, Politik und Krieg*. Osnabrück: Fibre.

Connor, Walker. (1972). Nation Building or Nation Destroying? *World Politics*, 24(3), 319–355.

Coser, Louis. (1956). *The Functions of Social Conflict*. Glencoe: The Free Press.

Dahrendorf, Ralph. (1954). Out of Utopia. *American Journal of Sociology*, 64, 115–127.

Eckert, Julia. (1999). *'Riots: That's Something that Happens in the Slums'. Land, städtische Unruhen und die Politik der Segregation (Bombay/Indien). Sozialanthropologisches Arbeitspapier 79*. Berlin: Das Arabische Buch.

Eckert, Julia, Georg Elwert, Kristóf Gosztonyi, & Thomas Zitelmann. (1999). *Konflikttreiber – Konfliktschlichter: Erste theoretische Ergebnisse einer vergleichenden Untersuchung in Bosnien, Bombay und Oromiya Regional State (Äthiopien). Sozialanthropologisches Arbeitspapier 75*. Berlin: Das Arabische Buch.

Elwert, Georg. (1973). *Wirtschaft und Herrschaft von Dãxome im 18. Jahrhundert*. München: Renner.

Elwert, Georg. (1997). Deutsche Nation. In Bernhard Schäfers & Wolfgang Zapf (Eds.), *Zur Gesellschaft Deutschlands* (pp. 123–134). Opladen: Leske & Budrich.

Elwert, Georg. (1999). Markets of Violence. In Georg Elwert, Stephan Feuchtwang & Dieter Neubert (Eds.), *Dynamics of Violence. Processes of Escalation and De-Escalation in Violent Group Conflicts* (pp. 85–102). Berlin: Duncker & Humblot.

Elwert, Georg. (2001a). Herausforderung durch das Fremde. In Wolfgang Fikentscher (Ed.), *Begegnungen und Konflikt* (pp. 132–144). München: Beck.

Elwert, Georg. (2002). Primordial Emotions and the Social Construction of We-Groups—Switching and Other Forgotten Features. In Günther Schleem (Ed.), *Imagined Differences: Hatred and the Construction of Identity*. Münster: Lit, in print.

Elwert, Georg, Stephan Feuchtwang, & Dieter/Neubert. (Eds.) (1999). *Dynamics of Violence. Processes of Escalation and De-Escalation in Violent Conflicts*. Berlin: Duncker und Humblot.

Engels, Friedrich. (1878). *Herrn Eugen Dühring's Umwälzung der Wissenschaft*. Leipzig: Genossenschaftsbuchdruckerei.

Erdheim, Mario. (1973). *Prestige und Kulturwandel*. Wiesbaden: Focus.

Evans-Pritchard, Edward. (1940a). *The Nuer. A Description of the Modes of Livelihood and Political Institutions of a Nilotic People*. Oxford: Clarendon.

Evans-Pritchard, Edward. (1940b). *The Political System of the Anuak*. London: London School of Economics.

Evans-Pritchard, Edward. (1957). Azande Warfare. *Anthropos*, 52, 239–262.

Evers, Hans-Dieter, & Tilman Schiel. (1988). *Strategische Gruppen: Vergleichende Studien zu Staat, Bürokratie und Klassenbildung in der Dritten Welt*. Berlin: Reimer.

Ferguson, Brian, & Neil Whitehead. (Eds.) (1992). *War in the Tribal Zone. Expanding States and Indigenous Warfare*. Santa Fe: School of American Research Press.

Forster, Georg. (1967) [1789]. *Werke in vier Bänden*. Gerhard Steiner (Ed.). Frankfurt a. M.: Insel Verlag.

Forster, Georg. (1985). *Georg Forsters Werke. Vol. 5*. Berlin: Akademie.

Gabbert, Wolfgang. (1999a). *Ethnizität und soziale Ungleichheit auf der Halbinsel Yucatán, Mexiko, 1500–1998. Habilitationsschrift*. Berlin: Fachbereich Politik und Sozialwissenschaften der Freien Universität.

Gabbert, Wolfgang. (1999b). Violence and Social Change in Highland Maya Communities, Chiapas, Mexico. *Iberoamerikanisches Archiv*, 25(3/4), 351–374.

Gabbert, Wolfgang. (2001). Staat, Paramilitärs und dörfliche Konflikte im Hochland von Chiapas, Mexiko. In Wolfgang Höpken & Michael Riekenberg (Eds.), *Politische und ethnische Gewalt in Südosteuropa und in Lateinamerika* (pp. 131–148). Köln: Böhlau.

Galtung, Johan. (1969). Violence, Peace, and Peace Research. *Journal of Peace Research, 6,* 106–112.

Galtung, Johan. (1978). Der besondere Beitrag der Friedensforschung zum Studium der Gewalt. In Kurt Röttgers & Hans Saner (Eds.), *Gewalt, Grundlagenprobleme in der Diskussion der Gewaltphänomene* (pp. 9–32). Basel, Stuttgart: Schwabe.

Galtung, Johan. (1990). Cultural Violence. *Journal of Peace Research, 27*(3), 291–305.

Gluckman, Max. (1956). *Custom and Conflict in Africa.* Oxford: Blackwell.

Gluckman, Max. (1963). *Order and Rebellion in Tribal Africa.* London: Cohen and West.

Gosztonyi, Kristof. (1999). *Der Konfliktschlichtungsprozess in Mostar (Bosnien): Zwischen internationalem Druck und lokaler Obstruktion. Sozialanthropologisches Arbeitspapier 78.* Berlin: Das Arabische Buch.

Gurr, Ted. (1994). Peoples against States. *International Studies Quarterly, 38*(3), 347–379.

Halbmayer, Ernst. (2000). Socio-Cosmological Context and Forms of Violence—War, Vendetta and Suicide Among the Yukpa of North-Western Venezuela. *Sociologus, 2,* 37–63.

Hallpike, Christopher. (1973). Functionalist Interpretation of Primitive Warfare. *Man, 8,* 451–470.

Hallpike, Christopher. (1977). *Bloodshed and Vengeance in the Papuan Mountains.* London. Oxford University Press.

Heine-Geldern, Robert. (1923). Südostasien. In Georg Buschan (Ed.), *Illustrierte Völkerkunde* (pp. 689–968). Stuttgart: Strecker und Schröder.

Helbling, Jürg. (1999). The Dynamics of War and Alliance among the Yanomami. In Georg Elwert, Stefan Feuchtwang & Dieter Neubert (Eds.), *Dynamics of Violence* (pp. 103–116). Berlin: Duncker und Humblot.

Hirschman, Albert O. (1970). *Exit, Voice and Loyalty. Responses to Decline in Firms Organizations and States.* Cambridge, Mass.: Harvard University Press.

Hirschman, Albert. (1994). Social Conflicts as Pillars of Democratic Market Society. *Political Theory, 22*(2), 203–218.

Hobbes, Thomas. (1965) [1651]. *Leviathan oder Wesen, Form und Gewalt des kirchlichen und bürgerlichen Staates.* Reinbek: Rowohlt.

Hobsbawm, Eric, & Terence Ranger. (Eds.) (1973). *The Invention of Tradition.* Oxford: Oxford University Press.

James, Wendy. (1995). *'Internal' Bodily Images and Disciplinary Practices: a Contributing Factor in Modern War Fare? Paper presented at the Conference: Feud, War, Genocide.* Berlin Academy of Sciences.

Jensen, Adolf. (1948). *Das religiöse Weltbild einer frühen Kultur.* Stuttgart: A. Schröder.

Kelman, Herbert. (1973). Violence without Moral Constraint. *Journal of Social Issues, 29,* 25–61.

Koch, Klaus. (1976). Konfliktmanagement und Rechtsethnologie. *Sociologus, 26*(2), 97–129.

Koehler, Jan. (2000). *Zur Organisation von Gewalt und der Austragung von Konflikten in Georgien.* Münster: Lit.

Krauthausen, Ciro. (1997). *Moderne Gewalten.* Frankfurt a. M., New York: Campus.

Kuper, Adam, & Audrey Richards. (Eds.) (1971). *Councils in Action.* Cambridge: Cambridge University Press.

Leach, Edmund. (1965). The Nature of War. *Disarmament and Arms Control, 3,* 165–183.

Lentz, Carola. (1998). *Die Konstruktion von Ethnizität: Eine politische Geschichte Nord-West Ghanas 1870–1990.* Köln: Rüdiger Köppe.

Lévi-Straus, Claude. (1971) [1958]. *Strukturale Anthropologie.* Frankfurt a. M.: Suhrkamp.

Lorenz, Konrad. (1966). *On Aggression.* New York: Harcourt, Brace and World.

Luhmann, Niklas. (1969). *Legitimation durch Verfahren.* Neuwied am Rhein: Luchterhand.

Luhmann, Niklas. (1974). Symbiotische Mechanismen. In Otthein Rammstedt (Ed.), *Gewaltverhältnisse und die Ohnmacht der Kritik* (pp. 107–131). Frankfurt a. M.: Suhrkamp.

Macek, Ivana. (2001). Predicament of War: Sarajevo Experiences and Ethics of War. In Ingo Schröder & Bettina Schmidt (Eds.), *Anthropology of Violence and Conflict* (pp. 197–224). London: Routledge.

Martius, Carl Friedrich Philipp von. (1867). *Zur Ethnographie Amerikas, zumal Brasiliens.* Leipzig: F. Fleischer.

Marx, Christoph. (2000). Folter und Rassismus. Südafrika während der Apartheid. In Peter Bursche, Götz Distelrath & Sven Lembke (Eds.), *Das Quälen des Körpers. Eine historische Anthropologie der Folter* (pp. 257–279). Köln: Böhlau.

Mayer, Kathrin, & Herfried Münkler. (1998). Zur Stiftung nationaler Identität in den Schriften italienischer Humanisten. In Herfried Münkler (Ed.), *Die Herausforderung durch das Fremde* (pp. 27–129). Berlin: Akademie.

Montagu, Ashley. (Ed.) (1968). *Man and Aggression.* Oxford and New York: Oxford University Press.

Mühlmann, Wilhelm E. (1940). *Krieg und Frieden*. Heidelberg: Winter.

Mühlmann, Wilhelm E. (1962). *Homo Creator. Abhandlungen zur Soziologie, Anthropologie und Ethnologie*. Wiesbaden: Harrassowitz.

Mühlmann, Wilhelm E. (1972). Krieg und Frieden. In Wilhelm Bernsdorf (Ed.), *Wörterbuch der Soziologie. Vol. 2* (pp. 475–479). Frankfurt a. M.: Fischer.

Müller, Salomon. (1839–1844). *Land- en Volkenkunde*. Leiden: Naturkundige commissie.

Nagata, Judith. (1974). What is Malay? Situational Selection of Ethnic Identity in a Plural Society. *American Ethnologist, 1*, 331–350.

Neubert, Dieter. (1999). Dynamics of Escalating Violence. In Georg Elwert, Stefan Feuchtwang & Dieter Neubert (Eds.), *Dynamics of Violence* (pp. 151–174). Berlin: Duncker & Humblot.

Neubert, Dieter, & Anna-Maria Brandstetter. (1996). Historische und gesellschaftliche Hintergründe des Konflikts in Ruanda. In Peter Meyns (Ed.), *Staat und Gesellschaft in Afrika. Erosions- und Reformprozesse* (pp. 409–424). Hamburg, Münster: Lit. Verlag.

Orywal, Erwin. (1986). *Die ethnischen Gruppen Afghanistans*. Wiesbaden: Reichert.

Orywal, Erwin. (1996). Krieg als Konfliktaustragungsstrategie—Zur Plausibilität von Kriegsursachentheorien aus kognitionsethnologischer Sicht. *Zeitschrift für Ethnologie, 121*(1), 1–48.

Orywal, Erwin, Aparnar Rao, & Michael Bollig. (Eds.) (1996). *Krieg und Kampf. Die Gewalt in unseren Köpfen*. Berlin: Reimer.

Otterbein, Keith. (1970). *The Evolution of War: a Cross-cultural Study*. New Haven: HRAF-Press.

Otterbein, Keith. (1973). The Anthropology of War. In John J. Honigmann (Ed.), *Handbook of Social and Cultural Anthropology* (pp. 923–958). Chicago: Rand McNally.

Peller, Annette. (2000). *Chiffrierte Körper—Disziplinierte Körper. Die Exzision der Vulva in ihrem sozial-kulturellen Kontext (Äthiopien). Dissertation*. Berlin: Fachbereich Politische und Sozialwissenschaften, Freie Universität.

Peristiany, Jean. (1966). *Honour and Shame. The Values of Mediterranean Society*. London: Weidenfeld and Nicolson.

Peters, Krijn, & Paul Richards. (1998). *Why We Fight: Voices of Youth Combattants in Sierra Leone*. Africa, 68, pp. 183–210.

Pike, Kenneth. (1967). *Language in Relation to a Unified Theory of Human Behavior*. The Hague: Mouton.

Pospisil, Leopold. (1958). Feud. *International Encyclopedia of the Social Sciences, 16*, 389–393.

Radcliffe-Brown, Alfred. (1952). *Structure and Function in Primitive Society*. London: Cohen and West.

Riches, David. (1991). Aggression, War, Violence: Space/Time and Paradigm. *Man, 26*(2), 281–298.

Rummel, Rudolph J. (1994). *Death by Government*. New Brunswick, N. J.: Transaction Publishers.

Sahlins, Marshall D. (1961). The Segmentary Lineage: an Organization of Predatory Expansion. *American Anthropologist, 63*, 322–345.

Scheffler, Thomas. (1991). Ethnizität und Gewalt im Vorderen und Mittleren Orient. In Thomas Scheffler (Ed.), *Ethnizität und Gewalt* (pp. 9–32). Hamburg: Deutsches Orientinstitut.

Scheffler, Thomas. (1995). Ethnoradikalismus: Zum Verhältnis von Ethnopolitik und Gewalt. In Gerhard Seewann (Ed.), *Minderheiten als Konfliktpotential in Ostmittel- und Südosteuropa* (pp. 9–47). München: Oldenbourg.

Schlee Günther. (1979). *Das Glaubens- und Sozialsystem der Rendille: Kamelnomaden Nordkenias*. Berlin: Reimer.

Schlee, Günther. (1990). Altersklassen und Veränderung der Lebenslaufalter bei den Rendille. In Georg Elwert, Martin Kohli & Harald Müller (Eds.), *Im Lauf der Zeit. Ethnographische Studien zur gesellschaftlichen Konstruktion von Lebenszeit* (pp. 69–82). Saabrücken: Breitenbach.

Schlee, Günther. (2000). Identitätskonstruktionen und Parteinahme: Überlegungen zur Konflikttheorie. *Sociologus, 1*, 64–89.

Schmidt, Bettina, & Ingo Schröder. (2001). Violent Imagineries and Violent Practices. In Bettina Schmidt & Ingo Schröder (Eds.), *Anthropology of Violence and Conflict* (pp. 1–24). London: Routledge.

Schwandner-Sievers, Stephanie. (1996). Zur Logik der Blutrache in Nordalbanien: Ehre, Symbolik und Gewaltlegitimation. *Sociologus, 45*(2), 109–129.

Schwandner-Sievers, Stephanie. (1999). Humiliation and Reconciliation in Northern Albania. The Logics of Feuding in Symbolic and Diachronic Perspectives. In Georg Elwert, Stephan Feuchtwang & Dieter Neubert (Eds.), Dynamics of Violence. *Processes of Escalation and De-Escalation in Violent Group Conflicts* (pp. 133–152). Berlin: Duncker and Humblot.

Searle, John. (1997). *Die Konstruktion der gesellschaftlichen Wirklichkeit. Zur Ontologie sozialer Tatsachen*. Reinbek: Rowohlt.

Sommer, Jörn. (2000). *Korrupte Zivilgesellschaft—Unterschlagungen und die Kontrolle dörflicher Eliten bei Bauern im Borgu (Bénin). Dissertation.* Berlin: Fachbereich Politische und Sozialwissenschaften, Freie Universität.

Spittler, Gerd. (1980). Konfliktaustragung in akephalen Gesellschaften: Selbsthilfe und Verhandlung. *Jahrbuch für Rechtssoziologie und Rechtstheorie, 6,* 142–164.

Strathern, Andrew. (1992). Let the Bow go Down. In Brian Ferguson & Neil L. Whitehead (Eds.), *War in the Tribal Zone. Expanding States and Indigenous Warfare* (pp. 229–250). Santa Fe: School of American Research Press.

Strecker, Ivo. (1999). The Temptations of War and the Struggle for Peace among the Hamar of Southern Ethiopia. In Georg Elwert, Stephan Feuchtwang & Dieter Neubert (Eds.), *Dynamics of Violence. Processes of Escalation and De-Escalation in Violent Group Conflicts* (pp. 227–259). Berlin: Duncker & Humblot.

Sumner, William. (1911). *War and Other Essays.* New Haven: Yale University Press.

Terray, Emmanuel. (Ed.) (1987). *L'État Contemporain en Afrique.* Paris: Harmattan.

Tillon, Germaine. (1997) [1946]. *Ravensbrück.* Paris: Seuil.

Tishkov, Valery. (Ed.) (1997). *Ethnicity, Nationalism and Conflict in and after the Soviet Union. The Mind Aflame. 2nd Edition.* Beverly Hills: Sage.

Tornay, Serge. (1984). Remarques sur le Principe Générationnel en Afrique Orientale. *Production Pastorale et Société, 15,* 87–97.

Tornay, Serge. (1986). Une Afrique Démasquée. Initiation et Sacrifice chez les Pasteurs d'Afrique Orientale. In Pierre Centlivres & Jacques Hainard (Eds.), *Les Rites de Passage Aujourd'hui* (pp. 69–92). Lausanne: L'Age d'Homme.

Trotha, Trutz von. (1999). Forms of Martial Power: Total Wars, Wars of Pacification and Raid. Some Observations on the Typology of Violence. In Georg Elwert, Stephan Feuchtwang & Dieter Neubert (Eds.), Dynamics of Violence. Processes of Escalation and De-Escalation in Violent Conflicts (pp. 35–61). Berlin: Duncker & Humblot.

Vayda, Andrew. (1961). Expansion and Warfare among Agriculturalists. *American Anthropologist, 63,* 346–358.

Vayda, Andrew. (Ed.) (1968). *Peoples and Cultures of the Pacific: An Anthropological Reader.* Garden City, NY: Natural History Press.

Voget, Fred W. (1964). Warfare and Integration of Crow Indian Culture. In Ward Goodenough (Ed.), *Explorations in Cultural Anthropology* (pp. 483–509). New York: Mc Graw-Hill.

Waldmann, Peter. (1999). Societies in Civil War. In Georg Elwert, Stephan Feuchtwang & Dieter Neubert (Eds.), *Dynamics of Violence. Processes of Escalation and De-Escalation in Violent Conflicts* (pp. 61–103). Berlin: Duncker & Humblot.

Weber, Max. (1922). *Wirtschaft und Gesellschaft.* Tübingen: Mohr.

White, Leslie. (1949). *The Science of Culture.* New York: Grove-Press.

Wicker, Hans-Rudolf. (1993). Macht schafft Wahrheit: Ein Essay zur systematischen Folter. In Thomas Fillitz, André Gingrich & Gabriele Rasuly-Paleczek (Eds.), *Kultur, Identität und Macht* (pp. 257–269). Frankfurt a. M.: Verlag für interkulturelle Kommunikation.

Wimmer, Andreas. (1995). Interethnische Konflikte: ein Beitrag zur Integration aktueller Forschungsansätze. *Kölner Zeitschrift für Soziologie und Sozialpsychologie, 47,* 464–493.

Wirz, Albert. (1982). *Krieg in Afrika—Die nachkolonialen Konflikte in Nigeria, Sudan, Tschad und Kongo.* Wiesbaden: Steiner.

Würth, Anna. (2000). *As-Sari'a fi Bab al-Yaman. Recht, Richter und Rechtspraxis.* Berlin: Duncker und Humblot.

Young, Frank. (1965). *Initiation Ceremonies: A Cross Cultural Study of Status Dramatization.* Indianapolis: Bobbs Merill.

Zitelmann, Thomas. (1990). Verzeitlichung und Lebenslauf. Die Alters- und Generationsklassenordnung (Gada) der Borana-Oromo. In Georg Elwert, Martin Kohli & Harald Müller (Eds.), *Im Lauf der Zeit. Ethnographische Studien zur gesellschaftlichen Konstruktion von Lebensaltern* (pp. 50–68). Saabrücken: Breitenbach.

Zitelmann, Thomas. (1998). Bomben in Addis Ababa. Nachricht, Gerücht, Selbstinformation. In Jan Koehler & Sonja Heyer (Eds.), *Anthropologie der Gewalt* (pp. 205–216). Berlin: VWF.

Zizek, Slavoj. (2001). Die Spur der Steine. Nach den Zerstörungen von Bamian: Das Taliban-Regime als unfreiwilliger Modernisierungseffekt. *Frankfurter Rundschau* vom 07. März, p. 19.

Civil Wars

Peter Waldmann

I. DEFINITION: HISTORICAL AND PRESENT-DAY SIGNIFICANCE

Civil wars are large-scale armed conflicts of substantial duration fought between two or more groups within a state in order to gain, divide, or fragment control of government. As well as civil wars fought for political objectives there are other types in which ethnic, religious, or economic reasons play an important part.

A defining feature of any war is the extensive, long-term use of violence. Conventional research has set a threshold of 1,000 fatalities per year as the point above which armed hostilities can be defined as war (cf. Small & Singer, 1982:55). More important than such numerical standards, though, are the structural features of warfare: the fact that large parts of the population are involved in the conflict, whether actively or as victims; that both sides follow planned and organized campaigns; that their actions—whatever their purpose—exhibit a degree of continuity and strategic consistency (Kende, 1971); and, finally, that the groups involved are such that one is not hopelessly inferior to the other. Large-scale punitive campaigns, massacres, and acts of genocide may be an integral part of a war or the consequence of one, but cannot be referred to as war in the narrower sense since war entails not only the intent to kill others but also the risk of being oneself the victim of violence (cf. van Creveld, 1991:159ff.).

Despite its general nature, our definition does supply criteria for distinguishing a civil war from other forms of internal violence. For example, *coups d'état* of the kind routinely seen in the Third World during the 1960s and 1970s may have been highly organized, planned enterprises, but were confined to a brief period and did not actively involve the mass of the people. Riots, rebellions, and armed disturbances within a state do often result in the mobilization of large numbers of people but for the most part lack a viable organization pursuing a longer-term strategy. The distinction between civil war and revolution is not an easy one: the decisive factor should probably be whether, in the

W. Heitmeyer and J. Hagan (eds.), *International Handbook of Violence Research*, 291–308.
© 2003 Kluwer Academic Publishers. Printed in the Netherlands.

interpretation of the event, more emphasis is attached to the aspect of dialectical social progress, an "acceleration" of history (Schulz, 1989), or to a radical and extremely costly internal feud.

The trigger of the current debate, however, is not so much the distinction between civil war and revolution as the question of the political and governmental aspects of civil wars. In the traditional view, still held by the *Arbeitsgemeinschaft Kriegsursachen-forschung* (German Association for Research into the Causes of Wars—AKUF) in Hamburg, for the term *war* to be used, it is necessary for the state and government troops to be involved in the hostilities. Otherwise, there is a risk that *any* kind of conflict, including private feuds, may be included in this category (Gantzel & Schwinghammer, 1995:31ff.; Gantzel, 1997:258).

By contrast with these politically based approaches, more recent studies maintain that many violent conflicts in the developing countries today defy the binary classification of "political/apolitical" or "public/private." One frequently cited example of a type of warfare independent of government involves the activities of the "warlord," a figure to be encountered in many parts of Africa, who has set up his own power structures outside or "below" the level of government and pursues a systematic campaign of looting and extortion against not only the local population but also passing traders and international aid organizations (Waldmann, 1998:30ff.). H. Münkler, making the point that the initiative in matters of violence has in many parts of the world passed to criminal gangs, private militias, drug cartels, and guerrilla bands, poses the question of whether war is still the preserve of states (Münkler, 2000). H. M. Enzensberger refers to "molecular civil war," which, he says, is not confined to the poorer regions of the world with weak governments but occurs wherever young men make violent attacks on one another with no discernible objective or purpose (Enzensberger, 1993). There is general agreement that we are confronted today by a new type of armed conflict, which cannot easily be viewed as a successor to conventional warfare directed at control of the state (Kaldor, 1999).

The definition proposed at the start of this paper takes account of these more recent developments by including the processes of fragmentation and dissolution of states and recognizing reasons for war which cannot be described as "political" in the narrower sense. It seems inadvisable to drop the reference to government altogether, because to do so would be to disregard the *de facto* and symbolic importance which attaches to the state, and will continue to do so in the foreseeable future, quite apart from the fact that the distinction between international and civil wars would also become redundant. The *Bürger* ("civilian") part of the German term for civil war, *Bürgerkrieg*, should not be taken too literally, since it is precisely the aim of many of the more recent civil wars to deny citizenship to part of the population of a state, or deprive them of it (a similar problem arises with the English term "civil war," since one of the most universal characteristics of modern civil wars is the uncivil manner in which they are fought) (cf. Keen, 1998:131ff.). In this article, the terms "civil," "internal," and "intranational" war are treated as synonymous.

Taking the historical view, periods dominated by wars between states have alternated with others in which civil wars represented the "norm" (Janssen, 1982). Long periods of European history, especially the era of the bloody wars of religion during the sixteenth and early seventeenth centuries, were dominated by the search for ways of stopping the civilian population tearing each other limb from limb and helping to assert the unchallenged authority of the state. In the eighteenth century, the focus then shifted to wars between states, one of the main means of consolidating monarchical power in the age of absolutism. During the first half of the twentieth century, the two world wars, which put all

Table II-2-4.1. Armed conflicts by type and region, 1945–1993

Type	State vs. state/ intervention	Secession/ resistance	Ideological/ factional	Total	Of which internal	
	N	N	N	N	N	%
Africa	7	21	16	44	37	84
Middle East	11	12	10	33	22	66
South Asia	4	10	4	18	14	78
Southeast Asia	5	11	9	25	20	80
East Asia	3	1	2	6	3	50
South America	1	—	8	9	8	89
Central America/Caribbean	4	—	10	14	10	71
Balkans/Eastern Europe	3	2	—	5	2	40
Former USSR	—	5	2	7	7	100
Western Europe	—	2	1	3	3	100
Total	38	64	62	164	126	77

Source: Holsti, 1996:22, presentation adapted.

other passages of violence in the shade, ensured that war was largely equated with violent international conflict. Nor did anything much happen during the long years of the Cold War to change this prevalent view. Wherever bloodshed and conflict flared up in Asia, Latin America, or Africa, the rival superpowers were always assumed to be in the background, pulling the strings. People could not see, or refused to see, that internal factors were increasingly determining the course of hostilities. This became clear only when many of these conflicts continued—or broke out again—even after the breakup of the Eastern Bloc.

The statistical recording of wars has now become an independent branch of research, the results varying depending on the period considered and the units of measurement employed. These fluctuations, however, do not affect the most important result to be inferred from K. Holsti's table: the great majority of wars that have taken place since the end of World War II (between 75 percent and 90 percent, depending on the method of counting) have been internal wars. Holsti's listing (Table II-2-4.1) has the advantage of disregarding the anticolonial wars of liberation during the 1950s and 1960s, a special type confined to one particular period. Even excluding this type, it is apparent that the theater for most wars has comprised the underdeveloped countries of Africa, the Middle East, and South and Southeast Asia, to which may recently be added the Balkans and the territory of the former Soviet Union. In the Americas, the majority of armed hostilities have taken place in Central America and the Caribbean. North America is unrepresented in the table, and Western Europe makes only scattered appearances.

It is now generally recognized that hopes that the end of the Cold War would herald an era of global peace have proven unfounded. A list recently published by *Projecten Interdisciplinair Onderzoek naar de Oorzaken van Mensenrechtenschendingen* (the Interdisciplinary Research Project on Root Causes of Human Rights Violations—PIOOM), an organization that reports regularly on worldwide trends in warfare, shows that there has been a further increase in the numbers of major and minor armed conflicts (Table II-2-4.2).

Table II-2-4.2. Number of armed conflicts from mid-1995 through mid-1999

	1995	1996	1997	1998	1999
High intensity conflict (HIC)	22	20	20	16	22
Low intensity conflict (LIC)	39	31	59	70	77
Violent political conflict (VPC)	40	44	45	114	151
Total	101	95	124	200	250

Source: Jongman, 1999/2000:29.

It can be assumed that the category of "high intensity conflict" is largely synonymous with war, and that most of the conflicts recorded are internal ones. What is particularly alarming is not so much the fact that the number of high intensity conflicts has again increased, after a temporary drop, but that the number of low intensity conflicts has virtually doubled since 1997. This gives cause for concern because experience shows that violent conflicts on a limited scale can all too swiftly escalate into all-out wars.

II. DEVELOPMENTS IN RESEARCH

Civil wars have always been a subject of particular interest to contemporary intellectuals: from the Peloponnesian War for supremacy in Greece (Thucydides), through the Roman civil wars after the fall of the Republic, and the tangle of civil wars in England, France, and Germany during the early modern era, to the American Civil War (1861–1865), the first total war in modern history (Förster, 1996), or the Spanish Civil War (1936–1939), which split the whole of Europe into two ideological camps. Even so, the state of comparative research into civil wars is far from satisfactory. In contrast, for example, to comparative research into revolutions, which resulted in important studies even before World War II, civil wars have remained a poor relation in terms of systematic research. It is only very recently that this situation has changed, a vital stimulus being provided by efforts to obtain the earliest possible warning of impending civil wars and take preventive action to contain them.

There are a number of reasons why research neglected civil wars for so many years. One lies in the very nature of the subject. Civil wars are not only extremely complex chains of events that are difficult to record in empirical terms but—because of their intrinsic dynamics and often inconclusive outcome—they also defy the theoretical approaches of causal or functional analysis customary in the comparative social sciences. Ultimately, each civil war seems to be a special case. Another factor is that they cannot be clearly assigned to any particular academic discipline. Whereas wars between nations are clearly the province of political scientists dealing in "international relations," responsibility for research into civil war lies not only with political scientists but also with sociologists, ethnologists, and historians—in other words, strictly speaking, with none of them. The balance of political power and the general climate of research that is closely associated with it may also have played a part. While the nation-state still enjoyed unchallenged sovereignty, the bulk of social scientists tended, when in doubt, to interpret violent internal clashes more as "vertical" power conflicts than as civil wars on the "horizontal" level. As has already been noted, during the Cold War the hand of the superpowers was seen everywhere and the local nature of violent rebellions and riots was played down (David, 1996/1997:552). And indeed, the frequent close interplay between external and internal causes of conflict (examples being the Vietnam War and the later invasion of Afghanistan by Soviet troops) does make it difficult to classify civil wars unambiguously. The increasing degree of transnational networking and the rise of globalization has meant, in any case, that from the 1980s onward it seemed to be only a matter of time before the distinction between international and intranational wars became redundant.

Nevertheless, it would be wrong to give the impression that the growing academic interest in civil wars during the 1990s had to start, as it were, from scratch. There are four identifiable earlier lines of research which these most recent efforts at a systematic recording and analysis of civil wars could follow.

The first of these comprises monographs on individual civil wars, most—though not all—of which were written by historians. This is a rich and meticulously prepared source of empirical material, though in almost every case these monographs are individual case studies which rarely make any claim to a more general, universal scope.

In a way at the opposite extreme from these case-by-case studies are the works of the "civil violence" researchers from the 1960s and 1970s. In the United States, this period is closely associated with the names of T. Gurr, I. and R. Feierabend and H. Eckstein, while the main exponent of this approach in Germany was E. Zimmermann (Eckstein, 1965; Gurr, 1970; Feierabend, Feierabend, & Gurr, 1972; Zimmermann, 1981). The specific background to these works was formed by the student protests that occurred during those years, additionally reinforced by race riots in the United States. The studies associated with the "civil violence" school share three features in common. The first is the central importance of social-psychological assumptions (such as the concept of relative deprivation). Secondly, and this is the main difference from the individual case studies, these works were all comparative studies covering numerous countries. Data on those countries were systematically collected with a view to using statistical methods to ascertain correlations between certain structures and developments on the one hand and the variables of frequency and intensity of violence on the other. The third characteristic was that, in this context, the concept of civil war arose only as a variation, involving the particularly widespread, organized, and longer-term use of violence, while otherwise remaining vague and insubstantial.

The theme of internal conflict was also approached from a completely different angle by a group of researchers, primarily sociologists and anthropologists, who looked at it from the standpoint of rebellious ethnic minorities. Here again, specific trends and events provided the stimulus, especially the unexpected "ethnic revival" from the 1970s onward. In both the 1970s and the 1980s, a great many works appeared, some of them dealing with individual cases and others primarily comparative, which investigated the causes and the development of ethnic protest in the course of time (Hechter, 1975; Esman, 1977; Waldmann, 1989). Initially, these studies were mainly confined to those marginal areas of Europe that had never been entirely subjugated by the central governments that theoretically controlled them (Corsica, Northern Ireland, the Basque country), but studies later extended to include the Balkans, the countries of Eastern Europe after their liberation from the Soviet yoke, and eventually the entire Third World, where ethnic conflict is now the most widespread type of civil war (Brown et al., 1997). This line of research, however, is concerned not only with organized mass violence—war, in other words—but also with the many variations of "low intensity war."

Fourthly, we have conventional research into war, which again usually deals with "civil war" under a separate heading. It is frequently emphasized here, however, that this distinction is a purely formal one, and that, structurally, there is no fundamental difference between international and intranational wars (as a representative of this approach see Gantzel, 1997:258). It follows that any serious investigation of the subject must begin with the question of whether civil wars have characteristics of their own that distinguish them from wars between nations.

III. GENERAL CHARACTERIZATION; SUBTYPES

In purely phenotypical terms, it is striking that civil wars generally last longer than international wars, that they are fought with exceptional savagery and brutality, and that peace settlements are achieved only with the greatest difficulty and often prove short-lived (Licklider, 1993:8; Walter, 1999b:1).

The fact that civil wars are fought with unusual ruthlessness is a basic concept that can be traced far back in history. Even in Caesar, we read that it was customary during the Roman civil war to compel recalcitrant cities to capitulate by destroying their granaries and seed, and depriving them of their water supply by diverting rivers and poisoning wells. One of the first civil wars of the modern age, in which the province of the Vendée, faithful to Church and King, rose to resist the revolutionary, centralizing Jacobins from Paris (1793–1797), gave rise to the term *la guerre à l'outrance*—war to the death (cf. Schulz, 1985:11). Similar accounts date from the American Civil War of some fifty years later, in which partisan warfare flared up behind the lines, featuring denunciations and extortion against the civilian population while the young men fighting for the opposite side were shot in the back, hanged or poisoned (Fellman, 1989). In more recent times, mass killings, mass rapes, and mass expulsions followed the collapse of the Yugoslav state, with particularly bloody ethnic clashes taking place in the struggle for supremacy in the central republic of Bosnia-Herzegovina, once again recalling Blaise Pascal's dictum that a country could never experience anything worse than civil war (Janssen, 1982:577). How reliable are these judgments, and what possible explanations are there for the unusual cruelty and bitterness generally associated with civil wars?

As yet, we have no firmly established academic discipline of civil war studies that might provide an answer to this question. Combining the scattered references, we come up with an outline explanation consisting of three time sequences: civil wars are particularly harsh and cruel first because of the common past shared by the parties to the conflict, secondly because of the specific features of the current conflict situation, and thirdly because of the prospects for the future conjured up by these events (cf. also Waldmann, 1998:18ff.).

Regarding the first point, the sharing of a common past, it is important to discard any idea that human hatred has been primarily or exclusively directed against virtual strangers. Frequently, the exact opposite is true. Georg Simmel called attention years ago to the fact that minor differences between closely associated and otherwise similar individuals or groups can give rise to particularly violent animosities (Simmel, 1968:204). Taking the point much further, H. M. Enzensberger's crisp summary was that the detested other always starts out as a neighbor, and it is only when larger communities have formed that the stranger beyond the frontiers becomes the declared enemy (Enzensberger, 1993:11). It is no coincidence that most acts of criminal violence are directed against a member of the perpetrator's own family or some other closely associated individual. Civil wars is often metaphorically equated with a family feud, in which men find themselves fighting against their own brothers or other kin. Geographical and social closeness does not necessarily generate sympathy, but it does result in specialized knowledge of one's neighbors' weaknesses and vulnerability. Only those who, like the Bosnian Serbs, had lived in the closest proximity with Muslims over many years could know that acts of rape would dishonor not only the victims but also their husbands and their entire families, making it impossible for them to remain in the vicinity.

Not only the past, however, but also the present conflict situation contains latent factors that help to increase the bitterness of the struggle. There are two possible configurations here: either one part of the population revolts against a reasonably intact central government to demand the radical restructuring of the state and/or more rights; or the state is caught up in a temporary or longer-term process of disintegration, so that there is no certainty what the future balance of power will be between groups that have hitherto been united under the central government. In the former case, where a group revolts against an intact state, there is an obvious imbalance of forces (on the following, see King, 1997:40ff.). A state which is still functional not only has greater financial, human, and military resources than the rebels but, in general, also enjoys the advantage of legitimacy as the established institution (Eberwein, 1997:271). In order to offset this superiority, the rebels need a higher level of commitment and a far greater than average spirit of self-sacrifice, while the representatives of government for their part will do all they can in the way of repression to prevent the rebels becoming able to fight a war on an equal footing. In general, then, the asymmetrical initial situation triggers dynamics of conflict which is difficult to control.

The alternative situation—where the collapse or sudden weakening of the governmental power gives rise to general fear and uncertainty as to the likely future course of events—has often been described as the "security dilemma" (Walter & Snyder, 1999). Whereas the power of the state, spanning all the various social groups and strata, previously guaranteed internal peace, this can no longer be taken for granted. The various groups become aware of their lack of protection and wonder how far they can trust other social groups not to take advantage of the new situation by seizing the residual machinery of state in a *coup d'état* or launching a violent attack upon them. The dilemma lies in the fact that the various groups' efforts to equip themselves with a minimal defense (by buying arms, raising militias, etc.) necessarily cause a deterioration in the internal social climate and increase the risk of an outbreak or escalation of armed hostilities (Snyder & Jervis, 1999:15).

The final factor contributing to the "all or nothing" civil war mentality is the prospect of the postwar future as it appears to all the participants. Apart from the special case of secession, they know that they will be left with no alternative but to continue living together within a state and finding some kind of compromise (Licklider, 1993:4ff.). In contrast to wars between states, in which the occupying power, in the short or long run, withdraws from the conquered territory to its own, this cannot happen in civil wars where both sides share one territory. In this case, victory or defeat will determine for many years to come which faction exercises control, holds the upper hand politically and economically, and shapes the identity of the country (Bowyer Bell, 1972:217ff.). Even in the event of a negotiated solution, the better prospects of political success will lie with whichever party has been able to weaken its opponents as much as possible, militarily and —not least—numerically.

Having considered the exceptional brutality that is the most striking general characteristic of civil wars (and at the same time offers a kaleidoscopic reflection of most of their other features), we are faced with the question of the subtypes into which this type of war is divided. A distinction is often made between antiregime wars and those fought for ethnic/ nationalistic autonomy or wars of secession (cf. Table II-2-4.1 and Ferdowsi, 1996:6). Whereas the former subtype is primarily a class war within a society, aimed at a fundamental reorganization of state and economy, the main focus of the latter is the balance of power between different ethnic groups (Scherrer, 1993). Although these two types of conflict can, in the classic case, be clearly distinguished from one another in terms of aims and leading collective actors, in fact they often merge into one another. In Latin America, for example, it is not unusual for protest movements ultimately driven by socioeconomic disadvantage to have an ethnic label attached to them in the interests of a better public image. The weakness of the binomial classification is that it allows only for politically motivated civil wars. It should be extended to include a third subtype, "community civil wars," which includes those ethnic, religious, racial, or economic disputes, often associated today with the massive use of violence, that take place below or outside the political arena.

A common procedure in the keeping of war records is to make distinctions by macroregions (cf. Table II-2-4.1). Although this approach is primarily suited to providing an overview of the quantitative geographical distribution of wars, it can also serve as a basis for assumptions about their presumed causes. Especially in connection with the classification referred to initially, it may very well make sense to inquire which type of civil war occurs particularly frequently in which region, and why. Whether this could be taken to the point of identifying separate African, Latin American, etc. types of civil war, as sometimes happens (Engel & Mehler, 1998:142), is however dubious.

A third proposed classification, only rarely discussed hitherto, distinguishes between regular and irregular civil wars. Essential criteria here are whether regular troops participate in the fighting, whether a political leadership and clear-cut front lines can be identified, whether certain basic rules of warfare are being observed, and whether political and military responsibilities are defined (cf. van Creveld, 1991:ch. 3). Civil wars have an inherent tendency to become increasingly irregular. On the other hand, we have recently seen civil wars, such as that in El Salvador, where a degree of coordinated political and military procedure was observed on both sides to the end. The distinction is mainly of interest in terms of a peace settlement to put an end to such conflicts, which is much easier to arrive at in regular wars than in irregular ones.

IV. CAUSES

The question of the origin of civil wars is a debated area of research, still containing many areas of uncertainty. The only point on which all agree is that monocausal theories generally prove inadequate; in addition, there is no apparent consensus on the optimum research strategy. In some cases, it seems doubtful whether it makes any sense at all to try to come up with a general theory of civil war and whether it would not be better to concentrate more on the analysis of subtypes such as ethnic/nationalistic conflicts (David, 1996/97:575). Nor is there any agreement about the degree of abstraction of the model explanations to be developed. For example, the explanatory formula favored by the AKUF, which holds that wars (including civil wars) since 1945 have ultimately arisen from the clash between bourgeois capitalist sociation on the one hand and traditional or prebourgeois community forms on the other, is criticized as being too general and reductionist (Albrecht, 1997:268). Another unresolved issue concerns the distinction between causal theories based on structures and those based on actors. The criticism advanced several decades ago by H. Eckstein—that most forms of research overemphasized structural data and disregarded the conduct of the actors in the process of the genesis of war—is as justified now as it was then (Eckstein, 1965:146ff.). A final problem is that most of the relevant studies deal with the subject of "violent conflict" in general, so that they are of only limited value in drawing conclusions about the narrower subject of civil wars.

Despite these shortcomings and points of contention, there are five sets of variables that can be identified here which, in the present writer's view, must exist in order for civil war to arise. Some are taken from existing research while others are the result of the author's own empirical research undertaken in Europe and Latin America (cf. Brown, 1997:3ff.; David, 1996/1997; Spelten, 1999; Waldmann, 1989; Waldmann, 1995:345ff.; Waldmann & Reinares, 1999).

The first complex of factors relates to the state. Civil wars break out where (and only where) the authority of the state has been greatly weakened or the state is in the process of dissolution (Holsti, 1996:ch. 6). This is the main reason for the concentration of civil wars in the underdeveloped regions: Africa, the Middle East, South and Southeast Asia, and more recently in the territory of the former Soviet Union as well. The states in these regions—often artificially created, corrupt, and lacking in strong foundations—have never been able to achieve a position of power comparable to that of the states of central and western Europe. This argument is directed at both the exterior and the interior of central government. As far as the external effect is concerned, very few of these states have been able to establish what Max Weber regards as the central feature of modern governance: a monopoly on the legitimate exercise of violence. But these countries are also poorly placed in terms of the inner allegiance of their populations to the government and state. In most cases, their true sympathies lie with a smaller social entity—the tribe, the clan, or the village, their own ethnic group, the local region—while the state and its bureaucracy are perceived as alien and hostile. This internal divide becomes even wider if the country's leaders try to impose obedience and loyalty. Both the absence of a monopoly on violence and the lack of governmental legitimacy in the underdeveloped regions makes them extremely prone to internal revolts and feuds.

Such conflicts, however, do not break out everywhere: they are especially likely in those societies with extreme internal tensions and social divides (Waldmann, 1995:347). These tensions and divisions may be social, religious, ethnic, or political in nature. Their significance is that, basically, there is no unified national population: the society concerned breaks down into a variety of social strata, macrogroups, or regions, each of which is mistrustful of the others. In the case of this feature, again, the objective situation is not in itself sufficient—it also has to be perceived by those concerned as an element of tension. The great majority of the world's states are multiethnic, and many of them suffer from extreme inequality in the distribution of income and wealth across society. This can result in conflicts, though it need not. It is only when the materially disadvantaged or the ethnic minorities perceive their situation as unjust and discriminatory that armed conflict may break out.

This kind of subjective perception of the situation is particularly likely when the various groups or strata already have a past record of repeated hostilities (Spelten, 1999:130). Experience of early violent clashes stored in the collective memory is not infrequently a contributory factor in conjuring up the same situation all over again. Communities below state level have long memories; in some circumstances, even decades of apparent calm are insufficient to wipe out the recollection of a bloody conflict of long ago or a shameful defeat. The Troubles in Northern Ireland, which have simmered over so many years, offer a good example of the difficulty of breaking free of antagonistic perceptions and behavior patterns once they have become historically engrained.

Social and political change is a fourth necessary condition. Even conditions of extreme social inequality and ethnic discrimination may be accepted without protest over long periods if the balance of power is clear and the disadvantaged have become accustomed to their lot. In most cases, dissatisfaction and the spirit of protest are aroused by structural changes—and, in some cases, external influences as well—that undermine the status quo and can rapidly escalate into a broader conflict (Waldmann, 1989:38ff.; 76). Such factors include, for example, a shift in the demographic ratio between rival groups, especially if resources are in short supply because of a high overall rate of population increase (Dießenbacher, 1998). They may also include the collapse of old sectors of the economy and the emergence of new ones, serious ecological damage, and the social decline of certain groups and classes. Social or political change can produce sudden effects that are nothing short of dramatic: the unexpected fall of the government or disintegration of the state, an influx of refugees from other countries, or massive external interference. In such situations, the rapid spread of fear and uncertainty can create precisely that explosive social climate known as the "security dilemma," referred to earlier (Walter, 1999b:304ff.).

Whether or not violence actually breaks out in such precarious situations depends to a large extent on the social and political elites (Brown, 1997:17ff.; David, 1996/1997:562ff.). They are capable of sowing the seeds of additional mistrust and either stoking the growing fires of hatred or suppressing the unrest; they may steer a course of confrontation or seek to come to terms with other subelites. The conduct of the elites is, in turn, significantly influenced by the strategic power calculations of important individuals, with political leaders perhaps wondering whether their disliked promoderation rivals can be neutralized by a selective escalation of the conflict. Quite often, however, the inherent dynamics of events, especially the wildfire spread of violence, may rapidly invalidate such initial calculations, with the result that those who instigated the conflict often find themselves worse off at the end than they were in the beginning.

It does appear important, in any event, that the motives and emotions of large groups among the population should coincide with the plans and interests of significant sections of the elites. Otherwise, it is unlikely that armed conflicts will escalate into civil wars.

This list of the five complexes of causal factors in itself says nothing about their time sequence, the process by which civil wars come into being. The first three are structural variables, whose effects are heightened by sociopolitical change and the reaction of the elites. If we then assume that more or less arbitrary events or developments can trigger the conflict, we arrive at a three-part classification of variables: structural causes; factors that promote or inhibit conflict; trigger events and immediate causes (Engel & Mehler, 1998:164).

In general terms, academic research has not yet given much thought to the genesis of conflict—which factor becomes particularly important at which time? As far as this question is concerned, a more recent, practical branch of conflict and civil war research may provide some assistance. This is research into prevention projects. Plans and proposals for prompt external action to preempt the threat of a massive outbreak of violence originally arose out of the failure of traditional forms of international crisis management during the wars in Somalia, Yugoslavia, and Rwanda, and are now enjoying a boom (Matthies, 1996). Such plans involve a far from simple sequence of operational steps: first the timely identification of the threat of an armed conflict; then the appropriate preparation of the briefing, to ensure that the warning message is taken seriously by politicians, international bodies, and the public; and finally the dispelling of reservations and the necessary work of persuasion to ensure that something is actually done. What mainly interests us in this context is the cognitive aspect of the multistage process (Krummenacher, Baechler, & Schmeidel, 1999).

When the aim is to anticipate the outbreak of violence, reference to general causal models containing a list of potential conflict-promoting and conflict-inhibiting factors has proven inadequate, especially since the original causes of such tensions are often quickly overtaken by the course of the conflict. What is also needed is a precise vision of the time sequence in which each successive stage of escalation follows the last, to identify the optimum timing for preventive action. Some of the teams working on these questions, such as the Swiss FAST (Early Analysis of Tensions and Identification of Facts) organization, have adopted a policy of direct monitoring of the course of events during critical phases ("real-time monitoring," cf. Krummenacher et al., 1999:93ff.; Baechler, 1997). At present, a rough three-part sequence grid is still accepted as satisfactory: a) conflicts which are resolved by lawful means; b) occasional resort to violence; c) outbreaks of massive violence. However, if efforts in this area continue, high-differentiation threshold models can be expected to evolve in the foreseeable future.

V. DIRECT EFFECTS AND STRUCTURAL CONSEQUENCES

Although there has been no shortage of attempts to elucidate the origins and genesis of civil wars, little attempt has been made hitherto to analyze their consequences systematically. The pages that follow provide a few key phrases and ideas in this connection, though these are as yet unsubstantiated by any broader empirical findings. It seems useful here to distinguish between the direct, short-term and the longer-term, structural effects of civil wars.

Civil warfare may escalate gradually, but it not infrequently begins with a single shock that abruptly polarizes society. This polarization has a social-psychological and a military/geographic aspect (Waldmann, 1995:349). As far as the former is concerned, deep gulfs suddenly open up between the various macrogroups or classes. Ancient fears are rekindled, past experience of mutual disappointments and betrayals are recalled. In this situation, those who argue for compromise and mutual trust may easily be dismissed as naïve, while the initiative passes to the hardliners who have an interest in escalating the conflict (Thucydides:262).

Collective moods might evaporate again; but it is the geographical and demographic consequences it entails that give the new situation an irreversible momentum. Each of the emerging potential parties to a civil war tries to secure territorial backing. Before long, the once united territory of the state has been split up among the rival groups. In general, each group selects as its geographical power base the territory where it previously enjoyed a demographic majority, while parts of the country in which it was numerically underrepresented tend to be abandoned. The general uncertainty, and the need not to concede any advantage in the new situation, gives these conflicts a special initial impetus and bitterness. At a later stage, however, when each group has firmly secured a part of the territory, such wars can congeal over long periods into positional struggles (Hanf, 1990:431ff.).

The splitting of the national territory into different areas of domination compels many people to leave their traditional homelands. Civil wars give rise to massive movements of refugees, with between a third and half of the population sometimes relocating (and in some cases doing so several times). This applies not only to ethnic/nationalistic wars (Lebanon or Bosnia-Herzegovina) but also to antiregime wars. In Colombia, for example, a major landowner will find it hard to stay on in a region that seems likely to be occupied by a Marxist guerrilla group. The currents of migration generally move away from the territory in which those affected, as a minority, have reason to fear repression toward a city or region where their faction has the upper hand. If fast-shifting front lines mean that there are no longer any safe areas within the country, the refugees may spill over the borders into neighboring countries, which then become at risk of being infected by the war (Cerny, 1998:58).

Violence is contagious. While many authors agree with this basic view, attempts to elucidate the escalating inherent dynamics of civil war have been rare. In some cases, this may be attributable to the same causes that were identified in section 3 as being responsible for the particular cruelty and bitterness of this type of war, such as the "security dilemma," which compels all parties involved in an unresolved initial situation to demonstrate their fighting potential or their unequal strength and represents the starting signal in a race to cause damage to each other. In addition, though, there are two other motive forces which ensure that once war has broken out it is sustained and perpetuated: themes of vengeance and retaliation, and substantial material interests of the kind to which research refers as "civil war economics."

While social anthropologists are fully familiar with the effectiveness of revenge as an institution to promote violence in traditional societies (Girard, 1972), social scientists working on contemporary societies largely exclude it from their calculations, as if the governmental prohibition on dueling and feuding had also eliminated the associated motive of violence. But on closer study of the bloody conflicts in Colombia, southern Africa and the former Yugoslavia, and Northern Ireland too, there is no mistaking the central role that the concept of vengeance, the idea of "unsettled accounts," the rule of "an eye for an eye" or "tit for tat" play in the thinking of mutually hostile ethnic groups. In many cases, this thinking is underpinned by a particular code of honor or exaggerated by religious ideas.

Material considerations provide the second driving force behind the continuation and escalation of violence. Irrespective of the political or ideological aims they pursue, rebel organizations need a minimal material resource base if they are to survive (Waldmann, 1995:354). They obtain such resources through "revolutionary taxes" imposed on the population, plundering campaigns against their enemies, and in some cases criminal raids. What was originally justified as a mere means to a supposedly noble end can easily become an end in itself. G. Elwert coined the term "violence markets" to alert us to a type of warlord who is also an entrepreneur, turning the use of violence into a business (Elwert, 1999). Similarly, in a recently published work, J. C. Rufin et al. showed that guerrilla bands are extremely inventive when it comes to turning a general climate of fear and uncertainty to economic advantage. Their methods of self-enrichment range from systematic plundering of the civilian population through highway robbery, protection rackets, and illegal trading in especially valuable and in some cases illegal goods (gold, diamonds, or drugs) to the exploitation of the generosity of exile communities and the unauthorized administration of international aid in cash or kind (Rufin, 1999ff.; cf. also Keen, 1998).

How important a part do external influences and activities play in determining the course of the conflict, whether in damping it down or inflaming it further? This question has deliberately not been touched on the preceding pages, because—in the present writer's view—there is no easy answer. During the Cold War era, it was assumed that Third World states could be controlled and manipulated from outside to an unlimited extent, but experience, painful in some cases (Somalia), has brought the realization that external influence can neither create the conditions for a civil war nor bring one to an ultimate conclusion. Ultimately, it is the parties to the civil war that determine events: at best, their desires and intentions can be pushed in one direction or the other by external pressure or offers of outside aid. If the purpose of outside intervention is to bring about peace as quickly as possible—something that can by no means be taken for granted—the prospects of doing so are greatest at the start of the conflict or when the warring parties begin to show signs of fatigue, not during the peak period of hostilities when the combatants have sunk their teeth into each other beyond recall (cf. section 6). Furthermore, as the above example of humanitarian aid demonstrates, even international activities based on the best of intentions may in fact produce the very opposite effect from that desired, serving the interests of the warlords and helping to perpetuate the armed conflict.

"Civil" or "internal" wars generally leave behind them a ruined economy and infrastructure, an empty treasury, and an impoverished population. The more developed a country was previously, the "more destructive" is the economic impact: it affects not only ports, roads, and industrial plant but also the services sector (banks and tourism, for example). The quality of public life is permanently impaired; schools and universities close; cafés and shops disappear; associations and clubs go into decline, because people have to deal with the more urgent considerations of survival. The effect of general impoverishment is all the more disturbing when various individuals and groups, the "war profiteers," clearly know how to profit from the general chaos and decline and thus enjoy lives of relative prosperity. Civil wars, then, do not automatically dismantle social barriers but merely shift them. The old upper class and upper middle class, whose qualifications and skills are geared to peacetime and no longer in demand, are replaced by groups who have risen socially from the ranks through their understanding of the mechanics of warfare or the war economy. The effects of such social conflicts on people's moral attitudes are unclear. Undoubtedly, many years of civil strife have an effect on the general perception of good and evil, and what is beneficial or damaging to the community. But lamentations about the moral collapse of societies afflicted by civil wars must be treated with a degree of caution. As confirmed by studies of the Lebanon and Northern Ireland, a superficial adjustment to the looser standards that prevail during civil wars does not necessarily mean that deeper-seated ethical and moral attitudes have been similarly affected (Hanf, 1990:581ff.; Waldmann, 1989:343ff.).

VI. ENDING THE WAR

Like efforts to nip wars in the bud by preventive action, the desire and repeated calls to help end them by way of a negotiated peace have produced a certain amount of literature. Since no war can or should last for ever, runs the argument, humanitarian considerations demand an effort to bring them to a rapid conclusion and work toward an early peace (Matthies, 1994:67). This somewhat optimistic view is opposed by those who warn against overestimating the viability of negotiated solutions (David, 1996/1997:567ff.). Which side is right?

The available empirical data tend to confirm the difficulty of bringing civil wars to a mutually acceptable conclusion. Of the armed conflicts that took place between 1940 and 1990, 55 percent of international wars but only 20 percent of internal hostilities were ended by negotiation. The majority were decided by victory and defeat, or ended as a result of one faction's withdrawal. Where a peace treaty has been concluded between the parties to a civil war, the end of hostilities has often proven short-lived. In half of the cases officially concluded by peace treaties, hostilities flared up again later (whereas this occurred in only 15 percent of cases decided by victory and defeat: cf. David, 1996/1997:568; Walter, 1999a:38ff., 59ff.). Examples of armistices or peace settlements which were not consistently observed can be found during the 1990s in Rwanda, Liberia, and Angola, and more recently in Northern Ireland and Congo Kinshasa.

Looking into the question of why negotiated solutions to civil wars are so difficult to achieve and often prove untenable, we find a number of explanatory factors (King, 1997:29ff.). The first is the efforts of the rebel leaders to safeguard their position of power at all costs. The prospect of having to embark upon an unpredictable process of political change in the event of a compromise quite often prompts them to cling to a hard-line attitude that consolidates existing antagonisms. The warring factions' lack of internal discipline and cohesion can also become a problem. As well as "doves," who are ready to negotiate, there is usually a party of intractable "hawks," stigmatizing any concession to the enemy as betrayal of the cause. Unless they can be persuaded or compelled to obey the leadership of their factions, which is ready to negotiate, the prospects of implementing the peace agreement are poor. In general, it would be a mistake to believe that the various factions soon become weary of armed hostilities and are simply waiting for a favorable opportunity to return to peacetime conditions as soon as possible (Krumwiede & Waldmann, 1998:327). Once they have adjusted to being on a war footing and settled into it, they—unlike the population at large—have no trouble in living with it and, as we saw in the previous section, off it. This applies particularly, as W. Zartman has shown, to the rebel camp (Marxist guerrilla bands or rebellious minority groups) for whom fighting the government can become their life's work (Zartman, 1993:25). For the same reason, the parties to the violence are usually all too willing to resume hostilities if the peace terms fail to meet their expectations. Confronted as they are by the uncertain prospects for their future once they have laid down their arms, and with no certainty of where their future livelihood is to come from, they may indeed find this the more attractive option.

Various lessons can be learned from this list of obstacles to peace agreements. On careful scrutiny of the relevant literature, there appear to be four basic conditions that have to be met if peace negotiations are to have some prospect of success more durable than a temporary armistice (cf. Licklider, 1993:14 and ch. 13; King, 1997:ch. 3; Krumwiede & Waldmann, 1998:325ff.; Walter, 1999b:305ff.). These conditions relate to the subject of negotiations, the parties to be involved in them, the correct timing, and the action that will have to be taken to implement the results of the negotiations.

It seems important to start by limiting the definition of the subject to be discussed. Is it just a matter of ending hostilities, or will the discussions also cover the rules that are to govern the future distribution of political power? Is the political autonomy of one part of the country an issue that can be addressed or one to be avoided? Will the negotiations be confined to the points that originally triggered the conflict, or should they also include subsequent problems generated by the conflict itself? Unless a minimum of consensus can be achieved regarding the points to be included in the negotiations, there is a high probability that the parties will find themselves talking at cross purposes and the negotiations will break up with nothing achieved. In general, it is assumed that interests and political positions are more negotiable than matters of ethnic or religious identity

(Krumwiede, 1998:54ff.); however, in view of the manipulative way in which many groups exploit the label of "ethnicity" or "religion," this assumption should be reviewed on a case-by-case basis.

Considering the difficulties mentioned above in creating a minimal interest in peace among the parties to the conflict, it is very important that all the relevant actors should be included in the peace talks. Even more important in this connection than those leaders who are already willing to compromise are the hardliners, because any signal from them that they are willing to concede has an incomparably greater exemplary effect than prospects for an agreement confined to the "doves" in the various camps. If the negotiated solution implies a major change of course in the military policy of one of the parties, it may be necessary to replace the leadership. Furthermore, the success of the negotiations depends less on the compatibility of the differing aims and interests as seen from the standpoint of a neutral third party than on whether the result will satisfy the participants themselves. Their consent to the agreement will be credible and lasting only if they see that the advantages of a conciliatory attitude will outweigh any resulting disadvantages, and especially if they are not expected to accept any radical reductions in power or income.

The willingness of the warring parties to reach agreement around the negotiating table increases, especially, when they see no further hope of gaining a military victory. There is, of course, always something ambivalent about military stalemates, because at the same time they offer an ideal pretext for continuing hostilities indefinitely where necessary (Waldmann, 1995:356). For this reason, W. Zartman, who proposed the thesis that a military balance of power was the necessary precondition for negotiated solutions, added that the situation must be a "hurting stalemate," one whose high cost meant that neither side could accept it for too long (Zartman, 1993:24ff.; Krumwiede, 1998:42ff.). Again, the warring factions' tolerance threshold for "costs" (military losses and loss of political prestige, political supporters, etc.) must not be underestimated, or their readiness to concede overestimated.

Just as it does at the outset of a civil war, so too at the point of transition from war to peace, a "security dilemma" recurs. Peace means disarmament, the surrender of fortified positions and occupied territories. How confident can one party be that the others will also adhere faithfully to the arrangements made, lay down their arms, and rely on peaceful coexistence in the future? This difficult situation, in the view of B. Walter, offers the international community one of its main opportunities to make itself useful and advance the peace process (Walter, 1999b:305ff.). After all, the objective now is not to influence the basic military policy decisions of the parties to the peace treaty but systematically to disseminate information on the current state of disarmament and to ensure that each party observes the undertakings entered into. Furthermore, the aim now is to rebuild that minimum of trust between the formerly hostile groups without which their future cohabitation under a single national roof is difficult to conceive.

All these conditions for an amicable negotiated settlement presuppose, however, that there are still political and military contacts, identifiable objectives and interests, and recognizable military formations and front lines—in other words, that the hostilities still retain something resembling regularity. By contrast, if violence has permeated every pore of a society, and is being used without restraint by what is now an unknown number of collective actors for their own purposes—in other words, if the forces of irregularity have clearly gained the upper hand—there will be little to be gained by peace talks, however often they may be convened and held (the author is thinking here of the specific case of Colombia, cf. Waldmann, 1997).

VII. DESIDERATA

Viewed in simplified terms, the still relatively new discipline of systematic civil war research breaks down into three main strands: studies primarily concerned with the causes and functions of civil wars; a second strand which focuses on procedures and structural changes during such wars and in their aftermath; and a third where the main issue is the possibility of preventing wars or bringing them to a swift and bloodless conclusion. The author's academic preference is for broader and deeper studies of the second type. The original causes and instigators of civil wars customarily fade into the background during hostilities, because the war is self-propagating, whereas its functions can be eagerly debated depending on one's own point of view. Before considering such general and comprehensive questions, it would be necessary to know more about the wars themselves: by what rules and through which stages of escalation they evolve, what the dynamics of violence will be once freed from the shackles of state control, how far they infect and affect the other structural areas of society, what part key actors and key moments play in these procedures, to what extent—alongside the frequently cited dynamics of violence—increasing fatigue and a desire for peace have dynamics of their own, etc. To date, we have only tentative answers to any of these questions, no real knowledge. If we could manage to accumulate such knowledge, then it would also be easier to prevent civil hostilities or control them more effectively than has been possible in the past.

REFERENCES

Albrecht, Ulrich. (1997). Neuartige Kriege? *Ethik und Sozialwissenschaften, 8*(3), 267–269.

Baechler, Günther. (1997). *FAST: Frühanalyse von Spannungen und Tatsachenermittlung.* Abschlußbericht zum Pilotprojekt FAST, Bern: SFS.

Bernecker, Walther L. (1998). 'Reconstruction' und Franquismus. Folgen und Wirkungen des US-amerikanischen und Spanischen Bürgerkriegs im Vergleich. In Heinrich Krumwiede & Peter Waldmann (Eds.), *Bürgerkriege: Folgen und Regulierungsmöglichkeiten* (pp. 133–154). Baden-Baden: Nomos Verlag.

Bowyer Bell, John B. (1972). Social Patterns and Lessons: The Irish Case. In Robin Higham (Ed.), *Civil Wars in the Twentieth Century* (pp. 217–228). Lexington: University Press of Kentucky.

Brown, Michael E. (1997). The Causes of Internal Conflict. In Michael E. Brown, Owen R. Coté, Jr., Sean M. Lynn-Jones & Steven E. Miller (Eds.), *Nationalism and Ethnic Conflict* (pp. 3–25). Cambridge/London: MIT Press.

Brown, Michael E., Owen R. Coté, Jr., Sean M. Lynn-Jones, Steven E. Miller (Eds.) (1997). *Nationalism and Ethnic Conflict.* Cambridge/London: MIT Press.

Burkhardt, Johannes. (1992). *Der Dreißigjährige Krieg.* Frankfurt: Suhrkamp.

Cerny, Philip G. (1998). Neomedievalism, Civil War and the New Security Dilemma: Globalisation as Durable Disorder. *Civil Wars, 1*(1), 36–64.

Creveld, Martin van. (1991). *The Transformation of War.* New York: The Free Press.

David, Steven R. (1996/1997). Internal War. Causes and Cures. *World Politics, 49*(3), 552–580.

Dießenbacher, Hartmut. (1998). *Kriege der Zukunft. Die Bevölkerungsexplosion gefährdet den Frieden.* München/Wien: Hanser.

Eberwein, Wolf-Dieter. (1997). Quantität und Qualität—beide gehören zusammen. *Ethik und Sozialwissenschaften, 8*(3), 270–272.

Eckstein, Harry. (1965). On the Etiology of Internal Wars. *History and Theory, 3*(2), pp. 133–163.

Elwert, Georg. (1998). Markets of Violence. *Sociologicus, 1* (Beiheft/Supplement), 85–102.

Engel, Ulf, & Andreas Mehler. (1998). Lücken schließen: Der Beitrag der Politikwissenschaft zur Analyse und Früherkennung gewaltsamer Konflikte in Afrika. In Ulf Engel & Andreas Mehler (Eds.), *Gewaltsame Konflikte und ihre Prävention in Afrika* (pp. 135–169). Hamburg: Institut für Afrikaforschung.

Enzensberger, Hans Magnus. (1993). *Aussichten auf den Bürgerkrieg.* Frankfurt: Suhrkamp.

Esman, Milton. ed. (1977). *Ethnic Conflict in the Western World.* Ithaca/London: Cornell University Press.

Feierabend, Ivo K., Rosalind Feierabend, & Ted Robert Gurr (Eds.) (1972). *Anger, Violence and Politics. Theories and Research*. Englewood Cliffs: Prentice-Hall.

Fellman, Michael. (1988). *Inside War. The Guerilla Conflict in Missouri during the American Civil War*. New York: Oxford University Press.

Ferdowsi, Mir A. (1996). *Dimensionen und Ursachen der Drittweltkriege—eine Bestandsaufnahme*. München: Arbeitspapiere zu Problemen der Internationalen Politik und der Entwicklungsländerforschung, No. 19.

Förster, Stig. (1996). Vom Volkskrieg zum totalen Krieg? Der Amerikanische Bürgerkrieg von 1861–1865, der Deutsch-Französische Krieg 1870/71 und die Anfänge moderner Kriegsführung. In Walter L. Bernecker & Volker Dotterweich (Eds.), *Deutschland in den internationalen Beziehungen des 19. und 20. Jahrhunderts* (pp. 71–92). München: Ernst Vögel.

Gantzel, Klaus Jürgen. (1997). Kriegsursachen—Tendenzen und Perspektiven. Ethik und Sozialwissenschaften. *Streitforum für Erwägungskultur, 8*(3), 257–266.

Gantzel, Klaus Jürgen, & Torsten Schwinghammer. (1995). *Die Kriege nach dem Zweiten Weltkrieg 1945–1992. Daten und Tendenzen*. Münster: Lit.

Girard, René. (1972). *Das Heilige und die Gewalt*. Frankfurt: Fischer.

Gurr, Ted Robert. (1978). *Why Men Rebel*. Princeton: Princeton University Press.

Gurr, Ted Robert, & Barbara Harff. (1994). *Ethnic Conflict in World Politics*. Boulder: Westview Press.

Hanf, Theodor. (1998). *Koexistenz im Krieg. Staatszerfall und Entstehung einer Nation*. Baden-Baden: Nomos Verlag.

Hechter, Michael. (1975). *Internal Colonialism. The Celtic Fringe in British National Development (1536–1966)*. London: Routledge and Kegan Paul.

Holsti, Kalevi J. (1996). *The State, War, and the State of War*. Cambridge: Cambridge University Press.

Horrowitz, Donald. (1985). *Ethnic Groups in Conflict*. Los Angeles: University of California Press.

Janssen, Wilhelm. (1982). Artikel Krieg. In Otto Brunner, Werner Conze & Reinhart Koselleck (Eds.), *Geschichtliche Grundbegriffe. Historisches Lexikon zur politisch-sozialen Sprache in Deutschland, Vol. 3* (pp. 567–615). Stuttgart: Klett-Cotta.

Jongman, Albert J. (1999/2008). Downward Trend in Armed Conflicts Reversed? *PIOOM Report, 9*(1), 28–34.

Kaldor, Mary. (1998). *New and Old Wars. Organized Violence in a Global Era*. Stanford: Stanford University Press.

Keane, John. (1996). *Reflections on Violence*. London and New York: Verso.

Keen, David. (1998). *The Economic Functions of Violence in Civil Wars*. Oxford/New York: Oxford University Press (Adelphi paper 320).

Kende, Istvan. (1971). Twenty-five Years of Local Wars. *Journal of Peace Research, 8*, 5–22.

King, Charles. (1997). *Ending Civil Wars*. Oxford/New York: Oxford University Press (Adelphi Paper 308).

Krummenacher, Heinz, Günther Baechler, & Susanne Schmeidl. (1998). Beitrag der Frühwarnung zur Krisenprävention. Möglichkeiten und Grenzen in Theorie und Praxis. In Friedensbericht, *Krisenprävention. Theorie und Praxis ziviler Konfliktbearbeitung* (pp. 77–97). Chur/Zürich: Rüegger.

Krumwiede, Heinrich. (1998). Regulierungsmöglichkeiten von Bürgerkriegen: Fragen und Hypothesen. In Krumwiede, Heinrich & Peter Waldmann (Eds.), *Bürgerkriege: Folgen und Regulierungsmöglichkeiten* (pp. 37–60). Baden-Baden: Nomos Verlag.

Krumwiede, Heinrich, & Peter Waldmann, Hrsg. (1998). *Bürgerkriege: Folgen und Regulierungsmöglichkeiten*. Baden-Baden: Nomos Verlag.

Licklider, Roy (Ed.) (1993). *Stopping the Killing. How Civil Wars End*. New York/London: New York University Press.

Licklider, Roy. (1995). The Consequences of Negotiated Settlements in Civil Wars. *American Political Science Review, 89*(3), 681–690.

Matthies, Volker. (1994). *Immer wieder Krieg? Wie Eindämmen? Beenden? Verhüten?* Opladen: Leske und Budrich.

Matthies, Volker. (1996). Vom reaktiven Krisenmanagement zur präventiven Konfliktbearbeitung? Aus Politik und Zeitgeschichte, Beilage zur Wochenzeitung. *Das Parlament, 33–34*/96, 19–28.

Münkler, Herfried. (2000). *Bleiben die Staaten die Herren des Krieges? Politisches Denken. Jahrbuch 2000* (pp. 16–34), Stuttgart/Weimar: Metzler.

Rufin, Jean-Cristophe. (1998). Kriegswirtschaft in internen Konflikten. In François Jean & Jean-Cristophe Rufin (Eds.), *Ökonomie der Bürgerkriege* (pp. 15–46). Hamburg: Hamburger Edition.

Rupesinghe, Kumar, & Sanam P. Anderlini. (1998). *Civil Wars, Civil Peace. An Introduction to Conflict Resolution*. London/Chicago: Pluto Press.

Scherrer, Christian P. (1993). Der Dritte Weltkrieg. Ethnizität und die Krise der Staaten in der Dritten Welt. *Der Überblick, 3*, 29–33.

Schulz, Gerhard. (1985). Die Irregulären: Guerilla, Partisanen und die Wandlungen des Krieges seit dem 18. Jahrhundert. Eine Einführung. In Gerhard Schulz (Ed.), *Partisanen und Volkskrieg. Zur Revolutionierung des Krieges im 20. Jahrhundert* (pp. 9–35). Göttingen: Vandenhoeck und Ruprecht.

Schulz, Gerhard. (1988). Zum historischen Wandel von Revolutionsbegriff und Revolutionsverständnis. In Dieter Langewiesche (Ed.), *Revolution und Krieg. Zur Dynamik historischen Wandels seit dem 18. Jahrhundert* (pp. 189–209). Paderborn: Schöningh.

Simmel, Georg. (1968). *Untersuchungen über die Formen der Vergesellschaftung*. Berlin: Duncker & Humblot.

Small, Melvin, & David Singer. (1982). *Resort to Arms. International and Civil Wars, 1876–1980*. Beverly Hills: Sage Publications.

Snyder, Jack, & Robert Jervis. (1998). Civil War and the Security Dilemma. In Barbara F. Walter & Jack Snyder (Eds.), *Civil Wars, Insecurity, and Intervention* (pp. 15–37). New York: Columbia University Press.

Spelten, Angelika. (1998). Präventive Maßnahmen in der Entwicklungszusammenarbeit. Indikatorenkatalog zur Bestimmung des Einsatzpunktes. In Friedensbericht, *Krisenprävention. Theorie und Praxis ziviler Konfliktbearbeitung* (pp. 121–136). Chur/Zürich: Rüegger.

Thukydides: *Der Peleponnesische Krieg*. Essen: Phaidon (without year specification).

Waldmann, Peter. (1988). *Ethnischer Radikalismus. Ursachen und Folgen gewaltsamer Minderheitenkonflikte*. Opladen: Westdeutscher Verlag.

Waldmann, Peter. (1995). Gesellschaften im Bürgerkrieg. Zur Eigendynamik entfesselter Gewalt. *Zeitschrift für Politik, 42*(4), 343–368.

Waldmann, Peter. (1997). Veralltäglichung von Gewalt: Das Beispiel Kolumbien. In Trutz von Trotha (Ed.), *Soziologie der Gewalt. Sonderheft der Kölner Zeitschrift für Soziologie und Sozialpsychologie* (pp. 141–161). Opladen: Westdeutscher Verlag.

Waldmann, Peter. (1998). Bürgerkrieg—Annäherung an einen schwer faßbaren Begriff. In Heinrich Krumwiede & Peter Waldmann (Eds.), *Bürgerkriege: Folgen und Regulierungsmöglichkeiten* (pp. 15–36). Baden-Baden: Nomos Verlag.

Waldmann, Peter, & Fernando Reinares (Eds.) (1998). *Sociedades en Guerra Civil. Conflictos Violentos de Europa y América Latina*. Barcelona: Paidos.

Walter, Barbara F. (1999a). Designing Transitions from Civil War. In Barbara F. Walter & Jack Snyder (Eds.), *Civil Wars, Insecurity and Intervention* (pp. 38–69). New York: Columbia University Press.

Walter, Barbara F. (1999b). Introduction/Conclusion. In Barbara F. Walter & Jack Snyder (Eds.), *Civil Wars, Insecurity and Intervention* (pp.1–12, 303–307). New York: Columbia University Press.

Walter, Barbara F., & Jack Snyder (Eds.) (1998). *Civil Wars, Insecurity and Intervention*. New York: Columbia University Press.

Zartman, William. (1985). *Ripe for Solution. Conflict and Intervention in Africa*. New York/Oxford: Oxford University Press.

Zartman, William. (1993). The Unfinished Agenda: Negotiating Internal Conflicts. In Roy Licklider (Ed.), *Stopping the Killing. How Civil Wars End* (pp. 20–36). New York/London: New York University Press.

Zimmermann, Ekkart. (1981). *Krisen, Staatsstreiche und Revolutionen, Theorien, Daten und neuere Forschungsansätze*. Opladen: Westdeutscher Verlag.

Terrorism

Fernando Reinares

I. INTRODUCTION

There are three basic traits which combined allow us to distinguish terrorism from other types of violent social interaction. First, an act of violence is to be considered terrorist when its psychical effects within a certain population or social aggregate, in terms of widespread emotional reactions such as fear and anxiety, likely to condition attitudes and behavior in a determined direction, are out of proportion with respect to its actual or potential material consequences, in terms of physical damage to both people and things (Aron, 1962). Secondly, for that violence to have such an impact, it must be systematic and rather unpredictable, usually directed against targets selected because of their symbolic relevance within a prevailing cultural frame and in a given institutional context (Hardman, 1962; Thornton, 1964; Walter, 1969). Thirdly, the harming of such targets is used to convey messages and threats that make terrorism a mechanism of both communication and social control (Roucek, 1962; Crelinsten, 1987).

Terrorism can thus be practiced by different actors, both individual or collective, and with an ample variety of purposes, genuinely political as well as nonpolitical. Nonpolitical expressions of terrorist activity may include, for instance, its actual employment with the fundamental intention of protecting illegal markets, hindering legal abortion practices or allegedly promoting animal rights. However, social science literature on the subject is primarily focused on *political* terrorism. This type of violence can be properly termed political if it is used with the intention to affect, in the short or long term, the structure and distribution of power within a given national society or on a wider scale. Political terrorism acquires an insurgent character if it attempts to change the established political order, and a vigilante orientation when used in order to preserve existing relations of power (Schmid & de Graaf, 1982). It is also possible to differentiate between a tactical, auxiliary use of terrorism on the one hand, and its rather more strategic or preferential utilization on the other (Bonanate, 1979).

W. Heitmeyer and J. Hagan (eds.), *International Handbook of Violence Research*, 309–321.
© 2003 Kluwer Academic Publishers. Printed in the Netherlands.

Throughout our age, terrorism has been and is practiced in the context of disputes confined to state polities, but also in the sphere of international relations (Stohl & Lopez, 1984; O'Sullivan, 1986; Laqueur, 1987; O'Kane, 1991). Concerning this latter domain, terrorism became a tactical device often employed by regular armies engaged in situations of warfare, as well as by a number of governments trying to advance their own national interests in a changing geopolitical scenario. As to the former, domestic or national scale, terrorism can be observed among the methods typically used, also on a more or less extended tactical basis, by nonresponsive authorities in order to establish and perpetuate a certain political order. State terror, for instance, is a common feature of totalitarian dictatorships (Arendt, 1966; Dallin & Breslauer, 1970; Tapia, 1980; Adelman, 1984). But terrorism as an auxiliary method is likely to be found in the course of processes intended to erode the stability of an established political regime, pursuing either reactionary or revolutionary objectives. More concretely, terrorist tactics have been used, since the late nineteenth century and throughout the twentieth century, in a large number of insurrectional processes, deployed by revolutionary parties, nationalist movements, guerrilla groups and even fundamentalist cults (Crenshaw, 1978; Bell, 1977; Mommsen & Hirschfeld, 1982; Chaliand, 1985; Perry, 1988).

However, a most prominent feature of terrorism in the context of advanced industrial societies, no doubt since the late 1960s, is the fact that some political organizations have adopted this type of violence as a predominant method in their repertoire of collective action (Reinares, 1998). Accordingly, these organizations are those we may define as terrorist organizations. Due to the illegal nature of their activities and the high risk they entail for those involved, such terrorist organizations usually operate clandestinely. In turn, illegality and secrecy tend to determine the relatively reduced size of these armed underground groups, rarely exceeding several dozens or, at the most, a few hundred members. They may nonetheless benefit from a significant amount of social acceptance or passive acquiescence, even if more often than not this amounts to only a small minority within their population of reference, particularly in consolidated liberal democracies.

By conceptualizing terrorist organizations along these lines, normative or evaluative considerations are excluded from the analytical delimitation of such phenomenon. Indeed, the emphasis lies on distinctive procedures, even acknowledged by many of those who have actually used terrorism, instead of alluding, as demarcation criteria, to the morality of armed activities undertaken by these clandestine groups, their main ideological orientations, the kind of political regime under which violence is produced, or the never precise threshold of popular support they may eventually mobilize. In addition, this conceptualization follows the sound advice of being consistent enough with conventional usage. Best known examples, past and present, of contemporary terrorist organizations are probably those of the ETA (Euskadi ta Askatasuna, Basqueland and Freedom) and GRAPO (Grupos Revolucionarios Antifascistas Primero de Octubre, First of October Antifascist Revolutionary Groups) in Spain; PIRA (Provisional Irish Republican Army) and the UFF (Ulster Freedom Fighters) in the United Kingdom; Brigate Rosse (Red Brigades) and Avanguardia Nazionale (National Vanguard) in Italy; Rote Armee Fraktion (Red Army Fraction) in Germany; Action Directe (Direct Action) and the FLNC (Fronte di Liberazione Naziunale di a Corsica, National Liberation Front of Corsica) in France; EO17N (Epanastatiki Organosi 17 Noemuri, 17 of November Revolutionary Organization) in Greece; the FLQ (Front de Libération du Québec, Liberation Front of Quebec) in Canada; the SLA (Symbionese Liberation Army) and Puerto Rican FALN (Fuerzas Armadas de Liberación Nacional, Armed Forces of National Liberation), as well as a number of neo-

Nazi militias in the United States of America; and the Rengo Sekigun (United Red Army) in Japan. Also, the ASALA (Armenian Secret Army for the Liberation of Armenia), the PFLP (Popular Front for the Liberation of Palestine) or the GIA (Groupes Islamiques Armés, Armed Islamic Groups) in Algeria.

II.   THEORETICAL APPROACHES AND EMPIRICAL RESULTS

Terrorism poses many questions of substantive and theoretical interest, both concerning its etiology, dynamics and consequences. As with other kinds of social and political phenomena, it can be explored at different levels of analysis: systemic, organizational and individual. At a systemic level of analysis, the study of terrorism focuses on the structural causes and consequences of such a form of political violence, including state reaction among the latter. Concerning the organizational or intermediate level of analysis, basic interrogants refer to the processes through which terrorist organizations are formed and to the factors determining their mobilization strategies. Empirical research at an individual level of analysis is mainly centered on the sociological profile, motivations and recruitment patterns of those who become terrorists. Needless to say, the phenomenon of terrorism may be examined from a plurality of complementary theoretical perspectives. Several recent books, first published or conveniently edited again during the last two decades, provide comprehensive approaches to the subject (Wilkinson, 1986; Rubenstein, 1987; Schmid, Stohl, & Jongman, 1988; Wardlaw, 1989; Weinberg & Davis, 1989; Guelke, 1995; Reinares, 1998; Waldmann, 1998).

Terrorism practiced by clandestine political organizations in the context of advanced industrial societies and elsewhere is one of a number of possible violent expressions of social conflict. However, the existence of politicized antagonisms is not a necessary nor a sufficient condition for terrorism. Indeed, it would be too simplistic and even misleading to explain the emergence of that violent phenomenon merely in terms of underlying strains such as those resulting from center and periphery cleavages within an established state, inequalities observed in the social structure of a given country, ideological positions divergent with respect to the form of government perceived as more adequate for a population, or hostilities between collectivities adherent to different religious beliefs. Therefore, attention must focus on additional political and cultural factors rendering terrorism more likely, as well as on certain precipitant circumstances typically intervening in the choice of such violence by political actors (Crenshaw, 1995). Nevertheless, despite undeniable links between terrorism and specific historical contexts, a general theory on the conditions which invariably produce that phenomenon would understandably be considered rather unfeasible.

The occurrence of either domestic or transnational terrorism since the end of World War II is often associated with relatively high levels of social development and economic modernization. In this sense, the globalization process has progressively disseminated worldwide a number of facilitating elements and vulnerability factors. Among these are mass transportation networks providing both easy mobility and accessible notorious targets, innovative technologies applied to a number of available weapons and explosives much appreciated by the terrorists, and sophisticated systems of information transmission as well as sensitized mass media communication offering new possibilities for resource mobilization, more concretely access to large national or international audiences (Redlick, 1979; Paletz & Schmid, 1992). Socioeconomic modernization also provides densely populated, heterogeneous urban and metropolitan areas where the disruptive potential of terrorism is considerably greater, at the same time that their perpetrators find it less difficult to live unnoticed (Grabosky, 1988). Finally, developed societies and functioning market economies are associated with a class and occupational structure which would tend to promote popular passivity and is seldom conducive to sustained mass movements in pursuit of radical sociopolitical transformations, but prone to insurgent terrorism instead (Targ, 1988).

Terrorism, however, regardless of the orientation toward an existing power distribution endorsed by those collective actors relying on it, does not seem to occur equally in the different polities known among industrialized societies, though situations of conflict likely to generate violence are more or less common to all of them. Even within a single country, however, the terrorist phenomenon often takes place cyclically, showing significant variations in its frequency and intensity over time. Therefore, it is plausible to suggest that both the emergence and evolution of terrorist organizations are to an important extent contingent upon the disposition of a number of systemic political factors, domestic as well as international, which may facilitate or otherwise constrain the calculated choice of a concrete violent repertoire as well as the subsequent dynamics of armed underground groups (Reinares, 1996). In other words, terrorism seems to be conditioned by the corresponding relevant configuration of what current theorizing on disruptive collective action in general defines as political opportunity structure.

In fact, the probability for insurgent terrorist organizations to emerge is considered technically greater in consolidated liberal democracies, since those who promote and practice such forms of violence may instrumentalize, for subversive purposes, existing and protected civil and political rights, whereas under totalitarian regimes the pervasive use of state power makes both expressions of peaceful protest and also of aggressive political dissent virtually impossible (Wilkinson, 1986; Reinares, 1998). However, terrorism against an established distribution of power seems to become even doubly likely in authoritarian dictatorships where paths to the legal expression of opposition are very restricted but official repression tends to be inefficient, as direct and permissive causes coincide (Crenshaw, 1981). This structural vulnerability toward the use of terrorism by underground groups would then be expected to increase when nontolerant polities undergo processes of liberalization and democratization.

How do terrorist organizations emerge? Empirical research on the dynamics of social conflict has stressed that peaceful collective mobilization tends to precede violent action. In this sense, a number of studies posit a relationship between social movements and protest cycles, on the one hand, and the formation of terrorist organizations on the other. According to most of these contributions, the relationship is one of wanted or unwanted continuity, a direct behavioral extension of nonviolent politics (Tarrow & della Porta, 1986; Reinares, 1990; Sprinzak, 1991). Alternatively however, it has been suggested that a sharp rupture exists between social movements and their eventual degeneration into terrorism, even if this process results from a deliberate decision taken by those actors involved (Wieviorka, 1988). Nevertheless, prior to becoming the predominant method of a collective action repertoire, terrorism is typically adopted as tactical innovation by certain weakened political groups, often small antisystem parties or radicalized social movement organizations embedded into a subculture where the use of violence as a method to affect the structure and distribution of power is justified. Commonly, these collective political actors are unable to reach influential stances through conventional procedures, see themselves affected by time constraints in order to benefit from immediate opportunity structures, or have been expelled from relevant public decision-making processes either as a result of open pluralistic competition or state repression (Baeyer-Katte & Claessens, 1982; Sprinzak, 1991; Weinberg, 1992).

Most terrorist organizations active in the past three decades in the context of industrial advanced societies and elsewhere disappeared shortly after their formation. But some others have survived for an average period of approximately ten years and a few of them even more than twenty. These variations in their life span reflect the differential ability observed among such armed underground groups to routinely mobilize those human, material and symbolic resources needed to advance alleged objectives or simply maintain themselves over time. Even though resources may also be provided from a variety of external sources, either governmental or nongovernmental, terrorist organizations normally behave so as to rely on those forcefully or willingly extracted from within their corresponding population of reference (Fetscher & Rohrmoser, 1981; Adams, 1986; Rapoport, 1988; della Porta, 1990; Wright, 1991). Accordingly, terrorist organizations design and develop mobilization strategies intended to produce widespread popular attitudes which range from passive tolerance to active support, thus engaging in what can be considered as a struggle over legitimacy (Burton, 1978; Gal Or, 1991; Hewitt, 1993; Funes, 1998a, 1998b).

Theory and research on the dynamics of terrorist organizations have also emphasized their proneness to subordinate political objectives and, explicitly or rather more often implicitly, choose group maintenance as main priority goal (Crenshaw, 1985; della Porta, 1995). This would imply, among other expected or unanticipated corollaries, certain operational changes, away from actions intended to advance alleged public ends and toward activities which have organizational subsistence as their predominant purpose. As clandestinity is an intervening variable, this is a shift which is likely to increase difficulties in both mobilization of resources and interaction of the underground group with the surrounding environment. This is why terrorist organizations often strive to create a subservient intermediation complex of small collective entities which may facilitate the performing of these crucial tasks. As has also been observed, the demise of terrorist organizations occurs mainly because of three factors: physical defeat of the extremist organization by the government as a result of domestic security policies implemented by the authorities, a collective decision to abandon the terrorist strategy perhaps prompted by political change or perceived social rejection, and organizational disintegration due, among other things, to the unsuccessful mobilization of resources or aggravated internal dissent (Crenshaw, 1991).

Who are the terrorists? According to research findings, they are basically young urban males, on average in their early twenties when recruited, extracted mainly from the middle classes during the formation of an armed clandestine group and outnumbered subsequently by activists with a working class background if the terrorist organization is to persist over a considerable period of time (Russell & Miller, 1977; Waldmann, 1989, 1998; Reinares, 1998, 2001). Though fundamental to our understanding of individual militancy in terrorist organizations, the issue of motivation is a difficult one to deal with. A concrete psychological perspective has insisted in seeing the terrorists in general, and women terrorists in particular, as people whose behavior is due to personality disorders such as narcissism or paranoia (Pearlstein, 1991; Robins & Post, 1997). However, most analysis does not follow this explanation, which is usually devoid of empirical evidence (Taylor, 1988; Reich, 1990). But mere adhesion to political goals, no matter how maximalist they may be, rarely alone explains why an individual decides to become member of a terrorist organization. Political objectives would normally be combined, though in varying proportions, with other motivations based on negative emotions and affective ties, on material and nonmaterial selective incentives, as well as on collective identity affirmation, before an individual decides to join a terrorist organization (Merkl, 1986; della Porta, 1992; Waldmann, 1993; White, 1993; Reinares, 2001). Secular and religious social norms pertaining to specific subcultures may also exist that, far from inhibiting aggressive behavior, stipulate rules for vengeance or retaliation, indicating more or less tentatively the circumstances under which these not only can but should be carried out, even in the form of terrorism (Jäger, Schmidtchen, & Süllwold, 1981; Rapoport, 1984; Rapoport & Alexander, 1989).

However, contemporary terrorism is not a form of political violence confined within the limits of particular state jurisdictions. It crosses established frontiers and has increasingly become an evolving transnational phenomenon. That happens either because terrorist organizations decide to mobilize resources outside the country of reference where they repeatedly carry out their armed activities, or because they deliberately look for targets in national territories other than the one they come from. These and other relocating circumstances, as well as the spread of terrorism through contagion or exchanges between armed organizations are often facilitated by the complexities of our world system and innovations associated with the globalization process (Hoffman, 1998). In addition, it is well known that some governments have relied on the use of terrorism as part of their foreign policy. International terrorism, now properly termed, commonly implies the sponsorship of clandestine organizations or undercover agents specialized in that form of violence, either directly or indirectly, by certain states thus trying to affect the stability of concrete national polities, entire geopolitical regions, or even a worldwide distribution of power (Slater & Stohl, 1988; Stohl & Lopez, 1988). Whereas some authors focus on the role played by former and current communist regimes, as well as radicalized non-Western authorities, in the promotion of international terrorism (Goren, 1984; Cline & Alexander, 1984), others have emphasized the responsibility of Western dictatorships and even of some liberal democracies (Herman, 1982; George, 1991).

The extent to which terrorism has been undergoing significant changes since the collapse of communism, so as to challenge our basic understanding of this phenomenon, was already subject to inquiry and debate during the 1990s. Enlarged collusion between terrorism and transnational organized crime, technological innovations applied to the practice of violence and mobilization of resources by armed underground groups, possible changes detected in the actual patterns of victimization, growing violent activity of political collective actors inspired by fundamentalist religious creeds both east and west, fanatical suicide bombings becoming perhaps the most dangerous terrorism of our time, reconstituted networks of international terrorism under both state and non-state sponsorship, as well as alternative organizational structures adopted in many countries by right-wing extremists and other radicalized movements likely to engage in terrorist action—all of these are among the most salient and important current trends in the subject matter being explored (Bjørgo, 1995; Hoffman, 1998; Kushner, 1998; Laqueur, 1999; Juergensmeyer, 2000; Taylor & Horgan, 2000).

Some recent analysis has exhibited remarkable insight into the basic characteristics of this new terrorism, particularly when interpreting its alleged overall increase in lethality, at least since the Cold War came to an end (Hoffman, 1998, 1999). As could be argued, this trend culminated with the astonishing incident of megaterrorism which took place on September 11, 2001. That day no doubt deserves a particular mention here, since these events have certainly modified our current perception of the terrorist phenomenon in general. Three commercial aircrafts following domestic flight routes, previously kidnapped by a group of Islamic fundamentalists determined to immolate themselves, were purposefully crashed into emblematic buildings of the United States' economic and military establishment, namely the World Trade Center in New York and the Pentagon in the city of Washington. Around three thousand people were killed in this catastrophic act of terrorism. In addition, the famous twin towers in Manhattan were completely destroyed and some important sections within the Department of Defense severely damaged. Alarm and fear became widespread not only among the American public but also among Western citizens in general and non-Western populations worldwide. There were immediate negative effects on the world's economic markets and international stability. This was all due to an act of megaterrorism, intentionally perpetrated on a global scale. This event, together with common organizational and operational patterns of change simultaneously observed in a significant number of terrorist groups across different countries, as well as accumulated evidence on the existence of a large, developed network of transnational terrorism, namely Al Qaeda (Gunaratna, 2002), indicate the ongoing globalization of terrorism.

A recurrent concern to many policymakers and academics is the potential use by terrorist organizations of unconventional weapons of mass destruction including chemical, biological and even nuclear components (Beres, 1979; Cameron, 1999; Gurr & Cole, 2000; Roberts, 2000; Tucker, 2000). This fear was in evidence before the dramatic appearance of megaterrorism, but it has certainly now been intensified, and yet the obvious catastrophic capabilities resulting from an innovative use of conventional weapons and explosives were surprisingly disregarded until very recently. Though the likelihood of a use of weapons of mass destruction has often been claimed in the absence of sufficient empirical evidence, focusing instead on issues of opportunity and capability, a qualitative move of domestic and international terrorism in that direction tends to be considered rather more probable when the decision to use such forms of violence is based on religious fanaticism, millenarian ideals or racist doctrines (Stern, 1999; Lifton, 1999). Arguably however, the more we talk about unconventional weapons of mass destruction, the less we may be strictly referring to the phenomenon of terrorism, insofar as those who promote and practice this type of violence would still look forward to an audience far greater than the actual number of casualties caused. However, the actual magnitude of this somewhat minded ratio may well depend on the scale on which terrorism is perpetrated, ranging from domestic to regional and even global scenarios.

III.   DESIDERATA

Progress in generic knowledge about terrorism has been evident since research on the subject was properly initiated nearly three decades ago. In addition to the relevant monographs and series of books on the theme, this field has two main international journals publishing mainly scholarly but also sound professional contributions, *Studies in Conflict and Terrorism* and *Terrorism and Political Violence*. However, social science studies on the subject are still characterized by limited theoretical advances and shortage of good empirical investigation. A more refined, integrated and cumulative theorizing, likely to allow the formulation of sound hypothesis, would undeniably contribute to expected major developments in the academic understanding of terrorism. Unfortunately though, there is still a persistent debate on the delimitation of this phenomenon and its analytical conceptualization. As with many other political concepts, terrorism continues to be a deeply contested term. Moreover, there is still a significant amount of highly tendentious publishing, far beyond the reasonable civic commitment of most scholars working in this field with the principles and procedures of liberal democracy. Nevertheless, middle range theories on the causes, dynamics and consequences of terrorism should rely on more firmly established theories, particularly in the domains of political science, sociology, social psychology, economics and international relations, on broader issues such as social conflict, political mobilization, collective action, political change, public policies, and the process of globalization.

Further research on terrorism, both quantitative and qualitative, is clearly required in all the areas of this field, though some are certainly more deficient than others. A current agenda should probably include, among its priorities at a systemic level of analysis, the development of differential analysis on the etiology and evolution of terrorism with respect to diverse models of democracy, as well as empirical studies on the societal effects of protracted terrorist campaigns and the domestic cleavages more likely to produce terrorism in the near future, both in advanced industrial societies and elsewhere. Concerning the organizational or intermediate level of analysis, more comparative research is needed, for instance, on the dynamics of terrorist groups, the variations in organizational structures, changing mobilization strategies observed, and behavioral innovations detected throughout terrorist trajectories. At an individual level of analysis, additional investigation is certainly required on the profile and motivations of those who join terrorist organizations, particularly with respect to the circumstances under which exit from these underground groups is more likely to occur, as well as on the biographical consequences of violent activism.

The study of antiterrorist policies should mainly focus on those interactions between institutions, actors, and public opinion affecting the government agenda, as far as the problem of terrorism is concerned, in the context of liberal democracies. In addition, research should address the formulation and effectiveness of different conciliatory, juridical, and police measures adopted in the context of these tolerant regimes with responsive elected political elites. State terror, as practiced today in a variety of existing repressive regimes, may indeed attract renewed attention from academics doing research in the field. The same is true of the use of terrorist tactics in situations of civil war or mass political violence. Transnational terrorism also requires informed research on continuities and changes observed in the phenomenon, including current trends in international terrorism, alleged links between cross-border organized crime and the financing of terrorist organizations, factors affecting the globalization of terrorism, structural and cultural conditions favoring the rise of megaterrorism, as well as on the problems associated with the formalization and implementation of both bilateral and multilateral international cooperative arrangements. This research is expected to be relevant for domestic and intergovernmental policy purposes.

IV.   APPROACHES TO PREVENTION AND CONTROL

Terrorism, as practiced by small clandestine organizations with the alleged intention of affecting the structure and distribution of power, both at a national or international level, has been particularly noticeable since the late 1960s. Though the duration and intensity of such lasting phenomenon varied from one country to the other, it has generally produced important political and social consequences. In spite of its limited scope when compared with other manifestations of organized collective violence, terrorism can nonetheless exert a severe impact on fundamental processes common to democratic regimes in the advanced industrial societies as well as elsewhere (Crenshaw, 1983; Furet, Liniers, & Raynaud, 1985; Wilkinson, 1986, 2000; Lodge, 1988; Holmes, 2001). For instance, sustained terrorist activity not only recurrently violates human rights, it also impedes the free exercise of civil liberties, alters the normal functioning of official institutions, hinders the management of public affairs by elected authorities, or disrupts the autonomous development of civil society. Combined with other factors likely to strain or overload the political system, terrorism becomes a risk, if not exactly a threat, to the stability of liberal democracies, in particular those undergoing a process of consolidation. Any legitimately constituted and responsive government is thus expected to readily and consistently confront such an aggressive challenge to both the existing tolerant political order and the monopoly of physical coercion over a given territory claimed by the state.

Even when the formation of terrorist organizations is typically preceded by disruptive collective mobilizations which undergo successive stages of radicalization, to the extent that some cautious proactive intervention is feasible for authorities concerned, democratic governments rather have to intervene once illegal violence has been dramatically initiated, then developing reactive as well as proactive responses. Still, terrorism poses serious dilemmas for executives trying to formulate and implement consistent policies aimed at preventing or neutralizing the phenomenon. Governmental responses, in the context of democratic regimes, are normally conditioned by currents of domestic public opinion, legal guarantees enjoyed by the citizens, the various state institutions involved and even those articulated interests ultimately active in the sector of internal security. As to the liberal democracies known in highly industrialized societies, antiterrorist policies have tended to include some strictly political decisions aimed at peacefully regulating violent social conflicts or affecting the internal cohesion of armed clandestine organizations, communicative action initiatives intended to educate the citizens and neutralize terrorist propaganda, the enactment of legislation intended to deter extremists from resorting to a repertoire of terrorism and favor law enforcement operations, and a number of other specialized responses to be undertaken by state security agencies; these latter two adopted in a context of increasing cooperation between countries due to the transnationalized character of the challenge (Finn, 1991; Vercher, 1992; Schmid & Crelinsten, 1993; Cettina, 1994; Chalk, 1996; Reinares, 1998, 2000; Jaime-Jiménez, 2002).

These various initiatives and measures, which sometimes lead to different results in terms of relative utility, depending on their own nature and the concrete situational conditions, often also display similarities as to their effectiveness across countries (Hewitt, 1984; Reinares, 1998). It may nevertheless be asserted that measures generally considered most useful against terrorism and at the same time least dangerous to the fabric of open societies are those taken under the rule of law and in accordance with the principles as well as the procedures of liberal democracies. Contemporary terrorism, though, is an evolving transnational phenomenon, as previously noted. Indeed, a phenomenon already influenced by the ongoing process of globalization. As a result, governmental antiterrorist policies applied within definite domestic boundaries are objectively constrained in their possible effects. The same basic argument could be applied with respect to unilateral military responses abroad or economic sanctions adopted by a single country in order to counter international or global terrorism. For this reason, and despite existing difficulties, bilateral or multilateral international cooperation, concerning security matters and other related issues, addressing both short and long-term goals, is of the greatest importance in the prevention and control of such actual or potential menace not only to the stability of concrete democratic regimes but to the balance of entire geopolitical regions, and even to world peace (Gal Or, 1985; Cassese, 1989). In this sense, a particularly promising collaborative arrangement between liberal democracies to prevent and fight terrorism has been formalized between member states of the European Union (Vercher, 1992; Chalk, 1996; Reinares, 2000). But the containment of a terrorism now ranging from the transnational to the global unavoidably requires far more enhanced cooperation among states.

REFERENCES

Adams, James. (1986). *The Financing of Terror*. London: New English Library.

Adelman, Jonathan R. (Ed.) (1984). *Terror and Communist Politics. The Role of Secret Police in Communist States*. Boulder: Westview Press.

Arendt, Hannah. (1966). *The Origins of Totalitarianism*. New York: Harcourt, Brace and World.

Aron, Raymond. (1962). *Paix et Guerre entre les Nations*. Paris: Calmann Levy.

Baeyer-Katte, Wanda von, & Dieter Claessens. (Eds.) (1982). *Analysen zum Terrorismus: Gruppenprozesse*. Opladen: Westdeutscher Verlag.

Bell, J. Bowyer. (1977). *Terror out of Zion: Irgun Zvai Leumi, LEHI and the Palestinian Underground, 1929–1949*. New York: St. Martin's Press.

Beres, Louis R. (1979). *Terrorism and Global Security: The Nuclear Threat*. Boulder: Westview Press.

Bjørgo, Tore. (Ed.) (1995). *Terror from the Extreme Right*. London: Frank Cass.

Bonanate, Luigi. (1979). Dimensioni del Terrorismo Politico. In Luigi Bonanate (Ed.), *Dimensioni del Terrorismo Politico* (pp. 99–179). Milano: Franco Angeli.

Burton, Frank. (1978). *The Politics of Legitimacy. Struggles in a Belfast Community*. London, Henley and Boston: Routledge and Kegan Paul.

Cameron, Gavin. (1999). *Nuclear Terrorism. A Threat Assessment for the 21st Century*. Basingstoke, Hampshire: Macmillan.

Cassese, Antonio. (1989). *Terrorism, Politics and Law*. Cambridge: Cambridge University Press.

Cettina, Nathalie. (1994). *Les Enjeux Organisationnels de la Lutte contre le Terrorisme*. Paris: Université Panthéon Assas.

Chaliand, Gérard. (1985). *Terrorismes et guérillas*. Paris: Flammarion.

Chalk, Peter. (1996). *West European Terrorism and Counterterrorism*. Basingstoke, Hampshire: Macmillan.

Cline, Ray S., & Yonah, Alexander. (1984). *Terrorism: the Soviet Connection*. New York: Crane Russak.

Crelinsten, Ronald. (1987). Terrorism as Political Communication: the Relationship between the Controller and the Controlled. In Paul Wilkinson & Alasdair M. Stewart (Eds.), *Contemporary Research on Terrorism* (pp. 3–23). Aberdeen: Aberdeen University Press.

Crenshaw, Martha. (1978). *Revolutionary Terrorism. The FLN in Algeria, 1954–1962*. Stanford: Hoover Institution Press.

Crenshaw, Martha. (1981). The Causes of Terrorism. *Comparative Politics, 13*, 379–399.

Crenshaw, Martha. (Ed.) (1983). *Terrorism, Legitimacy and Power. The Consequences of Political Violence*. Middletown: Wesleyan University Press.

Crenshaw, Martha. (1985). *An Organizational Approach to the Analysis of Political Terrorism* (pp. 465–489). Orbis, 29.

Crenshaw, Martha. (1991). How Terrorism Declines. In Clark McCauley (Ed.), *Terrorism Research and Public Policy* (pp. 69–87). London: Frank Cass.

Crenshaw, Martha. (Ed.) (1995). *Terrorism in Context*. University Park: Pennsylvania State University Press.

Dallin, Alexander, & George W. Breslauer. (1970). *Political Terror in Communist Systems*. Stanford: Stanford University Press.

Della Porta, Donatella. (1990). *Il Terrorismo di Sinistra*. Bologna: Il Mulino.

Della Porta, Donatella. (Ed.) (1992). *Social Movements and Violence: Participation in Underground Organizations*. Greenwich: JAI Press.

Della Porta, Donatella. (1995). *Social Movements, Political Violence and the State. A Comparative Analysis of Italy and Germany*. Cambridge: Cambridge University Press.

Finn, John E. (1991). *Constitutions in Crisis. Political Violence and the Rule of Law*. New York, Oxford: Oxford University Press.

Fetscher, Irving,& Günter Rohrmoser. (Eds.) (1981). *Analysen zum Terrorismus: Ideologien und Strategien*. Opladen: Westdeutscher Verlag.

Funes, María J. (1998a. Social Responses to Political Violence in the Basque Country. Peace Movements and Their Audience. *Journal of Conflict Resolution, 42*, 493–510.

Funes, María J. (1998b.) *La Salida del Silencio. Movilizaciones por la Paz en Euskadi 1986–1998*. Madrid: Akal Ediciones.

Furet, François, Antoine Liniers, & Philippe Raynaud. (1985). *Terrorisme et Démocratie*. Paris: Fayard.

Gal Or, Noemi. (1985). *International Cooperation to Suppress Terrorism*. London: Croom Helm.

Gal Or, Noemi. (Ed.) (1991). *Tolerating Terrorism in the West*. London, New York: Routledge.

George, Alexander. (Ed.) (1991). *Western State Terrorism*. Cambridge: Polity Press.

Goren, Roberta. (1984). *The Soviet Union and Terrorism*. London: Allen and Unwin.

Grabosky, Peter N. (1988). The Urban Context of Political Terrorism. In Michael Stohl (Ed.), *The Politics of Terrorism* (pp. 31–57). New York, Basel: Marcel Dekker.

Guelke, Adrian. (1995). *The Age of Terrorism and the International Political System*. London, New York: Tauris Academic Studies.

Gunaratna, Rohan. (2002). *Inside Al Qaeda. Global Network of Terror*. London: Hurst and Company.

Gurr, Nadine, & Benjamin Cole. (2000). *The New Face of Terrorism. Threats from Weapons of Mass Destruction*. London: I.B. Tauris.

Hardman, J. B. S. (1962). Terrorism. In Edwin R. Selignam (Ed.), *Encyclopedia of the Social Sciences, Vol. 14* (pp. 575–579). New York: Macmillan.

Herman, Edward. (1982). *The Real Terror Network*. Boston: South End Press.

Hewitt, Christopher. (1984). *The Effectiveness of Antiterrorist Policies*. Lanham: University Press of America.

Hewitt, Christopher. (1993). *Consequences of Political Violence*. Aldershot: Dartmouth.

Hoffman, Bruce. (1998). *Inside Terrorism*. London: Victor Gollancz.

Hoffman, Bruce. (1999). Terrorism Trends and Prospects. In Ian O. Lesser, Bruce Hoffman, John Arquilla, David Ronfeldt & Michele Zanini, *Countering the New Terrorism* (pp. 7–38). Santa Monica, California, Washington D.C.: RAND.

Holmes, Jennifer S. (2001). *Terrorism and Democratic Stability*. Manchester: Manchester University Press.

Jäger, Herbert, Gerhard Schmidtchen, & Liselotte Süllwold. (Eds.) (1981). *Analysen zum Terrorismus: Lebenslaufanalysen*. Opladen: Westdeutscher Verlag.

Jaime-Jiménez, Oscar. (2002). *Policía, Terrorismo y Cambio Político en España*. Valencia: Tirant lo Blanch.

Juergensmeyer, Mark. (2000). *Terror in the Mind of God: The Global Rise of Religious Violence*. Berkeley: University of California Press.

Kushner, Harvey W. (1998). *The Future of Terrorism: Violence in the New Millennium*. Thousand Oaks, California: Sage.

Laqueur, Walter. (1987). *The Age of Terrorism*. Boston: Little, Brown and Company.

Laqueur, Walter. (1999). *The New Terrorism. Fanaticism and the Arms of Mass Destruction*. New York: Oxford University Press.

Lifton, Robert J. (1999). *Destroying the World to Save It: Aum Shinrikyo, Apocalyptic Violence and the New Global Terrorism*. New York: Holt.

Lodge, Juliet. (Ed.) (1988). *The Threat of Terrorism*. Brighton: Wheatsheaf Books.

Merkl, Peter H. (Ed.) (1986). *Political Violence and Terror: Motifs and Motivations*. Berkeley: University of California Press.

Mommsen, Wolfgang J., & Gerhard Hirschfeld. (Eds.) (1982). *Social Protest, Violence and Terror in Nineteenth and Twentieth Century Europe*. London: Macmillan.

O'Kane, Rosemary. (1991). *The Revolutionary Reign of Terror: the Role of Violence in Political Change*. Aldershot, Hampshire: Elgar.

O'sullivan, Noel. (Ed.) (1986). *Terrorism, Ideology and Revolution: The Origins of Modern Political Violence*. Brighton: Wheatsheaf.

Pearlstein, Robert M. (1991). *The Mind of the Political Terrorist*. Wilmington, Delaware: Scholarly Resources.

Paletz, David L., & Alex P. Schmid. (Eds.) (1992). *Terrorism and the Media*. Newbury Park, London: Sage.

Perry, Duncan M. (1988). *The Politics of Terror. The Macedonian Liberation Movement 1893–1903*. Durham: Duke University Press.

Rapoport, David C. (1984). Fear and Trembling: Terror in Three Religious Traditions. *American Political Science Review, 78*, 658–677.

Rapoport, David C. (Ed.) (1988). *Inside Terrorist Organizations*. New York: Columbia University Press.

Rapoport, David C., & Yonah Alexander. (Eds.) (1989). *The Morality of Terrorism: Religious and Secular Justifications*. New York: Columbia University Press.

Redlick, Amy S. (1979). The Transnational Flow of Information as a Cause of Terrorism. In Yonah Alexander, David Carlton & Paul Wilkinson (Eds.), *Terrorism; Theory and Practice* (pp. 73–95). Boulder: Westview Press.

Reich, Walter. (Ed.) (1990). *Origins of Terrorism. Psychologies, Ideologies, Theologies, States of Mind*. Cambridge: Cambridge University Press.

Reinares, Fernando. (1990). Sociogénesis y Evolución del Terrorismo en España. In Salvador Giner (Ed.), *España: Sociedad y Política* (pp. 353–396). Madrid: Espasa Calpe.

Reinares, Fernando. (1996). The Political Conditioning of Collective Violence: Regime Change and Insurgent Terrorism in Spain. *Research on Democracy and Society*, *3*, 297–326.

Reinares, Fernando. (1998). *Terrorismo y Antiterrorismo*. Barcelona: Ediciones Paidós.

Reinares, Fernando. (Ed.) (2000). *European Democracies against Terrorism. Governmental Policies and Intergovernmental Cooperation*. Aldershot, Hampshire: Ashgate.

Reinares, Fernando. (2001). *Patriotas de la Muerte. Quiénes han militado en ETA y por qué*. Madrid: Taurus.

Roberts, Brad. (Ed.) (2000). *Hype or Reality? The New Terrorism and Mass Casualty Attacks*. Alexandria: The Chemical and Biological Arms Control Institute.

Robins, Robert S., & Jerrold M. Post. (1997). *Political Paranoia. The Psychopolitics of Hatred*. New Haven and London: Yale University Press.

Roucek, Joseph S. (1962). Sociological Elements of a Theory of Terror and Violence. *The American Journal of Economics and Sociology*, *21*, 165–172.

Rubenstein, Richard E. (1987). *Alchemists of Revolution. Terrorism in the Modern World*. New York: Basic Books.

Russell, Charles A., & Bowman H. Miller. (1977). Profile of a Terrorist. *Terrorism*, *1*, 17–34.

Schmid, Alex P., & Janny de Graaf. (1982). *Violence as Communication: Insurgent Terrorism and the Western News Media*. London, Beverly Hills: Sage.

Schmid, Alex P., Michael Stohl, & Albert J. Jongman. (1988). *Political Terrorism. A New Guide to Actors, Authors, Concepts, Data Bases, Theories and Literature*. Amsterdam: North Holland Publishing Company.

Schmid, Alex P., & Ronald D. Crelinsten. (Eds.) (1993). *Western Responses to Terrorism*. London: Frank Cass.

Slater, Robert O., & Michael Stohl. (Eds.) (1988). *Current Perspectives on International Terrorism*. London: Macmillan.

Sprinzak, Ehud. (1991). The Process of Delegitimization: Towards a Linkage Theory of Political Terrorism. In Clark McCauley (Ed.), *Terrorism Research and Public Policy* (pp. 50–68). London: Frank Cass.

Stern, Jessica. (1999). *The Ultimate Terrorists*. Cambridge: Harvard University Press.

Stohl, Michael, & George A. Lopez. (Eds.) (1984). *The State as Terrorist. The Dynamics of Governmental Violence and Repression*. Westport: Greenwood Press.

Stohl, Michael, & George A. Lopez. (Eds.) (1988). *Terrible beyond Endurance? The Foreign Policy of State Terrorism*. New York: Greenwood Press.

Tapia, Jorge A. (1980). *El Terrorismo de Estado. La Doctrina de la Seguridad Nacional en el Cono Sur*. México: Nueva Imagen.

Targ, Harry R. (1988). Societal Structure and Revolutionary Terrorism: A Preliminary Investigation. In Michael Stohl (Ed.), *The Politics of Terrorism* (pp. 127–151). New York, Basel: Marcel Dekker.

Tarrow, Sidney, & Donatella della Porta. (1986). Unwanted Children: Political Violence and the Cycle of Protest in Italy. *European Journal of Political Research*, *14*, 607–632.

Taylor, Maxwell. (1988). *The Terrorists*. London: Brassey's Defence Publishers.

Taylor, Maxwell, & John Horgan. (Eds.) (2000). *The Future of Terrorism*. London: Frank Cass.

Thornton, Thomas P. (1964). Terror as a Weapon of Political Agitation. In Harry Eckstein (Ed.), *Internal War: Problems and Approaches* (pp. 71–99). New York: Free Press.

Tucker, Jonathan B. (Ed.) (2000). *Toxic Terror: Assessing Terrorist Use of Chemical and Biological Weapons*. Cambridge, Massachusetts: Massachusetts Institute of Technology Press.

Vercher, Antonio. (1992). *Terrorism in Europe. An International Comparative Legal Analysis*. Oxford: Clarendon Press.

Waldmann, Peter. (1989). *Ethnischer Radikalismus. Ursachen und Folgen gewaltsamer Minderheitenkonflikte*. Opladen: Westdeutscher Verlag.

Waldmann, Peter. (1993). *Beruf Terrorist. Lebensläufe im Untergrund*. München: C. H. Beck.

Waldmann, Peter. (1998). *Terrorismus. Provokation der Macht*. München: Gerling Akademie.

Walter, Eugene V. (Ed.) (1969). *Terror and Resistance. A Study of Political Violence*. New York: Oxford University Press.

Wardlaw, Grant. (1989). *Political Terrorism. Theory, Tactics and Countermeasures. 2nd Edition*. Cambridge: Cambridge University Press.

Weinberg, Leonard. (Ed.) (1992). *Political Parties and Terrorist Groups*. London: Frank Cass.

Weinberg, Leonard, & Paul Davis. (1989). *Introduction to Political Terrorism*. New York: McGraw Hill.

White, Robert. (1993). *Provisional Irish Republicans: An Oral and Interpretive History*. Westport: Greenwood Press.

Wieviorka, Michel. (1988). *Sociétés et Terrorisme*. Paris: Fayard.

Wilkinson, Paul. (1986). *Terrorism and the Liberal State. 2nd Edition*. Basingstoke, Hampshire: Macmillan.

Wilkinson, Paul. (2000). *Terrorism versus Democracy: the Liberal State Response*. London: Frank Cass.

Wright, Joanne. (1991). *Terrorist Propaganda. The Red Army Faction and the Provisional IRA, 1968–1986*. Basingstoke, Hampshire: Macmillan.

Violence from Religious Groups

Jon Pahl

I. INTRODUCTION

Connections between religious groups and violence are widespread in history and in contemporary societies, but have only recently begun to receive systematic attention by social scientists (Candland, 1992). This oversight is due, in part, to what Edward Shils called "the blindness of the social sciences to tradition" (1981:14). Parochialism within the disciplines of theology and religious studies, and social scientific paradigms which assumed secularization and the Western separation of "church" and "state", have obscured the complex interactions between religious traditions and political and social activism, including the abilities of religious groups and members to inspire, legitimize, enact, and prevent violence.

"Religion" itself, of course, is a contested matter. Two schools of definition predominate. The first, following Mircea Eliade (1959), defines religion substantively by pointing to the experiences, practices, or beliefs held to be essential to or characteristic of religious groups, such as the sacred, rituals, or myth. A more situational and functional definition has found favor among recent theorists of religion. Anthropologist Clifford Geertz, for one influential example, identifies religion as a cultural system "of symbols which acts to establish powerful, pervasive, and long-lasting moods and motivations in [people] by formulating conceptions of a general order of existence and clothing these conceptions with such an aura of factuality that the moods and motivations seem uniquely realistic" (Geertz, 1973:90). The utility of the latter approach to religion is that it mandates comparative, systematic analysis, while excluding no subject (such as "the sacred") as a reified or untouchable domain. Such a cultural systems approach to religions also includes in its purview not only the great traditions of historic religious groups, but also new religious movements, and religious features of otherwise secular groups or movements. Seeing religion as a cultural system enables scholars to uncover and discuss such phenomena as civil religions, religious nationalism, and religiously-legitimated features of economic or

W. Heitmeyer and J. Hagan (eds.), *International Handbook of Violence Research*, 323–338.
© 2003 Kluwer Academic Publishers. Printed in the Netherlands.

political behavior, and therefore is especially fruitful for an analysis of violence from religious groups. For the sake of this essay, then, religion will be considered functionally, as a cultural system. Through use of religious symbols, people cohere into groups with identifiable boundaries, define for themselves social norms, and motivate themselves and others to engage in specific behaviors, including acts of violence.

Violence, of course, also admits of several definitions. Scholars generally distinguish between maximalist or minimalist approaches. Minimalists choose to limit the term "violence" to organized aggression or physical force, as in war, riots, or crime. Some minimalists further prefer to limit the term to illegitimate, or criminal, physical aggression. Maximalists, by contrast, prefer to extend the term "violence" to include overt and covert forms of cultural coercion, including both physical and symbolic action. Some maximalists describe particular language patterns (for instance hate speech) as violent, even though no overt physical aggression may accompany any given speech (or writing) act. Given the above definition of religion as a cultural system, a maximalist definition of "violence" is necessary to uncover the ways religious groups may, through their self-definition in symbolic processes, both move from symbolic to physical violence, on the one hand, and forestall physical violence through the mediation of symbolic processes, on the other.

For the sake of this essay, then, seven types or aspects of violence can be identified as connected in the research to religious systems. These seven are, of course, somewhat arbitrarily differentiated, but their organization into a hierarchy of intensity can help to clarify the complex relations between religious systems and various forms of force and coercion. At the most basic level is the ritual or symbolic violence found within the language and practices (e.g., myths and rituals) of nearly all religious groups. The specific ritual of sacrifice has received the most attention, but violent myths of cosmic or spiritual war, coercive rites of passage, ascetic disciplines or bodily mortification, and normative doctrinal boundaries or ascriptive identities are also features of many religious traditions. No simple causal link between such symbolic violence and actual aggression has been established, but many scholars suspect such a link. Clarifying its mechanism, however, awaits another generation of research.

A second level of intensity is the tendency of religions to divide the world into "insiders" and "outsiders", "pure" and "impure", or a thought pattern marked by dualism. On the one hand, this tendency may be a necessary component of any group identification: we define ourselves symbolically by marking what we are *not* as much as by marking what we are. Nevertheless, that this symbolic process is often found in cases of physical violence is well-established, in manifestations ranging from domestic and street crime to war. Again, though, the threshold at which, or mechanism by which, the dualism of "us" and "them" moves from symbolic to physical violence is not entirely clear. The same is true of the relationships—both preventative and catalytic, between religious and ethical systems and criminal or forensic violence to property or person—including theft, rape, and murder. On this third level of intensity, religious prohibition may forestall individual acts, but on the other hand, the same system may mandate or give license to such acts under certain circumstances.

A fourth level of intensity of violence from religious groups involves systemic persecution or punishment, either overt or covert, which is religiously sanctioned through stereotyping, ridicule, segregation, and abuse. Examples such as incarceration, torture, or capital punishment fall under this category, as do "softer" forms of persecution or punishment, all of which may receive warrant, or criticism from a particular religious group or tradition.

A fifth level of violence is systemic exclusion, or religiously-legitimized social violence, such as economic inequity or gender bias. Many religious groups denounce such inequities; others endorse them as necessary (or permissible) for religious or social order.

A sixth level of intensity is organized retaliatory violence, as in religiously-inspired terrorism or revolution. Teachings of revenge or vengeance in religious traditions often blend with acts of vengeance or revenge, on small and large scale, by individuals and groups.

Finally, religious groups have engaged in holy war, and have legitimized genocide. These collective acts of physical aggression and destruction—as the most intense, overt, and organized forms of violence—have received the most attention from historians and social scientists.

Needless to say, the interactions between religious systems and these various manifestations of violence are complex (see Freedman & McClymond, 1999). Many studies have explored the ways religious groups have legitimized and inspired violence, usually through particular case studies. Relatively few works have sought systematic explanations of the relationships between religions and violence as human or cultural systems. Fewer still are the works studying the peace-making or conflict-resolving potential of religions, although an argument could be made that religions have as often as not forestalled violence as caused it. In any event, the social sciences have not only been "blind" to traditions, then, but by neglecting the potential of religious groups and individuals as agents of peace-making and reconciliation, the social sciences may in fact have contributed to the continuing manipulation of religious symbols and groups for nationalist or other violent causes.

II. THEORETICAL APPROACHES AND EMPIRICAL RESULTS

1. Theoretical Approaches

Classical paradigms for the theoretical relationship between religion and violence continue to inform studies today in often subtle ways. Marx, Freud, Weber, and Durkheim inform all substantive discussions. Arguments shade in varying degrees on a continuum. The Marxist critique of religious systems as class-driven, oppressive "opiates" of the masses which mask material causes of conflict remains vital in academic circles, but has in recent years been tempered by the role of religion in economic and political liberation movements in Latin America, Poland, and South Africa. Freudian critiques of religion also endure, with religion depicted as an epiphenomenal and neurotic (if powerful) illusion for individuals who are otherwise discontented with civilization and its inevitable diversity and conflicts. Weberian analysis of the role of religion in legitimizing the State's monopoly on violence has become increasingly attractive since the end of the Cold War and the rise of political active religion (notably Islam) around the globe, and Durkheimian appreciation for religion's ability to cohere societies and cultures has taken on new salience as well. These paradigms are broadly drawn, of course, and the best works are informed by them all, but four broadly conceived and influential studies of the relationship between violence and religion fall neatly under these ideal types.

Robert McAfee Brown, writing primarily for an American Christian audience, encouraged moving "beyond conventional definitions of violence" (1987:28) to an understanding of violence as "any violation of personhood" (1987:29), with or without physical force. Drawing especially upon the works of Marxist-informed liberation theologians,

Brown suggested three manifestations of violence in connection with religion, beginning with the "first violence" of "injustice." Brown quoted Aquinas approvingly to ground this assertion: unjust laws "are acts of violence rather than laws" (1987:31). The second form of violence was what properly goes by the word—street crime, protest, or revolution, which Brown considered in many cases to be the understandable if not religiously justified response of people to situations of first violence or injustice. Finally, Robert McAfee Brown identified a third form of religiously-inspired violence, repression, as the overt or covert response of authorities to protest or revolt in the interest of maintaining order and vested power. As with early liberation theology generally, Brown's analysis was sympathetic to the Marxist critique of religion's (and especially American Christianity's) connection to violence: "Those who enjoy the benefits of the structures [of violence], and are rendered comfortable and secure by them, are to that degree implicated in the violence to which those structures lead" (Brown, 1987:38).

A second theory of the relationship between violence and religion has come from the pen of Rene Girard (1977), and has led to the establishment of the Colloquium on Violence and Religion, a scholarly group dedicated to exploring and applying the theory. Girard builds on Freud to highlight the epiphenomenal character of religion: religions are a response to rivalry, resulting from "mimetic desire," the learned imitation of another's desire for an object. Religions for Girard reduce to sacrifice, and sacrifice, Girard argues, temporarily placates rivalry by transferring its violence unto a "scapegoat," who turns the threat of violence of all against all into the unanimous violence of all against one. Religion thus restrains violence, but it does so *through* violence, and as it is institutionalized in myths and rituals which symbolically reenact and reinforce the scapegoating pattern over generations, the violent nature of religion's violence-reducing function is masked, forgotten, obscured, and repressed. Girard's debt to Freud is extensive and acknowledged.

A third theoretical paradigm for understanding the relationship between violence and religion, developed by Mark Juergensmeyer (1993), draws upon Weberian theory to develop the notions of "religious nationalism" and "cosmic war" as the culprits in religious legitimation of violence. Tracing patterns in recent movements in the Middle East, South Asia, and formerly Marxist states, Juergensmeyer identifies "religious nationalism" as the most inclusive way to describe the tendencies of people to "fuse their religious perspective with a broad prescription for their nation's political and social destiny"(Juergensmeyer, 1993:6). Religious nationalists reject secular ideas, but not secular politics, focus more on ideology than political structures, and tend to reject the separation of religion and politics as a peculiarly Western idea. On the question of why religious nationalists become violent, Juergensmeyer contends against Girard that "most acts of religious violence are less like sacrifice than they are like war" (1993:7). Religious nationalists become violent when they act upon a view of the world that mythologically imagines "[a] great encounter between cosmic forces—an ultimate good and evil, a divine truth and falsehood" (Juergensmeyer, 1993:155). A "rhetoric of cosmic war," then, can become "real" war when religious actors have access to political power and military instruments. Hence, "even though virtually all religions preach the virtues of non-violence, it is their ability to sanction violence that gives them political power" (Juergensmeyer, 1993:164).

Finally, R. Scott Appleby (2000) has most recently authored a book which depends, indirectly if not intentionally, on Durkheim's appreciation for the function of religion to cohere and solidify social orders. Drawing especially on his earlier studies of global fundamentalist movements, Appleby depicts violent religion as the exception rather then the rule: "Religious extremism—the civic and violent intolerance of outsiders—has become the response of choice for a disproportionately influential minority within traditional communities" (Appleby, 2000:58). "Weak religions", Appleby contends, are particularly susceptible to violence. Religions can be "weak" in two senses. Weak religions are, first, those which are "chronically vulnerable to manipulation by external agents" (Appleby, 2000:76), or even constantly reacting to changes extrinsic to the tradition itself (e.g., technological modernization). Religions may also be weak if they have been suppressed (e.g., under Communism), so that folk piety is marked by extensive "religious illiteracy." These two conditions—reactivity to extrinsic agents, and religious illiteracy, mark religious movements which have historically been susceptible to violence, suggests Appleby. Appleby is generally appreciative of traditional religions and their ability to unify cultural systems.

These four theoretical paradigms thus all point to what Appleby calls the "ambivalence" of religious groups on the question of violence. On the one hand, religions serve to unite humans in collectives which transcend and complement individual existence. Through symbols, metaphors, and practices which are highly valorized, religious groups endure across centuries and cultures in ways that political associations can only envy. Religions migrate, adapt, undergo extensive challenge and change, and yet have served for millennia to bond human beings with ties of both affectional and political power. On the other hand, religions divide humanity into competing tribal identities, defined over and against one another, which have often produced conflict. Indeed, because of the potential of symbols to be given "excessive" valorization (e.g., the notion of a supernatural sanction), religiously-inspired acts of violence have been among the bloodiest and most brutal in human history.

2. Empirical Results

Empirical studies understandably produce results which follow patterns set by their theoretical assumptions. Thus, whether a social scientist views religion as epiphenomenal, or as a cultural system in its own right, determines to a large degree what one finds in the evidence. Appleby has offered the most recent apology for the latter approach. He contends that "religious behavior is ... distinctive; failure to recognize motivations, purposes, and patterns that are peculiarly religious invites flawed analysis of the actors as well as the act" (Appleby, 2000:55). From this premise, Appleby argues that religious militancy and violence—whether in Buddhism, Christianity, Hinduism, Islam, Judaism, or Sikhism, has eight features. Focusing primarily on fundamentalism, but with an eye on more general trends, Appleby contends that religious militancy "begins as a reaction to the penetration of the religious community by secular or religious outsiders" (Appleby, 2000:87). Second, "the reaction takes the form of a selected retrieval of the sacred past, [for example] lines or passages from the holy book [or] traditional teachings of a guru or prophet ... for the purpose of legitimating an innovative ideology and program of action designed to protect and bolster the besieged 'fundamentals' of the religion and to fend off or conquer the outsider" (2000:87). Third, "fundamentalist movements form around male charismatic or authoritarian leaders ... and draw new members disproportionately from among young, educated, unemployed, or underemployed males" (2000:87). Fourth, these movements "impose strict codes of personal discipline, dress, diet, and other markers" (2000:88). Fifth, "ideologically, fundamentalists are both reactive against and interactive with secular modernity.... Having subordinated secular to sacred epistemology, fundamentalists feel free to engage and even develop new forms of computer and communications technology, scientific research, political organizations, and the like" (2000:88). Sixth, "fundamentalists remain dualists at heart; they imagine the world divided into unambiguous realms of light and darkness peopled by the elect and the reprobate, the pure and the impure, the orthodox and the infidel" (2000:88). Seventh, "fundamentalists tend to be 'exceptionalists' … [They] believe themselves to be living in a special dispensation—an unusual, extraordinary time of crisis, danger, or apocalyptic doom" (2000:88). Finally, the "ability of religion to inspire ecstasy—literally, to lift the believer psychologically out of a mundane environment—stands behind the distinctive logic of religious violence. As unpredictable and illogical as this violence may seem to outsiders, it falls within a pattern of asceticism leading to the ecstasy of self-sacrifice that runs as a continuous thread through most religions" (Appleby, 2000:91). Appleby's findings take into account movements in Europe, India, the Middle East, South Asia, North America, and Africa.

A similar catalog of markers for religious violence appears in Catherine Wessinger (2000). Wessinger focuses more narrowly than Appleby on "millennialist" groups, and while her list of "warning signs" for millennialist groups extends to thirteen characteristics, six predominate. Most generally, a millennialist or religious group is prone to violence if "catastrophic millennial beliefs combined with belief in reincarnation and with the members' conviction that the group is being persecuted" (Wessinger, 2000:276). "Social alienation", where group members feel and articulate that "one's home is not on this planet" (2000:276), is a second trigger for religious groups to turn violent. Third is a "radical dualistic view of good versus evil" (2000:277). "Resistance to investigation and withdrawal to an isolated refuge" (2000:277) is a fourth marker, and dependence upon a "charismatic leader" who demands "high exit costs" (2000:278) of members, and who gives "new identities to the followers" (2000:278–279) is a fifth. Finally, tendencies to violence appear when "relatively small acts of violence [are] repeated in a ritualistic manner so that the scale and intensity of the violence increases" (Wessinger, 2000:280–281). Wessinger bases her conclusion on a study of The Peoples' Temple Movement (Jonestown), the Branch Davidians (Waco), Aum Shinrikyo, the Montana Freemen, and a few other cases. Most are from the United States; all of them were recent (1978–present). Wessinger posits three categories of millennialist groups prone to violence: "fragile" groups that initiate violence due to internal weaknesses and cultural opposition; "assaulted groups" that are attacked by law enforcement agents because they are perceived as "dangerous;" and "revolutionary millennial movements possessing theologies of violence" (Wessinger, 2000:17–22).

With a few notable exceptions (Beuken & Kischel, 1997; Huntington, 1996), other studies tend to focus more narrowly on particular regions or groups. The recent conflict in the former Yugoslavia, for instance, has produced various findings about the role of religion. Historian Paul Mojzes concluded that the conflict was "ethnoreligious." It "did not begin as an explicitly religious war … but [has] ethnoreligious characteristics because ethnicity and religion have become so enmeshed that they cannot be separated" (Mojzes, 1994:125). Muslim, Orthodox, Catholic, and Protestant Christian groups all interacted in complex ways with Bosnian, Serbian, and Croatian identities to produce conflict whose fundamental causes were ethnonational, according to Mojzes. More recently, building on the work of Samuel Huntington (1996) and Mark Juergensmeyer (1987), Christopher Catherwood (1997) indicts "religious nationalism" as the origin of the conflicts in the Balkans (and other places). Religious factors, notably group "identity" and "imaginary kingdoms" led members of religious groups to act on nationalist ambitions in ways that led to violence. These mythic constructs of group "identity" and "imaginary kingdoms" were the symbolic constellations by means of which religious impulses fueled violence in the Balkans. Yet a third study, by Michael Sells (1996, in a series edited by Juergensmeyer), traces the conflict (Sells calls it "genocide") directly to "Slobodan Milosevic's 1989 call ... for a new spirit of religious war and crusade" (Sells, 1996:xviii). Finally, Mart Bax (1995) focuses on "lower levels of social integration" than the national, and finds religious attachment to place (specifically the pilgrimage site of Medjugorje) a key contributing factor in the recent violence in the region. These conflicting results point to the need for both rigorous examination of the particular data and clearer theoretical and methodological paradigms, before understanding of the relationships between violence and religious groupings can be gained. Appleby's distinction between "strong" and "weak" religions, in particular, holds promise for shedding light on the travail of religion in the regions made up of the former Yugoslavia. Years of official suppression invariably produce "weak" group identities (in Appleby's sense), liable to manipulation by demagogues seeking legitimacy.

The same ambiguity in theoretical approach and empirical findings holds true in studies of conflict across India, and more specifically between Muslims, Sikhs, and Hindus. Kumar Pramod traces the conflicts to "communalism," which exhibits (among other things) communal based nationality, communal competition, ruler-centric religious-based history, and ascriptive identities embedded in discrete social interactions and discourse (Pramod, 1992:21). Communalism emerges out of complex economic, social, political, and religious causes, and produces violence (most notably to date repeated rioting) through equally complex trigger events which appear to one party or another to "pollute" or "distort" sacred faith. Again, Appleby's conception of "weak" religious links uniting group identity would seem to explain this susceptibility of communal groups to "trigger events." More broadly, Sudhir Kakar has utilized a psychoanalytic perspective to argue that "group identities" and "subjective, experiential aspects of conflict" (1996:ix) are important to consider in the Hindu-Muslim violence of 1990. "Fantasies, social representations, and modes of moral reasoning about the outgroups ... motivate and rationalize arson, looting, rape, and killing" (Kakar, 1996:x). Whether one calls these social constructions of "group identity" or "subjective experience" "religion" or not, probably doesn't matter in the long run, but it would lend conceptual clarity if social scientists could agree on their theoretical paradigms.

Finally, the most focused interpretation of these conflicts comes from the pen of Stanley J. Tambiah (1996). Tambiah downplays religious or symbolic factors formally, describing the conflicts as "ethnonationalist" or "leveling," yet Tambiah also resorts to religious language to explain the destruction of property and life as action "in a public cause that absolves [the destroyers] of individual crime and guilt" (Tambiah, 1996:279). Clearly, terms such as "absolve" and "guilt" are drawn from the field of religion, although Tambiah does not treat them as such. According to Tambiah, leveling crowds of Hindu, Muslim, or Sikh militants display "jubilant and festive moods" (1996:279) when engaged in violence. This accords well with Appleby's emphasis on the "ecstasy" that religious ritual can produce. Tambiah claims that the thrill-seeking of leveling crowds occurs because their acts of violence "are of a piece with their collective identity, their temporary sense of homogeneity, equality, and physical intimacy, their sense of taking righteous action to level down the enemy's presumed advantage and claim their collective entitlements" (Tambiah, 1996:280). Again, Tambiah skirts explicitly religious language, but it is clear from his analysis that the riots take on a ritualized character, governed by what he calls a "moral economy," but which could more accurately be described as a "ritual structure" that helps to limit, if not contain, the violence. Other practices or traditions of religious violence in India, notably *sati,* or wife-burning, and the deep layers of symbolic violence in traditional texts like the *Bhagavad Gita*, have begun to receive serious attention for the origins, persistence, and function (Dumezil, 1971; Hawley, 1994; Littleton, 1982).

Elsewhere in Asia religious conflicts have similarly been treated in case studies, with few syntheses. Sri Lanka, as one of the few Buddhist countries beset by overtly religious violence, has received careful attention from Kapferer (1988), Tambiah (1992), and Southwold (1993). The subtle role of religion in legitimating state power in other areas of Southeast Asia has been described recently in ways that respect the complex dynamics through which an "officially" nonviolent religion like Buddhism can accommodate itself to force and coercion (Smith, 1978; Swearer, 1995). Violence in China has often been linked to ethnic or political causes, but at least in some notable cases more overtly religious motivations have been discerned by social scientists (Lifton, 1973; Lipman & Harrell, 1990; Shea, 1997; Shek, 1990). Similarly in Japan, with the notable exception of the samurai traditions, Shinto, and a few other sects such as Aum Shinrikyo (Reader, 2000), analyses of links between violence and religion have been rare (King, 1993). Most recently, violence in Indonesia and East Timor has begun to receive attention as rooted in religious conflict (Jardine, 1995).

Religious violence in the Middle East—and especially from Muslim groups—has received a disproportionate amount of attention; not all of it even-handed. Among the most balanced are those of Bruce Lawrence (1998) and John L. Esposito (1992). Esposito contends that "a series of world events ... have reinforced mutually destructive stereotypes in the Muslim world and in the West" (1992:vii). Esposito is critical both of those who perpetuate "images of a militant Islam ... as particularly prone to religious extremism, fanaticism, and warfare" (1992:viii) and of those who fail to see "authoritarianism and violence in the name of Islam" (1992:viii) as historic facts. In contrast, Esposito encourages a multifaceted understanding of Islam, open to the diversity within the tradition and seeking to engage "political realities dispassionately and constructively and to transcend stereotypes"(Esposito, 1992:ix). The three volumes of The Fundamentalism Project of The University of Chicago, edited by Martin E. Marty and R. Scott Appleby (1993), also provide wide-ranging, and generally balanced, social-scientific coverage of the links between violence and religion in the Middle East, including both Muslim and Jewish groups. *Volume 3: Fundamentalisms and the State: Remaking Politics, Economies, and Militance* is particularly pointed and focused. Chapters cover religious groups from Israel, Iran, Egypt, Lebanon, and elsewhere, along with more comparative essays (see Sprinzak, 1999).

Studies of violence from religious groups in Africa range from treatment of the episodic upheavals among African independent churches and traditionalist groups, to case studies of post-colonial religious conflict in places like Nigeria, Sudan, Algeria, and South Africa. The conflicts of Nigeria have been particularly well documented by Toyin Falola. Falola argues that "the struggle for political power [in Nigeria] has come to entail the manipulation of the symbols and beliefs of Islam and Christianity. Indeed, religion has become so important in recent history that no analysis of modern Nigerian politics in the last quarter of the twentieth-century can fail to consider it fully" (Falola, 1998:2). The South African situation poses a fascinating case study for the potential of religion as catalyst for both violence and nonviolence. Prior to the fall of apartheid, several works profiled the various roles of religious groups in creating and responding to Afrikaner rule (Balia, 1989; Chidester, 1991; Tlhagale & Mosala, 1987; Villa-Vicencio, 1987). On the cusp of the transformation of South Africa, a group of theologians produced the historic *Kairos Document* clearly linking apartheid to its religious causes, and suggesting an alternative way for religion in a new South Africa. The Kairos theologians, as they came to be called, developed their own version of the distinction utilized by Robert McAfee Brown (1987) between the "first" violence of state-sponsored injustice, which was perpetually violent, and the episodic "second" violence manifest in attempts of oppressed people to defend themselves. Some of the Kairos theologians also contributed to a wide-ranging but detailed social-scientific analysis of *People and Violence in South Africa* (McKendrick & Hoffmann, 1990) which described how the nation was "ravaged and despoiled by widespread violence" (1990:5). Since the release of Nelson Mandela and the establishment of a new democratic regime, a number of social scientists have described and analyzed the role of religion in that "nonviolent revolution" and its aftermath (Gifford, 1995; Graybill, 1998; Lubbe, 1994; Waldmeier, 1998). Case studies also exist documenting the relations between violence and religion in other African nations, notably Sudan (El-Affendi, 1991) and Algeria (Impagliazzo & Giro, 2000).

By far the most ink has been used to document violence in European history and among Christian cultures, especially in the United States. Beyond the earlier discussions of violence and religion in Yugoslavia, studies exist for nearly every imaginable period and region, although, again, few are syntheses. Historical treatments abound. Frend (1965) produced a classic history of *Martyrdom and Persecution in the Early Church* which documented the crucible of violence out of which Christianity arose and the turn of Christians from persecuted minority to established persecutors over time. Among the most notorious examples of Christian violence, of course, are the Inquisitions (Kamen, 1997; Peters, 1988), Crusades (Armstrong, 1988), wars of religion (Parrow, 1993), and anti-Semitism (Flannery, 1985; Moore, 1985). The special case of religion, violence, and German anti-Semitism during the Nazi regime is described in any number of studies, notably Cochrane (1962) and Ericksen and Heschel (1999). Catholic groups during the Third Reich receive special attention from Lewy (1964) and Zahn (1962). Particular light on the complex relations between Nazi ideology and religion is shed by the specialized studies of Quaker, gypsies, and Jehovah's Witnesses in Germany between 1939–1945 (Schmitt, 1997; Lewy, 2000).

Elsewhere in Europe, Northern Ireland has understandably been the focus of many recent studies (Irvine, 1991; Keogh & Haltzel, 1993; Kinahan, 1995; Lennon, 1995; Wells, 1999), but events in Latin America (Berryman, 1994; Bonino, 1975) and Poland (Szajkowski, 1983; Weigel, 1992) have also drawn the attention of social scientists concerned with the relationships between Christianity, violence, and nonviolence (see also van der Veer & Lehmann, 1999). Few of these studies generalize beyond their specific locales. One notable exception to that rule is Marc H. Ellis (1997), who in an interesting cross-cultural study has posited "barbarism" as the link between "religion" and "atrocity." For Ellis, religious systems characterized by devotion to a "god of death" (1997:8) (e.g., one who promotes martyrdom) predisposes some believers to acts of violence, whereas religious systems characterized by devotion to a "god of life" (1997:8) (e.g., one who promotes tolerance and compassion for victims of suffering) might promote peace and reconciliation. In another cross-cultural study, Regina Schwartz (1997) has even more pointedly than Ellis (1997) traced the origins of religious violence to the Western notion of monotheism, and especially the notion of "scarcity" monotheism often implies. Schwartz writes: "When everything is in short supply, it must all be competed for—land, prosperity, power, favor, even identity itself. In many biblical narratives, the one God is not imagined as infinitely giving, but as strangely withholding. Everyone does not receive divine blessings. Some are cursed" (Schwartz, 1997:xi). In short, argues Schwartz, violence from religious groups stems from scarcity (or perception of scarcity), competition, and the defense of an "exclusive" identity as a mark of possession of divine favor or chosenness. Combining Freud, Weber, and Marx, although in a literary rather than an empirical study,

Schwartz traces religious violence especially to the logic of monotheism, with a capitalist overlay. Along the same lines, Barrington Moore Jr. (2000) has recently traced links between ideologies of "moral purity" and "persecution" in somewhat randomly chosen historical examples.

In the United States, selected episodes of violence from religious groups have been well documented. In three large volumes, Richard Slotkin (1973) has traced the complicity of religious motives, and especially what he has called "the frontier myth," in the recurrent violence of American culture. In early America, literature on the conquest and "resettlement" of Native tribes is vast (Deloria, 1969), as is literature on the links between religion and the unique form of chattel slavery that developed in the United States (Butler, 1993). Studies also exist which document the religious roots of the persecution and execution of witches and women in New England (Hoffer, 1996; Taves, 1989), and broader currents of ideological exclusion and boundary formation in early America (Pahl, 1992). In the twentieth century, studies have focused on violence from religious groups opposed to legalized abortion (Gorney, 1998; Risen & Thomas, 1998; Solinger, 1998), religious legitimized violence against women and children (Adams & Fortune, 1995; Brown & Bohn, 1989), Christian violence against lesbians and gay men (Comstock, 1992; Herek & Berrill, 1992; Seow, 1996). Social scientists have also mapped the symbolic functions of youth gang violence (Spergel, 1995), the cultural origins of American nuclear policy (Boyer, 1985), lynching of African-Americans as ritual violence (Brundage, 1993), militias and other right-wing "Christian identity" groups (Abanes, 1996), and violence from millennial and sectarian groups like the "Peoples' Temple" and "Branch Davidians" (Levi, 1982; Wessinger, 2000).

III.   DESIDERATA

Scholars in religious studies have until recently favored the humanities and literary approaches to their topics, while social scientists have often avoided the topic of religion and tradition, seeking to reduce the complex symbolic processes at the basis of religious life to some more quantifiable or material substrata. This means that considerable work remains to be done to unearth empirically verifiable findings to explain the complex relations between religious groups and various manifestations of violence. Theoretical paradigms have remained largely beholden to classical approaches, although the best studies combine and cross methods. No new theory of the relationship between violence and religion has emerged since Girard, although Juergensmeyer and Appleby show promise of promoting such a paradigm shift in future works. Appleby's emphasis on the ambivalence of the sacred is a helpful corrective to approaches which highlight either the violence or nonviolence of religious systems and groups.

Within the seven levels or forms of intensity of violence identified previously in the article, some areas are in more need of work than others. Attention to key religious symbols and rituals other than sacrifice and myths of cosmic war would be an important first step, although no consensus exists on those two topics, either. How symbolic processes are linked to violence in forming "group identity," for instance, would appear to be a most promising direction for future research. Appleby's categories of "strong" and "weak" religious identification, for instance, could be linked to substantive symbolic processes such as moral formulations, behavioral codes, legal systems, theological images and metaphors (see Wessinger (2000) on millennialism, and Schwartz (1997) on scarcity and abundance), and other basic aspects of religious systems in ways that were both quantifiable and illuminating. Along with these linguistic elements, more attention could be paid to the presence of coercion and violence in rituals other than sacrifice, most notably in rites of passage, where violent "tests" of one kind or another are often offered potential initiates. Close studies of other ritual processes, such as ascetic practices (fasting, physical discipline, etc.), rituals of affliction in pilgrimage processes, and other even more austere forms of religiously inspired bodily mortification and modification, if not mutilation, would be informative. Similarly, the tendency of religious groups to create normative boundaries through heresy trials and other modes of censure or exclusion could use careful cross-cultural study. Finally, the relationship between religion and authoritarianism needs updated attention (Altemeyer, 1988). Generally, then, nearly the entire field of "symbolic analysis" of how religious language and practice inform, control, or escalate practices of violence remains open to social scientific investigation.

The second level of intensity of violence—the tendency of religious groups to divide the world into "insiders" and "outsiders," "pure" and "impure," is well-established as a phenomenon or element in violent situations (Aho, 1994; Moore, 2000; Volf, 1996). The specific mechanisms which trigger such formulations, however, and the specific events which incite ideologies of dualism to motivate individuals or groups to violent actions are less clear.

Relationships between belonging to a religious group and participation in behaviors from a third level of intensity of violence, namely street crime, vandalism, gang formation, rape, the drug trade and so forth also need closer analysis. Turpin and Kurtz (1997) have made an initial foray, but the field is ripe for both descriptive and prescriptive studies. Churches and other religious congregations are, obviously, potential allies of agencies involved in crime prevention. They also can serve to defend individuals wrongly accused, or to harbor dissidents. The pattern in scholarship here is replicated throughout the field: stronger links need to be drawn between the "macro"-level of analysis on which most scholars of religion have tended to operate, and the "micro"-level of policy and local initiative. This is true also of the ways in which religious groups contribute to (and/or oppose) the "legitimized" responses of society to crime, namely discipline and punishment. For example, advocates from religious traditions both for and against capital punishment or other forms of sanctioned violence can easily be located, but little analysis of how and why the various advocates arrive at their positions has been offered. Close attention to patterns of ridicule, stereotyping, segregation, and so forth would be helpful.

The fifth and sixth levels of intensity of violence—systemic exclusion and organized retaliatory violence in the name of religion—such as gender bias and racism, terrorism, and revolution in the name of religion, have been mapped in both popular and scholarly literature. The spectacular cases of racist activity and terrorist activity in the name of God have been documented by Fox (1999), Hoffman (1998), Ranstorp (1996), and Reich (1990); far less attention has been paid to the day-to-day manifestations of peace-making and reconciliation within and across religions. The best study of the relationship between religion and revolution dates from 1974, and is badly in need of updating (Lewy, 1974).

Finally, the examination of war and genocide in the name of religion has been advanced especially by the studies of Juergensmeyer (2000), although close cross-cultural studies are still much in need. Ferguson's study from 1977 bears examination, and Nardin (1996) has edited an influential volume that points toward a clearer picture than hitherto offered of at least the Western religious traditions and war.

IV.   APPROACHES OF PREVENTION

R. Scott Appleby (2000) has provided, again, the most systematic and recent overview of the peace-building potential of religious groups. Drawing on examples from Buddhism, Judaism, Islam, Christianity, and Hinduism, Appleby has developed a typology of peace-making from religious groups. Religions, he suggests, can be involved in violence prevention through "preventive diplomacy, education and training, election monitoring, conflict mediation, nonviolent protest and advocacy for structural reform, and withdrawing or providing moral legitimacy for a government in times of crisis" (Appleby, 2000:211). These interrelated activities indicate, to Appleby, not particular "stages" for religious groups involved in nonviolence, but a general "logic" to religious peacemaking across traditions. Individual examples such as Mohandas Gandhi, the Dalai Lama (1997), Martin Luther King Jr., Desmond Tutu, and Lech Walesa demonstrate the ability of belonging to a religious group to motivate peacemaking and nonviolence across cultures (see also Stassen, 1998).

Mark Juergensmeyer has also identified three ways religions can contribute to nonviolence. First, he argues, religions can promote violence through "an inner state or attitude of nondestructiveness and reverence for life" (1987:463). Juergensmeyer identifies this strand of religious nonviolence in the Jain, Buddhist, and Hindu traditions, primarily through the notion of *ahimsa*. Juergensmeyer also sees this attitude present, with different names, in particular African and Native American tribal societies, as well as among the Quakers and other pacifist Christian traditions, such as the Mennonites (Driedger & Kraybill, 1994). Juergensmeyer's second way for members of religious groups to promote nonviolence is to promulgate "an ideal of social harmony and peaceful living" (1987:463). The Hebrew concept of *shalom*, and the Islamic term *salam*, represent this ideal of peace also found in some archaic and tribal religious groupings (see also Wink, 1992). Finally, nonviolence from religious groups might be evident as "a response to conflict" (1987:463). Here Juergensmeyer points to the Christian notion of sacrificial love, the Jewish concept of martyrdom, and the Gandhian strategy of nonviolence as manifest examples (see also Bondurant, 1988).

In short, there are ample ideological and human resources within every major religious tradition that devotees could draw upon to mobilize supporters in the cause of nonviolence. As Appleby suggests, it is incumbent upon religious leaders, and students of religion, to communicate the depths of these traditions in such a way that the countervailing tendencies of "weak" religious groupings toward extremism and violence can be lessened, if not eliminated. Social scientists can certainly assist in this goal, by examining closely and critically the ambivalence of the sacred and the way human beings enact their devotion in society.

REFERENCES

Abanes, Richard. (1996). *American Militias: Rebellion, Racism, and Religion.* Downers Grove: InterVarsity Press.

Adams, Carol J., & Marie M. Fortune. (1995). *Violence against Women and Children: A Christian Theological Sourcebook.* Continuum Publishers.

Aho, James. (1994). *This Thing of Darkness: A Sociology of the Enemy.* Seattle: University of Washington Press.

Altemeyer, Bob. (1988). *Enemies of Freedom: Understanding Right-Wing Authoritarianism.* San Francisco: Jossey-Bass.

Appleby, R. Scott. (2000). *The Ambivalence of the Sacred: Religion, Violence, and Reconciliation.* Lanham, Boulder, New York, Oxford: Rowman and Littlefield.

Armstrong, Karen. (1988). *Holy War: The Crusades and Their Impact on Today's World*. New York: Anchor/ Doubleday.

Balia, Daryl M. (1989). *Christian Resistance to Apartheid: Ecumenism in South Africa, 1960–1987*. Hamburg: Verlag an der Lottbek.

Bax, Mart. (1995). *Medjugorje: Religion, Politics, and Violence in Rural Bosnia*. Amsterdam: VU University Press.

Berryman, Philip. (1994). *Stubborn Hope: Religion, Politics, and Revolution in Central America*. Maryknoll: Orbis Books.

Beuken, Wim, & Karl-Josef Kischel. (Eds.) (1997). *Religion as a Source of Violence*. London: SCM Press.

Bondurant, Joan V. (1988). *Conquest of Violence: The Gandhian Philosophy of Conflict*. Princeton: Princeton University Press.

Bonino, Jose Miguez. (1975). *Doing Theology in a Revolutionary Situation*. Philadelphia: Fortress.

Boyer, Paul. (1985). *By the Bomb's Early Light: American Thought and Culture at the Dawn of the Atomic Age*. New York: Pantheon Books.

Brown, Joanne Carlson, & Carole R. Bohn. (Eds.) (1989). *Christianity, Patriarchy, and Abuse: A Feminist Critique*. New York: Pilgrim Press.

Brown, Robert McAfee. (1987 [1973]). *Religion and Violence: A Primer for White Americans*. Philadelphia: Fortress.

Brundage, W. Fitzhugh. (1993). *Lynching in the New South: Georgia and Virginia, 1880–1930*. Urbana, Chicago: The University of Illinois Press.

Butler, Jon. (1993). *Awash in a Sea of Faith: Christianizing the American People*. Cambridge: Harvard University Press.

Candland, Christopher. (1992). *The Spirit of Violence: An Interdisciplinary Bibliography of Religion and Violence. Occasional Papers of the Harry Frank Guggenheim Foundation, Number 6*. New York: Harry Frank Guggenheim Foundation.

Catherwood, Christopher. (1997). *Why the Nations Rage*. London, Sydney, Auckland: Hodder and Stoughton.

Chidester, David. (1991). *Shots in the Streets: Violence and Religion in South Africa*. Boston: Beacon.

Cochrane, Arthur C. (1962). *The Church's Confession Under Hitler*. Philadelphia: Westminster.

Comstock, Gary David. (1992). *Violence Against Lesbians and Gay Men*. New York: Columbia University Press.

The Dalai Lama of Tibet. (1997). Lopen, Donald S., Jr. (Ed.), *The Joy of Living and Dying in Peace*. New York: Harper Collins.

Deloria, Vine. (1969). *Custer Died for Your Sins: An Indian Manifesto*. New York: Macmillan.

Driedger, Leo, & Donald B. Kraybill. (1994). *Mennonite Peacemaking: From Quietism to Activism*. Scottsdale: Herald Press.

Dumezil, Georges. (1971). *The Stakes of the Warrior*. Berkeley: The University of California Press.

El-Affendi, Abdelwahab. (1991). *Turabi's Revolution, Islam and Power in Sudan*. London: Grey Seal.

Eliade, Mircea. (1959). *The Sacred and the Profane: The Nature of Religion* (trans. by Willark Trask). New York: Harper and Row.

Ellis, Marc H. (1997). *Unholy Alliance: Religion and Atrocity in Our Time*. Minneapolis: Fortress.

Ericksen, Robert P., & Susannah Heschel. (1999). *Betrayal: German Churches and the Holocaust*. Minneapolis: Fortress Press.

Esposito, John L. (1992). *The Islamic Threat: Myth or Reality?* New York, Oxford: Oxford University Press.

Falola, Toyin. (1998). *Violence in Nigeria: The Crisis of Religious Politics and Secular Ideologies*. Rochester: The University of Rochester Press.

Ferguson, John. (1977). *War and Peace in the World's Religions*. London: Sheldon Press.

Flannery, Edward H. (1985). *The Anguish of the Jews: Twenty-Three Centuries of Anti-Semitism*. New York: Paulist.

Fox, Jonathan. (1999). Do Religious Institutions Support Violence or the Status Quo? *Studies in Conflict and Terrorism, 22*, 119–139.

Freedman, David Noel, & Michael J. McClymond. (1999). *Religious Traditions, Violence, and Nonviolence*. Encyclopedia of Violence, Peace, and Conflict. Volume 3. San Diego: Academic Press, pp. 229–239.

Frend, William Hugh Clifford. (1965). *Martyrdom and Persecution in the Early Church*. Grand Rapids: Baker Book House.

Geertz, Clifford. (1973). *The Interpretation of Cultures: Selected Essays*. New York: Basic Books.

Gifford, Paul. (Ed.) (1995). *The Christian Churches and the Democratization of Africa*. Leiden: E. J. Brill.

Girard, Rene. (1977). *Violence and the Sacred, tr. Patrick Gregory*. Baltimore: The Johns Hopkins University Press.

Gorney, Cynthia. (1998). *Articles of Faith: A Frontline History of the Abortion Wars*. New York: Simon and Schuster.

Graybill, Lyn S. (1998). South Africa's Truth and Reconciliation Commission: Ethical and Theological Perspectives. *Ethics and International Affairs*, *12*, 44–67.

Hawley, John Stratton. (Ed.) (1994). *Sati: The Blessing and the Curse—The Burning of Wives in India*. New York, Oxford: Oxford University Press.

Herek, Gregory M., & Kevin T. Berrill. (1992). *Hate Crimes: Confronting Violence against Lesbians and Gay Men*. Newbury Park: Sage Publications.

Hoffer, Peter Charles. (1996). *The Devil's Disciples: Makers of the Salem Witchcraft Trials*. Baltimore: The Johns Hopkins University Press.

Hoffman, Bruce. (1998). *Inside Terrorism*. New York: Columbia University Press.

Huntington, Samuel P. (1996). *The Clash of Civilizations and the Remaking of World Order*. New York: Simon and Schuster.

Impagliazzo, Marco, & Mario Giro. (2000). *Algeria Held Hostage: The Army, Fundamentalism, and the History of a Troublesome Peace*. Boulder: Westview Press.

Irvine, Maurice. (1991). *Northern Ireland: Faith and Faction*. London: Routledge.

Jardine, Matthew. (1995). *East Timor: Genocide in Paradise*. Tucson: Odonian Press.

Juergensmeyer, Mark. (1987). Nonviolence. In Eliade, Mircea (Ed.), *The Encyclopedia of Religion, Vol. 10* (pp. 463–468). New York: Macmillian.

Juergensmeyer, Mark. (1993). *The New Cold War? Religious Nationalism Confronts the Secular State*. Berkeley: The University of California Press.

Juergensmeyer, Mark. (2000). *Terror in the Mind of God: The Global Rise of Religious Violence (Comparative Studies in Religion and Society)*. Berkeley: The University of California Press.

Kairos Theologians. (1986). *The Kairos Document: Challenge to the Church. A Theological Comment on the Political Crisis in South Africa. Rev. 2nd Edition*. Grand Rapids: Eerdmans.

Kakar, Sudhir. (1996). *The Colors of Violence: Cultural Identities, Religion, and Conflict*. Chicago, London: The University of Chicago Press.

Kamen, Henry. (1997). *The Spanish Inquisition: An Historical Revision*. London: Weidenfeld and Nicolson.

Kapferer, Bruce. (1988). *Legends of People, Myths of State: Violence, Intolerance, and Political Culture in Sri Lanka and Australia*. Washington: Smithsonian Institution Press.

Keogh, Dermot, & Michael H. Haltzel. (Eds.) (1993). *Northern Ireland and the Politics of Reconciliation*. Cambridge: Press Syndicate of the University of Cambridge.

Kinahan, Timothy. (1995). *Where Do We Go from Here? Protestants and the Future of Northern Ireland*. Dublin: Columba.

King, Winston Lee. (1993). *Zen and the Way of the Sword: Arming the Samurai Psyche*. New York: Oxford.

Lawrence, Bruce B. (1998). *Shattering the Myth: Islam beyond Violence*. Princeton: Princeton University Press.

Lennon, Brian S. J. (1995). *After the Cease Fires: Catholics and the Future of Northern Ireland*. Dublin: Columba.

Levi, Ken. (1982). *Violence and Religious Commitment: Implications of Jim Jones's People's Temple Movement*. University Park, London: The Pennsylvania State University Press.

Lewy, Guenter. (1964). *The Catholic Church and Nazi Germany*. New York: McGraw-Hill.

Lewy, Guenter. (1974). *Religion and Revolution*. New York: Oxford University Press.

Lewy, Guenter. (2000). *The Nazi Persecution of the Gypsies*. New York: Oxford University Press.

Lifton, Robert J. (1973). *Revolutionary Immortality: Mao Tse-Tung and the Chinese Cultural Revolution*. New York: Random House.

Lipman, Jonathan N., & Stevan Harrell. (Eds.) (1990). *Violence in China: Essays in Culture and Counterculture*. Albany: State University of New York Press.

Littleton, C. Scott. (1982). *The Comparative Mythology: An Anthropological Assessment of the Theories of Georges Dumezil. 3rd Edition*. Berkeley: The University of California Press.

Lubbe, Gerrie. (Ed.) (1994). *A Decade of Interfaith Dialogue*. Johannesburg: The South African Chapter of the World Conference on Religions and Peace.

Marty, Martin E., & R. Scott Appleby. (Eds.) (1993). *Fundamentalisms and the State: Remaking Polities, Economies, and Militance. The Fundamentalism Project. Vol. 3*. Chicago, London: The University of Chicago Press.

McKendrick, Brian, & Wilma Hoffmann. (Eds.) (1990). *People and Violence in South Africa*. Cape Town: Oxford University Press.

Moore, Barrington, Jr. (2000). *Moral Purity and Persecution in History*. Princeton: Princeton University Press.

Moore, Robert Ian. (1985). *The Formation of a Persecuting Society: Power and Deviance in Western Europe, 950–1250*. New York: Basil Blackwell.

Mojzes, Paul. (1994). *Yugoslavian Inferno: Ethnoreligious Warfare in the Balkans*. New York: Continuum.

Nardin, Terry. (Ed.) (1996). *The Ethics of War and Peace: Religious and Secular Perspectives*. Princeton: Princeton University Press.

Pahl, Jon. (1992). *Paradox Lost: Free Will and Political Liberty in American Culture, 1630–1760*. Baltimore, London: The Johns Hopkins University Press.

Parrow, Kathleen Ann. (1993). *From Defense to Resistance: Justification of Violence during the French Wars of Religion*. Philadelphia: American Philosophical Association.

Peters, Edward. (1988). *Inquisition*. New York, London: The Free Press.

Pramod, Kumar. (1992). *Polluting Sacred Faith: A Study of Communalism and Violence in India*. Columbia: The University of Missouri Press.

Ranstorp, Magnus. (1996). Terrorism in the Name of Religion. *Journal of International Affairs, 50*, 41–62.

Reader, Ian. (2000). *Religious Violence in Contemporary Japan: The Case of Aum Shinrikyo*. Honolulu: University of Hawaii Press.

Reich, Walter. (Ed.) (1990). *Origins of Terrorism: Psychologies, Ideologies, Theologies, States of Mind*. Cambridge: Cambridge University Press.

Risen, James, & Judy L. Thomas. (1998). *Wrath of Angels: The American Abortion War*. New York: Basic Books.

Schmitt, Hans A. (1997). *Quakers and Nazis: Inner Light in Outer Darkness*. Columbia: The University of Missouri Press.

Schwartz, Regina. (1997). *The Curse of Cain: The Violent Legacy of Monotheism*. Chicago, London: The University of Chicago Press.

Sells, Michael A. (1996). *The Bridge Betrayed: Religion and Genocide in Bosnia*. Berkeley: The University of California Press.

Seow, Choon-Leong. (Ed.) (1996). *Homosexuality and Christian Community*. Louisville: Westminster John Knox Press.

Shea, Nina. (1997). *In the Lion's Den: A Shocking Account of Persecution and Martyrdom of Christians Today*. Nashville: Abingdon Press.

Shek, Richard. (1990). Sectarian Eschatology and Violence. In Jonathan M. Lipman & Stevan Harrell (Eds.), *Violence in China* (pp. 87–114). Albany: State University of New York Press.

Shils, Edward. (1981). *Tradition*. Chicago: The University of Chicago Press.

Slotkin, Richard. (1973). *Regeneration through Violence: The Mythology of the American Frontier, 1600–1860*. Middletown: Wesleyan University Press.

Smith, Bardwell L. (Ed.) (1978). *Religion and Legitimization of Power in Thailand, Laos, and Burma*. Chambersburg: Anima.

Solinger, Rickie. (1998). *Abortion Wars: A Half Century of Struggle, 1950–2000*. Berkeley: The University of California Press.

Southwold, Martin. (1993). Purity and Power in Buddhist Sri Lanka. In Mart Bax & Adrianus Koster (Eds.), *Power and Prayer: Religious and Political Processes in Past and Present* (pp. 201–214). Amsterdam: VU University Press.

Spergel, Irving A. (1995). *The Youth Gang Problem: A Community Approach*. New York: Oxford University Press.

Sprinzak, Ehud. (1999). *Brother against Brother: Violence and Extremism in Israeli Politics from Altalena to the Rabin Assassination*. New York: The Free Press.

Stassen, Glen. (Ed.) (1998). *Just Peacemaking: Ten Practices for Abolishing War*. Cleveland: Pilgrim Press.

Swearer, Donald K. (1995). *The Buddhist World of Southeast Asia*. Albany: State University of New York Press.

Szajkowski, Bogdan. (1983). *Next to God. Poland: Politics and Religion in Contemporary Poland*. New York: St Martin's Press.

Tambiah, Stanley. (1992). *Buddhism Betrayed? Religion, Politics, and Violence in Sri Lanka*. Chicago, London: The University of Chicago Press.

Tambiah, Stanley. (1996). *Leveling Crowds: Ethnonationalist Conflicts and Collective Violence in South Asia*. Berkeley, Los Angeles, London: University of California Press.

Taves, Ann. (Ed.) (1989). *Religion and Domestic Violence in Early New England: The Memoirs of Abigail Abbot Bailey*. Bloomington, Indianapolis: Indiana University Press.

Tlhagale, Buti, and Itumelend Mosala. (Eds.) (1987). *Hammering Swords into Plowshares: Essays in Honor of Archbishop Mpilo Desmond Tutu*. Grand Rapids: Eerdmans.

Turpin, Jennifer, & Lester R. Kurtz. (Eds.) (1997). *The Web of Violence: From Interpersonal to Global*. Urbana, Chicago: The University of Illinois Press.

Van der Veer, Peter, & Helmut Lehmann. (Eds.) (1999). *Nation and Religion: Perspectives on Europe and Asia*. Princeton: Princeton University Press.

Villa-Vicencio, Charles. (Ed.) (1987). *Theology and Violence: The South African Debate*. Grand Rapids: Eerdmans.

Volf, Miroslav. (1996). *Exclusion and Embrace: A Theological Exploration of Identity, Otherness and Reconciliation*. Nashville: Abingdon.

Waldmeier, Patti. (1998). *Anatomy of a Miracle: The End of Apartheid and the Birth of the New South Africa*. New York: Norton.

Weigel, George. (1992). *The Final Revolution: The Resistance Church and the Collapse of Communism*. New York: Oxford University Press.

Wells, Ronald A. (1999). *People behind the Peace: Community and Reconciliation in Northern Ireland*. Grand Rapids: Eerdmans.

Wink, Walter. (1992). *Engaging the Powers: Discernment and Resistance in a World of Domination*. Minneapolis: Fortress Press.

Wessinger, Catherine. (2000). *How the Millennium Comes Violently: From Jonestown to Heaven's Gate*. New York, London: Seven Bridges Press.

Zahn, Gordon C. (1962). *German Catholics and Hitler's Wars*. New York: Sheed and Ward.

Vigilantism

David Kowalewski

I. INTRODUCTION

In Los Angeles, a neighborhood-watch group forms to counter a recent rash of burglaries. In London, a group of skinheads rampages through a neighborhood in an spree of "Paki-bashing." In Nairobi, President Daniel Arap Moi sends out the youth wing of his ruling Kenya African National Union party to disrupt dissident demonstrations and harass opposition leaders.

These and similar events, often encountered in the news media, can all be classed as vigilante behaviors (see Brown, 1975, 1979, 1983; Culberson, 1990; Rosenbaum & Sederberg, 1976; Tucker, 1985). Vigilantism refers to the activities of private citizens, or government employees acting off-duty in their private capacity, designed to suppress deviance by other citizens. By deviance is meant the beliefs and behaviors of citizens which differ significantly from the established social norms of a community. By established social norms are meant those expected patterns of beliefs and behaviors professed by the ruling elites of a community. The deviance against which vigilantes mobilize may be of three types: criminal (e.g., neighborhood drug-dealing); cultural (e.g., hippie communes); or political (e.g., labor strikes) (see Kowalewski, 1996a, 1996b; Neeley, 1990).

Both vigilantes, and the deviants countered by vigilantes, may be acting individually or collectively. Individual vigilantes would include such persons as lone crime-fighters (e.g., Bernhard Goetz, the New York City "subway killer" who shot several would-be muggers), while collective vigilantes would include such formations as community groups combating threats to their property (e.g., white South African commandos formed to counter black African cattle-raiders). Individual deviants would comprise citizens such as urban homeless beggars; collective deviants would embrace groups such as student organizations dissenting against government repression.

Objectively, vigilantes occupy an ambivalent role in society, which may explain the subjective ambivalence with which they are often regarded by scholars and public alike.

W. Heitmeyer and J. Hagan (eds.), *International Handbook of Violence Research*, 339–349.
© 2003 Kluwer Academic Publishers. Printed in the Netherlands.

On the one hand, they act outside of established institutions, taking the law into their own hands. As such, they are often seen as playing a role of dubious social legitimacy. Ironically, they "act deviantly" in order to suppress deviance. On the other hand, since they do take the law into their own hands in order to uphold established norms, they are often seen as playing a legitimate social role. This borderline social legitimacy accounts for the seemingly contradictory labels which society puts on vigilantes, i.e., "parapolice" and "paramilitary," and "private police" and "private militia."

II. THEORETICAL APPROACHES AND EMPIRICAL FINDINGS

Despite the prevalence of vigilante groups around the world, there exists little research on the topic. Two reasons can be adduced for the lack of scholarly attention: (1) the short-lived nature of vigilante formations, and (2) the frontier theory which despite its inadequacies persisted as a popular paradigm discouraging theoretical development and research.

First, vigilante activities, to use Fernand Braudel's term, are almost always "firefly events," which arise suddenly and unexpectedly but then just as suddenly and unexpectedly disappear. Usually vigilantes are part-time sociopolitical amateurs, having little desire or opportunity for full-time counterdeviant activities and few skills for building any formidable organizations. Vigilante activities usually decline dramatically after initial enthusiasm wanes (Lungren, 1991). Further, the disruption caused by vigilante groups quickly provokes efforts by government and public alike to curtail their activities and disband their formations. Rarely if ever, therefore, do vigilante groups transform themselves into long-lasting social institutions. This lack of institutionalization, in turn, means little written documentation for scholars to examine. The lack of written records is further aggravated by the private and informal—and often illegal—nature of vigilante behaviors. Thus, social scientists have few incentives to research the groups while at the same time they face many difficulties.

Second, the long-prevailing social-scientific theory for explaining vigilantism, the frontier perspective, captured the imagination of scholars and public and discouraged further questioning. Scholars like Richard Brown in Strain of Violence (1975) and Roger McGrath in Gunfighters, Highwaymen, and Vigilantes (1984) provided vivid and detailed descriptions of private law-enforcement on the near-lawless frontier. Perhaps more importantly, however, the frontier theory proved seriously inadequate and left scholars without a useful conceptual handle for understanding vigilantism.

Developed in the United States to explain such groupings as lynch mobs and posses, the theory proposed that the lack of law-enforcement institutions in the American "wild west" left crime-besieged citizens with no alternative but to take the law into their own hands. Certainly there was some truth to the theory. The perceived ineffectiveness of law-enforcement always plays a role in the rise of vigilantism. In addition, remote rural frontier communities are often socially homogeneous, lacking the diversity of large cities; hence we might expect citizens in such locales to be less tolerant of deviants than their urban counterparts and thus more likely to turn to vigilantism.

Several problems with the frontier theory, however, quickly became apparent. In brief, the theory was too narrow in scope. First, it dealt only with vigilantism against criminal deviance and failed to include other types. For example, it is hard-pressed to account for the vigilante "GOON" squads mobilized by the Federal Bureau of Investigation (FBI) against the political dissidents of the American Indian Movement (Churchill & VanderWall, 1988, 1990). Second, the frontier theory, derived from the experience of the American "wild west," failed to account for the relative absence of vigilantism in other large remote regions of the world (e.g., Russian Siberia). Third, the frontier theory failed to explain numerous vigilante phenomena in nonfrontier regions. For example, it is unable to account for the vigilante groups which have attacked crack-houses in American urban neighborhoods. Fourth, the frontier theory assumed that vigilantes only arise autonomously and spontaneously in the absence of law enforcement, thereby ignoring the many instances of state-sponsored vigilantism, e.g., the mobilization of death squads by the Colombian military against suspected revolutionaries. Fifth, the frontier theory proved historically myopic. It predicts that the rapid disappearance of the frontier across the world will make vigilantes an extinct social species, as the requisite grounding erodes beneath their feet. Of course, no such thing has happened; vigilantism is alive, well, and thriving—despite the disappearing frontier.

The theoretical blinders of the frontier theory have caused most social scientists to ignore a wide array of vigilante activities across the world. Unfortunately for these scholars, vigilantism continues to rear its head almost everywhere and, if anything, has increased in frequency. Thus the need for a fresh theoretical perspective is urgent.

The countermovement perspective seems to fulfill this need. Useful delineations of the theory can be found in the author's "Counterinsurgent Vigilantism and Public Response" (1991), "Countermovement Vigilantism and Human Rights" (1996), and "Legality of State-Sponsored Vigilantism" (1996). Accordingly, vigilantes are best understood in terms of their dynamic interactions with growing numbers and activities of deviants. It is not so much the simple presence of deviants that provokes vigilantism, but rather their rapid growth in the form of a threatening movement, e.g., a crime epidemic, a cultural fad, or a wave of dissent. As such, vigilantes constitute a countermovement designed to push back a movement increasingly seen as threatening their way of life.

The rapidity of the growth of a deviant movement is key to understanding vigilante mobilization. It explains both the sudden rise of citizen grievances against deviants as well as the depletion of law-enforcement resources necessary to counter their activities. First, the rapid growth of deviance on citizens' turf allows them little social time to adjust to and assimilate the new beliefs and behaviors. Citizens feel besieged, unexpectedly, and have little conceptual equipment to understand the disruption. For example, the growth of demonstrations, marches, rallies, and other public activities by the American gay movement greatly unsettled the heterosexual public and soon led to an epidemic of "gay-bashing." In short, lack of public understanding in the face of rapidly growing deviance quickly becomes a set of grievances which can reach violent levels. Public fear—or to use perhaps a more accurate term, public panic—based on ignorance helps explain such strange vigilante phenomena as American parents attacking neighborhood school children who have contracted the AIDS virus.

Second, the rapid growth of deviance puts a severe strain on the resources of law-enforcement agencies. In the face of rapidly rising deviance, a society's police, courts, and military are usually unable to mobilize sufficient personnel, facilities, and equipment for timely response to the deviants. Governmental control resources are quickly depleted, while official frustration builds as deviants appear to be taking over the community. In Guatemala, for instance, counterinsurgency programs against the leftist movement have consumed up to one-third of the national budget. A growing movement stretches thin the personnel resources of coercive organs, thereby encouraging the search for auxiliary forces among the citizenry. Governments, therefore, often see vigilantes as a low-cost means of deviance-control.

Instances of vigilantism arising in response to growing deviance are legion. In the United States after World War I, for example, a strike wave prompted the "Red Scare" during which coercive organs used Pinkerton detectives and other private groups against the labor movement. An American Protective League worked to help the overloaded Bureau of Investigation against the Industrial Workers of the World and other unionists. In the 1960s, as dissent against the Vietnam War increased, the FBI formed the private Secret Army Organization as part of its counterdissident COINTELPRO program. The group broke into offices and terrorized journalists, professors, and other dissenters. In Chicago the FBI directed the Legion of Justice to vandalize the offices of the antiwar movement. In the 1980s, as dissent against the Reagan administration's policy in Central America grew, the FBI and National Security Council utilized the World Anti-Communist League and other private groups to harass dissenters and Central American refugees.

In the Soviet Union during the 1970s, the rise of the Human Rights Movement led the government to use civilian volunteer militias (druzhiny) against dissenters. During the late 1980s, the wave of national independence campaigns in non-Slavic republics led Slavs in these regions to form Interfront groups to fight against the movements. In Estonia, for example, the Soviet navy called on its radio listeners to form vigilante groups. Elsewhere, the uniformed police and military recruited squads of young Cossacks to join them on patrols.

In Haiti, following an attempt to overthrow President Francis "Papa Doc" Duvalier in 1958, a mass countermovement, the National Security Volunteers or Tontons Macoutes, was organized by the government. In El Salvador, Honduras, and Peru, the number of vigilante death squads grew in response to increases in leftist insurgency.

Private elites in particular, who have the most to lose from a breakdown of sociopolitical norms, develop elaborate normative and utilitarian justifications for vigilante mobilization. Vigilantism is touted as normatively justifiable to uphold threatened social norms, and utilitarianly justifiable to bolster overwhelmed law-enforcement agencies. Private elites feel that government has let them down—now it is their turn to act. They feel they have no other choice, and the vigilante choice is easily justified. For example, American private elites involved in exploiting natural resources have developed a vigilante ideology of "wise use" of the land in response to the rapid growth of the environmental movement which has threatened their profit-taking (Helvarg, 1997). During the war in Vietnam, young native economic elites participated in the U.S. Central Intelligence Agency's (CIA) Phoenix program against the leftist insurgency. In Colombia, large landowners hire vigilantes to repress the leaders of dissident agricultural workers.

Government officials for their part are often involved in promoting vigilantism, especially in response to political deviance which threatens their positions of power. Besieged themselves, they frequently take the initiative in forming such private groups as "police auxiliaries." A growth of political deviance indicates that a government has become alienated from its citizens. Hence governments, for political reasons, propagate the myth that vigilantism represents a spontaneous rising of the "majority" of citizens against a "minority" movement. This myth projects an image of public support for the government but opposition to the movement. In Central America, for example, governments have been the major sponsors of counterdeviant death squads. La Banda vigilantes in the Dominican Republic were openly supported by the government. The South African government mobilized Zulu tribesmen against the growing power of the dissident African National

Congress. Philippine President Corazon Aquino organized vigilante death squads against the growing threat of communist insurgents (Kowalewski, 1991a, 1991b). County sheriffs in the United States still offer generous monetary bounties to private entrepreneurs for capturing criminals.

In some instances, government officials deliberately recruit criminals, especially imprisoned ones, into vigilante groups to fight political deviance. Criminals are usually familiar with violence and arms, and are more than willing to use them. They are known to the police and military sponsors of vigilantism. Some individuals, undoubtedly, served previously as undercover agents for police to infiltrate deviant groups. Many are desensitized to physical violence. Political deviants often attack, verbally and physically, criminals for preying on citizens; vigilantism offers these criminals a legitimate means of revenge. In Colombia, for example, some vigilante groups are deployed by military officers and druglords specifically against those dissenters who are most openly critical of drug-trafficking. Criminals have been active in CIA-sponsored vigilante programs in Vietnam and the Philippines. South Korean corporations hire thugs from local gangs to serve in their Save Our Company Groups, led by military officers, to attack dissenting laborers. Drug traffickers and thieves are especially prevalent in the vigilante groups operating in the coca regions of Peru. In Brazil, government-backed private armies of large landlords are made up of ruffians and thugs. In return for their vigilante services, criminals receive not only commutation of their prison sentences but also a long-denied social legitimacy. It is quite a bargain: they can continue their antisocial behavior while simultaneously gaining social respect. For this reason, perhaps, criminals seem to be disproportionately attracted to countermovement groups.

Government officials, especially off-duty or retired police and military officers, in their roles as private citizens, also take the law into their own hands against deviants. American mythology is full of such examples, such as The Lone (Texas) Ranger, Dirty Harry, and the like. In Soviet Latvia, for example, a significant portion of vigilante Interfront members were retired military officers. In Guatemala, many vigilantes are ex-soldiers. In Brazil, off-duty police officers roam city streets at night killing street-children suspected of criminal activity (Huggins, 1991; Huggins & Mesquita, 1995).

The countermovement theory also sheds light on the dynamics of vigilante behaviors. Vigilante groups in fact appear as a mirror-image of the deviant movement they oppose. One of the most common ideas expressed by vigilantes is that, since deviance appears to be quickly taking over the community like a destructive blaze, they must "fight fire with fire." Thus, similar mobilization processes, such as extreme emotionality, proselytizing recruitment, initiation rites, rallies, rapidly changing tactics, and so on characterize both deviant movements and vigilante countermovements. Countermovements have as many earmarks of a raucous social campaign as do movements. In the Philippines, for example, vigilantism against the leftist New People's Army was preceded by large and noisy demonstrations, speeches by military officers, media blitzes, and the like (Kowalewski, 1992).

The countermovement theory also illuminates why certain social locales give birth to vigilantes. A cursory cross-national survey reveals that vigilantism is most commonly found in places with a tradition of popular sovereignty. Such places either lack an historical legacy of strong state sovereignty, or have developed a philosophy of populism directly opposed to state sovereignty. Popular sovereignty in such locales is often embodied in the political rights of the public to bear arms, make citizens' arrests, and other popular-policing powers. The more citizens feel they have rights vis-à-vis the state, the more likely they will form countermovements. Such countermovements are seen as having popular legitimacy, i.e., if the state derives its authority from the people, then it can just as easily lose it to them. In short, if it is citizens who give power to the state, then they can take it back. Indeed, under conditions of crisis in such locales, popular appropriation of political legitimacy is socially expected. Thus, the belief-system of popular sovereignty provides fertile ground for the growth of vigilante countermovements, which are seen as a form of spontaneous, grassroots, direct democracy. Vigilantism thus truly represents a "movement" of power back to the people. When a rapid growth of deviance clearly indicates a failure of state power, citizens assume their right to exercise that power themselves.

Deviance-besieged elites are quick to seize on this populist myth and manipulate it to their own advantage. Vigilantism functions as a symbol of democratic participation in coercion and hence provides legitimation for repressive elites. It also enables elites to close the social gap between themselves and nonelites, which of course is one of the major causes of growth in deviance.

The countermovement theory also sheds light on the violence usually associated with vigilantism. Vigilantes are among the most violent of all social formations. One only has to recall the behaviors of Salvadoran death squads, American Prohibitionists, and European skinheads to realize the physical toll which vigilantes take on their fellow citizens. In the United States, vigilantes at the Native-American Pine Ridge reservation physically assaulted, murdered, and "disappeared" dissidents. In the Soviet Union, injuries to human rights dissenters at demonstrations were more common when private vigilantes were present than when they were absent. Similarly, vigilante "Afghans"—veterans of the Soviet war in Afghanistan—attacked nationalist dissidents, burning and raping and killing as police stood by. In Vietnam, CIA-sponsored vigilantes in the Phoenix program killed some 20,000 people. Lebanese vigilantes have killed hundreds. Vigilantes are often described as sadistic because of their treatment of suspects. Torture by vigilante groups was common, for example, during counterinsurgency operations in Vietnam and Latin America.

Vigilante violence, further, becomes more indiscriminate over time, targeting deviants and nondeviants alike. Vigilantes quickly learn that, for their elite sponsors, countering a wave of deviance is more important than legal niceties. Minimal training and supervision allow vigilantes a wide latitude to act. Elite-sponsors, knowingly and unknowingly, encourage the expansion of vigilante violence by labeling opponents of the countermovement as "deviant sympathizers." Criminal elements, protected by elites, find they can freely commit abuses against suspects. Under pressure from elites to produce results, vigilantes often extend their net of victims to include mere suspects and their families, friends, classmates, colleagues, and neighbors. Some vigilantes use their power to settle scores with old enemies. In the end, violence may be randomly directed against citizens "just for fun" or to terrorize potential deviants. In Colombia, for example, vigilantes have killed numerous citizens in the broad category of so-called "social slag," including beggars, homosexuals, and prostitutes. In El Salvador, vigilantes have held entire villages responsible for harboring suspected dissidents; in some villages all the residents have been killed or forced to flee.

In turn, the deviants and at times the public, out of a need for self-protection, may respond in kind by forming violent counter-countermovements against the vigilantes. For example, the Deacons for Defense grew out of a need to counter the violence directed against African-American dissenters by the Ku Klux Klan. In the U.S. Pine Ridge reservation, Native-American dissidents formed special committees to force vigilantes out of their communities and threatened reprisals if attacks continued. In the Soviet Union, Latvian dissidents organized self-defense units against Interfront vigilantes. Dissident Soviet writers, after suffering attacks by vigilantes as police stood by, were assisted by the Sakharov Union of Democratic Afghan War Veterans as a means of defense against the violence. In the Philippines, as a response to vigilante assaults on religious base communities and labor unions, dissidents formed self-defense units. Guatemalan villagers formed CERJ, an organization designed to help citizens resist forcible recruitment into vigilante patrols.

Since deviants receive little or no governmental protection from vigilante attacks, they often feel themselves forced to attack vigilantes violently in turn. In Peru, for example, the Sendero Luminoso movement has assassinated peasant vigilantes who enlisted in the government-sponsored rondas campesinas (Burt & Panfici, 1992). In South Africa, supporters of the dissident African National Congress formed their own groups to attack the hostels of police-backed Inkatha vigilantes. In the Philippines, enraged deviants have killed vigilantes. As such, therefore, vigilantes often themselves become the victims of deviant violence. In a dynamic modeling simulation of vigilantism, it was found that vigilante violence raises the violence of deviants almost to a maximum level in all the models tested (Kowalewski & Hoover, 1995).

Yet when counter-countermovements strike back at vigilantes, the vigilantes are unable to rely on a retaliatory response against the attackers from law-enforcement agencies. Hence they feel they must respond violently in turn. Governments, in the face of growing deviance, lack the resources not only to protect citizens from deviants but also to protect counterdeviants. Countervigilante groups, therefore, are usually attacked by vigilantes. In Guatemala, for example, CERJ members have been labeled as subversive, abducted, tortured, and murdered. Thus the spiral of violence escalates.

Further, the coincidence of interest in deviance-control between law-enforcement officers and vigilantes quickly erodes, leading to violent clashes between the two groups. In the United States, for example, relations between the police and Guardian Angel vigilantes are often tense. Law-enforcement officers begin to resent vigilante encroachment on their turf, while vigilantes begin to think of that turf as their own. Shootouts between police and vigilantes have been reported in several countries (Kowalewski, 1991a, 1990). In sum, vigilantes almost always provoke more violence than they prevent.

Yet some types of vigilantes are more violent than others. Countercultural vigilantes are the least violent, since cultural deviants, while threatening social norms, rarely pose a direct and immediate threat to property or power. Countercriminal vigilantes rank second, since criminal deviants, while not representing a direct and immediate threat to power, do flaunt norms and threaten property. Finally, counterdissident vigilantes are certainly the most violent of all; political deviants directly and immediately threaten norms, property, and power, and thus the full array of established violence is usually mobilized to counter them.

The violence associated with vigilantism results directly from the mobilization processes of a countermovement. First, vigilantes react against a rapid growth of deviance and thus feel overwhelmed, acting not out of confidence but rather desperation. They feel they are fighting for their social (and perhaps physical) lives. Thus they often develop a self-image of soldiers in a war. Since they cannot count on physical protection from their resource-depleted government, they feel they must be tough on deviants. Further, since their goals are usually the same as government's, they feel they can be violent without incurring any legal sanctions. In short, they can act violently against deviants with judicial impunity. In Kenya's capital of Nairobi, for example, street crime has grown so rapidly that residents have re-named it "Nai-robbery." In this milieu, it is not uncommon for street mobs to seize suspected thieves and pummel them to death on the spot. No one has ever been jailed for this kind of vigilante street justice.

Second, governments besieged by a rapidly growing movement may not only encourage vigilante formations, but provide them with arms, logistical information, safe houses, and the like. Such support for unofficial law-enforcement, in turn, allows governments to bring violence to bear against deviance, while offering them a convenient way to "wash their hands" of the dirty work. In the Soviet Union, for example, vigilante "friends of the regime" were often deployed by the secret police to beat up drunks, dissidents, and other deviants, thereby serving as lighting rods for public criticism of the police for Stalinist brutality (Kowalewski, 1982). This "Pontius Pilate Syndrome" has characterized state-sponsored vigilantism across the world (Burt & Panfici, 1992; Kowalewski, 1992).

Third, countermovement vigilantes often display the same enthusiasm for their cause as movement deviants. Taking on the role of law-enforcement officers is seen as a rightful social mission. Vigilantes exhibit a quasi-religious fervor for their perceived calling from the people to counter deviants. Indeed, for this reason, extremist religious cults are often drawn to vigilante activity. In the Philippines, for example, groups of Christian cultists going by the name of "Tadtad" (chop-chop) cut up suspected communist guerrillas with bolo knives (Kowalewski, 1991b). Christian vigilantes have been used by the Philippine government to attack the Muslim movement in Mindanao. The Indonesian military used Muslim fanatics to help in its massacre of one-half million suspected leftists after its successful coup in 1965. In the United States, the Reagan administration used the youth of the Unification Church ("Moonies")—the Collegiate Association for Research of Principles—to provoke fights with dissidents on university campuses.

In all likelihood, vigilante violence will grow in the twenty-first century across the world. Under the combined pressures of exponential population growth, overurbanization, globalization, declining governmental legitimacy, shrinking public sectors and democratization, governments will be ill-equipped to cope with growing social diversity and perceived deviance. As such, besieged private citizens will increasingly be drawn to take it upon themselves to enforce prevailing norms against the flood of deviant beliefs and behaviors. Add to this social stew the increased availability of arms—of both minor and mass destruction—and one has the formula for vigilante violence on a major scale. The American militia movement, while perhaps not the wave of the future, is worth taking seriously and studying diligently (Dees, 1996).

III.   DESIDERATA

These considerations suggest avenues for future research. Whereas almost all existing scholarship on vigilantism is made up of uninational case-studies, the present article makes clear that vigilantism is prevalent across the world (Helvarg, 1997; Rosenbaum & Sederberg, 1976). A cross-national approach is likely to yield important insights concerning similarities and differences in vigilante violence in various contexts (see Huggins, 1991; Kowalewski, 1996a).

Given rapid globalization, moreover, a narrow uninational approach can no longer be justified. More and more countries are becoming more diverse, yet public tolerance of diversity has yet to grow apace. As a consequence, citizens increasingly see differences as deviance, and thus are more likely to engage in vigilante activity.

Future studies should pay special attention to global demographic change. Exponential population growth in less developed countries implies a huge bulge in the most crime-prone age-cohort (15–25 years old), which in turn predicts a dramatic crime wave in these countries. At the same time, rapid population growth strains governmental resources to the breaking point. Governments in these countries will be no more able to provide security for citizens than they are now able to provide food, shelter, water, roads, electricity, or other basic needs. Globalization processes, further, will make this crime wave increasingly cross-national. Illegal immigration by resource-rich criminals has become increasingly easy, yet national governments and especially the cross-national police apparatus, Interpol, lack the resources to deal with it. In short, criminals are rapidly becoming far more globalized and resource-endowed than police. This pattern suggests not only that criminals will soon run amok cross-nationally, if they are not doing so already, but that vigilante formations to counter them may soon become global as well.

Future studies of vigilantism should also pay close attention to changes in governmental legitimacy and democratization, especially popular sovereignty, across the world. According to a recent meta-analysis of global public opinion, national governments are losing legitimacy everywhere (Nye, 1997). Citizens increasingly feel that government is ineffective in solving their problems. This trend, along with the trend in global democratization, predict an increase in the extent to which citizens take the law into their own hands.

Future research should also avoid the historical myopia which characterized the frontier theory. It should consider, for example, the degree to which vigilantism will change as the global economy transits from agro-industrialism to the information age. Will vigilantes, for example, increasingly connect with each other cross-nationally on the Internet? Will vigilantism increasingly take the form of cyberterrorism? Will uneducated citizens, rendered economically irrelevant in the information age, take out their frustrations about poor job prospects against the flood of "deviant" immigrants who have left their own backward and overpopulated countries? In sum, future research on vigilantism will be most useful if it adopts a broad global-historical perspective.

IV. APPROACHES OF PREVENTION

Ultimately the responsibility for vigilante violence must be laid at the feet of governments. They fail to alleviate the poverty, inequality, and discrimination which spawn deviant movements against which vigilantes arise. They fail to foresee a rapid growth in deviance, thus failing to allocate the resources needed to control it. They usually fail to promote public tolerance of diversity, often promoting intolerance instead. They fail to maintain legitimacy, thus encouraging citizens to take the law into their own hands. They themselves often sponsor vigilante countermovements. They fail to curtail vigilante violence effectively. They fail to foresee that vigilante violence provokes even more violence against the vigilantes themselves, from deviants and law-enforcement officers alike. They even fail to see that vigilantes sometimes direct violence against them.

These failures suggest that government officials must take vigilantism far more seriously than they have in the past. Perhaps the bombing of the U.S. federal building in Oklahoma City by Timothy McVeigh, a known associate of several vigilante militia groups, will constitute a wake-up call to governments around the world. Governments, and especially law-enforcement agencies, need special training in the causes and consequences of vigilante violence.

The global human rights community can also play a strategic role in prevention. Although international organizations have been reluctant to interfere directly in national conflicts between governments and deviants, global involvement in such disputes has increased significantly in recent years (e.g., Namibia, the Balkans).

Human rights organizations can do three things: take prophylactic measures, form disbandment coalitions, and protect actual and potential victims. First, they can take measures to prevent vigilante groups from forming. Vigilantism is more likely at some times and places than others. Since vigilantism follows a sharp growth in deviance, such an increase offers rights organizations an early-warning signal to mobilize their resources. Local groups, seeing a rise of deviance in their nation, can alert the international community to mobilize its network to concentrate resources on that nation. Since vigilantes are most likely to arise in places with a tradition of popular sovereignty, rights organizations can focus on these locales as top-priority sites for their efforts. Using statistical time-series on nations' levels of vigilante violence, rights organizations can isolate those polities most prone to the phenomenon and concentrate attention there.

Rights organizations can make efforts to convince governments, deviant movements, potential vigilantes, and mass publics that vigilantism is in nobody's interest. Governments may be amenable to arguments that vigilantes create more disorder than they suppress. Deviant movements can be reminded that vigilantism responds to a rapid growth in their activities. Movements may well have an interest in a moratorium on their deviant behaviors in order to alleviate pressures on governments and potential vigilantes to respond with countermovements. Potential vigilantes may be amenable to arguments that they can be attacked by deviants and law-enforcement officers. Mass publics may be persuaded that vigilantes, while sometimes representing spontaneous risings of citizens, often result from calculated state-sponsorship. They can also be shown that vigilante groups attract antisocial elements to pursue their private agendas—usually with judicial impunity.

Second, if vigilante groups have already formed, rights organizations have numerous allies available for building a disbandment coalition. Among government agencies, rank-and-file police officers may be sympathetic to disbandment. Their turf is ultimately threatened by vigilante disorders, and they themselves may suffer vigilante attacks. Local government officials, their jurisdictions disrupted by vigilantes, may also be sympathetic. Prosecutors and judges find their authority undermined by vigilantes who operate beyond the law. Of course, the deviants themselves may well lend a hand. Finally, the mass public, their lives disrupted as much by vigilantes as by deviants, grow less supportive of vigilantism over time.

Building a disbandment coalition might start with international conferences to enlighten the global community about the social pathologies of vigilantism. Especially violent vigilante groups and their state-sponsors might be "put on trial" by international tribunals. A broad coalition of government sectors, citizen groups, and international organizations cannot be easily dismissed by vigilantes and their sponsors. Recently, for example, as part of the peace agreement between the Salvadoran government and the leftist movement, legislation was introduced into the national parliament to curtail vigilante formations.

Third, rights organizations can take measures to protect officials, deviants, and citizens from vigilante threats and attacks. In the short term, the principle of political asylum needs strengthening to include victims of vigilante violence, whether or not the vigilantes are state-sponsored. In addition, programs of judicial protection for victims, prosecutors and judges, witnesses, vigilante whistle-blowers and the like should be established. In the long term, rights organizations should strive to make antivigilantism a global norm by means of formal resolutions, diplomatic and economic sanctions against sponsoring governments, peacemaking interpositions, and allocations of resources for disbandment groups and refugees fleeing vigilante abuses. In sum, although powerful forces are operative in the formation of vigilante groups, even more powerful ones can be arrayed to make them an extinct social species.

REFERENCES

Brown, Richard. (1975). *Strain of Violence: Historical Studies of American Violence and Vigilantism.* New York: Oxford University Press.

Brown, Richard. (1979). American Vigilante Tradition. In Ted Robert Gurr & Hugh Davies Graham (Eds.), *Violence in America* (pp. 153–185). Beverly Hills: Sage.

Brown, Richard. (1983). *Vigilante Policing.* In Carl Klockars (Ed.), *Thinking about Police* (pp. 84–106). New York: McGraw-Hill.

Burt, Jo-Marie, & Aldo Panfici. (1992). *Peru: Caught in the Crossfire.* Jefferson City: Peru Peace Network – USA.

Churchill, Ward, & Jim VanderWall. (1988). *Agents of Repression.* Boston: South End.

Churchill, Ward, & Jim VanderWall. (1990). *COINTELPRO Papers.* Boston: South End.

Culberson, William. (1990. *Vigilantism: A Political History of Private Power in America.* New York: Greenwood.

Dees, Morris. (1996). *Gathering Storm: America's Militia Threat.* New York: HarperCollins.

Helvarg, David. (1997). *War against the Greens: The 'Wise Use' Movement, the New Right, and Anti-Environmental Violence.* San Francisco: Sierra Club Books.

Huggins, Martha. (1991). *Vigilantism and the State in Modern Latin America.* New York: Praeger.

Huggins, Martha, & Myriam Mesquita. (1995). Scapegoating Outsiders: The Murders of Street Youth in Modern Brazil. *Policing and Society, 5,* 265–280.

Kowalewski, David. (1982). Establishment Vigilantism and Political Dissent. *Armed Forces and Society, 9*(1), 83–97.

Kowalewski, David. (1990). Vigilante Counterinsurgency and Human Rights in the Philippines. *Human Rights Quarterly, 12*(2), 246–264.

Kowalewski, David. (1991a). Counterinsurgent Vigilantism and Public Response. *Sociological Perspectives, 34*(2), 127–144.

Kowalewski, David. (1991b). Cultism, Insurgency, and Vigilantism in the Philippines. *Sociological Analysis, 52*(3), 241–254.

Kowalewski, David. (1992). Counterinsurgent Paramilitarism. *Journal of Peace Research, 29*(1), 71–84.

Kowalewski, David. (1996a). Countermovement Vigilantism and Human Rights. *Crime, Law, and Social Change, 25,* 63–81.

Kowalewski, David. (1996b). The Legality of State-Sponsored Vigilantism. In David L. Cingranelli, (Ed.), *Human Rights and Developing Countries* (pp. 211–222). London: JAI Press.

Kowalewski, David, & Dean Hoover. (1995). *Dynamic Models of Conflict and Pacification.* London: Praeger.

Lungren, Daniel. (1991). *Neighborhood Watch Guide.* Sacramento: Crime and Violence Prevention Center, California Department of Justice.

McGrath, Roger. (1984). *Gunfighters, Highwaymen, and Vigilantes.* Berkeley: University of California Press.

Neeley, Richard. (1990). *Take back Your Neighborhood.* New York: Fine.

Nye, Joseph. (1997). In Government We Don't Trust. *Foreign Policy, 42*(Fall), 99–111.

Rosenbaum, H. Jon, & Peter Sederberg. (1976). *Vigilante Politics.* Philadelphia: University of Pennsylvania Press.

Tucker, William. (1985). *Vigilante.* New York: Stein and Dery.

Pogroms

WERNER BERGMANN

I. INTRODUCTION

It was not until the late 1980s that social sciences research into *political violence* first began to deal systematically with collective violence against the persons, lives, and property of ethnic groups, just as researchers into *ethnic conflicts*, conversely, had long paid little heed to the dynamics of violence (Brubaker & Laitin, 1998:423). As late as 1992, Jenkins and Schock were deploring the fact that a "huge empirical gap currently limits our understanding of ethnic antagonisms" (181). There were several reasons for this neglect: The sociological modernization theory, which saw a steady decline in the significance of ascriptive features; the selection of new social movements as paradigms of collective behavior; the problems experienced by sociologists in dealing with physical violence and emotions; and the treatment of ethnic conflicts as epiphenomena of economic interests and contradictions (Hanf, 1989:314).

The concept of "ethnic violence" covers a range of heterogeneous phenomena, and in many cases there are still no established theoretical and conceptual distinctions in this field (Waldmann, 1995:343). Brubaker and Laitin (1998:446) argue, as does Williams (1994:73), in favor of a disaggregated analysis of the heterogeneous phenomena lumped together as "ethnic violence."

The word "pogrom" (from the Russian, meaning storm or devastation) has a relatively short history. Its international currency dates back to the anti-Semitic excesses in Tsarist Russia during the years 1881–1883, but the phenomenon existed in the same form at a much earlier date and was by no means confined to Russia (Rogger, 1992). As John D. Klier points out in his seminal article "The pogrom paradigm in Russian history" (1992), the anti-Semitic pogroms in Russia were described by contemporaries as demonstrations, persecution, or struggle, and the government made use of the term *besporiadok* (unrest, riot) to emphasize the breach of public order. Then, during the twentieth century, the term began to develop along two separate lines. In the Soviet Union, the word lost its anti-

W. Heitmeyer and J. Hagan (eds.), *International Handbook of Violence Research*, 351–367.

Semitic connotation and came to be used for reactionary forms of political unrest and, from 1989, for outbreaks of interethnic violence; while in the West, the anti-Semitic overtones were retained and government orchestration or acquiescence was emphasized. In *Webster's Third New International Dictionary* (Springfield, IL, 1964), *pogrom* is defined as "an organized massacre and looting of helpless people, usually with the connivance of officials, specifically, such a massacre of Jews," while the *Oxford English Dictionary* (1933) also refers to an "organized massacre" in Russia, though not necessarily directed against Jews but meaning the "destruction or annihilation of any body or class." The dictionary considers "riots" to be typified by the use of violence and active violations of the rule of law by the populace. In German dictionaries, *pogrom* is defined in very general terms as "agitation involving violence against a group within the population," Jews being specifically mentioned as an afterthought (Brockhaus, 1980). By contrast, Klier stresses that common features of the waves of pogroms within Russia were their spontaneous and confused character, the absence of long-term aims, and their urban origin (1992:14), and more recent research has also found that they were not government-controlled. The feature of "government control" included in some definitions thus originates with a historically inaccurate judgment regarding the Russian pogroms, so pogroms have to be seen as a form of spontaneous riots. Paul R. Brass, however, follows the older interpretation and defines government participation as the feature that distinguishes riots from pogroms: "When it can be proved that the police and the state authorities more broadly are directly implicated in a 'riot' in which one community provides the principal or sole victims, then, of course, one is confronted with a pogrom, in which the victims were targeted by the state itself or its agents" (1996:26). In his discussion of the distinction, "riot or pogrom," he partially retracts his own proposed definition, since neither *riot* nor *pogrom* was able to express the dynamics of mass violence, which always contains elements of spontaneity together with elements of planning and organization. He reaches the conclusion that "it is quite fruitless in such situations to seek to define a situation precisely as either a riot or a pogrom" (1996:33). Even though the boundaries are fluid, he says, he would prefer to define pogroms as attacks on the persons and property of a particular ethnic, racial, or local group, in which the state and/ or its machinery participates to a significant extent but which is portrayed, by the government or some other body, as a riot (ibid.). In the present contribution, by contrast, the difference will be considered as lying not in the part played by the state but in the relative positions of power of the pogromists and the minority attacked. The part played by governmental violence can vary from the swift suppression of a pogrom through an inadequate or belated deployment of the forces of order to the (rare) extreme case of governmental encouragement and orchestration. The use of the term, then, is inconsistent in the literature, though there is agreement to the extent that pogroms are defined as a specific form of riot and should therefore be distinguished from massacres, on the one hand, and other forms of riots, on the other.

Researchers frequently fail to distinguish between "pogrom" and "massacre," using the definition "mass murder, often implicating the state (or allowed to be killed) some members of a collectivity or category, usually a communal group, class, or political faction" (Melson, 1992:26). L. Alex Swan, referring to the attacks by Whites on Blacks in St. Louis in 1917, also uses the term "massacre" (1980:91). Brass, discussing the excesses against Sikhs in New Delhi in November 1984, argues that the term used should be "massacre" rather than "riot," since the violence was the result of incitement and was planned and orchestrated (1996:14). In fact, it is not easy to distinguish between massacres and pogroms: both cases refer to a unilateral, *collective* assault on a largely defenseless group.

The differences lie in the fact that massacres are conducted by more highly organized and better armed assailants (often military or police units), their purpose being to wipe out all members of the target group (Levene, 1999:5), whereas the elements typical of a pogrom—a large group of attackers acting on a short-term basis within a local framework, and the destruction and looting of property—do not play a major part in such cases. Donald L. Horowitz (2000) regards the essential features of "deadly ethnic riots" as including their very irregular concentration in space and time, their relatively spontaneous nature (although not devoid of elements of organization and planning), the selection of the victims on the basis of their membership of a particular category, the expression of a passionate rejection of the other group, and the purposeless mutilation of the victims (quoted in Brubaker & Laitin, 1998:432). Similarly, he distinguishes this form of "mass civilian intergroup violence in which victims are chosen by their group membership" from other forms such as genocide, lynching, violent protest, feud, and civil war.

The German terms *Unruhe* (unrest) and *Ausschreitung* (riot, excess), like the English term *riot*, do not reflect the specific circumstances of conflict. As early as 1972, Gary T. Marx critically noted that, although a distinction had been drawn between riots, on the one hand, and revolutions and revolts, on the other, insufficient efforts were being made to deal systematically with various types of riots (1972:51). Frequently, the term "riot" or "race riot" is used to describe not only collective violence on the part of an ethnic group that perceives itself as disadvantaged, directed against the state or the majority within the population, but also a violent assault by the majority on an ethnic minority. Morris Janowitz (1968) proposed therefore that a distinction should be made between "commodity riots," in which the population rises up against the state and other "oppressors" to indulge in arson and looting, and "communal riots," in which one ethnic group attacks another ("interracial clash"). In the "property" or "commodity riots," violence against the person is practiced mainly by the police, whereas in "communal riots," the members of another ethnic group and their possessions are the target of the violence. McPhail, who adds the further categories of "police riots," "celebration riots," and "protest riots," distinguishes such riots on the basis of the participants, objective, forms of action, and causes (1994:3). Pogroms fall within the category of "communal riots," also referred to by Janowitz as "contested area riots" because they take the form of conflicts within the local area (1969:416). This, however, tells us nothing about the respective numbers and power relations of the ethnic groups involved. Swan (1980) has defined a historical sequence of types of riot applicable to the United States: conflicts between black and white began during the late nineteenth century with "White riots" (1890–1921), which can be viewed as pogroms practiced by the white majority against black migrants, to be followed by "White-Black riots," in which blacks and whites each attacked the other, and eventually "Black riots," beginning in the 1940s, which took the form of a rebellion by the disadvantaged minority. Susan Olzak (1992:186) also makes a distinction along these lines between ethnic conflicts, in which an ethnic majority attacks an ethnic minority, and conflicts between two ethnic minorities, though without proposing any terminological distinction. "Pogrom" evidently implies a significant difference in numbers or power between the attackers and the attacked. A different view of this is taken by Rösel, who also uses the term "pogroms" to refer to violent excesses between groups of approximately equal strength (1997:171ff.). There is as yet no consensus on terminology here among researchers.

Following on from the classification described above, and using a typology proposed by Roberta Senechal de la Roche, pogroms are defined as a *unilateral, nongovernmental* form of *collective* violence *initiated by the majority population* against a largely defenseless ethnic group, and occurring when the *majority* expect the state to provide them with no assistance in overcoming a (perceived) threat from the minority. By the *collective attribution* of a threat, the pogrom differs from forms of violence, such as lynching, which are directed against individual members of a minority, while the *imbalance of power* in favor of the rioters distinguishes pogroms from other forms of riot (food riots, race riots, or "communal riots" between evenly matched groups), and again the *low level of organization* separates them from vigilantism, terrorism, massacre, and genocide. This analytical separation is not always easy to apply empirically, because pogroms often occur in the context of international or civil wars or genocide, and vigilante groups may well organize pogroms in such a way that they develop into massacres. Under this definition, state-organized acts of violence such as the *Reichskristallnacht* (night of broken glass) of 1938 can be assigned to the pogrom category, admittedly as an extreme case. The fact that the National Socialists halfheartedly characterized this event as "popular fury," while referring to it internally by the more accurate term of "anti-Jewish action" ("Judenaktion") emphasizes that this was in fact the "stage-managing of a pogrom." This is not to disregard the fact that pogroms did develop at local level during *Kristallnacht* as a result of the spontaneous involvement of the populace (Benz, 2001). In the case of the medieval "plague pogroms" of 1348–1349, too, a terminological distinction must be made between pogroms resulting from civil uproar and collective executions of a town's Jewry by the authorities, which were not pogroms, although they are customarily classified under that general heading.

II. THEORETICAL APPROACHES AND EMPIRICAL RESULTS

1. Formative Conditions

Most case studies of pogroms hitherto have been undertaken in the context of minority or national histories. Important examples are German history of the nineteenth and twentieth centuries (Sterling, 1950; Katz, 1994; Rohrbacher, 1993; Hoffmann, 1994; Nonn, 1998), the outbreaks of pogroms from the 1880s onward in Russia (Berk, 1985; Aronson, 1990; Klier & Lambroza, 1992; Wynn, 1992), Southeast Asia (Basu, 1995; Kannangara, 1984; Kakar, 1996; Brass, 1996; Rösel, 1997), and the United States in the period between 1890 and World War I (Crowe, 1969; Senechal, 1990; Rudwick, 1964; Greenberg, 1992). For the period after World War II, there are studies of attacks on immigrant minorities (Panayi, 1991; Kushner, 1993). Attempts at a comparative study are rare (recently, Rogger, 1992; Wimmer, 1995; Brass, 1996; von Trotha, 1997; Rösel, 1997).

Brass recently pointed out the extent to which theoretical "narratives" from psychiatric, psychological, sociological, and criminological standpoints on the causes of collective episodes of violence pervade current ethnic relations as interpretative models, meaning that the choice of a typical explanation by politicians, journalists, or academics is a far-reaching political decision: "But the interpretive process is not only political, it also generates competing systems of knowledge concerning inter-ethnic relations, the sources of tension between members of ethnic groups, the causes of discrimination and prejudice, their social and economic bases, and the like" (1996:1). In his opinion, therefore, it is impossible to evolve a theory of riots or pogroms which takes a neutral stance toward the interests of those who try to interpret the events, uninfluenced by the prevalent ideological and academic paradigms. In every case, a theory of pogroms would have to include, alongside an analysis of events, the level of the debate among participants in and observers of those events (1996:2).

There has hitherto been no attempt to develop a theory of pogroms which specifies the general approaches to explain the origins of collective ethnic violence. In what follows, therefore, we merely consider the approaches whereby the origins and course of pogroms have been analyzed to date.

a) THEORIES OF COLLECTIVE BEHAVIOR: STRUCTURAL STRAINS. In his theory of collective behavior, which can be considered to follow on from the tradition of "theories of social disintegration or breakdown," Neil J. Smelser (1963) not only develops a theoretical framework but also makes his theory specific to the analysis of "hostile outbursts." He sees six factors that determine collective behavior: 1) structural conduciveness, 2) structural strain, 3) the growth and spread of a generalized belief, 4) precipitating factors, 5) mobilization of participants, and 6) deployment of social controls. These six factors are sequentially linked to form a "natural history of evolution," so that, in a "value-added" process, each succeeding factor presupposes the previous ones and, at the same time, each event or each situation can take effect only within the framework created by the other factors. Smelser formally defines a "hostile outburst" as "mobilization to action based on a hostile perception." The basic condition for this is structural conduciveness: a) the structure of responsibility in situations of tension, in other words the attribution of responsibility for undesirable circumstances and crises along existing or temporary boundaries between groups, ethnic and religious differences being central to pogroms; b) the existence of channels by which grievances can be aired, as a method of reducing strains; and c) opportunities for communication between those whose rights are adversely affected, the possibility of achieving the aims of the attack, and the territorial distribution of hostile groups. In the absence of social strains, this conduciveness remains latent. The most frequent form of strain results from the actual or impending existence of a disadvantage for one group (relative deprivation), but there are also normative strains and value conflicts between groups. This strain is further increased by the development of a hostile belief and generalized aggression, when it comes to be directed against particular groups. The precipitating factor, usually a trigger event which bars the way to peaceful protest or signals the failure of other forms of protest, confirms and exaggerates fears and antagonisms. A hostile outburst or the dissemination of hostile beliefs through rumors or selective agitation may themselves act as other precipitating factors. In the mobilization of participants, the existence of "leadership," the degree to which the participants were previously organized, ecological factors, and the actions of controlling social authorities play a central part in determining the form and course of the hostilities. Social control can act as a counterweight on all these levels. It depends upon the attitude of the bodies ultimately responsible for decisions and upon the executive institutions (the police or military) to what extent social control can prevent or contain the use of violence. Smelser's theory has greatly influenced researchers, though it has also been the subject of significant criticism. This criticism is directed, first, at its emphasis on objective factors and general behavioral characteristics (such as aggression), which seem, as it were, to have an impetus of their own, whereas the intentions underlying action and factors such as leadership and organization are insufficiently considered (Brass, 1996:12); and, second, against the normative bias, whereby the theory of collective behavior takes a positive view of violence for the purposes of social control, whereas the violent actions of the rioters are deemed to be deviant and destructive. A further criticism is that behavior in riot situations is much more structured and

Table II-2-8.1. Typology of "riots" according to Gary T. Marx

		Generalized belief present	
		Yes	No
		I	III
Collectively instrumental	Yes	Bread riots Luddites Prison riots	Riots misinterpreted by authorities
		II	IV
	No	Pogroms Communal riots	Riots during police strikes/ Riots in victory

Source: Marx, 1972:52.

standardized than is assumed, and is a much more specific response to problems, directed toward selected objectives. The more recent resource mobilization approach and the theory of political opportunity structures fundamentally challenge the assumption that relative deprivation and structural tension are sufficient conditions for collective action, emphasizing instead the significance of resources and favorable political contexts for mobilization. Recently, Gurr has endeavored to combine the two theoretical traditions in his analysis of ethnopolitical conflicts (1993:123ff.).

The "hostile outburst" as a type of collective behavior combines many different forms of collective violence. Gary T. Marx (1972), adopting aspects of Smelser's theory, tried to develop a typology of "riots" which takes due account of the type of conviction that legitimizes the action taken, the consequences of the collective outburst, the context of origin, the psychological profile of the actors, selectivity regarding the targets for attack, questions of planning and leadership, etc. (1972:52). Marx published a crosstable (see Fig. II-2-8.1, above), with generalized conviction along one axis and collective instrumental action along the other.

Marx makes an initial distinction between protest riots (I and II), where "higher" principles are at stake ("principled"), and issueless riots ("unprincipled," IV). The type II riot, which is what interests us here, is distinguished from type I in that its course is less controlled and less patterned, more damage is done, participants retain a lower level of self-control, and the customary phenomena of mass behavior (milling collective excitement) are more pronounced. Marx also recognizes a tendency for spontaneous unrest (II) to develop into the more highly organized type I. In his opinion, there are also differences in the type of generalized belief, the targets attacked, and the reaction of the controlling authorities. Features of pogroms and communal riots, therefore, are that the hostile beliefs tend to have a magical quality that short-circuits imagination and reality, that the participants tend to define themselves on the basis of ascriptive features, that the target for the attack is a weaker group or ethnic minority (whereas the target in the case of type I is a more powerful group), and that types II and IV result in less severe punishment under the law than type I. While Marx primarily ascribes the ghetto riots in the United States during the 1960s to type I, pogroms and communal riots are more diffuse in character. They deal in violence between ethnically, religiously, regionally, or ideologically different groups, while the state is a mere spectator. The generalized conviction defines the other group as aliens, outsiders, degenerates, subversives, or impure, and blames it for a variety of social problems and historical sins

(1972:55). Although elements of genuine competition and a clash of divergent lifestyles and values exist in this type as well, it is not so clearly directed against the source of the strains or aimed at changing public policy. More typical is what Smelser called a "short circuit": the leap from the level of general beliefs to an attack on specific actors. This typology fails to explain the difference between a pogrom and a "communal riot" in type II, though Marx's description fits better with the definition of "pogrom" proposed here.

b) COLLECTIVE VIOLENCE AS A FORM OF SOCIAL CONTROL. An attempt to explain collective violence in terms of the *theory of social control* was made by Roberta Senechal de la Roche (1996), who understands certain forms of violence as the exercise of social control. A group moves to self-help by violence when it defines a form of conduct as deviant and reacts to it. Senechal de la Roche analyzes the forms of unilateral, nongovernmental, collective violence, which include the pogrom. She distinguishes four types, depending on the degree of organization and whether the deviant behavior is attributed to an individual or a group: lynching (relatively unorganized and directed against individuals), pogrom/ riot (relatively unorganized and directed against a group), vigilantism (highly organized and directed against individuals), and terrorism (highly organized and directed against a group). The probability of these types of violence occurring and the severity of the violence vary according to the structure of the group relationships: collective violence displays a positive correlation with wide social distance, cultural distance (language or religion), a high level of functional independence between the groups concerned (economic and political cooperation), and wide differences in status (size of group, resources, classes). According to this theory, the selection of the type of violence is based on the degree of social polarization (consisting of the four group relations referred to above) and the continuity of the deviant behavior. Collective attribution is more likely to occur in cases of strong social polarization (pogroms or terrorism), while relatively unorganized violence is a more likely response to sporadic deviance. Pogrom violence is the form of violent social control that occurs when social polarization is high and, at the same time, the violations of standards by the other group are not a continuous phenomenon, in other words pogromists are "one-shotters" and not "repeat players" (1996:119).

c) "POWER APPROACH TO INTERGROUP HOSTILITY" OR "COMPETITIVE ETHNICITY" MODEL. The *conflict theory* regards rioting as an extreme form of the expression of ethnic conflicts: "We may say therefore, that race riots are extreme forms of racial conflict in which two racial groups struggle in a particular kind of political, social, economic and legal conflict setting, using riots as an alternative and ultimate technique to establish, maintain or change power relations in society" (Swan, 1980:220). Since pogroms are instituted by the dominant group, the aim of that group is generally not to bring about change, but to maintain or restore a particular social, economic, or political power situation and/ or to prevent the minority obtaining an advantage. According to the distinction between "backward-looking" and "forward-looking" riots proposed by George Rudé, pogroms fall under the first type (1964:214ff.). In American sociology, Herbert Blumer (1958) and Hubert Blalock (1967) took this question of power relationships and group positions as the starting point of the "power approach to intergroup hostility," also referred to as the "conflict" or "competitive ethnicity" model. "The power model views racial and ethnic groups as participants in ongoing competition for control of economic, political, and social structures and suggests that intergroup hostility and antagonism are natural products of that competition" (LeVine & Campbell, 1972:29). Hostility results from two conditions: the real or perceived threat from an "out-group" and, as its complement, identification with an "in-group" (Giles & Evans, 1986), because in the absence of these conditions the individual would react only to competitive circumstances and threats that affect him personally. The issue, then, is the *collective* good, in other words clashes of interests and individual conflicts are "collectivized" as ethnic antagonism (Rösel, 1997:163). In essence, dominant ethnic groups undergo this process as a result of the perception of a *collective threat* (whether it be to economic interest, cultural or political autonomy, or identity or existence as a whole) posed by an out-group. Empirical studies in the United States have identified two main factors for the perception of such a threat: "The numerical size of the subordinate group relative to the dominant group, and economic circumstances" (Quillian, 1995:586; Giles & Buckner, 1993). A collision between these two factors (for example, immigration combined with economic crisis) makes an ethnic conflict even more probable. The "power approach" thus predicts greater hostility either when identification with the group becomes stronger and/ or when competition between ethnic groups is exacerbated. In the past, this approach has been mainly used to explain racial prejudices but has not been applied to explain collective violence in the form of pogroms (recently Bergmann, 1998, see below). Susan Olzak has used it in an attempt to explain the frequency of lynching (1990). Critics have called for a modification of the theory: what is decisive in the case of ethnic conflicts, they say, is not objective competition but the perception of competition as illegitimate.

Olzak (1992) used an "event history analysis" and ecological theories of competition to explain the data on the cyclical occurrence of ethnic/ racial confrontations in nineteenth and twentieth century America. According to this analysis, the collapse of ethnic segregation combines with increased economic and political competition (resulting, for example, from a sharp increase in immigration and a shrinking economy) to trigger collective actions designed to exclude the other group by violence. Olzak, however, provides no more detailed classification of the type of ethnic conflict. This theory certainly encompasses a specific cause of conflict, but disregards the overall aspect of symbolic deprivation as a cause of ethnic conflicts.

Walter Korpi (1974) has proposed that the "political process approach," which focuses on the struggle for resources and the mobilization of power resources to explain collective violence, should be extended to include the "expectation achievement approach," which is concerned with motivational aspects. In his *power balance model of conflict*, the intervening variables of utility of reaching the goal, expectation of success, and relative deprivation play an intermediary part between the independent variables "difference in power resources" and the probability of conflict. This theory may help to explain the occurrence of pogroms, since it assumes that the probability of manifest conflict increases when the balance of power between groups shifts to the detriment of the more powerful group. Both where the balance of power is extremely uneven (as in the Indian caste system) and where it is even, conflicts are rare. If, however, a wide power gap between two groups narrows, then the dominant group experiences a form of "progressive deprivation" when the subordinate group achieves a rapid improvement in its situation. This deprivation increases the probability of conflict (Korpi, 1974:1576), particularly if the dominant group can expect a conflict to offer prospects of success for itself. This theory, though, says nothing about when and how such a conflict finds expression in violence. By adopting this approach, Korpi not only breaks with the earlier approaches, which assume a generally positive correlation between relative deprivation and conflict (Gurr, 1970; Davies, 1962), but also rejects the "political process model" (Snyder & Tilly, 1972), which regards not only the loss of power resources but also the gaining of such resources as a cause of conflict. If a weak group loses resources, or if the dominant group acquires additional ones, the probability of conflict is more likely to decrease than to increase.

In line with the call for types of conflict involving collective violence to be specified, Werner Bergmann (1998) makes an attempt to distinguish pogroms from race riots, food riots, or protest campaigns by social movements. According to his theory, three conditioning factors are central to the occurrence of pogroms: 1) a *change* in the equal or unequal position of groups, which is perceived as a threat by the dominant group; 2) the attitude of the state and its controlling authorities—in other words, the political opportunity structure; and 3) the ideological interpretation and heightening of the conflict.

Pogroms are characterized by a tripartite pattern of relations. The target for attack is another ethnic group, the role of the state as a third party being perceived as ambivalent, partly because the actors regard their efforts at self-help as legitimate and partly because they nevertheless "know" that they are breaking the state's monopoly of violence and that their actions are criminal. On the one hand, pogroms can be "protest pogroms," in which attacks are made upon the authorities of the state when they protect the attacked minority; on the other hand, they may be "loyalist" and intended to help the state to safeguard its supposed interests. On the basis of this tripartite relationship, the following changes in the balance of power may result in acts of violence:

1) Real or supposed demands for or improvements in status by the minority in regard to legal, political, economic, or symbolic status, or a quantitative shift in favor of the minority, result in a defensive reaction by the group threatened with the loss of power or status. The state plays a key role here as the central authority in the regulation of social conflicts and the preservation of collective goods.

2) Situations in which power shifts (revolution or civil war) or where there is a general loss of power at state level (as a result of political assassination, a system change, or a lost war), in which the power of the state to impose sanctions and its capacity to maintain its monopoly of power decrease, thus both making collective action less costly and apparently legitimizing self-help.

3) The power model must be extended to include those cases in which sources of danger whose roots lie in crises of society as a whole (war, famine, or epidemic) are attributed to the minority, in which originators are difficult to identify or deal with, and which are interpreted as intentional damage caused by a minority. This is the form described by Lewis Coser as "unreal conflict," in which a conflict situation is created with a substitute object (1956). This mechanism serves as a way of reinterpreting internal group conflicts as intergroup conflicts.

In order to analyze the phenomenon as a whole, a number of theories have to be combined. The "power approach to intergroup hostility" and the model of the political opportunity structure can provide the *formative conditions* for a situation of tension, but they say nothing about when that situation crosses the threshold to pogrom-style violence, nor can they explain the "unreal" ethnic conflicts. The power approach assumes that hostilities between ethnic groups are the result of competition for scarce resources, and that this simultaneously strengthens in-group identification. The probability of manifest conflict increases when (sudden) disadvantages are feared, and also when, on the other hand, there is a (residual) *power divide* in favor of the pogromists. The tension may be increased by: 1) An increase in numbers for one group (the result of immigration or emigration); 2) an increase in economic competition (relative economic status); 3) an increase in political power (for example, as a result of the statutory imposition of equality); 4) a higher level of identification with the in-group; or 5) the reinterpretation of internal group conflicts as intergroup conflicts. The competitive situation is regarded by this theory as "real," but must be translated into a perceived threat. The power approach has hitherto paid little attention to this process of transformation. It can be assumed that two factors influence the process of definition here: first, the assessment of a group's own resources (for example, political influence) to control the situation and favorable ambient conditions, and, second, the cognitive/ cultural dissemination of information by way of interpretations which define the situation as threatening to the group as a whole and so trigger processes of identification and growing solidarity. Culturalist analyses of the social construction of this perceived threat regard not only causes rooted in social psychology but also historic and cultural experience of the coexistence between groups as central factors. Defining a situation on the basis of earlier adverse experience may lead to the "security dilemma," in which the threat can be averted only by a preemptive strike against the enemy. The "framing concept" developed in the field of social movement research can be used to analyze this process of definition, linked to theories of prejudice derived from social psychology. If a threat is "constructed," Black's theory of social control (1983) states that collective, violent "self-help" may come into effect if 1) recourse to law and order is impossible or has failed; 2) a gap in status and power in favor of the "threatened" group exists; 3) there is a wide relational and cultural distance between the groups; 4) there is a low level of functional independence between the groups; and 5) the state (at all levels) fails to take preventive and reactive action to penalize the "self-help."

Collective "self-help" takes on the form of a pogrom if the actors' level of organization is low and the attacked group is accused collectively. Whether a violent assault escalates into a pogrom then depends essentially on the speed and scale of intervention by the controlling authorities.

d) THE CULTURALIST APPROACH: POGROMS AS RITUAL BEHAVIOR. While Smelser and Marx, in categorizing pogroms, emphasize their diffuse nature, Harvey E. Goldberg (1977), though also placing pogroms within unstructured phases of transition, stresses their ritualized character. Goldberg selected a *culturalist approach* for his analysis, based on the case study of an anti-Semitic pogrom in Tripoli (Libya) in 1945, and draws upon ethnological theories of symbolic activity as developed by Claude Lévi-Strauss and Victor Turner. He stresses the cultural and symbolic logic of collective action in pogroms, which displays parallels to ritual activity. Goldberg considers the causes of pogroms to lie in political tensions (anomie and economic frustration), but the conversion of these tensions into social reality follows a cultural pattern of behavior which determines the course of the pogrom and is familiar to both attackers and attacked. Goldberg analyzes the parallels between Smelser's theory of collective behavior and the theory of symbolic action. According to Smelser, the pogrom-type of action is a noninstitutionalized one, modifying or restoring a situation on the basis of a hostile conviction. Goldberg sees parallels with Turner's concept of "liminal" status, meaning the unstructured intermediate phase in a rite of passage. This concept would provide a better explanation of the occurrence of symbolic acts in pogrom situations than the mere assertion that they are "lacking in structure." Rites of passage also have the function of regulating both the achievement of a new status and the restoration of a previous one. The concept of generalized belief to be found in Smelser corresponds, according to Goldberg, to Turner's assumption that the normative and psychological aspects of the belief come together in symbolic action. This leads Goldberg to the argument that "during the 'liminal' states of political transition, cultural elements which are not salient in daily life are given symbolic emphasis and influence the course of collective outbursts" (1977:41). A sociopolitical analysis of social relations must be extended to include the symbolic aspect. According to this approach, the destructive activity involved in pogroms should a) not be described negatively as "unstructured" because there are existing cultural expectations among the actors regarding the course the action will take, and b) not simply be regarded as a random expression of aggression because it follows condensed symbolic forms which originate in existing cultural traditions that often emphasize the polarity of social categories, while c) the symbolic forms may simultaneously be aimed at the creation of a new order or the restoration of the old, and d) this symbolic aspect places pogroms in a historical context and hence gives them a significance extending beyond the individual motives of the participants (1977:52). A similar analytical approach was adopted by Peter Loewenberg when he analyzed *Reichskristallnacht* as a "degradation ritual" (1987). Another form of close link between "riots and rituals" has been observed, for example, by Natalie Zemon Davis (1973) and Peter van der Veer in their examination of conflicts between religious groups such as Catholics and Huguenots in France or Hindus and Muslims in India. Religious riots are often an extension of religious rituals, and in some cases their course, too, is ritualized. Both forms of action are regarded as rational and logical, and ascribed an important part in the creation of social identities. According to this theory, pogroms and rituals are linked in the "construction of 'communal' identities in public space" (van der Veer, 1996:154). In India, for example, processions serve as "rituals of provocation," which frequently end in riots. Riots, by this interpretation, represent a form of ritual group antagonism. Collective public violence in the form of riots and rituals, frequently a conflict over holy places, serves as a mechanism for drawing boundaries between (religious) groups, in that it "cleanses" the community of internal and external threats. In Davis's interpretation, pogroms are cultural phenomena or more precisely a form of ritual behavior whose core is "order" and the "purity of the community" (1973). Here, the culturalist theory coincides with assumptions of the "power approach," in which the necessity for group integration is also a central force behind ethnic conflicts.

2. The Dynamics of Pogroms

The dynamics of collective action in pogroms have hitherto been the subject of little detailed analysis. In some aspects, such as ecological preconditions (trigger event, location, time, weather), they follow the patterns familiar from research into (race) riots, but there are important differences, too.

The start, course, and severity of pogroms differ according to the pogromists' *degree of organization*. A continuum can be assumed here between the pole of a relatively highly organized form, which generally follows a very violent pattern, and the opposite pole of a spontaneous brawl involving a low level of violence. As far as the *outbreak* of pogrom-style violence is concerned, a low level of horizontal networking with the other party to the conflict plays an important part. In contrast, for example, to food riots during the early nineteenth century, where such networks existed and violence was contained by negotiation and custom ("protocols of riots"), fewer overlapping relationships exist between ethnic groups, and they are further reduced in the course of an escalating conflict. These circumstances explain the rapid onset of violence and its high level. The breaking-off of external communications contrasts with intensive local in-group communication, which is described as a "pogrom atmosphere": an emotionally charged situation intensified by agitation, experimental acts of violence, and rumor. The low level of information exchange ("information asymmetry") between ethnic groups means that people are poorly informed about the behavior patterns and membership of the other group, so that in the event of an incident the specific guilty party cannot be identified and the out-group is therefore punished in its entirety. This opens the way to a spiral of violence that can only be halted if the controlling authorities assist the out-group's efforts to identify and punish the guilty individual (in-group policing).

Whether a pogrom breaks out depends on a contingent *trigger event*, which manifests the group conflict and can serve as a starting point for collective action. In the case of pogroms, trigger events are those in which a threat to the majority is symbolized. Collective interpretation models are already available for the interpretation of such trigger events (for the significance of early socialization in such hostile concepts, cf. Kakar, 1996). The "outrageous event" triggers feelings of fury and vengeance, increases the density of communication, and results in the *de facto* acquisition of a "critical mass" of people prepared to participate in collective action (Oliver, Marwell, & Teixera, 1985). "Leadership" plays a part here: in many cases "ethnic ideologues" and "entrepreneurs" (Brass refers to "institutionalized riot systems," 1996:12) exploit a trigger event to bring about escalation, imposing a direction and a model on the joint action and having the ability to exert an escalating or de-escalating effect on the rank and file in the sense of "extremity shifts" (Bohstedt, 1994:263ff.).

In contrast to social movements, which deliberately mobilize their interlinked networks for action, pogroms require a populace that can be mobilized locally. McPhail has stressed the importance of *structural availability* for the processes of assembly and mobilization (1994:8ff.). It is not necessarily the case that violent conflict is intended here from the outset: it may be the result of a process of escalation beginning with routine conflicts between members of ethnic groups, or it may take the form of a substitute action, for example in connection with labor or food riots, strikes, or revolutionary movements (Wynn, 1992). Often, there are local level groups—factory workforces, student groups, hooligans, or nationalist organizations—which can serve *ad hoc* as a mass with the potential for action, act as organizers (for Kischinew Dahlke, 1951/52), and intend violence from the outset. The mob must also have a geographically identifiable target area: in other words, the minority must be concentrated in an ethnic colony or refugee hostel, possess identifiable business premises, or actually have gathered at a particular location.

Typical of pogroms is their *ripple effect*. Pogrom-style violence at one location becomes the most important trigger event for follow-up action. This applies not only to action at the point of origin but also to its substantial propagation over space and time (there were 259 pogroms in Russia from 1881–1883). As far as *diffusion* is concerned, both social density—in other words, the possibility of recruiting participants *en bloc*—and the density and channels of communication play an important part (Aronson, 1990). The pogrom spreads via rumors or flysheets or party newspapers. Today, the mass media, especially television, have (involuntarily) taken over this propagating function (electronic contagion). A successful pogrom serves as an action model which changes the cost-benefit ratio in favor of participation, since the risk of punishment decreases as the number of pogromists and the underreaction of the state increase, the diffuse acceptance of violence takes concrete form, and opportunities for profitable looting beckon. We know little as yet about these dynamics of escalation (Willems, 1997:467ff.); but in this case, a communicatively induced imitative behavior seems to enter into play, of a type we also see in other publicized events such as terrorist attacks and suicides.

Pogroms are *episodic* in character, since a "critical mass" cannot remain available for mobilization in the long term because the pogromists are often quick to complete their work of destruction, looting, and expulsion, and because the state cannot allow the situation of public disorder to last very long.

3. Aims and Effects of Action

Protest and movement research have ascribed a high degree of rationality to militant action by social movements and to race riots, and have largely glossed over emotional aspects. For such researchers, acts of civil violence arise from nonviolent forms, so that violence is seen only as a rational means of attaining objectives that may arise under certain circumstances. It is possible to list examples contrary to this view, which begin as acts of violence from the outset (lynching and pogroms). It is also necessary to ask whether the use of violence implies only a heightening of conflict, or whether violence should not be regarded as an independent mode of conflict expression (Brubaker & Laitin, 1998:425). The rational pursuit of interests may be insignificant, especially in cases of localized episodic violence (Rule, 1988:193). The sometimes excessive violence of pogroms is difficult to categorize simply as purposive or symbolic action without including forces of expression, the release of emotional tension and hostile aggression, demonstrations of power and strength, and the pleasure of violence. Pogromists often come from a subcultural milieu or criminal gangs (farmworkers and migrant laborers in Russia, skinheads), for which violence is much less an exceptional means to an end than an obsession. "They act to make their perceptions match their goal of violating—intimidating, assaulting, injuring or killing—another human being" (McPhail, 1994:23). There is a correlation between crime rates and phases of unrestrained collective violence, as there is between rioting and youth (Useem, 1998:224). The pogromists make no specific, limited demands of any kind; rather, violent action and its possible effects are inseparably linked, so that the actors are all the more successful in achieving the expulsion, deprivation, or humiliation of their victims when the level of violence is higher. Pogrom reports, therefore, are full of violent excesses (for India, see Rösel, 1997:170ff.). Evidently, the sense of governmental "authorization" helps to dispel inhibitory moral standards of conduct.

The action taken by the pogromists also includes a utilitarian component (improving or securing their group position), but its direct purpose is to ward off a perceived threat. Their aim is actually to get rid of the attacked group ("foreigners out!"), deprive them of their livelihood (looting and arson), degrade them ("down with ...!"), or even kill them ("death to ...!"). The pogrom is also an *indirect* call for government action against the minority and in favor of the pogromists themselves, and this is frequently successful (restrictions on inward migration or the promulgation of discriminatory legislation). The intended effects on the minority are to make them anxious and afraid and to damage their social situation to the point of destroying their economic livelihood, resulting in extreme cases in suicides or emigration.

III. CURRENT CONTROVERSIES AND
DESIDERATA

There has as yet been little interlinked research into pogroms, and the studies hitherto available are for the most part historical case studies with little theoretical orientation. This means that it is hardly possible to speak of a state of research with current controversies. Initially, therefore, pogrom research will have to focus on distinguishing pogroms from other, closely related forms of ethnic violence, along the lines of the disaggregation referred to earlier. There are indications here that the theories evolved in relation to social movements and race riots display certain utilitarian unilateralisms and fail to take adequate account of important aspects of pogroms (emotionalism, brutality, and spontaneity). This may result in a reassessment of discredited theories (for example, the "breakdown theories," Useem, 1998), particularly since the rational choice approach and the "bounded rationality explanations," apart the "free rider" problem, face problems in translating rational calculation to the level of specific action (McPhail, 1994:14ff.). It is necessary, therefore, to find explanatory approaches which are preoccupied less with the motives and characteristics of the actors and more with the interactive dynamics of collective violent action (Bohstedt, 1994:283ff.). This means focusing less on the causes than on the process dynamics of communication and action. Brass, among others, has criticized the fact that academic literature displays a tendency toward objectivization by emphasizing deep-seated structural causes (which, as it were, are the tinder that can be ignited by a spark to produce the conflagration of a pogrom) and ignoring two important influencing factors: the contribution made by hostile discourses and the role of certain individuals and groups as intermediaries in the conversion of "trigger events" into a pogrom (1996:6ff.). Brass suggests that the frequently reported "pogrom atmosphere" and the existence of prejudices should undoubtedly be viewed as contributory causes. Pogroms may be conditioned more by specific events and the form of group relationships than by structural factors such as economic crises, unemployment, and so on. The question of which group of factors are primary factors and which are secondary is still a subject of debate in research. Both in historical case studies and in theoretical works, it remains generally unclear how localized acts of violence result from changes in context (crisis or conflict). Historians tend to regard every pogrom as a specific local instance and to formulate only a loose link to the context, while sociologists take the reverse view, being more likely to analyze general structures and neglect the local actors (cf. Basu, 1995:35ff.). In the case of theories which emphasize the conditions of competition and exploitation, collective violence becomes a comprehensible even though possibly misguided reaction; these theories recognize neither responsibilities nor actors.

Also controversial is who the pogromists are. The mob or "riff-raff" theory regards socially marginalized and poorer sections of the population as vectors of violence, while another view considers that pogromists do not vary much from the population average. Empirical case studies confirm both these assumptions. The question of the identity of the actors also influences the hypotheses regarding their motives: a mob is customarily ascribed no far-reaching political aims, merely a destructive attitude that is driven by prejudice and aimed at self-enrichment, whereas the higher social classes are believed to hold deeper convictions and pursue more specific political aims (Brass, 1996:16ff.).

The numerous historical case studies offer a source of empirical verification or empirically induced theoretical development that has still not yet been fully exploited. Previously distinct fields of research, such as collective political violence and ethnicity/ ethnic conflicts, must be more closely related to one another. This means taking account not only of the sociological theories of collective action but also of new social psychology approaches (such as the social identity theory), and of research into nationalism/ ethnocentricity.

IV. APPROACHES TO PREVENTION

To my knowledge, there have not hitherto been any specifically pogrom-related approaches to prevention (regarding the conditions for amicable settlement of ethnic conflicts in general, cf. Hanf, 1989:331ff.; Montville, 1990).

Translated by Richard Sharp

REFERENCES

Aronson, I. Michael. (1990). *Troubled Waters. The Origins of the 1881 Anti-Jewish Pogroms in Russia*. Pittsburgh: University of Pittsburgh Press.

Basu, Amrita. (1995). Why Local Riots Are not Simply Local: Collective Violence and the State in Bijnor, India 1988–1993. *Theory and Society*, 24, 35–78.

Benz, Wolfgang. (2001). The November Pogrom of 1938. Participation, Applause, Disapproval. In Christhard Hoffmann, Werner Bergmann & Helmut W. Smith (Eds.), *Exclusionary Violence. Antisemitic Riots in Modern German History*. Ann Arbor: University of Michigan Press.

Bergmann, Werner. (1998). Pogrome: Eine spezifische Form kollektiver Gewalt. *Kölner Zeitschrift für Soziologie und Sozialpsychologie*, 50, 644–665.

Berk, Stephen M. (1985). *Year of Crisis, Year of Hope. Russian Jewry and the Pogroms of 1881–1882*. Westport, London: Greenwood Press.

Black, Donald. (1983). "Crime as Social Control." *American Sociological Review*, 48, 34–45.

Blalock, Hubert M. (1967). *Toward a Theory of Minority-Group Relations*. New York: Wiley.

Blumer, Herbert. (1958). Race Prejudice as a Sense of Group Position. *Pacific Sociological Review*, 1, 3–7.

Bohstedt, John. (1994). The Dynamics of Riots: Escalation and Diffusion/ Contagion. In Michael Potegal & John F. Knutson (Eds.), *The Dynamics of Aggression. Biological and Social Processes in Dyads and Groups* (pp. 257–306). Hillsdale: Erlbaum.

Brass, Paul R. (1996). Introduction: Discourses of Ethnicity, Communalism, and Violence. In Paul R. Brass (Ed.), *Riots and Pogroms* (pp. 1–55). Hampshire: Basingstoke.

Brubaker, Rogers, & David D. Laitin. (1998). Ethnic and Nationalist Violence. *Annual Review of Sociology*, 24, 423–452.

Coser, Lewis A. (1956). *The Functions of Social Conflict*. New York: The Free Press.

Crowe, Charles. (1969). Racial Massacre in Atlanta September 22, 1906. *Journal of Negro History*, 54, 150–173.

Dahlke, H. Otto. (1951/52). Race and Minority Riots. A Study in the Typology of Violence. *Social Forces*, 30, 419–425.

Davies, James C. (1962). Toward a Theory of Revolution. *American Journal of Sociology*, 27, 5–18.

Davis, Natalie Zemon. (1973). The Rites of Violence: Religious Riot in Sixteenth Century France. *Past and Present*, 59, 51–91.

Giles, Micheal W., & Arthur Evans. (1986). The Power Approach to Intergroup Hostility. *Journal of Conflict Resolution*, 30, 469–486.

Giles, Micheal W., & Melanie A. Buckner. (1993). David Duke and Black Threat: An Old Hypothesis Revisited. *Journal of Politics*, 55, 702–713.

Goldberg, Harvey E. (1977). Rites and Riots. The Tripolitanian Pogrom of 1945. *Plural Societies*, 8, 5–56.

Greenberg, Cheryl. (1992). The Politics of Disorder: Reexamining Harlem's Riots of 1935 and 1943. *Journal of Urban History*, 18, 395–441.

Gurr, Ted R. (1970). *Why Men Rebel.* Princeton: Princeton University Press.

Gurr, Ted R. (1993). *Minorities at Risk. A Global View of Ethnopolitical Conflict.* Washington: United States Institute of Peace Press.

Hanf, Theodor. (1989). The Prospects of Accommodation in Communal Conflicts: A Comparative Study. In Peter A. Döring, Horst Weishaupt & Manfred Weiß (Eds.), *Bildung in sozioökonomischer Sicht* (pp. 313–332). Köln: Böhlau.

Hoffmann, Christhard. (1994). Politische Kultur und Gewalt gegen Minderheiten. Die antisemitischen Ausschreitungen in Pommern und Westpreußen 1881. *Jahrbuch für Antisemitismusforschung, 3*, 93–120.

Horowitz, Donald L. (2000). *The Deadly Ethnic Riots.* Los Angeles: University of California Press.

Jenkins, J. Craig, & Kurt Schock. (1992). Global Structures and Political Processes in the Study of Domestic Political Conflict. *Annual Review of Sociology, 18*, 161–185.

Janowitz, Morris. (1968). *Social Control of Escalated Riots.* Chicago: University of Chicago Press.

Janowitz, Morris. (1969). Patterns of Collective Racial Violence. In Hugh Davies Graham & Ted R. Gurr (Eds.), *The History of Violence in America. Historical and Comparative Perspectives* (pp. 412–444). New York: Bantam Books.

Kakar, Sudhir. (1996). *The Colours of Violence: Cultural Identities, Religion and Conflict.* Chicago: University of Chicago Press.

Kannangara, A. P. (1984). The Riots of 1915 in Sri Lanka: A Study in the Roots of Communal Violence. *Past and Present, 102*, 130–165.

Katz, Jacob. (1994). *Die Hep-Hep-Verfolgungen des Jahres 1819.* Berlin: Metropol.

Klier, John D. (1992). The Pogrom Paradigm in Russian History. In John D. Klier & Shlomo Lambroza (Eds.), *Pogroms: Anti-Jewish Violence in Modern Russian History* (pp. 13–38). Cambridge, New York: Cambridge University Press.

Klier, John D., & Shlomo Lambroza. (Eds.) (1992). *Pogroms: Anti-Jewish Violence in Modern Russian History.* Cambridge, New York: Cambridge University Press.

Korpi, Walter. (1974). Conflict, Power and Relative Deprivation. *American Political Science Review, 38*, 1569–1578.

Kushner, Tony. (1993). Anti-Semitism and Austerity: the August 1947 Riots in Britain. In Panikos Panayi (Ed.), *Racial Violence in Britain 1840–1950* (pp. 149–168). Leicester: Leicester University Press.

LeVine, Robert A., & Donald T. Campbell. (1972). *Ethnocentrism: Theories of Conflict, Ethnic Attitudes and Group Behavior.* New York/ London: Wiley.

Levene, Mark. (Ed.) (1999). *Massacres in History.* London: Berghahn.

Loewenberg, Peter. (1987). The Kristallnacht as a Public Degradation Ritual. *Yearbook of the Leo Baeck Institute, 33*, 309–323.

Marx, Gary T. (1972). Issueless Riots. In James F. Short, Jr. & Marvin E. Wolfgang (Eds.), *Collective Violence* (pp. 47–59). Chicago, New York: Aldine-Atherton.

McPhail, Clark. (1994). Presidential Address. The Dark Side of Purpose: Individual and Collective Violence in Riots. *Sociological Quarterly, 35*, pp. 1–32.

Melson, Robert. (1992). *Revolution and Genocide. On the Origins of the Armenian Genocide and the Holocaust.* Chicago: University of Chicago Press.

Montville, Joseph V. (Ed.) (1990). *Conflict and Peacemaking in Multiethnic Societies.* Lexington: Lexington Books.

Nonn, Christoph. (1998). Zwischenfall in Konitz. Antisemitismus und Nationalismus im preußischen Osten um 1900. *Historische Zeitschrift, 266*, 387–418.

Oliver, Pamela, Gerald Marwell, & Ruy Teixera. (1985). A Theory of Critical Mass. I. Interdependence, Group Heterogeneity, and the Production of Collective Action. *American Journal of Sociology, 91*, 522–556.

Olzak, Susan. (1990). The Political Context of Competition: Lynching and Urban Racial Violence (1882–1914). *Social Forces, 69*, pp. 395–421.

Olzak, Susan. (1992). *The Dynamics of Ethnic Competition and Conflict.* Stanford: Stanford University Press

Panayi, Panikos. (1991). Middlesbrough 1961: A British Race Riot of the 1960s? *Social History, 16*, 139–153.

Quillian, Lincoln. (1995). Prejudice as a Response to Perceived Threat: Population Composition and Anti-Immigrant and Racial Prejudice in Europe. *American Sociological Review, 60*, 586–611.

Rösel, Jakob. (1997). Vom ethnischen Antagonismus zum ethnischen Bürgerkrieg. Antagonismus, Erinnerung und Gewalt in ethnischen Konflikten. In Trutz von Trotha (Ed.), *Soziologie der Gewalt* (pp. 162–182). Opladen: Westdeutscher Verlag.

Rogger, Hans. (1992). Conclusion and Overview. In John D. Klier & Shlomo Lambroza (Eds.), *Pogroms: Anti-Jewish Violence in Modern Russian History* (pp. 314–372). Cambridge, New York: Cambridge University Press.

Rohrbacher, Stefan. (1993). *Gewalt im Biedermeier. Antijüdische Ausschreitungen in Vormärz und Revolution (1815–1848/49)*. Frankfurt, New York: Campus.

Rudé, George. (1964). *The Crowd in History. A Study of Popular Disturbances in France and England, 1730–1848*. New York: Wiley.

Rudwick, Elliott. (1964). *Race Riot at East St. Louis, July 2, 1917*. Urbana: University of Illinois Press.

Rule, James. (1988). *Theories of Civil Violence*. Berkeley: University of California Press.

Senechal de la Roche, Roberta. (1990). *The Sociogenesis of a Race Riot: Springfield, Illinois, in 1908*. Urbana: University of Illinois Press.

Senechal de la Roche, Roberta. (1996). Collective Violence as Social Control. *Sociological Forum, 11*, 97–128.

Smelser, Neil J. (1963). *Theory of Collective Behavior*. New York: The Free Press.

Snyder, David, & Charles Tilly. (1972). Hardship and Collective Violence in France, 1830 to 1960. *American Sociological Review, 37*, 520–532.

Sterling, Eleonore. (1950). Anti-Jewish Riots in Germany in 1819. *Historia Judaica, 12*, 105–142.

Swan, L. Alex. (1980). *The Politics of Riot Behavior*. Washington: University Press of America.

Trotha, Trutz von. (Ed.) (1997). *Soziologie der Gewalt*. Opladen: Westdeutscher Verlag.

Useem, Bert. (1998). Breakdown Theories of Collective Action. *Annual Review of Sociology, 24*, 215–238.

Van der Veer, Peter. (1996). Riots and Rituals: The Construction of Violence and Public Space in Hindu Nationalism. In Paul R. Brass (Ed.), *Riots and Pogroms* (pp. 154–176). Hampshire: Basingstoke.

Waldmann, Peter. (1995). Gesellschaften im Bürgerkrieg. Zur Eigendynamik entfesselter Gewalt. *Zeitschrift für Politik, 42*, 343–368.

Willems, Helmut. (1997). *Jugendunruhen und Protestbewegungen. Eine Studie zur Dynamik innergesellschaftlicher Konflikte in vier europäischen Ländern*. Opladen: Leske & Budrich.

Williams, Robin W., Jr. (1994). The Sociology of Ethnic Conflicts: Comparative International Perspectives. *Annual Review of Sociology, 20*, 49–79.

Wimmer, Andreas. (1995). Interethnische Konflikte. Ein Beitrag zur Integration aktueller Forschungsansätze. *Kölner Zeitschrift für Soziologie und Sozialpsychologie, 47*, 464–493.

Wynn, Charters. (1992). *Workers, Strikes, and Pogroms. The Donbass-Dnepr Bend in Late Imperial Russia 1870–1905*. Princeton: Princeton University Press.

Violence and New Social Movements

Dieter Rucht

I. INTRODUCTION

Some writers in the field have a very broad concept of what constitutes violence. In the theory of "structural violence" (Johan Galtung), social conditions that result in massive social discrimination and injustice are a form of violence. Similarly, even relatively harmless forms of civil disobedience, such as short-term sit-ins, are sometimes included within the definition of violence. These broad interpretations mean that the concept of violence is ill defined and, ultimately, useless. It is preferable to adopt a definition of violence closely based on the everyday understanding of the term. *Violence* means intentionally caused or carelessly accepted damage to/destruction of property or the injuring/killing of people (Graham & Gurr, 1969; Neidhardt, 1986). Even so, problems of definition remain, as in the case of minor damage to property (such as graffiti), the holding of individuals against their expressed will, or the exertion of huge mental pressure which—in some forms of torture—can in extreme cases result in destruction of the personality. The first of these examples should be excluded from the concept of violence, and the third included, while the second can probably not be classified meaningfully unless the circumstances are known. In general terms, it may be said that the understanding of violence is culture-dependent. Whereas, for example, female circumcision is a generally accepted social practice in some parts of Africa, it is perceived by many Western observers as a cruel form of mutilation and an unambiguous act of violence within the definition adopted here.

A further inconsistency lies in the classification of violations of rules, such as occur in the context of social movements. The acts of *confrontation* practiced by many movements lie below the threshold of violence. They are intentional breaches of rules which—unlike such manifestations as protest meetings, picketing, and hunger strikes—interfere with other people's freedom of action, or make it difficult or impossible for them to do as they wish or go where they wish, but are not intended to cause physical harm to property or persons. In English-speaking countries, the term "direct action" is often used for this,

W. Heitmeyer and J. Hagan (eds.), *International Handbook of Violence Research*, 369–382.

and direct action is frequently illegal, though not by definition. Acts of *civil disobedience* are a special instance of illegal direct action, associated with strict conditions (including the fruitless exhaustion of all legal means, strict self-discipline, preventive measures to avoid escalation, no attempt to conceal individual identities, and the acceptance of legal penalties).

Violence is not an intrinsic feature of social movements. Some movements are avowedly nonviolent; others use violence as a tactical weapon to be employed only under the most extreme circumstances; for others again, violence is a natural and necessary resource in the struggle. Where social movements do make use of violence, its ultimate purpose is to achieve social or political aims, which can include the use of violence to attract attention, to strengthen one's own position, to eliminate internal competition, or as a defense against attacks from outside. Whether terrorist groups, which use violence without hesitation, should be included among social movements depends on the basic concept of a movement adopted.

A *social movement* is "an action system, formed for a certain period of time and based on collective identity, of mobilized networks of groups and organizations which aim to bring about, prevent, or reverse social change by means of protest—if necessary, violent protest" (Rucht, 1994:76 ff.). Social movements, then, may include formal organizations but are not themselves organizations. Features of organizations include a clearly defined membership, a charter or statutes, binding agendas, and—in most cases—hierarchical structures. The boundaries between social and political movements in modern societies are fluid, so that Jenkins (1981), for example, refers to "sociopolitical movements."

The concept of *new social movements* ("NSMs") came to the fore during the 1970s, initially in France and Italy. By 1980 it had spread to other Western European countries, and the term later came to be used in the United States, Eastern Europe, and Latin America. The adjective "new" is used to distinguish these movements from "old" movements, in particular the labor movement. We find similar distinctions used in the names of artistic movements, such as Art Nouveau. In many ways, NSMs follow the tradition established by the labor movement. They too are basically emancipatory, prodemocratic, and egalitarian, in sharp contradistinction to right-wing radical groups. In contrast to the labor movement, however, the direct focal points of NSMs are not to be found in the sphere of production. The central issues for the NSMs are rather peace and disarmament, democracy and participation, human and civil rights, the Third World, equal rights for women, the protection of minorities, ecology, and urban renewal. The individual movements that pursue these aims recruit primarily from the middle classes. The substructure of NSMs consists mainly not of large-scale formal organizations but of networks of different types of groups, including informal local or regional groups. Prominent leaders who might rely on personal charisma or the power of an organization are of minor significance. Strategically, a typical feature is that NSMs try to bring about change not through revolution but through more or less radical reforms. It follows that the use of violence plays a minor part in the activities of the NSMs.

Researchers are divided on whether the real origins of the NSMs lie in the New Left of the 1960s (including the extraparliamentary opposition and student revolt). There are arguments in favor of regarding the New Left as an independent complex of movements bridging the gap, in both time and content, between the labor movement or Old Left on the one hand and the NSMs on the other. Unlike the majority of NSMs, the New Left shared with the labor movement a radical critique of capitalism and the desire for revolutionary change, but rejected the latter's rigid organizational models and self-righteous attitudes. In its antiauthoritarian actions, spontaneity, emphasis on the subjective factor, and radical critique of modern civilization, the New Left anticipated the positions adopted—mostly in diluted form—by the NSMs. A good many groups within the NSMs originated directly from the New Left and the student movement, but typically refused to participate in the ideological trench warfare that marked the period of collapse of the student movement. On the whole, the NSMs that came into existence during the late 1960s and early 1970s pursued an independent path, avoiding both the last sectarian vestiges of the student movement and those forces of reform that had migrated into the left-wing and liberal parties and trusted in the self-renewal of establishment politics.

The NSMs are a loose association of partly overlapping individual movements, which are sometimes also described as a left-wing libertarian movements family (della Porta & Rucht, 1995). Between and within the individual movements, there are differing preferences on policy and strategy, a point that becomes notably apparent in their attitude to the issue of violence. On one side of the spectrum are legalists, for whom even civil disobedience goes too far. On the other are the street fighters of groups like the anti-imperial *Autonomen* ("autonomists") in Germany, who are prepared for violence. Although they do not resort to the tactics of terrorism, they do have a certain sympathy for the underground groups of the radical left—such as, in Germany, the "Revolutionäre Zellen" (Revolutionary Cells) and its feminist auxiliary "Rote Zora" (Red Zora).

II. THEORETICAL APPROACHES AND EMPIRICAL RESULTS

1. Theories of New Social Movements

There is a large body of research in the social sciences on the causes, manifestations, and effects of social movements in general and the NSMs in particular. Most of it originates from the disciplines of sociology and political science. The theoretical debate on the NSMs initially evolved in different directions in the United States and in Europe (Klandermans, 1991).

The older theory of social movements, based primarily in the United States and inspired by mass psychology, the sociology of conflict, and the collective-behavior theories of structural functionalism and symbolic interaction (Marx & Wood, 1975), had become insignificant even while the NSMs were still in their formative phase. Because of the relatively high degree of specialization in U.S. research, individual aspects of social movements—such as questions of organization, recruitment, and strategy—had been the main focus since the 1970s. These in turn provided the basis for corresponding "medium-range" theories, such as the approach dealing with the mobilization of resources (Edwards & McCarthy, 1992). An additional part was played by microsociological theories (relative deprivation, rational choice), which dealt primarily with the motives and reasons for individual commitment. U.S. research was concerned not only with the civil rights movement, the New Left, and the NSMs, but also took into consideration, for example, agrarian and religious movements.

In Europe, an academic discipline of social movements only really began in the 1970s, works prior to that date being few and scattered. It first developed in connection with the NSMs, with its main emphasis on macrostructural attempts to explain the origins and evolutionary dynamics of NSMs. Whereas U.S. research at this time was concerned

primarily with the "how" of social movements—aspects of organization and mobilization—European research concentrated on the "why," questions relating to the origin of
social movements in the context of overall social change (Melucci, 1984:821). It was only
later that European research into social movements broadened its horizons to include other
movements and general issues relating to social movements.

From about the mid-1980s onward, American and European researchers began to
become more aware of each other, so that the profiles of research in the two continents
each affected and influenced the other, a process outwardly manifested in joint conferences and publications (Klandermans, Kriesi, & Tarrow, 1988; McAdam, McCarthy, &
Zald, 1996). This process was also apparent in theoretical approaches, between which
there were now virtually no geographical differences.

As far as (new) social movements are concerned, it is possible to identify four relatively new approaches (see below) that have recently been supplemented by greater efforts at integration. None of these approaches specifically addresses questions relating to
the use of violence, a problem that tends to be dealt with more outside the field of genuine
social movement research, for example in the context of theories of relative deprivation,
research into extremism, or a form of conflict research specifically tailored to violent
phenomena (Eckstein, 1980; Rule, 1988). As all the above approaches are dealt with by
other articles in this volume, we will confine ourselves here to specific investigations of
social movements and—insofar as this exists at all—their consideration of violence in the
context of (new) social movements.

a. *Macrostructural explanations* interpret the origins and specific profile of NSMs against
a background of overall social processes and situations (e.g., Touraine, 1984; Melucci,
1984). Setting out from different premises of grand social theory, they deal either with
advancing processes of modernization or with the transition to a "postindustrial", "programmed", "postmodern", or "post-Fordist" society. According to these theories, the associated transformations result in structural problems and strains but also in greater
opportunities for action on the part of certain groups that form the mobilization potential
for NSMs. In some cases, these approaches also consider the influence of specific political
conditions. Thus, for example, the closure or intransigence of the political establishment—
in the context of neocorporatist arrangements or the blocking of reform—are held responsible for the mobilization of NSMs in a form that demands greater participation and
introduces neglected problems to the political agenda. Violent phenomena receive no special attention in the course of these approaches. Implicitly, however, the majority of such
theories assume that NSMs become radical to the extent that the problems they raise are
ignored by the established powers and the movements are structurally marginalized from
political debate and the decision-making process.

b. *Resource mobilization approaches*, which are presented in more detail in della Porta's
article in this volume, do not associate macrostructural situations with the emergence of
social movements. Instead, they start from the assumption that problems and strains exist
in all societies at every stage, without necessarily leading to collective action. The critical
factor for such action is rather that tangible and intangible resources are mobilized by
movement organizations and, especially, the "social movement entrepreneurs" who work
within them. Explicitly in the case of the United States, but implicitly for the Western
world as a whole, it is assumed that such resources are increasingly available and that the
social movement sector is becoming professionalized (McCarthy & Zald, 1973).

Categorically, movements are not distinguished from interest groups or parties. Nor is there much discussion of the special features of particular types of movement (such as NSMs) or the conditions for the use of different options for action (such as the use of violence). The work done by Tilly (1978) is an exception here. But if the premises of the resource mobilization approach were to be applied to phenomena of collective violence, their increase or decrease could not be explained in terms of objective or subjective deprivation. What would be needed, rather, would be an "organization" of violence, making it possible to convert the latent potential for action into manifest acts of violence, violence—like any form of social and political mobilization—being conceived as what Lipsky (1968) calls a strategically deployed resource and not, for example, a spontaneous eruption of rage and hatred.

c. Political process and political opportunity approaches have separate roots but share certain common ground and have increasingly come to overlap. The former type, represented for example by McAdam (1982), sees itself as an extension of the resource mobilization approaches. In addition to the need for mobilizing movement organizations, it also emphasizes the dynamics of interaction between movements and their relevant reference groups. Only this can provide an explanation for the rise or fall of mobilization, radicalization, or deradicalization of action. Here again, developments and problem situations in society as a whole remain in the background. It is only in the sociohistorical works of Tilly (1978) that developments such as industrialization and urbanization are discussed as factors possibly influencing social movements and collective violence.

Political opportunity approaches concentrate on factors which exert a positive or negative influence on the nature and extent of mobilization and hence, indirectly, on the effects of social movements (for example, access to the political decision-making system, consensus or dissensus among elites, allies, state repression). A distinction can be made here between the more stable and the more variable opportunities. When we consider changing opportunities that can also be influenced by movements, the difference between these approaches and the political process ones shrinks. Some authors have suggested that the concept of political opportunity structures should be extended to include cultural and other opportunities (Brand, 1985) or incorporated into a more comprehensive model of context structures (Rucht, 1994). These ideas have hitherto been applied primarily with an eye to NSMs, although they are certainly not tailored to these particular actors.

It has been pointed out that different movements or campaigns within the same society are in each case partly influenced by specific opportunities. Although these ideas have not been systematically applied to structures that promote or prevent violence, it is still an obvious assumption that in highly repressive systems the likely cost deters acts of political violence, so that only very moderate or extremely subtle forms of protest are encountered. By contrast, very open, liberal systems take the wind from the sails of protest, and especially of violent protest.

d. Framing theories and identity-oriented approaches are independent of each other but have areas of overlap. "Frames," borrowing Erving Goffman's term, means frameworks of interpretation which movements and protest groups use to try to demonstrate that a situation of which they are critical is a matter of urgency, to identify the causes or those responsible, and where possible to propose solutions (Snow et al., 1986). A further important aspect of framing is the self-image of those involved in collective action, who try to present themselves—usually by way of negative contrast with their political opponents—as competent and credible.

In partial association with framing theories, approaches have been evolved which specifically address cultural aspects and the mechanisms by which movements assert their identity. Self-portrayal emphasized by symbols, language, and clothing, and by the collective practice of protest too, plays an important part in creating an identity both within the group and for the benefit of outsiders, and in the case of very expressive or culturally oriented movements, this function can actually become the central focus of action. Approaches to this area, however, have so far suffered from theoretical underexposure. They generally confine themselves to illustrative references to the significance of identity politics, and in some cases pay particular attention to very expressive or identity-oriented groups, such as the gay movement or youth subcultures. In this connection, the practices of radical or potentially violent groups would also be of interest, because these are particularly concerned to set themselves apart, in symbolic and often ritualistic ways, from the majority culture and in some cases even from the moderate groups in the broader field of social movements. In Germany, for example, the "autonomists," a network of undogmatic anticapitalist groups, are to be seen at major demonstrations as a "black block," identifiable by dark leather clothing and radical slogans ("Kampf dem Schweinesystem" [Fight the pig system]). The occasional covering of faces—illegal in Germany—is probably not just designed to make prosecution more difficult but also gives activists a warlike image which is in line with their interpretation of the situation as a battlefield.

Sorting through the approaches described above, we can see that their relationship to each other is more complementary than competitive. They address different questions and, in most cases, do so at different levels of analysis (the micro-, meso-, and macrodimension). As a result, there have been frequent calls for closer association or even *integration* of these approaches, and those calls have also produced more specific proposals (Neidhardt & Rucht, 1993; McAdam et al., 1996; Tarrow, 1998). This kind of combination of different aspects and levels could also prove fruitful with regard to the question of violence in the context of (new) social movements. The field within the social sciences that specializes in phenomena of collective violence (terrorism, extremism) has hardly considered social movement research theory. Exceptions to this, however, are a number of more recent works on right-wing radicalism, which have also made use of certain concepts that were developed primarily with an eye to NSMs (Bergmann, 1994; Koopmans & Rucht, 1996; Minkenberg, 1998).

2. Empirical Findings

Even though the NSMs in some cases propagate notions of a better society very different from the status quo, the idea of a revolutionary acquisition of power such as characterized sections of the New Left remains alien to them. The basic tendency of most groups within the NSMs is reformist. Consequently, most of their protest activity falls short of lawbreaking and violence, although confrontational and even violent action is no rarity.

Protest event data based on analyses of the content of national newspapers give some idea of the proportions of confrontational and violent protest. According to the study by Kriesi et al. (1995:50), which dealt with four European countries in the period from 1975 through 1989, confrontational protest as a proportion of all protests by NSMs was highest in the Netherlands at 30.9% (Germany 19.1%, France 17.0%, Switzerland 12.6%). Statistics on violent protest show France in the lead at 22.5%, followed by Switzerland (14.7%), Germany (14.3%) and the Netherlands (12.3%). If a distinction is made between moderate and severe violence, the occurrence of severe violence is far higher in France, at 17.6%, than in the other countries (Germany 7.0%, Netherlands 5.7%, Switzerland 3.9%).

A time series also exists covering protests for the Federal Republic of Germany from 1950 through 1994, protests taking place in the territory of the (former) GDR also being included from 1989 onward (source: Prodat project, Wissenschaftszentrum Berlin/Rucht; cf. also Neidhardt & Rucht, 1999). If we consider only NSM protests from 1970 onward, the proportion of confrontational protests is 15.0% and violent protests 8.8%. In the 1970s, the proportion of confrontational protest was considerably lower than during subsequent periods at 9.8% (1980–1989, 17.3%; 1990–1994, 16.7%). The same is true of violent protests, where the proportion increased from 4.5% in the 1970s to 11.2% in the 1980s and 9.3% in the first half of the 1990s. A breakdown by subject shows high proportions of confrontational protest on the issues of infrastructure (50.8%) and nuclear power (21.7%), and high proportions of violent action in protests in favor of leftist ideologies (17.5%), ecology (11.2%), democracy/human rights (9.8%), and the Third World (8.8%), and those against nuclear power (8.0%). The lowest proportion of violence is to be found in protests in favor of immigrants (4.7%), peace (5.4%) and women (5.5%).

According to the Ministry of Internal Affairs of the Federal Republic of Germany, the average number of demonstrations recorded each year from 1968 through 1994 was slightly more than 5,000, of which 4.7% were classified as "unpeaceful." There is no breakdown by different subject areas. Taking the Prodat project as a basis, the NSMs represent nearly 60% of all protest activity in the period from 1968 through 1994.

Viewed as a whole, these figures show that the percentages of confrontational and violent action fluctuated substantially from state to state, movement to movement, and stage to stage. In the broader national comparison, there is a strong impression that, especially, the tendency to severe violence is less pronounced in relatively open and responsive systems (such as Scandinavia, the Netherlands, and Switzerland) than in a corporatist system (such as the Federal Republic of Germany) or a centralist system (such as France). The French political system, in particular, seems to offer groups in civil society too little opportunity to influence events (for example, through the representation of protest parties in parliament, lobbying, or action before the administrative courts), so that the discontent among opposition groups initially builds up with no recognizable external signs and then— as in an overpressurized boiler—finds an explosive outlet. This pattern was apparent not only in the student revolts of May 1968 and the NSMs that followed, but also in protests by farmers, wine producers, fishermen, truck drivers, and miners. Militant protest is fueled by the knowledge that it has frequently been successful in winning concessions from the government in the past. Similar lessons were learned, under very different circumstances, by the Afro-American residents of North America's urban ghettoes, whose uprisings—as later research demonstrated—were by no means an expression of social rootlessness, anomie, and blind destructive rage but were often prompted by the calculated belief that this appeared to be the only way of attracting public attention and bringing about an improvement in their social situation (Skolnick, 1969; McPhail, 1991).

Thematically, violent protest by the NSMs is scattered over many areas. Violence is concentrated in conflict over the urban infrastructure and construction projects (especially squats and urban renewal), youth centers, large-scale industrial engineering projects (especially nuclear facilities), road building, genetic engineering, animal rights, military facilities and rituals (such as the swearing-in of recruits), conferences by international institutions such as the World Bank and the International Monetary Fund, ethnic problems, and the struggle against the radical right. In addition, where regionalist movements are associated with the NSMs (as in France and Spain), the tendency to violence is noticeably above average.

The *social vectors* of violence are most often seen to be young males, while students typically tend to favor confrontational means, though less frequently resorting to violence. Among the violent participants, some are young people representing a definite political ideology. In addition, also apolitical young people who are merely in search of space (in squats, for example, or self-administered youth centers), become involved in the dynamics of conflict, and then resort to violence either in the belief that they are legitimately defending their territory or simply for kicks.

Organizational vectors of violence are almost without exception small, informal groups, in most cases associated within loose networks. Among such groups, those with a propensity for militancy and violence during the 1970s were mainly communist (Maoist or Trotskyite) and—in a few countries—anarchist groups, while from the 1980s onward this tendency became the particular preserve of the undogmatic anticapitalist "autonomists." They perceive the imperialist/capitalist system as their enemy, along with militarism, neofascism, and the patriarchal system. Often, events which attract the attention of the public—the swearing-in of recruits, May Day celebrations, state visits by foreign politicians, and international conferences—provide an opportunity for skirmishes with the authority of the state. In some cases, the provocative appearance and postures of subcultural groups, such as punks, is in itself sufficient to cause clashes which, in certain conditions, escalate into acts of violence. Inappropriate response or intervention by the police may also trigger a violent reaction by the demonstrators (Neidhardt, 1989). Additionally, in the 1990s, direct confrontation with right-wing radical groups developed into another theater of conflict with the potential for violence, involving groups of young immigrants as well as "antifascist" circles. Large NSM member organizations steer clear of violence, though a good many such organizations, such as Greenpeace, are quite prepared to resort to unlawful actions, including forms of civil disobedience, while emphasizing their strict adherence to the principle of nonviolence.

The *spectrum of violent action* is a broad one. At the bottom end of the scale comes damage to property. This may take the form of an attempt to gain access to a building or site (by breaking open doors or tearing down fences) or of material damage that is primarily symbolic in nature. Examples of this include the breaking of bank windows in anticapitalist demonstrations, the desecration of a war memorial, or the puncturing of police car tires. There is no limit to the potential level of damage. It can also take on a new, functional quality by significantly obstructing certain activities or building projects, or even delaying them for long periods. Radical animal rights protesters in Scandinavia broke open the cages of fur farms and released the animals into the wild; opponents of field trials of genetically modified plants have destroyed experimental crops; groups protesting against new highways in Britain have undermined access roads and built barricades; conservationists in America have tried to prevent the felling of ecologically valuable trees by driving spikes into the trunks to damage the chainsaws; peace activists in both the United States and Germany have forced entry to military facilities and attacked missiles with hammers; antinuclear protesters in various countries have destroyed construction machinery, short-circuited railroad power cables, sawn down pylons, and set fires; ecologists in the Basque country cut the cable of a materials handling installation to prevent the building of a dam.

Similarly, violence against the person can come anywhere on a scale of intensity ranging from jostling through more or less severe injury to murder, though fatalities are rare. In Germany, for example, left-wing radical activists stabbed a right-wing radical.

Similarly, a member of the movement opposed to the expansion of Frankfurt airport shot two police officers. Acts such as these create deep disturbance within the movement concerned and are the subject of bitter internal criticism.

The question of the *conditions that cause and trigger* such acts of violence has preoccupied public opinion, "internal security" experts, and social scientists alike, though none of them have arrived at any convincing explanations, let alone valid predictions or effective preventive measures. There are certainly no arguments to suggest that violence occurs randomly within the framework of social movements. In individual cases, therefore, it is perfectly possible in retrospect to identify a number of factors that were conducive to violence. On the other hand, the use of violence is subject to an extremely multilayered and complex structure of conditions which is difficult to summarize in terms of simple principles, so that surprises must be expected.

Factors which tend to promote or reduce violence can be located on a number of levels. One apparently obvious condition—the objective scale of social problems, injustice, and repression—is very rarely directly related to the occurrence or intensity of violence, as has been demonstrated by a great many studies—beginning with the Luddites in Europe and continuing through ghetto uprisings in the United States to peasant revolutions in Third World countries. According to the theories of relative deprivation, problems only become relevant to action and a potential cause of violence when they appear to become intolerable, on scales of expectation that may relate to comparison groups but also to past or predicted future situations (Davis, 1969; Gurr, 1970). The empirical basis for these theories, however, remains controversial (Brush, 1996), particularly because, in many cases, generalized indicators are derived from surveys which were not actually designed for that particular purpose at all. An additional problem in the context of political violence is that the actors are either difficult to identify or reluctant to provide information. Even if these obstacles can be overcome, those questioned can provide only retrospective justifications for their actions, and thus only an inadequate reflection of the tangle of actual motives. Studies on relative deprivation have also largely ignored the fact that the mobilization of protest (including mobilization to violent action) is partly determined by subjectively perceived prospects of success and risk calculations.

Overall, explanations of collective violence that address the subject purely on the subjective level and are committed to methodological individualism prove to be inadequate. Not only do they disregard group dynamic processes and interactive escalations of violence (see Gamson, Fireman, & Rytina, 1982; della Porta, 1995), but they also overlook situations of collective violence in which rage and bitterness sweep aside any objective cost/benefit calculation. In addition, all previous attempts, including those made by research on terrorism, to develop a composite perpetrator profile from demographic characteristics or features typical of socialization can be regarded as failures. For the specific case of the NSMs, in any case, no such studies exist. Thus attention shifts to other sets of factors located on the macro- and mesosocial levels.

As far as the macrosocial level is concerned, it can be said that whole societies are characterized by a greater or lesser level of civility in the resolution of conflicts. An important indicator of conflict cultures in a specific society is how politicians and the police deal with protest groups. Groups that make similar demands and practice similar forms of action encounter very different treatment in different countries. Massive clashes between police and demonstrators, leaving many dead, as occurred in Paris in 1961, Mexico City in 1968, and Peking in 1989, are hardly conceivable in certain other countries such as the Netherlands, Switzerland or Finland. Countries such as these are notable for numerous features and mechanisms that tend to restrict violence. They include: (1) liberal cultures which view political conflict as the norm, (2) political systems that are capable of reform and take their critics seriously rather curtly marginalizing them, (3) liberal laws, including regulations on the protection of minorities, (4) a criminal-law treatment of politically motivated lawbreaking that considers the reasons as well as the consequences, and (5) a flexible police attitude toward protest groups, which in some cases and temporarily accepts minor violations in order to prevent an escalation of violence.

The last two factors are particularly important when we recall that NSM activists rarely resort to violent means eagerly and indiscriminately. As numerous individual case studies show, violence among NSMs is often the result of situational and interactive dynamics in which a number of factors combine synergistically. Those factors include: First, a previous history of conflict in which protest actors have been actively marginalized or ignored. Secondly, the independence and isolation of militant groups who have alienated themselves even from the moderate protest groups who are their potential allies, perhaps accusing them of "betrayal of the cause" and hoping to compensate for a lack of numbers with more radical forms of action. A third element, finally, is insensitive policing. For example, it sometimes occurs even in the run-up to protests that "information" about impending violence passed to the press generates a climate of hostility, disproportionate "preventive" action is taken, or the provocations emanating from protest groups, which are often purely symbolic, are treated with inappropriate severity. In some cases, press observers and innocent bystanders are beaten up, sometimes without regard to whether the demonstrators are violent or peaceful. As empirical reports have shown, such attacks may be a key factor in persuading previously peaceable individuals to abandon their restraint and become politically radical.

Even though factors such as these may promote the use of violence within NSMs, those responsible for political violence are rarely viewed as victims of special circumstances or motivated by mere reaction. In the great majority of clashes between police and demonstrators, it is the latter who start the violence. Some political groups embark on a calculated and proactive course of conflict—a conflict that derives its drama from simplifications and exaggerations in which a group overstates its own mission as that of a political avant-garde, while moderate protest groups are accused either of being politically unaware or of lacking the courage of their convictions. This interpretation of the situation also includes the actively induced confirmation of the repressive nature of the "system." Provocation of the police is the preferred way of achieving this. Interviews with members of the "autonomists" recorded on various occasions suggest that skirmishing with the police can take on the dimensions of a kind of sport and add considerably to their enjoyment.

Groups which take a skeptical view of the use of violence within their own movement, or reject it in principle, adopt different attitudes in their practical dealings with militant activists. One possible reaction by nonviolent groups is to defend an excessive principle of tolerance ("everyone has his own way of protesting"), so that while not approving acts of violence they do express understanding for them or regard them as a not unwelcome means of enhancing their own negotiating position by way of a "radical flank effect" (Haines, 1984). A second reaction is for the group to distance itself from potentially violent activists, including withdrawal from jointly planned activities which begin to look as if they may lead to violence, or strict segregation in different processions or other protest activities. This happens particularly when moderate protest groups fear that their cause will be damaged as soon as it becomes associated with violence, with public sympathy being alienated and the focus of debate shifting away from the reasons for protest to the circumstances and forms of violence. A third position is adopted by those groups which actively and firmly defend the principle of total nonviolence, seek to exert a moderating influence on potentially violent groups, and during actual protest events even take a position between the two front lines, militants on the one hand and police on the other, acting as a human buffer to prevent attacks by either side. In the drama of their world view, many of these nonviolent groups, protagonists of the idea of a "grassroots revolution," are not far behind the autonomists, since their ranks include not only Christian socialists but also committed anticapitalists and anarchists. In contrast to potentially violent groups, however, they do not believe that the objective of a "good" society, however they may picture it, can sanctify the use of violence and, indeed, consider that it may tend to escalate levels of aggression and violence.

III. DESIDERATA

There is, admittedly, a lively political debate on violence in (new) social movements, though hardly an intensive academic one. The broader field of research into violence has paid little attention to the specific contexts of collective and political violence, with the exception of terrorism studies and research into youth violence. Where violence within social movements has been addressed by the social sciences, the aim has been much more to describe it than to explain it. And even the description has been confined to relatively general overviews of individual countries (Rucht, 1999) or portraits of particular violence-prone groups. As a result, many basic questions remain unanswered. For example, we do not know:

- whether violence among NSMs in Western countries is increasing or decreasing,
- the relative importance of internal factors by comparison with context factors in the occurrence of violence,
- what combinations of factors particularly encourage or restrain the use of violence,
- whether the institutionalization of a movement encourages more radical tendencies on the fringes of that movement,
- whether the formation of protest parties, or even their parliamentary representation, restrains the tendency to violence among movements with related aims, or
- whether violence becomes more pronounced in identifiable periods (such as phases when mass mobilization is decreasing or repression by the state is increasing).

These deficiencies mean that there are no real academic controversies in this field, while at the same time interpretations based on everyday life and political theories proliferate.

IV. APPROACHES TO PREVENTION

There are no thorough academic theories on the prevention of violence by NSMs, because, after all, the critical causative factors are largely unknown. In journalistic and (party) political debate, of course, we do find patterns of interpretation and proposed solutions of the kind familiar from the context of terrorist groups, drug problems, and crime. Conservative groups, for example, are inclined to exaggerate the level of political violence among NSMs. According to this current of opinion, a general loss of values and guiding principles together with the laxity of the prosecuting authorities are responsible for the high level of political violence. The remedy is seen as lying in a return to civic virtues and a strategy of zero tolerance on the part of the courts and the police. The mirror image of this view, at the left and liberal end of the spectrum, is to see the scale of the problem as being much smaller. Unresolved tensions and unsolved problems in society as a whole are seen as the critical causes of politically motivated violence. Logically, those who hold this view argue in favor of a policy of openness to reform and relative tolerance, at least in dealing with those violence-prone groups that are regarded as "reasonable" and whose militancy is considered an expression of a phase of emotional behavior specific to youth. In a period when conflicts with protest groups are becoming more acute, parliamentary commissions of inquiry and other advisory bodies are being set up, their composition largely proportionate to the size of the political parties. The end result generally takes the form of middle-of-the-road reports and lists of recommendations (e.g., Schwind, Baumann, & Lösel, 1990 in the case of Germany), which are forgotten as soon as the conflicts or the public debate they trigger have died down, if not before. Any continuous and cumulative study of violence within society, the essential basis for a promising preventive strategy, exists only in embryo. Only a few academic institutions in the West are active in this field, and even that activity is strongly influenced by short-term preferences geared to the possibility of obtaining project finance.

Overall, though, there do seem to be a number of trends which, collectively, hold out the promise of damping down rather than inflaming the willingness to resort to political violence—other things being equal, of course. The first is a gradual reversal of police strategies, which are becoming generally more flexible and appropriate to the particular situation (della Porta & Reiter, 1998). A relatively long retrospective analysis is necessary to make it clear that the scope for disproportionate attacks by the police, such as marked the demonstrations against the visit by the Shah of Persia to Berlin in June 1967 or the 1968 Democratic Party Congress in Chicago, has become narrower. It is hardly conceivable today that a chief of police—as in Berlin in 1967—would publicly advocate his home-spun "liver sausage tactics" for dealing with demonstrators (fill the "sausage" with demonstrators then "tie it off at both ends and stick a fork in the middle").

Secondly, as an important influence on the change in police strategy, a more liberal political climate has become established in most Western countries. Protest, even in its confrontational and moderately violent forms, is no longer perceived in simplistic terms as an attack against the heart of the nation or the beginning of the end of democracy. The attempts by sections of the "bourgeois" press to whip up popular frenzy, seen for example as recently as the press response to the student movement, have given way to a generally more discriminating form of reporting, more in line with professional standards of journalism. Even anticapitalist and far from peaceful protests such as marked the conference of the World Trade Organization in Seattle in December 1999, or the International Monetary Fund conference in Washington, D.C., in the Spring of 2000, received relatively objective coverage from most of the media.

Learning curves, both among the NSMs and among establishment politicians, have helped to soften the rigid battle lines. For one thing, more pragmatic and technically sound demands have replaced the uncompromising tendency inherent in statements such as: "we want it all, and we want it here and now." It is increasingly clear, even to radical protesters, that a spirit of compromise and patience is essential. The shutting-down of nuclear power plants is not something that can be achieved overnight; equal opportunities for women cannot be guaranteed by legislation alone; the police and judiciary are not mere tools of the state but are also used to protect the protesters' own demonstrations or punish the activities of the radical right.

On the other hand, some politicians—even those who did not themselves come up through the NSMs—have embarked upon a learning process as well. Protesters may have a good point, even if they do look somewhat disreputable; political demands that initially appear naïve may, after a lapse of time, become part of the general ethos of the establishment parties; the unconditional repression of militant protest may prove counterproductive.

This, of course, does nothing to eradicate the deeper causes of NSM protest. Areas where this becomes particularly apparent include the "millennium" themes of ecology and women's equality. Despite constant mobilization, despite increased public awareness of the problem, despite a wealth of legislation, programs, and specific measures, there are still grounds for protest. And then there are other problems, some old, some new, the scale of which was not previously apparent, ranging from the growing worldwide political imbalance between rich and poor to the unknown long-term effects of experiments in genetic engineering. The new social movements have become middle-aged, and they may have lost something of their drama, but there has probably been little change in their ability to mobilize opinion. There is no reason to expect that the NSMs will suddenly fall gently asleep or make themselves superfluous by their own successes; nor is it probable that "friendly" protest will become the exclusive substitute for violent action.

Translated by Richard Sharp

REFERENCES

Bergmann, Werner. (1994). Ein Versuch, die extreme Rechte als soziale Bewegung zu beschreiben. In Werner Bergmann & Erb Rainer (Eds.), *Neonazismus und rechte Subkultur* (pp. 183–207). Berlin: Metropol.

Brand, Karl-Werner. (1985). Vergleichendes Resümee. In Karl-Werner Brand (Ed.), *Neue soziale Bewegungen in Westeuropa und den USA* (pp. 306–334). Frankfurt: Campus.

Brush, Steven. (1996). Dynamics of Theory Change in the Social Sciences: Relative Deprivation and Collective Violence. *Journal of Conflict Resolution, 40*, 523–545.

Bundesministerium des Innern. der Bundesrepublik Deutschland (Eds.) (1968–1994). *Jahresstatistik des Demonstrationsgeschehens. Lose Blätter mit Tabellen und Listen, erhältlich vom Inspekteur der Bereitschaftspolizeien der Länder.* Berlin.

Davis, James Chowning. (1969). The J-Curve of Rising and Declining Satisfactions as a Cause of Revolution and Rebellion. In Graham D.H. Davis & Ted R. Gurr (Eds.), *The History of Violence in America* (pp. 415–436). New York: Preager.

Della Porta, Donatella. (1995). *Social Movements, Political Violence, and the State: A Comparative Analysis of Italy and Germany.* Cambridge: Cambridge University Press.

Della Porta, Donatella, & Herbert Reiter (Eds.) (1998). *Policing Protest: The Control of Mass Demonstrations in Western Democracies.* Minneapolis: The University of Minnesota Press.

Della Porta, Donatella, & Dieter Rucht. (1995). Left-Libertarian Movements in Context: A Comparison of Italy and West Germany, 1965–1990. In Bert Klandermans & Craig Jenkins (Eds.), *The Politics of Social Protest: Comparative Perspectives on States and Social Movements* (pp. 229–272). Minneapolis, St. Paul: University of Minnesota Press.

Eckstein, Harry. (1980). Theoretical Approaches to Explaining Collective Violence. In Ted R. Gurr (Ed.), *Handbook of Political Conflict. Theory and Research* (pp. 135–166). New York: The Free Press.

Edwards, Bob, & John D. McCarthy. (1992). Social Movement Schools. *Sociological Forum, 7(3)*, 541–550.

Gamson, William A., Bruce Fireman, & Steven Rytina. (1982). *Encounters with Unjust Authority.* Homewood: Dorsey.

Graham, Hugh, & Ted R. Gurr. (1969). *Violence in America: Historical and Comparative Perspective.* New York: Praeger.

Gurr, Ted R. (1970). *Why Men Rebel.* Princeton: Princeton University Press.

Haines, Herbert H. (1984). Black Radicalization and the Funding of Civil Rights: 1957–1970. *Social Problems, 32*, 31–41.

Jenkins, Craig. (1981). Sociopolitical Movements. In Samuel L. Long (Ed.), *Handbook of Political Behavior.* *Vol. 4* (pp. 81–153). New York, London: Plenum Press.

Klandermans, Bert. (1991). New Social Movements and Resource Mobilization: The European and the American Approach Revisited. In Dieter Rucht (Ed.), *Research on Social Movements: The State of the Art in Western Europe and the USA* (pp. 17–44). Frankfurt, Boulder: Campus and Westview Press.

Klandermans, Bert, Hanspeter Kriesi, & Sidney Tarrow (Eds.) (1988). *From Structure to Action: Comparing Social Movement Research across Cultures.* Greenwich: JAI Press.

Koopmans, Ruud, & Dieter Rucht. (1996). Rechtsradikalismus als soziale Bewegung? In Jürgen W. Falter, Hans-Gerd Jaschke & Jürgen R. Winkler (Eds.), *Rechtsextremismus. Ergebnisse und Perspektiven der Forschung. Sonderheft 27 der Politischen Vierteljahresschrift* (pp. 265–287). Opladen: Westdeutscher Verlag.

Kriesi, Hanspeter, Ruud Koopmans, Jan Willem Duyvendak, & Marco G. Giugni. (1995). *New Social Movements in Western Europe: A Comparative Analysis.* Minneapolis: University of Minnesota Press.

Lipsky, Michael. (1968). Protest as a Political Resource. *The American Political Science Review, 62,* 1144–1158.

Marx, Gary T., & James L. Wood. (1975). Strands of Theory and Research on Collective Behavior. *Annual Review of Sociology, 1,* 368–428.

McAdam, Doug, John McCarthy, & Mayer N. Zald (Eds.) (1996). *Comparative Perspectives on Social Movements: Political Opportunities, Mobilization Structures, and Cultural Framings.* Cambridge: Cambridge University Press.

McAdam, Doug. (1982). *Political Process and the Development of Black Insurgency, 1930–1970.* Chicago, London: The University of Chicago Press.

McCarthy, John D., & Mayer N. Zald. (1973). *The Trend of Social Movements in America: Professionalization and Resource Mobilization.* Morriston: General Learning Press.

McPhail, Clark. (1991). *The Myth of the Madding Crowd.* New York: Aldine de Gruyter.

Melucci, Alberto. (1984). An End to Social Movements? Introductory Paper to the Sessions on 'New Social Movements and Change in Organizational Forms.' *Social Science Information, 24(4/ 5),* 819–835.

Minkenberg, Michael. (1998). *Die neue radikale Rechte im Vergleich. USA, Frankreich, Deutschland.* Opladen: Westdeutscher Verlag.

Neidhardt, Friedhelm. (1986). Gewalt – Soziale Bedeutungen und sozialwissenschaftliche Bestimmungen des Begriffs." In Bundeskriminalamt (Ed.), *Was ist Gewalt? Auseinandersetzungen mit einem Begriff. Vol. I: Strafrechtliche und sozialwissenschaftliche Darlegungen* (pp. 109–147). Wiesbaden: Bundeskriminalamt.

Neidhardt, Friedhelm. (1989). Gewalt und Gegengewalt. Steigt die Bereitschaft zu Gewaltaktionen bei zunehmender staatlicher Kontrolle und Repression? In Wilhelm Heitmeyer, Kurt Möller & Heinz Sünker (Eds.), *Jugend – Staat – Gewalt* (pp. 233–243). Weinheim, München: Juventa.

Neidhardt, Friedhelm, & Dieter Rucht. (1993). Auf dem Weg in die 'Bewegungsgesellschaft'? Über die Stabilisierbarkeit sozialer Bewegungen. *Soziale Welt, 44(3),* 305–326.

Neidhardt, Friedhelm, & Dieter Rucht. (1999). Protest und Protestgeschichte in der Bundesrepublik 1950–1994. In Max Kaase & Günther Schmid (Eds.), *Demokratie in der Bewährungsprobe. Jahrbuch 1999 des WZB* (pp. 129–164). Berlin: Edition Sigma.

Rucht, Dieter. (1994). *Modernisierung und neue soziale Bewegungen. Deutschland, Frankreich und USA im Vergleich.* Frankfurt: Campus Verlag.

Rucht, Dieter. (1999). Konfrontation und Gewalt. Verlauf, Struktur und Bedingungen unfriedlicher politischer Proteste in der Bundesrepublik. In Jürgen Gerhards & Ronald Hitzler (Eds.), *Die Eigenwilligkeit und Rationalität sozialer Prozesse. Festschrift zum 65. Geburtstag von Friedhelm Neidhardt* (pp. 352–378). Opladen: Westdeutscher Verlag.

Rule, James R. (1988). *Theories of Civil Violence.* Berkeley: University of California Press.

Schwind, Hans-Dieter, Jürgen Baumann, & Friedrich Lösel (Eds.) (1990). *Ursachen, Prävention und Kontrolle von Gewalt.* Berlin: Duncker und Humblot.

Skolnick, Jerome H. (Director). (1969). *The Politics of Protest. Task Force on Violent Aspects of Protest and Confrontation of the National Commission of the Causes and Prevention of Violence.* New York: Simon and Schuster.

Snow, David A., E. Bourke Rochford, Steven K. Worden, & Robert D. Benford. (1986). Frame Alignment Processes, Micromobilization, and Movement Participation. *American Sociological Review, 51(4),* 464–481.

Tarrow, Sidney. (1998). *Power in Movement: Social Movements and Contentious Politics. 2nd Edition.* Cambridge: Cambridge University Press.

Tilly, Charles. (1978). *From Mobilization to Revolution.* Reading: Addison-Wesley.

Touraine, Alain. (1984). Les mouvements sociaux: objet particulier ou problème central de l'analyse sociologique? *Revue Française de Sociologie, 25(1),* 3–19.

Violence and the New Left

Donatella della Porta

I. DEFINITION OF KEY TERMS

In its everyday use, "violence" refers to "acting with or characterized by great physical force, so as to injure, damaging or destroy; [or] ... force unlawfully or callously used" (Webster's New World Dictionary of the American Language, second college edition, 1979). *Violence* is therefore the use of great *physical force* oriented at producing damage. In the same vein, the classical social science definition of violence refers to "behavior designed to inflict physical injury on people or damage to property" (Graham & Gurr, 1969:XVII), or "any observable interaction in the course of which persons or objects are seized or physically damaged in spite of resistance" (Tilly, 1978:176).

Political violence then is the use of physical force in order to damage a political adversary. If we leave aside state or state-sponsored violence, political violence consists, therefore, of "collective attacks within a political community against a political regime" (Gurr, 1970:3–4). In these situations, violence may emerge intentionally or accidentally: "[as the] deliberate infliction or threat of infliction of physical injury or damage for political ends," or as violence "which occurs unintentionally in the course of severe political conflict" (Wilkinson, 1986:30). In general, political violence consists of those repertoires of collective action that involve great physical force and cause damage to an adversary in order to impose political aims.

The understanding of both "great" and "damage" is however highly subjective. A certain degree of physical force is involved in forms of collective action that are usually not considered violent per se; moreover, all collective actions seek to damage a more or less visible adversary. For example, a picket line displays (sometimes great) physical force and seeks to damage the factory owner's interests, but it is debatable as to whether picketing per se constitutes violent action.

We need therefore to find some thresholds beyond which the use of physical force, and the consequently suffered damages, may be considered as violent. The second part of

---

W. Heitmeyer and J. Hagan (eds.), *International Handbook of Violence Research*, 383–398.

Webster's definition only partially resolves the problem by introducing the terms "unlawful" or "callous use" of force or power. Political violence is generally understood as behavior that *violates* the prevailing definition of legitimate political action. Operationally, however, the degree of legitimacy is not easy to measure. "Callous" is too vague a term to define illegitimacy, and "unlawful" is also questionable. Protest actions are, for instance, by definition uninstitutionalized, disruptive forms of collective action, and some of them—including picketing—have long been unlawful, even if tolerated and semi-institutionalized. In the prevailing political culture, however, not all unlawful protests are considered violent.

Any understanding of a concept such as political violence is in fact historically bound. An operational definition of political violence needs therefore to start from the specific historical forms of violence addressed by research. This chapter focuses on the political violence that emerged from within the left-libertarian social movement family during the cycle of protest of the late sixties and early seventies, with particular reference to the New Left. A *social movement* can be defined as "(1) informal networks, based (2) on shared belief and solidarity, which mobilize around (3) conflictual issues, through (4) the frequent use of various forms of protest" (della Porta & Diani, 1999:16). In each society, there are movements that, regardless of their specific or individual goals, have similar basic demands and a common constituency: these sets of coexisting movements constitute *movement families* (della Porta & Rucht, 1995). Movement families emerge during periods of particular turmoil, when protest activity intensifies, new repertoires of collective action are created, and unconventional action spreads to different social sectors: these periods represent the peaks of *protest cycles* (Tarrow, 1989:13–14). By *left-libertarian* movement family, we understand a set of movements that combined the call for justice and equality, proper to the traditional Left, with the attention to the individual freedom.

The *New Left* was composed of a network of organizations that shared a critique of traditional left-wing discourse, and an attempt at adapting Marxism to the new, postindustrial society. Since the beginning of the sixties, many small groups focused on "a concept of a 'Third Way' between state socialism and capitalism, a nondogmatic Marxism, or an eclectic radicalism" (Flacks, 1998:155). As such, this represented a moment of passage from the Old Left to the left-libertarian movements. Although the New Left—and the left-libertarian movements that followed—remained mainly peaceful, violence often emerged in the late sixties and early seventies as an effect of the escalation of mass demonstrations and symbolic provocations. In some countries, terrorist organizations developed from inside the groups that had coalesced around the New-Leftist discourse.

In this context, political violence was a particular repertoire of collective action that involved a considerable use of physical force, considered at that time as illegitimate in the dominant culture. It included forms of action such as *attacks on property*, when damage or theft of property is the main goal; *rioting*, when unorganized disorder leads to damage to property; *violent confrontation*, when members of opposing political groups clash with one another; *clashes with the police*, when protesters interact violently with the police; *violent attacks directed against persons*, when one political group attacks another group, or members of the elite or the public, causing injuries or deaths; *random violent attacks*, when organized violence is directed against persons regardless of their political or social identities; *armed seizure of places or people*, including armed trespassing, holdups, and hijacking. In all these forms of action, the main objective is a de facto display of physical force (della Porta & Tarrow, 1986:614).

II.   THEORETICAL APPROACHES AND EMPIRICAL RESULTS

Although political violence is not an established field of study in mainstream political science and sociology, attention to the phenomenon developed on sporadic occasions—especially when violence emerged as a dramatic problem in the political system. This was the case with the first research on revolutions in the nineteenth century, the tragedy of fascism in the first half of the last century, and the urban riots of the sixties. The wave of protest involving the New Left at the end of the sixties and the beginning of the seventies was one of these occasions, and the different streams traditionally established in the social sciences as well as new approaches attempted to provide an explanation for the phenomenon. Explanations have been divided into a breakdown approach and a resource mobilization approach (Oberschall, 1978). While the former stresses the individual and social pathologies that bring about conflict as a destruction of previous order, the latter assumes conflict as an inherent characteristic of any society, focusing on how and when interests mobilize (Tilly, 1978).

1.   The "Breakdown" Approach

Violence has traditionally been considered as a pathological form of politics, a sign of the failure of peaceful means of dealing with the confrontation of opinions and decision making upon which democracies are based. In the sixties, the reemergence of violent conflicts, in particular in societies that had appeared to be pacified and satisfied by the economic success of the decades that had followed the end of World War II, puzzled politicians as well as political scientists. The first reaction was usually to consider recourse to the most disruptive forms of protest as a sign of individual "misadaptation," whose roots where looked for in a malfunctioning of the social system and/or irrational psychological mechanisms. Referring, more or less explicitly, to Durkheim's concept of anomia, many authors saw social movements as an effect of individual disorientation and the destruction of social life deriving from the growing gap between the degree of differentiation and the degree of social regulation (Tilly, 1978:17). Although they had different emphasis, various approaches converged in the analysis of movements as a by-product of the "breakdown" of social norms and institutions.

a. The Structural-Functionalist School.   Many interpretations referred, more or less explicitly, to the structural-functionalist school. Among the scholars belonging to that school, Neil Smelser, who had dedicated considerable attention to collective behavior, considered "wild rumors, crazes, panics, riots, and revolutions" (Smelser, 1964:1) as side effects of over-rapid social transformations. According to Smelser, in a system made up of balanced subsystems, collective behavior reveals tensions that homeostatic balancing mechanisms cannot, temporarily, absorb. At times of rapid, large-scale transformations, the emergence of collective behaviors—religious cults, secret societies, political sects, economic utopias—reflected the inability of institutions and social control mechanisms to reproduce social cohesion. At the same time, they were attempts by the society to react to crisis situations through the development of shared beliefs on the basis of which to found new collective solidarity. Within a functionalist perspective, many cross-national comparative studies located the causes for high levels of domestic violence in strains at the macro level.

Following Neil Smelser, various scholars of domestic conflict explained violence by looking at *imbalances in different subsystems,* citing such conjunctural conditions as the intermediate stages of economic development, the crises of modernization, periods of ineffective state coercion, and rapid cultural change (for a review of these models, see Eckstein, 1980). In line with the theory of mass society, political violence was considered to be an effect of the decline of strong traditional solidarity and the atomization of the individual (Kornhauser, 1959). Political extremism was in fact associated with those who were uprooted from social ties and the loss of norms. A lack of social integration in the system, or systemic difficulties in transmitting social values produced anomic behaviors and, with these, increasing vulnerability to the appeal of political radicalism.

Comparative research on political violence in the late sixties and early seventies has often referred to some index of economic inequalities and related them to measures of political violence (for a critique, see White, 1989:1277–1282). Between the end of the sixties and the beginning of the seventies, the normative conflicts related with fast modernization, the contradiction between an old educational system and the new demands coming from society, and the economic "stagflation" that followed the economic boom were all considered as signs of strains that could debauch in violence.

b. Relative Deprivation Approach. Another line of thought usually considered as part of a "breakdown" approach focuses on the psychological mechanisms that account for violence. Some scholars have analyzed individual political participation at a micro-analytic level focusing on the *psychological characteristics* of militants. Drawing on so-called mass theory, several studies assume that individuals who resort to the use of political violence are likely to be socially uprooted (Kornhauser, 1959). Radical personalities are defined—according to LeBon's description of the "psychologies des foules" (1896) and Hoffe's notion of the "true believer" (1951)—as frustrated individuals, blindly obedient to a leader or following the mass, content to lose their "unwanted" selves. The more radical—or "deviant"—the forms of collective action, the greater the likelihood that scholarly analysis would concentrate on assumed psychopathologies. The militants of underground organizations have in fact often been defined as infantile, mentally distressed, and terrorized by the external world, as defeated people seeking to compensate for their failures by excluding themselves from society or seeking for revenge (for a critical review, see Wilkinson, 1979).

The most sophisticated analyses of psychological motivations converged in the so-called *relative deprivation approach.* The main exponent of this approach, Ted Robert Gurr, developed his theory in *Why Men Rebel,* published in 1970. According to Gurr, violence derives from high levels of discontent. In particular, at the individual level, aggressive reactions follow frustration. In a society, violence is therefore likely to develop when there is a widespread relative deprivation, defined as "a perceived discrepancy between men's value expectations and their value capabilities." In this approach, "value expectations are the goods and conditions of life to which people believe they are rightfully entitled," and "value capabilities are the goods and conditions they think they are capable of attaining or maintaining" (Gurr, 1970:13). Relative deprivation spreads with all structural conditions that increase the level of expectation without increasing capabilities: for instance, gains for other groups or a sudden disillusion. The political expression of such frustration is influenced by other societal conditions, such as cultural acceptance of aggression as a political means, past success of political violence, the degree of legitimation of the state as well as its capacity for repression.

These interpretations were applied to the New Left. The French May was described as "the responsibility of the generation that in 1968 was between thirty and forty years old: impatient assistants that wanted to became professors, second-order intellectuals ready to exploit their occasion, frustrated individuals that could not win in the order and were now playing the card of disorder" (cit. in Bongiovanni, 1991:108). Even an intellectual such as Raymond Aron (1968) described the movement as an irrational fever that debauched in a collective psychodrama.

A first critique of this trend of studies addresses their empirical validity. First of all, as a critic observed, "[m]uch of the sociological work involved an ex-post facto examination of the outcropping of collective action, without systematically asking whether grievances at the individual or aggregate level had systematically changed" (Zald, 1992:328–329). Even research at the micro level—focusing on the biographical and psychological characteristics of *radical activists*—has indicated that political violence is *not* the consequence of pathological personalities or international conspiracies. Leaving aside their much-debated empirical validity, the structural-functionalist as well as relative deprivation approach share a total disinterest in the institutional aspect of political life. In their theory, uprooting and psychological strain "translate" into political violence, which appears therefore as a spontaneous, unorganized phenomenon. As James Coleman noted (1990:479), the hypothesis that revolts follow on automatically from situations of frustration, rootlessness, deprivation, and social crisis reduces collective action to an agglomeration of individual behaviors. This perspective ignores the importance of the dynamics by which feelings experienced at the individual level give rise to phenomena such as social movements or revolutions. A main critique concerned the view of disruptive action as reactive behavior, incapable of strategic rationality and isolated from the conflicts it sought to express.

2. Resource Mobilization

In deliberate contrast to this way of conceptualizing social movements, in the 1970s American sociologists developed a current of research centered on the analysis of processes by which the resources necessary for collective action are mobilized. In their view, collective movements constitute an extension of the conventional forms of political action; the protagonists act in a rational way, following their interests; organizations and movement "entrepreneurs" play an essential role in the mobilization of collective resources on which action is founded. Movements are therefore part of the normal political process. In the social movement studies of the seventies and the eighties, protest is not considered as the product of temporary strains, but of the conflicts structurally inherent in society. These conflicts, however, do not automatically produce collective action. As one of the proponents of the resource mobilization approach observed, "behavior entails costs; therefore grievances or deprivation do not automatically or easily translate into social movement activities, especially high-risk social movement activity" (Zald, 1992:332). In order for collective action to take place, collective actors must organize, collective identities be created, and organizations founded. As any other collective actor, social movements have to motivate their followers, and since the latter are rational beings, they need to distribute selective incentive. Stressing the external obstacles and incentives, numerous contributions to research have examined the variety of resources to be mobilized, the links which social movements have with their allies, the tactics used by society to control or incorporate collective action, and its results.

In order to explain violence, it is therefore necessary to look at the ways in which these collective actors operate, at the methods they adopt to acquire resources and mobilize support, both within and outside their adherents' group. It is worth noting, however, that—with few noteworthy exceptions (see Tilly, 1978)—the new approaches to social movements pay little attention to political violence. As was observed in a recent review of the literature, "the relationships among levels of violence and conflict, types of grievances, and the key variables of resource mobilization (resources, organization, opportunities) remain underdeveloped" (McClurg Mueller, 1992:18).

Although violence never became a main concern for social movement studies, some research on case studies, and even some cross-national research, has developed recently, focusing on the political and organizational resources that pushed movement organizations to adopt violent repertoires. Many of these studies focus on the explanation of violence during the evolution of the student movement and the New Left.

Political violence is a very complex phenomenon. Most empirical studies on political violence refer to one of three analytical levels: the system, the group, or the individual (corresponding, respectively, to the macro, meso, and micro levels of analysis). They address one of three questions: a) in what type of society is political violence most likely to develop—that is, what environmental conditions foster political violence?; b) which groups are most likely to use violent repertoires—that is, which characteristics of political organizations eventually lead them to adopt the most extreme forms of political violence?; c) which individuals are most likely to resort to political violence? Although the existing macro, meso, and micro analyses have generated interesting suggestions, on the environmental preconditions for violence, the characteristics of violent groups, and individual commitment to violence, for example, their focus on a single analytic level has certain disadvantages. The macro analysis fails to consider the intermediate processes between general structures and individual behavior. The meso analysis gives us a voluntaristic interpretation of violence as a strategic choice carried out by single groups or organizations. And the micro analysis tends to attribute this political phenomenon to purely psychological factors.

In what follows, I shall try to develop a more complex explanation, taking into account the three mentioned levels. Although an attempt will be made to integrate all three levels, the analysis of the macro level is more relevant for the study of the political process (see *a*), the micro level for an analysis of frames and identity building (see *b*), and the meso level for an analysis of organizational dynamics (see *c*).

a. The Political Process and Violence. Some of the scholars who shared a rational view of collective action focused on the political and institutional environment—the "macro" conditions—in which social movements operate. The central focus of this "political process" approach is the relationship between institutional political actors and protest. The political opportunities include the institutional features of a regime (such as the geographical and functional division of power) as well as conjunctural factors, the degree of stability or instability of political alignments, the availability and strategic posture of potential allies, and political conflicts between and within elites (Tarrow, 1989:35; Kriesi et al., 1995).

Within this approach, the political opportunities influence the repertoires of collective action. A main hypothesis is that the most radical repertoires develop when the political system is closed to the demands of the challengers. Centralized institutions, an exclusionary tradition, weakness of alliances, and strength of opponents are all conditions that often push toward an escalation of the forms of protest.

In the late sixties and early seventies, political violence developed directly from interactions between social movements and the state, during processes of escalation. In many countries, the student protest started inside the university, and then spread to the external society. During this evolution, the forms of action became more radical, in particular during physical confrontation with the police and countermovements. At the beginning of their protest, the students used forms of action that combined traditional means of exerting pressure with more innovatory forms of action. The most widespread form of disruptive protest in the first years of the student movement were university occupations—which, in the words of a historian and former activist, expressed "the attempt to 'retire into oneself,' to be separated from the dominant society, the search for a place (not only in the symbolic sense, but also in a very real one) where to live in full autonomy and freedom, surrounded by a peer community, and on the basis of a different and original value system" (Ortoleva, 1988:47). As Tarrow noted for the Italian case—but this may be easily generalized also to other countries—"[t]he main forms of action that the students used were the occupation, which was notably non-violent, and the public march, the classical form of political mobilization in democracies... Little violence occurred in the schools themselves" (Tarrow, 1989:300–301).

The repertoire of action and the ideology of the protest gradually changed as the movement interacted with other groups and with the state. First, a spontaneous type of violence developed especially when the police intervened to clear the university from the "occupants," and the students tried then to reconquer the lost spaces. Pushed outside of the university, the activists often went "in the street," where they again met the police, or—sometimes—countermovements, such as neofascists in Italy. During the clashes in the street, the "need for self-defense" became a relevant, albeit contested, issue.

In the sixties, however, violence was mainly unspecialized, unplanned and occurred during mass demonstrations, usually triggered by confrontations with neofascists or the police, and it was justified as "defense" against attacks from outside. For instance, in Italy "[d]uring the intensive peak of the cycle, from 1967 to 1969... violence occurred most often in the context of large peaceful or confrontational gatherings: in clashes with police who were barring demonstrators way or charging them... and when an opposing band tried to break up a peaceful mass meeting" (Tarrow, 1989:305).

It was especially during the declining phase of mobilization that violence escalated. The quantitative data on protest in Italy shows that the more spontaneous violence of the beginning of the cycle tended to be substituted by semimilitary forms of violence: "As far as the gravity of the effects is concerned, the more violent and directed forms of violence—attacks on persons—grew continuously up to the end of the cycle, while violence directed at persons or things increased as the total magnitude of conflict declined" (della Porta & Tarrow, 1986:618). Not only in Italy, by the beginning of the seventies, the concept of "defensive violence" was losing its appeal, while small group forms of violence increased (della Porta & Tarrow, 1986: 619).

Radicalization happened, first of all, during the interactions between the movement organization and the state, following a process that McAdam (1983) has called *tactical interactions*. Social movements, as well as state institutions, rely upon tactical innovation—that is, they change their tactics in order to be able to mobilize as their adversaries learn to respond to their previous forms of protest. The process of innovation and adaptation, in other words, is reciprocal, each side responding to the other. Between the end of the sixties and the beginning of the seventies, violence grew in the course of experimentation with different tactics, as both adversaries tested "hard" techniques.

It was not only encounters between the movements and the state apparatuses that produced escalation, via tactical adaptation. The very conditions that favored the escalation of violence in the New Left often stimulated *radical countermovements* as well. This development was characteristic especially of countries such as Italy or Germany, with a recent historical experience with fascism. Here, harsh physical clashes multiplied during the protest cycle between young members of the right wing and left wing, while alleged police sympathy for the radical Right further delegitimized the state in the eyes of the militants.

b. Violence, Identity, and Frames. In order to understand political violence, the structural approach has indeed to be combined with a constructionist approach that explains the "mediating processes through which people attribute meaning to events and interpret situations" (Klandermans, 1992:77). The linkages between the macro (social and political conditions) and the micro (individual behavior) have to be specified. To understand why an individual would choose to join a radical organization, we need to draw on concepts such as *social network*—the sets of social and affective ties an individual belongs to; *collective identity*—the importance of a collective definition in the structure of the ego; *collective action frames*—that justify protest action; and *incentives*—that motivate individual commitment. Research on social movements shows that movement organizations—which have a low level of material resources—have to rely mainly on nonmaterial incentives: the emotional fulfillment that comes from group solidarity, the psychological fulfillment derived from a strong collective identity, and the ethical fulfillment produced by acting for a cause. During face-to-face interactions, interpersonal life circles determine collective action frames (Snow et al., 1986). The solidarity and proximity—that derive both from preexisting social networks and organizational forms that maximize face-to-face interaction—characterize the relationships through which meaning is constructed and identities are created.

In fact, in the late sixties and the seventies, the escalation in repertoires of action developed together with an ideological radicalization. In its evolution, the very identity of the student movement changed. In the beginning, the student movement demanded the reform of the university, soon expanding to a cultural critique of capitalist society as well as demands for broad political change. The discourse went in two different directions. First of all, the students protested against the authoritarianism of the elite university structure—a residual of the past. Second, they asked for an effective "right to study," framing their demands inside an egalitarian discourse. Inside the universities, during the occupation or the so-called countercourses, they tried to develop a new way of studying. The protest inside the university, however, rapidly escalated into a cultural critique of capitalist society and, especially, a demand for far-reaching political changes. The more the movement felt itself to be a victim of state repression, the more the government became the political counterpart in a conflict that went well beyond the system of education.

Even if—to a larger or lesser extent—combined with reform, repression had dramatic effects on the social movement. For the activists, the brutality of the police was the most visible response of the state. While policy reform took years to materialize, the police charges became—in the late sixties—a direct experience for thousands of young activists. Police actions of this sort *delegitimized the state* in the eyes of the activists by creating "injustice frames" (Gamson et al., 1982). In Italy, the militants perceived the neofascist massacre of Piazza Fontana—in which Italian secret services were believed to be involved—as a watershed. In West Germany, the attempt on the life of the student movement leader Rudi Dutschke galvanized the militants, and reduced confidence in the

Rechtsstaat among young activists (Fetscher, 1983:192–196). In a similar way, the process of Burgos in Spain (Jáuregui Bereciartu, 1981; Ibarra, 1989) or Bloody Sunday in Ireland (White, 1993) represented a point of nonreturn for many militants in the social movements, symbolizing the betrayal of democratic rules by the state institutions themselves, and justifying the need to take up arms against an unjust and brutal system. Moreover, *state "repression" created martyrs and myths*: for example, Benno Ohnesorg, killed by police during a protest against the Shah of Iran's visit to Berlin, or the "battle" with the police in Valle Giulia in Rome, which took on a legendary quality for Italian activists.

The ideological frames through which the militants interpreted their daily encounters with political violence tended to dramatize the significance of these events. Memories of police brutalities or the allegedly inhuman treatment of "political prisoners" undermined confidence in democracy. The state became the fascist state of the bourgeoisie. Police charges were viewed as evidence of an imminent fascist evolution of the state. Street fights with young political opponents became episodes in a civil war. Violent encounters with the police were perceived as a stage in the social revolution. Those militants who eventually chose, or were drawn into, the underground then developed a freedom-fighter identity, seeing themselves as members of an embattled community of idealistic and altruistic people fighting a heroic war against "evil."

Feeling excluded from the political system, the movement escalated its demands, both symbolically, with the elaboration of radical frames of meaning and a revolutionary rhetoric, and practically, with the development of a "meta-conflict" about the very nature of democracy. What the protesters demanded, in fact, was not only a modernization of the university system and also not only more or less revolutionary policy changes. The very forms of the protest challenged the representative conception of democracy that had dominated until then. The meta-issue around which the opposite front polarized concerned the very right to protest, the degree of participation that a democracy had to permit besides electoral participation, and the citizens' right to intervene in politics, beyond the choice of representatives.

In this "politicization" of the social conflict, the students were able to pick up some frames that were well developed in at least part of the left-wing culture. Although ideology per se is not the cause of violence, it may work as a facilitator, especially when other environmental conditions trigger escalation. In the New Left, many groups shared an anti-imperialist frame that stressed the positive role of radical vanguards. The appeal of the "guerrilla" spread with the myth of Che Guevara, the hope for a revolution was fueled by the writings of the Chinese leader Mao Tse Tung, the need for a violent upsurge developed with the radical wing of the Palestine liberation movement, which drew on the same ideological sources. While classical Marxist theory emphasizes the necessity of building a base of support in the working class, the New Left was fascinated by the action of small groups of armed people able to mobilize the masses against Western colonialism and local tyrants. The urban guerrilla in Latin America was taken as an example of the exemplary role of "revolutionary" acts by enlightened leaders. Anti-imperialistic frames spread in at least part of the New Left: "The key elements were: an adherence to the 'one war' theory of imperialism, in which all resistance movements were linked together in opposition to the presumed unity and common interests of all imperialist powers; deference to a Third World vanguard that provided models for success through rural or urban guerrilla activity or dramatic symbolic actions; and belief that violence in the form of 'armed struggle' was the necessary centerpiece of a serious revolutionary movement" (Zwerman, Steinhof, & della Porta, 2000).

The search to free oneself from the control of an oppressive society pushed toward an emphasis on the construction of the "new human being." Some analysts stressed in fact the search for "old virtues," such as courage, abnegation, and the refusal of consumerism (Ortoleva, 1988:105). It was also in competition with the Old Left that the discourse became more and more radical. Simultaneously, the New Left emphasized both innovation and the "return to the original state." In order to innovate, the New Left frequently emphasized the need to act, against the renunciation of the Old Left, and the "all-and-now" against the postponement of the revolution. The "return to the origins" brought about the stress on the antagonistic identity of the movement, the refusal to compromise, the stress on "purism." Verbal inflation was a way to legitimize a new subject, expressing a sense of urgency that is typical of the formation of new identities.

The more radical the group, the more isolated from the movement culture it became, and the more the members' shared risks intensified the "us versus them" mentality. The activists' acceptance of violence grew along with their emotional investment in politics, and their emotional investment grew with their experience of violence. Stronger solidarity within radical groups coincided with intensified hatred for opponents—members of right-wing groups, and also the police—who, in the militants' eyes, became progressively dehumanized. Daily fights thus created a rationale for violence and "militarized" the activists' attitudes, diffusing a kind of "battle spirit" toward politics. At the same time, the militants' commitment to politics deepened.

Affective ties with friends-comrades were ultimately vital in recruitment to clandestine organizations (della Porta, 1992; Waldmann, 1993). Recruitment to underground organizations was often "block recruitment," involving networks of peer groups. In this way, the affective and cognitive dynamics of group solidarity smooth the entrance into the "armed struggle," reducing the perception of an individual choice and of personal responsibilities. In the ethnically based terrorist groups, traditional meeting places and associations— such as the gastronomic societies or the alpine groups in the Basque case (Wieviorka, 1988)—provide a reservoir for recruitment to the underground. In a similar way, recruitment was eased by organizational networks surviving from a previous phase of military conflict— such as the Irish Republican Army (IRA) in Northern Ireland (White, 1993)—as well as by family bonds with previous generations of militants. In ideological terrorism, networks of friendship are constituted in small radical groups, active inside prevalently pacific social movements: the Red Brigades and Front Line in Italy (della Porta, 1990, 1995) or the Red Army Fraction and the Revolutionary Cells in the Federal Republic of Germany (Neidhardt, 1981; della Porta, 1995) emerged from splits inside radical groups active during long protest cycles. The decision to form underground groups was taken by small networks of people with such dense ties with each other that they often refer to their own group as a "family."

Social networks also provided important constraints against "breaking the contract": the group relationship was in fact so intense, and individual identities so embedded in the group, that the members believed it was impossible to live outside it. This communal solidarity affected the militants' cognitive processes insofar as all the information individuals received was filtered through the group, which defined the external reality by providing shared master frames of meaning. Moreover, they helped to ensure internal conformity. The emphasis on cognitive coherence was all the more important since the process of individual socialization in radical organizations involved a dramatic change in the militants' images of the external world.

The image of external reality, however, was not only the product of small group dynamics: in the social construction of reality, the frames of meaning provided by the cliques of comrade-friends interacted with the reality of everyday experience. The militants' immersion in violence distorted their perceptions of external reality: direct experiences of violence produced, in fact, frames of meaning that justified violence. Internalizing the use of violence as "right" increased an individual's propensity to take part in violent confrontations.

c. Organizational Competition and Radicalization. Resource mobilization theorists defined collective movement as a rational, purposeful, and organized action. Social movement organizations represent—at the "meso" levels—the collective entrepreneurs of protest. According to this perspective, protest actions derive from a calculation of the costs and benefits, influenced by the presence of resources—in particular by organization and by the strategic interactions necessary for the development of a social movement. In a historical situation in which feelings of unease, differences of opinion, conflicts of interest, and opposing ideologies are always present, the emergence of collective action cannot be explained simply as having been caused by these elements. It is not enough to discover the existence of tensions and structural conflicts, but necessary also to study the conditions that enable discontent to be transformed into mobilization. The fundamental tenet of this approach is that the capacity for mobilization depends on the material resources (work, money, concrete benefits, services) as well as the nonmaterial resources (authority, moral engagement, faith, friendship) available to the group. These resources are distributed across multiple objectives according to a rational calculation of costs and benefits. Beyond the existence of tensions, mobilization derives from the way in which social movements are able to organize discontent, reduce the costs of action, utilize and create solidarity networks, share incentives among members, and achieve external consensus.

The type and nature of the resources available explain the tactical choices made by movements and the consequences of collective action on the social and political system. Some case studies developed within the resource mobilization perspective tried in fact to explain why, during cycles of protest, small radical organizations espousing violence evolved within and then broke away from the larger, nonviolent, social movement organizations. Exploiting environmental conditions conducive to militancy, these groups underwent further radicalization and eventually created new resources and occasions for violence. These radical groups, in other words, themselves become agents, or entrepreneurs, for the propagation of violence.

In the New Left, organized violence—and the groups that specialized in violent repertoires—developed gradually. A characteristic of a social movement is that it is formed by networks of groups of various sizes and structurations. This loosely structured set of interaction usually plays a positive role in the development of a movement, allowing it to spread in different environments and survive repression. Cooperation among different groups is a fundamental element for mobilizing a vast and widespread constituency. The presence of many organizations is however also a sort of tension, as groups tend to compete with each other for members and resources (Zald & McCarthy, 1980).

The New Left was also formed by a wide net of organizations—groups of people organized around a journal, collectives intervening in a university, youth circles active in the metropolis. In the beginning, the various groups survived near to each other, cooperating informally in the construction of a common identity. During periods of high mobilization, however, the contacts between groups intensified. They brought about, first of all, the creation of ad hoc committees for the coordination of action campaigns. Later on, however, these interactions produced the birth of more formal organizations, often structured at the national level. Differing in size, these groups shared the attempt to build a party-like structure. They founded chapters in different cities, elected central committees, printed newspapers, and distributed membership cards. Moreover, they elaborated ideologically based, exclusive identities. Membership in one organization excluded membership in another—and organizational membership became more important than the sense of belonging to the movement at large.

The decline of student mobilization, and the consequent reduction in available resources, led to increased competition among the several (formal and informal) networks that constituted the New Left. A first result of the decline in mobilization was that the surviving movement organizations concentrated on retaining the loyalty of their members and focused on recruiting individuals already involved in the movement family instead of potential supporters from outside the movement. To face the internal competition, the political networks that had arisen in the movement family had to alter their structures. Competition thus set off a process of internal differentiation. Like rival companies vying for a share of the market, each political organization had to distinguish its "product" from that of the others in order to occupy the "niche" in the market where its products were most in demand.

During the fights with right-wing radicals and/or the police, a number of radical organizations constructed semi-clandestine structures, established specifically to plan and carry out violent actions. Several kinds of factors—organizational, psychological, and accidental—prepared some of the semimilitary organizations for complete clandestinity. The most militant groups had attracted militants already experienced in the use of violent forms of political action; because of their particular socialization, their concept of politics was based more on direct forms of action than on bargaining processes. In most of the radical groups, attempts to sustain both a public (legal) and clandestine (military) organization failed. The military wings often split off and experimented with different violent strategies. In the process, these groups underwent a special sort of bureaucratization—a spiral of radicalization, consequent isolation, and further radicalization—in which they became increasingly ingrown, abandoning the language and imagery they shared with the movement subculture. Caught up in their own self-constructed, "alternative" version of reality—particularly their identification with a military opposition to the state—members of these groups lost a sense of external reality and the ability to foresee the consequences of their actions. These conditions made the small radical groups "ripe" for the shift to clandestinity, which was generally *precipitated by a violent chance event* that propelled the members underground in order to escape arrest or some other form of what they perceived as state repression.

This *internal dynamics* took over completely once the extremist groups went underground. Although even the underground groups felt the need to try to adapt their strategies to changing external reality, the moves they made drastically reduced their range of possible choices and further weakened the group's sense of reality. The very choice of clandestinity forced them into a losing military conflict with the much more powerful state apparatuses. As this conflict became more and more brutal, most radical groups lost the little solidarity they had when they were first organized. Thus, they gradually gave up externally oriented goals in order to concentrate on mere organizational survival. The struggle to find resources for survival (money, hideouts, etc.) further isolated the clandestine groups, even from the movements in which they had arisen. Groups as different as the Italian Red Brigades and the German Red Army Fraction (della Porta, 1995), the Argentine Montoneros (Moyano, 1995; Gillespie, 1982) and the Red Japanese Army (Steinhoff,

1991), the Peruvian Shining Path (Palmer, 1995) and the Weather Underground in the U.S. (Zwerman, Steinhoff, & della Porta, 2000), followed a similar pattern of evolution that brought them to turn more and more inward, progressively losing touch with the other political actors. Increasingly, they used a military frame to define themselves and their adversary. Bloody internal purges, including the assassinations of their own military accused of betrayal or "deviations" from the "right line," often ensued from a definition of the "inside" as an heroic elite, and the "outside" as an absolute enemy. Each successive turn of the spiral reduced the group's strategic options, making it a prisoner of its own version of reality. Violence was therefore the result of internal organizational competition that brought different strategic choices. In the evolution of the New Left, some organizations institutionalized, others became kinds of *violent entrepreneurs*, consuming but also reproducing resources for violence in their environment. The choices made by the radical organizations corresponded in part to their *search for a niche in order to face competition* in their environment—among marginal social strata, or the radicalized militants of the fundamentalist movements of crisis. Spirals of *encapsulation* reduced the organizational contact with the external world.

III. DESIDERATA

According to an influential scholar in the field, the "state of the art" of empirical studies on political violence was, still in the eighties, characterized by "a disturbing lack of good empirically-grounded research" (Gurr, 1988:115). Research on political violence has oscillated between multicase, cross-national comparisons, and organizational case studies. On the one hand, the cross-national analysis of many national cases has generally produced poor results because most of the available indicators of political violence are unreliable and not comparable. On the other hand, case studies have produced an ideographic, noncumulative body of knowledge that is difficult to integrate into more general analyses because of the lack of a common theoretical framework. What is missing, then, is an intermediate approach between the (often unreliable) large-scale comparisons and the idiosyncratic case studies. Notwithstanding recent improvements in our knowledge of the field, there is still a strong need for theoretically relevant research.

Political violence is quite an abstract concept. In technical terms, this means that it has in general a large number of connotations—that a range of phenomena is involved. Comparative analysis allows us gradually to enlarge our range of knowledge. Cross-national comparative research should therefore provide perspectives for results yielded by one national case study, and verify the extent to which these results can be generalized to other regions or historical periods. We need, however, a gradual program of research, that starts from an understanding of specific historical forms of violence, before trying to develop more generalizable hypotheses. Rule (1988:256) correctly noted that "[t]he idea that there must exist underlying causes for civil violence *in general*—or invariant characteristics of its participants, organizations or settings—deserves much skepticism. To be sure, we have no proof of the opposite position, for these are not matters that can be proved in advance. But it would be wiser to proceed from the more prudent assumptions that, for civil violence as for other things, what appears as 'the same' effect may proceed from a variety of causes, and that 'the same' causal influences may yield a variety of different effects in various settings."

In order to develop a more complex explanation of political violence, we need a model in which the systemic, organizational, and individual perspectives—in other words, environmental conditions, group dynamics, and individual motivations—are all taken into account. For although political violence, as a political phenomenon, is certainly influenced by the conditions of the political system from which it emerges, it is, at least in most industrial democracies, a phenomenon involving fairly small organizations, whose dynamics inevitably influence its development. Moreover, like other forms of deviant behavior, political violence generated changes in individuals' value systems and perceptions of external reality that in turn affected the organization as a whole. Thus, different analytical levels may be said to "dominate" different stages of the evolution of radical groups.

Political violence involves long-lasting dynamics. The traditional reasoning tends to look for causes for violence: social, economic, political, cultural variables are discussed as preconditions for protest escalation. As we mentioned, however, political violence interacts with its environment, not only "using" but also "producing" resources for radicalization. Understanding political violence involves therefore the development of interacting models, in which we have to take into account both the environmental conditions that facilitate the choice of violent repertoires and also the effects that violence produces in its environment—in part reproducing in time the conditions for its very development. In the interactions that allow violence to develop, we find simultaneously strategic actions and also vicious circles with unplanned results.

IV. APPROACHES OF PREVENTION

The development of violence in the New Left has been attributed to an escalation of forms of action, determined by the initial closure of the political elites to new demands. The New Left belonged to this phase of radicalization—so much so that it disappeared in the eighties, leaving room for left-libertarian movements that generally rejected the use of violence. This evolution was facilitated by some reforms, but especially by the acceptance of a conception of democracy that left more space for "participation from below." From being considered mainly "antidemocratic," protest is now accepted as a legitimate, even a "positive" form of citizens' involvement. The policing of protest became—by and large—more tolerant; techniques of "de-escalation" were consciously developed both by police officials and by demonstrators: the "right to demonstrate" has become more and more a right of citizenship. If the first reactions to the left-libertarian movements included a good deal of fear, the democratic regimes eventually demonstrated their adaptive capacity, instituting policy reforms while extending political rights. Further, the later history of the left-libertarian movements showed that the concerns and demands of these movements were not anti-systemic. Indeed, it was not so much the radicalism of the movements' demands as the difficulty of the established institutions in recognizing new democratic actors that led to the escalations of the seventies. Yet even in the seventies, the adaptive, integrative process had already begun (though its deradicalizing impact on the movement family was counterbalanced by repression of the movements' radical fringes). In the eighties, inclusive attitudes finally prevailed (and came to be seen as prevailing), helping to deradicalize political conflicts. Former movement activists entered established politics, and the very conception of democracy evolved to such an extent that we can reasonably speak of a change in the political regime or, at least, of the final stage of consolidation of democracy. And a new collective actor—called social movement—was admitted to "normal" politics.

De-escalation also required deep changes in the social movement strategies. As we mentioned, political violence was only a side effect of movements that remained mainly pacific. Moreover, radicalization—with its visible effects of isolation and marginalization—also contributed to an open debate on the legitimate forms of action. Whereas in the late sixties, violence was often considered as a legitimate means, although it was seldom practiced, later the criticism of violence became more explicit, and came to involve both a negative judgment of its "instrumental" value, and also moral condemnation. Nonviolence spread as a conscious, legitimated technique of protest, while violence was more and more stigmatized. Moreover, the movements of the left-libertarian family underwent a deep change in their organizational structures. In particular, the exclusive conception of membership—that had produced harsh ideological battles—was replaced by a more inclusive understanding. Overlapping and crosscutting membership became a dominant form.

Of course, political violence did not disappear. On the contrary, there is always the risk that it will develop on the margins of large peaceful movements. The fact that political violence is more and more stigmatized in the social movements often isolates the small groups that use more radical repertoires, reducing the opportunities for mediation. Also state responses tend to increase the polarization between those who are considered as "good protesters"—and channeled inside the political institutions—and those "bad protesters" whose "bad manners" are taken as a sign of a refusal of any compromise (della Porta & Reiter, 1998). Violence, therefore, is now more and more seen as "unpolitical"—and dealt with only as a social problem with the risk of reproducing a dynamic of escalation.

REFERENCES

Aron, Raymond. (1968). *La Révolution Introuvable*. Paris: Fayard.

Bongiovanni, Bruno. (1991). Attraverso le Interpretazioni del Maggio Francese. In Aldo Agosti, Luisa Passerini & Nicola Tranfaglia (Eds.), *La Cultura e i Loghi del '68* (pp. 193–123). Milano: Angeli.

Coleman, James. (1990). *The Foundations of Social Theory*. Cambridge: Belknap.

Della Porta, Donatella. (1990). *Il Terrorismo di Sinistra in Italia*. Bologna: Il Mulino.

Della Porta, Donatella. (Ed.) (1992). *Social Movement and Violence: Participation in Underground Organisations*. Greenwich: Jai Press.

Della Porta, Donatella. (1995). *Social Movements, Political Violence and the State*. New York: Cambridge University Press.

Della Porta, Donatella, & Sidney Tarrow. (1986). Unwanted Children. Political Violence and the Cycle of Protest in Italy. 1966–1973. *European Journal of Political Research, 14*, 607–632.

Della Porta, Donatella, & Dieter Rucht. (1995). Social Movement Sectors in Context: A Comparison of Italy and West Germany, 1965–1990. In J. Craig Jenkins & Bert Klandermans (Eds.), *The Politics of Social Protest* (pp. 229–272). Minneapolis: Minnesota University Press.

Della Porta, Donatella, & Herbert Reiter (Eds.) (1998). *Policing Protest: The Control of Mass Demonstrations in Western Democracies*. Minneapolis: The University of Minnesota Press.

Della Porta, Donatella, & Mario Diani. (1999). *Social Movements: An Introduction*. Oxford: Blackwell.

Eckstein, Harry. (1980). Theoretical Approaches to Explaining Collective Political Violence. In Ted R. Gurr (Ed.), *Handbook of Political Conflict* (pp. 135–166). New York: Free Press.

Fetscher, Iring. (1983). Violenza Politica nella Repubblica Federale Tedesca. Motivazioni Interazione Reazione. In Donatella della Porta & Gianfranco Pasquino (Eds.), *Terrorismo e Violenza Politica. Tre Casi a Confronto: Stati Uniti, Germania, Giappone* (pp. 163–206). Bologna: Il Mulino.

Flacks, Richard. (1998). Die philosophischen und politischen Ursprünge der amerikanischen New Left. In Ingrid Gilcher-Holtey (Ed.) (1968), *Vom Ereignis zum Gegenstand der Geschichtswissenschaft* (pp. 151–167). Göttingen: Vandenhoeck & Ruprecht.

Gamson, William A., Bruce Fireman, & Steven Rytina. (1982). *Encounters with Unjust Authorities*. Homewood: Dorsey Press.

Gillespie, Richard. (1982). *Soldiers of Peron: Argentina's Montoneros*. New York: Oxford University Press.

Graham, Hugh, & Ted R. Gurr. (1969). *Violence in America: Historical and Comparative Perspective*. New York: Praeger.

Gurr, Ted R. (1970). *Why Men Rebel*. Princeton: Princeton University Press.

Gurr, Ted R. (1988). Empirical Research on Political Terrorism: The State of the Art and How It Might Be Improved. In Robert O. Slater & Michael Stohl (Eds.), *Current Perspectives on International Terrorism* (pp. 115–154). London: Macmillan.

Hoffer, Eric. (1951). *The True Believer: Thoughts on the Nature of Mass Movement*. New York: Harper and Brothers.

Ibarra, Pedro. (1989). *La Evolucion Estrategica de Eta*. Donostia: Kriselu.

Jáuregui Bereciartu, Gurutz. (1981). *Ideología y Estrategia Política de Eta (1959–1968)*. Madrid: Siglo XXI.

Klandermans, Bert G. (1992). The Social Construction of Protest and Multiorganizational Fields. In: Aldon D. Morris & Carol McClurg Mueller (Eds.), *Frontiers in Social Movement Theory* (pp. 77–103). New Haven: Yale University Press.

Kornhauser, Arthur. (1959). *The Politics of Mass Society*. Glencoe: The Free Press.

Kriesi, Hanspeter, Ruud Koopman, Jan-Willem Duyvendak, Marco Giugni, & Hein-Anton van der Heijden. (1995). *New Social Movements in Western Europe*. Minneapolis: The University of Minnesota Press.

LeBon, Gustave. (1896). *The Crowd: A Study of the Popular Mind*. London: Ernest Benn.

McAdam, Doug. (1983). Tactical Innovation and the Pace of Insurgency. *American Sociological Review, 48,* 735–754.

McClurg Mueller, Carol. (1992). Building Social Movement Theory. In Aldon D. Morris & Carol McClurg Mueller (Eds.), *Frontiers in Social Movement Theory* (pp. 3–25). New Haven: Yale University Press.

Moyano, Maria J. 1995). *Argentina's Lost Patrol: Armed Struggle, 1969–1979*. New Haven: Yale University Press.

Neidhardt, Friedhelm. (1981). Über Zufall, Eigendynamik und Institutionalisierbarkeit absurder Prozesse. Notizen am Beispiel der Entstehung und Einrichtung einer terroristischen Gruppe. In Heinz von Alemann & Hans Peter Thurn (Eds.), *Soziologie in weltbürgerlicher Absicht* (pp. 243–257). Opladen: Westdeutscher Verlag.

Oberschall, Anthony. (1978). Theories of Social Conflict. *Annual Review of Sociology, 4,* 291–315.

Ortoleva, Giuseppe. (1988). *Saggio sui Movimenti del 1968 in Europa e in America*. Roma: Editori Riuniti.

Palmer, David Scott. (1995). The Revolutionary Terrorism of Peru's Shining Path. In Martha Crenshaw (Ed.), *Terrorism in Context* (pp. 249–307). Philadelphia: Penn State Press.

Rule, James R. (1988). *Theories of Civil Violence*. Berkeley: University of California Press.

Smelser, Neil J. (1964). *Theory of Collective Behaviour*. London: Routledge and Kegan Paul.

Snow, David A., E. Burk Rochford, Steven K. Worden, & Robert D. Benford. (1986). Frame Alignment Processes, Micromobilization, and Movement Participation. *American Sociological Review, 51,* 464–481.

Steinhoff, Patricia. (1991). *Nihon Sekigunha: Sono Shakaigakuteki Monogatari (Japan Red Army Faction: A Sociological Tale)*. Tokyo: Kawade Shobo Shinsha.

Tarrow, Sidney. (1989). *Democracy and Disorder. Protest and Politics in Italy 1965–1975*. Oxford: Clarendon Press.

Tilly, Charles. (1978). *From Mobilisation to Revolution*. Reading, Mass.: Addison Wesley.

Waldmann, Peter (Ed.) (1993). *Beruf: Terrorist. Lebensläufe im Untergrund*. München, Beck Verlag.

White, Robert W. (1989). From Peaceful Protest to Guerrilla War: Micromobilization of the Provisional Irish Republican Army. *American Journal of Sociology, 94,* 1277–1302.

White, Robert W. (1993). *Provisional Irish Republicans: An Oral and Interpretative History*. Westport: Greenwood Press.

Wieviorka, Michel. (1988). *Société et Terrorisme*. Paris. Fayard.

Wilkinson, Paul. (1979). Social Scientific Theory and Civil Violence. In Alexander Yona, David Carlton & Paul Wilkinson (Eds.), *Terrorism: Theory and Practice* (pp. 326–346). Boulder: Westview Press.

Wilkinson, Paul. (1986). *Terrorism and the Liberal State. 2nd Edition*. London: Macmillan.

Zald, Mayer N. (1992). Looking Backward to Look Forward: Reflections on the Past and Future of the Resource Mobilization Research Program. In Aldon D. Morris & Carol McClurg Mueller (Eds.), *Frontiers in Social Movement Theory* (pp. 326–346). New Haven: Yale University Press.

Zald, Mayer N., & John McCarthy. (1980). Social Movement Industries: Competition and Cooperation Among Movement Organizations. In Louis Kriesberg (Ed.), *Research in Social Movements, Conflict and Change. Vol. III* (pp. 1–20). Greenwich: JAI Press.

Zwerman, Gilda, Patricia G. Steinhoff, & Donatella della Porta. (2000). Disappearing Social Movements: Clandestinity in the Cycle of New Left Protest in the U.S., Japan, Germany and Italy. *Mobilization, 5*(1), 83–100.

Right-Wing Extremist Violence

WILHELM HEITMEYER

I. INTRODUCTION

Over the last few decades, rapid and far-reaching processes of social modernization, the redefining of the structures of nation states, and powerful thrusts toward globalization among Western societies have provided the background to a highly diverse, variable, and self-contradictory increase in right-wing extremism and the violence associated with it.

Right-wing extremism (in the sense of the availability of political parties and movements) and right-wing extremist violence[1] not only represent a growing threat to ideologically targeted groups among the population, but are also poisoning the democratic fabric of liberal societies.

The recent trends in right-wing extremism and current status reports and analyses on right-wing extremist violence form the central focus of this chapter. The *Analytical Framework* (section II) begins with a discussion of the available range of right-wing political options (cf. section II, Fig. II-2-11.1) and their core ideological elements (cf. section II, Fig. II-2-11.2), and then moves on to single out the individual structural elements for the analysis of right-wing extremist violence (cf. section II, Fig. II-2-11.3).

---

[1] The problem of right-wing extremist violence calls for a special preliminary comment. This is necessary because this type of violence, in its National Socialist manifestation, is associated with one particular event of the twentieth century, the Holocaust, one of the principal reasons why the previous century will go down in the annals of world history as an age of extreme violence (cf. Hobsbawm, 1994). Yet it would be wrong to see the present-day phenomena as a mere continuation of the violence that led to that disaster. One reason for this is that right-wing extremist violence is certainly not an exclusively German problem. For that reason, the phenomenon is placed in an international context and, at the same time, viewed against a background of the economic, social, and political trends in modern Western societies. This, however, means that the history of political violence in Germany (cf. Schumann, 1997) and the Holocaust cannot be included in this chapter (but cf. Longerich in this volume). Similarly, this approach means that extreme right-wing violence in ethnic civil wars, as seen in the former Yugoslavia during the second half of the 1990s, and the violence of far-right murder squads of the type seen in South America (cf. Tobler & Waldmann, 1991), are not considered here.

W. Heitmeyer and J. Hagan (eds.), *International Handbook of Violence Research*, 399–436.
© 2003 Kluwer Academic Publishers. Printed in the Netherlands.

A second focus of this chapter is the broad range of *Theoretical Approaches to an Explanation* (cf. section III), which will endeavor to examine the relevance of the various theories relating to right-wing extremist violence and the extent to which they offer an explanation.

The third part (cf. section IV) centers on *Empirical Studies* of right-wing extremism. They concentrate especially on structural elements and are linked to theoretical approaches to explaining different categories, extents, processes, and dynamics of right-wing extremist violence. The presentation of the contexts of violence is organized here to analyze, by stages, first the situational dynamics (cf. section IV, Fig. II-2-11.4), then the sociospatial configurations, and finally regional and national dimensions of right-wing extremism.

II.   ANALYTICAL FRAMEWORK

1.   Definitions and Structural Elements

A conceptual definition of the field of study seems to be best approached in stages. The starting point must be the concept of violence. It defies any unambiguous definition (cf. Imbusch in this volume): for example, even if the emphasis is placed on a physical assault upon personal integrity and freedom from injury, then the terrorizing of individuals, together with the resulting traumatization of the individual (cf. van der Kolk and Streeck-Fischer in this volume), and constraints upon social freedom (of movement) are also relevant, because the perpetrator is forcibly imposing his own will on that of his victim.

If the *concept of violence* covers not only physical injury and killing but also *coercion* or the *threat* of injury, then the mental aspect is part of the concept, because these elements do not represent "externally" visible indicators that can be perceived intersubjectively.

This, however, is where *political* violence comes to the fore. As a result, the central issue becomes the *collective* struggle for *power* and *domination*. That struggle always takes the form of *conflict*. In view of this, it is appropriate to direct analysis toward political *interaction contexts*, in which different groups of protagonists, such as right-wing groups and their opponents together with "observer groups" and institutions, interact, resolve violent conflicts, accept fatalities or even deliberately commit murders, and practice coercion against other people, thus damaging their mental integrity.

Before we look more closely at right-wing extremist violence, it is important for the purposes of the international debate to begin by noting the unclear dividing lines between racist and xenophobic violence, on the one hand, and right-wing extremist violence, on the other. The purpose of racist violence is usually the nonspecific demonstration of power in a particular situation ("Pakistani bashing," for example), while right-wing extremist violence, being ideologically driven, functions with a view to sustainable demonstrations of power in public social spaces or in social and political institutions. These points are important because, in countries where electoral law means that right-wing extremist groups have no prospects of success (such as the United Kingdom), their violence is not regarded in political circles as being right-wing extremist, in other words as being directed against the political system, so that no such problem appears to exist. Yet that is by no means the case: all that happens is that the same violence occurs under other names and in other forms.

The next step toward classification relates to *right-wing extremist* violence as a variant of political violence. This makes it necessary to consider political ideologies as legitimations; to shift the focus of analysis to organizations, perpetrator groups, victim groups, and the contexts of acts. Before taking that step, we first need to define the boundaries of "right-wing extremism" and set out the core elements of the ideological and political concept. In attempting this, we find that there is no consensus on a definition (cf. the survey in Mudde, 1995). One reason for this is that there are competing concepts, moving the boundaries of the frame in different directions, such as (neo-)fascism, right-wing radicalism, (neo-)Nazism, etc. (cf. Heitmeyer, 1987:13–16).

In this chapter, the term "right-wing extremism" is preferred, because it encompasses the most important overlaps in the broad spectrum ranging from right-wing populism bordering on ultraconservative democratic forms at one end, to neo-Nazism at the other, as a variant that carries a particularly heavy historical charge. If we survey the ideological components of right-wing extremism, it becomes apparent that they may be directed both toward the structure of the political system and toward the organization of social coexistence. If the attempt to frame and delimit the concept ideologically draws upon the empirically identifiable thrusts of violence—against institutions of government in the United States, for example—or the victim groups, who are for the most part weaker individuals or foreigners, the most obvious definition becomes a *politico-institutional* one, according to which right-wing extremism is directed against a parliamentary, pluralistic, and democratic system. If that is the case, representatives of that system also come within the sights of violent right-wing extremist groups: politicians, police officers. Secondly, two elements are central to the *sociological* concept of right-wing extremism: ideologies of inequality on the one hand, such as exaggerated nationalism, racist denigration, and totalitarian views of the law, are associated with varying levels of acceptance of violence on the other (cf. Heitmeyer, 1987).

The survey of the political spectrum that follows provides a summary of the action contexts to be taken into account here, the available options, targets, and objectives of right-wing extremism (cf. Fig. II-2-11.1). In a subsequent step (cf. Fig. II-2-11.3), we then move on to examine right-wing extremist violence, which in this context is merely one aspect among several.

Ideologies of inequality are central to the political options available to right-wing extremist groups. The issue here is the demonstration of power: the superiority of one's own group and the inferiority, depersonalization, and dehumanization of other groups and their members. One appropriate field of inquiry is to consider a broad spectrum of "group-focused enmity" (cf. Fig. II-2-11.2), which is directed not only against those who are ethnically/culturally or religiously different but even against those who are "the same" but are defined as "deviant" from the standpoint of the right-wing extremist ideology of inequality.

Right-wing extremist constructs of reality (cf. Funke et al., 1999) can also be demonstrated empirically and provide the basis of legitimation for lowering inhibitions against violence, the selection of specific groups of victims, acts of violence within specific opportunity structures, and the establishment of illegitimate power. Within these definition frameworks can also be included attacks on cultural and religious symbols and objects (such as mosques, Jewish cemeteries, memorials to victims, etc.) pertaining to the groups of victims that are regarded as hostile or unequal, because this violence against objects (in the form of ideologically justified iconoclastic vandalism) is fundamentally designed to destroy the self-image and self-awareness of the victims and prevent them from living their lives free of fear.

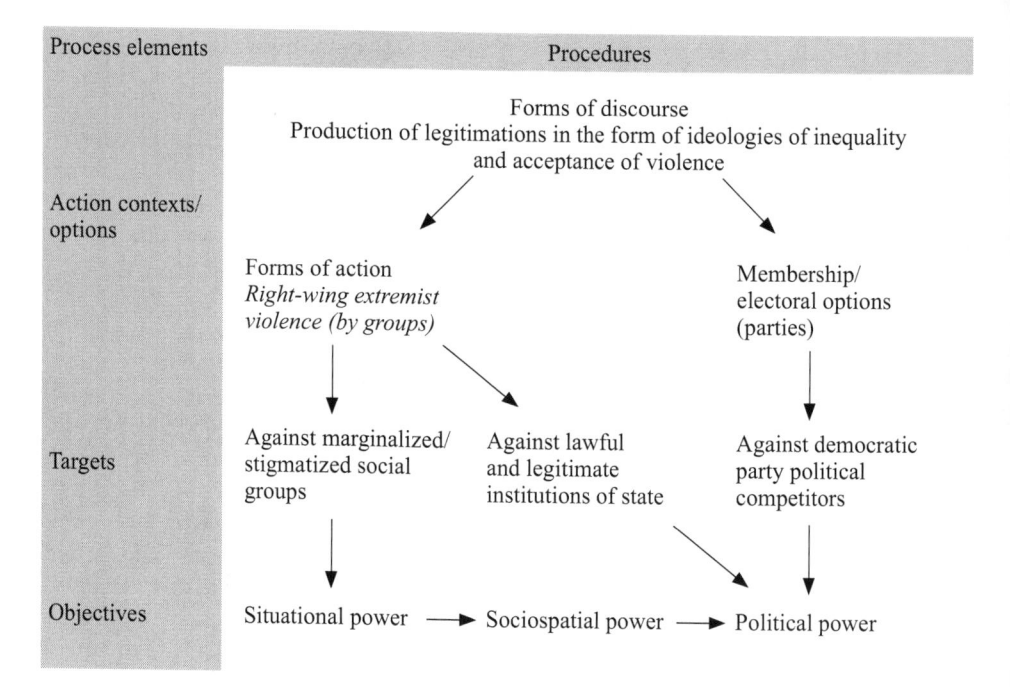

FIGURE II-2-11.1. Overall context, options, targets, and objectives of right-wing extremism.

Syndrome elements	Core content
Racism	Denigration of others based on assessment of biological differences ("natural" superiority of own group)
Anti-Semitism	Denigration of people of Jewish origin or faith
Ethnocentrism	Self-aggrandizement by laying claim to cultural and economic achievement (differences of development)
Xenophobia	Defense against competition for position, jobs, etc. based on different ethnic origin
Heterophobia	Fear and denigration of deviation from the "norm" (rejection of "difference": homosexuals, lesbians, the homeless, Muslims)
Rights of Precedence	Insistence on spatial/temporal precedence over "newcomers"

FIGURE II-2-11.2. Components of ideologies of inequality: group-focused enmity. (*Source*: adapted from Heitmeyer, 1994:31.)

Whichever approach is adopted to the analysis of the whole complex of "right-wing extremism" as a mental attitude, political movement, or form of group violence, there are four central research aspects that must be primarily borne in mind:

a) A *multidisciplinary approach* is necessary, in order, *inter alia*, to link social-psychological factors to sociological structural analyses so that *relationships* are elucidated (cf. *inter alios* Husbands, 1993; Stöss, 1994; Winkler, 1996);

b) *multilevel analyses* (macro-, meso- and microapproaches) are needed, offering as they do the only way of shedding appropriate light on *cause-effect processes* (cf. *inter alios* Heitmeyer, 1994; Kühnel, 1998);

c) *internationally* comparative research must be taken into account, to allow the various *patterns of development* to be studied (cf. *inter alios* Kaplan & Weinberg, 1998; Minkenberg, 1998);

d) the basic assumption of a *context of political interaction* is a necessary starting point for a proper understanding of *dynamics* and *mobilization* (cf. Koopmans, 1998; Perry, 2001).

These four aspects need to be synthesized in the further course of research, to enable phenomena to be analyzed and explained in various *contexts*.

2. The Right-Wing Extremist Spectrum in the Context of Political Interaction

Right-wing extremist violence cannot be viewed in isolation but must first be examined in the context of the structures of political choice that exist in the societies in question.

The first of these is the choice of discourse within the right-wing spectrum. This is provided by intellectual elites who develop and put forward ideological choices that specialize in historical revisionism—for example, of National Socialism in Germany, Holocaust denial (e.g., Irving, 1977), or highly controversial assessments of Fascism in Italy or of the Vichy regime in France. Another form is evinced by a "New Right," which more or less divorces itself from that period of history and promotes, for example, an ideological stock containing fragments of social Darwinism, or develops theories of ethnopluralism (where every group has its "own" place) (e.g., Benoist, 1977, 1999; Weißmann, 2000).

Elements of these ideological products amenable to popularization are reworked to provide *options of belonging*, for example to the relevant far right parties, and *electoral options*, and in some cases they are radicalized as well. A wide range of party political variations is associated with this diversity, from populist right-wing "bridging" parties, with their overlaps with conservative democratic organizations, through traditional shades of right-wing extremism (with historical points of contact) to neo-Nazi parties aiming to replicate historical events.

The right-wing extremist *action options*, frequently associated with hostile demonstrations and a use of violence that may be either tactical (to seize territorial power in certain neighborhoods, for example) or expressive (to demonstrate power over individuals in given situations), are in some cases covertly linked to the equivalent party political options.

The complex range of options provided by right-wing extremism has taken very different forms in individual societies, reflecting the differences in their historical and political development and the evolution of their social structures (cf. Betz, 1994; von Beyme, 1996; Bjørgo, 1997; Bowling, 1998; van Donselaar, 1993; Hockenos, 1993; Kaplan, 1995; Koopmans & Kriesi, 1997; Kürti, 1998; Mayer & Perrineau, 1996; Minkenberg, 1998; Pfahl-Traughber, 1995). These differences extend to the targets selected.

We are primarily concerned here with those forms of action that are linked to acts of violence, always bearing in mind the legitimizing functions of the discourse, membership, and electoral options within the internal interaction context of right-wing extremism.

3. The Analytical Concept for Right-Wing Extremist Violence and the Beliefs of Groups

Against the background of a definition framework, we now have to picture a complex ana-lytical concept. This has to extend over three levels and identify the very heart of the subject under discussion. It arises from the *right-wing extremist violence practiced by groups in the public arena*. This heart is located on the *mesolevel* of the analysis. It is framed by the *microlevel* of individual behavior, because explanations have to be found not only for the scale of the *individual capacity for violence* and for the processes by which it comes into being (is learned, in other words) but also for the motives for adopting and approving the *ideological patterns*, in other words the facets of an ideology of inequality. Finally, the third level is concerned with the *background processes*, so that on the *macrolevel* the social-struc-ture factors and the developments in the political and economic systems are demonstrated.

In the context of structural developments, there are three central elements to be taken into account: first, the *conditions of action* (i.e., opportunity structures and the equipment/ facilities available to groups); secondly, the *protagonists* (and their individual propensities to violence together with the group-dynamic composition of the group); and thirdly, the *action groups that are relevant to the process* (for the dynamics of escalation or de-escalation).

This analytical concept has to be applied with care, because distinctions have to be made between *individual situations of violence* (for isolated demonstrations of power), the *sociospatial density* of violent situations (for the occupation of local territory), and what are referred to as *"waves of violence"* (throughout a society, for example). The signifi-cance pertaining to each of the individual analytical elements varies in accordance with focus. Thus, for example, the reporting of violence in the media is more significant to our understanding of waves of violence than to the analysis of the microsituation of an indi-vidual violent act.

Taking due account of these requirements means giving thought to simple *analyses of relationships* as well as portraying *interactions*, in other words reciprocal influences at protagonist level, because the configurations of right-wing extremist group violence are set within a complex context. Unless this view is adopted, there is no way of explaining the *processes* of brutalization or the statistical cycles of linear and nonlinear increases and decreases in violence. Figure II-2-11.3 illustrates this structure.

The *choice* and *configuration* are indicative of a complex pattern, whose *origin*, *dissemination*, and in some cases *cycles* of escalation are determined by the interplay of many factors of an interaction context within society that is political in the sense of being geared to power, domination, and conflict.

As the subject of right-wing extremist violence to be studied here is concerned with *processes* of origination, dissemination, increase, escalation, and decrease, it seems ap-propriate to organize the review in such a way that violence is analyzed within the frame-work of a context of political interaction[2] (cf. Heitmeyer, 1999).

In that context, it is necessary to study not only the process results that reinforce the escalating activities of violent groups but also those that may serve to inhibit them. The second issue relates to ways in which the social, economic, political, and mass-media

---

[2] The same perspective is also adopted by Perry in analyzing American hate crimes: "Hate is, in fact, an assault against all members of stigmatized and marginalized communities. Hate crime—often referred to as 'ethnoviolence'—is much more than the act of mean-spirited bigots. It is embedded in the structural and cultural context within which groups interact. ... It does not occur in a social or cultural vacuum; rather, it is a socially situated, dynamic process, involving context and actors, structure, and agency" (Perry, 2001:1).

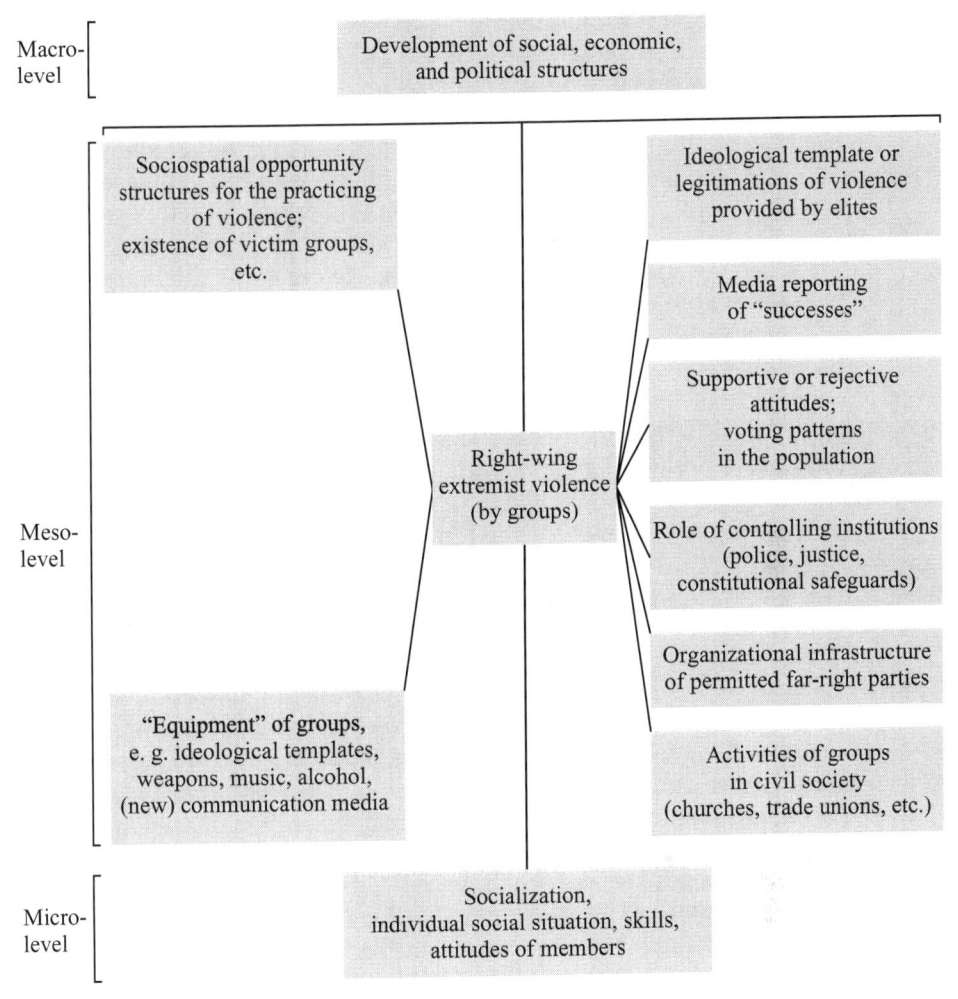

Macro-level — Development of social, economic, and political structures

Meso-level
- Sociospatial opportunity structures for the practicing of violence; existence of victim groups, etc.
- Ideological template or legitimations of violence provided by elites
- Media reporting of "successes"
- Supportive or rejective attitudes; voting patterns in the population
- Right-wing extremist violence (by groups)
- Role of controlling institutions (police, justice, constitutional safeguards)
- Organizational infrastructure of permitted far-right parties
- "Equipment" of groups, e. g. ideological templates, weapons, music, alcohol, (new) communication media
- Activities of groups in civil society (churches, trade unions, etc.)

Micro-level — Socialization, individual social situation, skills, attitudes of members

FIGURE II-2-11.3.   Structural model for the analysis of right-wing extremist violence.

actor groups influence or paralyze each other, demonstrate indifference, or even mobilize counterforces and bring about changes in the groups that make up civil society or in the institutions of socialization or control.

On that basis, an appropriate analytical model must achieve the integration of several levels and, apart from root causes, also take account of the factors of the *dynamics* of violence.

At the center (cf. Fig. II-2-11.3) stands collective violence: apart from individual perpetrators (such as the 1980 attack at the Munich *Oktoberfest* in Germany, which cost thirteen lives), right-wing extremist violence is typically group violence, which takes a variety of ideological forms, each pursuing a different variant of power. Seven such variants can be identified:

- *Opportunity-dependent violence by (youth) gangs*
  As a rule, the violence is not strategically motivated, but is based on an unfocused hatred of those who are "different." It manifests itself as the forcible demonstra-

tion of superiority when situations and moods are favorable. This variant mainly takes the form of "street violence" (cf. Bjørgo, 1997; Wagner, 1998).

- *Subcultural violence*
  This type of violence usually exists within a youth culture environment and is directed against others who have no institutionalized power interests of their own. As a result of its habitual setting, it usually goes further than the situation-dependent practice of violence, and is actively sought. Skinheads belong to this category (cf. Hockenos, 1993, Hamm, 1993, Wieviorka et al., 1992, Heitmann, 1997).

- *Organized, party-political right-wing extremist violence*
  This form is strategically based on planned action and is political in the narrower sense, so that violence is also used as a means to seek institutionalized power. Its targets include not only those who are "different" but also the representatives of institutions (politicians, journalists, and trade union members). Examples of parties that fall within this spectrum include the British National Party (BNP) in the United Kingdom, the *Nationaldemokratische Partei Deutschlands* (National Democratic Party of Germany—NPD) and its youth organization, the *Junge Nationaldemokraten* (Young National Democrats—JN) (cf. Hoffmann, 1999), and the former neo-Nazi groups—banned in Germany since the mid-1990s and now going by the name of *Freie Kameradschaften* (Free Comrades' Associations), which cooperate, in some cases covertly, with the NPD. A Swedish example is the *Nationalsocialistik Front* (National Socialist Front—NSF) (cf. Lööw, 1995). Parties active in the United States include the NSDAP-AO (the Nazi Party "Foreign and Development Association") and the National Alliance (NA). Also linked to many organizations of this type, though not itself run as a political party, is the Swedish group *Vit Ariskt Motstand* (White Aryan Resistance—VAM), which sees itself as a vanguard of revolution.

- *Religiously oriented right-wing extremist groups*
  The mainsprings of this variation are in most cases pure racism and anti-Semitism. It includes groups such as White Aryan Resistance (WAR), a prototype of "leaderless resistance" (Grumke, 2001:124), an important organizational principle for the formation of small, autonomous cells. The "World Church of the Creator" (WCOTC) can also be considered part of this spectrum, while outlying areas include variants of the "Christian Identity" churches.

- *The Ku Klux Klan*
  In a category of its own in the United States is the Ku Klux Klan, by far the oldest right-wing extremist organization, which, too, is driven by racism and anti-Semitism and, despite falling membership, is regularly responsible for outbreaks of violence (Kaplan, 1995).

- *Terrorist violence with a far-right background*
  Violence by conspiratorial groups is directed not only against those who are "different" but also, with varying intensity, against the state. Their intention is to challenge authority through the power of the bomb, without themselves having any ambitions for power. This variant has hitherto appeared only in embryonic form in Europe—as in the case of the Combat 18 group in the United Kingdom—and is to be found in some American militias (cf. Dees, 1996; Stern, 1996; Kaplan & Weinberg, 1998).

- *Right-wing extremist pogroms*
  This form of violence is not explicitly group-driven, but is based on accumulated or even deliberately harnessed tensions directed against helpless "others" by fac-

tions acting in a largely unstructured way. Such violence is usually eruptive in nature, because opportunities for "background elites" to exert any influence are generally limited (cf. also Bergmann in this volume).

A comparison between European and United States variants also reveals substantial differences. In American right-wing extremism, for example, political parties are less important than they are in Europe, whereas a much greater part is played by those organizations that are often collectively classified as "hate groups." A related point here is that some types of group, such as militias and the Ku Klux Klan, have no European counterparts. Neo-Nazi groups dominate the European scene, whereas militant religious groups and churches are particularly prominent in the United States. Skinheads are active on both sides of the Atlantic, but are more significant in the Old World.

In most cases, we have only estimates of the numerical strengths of these groups and their memberships in the various countries. One reason for this is that some groups have no formal membership arrangements; another is that their activities are largely secretive. In any case, numbers and membership allow only indirect conclusions regarding the quality and frequency of violence. The German example demonstrates this: At the end of 2000, there were 144 right-wing extremist organizations or groups with an estimated membership of 51,000 (cf. Bundesministerium des Innern and Bundesministerium der Justiz, 2001:280). While the *Bundesamt für Verfassungsschutz* (German Federal Office for the Protection of the Constitution) considered that estimated numbers had been falling slightly, the potential numbers of pro-violence right-wing extremists had risen steadily, from 6,200 in 1995 to 9,700 in 2000 (2001:3). Between 1990 and 2000, these groups became younger, more militant, more violent, and more action-oriented (ibid., 26). Similar trends on the potentially violent side of right-wing extremism have also been reported from other countries. In Sweden, the hard core of right-wing extremism is estimated to number some 500 individuals, and the development of a terrorist variant is no longer ruled out, and there were first indications of this kind in Germany in 2003 (Munich; Kameradschaft Sued). In the United States, there are similar problems with the reporting of the number of groups, their membership rates, and the question whether those figures are rising or falling (cf. section IV. 3).

III. THE SPECTRUM OF THEORETICAL APPROACHES TO AN EXPLANATION

In contrast to violent crime, which encompasses a subject area that is relatively clearly defined, and to which many theories refer (cf. Albrecht in this volume), theories on right-wing extremism are directed toward a political phenomenon within which violence is only one aspect. There is as yet no specific theory to explain right-wing extremist violence. There are various reasons for this. One is that right-wing extremist violence is to some extent a part of a process of escalation designed to demonstrate and/or gain political power. Another reason is that it is not always possible to draw a precise line of demarcation between this politically motivated violence and nonpolitical (crimes of) violence, because the same actors—many of them young—are often prominent in both cases.

In view of these problems, the obvious approach now seems to be to put forward theories oriented toward different *manifestations* of the origin and evolution of right-wing extremist violence.

The first point to consider is the *origin* of individual attitudes to the *acceptance of ideologies of inequality* (i.e., the facets of attitudes of enmity; cf. section II, Fig. II-2-11.2) and the *development of behavioral tendencies* (i.e., the propensity to violence). They are based partly on individual motives and partly on the forms of discourse offered by the far-right spectrum. Approaches here are based on *theories of learning, social psychology, socialization,* and *deprivation.*

Secondly, both the causes of the *dissemination* of individual attitudes and the motives for *transitions to collective action* need to be illustrated. Relevant approaches in this context are those based on *political culture*, which describe the evolution of trust or mistrust of the democratic system. Concepts of media theories and elite theories can be associated with these, because they focus on issues of dissemination and are able to characterize the social "climate." They have to be considered in connection with the range of "belonging" options and electoral choices offered by the right-wing extremist spectrum.

Thirdly, situational and sociospatial *escalation dynamics* need to be addressed; these focus on the collective actions of groups. At this point, ideas based on *subculture theories* and *conflict theories* can be deployed. They will be discussed in the context of the action options offered by the right-wing extremist camp, the core of which is violent action. Consequently, *criminological approaches* to the explanation of violence are appropriate here.

Fourthly, the reasons for the *propagation of waves of violence* in a society must be highlighted. Considerations based on *media theory* and *movement theory* are particularly useful here.

Fifthly and lastly, the very general question arises of how such a *pattern of development in the modern age* could possibly have occurred again toward the end of the twentieth century after the experiences of the Holocaust. An answer to this question may be provided by theories that endeavor to incorporate the four stages of development described into a complex concept embracing several analytical levels.

Having linked manifestations to theoretical approaches, we can now move on to present the basic outlines of those approaches.

- *Social-psychological* approaches emphasize the individual processing of social experiences to create political attitudes and behavior patterns. In the context of acts of right-wing extremist violence and the associated ideologies, a prominent source is the classical theory of pathological authoritarianism (cf. Adorno et al., 1950) and its subsequent developments (cf. Altemeyer, 1996, whose theory of learning owes more to Bandura). Whereas this approach centers on the mentalities of individuals, the theory of social identity (cf. Tajfel, 1981) focuses on the description of ingroup-outgroup relations, whose relevance lies in the explanation of the lowering of the thresholds of violence (cf. the overview in Zick, 1997).

- *Socialization theory approaches* concentrate on the development of social and political attitudes to outsiders, on skills in dealing with everyday routine, for example gaining recognition and learning to handle problems such as conflicts, and on the learning of the capacity for violence. These approaches concentrate primarily on the stages of childhood and young adulthood. They transform classical theories such as authoritarianism to this period of development (cf. Hopf et al., 1995), emphasize the special part played by anomie (Boehnke, Hagan, & Merkens, 1998:124), and highlight the processes by which everyday problems (such as adolescent difficulties with integration and recognition) are converted to political options (cf. Heitmeyer, 1993). Other analyses emphasize new concepts that link up to the imperatives of cutthroat modern market processes (cf. Hagan et al., 1999). Clarification of the issue of the capacity for violence can also be provided by theories of learning, with their elements of imitation, observation, and reinforcement (cf. Bandura, 1973). These approaches, then, are concerned with the elucidation of willingness to act (to legitimize violence) and ability to act (to practice violence), which are acquired in the process of socialization (cf. Möller, 2000).

- *Subculture theory approaches* emphasize the role of the group and its attractiveness to certain target individuals (Jaschke, 1982). These center first on specific socialization careers and their relationship to violence and secondly on the relationship to the democratic political culture. The intra-group-dynamic processes are also analyzed; these influence the transition from individual propensities toward violence to collective violent action (Hamm, 1993).

- *Criminological theories* are particularly informative where it is impossible to separate political motivations to achieve power and dominance from the aims of situational superiority or mere destruction (cf. Albrecht in this volume). In this area, the various explanations provided by strain, control, and labeling theories or Marxist-oriented approaches of "critical criminology" need to be taken into account (cf. also Perry, 2001:39–41 on the phenomenon of hate crimes).

- *Movement theory concepts* try to explain why collective action (organized group violence or pogroms) comes about, since neither specific socialization experience nor individual relative deprivation transposes seamlessly into xenophobic or right-wing extremist postures. Movement theory approaches only come into play when a network of groups and organizations exists which offer interpretations and so link individual problem situations to the aims of the movement as a way of achieving mobilization. Structural strains, collective identity, framing, resource mobilization, and political opportunity structures represent not only competing approaches but also the framework for an integrated concept (cf. McAdam, Tarrow, & Tilly, 1996; Hellmann, 1998).

- *Conflict theory approaches* emphasize the clash between majorities and minorities in local contexts, where, in particular, situations in which groups are excessively challenged result in an increase in xenophobic attitudes. In conflicts involving immigration, for example, acceptance of violence acquires a political sense and a new dynamism (cf. Willems et al., 1993).

- *Deprivation theory approaches* emphasize the degree of disadvantage in society, by *absolute* standards, associated with poverty and destitution, and the *relative* disadvantage which, according to the classic approach adopted by Ted R. Gurr (1972), occurs as a result of a social inequality that is *perceived* as unjust in relation to the distribution of tangible and intangible goods and assets. It is assumed that there are direct connections with aggression and violence, especially at the level of the individual.

- *Political culture approaches* target the attractions or failures of the democratic system, corresponding opportunities for participation, and state benefits. Loss of confidence in or ties with political parties, social milieus, and the institutions of society provide the points of reference for explanations here (cf. Stöss, 1989; Sprinzak, 1995; Minkenberg, 1998).

- *Continuity theory approaches* are often committed to the Marxist analysis of society and draw historical lines of connection. They attribute the existence and spread of right-wing extremist violence to the failure to critically come to terms with fascism or National Socialism and to an inadequate democratic culture (cf. Kühnl, 1990).
- *Modernization theory approaches* take as their starting point the processes of social change and their individual, social, and political repercussions in terms of problems of integration and disintegration (cf. Heitmeyer, 1994; Anhut & Heitmeyer, 2000). This approach provides an explanation of the conditions that cause individuals or groups to regard it—because of structural access problems, uncertainties, and collapse of recognition—as "necessary" and appropriate to perceive the options offered by the far right as attractive explanations of their own situations and so turn to right-wing extremist groups (cf. in the case of France, *inter alios*, Wieviorka, 1999:52–72).

These alternative theories are of varying *significance* for the purposes of explaining the development of right-wing extremist violence. Socialization theories concentrate especially on explaining dispositions acquired at an early age, subculture theories may elucidate the habitualization of specific behavior within groups, movement theory approaches place the emphasis on mobilization, while approaches based on theories of modernization, deprivation, and political culture attach more importance to the reasons for turning to right-wing extremist groups.

Because these theories have different areas of emphasis, they also differ in *scope*. Thus, a residual problem with theories structurally based on conditions of social strain and on crises (cf. Neidhardt, 1985:198) is the inadequate explanation of situational action dynamics. Conflict theory approaches, in turn, are very limited in their explanation of long-term trends. For this reason, it is necessary to develop combinations of theories or integrative draft theories that encompass several levels and refer to different settings (short-term events and long-term trends).

In the further course of this account, relevant empirical results are in each case associated with specific explanations, or problems of explanation, that can essentially be related to one or more of these basic theoretical concepts.

IV.   RIGHT-WING EXTREMIST VIOLENCE: DYNAMICS, DISTRIBUTIONS, EXTENTS, AND THEIR EXPLANATIONS

The presentation of right-wing extremist violence in this chapter is based on a socioecological zoning model—in other words, different contexts are presented which in each case are representative of their more comprehensive variants. The first issue, therefore, is the situational context with the specific dynamics of violence: what course does the violence follow (section IV. 1)? The next context is sociospatial: where does the violence take place (section IV. 2)? Thirdly, and finally, the degree of dissemination in regional and/or national contexts is considered, to make it possible to estimate the level of jeopardy for Western societies that perceive themselves as democratic and for eastern European transitional societies (section IV. 3).

1. Contexts of Violence: Situational Dynamics

The causes of developments of right-wing extremist violence can be analyzed with reference to two paradigms. One is the *personal* approach, which focuses on the perpetrators, so that theories based on anthropology and on individual and social psychology become relevant. The alternative approach is one that regards the individual as an element in a social constellation and places greater emphasis on the *interactive* nature of violence.

A further analytical approach requires that violence be analyzed within different *contexts*. The approach selected here is one that analyses the *interactive* nature of violence with a view to explaining both the *origin* and the (qualitative and quantitative) *development* of right-wing extremist violence. The first step here is to consider the *situational* context. In that context, analysis looks at the process from the emergence of attitudes and a willingness to act in the individual's area of socialization with political choices to opportunity structures and to violent escalation by groups. This process comprises five necessary elements (cf. Fig. II-2-11.4—the SOLIE chart) and applies only to the first three of the identified variants of violent groups.

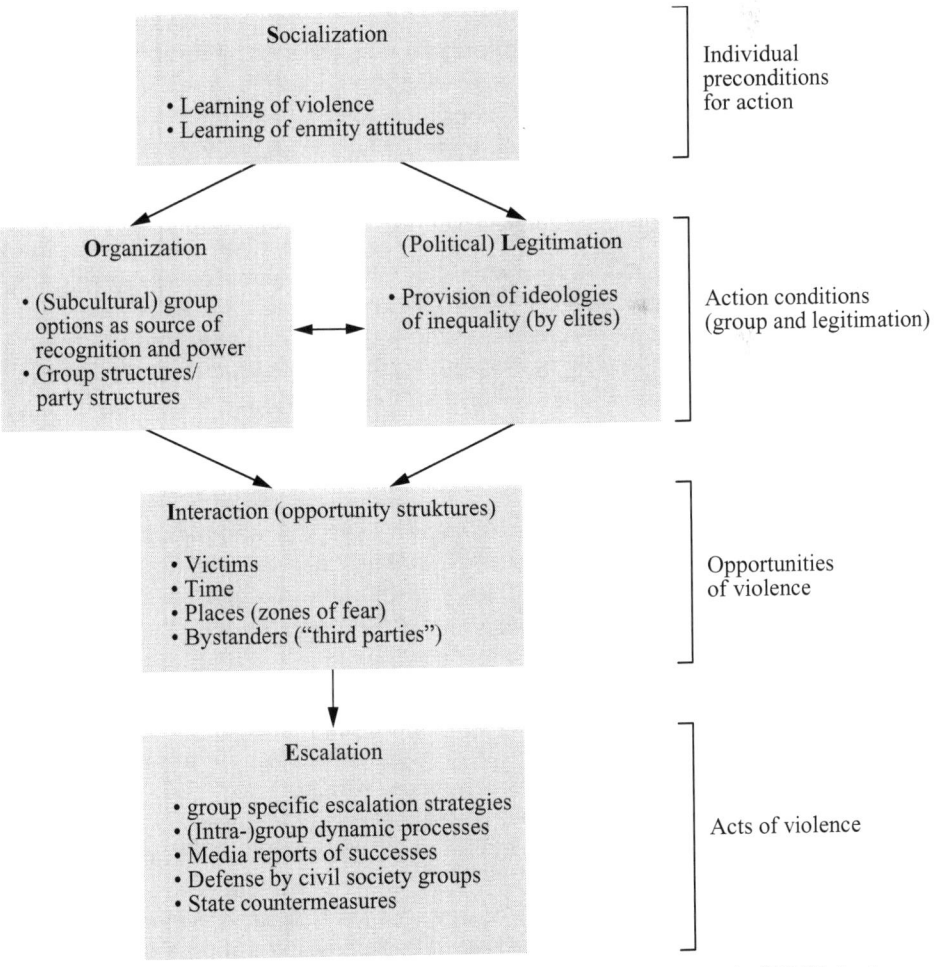

FIGURE II-2-11.4. **Process model for analyzing constellations of violence: the SOLIE chart.**

The SOLIE chart illustrates the relevant conditions and contexts of action and the escalation factors in such a way as to display fundamental relationships on which approaches to explanations are based. For analytical reasons, the five fundamental elements (Socialization, Organization, Legitimation, Interaction und Escalation) are each dealt with separately. Even so, none of these elements can be absent from any explanation, as they form a closely related whole.

This process model is based on preconditions of socialization, which include individual violence learning processes and the individual learning of attitudes of enmity. They remain an individual and private matter until such time as publicly relevant legitimation is provided by elites, and organizations exist in the form of options for action or mobilization. They become relevant to action only when opportunity structures exist, that is, the possibility of interactions to enable the postulates of attitude and action to escalate into violence (cf. also Bjørgo, 1993:43). Here again, nothing can be assumed to take place automatically. This also points to the existence of gaps in research to elucidate the logic involved, because within this process the various elements (cf. also structural model, section II, Fig. II-2-11.3) fulfill different functions in relation to the practice of violence.

a. Socialization: Individual Preconditions for Action. The individual capacity for violence is not conceivable in the absence of specific socialization experiences that occur in the course of dealing with social conditions, so that both attitudes of enmity and the effectiveness of violence are learned. Particularly relevant here are family, school, peer groups, and the media.

In the academic debate, there are two particularly contentious issues as far as family influences are concerned. The first is whether the origins of right-wing extremist attitudes and violence can be associated with a problematic family background. Such problem areas include experience of broken homes, cold emotional relationships, and experience of violence within the family. While specific configurations of stress are regularly cited in German studies (cf. *inter alios* Heitmeyer & Müller, 1995; Hopf *et al.*, 1995:129; Mentzel, 1998; Möller, 2000; Wetzels & Greve, 2001), Hamm (1993:114) does not identify any particular family problem situations in his study of American skinheads. He does not regard the family experience as a significant predictor of right-wing extremist violence or terrorism. The second controversial issue focuses on the extent to which parents pass on ideological positions. In particular, the Swiss study by Fend (1994:144) emphasizes that in this context the role of the family is underestimated and that of school overestimated. A largely uncontested point is the great influence attributed to peer groups in the development both of right-wing extremist attitudes and of the propensity for violence. By contrast, the mass media cannot be shown to produce any direct causative effect connected with right-wing extremist attitudes and actions. Their effects are more apparent as trigger and escalation factors (cf. Lukesch in this volume).

Studies of groups of individuals, usually male perpetrators of violence in the far-right camp, suggest certain common characteristics (Willems et al., 1993; Merkl, 1997; Bjørgo, 1998; Lööw, 1995; Perry, 2001:30). The age structure is centered on the 16–26 bracket, although the average age is far higher in such cases as the American militias and terrorist forms of violence.

There is no significant difference between the sexes where xenophobic or right-wing extremist views are concerned, and the role of girls and women as "bystanders" should not be underestimated here.

Conclusions are also generally consistent as far as education levels are concerned. Most perpetrators of violence have only poor educational qualifications. Where researchers differ is on the extent and significance of employment, or the lack of it, as a factor in the development of right-wing extremist attitudes and violence. As far as formal employment status is concerned, it is apparent that in Europe, in terms of the total number of unemployed and the comparable age-group, a disproportionately high percentage of the perpetrators are indeed unemployed. At the same time, however, this finding suggests that this factor is of limited significance. It seems likely that a more influential factor is the precarious nature of employments as such and the associated fears and anxieties (cf. on skinheads, for example, Heitmann, 1997:93), insofar as employment is regarded as a central factor in social integration and a source of social recognition.

b. ORGANIZATION AND POLITICAL LEGITIMATION: CONDITIONS FOR VIOLENT ACTION. Groups play a special part in the career of the individual, in determining his capacity for action and ability to gain recognition or power. Preconditions of learning and sociospatial contexts determine which groups are sought out, which group options are accepted, and which intra-group-dynamic processes are relevant to the activation of the potential for violence. This activation is dependent on the provision of ideologies by elites, who offer discourse options that lower the thresholds of violence. Also necessary to this lowering process is perceived approval of prejudice against minorities (as potential target objects) within the population, in other words within the direct range of experience of the group participants, and thus the quality of the political culture.

The first fundamentally important factor here is the relationship between ideology and violence, which depends on the degree of politicization of the various groups. Among ideologically unified groups, the function of violence is to enforce an ideology as a way of obtaining political power. In such cases, violence is deployed strategically. Such groups are generally distinct from those comprising mainly young people and teenagers, where the emphasis is more on territorial power over social spaces. Expressive violence is more dominant here, and fragments of ideology—in some cases with changed content—are invoked as a justification.

With regard to the distribution of the frequency of violence among the various violent groups, the clear emphasis in Europe is on opportunity-dependent violence practiced by politically unorganized groups. By contrast, the particularly brutal perpetrators of violence are to be found among the skinheads, who in turn, according to the American studies by Hamm (1993:62), can be clearly distinguished from the street gangs. Hamm also points out that—in contrast to Europe—"most terrorist skinheads do not look like skinheads at all" (Hamm, 1993:130). They are identifiable in the United States not by their boots (Doc Martens) but by .357 Smith & Wessons and beer. Hamm associates this with the view that skinheads in the United States represent a subculture "whose rituals und symbols reveal a basic truth about the values of society at large" (Hamm, 1993:215).

Very different types of perpetrators can be identified among the groups that have been responsible for violence against immigrants and dissidents in Germany. Willems et al. (1993:200–207) identify four of these types: a) the follower, b) the criminal youth ("thug" type), c) the xenophobe or ethnocentrist, and finally d) the ideologically motivated right-wing extremist type. These types differ recognizably in their political views and in their propensity to violence. There is a corresponding variation in the processes by which members join and leave the groups, and no clear patterns have yet been identified here (cf. also Bjørgo, 1998:234; Möller, 2000).

c. INTERACTION: OPPORTUNITY STRUCTURES.   Violence takes place in social situations that are determined by different power constellations within which perpetrators and victims (have to) act. These situations are typified by a specific fabric of interaction.

What Levin and McDevitt (1993) say about the American variants of hate-crime violence is also applicable to Europe in the context of the act of violence. In most cases, it involves excessive brutality: the victims have no personal contacts with the perpetrators, the victims are interchangeable, and the situations are such that the perpetrators have numerical superiority (cf. also Perry, 2001:29). The violence of organized groups or terrorist attacks, which is usually strategically planned, is structured differently: it generally takes an anonymous form, preferring arson or bombings to direct physical confrontation with the victims. The victims vary accordingly: thus the main targets of American militias are consistent with their hatred of government: federal officials, judges, district attorneys, etc.

In the European context, at least, xenophobic right-wing extremist violence by youth gangs generally takes place in the vicinity of where they live (Mentzel, 1998:311)—in other words, in a familiar environment. By contrast, the geographical location of subcultural violence is more likely to be linked to opportunities arising from organized musical events or drinking festivals, which means that the frequency of violence rises at weekends.

In general, these interaction dynamics have not yet been sufficiently systematically elucidated, and often have to be reconstructed from police records, resulting in problems of validity.

d. ESCALATION: THE DYNAMICS OF VIOLENCE.   One form of escalation is microsocial: within a limited context of interaction, violence intensifies to the point where victims are killed—in other words, acts of violence "run out of control," and the targets of the attacks are individually "dehumanized." In the mesosocial variant, by contrast, the escalation spills over onto the attacked group through the agency of labeling media (cf. Brosius & Esser, 1995) or the exceeding of thresholds.

Group "equipment" plays an important part in the practice/prevention or escalation/ de-escalation of violence (cf. Eckert and Willems in this volume). The availability of alcohol and/or music, e.g., skinhead concerts (Searchlight et al., 1999; Trüller, 1999), and rituals (cf. Lööw, 1998), all increase internal cohesion and provide functionalizable trigger factors to release the potential for violence. The new communications media (Schröder, 1995) provide improved opportunities for organization, mobilization, and mobility, and the possibility of international networking (e.g., in the case of skinheads, "Blood & Honour").

In the social and political environment, the greatest contribution made by right-wing extremist parties is the potential for organizational support. A society's elites also contribute to the legitimation of an ideology of inequality by the way in which they "grade" or value immigrants (for example, as "useful" or "useless") and so build up the potential encouragement of violent action.

Media reporting—especially of "successes"—on particular right-wing events, too, always serves to disseminate the positions of elites and confirms the status of the groups as factors to be taken seriously, which in turn may be propitious for escalation. In Germany in 1992/93, for example, reports in the mass media covering tragic arson attacks on asylum-seekers' hostels were rapidly followed by an increased number of similar attacks (cf. Koopmans, 1996:205). "First, the perpetrators learned from the media that violence was a promising approach to solving problems; then they learned that they could rely almost automatically on extensive media coverage. Almost by reflex, the media now pounced on any forms of violence by the right.... As a result, they gave this "new movement" a collective significance that invested it with an identity.... Since every copycat criminal wanted to be part of this new high-profile movement, and could even expect anonymous distinction, the reporting generated a high level of motivation for the perpetrators of violence" (Brosius & Esser, 1996:216). In his comparative survey of various empirical studies of the effects of the mass media, Weiss (1997) concluded that a particularly important part was played by the clearer definition of problems (for example in regard to asylum seekers).

The degree of dissemination can be explained within the framework of a threshold model (Lüdemann & Erzberger, 1994). This model serves to elucidate processes of transition between attitudes and collective acts of violence. The underlying concept is the assumption that different categories of incentives produce different effects on different subgroups within a collective. For example, because it is assumed with regard to the relatively small group of ringleaders that their actions will be dominated by the effects of internal stimuli (boosting of the ego, etc.), the assumption that applies to the numerically larger groups of followers and doubters is that their willingness to act violently is primarily the result of external stimuli, and thus does not take effect until certain thresholds have been exceeded. In particular, the subjective calculation of the likelihood of penalties seems to be a direct function of the number of persons already taking (violent) action, so that the willingness to engage in violence must also be regarded as dependent on majority and minority attitudes.

The patterns of attitudes and overt contrasting positions among the population determine the extent to which the groups derive potential motivation from them. Problems are caused by feedback and booster effects provided by some sectors of the population, for example in connection with conflicts over asylum seekers. They play a part in escalation and mobilization when the violent groups can see themselves as acting (as a "national vanguard") on behalf of silent groups among the population. Ultimately, the density of control exercised by government institutions is of central importance to the use of violence—either overreaction or underreaction can help to escalate the violence (cf. also Neidhardt, 1989). The main effect here is to change the cost and risk structures of violence. From the game theory standpoint, a successful advance guard eliminates the risks of action, so that even potentially violent groups that are wary of risk are then mobilized (cf. Willems, 1996:37 and Eckert and Willems in this volume).

The theory of "split delegitimization" in relation to the escalation of the use of right-wing extremist violence is relevant to the case of the United States, and to some extent Sweden also—particularly because its central targets there include not just alien groups, as is usually the case in Europe, but the state as well. Sprinzak's (1995) theory identifies three levels. The crisis of confidence is followed by a radicalization in the form of a conflict of legitimacy, in which the political system is called into question (because of "Zionist infiltration"). On the third level, the crisis of legitimation broadens to include every individual associated with the system, extending beyond depersonalization and dehumanization to include actual violence against such persons (branded as "traitors"), which can now be justified as a blow struck against the hated system (cf. also Grumke, 2001:208).

2. Contexts of Violence: Sociospatial Constellations

In addition to direct, destructive violence against alien or hated individuals (the particular preference of terrorist groups), the "struggle for territory" is of central significance to unorganized gangs, subcultural groups, and party political organizations. Demonstrations of power through violence in the situational context of the act of violence itself are now employed as means for exercising power over social spaces and creating "zones of fear" (no-go-areas).

An examination of the distribution of such violence in social spaces—meaning specific locations, blocks, districts, or towns—reveals considerable international variations. These are partly a reflection of the settlement structures of different societies. Thus, it is no surprise that Bjørgo concludes that most attacks in the Scandinavian countries occur in small towns and communities (1998:139). Willems et al. (1993) similarly recorded that the majority of attacks on foreigners in Germany took place in smaller towns, especially in the former East Germany, which in 1998 accounted for only 21 percent of the national population but some 46 percent of violent acts of this type. By 1999, the latter figure had risen to 51 percent (cf. Bundesamt für Verfassungsschutz, 2001).

One explanation is that immigrants are more alien to such areas, combined with social and cultural homogeneity. It should also be borne in mind that the pattern of human settlement in eastern Germany is very much dominated by small towns, so that these findings could be said to be structurally preprogrammed. In North Rhine-Westphalia (comparable in size of population to the whole of East Germany) about 60 percent of acts of violence in 1996 were committed in cities of more than 100,000 population. There has still been no explanation of this phenomenon, though a critical factor is probably the democratic quality of the political interaction fabric (cf. section II, Fig. II-2-11.3) in the various towns and communities and the extent to which a "reflexive and reactive urban society" confronts the activities of the right-wing extremist groups in the social spaces (cf. in the case of Sweden Blomgren, 1999)—or whether the institutions are "blank" (Heitmeyer, 1999:72).

In the United Kingdom, too, the public space has become a battleground orchestrated by the far right, resulting in sporadic riots. One tactic adopted by the right-wing extremists in urban districts settled by immigrants (parts of Birmingham, Leeds, and Bradford in 2001) is to provoke the discharge of the latent tensions between ethnic groups (usually the result of insufficient integration on the part of younger immigrants), to maneuver the immigrants into violent confrontations with the police, and (with the assistance of the media) to display publicly their potential for violence (cf. also Cantle Report, 2001).

Another variant is to be found in France, where the areas of violent struggle for territory and recognition develop within the distinctive structure of the monotonous *banlieues* (suburbs), dominated by nonideological right-wing extremist violence (cf. Wieviorka et al., 1992; Dubet, 1997; Dubet in this volume).

In Italy's case, a different social space has been playing a critical role for some years now. It comprises the football grounds of the big professional clubs, where displays of racist and, in some cases, right-wing extremist ideology are staged, together with demonstrations of violent domination by *ultras*, groups of hooligans with a particular taste for violence (cf. Podaliri & Balestri, 1998; di Roversi & Balestri, 1999).

In the United States, with its numerous right-wing extremist groups, the picture is again different. These groups are not uniformly distributed across the country: the Ku Klux Klan, for example, is active in the South, while neo-Nazi groups are mainly to be found in the Midwest. Another characteristic feature is that neo-Nazi groups and skinheads are more likely to be encountered in the major cities, while far-right religious groups are active in rural and small-town settings. Prospects for the mobilization of large groups are less good in America, but the danger lies in the high level of mobilization offered by a shared core of ideological beliefs, the collective identity of the groups, and the availability of "binders" in the form of conspiracy theories and access to weapons (cf. Weinberg, 1998; Grumke, 2001).

The escalation dynamics evident in the situational context also exists in the sociospatial context. Whereas there are generally few participants in actual violence in the situational context, the situation with social spaces is different. This, too, is where mobilization effects become important. The processes of escalation and mobilization may occupy a short, intensive period of time, as in the case of the British riots, which take place in the full spotlight of media coverage, but they may also take place at indeterminate periods. One example of the latter process could be seen in Germany—and especially in the East—during the early 1990s (cf. Heitmeyer, 1999:67–71).

In these interaction sequences, which are associated with the expansion of power at every level of escalation, it is possible to identify four central stages, in each of which the relevant actor groups—the media, civil society groups, the state authorities (cf. section II, Fig. II-2-11.3)—differ in their respective relevance as factors that may foster or prevent the success of right-wing extremist violence.

- The first stage is generally *provocation gains*, meaning that the groups have to establish themselves as factors to be taken seriously. The media play a crucial part in this process, but low-density control is also propitious, as is the effect of liberal legislation.
- The second stage comprises *clearance gains*, meaning that groups which are unpopular or the target of hate are forced to leave their homes (for example, asylum seekers).
- The third stage is *territorial gains*, meaning that the exercise of power becomes visible in public places such as shopping malls or railroad station forecourts. The effect here is the establishment of "zones of fear" that no longer affect foreigners alone but also some segments of the "indigenous" population.
- Finally, the fourth stage is the establishment of new acceptances. This involves *normality gains*, meaning that the marginalization of certain groups is no longer perceived as a problem. This may come about because actual violence becomes less frequent at this stage, since some sections of the population are now completely absent from the areas concerned.

Different degrees of danger characterize each of these different stages. Clearance gains mainly affect selected individuals and groups. Territorial gains threaten the whole climate of public opinion. And by the time of the normality gains, if not before, the democratic culture of a society, together with questions of power and dominance, has been called into question.

The great importance attached to the local or regional space as an opportunity to "fight for the streets" is also apparent in the quantitatively recorded protest data (1985–1992) on right-wing extremists in Germany (cf. Rucht, 1996), and contrasts with the state targets favored by their equivalents in the United States, for example, or some variants in Sweden.

The full picture—how the pattern of violence escalates situationally at the relevant locations, how cyclical mobilization effects come about which result in waves of violence and eventually result in these stages of expansion of power—has not been fully explained. Conflict theory approaches, for example, no longer apply where the identified reason for violence ceases to exist, while movement theory approaches have so far been confronted by the problem of classifying the various alternative forms of right-wing extremist violence as a coherent "movement," so as to enable the theoretically complex assumptions to be applied to the recorded phenomena.

3.   Contexts of Violence: Regional and National Dimensions of Violence

Following the discussion of the dynamics of violence in situational and sociospatial contexts, the next stage of the analysis is concerned with current situations and trends in
national and regional contexts (Western Europe, Eastern Europe, and the United States).

3.1.   THE WESTERN EUROPEAN CONTEXT

a) Attitudes as a Background to Legitimation.   The underlying concept adopted here for
the analysis of right-wing extremist violence is the assumption that such violence cannot
be viewed in isolation from social trends and the patterns of attitudes existing among the
population (cf. Fig. II-2-11.3). This, then, calls for a presentation of the prevalence of
those attitudes that are propitious to racist or xenophobic positions and reflect the quality
of interethnic relations. They are important because these subjects are among the central
political areas of the far-right spectrum and the votes of the population are used as potential legitimations for violence.

To date, there has been no thorough research using a comparative approach and
clearly defined predictors. In addition, for methodological reasons, only limited conclusions are possible regarding trends in the countries of the European Union, referring to the
dates at which the three Eurobarometer surveys were carried out. In 1989, only 37 percent
of those questioned shared the view that there were "too many" representatives of ethnic
minorities or people of different nationalities and cultures in Europe, but by 1997 this
figure had risen to 41 percent. In 1997, moreover, about 33 percent of people classified
themselves as "quite racist" or "very racist" (cf. Table II-2-11.1). At the same time, the
number of people regarding the fight against racism as important is gradually declining
(from 36 percent in 1989 to 22 percent in 1997), which certainly fits the pattern and can be
interpreted as creeping normalization of xenophobic attitudes. For the period 1997–2000
(the third survey), Thalhammer et al. recorded a contradictory trend: "On the one hand,
many EU citizens favor policies designed to improve the coexistence of majorities and
minorities. Support for such policies has increased over the past three years. On the other
hand, a majority of Europeans have voiced concern over minorities because they fear
minorities are threatening social peace and welfare; this percentage increased over the
period 1997–2000. People are worried about unemployment, a loss of social welfare and a
drop in educational standards. A small, but relevant minority of Europeans feels personally disturbed by the existence of minorities" (2001:11).

The increasing insecurity and in many cases, xenophobic attitudes (cf. Table II-2-
11.1) provide an underlying legitimation for violence by right-wing groups, as they see
themselves as the self-appointed "enforcers of the popular will." At the same time, this
association is not automatic, because attitudes among the population can be channeled
through political representation.

The first point that becomes apparent here is that the spectrum of discourse, membership, and electoral choices in Europe has broadened, ranging from right-wing populism
to right-wing extremist variants. This can point to a basis in the attitudes of the population and, in some cases, to influence on government policy or participation in government. This is particularly true of right-wing populist parties, such as Austria's *Freiheitliche
Partei* (Freedom Party—FPÖ) and the party alliances in Italy: *Forza Italia*, *Lega Nord*
(Northern League), and *Allianza Nationale* (National Alliance). The emergence of the
Fremskrittsparti (Progress Party—FrP) in Norway and the *Dansk Folkeparti* (Danish
People's Party—DF) in Denmark influence the activities of government, either directly

Table II-2-11.1. Results of the Eurobarometer Survey

	1997			2000		
	tend to agree	tend to disagree	don't know	tend to agree	tend to disagree	don't know
Greece	66	27	8	77	19	3
Danmark	60	33	8	60	33	7
Belgium	59	31	10	56	35	9
France	46	45	10	51	41	8
Germany	41	37	22	46	34	19
Portugal*	45	38	17	45	41	14
Netherlands	34	59	7	45	44	11
Austria	45	37	18	44	39	17
Ireland	16	61	23	42	43	14
Luxembourg	29	57	14	40	47	13
Italy	28	56	16	38	46	16
Spain	27	55	19	34	56	11
United Kingdom	33	50	18	32	48	20
Finland	24	67	9	32	61	8
Sweden	21	65	15	24	66	10
EU	37	47	16	42	43	15

* Results are not comparable with the results from the other countries.

Source: Thalhammer et al., 2001:53.

through success at the ballot box or indirectly through the counteractivities of government to prevent such successes.

Secondly, however, electoral systems can minimize the direct influence of these right-wing populist or extremist groups and parties on the activities of government, as happens in the United Kingdom (in the case of the British National Party) and in France. A third factor is the degree of fragmentation existing within the party political camp across the range from populist to extremist. This is particularly the case in Germany with its NPD, *Republikaner*, and *Deutsche Volksunion* (German People's Union), and is also apparent in the divisions within the *Front National* (National Front—FN) in France.

The *increases* in xenophobic attitudes and the successes of these parties in attracting attention to themselves, gaining votes, and in some cases gaining power, are interpreted in various ways. At the heart of these interpretations are approaches based on modernization and deprivation theories, which are linked to research on political culture. Thus, Perrineau (1988) explains the success of the FN in France as a "political echo of urban anomie" based on feelings of deprivation (2001:199ff.), which produce a marginalizing national populism as a response to headlong processes of change. In a multifactor approach to explaining the trend in Austria, Ulram (2001:221f.) emphasizes both the syndrome of an authoritarian disenchantment with the system and an "anxious materialism," meaning the fear of loss of status, as important elements. In the case of Germany, the integration/disintegration dynamics and experiences and anxieties associated with it are emphasized by Heitmeyer (1994), Heitmeyer et al. (1995), and Anhut and Heitmeyer (2000), these factors having become particularly apparent as a result of developments in eastern Germany—the former GDR. Other authors, such as Willems et al. (1993), consider relative deprivation theory in combination with aspects of conflict theory to be particularly effective. Betz (2001:168) attributes the rise of radically right-wing populist groupings since the 1980s to the conflicting influences of neoliberal offensive (with its disintegrative social trends), dissatisfaction with es-

TABLE II-2-11.2.   Lethal violence[1], based on police statistics vs. other sources

	1995	1996	1997	1998	1999	Total
Austria	4[2]/4	0/0	1/0	0/1	0/0	5/5
Belgium	.../...	.../...	.../...	.../2[3]	.../...	.../2
Denmark	.../...	.../...	.../...	.../...	.../...	.../...
Finland[4]	1/...	0/...	0/...	0/...	0/...	1/...
France	8/...	0/...	1/...	0/1[5]	1/...	10/1
Germany	3/45[6]	6/20	9/14	0/7	0/7	18/93
Greece	0/...	0/1[7]	0/...	0/1[7]	0/...	.../2
Ireland	.../...	.../...	.../...	.../...	.../...	0/...
Italy	0/...	0/...	0/...	0/1[8]	0/...	0/1
Luxembourg	0/...	0/...	0/...	0/...	0/...	0/...
Netherlands	0/...	0/...	1[9]/...	0/1[10]	.../...	1/1
Portugal	1/...	0/...	0/...	0/...	0/...	1/...
Spain	0/...	0/...	0/1[11]	0/1[12]	0/...	0/2
Sweden	4/...	0/...	0/...	0/...	5[13]/...	9/...
UK	1/1	2/3	4/2	3/4	6/6	16/16[14]

[1] Includes homicide, murder, manslaughter, and assaults, arson and police violence leading to death. The first number denotes police data and the second NGO data.
[2] Four Roma were killed with an explosive. In 1998, death of an asylum seeker arising out of confrontation with the police at a frontier crossing point (CARF, 1999:1).
[3] CARF: A Nigerian deportee suffocated, and a Nigerian asylum seeker died after being refused medical treatment.
[4] Pekonen et al. (1999:16). Case of a racist nature.
[5] CARF: Death of an asylum seeker arising out of confrontation at a frontier crossing-point in France.
[6] Rechte Gewalt. Der Tagespiegel Online and Antirassistische Initiative Berlin (2001). In 2000, the police data included 3 cases, and Tagespiegel data 7 cases of right-wing, xenophobic or anti-Semitic violence.
[7] Greek Helsinki Monitor (2000:10–11). Two Roms, A. Mouratis, and angelos Celal, were killed by policemen in 1996 and 1998.
[8] CARF: Undocumented Moroccan worker dies in disputed circumstances in a Sicilian reception centre.
[9] Police data include homicide cases (doodslaag) with racist, right-wing extremist or anti-Semitic motivation; van Donselaar (2000:29).
[10] CARF: An Algerian shot dead by the police in an asylum centre in Nijmenen in disputed circumstances.
[11] Police data include homicide (homicidios)/other agency data include lethal violence by the extreme right on immigrants, other 10 victims were mostly young native men (Instituto de Migraciones y Servicios Sociales 2001).
[12] CARF: A Basque football fan stabbed to death by skinheads in Madrid.
[13] Swedish Security Police 1995 (App. 1) and 1999:19. Cases of a xenophobic or racist nature in the category majority against minority, and racist, anti-Semitic and ideological crimes linked to the White Power movement.
[14] IRR (2000a) documented 16 murders, and Home Office reported a total of 16 homicides with a racist element.
Source: Virtanen, 2001:20.

tablished political parties, and an antiliberal countermovement to preserve national identity. He attributes the situation to political conflicts in an age of social fragmentation (Betz, 1994:169). The trends and processes identified in the copious literature provide the political, sociocultural, and economic background for right-wing extremist violence.

b. Dimensions and Extent of Violence. There are significant problems with forming any soundly based assessment of the extent of the violence. Even at the descriptive level, there are national variations in concepts and theory. For example, Witte (1995:490) points out that activities are described in the United Kingdom as "racial violence," in Germany and the Netherlands as "right-wing extremist violence," in Germany as "neo-Nazi violence" and "antiforeigner violence," in Scandinavia as "anti-immigrant violence," and in France and

TABLE II-2-11.3. **Violent assaults against a person**[1]

	1995	1996	1997	1998	1999	Total
Austria[2]	189	99	105	109	212	714
Belgium	...	...	...	...	...	...
Denmark[3]	...	...	...	26	33	59
Finland	...	...	75	157	156	388
France[4]	41	32	36	27	36	172
Germany[5]	899	837	1,104	1,005	1,040	4,885
Greece	...	...	...	...	...	...
Ireland	...	...	...	...	...	...
Italy[6]	7	30	11	3	0	51
Luxembourg	0	0	0	0	0	0
Netherlands[7]	13	19	36	41	...	109
Portugal	...	...	...	...	...	...
Spain[8]	29	22	26	27	44	148
Sweden[9]	332	458	380	564	584	2,318
UK[10]	...	3,014	...	...	6,962	9,976

[1] Includes aggravated assault, assault, bodily injury, attempted aggravated assault, attempted murder and attempted manslaughter. The data is mainly based on the offences reported to the police.
[2] Includes data on violent assaults (*tätliche Angriffe, Anzeigen nach § 283 StGB*), bodily injury (*Körperverletzungen*) and damage to property (*Sachbeschädigung; Sonstige Anzeigen StGB*).
[3] Includes violence to a person reported to the police. In 1999, 15 cases out of 33 lead to charges.
[4] Includes data on violent assaults (*violence*) with racist, xenophobic or anti-Semitic motivation.
[5] Includes data on violent assaults with bodily injury (*Körperverletzungen*), attempted homicide with a proven or suspected right-extremist, xenophobic or anti-Semitic background.
[6] Includes court convictions based on racial grounds.
[7] Includes assaults (*mishandeling*) with racist, right-wing extremist or anti-Semitic motivation.
[8] Includes assaults with and without bodily injuries (*ataques c/incendio and lesiones*).
[9] Includes assault (*misshandel*), aggravated assault, and attempted murder of a xenophobic or racist nature, clear and doubtful incidents in the category majority against minority, and racist, anti-Semitic, and ideological offences linked to the White Power movement.
[10] Includes racially motivated violent assaults in 1996, and racially aggravated other woulding and common assault in England and Wales since 1 April 1999.
Source: Virtanen, 2001:24.

TABLE II-2-11.4.   Racial incidents recorded by the police in England and Wales

1984	1985	1986	1987	1988	1989	1990	1991	1992	1993	1993/ 1994	1994/ 1995	1995/ 1996
1,329	1,626	4,519	2,965	4,383	5,044	6,339	7,782	7,734	9,218	10,997	11,878	12,199

Source: Bowling 1998:6.

the Netherlands as "racist violence." In the United States, the term "right-wing extremist violence" is also current, though the most popular term is "hate crime." These different uses of terminology have a profound impact on the reporting of the extent of violence in the various countries. It therefore seems advisable to use the broadest term, enmity violence, so as not to exclude particular groups of victims (cf. section II, Fig. II-2-11.2). This extension, however, involves a new set of problems. The recording of right-wing extremist violence is extremely unsatisfactory, because its extent is critically affected not only by variations in definition but also by the institutions recording it. One significant reflection of this is the compilation of officially recorded incidents of racial violence. Both the sources and the variants of violence vary greatly, from bodily assault through bombings to lethal violence. These reporting difficulties are apparent again when it comes to reporting the number of fatalities caused by this violence. For example, in the period from 1989 through 1999 in Germany, official figures tell us that twenty-three people, mostly of foreign origin, were killed by acts of right-wing extremist violence. However, studies by journalists and researchers record over ninety victims (cf. Jansen, 2000; Bundesministerium des Innern and Bundesministerium der Justiz, 2001).The official count failed to record homeless people kicked to death by skinhead groups, for example, because there was allegedly no apparent political

TABLE II-2-11.5.   Racist violence and right-wing extremist violence in the Netherlands, 1996–2000

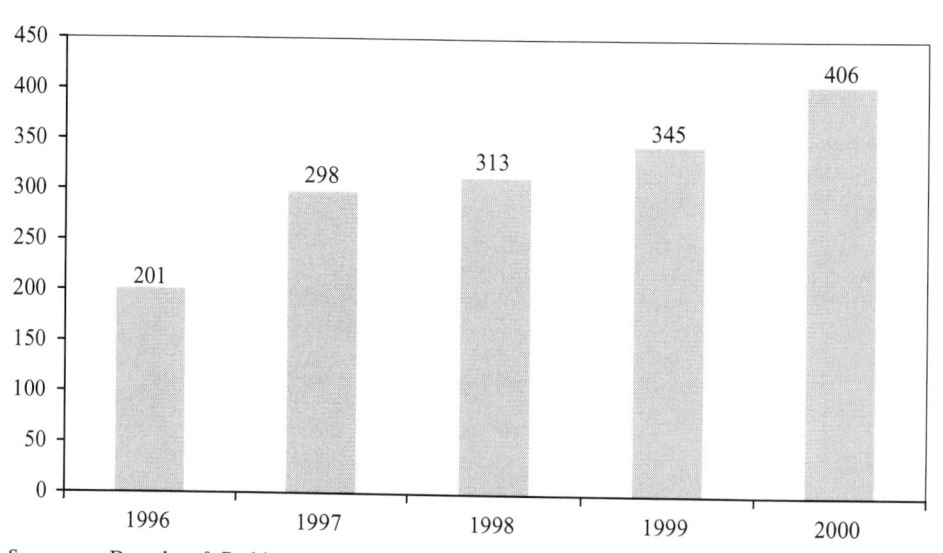

Source: van Donselaar & Rodrigues, 2001:12.

motive. Thus, the reporting of racially motivated or right-wing extremist violence is confronted by serious problems. These are also expressed in the *European Statistical Atlas on Racial Violence 1995–2000*, first produced by Virtanen (2001). The author rightly emphasizes the great difficulties of comparisons between the fifteen states of the European Community, and is obliged to annotate the statistics in some detail. He cautions the reader against attaching too much importance to the differences shown in the tables below recording instances of lethal violence (cf. Table II-2-11.2) and violent attacks (cf. Table II-2-11.3).

The figures for recorded incidents in England and Wales (cf. Table II-2-11.4) again give a different picture from Virtanen's study (cf. Table II-2-11.3), depending on the category recorded. They also document the continuous increase in such incidents.

The Netherlands provides another example that clearly illustrates the problems. Virtanen (2001) arrived at the results of his international comparative study on the basis of official data. However, the results (Table II-2-11.5) presented from an academic perspective by van Donselaar and Rodrigues (2001:12) show a greater frequency and more continuous rise; the authors add a note to the effect that these figures represent only the tip of the iceberg.

If France is added, as a third example (Table II-2-11.6), the consequences of a re-

TABLE II-2-11.6. **Racist acts and violence in France**

Year	Threats	Acts	Injuries	Deaths
1980	20	35	10	—
1981	23	23	2	—
1982	5	43	11	—
1983	96	68	33	5
1984	102	53	16	4
1985	98	70	29	5
1986	95	54	11	3
1987	80	46	31	3
1988	135	64	51	3
1989	237	54	31	1
1990	283	51	35	1
1991	318	52	14	—
1992	141	32	17	—
1993	134	37	33	—
1994	171	36	28	2
1995	445	19	2	6
1996	206	9	4	0
1997	121	6	2	1
1998	91	8	4	0
1999	89	13	7	0
2000	119	16	4	0

Source: Commission nationale, 1996:433–436; Commission nationale, 2001:28–29, updated by the author from 1995.

strictive choice of terminology become apparent. In view of the circumstances of violence in the French suburbs, in particular, the official statistics seem to be distorted (cf. also Witte, 1995:493 and Bjørgo in this volume).

The recording problem here is that, in general, government sources underestimate the extent of such activities, if they are recorded at all, while nongovernmental organizations (which include victim organizations) usually return higher figures. This rule also applies to the comparable problem of hate crimes in the United States (Perry, 2001:13).

Academic studies cannot correct these distortions satisfactorily, because they usually depend on figures recorded by the police and the counting methods used to produce those figures; to date, there has been no sophisticated, comparative, and independent research into the gray areas of right-wing extremist violence or regular victim studies. Until such gaps in research have been closed, comparisons will remain contentious. This also applies to the study by Koopmans (1996), who, in his comparative analysis of right-wing extremist and racist violence in eight European countries, reached the conclusion that Germany was not a "special case." But Germany is in the group with the highest rates of violence; Switzerland and the United Kingdom, too, produce comparable data for the period studied, 1988–1993 (for a critical view, cf. Bjørgo in this volume).

Apart from these problems of comparison, the risks for the potential victim groups of the ideology of inequality are especially great when *waves* of xenophobic violence sweep through societies. Merkl (1995:98f.) has identified phases of this kind in Western Europe: France in 1961, 1973, 1982 and during the later 1980s; Britain in the early 1970s and early 1980s; the Netherlands in the 1970s and early 1980s and in 1992; Sweden in 1989–1991 and Germany in 1991–1993.

The circumstances governing the times at which such waves begin to peak are far from clear. In addition to the cyclical pattern of the waves, there is also evidence of a combined pattern of wave movement and continuous increase—i.e., after a wave, the level of violence remains at a higher level than it was before the wave, or continues to rise. Germany provides one example of this kind of pattern. The rapid increase in violence during the early 1990s coincided both with the sharp rise in the number of asylum seekers in Germany (from some 74,000 in 1985 to approximately 440,000 in 1992), and with the reunification of the two German states and societies and the pressure for social modernization this generated, especially in the east. The data given below (cf. Table II-2-11.7) reflect this pattern of violence. They make it clear that the level of right-wing extremist crimes (propaganda offenses and violence) has risen continuously since the end of the 1980s.

After the asylum problem was "solved" by restrictive legislation with high barriers to access, the rate of violence began to rise again from 1996, and here again the way in which these data were recorded means that they must be treated with considerable caution. The cyclical trend curve can also be used to show the scope of different approaches to an explanation. What is striking is that the trend shows two continuous increases: both rates of violence and propaganda/incitement offenses. Another unusual factor is the extreme increase between 1991 and 1993. At least three approaches can provide a credible explanation here.

- The long-term increase in right-wing extremist violence can be explained by the *modernization theory* approach, because the rapid pace of social change and the inbuilt experiences and fears of social disintegration are particularly significant here. They are compensated for by the expression of ideologies of inequality directed at specific groups, which in turn provide important preconditions for the legitimation and use of violence. The increase in violence since 1996, which,

TABLE II-2-11.7.   Absolute changes in right-wing extremist crimes and acts of violence in Germany

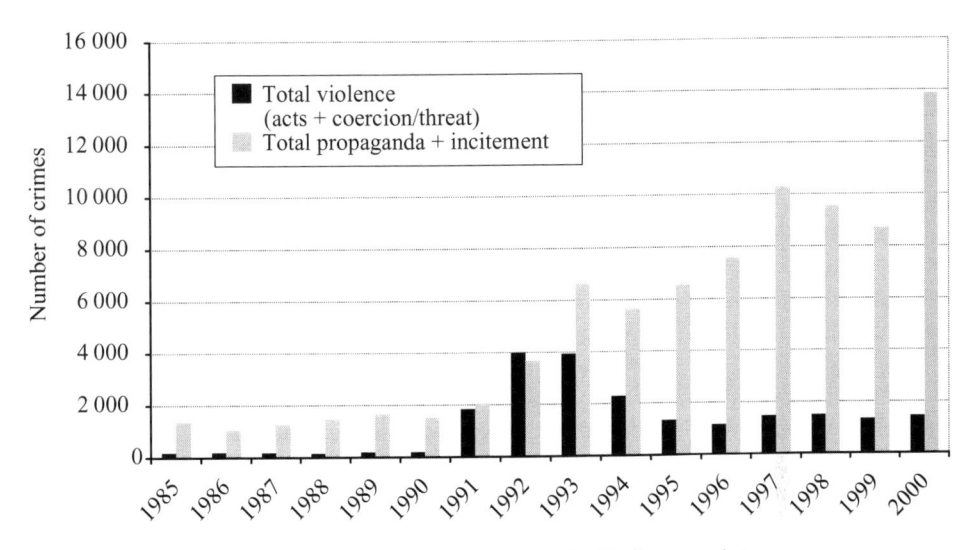

Source: Own calculations based on the annual reports of Deutscher Verfassungsschutz.

incidentally, was associated with a renewed increase in xenophobic political attitudes after years of decline, also went hand in hand with a proportionately higher increase in the rate of violence (per 100,000 population) in eastern Germany, where the duress of modernization, and fears and experiences of professional and social disintegration, were especially pronounced.

- The *conflict theory approach* considers the increase in violence as the expression of conflicts associated with immigration and, especially, the rise in the number of asylum seekers, which resulted in problems in cities, urban districts, and communities. This assumption seems self-evident, but it applies only to a very brief period, because the decrease in numbers of asylum seekers and the introduction of restrictive legislation saw an initial decrease in the frequency of violence because the alleged cause—the large numbers of asylum seekers—no longer existed. The frequency of violence began to rise again in 1996, and indeed climbed to a far higher level than before the period of increased demand for asylum. It follows that the explanatory scope of the conflict theory approach is confined to a brief period.

- In addition to the cyclical pattern of violence, there has been a generally continuous increase in the frequency of propaganda and incitement offenses among the public. From the *political culture theory* standpoint, this means that right-wing extremist activities are meeting with an increasingly sympathetic response from the general population, and their frequency increases because some sectors of the public are no longer loyal to democratic parties and have lost confidence in the democratic system.

In the case of Germany, it is clear that the scope of individual analytical approaches is limited, so that a reasonable analysis of these trends requires a combination of theories. Such combinations are themselves controversial, however. If, for example, multilevel approaches, beginning with the macrolevel and referring to conditions of structural tension, are applied, the problem arises that not all those people who are exposed to those situations think in right-wing extremist terms or become violent. The question is, then, how these tensions become manifest in individual dissatisfaction. This results in the use of relative deprivation approaches, the intention being to use reference group theories to explain why certain individuals turn against foreigners. Rational choice theories should then help to explain violence, assuming that the individuals expect to derive a benefit from acts of violence that will result in the reduction of their dissatisfaction and improved ability to cope with situations of structural tension (cf. Bundesministerium des Innern and Bundesministerium der Justiz, 2001:264). The question of group violence, with its incalculable intra-group-dynamic processes, cannot be convincingly explained with the aid of rational choice theories, because violent situations generate highly emotionalized dynamics of their own, which is hard to control by rational means, but is more dependent on uncontrollable situational effects, especially when alcohol is involved.

To summarize, the following conclusions can be drawn for Western Europe regarding the *relationship* between attitudes among the population in various countries, membership and electoral successes of right-wing populist parties, and right-wing extremist violence:

- A violent form of right-wing extremism is more likely to develop where there is no political representation through political parties or channeling mechanisms in the form of electoral successes at national level (Koopmans, 1996). This applies to Sweden, the United Kingdom, Germany, and some militias in the United States. On the other hand, it does not apply to Austria, where a right-wing populist alternative is available, or to France, which has right-wing extremist political parties. In France, the FN has an ambivalent relationship to violence. On the one hand, it avoids direct incitement to violence; on the other, it purveys "hate speech" (Wieviorka, 1999:40). Italy is to some extent an exception to these trends, as not only are right-wing populist parties successful there (cf. Betz, 1994; Biorcio, 2001), but violent, racist hooligans have been becoming a more significant factor for some years.

- Right-wing extremist violence can exist or develop without electoral successes for the far right, but can never survive without xenophobic and right-wing populist moods and attitudes among the population. Hypotheses that reassuringly refer to the fact that democratic parties are effective because they integrate groups of individuals that hold such attitudes are to be treated with caution. Findings from research into political culture have for some time been suggesting that party loyalty is on the wane (Decker, 2000:329), and electoral support (tactical in some cases) for democratic parties may go hand in hand with attitudes of enmity (toward immigrants, for example) in everyday life.

- The greater the level of violence perpetrated by right-wing extremist groups, the lower is the political weight attaching to legitimate power-sharing. As a result, we see not only spectacular cycles of violence but also instances of creeping "normalization" of violence against selected groups, associated with situational personal power over weaker individuals (usually of foreign origin) and/or short-lived illegitimate territorial power (cf. section IV. 2).

- Political *marginalization* of right-wing extremist parties and groups produces variable results. In some cases it leads to *fragmentation* of the extreme right (cf. Camus, 2000), as in Germany, while in others it may lead to *radicalization*, as in Sweden, which manifests itself in political murders, incitements to murder on the

Internet, and the procurement of arms, which must all be considered preliminaries to right-wing terrorism.

3.2. The Eastern European Context.   This context can be described only briefly, because, for ideological reasons, no research into right-wing extremism took place during the existence of the Eastern Bloc. It was only after the collapse of the Communist camp that nationalistic and even right-wing extremist parties began to come more into public view in the various countries of the former Eastern Bloc. It should be recalled here that there was a very diverse tradition of anti-Semitism in Poland, and also that it existed on an organized basis in Hungary and the Czech Republic. Hockenos (1993) has analyzed the violent forms (especially skinhead violence in the Czech Republic). Their numbers are also increasing (6,200 in 2001, representing an approximately 25 percent increase over the previous year), as is the number of crimes committed by them. Apart from propaganda offenses, the violence—in contrast to other European countries—is directed primarily against the Sinti and Roma minorities (cf. Reemtsma, 1993; Kürti, 1998).

The main reason for this is that although there is virtually no immigration into those countries, there are still national minorities, who are increasingly becoming the targets of violence in the course of advancing liberalization, on the one hand, and the relaxation of government control, on the other. Here again, the modernization of society is changing the social structures and exerting considerable pressure to secure social status and property, which results in hostility toward weaker groups that may escalate into violence.

3.3. Mobilization Potentials and Right-Wing Extremist Violence in the United States Context.   Patterns of development in the United States are extremely complex. Taking the same starting point as was used for the European situation, attitudes among the population, reveals contradictory trends. The studies undertaken by Schuman et al. (1997) provide evidence, in long-term trends from the early 1960s to the mid-1990s, of a dramatic change for the better in "racial attitudes," for example as regards the exclusion of blacks from residential districts or marriage between black and white.

At the same time, the "hate crime" data gathered between 1991 and 1998 show a variable but significant increase (cf. Table II-2-11.8), no reasons to explain this being supplied. It is not clear which groups are responsible for such crimes, or whether they can be considered part of the right-wing extremist camp at all. It is also unclear whether the recorded rise is based on greater awareness or an actual increase in incidents. Another point to bear in mind here is that reports from official sources (such as the FBI's UCR project), as in Europe, produce lower figures than those quoted by private agencies (cf. Perry, 2001:13).

The data given in Table II-2-11.8 show that there is potential for both mobilization and action in the United States, some of which is absorbed within rightist political institutions that are integrated into the political system. This also explains why the extreme right in the United States has remained relatively weak in numbers.

Politically, the American extreme right is motivated by the ideologies of inequality mentioned earlier (cf. section II, Fig. II-2-11.2). Racism and anti-Semitism are prominent and are supplemented by religious classifications. On the other hand, there are overlaps with the extreme exaltation of national values—an extreme form of ethnocentrism, as it were. This ideological mindset, which uses the "Jewish enemy" as the seed of the crystal and indulges in biological racism (for the salvation of the white race), is associated with an objective that unites many groups: the enemy is the state, as an organization under Zionist

TABLE II-2-11.8. Hate crime by bias motivation (1991–1998) in the United States

	1991	1992	1993	1994	1995	1996	1997	1998
Race	2,963 (62.3%)	4,025 (60.8%)	4,732 (62.4%)	3,545 (59.8%)	4,831 (60.8%)	5,396 (61.6%)	5,898 (59.9%)	5,360 (58.3%)
Ethnicity	450 (9.5%)	669 (10.1%)	697 (9.2%)	638 (10.8%)	814 (10.2%)	940 (10.7%)	1,083 (11.0%)	919 (10.0%)
Religion	917 (19.3%)	1,162 (17.5%)	1,298 (17.1%)	1,062 (18.0%)	1,277 (16.1%)	1,461 (16.0%)	1,483 (15.1%)	1,475 (16.0%)
Sexual orientation	425 (8.9%)	767 (11.6%)	860 (11.3%)	685 (11.5%)	1,019 (12.8%)	1,016 (11.6%)	1,375 (14.0%)	1,439 (15.7%)

Original source: Federal Bureau of Investigation, 1992, 1993, 1994, 1995, 1996, 1997, 1998, 1999.
Source: Perry, 2001:15 (only the main categories from the original table have been reproduced).

control (Zionist Occupied Government—ZOG), which must be fought with every weapon that hatred and violence can offer. Conspiracy theories act as a binding and escalating factor. As a result, it is unsurprising that some groups have declared "war" upon the state and its institutions (as with the Oklahoma City bombing of 1995) (cf. Kaplan & Weinberg, 1998:59ff.). They benefit from the fact that the legal obstacles to such operations are significantly lower than in Europe, and the cult of bearing arms forms part of the normal set of standards of American society. Kaplan and Weinberg (1998:63) therefore adopt the view that no other Western democracy is confronted with the same level of violent threat as that posed by American right-wing extremist groups, to government institutions in particular, but also to banks, hospitals, and members of ethnic or religious minorities.

Whether this appraisal is justified depends both on the quality of the individual groups and on their numerical strengths. There is no clarity at all on this, however, as there are no government authorities to record them (comparable to, for example, the Verfassungsschutz in Germany). Information from private monitoring institutions is contradictory and often based on estimates.

The Southern Poverty Law Center (SPLC Klanwatch Project) regularly publishes data on trends (cf. George & Wilcox, 1996). In 1999, those data showed 457 registered active "hate groups," including Christian Identity, neo-Nazi groups, the Ku Klux Klan, and skinheads (cf. also Perry, 2001). In the same year, 1999, the SPLC also recorded 217 active "patriot groups," of which 68 were classified as militias, the divisions between right-wing extremist and "ultrapatriotic" attitudes often being fluid (cf. George & Wilcox, 1996). Overall, the authorities assume that both potential and active numbers are underestimated—one example of this problem would be the group Aryan Nations, for which numbers of local adherents cannot be recorded.

More important than the numerical trends, which cannot be satisfactorily clarified (cf. Levin and McDevitt, 1999:97 and McDevitt and Williamson in this volume) is the question of the groups' attitude to violence. The analysis by Grumke (2001:214) provides an informative overview here (cf. Table II-2-11.9).

The conclusion is clear: violence as a political means is consistently either accepted or openly endorsed by all nine types of right-wing extremist organization studied (Grumke, 2001:213). Violence is often perceived here as a remedy and a last resort in the battle for the fate of the white race.

TABLE II-2-11.9. Acceptance of violence among American right-wing extremists

	CJJ/AN	LPCC	NSDAP/AO	NA	WAR	WCOTC	Skin-heads	Militias	KKK
Violence as a political means	+	–	+	+/++	++	++	++	+	+/++
Oklahoma City bombing	+	–	n/a	+	++	++	n/a	–/+	–/+
Aryan Revolution	+/++	+	+	+/++	++	++	+/++	+	+

Key ++ = openly endorsed, + = accepted, – = rejected,
n/a = no answer or no reliable finding

Organizations
CJJC/AN	Church of Jesus Christ-Christian and Aryan Nations
LPCC	LaPorte Church of Christ
NSDAP/AO	German National Socialist Party/*Auslands-Organisation*
NA	National Alliance
WAR	White Aryan Resistance
WCOTC	World Church of the Creator
Skinheads	
Militias	
KKK	Ku Klux Klan

Source: Grumke, 2001:214.

On reviewing trends within the right-wing extremist spectrum in the United States, there are three aspects to be discussed. First, does a Euro-American connection seem likely? Kaplan and Weinberg (1998:195) estimate that links have been intensified via the Internet (cf. also Bös, 2001). Contact points include the "Thule network" in Germany and "Stormfront" and "Voice of Freedom" in the United States. There are ideological barriers to be overcome in some cases, because the "American way of life" is seen by some European right-wing extremists as precisely the kind of decadence against which their own "national" struggle is supposed to be directed. On the other hand, the hatred of Jewish influence in society and government is an important connecting link in the chain of ideological networking.

The second question is one of political significance. Individual studies have shown that the mobilization potential existing in the United States for an ethnocentrically oriented extreme right (cf. Minkenberg, 1998:168–205) "is of little benefit to the proviolence, openly racist, antisystem and ritualistic extreme right" (Grumke, 2001:81). But when there are no prospects of expressing fundamental opposition by infiltrating the mainstream, so that no opportunities exist for gaining access to the mechanisms of political decision, only two options for action remain: resignation or radicalization of the "Aryan Revolution." The latter variant is observed by the Southern Law Center. Morris Dees writes: "The hate groups of today have become smaller, more Nazi, and more revolutionary. That makes them dangerous. So the risk of domestic terrorism certainly lives on." A similar trend is also noted by Kaplan and Weinberg (1998:73), who regard right-wing radicalism as characterized by a "radical holy war," combined with increasingly independent, autonomous small groups and extensive weaponry.

Thirdly, these findings broaden out to raise new questions in the light of "September 11th" and the resulting movement toward "ultrapatriotism" in the United States. It is completely unclear here whether, and to what extent, the effects of this are favorable or unfavorable to right-wing extremist groups.

V. SUMMARY: DESIDERATA AND PROSPECTS FOR THE DEVELOPMENT OF THEORIES

Problems relating to the status of empirical research, analytical desiderata, and theoretical prospects will be summarized against the background of increasing academic interest in the study of right-wing extremist violence.

a) As far as *empirical research* is concerned, the status of data quality is clear. There are numerous problems with categorizing and classifying individual manifestations of violence as right-wing extremism. Consequently, the recording of data is often influenced by the political interests of governmental institutions (in minimizing the extent of the problem or dramatizing it). There is no such thing as a reasonably realistic view of the true dimensions of right-wing radicalism. As a result, comparative research, too, is made virtually impossible. This is one of the main reasons why the research is so contradictory and inconsistent. Thus, on the one hand, there are many indications that acceptance of immigrants or ethnic minorities is increasing, while on the other there are some countries where right-wing extremism or right-wing populism is enjoying more and more success. There are also signs in various areas of an increasing willingness to use violence that makes use of right-wing extremist ideology. There are worrying trends in some countries, moreover, where what is changing is not the extent of right-wing extremist violence but the quality of violence, with a tendency toward increasing brutalization, so that terrorist variants of right-wing extremism cannot be ruled out in the future. In the interests of greater clarity, an obvious step is to increase research into gray areas, which will at least complement effectively the results of police inquiries. This should be associated with long-term studies designed not only to improve the quality of explanations (with hindsight) but also to permit forecasting. Such prospects are limited, however, because it is not apparent at present whether it will be possible to provide systematic overviews of the manifold causes of outbreaks of collective violence.

b) An overview of the *analytical approaches* shows that one clear research desideratum lies in the development of multilevel analyses, to link up the *manifestations* of right-wing extremist violence described from the preconditions of socialization to endemic violence, and explain them in terms of the various patterns of linear, nonlinear, and two-way processes. Relationship analyses alone is not sufficient to trace the remolding of individual attitudes into collective violent action; this also requires increased understanding of the interaction processes between individual actors. Such interaction processes have not been sufficiently studied in the past; advances in knowledge can no longer be expected to result from individual research projects alone but require interdisciplinary research alliances. This new strategy in research is all the more necessary as Europe develops toward multiethnic societies, in which new groups with a propensity to violence appear on the stage (from migrant communities, for example) and new interaction patterns can be expected in specified sociospatial contexts.

c) The *theoretical picture* as far as right-wing extremist violence is concerned is now multifaceted, but still typified by two central problems. The question of the validity of theories in different contexts is still open to debate—can "European" theories also be helpful in the American context and vice versa?—as is the scope of individual theories in a particular subject area. There are two ways forward that would be worth investigating. First, more work could be done on empirically designed theoretical comparisons, making these more extensive than the preliminary approaches to date. Secondly, future research should ensure the possibility of connection between different theories, as a way of addressing both the multilevel problem and the issues of validity and scope.

Future theoretical development must adopt a *two-dimensional* approach. One dimension will have to cover the *manifestations* of the trend, which can be compressed to form stages (cf. section II, Fig. II-2-11.4), from the *origins* of vague individual attitudes of enmity and acceptance of violence, through *politicization*, in the sense of organization into groups (i.e., participation in collective action), to *escalation* (in the sense of situational and sociospatial violence), and nationwide *dissemination* (i.e., endemic violence or "waves" of violence).

    The second dimension relates to the *levels*. In this case, structural factors of the *macrolevel* (i.e., *social trends*) that help to explain the origin and propagation of ideologies must be combined with *individual factors* of the *microlevel*, in order eventually to link these to analyses on the *mesolevel* of *collective violent acts* and so explain politicization and possible escalation.

    The disintegration approach (cf. Albrecht in this volume) can be developed into a framework theory whose basic assumptions encompass several analytical levels and hence provide possible points of connection between the individual theories (cf. section III). Disintegration relates to the unredeemed contributions made by social institutions and communities to securing the fundamentals of existence, social recognition, and personal safety and integrity. Recognition circumstances and power interests function as central categories of this approach. The processes by which these evolve and are safeguarded, threatened, violated, and restored are particularly significant, arising as they do from perceived or experienced problems with access to the economic system, inadequate participation in the politico-institutional system, and membership of communities. As a result, problem *locations* and problem *qualities* can be identified and structural factors linked to individual experiences.

    The approach is in principle a twin-track one. First, there is the *basic assumption of deficit theory*, that people develop ethnicizing or xenophobic attitudes from a position of relative impotence and disadvantage (in the sense of the *theory of relative deprivation*) as a reaction to enforced economic, politico-institutional, and social fears or experiences of disintegration and the associated threats to or loss of recognition. These attitudes can help right-wing extremist groups to be seen as new, integrating units with their own sources of recognition, one of which is violence. The issues are *status* and *recognition* at the expense of weaker individuals, enemies, and foreigners.

    The second basic assumption is based on *action and ideology criticism*. This basic assumption leaves aside fears and experiences of disintegration and emphasizes the kinds of situations in which individuals and groups, from positions of perceived or established power, contribute to denigration and discrimination or to images of an enemy that produce a *disintegrative effect* and result in the lowering of thresholds of violence. The issue in these situations is the increase of power.

The disintegration approach provides a "theory-organizing" framework to explain the *manifestations*. With regard to the *origins* of ideologies of inequality and acceptance of violence, the approach adopts *socialization theory* arguments on the microlevel, by citing early injuries to recognition which determine the quest for security and superiority and combine high levels of anomie and insecurity with authoritarian reflexes.

For the stage of *politicization*, which is linked to losses of confidence in the political system, assumptions of *politico-cultural approaches* (including assumptions of delegitimation) are applied. As compensation for (perceived or experienced) threats to status is important at this stage, damage to integration and recognition makes it natural that violence-prone ingroup/outgroup distinctions (in the sense of the *social identity theory*) should become sharper and, as a result, groups and communities with a high level of internal integration (in accordance with assumptions of *subculture theory*) become more important.

The *escalation stage*, in the light of the framework approach, is linked to potentially recognition-enhancing opportunities to demonstrate (new) power in violent situations or with regard to certain territories, which are most likely to be pursued by groups that are successful in creating clear scapegoats for their own situation or scenarios of threat that act as triggers of violence. *Conflict theory* can be applied here. To what extent individuals indulge in such escalations depends on numerous factors (such as reference group orientation, comparative processes, etc.), which can be introduced, in particular, by *social-psychological* approaches.

If it proves impossible to meet these challenges to research—empirical surveys, existing analytical approaches, and the limitations of previous explanations—then they will prevent comparative research and provide no constructive indication of practical forms of intervention by government institutions or the actors of civil society.

VI. REFERENCES

Adorno, Theodor W., Else Frenkel-Brunswik, Daniel J. Levinson, & R. Nevitt Sanford. (1950). *The Authoritarian Personality. Studies in Prejudice.* New York: Harper & Row.

Altemeyer, Bob. (1996). *The Authoritarian Specter.* Cambridge, MA, Harvard University Press.

Anhut, Reimund, & Wilhelm Heitmeyer. (2000). Desintegration, Konflikt und Ethnisierung. Eine Problemanalyse und theoretische Rahmenkonzeption. In Wilhelm Heitmeyer & Reimund Anhut (Eds.), *Bedrohte Stadtgesellschaft. Soziale Desintegrationsprozesse und ethnisch-kulturelle Konfliktkonstellationen* (pp. 17–75). Weinheim, München: Juventa.

Bandura, Albert. (1973). *Aggression. A Social Learning Analysis.* Englewood Cliffs: Prentice-Hall.

Benoist, Alain de. (1977). *Vu de droite. Anthologie critique des idées contemporaines.* Paris: Copernic.

Benoist, Alain de. (1999). *Aufstand der Kulturen. Europäisches Manifest für das 21. Jahrhundert.* Berlin: Edition 'Junge Freiheit'.

Betz, Hans-Georg. (1994). *Radical Right-Wing Populism in Western Europe.* Houndsmills and London: MacMillan Press.

Betz, Hans-Georg. (2001). Radikaler Rechtspopulismus im Spannungsfeld zwischen neoliberalistischen Wirtschaftskonzepten und antiliberaler autoritärer Ideologie. In Dietmar Loch & Wilhelm Heitmeyer (Eds.), *Schattenseiten der Globalisierung. Rechtsradikalismus, Rechtspopulismus und separatistischer Regionalismus in westlichen Demokratien* (pp. 186–205). Frankfurt a. M.: Suhrkamp.

Beyme, Klaus von. (1996). Rechtsextremismus in Osteuropa. In Jürgen W. Falter, Hans-Gerd Jaschke & Jürgen R. Winkler (Eds.), *Rechtsextremismus. Ergebnisse und Perspektiven der Forschung. Politische Vierteljahresschrift. Sonderheft 27* (pp. 423–442). Opladen: Westdeutscher Verlag.

Biorcio, Roberto. (2001). Separatistischer Regionalismus in einer reichen Region: die Lega Nord. In Dietmar Loch & Wilhelm Heitmeyer (Eds.), *Schattenseiten der Globalisierung. Rechtsradikalismus,*

Rechtspopulismus und separatistischer Regionalismus in westlichen Demokratien (pp. 246–273). Frankfurt a. M.: Suhrkamp.

Bjørgo, Tore. (1993). *Terrorist Violence against Immigrants and Refugees in Scandinavia: Patterns and Motives.* In Tore Bjørgo & Rob Witte (Eds.), *Racist Violence in Europe* (pp. 29–45). New York: St. Martins Press.

Bjørgo, Tore. (1997). *Racist and Right-Wing Violence in Scandinavia. Patterns, Perpetrators and Responses.* Sweden: Tano Aschehoug.

Bjørgo, Tore. (1998). Entry, Bridge-Burning, and Exit Options: What Happens to Young People Who Join Racist Groups—and Want to Leave? In Jeffrey Kaplan & Tore Bjørgo (Eds.), *Nation and Race. The Developing Euro-American Racist Subculture* (pp. 231–258). Boston: Northeastern University Press.

Blomgren, Anna-Maria. (1999). *Vad gör samhället? Offentlig politik mot rasistiskt och främlingsfientligt vald i Vänerborg, Trollhättan och Uddevalla. [What is Done by Society? Public Policy against Racial and Xenophobic Violence in Vänersborg. Trollhättan and Uddevalla.]* Stockholm: CEIFO, Stockholm University.

Boehnke, Klaus, John Hagan, & Hans Merkens. (1998). Right-Wing Extremism among German Adolescents: Risk Factors and Protective Factors. *Applied Psychology: An International Review, 47*(1), pp. 109–126.

Bös, Matthias. (2001). 'Community-Building' im Internet: Entgrenzung und neue Grenzverläufe für politischen Extremismus in der globalen Kommunikation. In Dietmar Loch & Wilhelm Heitmeyer (Eds.), *Schattenseiten der Globalisierung. Rechtsradikalismus, Rechtspopulismus und separatistischer Regionalismus in westlichen Demokratien* (pp. 381–396). Frankfurt a. M.: Suhrkamp.

Bowling, Benjamin. (1998). *Violent Racism. Victimization, Policing and Social Context.* Oxford: Oxford University Press.

Brosius, Hans-Bernd, & Frank Esser. (1996). Massenmedien und fremdenfeindliche Gewalt. In Jürgen W. Falter, Hans-Gerd Jaschke & Jürgen R. Winkler (Eds.), *Rechtsextremismus. Ergebnisse und Perspektiven der Forschung. Politische Vierteljahresschrift, Sonderheft 27,* (pp. 204–218). Opladen: Westdeutscher Verlag.

Brosius, Hans-Bernd, & Frank Esser. (1995). *Eskalation durch Berichterstattung. Massenmedien und fremdenfeindliche Gewalt.* Opladen: Westdeutscher Verlag.

Bundesministerium des Innern/Bundesministeriums der Justiz (Ed.) (2001). *Erster Periodischer Sicherheitsbericht.* Berlin (Juli).

Bundesamt für Verfassungsschutz. (2001). *Ein Jahrzehnt rechtsextremistischer Politik. Strukturdaten—Ideologie—Agitation—Perspektiven 1990–2000.* Köln.

Camus, Jean-Yves. (2000). Europas extreme Rechte zwischen Marginalisierung und Salonfähigkeit. *Le Monde diplomatique/die tageszeitung,* März 2000, 4–5.

Cantle, Ted (Chair). (2001). *Community Cohesion: A Report of the Independent Review Team. Home Office. Building a Safe, Just and Tolerant Society.* (Great Britain).

Commission nationale consultative des Droits de l'Homme. (1996). *La lutte contre le racisme.* Paris : La Documentation française.

Commission nationale consultative des Droits de l'Homme. (2001). *La lutte contre le Racisme et la Xénophobie.* Paris : La Documentation française.

Decker, Frank. (2000). *Parteien unter Druck. Der neue Rechtspopulismus in den westlichen Demokratien.* Opladen: Leske & Budrich.

Dees, Morris, with Corcorau, James. (1996). *Gathering Storm. America's Militia Threat.* New York: Harper Collins Publishers.

Donselaar, Jaap van. (1993). The Extreme Right and Racist Violence in the Netherlands. In Tore Bjørgo & Rob Witte (Eds.), *Racist Violence in Europe* (pp. 46–61). Basingstoke, New York: MacMillan, St. Andrew Press.

Donselaar, Jaap van, & Peter R. Rodrigues. (2001). *Monitor racisme en extreem-rechts; vierde rapportage.* Amsterdam: Anne Frank Stichting.

Dubet, Francois. (1997). Die Logik der Jugendgewalt. Das Beispiel der französischen Vorstädte. In Trutz von Trotha (Ed.), *Soziologie der Gewalt. Kölner Zeitschrift für Soziologie und Sozialpsychologie. Sonderheft 37,* 220–234.

Eurobarometer. (1997). *Racism and Xenophobia in Europe. Eurobarometer Opinion Poll no 47.1.* Luxembourg (European Commission).

Fend, Helmut. (1994). Ausländerfeindlich-nationalistische Weltbilder und Aggressionsbereitschaft bei Jugendlichen in Deutschland und der Schweiz—kontextuelle und personale Antecedensbedingung. *Zeitschrift für Sozialisationsforschung und Erziehungssoziologie, 2,* 131–162.

Funke, Friedrich, Wolfgang Frindte, Susanne Jacob, & Jörg Neumann. (1999). Rechtsextreme Wirklichkeitskonstruktion. In Wolfgang Frindte (Ed.), *Fremde, Freunde, Feindlichkeiten* (pp. 70–82). Opladen, Wiesbaden: Westdeutscher Verlag.

George, John, & Laird Wilcox. (1996). *American Extremists: Militias, Supremacists, Klansmen, Communists, and Others.* New York: Prometheus Books.

Grumke, Thomas. (2001). *Rechtsextremismus in den USA.* Opladen: Leske & Budrich.

Gurr, Ted R. (1972). *Why Men Rebel.* New Jersey: Princeton University Press.

Hagan, John, Susanne Rippl, Klaus Boehnke, & Hans Merkens. (1999). The Interest in Evil: Hierarchic Self-Interest and Right-Wing Extremism among East and West German Youth. *Social Science Research, 28,* 162–183.

Hamm, Mark S. (1993). *American Skinheads. The Criminology and Control of Hate Crime.* Westport, Connecticut, London: Praeger.

Heitmann, Helmut. (1997). Die Skinhead Studie. In Klaus Farin (Ed.), *Die Skins. Mythos und Realität* (pp. 69–95). Berlin: Links Verlag.

Heitmeyer, Wilhelm. (1987). *Rechtsextremistische Orientierungen bei Jugendlichen.* Weinheim, München: Juventa.

Heitmeyer, Wilhelm. (1993). Hostility and Violence towards Foreigners in Germany. In Tore Bjørgo & Rob Witte (Eds.), *Racist Violence in Europe* (pp. 17–28). New York: St. Martin's Press.

Heitmeyer, Wilhelm. (1994). Das Desintegrations-Theorem. Ein Erklärungsansatz zu fremdenfeindlich motivierter, rechtsextremistischer Gewalt und zur Lähmung gesellschaftlicher Institutionen. In Wilhelm Heitmeyer (Ed.), *Das Gewalt-Dilemma. Gesellschaftliche Reaktionen auf fremdenfeindliche Gewalt und Rechtsextremismus* (pp. 29–72). Frankfurt a. M.: Suhrkamp.

Heitmeyer, Wilhelm. (1999). Sozialräumliche Machtversuche des ostdeutschen Rechtsextremismus—Zum Problem unzureichender politischer Gegenöffentlichkeit in Städten und Kommunen. In: Peter E. Kalb, Karin Sitte & Christian Petry (Eds.), *Rechtsextremistische Jugendliche—was tun?* (pp. 47–79) Weinheim, Basel: Beltz.

Heitmeyer, Wilhelm, Birgit Collmann, Jutta Conrads, Ingo Matuschek, Dietmar Kraul, Wolfgang Kühnel, Renate Möller, & Matthias Ulbrich-Herrmann. (1995). *Gewalt. Schattenseiten der Individualisierung bei Jugendlichen aus unterschiedlichen Milieus.* Weinheim, München: Juventa.

Heitmeyer, Wilhelm, & Joachim Müller. (1995). *Fremdenfeindliche Gewalt junger Menschen. Biographische Hintergründe, soziale Situationskontexte und die Bedeutung strafrechtlicher Sanktionen.* Bonn: Forum Verlag.

Hellmann, Kai-Uwe. (1998). Paradigmen der Bewegungsforschung. Forschungs- und Erklärungsansätze – ein Überblick. In Kai-Uwe Hellmann & Ruud Koopmans (Eds.), *Paradigmen der Bewegungsforschung. Entstehung und Entwicklung von neuen sozialen Bewegungen und Rechtsextremismus* (pp. 9–30). Opladen, Wiesbaden: Westdeutscher Verlag.

Hobsbawn, Eric. (1994). *Age of Extremes. The Short Twentieth Century 1914–1991.* London: Michael Joseph.

Hockenos, Paul. (1993). *Free to Hate. The Rise of the Right in Post-Communist Eastern Europe.* New York, London: Routledge.

Hoffmann, Uwe. (1999). *Die NPD. Entwicklung, Ideologie und Struktur.* Frankfurt a. M.: Lang.

Hopf, Christel, Peter Rieker, Martina Sanden-Marens, & Christiane Schmidt. (1995). *Familie und Rechtsextremismus. Familiale Sozialisation und rechtsextreme Orientierungen junger Männer.* Weinheim, München: Juventa.

Husbands, Christopher T. (1993). Racism and Racist Violence: Some Theories and Policy Perspectives. In Tore Bjørgo & Rob Witte (Eds.), *Racist Violence in Europe* (pp. 113–127). New York: St. Martin's Press.

Irving, David. (1977). *Hitler's War.* London: Hodder and Stoughton.

Jansen, Frank. (2000). *Todesopfer rechter Gewalt seit der Vereinigung—eine Bilanz. Sonderdruck 'Der Tagesspiegel',* 09/22/2000, Berlin.

Jaschke, Hans-Gerd. (1982). Subkulturanalysen. Anmerkungen zu einem neuen Ansatz in der Diskussion um rechtsextreme Jugendliche. In Peter Dudek & Hans-Gerd Jaschke, *Jugend rechtsaußen. Analysen, Essays, Kritik.* Bensheim: Lamuv.

Kaplan, Jeffrey. (1995). Right Wing Violence in North America. In Tore Bjørgo (Ed.), *Terror from the Extreme Right* (pp. 44–95). London: Frank Cass.

Kaplan, Jeffrey, & Leonhard Weinberg. (1998). *The Emergence of a Euro-American Radical Right.* New Brunswick, New Jersey, London: Rutgers University Press.

Koopmans, Ruud. (1996). Explaining the Rise of Racist and Extreme Right Violence in Western Europe: Grievance or Opportunities? *European Journal of Political Research, 30,* 185–216.

Koopmans, Ruud. (1998). Rechtsextremismus, fremdenfeindliche Mobilisierung und Einwanderungspolitik. Bewegungsanalyse unter dem Gesichtspunkt politischer Gelegenheitsstrukturen. In Kai-Uwe Hellmann & Ruud Koopmans (Eds.), *Paradigmen der Bewegungsforschung. Entstehung und Entwicklung von neuen sozialen Bewegungen und Rechtsextremismus* (pp. 198–212). Opladen, Wiesbaden: Westdeutscher Verlag.

Koopmans, Ruud, & Hanspeter Kriesi. (1997). *Citizenship, National Identity and the Mobilization of the Extreme Right. A Comparison of France, Germany, the Netherlands and Switzerland* (pp. 97–101). Science Center Berlin, Research Unit: The Public and Social Movements, FS III.

Kühnel, Wolfgang. (1998). Hitler's Grandchildren? The Reemergence of a Right-Wing Social Movement in Germany. In Jeffrey Kaplan & Tore Bjørgo (Eds.), *Nation and Race. The Developing Euro-American Racist Subculture* (pp. 148–201). Boston: Northeastern University Press.

Kühnl, Reinhard. (1990). *Gefahr von rechts. Vergangenheit und Gegenwart der extremen Rechten.* Heilbronn: Distel-Verlag.

Kürti, László. (1998). Racism and the Extreme Right and Anti-Gypsy Sentiments in East Central Europe. In Charles Westin (Ed.), *Racism, Ideology and Political Organisation* (pp. 217–254). Edsbruk: CEIFO.

Levin, Jack, & Jack McDevitt. (1993). *Hate Crimes: The Rising Tide of Bigotry and Bloodshed.* New York: Plenum.

Levin, Jack, & Jack McDevitt. (1999). Hate Crime. In *Encyclopedia of Violence, Race, Conflict. Vol. 2* (pp. 89–101). San Diego et al: Academic Press.

Lööw, Helene. (1995). Racist Violence and Criminal Behaviour in Sweden: Mythos and Reality. In Tore Bjørgo (Ed.), *Terror From the Extreme Right* (pp. 116–161). London: Frank Cass.

Lööw, Helene. (1998). *Nazism I Sverige 1980–1997. Den rasistiska undergroundrörelsen: musiken, mytherna, riterna. [Nazism in Sweden 1980–1997. The Racial Underground Movement: The Music, the Myths, the Rites.]* Stockholm: Ordfront.

Lüdemann, Christian, & Christian Erzberger. (1994). Fremdenfeindliche Gewalt in Deutschland. Zur zeitlichen Entwicklung und Erklärung von Eskalationsprozessen. *Zeitschrift für Rechtssoziologie, 15,* 169–190.

Mayer, Nonna, & Pascal Perrineau (Eds.) (1996). *Le Front national à découvert.* Paris: Presses de la Fondation nationale des Sciences politiques.

McAdam, Dong, Sidney Tarrow, & Charles Tilly. (1996). Top Map Contentions Politics. *Mobilisation, 1*(1), 17–34.

Mentzel, Thomas. (1998). *Rechtsextremistische Gewalttaten von Jugendlichen und Heranwachsenden in den neuen Bundesländern. Eine empirische Untersuchung von Erscheinungsformen und Ursachen am Beispiel des Bundeslandes Sachsen-Anhalt.* München: Fink.

Merkl, Peter H. (1995). Radical Right Parties in Europe and Anti-Foreign Violence: A Comparative Essay. In Tore Bjørgo (Ed.), *Terror from the Extreme Right* (pp. 96–118). London: Frank Cass.

Merkl, Peter H. (1997). Why Are They So Strong Now? In Peter H.Merkl & Leonhard Weinberg (Eds.), *The Revival of Right-Wing Extremism in the 1990s* (pp. 17–46). London: Frank Cass.

Minkenberg, Michael. (1998). *Die neue radikale Rechte im Vergleich. USA, Frankreich, Deutschland.* Opladen: Westdeutscher Verlag.

Möller, Kurt. (2000). *Rechte Kids. Eine Langzeitstudie über Auf- und Abbau rechtsextremistischer Orientierungen bei 13- bis 15jährigen.* Weinheim, München: Juventa.

Mudde, Cas. (1995). Right-Wing Extremism Analyzed. *European Journal of Political Research, 27,* 203–224.

Neidhardt, Friedhelm. (1985). Einige Ideen zu einer allgemeinen Theorie sozialer Bewegungen. In Stefan Hradil (Ed.), *Sozialstruktur im Umbruch* (pp. 193–204). Opladen: Leske & Budrich.

Neidhardt, Friedhelm. (1989). Gewalt und Gegengewalt. In Wilhelm Heitmeyer, Kurt Möller & Heinz Sünker (Eds.), *Jugend-Staat-Gewalt* (pp. 233–243). Weinheim, München: Juventa.

Perrineau, Pascal. (1988). Front national: l'écho politique de l'anomie urbaine. *La France en politique, Sonderheft von Esprit,* mars–avril, 22–38.

Perrineau, Pascal. (2001). Die Faktoren der Wahldynamik des Front national. In Dietmar Loch & Wilhelm Heitmeyer (Eds.), *Schattenseiten der Globalisierung. Rechtsradikalismus, Rechtspopulismus und separatistischer Regionalismus in westlichen Demokratien* (pp. 186–205). Frankfurt a. M.: Suhrkamp.

Perry, Barbara. (2001). *In the Name of Hate. Understanding Hate Crimes.* New York, London: Routledge.

Pfahl-Traughber, Armin. (1995). *Rechtsextremismus. Eine kritische Bestandsaufnahme nach der Wiedervereinigung.* Bonn: Bouvier.

Podaliri, Carlo, & Carlo Balestri. (1998). Racism and Football Culture in Italy. In Adam Brown (Ed.), *Fanatics! Football and Popular Culture in Europe* (pp. 88–100). London: Routledge.

Reemtsma, Katrin. (1993). Between Freedom and Persecution: Roma in Romania. In Tore Bjørgo & Rob Witte (Eds.), *Racist Violence in Europe* (pp. 194–206). New York: St. Martin's Press.

Roversi, Antonio di, & Carlo Ballestri. (1999). Gli Ultras oggi. Declino o cambiamento? *POLIS,* Bologna, 453–468.

Rucht, Dieter. (1996). Recent Right-Wing Radicalism in Germany: Its Development and Resonance in the Public and Social Sciences. *Research on Democracy and Society, 3,* 225–274.

Schröder, Burkhard. (1995). *Neonazis und Computernetze—wie Rechtsradikale neue Kommunikationsformen nutzen.* Reinbek bei Hamburg: Rowohlt.

Schuman, Howard, Charlotte Steek, Laurence Bobo, & Maria Krysan. (1997). *Racial Attitudes in America: Trends and Interpretations.* Cambridge, MA and London: Harvard University Press.

Schumann, Dirk. (1997). Gewalt als Grenzüberschreitung: Überlegungen zur Sozialgeschichte der Gewalt im 19. und 20. Jahrhundert. *Archiv für Sozialgeschichte, 37,* 383–395.

Searchlight et al. (Ed.) (1999). *White Noise. Rechts-Rock, Skinhead Musik, Blood & Honour-Einblicke in die internationale Neonazi-Musik-Szene.* Hamburg/Münster: UNRAST-Verlag.

Sprinzak, Ehud. (1995). Right-Wing Terrorism in a Comparative Perspective: The Case of Split Delegitimization. In Tore Bjørgo (Ed.), *Terror from the Extreme Right* (pp. 17–43). London: Frank Cass.

Stern, Kenneth S. (1996). *A Force Upon The Plain. The American Militia Movement and the Politics of Hate.* New York et al.: Simon & Schuster.

Stöss, Richard. (1989). *Die extreme Rechte in der Bundesrepublik. Entwicklung, Ursachen, Gegenmaßnahmen.* Opladen: Westdeutscher Verlag.

Stöss, Richard. (1994). Forschungs- und Erklärungsansätze—ein Überblick. In Wolfgang Kowalsky & Wolfgang Schroeder (Eds.), *Rechtsextremismus. Einführung und Forschungsbilanz* (pp. 23–68). Opladen: Westdeutscher Verlag.

Tajfel, Henri. (1981). *Human Groups and Social Categories.* Cambridge: University Press.

Thalhammer, Eva et al. (2001). *Attitudes towards Minority Groups in the European Union. A Special Analysis of the Eurobarometer 2000 Survey on Behalf of the European Monitoring Centre on Racism and Xenophobia.* Vienna: EUMC.

Tobler, Hans Werner, & Peter Waldmann (Eds.) (1991). *Staatliche und parastaatliche Gewalt in Lateinamerika.* Frankfurt a. M.: Vervuert.

Trüller, Dirk. (1999). Die Macht der Gefühle—Gefühle der Macht. Gewaltphantasien und Emotionalität in der Musikszene rechter Skins. In Sighard Neckel & Michael Schwab-Trapp (Eds.), *Ordnungen der Gewalt. Beiträge zu einer politischen Soziologie der Gewalt und des Krieges* (pp. 55–69). Opladen: Leske & Budrich.

Ulram, Peter A. (2001). Sozialprofil und Wahlmotive der FPÖ-Wähler: Zur Modernität des Rechtspopulismus am Beispiel des Phänomens Haider. In Dietmar Loch & Wilhelm Heitmeyer (Eds.), *Schattenseiten der Globalisierung. Rechtsradikalismus, Rechtspopulismus und separatistischer Regionalismus in westlichen Demokratien* (pp. 206–226). Frankfurt a. M.: Suhrkamp.

Virtanen, Timo. (2001). *The European Statistical Atlas on Racial Violence 1995–2000.* European Monitoring Centre on Racism and Xenophobia (Ed.): Vienna.

Wagner, Bernd. (1998). *Rechtsextremismus und kulturelle Subversion in den neuen Ländern.* Berlin: Zentrum Demokratische Kultur.

Weinberg, Leonhard. (1998). An Overview of Right-Wing Extremism in the Western World: A Study of Convergence, Linkage and Identity. In Jeffrey Kaplan & Tore Bjørgo (Eds.), *Nation and Race. The Developing Euro-American Racist Subculture* (pp. 3–33). Boston: Northeastern University Press.

Weiss, Hans-Jürgen. (1997). Extreme Right-Wing Racial Violence—An Effect of the Mass Media? *Communications, 22*(1), 57–68.

Weißmann, Karlheinz. (2000). *Alles, was recht(s) ist. Ideen, Köpfe und Perspektiven der politischen Rechten.* Graz: Stocker.

Wetzels, Peter, & Werner Greve. (2001). Fremdenfeindliche Gewalt-Bedingungen und Reaktionen. *Zeitschrift für Politische Psychologie, 9,* 7–22.

Wieviorka, Michel. (1999). *Violence en France.* Paris: Éditions Du Seuil.

Wieviorka, Michel, Philippe Bataille, Daniel Jacquin, Danilo Martuccelli, Angelina Peralva, & Paul Zawadzki. (1992). *La France Raciste.* Paris: Éditions du Seuil.

Willems, Helmut. (1996). Mobilisierungseffekte und Eskalationsprozesse. Entwicklung und Diffusion der kollektiven Gewalt gegen Fremde. *Berliner Debatte INITIAL, 1,* 34–42.

Willems, Helmut, Roland Eckert, Stefanie Würtz, & Linda Steinmetz. (1993). *Fremdenfeindliche Gewalt. Einstellungen, Täter, Konflikteskalation.* Opladen: Leske & Budrich.

Winkler, Jürgen R. (1996). Bausteine einer allgemeinen Theorie des Rechtsextremismus. Zur Stellung und Integration von Persönlichkeits- und Umweltfaktoren. In Jürgen W. Falter, Hans-Gerd Jaschke & Jürgen R. Winkler (Eds.), *Rechtsextremismus. Ergebnisse und Perspektiven der Forschung* (pp. 25–48). Opladen: Westdeutscher Verlag.

Witte, Rob. (1995). Racist Violence in Western Europe. *New Community, 21*(4), 489–500.

Zick, Andreas. (1997). *Vorurteile und Rassismus. Eine sozialpsychologische Analyse.* Münster et al.: Waxmann.

Large-Scale Violence as Contentious Politics

CHARLES TILLY*

I. THE CONCEPTION

Political theorists and fearful citizens alike often draw a deep distinction between violence and politics. As Hannah Arendt put it:

> Power springs up whenever people get together and act in concert, but it derives its legitimacy from the initial getting together rather than from any action that then may follow. Legitimacy, when challenged, bases itself on an appeal to the past, while justification relates to an end that lies in the future. Violence can be justifiable, but it never will be legitimate. Its justification loses in plausibility the farther its intended end recedes into the future. No one questions the use of violence in self-defense, because the danger is not only clear but also present, and the end justifying the means is immediate (Arendt, 1969:52).

Later, Arendt summed up: "Power and violence are opposites; where the one rules absolutely, the other is absent ... Violence can destroy power; it is utterly incapable of creating it" (Arendt, 1969:56; see Mayer, 2000:82–84).

A few years after Arendt, a French presidential commission reported its own inquiry into violence. Like Arendt, the commission wanted to distinguish force from violence:

> Common sense often equates [violence] with force and aggressiveness. But that equation is wrong. Force, neutral in its potential, can pursue any end; violence implies infringement of accepted norms ... Violence is not a simple expression of force or exteriorization of aggressiveness. It takes place in an incessant play of antitheses and oppositions, at the center of the oppo-

* Thanks to Peter Bearman for reminding me of Ulf Hannerz's work as a resource for this paper. I owe my meager knowledge of genocide to collaboration with Bruce Jones. Bruce does not, however, bear any responsibility for my errors. As usual, Sidney Tarrow's unforgiving criticism has caused significant revisions to earlier versions of the paper.

W. Heitmeyer and J. Hagan (eds.), *International Handbook of Violence Research*, 437–454.

sition between individual and society, as well as among individuals (Peyrefitte et al., 1977: I, 35–36).

Faced with the task of defining violence precisely, France's violence commissioners finally threw up their hands. But they made clear that violence consisted of force used wrongly, and that a civilized government had an obligation to suppress it. To suppress violence, they reasoned, was to restore normal politics. After all, President Giscard d'Estaing had appointed his commission to advise the government in that very effort. Thus the commissioners implicitly endorsed two widely held principles: 1) violence exists in separation from ordinary politics, and 2) violence and ordinary politics spring from different causes. Call 1 and 2 principles of *separation* and of *heterogeneity*.

My plan here is not to assess the general validity of those two principles over all types of violent acts. It is instead to challenge their applicability to large-scale violence. Although the circumstances that produce large-scale violence have some distinctive properties, in general they belong to the realm of contentious politics. The same sorts of mechanisms and processes that cause change and variation in nonviolent making of political claims also cause change and variation in violent claim-making. In the case of large-scale violence, the principles of separation and heterogeneity fail. Or at least so I shall argue.

Large-scale violence, for present purposes, refers to episodic social interaction that:

- involves at least two distinguishable collective actors
- extends over at least two adjacent days and localities
- immediately inflicts physical damage (including forcible seizure of persons or objects over restraint or resistance) on persons and/or objects
- results at least in part from coordination among persons who perform the damaging acts

The minima are arbitrary and unimportant. Although scale effects surely appear in collective violence—violent events engaging a whole country, for example, have somewhat different properties, on average, from those involving no more than adjacent neighborhoods—those effects matter little for this paper's main arguments. Raising the minimum number of actors to five or the minimum scale to a month plus a whole region would, for example, simply exclude transitory and localized events without much altering the explanatory problem.

Yet the definition does exclude a number of phenomena people commonly call violence. At one edge, the definition excludes strictly individual, private, impulsive, and/or accidental damage to persons or objects. At the other, it excludes long-term, incremental damage such as communication of infectious disease, cumulative wear and tear, exposure to toxic substances, the daily brutalization of imprisonment, military service, or slavery, and death hastened by neglect or social pressure. Throughout its range, the definition also excludes insult, hate, discrimination, anguish, and ostracism except insofar as they appear in the course of interactions producing physical damage; insult, hate, discrimination, anguish, and ostracism in themselves do not qualify as violence. Nevertheless, large-scale violence so defined includes an immense array of social interactions, from major gang fights to international wars.

How shall we map that array? Assuming episodic interaction, at least a little communication among actors, and some minimum of physical damage to persons or objects, Table II-2-12.1 combines the extent of coordination among damage-doers and the salience of damage in the overall pattern of interaction to produce a crude typology of large-scale violence. "Low" coordination means individualized action with little collective planning

TABLE II-2-12.1. A typology of large-scale violence

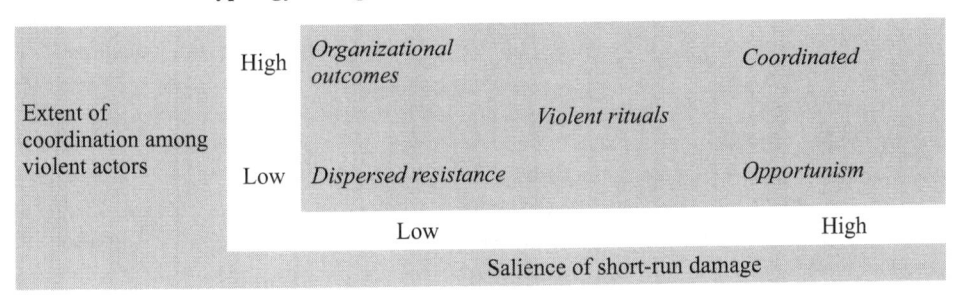

and signaling. "High" coordination means activation of differentiated, bounded organizational structure with extensive planning and signaling. "Low" salience of damage means that most of the social interaction involved produces no short-term physical harm. "High" salience means interaction strongly concentrated on physical harm.

Within the coordination-salience space we can conveniently distinguish five locations. Moving in a clockwise spiral, they are:

- *dispersed resistance*: in the course of widespread small-scale and generally non-violent interaction, a number of participants respond to obstacles, challenges, or restraints by means of damaging acts; examples include sabotage, clandestine attacks on symbolic objects or places, assaults of governmental agents, and arson
- *organizational outcomes*: various forms of collective action generate resistance or rivalry to which one or more parties respond by actions that damage persons and/or objects; examples include demonstrations, protection rackets, governmental repression, and military coups, all of which frequently occur with no more than threats of violence, but sometimes produce physical damage
- *coordinated destruction*: persons or organizations that specialize in the deployment of coercive means undertake a program of damage to persons and/or objects; examples include war, collective self-immolation, some kinds of terrorism, genocide, and politicide—the programmed annihilation of a political category's members
- *opportunism*: as a consequence of shielding from routine surveillance and repression, individuals or clusters of individuals use immediately damaging means to pursue generally forbidden ends; examples include looting, gang rape, revenge killing, and some sorts of military pillage
- *violent rituals*: two or more relatively well defined and coordinated groups follow a known interaction script entailing the infliction of damage on themselves or others as they compete for priority within a recognized arena; examples include gang rivalries, contact sports, some election battles, and some struggles among supporters of sporting teams or entertainment stars

These crude types overlap, for example in the activities of mercenaries, who often alternate between concerted battle (coordinated destruction) and individual looting or rape (opportunism). Similarly, the various practices known as terrorism show up throughout the diagram—as clandestine resistance, as a by-product of peaceful claim-making in highly repressive regimes, as part of genocide, as opportunistic elimination of old enemies, and as ritual shows of strength. It is nevertheless useful to retain the five-part division, both because within each area thus delineated social scientists have accumulated at least a modi-cum of systematic knowledge and because the five zones correspond to rather different varieties of contentious politics. The challenge is to show that similar mechanisms and processes explain diverse forms of violent contention.

Contentious politics means *episodic, collective interaction among makers of claims and their objects when a) at least one government is a claimant, an object of claims, or a party to the claims and b) the claims would, if realized, affect the interests of at least one of the claimants.* Roughly translated, the definition refers to collective political struggle. Contentious politics excludes individual patron–client relations, everyday operation of bureaucracies, ordinary compliance with legal procedures, uncontested transfer of resources (e.g., taxes, personal information, and military manpower) to governmental agencies, and routine implementation of governmental programs. Yet it includes a significant share of public politics in all sorts of regimes.

My claim is double:

1. Almost all large-scale violence meeting my earlier definition also qualifies as contentious politics thus defined.
2. The same sorts of processes and mechanisms that explain nonviolent contentious politics also explain its visibly violent versions.

I have, of course, favored the first proposition to some extent by defining large-scale violence in terms of collective actors. The only serious effect of that restriction, however, is to eliminate some forms of dispersed resistance and opportunism—those extreme cases where one side of a two-sided struggle consists entirely of individuals acting independ-ently of each other. I claim, in fact, that such cases are either rare or nonexistent; both resistance and opportunism actually depend on some minimum of interpersonal coordina-tion. The most interesting possible exceptions to both propositions concern violent rituals: potlatches, penitential processions, shooting contests, military maneuvers, contact sports, and similar scripted deployments of destructive means. While conceding that violent ritu-als occur at the margins of contentious politics, I claim that they share a number of prop-erties with their less ritualized cousins. Later sections of the paper identify some of those common properties.

Assimilating large-scale violence to contentious politics goes beyond definitional sleight of hand. It follows from a general explanatory program that has recently been emerging among students of social movements, revolution, democratization, war, and other conflict-filled forms of politics (see e.g., Jackson & Nexon, 1999, McAdam, Tarrow, & Tilly, 1997, Stroschein, 2000, Tarrow, 1998). We can call the program DOC: Dynamics of Contention. The DOC program involves these steps:

- Recognize that in principle contention ranges among wars, revolutions, social movements, industrial conflict, and a number of other forms of interaction that analysts have ordinarily conceived of as *sui generis*.
- Elaborate concepts calling attention to these similarities; call upon the major con-cepts developed out of the study of social movements in Western democracies since the 1960s to make a start.
- Improve on those concepts by critique and autocritique, then by applying the product of critique and autocritique to other settings and periods of history.
- Across these settings and periods, look for causal analogies not among whole phenomena but among mechanisms revealed within these phenomena—for ex-

ample, parallels between the mechanisms of brokerage in social movement cycles and revolutionary situations.

- Give particular attention to relational mechanisms such as brokerage rather than cognitive and environmental mechanisms (e.g., cognitive dissonance and environmental depletion), since relational mechanisms account for many changes in scale, form, and organization of interaction that analysts have attempted to explain by means of cognitive and environmental mechanisms.
- Having identified robust relational mechanisms, specify their connections with cognitive and environmental mechanisms.
- Examine how these causal mechanisms combine into longer chains of political processes. From identification of such processes, create not general theories of contention but partial theories corresponding to these robust causal analogies.
- Move away from attempting to explain whole episodes of contentious politics (such as the French Revolution or the American civil rights movement) in favor of using episodes as viewing screens for detection of analogous mechanisms and processes.
- Establish scope conditions with regard to time, space, and social setting under which such partial theories hold and those in which they do not.
- Treat discontinuities in those scope conditions—for example, the discovery that explanations built into social movement theories coming from liberal democracies apply badly outside such regimes—not as cultural roadblocks but as challenges to undertake new theories and comparisons.

The program centers on identification and analysis of mechanisms, classes of recurrent events that alter connections among specified sets of elements. It involves grouping mechanisms into robust processes, combinations and sequences of mechanisms that occur in essentially the same way with similar effects in a wide variety of circumstances. It calls for breaking complex episodes into crucial mechanisms and processes, thus explaining distinctive features of those episodes without supposing that whole classes of episodes—revolutions, social movements, nationalist mobilizations, and so on—conform to general laws.

Applied to large-scale violence, the DOC program helps identify crucial connections between violent and nonviolent making of claims. Let me illustrate some of those connections by following another spiral among dispersed resistance, organizational outcomes, coordinated destruction, opportunism, and violent rituals. In each case, the point will be to describe the operation of a few important general causal mechanisms in the production of a particular sort of violent interaction. Consistent with DOC precepts, my analysis will resist all temptation to formulate a general model of violence. Instead, it will pursue partial causal analogies among ostensibly different sorts of violent interaction.

1. Dispersed Resistance

We can speak of dispersed resistance when in the course of widespread small-scale and generally nonviolent interaction, a number of participants respond to obstacles, challenges, or restraints by means of damaging actions. Inspired by Marc Bloch, A.V. Chayanov, Richard Cobb, E.P. Thompson and, later, Antonio Gramsci, political ethnographer James Scott has been studying dispersed resistance since the 1970s. One of Scott's recent syntheses describes peasant resistance to the introduction of power combines in the rice-growing Malaysian village he has long studied:

When, in 1976, combine harvesters began to make serious inroads into the wages of poor villagers, the entire region experienced a rash of machine-breaking and sabotage reminiscent of the 1930s in England. The provincial authorities called it "vandalism" and "theft," but it was clear that there was a fairly generalised nocturnal campaign to prevent the use of combines. Batteries were removed from the machines and thrown into irrigation ditches; carburettors (*sic*) and other vital parts such as distributors were smashed; sand and mud were introduced into the gas tanks; various objects (stones, wire, nails) were used to jam the augers; coconut trees were felled across the combine's path; and at least two machines were destroyed by arson. Two aspects of this resistance deserve emphasis. First, it was clear that the goal of the saboteurs was never simple theft, for nothing was actually stolen. Second, all of the sabotage was carried out at night by individuals or small groups acting anonymously. They were, furthermore, shielded by their fellow villagers who, even if they knew who was involved, claimed total ignorance when the police came to investigate (Scott, 2000:200).

Most of the time, Scott emphasizes, the same peasants maintained decorous, deferential public relations to the same landlords despite incessantly muttering among themselves, dragging their feet, stealing rice from the landlords' fields, and otherwise deploying what Scott calls "weapons of the weak" (Scott, 1985). Although landlords would not have hesitated to prosecute a machine-breaker or thief caught red-handed, they found themselves caught in a confining set of relations that would cost them standing, influence, and access to labor if they engaged in vindictive violence or generated open rebellion. At work was a very general relational mechanism we might call *polyvalent performance*: individual or collective presentation of gestures simultaneously to two or more audiences in ways that code differently within the audiences (Tilly, 1999).

Polyvalent performance figures widely in contentious politics, violent or not. It facilitates coordination of interaction among groups that maintain differing, or even hostile, programs and world-views. Sometimes participants on both sides of polyvalent performance recognize their participation in a double game, but maintain their relations by refusing to acknowledge that duality openly. The polyvalent performance of working by rule to undermine overzealous bosses gains its effectiveness precisely from resonance in two registers, both of them audible to each side. Polyvalence matters to large-scale violence because it provides a bridge crossed by parties that collaborate in some times and circumstances but clash violently in other times and circumstances. That happens, obviously, not in dispersed resistance alone, but also in organizational outcomes, coordinated destruction, opportunism, and violent rituals.

Scott's analysis also identifies a number of other causal mechanisms well known to students of contentious politics. They include 1) *sabotage*, the clandestine attack on means of producing or reproducing some oppressive forms of interaction; 2) *category shift*, direct reinforcement of known boundaries separating one set of persons or social locations from another, thus increasing the salience of identities and practices associated with that pair of categories while diminishing the salience of other identities and practices that are also available to some or all participants; 3) *signaling spirals*, in which people detect and communicate the availability and feasibility of ostensibly risky practices. We will encounter similar causal mechanisms in other kinds of large-scale violence.

2. Organizational Outcomes

In the forms of large-scale violence, which I am calling organizational outcomes, various forms of collective action generate resistance or rivalry to which one or more parties respond by actions that damage persons and/or objects. Organizational processes often generate large-scale collective violence in the course of two different sequences:

a. *Imposition-Resistance:* Authorities (governmental or otherwise) try to impose an innovation that threatens valued programs within previously compliant subordinate populations; scattered resistance to the innovation signals both the possibility of resistance and the incapacity of the authorities to suppress that resistance; centers of resistance connect and consolidate; repression and resistance interact to generate damage-producing interaction. Common examples are new taxes in existing polities, technological changes in industries, and installation of uniform cultural practices (e.g., national languages) in the presence of distinctive minorities.

b. *Authority Failure:* Previously solid authorities visibly demonstrate either their failing capacity or their increasing unreadiness to fulfill earlier commitments; previously cooperative subjects demand guarantees backing those earlier commitments; when authorities fail to offer adequate guarantees, subjects begin to withdraw support and collaboration; authorities repress ineffectually; withdrawal and resistance generalize, then repression and resistance interact to generate damage-producing interaction. Relevant cases include the concentration of military desertions, civilian strikes, popular rebellions, and revolutions in periods when national armies suffer spectacular defeats in war, as well as the surging of collective demands for recompense of both veterans and civilians in postwar periods of military demobilization.

The two robust processes share a number of causal mechanisms, but assemble them somewhat differently. They also sometimes combine in complex episodes.

Consider the wave of demands for local and regional political autonomy that swept over France during the spring of 1871. After the Second Empire's legalization of strikes (1864) and considerable relaxation of restrictions on assembly and association (1868), French workers and radicals greatly expanded their publicly visible contention. As had already happened during the Second Republic (1848–1851) and in the failed resistance to Louis Napoleon's coup, widespread webs of association with much sending of delegates and addresses from place to place provided bases of coordination for collective action at larger than local scales. They also underlay a popular program of federalism that occupied a middle ground between the radical decentralizing programs of anarchists and the hierarchical structures of many revolutionary organizations.

The war with Prussia that began in July 1870 raised the political stakes and sharpened divisions within the republican opposition. Especially when Prussia gained a massive military advantage and began to fight on French soil, activists divided between those who supported the war effort and those who gave priority to internationalist, autonomist, or anarchist programs. As French national military forces lurched from disaster to disaster, however, temporary alliances formed between those who criticized the government for incompetence and those who complained about its oppression. In parallel with many other revolutionary movements in France and elsewhere, radical programs gained support as a function of the central government's war-driven vulnerability.

The Parisian declaration of a Commune on 28 March 1871 followed months of campaigning by Parisian radicals for such a move and numerous attempts—some successful—to establish radical autonomous governments in smaller French cities. Arrondissement-based National Guard units doubled by local committees formed the structure of Parisian government. At the top stood a municipal government consisting of delegates from arrondissements and a National Guard central committee likewise formed by election. These twinned organizations overhauled municipal administration, created public services, and coordinated the city's defense against encircling German and French troops. A third kind of structure—the popular club—played no formal part in government but beginning in the fall of 1870 became a central forum for discussion of public affairs and mobilization of collective claim-making.

Soon after the Commune's formation, national troops started dislodging Parisian National Guard units from the city's external forts and continued to bombard the city with artillery. By the time of their entry into Paris through a damaged and unguarded gate on 21 May, national forces had retaken all the external posts and shut Parisian forces within the city.

Meanwhile parallel (and sometimes prior) movements for political autonomy were occurring in Lyon, Toulouse, Marseille, Saint-Etienne, Grenoble, and other French cities. As Ronald Aminzade summarizes:

> The key event that triggered a revolutionary crisis in France in 1870 was defeat in the Franco-Prussian War and the capture of Louis Napoleon Bonaparte by Prussian troops. Events at the national and international level explain the emergence of a revolutionary crisis that made possible the development of local revolutionary communes. The rhythm of revolution at the local level can also be understood in terms of supralocal forces, since in all cities it followed a pattern marked by major surges in revolutionary activity following the proclamation of the Third Republic in September, the war defeats of late October, the January armistice and subsequent February election of a conservative National Assembly, and the declaration of the Paris commune in March. The outcomes of the local revolutions that preceded the Paris commune of 1871 were also, in large part, determined by supralocal forces, especially the dispatch of Versailles troops to crush provincial municipal insurrections. But national and international factors cannot explain why revolutionary communes emerged in some cities but not others, because urban revolutionary upheavals were closely tied to different local histories of Republican party formation (Aminzade, 1993:210).

Such complex episodes offer a feast of significant causal mechanisms. The Commune's crucial recurrent mechanisms include activation of brokerage (linkage of previously disconnected parties to each other or to some external social site), multiple instances of certification (validation of actors, their performances, and their claims by external authorities, with de-certification of its weighty complement), not to mention object shift (alteration in relations between claimants and objects of claims, for example when feuding clans unite against intervening state authorities). Let me single out from that plethora an interesting pair of mechanisms that made a significant difference to how the entire episode unfolded.

The first is *network activation*, the second *failed repression*. In Paris and other cities, citizens organized their self-defense against German occupation through interlocking political clubs, local committees, and National Guard units, which in turn built in part on previously existing craft and neighborhood networks. In the face of challenges from both German and French authorities, Parisians and others built communication and resistance within those networks. Failed repression—deliberate deployment of conditional threats to harm, followed by failure to deliver effective harm when the objects of threats did not meet the stipulated conditions—repeatedly galvanized local populations against the regime, simultaneously accelerating evasion and direct resistance.

Network activation and failed repression interacted. Exiled to Bordeaux in retreat from Parisian threats and German advances, the French regime issued a series of ineffectual edicts. It cut off National Guard stipends and called for Parisians to resume payment of their long-suspended rents. Then before dawn on 18 March 1871, prime minister Adolphe Thiers dispatched national troops to seize the National Guard's cannon. That failed attempt mobilized much of the Parisian population, precipitated the killing of two national army generals in Montmartre, and soon led to the National Guard Central Committee's occupation of the Hôtel de Ville, Paris's city hall and seat of government. Within ten days, improvised authorities had held elections, brought in a revolutionary government, and declared Paris an autonomous Commune. This famous series of events began and ended with large-scale violence. And it resulted in part from the intersection of two very general political mechanisms: network activation and failed repression.

The Commune's last phase—the street by street reconquest and destruction of Paris by France's national army—moved out of organizational outcomes over into coordinated destruction. The early stages of that reconquest resembled war, the late stages politicide. But at either stage, organizations that specialized in the deployment of coercive means undertook programs of damage to persons and objects.

3. Coordinated Destruction

In coordinated destruction, persons or organizations specializing in the deployment of coercive means undertake a program of damage to persons and/or objects. Taking our cue from the Franco-Prussian War and the Paris Commune, we might easily move into more general discussions of interstate war, civil war, and some forms of governmental repression as coordinated destruction. To increase the range of our discussion, however, let us turn to a variety of large-scale violence about which we understand even less: genocide.

Considering its prevalence around much of the globe since World War I, genocide has attracted surprisingly little attention from students of war, military organization, states, security studies, international relations, conflict resolution, and contentious politics. State-incited mass killing of people concentrated in a single social category—genocide—has remained the province of case specialists, an occasional political philosopher, and participants in the new, small field of comparative genocide studies. Others ritually condemn genocide as vicious, vile, and virtually incomprehensible, but contribute nothing to describing, explaining, or preventing it. Given the apparent expansion of genocide during the twentieth century, that is a pity, perhaps a disgrace.

Let us take Somalia, Burundi, and Rwanda as cases in point. All three are poor countries that in recent years have frequently lived under minority rule. Indeed, large-scale violence has occurred in Somalia, Burundi, and Rwanda chiefly in times when a minority attempted to preserve its power by fomenting attacks on great numbers of the majority population. In each case, furthermore, the ostensibly dominant minority actually split into at least two competing segments, with genocide resulting in part from that split within the elite. In Burundi, rivalry between Bagaza and Buyoya factions, in Rwanda rivalry between Bagogwe clan members from the northwest and others, and in Somalia rivalry among multiple clans have all contributed to lethal attacks on whole categories of the national population. In all of them, finally, military forces nominally attached to the central state have helped organize and execute genocidal programs.

Somalia's Siyaad Barre kept his Darod clan-family in power first by buying off heads of rival clans with patronage, then by pitting one clan against another. The second tactic worked well, until the Cold War's decline in the late 1980s reduced Soviet military backing for Barre's regime, and emboldened neighboring powers began to supply arms to various segments of Barre's opposition. Segmented civil war ensued, with incessant shifts of coalitions among clans. In addition to many battle deaths, Somalia then experienced lethal famines and epidemics as a direct consequence of interruptions to food distribution and preventive medicine. Under these conditions, even the United States was unable to promote a stable system of rule in Somalia. As it turns out, mass deaths resulted from inter-clan competition, but not from a state-centered campaign to extirpate members of a single ethnic category. Somalia's experience therefore qualifies as large-scale violence, but not quite as genocide.

Burundi was different. There, Tutsi groups have dominated the state in the face of a Hutu majority most of the time since independence. In 1972, an uprising begun by Hutu elites precipitated state reprisals against educated Hutus. The national army organized a campaign of killing that eventually produced around 100 thousand Hutu deaths. Similarly, in 1988 the army mounted a campaign against Hutu-based guerrilla forces that broadened into killing of thousands of Hutus. Meanwhile, within the dominant Tutsi, a 1987 coup transferred power from President Bagaza to Pierre Buyoya. Buyoya liberalized the regime to some extent, leading to a general election of 1993 in which a Hutu-dominated party temporarily came to power. The relatively free Burundian election of June 1993 brought a Hutu to the presidency for the first time.

Although the new president, Melchior Ndadaye, appointed a Tutsi prime minister and proceeded cautiously in advancing his own party's interests, leaders of the predominantly Tutsi Burundian army soon assassinated Ndadaye. Under international pressure, the soldiers then returned to barracks and restored power to a civilian government. Soon, however, Hutu activists were massacring Burundian Tutsi, whereupon the army began fierce reprisals, chiefly against Hutu. The conflict produced between thirty-five and fifty thousand Burundian deaths in a single week and accomplished a partial coup. The episode has at least as much in common with a run-of-the-mill military coup as it does with the massive Rwandan genocide of 1994. From 1994 onward, Burundi's lethal conflicts continued, but increasingly took on the character of civil war, with significant support for different factions from outside the country. Burundi alternated between genocide and civil war, as factions within both the Hutu and Tutsi categories sometimes fought each other.

In both Burundi and Rwanda, the categories "Hutu" and "Tutsi" only became relatively well defined in the course of Belgian colonial rule, and even then designated class and power as much as kinship or genetic origin. (Compare distinctions among *indios, mestizos, and latinos or blancos* in Central America.) In Rwanda, colonial authorities clearly favored those they recognized as Tutsi and ruled with their collaboration. Toward the end of Belgium's colonial control, however, two crucial things happened: radical anticolonial activists emerged disproportionately from the Tutsi elite, and the colonial regime correspondingly began to balance toward Hutu intellectual leaders. As independence approached, politicians on both side of the divide mobilized followings in ethnic terms. An initial Tutsi attempt to exterminate leaders of their Hutu opposition (1959) generated a Hutu response in which tens of thousands of Tutsi died, and many more fled the country. Between 1962 and 1964, perhaps 20,000 Tutsi lost their lives, and something like 200,000 Tutsi (40–70 percent of the surviving Tutsis in Rwanda) exited (Uvin, 1998:20). Tutsi refugees settled mainly in Uganda and established military control of Rwandan territory near the Ugandan border.

From that point to the 1990s, Hutu regional factions struggled for control of the state; the *Akazu* faction (closely associated with President Habyarimana's wife and based especially on power-holders from the president's home region in the northwest) won a dominant position. In reaction to invasion by second-generation Tutsis from Uganda, the

Akazu organized step-by-step extermination, first of Tutsi, then increasingly of Hutu who did not join the extermination effort. That spiraling genocide eventually killed close to a million civilians, until the Tutsi-based exile armies drove *Akazu* forces out of Rwanda. Once again civil war and genocide intersected. As in Somalia and Burundi, great powers and international forces did not intervene with any effectiveness until the massacres were spiraling downward. The investigators of Human Rights Watch summed it up this way:

> This genocide resulted from the deliberate choice of a modern elite to foster hatred and fear to keep itself in power. This small, privileged group first set the majority against the minority to counter a growing political opposition within Rwanda. Then, faced with RPF [Rwandan Patriotic Front] success on the battlefield and at the negotiating table, these few powerholders transformed the strategy of ethnic division into genocide. They believed that the extermination campaign would restore the solidarity of the Hutu under their leadership and help them win the war, or at least improve their chances of negotiating a favorable peace. They seized control of the state and used its machinery and its authority to carry out the slaughter.
>
> Like the organizers, the killers who executed the genocide were not demons nor automatons responding to ineluctable forces. They were people who chose to do evil. Tens of thousands, swayed by fear, hatred, or hope of profit, made the choice quickly and easily. They were the first to kill, rape, rob and destroy. They attacked Tutsi frequently and until the very end, without doubt or remorse. Many made their victims suffer horribly and enjoyed doing so.
>
> Hundreds of thousands of others chose to participate in the genocide reluctantly, some only under duress or in fear of their own lives. Unlike the zealots who never questioned their original choice, these people had to decide repeatedly whether or not to participate, each time weighing the kind of action planned, the identity of the proposed victim, the rewards of participating and the likely costs of not participating. Because attacks were incited or ordered by supposedly legitimate authorities, those with misgivings found it easier to commit crimes and to believe or pretend to believe they had done no wrong (Des Forges et al., 1999:1–2).

Age-old hatreds do not explain the political struggles that produced so much death in Somalia, Burundi, and Rwanda. Nor does a simple division between privileged rulers and rebellious subjects describe the deadly alignments. In fact, the term genocide only applies to certain phases of these complex conflicts. Mechanisms of category formation and category transformation obviously conditioned politics in all three countries. Less obviously, the crucial mechanisms generating coordinated destruction combined divide-and-rule maneuvers on the part of current power-holders, brokerage on the part of opposition leaders, and polarization that erased the middle ground between rank and file members of increasingly distinct categories. The mechanisms of divide and rule, brokerage, and polarization occur widely throughout a great variety of contentious politics. Saying so, to be sure, does not explain these bloody episodes. But it does help specify what must be explained. The explanatory problem greatly resembles those we encounter elsewhere in the study of contentious politics.

4. Opportunism

Opportunism is the version of large-scale violence that occurs when, as a consequence of shielding from routine surveillance and repression, individuals or clusters of individuals use immediately damaging means to pursue generally forbidden ends. Plenty of opportunistic violence occurred in Somalia, Burundi, and Rwanda as civil war and genocide took their deadly tolls. Let us turn, however, to a rather different example: the looting and burning that often occurs at the temporal and geographic edges of those urban uprisings authorities usually call "riots."

American ghetto rebellions of the 1960s provide graphic examples. They commonly began as confrontations between police and local residents in the course of a routine police action that went awry. The vast Los Angeles conflagration of August 1965 began, for example, with the Highway Patrol arrest of Marquette Fry, who was speeding his Buick after having a few drinks with friends, a block from his home in Watts. A large street confrontation ensued, with multiple arrests and plenty of additional police. As the police drove away from that first incident, one of the spectators (who had experienced rough treatment from police on earlier occasions) threw a soda bottle at a police car. Then:

> Rocks, bottles, pieces of wood and iron—whatever missiles came to hand—were projected against the sides and windows of the bus and automobiles that, halted for the past 20 minutes by the jammed street, unwittingly started through the gauntlet. The people had not been able to overcome the power of the police. But they could, and would, vent their fury on other white people. The white people who used the police to keep them from asserting their rights (Conot, 1967:29).

As the conflict spread, open confrontations between police, then National Guard, and Los Angeles citizens occurred through much of the Watts area. In between those street battles occurred widespread smashing, burning, and looting of neighborhood stores. Although parts of the Watts conflict qualify as organizational outcome and coordinated destruction, these activities in the interstices qualify as opportunism.

A few years after Watts, Swedish ethnographer Ulf Hannerz spent two years (August 1966 to July 1968) in a predominantly black neighborhood of Washington, D.C., learning about ghetto life. When the news of Martin Luther King's assassination reached that neighborhood, crowds gathered, and local people attacked police who arrived to establish control over the streets. For two days, looting and burning occurred. On the second day (Friday):

> Some groups went downtown but looting there was rather limited—as we have noted once before, it was particularly men's fashion stores that were hit—and there was hardly any burning outside the ghetto, where most of it continued to be concentrated on the main shopping streets. Some groups seemed to concentrate on going around "opening up" stores which had closed early—that is, they broke doors and windows to leave the way in open to looters. This made it possible for a great many to join in who had qualms about taking the first step themselves. One young mother said afterwards:
>
> "Well, you could see all the stuff lying there and all those people going in and out, and somebody was gonna take it, so I thought I could as well get some for myself." (Hannerz, 1969:173)

Fire-bombers aimed chiefly at white-owned businesses, but in a high-density area where many black tenants lived in apartments above such businesses, fire wiped out many black businesses and residences as well.

Opportunism of this sort often incites observers, analysts, and critics to concentrate on motives, hence on morality, thence on rights and obligations: If people smash, burn, and steal, can they speak seriously about demanding their rights? As Hannah Arendt argues, those are indeed important questions for political philosophy. In the perspective of contentious politics, however, it is striking how much causal process opportunism shares with dispersed resistance, organizational outcomes, and coordinated destruction. In the American cases at hand, we see familiar mechanisms of:

- activation of available we/they categories
- response to weakened, distracted, or failed repression
- signaling spirals that communicate the current feasibility and effectiveness of generally risky practices, and thereby alter the readiness of participants to face the risks in question

- selective retaliation for previously experienced wrongs

All of these mechanisms occur widely through the entire array of large-scale violence. To say so is not to say that all participants in large-scale violence share the resentment of black people in Los Angeles and Washington during the 1960s. On the contrary, it is to say that the cognitive mechanisms generating resentment in Los Angeles and Washington interact with relational and environmental mechanisms coupled with quite different cognitive mechanisms in other forms of contentious politics.

5. Violent Rituals

In violent rituals, two or more relatively well defined and coordinated groups follow a known interaction script entailing the infliction of damage on themselves or others as they compete for priority within a recognized arena. Students of violence and of contentious politics have generally avoided violent rituals as a separate genre—as sport, initiation, or display, perhaps, but not as serious politics. Some time ago, however, Richard Trexler pointed out the political stakes of Florentine public rituals about the same time that Karen and Jeffery Paige were making a more general case for coming-of-age rituals as political contests (Trexler, 1981; Paige & Paige, 1981). In both cases, failures to bring out adequate followings reduced future credibility and alliance value of the principals.

Most such rituals, to be sure, fall short of violence. But a subclass of them either incorporate violent practices into their scripts or frequently generate violent encounters as an outcome of struggles for precedence and for recognition of precedence. By-product encounters (e.g., battles between volunteer fire companies or between village age-grades) overlap our categories of dispersed resistance and organizational outcomes. Scripted violent practices (e.g., contact sports) look more like coordinated destruction. Yet it is worth giving that heterogeneous middle zone its own name—violent rituals—and separate attention.

Consider two very different examples: the potlatch of Canadian-American Northwest Coast populations and the flagellant confraternities of medieval and Renaissance Italy. Because Franz Boas founded a whole school of anthropology on study of Northwest Coast populations, anthropologists have frequently reasoned about the potlatch. In the form that crystallized after 1849 among the people Boas called Kwakiutl, potlatch designated great public displays and giveaways of wealth. In particular, performers of potlatch gave away large numbers of blankets bought from the Hudson's Bay Company and bestowed or destroyed copper shields worth a currently known number of blankets in the Kwakiutl exchange system. Potlatch may have developed from pre-1849 routines of slave-trading and warfare along the Northwest Coast (Wolf, 1999:121). In any case, the scale of potlatch escalated up to 1921, when the Canadian government stepped in to ban such a destructive procedure.

In a recent review of the ceremonial practice, Eric Wolf has linked escalation of potlatch to a survival crisis doubled with increased competition for high standing among kin groups. Coppers were rising rapidly in value, partly as a result of intensifying competition and partly as a consequence of inflation—as Kwakiutl adults moved increasingly into capitalist markets, more and more bought Hudson's Bay blankets, and the ratio of blankets to coppers increased. Destruction and reconstitution of any particular copper made it even more valuable. (If this seems strange, consider the fact that in today's world of art collectors, prices of some artists rise rapidly as a result of promotion and competition, but absolute prices of sculptures and paintings hardly ever decline.)

As suggested by the analyses of Trexler and of Paige and Paige, potlatches definitely marked ritual transitions, especially marriages between members of high-ranking kinship groups. Most dramatic was the ritual destruction of copper shields:

> These shields were equated with hundreds and thousands of blankets in distributive events, but they reached an evaluative climax when they were ritually destroyed or thrown into the sea. Throwing a copper into the sea transferred vital force to the fish-people. Melting down a copper in fire conveyed vital energy to the sky spirits. "Killing" a copper by breaking it up simulated the death of the vitality contained in it; riveting the pieces together once more, however, was understood as a transformation that multiplied its power to redistribute vital forces among human beings (Wolf, 1999:121).

In the Kwakiutl potlatch, violent ritual unquestionably partook of contentious politics. It connected, indeed, with a very general political phenomenon: the politics of reputation, in which successful or unsuccessful public defense of perquisites, precedence, and honor affects the readiness of witnesses, patrons, and clients to commit future enterprises to one or another of the contestants.

Italy's flagellant confraternities seem a far cry from Kwakiutl potlatches. Still, the two phenomena not only belong to the world of violent ritual but also share some political properties. Religious confraternities proliferated in Italy during the later Middle Ages. Chiefly restricted to relatively high-ranking males, they combined devotion, service, and public display in varying degrees. From 1260 onward a flagellant movement accelerated. Whatever other devotion, service, and public display they engaged in, they undertook penitential public self-flagellation as part of their regular activity. The Genoese *casacce*, for example, formed in the thirteenth century, continued their activity unabated into the eighteenth century, and did not disappear definitively until the nineteenth. During the fifteenth and sixteenth centuries:

> According to the chronicler Giustianiani, their principal collaborative ritual was the Good Friday procession. Five thousand confratelli clothed in sackcloth traversed the streets in total silence calling at churches and beating themselves until the blood ran in a spectacle which moved the sinful and the pious alike . . . The success of the Eucharistic cult in the fifteenth century had led the flagellant confraternities to move their main public ritual from Good Friday to Holy Thursday. The visit to the sepulchre in San Lorenzo led to bouts of fierce competition among the casacce, which centered not only on the rival displays of coffers, vestments, singing and crucifixes, but often ended in fighting which led to violent assault and even on occasion murder (Bernardi, 2000:238).

Thus Genoa's violent rituals neighbored on organizational outcomes, perhaps sometimes on coordinated destruction as well. Although no one would mistake a penitential procession for a potlatch, they had in common heavy scripting, reinforcement of solidarity within each performing group, competitive public display of standing, and significant consequences for that standing. In these regards they also bear resemblances to contact sports, violent election battles, gang rivalries, and some struggles among supporters of sporting teams or entertainment stars. The mechanisms they involve include such familiar ones as competitive display, polarization, and activation of we/they categories. Ritualized as these interactions may be, they belong at least in part to the world of contentious politics.

II. WHAT'S UP, DOC?

The DOC (dynamics of contention) program sensitizes us to similarities among very different kinds of large-scale violence. Those similarities do not rest on parallel attitudes, emotions, or impulses. Nor do they constitute a General Model of political violence. Instead, they identify partial causal analogies: similar mechanisms operating in similar ways in very different contexts, with contrasting global outcomes. In earlier analyses of violence (e.g., Tilly, 1975), I despaired of identifying any common properties across the full range of collective violence, but formulated by-product explanations of the violent conflicts I knew best: tax rebellions, struggles over food, militant marches, and so on. I argued that collective violence generally emerged from social interactions that were not intrinsically violent, and that frequently occurred without generating violence. Most people, for example, paid their taxes without attacking tax collectors, most pressure on price-gouging factors, millers, and bakers operated in nonviolent ways, and most marches went on without fights or physical intervention by the police.

That was a mistake, although not an entirely stupid mistake. By-product arguments identify significant features of the episodes this paper has clumped together under the headings of organizational outcomes and dispersed resistance, which were indeed the forms

TABLE II-2-12.2. Mechanisms in large-scale violence

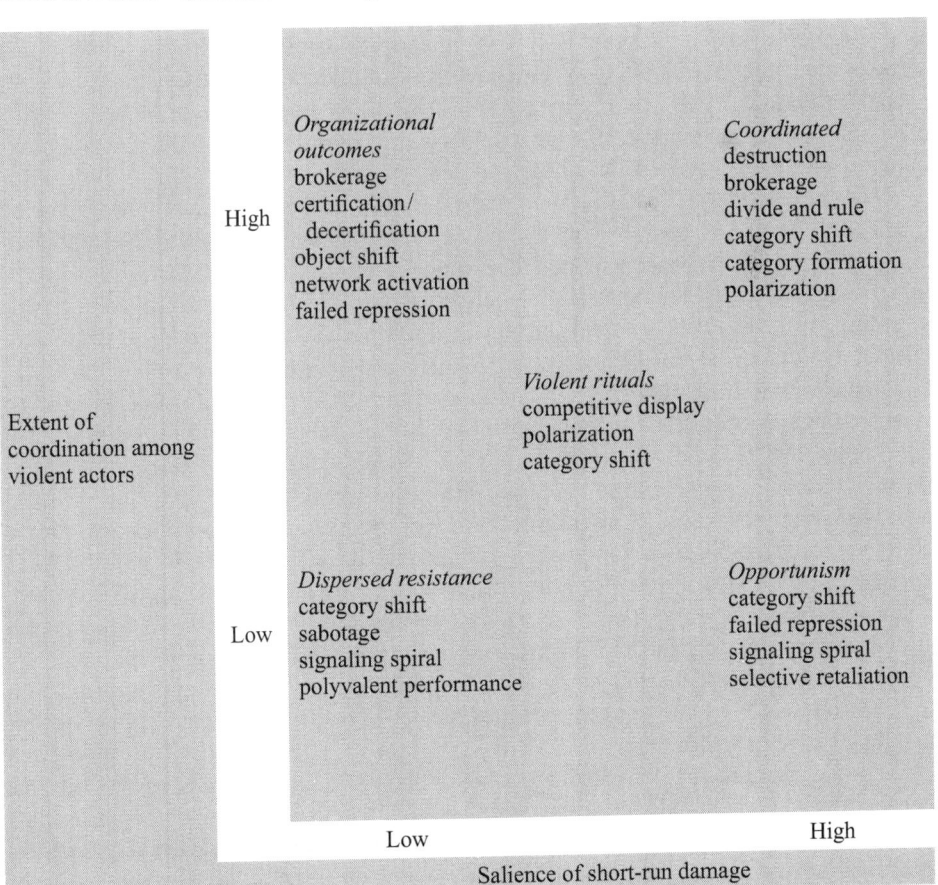

of collective violence I had been studying closely. Those arguments provided insight into the left-hand side of Table II-2-12.1, especially its upper half. They did not, however, capture significant features of violent rituals, coordinated destruction, and opportunism. They neglected the diagram's center and right-hand side as well as obscuring some features of its lower half.

As we move into forms of large-scale violence in which short-run damage becomes more salient, we also move into the world of specialists in violence—violent entrepreneurs as Vadim Volkov (1999) calls them, managers of institutionalized riot systems as Paul Brass (1996) calls them, soldiers, paramilitaries, police, mercenaries, mafiosi, thugs, or bodyguards as we meet them in other contexts. As we move farther down the space into territories where less and less coordination occurs among violent actors, we enter a world in which signals concerning the vulnerability of authorities become increasingly crucial precipitants of violent interaction.

Table II-2-12.2 makes that point by locating various mechanisms we have encountered in the coordination-salience space. Consistent with DOC principles, it declares that the relative prominence of causal mechanisms varies significantly according to type of large-scale violence. Brokerage, for example, figures more prominently in highly coordinated forms of political violence—organizational outcomes and coordinated destruction—than in the more fragmented violence of dispersed resistance and opportunism. That discovery will not much surprise students of contentious politics, but it confirms once again the intimate interaction of violent and nonviolent political processes. Category shifts (activation of available but previously less salient boundaries, plus relations within and across the boundaries) couple with signaling spirals (in which people detect and communicate the availability and feasibility of ostensibly risky practices) more regularly in the zone of low coordination among violent actors. Such contrasts point to the value of looking closely at recurrent causal mechanisms.

Let no one mistake what is going on here. In no sense have I drawn my arguments inductively from cool comparisons among cases or matched hypotheses with unbiased arrays of evidence. I have constructed the typology, selected the cases, then glossed them in my own vocabulary. I have pointed selectively to some of the many causal mechanisms generating five somewhat different clusters of large-scale violence, arguing—but not demonstrating—that those mechanisms vary systematically in prominence from one location to another within Table II-2-12.2's coordination-salience space. My effort amounts to an exercise in theory construction, an application of DOC thinking to forms of politics that have not often been so doctored. At best, any such exercise will elicit objections, reformulations, countercases, and new empirical investigations. That is my hope.

An ambitious research program follows. That program does not consist of finding comprehensive explanations for whole episodes such as the Paris Commune or the Watts uprising. Nor does it consist of identifying common properties of the clusters I have provisionally distinguished: dispersed resistance, organizational outcomes, coordinated destruction, opportunism, and violent ritual. Instead, it entails identifying and explaining particular robust causal mechanisms and processes through their investigation across multiple episodes—for example, a more serious pursuit of category shifts and signaling spirals than I have provided here.

In the medium run, paradoxically, theory and research must return to differences between violent and nonviolent forms of contention. Not that we should now resuscitate the principles of separation and heterogeneity. On the contrary, we need more careful specification of political processes promoting violent outcomes, as well as examination of what happens once violence occurs. It seems likely, for example, that the appearance of physical damage in the course of a previously nonviolent interaction alters signaling of threat and opportunity, thus changing the probability of polarization, defection, violent retaliation, and object shift. Just such contingent shifts in the direction of contention deserve closer attention than general models can ever give them.

In the long run, the DOC enterprise should replace the crude typology this paper has employed with two other sorts of taxonomy: 1) Causally similar political processes that under specified conditions generate large-scale violence. 2) Socially constructed categories having meaning precisely because their recognition by participants and observers activates certain routines, in the way that legally labeling an event as genocide activates international sanctions. Until students of large-scale violence get a better grip on causal mechanisms and processes, however, no typology should inhibit comparisons over apparently distinctive forms of violence.

At the risk of tedium, let me therefore warn against three possible misreadings of my analysis. First, the various mechanisms I have identified do not figure as necessary, much less sufficient, conditions for the types of large-scale violence with which I have paired them.

Second, although a given mechanism typically operates more prominently in some kinds of violence than others, all of them appear in more than one sort of large-scale violence.

Third, in no sense do the five clusters of mechanisms constitute exhaustive general models of their particular portions of the coordination-salience space, of large-scale violence, or of contentious politics as a whole.

Here, then, is my chief claim: most forms of large-scale violence belong to contentious politics and spring from the same causal mechanisms and processes as nonviolent contentious politics. Neither the principle of separation nor the principle of heterogeneity holds up to close scrutiny. Thinking of violence as a distinct realm of human experience erects obstacles to valid explanations of violent interaction on the large scale.

REFERENCES

Aminzade, Ronald. (1993). *Ballots and Barricades. Class Formation and Republic Politics in France, 1830–1871*. Princeton: Princeton University Press.

Arendt, Hannah. (1969). *On Violence*. New York: Harcourt, Brace & World.

Bernardi, Claudio. (2000). Corpus Domini: Ritual Metamorphoses and Social Changes in Sixteenth and Seventeenth-Century Genoa. In Nicholas Terpstra (Ed.), *The Politics of Ritual Kinship. Confraternities and Social Order in Early Modern Italy* (pp. 228–242). Cambridge: Cambridge University Press.

Brass, Paul R. (Ed.) (1996). *Riots and Pogroms*. New York: New York University Press.

Conot, Robert. (1967). *Rivers of Blood, Years of Darkness*. New York: Bantam.

Des Forges, Alison. (1999). *Leave None to Tell the Story. Genocide in Rwanda*. New York: Human Rights Watch.

Hannerz, Ulf. (1969). *Soulside. Inquiries into Ghetto Culture and Community*. New York: Columbia University Press.

Jackson, Patrick, & Daniel Nexon. (1999). Relations before States: Substance, Process, and the Study of World Politics. *European Journal of International Relations, 5*, 291–332.

Mayer, Arno J. (2000). *The Furies. Violence and Terror in the French and Russian Revolutions*. Princeton: Princeton University Press.

McAdam, Doug, Sidney Tarrow, & Charles Tilly. (1997). Toward an Integrated Perspective on Social Movements and Revolutions. In Mark Irving Lichbach & Alan S. Zuckerman (Eds.), *Comparative Politics* (pp. 142–173). Cambridge: Cambridge University Press.

Paige, Karen, and Jeffery Paige. (1981). *The Politics of Reproductive Ritual.* Berkeley: University of California Press.

Peyrefitte, Alain. (1977). *Réponses à la Violence. Rapport du Comité d'Etudes sur la Violence, la Criminalité et la Délinquance.* Paris: Presses Pocket.

Scott, James C. (1985). *Weapons of the Weak. Everyday Forms of Peasant Resistance.* New Haven: Yale University Press.

Scott, James C. (2000). The Moral Economy as an Argument and as a Fight. In Adrian Randall & Andrew Charlesworth (Eds.), *Moral Economy and Popular Protest. Crowds, Conflict and Authority* (pp. 187–208). London: Macmillan.

Stroschein, Sherrill. (2000). *Contention and Coexistence: Hungarian Minorities and Inter-Ethnic Relations in Romania, Slovakia, and Ukraine.* Unpublished doctoral dissertation in political science, Columbia University.

Tarrow, Sidney. (1998). *Power in Movement. 2nd Edition.* Cambridge: Cambridge University Press.

Tilly, Charles. (1975). Revolutions and Collective Violence. In Fred I. Greenstein & Nelon W. Polsby (Eds.), *Handbook of Political Science. Vol. 3: Macropolitical Theory* (pp. 483–555). Reading: Addison-Wesley.

Tilly, Charles. (1999). Power—Top Down and Bottom Up. *Journal of Political Philosophy, 7,* 306–328.

Trexler, Richard C. (1981). *Public Life in Renaissance Florence.* New York: Academic Press.

Uvin, Peter. (1998). *Aiding Violence. The Development Enterprise in Rwanda.* West Hartford: Kumarian Press.

Volkov, Vadim. (1999). Violent Entrepreneurship in Post-Communist Russia. *Europe-Asia Studies, 51,* 741–754.

Wolf, Eric R. (1999). *Envisioning Power: Ideologies of Dominance and Crisis.* Berkeley: University of California Press.

VIOLENT INDIVIDUALS: PERPETRATORS AND MOTIVES

PART II-3-1

PROCESSES OF LEARNING AND SOCIALIZATION

The Social Psychology of Aggression and Violence

James T. Tedeschi

I. INTRODUCTION

Most of the research in social psychology on harm doing behavior is conceived as aggression. There is no separate basic research area on violence, although sometimes high levels of aggression or inflicting physical harm are referred to as violence. The same causal factors that instigate aggressive behavior are assumed to also generate violent behavior. Examination of recent textbooks in social psychology indicate that they all have a chapter on aggression, but violence is only mentioned as a descriptive term referring to content of television programs or violent crimes. Applied researchers do of course study spouse and child abuse, sexual coercion, the effects of depictions of violence in the mass media, assaults and homicides, and (less often) terrorism, but no cohesive scientific theory of violence has been offered.

Social psychologists tend to focus on individuals in face-to-face interactions and to neglect larger scale conflicts between groups of people, such as riots and revolutions. Nevertheless, there are a few case studies of hooliganism at soccer games and experiments examining intergroup conflicts. There is a body of research that focuses on factors that might be implicated in violence, such as stereotyping of outgroup members and the tendency to view the conduct of one's own group as legitimate and the same conduct when carried out by an outgroup as illegitimate. Stereotyping and prejudice, divergent perspectives, and ingroup and outgroup biases, are extensively studied in social psychology, but the role of these cognitive factors in bringing about violent behavior has not been subjected to systematic empirical evaluation.

The evolution of theories of aggression will be described as an historical background understanding research directions in various fields of psychology, including cognitive, developmental and social psychology. A selective review of the current research on ag-

W. Heitmeyer and J. Hagan (eds.), *International Handbook of Violence Research*, 459–478.

gression indicates that divergent perspectives of alleged perpetrator and alleged victim may be important for understanding the dynamics of aggressive encounters. Furthermore, aggressive people have been shown to have hostility attribution biases. In other areas of research there is little agreement about mediators and moderators of aggressive behavior. There is sharp disagreement about the role of emotions, especially anger, in generating aggressive behavior. Controversies also exist with regard to the effects of viewing violence on television, the impact of pornography on violence toward women, and the role that alcohol plays in aggressive behavior.

II. THEORIES OF AGGRESSION IN SOCIAL PSYCHOLOGY

The laboratory study of human aggression was stimulated by frustration-aggression theory in the 1940s. Subsequent tests of the theory revealed shortcomings, which were addressed by the learning theories of Buss (1961) and Bandura (1973), and Berkowitz's (1989) reconceptualization of frustration-aggression theory as emotional aggression. Since much of the laboratory research on aggression has been theory relevant, it is appropriate to briefly describe the theories and some of the research each has generated.

1. Frustration-Aggression Theory

Laboratory research on aggression was limited primarily to examining biological factors until the 1940s. For example, Kuo (1930) found that cats do not have an instinct to kill mice or rats. The experience of kittens, particularly in observing the predatory behavior of their mothers, was the determining factor in whether the kittens would kill and eat rodents. The promulgation of frustration-aggression theory (Dollard et al., 1939) stimulated psychologists to carry out experiments on aggression. The five authors specialized in different areas of psychology, including clinical, social, biological, learning, and developmental psychology. They applied Clark Hull's (1952) behavior theory to Freud's (1938) interpretation of aggressive behavior. According to frustration-aggression theory, frustration, defined as an interference in obtaining a goal when an organism is striving to obtain the goal, automatically—because of biological prewiring—creates aggressive energy or drive. Aggressive drive instigates aggressive behavior, which usually is directed at the frustrating agent. Aggressive behavior reduces aggressive drive, a process referred to as catharsis. Drive reduction is reinforcing, and therefore aggressive behavior is self-reinforcing. The organism's aggressive behavior, like any other behavior, is shaped by rewards and punishments. If aggressive behavior is punished or the organism learns to expect punishment for engaging in it, the organism will be inhibited. Whenever the organism does not perform an instigated aggressive behavior, the aggressive drive remains. This drive state may lead the organism to engage in displaced aggression which may take the form of some other noninhibited aggressive behavior against the frustrating agent (i.e., response generalization) or aggression against a substitute person who is in some way similar to the frustrating agent (i.e., stimulus generalization).

a. DIRECT EFFECT OF FRUSTRATION ON AGGRESSION. Laboratory research tested three major aspects of frustration-aggression theory: (1) the direct effects of frustration on aggression, (2) whether performing aggressive behavior is cathartic, and (3) displacement of aggression toward substitute targets. The research on the direct effects of frustration produced mixed results. Frustration in the form of task failure (Buss, 1966) or time-out from positive reinforcements (Jegard & Walters, 1960) did not cause human subjects to be more aggressive toward another person. On the other hand, when the individual is insulted, given high levels of shock by another person, or treated unjustly, increased aggression does occur (Berkowitz, 1965; Buss, 1961; Geen, 1968, Gentry, 1970). A distinction was made between arbitrary and justified frustration in an attempt to understand contradictory results (Pastore, 1952; Cohen, 1955). The idea was that a person would become angry only when experiencing arbitrary frustration, but not when the frustrating agent was justified in interfering with the person's attempt to achieve a goal. Thus, if task failure or time-outs from positive reinforcements did not cause aggression, it might be because the frustration was justified.

Overall, the evidence does not support a direct relationship between frustration and aggression. Not only has research indicated a variety of frustrating conditions that are not associated with aggression, but related research indicates that frustration may cause other forms of behavior, such as depression or learned helplessness. It has also been said that frustration is the mother of all invention. Furthermore, some forms of frustration, such as playing golf or climbing cliffs, may be exciting and fun. In place of the term frustration more precise terms , such as attack, withdrawal of reinforcement, and delay of reinforcement, have become commonplace. Bandura (1973) has shown that these more precisely defined conditions lead to different behavioral outcomes.

b. CATHARSIS. Early tests of the catharsis hypothesis interpreted aggressive drive as autonomic nervous system (ANS) activity, which was measured in the form of heart rate, respiration rate, and so on. In a series of experiments Hokanson (1970) found that frustration in the form of insults from another person caused increased ANS arousal, and delivering electric shocks to that person reduced ANS arousal. However, in this research subjects were only allowed to give more or less shocks to the other person, and did not have an option to behave in other ways. When subjects received shocks from another person who was said to have had the opportunity to choose to give a token reward or to pass on a given trial, males reciprocated by giving shocks back. However, female subjects tended to respond to shocks with conciliatory behavior. Both males and females showed the increased ANS arousal when receiving shocks, and reduction in ANS arousal after their aggressive or conciliatory behavior. Apparently, there is a reduction of arousal when any behavior sequence is completed, and it is not specific to catharsis produced by aggressive behavior.

An implication of the catharsis hypothesis is that when an aggressive behavior is performed, and drive reduction occurs, the organism would be less aggressive if given an immediate opportunity to again aggress against a frustrating agent. However, reviews of the literature (e.g., Geen & Quanty, 1977) indicate that performing an aggressive response increases aggressiveness.

c. DISPLACEMENT OF AGGRESSION. A displacement effect has been reliably demonstrated (Tedeschi & Norman, 1985). For example, Doob and Wood (1972) had a confederate annoy subjects and then gave some of them an opportunity to shock him, while others were given an opportunity to shock a third party. The third party was shocked just as much as the annoying person. The interpretation by frustration-aggression theory is that subjects aggressed against the innocent third party because aggressive drive had built up and needed to be released or reduced by aggressive behavior. However, the evidence does not support a catharsis process. Thus, frustration-aggression theory, which we know to be inadequate, has produced a reliable phenomenon (displacement), but the explanation for it cannot be correct.

2.   Buss's Theory of Instrumental Aggression

Buss (1961) explained aggression in terms of instrumental conditioning. Research has shown that reinforcements do increase both the frequency and intensity of aggressive behavior (Geen & Pigg, 1970; Geen & Stonner, 1971). Frustration may lead to aggression, if that is the response that it associated with such an antecedent condition and subsequently reinforced. Buss also considered anger and personality as factors that need to be considered in explaining aggressive behavior. He indicated that anger increases the intensity but not the form of response performed by a person. Hostility is an attitude that develops out of negative experiences and persists over time, and may motivate aggressive acts of vengeance. Buss and Durkee (1957) developed a Hostility Inventory, which has been used in numerous research projects with varying success in predicting aggressive behavior. Buss believed that people had certain temperaments, perhaps determined largely by genetic endowment, that remained relatively unchanged throughout the life span. Impulsiveness, activity level, independence, and intensity of actions were temperament types that he associated with aggressive behavior. Thus, Buss brought emotions and personality into the empirical study of human aggression. A shortcoming of Buss's theory is that it views the individual as pushed by historical forces (i.e., past reinforcements). Habit patterns are simply tripped off by cues in the environment. Newer, cognitively oriented learning theories have since emerged in which individuals are viewed as examining choice alternatives and making decisions based on anticipated future outcomes.

3.   Bandura's Social Learning Theory

Bandura (1983) proposed a cognitively oriented social learning theory of aggressive behavior. According to this theory individuals learn aggressive behavior by observing models who act in aggressive ways. Imitation of the model's aggressive behavior is likely when the model's behavior is reinforced. Vicarious learning involves four interrelated processes (Bandura, 1983). First, the observer must pay attention to the cues, responses and outcomes associated with the modeled event. Second, an encoding of the observation must occur. Third, the encoded cognitive processes must be transformed into the imitative response. And, last, the learned response will be performed if the appropriate incentive conditions are present. It should be noted that an important distinction for Bandura is between learning a behavior pattern and performing it. The encoding process represents the learning of the behavior, while the incentive conditions elicit the performance of it.
     Bandura developed a set of procedures to investigate modeling of aggression in which children observed an adult hit, kick, and yell at a large plastic clown (Bobo). Studies have shown that children more often imitate the model's behavior if the model was reinforced, and are inhibited from imitating when the model was condemned (e.g., Hicks, 1968a). Furthermore, it has been found that children recall and repeat aggressive behavior

several months after observing aggressive behavior by a model (Hicks, 1968b). Characteristics of the model are important in determining whether the individual will pay attention to the model's conduct and the influence that the model has on the subsequent imitative responses of the observer. For example, children more often imitated the aggressive behavior of a high status teacher than a low status teacher (Grusec & Mischel, 1966).

Bandura's theory stimulated research on the effects of corporal punishment by parents on their children. By using punishment parents serve as a model to the child, and if the punishment is effective in controlling the child, the parents' aggressive behavior is reinforced. While the child may be inhibited by fear of retaliation from acting aggressively toward the parents, they may use aggressive behavior to control others. This reasoning was supported by research showing that children who experience corporal punishment from parents engage in more fighting than control children (Bandura & Walters, 1963; Hoffman, 1970). To take this reasoning a step further it might be hypothesized that parents who abuse their children may have learned the behavior by observing their own parents. That is, abusive parents may have been abused when they were children. Examination of this intergenerational hypothesis has shown that a small percentage of abusive parents report that they were abused as children (Gil, 1973). In addition to interview studies involving retrospective reports, prospective studies in which abused children are followed over time have found a relationship between child abuse and violent behavior later in life (McCord, 1983; Widom, 1989). However, caution needs to be used in interpreting modeling as a cause of aggressive behavior from these correlational studies. A series of studies indicate that any form of parental maltreatment, whether it be neglect, sexual abuse, or physical abuse, is associated with a likelihood of having a criminal record and other forms of misbehavior (McCord, 1983; Matt, 1992). A meta-analysis of the effects of family experiences on delinquency and conduct disorders found that harsh discipline was not an important predictor of misbehavior (Loeber & Schmaling, 1985).

The emphasis of learning theories, such as those of Buss and Bandura, is on the acquisition and performance of responses, sometimes referred to as skills by Bandura. In Bobo experiments children learn to punch, kick, and yell, responses that when aimed at another child can do harm. Aside from Buss's acknowledgement of the presence of social norms, there is very little in these theories about the social context of behavior. Other people are simply stimuli, serving as cues to elicit or perhaps to inhibit aggressive behavior, depending on the reinforcement history of the individual or the encodings of cue-response-outcome contingencies learned from observing models. The developments in aggression research in the 1980s and 1990s were in the direction of examining cognitive, emotional, and social factors that might be involved in aggressive behavior.

4. Berkowitz's Theory of Emotional Aggression

Berkowitz (1993) has developed a theory of emotional aggression that has dominated social psychological research on aggression for several decades (see Geen, 1990). According to Berkowitz (1993), there are two systems of aggression—emotional and instrumental. Emotional aggression is based on innate tendencies of organisms to respond aggressively (or by flight) to aversive stimulation. Aversive stimuli produce negative affect in individuals, and the negative affect creates a desire to hurt, which, in turn, instigates aggressive behavior. This innate system is modifiable by experience and may be indirectly affected by emotions and cognitions. Aversive stimuli may prime negative thoughts and feelings, adding to the intensity of negative affect experienced by the individual, and the intensity of aggressive behavior. Anger does not instigate aggression, but may be a parallel process. Anger does not cause aggression, but it does induce negative thoughts and feelings that adds to negative affect. Thus, anger may facilitate aggression, but it is not an instigator.

While emotional aggression is aimed at hurting the target, instrumental aggression is simply a means of achieving others goals that might require hurting a target. For example, a robber's goal is to get the loot and not to harm the victim. However, harming the victim may be a necessary aspect of getting the loot. As the organism gains experience, its behavior is increasingly guided by environmental cues. Instrumental aggression is grafted onto the more primitive or basic system of emotional aggression. As a consequence, emotional aggression becomes less likely to be automatic, but instead is given expression only to appropriate cues.

Over the past four decades there has been a vigorous investigation of Berkowitz's theory of emotional aggression. It has been found that exposure to noise, air pollution, high population density, and personal space invasions may increase aggressive behavior (Mueller, 1983). However, these conditions facilitate or intensify aggression only when some other factor instigates it (Zillmann, 1983). Thus, exposure to noise or air pollution do not cause people to become aggressive, but when a person is instigated to be aggressive, its intensity will be greater if aversive physical stimuli are present.

A series of studies examined the role of cues in aggressive behavior. In one study a person identified as a boxer or a speech major insulted subjects (Berkowitz, 1965), who then were exposed to either a film depicting a violent boxing scene or a film about canal boats. In the guise of evaluating a work product of the other person, subjects were most aggressive when they had been insulted, the other person was a boxer, and they had viewed a violent boxing scene. Witnessing the fight scene had no impact on the aggressiveness of participants if they had not been first insulted by the other person. It is not clear whether this kind of result supports Berkowitz's theory. If viewing the fight film created more negative affect in the participants than watching boats float down a canal, then there should have been some impact of the fight film on aggressive behavior whether or not the confederate had insulted them. On the other hand, it might be argued that viewing the film after one has been angered might lead to different associated thoughts than watching it without being angered first. Thus, associated cognitions primed by the fight film might have created more negative affect in the insult condition. Another possibility is that the responses of participants merely reflect what they believe the experimenter wants them to do. A person who has just been insulted by a boxer, then is given a fight film to view, and then is given an opportunity to deliver electric shocks to the boxer may believe that the experimenter expects them to use more rather than less shocks—which is the only choice participants have in the situation.

Weapons are cues that prime negative thoughts in most people. According to Berkowitz's theory, the mere presence of weapons may make people more aggressive. Not only do people pull the triggers of guns, but the trigger can pull the finger (Berkowitz, 1981:12). A number of experiments have been carried out in which guns, knives and other weapons are placed directly on an apparatus which is used by participants to deliver electric shocks to another person. The results of some of these studies appear to support the hypothesis that the presence of weapons increases aggression. However, there are a significant number of weapons related studies that have produced null or even reverse effects (see Tedeschi & Felson, 1994:60–65).

5. Social Interactionist Theory

In a radical departure from more traditional approaches, the social interactionist theory proposes that the concept of aggression should be abandoned as a scientific concept (Tedeschi, Smith, & Brown, 1974). An alternative language of coercive actions is preferred and is used to integrate aggression research into a more general theory of power and influence. The types of coercive actions include threats, punishments, and bodily force. The theoretical question to be answered is why people choose to use threats, punishments, and/or bodily force against one another. The social interactionist theory (Tedeschi & Felson, 1994) proposes that there are three basic motives for the use of coercive actions: social control, justice, and identity. One of the implications of this viewpoint is that the typical methods of studying aggression in the laboratory may underrepresent the construct of aggression, or possibly may not even be interpretable as aggression (Tedeschi & Quigley, 1996, 2000).

a. Conceptual Issues.   The concept of aggression is an observational term which purportedly identifies a common attribute that all such responses have. The most accepted definition of aggression is that it refers to any behavior that the actor performs with an intent to do harm. In an analysis of this definition Tedeschi, Melburg, and Rosenfeld (1981) argued that no aggression theorist has defined intent and seldom are the intentions of participants in aggression experiments assessed. Furthermore, there is an implicit value judgment made when identifying aggressive behaviors. It is usual to distinguish between legitimate and illegitimate forms of aggression. For example, it is legitimate for a judge to impose a fine on a traffic violator or for a parent to punish disobedience by a child, but it is illegitimate for a person to rob a victim of money or for a motorist to punish another motorist for violation of traffic laws. Since what is considered legitimate or illegitimate varies across people within a society and between cultures, the distinction is a subjective one. This is important because aggression theorists are clearly concerned with explaining illegitimate forms of aggression, and therefore must use their subjective values to identify the appropriate responses. It is typically assumed that the causes of legitimate and illegitimate forms of aggression are different. According to social interactionist theory, there is no necessity for distinguishing between legitimate and illegitimate threats, punishments, or bodily force because the essential motives that explain their use are the same. A judge who punishes a traffic violator and a motorist who punishes another motorist both have the motive to punish someone who violated a rule—that is, a justice motive.

b. Social Control Motivation.   Social control motivation is one of the three basic motives for engaging in coercive actions. It is assumed by social interactionist theory that people are reward-seeking and punishment-avoiding organisms, and that most reinforcements are mediated by other people. For example, if we want money, we must somehow convince someone to give it to us, and if we want love, we must make ourselves lovable to someone. In other words, if we are going to achieve our goals, we must influence others to do what we need them to do so that we can have what we want. The primary concern of a person motivated by social control is to gain compliance from target persons. Of course there are many ways to influence others, including persuasion, offers of exchange, promises, forming of alliances, and modeling. Stronger techniques include the use of threats, punishments, and bodily force. It is proposed that coercive actions are used when the actor believes that other forms of influence will not work and the actor is not willing to forgo the interpersonal goal. Among the conditions that undermine confidence in positive forms of influence, and hence increase the likelihood of coercion, are the lack of social skills, intelligence, education, or possession of resources that would allow a person to effectively use them. A person with low intelligence or who is inarticulate cannot form effective persuasive messages, and a person without resources cannot offer exchanges or make believable promises. Consistent with this explanation is the fact that violent criminals have lower intelligence than nonviolent criminals (Wilson & Herrnstein, 1985) and that inarticulateness is related to spouse abuse (Infante, Chandler, & Rudd, 1989). Conflict also undermines the confidence that positive forms of influence will work since the parties know that each is motivated to obtain a resource that both desire. The lack of trust that is inspired by knowledge that each is acting out of self-interest may place the individual into a situation of letting the other person have the desired resource or of using coercive means to attain it (Deutsch, 1969). The scarcity and value of resources in conflicts are related to their intensity, and the likelihood that coercion will be used.

c. JUSTICE MOTIVATION. When a perceived injustice occurs to a victim or to others who are socially identified with the victim, the emotion of anger is experienced and the motive for restoring or imposing justice on the perpetrator is aroused. The injustice may represent what is perceived as an unfair distribution of positive or negative resources, privileges, or responsibilities, or some set of procedures for making decisions that are perceived as unfair, or violation of norms of how people ought to treat one another. A person who is motivated to restore justice may do nothing, may reconsider the event and decide that the purported perpetrator is not responsible for an injustice (remove blame), may forgive the perpetrator, may make a demand that the perpetrator make restitution or offer an apology, or may punish the perpetrator.

The grievant may do nothing when the costs of acting are perceived as high, as for example might be the case when an employee believes her supervisor treated her unfairly. Expressing anger and demanding some change in the supervisor's behavior could be costly in terms of job security and advancement. If the perpetrator provides explanations that excuse or justify his conduct, the grievant may remove blame, and the injustice no longer exists. Research has shown that accounts of what has been perceived as misconduct can be effective in revising judgments by others (cf. McLaughlin, Cody, & Read, 1992). The use of apologies and remorse by a perpetrator may induce a grievant to forgive previous unjust actions and reduce the likelihood that punitive actions will be taken (Ohbuchi, Kameda, & Agarie, 1989). If the perpetrator agrees to demands for restitution or an apology, the grievant may feel that the episode has been satisfactorily closed, but if the perpetrator resists such demands, there is the possibility that the conflict between the two parties will escalate. The grievant may follow the biblical law of lex talionis and impose a harm on the perpetrator which is modulated to be about equivalent to the degree of harm done by the prior unjust action. The tit for tat behavior of participants in laboratory experiments, which has been interpreted as retaliatory behavior, has been interpreted as a desire to restore justice (Donnerstein & Hatfield, 1982).

d. IDENTITY MOTIVATION. The third motive for engaging in coercive actions, according to social interactionist theory, is the desire to assert or to protect identities. A person may try to establish a reputation as being tough by provoking others into fights (Toch,

1993) or by acting as a bully against whipping boys (Olweus, 1978). These proactive actions are typically staged in front of audiences to build the desired reputation. The individual desires an identity as tough, courageous, or bad because it serves his social control interests by gaining compliance from those who are afraid of him. A person may also act to defend his identities when it is perceived that another person has threatened or attacked them. When an affront is perceived, a character contest may ensue (Goffman, 1955). Actions that are perceived as showing disrespect or attacking valued identities will motivate the target to save face. If the target does nothing, she will look weak, ineffective, and perhaps as assenting to the affronts that have occurred, and it may encourage subsequent disrespect from the offender and by third parties. Thus, the target is highly motivated to turn the tables by putting the offender down by the use of insults. While this may put the person one up in the relationship, the other party is now motivated to counterattack, and an escalation process occurs which may lead to violence (Felson & Steadman, 1983; Luckenbill, 1977).

e. OVERDETERMINATION. The course of a coercive episode may involve all three motives proposed by social interactionist theory (Ohbuchi, Fukushima, & Tedeschi, 1999), although they may occur at different points in the episode or be present in different degrees at any particular time. For example, an episode may begin with an attempt at social control through persuasion, which the target person resists. Perhaps it is important for the source to obtain compliance from the target and so a stronger demand is made. The target person may interpret such a demand as a form of disrespect and respond by insulting the source. Each person may interpret the other's behavior as unfair or unjust. Thus, a failed attempt at social control may lead to a character contest and perceptions of injustice, and the processes that are associated with justice and identity motivations. The presence of multiple motives is a form of overdetermination that may intensify the behaviors performed by the person.

f. LIMITATIONS OF CURRENT RESEARCH PARADIGMS. The dynamic character of most coercive episodes are not captured by experiments that basically maintain a stimulus-response character. Most research has a confederate insult or deliver noxious stimuli to a participant, who is then given an opportunity to deliver noxious stimuli to the confederate. The participant is under strong constraints imposed by the instructions of the experimenter. In most cases the instruction is that they must administer noxious stimuli to another person, and the measure of aggression is how much is administered. Viewed in this way it may be said that the main instigation to aggression found in social psychological research is obedience to authority (cf. Milgram, 1974). It may be questioned whether this obedient behavior is aggression (Gottfredson & Hirschi, 1990).

Research on aggression is conducted by giving participants cover stories that they are to act as teachers and use the noxious stimuli to punish the other person's errors (and presumably help them learn), or that they are to evaluate the work product of another person by giving one to ten shocks, which represents a rating scale from excellent to poor. Still another set of procedures sets up the exchange of shocks as a competitive game. These cover stories act as frames within which the meaning of actions are modified. While in the teacher/learner frame, giving shocks to a learner who makes errors may do harm, the participants' motive may be to help the other person to learn. But a critical component of the definition of aggression is that the actor has the intent to do harm. Similarly, if the participant believes that giving shocks is necessary for giving a rating, then the goal of giving a shock is not to harm the other person, although of course that may happen, but rather it is to obey the experimenter and do the best job of evaluation one can do.

Tedeschi and Quigley (1996, 2000) strongly recommend that researchers should investigate the construct validity of the major empirical paradigms for studying aggression, and that modifications be made to give participants more freedom in deciding whether to harm others. They note that aggression researchers seldom study threats or the recursive nature of coercive episodes. Evaluation of the processes proposed by social interactionist theory will require the invention of new procedures for studying coercive behavior.

III. CURRENT RESEARCH AND CONTROVERSIES IN THE DISCIPLINE

Eddies of research on aggression have emerged in developmental, cognitive, and personality psychology. No general theory has emerged from these sometimes isolated studies, but they have identified components to an overall process that leads to aggressive conduct. It will be useful, then, to examine an hostility attribution bias, divergent perspectives, and excitation transfer as processes that contribute to an understanding of human aggression. In response to salient and important social problems, social psychologists have also examined the impact of pornography on aggression toward women, the effect of violent programs on the mass media on viewers' aggression, and the effects of alcohol consumption on aggressive behavior. The research on these applied areas have generated controversies within the discipline.

1.   Hostility Attribution Bias and Divergent Perspectives

Toch (1969) studied violent men who were in prison and observed that they often engaged in what they believed were preemptive attacks. These men had a paranoid style of attributions with a tendency to infer hostile intentions by others. Parents who attribute their children's misbehaviors or failures to willful disobedience are more likely to be abusive (Frodi & Lamb, 1980). Institutionalized, aggressive boys display a tendency to attribute hostility to other boys (Nasby, Hayden, & DePaulo, 1980).

In their study of elementary school children Dodge and Newman (1981) found that aggressive children made more hostile attributions about fictitious others and remembered hostile information better than did nonaggressive children. In a subsequent study, Dodge and Somberg (1987) found that attributions of hostility toward another led to direct aggressive actions toward him. If the target strikes back, the retaliation can be interpreted as verifying the original hostility attribution, and the circle is closed. While some people may have a more paranoid attributive style than others, most observers tend to weigh negative information about an actor more heavily than positive information, and this tendency may contribute to attributions of blame under ambiguous circumstances (Kanouse & Hanson, 1971).

The perspective of the person involved in an aggressive episode affects the attributions that are made about the other actor. For example, Mummendey, Linneweber, and Löschper (1984) assigned participants roles as actors or recipients of actions. Actors viewed their actions as provoked, while recipients perceived attacks as unprovoked. Interviews of married couples indicated that husbands and wives have very different memories of what the other person experienced as a serious transgression (Mikula & Heimgartner, 1992). Blaming others may be a form of self-justification, but divergences may be a product of a fundamental attribution error (Ross, 1977). In general actors tend to view their own behavior as constrained by environmental forces, while observers tend to perceive actors as first causes of their actions.

Hostility attribution bias, divergent perspectives, attributions of blame, and a negativity bias probably contribute to negative reactions toward another person. This reaction may produce a further reaction from the other person, and a conflict spiral and aggressive behavior may be the outcome. Combined with scripts about how to react to negative actions of others or habitual responses to conflict, cognitive processes contribute to the likelihood of aggressive behavior.

2. Emotions and Aggression

Psychologists have strong differences about what emotions are, what arouses them, and what effects they have. One view is that there is some primitive level of emotional reaction, such as flight or fight dispositions, which is enriched, interpreted, and guided by cognitive mechanisms (Berkowitz & Heimer, 1989). Another view is that emotions are constructed and can be understood only by consideration of language, attributions, and appraisals (Averill, 1983). Still another approach considers social norms as providing the basis for interpreting and expressing emotions. Eclectic approaches combine each of these levels of analysis, giving more or less weight to one or another of the processes. These wide differences in describing what an emotion is may have stunted the development of research on emotions and aggression, which has been limited primarily to the study of anger and aggression.

Zillmann (1983) has proposed that the intensity of anger is associated with the degree of autonomic arousal that the individual experiences. He proposed a process of excitation arousal to explain why people sometimes seem to overreact to provocations or frustrations that they experience. A person might be aroused in numerous ways—by watching an exciting film or by riding a bicycle, for example. The arousal dissipates over time but a residual amount may still be present when the individual is no longer aware of its presence. If at such a time the individual is angered, there will be a greater intensity of anger than would have been experienced if the residual arousal had not been present. Because for Zillmann aggression is often learned as a response in anger producing situations, heightened anger leads to more intense aggression. Thus, excitation transfer is a process by which physiological arousal may summate across situations to produce enhanced aggressive behavior. It would be fair to say that the majority of aggression researchers have been convinced by Zillmann's research. However, Tedeschi and Felson (1994:75–83) examined his evidence and raised questions about Zillmann's procedures, specific patterns of results in experiments, and about the problems associated with experimental manipulations of conditions to produce different levels of arousal. For example, the basic idea of excitation transfer is that there is residual arousal available when a person is angered. However, most of the research has first angered the participants and then had them watch pornographic films or ride bicycles. Also, whenever a manipulation creates different levels of arousal, it presumably also induces different cognitions. Thus, all of the studies done to investigate excitation transfer might also be interpreted as due to ideas, expectations, or other interpretations of conditions made by participants.

Berkowitz and Heimer (1989) proposed that anger and aggression are parallel processes. Negative affect, negative ideas or cognitions, and aggressive response tendencies may be associated as nodes in a network so that when one is activated, they tend to reverberate and activate associated nodes. Aversive stimuli may bring about negative ideas and anger, and also instigate aggressive responses. These nodes are elements of the same syndrome and produced by the same antecedent condition—aversive stimuli. Thus, anger does not cause aggression, although sometimes they occur together.

Averill (1983) and Tavris (1982) have proposed that expressions of anger only sometimes lead to aggressive behavior, but usually have constructive outcomes. Presumably, the constructive or destructive outcomes that anger may have depend upon how it is expressed. And, how anger is expressed is probably a learned behavior. Tedeschi and Felson (1994) have proposed that anger produces justice motivation. When a negative event is blamed on another actor, the victim is angered, and anger produces a desire to remedy the injustice. In their social interactionist theory Tedeschi and Felson (1994) attempted to state some of the conditions in which an angered person is likely to engage in aggressive behavior.

There is evidence to support all of the above theories, but many anomalous findings have also been obtained. It will be some time before the relationship between anger and aggression is clarified. Even less is known about the impact of other social emotions, such as jealousy, humiliation, envy, and fear, on aggressive behavior. For more information on this topic, the reader might turn to the chapter by Baumeister in this volume

3.   Television Violence and Aggression

The Bobo studies carried out to examine Bandura's social learning theory indicated that a model's aggressive behavior could induce imitative responses by the observer. Because many of the characters in movies and television programs are rewarded for aggressive behavior, it could be asked whether viewers are likely to become more aggressive themselves. Three approaches have been used to study the effects of viewing mass media violence on aggressive behavior: laboratory studies, longitudinal studies, and field studies. Meta-analyses have found that effects in laboratory studies have been reliable and substantial (Andison, 1977; Hearold, 1986). The National Institute of Health (1982) and the American Psychological Association (1993) have publicly concluded that there is a significant relationship between viewing violence on television and aggressive behavior. Yet, a few psychologists remain unconvinced.

The generalizability of laboratory findings has been questioned. One argument is that the use of noxious stimuli in laboratory experiments is rationalized to participants as ratings or teaching procedures, or as a competitive game that is being played with another person. Experimenters legitimate, encourage, and even demand that participants administer electric shocks or noxious noise to another person. It is not clear that without the legitimations of a high status person or the permissive social climate that presenting such programs creates that viewing violent programs would have the same effects (Cook, Kendzierski & Thomas, 1983; Freedman, 1984). A second argument is that violent programs are shown to research participants apart from the context of other programs that are available outside the laboratory. This selectivity itself may enhance the effects on viewer aggression that are found. A third argument is that demand cues are strong in these studies. As was mentioned when we examined Berkowitz's cue-arousal experiments, the sequencing of events that include insult, an aggressive cue (such as guns or another person identified as a boxer), watching a violent film, and finally directions to give shocks to another person may indicate to participants that they should deliver more shock rather than less shock. The film is an added component that may serve to communicate what the experiment would like participants to do. It is noteworthy that watching violent films in laboratory studies typically has no effect on aggressive behavior unless the participants have first been insulted or otherwise attacked.

The most important problem associated with the research on television violence is that it has not shown which processes or mechanisms are activated by viewing violence and how such viewing gets converted into aggressive behavior. While most studies show a small but significant relationship, they do not establish a causal one. A number of processes have been suggested, including modeling, cultural spillover, priming, desensitization, and unrealistic fear. Modeling can explain the fact that airline hijackings, civil disorders, and suicides tend to increase after a highly publicized instance takes place. However, these contagion effects reflect news events and not fictional ones, and it needs to be established that viewing fictional forms of violence induces imitative behavior. Straus (1991) proposed that viewing fictional programs may create legitimation for violence that spill over into everyday life. Very little research has been carried out to examine this process.

We have seen that Berkowitz's neoassociationist model incorporates the idea that aggressive stimuli prime hostile thoughts and contribute to negative affect, thereby increasing aggressive behavior. Huesmann (1982) proposed that viewers of television programs learn scripts about how to behave in various situations. Later when placed in similar circumstances, or perhaps in seeking out such circumstances, the scripts are activated in the form of aggressive or violent conduct. There is scattered evidence that can be interpreted as priming of aggressive or scripted forms of violence, but it is inadequate to draw any firm conclusions about these processes.

Still another process that has been proposed is that observing so many thousands of murders over the years, viewers become desensitized to the plight of victims. A desensitized person no longer is aroused by viewing a murder, and has little or no sympathy for the victim. This indifference to suffering may make it easier for a desensitized person to hurt others. There is some evidence that desensitization results from frequent viewing of television violence (cf. Rule & Ferguson, 1986), but no evidence that desensitization makes people more aggressive. Insofar as television distorts the real world and makes it appear more dangerous than it is, people may develop unrealistic fear of others. This distrust may lead them to make hostile attribution biases and engage in preemptive actions. While there is some evidence that people who watch a lot of television do have unrealistic fears, there is little or no evidence that unrealistic fear resulting from viewing television leads to aggressive behavior.

Until social psychologists pin down the causal processes that allegedly mediate the impact of viewing violence on television on aggressive behavior, it would be premature to conclude that there is a causal relationship. On the other hand, given the grave import of such a relationship, if it exists, policy makers appear willing to err in the direction of assuming that it does.

4. Pornography and Aggression

Sigmund Freud (1933) speculated that sadistic and masochistic behaviors frequently occur in normal sexual relations. Research done with male animals has demonstrated that concentrations of testosterone are associated with both sexual and aggressive behaviors (Bernstein, Gordon, & Rose, 1983)[1]. One possible implication of a connection between sex and aggression is that viewing pornography may increase the amount of aggression by men against women.

Several early studies indicated that subjects who are provoked and then shown an erotic film are more aggressive than provoked subjects who have seen a neutral film or no film (e.g., Zillmann, 1971; Meyer, 1972). On the other hand, it has also been found that exposure to pictures of nude women lowered the aggressiveness of provoked subjects (e.g., Baron, 1974). These inconsistent early studies did not focus on male aggressiveness toward women, however. More systematic studies were undertaken to determine whether observing pornographic films can make male subjects more aggressive against female than against male victims. The usual finding in laboratory studies of aggression is that both men and women are more aggressive toward men than women (e.g., Taylor & Epstein, 1967).

No clear pattern of results has been obtained across studies of pornography and aggression. A greater amount of aggressiveness by men toward women as compared to other men has been shown only under two specific conditions: when the male participants are angered and either the pornographic film contains violence, or a depicted victim of rape confirms a rape myth by showing a pleasurable response to the violence (cf. Donnerstein & Linz, 1986). Since it had already been established that viewing violent films can increase the intensity of aggressive behavior by already angered subjects, it may be the violence and not the sexual content of the film that facilitates aggression. The victim's response to the violence might also serve as a demand cue to subjects about the responsiveness of women to being hurt. If so, a positive response to violence in the film might have served as a cue that they are expected to give more shocks, and a negative response to violence in the film might serve as an inhibitory cue to give fewer shocks to a female target.

It has been argued that the effects of viewing pornography on aggression may be indirect. Negative attitudes toward women may be fostered by depictions of women as sexual playthings, and sexist attitudes may increase the likelihood of sexual coercion (MacKinnon, 1984). A few studies have shown that viewing pornography may be associated with less favorable attitudes toward women (e.g., Malamuth, 1986), but the link from attitudes to aggressive behavior has not been established. Furthermore, Reiss (1986) reported that men who were interested in pornography had more liberal attitudes toward women.

5.   Alcohol and Aggression

Alcohol is associated with criminal assaults (Martin & Bachman, 1997) and homicides (Shupe, 1954; Virkkunen, 1974). Reviews of research also indicate a reliable impact of alcohol on aggressive behavior in laboratory experiments (Bushman & Cooper, 1990; Ito, Miller, & Pollock, 1996). Despite intense investigation of the alcohol-aggression relationship, it is not known at this time what specific mechanism mediates it. A physiological perspective suggests that psycho-pharmacological effects on cognitive functioning may be responsible for the relationship, while a cultural perspective suggests that the symbolic meaning of drinking may create self-fulfilling behavior.

---

[1] There is no convincing evidence that testosterone affects aggressive behavior in humans (cf. Svare & Kinsley, 1987).

a. PSYCHOPHARMACOLOGICAL EFFECTS. Imbibing a small amount of alcohol may produce physiological arousal, but larger doses produce sedative effects and reduced responsiveness to stressful stimuli (Wallgren & Barry, 1970; Levenson et al., 1980). Since it has been well established that arousal may intensify aggressive behavior, it could be suggested that low doses of alcohol would lead to more aggression than imbibing larger amounts. However, Taylor and Gammon (1975) found that subjects who ingested larger doses of bourbon or vodka were more aggressive than subjects who drank a lesser amount. In general no clear relationship has been found between the arousal effects of alcohol and aggression.

One proposed pharmacological effect on cognition is that inebriated persons may be less sensitive to the contingencies involved in interpersonal behavior. For example, Zeichner and Pihl (1979) showed sober persons reduce their use of aversive stimuli against another person when the other person used a tit-for-tat strategy of responsiveness as compared to a condition where there was no such contingency. However, inebriated persons aggressively administered aversive stimuli in both conditions, despite the fact that doing so led to receiving more aversive stimuli from the other person. This effect may be associated with a failure to perceive inhibitory cues. Steele and Southwick (1985) proposed that when there is strong instigation to aggression and salient inhibitory cues (a condition they refer to as inhibitory conflict), drinking may have a disinhibitory effect. In a meta-analysis of relevant studies, they found support for their hypothesis. However, a direct experimental test of the inhibitory conflict hypothesis would be desirable.

Ingestion of alcohol may make it more difficult for a person to interpret social situations, a condition of ambiguity that may trigger the negative inferences of persons with a hostile attribution bias. Support for this hypothesis was found by Schmutte, Leonard, and Taylor (1979). Subjects faced variable levels of shock from another player in a competitive game. Those who had been drinking estimated that the level of shock they would receive as greater than did control subjects. Despite attributing a higher intent to do harm to the other person, subjects who had been drinking did not act more aggressively than did control subjects.

b. Cultural Effects

There are cultural differences in the effects of alcohol consumption on social behavior (MacAndrew & Edgerton, 1969). In Japan, for example, alcohol is associated with congenial social relations rather than aggressiveness. Such cultural differences throw doubt on any psychopharmacological explanation for the effects of alcohol consumption. In the United States drinking evokes stereotypes and expectancies related to aggressive conduct. In a survey of 400 respondents, it was found that moderate drinkers report that drinking gives them a feeling of power and makes them more assertive, and reduces tension and anxiety (Brown et al., 1980). If these beliefs get converted into self-fulfilling behaviors, the result could be greater aggressiveness.

In support of an expectancy hypothesis, subjects in placebo conditions have been shown to be more aggressive than control subjects (Lang et al., 1975; Zeichner & Pihl, 1979). However, a meta-analysis of experiments comparing placebo and alcohol conditions found no overall difference between placebo and control groups (Bushman & Cooper, 1990). Placebo conditions may not be the best way to examine alcohol expectancy effects. There may be strong individual differences in alcohol-related expectancies, and self-fulfilling prophesies leading to aggressive behavior may occur only when a particular set of schemata exist. Tedeschi and Felson (1994) suggested that expectancies may be channeled through aspects of identity. For example, males who desire a macho identity and who believe that drinking transforms them into more dynamic, courageous, and assertive persons, may be less polite to others, and their offensive conduct may precipitate conflicts. Given expectations of how they should act (i.e., how men should act), especially in honor-based cultures (cf. Nisbett & Cohen, 1996), they may also be more confrontive and less likely to be conciliatory in conflict situations.

IV. CONCLUSION

Future research on aggression will probably try to resolve controversies that exist in the present literature. There is also a growing literature on the development of the deviant and aggressive personality, which appears to be a trait developed early in life based on the individual's neurophysiological predispositions and negative social experiences. It is important that the methods of doing research be enriched to examine the way aggressive episodes evolve, escalate, and terminate. The older methods of manipulating stimuli and measuring response outputs under highly constrained conditions have not tested models that include cognitive, emotional, and motivational components. The nonrecursive nature of the existing methods is too static to capture the dynamics of aggressive episodes. In addition, researchers of aggression should expand the scope of phenomena included in their domain of interest. Reactions to injustice, attacks on identity, conflict management, anger control, power relations, and the use of threats and punishments to control the behavior of others are just some of the topics that have been neglected by traditional approaches to studying the social psychology of aggression.

REFERENCES

American Psychological Association. (1993). *Violence and Youth: Psychology's Response. Vol. I: Summary Report of the American Psychological Association Commission on Violence and Youth.* Washington: American Psychological Association.

Andison, F. Scott. (1977). TV Violence and Viewer Aggression: A Cumulation of Study Results: 1956–1976. *Public Opinion Quarterly, 41,* 314–333.

Averill, James R. (1983). Studies on Anger and Aggression: Implications for Theories of Emotion. *American Psychologist, 38,* 1145–1160.

Bandura, Albert. (1973). *Aggression: A Social Learning Analysis.* Englewood Cliffs: Prentice-Hall.

Bandura, Albert. (1983). Psychological Mechanisms of Aggression. In Russell G. Geen & Edward I. Donnerstein (Eds.), *Aggression: Theoretical and Empirical Reviews. Vol. 1* (pp. 1–40). New York: Academic Press.

Bandura, Albert, & Richard H. Walters. (1963). *Social Learning and Personality Development.* New York: Holt, Rinehart & Winston.

Baron, Robert A. (1974). The Aggression-Inhibiting Influence of Heightened Sexual Arousal. *Journal of Personality and Social Psychology, 30,* 318–322.

Berkowitz, Leonard. (1965). The Concept of Aggressive Drive: Some Additional Considerations. In Leonard Berkowitz (Ed.), *Advances in Experimental Social Psychology. Vol. 2* (pp. 301–329). New York: Academic Press.

Berkowitz, Leonard. (1981). How Guns Control Us. *Psychology Today, 15,* 11–12.

Berkowitz, Leonard. (1989). The Frustration-Aggression Hypothesis: An Examination and Reformulation. *Psychological Bulletin, 106,* 59–73.

Berkowitz, Leonard. (1993). *Aggression: Its Causes, Consequences, and Control.* New York: McGraw-Hill.

Berkowitz, Leonard, & Karen Heimer. (1989). On the Construction of the Anger Experience: Aversive Events and Negative Priming in the Formation of Feelings. In Leonard Berkowitz (Ed.), *Advances in Experimental Social Psychology. Vol. 22* (pp. 1–37). New York: Academic Press.

Bernstein, Irwin S., Thomas P. Gordon, & Robert M. Rose. (1983). The Interaction of Hormones, Behavior, and Social Context in Nonhuman Primates. In Bruce Svare (Ed.), *Hormones and Aggressive Behavior* (pp. 535–562). New York: Plenum.

Brown, Sandra A., Mark S. Goldman, Andres Inn, & Lynn R. Anderson. (1980). Expectations of Reinforcement from Alcohol: Their Domain and Relation to Drinking Patterns. *Journal of Counseling and Clinical Psychology, 48*, 419–426.

Bushman, Brad J., & Harris M. Cooper. (1990). Effects of Alcohol on Human Aggression: An Integrative Research Review. *Psychological Bulletin, 107*, 341–354.

Buss, Arnold H. (1961). *The Psychology of Aggression*. New York: Wiley.

Buss, Arnold H. (1966). Instrumentality of Aggression, Feedback, and Frustration as Determinants of Physical Aggression. *Journal of Personality and Social Psychology, 3*, 153–162.

Buss, Arnold H. & Ann Durkee. (1957). An Inventory for Assessing Different Kinds of Hostility. *Journal of Consulting Psychology, 21*, 343–349.

Cohen, Albert. (1955). *Delinquent Boys*. New York: Free Press.

Cook, Thomas D., Deborah A. Kendzierski, & Stephen V. Thomas. (1983). The Implicit Assumptions of Television: An Analysis of the 1982 NIMH Report on Television and Behavior. *Public Opinion Quarterly, 47*, 161–201.

Deutsch, Morton. (1969). Socially Relevant Science: Reflections on Some Studies of Inter-personal Conflict. *American Psychologist, 24*, 1076–1092.

Dodge, Kenneth A., & Joseph P. Newman. (1981). Biased Decision-Making Processes in Aggressive Boys. *Journal of Abnormal Psychology, 90*, 375–379.

Dodge, Kenneth A., & Daniel R. Somberg. (1987). Hostile Attributional Biases among Aggressive Boys are Exacerbated under Conditions of Threats to Self. *Child Development, 58*, 213–224.

Dollard, John, Leonard Doob, Neal E. Miller, O. Hobart Mowrer, & David R. Sears. (1939). *Frustration and Aggression*. New Haven: Yale University Press.

Donnerstein, Edward, & Elaine Hatfield. (1982). Aggression and Inequity. In Jerald Greenberg & Ronald L. Cohen (Eds.), *Equity and Justice in Social Behavior* (pp. 309–336). New York: Academic Press.

Donnerstein, Edward, & Daniel Linz. (1986). Mass Media Sexual Violence and Male Viewers. *American Behavioral Scientist, 29*, 601–618.

Doob, Anthony N., & Loraine Wood. (1972). Catharsis and Aggression: The Effects of Annoyance and Retaliation on Aggressive Behavior. *Journal of Personality and Social Psychology, 22*, 156–162.

Felson, Richard B., & Henry J. Steadman. (1983). Situational Factors in Disputes Leading to Criminal Violence. *Criminology, 21*, 59–74.

Freedman, Jonathan L. (1984). Effects of Television Violence on Aggressiveness. *Psychological Bulletin, 96*, 227–246.

Freud, Sigmund. (1933). *New Introductory Lectures on Psychoanalysis*. New York: Norton.

Freud, Sigmund. (1938). *Basic Writings of Sigmund Freud*. Translated and edited, with an introduction, by A. A. Brill. New York: Modern Library.

Frodi, Ann M., & Michael E. Lamb. (1980). Child Abusers' Responses to Infant Smiles and Cries. *Child Development, 51*, 238–241.

Geen, Russell G. (1968). Effects of Frustration, Attack, and Prior Training in Aggressiveness upon Aggressive Behavior. *Journal of Personality and Social Psychology, 9*, 316–321.

Geen, Russell G. (1990). *Human Aggression*. Pacific Grove: Brooks/Cole.

Geen, Russell G., & Roger Pigg. (1970). Acquisition of an Aggressive Response and Its Generalization to Verbal Behavior. *Journal of Personality and Social Psychology, 15*, 165–170.

Geen, Russell G., & David Stonner. (1971). The Effects of Aggressiveness Habit Strength upon Behavior in the Presence of Aggression-Related Stimuli. *Journal of Personality and Social Psychology, 17*, 149–153.

Geen, Russell G., & Michael B. Quanty. (1977). The Catharsis of Aggression: An Evaluation of a Hypothesis. In Leonard Berkowitz (Ed.), *Advances in Experimental Social Psychology. Vol. 10* (pp. 2–39). New York: Academic Press.

Gentry, William D. (1970). Effects of Frustration, Attack, and Prior Aggressive Training on Overt Aggression and Vascular Processes. *Journal of Personality and Social Psychology, 16*, 718–725.

Gil, David G. (1973). *Violence against Children: Physical Child Abuse in the United States*. Cambridge: Harvard University Press.

Goffman, Erving. (1955). On Face-Work: An Analysis of Ritual Elements in Social Interaction. *Psychiatry, 18,* 213–231.

Gottfredson, Michael R. & Travis Hirschi. (1990). *A General Theory of Crime.* Stanford: Stanford University Press.

Grusec, Joan, & Walter Mischel. (1966). Model's Characteristics as Determinants of Social Learning. *Journal of Personality and Social Psychology, 4,* 211–215.

Hearold, Susan. (1986). A Synthesis of 1043 Effects of Television on Social Behavior. In George Comstock (Ed.), *Public Communication and Behavior. Vol. 1* (pp. 65–133). San Diego: Academic Press.

Hicks, David J. (1968a). Effects of Co-Observer's Sanctions and Adult Presence on Imitative Aggression. *Child Development, 39,* 303–309.

Hicks, David J. (1968b). Short and Long-Term Retention of Affectively Varied Modeled Behavior. *Psychonomic Science, 11,* 369–370.

Hoffman, Martin L. (1970). Moral Development. In Paul H. Mussen (Ed.), *Carmichael' Manual of Child Psychology. Vol. 11* (pp. 261–359). New York: Wiley.

Hokanson, Jack E. (1970). Psycholophysiological Evaluation of the Catharsis Hypothesis. In Edwin I. Megargee & Jack E. Hokanson (Eds.), *The Dynamics of Aggression* (pp. 74–86). New York: Harper & Row.

Huesmann, L. R. (1982). Television Violence and Aggressive Behavior. In David Pearl, Lorraine Bouthilet & Joyce Lazar (Eds.), *Television and Behavior: Ten Years of Scientific Progress and Implications for the Eighties. Vol. 2: Technical Reviews* (pp. 220–256). Washington: National Institute of Mental Health.

Hull, Clark L. (1952). *A Behavior System.* New Haven: Yale University Press.

Infante, Dominic A., Teresa A. Chandler, & Jill E. Rudd. (1989). Test of an Argumentative Skill Deficiency Model of Interspousal Violence. *Communication Monographs, 56,* 163–177.

Ito, Tiffany A., Norman Miller, & Vicki E. Pollock. (1996). Alcohol and Aggression: A Meta-Analysis on the Moderating Effects of Inhibitory Cues, Triggering Events, and Self-Focused Attention. *Psychological-Bulletin, 120,* 60–82.

Jegard, Suzanne, & Richard Walters. (1960). A Study of Some Determinants of Aggression in Young Children. *Child Development, 31,* 739–747.

Kanouse, David E., & L. Reid Hanson. (1971). Negativity in Evaluations. In Edward E. Jones, David E. Kanouse, Harold H. Kelley, Richard E. Nisbett, Stuart Valins & Bernard Weiner (Eds.), *Attribution: Perceiving the Causes of Behavior* (pp. 47–62). Morristown: General Learning Press.

Kuo, Zing-Yang. (1930). The Genesis of the Cat's Response toward the Rat. *Journal of Comparative Psychology, 11,* 1–35.

Lang, Alan R., Daniel J. Goeckner, Vincent J. Adesso, & G. Alan Marlatt. (1975). Effects of Alcohol on Aggression in Male Social Drinkers. *Journal of Abnormal Psychology, 84,* 508–518.

Levenson, Robert W., Kenneth J. Sher, Linda M. Grossman, Joseph Newman, & David B. Newlin. (1980). Alcohol and Stress Response Dampening: Pharmacological Effects, Expectancy, and Tension Reduction. *Journal of Abnormal Psychology, 89,* 528–538.

Loeber, Rolf, & Karen B. Schmaling. (1985). Empirical Evidence for Overt and Covert Patterns of Antisocial Conduct Problems: A Meta-Analysis. *Journal of Abnormal Child Psychology, 13,* 337–353.

Luckenbill, David F. (1977). Criminal Homicide as a Situated Transaction. *Social Problems, 25,* 176–186.

MacAndrew, Craig, & Robert B. Edgerton. (1969). *Drunken Comportment: A Social Explanation.* Chicago: Aldine.

MacKinnon, Catharine. (1984). Not a Moral Issue. *Yale Law and Policy Review, 2,* 321–345.

Malamuth, Neil M. (1986). Predictors of Naturalistic Sexual Aggression. *Journal of Personality and Social Psychology, 50,* 953–962.

Martin, Susan Ehrlich, & Ronet Bachman. (1997). The Relationship of Alcohol to Injury in Assault Cases. In Marc Galanter, et al. *Alcohol and Violence: Epidemiology, Neurobiology, Psychology, Family Issues. Recent Developments in Alcoholism. Vol. 13* (pp. 41–56). New York: Plenum Press.

Matt, Charles. (1992). *Violence and Delinquency in Abused and Neglected Emotionally Disturbed Children.* Unpublished Master's Thesis. State University of New York at Albany.

McCord, Joan. (1983). A Forty Year Perspective on Effects of Child Abuse and Neglect. *Child Abuse and Neglect, 7,* 265–270.

McLaughlin, Margaret L., Michael J. Cody, & Stephen J. Read (Eds.) (1992). *Explaining Oneself to Others: Reason Giving in a Social Context.* Hillsdale: Erlbaum.

Meyer, Timothy P. (1972). The Effects of Sexually Arousing and Violent Films on Aggression Behavior. *Journal of Sex Research, 8,* 324–331.

Mikula, Gerald, & Arno Heimgartner. (1992). *Experiences of Injustice in Intimate Relationships.* Unpublished manuscript, University of Graz, Austria.

Milgram, Stanley. (1974). *Obedience to Authority: An Experimental View*. New York: Harper & Row.

Mueller, Charles W. (1983). Environmental Stressors and Aggressive Behavior. In Russell G. Geen & Edward I. Donnerstein (Eds.), *Aggression: Theoretical and Empirical Reviews. Vol. 2* (pp. 51–76). New York: Academic Press.

Mummendey, Amélie, Volker Linneweber, & Gabi Löschper. (1984). Actor or Victim of Aggression. Divergent Perspectives—Divergent Evaluations. *European Journal of Social Psychology, 14,* 291–311.

Nasby, William, Brian Hayden, & Bella M. DePaulo. (1980). Attributional Bias among Aggressive Boys to Interpret Unambiguous Social Stimuli as Displays of Hostility. *Journal of Abnormal Psychology, 89,* 459–468.

National Institute of Mental Health. (1982). *Television and Behavior: Ten Years of Scientific Progress and Implications for the Eighties. Vol. 1, Summary Report.* Washington: United States Government Printing Office.

Nisbett, Richard E., & Dov Cohen. (1996). *Culture of Honor: The Psychology of Violence in the South.* Boulder: Westview Press

Ohbuchi, Ken-Ichi, Masuvo Kameda, & Nariyuki Agarie. (1989). Apology as Aggression Control: Its Role in Mediating Appraisal of and Response to Harm. *Journal of Personality and Social Psychology, 56,* 219–227.

Ohbuchi, Ken-Ichi, Osamu Fukushima, & James T. Tedeschi. (1999). Cultural Values in Conflict Management: Goal Orientation, Goal Attainment, and Tactical Decision. *Journal of Cross-Cultural Psychology, 30,* 51–71.

Olweus, Dan. (1978). *Aggression in the Schools: Bullies and Whipping Boys.* Washington: Hemisphere.

Pastore, Nicholas. (1952). The Role of Arbitrariness in the Frustration-Aggression Hypothesis. *Journal of Abnormal and Social Psychology, 47,* 728–731.

Reiss, Ira L. (1986). *Journey into Sexuality: An Exploratory Voyage.* Englewood Cliffs: Prentice Hall.

Ross, Lee. (1977). The Intuitive Psychologist and His Shortcomings: Distortions in the Attribution Process. In Leonard Berkowitz (Ed.), *Advances in Experimental Social Psychology. Vol. 10* (pp. 174–221). New York: Academic Press.

Rule, Brendan G., & Tamara J. Ferguson. (1986). The Effects of Media Violence on Attitudes, Emotions, and Cognitions. *Journal of Social Issues, 42,* 29–50.

Schmutte, Gregory T, Kenneth E. Leonard, & Stuart P. Taylor. (1979). Alcohol and Expectations of Attack. *Psychological Reports, 45,* 163–167.

Shupe, Lloyd M. (1954). Alcohol and Crime: A Study of the Urine-Alcohol Concentration Found in 882 Persons Arrested During or Immediately after the Commission of a Felony. *Journal of Criminal Law & Criminology, 44,* 661–664.

Steele, Claude M., & Lillian Southwick. (1985). Alcohol and Social Behavior I: The Psychology of Drunken Excess. *Journal of Personality and Social Psychology, 48,* 18–34.

Straus, Murray A. (1991). Discipline and Deviance: Physical Punishment of Children and Violence and Other Crime in Adulthood. *Social Problems, 38,* 133–153.

Svare, Bruce, & Craig H. Kinsley. (1987). Hormones and Sex-Related Behavior. In Katherine Kelley (Ed.), *Females, Males and Sexuality: Theories and Research* (pp. 13–58). Albany: State University of New York Press.

Tavris, Carole. (1982). *Anger: The Misunderstood Emotion.* New York: Simon & Schuster.

Taylor, Stuart P., & Seymour Epstein. (1967). Aggression as a Function of the Interaction of the Sex of the Aggressor and the Sex of the Victim. *Journal of Personality, 35,* 474–485.

Taylor, Stuart P., & Charles B. Gammon. (1975). Effects of Type and Dose of Alcohol on Human Physical Aggression. *Journal of Personality and Social Psychology, 32,* 169–175.

Tedeschi, James T., Bob B. Smith, III, & Robert C. Brown, Jr. (1974). A Reinterpretation of Research on Aggression. *Psychological Bulletin, 89,* 540–563.

Tedeschi, James T., Valerie Melburg, & Paul Rosenfeld. (1981). Is the Concept of Aggression Useful? In Paul Brain & David Benton (Eds.), *A Multi-Disciplinary Approach to Aggression Research* (pp. 23–37). Elsenier North Holland: Biomedical Press.

Tedeschi, James T., & Nancy Norman. (1985). Social Mechanisms of Displaced Aggression. In Edward J. Lawler (Ed.), *Advances in Group Processes: Theory and Research. Vol. 2* (pp. 29–56). Greenwich: JAI Press.

Tedeschi, James T., & Richard B. Felson. (1994). *Violence, Aggression and Coercive Actions.* Washington: American Psychological Association.

Tedeschi, James T., & Brian M. Quigley. (1996). Limitations of Laboratory Paradigms for Studying Aggression. *Aggression and Violent Behavior: A Review Journal, 1,* 163–177.

Tedeschi, James T., & Brian M. Quigley. (2000). A Further Comment on the Construct Validity of Laboratory Aggression Paradigms: A Response to Giancola and Chermack. *Aggression and Violent Behavior: A Review Journal, 5*, 127–136.

Toch, Hans H. (1969). *Violent Men: An Inquiry into the Psychology of Violence.* Chicago: Aldine-Atherton.

Toch, Hans H. (1993). Good Violence and Bad Violence: Self-Presentations of Aggressors through Accounts and War Stories. In Richard B. Felson & James T. Tedeschi (Eds.), *Aggression and Violence: Social Interactionist Perspectives* (pp. 193–208). Washington: American Psychological Association.

Virkkunen, M. (1974). Alcohol as a Factor Precipitating Aggression and Conflict Behavior Leading to Homicide. *British Journal of Addictions, 69*, 149–154.

Wallgren, Henrik, & Herbert B. Barry, III. (1970). *Actions of Alcohol: Biochemical, Physiological, and Psychological Aspects. Vol. 1.* Amsterdam: Elsevier.

Widom, Cathy S. (1989). Does Violence Beget Violence? A Critical Examination of the Literature. *Psychological Bulletin, 106*, 3–28.

Wilson, James Q., & Richard J. Herrnstein. (1985). *Crime and Human Nature.* New York: Simon & Schuster.

Zeichner, Amos, & R. O. Pihl. (1979). Effects of Alcohol and Behavior Contingencies on Human Aggression. *Journal of Abnormal Psychology, 88*, 153–160.

Zillmann, Dolf. (1971). Excitation Transfer in Communication-Mediated Aggressive Behavior. *Journal of Experimental Social Psychology, 7*, 419–434.

Zillmann, Dolf. (1983). Arousal and Aggression. In Russell G. Geen & Edward I. Donnerstein (Eds.), *Aggression: Theoretical and Empirical Reviews. Vol. 1* (pp. 75–101). New York: Academic Press.

Emotions and Aggressiveness

Roy F. Baumeister and Brad J. Bushman

I. INTRODUCTION

Emotions constitute an important category of the psychological causes of aggression and violence. Although it would be absurd to suggest that emotions are the sole or primary causes of aggression, they constitute a very important and proximal factor. Ultimately, violent acts consist of individual human beings inflicting harm on other human beings. The emotional states of the perpetrators at those moments can have a decisive effect on the degree of violence and even on whether any aggression occurs at all.

For present purposes, aggression is defined as any behavior that is intended to harm another person. It is understood that the victim wishes to avoid harm; in cases where the victim desires the harm, the behavior is not considered aggression. Emotion, meanwhile, is understood as a subjective state, typically marked by a temporary change in arousal levels and an evaluative response to some event. Thus, whereas aggression is a behavior, emotion is a feeling state, and so the links between aggression and behavior involve relationships between objective actions and subjective feelings.

The effects of emotion are far from uniform, as this review will make clear. Some emotions (such as anger and frustration) instigate and increase aggression. Others (such as guilt) tend to deter aggression.

Although no one denies that emotions can play an important role in causing aggression, the debates have been frequent and fierce as to just how that role is played. The causal processes by which emotion affects aggression have begun to emerge from years of research, and no one theory or mechanism has a monopoly on the facts in this topic. Rather, the current state of knowledge indicates that an assortment of different causal processes and mechanisms must be recognized. It is also very conceivable that further work, especially in connection with new advances in the theoretical understanding of emotion, will reveal new, additional processes by which emotions affect aggression. Although further advances may be anticipated, many particular conclusions are fairly solid and clear at this point.

W. Heitmeyer and J. Hagan (eds.), *International Handbook of Violence Research*, 479–493.
© 2003 Kluwer Academic Publishers. Printed in the Netherlands.

II. EMOTIONS AS CAUSES OF AGGRESSION

1. Frustration and Aggression

In their seminal book *Frustration and Aggression*, Dollard, Doob, Miller, Mowrer, and Sears (1939) proposed the frustration-aggression hypothesis. They summarized their two main points on the book's first page: (a) "the occurrence of aggressive behavior always presupposes the existence of frustration" (p. 1), and (b) "the existence of frustration always leads to some form of aggression" (p. 1). They defined frustration as "an interference with the occurrence of an instigated goal response at its proper time in the behavior sequence" (p. 7). In simpler words, an event is frustrating if it interferes with one's ability to achieve a goal.

Dollard and his colleagues formulated the frustration-aggression hypothesis from the early writings of Sigmund Freud (1934 [1917]). Freud believed that people are primarily motivated to seek pleasure and avoid pain. People were presumed to be frustrated when their pleasure-seeking or pain-avoiding behavior was blocked. Freud regarded aggression as the "primordial reaction" to frustration. Later, Freud revised his opinions and began to propose that some aggression derives from an innate drive or instinct (e.g., Freud, 1961 [1920]; 1930). The view that aggression is innate and instinctual has remained controversial, and proposing innate or instinctual sources of behavior was anathema to many American academic psychologists, who wanted to emphasize learning and social experiences as the crucial determinants. Hence the strong statements by Dollard and his colleagues: By insisting that frustration always preceded aggression, they offered a formula that dispensed with any need to postulate an aggressive instinct. The widespread reality of aggression could be understood by invoking frustration everywhere.

Dollard and his colleagues identified three factors that contribute to the magnitude of the frustration and the subsequent aggression (Dollard et al., 1939:28–32). The first was the strength of instigation to the frustrated response. In plain terms, the more strongly the person wanted something, the more frustrated he or she is over being denied it. The second was the degree of interference with the frustrated response. A small hindering is less frustrating than a total blockage. The third moderator was the number of frustrated-response sequences. Being repeatedly or frequently thwarted should produce more frustration (and hence more aggression) than being thwarted only once.

Research studies were cited to support the three contributors to frustration. The first factor (strength of desire) had been studied in various ways. In one memorable study (Sears & Sears, 1940), researchers took a bottle of milk away from a hungry 5-month-old baby, either after the baby had consumed only 0.5 ounces, after the baby had consumed 2.5 ounces, or after the baby had consumed 4.5 ounces. The more the baby had been able to achieve some degree of satisfaction, the less frustrated it was (and the less it protested through crying) when further satisfaction was arbitrarily thwarted.

The second moderator discussed by Dollard and his colleagues was the degree of interference with the frustrated response. In one classic study, Hovland and Sears (1940) found that the number of lynchings in 14 southern states was negatively correlated with economic conditions ($r = -.67$). Thus, the less money farmers could get for their cotton, the more frustrated they were presumed to be, and so the more violent they became in terms of extralegal aggression. More recent analyses of these data using time series analysis have confirmed this finding, although the relation was weaker than what Hovland and Sears reported (Hepworth & West, 1988).

The third factor involved the number of frustrated-response sequences, which was hypothesized to influence the strength of the aggressive response. Dollard and his colleagues (1939) posited that minor frustrations add together to produce more aggression than would be observed from the frustration that occurs immediately before the aggressive response. To support their claim, they cited sleep deprivation studies in which minor frustrations have been shown to bring about "explosions of wrath" (Katz & Landis, 1935:32). The more the person was deprived of sleep, the greater proneness to aggressive outbursts.

Over the years it became obvious that Dollard and his colleagues had substantially overstated the case. Miller (1941), one of the original authors of *Frustration and Aggression*, was himself quick to revise the assertion that frustration *always* leads to aggression. Even though research has continued to confirm that frustration is one important cause of aggression, it is not the only cause, nor does it invariably produce aggression. As Berkowitz (1989) summarized the data, frustration is neither necessary nor sufficient to cause aggression. Most people do not get everything they want, and so in a sense they are repeatedly frustrated, but the majority of these frustrations do not lead to aggression. Furthermore, some forms of aggression do not depend on frustration.

Recognizing that frustration only sometimes causes aggression has led many researchers to search for moderators. Frustrations that appear arbitrary, intentional, and unjustified elicit the most aggression. In contrast, frustrations that seem expected and understandable, or that were not intended, or that can be recognized as legitimate are much less likely to produce aggression.

2. Unpleasant Emotions in General

A broad reformulation of the frustration-aggression hypothesis was proposed by Berkowitz (1989). Recognizing that many acts of aggression do not follow from any apparent frustration, he shifted the analysis to focus on negative affect (that is, unpleasant emotions). In his view, the reason frustration often succeeds in causing aggression is that being thwarted causes these states of negative affect to arise, and these cause aggression. In a sweeping statement, he proposed that all forms of negative affect cause aggression.

Berkowitz's theory is thus the broadest statement about the link between emotions and aggressiveness. From Berkowitz's perspective, any sort of bad feeling is likely to increase aggressive tendencies. Hence not only frustration but any sort of aversive event can lead to aggression, as long as it generates emotional distress or bad moods (Berkowitz, 1983, 1989, 1990, 1993). Aversive events can be either nonsocial (e.g., physical pain, extreme temperatures, loud noises, unpleasant odors, smoke) or social (e.g., interpersonal frustration and provocation). In his studies, people who were subjected to the mildly painful experience of holding their hands in ice water were later more aggressive than others, even though the aggression had no meaningful connection to the ice water.

Negative affect produced by unpleasant experiences, in turn, automatically stimulates various thoughts, memories, expressive motor reactions, and physiological responses associated with both fight and flight tendencies. The fight associations give rise to rudimentary feelings of anger, whereas the flight associations give rise to rudimentary feelings of fear.

Berkowitz's theory assumes that cues present during an aversive event become associated with the event and with the thoughts, memories, expressive motor reactions, and physiological responses triggered by the event. In addition, however, his theory invokes higher order cognitive processes, such as appraisal and attribution processes. If people are motivated to do so, they may use higher order cognitive processes to further analyze their situation. For example, they may think about how they feel, make causal attributions for what led them to feel this way, and consider the consequences of acting on their feelings. This more deliberate thought produces more clearly differentiated feelings of anger, fear, or both. It can also suppress or enhance the action tendencies associated with these feelings.

As a novel integration of affective and cognitive processes, Berkowitz's theory represents an important new conception of aggression. Critics suggest however that it may be too broad to say that all negative affect leads to aggression. There is a broad range of bad moods and aversive emotional states, and many of them have not been shown to cause aggression. Berkowitz extrapolated from a limited range of findings to propose the generalization that all negative affect stimulates aggression, but this must be recognized as an extrapolation rather than a proven fact. In any case, the next generation of research can build on Berkowitz's theory to determine more precisely which negative emotional states cause aggression and under what circumstances they do so.

3. Anger

Anger is associated with aggression in popular beliefs, and in this case the beliefs are correct: Anger does increase the likelihood and the severity of aggression. Indeed, aggression is sufficiently important that many studies of aggression include an anger instigation without even mentioning it. The reason is that many other variables only produce aggression in combination with anger. For example, non-angry people who drink alcohol do not typically become more aggressive, but when alcohol combines with anger the result is a higher level of aggression than anger alone will produce (Bushman, 1997; Bushman & Cooper, 1990). Likewise, film violence alone fails to produce an increase in aggression, but film violence combined with anger can produce elevated levels of aggression under certain circumstances (Berkowitz & Geen, 1966; Geen & Berkowitz, 1967). In other words, alcohol and film violence only cause aggression in combination with anger. Researchers who are interested in the effects of alcohol or film violence therefore induce anger in their research participants, even though the researchers are not specifically interested in the effects of anger.

As with frustration, the link between anger and aggression should not be overstated. A great deal of anger occurs without producing aggression, and some aggression occurs in the absence of anger. Thus, anger is neither necessary nor sufficient to cause aggression (see Averill, 1982; Tavris, 1989). Still, it is an important and powerful cause.

Current research sorts emotions into four categories, defined by crossing pleasant versus unpleasant feelings with high versus low arousal. Anger falls in the unpleasant, high arousal category. It thus both feels bad and energizes the person. Angry people are thus highly motivated to take action, because the unpleasantness makes people want to do something to bring about a change, and the high arousal contributes to initiative.

The other side of the energizing aspect of anger, however, is that this contributes to making people feel strong and powerful. Anger can thus be a powerful force to help people stand up for what is right. The civil rights movement, the feminist movement, and other causes probably benefited from anger and the resultant willingness to take action.

Anger is also potentially potent in interpersonal relations. Anger can intimidate other people, especially because many people seek to avoid overt conflict. Gaining a reputation for violent rages can serve the individual's long-term goals, if other people start cooperating with one's wishes in order to prevent anger. Anger can serve a social function by providing an advance warning of possible aggression, thereby enabling other people to resolve the conflict and smooth things over before the angry person turns violent. Some people exploit this function effectively and use incipient anger to get others to go along with their wishes.

Ultimately, these considerations suggest that anger can actually play a positive role in interpersonal relations, contrary to the very negative assessments drawn by some experts such as Tavris (1989). Anger may serve as a sign of potential aggressive activity. If other people respond to the anger by addressing the conflict, they may be able to resolve it without its leading to violence. In contrast, if anger did not exist, conflict might lead directly to aggression without any advance warning, and this would increase the total amount of harm and injury in the world. These remarks are speculative, however.

4. Shame and Humiliation

An important set of emotional causes of violence and aggression consists of the feelings that arise when one's pride, reputation, or self-esteem is impugned by others. Threats to self-esteem set off feelings of anger and shame, and aggressive responses are especially likely.

To understand the emotional patterns and their effects on aggression, it is necessary to appreciate the distinction between shame and guilt. Tangney (1991, 1995) has built on earlier work by Lewis (1971) to establish this distinction precisely. Both shame and guilt involve aversive emotional states that arise in connection with one's misdeeds. The crucial difference is that guilt focuses on the act, whereas shame focuses on the self. Guilt may bring considerable regret and remorse over what one has done, and the guilty person certainly sees the action as having been wrong or undesirable, but the bad feelings do not generalize to the self as a whole. In contrast, shame entails the feeling that one is a bad person, with the recent misdeed being merely one sign or confirmation.

Shame thus involves a global condemnation of the self, coming usually in the wake of some misdeed or the exposure thereof. Shame may also become acute when some other person calls attention to possible or alleged shortcomings in the self.

Shame evokes a variety of responses, only some of which are aggressive. Shame is often experienced as an unsolvable problem—after all, if the whole self is bad, there is not much that can be easily done. In this respect, shame contrasts sharply with guilt, because guilt focuses narrowly on a specific action, and its ill effects can often be addressed. Guilt therefore motivates people to apologize, make amends, resolve to change their future behavior, or in other ways repair any interpersonal damage that may have been done (see Baumeister, Stillwell, & Heatherton, 1994). Shame, in contrast, creates a sense of helplessness, and so the person may withdraw and hide from social contact. Alternatively, shame may cause the person to lash out aggressively.

The transformation of shame into anger was the focus of work by Tangney, Wagner, Fletcher, and Gramzow (1992). In their work, shame-prone people reported higher levels of anger arousal, suspiciousness toward others, resentment, and irritability. Shame-prone people were more likely than others to shift the blame for problems onto other people, away from themselves. Shame-prone people reported a pronounced tendency to engage in indirect hostility toward others, although shame-proneness did not correlate with self-reported assaultive tendencies or other measures of direct aggression. Shame was linked with many measures of trait anger and angry dispositions.

The authors favored the interpretation that shame leads to anger and aggression. In their view, shame is highly aversive and is experienced as unfair, in part because it condemns the whole self as bad, which strikes the person as an excessive response to an individual misdeed. The shamed person may therefore regard other people as the source of unfair treatment and become indignant and angry toward them. In essence, the shamed person feels acutely bad and refuses to accept that bad feeling, blames his or her own distress on others, and becomes angry and potentially aggressive toward them (see also Retzinger, 1991).

The link between shame and aggression had contributed to the view, once widespread, that low self-esteem was a significant cause of aggression. The belief was that people with low self-esteem were especially prone to experience bad feelings about the self and therefore would be most likely to exhibit aggressive, violent reactions. The link is more apparent than real; after all, the key for aggression is that the person is unwilling to feel shame, and people with high rather than low self-esteem may be more unwilling to accept shame. Although precious little data and no major theoretical statement can be found in the literature to articulate the view that low self-esteem causes aggression, the assumption was widely cited and repeated.

A review of the literature by Baumeister, Smart, and Boden (1996) rejected the belief that low self-esteem causes aggression, however. These authors found that the self-images of aggressive, violent people were typically quite favorable, contrary to the assumption that low self-esteem would be widespread among them. Where groups differed in their average self-esteem, the more aggressive group was typically the one with higher self-esteem. Violent groups and violent individuals often expressed strong views of their superiority over others.

Baumeister et al. (1996) concluded that threatened egotism was the most important link between self-appraisal and aggression. That is, violent and aggressive behavior was most likely when people hold a favorable opinion of themselves and then encounter someone else who disputes that favorable opinion, such as by delivering an insult or showing disrespect. The insulted person may therefore attack the source of the insult, as a way of rejecting the threat to his or her self-esteem and avoiding any loss of self-esteem.

The threatened egotism hypothesis received support in laboratory work by Bushman and Baumeister (1998). In two studies, participants were randomly praised or insulted and then had an opportunity to aggress against the source of evaluation or against another person. The researchers also assessed people's self-appraisals with measures of self-esteem and narcissism. Narcissism is a newly popular trait construct that refers to feelings of personal superiority, an inflated sense of entitlement, and self-admiration. The term comes from the mythical Greek character Narcissus who fell in love with his own image reflected in the water. The view that low self-esteem would cause aggression received no support whatsoever, and in fact different measures of self-esteem in different studies consistently yielded no significant results. In contrast, people who scored high on narcissism responded to insults with exceptionally high levels of aggression (but only toward the person who had insulted them, not toward innocent third parties).

The threatened egotism view, as well as the important mediation by emotional responses such as shame, was further attested in questionnaire studies by Kernis, Granneman, and Barclay (1989). These authors not only measured participants' level of self-esteem but also assessed the stability of self-esteem, defined in terms of how much a person's self-esteem score fluctuated from one occasion to another. They found people with high self-esteem scored at both extremes on an inventory of hostility. Specifically, people with high but unstable self-esteem exhibited the highest levels of hostility. In contrast, people with stable high self-esteem were the least hostile and aggressive.

The implication of Kernis et al.'s work is thus that unstable high self-esteem is an important predisposition to hostility. By definition, these people have favorable opinions of themselves, but these favorable opinions are vulnerable to events that might raise or lower them, and so criticism or disrespect holds the potential to cause a loss in self-esteem. Losses of self-esteem typically evoke negative emotional responses such as shame, and so these people become aggressive as a way of warding off these very unpleasant feelings. The findings of Kernis et al. overlap with the conclusions of Bushman and Baumeister (1998), because other work has confirmed that narcissists tend to fall in the category of having high, unstable self-esteem (Rhodewalt, Madrian, & Cheney, 1998)—precisely the category of people who are most hostile and aggressive.

Thus, experiences that reflect badly on the self evoke very negative emotions such as shame and anger. An increase in aggressive tendencies is a common result.

III. OTHER THEORIES ABOUT AGGRESSION AND EMOTION

1. Catharsis

One of the most influential theories about the links between aggression and emotion is based on the concept of catharsis. The first recorded usage of the term was in Aristotle's *Poetics* (Aristotle, 1970), in which he proposed that the audience of a play will experience an emotional purging as a result of the drama they witness. The term literally means cleansing or purging.

The central point of the catharsis theory of aggression is that negative emotions such as anger may build up over time but can be released and removed from the person's mind and body by participating in aggressive acts. In this view, hostile feelings are either kept inside or let out through aggressive activity. Keeping them inside is considered unhealthy, whereas aggression is a helpful way to get rid of them. Two important consequences of aggression are central to the catharsis theory. First, getting rid of the bad feelings (even by means of aggression) is good for you. Second, aggressive tendencies are reduced by means of aggressive acts, because the toxic emotions and impulses that are released by aggressive action are removed from the self, and so the subsequent urge to aggress is diminished.

Catharsis is an especially important concept in relation to theories that regard aggression as innate or instinctual. Such views assume that aggressive tendencies will build up over time regardless of what happens in one's surroundings, because aggression derives from natural and innate drives. By refusing to aggress, the person will keep these impulses inside, where they may be harmful. Finding ways to express them is natural and healthy.

In psychology, the most influential statement of the catharsis theory was by Freud. In one of his earliest writings, he and Breuer proposed that the treatment of hysteria required the discharge of the emotional state that was previously associated with the trauma (Breuer & Freud, 1955 [1893–1895]). For interpersonal traumas such as being insulted, emotional catharsis could be achieved through direct aggression. They believed that expressing hostility was better than bottling it up inside. Substitute targets were also effective for catharsis.

Other psychologists have agreed with Freud's position. Dollard et al. asserted that

"The expression of any act of aggression is a catharsis that reduces the instigation to all other acts of aggression" (1939:53). Even today, popular psychologists like to assert that expressing aggression (preferably by seemingly innocuous means such as hitting a pillow) will reduce aggressive tendencies (e.g., Lee, 1993). In some therapies, couples are encouraged to hit each other with foam bats that do not cause injury. An important extension of catharsis theory has proposed that viewing violence can provide release, and so it is supposedly healthy and socially beneficial to watch violent movies, which are predicted to lead to reductions in actual aggressive actions.

Research findings have not supported the theory of catharsis, and in fact most findings point clearly and strongly in the opposite direction. The central prediction is that aggressive acts should produce a reduction in subsequent aggressive behavior. In most studies, aggressive acts lead to no reduction and often even produce an increase in subsequent aggressive behavior.

For example, in one early study (Hornberger, 1959) people were insulted by an experimental confederate, which made them angry at him. By random assignment, half the subjects were encouraged to pound nails into a block of wood, which is just the sort of aggressive outlet that many therapists and advisors recommend. The others did not have any opportunity to vent their anger. Later, people were given an opportunity to display aggression against the confederate directly by giving him a bad evaluation. The catharsis theory predicted that the people who had vented their anger by pounding nails should have been less critical of the confederate than the other participants, because pounding nails should have drained off some of their aggression. The opposite was found: The people who pounded the nails were more critical and aggressive toward the confederate.

Similar findings emerged from many subsequent studies, including ones in which people expressed their aggression directly at the target of their hostility and ones in which substitute targets were used. The evidence consistently failed to show any support for the catharsis theory. Likewise, the belief that viewing violence (such as in violent movies) will release aggression and produce a reduction in aggressive behavior has been repeatedly contradicted. If anything, the opposite finding is more common: Acting aggressively or viewing aggressive movies produces an increase in subsequent aggression, rather than a decrease as the catharsis theory would predict. A review of many findings by Geen and Quanty (1977) concluded that the catharsis theory is simply wrong. Geen and Quanty's paper is still recognized by many authorities as the definitive work on the topic.

There is however an emotional dimension to aggressive behavior that has been neglected in much of the catharsis research. Bushman, Baumeister, and Stack (1999) found that people sometimes do actually feel better after engaging in aggressive acts. This may help explain why the catharsis hypothesis continues to be popular and to be asserted as true despite the many contrary findings. Aggression feels good to angry people, at least sometimes, and they may mistake this improvement in their emotional state for some genuine satisfaction or benefit akin to catharsis. In reality, however, these emotional benefits do not produce any reduction in aggressive activity.

The fact that people may start to believe in the catharsis theory raises the possibility that it might be true for some people under some circumstances. Indeed, believing in the benefits of catharsis might create a self-fulfilling prophecy, by which the expected reduction in aggressive feelings following aggression actually occurs because it is expected. Contrary to that view, however, Bushman et al. (1999) found that even people who believed in the benefits of catharsis (and who were told that it was true) still exhibited an increase in aggressive behavior after venting.

Venting one's anger, in short, is not a productive or socially beneficial exercise. The view of hostile feelings and impulses as some kind of toxin or other substance that must be purged from the body through aggressive action appears to be false. If anything, aggression is increased after people act out their aggressions or even after they watch aggression on film. The theory of aggressive catharsis was plausible and even appealing in some ways, but it should be regarded as incorrect.

2. Emotion and Self-Control

Another very important link between emotion and aggressiveness involves self-control. The relevance of self-control to aggression has begun to emerge from studies in recent years. Possibly the most sweeping and influential statement of that link was in the criminological work by Gottfredson and Hirschi (1990), whose book *A General Theory of Crime* concluded that low self-control is the single most important factor for understanding criminal and violent behavior. A similar conclusion was reached from different evidence by Baumeister (1997), who acknowledged the wide assortment of factors that have been shown to cause violence and concluded that the traditional question of "Why does violence occur?" should be at least partly supplanted by the question "Why isn't there more violence than there is?" The answer, he proposed, is that people have internal restraints (i.e., self-control) that prevent them from acting on their violent impulses.

Viewed in that way, the proximal cause of a great deal of violent, aggressive behavior is a breakdown in self-control. Frustration, disrespect, poverty, relative deprivation, heat, aggressive cues, media violence, and other factors may give rise to violent tendencies and impulses, but people restrain themselves from acting on them—except when self-control is impaired.

Emotional distress is generally recognized as a powerful impediment to effective self-control (see Baumeister, Heatherton, & Tice, 1994, for review). When people are upset, they lose or abandon their ordinary ability to regulate their behavior properly. Several effects of emotional distress appear to contribute to these breakdowns in self-control, which can then allow aggressive behavior to emerge.

One means by which emotional distress can impair self-control is that it curtails decision making, leading to a penchant for high-risk, high-payoff courses of action—a category of action that often includes aggression. In a series of studies, Leith and Baumeister (1996) offered research participants a choice between several options that varied in their level of risk. The choice was specifically structured so that choosing the low-risk option was objectively the better decision, as reflected in a higher expected value of outcome. Most participants seem to have recognized this and chose the low-risk option, but participants who were experiencing emotional distress (induced by random assignment) shifted over to exhibit strong preferences for the high-risk, high-payoff option. These shifts in choice patterns were mediated by a tendency to not think through all the possible outcomes and contingencies. Instead, people who were upset simply jumped at the chance to do something that seemed appealing. Although this work did not specifically include measures of aggression, it seems clear that aggression is often a high-risk option in many situations, because attacking someone carries the risk that one may be injured or killed (or may incur other costs, such as arrest). Angry or upset people may therefore give in to violent impulses without pausing to consider the potential downside of their risky behavior.

Another way that emotional distress contributes to aggression is based on the self-control of emotion. Sometimes people give priority to their feelings and the prospect of feeling better, as opposed to doing what might be best in the long run. In a conflict situation, for example, a person may feel like using aggression or force to get their way, but in recognition of the potential dangers and drawbacks of aggression the person may hold back. Emotionally upset people may however believe that attacking their opponent would make them feel better, and so they may aggress as a means of regulating their emotions (i.e., bringing about an improvement in mood). In essence, they decide to regulate their feelings rather than regulate their aggressive impulses and behavior.

Support for the affect regulation theory of aggression was found by Bushman, Baumeister, and Phillips (2000) in a series of laboratory studies. Participants were angered by means of having a confederate ostensibly give them an insulting, critical evaluation. In one study, half the participants were led to believe that aggressing would make them feel better, such as by causing a catharsis that would purge their unpleasant, angry feelings. In another, participants' own naturally occurring beliefs in the benefits of expressing one's anger were assessed. One finding was that people showed higher aggression when they believed that aggression would make them feel better.

The crucial manipulation, however, involved telling some participants that their emotional states were "frozen" and thus not subject to change. This was accomplished by giving them a pill and informing them (falsely) that the pill (actually vitamin B6) had been shown to have mood effects that consisted of fixing one's mood so that it would remain unchangeable for an hour or so. This manipulation effectively makes affect regulation impossible: Nothing you do will cheer you up. This manipulation eliminated the aggressive responses to the insult. Even people who believed that aggression normally makes a person feel better refrained from aggression when they had been told that their moods were not changeable.

Taken together, these findings indicate that people sometimes aggress as a way of improving their mood and emotional state. Some people believe that expressing their anger, even by means of aggressive behavior, will help them purge their bad feelings and end up in a more pleasant state. These people are normally prone to deal with their feelings of anger and hostility by attacking the person whom they hold responsible. But if they believe that their emotions have been artificially frozen so as to be immune to change, they cease to aggress. When affect regulation is supposedly impossible, aggression is diminished.

3. Guilt

Guilt is an important cause of prosocial behavior and an important potential restraint on aggression. Although a misreading of psychodynamic theories caused many people during the twentieth century to regard guilt as an antisocial, pathological feeling that caused neurosis while accomplishing little of value, the weight of expert opinion has shifted substantially toward a more favorable view of guilt in light of studies that attested to its positive effects.

Guilt appears to be strongly linked to empathy and to the desire to maintain good interpersonal relationships (Hoffman, 1982; Tangney, 1991). The prototype cause of guilt is causing harm or suffering to somebody one cares about (Baumeister, Stillwell, & Heatherton, 1994). Thus, because aggression is often a central means of causing such suffering, guilt may be an important mechanism for punishing and preventing such aggression. To the extent that people wish to avoid guilt, they should refrain from aggressing and causing harm to other people.

Assorted evidence confirms the value of guilt for reducing aggression. Tangney, Wagner, Fletcher, and Gramzow (1992) showed that when guilt-prone tendencies were corrected for shame tendencies, the residual "shame-free guilt" (p. 673) was associated with lower levels of anger, hostility, resentment, and even lower self-reports of assaultive behavior toward others. Apparently, guilt prevents aggression.

Even more dramatic evidence comes from studies of people who seem to lack any sense of guilt. These people, typically known as psychopaths, are notoriously prone to criminal and violent behavior. In one of the leading works on these people, Hare (1993) estimated that psychopaths make up less than 1% of the population but account for 50% of serious crimes. Hare insisted that these people are not mentally ill in the usual sense, because they can function effectively in society and are well aware of its norms, rules, and expectations. They know the difference between right and wrong, but they simply do not care all that much about it. In a sense, they are ruthless pragmatists who are willing to victimize others for the sake of their own self-interest. Lacking a sense of guilt, they do not feel any distress or inner turmoil over bringing suffering to others (even others who have been close to them). That aptly captures what comes from a lack of guilt. Guilt is an important force that causes people to respect the welfare of others and feel bad whenever they cause others to suffer.

Guilt appears to arise most strongly in the context of close relationships, and indeed some studies suggest that guilt is more strongly linked than other emotions to close relationship contexts (Baumeister, Reis, & Delespaul, 1995). For example, people may feel fear toward strangers, and the same goes for irritation, but guilt is mostly reserved for partners in relationships. Hence guilt will be most effective at discouraging aggression between people who know each other.

In practice, the power of guilt for restraining and discouraging aggression entails that aggressors must often find a way to deal with their guilt. Psychopaths may be able to inflict harm without feeling bad, but most people are prone to feel moderate to acute guilt when they hurt someone. Baumeister (1997) surveyed an assortment of techniques that aggressors use to minimize their feelings of guilt. Some aggressors seek to distance themselves from their victims by regarding them as thoroughly unrelated and dissimilar to the self, even to the extent of speaking of victims as less than human. Others downplay the amount that the victim suffered and regard their aggressive acts as trivial or ephemeral matters. Others rely on complex rationalizations that justify their actions or depict the aggression as having benefited the victim. Others deny their responsibility by insisting they had no choice. Many others use alcohol to escape from full awareness of what they were doing.

4. Sadistic Pleasure

The notion of sadism points toward a link between aggression and emotion that is quite different from what we have considered thus far. Sadism implies that the perpetrator actually enjoys inflicting harm and gets pleasure from the victim's suffering. Thus, the quest for positive, pleasant emotional states may cause sadists to behave aggressively. This stands in sharp contrast to the pattern we noted with guilt. Guilt constitutes an impediment to aggression, and so avoiding guilt often motivates an attempt to ignore or minimize the victim's suffering. The sadist, however, is precisely motivated to maximize that suffering and derive pleasure by focusing on it.

Sadism is an important theme in many victims' accounts. They often emphasize that the persons who were harming them were doing so because they enjoyed it. Laughter or other apparent signs of pleasure are very salient to victims. Still, these accounts cannot be fully trusted, because victims are prone to assimilate their tormentors' actions to the culturally dominant images of evil, which often include sadistic pleasure (Baumeister, 1997; Dower, 1986).

Perpetrators' accounts generally offer far less evidence of sadism. Still, there is some evidence, and it seems sufficiently widespread that one must conclude that some degree of sadism exists. Several observations suggest that a small minority of perpetrators actually get pleasure from causing their victims to suffer. For example, Groth (1979) concluded that about 5% of rapists fall into this sadistic category. Toch's (1993 [1969]) classic study of violent men concluded that about 6% were sadistic in the sense of enjoying the victim's suffering. Toch explained that most bullies would be aggressive until the victim would give in and show signs of weakness and suffering, whereupon the attackers would stop. The sadistic minority, however, would increase their tormenting behaviors instead of stopping at that point.

The idea that perpetrators enjoy inflicting suffering supports popular mythology of evil (such as reflected in movies and cartoons), but it seems contradicted by evidence that perpetrators typically experience considerable distress over hurting others. Browning's (1992) account of German reserve policemen assigned to kill Jews in Poland, for example, reports that the initial assignments produced extremely negative reactions, including anxiety attacks, nightmares, and gastrointestinal disturbances. Later, however, the men appeared to become desensitized to the killing duties and were better able to take them in stride. He did not, however, find much evidence that the men came to actually enjoy these assignments.

One possible explanation for the emergence of sadism would be based on opponent-process theory (Solomon & Corbit, 1974; Solomon, 1980). This theory is based on human homeostatic mechanisms, and so any departure from the normal state sets off an opposite process designed to restore the original status quo. If the experience is repeated many times, the second (opponent) process becomes stronger and the initial reaction becomes weaker. Thus, when an out-of-shape person runs up a flight of stairs, the body responds by making the person breathe faster and by pumping more blood. Then, when running ceases, the opponent processes gradually slow the breathing and pulse to their normal, resting levels. If the person runs every day, the speedup in breathing and pulse become less pronounced, and the restoration becomes quicker and more efficient. This theory helps explain how people can learn to enjoy such paradoxical experiences as falling (e.g., in bungee jumping or skydiving), which evoke some of the most natural and deeply rooted fears in the human psyche. The terror of falling evokes a pleasant, even euphoric reaction to restore the ordinary state, and after repeated jumps the person may experience relatively little terror but a pronounced euphoria.

Applied to violence, opponent-process theory would suggest that the initial feelings of nausea, revulsion, and other distress are initially very salient and powerful, while the more positive feelings the body needs to offset those feelings start off being slow and inefficient. Through repeated participation in violent acts, however, the person is likely to find that the initial, negative state diminishes in power, whereas the compensatory (and pleasant) process becomes stronger. Ultimately the person may begin to find that inflicting harm on others becomes positively appealing because of the rising predominance of the positive, pleasant feelings. To be sure, most people would still be restrained by guilt and would probably not permit themselves to acknowledge that they enjoyed inflicting harm.

But people with a relatively weak sense of guilt might be susceptible to recognizing that they have learned to enjoy harming others, and these individuals could develop into full-blown sadists (Baumeister, 1997).

Sadistic pleasure through enjoyment of a victim's suffering is not the only possible mechanism by which positive affective states can be gotten from aggressive action. Another important category involves excitement and thrills (see Baumeister & Campbell, 1999). Committing violent acts is often very exciting. Such excitement may appeal especially to people who find life boring, because the thrills of crime and violence may constitute a powerful antidote to boredom.

A memorable analysis of the quest for "sneaky thrills" was provided by Katz (1988) in his book *Seductions of Crime*. Even such seemingly minor crimes of shoplifting may appeal to people more because the episode is emotionally compelling and banishes boredom. Katz found that shoplifters often did not value the items they stole and either discarded them or put them away and forgot about them after the event, but they retained vivid memories of the suspense and excitement that accompanied the theft itself. The emotional experience was thus what they wanted, more than the item they stole. Their accounts emphasized the exciting process of planning the theft, the fear of getting caught while attempting to leave the store, and the euphoric sense of victory that came upon the success of their mission. Apter (1992) and other writers have similarly emphasized how the quest for excitement can lead people to court danger, including through criminal and violent activity.

Viewing aggression as a potential source of emotional gratification that provides thrills and excitement and banishes boredom can help predict what kinds of individuals are more likely to engage in it. People with sensation-seeking or thrill-seeking temperaments would be prominent candidates, as would people whose ordinary lives lack alternative sources of excitement. Some observers have noted that adolescents are likely to qualify on both counts, insofar as they regard school and adult-supervised activities as endlessly boring (e.g., Larkin, 1979), but are in a developmental phase where the desire for affectively intense experiences is unusually powerful (e.g., Baldwin, 1985). The relatively high rates of criminal and aggressive behavior (especially of the exuberant, thrill-seeking type) among adolescents provides some support for that approach, as does the frequent combination of aggressive, antisocial behavior with alcohol or drug abuse.

IV. CONCLUSION

Emotion has multiple links to aggressive behavior. Two major theories have dominated the twentieth century, namely frustration-aggression and catharsis. The catharsis theory has been proven wrong, whereas the frustration theory has evolved into broader formulations about how various states of negative emotion instigate aggression. Anger and shame have been particularly linked to aggression.

Meanwhile, new evidence points to other connections. Emotional distress impairs self-control, and loss of self-control is a widespread proximal cause of aggression. Angry people feel better when they aggress, and some people appear to engage in aggression because they are seeking this emotional benefit. Some people seem to learn to gain sadistic pleasure from aggression, although the emotional processes that produce such pleasures remain at the stage of mere theory. Last, it is important to recognize that not all emotions contribute to increasing aggression. Guilt, at least, appears to have some power to restrain and prevent aggression.

REFERENCES

Apter, Michael J. (1992). *The Dangerous Edge: The Psychology of Excitement*. New York: The Free Press.

Aristotle. (1970). *Poetics*. Ann Arbor: University of Michigan Press.

Averill, James. (1982). *Anger and Aggression: An Essay on Emotion*. New York: Springer-Verlag.

Baldwin, John D. (1985). Thrill and Adventure Seeking and the Age Distribution of Crime: Comment on Hirschi and Gottfredson. *American Journal of Sociology, 90*, 1326–1330.

Baumeister, Roy F. (1997). *Evil: Inside Human Violence and Cruelty*. New York: W. H. Freeman.

Baumeister, Roy F., Todd F. Heatherton, & Dianne M. Tice. (1994). *Losing Control: How and Why People Fail at Self-regulation*. San Diego: Academic Press.

Baumeister, Roy F., Arlene M. Stillwell, & Todd F. Heatherton. (1994). Guilt: An Interpersonal Approach. *Psychological Bulletin, 115*, 243–267.

Baumeister, Roy F., Harry T. Reis, & Phillippe A. E. G. Delespaul. (1995). Subjective and Experiential Correlates of Guilt in Everyday Life. *Personality and Social Psychology Bulletin, 21*, 1256–1268.

Baumeister, Roy F., Laura Smart, & Joseph M. Boden. (1996). Relation of Threatened Egotism to Violence and Aggression: The Dark Side of High Self-esteem. *Psychological Review, 103*, 5–33.

Baumeister, Roy F., & W. Keith Campbell. (1999). The Intrinsic Appeal of Evil: Sadism, Sensational Thrills, and Threatened Egotism. *Personality and Social Psychology Review, 3*, 210–221.

Berkowitz, Leonard. (1983). Aversively Stimulated Aggression: Some Parallels and Differences in Research with Animals and Humans. *American Psychologist, 38*, 1135–114.

Berkowitz, Leonard. (1989). Frustration-aggression Hypothesis: Examination and Reformulation. *Psychological Bulletin, 106*, 59–73.

Berkowitz, Leonard. (1990). On the Formation and Regulation of Anger and Aggression: A Cognitive Neoassociationistic Analysis. *American Psychologist, 45*, 494–503.

Berkowitz, Leonard. (1993). *Aggression: Its Causes, Consequences, and Control*. New York: McGraw-Hill.

Berkowitz, Leonard, & Russell G. Geen. (1966). Film Violence and the Cue Properties of Available Targets. *Journal of Personality and Social Psychology, 3*, 525–530.

Breuer, Josef, & Sigmund Freud. (1955). *Studies on Hysteria. Standard Edition of the Complete Works of Sigmund Freud, James Strachey (trans.). Vol. II*. London: Hogarth. [1893–1895]

Browning, Christopher R. (1992). *Ordinary Men: Reserve Police Battalion 101 and the Final Solution in Poland*. New York: Harper Collins.

Bushman, Brad J. (1997). Effects of Alcohol on Human Aggression: Validity of Proposed Explanations. In Marc Galanter (Ed.), *Recent Developments in Alcoholism: Alcohol and Violence. Vol. 13* (pp. 227–243). New York: Plenum.

Bushman, Brad J., & Harris M. Cooper. (1990). Effects of Alcohol on Human Aggression: An Integrative Research Review. *Psychological Bulletin, 107*, 341–354.

Bushman, Brad J., & Roy F. Baumeister. (1998). Threatened Egotism, Narcissism, Self-esteem, and Direct and Displaced Aggression: Does Self-love or Self-hate Lead to Violence? *Journal of Personality and Social Psychology, 75*, 219–229.

Bushman, Brad J., Roy F. Baumeister, & Angela D. Stack. (1999). Catharsis, Aggression, and Persuasive Influence: Self-fulfilling or Self-defeating Prophecies? *Journal of Personality and Social Psychology, 76*, 367–376.

Bushman, Brad J., Roy F. Baumeister, & Collen M. Phillips. (2001). Do People Aggress to Improve Their Mood? Catharsis Beliefs, Affect Regulation Opportunity, and Aggressive Responding. *Journal of Personality and Social Psychology, 81*, 17–32.

Dollard, John, Leonard Doob, Neal Miller, Oliver Mowrer, & Robert Sears. (1939). *Frustration and Aggression*. New Haven: Yale University Press.

Dower, John W. (1986). *War Without Mercy: Race and Power in the Pacific War*. New York: Pantheon.

Freud, Sigmund. (1930). *Civilization and Its Discontents*. London: Hogarth Press.

Freud, Sigmund. (1934). *Mourning and Melancholia. Reprinted in Collected Papers. Vol. IV*. [1917] London: Hogarth Press.

Freud, Sigmund. (1961). *Beyond the Pleasure Principle*. [1920] London: Norton.

Geen, Russell G., & Leonard Berkowitz. (1967). Some Conditions Facilitating the Occurrence of Aggression after the Observation of Violence. *Journal of Personality, 35*, 666–676.

Geen, Russell G., & Michael B. Quanty. (1977). The Catharsis of Aggression: An Evaluation of a Hypothesis. In Leonard Berkowitz (Ed.), *Advances in Experimental Social Psychology. Vol. 10* (pp. 1–37). New York: Academic Press.

Gottfredson, Michael R., & Travis Hirschi. (1990). *A General Theory of Crime*. Stanford: Stanford University Press.

Groth, A. Nicholas. (1979). *Men Who Rape: The Psychology of the Offender*. New York: Plenum.

Hare, Robert. (1993). *Without Conscience: The Disturbing World of the Psychopaths among us*. New York: Simon & Schuster/Pocket.

Hepworth, Joseph T., & Stephen G. West. (1988). Lynchings and the Economy: A Time-series Reanalysis of Hovland and Sears (1940). *Journal of Personality and Social Psychology*, *55*, 239–247.

Hoffman, Martin L. (1982). Development of Prosocial Motivation: Empathy and Guilt. In Nancy Eisenberg (Ed.), *The Development of Prosocial Behavior* (pp. 281–313). New York: Academic Press.

Hornberger, Robert H. (1959). The Differential Reduction of Aggressive Responses as a Function of Interpolated Activities. *American Psychologist*, *14*, p. 354.

Hovland, Carl I., & Robert Sears. (1940). Minor Studies of Aggression: Correlation of Lynchings with Economic Indices. *Journal of Psychology*, *9*, 301–310.

Katz, Jack. (1988). *Seductions of Crime: Moral and Sensual Attractions in Doing Evil*. New York: Basic Books.

Katz, S. E., & Carney Landis. (1935). Psychologic and Physiologic Phenomena During a Prolonged Vigil. *Archives of Neurology and Psychiatry*, *34*, 307–317.

Kernis, Michael H., Bruce D. Grannemann, & Lynda C. Barclay. (1989). Stability and Level of Self-esteem as Predictors of Anger Arousal and Hostility. *Journal of Personality and Social Psychology*, *56*, 1013–1022.

Larkin, Ralph W. (1979). *Suburban Youth in Cultural Crisis*. New York: Oxford University Press.

Lee, James H. (1993). *Facing the Fire: Experiencing and Expressing Anger Appropriately*. New York: Bantam.

Leith, Karen P., & Roy F. Baumeister. (1996). Why Do Bad Moods Increase Self-defeating Behavior? Emotion, Risk Taking, and Self-regulation. *Journal of Personality and Social Psychology*, *71*, 1250–1267.

Lewis, Helen Block. (1971). *Shame and Guilt in Neurosis*. New York: International Universities Press.

Miller, Neal E. (1941). The Frustration-aggression Hypothesis. *Psychological Review*, *48*, 337–342.

Retzinger, Suzanne M. (1991). *Violent Emotions*. Newbury Park: Sage.

Rhodewalt, Frederick, Jennifer C. Madrian, & Sharon Cheney. (1998). Narcissism, Self-knowledge Organization, and Emotional Reactivity: The Effects of Daily Experiences on Self-esteem and Affect. *Personality and Social Psychology Bulletin*, *24*, 75–86.

Sears, Robert R., & Pauline S. Sears. (1940). Minor Studies of Aggression: V. Strength of Frustration Reaction as a Function of Strength of Drive. *Journal of Psychology*, *9*, 297–300.

Solomon, Richard L. (1980). The Opponent-process Theory of Acquired Motivations: The Costs of Pleasure and the Benefits of Pain. *American Psychologist*, *35*, 691–712.

Solomon, Richard L., & John D. Corbit. (1974). An Opponent-process Theory of Motivation: I. Temporal Dynamics of Affect. *Psychological Review*, *81*, 119–145.

Tangney, June P. (1991). Moral Affect: The Good, the Bad, and the Ugly. *Journal of Personality and Social Psychology*, *61*, 598–607.

Tangney, June P. (1995). Shame and Guilt in Interpersonal Relationships. In June Price Tangney & Kurt W. Fischer (Eds.), *The Self-conscious Emotions* (pp. 114–139). New York: Guilford.

Tangney, June P., Patricia E. Wagner, Carey Fletcher, & Richard Gramzow. (1992). Shamed into Anger? The Relation of Shame and Guilt to Anger and Self-reported Aggression. *Journal of Personality and Social Psychology*, *62*, 669–675.

Tavris, Carol. (1989). *Anger: The Misunderstood Emotion*. New York: Simon & Shuster (Touchstone).

Toch, Hans. (1993). *Violent Men: An Inquiry into the Psychology of Violence*. Washington: American Psychological Association. [1969].

Learning of Aggression in the Home and the Peer Group

Ernest V. E. Hodges, Noel A. Card and Jenny Isaacs

I. INTRODUCTION

As the chapters in this book illustrate, aggression and violence are serious problems in our society. In searching for the roots of aggression in individuals, one must look to the early lives of children. Individual differences in levels of aggression emerge early in life and are highly stable across development. While there is undeniable evidence that individual differences in aggression are due in no small part to innate (biological or genetic) factors, there is also overwhelming evidence that aggression is in large part learned through a child's interaction with the environment. This chapter will focus on two contexts largely responsible for a child's learning of aggression—the home and the peer group.

II. THEORIES OF AGGRESSION IN CHILDREN

Over the last several decades, developmental psychologists have proposed several theories of childhood aggression. We will briefly describe three of these theories that have been most widely used and have received the most empirical support.

1. Bandura's Social-cognitive Learning Theory

According to Bandura's (1986) social-cognitive learning theory, mental representations of social interactions determine a child's subsequent behavior. Children initially acquire an aggressive repertoire through the simple observation of aggressive models. By viewing

W. Heitmeyer and J. Hagan (eds.), *International Handbook of Violence Research*, 495–509.

others being rewarded for engaging in aggressive acts, children may feel that they too will be rewarded for such behavior. Aggression is maintained and strengthened when children imitating these models are themselves reinforced for their aggressive behavior. The positive outcomes received through an aggressive act may become encoded into memory and be used to generate more abstract rules for conduct, such as "I can get what I want by using physical force."

Social-cognitive learning theory views aggression as a learned response to an arousing event. This relation, however, is mediated by three social-cognitive evaluations: self-efficacy for aggression, outcome expectations for aggression, and values of outcomes obtained through aggression. That these social cognitions underlie aggressive behavior has repeatedly received empirical support (e.g., Boldizar, Perry, & Perry, 1989; Egan, Monson, & Perry, 1998).

2. Dodge's Social Information-Processing Model

Dodge has proposed a social information-processing model of children's social adjustment comprised of six parallel steps (Crick & Dodge, 1994). The perpetuation of aggression rests on deficits and biases in various steps of this cognitive process.

The first step is encoding, and involves the sensory encoding of social and internal cues. Aggressive children attend to fewer cues and selectively attend to hostile cues. The second step is the Interpretation of Social Cues. During this step meaningful interpretations are attached to the encoded information. Aggressive children display a hostile attributional bias, meaning that they interpret the ambiguous social behavior of others as being hostile in intent. The third step is the Clarification of Goals. Here the child either selects a goal or continues to follow through with a prior goal. Aggressive children tend to select goals based on domination and control rather than on the formation and preservation of interpersonal relationships. The fourth step, Response Access and Construction, requires the child to search for previously learned social behaviors or to create new responses to fit emergent needs. Aggressive children tend to generate fewer potential responses to provocation and tend to produce responses that are more hostile in nature. During the fifth step, Response Evaluation and Decision, the child evaluates the potential outcomes of a response, their ability to effectively enact the response, and the appropriateness of the response (this step is similar to components of Bandura's social-cognitive learning theory). The sixth step, Behavioral Enactment, entails the actual performance of the selected response.

3. Patterson's Conflict Model

Patterson (1982) has proposed a model that emphasizes the process by which aggression is learned within conflict situations. According to this model, how parents manage the inevitable conflicts that arise between themselves and their children is central to the learning of aggression. When parents are unable to stop the child from escalating the intensity of conflict, and when they at least intermittently reinforce the child's coercive behavior, the child learns that escalation is a viable method of resolving conflict. When this conflict strategy is applied to interactions with similar age siblings or peers, and if it is also reinforced in these contexts (at least intermittently), this conflict escalation is likely to include acts of aggression.

There is substantial empirical evidence to support this theory. Comparisons of aggressive and nonaggressive boys' interactions with family members reveal that aversive exchanges are longer and more intense for aggressive children, that parents of aggressive children start more conflicts with their children and handle these conflicts less competently than parents of nonaggressive children, and that parents of aggressive children handle sibling conflict less effectively than parents of nonaggressive children (Patterson, 1982).

III. TWO LEARNING CONTEXTS

1. Learning of Aggression in the Home Context

Several aspects of the family environment have been repeatedly examined by developmental researchers, including parental permissiveness and monitoring, warmth versus negativity, rejection, inconsistent discipline, parental aggression and physical punishment, and marital conflict (for reviews see Coie & Dodge, 1998; Perry, Perry, & Boldizar, 1990). Many of these aspects have been incorporated into more overarching views, including parenting style typologies, attachment theory, and Patterson's conflict model.

a. PARENTAL PERMISSIVENESS AND MONITORING. Parents of aggressive children, compared with parents of nonaggressive children, are more permissive in several ways. They fail to set limits on their children's behavior, are ineffective in stopping their children's deviant behavior, and seldom follow through on the punishments they do impose on their children. It is likely the case that children whose parents are permissive of aggression, compared with parents who discipline aggression, do not develop the inhibition of aggression normally learned by their nonaggressive peers.

Compared with parents of nonaggressive children, parents of aggressive children are less aware of their children's whereabouts, activities, and social contacts. Low parental monitoring results in parents' failure to punish inappropriate behavior, and the loss of opportunity for parents to teach more prosocial solutions. In adolescence, low parental monitoring is also related to delinquent behavior (Griffin et al., 2000), suggesting that parental monitoring may also be important in preventing the transition from childhood aggression to adolescent delinquency.

b. PARENTAL WARMTH VERSUS NEGATIVITY. Parental warmth has received considerable attention as a factor in childhood aggression. The relation between parental warmth/negativity and childhood aggression can be interpreted in terms of social-cognitive learning theory—for a parent to induce the child to follow parental standards for behavior, the parent-child interaction must be reinforcing to the child. Parents who are warm to their child will be able to reinforce desired behavior through continued interaction, and punish inappropriate behavior, such as aggression, through the withdrawal of that warmth. In contrast, parents who are negative are not able to use continued interaction as a positive reinforcer.

c. PARENTAL REJECTION. Aggressive children report a history of parental rejection. More important than the parent's actual rejection toward the child may be the child's *perception* of rejection (McHale, Johnson, & Sinclair, 1999). Although the mechanisms through which perceived rejection leads to aggression are not well explored, one possibility might be the development of a hostile attribution bias. In other words, the child's perception of rejection may teach the child to view the behavior and motives of others more negatively, and in some cases, as more hostile. However, although parental rejection may contribute to the development of aggression, the child's aggression may also contribute substantially to being rejected by the parents. Thus, parental rejection and childhood aggression may have reciprocal influences, with each reinforcing the enactment of the other.

d. INCONSISTENT DISCIPLINE. Children are more aggressive when a parent inconsistently punishes aggression, or when one parent enforces standards against aggression while the other does not. Not only do parents of aggressive children negatively reinforce their children's aversive behavior (i.e., discontinuing demands on the child when they behave aversively), but they are less likely than parents of nonaggressive children to reinforce prosocial behavior (Snyder & Patterson, 1995). However, aggressive children also reinforce the withdrawal of imposed discipline by their mothers more than nonaggressive boys, suggesting that, like parental rejection, the relation between childhood aggression and inconsistent discipline is bidirectional.

e. PARENTAL AGGRESSION AND PHYSICAL PUNISHMENT. Aggressive children more often come from homes in which at least one of the parents is aggressive. Adult criminals report histories of parents who frequently lost their temper, smashed things, had criminal histories, and were abusive. This use of aggression by parents may serve as a model for children's use of aggression. Aggression by one parent against the other, against other adults, or against siblings all are associated with children's learning of aggression.

A special case of this parental aggression is when it is directed toward the child. Not only may this aggression serve as a model for the child's aggression, but it can also lead the child to perceive rejection by the abusing parent and to develop a hostile attributional tendency (Dodge, Bates, & Pettit, 1990). The evidence of mild physical punishment leading to childhood aggression, however, is mixed. Concurrent associations between physical punishment and aggression in third graders reveal a positive relationship (high punishment was related to high levels of aggression) among children classified as having low identification with their parents, and a negative relationship among children classified as highly identified with their parents. Later examinations of this sample showed no relationship between physical punishment and aggression ten years later, but did find that physical punishment in third grade predicted antisocial behavior at age thirty (Eron, Huesmann, & Zelli, 1991). Similar to parental aggression, physical punishment may serve to model physical aggression as a source of conflict management, and may promote cognitions that physical domination is a means to acquire what one desires.

f. MARITAL CONFLICT. The method by which parents handle marital conflict can be an important factor in children's learning of aggression. Compared to children with peaceful parents, children who's parents engage in frequent, lengthy, and intense disputes are more likely to behave aggressively both at home and at school (MacKinnon-Lewis et al., 1997). What may be more important is not the presence of conflict, but the method by which conflict is handled. Angry intensification of conflict, especially if to the point of physical aggression, is likely to serve as an inappropriate model of conflict resolution for children. On the other hand, peaceful, cooperative conflict management might teach children appropriate conflict management strategies. Thus, appropriate management of conflict may be even more valuable than the absence of conflict.

g. PARENTING STYLES AND CHILDHOOD AGGRESSION. Many of the above parenting characteristics are encompassed by the parenting styles described by Baumrind (1971). Observing preschoolers and their parents, Baumrind delineated three patterns of parenting behavior: authoritative parenting, in which parents are warm and responsive to the child, yet place limits and controls on the child's behavior; authoritarian parenting, in which parents place strict limits on the child's behavior, with violation of these limits harshly punished, and in which there is little parental warmth or communication with the child; and permissive parenting, in which parents are warm and nurturing without placing limits on the child's behavior. Maccoby and Martin (1983) modified Baumrind's typology by fitting these styles to a two-dimensional classification based on the combination of responsive versus rejecting and restrictive versus permissive. In this schema, authoritative parenting is associated with responsiveness and restriction, authoritarian parenting with rejection and restriction, and permissive parenting with responsiveness and permissiveness. This classification also suggests a fourth style, disengaged parenting, marked by rejection and permissiveness. This parenting style is associated with insecure attachment in children and alcohol use, truancy, and arrests in adolescence (Baumrind, 1991).

Aside from the addition of a fourth parenting style important in understanding the learning of aggression and antisocial behavior, Maccoby and Martin's (1983) classification suggests an important topic for understanding parental factors. The two dimensional classification illuminates the importance of examining parenting factors in combination, rather than independently. In some studies (e.g., Hinde, Tamplin, & Barrett, 1993), researchers have failed to find associations between children's aggression and individual aspects of parenting, but have found associations when examining the patterns, or interactions, of these aspects. Thus, these parenting styles described by Baumrind and others serve as a taxonomy of the many patterns or interactions of the parenting aspects described in this section.

h. ATTACHMENT SECURITY AND CHILDHOOD AGGRESSION. Attachment theory posits that infants have an innate, evolutionarily adaptive tendency to form attachment bonds to caregivers, which serve to maintain a balance between the infant's exploration of its environment and the maintenance of proximity to the caregiver in times of perceived danger (Bowlby, 1969). Ainsworth (e.g., Ainsworth et al., 1978) has demonstrated that there are individual differences in attachment styles, depending on the history of caregiver availability and responsiveness. Three attachment styles were originally proposed by Ainsworth: "secure", "avoidant", and "resistant"; while a fourth style was later added, "disorganized/disoriented" (for a review see Lyons-Ruth & Jacobovitz, 1999). Secure attachment is related to a history of warm and consistent parenting, while avoidant attachment is related to parental negativity and rejection, resistant attachment to inconsistent parenting, and disorganized attachment to parental neglect or abuse.

Although attachment bonds initially form during infancy, individual differences in attachment strategies extend throughout the life span, and have been shown to relate to many aspects of development, including the development of aggression. Based upon attachment classifications using the three category system, children's avoidant attachment style toward their mother predicts later aggression toward peers (e.g., Hodges, Finnegan,

& Perry, 1999), though other studies have failed to replicate these findings. Use of the four category classification, however, has shown that the disorganized/disoriented style is more predictive of aggression, though the relation between this style and aggression has also not been found in several studies (Lyons-Ruth & Jacobovitz, 1999). The trend in this area of research has been that relations between attachment security and aggression are found in samples that are primarily low socioeconomic status, single-parent families, but not in samples that are middle class, two-parent families. This suggests that secure attachment may act as a buffer against a familial risk factor (i.e., low income, single-parent), or, alternatively, that having a financially stable, two-parent family is a buffer against the risk factor of insecure attachment.

i. PATTERSON'S CONFLICT MODEL. Patterson's conflict model, described earlier, incorporates many of the aspects of the family environment described in this section. Inconsistent discipline is most closely associated with this model, in that it intermittently reinforces the child's escalation of conflict. Parental negativity, rejection, and aggression toward the child may act as initiators of conflict, to which the child is likely to behave aversively. Low parental monitoring and warmth, as well as marital conflict, provide conditions in which the child's escalation of conflict is more likely to succeed in ending the conflict, reinforcing this aversive strategy of conflict management. The presence of siblings also affords the child a similar-age peer with whom to further enact this escalation, and the family factors described (e.g., low monitoring, marital conflict) are associated with parents' failure to properly manage these sibling conflicts (MacKinnon-Lewis et al., 1997).

2. Learning of Aggression in the Peer Context

Children who initially learn to behave aggressively in the home may discontinue their aggression when they enter the peer context, or they may increase their aggressive tendencies. Alternatively, children who do not learn aggression in the home context may develop aggressive behavior in the environment of their peers. This section will focus on several aspects of the peer context that are related to the development of aggressive behavior. These include social factors such as peer rejection and victimization, the environment of the peer context in terms of social norms, and the characteristics of peers with whom a child forms dyadic relationships.

a. PEER REJECTION. Although a majority of the studies of aggression and peer rejection have been correlational, resulting in ambiguity of whether rejection leads to aggression or vice-versa, some studies have suggested that aggression can serve as an antecedent of peer rejection (e.g., Dodge, 1983). Thus, the anticipated threat of peer rejection may deter some children from behaving aggressively.

In addition to being a consequence of aggression, rejection by peers can also lead to later aggression and antisocial behavior. This increase in aggression may be due in large part to the fact that these rejected children interpret the actions of their peers as more hostile (i.e., increases their hostile attribution biases; Dodge et al., 1990). Further, peer rejection in childhood predicts adolescent antisocial behavior beyond that predicted by childhood aggression alone (Coie et al., 1992), suggesting both that peer rejection independently affects engagement in antisocial activities (perhaps via association with an antisocial peer group, as described below; Patterson, DeBaryshe, & Ramsey, 1989) and that these effects can be long lasting.

b. Peer Victimization. The relationship between childhood aggression and peer victimization is complex. Numerous studies have shown that concurrent measures of aggression and peer victimization are uncorrelated (e.g., Perry, Kusel, & Perry, 1988). However, a more thorough examination of this relationship reveals that victimization by one's peers may act as either a deterrent against aggressive behavior or as a promoter of alternative forms of aggression. The processes by which peer victimization leads to decreases in aggression were demonstrated by Egan and colleagues (1998). Across a six-month period, victimization was predictive of decreases in children's aggression, though this effect was small. Peer victimization may play a greater role in the development of aggression in its interaction with other characteristics of the individual. Among boys, favorable cognitions about aggression predicted later aggression only among those who were not victimized by their peers, suggesting that when contemplating aggression, the experience of victimization can inhibit the enactment of the behavior.

Another consequence of peer victimization for those who are also aggressive may be the shifting to other forms of aggression. Aggressive victims, those children who attempt to aggress against their peers but who are also victimized by their peers, may come to realize that they are not able to effectively aggress in traditional ways—these children have been characterized as "ineffectual aggressors" in contrast to nonvictimized aggressors, who have been characterized as "effectual aggressors" (Perry, Perry, & Kennedy, 1992). Despite their ineffectual use of aggression, aggressive victims persist in their attempts to dominate their peers, and are likely to turn to other methods by which they believe they can effectively do so. Perhaps the most frightening alternative these aggressive victims may select is the use of weapons. Reports of school shootings in the United States have offered descriptions of these weapon carriers as rejected, victimized by their peers, and as having aggressive tendencies. While little research has yet explored these children prospectively, it has been shown that as early as middle school, these aggressive children who are also victimized have more favorable cognitions about carrying weapons to school than their peers (Isaacs, Card, & Hodges, 2000). Thus, while peer victimization may be a deterrent against aggressive behavior for some children, it may also serve to escalate aggression into more drastic and dangerous forms.

c. Social Norms of the Peer Context. Aggression does not occur solely as a result of the characteristics of the aggressor, or even the characteristics of the aggressor and victim. Aggressive behavior is also a group phenomenon, with nearly all children playing roles, if not as the aggressor or victim, than as assistants or reinforcers of the aggressor or as protectors of the victim (Salmivalli, Huttunen, & Lagerspetz, 1997). This group phenomenon of aggressive behavior influences the enactment of aggression in several ways, including weakening the inhibitions against aggression, distributing the responsibility for an individual's aggressive acts, and changing perceptions of the victims of aggression (Olweus, 1991). Thus, the larger peer group's attitudes about aggression influences the level of aggression by its members.

The peer group's attitudes toward specific targets may also influence children's aggressive behavior. Aggressive children do not distribute their aggression evenly across the peer group, but rather select specific targets for aggression (Perry et al., 1988). These victimized children tend to have certain characteristics which have been demonstrated to precede their victimization, including physical weakness, internalizing problems (i.e., crying and appearing anxious), and poor social skills (Hodges & Perry, 1999). Both aggressive and nonaggressive children expect more tangible rewards, more suffering and submission, and less retaliation when contemplating aggression against victimized versus nonvictimized children, and they are less concerned with hurting the victim or that the victim might attempt to retaliate (Perry, Willard, & Perry, 1990). This "legitimization" of aggression against a subsample of children may reinforce aggressors' attacks against these victims. Indeed, the general peer group may express little concern about children aggressing against these victims. This is reflected by findings that victimized children have few friends or have friends who are either unable or unwilling to defend the victim against aggression (Hodges et al., 1999), and that a large proportion of the peer group dislikes these children (Perry et al., 1988). Recalling the distinction between effectual and ineffectual aggressors, it has been demonstrated that effectual aggressors are selective in their targets of aggression, attacking those perceived as victimized by the peer group, while ineffectual aggressors are nonselective in their attacks, aggressing against targets throughout the peer group (Card, Isaacs, & Hodges, 2000a). Effectual aggressors are not punished by the peer group for their aggression, and in fact may be rewarded (through peer acceptance), while ineffectual aggressors are punished by the peer group (through rejection and victimization). It is unknown why these ineffectual aggressors continue to behave aggressively in the face of this punishment, though recent research suggests that they are emotionally dysregulated (Pope & Bierman, 1999), which may prevent them from accurately perceiving or considering the social norms of their peer group when engaged in conflict situations.

d. DYADIC RELATIONSHIPS OF AGGRESSIVE CHILDREN.   Despite the fact that many aggressive children are rejected by the larger peer group, these children have as many friends as their nonaggressive peers (Cairns & Cairns, 1994). Moreover, an examination of the characteristics of aggressive children's friends suggests that they too are aggressive. Aggressive friendship dyads can serve to promote each member's aggression and antisocial behavior (Dishion, McCord, & Poulin, 1999). Aggressive children also form friendships with children who assist and/or reinforce their aggression (Salmivalli et al., 1997). Within groups of boys consisting of aggressive members, highly aggressive boys are viewed more favorably than they are within groups of low aggressive members (Wright, Giammarino, & Parad, 1986). Children's aggressive behavior, then, is most likely to be reinforced by their aggressive friends and members of their peer network, those peers whose opinion is likely to be most valued by the aggressive child.

Although children's friendships have been well studied, virtually no attention has been given to children's inimical relationships. This is unfortunate, as it might be expected that aggression occurs more often within interpersonal relationships based on disliking. Given that aggressive children are often disliked by the general peer group (Dodge, 1983), it is not surprising that delinquent children have more enemies than nondelinquent children (Aloise-Young & Hennigan, 2000). In ambiguous situations, children are more likely to evaluate an enemy's behavior as hostile than a friend or neutral peer's behavior (Ray & Cohen, 1997), suggesting that incidences of aggression are likely to occur when enemies interact. Finally, findings that children who have enemies who are aggressive, strong, and nonvictimized are more victimized (Card, Isaacs & Hodges, 2000b), are consistent with the hypothesis that aggression occurs within inimical relationships. Although studies of children's inimical relationships are limited, the findings of these few studies suggest the importance of examining these negative interpersonal relationships when studying childhood aggression.

3.   Integration: Continuity of Aggression from the Home to Peer Context

Although we have described different mechanisms by which aggression is learned in the home and peer context, the two contexts are by no means independent. In this section, we will describe some of the pathways through which the continuity of aggression in the home and peer contexts may be established and maintained.

The continuity of aggression across these contexts can be partially understood within the social-cognitive models of Bandura and Dodge described earlier in this chapter. Because children have the ability to seek out their own environments, to differentially respond to their environment, and to elicit different responses from their environment, the social cognitions learned in one environment are likely to be applied and reinforced in other environments (Bandura, 1986). For example, a child who learns aggressive cognitions in the home is likely to seek out aggressive peers, to perceive situations and the actions of their peers as deserved of aggression, and to elicit and escalate conflicts with their peers. This process can also occur in the transfer of aggression learned in the peer context to the home. These processes described within Bandura's social-cognitive learning theory can also be applied to Dodge's social information-processing model. For instance, the effects of physical abuse in the home on later delinquency in the peer context is partially mediated by encoding errors, hostile attribution biases, more frequent accessing of aggressive responses, and favorable evaluations of aggressive responses (Dodge et al., 1995).

When discussing factors associated with the learning of aggression in the home, we described findings that avoidant or disorganized attachment styles, at least with some populations, are associated with later aggression in the peer context. Although early attachment bonds are with a child's primary caregiver (often the mother), there is a tendency to form similar attachment styles with others. Not only is avoidant attachment with parents predictive of externalizing problems (including aggression), but children's attachment style with their parents is related to their attachment style with best friends (Hodges, Finnegan, & Perry, 1999). Thus, another source of continuity of aggression between the home and peer context may be mediated through the continuity of attachment styles.

Perhaps the most comprehensive model provided to explain the continuity of aggression from the home to the peer context is provided by Patterson et al. (1989). First, the learning of aggression in coercive homes leads to early conduct problems. These initial conduct problems, when enacted in the peer context, lead to rejection by peers and academic failure in school. These two factors, in turn, predict membership in deviant peer groups, which then exacerbates initial conduct problems into more serious delinquency in both the home and peer group. Here again, both the home and peer context affect this process—rejection by nondeviant peers forces the child to affiliate with other rejected delinquents, and the failure of parents to adequately monitor the child's behavior allows this affiliation and the resulting escalation of delinquency.

IV. AGGRESSION AND ANTISOCIAL BEHAVIOR: DEVELOPMENTAL TRAJECTORIES

Throughout this chapter we have focused primarily on the learning of aggressive behavior, rather than violence. In part, this is reflective of the focus of developmental psychology research. However, aggression can be viewed as a necessary, but not sufficient, factor in predicting later acts of violence. In order to study this connection, researchers have conducted several long-term longitudinal studies. In this section we highlight some findings from these studies and discuss the relations between aggression and later violent behavior.

1. Early Aggression as a Predictor of Later Aggression and Violence

Numerous longitudinal studies have shown that aggression is highly stable from childhood to adulthood. In a review of 16 longitudinal studies, Olweus (1979) found that aggression among males was as stable across time as such traits as intelligence. A review of 6 studies showed that this stability is as high for females (Olweus, 1981).

In considering the relationship between childhood aggression and adult violence, it is important to keep in mind the concept of *heterotypic continuity*. This refers to the continuity of an underlying trait or disposition that may be behaviorally manifested in a variety of ways across development. Thus, children who are aggressive may become adolescents who carry weapons and are involved with gangs, who may in turn become adults who assault others, commit violent crimes, and abuse their spouses and children. Indeed, evidence has supported many of these contentions (for a review see Coie & Dodge, 1998). However, it is equally important to consider that a majority of youths who exhibit aggressive behavior do not become violent adults. Indeed, during adolescence, a certain level of aggression and antisocial behavior is considered normative. Moffitt (1993) provided a taxonomy for distinguishing individuals who engage in age-normative aggression and antisocial behavior and those who are likely to continue antisocial behavior into adulthood.

2. Moffitt's Taxonomy

Moffitt (1993) distinguished between two trajectories of antisocial behavior: adolescent-limited and life-course-persistent. The prevalence of antisocial behavior is very low prior to age seven, increases dramatically until about age seventeen, then declines back to a low level by age twenty-five. Furthermore, those individuals engaging in antisocial behavior prior to adolescence are likely to be the same individuals engaging in antisocial behavior after adolescence. In fact, from age three to fifteen, 68 percent of the stability of antisocial behavior could be attributed to just 5 percent of the boys. It was these individual differences in the stability of antisocial behavior that Moffitt used to classify developmental trajectories: those individuals who exhibited antisocial behavior in childhood, adolescence, and adulthood are considered life-course-persistent, while those exhibiting antisocial behavior only during adolescence are considered adolescent-limited. However, during adolescence, the life-course-persistent and adolescent-limited groups were indistinguishable in their levels of antisocial behavior, demonstrating the limitations of studying antisocial behavior in absence of developmental histories.

Life-course-persistent individuals exhibit antisocial behavior early in their lives, in the forms of childhood aggression and antisocial acts such as truancy, theft, and vandalism, and across contexts (i.e., at home, at school, in the neighborhood). Moffitt reviewed evidence that these individuals have biological risks (e.g., neuropsychological deficits, difficult temperament) that interact with environmental risks (e.g., low socioeconomic neighborhoods, family and parental factors). This interaction leads not only to early antisocial behavior, but results in these children becoming ensnared in a deviant lifestyle and failing to learn prosocial skills. Thus, the continuity of antisocial behavior is maintained not only by the learning of aggression and antisocial behavior, but the failure to learn conflict resolution skills, academic skills that might secure a legitimate job and the opportunity to interact with nondeviant individuals.

Adolescent-limited individuals, in contrast to life-course-persistent delinquents, do not commit antisocial acts during childhood (though it seems likely that they do engage in normative levels of childhood aggression), and discontinue their antisocial behavior upon entering adulthood. Moffitt claimed that these adolescent-limited individuals feel a "maturity gap" during adolescence when they are biologically adults, yet are offered few of the rewards of adulthood (e.g., independence from parents, financial rewards, sexual experiences). The life-course-persistent delinquents are perceived to have these adult rewards, and the adolescent-limited delinquents turn to them as role models for antisocial behavior aimed at obtaining these rewards. In contrast to the life-course-persistent delinquents, however, these individuals are able to desist in their antisocial behavior after adolescence because they have, prior to reaching adolescence, learned adaptive prosocial behaviors, such as effective conflict resolution skills, the ability to interact with nondeviant individuals, and have adequate academic success to secure satisfying jobs upon entering adulthood.

3. Future Directions

Moffitt's taxonomy, and the longitudinal studies on which it is based, demonstrate the importance of studying the developmental histories of those who are aggressive and/or antisocial. Nagin and Tremblay (1999) recently demonstrated that distinct developmental trajectories exist for physical aggression, oppositional behaviors, and hyperactivity—characteristics that are highly related in cross sectional studies. Further, these distinct trajectories were differentially predictive of adolescent outcomes, with physical aggression trajectories most predictive of adolescent violence. This study illustrates that characteristics that show high concurrent correlations may have different developmental trajectories in terms of their histories, later outcomes, and antecedent conditions. Future research is needed that attempts to unravel the social learning histories of children who follow these distinct trajectories.

V. LEARNING OF AGGRESSION IN THE HOME AND PEER GROUP: SUMMARY AND FUTURE DIRECTIONS

We have examined familial and peer factors associated with the development of aggression. Numerous family factors have been discovered, many of which can be incorporated into existing theories of parenting styles, attachment, and conflict models. We have also shown that aggression is highly influenced by the peer group. This influence can be examined through social factors, such as rejection and victimization, through peer group norms, and through children's dyadic relationships. It is likely that the development of new models of family and peer socialization will contribute to the understanding of childhood aggression, and that the further study of aggression will contribute to developmental psychologists' understanding of family and peer group processes.

With our increased knowledge of childhood aggression, developmental researchers have increasingly recognized that aggression is not a homogeneous construct. Aggression has long been differentiated in terms of its functions into proactive and reactive aggression, each with distinct underlying cognitions (Dodge & Coie, 1987). However, these measures of proactive and reactive aggression are highly correlated, drawing into question the utility of differentiating aggression in terms of function. More recently, the increased emphasis on relational aggression (e.g., Crick & Grotpeter, 1995) has spurred the study of various forms of aggression (i.e., physical, verbal, and social/relational) and highlighted the necessity of considering gender when studying childhood aggression. Studies have demonstrated distinct outcomes for boys and girls associated with these various forms of aggression (Crick, 1997), as well as distinct underlying cognitions (Crick & Werner, 1998). Unfortunately, a majority of the studies of childhood aggression, including most of those reviewed in this chapter, have either assessed only physical aggression or have not differentiated these forms of aggression. Thus, it is unclear to what extent the mechanisms by which aggression is learned in the home and peer group examined in this chapter differentially apply to the learning of these various forms of aggression. An important task for developmental researchers in the coming years is to examine the degree to which these different forms of aggression differentially develop, lead to different outcomes, and can be most effectively treated. Examination of the heterogeneous nature of aggression from a developmental trajectories approach may help clarify these questions.

VI.   INTERVENTIONS: CAN AGGRESSION BE UNLEARNED?

Because aggression and violence pose serious problems for society, numerous interventions have been designed and applied. Rather than discuss specific intervention techniques, we will describe three broad goals of interventions that are relevant to the material discussed in this chapter: interventions focusing on the individual, the family, and the peer context.

Interventions at the individual level typically apply behavior modification or attempt to change the cognitions underlying aggression. Behavior modification involves the selective punishment of aggressive behaviors and reinforcement of prosocial alternatives (e.g., Kazdin, 1989). This technique is most effective when applied in the contexts in which aggression occurs, so that it is preferable that parents and/or teachers are responsible for this reinforcement in the home and school, respectively. Problem-solving skills training (e.g., Kendall & Braswell, 1985) aims to restructure the cognitions underlying aggressive behavior. Such techniques include helping children generate more potential responses to provocation, or to devalue outcomes obtained through aggression.

Interventions at the family level aim either to change the nature of parent–child interventions, or to reduce the level of conflict or the management of conflict within the family. Patterson (1982) has described a family intervention aimed at teaching parents proper child-rearing practices that reduces conflict and the escalation of conflict when it occurs. This intervention has been found to be effective both immediately after intervention and at one-year follow-up.

A majority of interventions at the peer level have been within schools. Goals of these interventions are to increase school personnel's knowledge of aggression, to provide school personnel with methods of reducing aggression (e.g., clear limit setting, increased monitoring), and to promote an environment in which aggression is not considered an appropriate behavior among the students. This last strategy is especially relevant to the material discussed in this chapter—negative social norms and less reinforcement from friends for aggression is likely to change outcome expectations and values for aggressive behavior. This type of strategy has been demonstrated effective in large samples of children and adolescents (e.g., Olweus, 1991).

Although each of these approaches has demonstrated some degree of effectiveness with many aggressive children, interventions are largely unable to help life-course-persistent individuals (Moffitt, 1993). For these individuals, it may be necessary to identify and intervene early, before the biological predisposition for aggression is reinforced by environmental factors in the family and peer group. Recent research (Aguilar et al., 2000) has offered some insight as to how this can be done, though more work is needed.

REFERENCES

Aguilar, Benjamin, L. Alan Sroufe, Byron Egeland, & Elizabeth Carlson. (2000). Distinguishing the Early-Onset/Persistent and Adolescence-Onset Antisocial Behavior Types: From Birth to 16 Years. *Development and Psychopathology, 12*, 109–132.

Ainsworth, Mary D. S., Mary C. Blehar, Everett Waters, & Sally Wall. (1978). *Patterns of Attachment: A Psychological Study of the Strange Situation.* Hillsdale: Erlbaum.

Aloise-Young, Patricia, & Karen Hennigan. (2000) *Friends, Enemies, and Delinquency during Early Adolescence. Poster Presented at the Biennial Meeting of the Society for Research on Adolescence, March, 2000.* Chicago, IL.

Bandura, Albert. (1986). *Social Foundations of Thought and Action.* Englewood Cliffs: Prentice-Hall.

Baumrind, Diana. (1971). Current Patterns of Parental Authority. *Developmental Psychology Monographs, 4*, 1–103.

Baumrind, Diana. (1991). Parenting Styles and Adolescent Development. In Richard M. Lerner, Anne C. Peterson & Jeanne Brooks-Gunn (Eds.), *The Encyclopedia of Adolescence* (pp. 746–758). New York: Garland.

Boldizar, Janet P., David G. Perry, & Louise C. Perry. (1989). Outcome Values and Aggression. *Child Development, 60*, 571–579.

Bowlby, John. (1969). *Attachment and Loss. Vol. 1: Attachment.* New York: Basic Books.

Cairns, Robert B., & Beverley D. Cairns. (1994). *Lifelines and Risks: Pathways of Youth in Our Time.* New York: Cambridge University Press.

Card, Noel A., Jenny Isaacs, & Ernest V. E. Hodges. (2000a). *Dynamics of Interpersonal Aggression in the School Context: Who Aggresses against Whom? In Adrienne Nishina & Jaana Juvonen, Chairs, Harassment Across Diverse Contexts. Poster Symposium Presented at the Biennial Meeting of the Society for Research on Adolescence, March, 2000.* Chicago, IL.

Card, Noel A., Jenny Isaacs, & Ernest V. E. Hodges. (2000b). *The Hazards of Developing Enemies: Relations with Peer Victimization. Poster Presented at the 108th Annual Meeting of the American Psychological Association, August, 2000.* Washington, D.C.

Coie, John D., & Kenneth A. Dodge. (1998). Aggression and Antisocial Behavior. In William Damon (Series Ed.), & Nancy Eisenberg (Ed.), *Handbook of Child Psychology: Vol. 3, Social, Emotional, and Personality Development* (pp. 547–641). New York: Wiley.

Coie, John D., John E. Lochman, Robert Terry, & Clarine Hyman. (1992). Predicting Early Adolescent Disorder from Childhood Aggression and Peer Rejection. *Journal of Consulting and Clinical Psychology, 60*, 783–792.

Crick, Nicki R. (1997). Engagement in Gender Normative versus Nonnormative Forms of Aggression: Links to Social-Psychological Adjustment. *Developmental Psychology, 33*, 579–588.

Crick, Nicki R., & Kenneth A. Dodge. (1994). A Review and Reformation of Social Information-Processing Mechanisms in Children's Social Adjustment. *Psychological Bulletin, 115*, 74–101.

Crick, Nicki R., & Jennifer K. Grotpeter. (1995). Relational Aggression, Gender, and Social-Psychological Adjustment. *Child Development, 66*, 710–722.

Crick, Nicki R., & Nicole E. Werner. (1998). Response Decision Processes in Relational and Overt Aggression. *Child Development, 69*, 1630–1639.

Dishion, Thomas J., Joan McCord, & Francois Poulin. (1999). When Interventions Harm: Peer Groups and Problem Behavior. *American Psychologist, 54*, 755–764.

Dodge, Kenneth A. (1983). Behavioral Antecedents of Peer Social Status. *Child Development, 54*, 1386–1399.

Dodge, Kenneth A., John E. Bates, & Gregory S. Pettit. (1990). Mechanisms in the Cycle of Violence. *Science, 250*, 1678–1683.

Dodge, Kenneth A., & John D. Coie. (1987). Social Information-Processing Factors in Reactive and Proactive Aggression in Children's Peer Groups. *Journal of Personality and Social Psychology, 53*, 1146–1158.

Dodge, Kenneth A., Gregory S. Pettit, John E. Bates, & Ernest Valente. (1995). Social Information-Processing Patterns Partially Mediate the Effects of Early Physical Abuse on Later Conduct Problems. *Journal of Abnormal Psychology, 104*, 632–643.

Egan, Susan K., Thomas C. Monson, & David G. Perry. (1998). Social-Cognitive Influences on Change in Aggression over Time. *Developmental Psychology, 34*, 996–1006.

Eron, Leonard D., L. Rowell Huesmann, & Arnaldo Zelli. (1991). The Role of Parental Variables in the Learning of Aggression. In Debra J. Pepler & Kenneth H. Rubin (Eds.), *The Development and Treatment of Childhood Aggression* (pp. 169–188). Hillside: Lawrence Erlbaum Associates.

Griffin, Kenneth W., Gilbert J. Botvin, Lawrence M. Scheier, Tracy Diaz, & Nicole L. Miller. (2000). Parenting Practices as Predictors of Substance Use, Delinquency, and Aggression among Urban Minority Youth: Moderating Effects of Family Structure and Gender. *Psychology of Addictive Behaviors, 14*, 174–184.

Hinde, Robert A., Alison Tamplin, & Jane Barrett. (1993). Home Correlates of Aggression in Pre-School. *Aggressive Behavior, 19*, 85–105.

Hodges, Ernest V. E., Michel Boivin, Frank Vitaro, & William M. Bukowski. (1999). The Power of Friendship: Protection against an Escalating Cycle of Peer Victimization. *Developmental Psychology, 35*, 94–101.

Hodges, Ernest V. E., Regina A. Finnegan, & David G. Perry. (1999). Skewed Autonomy-Relatedness and Preadolescent's Conceptions of Their Relationships with Mother, Father, and Best Friend. *Developmental Psychology, 35*, 737–748.

Hodges, Ernest V. E., & David G. Perry. (1999). Personal and Interpersonal Antecedents and Consequences of Victimization by Peers. *Journal of Personality and Social Psychology, 76*, 677–685.

Isaacs, Jenny, Noel A. Card, & Ernest V. E. Hodges. (2000). *Aggression, Peer Victimization, Social Cognitions, and Weapon Carrying in Schools. Paper Presented at the 12th Annual Meeting of the American Psychological Society, June, 2000.* Miami, FL.

Kazdin, Alan E. (1989). *Behavior Modification in Applied Settings.* Pacific Grove: Brooks/Cole.

Kendall, Phillip C., & Lauren Braswell. (1985). *Cognitive-Behavioral Therapy for Impulsive Children.* New York: Guilford.

Lyons-Ruth, Karlen, & Deborah Jacobovitz. (1999). Attachment Disorganization: Unresolved Loss, Relational Loss, and Lapses in Behavioral and Attentional Strategies. In Jude Cassidy & Phillip R. Shaver (Eds.), *Handbook of Attachment* (pp. 520–554). New York: Guilford Press.

Maccoby, Eleanor E., & John A. Martin. (1983). Socialization in the Context of the Family: Parent-Child Interaction. In Paul H. Mussen (Series Ed.) and E. Mavis Hetherington (Ed.), *Handbook of Child Psychology: Vol. 4. Socialization, Personality, and Social Development* (pp. 1–101). New York: Wiley.

MacKinnon-Lewis, Carol, Rebecca Starnes, Brenda Volling, & Stephen Johnson. (1997). Perceptions of Parenting as Predictors of Boys' Sibling and Peer Relations. *Developmental Psychology, 33*, 1024–1031.

McHale, James P., Dannie Johnson, & Robert Sinclair. (1999). Family Dynamics, Preschoolers' Family Representations, and Preschool Peer Relationships. *Early Education and Development, 10*, 373–401.

Moffitt, Terrie E. (1993). Adolescence-Limited and Life-Course-Persistent Antisocial Behavior: A Developmental Taxonomy. *Psychological Review, 100*, 674–701.

Nagin, Daniel, & Richard E. Tremblay. (1999). Trajectories of Boys' Physical Aggression, Opposition, and Hyperactivity on the Path to Physically Violent and Nonviolent Juvenile Delinquency. *Child Development, 70*, 1181–1196.

Olweus, Dan. (1979). Stability of Aggressive Reaction Patterns in Males: A Review. *Psychological Bulletin, 86*, 852–875.

Olweus, Dan. (1981). Continuity in Aggressive and Inhibited, Withdrawn Behavior Patterns. *Psychiatry and Social Sciences, 1,* 141–159.

Olweus, Dan. (1991). Bully/Victim Problems among Schoolchildren: Basic Facts and Effects of a School Based Intervention Program. In Debra J. Pepler & Kenneth H. Rubin (Eds.), *The Development and Treatment of Childhood Aggression* (pp. 411–448). Hillside: Lawrence Erlbaum Associates.

Patterson, Gerald R. (1982). *Coercive Family Processes*. Eugene: Castalia.

Patterson, Gerald R., Barbara D. DeBaryshe, & Elizabeth Ramsey. (1989). A Developmental Perspective on Antisocial Behavior. *American Psychologist, 44,* 329–335.

Perry, David G., Sara J. Kusel, Louise C. Perry. (1988). Victims of Peer Aggression. *Developmental Psychology, 24,* 807–814.

Perry, David G., Louise C. Perry, & Janet P. Boldizar. (1990). Learning of Aggression. In Michael Lewis & Suzanne Miller (Eds.), *Handbook of Developmental Psychopathology* (pp. 135–146). New York: Plenum Press.

Perry, David G., Louise C. Perry, & Elizabeth Kennedy. (1992). Conflict and the Development of Antisocial Behavior. In Carolyn U. Schantz & Willard W. Hartup (Eds.), *Conflict in Child and Adolescent Development* (pp. 301–329). New York: Cambridge University Press.

Perry, David G., Jean C. Willard, & Louise C. Perry. (1990). Peers' Perceptions of the Consequences that Victimized Children Provide Aggressors. *Child Development, 61,* 1310–1325.

Pope, Alice W., & Karen L. Bierman. (1999). Predicting Adolescent Peer Problems and Antisocial Activities: The Relative Roles of Aggression and Dysregulation. *Developmental Psychology, 35,* 335–346.

Ray, Glen E., & Robert Cohen. (1997). Children's Evaluations of Provocation between Peers. *Aggressive Behavior, 23,* 417–431.

Salmivalli, Christina, Arja Huttunen, & Kirsti M. J. Lagerspetz. (1997). Peer Networks and Bullying in Schools. *Scandinavian Journal of Psychology, 38,* 305–312.

Snyder, James J., & Gerald R. Patterson. (1995). Individual Differences in Social Aggression: A Test of a Reinforcement Model of Socialization in the Natural Environment. *Behavior Therapy, 26,* 371–391.

Wright, Jack C., Mary Giammarino, & Harry W. Parad. (1986). Social Status in Small Groups: Individual-Group Similarity and the Social 'Misfit'. *Journal of Personality and Social Psychology, 50,* 523–536.

Violence and the Media[1]

HELMUT LUKESCH

I. INTRODUCTION: TYPES OF VIOLENCE IN THE MEDIA

Etymologically, the German word for violence—*Gewalt*—can mean three different things (Brockhaus, 1969/1970; Krey et al., 1986): first, the "use of compulsion" (e.g., in the form of "crude" violence or unlawful "violent" behavior), secondly, a more neutral meaning of "force," "strength," or "momentum" (as in *Redegewalt*, forceful speech), and finally, thirdly, the additional meaning of "power" in the sense of authority (e.g., authority to act, parental authority, governmental authority). What all three meanings seem to have in common is the assertion of a third party's will over the inclination of the person at whom the act of *Gewalt* is directed (Eibl-Eibesfeld, 1990). In the first case, that assertion of the will is regarded as illegitimate, and in the third as legitimate (though the basis for its legitimacy will not be a subject for discussion in the specific context).

These meanings of *Gewalt* differ from the everyday understanding of violence. Thus, Scheungrab (1993), for example, in the course of a number of interview studies, attempted to ascertain what young people understood by "violence in film." His resulting findings regarding the everyday psychological understanding of violence showed that it related primarily to *the use of physical means of violence* (typical answers were "someone is beaten to a pulp or gets his head chopped off," "if a person is treated cruelly, cut to pieces or something like that," etc.). In some cases the reference point was *how extreme the act was*: thus, if the acts in question were not particularly brutal, they were not interpreted as violence ("actual bloodshed ... if the director shows a person being slowly tortured," "not a brawl, then, and not a stabbing either, those are just ordinary (!) disagreements"). In specific cases, the use of *mental violence* was also taken as a reference point (for example,

---

[1]Reprinted from: Angenendt, Steffen, & Wilhelm Kempf (Eds.) (2000). *Konflikt und Gewalt: Ursachen, Entwicklungstendenzen, Perspektiven* (pp. 157–188). Münster: Agenda.

W. Heitmeyer and J. Hagan (eds.), *International Handbook of Violence Research*, 511–541.

"it doesn't have to be physical, it can also be mental cruelty ... I think locking someone up or taunting them is really brutal," "just holding a gun to a person's head or something like that can be violent as well"). *Violence against property* is sometimes explicitly excluded from the concept of violence (e.g., "violence always means violence against people, not the destruction of things"). This view evidently overlooks the point that "things" are owned by people, or at least by society, so that damage to property (vandalism) does indeed involve the violation of other people's rights. A few respondents showed a degree of sensitivity toward acts of violence, evaluating the *significance of the act in terms of advancing the action of the film* ("so violence for me begins where the plot of a film is relegated to the background ... and you see nothing except shootings and killings or even just beatings"). The area of *structural violence* (meaning violence in the sense of unjust circumstances, the unfair distribution of opportunities in life, damage to the interests of others caused, for example, by atmospheric or water pollution), was never spontaneously mentioned.

Früh (1995:178) showed that the same event can be perceived by different persons as reflecting different levels of violence. According to his assessments, based on the evaluation of sequences from films, it can be concluded that violence shown directly is perceived as more violent than reported violence, that physical violence is interpreted as more violent than acts of mental violence, that real violence is seen as a higher level of violence than fictional violence, and that violence against people is classified as more serious than violence against property. Violence in a humorous context (slapstick, comedy, and low-grade films, and in cartoons as well) is also perceived as violence. Structural violence (such as environmental pollution) is again assessed as having a relatively low violent content. In general, older respondents and women consider the level of violence shown to be more intense; level of education, on the other hand, seems to make little difference.

Basically, this everyday understanding of the concept of violence largely equates it with the concept of aggression, in the sense that any kind of deliberately harmful behavior, or at least any kind of behavior calculated to cause harm (Selg, Mees, & Berg, 1988), once it exceeds a certain threshold, is understood as violence. This kind of use of the term, in the present context, has the advantages that (1) all lawbreaking directed against persons or property and penalized by criminal law can be included, as can forms of behavior which (2) are experienced as harmful, annoying, threatening, frightening, etc., even if they fall short of the threshold at which they become punishable by law. (3) In the context of the media, this term becomes still broader, in the sense that even the effects of violence not caused by human agency (accidents or natural disasters) are seen as additional forms of violence (Krüger, 1994:72).

The types of violence reported in the media (see Fig. II-3-1-4.1) relate in some cases to events in the real world,[2] while in others they are literary fictions.

   1. One point to be noted is that even the documentation of real violence is influenced by creative elements. The presentation of real violence is not a mere image

---

[2] The question of whether the presentation of real violence should in principle be restricted is a difficult one to answer. According to Rödding (1994), it seems clear that any act of violence portrayed in the media is an offence against Section 1 GG (*Grundgesetz*, the Basic Law or constitution of the Federal Republic of Germany), which provides that "Human dignity shall be inviolable." On the other hand, we do not live in a nonviolent world: therefore the reporting of acts of violence is part of press freedom. Rödding considers that the limit is exceeded when people are treated as things and lengthy scenes of torture are portrayed to satisfy sensation-seekers. But who is to determine when that happens? In the world of fiction, by contrast, no subjective basic rights are being violated, so the issue here is not freedom of the press but freedom of opinion or artistic freedom.

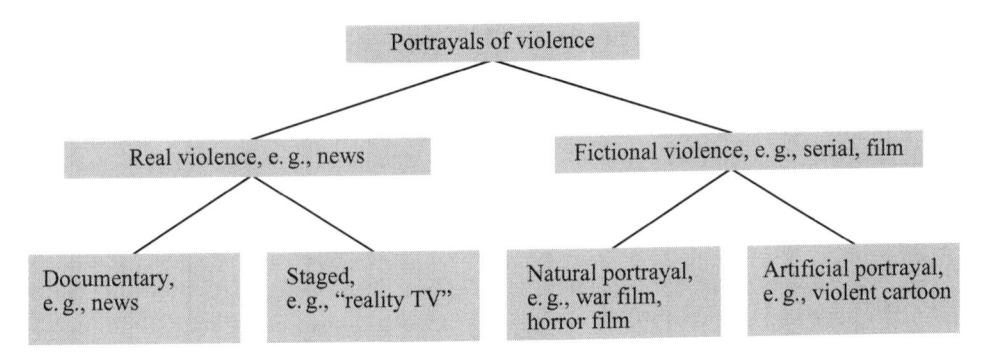

FIGURE II-3-1-4.1. Distinctions in the media's presentation of violence. *Source*: after Krüger (1994:72)* and Kepplinger and Dahlem (1990:384). *No attempt will be made here to consider the additional distinction introduced between simple portrayals and those that legitimize violence, because this is not a fundamental category but an additional, quantitatively variable aspect, which to a greater or lesser extent can be ascribed to all presentations of violence. Nor is it possible to deal here with all distinctions possible in terms of the structure of violence (Groebel and Gleich 1993:44).

of a social reality but always a creative image of a real social process (apart from "canards" and deliberately staged violence, which are admittedly entirely commonplace media fodder).[3] This staging has become very apparent in reconstructed reports on real events ("reality TV").[4] But even in documentary productions, visual commentary (selection of events, camera angles, cutting, and slow motion) and verbal commentary (the use of language with negative or positive overtones to qualify violent events) can be used to influence the way an event is perceived (Kepplinger, 1987; Kepplinger & Giesselmann, 1993). The incorporation of entertainment aspects into a news context ("infotainment") and the use of (almost) real events for entertainment purposes ("entermation") have been used here in pursuit of the short-term maximization of audience figures, at the expense of a possibly far-reaching change in both fields. In addition, news reports are not unrelated events; a single event is reported over an extended period. This can result in a sequence of action with a range of possible effects, not unlike the plot of a drama.[5]

2. Fictional media products with violent or other content are (almost) always artificially generated virtual realities that can deviate as much as their authors wish from the reality of the existing natural world. Hitherto, the diversity of the means

[3] Probably the best known example in Germany is the forgery of the "Hitler Diaries" by Konrad Kujau, which took in the magazine *Stern*. Mention should also be made, though, of the forged television reports produced by the German journalist Michael Born, which were sold to *stern-tv* among others. Even the production of videos on the fictional private lives of celebrities actually happens: one example being the case of the Princess of Wales foisted off on the British *Sun* newspaper. But, as always, the 'gray area' remains gray. With a sufficiently powerful graphics program, anyone today can be spliced into a video film to create new and apparently real images.

[4] Jonas and Neuberger (1996) have produced a detailed content analysis of programs of this type.

[5] In 1991, we used the Bogardus scale to carry out a pilot study of social distance from various nations, incorporating the factor of sex (in other words, social distance from a Dutchman/a Dutchwoman, a Jew/a Jewess, etc.). As was only to be expected in the context of the civil war in Bosnia, respondents felt themselves most remote socially from a Serbian man.

of media production, beginning with pictures and print, has broadened to include first the audio media and audiovisual data storage media and then the borderline area of interactive computer games and relatively realistic forms of experiencing cyberspace through whole-body activity (Lukesch, 1997:9); each of these media can use its own code to convey the subject of violence to the person experiencing it. Here again, hybrid products are possible: for example, the series "Faces of Death," in which real killings, failed stunts with grave consequences, motor-racing accidents, etc., have been spliced together into feature film length and offered as entertainment, complete with inane commentary. Similarly, it is not obvious to every viewer that the TV program "Wrestling" is not reporting real fights but come under the heading of staged, fictional violence.

In addressing the subject of violence in the media, questions that may be asked include the following:

1. To what extent is violent material offered by the media? This question can be answered relatively precisely as far as television is concerned on the basis of a content analysis (Groebel & Gleich, 1993; Krüger, 1994; Wilson et al., 1997). Früh (1995:173) admittedly regards the necessary "normative" (meaning conceptual and analytical) definitions of violence as problematic in content analyses, because the possibility exists that acts that were not conceived as violent may very well be perceived as violent by the recipient or, conversely, an act of violence may subjectively be perceived as harmless; in our view, however, such unclear areas are no problem, as we are not concerned with the reconstruction of subjective theories of violence.
2. The next question deals with the way in which violent content is perceived by different user groups. The content offered and the way that content is utilized by the various groups of recipients are obviously not identical, though they are related, in that the media want to sell their products at a profit and must therefore take account of, or create, their audience's requirements.
3. There is no escaping the next question: does the way in which this product sector is used also result in predictable effects on audiences?[6] As noted by Groebel and Gleich (1993:13), such content does have the "potential from which possible effects may arise." Content analyses can justify assumptions about potential effects (in the sense of explaining or predicting individual events; Lukesch, 1997:35f.) only insofar as they specify, within the framework of Hempel and Oppenheim's explanatory model (Stegmüller, 1969), the marginal or antecedent conditions under which the "laws" stated by a theory claim to be valid. The view that "what is not identified by the public as violent media content cannot produce the same effect as violent media content" (Früh, 1995:173) seems problematic. This statement disregards the possibility of latent learning or the learning of possible forms of action without the need also to encode them semantically.

[6]In this context, we merely refer in passing to the farther-reaching questions of whether the findings of researchers on the effects of the media allow conclusions to be drawn regarding the prevention of violent dispositions or whether such recommendations can be made on the basis of other areas of knowledge of technological change (Patry & Perrez, 1982).

II.   REAL AND FICTIONAL VIOLENT
TELEVISION CONTENT

1.   Content and Its Use

a. Fictional Violent Content in the Media and Its Uses.   It is a specific property of film that violent acts (unlike prosocial topics) can easily be pictorialised and used to create excitement. The quest for excitement, and its management, are in turn essential motives for turning to the media (Hassanein, 1995:56; Brosius & Schmitt, 1994). As a result of the demand for television programs that can be produced economically, therefore, films with a high content of violence have become very widely distributed. In the United States, this quickly resulted in complaints that television showed too much crime. As a result, since the 1950s, the content of violence in television programs has been studied objectively with methods of content analysis (Gerbner & Gross, 1973).

In a recent analysis, Hickey (1992; quoted in Groebel & Gleich, 1993:40) gave the following count for a single day's content on ten American television stations: 1,846 acts of aggression, with 175 scenes in which the use of violence culminated in the death of an adversary, 389 scenes showed grievous bodily harm, 362 portrayed shootings and 673 showed fights, beatings, and serious threats. In new types of program (music videos, film trailers, and reality TV), there was a significant increase in scenes of violence. Each broadcaster showed ten acts of violence per hour, one third of which were life-threatening assaults. Until very recently, the United States has broadcast the most violent programs of any country, followed by Japan (Huesmann & Eron, 1986:21; Iwao, de Sola Pool, & Hagiwara, 1981:31).

The latest "National Television Violence Study" (Wilson et al., 1997:5) also contains the following conclusions: "(1) the context in which most violence is presented on television poses risks for viewers; (2) the negative consequences of violence are not often portrayed in violent programming; (3) perpetrators go unpunished in most scenes of violence; (4) violent programs rarely employ an antiviolent theme; and (5) on the positive side, television violence is usually not explicit or graphic."

As far as America is concerned, then, there is already a long tradition of analyzing television program content. The German television scene, however, has been the subject of systematic analysis only in recent years. According to these studies, however, the levels of violence in German television, too, are not insignificant.

The study by Groebel and Gleich (1993; cf. Table II-3-1-4.1) of the most important channels in 1991 makes it clear that at least mild forms of violence—such as threats, beatings, shouting, and violent, aggressive gestures—are encountered in half of all programs. To put it another way, five acts of aggression are shown every hour; and extreme forms of violence are sufficiently represented in the form of 481 murders screened each week. As the authors say, "the taking of human life has in some cases become an automatic part of the program" (Groebel & Gleich, 1993:73). The fact that the proportion of violence is particularly high in programs broadcast by the private-sector channels is explained by the fact that these screen a great many American imports, for cost reasons, and use this method of generating excitement in an attempt to boost their share of the all-important advertising revenue.

In addition, mention should be made of a few findings from the qualitative analysis of the acts of violence, which could be significant in terms of the potential effects of televised violence (Groebel & Gleich, 1993:83f.): most acts of violence comprise bodily

TABLE II-3-1-4.1.   Acts of aggression on German television

Channel	Violence shown (as percent of all programming time)	Percent aggression before prime time	Frequency of murders/week
ARD	6.7	7.9	40
ZDF	7.2	5.5	48
ARD/ZDF (a. m.)	2.1	—	13
SAT 1	7.3	3.9	62
RTL+	10.7	22.8	93
TELE 5	11.7	7.9	93
Pro 7	12.7	52.0	132

Source: Groebel and Gleich, 1993:68, 72, 81.

attacks (32 percent), with use of firearms (20.9 percent). Two thirds of all acts are motivated by factors not immediately apparent from the context, and the "aggression seems very often to be a way of achieving certain aims or resolving conflicts" (Groebel & Gleich, 1993:89). In the majority of cases (74.7 percent) the aggression entailed no consequences for the aggressor, who is more likely to experience satisfaction (10.4 percent) than punishment (6.6 percent) or other consequences (4.3 percent). In addition, "frequently, there is no obvious empathy with the victims' sufferings and feelings" (Groebel & Gleich, 1993:93).

Media violence is a global reality, and the rewarding aspects of the violence shown are a particularly strong contributory factor in the development of a "global aggressive culture" (Groebel, 1998:217).

Krüger (1996) presented a similar study for children. This showed that 3.7 percent of total air time for all stations examined was taken up by acts of violence, transmitted mainly by the channels Pro 7 (33.2 percent), RTL 2 (19.0 percent), RTL (15.2 percent) and Sat 1 (12.9 percent); ARD (10.4 percent) and ZDF (9.4 percent) account for comparable proportions of this overall content of violence. The more tightly the definition of violence is worded (cf. footnote 10), the greater Pro 7's share. If the programs analyzed are restricted to those with an audience share of over 4 percent in the target group of children, the violent sequences in these more frequently seen transmissions rise to 5.6 percent of airtime. In other words, violence seems to be attractive to children and leads to selective viewing. Over 90 percent of the violence seen by children is screened by the private-sector TV channels (Pro 7 again occupying first place, with a proportion of 44.5 percent). As children largely avoid watching informative programs, most of the violence they experience is fictional; an exception here is RTL, where reality TV and tabloid-style broadcasts are still relatively popular with children, so that 27.2 percent of the violence shown on this channel is to be found in nonfictional programs (especially reality TV). Children, however, tend to avoid extreme levels of realistic violence ("hard violence").

In 1998, the UNESCO study on media violence and children, conducted in twenty-three countries, presented its first results (Groebel, 1998). The study confirmed that television was the most frequently used medium, irrespective of national boundaries. Worldwide, 88 percent of children were familiar with the actor Arnold Schwarzenegger in his "Terminator" role. In countries with a highly aggressive environment, 51 percent of all children questioned wanted to be like Schwarzenegger; in less violent countries, the figure is still as high as 35 percent.

The various other types of media outlet provide a great deal of additional violence for audiences, especially children and young people.[7] Of these, video is one means of distribution that has long been regarded with a degree of concern—after all, there are over 16,000 video films available for rent in Germany, a substantial proportion of which are products that have been classified as endangering young people;[8] the June 1998 *Jugendmedienschutz* (Media and the Protection of the Young—"JMS") report listed 2,686 video films and 369 computer games that had been blacklisted; 138 data storage products had been impounded for portraying violence that expressed contempt for humanity and 157 media products for hard pornography.

Despite the restrictions on distribution caused by blacklisting, these products continue to find their market—consumption of violent films is still flourishing. According to representative data provided by Weiß (1993), the proportion of eighth/ninth grade children in Germany who could be classified as "extreme" viewers of violence (which by the definition used means those who have seen more than fifty horror films or violent films) rose between 1989 and 1992 from 6.8 to 10 percent, while the segment of "regular viewers" (children who have seen eleven to fifty such films) rose from 10 percent to 12 percent. The increase was particularly noticeable among pupils attending secondary schools that prepare for vocational training rather than for university. In addition, the age at which children first view violent films seems to have moved down into the elementary school range: nearly half of all children saw their first horror film or violent film before the age of nine. Those who later became "excessive" viewers also made an earlier start on watching this kind of film. Across the whole sample, one third of the films first seen were blacklisted, meaning that the *Bundesprüfstelle für jugendgefährdende Schriften* (Federal Review Board for Publications Harmful to the Young—"BPS") had banned the distribution of these films to children and young people, while 15 percent had been impounded, meaning that they should no longer have been available on the market at all.

According to our trend data (Lukesch et al., 1989b: 73; 1989a: 132), about one third of all those under the age of eighteen spontaneously named blacklisted videos among their favorites. If selective sampling is used, this proportion becomes significantly higher still: rising, for example, to 57 percent (Scheungrab, 1989:263) among male *Berufsschule* (vocational school) students, and 62 percent among children/young people growing up in homes (Froschhammer, 1992). The eastern regions of Germany have already caught up with or overtaken those in the west (about 45 percent viewing blacklisted videos and 10 percent impounded videos; Lukesch, 1992).

---

[7] Adults in Germany are not subject to any control (cf. the prohibition of censorship in Section 5 GG) in their consumption of media violence (with the exception of products deemed to undermine the social ethic such as hard pornography [including child pornography, among other forms], violence that degrades human beings, glorification of National Socialism, or an offense against the safeguarding of personal honor), so that there is no motivation to carry out user studies of this kind among adults. On the other hand, it would be completely mistaken to regard children as the only group potentially at risk from the influence of media violence (Huesmann et al., 1997:189); in fact, no age-group is immune to these influences.

[8] Situations whose depiction is considered to be a threat to the young are: (1) extreme portrayals of violence in the media (e.g., vigilante-style justice), (2) glorification of the Nazi ideology, (3) incitement to racial hatred, (4) glorification of war, (5) discrimination against women and (6) pornography (it must be borne in mind here that even 'soft' pornography is classified as a severe risk to young people and therefore automatically placed on the index).

However, films with some claim to artistic merit are also marketing more and more violent action (for example, *Pulp Fiction, Robocop, Die Hard, Natural Born Killers, The Silence of the Lambs*). Van der Voort and Beentjes (1997:88) use the term "ultraviolent" films here; in this case, again, a great many rationalizations have been produced (using catchphrases such as "esthetics of violence" or viewing excessive portrayals of violence as a form of "media criticism" or "ironic treatment of media reality").

As viewing data from Germany confirm, legislation alone can produce only a limited effect. Even so, it is not useless either, as has sometimes been suggested (cf. the questionable argument that prohibiting something is in itself an incentive to use it); a law that imposes punishment for particular activities can never be a guarantee that those activities will cease. It would be nonsensical, though, to assert that the only reason people break the speed limit, for example, is because the speed limit is there. Statutory regulation at least sends out a signal to law-abiding citizens.

b. REAL VIOLENCE IN THE MEDIA AND ITS CONSUMPTION. As regards the presentation of real violence on television, again, the study by Groebel and Gleich (1993:74f.) is informative (cf. Table II-3-1-4.2). In terms of the program categories analyzed across the available TV spectrum, the portrayal of real violence again fluctuates greatly from channel to channel. The highest levels of violence in German news broadcasting are to be found on the private-sector channel RTL, where the proportion (portrayal of physical violence) is in some cases seven times higher than on ARD or ZDF.

Quantitative differences in the proportions of violence exist by comparison with fictional programs (films and serials), the levels of violence in these genres being much higher than in the documentary genre; news programs account for only 10 percent of all acts of violence shown, while if documentaries and factual programs are included this figures rises to nearly 15 percent. These differences have also been found in studies conducted in other countries, the content of violence in fictional and nonfictional television again varying from country to country (American productions contain particularly high levels of violence; cf. also Dorfman et al., 1997; Mustonen, 1997).

In the news sector, the acts of violence shown relate mainly to warfare (24.3 percent), ethnic and minority conflicts (29.8 percent), reporting of crime, organized and otherwise (18.3 percent), political disputes (16.6 percent), and terrorism (6.4 percent), leaving an "others" category of 4.7 percent. Frequently, where violence (e.g., crime) is portrayed,

TABLE II-3-1-4.2.   **Levels of violence in news and documentary broadcasting***

Channel	Violence (general)		Violence (physical)	
	News	Info/Doc	News	Info/Doc
ARD	8.1 %	5.8 %	1.4 %	0.5 %
ZDF	11.3 %	4.1 %	0.7 %	1.3 %
SAT 1	12.3 %	3.8 %	2.5 %	2.7 %
RTL+	15.4 %	2.0 %	7.6 %	1.9 %
TELE 5	9.4 %	2.8 %	0.3 %	1.4 %
Pro 7	10.2 %	13.5 %	2.6 %	—

*Percentages based on total time per channel and genre.
Source: Groebel and Gleich 1993:76.

there is no reference to any explanatory context, for example along the lines that violent crime is not a product of chance but takes place in accordance with particular social patterns (Dorfman et al., 1997). There are significant differences in the quality of the presentation of violence by comparison with the fictional genres: although even here 55.3 percent of all acts of violence entail no consequences for the aggressor, there are 39.5 percent of cases in which punishment is shown and in 5.3 percent the perpetrator even shows remorse. The victim's standpoint is also underrepresented in news reporting. If news reports are cut like fast-motion action video clips, it is difficult really to experience the suffering portrayed (as a result of war, famine, or disaster); in order to enable the viewer to empathize, however, victims should be identifiable as human beings in their pain. Here again, of course, reasonable limits would have to be observed.

Krüger (1994) produced a study from a rather different angle, based on the year 1993. This covered the genres of information (news and political and nonpolitical factual programs) and reality TV, and dealt with four ascending levels of the presentation of violence.[9] In terms of identified acts of violence (proportion of information/reality TV airtime taken up by portrayals of violence) the study agrees almost completely with the estimate of Groebel and Gleich (1993, see above): 9 percent of the content of information/reality TV is made up of portrayals of violence, although only 0.9 percent of the acts analyzed meet the "hard violence" criterion. The proportion of violence on RTL is 17.6 percent, far higher than on ARD (6.8 percent), ZDF (6.2 percent), or Sat.1 (9.3 percent); the order is unchanged when the focus is shifted to individual levels of violence. The relatively high proportion of violence in private-sector information broadcasts is attributable to the extremely high content of violence in the subcategory of reality TV (a form of broadcasting that is almost entirely absent from the public-sector broadcasting channels in Germany, apart from the series *Aktenzeichen XY*). "Hard violence" on the public-sector channels is primarily concerned with political information "realistically/authentically presented in the interests of information;" on reality TV, however, the emphasis is on staged and emotionally charged portrayals, intended "primarily to create emotional excitement and attention" (Groebel & Gleich, 1993:80).

It is interesting that similar results also apply to American television (Wartella et al., 1997): of the realistic categories of program, "only" 38 percent contain visual portrayals of violence, while violence is discussed in another 18 percent of programs; the public-sector TV channels broadcast less violence than the private-sector ones, and the authors recommend greater use of warning notices and the broadcasting of violence at later times.

2. Effects of Consumption of Media Violence

a. GENERAL ASSUMPTIONS.   There is already a widespread belief that the many forms of permitted and approved violence in society (violence in the home, for example, committed by abusive mothers, at school, and in the mass media) are creating habituation to violence and resulting in it being seen as a normal means of resolving conflict (Remschmidt et al., 1990:198):

[9]The following distinctions were made: (1) all portrayals of violence including at least one visible violent element (perpetrator, act/event, victim/person affected, damage), (2) portrayals of violence including victims/persons affected, (3) portrayals of violence with a visible act/event, (4) portrayals of 'hard violence', meaning that the act/event is seen, death/destruction or dead/injured people are seen, and the intensity of the violence, damage, or cruelty is very pronounced.

Dramatic, unusually spectacular portrayals of violence encourage, stimulate, and justify the use of violence. Even if the violence portrayed is not directly imitated, the constant flooding of the consciousness with violent stimuli leads to the trivialization of violence, which becomes an everyday event, not to be regarded as unusual or avoided. In their conflict resolution models, the justifiable anticipatory or even preventive use of violence is encouraged ... The constant portrayal of violence is a stimulus to increased consumption of violence (Remschmidt et al., 1990:203).

Many assumptions regarding the effects of violent media content have been formulated in more or less random and unrelated theories (cf. Fig. II-3-1-4.2). These theories have been built up from individual observations and studies on an arbitrary basis, without any effort to provide a linking framework theory, and can be used by those interested in the debate to support any and all points of view. Selg (1987) pointed out at an early date that this boosted a trivializing interpretation of the results of research into the effects of violence, an interpretation that is beneficial to the interests of the media institutions.

1. Catharsis thesis:[10] In this case we have a reference to the Aristotelian "theory" of classical tragedy regarding the purgative effect of observing violence; viewers of violence as portrayed by the media will supposedly be freed of their darker emotions by the vicarious working-off of negative tendencies. But violence as portrayed by the media generally does not produce any cathartic effect (Charlton, 1972:165; Andison, 1977). The vicarious aggression catharsis hypothesis (Feshbach, 1961), even under specific preconditions (such as previous annoyance and no opportunity for revenge on the person who caused it), is so sweeping in its generalizations that it is regarded as one of the best-refuted assertions of media research (Lukesch & Schauf, 1990).

2. Inhibition thesis: This observation, dating back to Berkowitz and Rawlings (1963), focuses on the finding that some people are deterred by the sight of violence (on this point, cf. also the differential effect identified by Brosius (1987) that watching a horror film tends to make older viewers less willing to legitimize violence, whereas this is not the case with younger viewers). Berkowitz and Rawlings (1963) attributed this to an increase in fear of aggression (this finding, incidentally, would be phenomenologically indistinguishable from a cathartic effect).

3. Stimulation thesis: In its simplest form, this assumes an increase in the viewer's own violent behavior, or propensity to it, as a result of viewing violence, along the lines of "like breeds like." This assumption, often alternatively circulated in the guise of the imitation thesis, disregards all the diverse knowledge available on differential media effects. In its simplicity, then, this thesis too is easily refuted—which may be one of the reasons why it is constantly being addressed.

4. Habituation or acclimatization thesis: This theory dwells on the habituation effects of violence; watching violence blunts the sensitivities toward the frightening acts of violence displayed in the media, and violence thus becomes routine. Here again, there are authors who try to find a favorable side to this effect—violent imagery, they say, would thus no longer be able to trigger the emotionalizing effects that depress the viewers.

---

[10] The word "catharsis," incidentally, is used in different ways. This diversity of meaning may again lead laymen to the conclusion that there might after all be something in the catharsis thesis (for example, releasing of emotional tension through physical action), and this conviction may then in turn be misapplied to the watching of violent media content in the belief that it produces a cathartic effect.

5. Imitation thesis: This psychoanalytically based thesis, which has its roots in the early days of psychology and holds that processes of imitation or identification allow the viewer to identify with the action and an attractive protagonist (the distinctions between anaclitic and aggressive identification may be noted here in passing), also seems to be referred to constantly because it is so self-evidently refutable. The customary argument is that despite tens of thousands of murders portrayed in the media, consumers of media violence have themselves committed such an act only in extremely rare cases. Even so, there are verifiable individual cases in which directly imitative acts can be assumed (an example being the killing of a small child by two ten-year-olds in Liverpool in 1993).

6. The thesis of ineffectiveness of media violence: Because of the diversity of the statements on record, it is tempting to reason that no conclusions whatsoever can be drawn regarding the effects of the media. This is a very popular point of view with the representatives of the media, since it implies that they have no need to take responsibility for their products.

The "social cognitive theory of mass communication" (Bandura, 1989) provides a framework within which these unrelated individual theses can be integrated. There is room, too, for all the differential effects (such as the advancement of the "double-dose theory," whereby the mass media could only produce an effect that additionally reinforces the learning conditions of genuine experience, or the inclusion of value orientations that may be important for an assessment of presented model behavior, for example the fact that sympathy with the victims of an act of violence may inhibit aggression). It is clear, too, however, that this complex theory cannot be tested in its entirety but only in some of its aspects (for further analyses of aggression theory, cf. Kleiter, 1997).

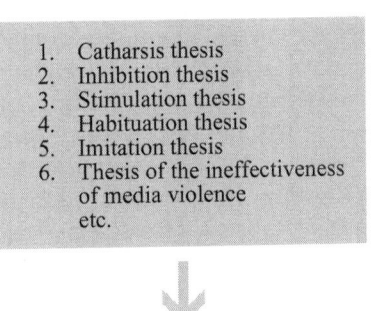

1. Catharsis thesis
2. Inhibition thesis
3. Stimulation thesis
4. Habituation thesis
5. Imitation thesis
6. Thesis of the ineffectiveness of media violence
   etc.

Social cognitive theory of mass communication (Bandura 1989)

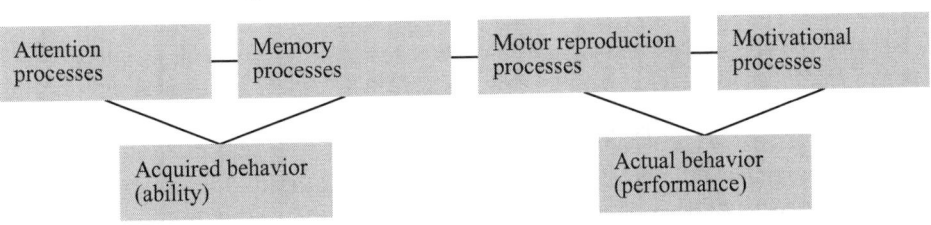

Attention processes — Memory processes — Motor reproduction processes — Motivational processes

Acquired behavior (ability)

Actual behavior (performance)

FIGURE II-3-1-4.2. From the individual theses on the effects of media portrayals of violence to the social cognitive theory of mass communication.

(1) Catharsis thesis
(2) Inhibition thesis
(3) Stimulation thesis
(4) Habituation thesis
(5) Imitation thesis
(6) Thesis of the ineffectiveness of media violence
    etc.

In the social cognitive theory of mass communication, it is assumed that four complexes of conditions intervene between a model event (whether this be the action of a real person or merely of a fictional one who is conveyed to a recipient by text or film) and a possible modeling performance (cf. Fig. II-3-1-4.2). Depending on the course taken by these processes, the ability to behave in a particular way is acquired, or imitative acts at a behavioral level are stimulated, or no learning process takes place at all (for example, if the modeled action is already a fixed part of a person's repertoire and conditions that are important for the performance of the behavior have turned out unsatisfactorily).

As an essential precondition for learning, a potential model must first attract *attention* to itself. (a) This requires the model person to meet numerous conditions (for example, persons of high social status are accorded greater attention than models of lesser status; similarly, behavior that stands out strongly from that of others in line with the figure-ground principle is also more clearly perceived; attractiveness, in the sense of possessing important characteristics desired by the observer, again increases the level of attention); (b) not every observer (meaning the viewer or reader of or listener to a media message) sees and hears the same message (for example, a timorous person will have a tendency to stimulus selection; a recipient with greater cognitive complexity is capable of more differentiated perceptions because of better prior knowledge; motivational dispositions and current motivations initiate selection and interference processes); (c) the structure of social interaction is also significant (which types of behavior are most commonly encountered in a social group or a mass medium).

How much of the material perceived in the course of these observations remains in long-term memory depends on *processes of retention and information processing*. Some of the acts presented are symbolically coded (by being given names, for example) and transformed into more or less easily memorable cognitive schemes: the modeled event has to be classified within existing cognitive structures. In such cases, the observer and his memory structures play an extremely active part. Elaborated repetitions (enrichment with meanings, including the results of daydreams, for example) may have the specific effect of changing originally existing information. Modeled action schemes that can be repeated on a motor level thus become particularly difficult to forget.

Processes of attention and memory make it possible to acquire the competence to perform a particular behavior pattern (we know, for example, from watching the film *California* how to slaughter a gas-station attendant); but this in itself still falls far short of translating the appropriate knowledge into action. Action first has to be practiced in the form of *motor reproduction processes* (which can also take place on a cognitive level, cf. the method of mental training and other forms of fantasy activity). It is helpful here to have the necessary physical capabilities, recourse to the partial reactions necessary to perform an action, and differentiated feedback conditions (capacity for self-perception or external feedback on the accuracy of an imitative act).

Ultimately, the overt performance of learned actions depends upon *reinforcement or motivational processes*. It is customary to refer first here to the influence (a) of vicarious reinforcement (for example, has the model for one's behavior been reinforced, has it been able to achieve important goals?).[11] Then, possible (b) self-rewarding and/or self-penalizing mechanisms (known as "intrinsic incentives") have to be taken into account: because people want to live in conformity with their value systems (or individual standards), different evaluations may mean that the identical modeled behavior possesses a completely different personal valence. People may reward themselves (for example in the form of a positive self-evaluation), depending on whether or not they have complied with such standards, or they may penalize themselves (for example, in the form of self-criticism). Finally, in the performance of behavior, consideration must also be given to (c) external processes of reinforcement by genuinely existing third parties. All these conditions may also be cognitively anticipated, because it is assumed that *efficiency expectations* (am I able to perform the behavior?) intervene between persons and their behavior and that *outcome expectations* (does a particular action also lead to the intended result?) are essential in determining an action and its possible outcome.

Whether an imitative performance ultimately comes about is, under the theory outlined above, a highly complex process.

That process cannot be sufficiently reproduced by the concepts (derived from psychoanalysis) of imitation and identification.[12] Many other terms have also been used in an attempt to capture the processes outlined here. This is associated, in part, with theoretical traditions from various disciplines. For example, Phillips (1983) refers from the sociological standpoint to a suggestion process, or image transfer phenomena are sometimes assumed in the field of advertising research. Basically, these concepts fail to capture the differentiated nature of the processes referred to in the social cognitive theory of mass communication; at best, they touch upon partial components of model learning.

b. Effects of the Use of Fictional Violent Media Content. Depending on the recipients' prior experience and predispositions, the reception of media violence can be shown to act in two major ways:

(1) For recipients with little experience of violence (who are generally more likely to be girls than boys and more likely to be younger children than older children or persons with a value system that does not legitimize acts of violence), in other words, as a whole, for recipients who have not yet undergone a process of habituation to violence, the large-scale consumption of violence leads to increased anxiety and depression (Cantor, 1991). This effect was first demonstrated on children in the classic study by Himmelweit, Oppenheim, and Vince (1958), and has been continued in a number of further findings

---

[11] Vicarious reinforcement has a primarily *informative function* and serves the purpose of environmental discrimination: for example, it is possible to distinguish between those situations in which activity meets with social approval and those where it meets with disapproval. However, it also produces *incentive effects* for the observer (anticipation of reward for identical behavior). In addition, *vicarious conditioning effects*, in accordance with the classical or operant paradigms, can arise as a result (for example, anxiety triggers can be acquired vicariously). Vicarious reinforcements may in some circumstances bring about a *modification of the appearance of the model* (penalties experienced reduce its prestige, rewards enhance its status). Finally, vicarious reinforcements also have their consequences for the *reinforcer:* depending on the observer's assessment of the legitimacy of reinforcements undertaken, the evaluation of the person performing the reinforcement changes.

[12] 'Imitation' is understood as meaning the replication of individual forms of behavior, which is sustained by extrinsic reward; the presence of the model is important here. The concept of 'identification' relates to the adoption of behavior patterns, this process being maintained by intrinsic conditions. The model is, as it were, a charismatic person to whom one would like to be similar. It follows that the acts caused by identification also take place in the absence of the model.

from surveys (Brosius & Hartmann, 1988; Rieseberg & Martin-Newe, 1988; Melchers & Seifert, 1984) and in controlled experimental studies (Gruber, 1993; Mezger-Brewka, 1993; for a summary, cf. Cantor, 1996).

However, anxiety and aggression—as ethological conceptions are sufficient to show—are related reaction cycles. This experience has also been transposed to the field of the media, insofar as it has been assumed that massive anxieties may lie behind media-induced aggression symptoms (Luca-Krüger, 1988). This assumption, first tested against individual observations, was subsequently confirmed in an evaluation method based on path analysis by Hopf and Weiß (1996); the latter showed that although aggressive personality dispositions are quite critically determined by the extent of consumption of horror and violence, nevertheless high levels of anxiety (especially guilt anxiety) also contribute to increased aggression. In addition, repeated exposure to frightening images can initiate a process of habituation which may also result in inurement to violence in everyday life (Drabman & Thomas, 1974).

(2) Innumerable (a) field studies, (b) experimental studies, and (c) summarizing meta-analyses exist on the aggression-increasing effect of fictional portrayals of violence.

(2a) Even the earliest studies from the first years of television, when media effects could still be tested with pre-posttest designs, suggest that portrayals of violence in the media have the effect of increasing aggression. For example, Himmelweit et al. (1958) found that portrayals of violence result in aggressive behavior in emotionally disturbed children, while in other children they trigger feelings of anxiety. Apart from the fact that the direct triggering of aggression affects only a small proportion of children, the authors believe that exposure to portrayals of violence eventually creates in children and young people the impression that violence in everyday life is a normal (and especially masculine) means of conflict resolution. Similar results were arrived at by Schramm, Lyle, and Parker in the United States (1961) and Furu (1971) in Japan. Probably the last study that was able to make use of these methods came from Canada, where Joy, Kimball, and Zabrack (1986), in the Notel, Unitel, and Multitel study (Williams, 1986), demonstrated the aggression-increasing effect of the introduction of television in a field experiment, noting that the effect in question occurred irrespective of the children's original level of aggression or their sex. They too see the general acceptance of violence and aggression produced by the programs in question as the most important causal mechanism.

Another way of verifying the effects of the consumption of violent media content is the longitudinal assessment of media and aggression indicators and their evaluation on the basis of causal analysis with the aid of cross-lagged panel correlations or structural equation models. A classic study using these methods is that of Eron et al. (1972). It was shown here that the preference for violent programs in the third year of school was the best predictor of aggressive behavior ten years later. Viemerö (1996) used a longitudinal study to show the significant contribution made by consumption of violent TV programs (as a separable component of an aggressive socialization atmosphere) on subsequent criminality. Other field studies are confined to cross-sectional data collection (Lamnek, 1995), but have recently attempted causal interpretations of correlative results (Lukesch, 1990) by testing the fit to model concepts, or excluding the effects of other possible intervening variables (such as social stratum, sex, etc.) by means of various statistical techniques (Lukesch, 1988).

A significant study of the long-term influence of televised violence on young males was undertaken by Belson (1978) in London. His results support the hypothesis that a high level of consumption of televised violence leads to an increase in acts of relatively serious violence. Interpretatively, Belson (1978) attributes his results to a process of demolition of the inhibitions acquired by socialization, a process that takes place not on a conscious level but subliminally.[13] In this context, particular forms of violence have proven especially stimulating, such as:

- morally justified violence (i.e., violence for a beneficial purpose; Berkowitz & Rawlings, 1963; Berkowitz, Corwin, & Heironimus, 1963),[14]
- the likeable aggressor,
- the portrayal of the victims as cowardly and treacherous,
- violence in the context of close social relationships,
- the rewarding of acts of violence,
- violence with no close relationship to the narrative structure of a film,
- a Western with excessive scenes of violence,
- the highly realistic portrayal of violence in a fictional plot,
- the absence of positive nonviolent countermodels and
- the establishment of great similarity between the situation of the aggressive model and the viewer, and, in the same way, between the victim of violence portrayed on film and a real person (Berkowitz & Geen, 1966).

Lukesch et al. (1989a:329) gathered various measurements with procedures based on the same methodological tradition that were also indicative of the past extent of reception of television, cinema, and video violence, and related them to aggression indicators. It is striking that the indicators of violence for video and cinema explain more variance in the dependent variables than the consumption of television violence. Special features of the content and a situation in which the violence is received amid a peer group that appreciates acts of violence may be held responsible for these differential media effects. Real-life circumstances (social stratum, age, sex) admittedly reduce the closeness of the relationships found but do not eliminate them altogether. Correlations (after testing bidirectional relations using a two-stage least-square procedure) also permit a causal interpretation, in the sense that this quality of video consumption has a causative significance for the subjects' aggression. Other long-term effects of consumption of video violence, in particular, may be seen in an "underdevelopment of social and human skills" (Rieseberg & Martin-Newe, 1988:78) and a lasting personality change in the sense of increased excitability, aggressive ego assertion, and spontaneous aggression (Weiß, 1990). The multivariate studies of Kleiter (1994) can be similarly assessed.[15]

[13] This is an important aspect for research methods: personality-impairing effects (for example in the stimulation of anxiety by the media) are close to consciousness; people feel disturbed and adversely affected by them; personality-enhancing effects that are perceived as pleasant (such as the feeling of strength gained from identification with a perpetrator of justified violence), which ultimately increase aggression, are not directly apparent to the recipient, meaning that they cannot be objectivized by survey techniques but have to be detected by means of other, empirical testing systems.

[14] Violence is, moreover, seen as less serious in a justifying context than in a nonjustifying one (Moore & Cockerton, 1996).

[15] "so one cannot say that 'screen violence makes our children aggressive', but one can certainly say 'screen violence encourages the propensity to aggressive conduct among a very particular group of children'—and does so quite clearly in certain constellations of additional moderator parameters or in the context of particular types. However, it does not follow from this, conversely, that for the subgroups in question the consumption of on-screen aggression is merely an independent additive or catalyst or merely a harbinger of previously existing aggression, with no active function. The film is not 'innocent.' What happens is that the aggression seen on screen reacts with a cumulative vicious-circle effect on a threshold displacement of increasing tolerance for aggression and may also simply result in an increase in aggressive behavior via processes of imitation" (Kleiter, 1994:53).

(2b)   The experimental analysis of the effects of violent films is linked to the work of the research team centered on Bandura. Aggression-imitating effects of violent models were examined in numerous experiments. Findings that can be simplistically summarized to form a stimulation thesis and interpreted in the context of social cognitive learning theory (Bandura, 1989) are available both for children (Bandura, Ross, & Ross, 1961; Bandura & Houston, 1961) and for adults (Walters & Thomas, 1962, 1963).

The form of the paradigmatic research design for children is that, following a base-line assessment, a model person performs aggressive acts against a doll that are new to the children. The children are then mildly frustrated, left alone in a playroom, and observed. Children who have been able to look at an aggressive model generally react more aggressively in this play phase than children in a control group. The effects do not merely arise directly in the context of the experiment but—at least as far as their representation in memory is concerned—are more long term (Hicks, 1968).

The experimental conditions have been varied in many ways and worked out to give a process model of the acquisition and performance of modeled behaviors (Bandura, 1989; cf. Fig. II-3-1-4.2). Mussen and Rutherford (1961), for example, observed that even the perception of acts of violence in pictures increases the aggressive conduct of first-grade pupils in permissive situations. Pass (1983) confirmed the aggression-stimulating effect on preschool children of short violent stories played on an audiotape. Charlton (1972) and Charlton et al. (1974) tested various model conditions using a Western series (*Gunsmoke*). It proved possible to demonstrate an increase in the propensity toward aggression after a screening of unpunished aggressive behavior models; an interaction effect with the domestic environment also occurred, in that, where domestic circumstances were unfavorable, even the screening of the punishment of aggressive behavior was reflected in an increase in the propensity toward violence, albeit a lesser increase. This finding can again be interpreted on the lines of the "double-dose theory," whereby the effect of violent media consumption is particularly noticeable in children who are confronted with real models of violence (Gerbner et al., 1980; Heath, Kruttschnitt, & Ward, 1986).

An effect study specifically geared to the video medium was published by Brosius (1987). The study was designed to examine the effects of consuming an unrealistic horror film and a realistic violent film. The question asked was whether, after viewing such films, the "legitimization of violence," as a significant precondition for aggressive personal behavior, changed. The result was as follows: in the case of the unrealistic horror film, willingness to accept violence increases after viewing the film. The effect persists over a prolonged period. The portrayal of realistic violence has no effect in the short term, while in the longer term it actually reduces acceptance of violence. This, however, must be seen in the context of the participants' ages: in all cases, in fact, the effect on younger viewers tends to be to increase acceptance of violence. It is only among older viewers that, where violence is realistically depicted, its acceptance is reduced after the screening of the film. The increase in legitimized violence in the case of the unrealistic zombie film can be attributed, among this group, to irritation, while its decrease after the realistic film can be attributed to concern.

A brief reference should also be made to interrelationships between media consumption and delinquency (for a summary, see Lukesch & Scheungrab, 1995). Using important criminological variables, Scheungrab (1990) differentiated the relationship between media consumption and delinquency among male vocational school students. As might be expected, close negative relationships existed between the acceptance of unlawful means and the preference for violence via television or video, or the number of blacklisted videos consumed. Inverse relationships were demonstrated for the acceptance of social stand-ards. In addition, participants with a high preference for video violence estimated the probability of being caught for criminal acts (subjective risk of delinquency) as less than those with a low preference for violence. The negative valence of sanctioning is also seen as less significant by those with a strong preference for violence than those with a weaker one. A causal model, taking into account family climate, structural features of family life, and aspects of communication, used media experience to demonstrate the high signifi-cance of video consumption, especially in its violent variation, for features favoring delin-quency, by comparison with other media (television, comics, books).

Finally, reference should be made to the direct effect of violent, horror, and porno-graphic videos in triggering acts of violence and sexual offences (Klosinski, 1987; Groebel, 1989). In individual cases, it can be assumed that observed acts of delinquency have been directly transposed into personal behavior (Glogauer, 1991). Although such direct transpositions of screened models are very rare and emerge only in a certain group of young people or adults, it is in the nature of a mass medium that such instances are not unique. Possible explanations for this are offered by identification with norm-violat-ing cinematic models, the neutralization techniques offered by these in films (Sykes & Matza, 1974), the reduction in the risks of delinquency suggested by the films, the por-trayal of the low relevance of sanctioning, and the acceptance of unlawful means (Scheungrab, 1990).[16]

(2c)   The studies mentioned are merely illustrative examples. It is clear that, in view of the very large number of studies available, some exist which do not demonstrate any such effect. This results simply from the logic of testing, which assumes a hypothesis to be confirmed provided that the percentage of findings contrary to that hypothesis does not exceed the 5 percent significance level.[17] The relevant reviews and meta-analyses there-fore need to be taken into consideration to supplement these individual studies. Thus, for example, Selg ("Risikothese," 1993, 1990), Roberts and Bachen (1981), Comstock et al. (1978), and Andison (1977) have found that, as far as the medium of television is con-cerned, portrayals of violence have a generally aggression-stimulating effect on children and young people. Huesmann, Moise, and Podolski (1997) also include violent video games and music videos in their analysis, saying that less powerful effects have been verified in

[16] The argument that "I too have seen such films and I haven't turned violent," which seems convincing in terms of everyday psychology, is an oversimplification. The performance of an act of violence obviously requires a number of situational circumstances (a topical conflict, a potential victim, propitious circumstances such as a violent group or loss of inhibitions through alcohol consumption) in addition to the appropriate personality dispositions on which the media are one influence (cf. on this point the results of research into personality structures propitious to delinquency; see above, and Lamnek, 1979; Lösel, 1975).

[17] This simple fact is regularly forgotten by those who would claim that the media have no social responsibility. An illustrative example of this is supplied by Kunczik (1995), where he describes two studies that were unable to demonstrate any aggression-promoting effects as "exceptionally thorough panel studies" (Kunczik, 1995:86) and tries to infer from this the conclusion of a "confused research situation." Also interesting is his argument that certain problems have been the subject of only a single study and no follow-up investigations, replications, or attempts at refutation, while at the same time he complains of the barrenness of research, which he says always examines short-term effects in the laboratory (Kunczik, 1995:106). This argument, again, is simplistic and simply mistaken (Wood et al., 1991), because there are a sufficient number of studies that have demonstrated the aggression-increasing potential of violent films in interaction with friends, adults, etc., in unrestricted social situations. In addition, this article contains an irrational attack on content analyses, which are dismissed, contrary to better judgment, as "body counting." Although the subtitle of this article is "On the current state of the debate," the latest studies, especially the relevant meta-analyses, are not included.

the case of the latter media than in that of violent drama. The mechanisms referred to here relate, according to their analysis, to the learning of (1) behavior through observation (2) thinking patterns, (3) cognitive justification processes, (4) cognitive priming processes (e.g., stimulation of aggressive thoughts), (5) emotional and cognitive desensitization toward violence, and (6) emergence and transfer of arousal.

In addition to these narrative summaries, particular mention must be made of the meta-analysis by Hearold (1986). This confirmed that antisocial media content had a significant effect on the recipients' antisocial behavior, the effects being much stronger in boys from the ages of six to eight than in girls, and effects being ascertained in the sense of a generalization to numerous and not merely specific dependent measurements (further meta-analyses with similar results have been produced by Andison (1977), Paik and Comstock (1994) and Wood, Wong and Chachere (1991).[18]

Summarizing these findings again, a distinction can be made between two aspects of the effects of violent media content: first, an increase in the propensity toward violence, and secondly the triggering of anxieties and their perpetuation in the sense of a threatening perception of the environment. It remains open to debate under which conditions each of these aspects is dominant. The key to answering this question lies partly in individual learning histories: if early and optimally dosed habituation conditions in respect of violent film consumption existed, the threshold above which a pleasantly exciting media event becomes one that creates a traumatizing impression was never crossed,[19] and if no counteracting stimuli, promoting empathy and moral development, came from the recipient's environment, then progressive habituation to violent images may take place. Such a development is also supported by early exposure to more harmless forms of violence, as seen, for example, on television. It is also promoted by a life world that reacts approvingly to audiovisual violence and itself actually contains such forms of conduct as part of its culture (for example, male peer groups). If these conditions—especially the small doses of graded habituation—do not exist, meaning that the media consumer is overexposed, the effect switches over toward the second aspect. It conforms to existing gender stereotypes that this is more often the case with forms of socialization of girls. This will usually result in a shunning effect, meaning that the provocation of anxiety can be eliminated in the short term. By contrast, experiences above a threshold that cannot be precisely determined will require longer-term processes of adaptation because of the traumatization that sets in.

c. EFFECTS OF THE USE OF REAL MEDIA VIOLENCE. *The "Bad News" Orientation of the Media.* As far as the information domain is concerned, it must be emphasized

---

[18] "Our results demonstrate that media violence enhances children's and adolescents' aggression in interactions with strangers, classmates, and friends. Our findings cannot be dismissed as representing artificial experimental constructions because the studies included in our review evaluated media exposure on aggression as it naturally emerged in unconstrained social interaction" (Wood et al., 1991:380).

[19] Reference should also be made here to the anxiety/pleasure thesis that dates back to Balint (1959). As we know, it is particularly exciting for children, and for adults too, to be exposed to a situation of danger but in the knowledge that nothing bad can happen. The visual media are particularly good at bringing about this kind of nervous thrill, because, after all, one is never exposed to any real danger and, indeed, always has the option of shutting one's eyes to the images or leaving the movie theater. It is only when this tightrope walk goes wrong (meaning, in the case of the media, if the images produce an excessive effect) that a psychologically traumatizing fall can result.

that images are in the nature of products. They acquire a high value if they document, or at least illustrate, events transcending daily routine.[20] For journalists (and others responsible for the media) the information value of scenes and reports of real violence (involving demonstrations, sports events, or crime) is particularly high. This also suits the recipients, since in their case attentiveness and subsequent information analysis processes are particularly highly developed in the case of negative news film (Lang, Newhagen, & Reeves, 1996). The media also use a language in which violent expressions are entirely commonplace (in sports reporting, for example, they refer to a "counterattack" or a "football war," etc. (Kerner et al., 1990:546); in the case of asylum seekers, turns of phrase such as "onslaught" or "invasion" are used (Brosius & Esser, 1995:215). The media themselves thus become part of the (non)culture of violence.

In a report on a demonstration, for example, the 99 percent of peaceful demonstrators have much less chance of featuring in the media than the other, violent 1 percent. Lösel et al. (1990:39) consider that, because of this specific peculiarity of the press, it seems almost normal and inevitable for demonstrations to escalate into violence, "and in addition peaceful demonstrators may, because of the stereotype of violent actions promoted by the media, be stigmatized in their social environment and driven out toward militant subcultures."

Particular cause for concern arises when—for example, in connection with the reporting of crime, which is exaggerated in any case—certain minority groups (foreigners, asylum seekers, or Muslims) are portrayed as particularly dangerous and culpable. This kind of demonization is, in turn, a precondition for the use of violence against these minorities (in this connection, consider the neutralization techniques that precede a possible act in the realms of fiction). The subsequent act, then, requires a justification that provides absolution, and this is contributed by media reporting.

This fundamental journalistic attitude, motivated by the desire for profits (advertising revenue, high-selling newspaper headlines) can result in a media-driven escalation of violence (Brosius & Esser, 1995), which neither the ordinary citizen nor the politicians can escape. Even politicians are affected by the interpretation of social realities as portrayed in the media, because they have to rely on the information provided by journalists and may feel driven to act (for example by deploying additional police or advocating draft legislation) by their electorate's anticipated reactions, even if a considered view suggests that there is no reason to do so.

Exploitation of the Media by Violent Factions. The powerful media focus on acts of violence entails the risk that media reporting may be abused as a platform by politically oriented protest groups (organized squatters, protesters against shipments of nuclear waste, right-wing radicals, and skinheads), criminal gangs (Schneider, 1990:305 gives an example from New Zealand), or groups of fans with violent propensities (hooligans; on this point, cf. Weis, Alt, & Gingeleit, 1990). Either such groups may themselves instigate outbreaks of violence or, in the political context, they may stage a strategy of provocation against the police, causing the latter to resort to violence. In the political arena, such meth-

---

[20] Winterhoff-Spurk (1994:58) lists the following "news value factors" based on American TV research: "(1) The story must be personalized or personalizable. (2) The story must be dramatic, conflictual, and ideally violent. (3) The story must contain 'action' elements or at least observable events. (4) The story must be new and/or deviant from the norm. (5) The story must pick up certain almost archetypal long-term themes ... The constraints of the 'news business' involve an obvious temptation to invent or—worse still—stage such events if they seem reluctant to happen of their own accord."

ods are to be found mainly among groups who are assumed to see no way of achieving their aims by the institutional route (Eckert et al., 1990:345).

The staging of violence in the form of pseudo-events, i.e., events that are created primarily or exclusively for reporting purposes, is a highly suitable way of drawing the attention of society as a whole, inexpensively and with a high degree of predictability, to groups who feel that they, or their interests, are excluded from the "normal" process of political mediation (Eckert et al., 1990:377)

Similar considerations apply to groups of fans, who are well aware of their value as a subject of sensationalist reporting and so provide the cameras with the expected material.[21]

Finally, the media enthusiastically exploit lawyers for the accused, not only in cases of politically motivated violence but also in connection with unusual crimes (such as child murder with a sexual angle), because it seems to be particularly attractive to demonize the authorities (Wassermann et al., 1990:775) or demonstrate their ineptitude. The interplay between journalists and lawyers may find expression in premature evaluations of evidence and partial assumptions regarding the outcome of the trial, thus exerting an influence on the course of a trial through a created audience.

"Scary World" Hypothesis.   Among recipients, so it has been assumed, the specific tendency of the press to focus on negative events—"only bad news is good news"—may result in a negative world image. This empirically based dependence between highly intensive television consumption and the development of a degraded view of the world, postulated by Gerbner and Gross (1981) as the "scary world" hypothesis, has repeatedly attracted the attention of researchers. In a relatively recent survey, Cheung and Chan (1996) found that television produced cultivation effects of this kind in terms of materialistic attitudes and a trivialization of moral values.

However, account must be taken of a differentiation pointed out by Winterhoff-Spurk (1989): the recipient seems fundamentally capable of making a distinction between various areas of experience, mental images of which are then filed in one memory for personal reality, one for media reality, and one for media fiction. This memory metaphor would be misleading, however, if one were to assume that the memories are three separate containers with no communication between them; to the contrary, even if, as a rule, a distinction can be made between the threatening content of the immediate environment (= personal reality experience) and threats in the outside world (e.g., jeopardy in a war zone or as a result of crime = transmission of media reality experience), nevertheless, here again, correlations can be confirmed between media consumption (for example, frequency of use of television news broadcasting) and subjectively experienced general anxiety or fear of victimization, the advocacy of security measures, and the demand for greater law and order (Taschler-Pollacek & Lukesch, 1990). Similarly, transfer effects, reality confusions, and interactions between media fiction and personal reality experiences are conceivable.

Different Effects of Media Messages on Different Recipients.   The reporting of violent events does not produce the same effect on every recipient; that much is generally known.

---

[21]These staged events, however, are not confined to the political arena. The entertainment world also provides a sufficiency of events that take place only because the cameras are running, or are motivated by the hope of securing an appearance on television (for example, a mother knocks over the chair containing her spinach-smeared baby while the father stands by with camera at the ready, hoping to find a slot for the film on German TV channels such as *Pleiten, Pech und Pannen* [Flops, Bad Luck and Mishaps]).

Clearly, there are many features that differentiate people (examples being age, sex, socialization history, level of development, intelligence, values, and current well-being), and those features also affect the way in which a media message is received and processed. This point has been made emphatically and repeatedly by Herta Sturm (1989), who bases her *recipient-oriented approach to media research*, to use her own term, primarily on interactive effects with formal structural features of the media. This provides at least an indication of the *possible* effects of media messages on individuals. Which of those possibilities become reality, and in what way, depends on features of the message and the social situation as well as on the activities of the recipient. These relations have been described and tested both in earlier persuasion research and in the more recent social cognitive theory of the mass media (for a summary, cf. Lukesch, 1997).

Kepplinger and Giesselmann (1993) show in an experimental study—and in involuntary agreement with the social cognitive learning theory of the effects of the mass media (Bandura, 1989)—that the recipients' previous attitudes have a marked effect on the evaluation of actions: sympathizers with demonstrators take a particularly negative view of the police when demonstrators are portrayed as victims of police brutality, while believers in the authority of the state take the opposite view. In these cases, documentaries have the effect of consolidating existing images of the enemy and so possibly help to intensify conflicts. Comparable attribution patterns toward violent news content were found in the United States to be dependent on race (black versus white) and sex (Johnson et al., 1997).

This differential potency of effect recurs in other cases, too. For example, violent films also possess an affinity to the models, values, and objectives existing in youth subcultures. Lukesch and Habereder (1989:138; similarly Weiß, 1994:266; 1997) found, among other things, a close correlation between frequency of video consumption, especially that of blacklisted videos, and support for nationalistic orientations. In the same way, there are youth cultures which, because of their values, consume significantly less violence (demonstrated, for example, in the case of adherents of the ecological movement or initiative groups; cf. also Lukesch et al., 1989b:191f.). In view of these results, it can be assumed that the ideas conveyed in violent films reinforce and build upon matching preexisting ideologies. To put it in positive terms, this also means that some value orientations may be incompatible with this use of leisure and may also be capable of providing immunization against the messages of violent films.

A differential relationship can also be substantiated between violent content in television news broadcasting and anxiety reactions (in children) (Cantor & Nathanson, 1996): about one third of all children are confused by such content (especially by violence between foreigners, reports of foreign wars, famine, and natural disasters), and reverse age trends (increase in anxiety reactions to violence between foreigners, decrease in fear reactions to reports on natural disasters) can be demonstrated.

Imitative Acts. We have already referred, in the explanation of the social cognitive theory of the effects of the mass media, to many moderating conditions that intervene between the presentation of an act by a model and a corresponding act by an observer. Nevertheless, reference should be made to a few examples in which a connection exists between the model event and the act; there is no need to establish clearly which intermediary processes played a part in the individual case.

Phillips (1983) was able to confirm a link between the televising of heavyweight boxing and cases of unlawful killing (which peaked on the third day after a title fight). The wider the range of a broadcast, the more significant the increase. The results of social cognitive learning theory are also partially confirmed here: there is a similarity between the loser of the fight and those killed in real life (if the loser was black, the killing of blacks increases, while if he was white, the number of white victims increases). In addition, boxing matches are ideal triggers of violence, because they justify it, indeed reward it, and do not criticize it. In exactly the same way, Phillips and Henshley (1984) were able to show that the punishment of aggression (in the form of real executions and guilty verdicts in murder trials) produces a deterrent effect as far as such acts are concerned (cf. also Stack, 1987). All this evidence does not mean that other influences do not play an important part in an act; as always, the processes involved are driven by multiple causes and cannot be explained solely by the interaction between features of individuals and situations.

Another well researched area is skyjacking. According to Holden (1986), every successful hijack triggers approximately two imitations during the six weeks that follow. The criterion "successful" is important: the hijackers must have succeeded in achieving their financial or political goals through the hijack.

Similarly, valuation methods based on time-series analysis have demonstrated that media reporting of acts of terrorism produces trigger effects (Brosius & Weimann, 1991). Here again, there seems to be extensive empirical support for this relation (Brosius & Weimann, 1991).

The interaction between reporting and acts of xenophobic violence has been analyzed by Brosius and Esser (1995). They found a striking increase in the frequency of xenophobic criminal offences in Germany during the two months following high-profile offences (in the cities of Hoyerswerda, Rostock, Mölln, and Solingen); naturally, reporting (in national newspapers and on television) focuses heavily on these acts. These parallels, however, are not in themselves sufficient to prove that the media, through their reporting, prompted an escalation of the violence. But taking account of general social trends (increasing numbers of immigrants, change in the climate of opinion toward immigrants, increasing proneness to violence among social problem groups), it has been possible to show that persons who were already prone to violence were prompted by such reports to commit xenophobic offences of their own:

> The perpetrators were probably motivated by at least three aspects. First, the high media profile ... provided them with an incentive to commit offences for themselves ... At least within their own reference group, they were guaranteed "honor and glory." Secondly, the nature of the reporting lowered possible inhibition thresholds in line with social learning theory ... Thirdly, the xenophobic actions were successful from the perpetrators' point of view in that they caused the relocation of the asylum seekers (Hoyerswerda, Rostock) (Brosius & Esser, 1995:193).

The authors attribute an escalating effect on violence to the structural properties of the media system (massive and unanimous reporting), to a number of significant circumstances (the fact that the perpetrators are "rewarded" by the fact that viewers are shown to approve, the impotence of the police to punish the crimes committed, and instrumental success in the form of relocation of the asylum seekers), and to the way the primary reporting is processed among groups that are already xenophobic.

The Role of the "Opinion Makers".   In the processing and dissemination of information, journalists, in their efforts to give their product greater news value by increasing the content of violence, are not the only influence to be considered. Associations, political parties, citizens' movements, "pressure groups," and so forth, also try to influence public opinion. But larger organizations too, even governments, try to use the media to gain publicity for their important messages. It is especially those who wield power who regard the mass communication system as having "outstanding potential for exploitation" (Langenbucher, 1979:9). Those who know how to play the instrument of the press—in other words, to provide attractive content—hold much stronger cards in a media democracy than other groups.[22]

In Germany, the federal government has set up its own machinery for analyzing published opinion and polishing its own image, in the form of the *Bundespresseamt* (Federal Press Office or BPA), which is under the direct control of the German Chancellery (Böckelmann & Nahr, 1979). It is in the nature of things that this may involve the blurring of boundaries between information and tendentious whitewashing. Such attempts to exert influence through state-sponsored public relations exercises (Koschwik, 1988; Kunczik, 1990) or "psychological warfare" can become massively manipulative.

One notable example of this was reporting during the Gulf War. In this case, no picture was left to chance by the American military ("surgical strikes" by accurately targeted cruise missiles). It was of course possible to predict the countermeasures taken by Saddam Hussein in publishing images of the population's sufferings as a result of the hostilities—as always, children, weeping women, and the despairing elderly (Buhl, 1991). In the Western media, invented footage showing the alleged slaughter of new-born babies by the Iraqi soldiery in hospital incubators was also used as a *measure of psychological warfare*; as subsequently transpired, the reporter was anything but a hospital nurse, being a member of the Kuwaiti royal house.

An extreme form of such attempts to influence public opinion is practiced by secret services. The routine *disinformation measures* and the associated attempt to "demonize the enemy" are difficult to penetrate, and it often takes years before this kind of abuse of information is uncovered.

An illustrative example of this was the rumor that the AIDS virus had been developed and released by an American research laboratory. This allegation was made in 1983 in an anonymous reader's letter to a pro-Moscow Indian newspaper, and triggered a chain reaction of reciprocally escalating reports in the Soviet Union. Details varied in accordance with the powers of the editors' imaginations. These reports were also taken up by the press in other countries (particularly frequently in Africa). Scientists, however, even in the Soviet Union, clearly recognized the impossibility of producing the AIDS virus synthetically (*NZZ*, November 6, 1987).[23]

There are many other examples of the exploitation of the media, especially in the political arena, which cannot be discussed at length (in American elections, for example, it is customary to publicize titillating details of the private lives of prominent politicians shortly before the candidates are due to make important appearances, or merely to claim that such details exist, on the principle of *aliquid semper haeret*, mud sticks). Opinion makers of this kind are very well aware of the entertainment value of a news item and, because news is a commodity, they can be sure that the media will pass the stories on to the public.

---

[22] Dagobert Lindlau, a long-serving editor in chief of Germany's Bayerischer Rundfunk, once wrote that television had become "the henchman of unrealistic, delusion systems;" "public life has been degraded into a marathon public relations exercise. Advertising has become socially acceptable everywhere, and with it the venial Big Lie" (quoted in Langenbucher, 1979:16).

[23] *NZZ: Neue Zürcher Zeitung* (Switzerland).

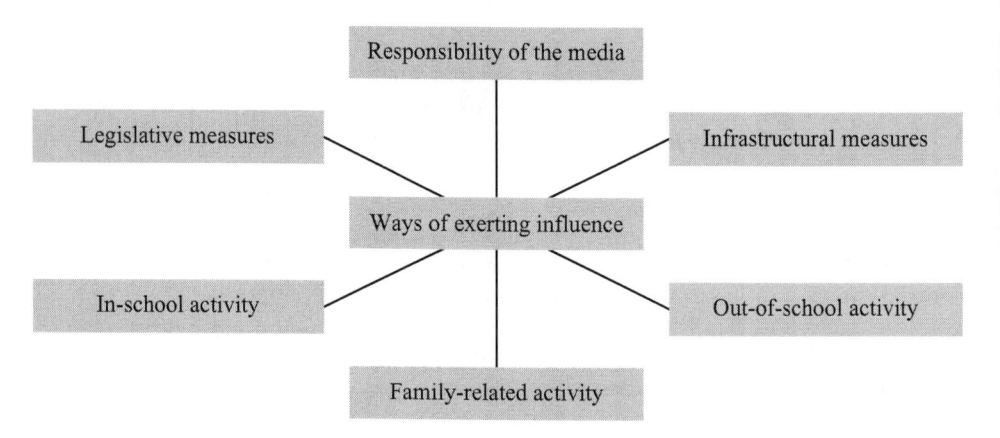

Figure II-3-1-4.3. **Ways of exerting influence on media consumption (especially consumption by children and young people).**

III.   WAYS OF CHANGING AND INFLUENCING BEHAVIOR

The media enjoy a high level of constitutional protection (cf. GG, Section 5(1)). Behind this protective screen, the media have evolved a life of their own, governed not so much by the criteria of responsible journalism or artistic standards as by the principles of profit making and profit maximization. As many examples have demonstrated, a focus on violence increases the publicity value of a news item or, in the fictional sphere, offers a simple way of making a course of action more exciting. As a basic matter of survival, the media will be unwilling to renounce the use of these tools. As a consequence, they have become part of the social "culture" of violence, even if those responsible are reluctant to see it in those terms, rationalizing their output in many different ways.

On the other hand, it would be conceivable, at least in principle, to expect the various social institutions to look for ways of intervening to remedy the problem. In principle, too, there are many conceivable forms of action that could be taken to influence the provision and consumption of violence in the media (especially fictional violence) (cf. Fig. II-3-1-4.3). A fundamental consideration here is that all the conditions that have an effect should be considered and that none of the institutions addressed should be exempted from responsibility; it should also be realized that mutual recriminations are an obstacle to possible solutions. They are, of course, a great relief: whoever one is talking to, one can lay the problem on the shoulders of "the others."

1. *Responsibility of the legislator:* Many of the trends reflecting the effects of the consumption of fictional violence could, and still can, prompt preventive action by the legislator. It could even be said that research into the effects of portrayals of violence in the media is better undertaken here than in the context of educational activities, since knowing how something came about does not necessarily lead to knowing how to change it. It can also be assumed that any new technological development will also be "abused" (cf. the Internet). It seems to be a regular temptation for producers and service providers to test—or push back—the boundaries of what a society will still accept. Remschmidt et al. (1990:266)

call for a dramatic reduction in portrayals of violence in the media as long as violence is still being used, almost as a matter of course, to increase the attractiveness of the program. This problem also has a European or international dimension (for example, satellite channels can be received irrespective of national frontiers), which means that international cooperation is needed.

2. *Responsibility of the media:* The principle guiding the activities of those responsible for the media should not be simply the avoidance of obvious violations of the law. Although there is, as yet, no product liability in the media sector, standards of voluntary restraint can be developed whereby not everything that can possibly be produced is actually produced and placed on the market. The customary press standards are in constant danger of being ignored in the interests of improved sales. Since the mass media can also encourage what can be regarded as positive social conduct (Hearold, 1986), this opportunity too should be utilized. It is worth pointing out here the interactive effect between film promotion policy and media production. One consequence of this would be to make it impossible simply to take over cut-price offers from the United States. In addition, systematic monitoring of programs should be introduced, allowing an independent disclosure, based on social sciences criteria, of a content analysis of important aspects portrayed in the programs (this is not a reference to *Freiwillige Selbstkontrolle Fernsehen* (Voluntary Self-Regulation of Television—FSF).

3. *Infrastructural measures:* One of the reasons for indiscriminate media consumption is the unavailability of alternative leisure-time pursuits (consider, for example, the living and traffic conditions in major conurbations). We know that the many stimuli provided by the ecological environment tends to reduce excessive television viewing (Schneewind, Beckmann, & Engfer, 1983). From this angle, town planning and development also have an influence on use of the media. This even extends to the planning of accommodation (for example, open-plan living and eating areas have made it possible to eat while watching television; Lukesch et al., 1989b).

4. *In-school measures:* As far as schools are concerned, attention has often been drawn to the many disciplines of media education. Hell (1988:8, 117f.) distinguishes four lines of action in media education: (a) media analysis (the planning, effect, and predictive criteria of media), (b) media production, (c) media reflection (reflection of media reception and media consumption taking due account of alternative leisure-time activities), and (d) working with parents. The possibilities are limited, however, when we still have no independent school subjects for this, no coordinated interaction between existing school subjects, and no specialist training for teachers. In addition, teachers are increasingly refusing to take responsibility for improving circumstances for which others are responsible.

5. *Out-of-school activities:* In youth groups, etc., (a) receptive media work can also be done; (b) projects can be undertaken as individual activities (for example, setting up a children's cinema with an appropriate range of films and activities, children's film weeks, etc.), and (c) active media work can be made available (for example, offering opportunities to record videos, radio features, etc. at youth meetings, etc.). An essential condition here is for staff to be competent and have the corresponding interests.

6. *Working with parents:* Media use takes place primarily within the family group. Some parents provide media education intuitively, and others deliberately, but

many can be assumed to apply a "laissez faire" policy. In this case, measures for working with parents could be initiated by institutions (for example, schools, kindergartens, and even the media themselves, including the mass-circulation program magazines).

As long as the media retain only a half-hearted commitment to acknowledging their responsibility (compare the laborious process of recognition and application of ecological standards), the propagation of such activities will, however, be no more than a token gesture.

Translated by Richard Sharp

REFERENCES

Andison, F. Scott. (1977). TV Violence and Viewer Aggression: A Cumulation of Study Results 1956–1976. *Public Opinion Quarterly, 41*, 314–331.

Balint, Michael. (1959). *Angstlust und Regression. Beitrag zur psychologischen Typenlehre.* Stuttgart: Klett.

Bandura, Albert. (1989). Die sozial-kognitive Theorie der Massenkommunikation. In Jo Groebel & Peter Winterhoff-Spurk (Eds.), *Empirische Medienpsychologie* (pp. 7–32). München: Psychologie Verlags Union.

Bandura, Albert, & Aletha C. Houston. (1961). Identification as a Process of Incidental Learning. *Journal of Abnormal and Social Psychology, 63*, 311–338.

Bandura, Albert, Dorothea Ross, & Sheila A. Ross. (1961). Imitation of Film-Mediated Aggressive Models. *Journal of Abnormal and Social Psychology, 63*, 575–582.

Belson, William A. (1978). *Television and the Adolescent Boy.* Westmead, England: Saxon House.

Berkowitz, Leonard, & Russel G. Geen. (1966). Film Violence and Cue Properties of Available Targets. *Journal of Personality and Social Psychology, 3*, 525–530.

Berkowitz, Leonard, & Edna Rawlings. (1963). Effects of Film Violence on Inhibition against Subsequent Aggression. *Journal of Abnormal and Social Psychology, 66*, 405–412.

Berkowitz, Leonard, Ronald Corwin, & Mark Heironimus. (1963). Film Violence and Aggressive Tendencies. *Public Opinion Quarterly, 27*, 217–229.

Böckelmann, Frank, & Günther Nahr. (1979). *Staatliche Öffentlichkeitsarbeit im Wandel der politischen Kommunikation.* Berlin: Spiess.

Brockhaus (Ed.) (1969/1970). *Brockhaus Enzyklopädie. Vols. 7, 11.* Wiesbaden: Brockhaus-Verlag.

Brosius, Hans-Bernd. (1987). Auswirkungen der Rezeption von Horror-Videos auf die Legitimation von aggressiven Handlungen. *Rundfunk und Fernsehen, 35*, 71–91.

Brosius, Hans-Bernd, & Thomas Hartmann. (1988). Erfahrungen mit Horror-Videos bei Schülern unterschiedlicher Schultypen. Eine Umfrage unter 12–15-jährigen Schülern. *Communications, 14*, 91–112.

Brosius, Hans-Bernd, & Gabriel Weimann. (1991). The Contagiousness of Mass Mediated Terrorism. *European Journal of Communication, 6*, 63–75.

Brosius, Hans-Bernd, & Iris Schmitt. (1994). Nervenkitzel oder Gruppendruck? Determinanten für die Beliebtheit von Horrorvideos bei Jugendlichen. In Helmut Lukesch (Ed.), *'Wenn Gewalt zur Unterhaltung wird ...' Beiträge zur Nutzung und Wirkung von Gewaltdarstellungen in audiovisuellen Medien (Reihe Medienforschung, Band 3)* (pp. 11–52). Regensburg: Roderer.

Brosius, Hans-Bernd, & Frank Esser. (1995). *Eskalation durch Berichterstattung? Massenmedien und fremdenfeindliche Gewalt.* Opladen: Westdeutscher Verlag.

Buhl, Dieter. (1991). Die Macht der Zensur. Medien und der Krieg. *Die Zeit*, January 25, 1991.

Cantor, Joanne. (1991). Fright Responses to Mass Media Productions. In Jenings Bryant & Dolf Zillmann (Eds.), *Responding to the Screen: Reception and Reaction Processes* (pp. 169–197). Hillsdale, NJ.: Erlbaum.

Cantor, Joanne. (1996). Television and Children's Fear. In Tannis MacBeth Williams (Ed.), *Tuning in to Young Viewers. Social Science Perspectives on Television* (pp. 87–116). Thousand Oaks: Sage.

Cantor, Joanne, & Amy I. Nathanson. (1996). Children's Fright Reactions to Television News. *Journal of Communication, 46*, 139–152.

Charlton, Michael. (1972). *Untersuchung zur Auswirkung aggressiver Filmmodelle auf Einstellungen und Verhaltensweisen von Schülern.* Unpublished Dissertation, Universität Hamburg.

Charlton, Michael, Elsa Liebelt, Jutta Sültz, & Anne-Marie Tausch. (1974). Auswirkungen von Verhaltensmodellen aus einem Fernsehwestern auf Gruppenarbeitsverhalten und Aggressionsbereitschaft von Grundschülern. *Psychologie in Erziehung und Unterricht, 21,* 164–175.

Cheung, Chan-Kin, & Chi-Fai Chan. (1996). Television Viewing and Mean World Value in Hong Kong's Adolescents. *Social Behavior and Personality, 24,* 351–364.

Comstock, George A., Steven Chaffee, Natan Katzmann, Maxwell McCombs, & Donald Roberts. (1978). *Television and Human Behavior.* New York: Columbia University.

Dorfman, Lori, Katie Woodruff, Vivian Chavez, & Lawrence Wallack. (1997). Youth and Violence on Local Television News in California. *American Journal of Public Health, 87,* 1311–1316.

Drabman, Ronald S., & Margaret H. Thomas. (1974). Does Media Violence Increase Children's Tolerance of Real-Life Violence? *Developmental Psychology, 10,* 418–421.

Eckert, Roland, Max Kaase, Friedhelm Neidhardt, & Helmut Willems. (1990). Ursachen, Prävention und Kontrolle von Gewalt aus soziologischer Sicht. In Hans-Dieter Schwind & Jürgen Baumann (Eds.), *Ursachen, Prävention und Kontrolle von Gewalt. Vol. 2* (pp. 293–414). Berlin: Duncker & Humblot.

Eibl-Eibesfeld, Irenäus. (1990). Gewaltbereitschaft aus ethologischer Sicht. In Klaus Rolinski & Irenäus Eibl-Eibesfeld (Eds.), *Gewalt in unserer Gesellschaft. Gutachten für das Bayerische Staatsministerium des Inneren* (pp. 59–86). Berlin: Duncker & Humblot.

Eron, Leonhard D., L. Rowell Huesmann, Monroe M. Lefkowitz, & Leopold O. Walder. (1972). Does Television Violence Cause Aggression? *American Psychologist, 27,* 253–263.

Feshbach, Seymor. (1961). The Stimulating versus Cathartic Effect of a Vicarious Aggressive Activity. *Journal of Abnormal and Social Psychology, 63,* 381–385.

Froschhammer, Hubert. (1992). *Die Untersuchung von Beziehungen zwischen audiovisuellen Medien und Delinquenz unter besonderer Berücksichtigung ausgewählter kriminologischer Variablen bei jugendlichen Heiminsassen. Unveröff.* Diplomarbeit, Universität Regensburg.

Früh, Werner. (1995). Die Rezeption von Fernsehgewalt. *Media Perspektiven, 45,* 172–185.

Furu, Takeo. (1971). *The Function of Television for Children and Adolescents.* Tokyo: Sophia University (Monumenta Nipponica).

Gerbner, George, & Larry Gross. (1973). *Violence Profile No. 5. Trends in Network Television Drama and Viewer Conceptions of Social Reality.* Philadelphia: University of Pennsylvania.

Gerbner, George, & Larry Gross. (1981). Die 'angsterregende Welt' des Vielsehers. *Fernsehen und Bildung, 15,* 16–42.

Gerbner, George, Larry Gross, Michael Morgan, & Nancy Signorelli. (1980). The 'Mainstreaming' of America: Violence Profile No. 11. *Journal of Communication, 30,* 10–29.

Glogauer, Walter. (1991). *Kriminalisierung von Kindern und Jugendlichen durch Medien. Wirkungen gewalttätiger, sexueller, pornographischer und satanischer Darstellungen.* Baden-Baden: Nomos.

Groebel, Jo. (1989). Fernsehen, Video und Schülerkriminalität. In Siegfried Bäuerle (Ed.), *Kriminalität bei Schülern* (pp. 154–159). Stuttgart: Verlag für Angewandte Psychologie.

Groebel, Jo. (1998). Media Violence and Children. *Educational Media International (EMI), 35,* 216–227.

Groebel, Jo, & Uli Gleich. (1993). *Gewaltprofil des deutschen Fernsehprogramms. Eine Analyse des Angebots privater und öffentlich-rechtlicher Sender.* Opladen: Leske & Budrich.

Gruber, Irene. (1993). *Die Abbildung emotionalisierender Effekte eines Gewaltfilmes mit der Methode des Katathymen Bilderlebens.* Unveröff. Diplomarbeit, Universität Regensburg.

Hassanein, Hanaa. (1995). *A Study of Television Viewing Motivation and Academic Achievement among Secondary School Students in Assiut—Egypt.* Regensburg: Roderer.

Hearold, Susan. (1986). A Synthesis of 1043 Effects of Television on Social Behavior. *Public Communication and Behavior, 1,* 65–133.

Heath, Linda, Candace Kruttschnitt, & David Ward. (1986). Television and Violent Criminal Behavior: Beyond the Bobo Doll. *Victims and Violence, 1,* 177–190.

Hell, Peter W. (Ed.) (1988). *Gefährdung durch Video. Pädagogische Handlungsmöglichkeiten. Modellversuch der Akademie für Lehrerfortbildung Dillingen.* München: Manz.

Hicks, David. (1968). Short- and Long-Term Retention of Affectively Varied Modeled Behavior. *Psychonomic Science, 11,* 369–370.

Himmelweit, Hilde, Abraham N. Oppenheim, & Pamela Vince. (1958). *Television and the Child.* London: Oxford University Press.

Holden, Robert T. (1986). The Contagiousness of Aircraft Hijackings. *American Journal of Sociology, 91,* 874–904.

Hopf, Werner, & Rudolf H. Weiß. (1996). Horror- und Gewaltkonsum bei Jugendlichen. Eine Untersuchung von Sprachproben von Videokonsumenten mit der Gottschalk-Gleser-Sprachinhaltsanalyse. *Praxis der Kinderpsychologie und Kinderpsychiatrie, 45*, 179–185.

Huesmann, L. Rowell, & Leonard D. Eron (Eds.) (1986). *Television and the Aggressive Child: A Cross-National Comparison.* Hillsdale: Erlbaum.

Huesmann, L. Rowell, Jessica F. Moise, & Cheryl-Lynn Podolski. (1997). The Effects of Media Violence on the Development of Antisocial Behavior. In David Stoff & James Breiling (Eds.), *Handbook of Antisocial Behavior* (pp. 181–193). New York: Wiley.

Iwao, Sumiko, Ithiel de Sola Pool, & Shigeru Hagiwara. (1981). Japanese and U.S. Media: Some Cross-Cultural Insights into TV Violence. *Journal of Communication, 31*, 28–36.

Johnson, James D., Mike S. Adams, William Hall, & Leslie Ashburn. (1997). Race, Media, and Violence: Differential Racial Effects of Exposure to Violent News Stories. Basic and Applied *Social Psychology, 19*, 81–90.

Jonas, Markus, & Christoph Neuberger. (1996). Unterhaltung durch Realitätsdarstellungen: 'Reality TV' als neue Programmform. *Publizistik, 41*, 187–203.

Joy, Lesley A., Meredith M. Kimball, & Merle L. Zabrack. (1986). Television and Children's Aggressive Behavior. In Tanis MacBeth Williams (Ed.), *The Impact of Television. A Natural Experiment in Three Communities* (pp. 303–360). Orlando: Academic Press.

Kepplinger, Hans Mathias. (1987). *Darstellungseffekte. Experimentelle Untersuchungen zur Wirkung von Pressefotos und Fernsehfilmen.* Freiburg: Alber.

Kepplinger, Hans Mathias, & Stefan Dahlem. (1990). Medieninhalte und Gewaltanwendung. In Hans-Dieter Schwind, Jürgen Baumann, Friedrich Lösel, et al. (Eds.), *Ursachen, Prävention und Kontrolle von Gewalt. Vol. III. Sondergutachten* (pp. 382–396). Berlin: Duncker und Humblot.

Kepplinger, Hans Mathias, & Thea Giesselmann. (1993). Die Wirkung von Gewaltdarstellungen in der aktuellen Fernsehberichterstattung. Eine konflikttheoretische Analyse. *Medienpsychologie, 5*, 160–189.

Kerner, Hans-Jürgen, Günther Kaiser, Arthur Kreuzer, & Christian Pfeiffer. (1990). Ursachen, Prävention und Kontrolle von Gewalt aus kriminologischer Sicht. In Hans-Dieter Schwind & Jürgen Baumann (Eds.), *Ursachen, Prävention und Kontrolle von Gewalt. Vol. II* (pp. 415–606). Berlin: Duncker und Humblot.

Kleiter, Ekkehard F. (1994). Aggression und Gewalt in Filmen und aggressiv-gewalttätiges Verhalten von Schülern. Darstellung einer empirischen Pilotstudie. *Empirische Pädagogik, 8*, 3–57.

Kleiter, Ekkehard F. (1997). *Film und Aggression–Aggressionspsychologie. Theorie und empirische Ergebnisse mit einem Beitrag zur Allgemeinen Aggressionspsychologie.* Weinheim: Deutscher Studien Verlag.

Klosinski, Günther. (1987). Beitrag zur Beziehung von Video-Filmkonsum und Kriminalität in der Adoleszenz. *Praxis der Kinderpsychologie und Kinderpsychiatrie, 36*, 66–71.

Koschwik, Hansjürgen. (1988). Der verdeckte Kampf. *Publizistik, 33*, 71–88.

Krey, Volker (in Cooperation with Norbert Arenz und Klaus Freudenberg). (1986). Zum Gewaltbegriff im Strafrecht. 1. Teil. Probleme der Nötigung mit Gewalt. In: Bundeskriminalamt Wiesbaden (Ed.), *Was ist Gewalt? Band 1. Strafrechtliche und sozialwissenschaftliche Darlegungen* (pp. 111–106). Wiesbaden.

Krüger, Udo Michael. (1994). Gewalt in Informationssendungen und Reality TV. *Media Perspektiven, 2*, 72–85.

Krüger, Udo Michael. (1996). Gewalt in von Kindern genutzten Fernsehsendungen. *Media Perspektiven, 3*, 114–133.

Kunczik, Michael. (1990). *Die manipulierte Meinung.* Köln: Böhlau.

Kunczik, Michael. (1995). Wirkungen von Gewaltdarstellungen. Zum aktuellen Stand der Diskussion. In Ekkehard Mochmann & Uta Gerhardt (Eds.), *Gewalt in Deutschland* (pp. 79–106). München: Oldenbourg.

Lamnek, Siegfried. (1979). *Theorien abweichenden Verhaltens.* München: Fink.

Lamnek, Siegfried. (1995). Gewalt in Massenmedien und Gewalt von Schülern. In Siegfried Lamnek (Ed.), *Jugend und Gewalt. Devianz und Kriminalität in Ost und West* (pp. 225–256). Opladen: Leske und Budrich.

Lang, Annie, John Newhagen, & Byron Reeves. (1996). Negative Video as Structure: Emotion, Attention, Capacity, and Memory. *Journal of Broadcasting and Electronic Media, 40*, 460–477.

Langenbucher, Wolfgang R. (1979). Einleitung. In Wolfgang R. Langenbucher (Ed.), *Politik und öffentliche Kommunikation. Über öffentliche Meinungsbildung* (pp. 7–26). München: Piper.

Lösel, Friedrich. (1975). *Handlungskontrolle und Jugenddelinquenz. Persönlichkeitspsychologische Erklärungsansätze delinquenten Verhaltens.* Stuttgart: Enke.

Lösel, Friedrich, Herbert Selg, Ursula Scheider, & Elisabeth Müller-Luckmann. (1990). Ursachen, Prävention und Kontrolle von Gewalt aus psychologischer Sicht. In Hans-Dieter Schwind & Jürgen Baumann (Eds.), *Ursachen, Prävention und Kontrolle von Gewalt. Vol. II* (pp. 1–156). Berlin: Duncker und Humblot.

Luca-Krüger, Renate. (1988). 'Das Gute soll gewinnen'. Gewaltvideos im Erleben weiblicher und männlicher Jugendlicher. *Publizistik, 33*, 481–492.

Lukesch, Helmut. (1988). Mass Media Use, Deviant Behavior and Delinquency. *Communications, 14*, 53–64.

Lukesch, Helmut. (1990). Video Violence and Aggression. *German Journal of Psychology, 13*, 293–300.

Lukesch, Helmut. (1992). Aktuelle Videokonsumgewohnheiten bei Kindern und Jugendlichen in den fünf neuen Bundesländern. *BPS-Info der Bundesprüfstelle für jugendgefährdende Schriften, 1*, 3–5.

Lukesch, Helmut. (1997). Medien und ihre Wirkungen. Eine Einführung. Sammelwerk Medienzeit (Eds.). *Bayerisches Staatsministerium für Unterricht Kultus, Wissenschaft und Kunst.* Donauwörth: Auer.

Lukesch, Helmut, & Sabine Habereder. (1989). Die Nutzung indizierter und konfiszierter Videofilme durch Jugendliche nach Änderung der Jugendschutzbestimmungen. *Psychologie in Erziehung und Unterricht, 36*, 134–139.

Lukesch, Helmut, Karl Heinz Kischkel, Anne Amann, Sieglinde Birner, Mechthild Hirte, Rainer Kern, Renate Mossburger, Luise Müller, Bärbel Schubert, & Hans Schuller. (1989a). *Jugendmedienstudie.* Regensburg: Roderer.

Lukesch, Helmut, Hans Kägi, Gerlinde Karger, & Heidrun Taschler-Pollacek. (1989b). *Video im Alltag der Jugend. Quantitative und qualitative Aspekte des Videokonsums, des Videospielens und der Nutzung anderer Medien bei Kindern, Jugendlichen und jungen Erwachsenen.* Regensburg: Roderer.

Lukesch, Helmut, & Marianne Schauf. (1990). Können Filme stellvertretende Aggressionskatharsis bewirken? *Psychologie in Erziehung und Unterricht, 37*, 38–46.

Lukesch, Helmut, & Michael Scheungrab. (1995). Beiträge der Massenmedien zur Delinquenzgenese Jugendlicher. *Gruppendynamik, 26*, 63–87.

Melchers, Christoph B., & Werner Seifert. (1984). '... das Bild ist jetzt noch nicht weg'. Psychologische Untersuchungen und Überlegungen zum Video-Horror. *Medium, 14*, 6, 21–31.

Mezger-Brewka, Jutta. (1993). *Die Abbildung emotionalisierender Effekte eines Horrorfilms mit der Methode des Katathymen Bilderlebens.* Unveröff. Diplomarbeit, Universität Regensburg.

Moore, Simon R., & Tracey Cockerton. (1996). Viewers' Ratings of Violence Presented in Justified and Unjustified Contexts. *Psychological Reports, 79*, 931–935.

Mussen, Paul, & Eldred Rutherford. (1961). Effects of Aggressive Cartoons on Children's Aggressive Play. *Journal of Abnormal and Social Psychology, 62*, 461–464.

Mustonen, Ann. (1997). Nature of Screen Violence and its Relation to Program Popularity. *Aggressive Behavior, 23*, 281–292.

Paik, Haejung, & George Comstock. (1994). The Effects of Television Violence on Anti-Social Behavior: A Meta-Analysis. *Communication Research, 21*, 516–546.

Pass, Helmut. (1983). Nachahmung von verbal übermittelten Modellen aggressiver und prosozialer Interaktionen. Eine experimentelle Analyse. *Psychologie in Erziehung und Unterricht, 30*, 40–45.

Patry, Jean-Luc, & Meinrad Perrez. (1982). Entstehungs-, Erklärungs- und Anwendungszusammenhang technologischer Regeln. In Jean-Luc Patry (Ed.), *Feldforschung* (pp. 389–412). Bern: Huber.

Phillips, David P. (1983). The Impact of Mass Media Violence on U.S. Homicides. *American Sociological Review, 48*, 560–568.

Phillips, David P., & John E. Henshley. (1984). When Violence is Rewarded or Punished: The Impact of Mass Media Stories on Homicide. *Journal of Communication, 34*, 101–116.

Remschmidt, Helmut, Friedrich Hacker, Elisabeth Müller-Luckmann, Martin H. Schmidt, & Peter Strunk. (1990). Ursachen, Prävention und Kontrolle von Gewalt aus psychiatrischer Sicht. In Hans-Dieter Schwind & Jürgen Baumann (Eds.), *Ursachen, Prävention und Kontrolle von Gewalt Vol. II* (pp. 157–292). Berlin: Duncker und Humblot.

Rieseberg, Angela, & Ursula Martin-Newe. (1988). *Macho-, Monster-, Medienfreizeit.* Pfaffenweiler: Centaurus.

Roberts, Donald F., & Christine M. Bachen. (1981). Mass Communication Effects. *Annual Review of Psychology, 32*, 307–356.

Rödding, Gerhard. (1994). Menschenwürde und Gewaltdarstellung im Fernsehen. *Medienpsychologie, 6*, 323–341.

Scheungrab, Michael. (1989). Videokonsum von Jugendlichen und jungen Erwachsenen—Neuere empirische Befunde zur Verbreitung und Nutzung des Mediums Video. *Empirische Pädagogik, 3*, 257–269.

Scheungrab, Michael. (1990). Die Abbildung von Beziehungen zwischen Medienkonsum und Delinquenz im Rahmen kausalanalytischer Modelle. In Helmut Lukesch (Ed.), *'Wenn Gewalt zur Unterhaltung wird ...'* (pp. 119–148). Regensburg: Roderer.

Scheungrab, Michael. (1993). *Filmkonsum und Delinquenz. Ergebnisse einer Interviewstudie mit straffälligen und nicht-straffälligen Jugendlichen und jungen Erwachsenen.* Regensburg: Roderer.

Schneider, Hans Joachim. (1990). Zusammenfassung des Berichts des 'Ministerial Committee of Inquiry into Violence' (Neuseeland). In Hans-Dieter Schwind & Jürgen Baumann (Eds.), *Ursachen, Prävention und Kontrolle von Gewalt. Vol. III. Sondergutachten* (pp. 293–313). Berlin: Duncker und Humblot.

Schneewind, Klaus A., Michael Beckmann, & Anette Engfer (Eds.) (1983). *Eltern und Kinder.* Stuttgart. Kohlhammer.

Schramm, Wilbur, Jack Lyle, & Edwin B. Parker. (1961). *Television in the Lives of Our Children.* Stanford, Calif.: Stanford University Press.

Selg, Herbert. (1987). Zur Verharmlosung der Wirkung brutaler Medieninhalte auf Kinder und Jugendliche. *Sozialpädiatrie in Praxis und Klinik, 9,* 442–444.

Selg, Herbert. (1990). Gewaltdarstellungen in Medien und ihre Auswirkungen auf Kinder und Jugendliche. *Zeitschrift für Kinder- und Jugendpsychiatrie, 18,* 152–156.

Selg, Herbert. (1993). Fördern Medien die Gewaltbereitschaft? In Hans-Georg Wehling (Ed.), *Aggression und Gewalt* (pp. 74–84). Stuttgart: Kohlhammer.

Selg, Herbert, Ulrich Mees, & Detlev Berg. (1988). *Psychologie der menschlichen Aggressivität.* Göttingen: Hogrefe.

Stack, Steven. (1987). Publicized Executions and Homicide, 1950–1980. *American Sociological Review, 52,* 532–540.

Stegmüller, Wolfgang. (1969). *Wissenschaftliche Erklärung und Begründung.* Berlin: Springer.

Sturm, Herta. (1989). Medienwirkungen—Ein Produkt der Beziehungen zwischen Rezipient und Medium. In Jo Groebel & Peter Winterhoff-Spurk (Eds.), *Empirische Medienpsychologie* (pp. 33–44). München: Psychologie Verlags Union.

Sykes, E. Gresham, & David Matza. (1974). Techniken der Neutralisierung: Eine Theorie der Delinquenz. In Fritz Sack & René König (Eds.), *Kriminalsoziologie* (pp. 360–371). Frankfurt: Akademische Verlagsgesellschaft.

Taschler-Pollacek, Heidrun, & Helmut Lukesch. (1990). Viktimisierungsangst als Folge des Fernsehkonsums? Eine Studie an älteren Frauen. *Publizistik, 35,* 443–453.

van der Voort, Tom H. A., & Johannes J. W. Beentjes. (1997). Effects of Extremely Violent Audiovisual Products on Young People's Aggressive Behavior and Emotional Reactions. In Peter Winterhoff-Spurk & Tom H. A. van der Voort (Eds.), *New Horizons in Media* (pp. 87–104). Opladen: Westdeutscher Verlag.

Viemerö, Vappu. (1996). Factors in Childhood that Predict Later Criminal Behavior. *Aggressive Behavior, 22,* 87–97.

Walters, Richard H., & Edward Llewellyn Thomas. (1962). Enhancement of Punitive Behavior by Audio-Visual Displays. *Science, 136,* 872–873.

Walters, Richard H., & Edward Llewellyn Thomas. (1963). Enhancement of Punitiveness by Visual and Audio-Visual Displays. *Canadian Journal of Psychology, 17,* 244–255.

Wartella, Ellen, Dominic Lasorsa, Wayne Danielson, Adriana Olivarez, Rafael Lopez, & Marlies Klijn. (1997). *National Television Violence Study, Part II: Television Violence in 'Reality' Programming: University of Texas at Austin Study.* Thousand Oaks: Sage.

Wassermann, Richard, Reinhard Böttcher, Gernot Steinhilper, & Gerhard Völz. (1990). Verhinderung und Bekämpfung von Gewalt aus der Sicht der Strafrechtspraxis. In Hans-Dieter Schwind & Jürgen Baumann (Eds.), *Ursachen, Prävention und Kontrolle von Gewalt. Vol. II* (pp. 762–856). Berlin: Duncker und Humblot.

Weis, Kurt, Christian Alt, & Frank Gingeleit. (1990). Probleme der Fanausschreitungen und ihrer Eindämmung. In Hans-Dieter Schwind & Jürgen Baumann (Eds.), *Ursachen, Prävention und Kontrolle von Gewalt. Vol. III. Sondergutachten* (pp. 575–670). Berlin: Duncker und Humblot.

Weiß, Rudolf H. (1990). Horror-Gewalt-Video-Konsum bei Jugendlichen. Gefühlsreaktionen—Persönlichkeit—Identifikation Täter/Opfer. In Helmut Lukesch (Ed.), *'Wenn Gewalt zur Unterhaltung wird ...'. Beiträge zur Nutzung und Wirkung von Gewaltdarstellungen in audiovisuellen Medien* (pp. 47–91). Regensburg: Roderer.

Weiß, Rudolf H. (1993). *Gewaltmedienkonsum—Video-Gewalt 1992. Eine Feldstudie April bis Juli 1992. Befragung von 12–16 jährigen Schülern aus 6.–9. Klassen im Bezirk des Oberschulamtes Stuttgart.* Stuttgart: Oberschulamt.

Weiß, Rudolf H. (1994). Von der Gewalt fasziniert—Gewaltmedienkonsum und seine Auswirkungen auf die jugendliche Psyche (insbesondere Aggressivität und Sozialverhalten). In Christoph Hanckel, Helmut Heipe & Udo Kalweit (Eds.), *Psychologie macht Schule. Kongressbericht der 10. Bundeskonferenz für Schulpsychologie1992 in Heidelberg* (pp. 256–272). Bonn: Deutscher Psychologen Verlag.

Weiß, Rudolf H. (1997). Gewaltmedienkonsum und Rechtsradikalismus bei Jugendlichen in Baden-Württemberg und Sachsen. Faktoren- und kausalanalytische Überprüfung eines vermuteten Zusammenhangs oder 'Wie kommt das nur in diese Köpfe rein?'. In Frank Baumgärtel, Friedrich W. Willer & Ulrich Winterfeld (Eds.), *Innovation und Erfahrung* (pp. 95–115). Bonn: Deutscher Psychologen Verlag.

Williams, Tanis MacBeth (Ed.) (1986). *The Impact of Television. A Natural Experiment in Three Communities.* Orlando: Academic Press.

Wilson, Barbara J., Dale Kunkel, Daniel Linz, James W. Potter, Edward Donnerstein, Stacy L. Smith, Eva Blumenthal, & Timothy Gray. (1997). *National Television Violence Study, Part I: Violence in Television Programming Overall: University of California, Santa Barbara Study.* Thousand Oaks: Sage.

Winterhoff-Spurk, Peter. (1989). *Fernsehen und Weltwissen.* Opladen: Westdeutscher Verlag.

Winterhoff-Spurk, Peter. (1994). Gewalt in Fernsehnachrichten. In Michael Jäckel & Peter Winterhoff-Spurk, (Eds.), *Politik und Medien. Analysen zur Entwicklung der politischen Kommunikation* (pp. 55–69). Berlin: Vistas.

Wood, Wendy, Frank Y. Wong, & J. Gregory Chachere. (1991). Effects of Media Violence on Viewers Aggression in Unconstrained Social Interactions. *Psychological Bulletin, 109,* 371–383.

Patterns and Explanations of Direct Physical and Indirect Nonphysical Aggression in Childhood

HOLLY FOSTER AND JOHN HAGAN

I. SOCIAL STRUCTURE AND BEHAVIOR

Research on childhood aggression has shown that the *form* of the behavior measured matters for conclusions regarding social location effects, including gender and age differences. Although aggression has been differentiated in psychological research, the need to clarify the roles of a broad range of structural effects (e.g., family and community characteristics), in addition to age and gender, across levels of analyses on specific outcomes remains. The inclusion of these multilevel risks together would more fully capture sociogenic influences on aggression. Sociological research, in contrast, has emphasized how social structure and processes affect psychological and other life course outcomes (Pearlin, 1989; Aneshensel, Rutter, & Lachenbruch, 1991; Sampson & Laub, [1993] 1995). However, research on child well-being in sociology has tended to investigate how environmental features may affect more composite outcomes (e.g., externalizing or internalizing behavior problems)[1], or among older youth, specific outcomes like predatory delinquency, while qualitative distinctions in aggression have received little attention.

Within unequal social structures, behavioral responses, including aggression, may be considered as adaptations to environmental constraints and opportunities (Merton, 1938; Patillo-McCoy, 1999; Suttles, 1968). These adaptations are in turn also affected by social

---

[1] Externalizing behavior "refers to behavior that is troubling to others—especially aggressive and antisocial behavior" (Menaghan, 1999:316). Internalizing behavior "... is marked by withdrawal from interaction, anxiety, and depressed mood" (Menaghan, 1999:316). Externalizing problems involve behaviors that are expressed outwardly, while internalizing problems involve more problematic inward feelings (Rosenfield, 1999:354).

W. Heitmeyer and J. Hagan (eds.), *International Handbook of Violence Research*, 543–565.

structure. For example, gender role socialization occurs within social structure, and as Heimer also indicates in research on violence: "... the specific form of these acts varies with position in the power-structure" (1995:143).

Along these lines, research in mental health compares structural sources of substance use and dependence that are behaviors more common among males with affective or anxiety disorders that are more common among females (Aneshensel et al., 1991). Aneshensel and colleagues (1991) find that among women stress increases affective or anxiety disorders and that among men stress increases substance abuse/ dependence. They then draw the conclusion that "(m)en and women appear to be similarly affected by the types of stressful events and circumstances considered here, but these effects are manifest as different types of disorder" (Aneshensel et al., 1991:174). As has been recently concluded, rates of psychopathology across men and women do not differ but *types* do (Rosenfield, 1999). It follows that including only one type of mental health problem may yield unclear conclusions regarding the implications of social structural location.

We suggest that the significance of this framework can be more broadly appreciated through its application to the study of aggression. Including only one form of aggression that may be more sensitive to the behaviors of males or females potentially obscures conclusions regarding contextual influences. We argue that the full implications of structural inequalities including family and neighborhood conditions on children's behaviors can be more effectively assessed through a comparative approach that includes the potentially gendered manifestations of indirect nonphysical and direct physical aggression. Furthermore, research may not fully capture the effects of social structural locations on children and youth by operationalizing only more mainstream sociological outcomes, such as physical aggression.

In this chapter, we review research on various forms of aggression and the patterning and explanations of these behaviors. We consider whether the identified risk factors are common across or unique to each type of aggression. Finally, the consequences of both forms of aggression for child well-being are considered. Given the implications of early childhood aggression for later personal and intergenerational disadvantages (Caspi et al., 1998; Kokko & Pulkkinen, 2000; Pepler & Sedighdeilami, 1998; Sampson & Laub, 1995; Serbin et al., 1991; Tremblay et al., 1996) and for violence, also a public health problem (Ellickson & McGuigan, 2000), this endeavor may yield more detailed information to identify preventive interventions to reduce risks to the broader society (Elliott, Hagan, & McCord, 1998; Levine & Rosich, 1996).

II. FORMS OF AGGRESSIVE BEHAVIOR

Qualitative differences in the forms of aggression distinguish relational, social, or indirect aggression, physical aggression, and verbal aggression (Tremblay, 1991), with recent literature bringing back in the concept of displaced aggression (Marcus-Newhall et al., 2000). Aggression has been distinguished from violence, where the former "... is defined as those acts that inflict bodily or mental harm on others," and the latter "... is defined as those aggressive acts causing serious harm, such as aggravated assault, rape, robbery, and homicide" (Loeber & Stouthamer-Loeber, 1998:242). This definition separates types of behavior by severity and includes both bodily and mental harm as results of acts of aggression. Aggression is itself a heterogeneous category that includes different forms and functions of behavior that vary over life stage (Buss, 1961; Coie & Dodge, 1998; Little et al., 2000; Rys & Bear, 1997).

The distinction between overt and covert behaviors has been used to distinguish more aggressive and violent behaviors from property damage and theft (see review in Loeber & Stouthamer-Loeber, 1998:247), but has also been applied to research on forms of aggression. Physical and direct verbal aggression have been combined in some research as 'overt aggression' (Crick & Grotpeter, 1995) including "... behaviors that harm others through physical damage or through the threat of such damage" (Crick, 1997:610), while the more relational and indirect forms constitute 'covert aggression' (Owens, Shute, & Slee, 2000; Rutter, Giller, & Hagell, 1998:149; Tomada & Schneider, 1997:601). As patterns by gender for direct verbal aggression differ from those of relational and physical aggression, it may be that comparisons combining physical and verbal aggression into one measure are less clear for discerning the effects of social structure. For example, in cohorts of eight and eighteen year old Finnish students, significant differences in verbal aggression were found between males and females, however, differences in verbal aggression were not significant in the eleven and fifteen-year-olds cohorts (Bjorkqvist, Osterman, & Kaukiainen, 1992; Lagerspetz, Bjorkqvist, & Peltonen, 1988).

Tremblay (1991) argues for finer distinctions in the content of the study of aggression, rather than the use of more composite outcomes of behavior problems. The distinctions provided in this research have not yet been incorporated into sociological perspectives examining child well-being. It has been suggested that even research focused only on one type of aggression (e.g., physical) may actually combine items measuring different domains of behavior (Loeber & Hay, 1997; Tremblay, 1991:72). Physical aggression has been more specifically defined as "... a category of behavior that causes or threatens physical harm to others" (Loeber & Hay, 1997:373) and as "physical acts oriented toward another person which could inflict physical harm" (Baillargeon, Tremblay & Willms, 1999). Common features of aggressive acts are that they include the potential for harm, they are intentional, may involve arousal, and must be aversive to the victim (see review in Coie & Dodge, 1998:783–784). The functions of physical aggression have been identified as both reactive and proactive, where the former may be "a response to antecedent conditions such as goal blocking and provocation, and responses that are primarily interpersonal and hostile in nature ...," and the latter may occur "... in anticipation of self-serving outcomes" (Coie & Dodge, 1998:784; see also Poulin & Boivin, 2000).

Finer distinctions have been drawn among the concepts of indirect, social, and relational aggression, addressing the 'directness' of the behavior, which is clearer in physical aggression research. Consistent with the definition of physical aggression, indirect aggression involves anger and actual or potential harm in the form of a damaged reputation, damaged relationships, and psychological harm (see Coie & Dodge, 1998:791; Crick, Bigbee, & Howes, 1996; Lagerspetz et al., 1988:405; Rutter et al., 1998:148). A comprehensive definition of indirect aggression indicates that it is "... a behavior that aims to hurt someone without the use of physical aggression" (Tremblay, 1999:58) and "refers to manipulations by the child that are intended to harm or deprive another person while evading direct confrontation" (Tremblay et al., 1996:129). Psychological research on indirect aggression dates back to research by Buss (1961) and Feshbach (1969). Indirect aggression was originally defined as including both verbal (e.g., "spreading nasty gossip") and physical behaviors (e.g., "a man sets fire to his neighbors home") (Buss, 1961:8). Behind both of these forms of indirect aggression is a motive to deliver noxious stimuli to a target person, but to also avoid detection (Buss, 1961:8). In the first instance, the victim is hurt through the use of others, and in the latter example, the person is not him/herself injured but the harm is administered through his or her objects.

A number of operationalizations and conceptualizations of indirect aggression have been discussed (Bjorkqvist, 1994). Research has predominantly focused on the more covert interpersonal aspects of aggression using social relationships. This is the form of indirect aggression investigated in most of the psychological research on children and youth. More specifically, indirect aggression "... includes circumventory behavior that exploits social relations among peers in order to harm the person at whom the anger is directed" (Bjorkqvist, Lagerspetz, & Kaukiainen, 1992:118). These behaviors involve the manipulation of friendship patterns, where "peers may be used as a means or vehicles for harming the victim" (Lagerspetz et al., 1988:405). Indirect aggression includes verbal "behind the back behavior," and also the manipulation of relationships, for example, "gets others to dislike the person" (Bjorkqvist, Lagerspetz, & Kaukiainen, 1992:52, 55). As the previous example indicates, verbal aggression can also be distinguished as direct (e.g., insults) and indirect aggression (e.g., gossip) (Bjorkqvist, Lagerspetz, & Kaukiainen, 1992). A recent study also proposed reactive and proactive forms of indirect aggression (Little et al., 2000). A broader definition of indirect aggression that has been used in some recent research is more consistent with Buss's earlier definition (1961) in considering "... indirect aggression to be a behavior intended to harm another living being that is delivered circuitously, through another person or object" (Richardson & Green, 1999:426; Walker, Richardson, & Green, 2000).

More subtle distinctions have also been drawn between relational and indirect aggression, however, both include the feature of the manipulation of the social structure of relations among individuals with the intent to harm (see also Rys & Bear, 1997; Xie et al., 2000). Research using both of these concepts has shown similar findings. Relational aggression includes those behaviors in which "... harm to others occurs through manipulation or control of their relationships with others" (e.g., "When mad, gets even by keeping the person from being in their group of friends;" "When mad at a person, ignores them and stops talking to them;" "Tries to keep other people from being in their group during activity or play time;" "Tells friends they will stop liking them unless they do what they say") (Crick & Grotpeter, 1995:713). This form of aggression uses acceptance or friendship as a way to control others (Crick & Grotpeter, 1995; Crick et al., 1996; Crick, 1997:610; Tomada & Schneider, 1997; Rys & Bear, 1997:102).

Finally, the broadest definition of these more relational forms of aggression may be captured with the concept of "social aggression," which:

> ... is directed toward damaging another's self-esteem, social status, or both, and may take forms such as verbal rejection, negative facial expressions or body movements, or more indirect forms such as slanderous rumors or social exclusion. We prefer the term social aggression because it aptly describes a class of behaviors that belong together because they serve the same function in ongoing social interaction: to hurt another person by doing harm to her self-concept or social standing (Galen & Underwood, 1997:589).

The above definition of social aggression includes both direct and indirect forms of more interpersonal and nonphysical aggression (e.g., facial expressions and gestures) and informs a modified scale of 'relational aggression' originally designed by Crick and Grotpeter (1996) (Paquette & Underwood, 1999:250). Others use this term to refer more to social ostracism and the alienation of affection (Cairns et al., 1989:321). In keeping with the other forms of aggression, both definitions of socially aggressive behaviors share in common their intent to control others and to induce harm (Galen & Underwood, 1997).

Most recently, reviews on relational aggression have differentiated the type of behavior that may indicate an aggressive act by the developmental stage of the child. For example, in the preschool and early childhood period, these acts may be an immediate response to a current transgression (Crick et al., 2001:200). The form of the aggressive act may involve directly telling the peer that they may not play with the aggressor, unless they do what s/he wants. In middle childhood, these acts are developed with more covert expression coinciding with the development of children's cognitive skills (Crick et al., 2001:200). Examples of relational aggression at this developmental stage may include "spreading rumors," "pretending not to see the target child or not inviting the target child to participate," or "writing nasty notes or talking behind the targets back." These acts may be in response to current or past transgressions (Crick et al., 2001:200). In adolescence, the relationally aggressive acts may also involve both male and female peers rather than same-sex peers characteristic of children's peer groups. These acts may include the behaviors of "dissing" or "trashing" the target child. The content of the rumors also develops in this developmental stage to include "gossip about one's sexual orientation or frequency of sexual partners" (Morales et al., 2000 cited in Crick et al., 2001:201). Finally, relational aggression may be practiced in romantic relationships through the manipulation of sexual confidences and fidelity issues (e.g., stealing a dating partner, trying to ruin one's reputation, "cheating," and trying the make the victim jealous) (see Morales et al., 2000 cited in Crick & Rose, 2000:201).

III. METHODOLOGICAL ISSUES IN PAST RESEARCH

Studies assessing the psychometric properties of the aggression scales have found distinctions among indirect and physical aggression, both within and across raters. The use of self-reports may be a particular challenge as people may not rate their own behaviors as 'indirectly aggressive' due to social desirability biases (Osterman et al., 1998), or they may not be aware of it, in that these behaviors may be seen as "simply telling the truth" (Lagerspetz et al., 1988:413). The reporting of aggressive behaviors may suffer from response biases and also present the challenge of incorporating especially young children into research (Bjorkqvist, Osterman, & Kaukiainen, 1992:53). Unlike physical aggression, which can be directly observed, most forms of indirect aggression also require knowledge of subtleties and group social dynamics. However, combinations of raters including peer, teacher, self, and parental reports have been used to study indirect and physical aggression among predominantly school-age children.

In addition to the various quantitative methodologies used, qualitative research has also found themes of indirect aggression, especially in accounts of female adolescent conflicts (see Owens et al., 2000; Taylor, Gilligan, & Sullivan, 1995). The use of peer nominations from students in school settings has been favored in the research on indirect and relational aggression, with additional later research including self-reported responses to vignettes, and parental, teacher, and self reports on national community surveys (see Bjorkqvist, Osterman, & Kaukiainen, 1992; Pepler & Sedighdeilami, 1998; Tremblay et al., 1996). Laboratory observations of children's play sessions and children's analyses of videotaped samples of aggression are recent innovations in the study of social aggression where facial expressions thought to display contempt were rated (Galen & Underwood, 1997). However, these research designs are less informative on familial and community processes.

Within-rater correlations have been reported for children between direct and indirect aggression. Analyses of the factor structure of a set of peer-assessed items yielded distinctions between overt and relational aggression using the Children's Social Behavior Scale (CSBS-P) in a sample of third to sixth graders (Crick & Grotpeter, 1995), with an intercorrelation of r = 0.54, p < 0.01 (Crick & Grotpeter, 1995:715). The correlations and factor structure indicate that the constructs are related but distinct. The Direct and Indirect Aggression Scale (DIAS) asked for ratings on the frequency of the occurrence of specific items and were preceded by the question: "What do they/I do when angry with another girl/boy in the class?" (Lagerspetz et al., 1988:405). The separate factors of direct (includes physical and verbal items) and indirect aggression were found among the eight and eleven to twelve-year-olds cohorts, while indirect, direct physical, and direct verbal aggression were distinguished among the fifteen-year-olds cohort (Bjorkqvist, Lagerspetz, & Kaukiainen, 1992:125). The DIAS was also used with a pooled sample across the four countries of Finland, Israel, Italy, and Poland. This cross-national sample yielded internal consistencies on the aggression scales with Cronbach's alpha reliability coefficients in the 0.8 to 0.9 range (Osterman et al., 1998).

Inter-relations between forms of aggressive behavior have also been investigated across age-groups, although the correlations vary by the rater. For example, in a study of preschool children using the Preschool Social Behavior Scale with teachers (PSBS-T), separate factors for both relational and overt aggression were found, each with Cronbach's alpha reliabilities greater than 0.90. These teacher-reported scales were related at 0.70 for both boys and girls, indicating strongly intercorrelated factors (Crick, Casas, & Mosher, 1997). However, a technique with preschoolers that asks children to point at photographs to identify peers (Preschool Social Behavior Scale-Peers) yielded factors for relational and overt aggression (α = 0.70), with peer correlations found to be more distinctive than the teacher reports (r = 0.37 for girls and r = 0.46 for boys) (Crick et al., 1997). Drawing on eight investigations of about 1,000 people aged twelve to ninety, another scale was used to measure direct and indirect aggression, the "Richardson Conflict Response Questionnaire" (RCRQ); correlations were found to range between forms of aggression at 0.07 (among college students) to 0.61 (among seventh graders) (Walker et al., 2000:150). They report an average correlation between direct and indirect aggression in these studies of 0.42 (Walker et al., 2000:150).

Across-rater analyses have shown fairly consistent intercorrelations among peer and teacher reports of overt and relational aggression, with the magnitude of these coefficients varying to some degree with age and gender (Crick, 1996; see also Little et al., 2000). Correlations between peer and teacher correlations among nine to twelve-year-olds for relational aggression were found at 0.57 for boys (p < 0.001) and 0.63 for girls (p < 0.001), and for overt aggression at 0.69 for boys (p < 0.001), and 0.74 for girls (p < 0.001) (Crick, 1996:2320–2321). Peer and teacher reports were intercorrelated at 0.52 in Rys and Bear's (1997) sample of third to sixth graders. Among an Italian sample of adolescents, peer and teacher reports correlated at 0.20 for both overt and relational aggression for girls, but a smaller nonsignificant correlation was observed for boys (Tomada & Schneider, 1997:606). These between-rater correlations show some age dependency with peer-teacher ratings among preschoolers (3.5–5 years old) in the United States of 0.30 for both boys and girls for overt aggression, and 0.42, p < 0.01 for peer-teacher reports for girls on relational aggression, which was 0.11 and not significant for boys (Crick et al., 1997). These across-rater findings suggest some clearer observability of indirect aggression in girls. Overall, there is more concordance between self and peer reports among direct than indirect behaviors (Lagerspetz et al., 1988; Bjorkqvist, Lagerspetz, & Kaukiainen, 1992; Richardson & Green, 1997 cited in Walker et al., 2000). Additionally, when using longitudinal data collected at three time points over the academic year on third through sixth graders, both forms of aggression were found to be stable with correlations between the time one and two and time one and three assessments of over 0.50 for both boys and girls (Crick, 1996).

The literature on physical and interpersonal aggression indicates some convergence in findings across studies in terms of measurement characteristics. Inter-rater agreement in the middle childhood years is within ranges established by a meta-analysis of the more commonly used scales of internalizing and externalizing behavior problems (Achenbach, McConaughy, & Howell, 1987; see also Rys & Bear, 1997). The use of parental reports additionally permits the inclusion of preschool-age children and behavior in noninstitutional settings (see Tremblay et al., 1996). As parents may be in the position to observe children or gain information on children's behavior across settings, they may be the most important source of information on younger children. Parent-reported assessments of indirect and physical aggression were used with younger children in the Canadian National Longitudinal Survey of Children and Youth (NLSCY) (see Tremblay et al., 1996; Tremblay et al., 2001; Foster, 2001; Foster et al., 2001). The results of research with this study will be examined in detail in the following sections of this review. The continued triangulation of methodologies will further establish the validity and reliability of measures of aggression.

IV. EXPLANATIONS OF CHILDHOOD AGGRESSION

Although the influences of individual level factors, including biological influences, have been supported by empirical literature on the development and persistence of antisocial behavior (for reviews see Coie and Dodge, 1998; Hill & Maughan, 2001; Loeber & Hay, 1997; Parke & Slaby, 1983; Rutter et al., 1998), we draw primarily on structural perspectives to examine variations in aggressive behavior. We add to the current literature a more detailed and multileveled consideration of social structural and processual effects. Social structure involves both external constraints and internalized expectations (see Risman, 1998). Social structural approaches to explaining behavior may favor individual characteristics (e.g., gender and age categories), environmental contexts, and/or social network structure (Bates & Peacock, 1989; Wellman & Berkowitz, 1988). Social structural factors have also been differentiated from and may be antecedent to processual variables, such as parenting practices (Sampson & Laub, 1995:69). Environmental characteristics have been found to affect the development of antisocial behavior, net of individual variables (Rutter et al., 1998). In the following section, we review the findings on gender and age trends in aggressive behavior as these indicators of social structural location have received the most investigation and indicate some common and conflicting patterns.

1. Gender as Structure

The relationship between gender and delinquency among youth has been examined in power-control theory, feminist scholarship, and a structural symbolic interactionist perspective (Chesney-Lind, 1998; Hagan et al., 1989; Heimer, 1995; McCarthy, Hagan & Woodward, 1999; Sims Blackwell, 2000). Further, gender and violent delinquency has been recently examined in a reformulated version of differential association theory (Heimer & De Coster, 1999). Structural and cultural factors have been examined as explanations of gender differences of these behaviors (e.g., class, gender definitions, definitions of violence). While yielding insight into gender differences *within* a realm of behaviors, it may be additionally useful to assess the implications of structural location (i.e., gender differences) by comparing males and females *across* behaviors. We are also concerned with variation in younger *children's* behaviors rather than the delinquent behaviors of adolescents. Insight into the subtleties of gender inequalities of the broader society may be found in examining children's behavioral manifestations and adaptations.

2. Patterns of Aggression by Gender

Research on the forms of aggression may also contribute to our understanding of the timing of when in the life course gender differences appear. Although research on depression has indicated a change in patterns of the gender differences occurring in early adolescence (Cairney, 1998; Cyranowski, Young, & Shear, 2000), with females developing higher levels than males at this life stage, *childhood* has been found to be the stage where aggressive behaviors are first differentiated by gender. Research on children has suggested that gender differences and similarities may be overlooked as a result of measuring only physical aggression in this age-group (see Crick & Grotpeter, 1995). Research has suggested a qualitative difference in the form or type of aggression by gender (Coie & Dodge, 1998:791; Crick & Grotpeter, 1995). This literature suggests a common purpose is achieved with strategies of indirect and direct physical forms of aggression, but the expression is affected by gender and other factors. The earliest research study on gender differences in aggression taking form into account indicated greater levels of indirect aggression for females than males[2] (Feshbach, 1969). This research pattern has been supported by subsequent research; however, variation emerges with samples from different countries, age-groups, and raters (Little et al., 2000).

Gender differences in physical aggression have been found to first emerge in the early school years between the ages of three to six years old (Coie & Dodge, 1998:791; Loeber & Hay, 1997:375). A study of preschoolers used specialized techniques to gain information about forms of aggression with a young sample of children (3.5–5 years old) (Crick et al., 1997). Items operationalizing relational aggression studied largely among elementary schools students were also adapted for age-specific use (e.g., "tells a peer that they won't be invited to their birthday party unless he or she does what the child wants"). Gender differences among preschoolers were found using teacher reports, with females showing higher levels of relational aggression than males, and males showing higher levels of overt aggression than females (Crick et al., 1997:583). However, peer reports of aggression did not show gender differences.

Including children aged four to eleven years olds, a recent Canadian study with a community cross-sectional sample found that at every year of age boys show higher levels

---

[2]However, subsequent studies have continued to examine gender differences as the conceptualization and measurement of indirect aggression has evolved over time. These early analyses examined behavior by boys and girls to a "newcomer" to the group, rather than sustained friendships (see Bjorkqvist, Osterman, & Kaukiainen, 1992:53).

of physical aggression than girls, and that the frequency of physical aggression may stabilize or decrease with age (Tremblay et al., 1996; Tremblay, 1999; see also Nagin & Tremblay, 1999). At each age, girls show higher levels of indirect aggression than boys, and indirect aggression increases for both groups with age. This study used parental reports of child aggression.

Content analyses of the presence of themes in narrative self-report data found that girls reported fewer incidents of social aggression in relationships with girls in early childhood than adolescence, whereas males reported few relationally aggressive incidents with boys at any time from grades four through seven (Cairns et al., 1989:322). Reports of physical aggression showed stability in male-aggressor, male-target aggression but a decline in male–female, female–male, and female–female physical aggression (Cairns et al., 1989:323). Teacher and self-reports of physical aggression show declining developmental trends for both boys and girls (Cairns et al., 1989:324).

Using categorical groupings of children's scores divided at one standard deviation above the mean, children were considered members of the relationally aggressive, overtly aggressive, and nonaggressive groups (Crick & Grotpeter, 1995:716). Most children were identified as nonaggressive using the categorical groupings, and a similar percentage of boys and girls were identified as aggressive. However, boys were found to be aggressive in terms of overt criteria, and girls in terms of relational criteria. A fourth group of children were identified as members of both the overtly and relationally aggressive group with the categorical criteria.

Using mean differences in peer-nominated continuous scores, females were found to have higher levels than males on relational aggression, and males were found to have higher levels than females on overt aggression (Crick & Grotpeter, 1995:716). This same pattern in gender differences was found with self-reports by these third to sixth graders of their own aggressive behaviors (Crick & Grotpeter, 1995:718). Similarly, with a larger sample of children in this age range, boys were found to display higher levels of peer nominated overt aggression than girls, while girls showed higher levels of relational aggression than boys (Crick et al., 1997:613). In contrast, a separate study using the same age-group and methodology as Crick and Grotpeter (1995) found no gender differences in relational aggression, until they used categorical groupings (Rys & Bear, 1997:95–96). In this study, females showed less overt aggression than males (including both verbal and physical aggression) (Rys & Bear, 1997).

A comparative study used the same instrument with a sample of third and fourth graders in Italy. With this sample, Tomada and Schneider (1997) found that males actually had slightly higher mean scores than females using peer reports on relational aggression, and that boys also had higher levels of overt aggression than females. The teacher reports showed no gender differences for either form of aggression. When dichotomized groupings were formed using the criteria of scores one standard deviation above the mean, fairly similar, but slightly higher percentages of boys than girls were categorized as relationally aggressive. Males were also more likely to be classified as overtly aggressive than females. Little et al. (2000) investigated overt, relational, proactive and reactive aggression with almost two thousand adolescents in Germany from grades five through ten. With self-report data, they found either no difference by gender or higher levels of relational aggression for males than females (Little et al., 2000). These results suggest the need for further research to consider both cultural context and reporting biases by gender to clarify gender related trends.

With a group of children from a school sample of fifth graders from Finland, aged eleven to twelve, using peer report data, males were found to show higher levels of direct means of aggression, and females showed higher mean scores on indirect aggression than males (Lagerspetz et al., 1988:410). A separate study of Finish eight-year-olds found the same factor structure differentiating direct and indirect aggression. However, gender differences in mean levels on these scales were not found at age eight. An analysis of fifteen-year-olds in the ninth grade differentiated verbal from physical aggression and found no gender differences among the former, although males had higher levels of physical aggression than females. At age fifteen, females showed higher levels of indirect aggression than males (Bjorkqvist, Lagerspetz and Kaukiainen, 1992; Lagerspetz & Bjorkqvist, 1994). In the eighteen-year-olds cohort, girls continued to show higher levels of indirect aggression than males (Bjorkqvist, Osterman, & Kaukiainen, 1992; Lagerspetz & Bjorkqvist, 1994:142). Comparing the trends by age-group, a review concludes that indirect aggression may peak around age eleven (Bjorkqvist, Osterman, & Kaukiainen, 1992).

The gender trends identified in Finland have been further supported in a cross-national study of eight, eleven, and fifteen-year-olds from Finland, Israel, Italy, and Poland. This study similarly used peer report data with a "Direct and Indirect Aggression Scale" (DIAS), assessing on how peers behave when angry with, or in conflict with, another person. For each age-group of girls, indirect aggression was the most used strategy, followed by verbal and physical aggression. For boys, indirect aggression was the least used strategy across these age-groups, with physical and verbal strategies more prevalent.

A self-report victimization component of the DIAS scale similarly indicated that boys experienced indirect aggression as the least likely form of aggression, while verbal aggression and physical aggression were more likely to be experienced (Osterman et al., 1998). Girls showed more verbal aggression than indirect or physical aggression at age eleven. By age fifteen, girls reported more indirect aggression than verbal or physical aggression, a result consistent with the peer report data (Osterman et al., 1998). Males showed a slight decrease in physical and increase in verbal aggression between the eight to fifteen-year-olds cohorts (Osterman et al., 1998).

The findings indicate the changes in indirect and physical aggression over the life course, and also highlight the complexity of peer, teacher, parent, and observational reports with children. Taken together, the range of evidence over the age-groups and samples indicates higher relational aggression among females in other-reports of younger children's behavior and greater levels of male physical aggression.

3. Explanations for Patterns by Gender

Theories of social structure may be used to guide an integration of the empirical findings on aggression. Gender is conceptualized as a source of social structure in Risman's broader sociological theory of gender relations (1998). Her multilevel theory spans three levels of analysis and "... treats gender itself as built into social life via socialization, interaction, and institutional organization" (Risman, 1998:13). Gender differences are explained through the individual level of analysis with the formation of "gendered selves," where children learn gender role norms and adapt their strategies of behavior within structural conditions, and the "interactional" level of analysis including parent, peer, and teacher expectations for behavior (see Crick et al., 1996; Crick, 1997). The concept of the interactional context can be expanded to include social network structure, drawing from a network theory of gender (Smith-Lovin & McPherson, 1993). Finally, the "institutional" or third level of analysis examines how gender relations are organized in the broader society. Broader contexts including the neighborhood may influence and organize gendered behavior (Risman, 1998; Joyner, 2000). This multilevel theory is consistent with, but more explicit than explanations of gender differences in antisocial behavior that include cognitive (see Bjorkqvist, 1994:179, 181) and gender role normative strategies, and also cultural representations of aggression (Rutter et al., 1998).

The third level of analysis in Risman's theory is consistent with related explanations in other areas of sociology concerning how structural inequalities by gender and differential access to power in society becomes manifest through forms of behavior. In a broader societal context of gender inequalities, children may find it easier to aggress according to gender role expectations (see Crick et al., 1996). This explanation of adaptations to societal inequalities is similar to the observations by Suttles (1968) in Chicago in the 1960s on how ethnic group inequalities encouraged adaptation to unsafe environments through the negotiation of space.

Gender role socialization guides the expression of anger in gender appropriate ways (Lagerspetz et al., 1988). Males are seen to value instrumentality and physical dominance, while girls may be more likely to value relational ties, including establishing intimate connections with others (Crick & Grotpeter, 1995; Taylor et al., 1995). Analyses of children's responses to vignettes indicate that girls see social and physical aggression as equally hurtful, but boys show a higher mean rating of perceived hurtfulness of the physically aggressive vignettes than the socially aggressive vignettes (Crick et al., 1996). Children's strategies may be chosen on the basis of the probability that they are likely to inflict harm (aggress) by disrupting valued goals (Crick & Grotpeter, 1995:710; Crick et al., 1996:2317–2318). Girls, according to this view, would be more likely than boys to engage in relational harm, while boys would be more overt in their strategies. Also, consistent with gender role expectations, girls may be more likely to incur sanctions if they act in physically aggressive ways, while boys may incur sanctions if they do not (Richardson & Green, 1999). This research is consistent with both the "gendered selves" and the "interactional" levels of analysis in Risman's theory.

A consideration of Risman's interactional context also raises the issue of how microcontextual considerations affect behavior. Interactional expectations may influence the form of aggressive behavior through gender norms. However, research on indirect aggression has begun to examine some further microcontextual features, for example, the gender of the target and the aggressor, the relationship type, and the conflict setting (Bjorkqvist, 1994: 178; Richardson & Green, 1999; Sumrall, Ray, & Tidwell, 2000). For example, the relationship of the aggressor to the target influences attributions and reactions regarding indirect aggression (Galen & Underwood, 1997; Richardson & Green, 1999; Sumrall et al., 2000). Using a series of hypothetical vignettes with a sample of second through fifth grade girls in a public elementary school, it was found that older girls attributed more hostile intent to the indirect aggressive acts; however, this was contingent on the social content of the relationship. Older girls saw indirect aggression from an enemy as involving more negative intent than if the same situation had involved their best friend. Girls showed less anger if the behavior came from a best friend, rather than an enemy, suggesting some leeway in interpretation based on prior relationship information (Sumrall et al., 2000). We suggest that future research could expand upon this research through considering other aspects of context.

4. Gender and Social Network Structure

Another aspect of social structure, social networks, affects gender differences in child-hood behaviors and later life course outcomes. A strength of the social network focus involves the empirical operationalization of the social structure of the group; however, this approach requires attention to classrooms in schools and thus limited samples.

Gender differences in homophily in play patterns have been observed to emerge around the time of school entry (Smith-Lovin & McPherson, 1993:230–233). Studies of children's playgroups have found that there are network size differences by gender, with girls playing in smaller groups than boys. An aspect that serves to reinforce these early differences between boys and girls is 'intransivity'.[3] As children age, these patterns result in size and composition differences in networks:

> Simple, small tendencies toward homophily and differences in resolving problems in the struc-
> ture of their relationships mean that boys and girls will move toward very different social cir-
> cles. Their worlds become gender segregated with boys in larger, more heterogeneous cliques
> (Smith-Lovin & McPherson, 1993:231).

As these networks become more homophilous by gender, males and females be-come more differentiated in terms of social structural location. These network differences in turn lead to different patterns of contact for males and females (Smith-Lovin & McPherson, 1993:233).

The focus of the network theory of gender is on life course inequalities that emerge over time with the accumulation of differences over the school years and beyond, in vol-untary organizations and paid work network structures, opportunities, the development of weak but potentially resourceful ties, and also subsequent knowledge and effectiveness (Smith-Lovin & McPherson, 1993:232; Ridgeway & Smith-Lovin, 1999:240).

The literature also shows a tight or close-knit network structure to be characteristic of indirect aggression. This type of network structure is related to being female in child-hood. Studies have found gender homophily in ego networks begins in early childhood (Ridgeway & Smith-Lovin, 1999; Smith-Lovin & McPherson, 1993:229,230). Male and female differences in network structure emerge in the school years (Smith-Lovin & McPherson, 1993:229). Connected to the gender patterns reported earlier, results from Finland indicated no gender differences in aggression at age eight, while females showed more indirect aggression than males at age fifteen. Males in this research also showed larger networks than females at ten to eleven years old (Lagerspetz et al., 1988:410), but no significant differences were found in friendship structure for the eight-year-olds co-hort. At age fifteen, females were more likely than males to be in dyads, and males were more likely than females to be in groups of greater than two or alone (Bjorkqvist, Lagerspetz, & Kaukiainen, 1992:123).

This research indicates some association between the form of network structure and the form of aggression. While dense network structures may provide more opportunity for social support (Smith-Lovin & McPherson, 1993:226), these environments also have a potential for interpersonal harm, as the relationship structure involves social vulnerability (see also Portes, 1998). This research becomes more complex among adolescents. Cairns et al. (1988) and others have studied network structure and physical aggression in some

---

[3] This is the situation where in a triad (ABC), A likes B, B likes C, but A does not like C. Boys tend to resolve this by developing a liking relationship to C, while girls are more likely to delete the link to B (cease liking) (Smith-Lovin & McPherson, 1993:231).

detail, finding that aggression may be a basis for homophily (or similarity) in early adolescence (see Cairns et al., 1988).

5. Other Risk Factors for Childhood Aggression: Common or Unique Across Forms?

Comprehensive reviews of childhood aggression and youth violence suggest the necessity of considering different levels (i.e., individual, familial, and environmental/societal), and domains of risk factors (Coie & Dodge, 1998; Herrenkohl et al., 2000; Rutter et al., 1998). We included a range of structural (e.g., family structure) and processual risks (e.g., parenting) for childhood aggression (Loeber & Stouthamer-Loeber, 1986; Maccoby & Martin, 1983; Sampson & Laub, 1995) in our research with the Canadian National Longitudinal Survey of Children and Youth, which we summarize below. We also summarize the findings of two other studies with the first cycle of the Canadian NLSCY, as they include both indirect and physical aggression.[4] Rather than assessing quantitative combinations of risk in composite risk measures, we focus instead on the question of which of the multilevel risk factors are associated with both types of aggression.

a. FAMILY STRUCTURAL FACTORS. While studies have investigated the structural antecedents of physical aggression, a fairly recent article observes: "… no information has yet been generated on the correlates of relational aggression …" (Crick & Grotpeter, 1995). However, among four to eleven-year-olds in the NLSCY, Tremblay and colleagues (1996) found that lower socioeconomic status (SES) (based on parental education, occupational status, and household income) is associated with higher levels of both forms of aggression.[5] Boys and girls from the lowest of six socioeconomic categories had higher mean physical aggression scores than those in higher SES categories. In all categories, males had higher mean scores than females, with the greatest difference at the lowest SES categories. Similarly, boys and girls from the lowest SES categories had higher mean scores on indirect aggression than those at higher SES categories. Girls had higher mean scores than boys at all SES levels. These results indicate a structural influence of SES net of control variables with very young children (Tremblay et al., 1996:130–131).

Tremblay and colleagues (1996) used multilevel models in their analyses of children nested in families.[6] Among those four to eleven years old, living with at least one biological parent (N = 16,021 children from 10,287 families) in either two-parent or single-parent homes, 38 percent of the variability in physical aggression was explained by family membership. Similarly, 43 percent of the total variance in indirect aggression was explained by family membership. These results highlight the importance of familial contributions to aggression.

---

[4]See also Boyle and Lipman (1998), Sprott and Doob (1998), and Wade, Pevalin, and Brannigan (1999) on related research on behavioral outcomes with the NLSCY.

[5]The measure of indirect aggression in the NLSCY is closest to that used in the work of the Finnish researchers, Bjorkqvist, Lagerspetz and colleagues, and involves mainly interpersonal relations (HRDC and Statistics Canada, 1995).

[6]In the first cycle of the NLSCY, other children were included from the same household as the target child if they were also in the eligible age range, up to four per household (Human Resources Development Canada and Statistics Canada, 1995).

More detailed information on aggression and SES was found in this research with the observation that the total variation in physical aggression between families increased from higher SES families to lower SES families. This is explained to indicate that:

> ... although average levels of expressed physical aggression are higher at lower SES levels, there is more variation in the use of aggression between children from lower SES families. In other words, family influences on aggressive behavior are greater among families of lower SES than among families of higher SES (Tremblay et al., 1996:132).

These patterns were also replicated for indirect aggression.

Research on the implications of family structure in general indicates that single-parent families may be more exposed (rather than differentially vulnerable) to stressors than two-parent families (Avison, 1999). In our research using multileveled models with the NLSCY sample, we examined the implications for children of living in single-parent families, or with two parents in a blended or reconstituted family, to living with two biological parents on both indirect and physical aggression, net of other factors. We found that both single-parent and blended family status increased the level of indirect aggression, while only single-parent family status increased physical aggression compared to living in a two-parent biological family. A hypothesis test for the equality of the effects on indirect aggression was rejected indicating that blended family forms may put children at greater risk of indirect aggression than single-parent family status (Foster, 2001; Foster et al., 2001; Tremblay et al., 2001).

As other research has linked child problem behavior to teen parenting or the age of the biological mother at her first birth (Nagin, Pogarsky, & Farrington, 1997), housing conditions, and a large family size or number of siblings (Boyle & Lipman, 1998; Coie & Dodge, 1998; Loeber & Hay, 1997; Rutter et al., 1998:181–193,199–202), we also investigated these risks. We found with the NLSCY that the biological mother's age at first birth protected against both indirect and physical aggression (Foster, 2001; Foster et al., 2001; Tremblay et al., 2001). More siblings increased physical aggression but not indirect aggression. We also hypothesized that home ownership and the length of time lived in the community would protect against aggression in providing family social capital as a resource for child-rearing (Coleman, 1988; Sampson, 1997; Hagan, 1994; Hagan, MacMillan & Wheaton, 1996). In the full multivariate models, home ownership had little impact on either physical or indirect aggression. However, the number of years the family lived at the current address was protective against physical but not indirect aggression. These structural factors may also influence the likelihood of a family living in a disadvantaged environment, indicating the need to control on these variables when assessing other contextual effects.

b. FAMILY PROCESSUAL FACTORS. Research has also indicated that the parenting dimensions of harshness, punitiveness, neglect, inconsistent parenting, lack of warmth, and a lack of supervision are associated with child behavior problems (see Coie & Dodge, 1998; Loeber & Stouthamer-Loeber, 1986; Loeber & Hay, 1997; McLeod, Kruttschnitt, & Dornfeld, 1994; Sampson, 1992, 1997; Sampson & Laub, 1994, 1995; Rutter et al., 1998). Exposure to violence in the home and community also elevate behavior problems in children (see Garbarino et al., 1992; Margolin & Gordis, 2000). Parental mental health problems have also been found to be influential on child behavior (Avison, 1999; Downey & Coyne, 1990; Ge et al., 1995). Although parental behavior affects children's behavior, models of bi-directional effects indicate there is reciprocality in this relationship (Ge et al., 1995; Kandel & Wu, 1995). However, for young children, there is reasonable evidence that the effect of parents on children holds net of the reciprocal effect (see Kandel & Wu, 1995).

In the first analyses of the NLSCY data to examine family, sibling, and peer contextual effects on both indirect and physical aggression, Pepler and Sedighdeilami (1998) found that among ten to eleven-year-olds, a total aggression score (combining physical and indirect aggression) was associated with familial environmental variables.[7] Exposure to family violence, ineffective parenting, parent–child conflict, and sibling conflict scores were higher among the aggressive compared to nonaggressive children. In multiple regression analyses using parent-rated aggression scores with child-rated risk factors, it was found that parent–child conflict and a range of peer-related interaction variables increased aggression. Using a child-rated total aggression score with parent-reported risk factors, exposure to family violence was found to increase aggression, while parent–child conflict and sibling conflict had conditional effects (Pepler & Sedighdeilami, 1998:35). Correlations presented separately for the family risk factor variables and each of indirect and physical aggression scores indicated that family violence, ineffective parenting, parent–child conflict (parent rating), parent–child conflict (child rating), sibling conflict (parent rating), and sibling conflict (child rating) related to each of physical and indirect aggression reports considered separately for boys and girls, rated by parent and child reports. An exception was the nonsignificant correlation reported for the effect of family violence on child ratings of indirect aggression for males only.

Similar to this research, we also found with the NLSCY data that hostile and punitive parenting increased both indirect and physical aggression. Positive interaction decreased indirect aggression but slightly increased physical aggression. Consistent parenting decreased both forms of aggression, while exposure to violence in the home increased indirect and physical aggression. The level of depression of the person most knowledgeable about the child increased both forms of aggression (Foster, 2001; Foster et al., 2001; Tremblay et al., 2001). These findings suggest a range of common processual risk factors to both forms of aggression, with the exception of the direction of the effect of positive interaction.

Although these findings on indirect and direct aggression show some consistency, we note that more research is required given the observation of a recent summary on relational aggression:

> ... studies of family socialization practices indicate that the coercive, highly conflictual, and nonaffectionate family patterns that often characterize the homes of physically aggressive children (for a review see Coie & Dodge, 1998) are not particularly descriptive of the family relationships of relationally aggressive children, whose family relationships are instead more likely to be overly close and enmeshed (Grotpeter & Crick, 1998) (Crick & Rose, 2000:159).

The reasons for the differences across studies regarding the commonalities of risk factors across types of aggression are not yet clear as some of this research on family process is recent and not yet published. We have also noted several family structural features that act as unique risks for each type of aggression.

---

[7] This study uses the information on physical and indirect aggression and risk factors available from parents and the children themselves for the 10–11 year old age-group, decreasing common method variance.

6. Multileveled Explanations of Aggression: Adding Community Characteristics

The contribution of other environmental influences along with other known structural risk factors may inform what combinations of risks influence either form of aggression (see Kupersmidt et al., 1995). As recent research has observed, "... results clearly indicate that social aggression hurts girls and that future research should address the social contexts in which socially aggressive behavior occurs" (Galen & Underwood, 1997:598). We suggest that further specification of the features of the contexts in which children are socialized (e.g., neighborhoods) could be expanded in research on forms and gender differences in aggression.

Recent overviews of neighborhood effects research (Brooks-Gunn, Duncan, & Aber, 1997a, 1997b; Leventhal & Brooks-Gunn, 2000) summarize which features of neighborhoods act as risk factors for child and youth behaviors. Socioeconomic factors are influential at earlier ages with additional aspects of neighborhoods becoming salient for older children. Cognitive-academic performance is most clearly related to the socioeconomic attributes of neighborhood environments; however, behavior problems appear to be more consistently associated with other factors captured by the concept of "concentration effects" (Wilson, 1987), including associated levels of joblessness and neighborhood family structure in disadvantaged areas. The literature indicates that:

> Across all of the outcomes, SES appeared to matter most, although the particular indicator of SES that mattered most varied by outcome. The strongest evidence was provided for the importance of high-SES neighborhoods for achievement outcomes among both children and adolescents. Low-SES neighborhoods and residential stability mattered most for adolescent juvenile delinquency. Low-SES neighborhoods also seemed to be associated with young children's externalizing behavior problems ... (Leventhal & Brooks-Gunn, 2000:328).

By including a range of behaviors (i.e., including indirect aggression), future neighborhood effects research may clarify whether neighborhood effects are gendered or are in part an artifact of the sensitivity of the included outcome measures (Mirowsky & Ross, 1995).

Qualitative research has begun to draw attention to contextual disadvantage and indirect aggression (Anderson, 1997). This ethnographic research on neighborhood disadvantage has provided some insight into gendered manifestations of the linkages between the "code of the streets" and the necessity of aggression to protect one's reputation as a requirement for daily negotiation of the environment. Among males, this is accomplished through physical aggression. Among females however, this negotiation of the environment may include more indirect means. As Anderson observes:

> A major cause of conflicts among girls is "he say, she say." This practice begins in the early school years and continues through high school. It occurs when "people," particularly girls, talk about others, thus putting their "business in the streets." Usually one girl will say something negative about another in the group, most often behind the person's back. The remarks will then get back to the person talked about. She may retaliate or her friends may feel required to "take up for" her. In essence, this is a form of group gossiping in which individuals are negatively assessed and evaluated. As with most gossip, the things said may or may not be true, but the point is such imputations can cast aspersions on a person's good name. The accused is required to defend herself against the slander, which can result in arguments and fights, often over little of real substance. Here again is the problem of low self-esteem, which encourages youngsters to be highly sensitive to slights and to be vulnerable to feeling dissed. To avenge the dissing, a fight is usually necessary (Anderson, 1997:26).

The above quotation links gender and neighborhood conditions. Context is implicated in this quotation with the structural conditions promoting cultural codes that reinforce "respect" on the streets, accomplished by physical means for males, and by reputation, interpersonal relations, and potentially physical means for females. These observations suggest expanding current sociological research on children's and youth's outcomes to include more sensitive measures of aggression that may better assess how behavior is manifest by gender. Both relational and physical aggression may be seen as "self-protective" strategies in disadvantaged contexts. In terms of the prevention of serious physical violence, it may also be advantageous to consider indirect aggression as *precursor*, possibly identifying a point of intervention. As has also been observed: "[o]ften if a girl is attacked or feels slighted, she will get a brother, uncle, or cousin to do her fighting for her. Increasingly, however, girls are doing their own fighting and are even asking their male relatives to teach them how to fight" (Anderson, 1997: 26).

In a recent review, Crick and Rose (2000) similarly draw attention to the need to consider relational aggression across samples:

> ... in a study of relational aggression (Crick & Grotpeter, 1995), the sample included schools from a largely working class town and comprised approximately 40 percent African-American children. In this study and others, we found that relational aggression is not unique to white, middle-class girls (or boys). These findings are consistent with work by Goodwin (1990, 1997), who has shown that African-American girls in a working-class neighborhood engage in "he said, she said" disputes that involve acts of relational aggression (Crick & Rose, 2000:165).

These observations, along with Anderson's reference of putting their "business in the streets" highlights the greater visibility of direct and indirect or relational aggression that an increased amount of time spent in public spaces imposes on economically disadvantaged youth (Stinchcombe, 1963). The implication is that even if disadvantaged youth engage in no more indirect aggression than others, they may be more publicly visible in doing so. These studies indicate how gendered forms of aggression may become visible and may overlap in disadvantaged neighborhoods.

Recent research with the community sample used in the National Longitudinal Survey of Children and Youth considered how the broader neighborhood context may affect *both* indirect and direct aggression (Foster, 2001; Foster et al., 2001: Tremblay et al., 2001). This study examined how subjective and objective features of the neighborhood context affect children's aggression levels.[8]

We used three level hierarchical linear models to examine individual, family, and neighborhood effects in our analyses of the NLSCY data on indirect and physical aggression. Similar to the research of Tremblay et al. (1996), we found that among four to eleven-year-olds, 47 percent of the variability in indirect aggression was between-families while an additional three percent is between census tracts. Fifty percent of the variability is between-individuals. Forty-two percent of the variability in physical aggression is between-families with five percent due to between-neighborhood differences. Among two to eleven-year-olds, 6 percent of the variance was explained by between-tract variability. These between-neighborhood intraclass correlations are within the range of those found for other behavioral outcomes of children and youth, where neighborhoods account for up to 10 percent of the variance (see Leventhal & Brooks-Gunn, 2000).

---

[8] The subjective measure assessed the person most knowledgeable about the child's (PMK's) perceptions of physical and social problem in the neighborhood. The objective measures used census tract and enumeration area characteristics (see Law & Willms, 1999) from the Canadian Census.

After examining both the main effects of the neighborhood and the models where familial factors were found to mediate the neighborhood effects, we found that the objective effects of neighborhoods tended to be explained by family factors. However, a robust finding regarding the subjective effects of neighborhood on *both* indirect and physical aggression held in all models, net of controls. We conclude from this research that living in neighborhoods perceived to have more social and physical problems is associated with higher levels of both indirect and physical aggression.

The need to assess the relative stressors of those in the family and those beyond the household, to see if broader contexts additionally matter and to better identify stressors in children's and adolescent's lives, and how community factors and parenting may combine, has recently been highlighted as a direction for further research (Menaghan, 1999:326–327). Our research indicates the prominence of family processes on both forms of aggression over neighborhood factors in explaining children's behavior problems (see also Brooks-Gunn et al., 1997a; Klebanov et al., 1997; Leventhal & Brooks-Gunn, 2000). Continued research with the longitudinal NLSCY would illuminate how these factors relatively affect aggression over time.

7. Consequences of Forms of Aggression for Aggressors and Victims

Some of the short and long-term implications of childhood aggression and victimization have been investigated (MacMillan, 2000; Sampson & Laub, 1995). Research on both physical and indirect aggression indicates problematic outcomes for child aggressors and victims (see Paquette & Underwood, 1999). While physical victimization has received the most research attention (but see Crick & Rose, 2000), the impact of indirect or relational aggression has also been found to be consequential both in terms of children's sociometric status (e.g., peer rejection) (Crick & Grotpeter, 1995:718,719; Crick, 1996, 1997; Crick & Bigbee, 1998:584; Rys & Bear, 1997:88; Tomada & Schneider, 1997; Werner & Crick, 1999) and social psychological outcomes, including depression (Crick et al., 1997:584), bulimic symptoms and antisocial and borderline personality features (Werner & Crick, 1999:620), and negative self-concept (Paquette & Underwood, 1999). Qualitative research has found that children report participating in relational aggression as they seek to avoid becoming targets themselves, and this behavior can create intimacy and inclusion among group members (see Owens et al., 2000:80). Recognition of the consequences of both physical and indirect forms of aggression may protect children's and adolescents' short and long-term well-being.

V. SUMMARY

We had three objectives in this chapter. The first was to define and differentiate types of childhood aggression. Second, we summarized a range of risk factors for aggression, emphasizing age and gender influences, and noted some points of inconsistency in current research. Finally, we suggested that quantitative research on the forms of aggression need to incorporate contextual neighborhood and family factors. We summarized some preliminary findings regarding family, peer, and neighborhood effects on both physical and indirect aggression from a major Canadian study. In keeping with the theme of this volume, we drew upon cross-cultural research where possible and noted the potential for both indirect and prior physical aggression to act as precursors to later more violent acts.

REFERENCES

Achenbach, Thomas M., Stephanie McConaughy, & Catherine T. Howell. (1987). Child/Adolescent Behavioral and Emotional Problems: Implications of Cross-Informant Correlations for Situational Specificity. *Psychological Bulletin, 101*, 213–232.

Anderson, Elijah. (1997). Violence and the Inner City Street Code. In Joan McCord (Ed.), *Violence and Childhood in the Inner City* (pp. 1–30). Cambridge: Cambridge University Press.

Aneshensel, Carol S., Carolyn M. Rutter, & Peter A. Lachenbruch. (1991). Social Structure, Stress, and Mental Health: Competing Conceptual and Analytic Models. *American Sociological Review, 56*, 166–178.

Avison, William R. (1999). Family Structure and Processes. In Allan V. Horwitz & Teresa L. Scheid (Eds.), *A Handbook for the Study of Mental Health: Social Contexts, Theories, and Systems* (pp. 228–240). Cambridge, U.K.: Cambridge University Press.

Baillargeon, Raymond, Richard E. Tremblay, & J. Douglas Willms. (1999). *The Prevalence of Physical Aggression in Canadian Children: A Multi-Group Latent Class Analysis of Data from the First Collection Cycle (1994–1995) of the NLSCY. Technical Document T-00-2E.* Ottawa, Ontario, Canada: Applied Research Branch, Strategic Policy, Human Resources Development Canada.

Bates, Frederick L., & Walter Gillis Peacock. (1989). Conceptualizing Social Structure: The Misuse of Classification in Structural Modeling. *American Sociological Review, 54*, 565–577.

Bjorkqvist, Kaj. (1994). Sex Differences in Physical, Verbal, and Indirect Aggression: A Review of Recent Research. *Sex Roles, 30*, 177–188.

Bjorkqvist, Kaj, Kirsti M. J. Lagerspetz, & Ari Kaukiainen. (1992). Do Girls Manipulate and Boys Fight? Developmental Trends in Regard to Direct and Indirect Aggression. *Aggressive Behavior, 18*, 117–127.

Bjorkqvist, Kaj, Karin Osterman, & Ari Kaukiainen. (1992). The Development of Direct and Indirect Aggressive Strategies in Males and Females. In Kaj Bjorkqvist & Pirkko Niemela (Eds.), *Of Mice and Women: Aspects of Female Aggression* (pp. 51–64). New York: Academic Press.

Boyle, Michael H., & Ellen L. Lipman. (1998). *Do Places Matter? A Multilevel Analysis of Geographic Variations in Child Behaviour in Canada. Working Paper W-98-16E.* Applied Research Branch, Strategic Policy, Human Resources Development Canada.

Brooks-Gunn, Jeanne, Greg. J. Duncan, & J. Lawrence Aber (Eds.) (1997a). *Neighborhood Poverty: Context and Consequences for Children. Volume I.* New York: Russell Sage Foundation.

Brooks-Gunn, Jeanne, Greg. J. Duncan, & J. Lawrence Aber (Eds.) (1997b). *Neighborhood Poverty: Context and Consequences for Children. Volume II.* New York: Russell Sage Foundation.

Buss, Arnold H. (1961). The Psychology of Aggression. New York: John Wiley and Sons.

Cairns, Robert B., Beverly D. Cairns, Holly J. Neckerman, Scott D. Gest, & Jean-Louis Gariepy. (1988). Social Networks and Aggressive Behavior: Peer Support or Peer Rejection. *Developmental Psychology, 24*, 815–823.

Cairns, Robert B., Beverly D. Cairns, Holly J. Neckerman, Lynda L. Ferguson, & Jen-Louis Gariepy. (1989). Growth and Aggression: 1. Childhood to Early Adolescence. *Developmental Psychology, 25*, 320–330.

Cairney, John. (1998). Gender Differences in the Prevalence of Depression among Canadian Adolescents. *Canadian Journal of Public Health, 89*, 181–182.

Caspi, Avshalom, Bradley R. Entner Wright, Terrie E. Moffitt, & Phil A. Silva. (1998). Early Failure in the Labor Market: Childhood and Adolescent Predictors of Unemployment in the Transition to Adulthood. *American Sociological Review, 63*, 424–451.

Chesney-Lind, Meda. (1998). *Girls, Delinquency, and Juvenile Justice, 2nd Edition.* New York: West/Wadsworth.

Coie, John D., & Kenneth A. Dodge. (1998). Aggression and Antisocial Behavior. In William Damon and Nancy Eisenberg (Eds.), *Handbook of Child Psychology. Volume 3. Social, Emotional, and Personality Development* (pp 779–862). New York: John Wiley & Sons.

Coleman, James S. (1988). Social Capital in the Creation of Human Capital. *American Journal of Sociology, 94*, 95–120.

Crick, Nicki R. (1996). The Role of Overt Aggression, Relational Aggression, and Prosocial Behavior in the Prediction of Children's Future Social Adjustment. *Child Development, 67*, 2317–2327.

Crick, Nicki R. (1997). Engagement in Gender Normative versus Non-Normative Forms of Aggression: Links to Social-Psychological Adjustment. *Developmental Psychology, 33*, 610–617.

Crick, Nicki R., & Maureen A. Bigbee. (1998). Relational and Overt Forms of Peer Victimization: A Multi-Informant Approach. *Journal of Consulting and Clinical Psychology, 66*, 337–347.

Crick, Nicki R., Maureen A. Bigbee, & Cynthia Howes. (1996). Gender Differences in Children's Normative Beliefs about Aggression: How Do I Hurt Thee? Let Me Count the Ways. *Child Development, 67*, 1003–1014.

Crick, Nicki R., Juan F. Casas, & Monique Mosher. (1997). Relational and Overt Aggression in Preschool. *Developmental Psychology, 33*, 579–588.

Crick, Nicki R., & Jennifer K. Grotpeter. (1995). Relational Aggression, Gender, and Social-Psychological Adjustment. *Child Development, 66*, 710–722.

Crick, Nicki R., & Amanda J. Rose. (2000). Toward a Gender-Balanced Approach to the Study of Social-Emotional Development: A Look at Relational Aggression. In Patricia H. Miller & Ellin Kofsky Scholnick (Eds.), *Toward a Feminist Developmental Psychology* (pp. 153–168). New York: Routledge.

Crick, Nicki R., David A. Nelson, Julie R. Morales, Crystal Cullerton-Sen, Juan F. Casas, & Susan E. Hickman. (2001). Relational Victimization in Childhood and Adolescence: I Hurt You Through the Grapevine. In Jaana Juvonen & Sandra Graham (Eds.), *Peer Harassment in School: The Plight of the Vulnerable and Victimized* (pp. 196–214). New York: The Guildford Press.

Cyranowski, Jill M., Elizabeth Young, & M. Katherine Shear. (2000). Adolescent Onset of the Gender Difference in Lifetime Rates of Major Depression: A Theoretical Model. *Archives of General Psychiatry, 57*, 21–27.

Downey, Geraldine, & James C. Coyne. (1990). Children of Depressed Parents: An Integrative Review. *Psychological Bulletin, 108*, 50–76.

Ellickson, Phyllis L., & Kimberly A. McGuigan. (2000). Early Predictors of Adolescent Violence. *American Journal of Public Health, 90*, 566–572.

Elliott, Delbert, John Hagan, & Joan McCord. (1998). *Youth Violence: Children at Risk*. Washington, D.C.: American Sociological Association.

Feshbach, Norma D. (1969). Sex Differences in Children's Models of Aggressive Responses toward Outsiders. *Merrill-Palmer Quarterly, 15*, 249–258.

Foster, Holly. (2001). *Neighborhood and Family Effects on Childhood Gendered Aggression*. Unpublished Ph.D. Dissertation. University of Toronto, Toronto, Ontario, Canada.

Foster, Holly, John Hagan, Richard E. Tremblay, & Bernard Boulerice. (2001). *Neighborhood and Family Contexts of Gendered Aggression among Children*. Unpublished Manuscript.

Galen, Britt Rachelle, & Marion K. Underwood. (1997). A Developmental Investigation of Social Aggression among Children. *Developmental Psychology, 33*, 589–600.

Garbarino, James, Nancy Dubrow, Kathleen Kostelny, & Carole Pardo. (1992). *Children in Danger: Coping with the Consequences of Community Violence*. San Francisco: Jossey-Bass.

Ge, Xiaojia, Rand D. Conger, Frederick O. Lorenz, Michael Shanahan, & Glen Elder. (1995). Mutual Influences in Parent and Adolescent Distress. *Developmental Psychology, 31*, 406–419.

Goodwin, M. H. (1990). *He Said, She Said: Talk as Social Organization Among Black Children*. Bloomington, Indiana: Indiana University Press.

Goodwin, Marjorie Harness (1997). Crafting Activities: Building Social Organization through Language in Girls' and Boys' Groups. In Charles T. Snowden & Martine Hausberger (Eds.), *Social Influences on Vocal Development* (pp. 328–341). Cambridge, UK: Cambridge University Press.

Grotpeter, Jennifer K., & Nicki R. Crick. (1998). *Relational Aggression, Physical Aggression, and Family Relationships*. Unpublished Manuscript, University of Minnesota, Twin Cities.

Hagan, John. (1994). *Crime and Disrepute*. Thousand Oaks, California: Pine Forge Press.

Hagan, John, Celesta Albonetti, Duan Alwin, A. R. Gillis, John Hewitt, Alberto Palloni, Patricia Parker, Ruth Peterson, & John Simpson. (1989). *Structural Criminology*. New Brunswick, NJ: Rutgers University Press.

Hagan, John, Ross MacMillan, & Blair Wheaton. (1996). New Kid in Town: Social Capital and the Life Course Effects of Family Migration on Children. *American Sociological Review, 61*, 368–385.

Heimer, Karen. (1995). Gender, Race, and the Pathways to Delinquency: An Interactionist Explanation. In John Hagan & Ruth D. Peterson (Eds.), *Crime and Inequality* (pp. 140–173). Stanford, California: Stanford University Press.

Heimer, Karen, & Stacy De Coster. (1999). The Gendering of Violent Delinquency. *Criminology, 37*, 277–312.

Herrenkohl, Todd I., Eugene Maguin, Karl G. Hill, J. David Hawkins, Robert D. Abbott, & Richard F. Catalano. (2000). Developmental Risk Factors for Youth Violence. *Journal of Adolescent Health, 26*, 176–186.

Hill, Jonathan, & Barbara Maughan. (2001). *Conduct Disorders in Childhood and Adolescence*. Cambridge, UK: Cambridge University Press.

Human Resources Development Canada and Statistics Canada. (1995). *National Longitudinal Survey of Children. Overview of Survey Instruments for 1994–1995 Data Collection, Cycle 1. NLSC Project team. What Works for Children-Information Development Program*. Ottawa, Canada: The Team.

Joyner, Jason. (2000). *What Happened to Gender in Studies of Neighborhood Effects? Theorizing Gender within and across Local Communities*. Paper Abstract from Southern Sociological Association Meetings retrieved from Sociological Abstracts, Silver Platter Data Bases.

Kandel, Denise B., & Ping Wu. (1995). Disentangling Mother-Child Effects in the Development of Antisocial Behavior. In Joan McCord (Ed.), *Coercion and Punishment in Long-Term Perspectives* (pp. 106–123). Cambridge, UK: Cambridge University Press.

Klebanov, Pamela K., Jeanne Brooks-Gunn, P. Lindsay Chase-Lansdale, & Rachel A. Gordon. (1997). Are Neighborhood Effects on Young Children Mediated by the Home Environment? In Jeanne Brooks-Gunn, Greg J. Duncan & J. Lawrence Aber (Eds.), *Neighborhood Poverty: Volume I. Context and Consequences for Children* (pp. 119–145). New York: Russell Sage Foundation.

Kokko, Katja, & Lea Pulkkinen. (2000). Aggression in Childhood and Long-Term Unemployment in Adulthood: A Cycle of Maladaptation and Some Protective Factors. *Developmental Psychology, 36*, 463–472.

Kupersmidt, Janis B., Pamela C. Griesler, Melissa E. DeRosier, Charlotte J. Patterson, Paul W. Davis. (1995). Childhood Aggression and Peer Relations in the Context of Family and Neighborhood Factors. *Child Development, 66*, 360–375.

Lagerspetz, Kirsti M. J., Kaj Bjorkqvist, & Tarja Peltonen. (1988). Is Indirect Aggression Typical of Females? Gender Differences in Aggressiveness in 11–12 Year-Old Children. *Aggressive Behavior, 14*, 403–414.

Lagerspetz, Kirsti M. J., & Kaj Bjorkqvist. (1994). Indirect Aggression in Boys and Girls. In L. Rowell Huesmann (Ed.), *Aggressive Behavior: Current Perspectives* (pp. 131–150). New York: Plenum Press.

Law, Jane, & J. Douglas Willms. (1998). Applied Research Branch Technical Paper Series [T-98-4]. Ottawa, Ontario. Applied Research Branch, Human Resources Development Canada, and forthcoming publication: A Clustering of Enumeration Areas Based on Socioeconomic Status, Chapter 4. In J. Douglas Willms (Ed.), *Vulnerable Children: Findings From Canada's Longitudinal Study of Children and Youth*.

Leventhal, Tama, & Jeanne Brooks-Gunn. (2000). The Neighborhoods They Live In: The Effects of Neighborhood Residence on Child and Adolescent Outcomes. *Psychological Bulletin, 126*, 309–337.

Levine, Felice J., & Katherine J. Rosich. (1996). *Social Causes of Violence: Crafting a Science Agenda*. Washington, DC: American Sociological Association.

Little, Todd, Stephanie M. Jones, Christopher C. Henrich, & Patricia H. Hawley. (2000). *Toward a Unified Model of Aggression: Integrating Form and Function*. Paper presented at the Society for Research on Adolescence, Chicago, Illinois.

Loeber, Rolf, & Dale Hay. (1997). Key Issues in the Development of Aggression and Violence from Childhood to Early Adulthood. *Annual Review of Psychology, 48*, 371–410.

Loeber, Rolf, & Magda Stouthamer-Loeber. (1986). Family Factors as Correlates and Predictors of Juvenile Conduct Problems and Delinquency. In Michael Tonry & Norval Morris (Eds.), *Crime and Justice: An Annual Review of Research, Vol. 7* (pp. 129–149). Chicago: University of Chicago Press.

Loeber, Rolf, & Magda Stouthamer-Loeber. (1998). Development of Juvenile Aggression and Violence: Some Common Misconceptions and Controversies. *American Psychologist, 53*, 242–259.

Maccoby, Eleanor E., & John A. Martin. (1983). Socialization in the Context of the Family: Parent-Child Interaction. In E. Mavis Hetherington (Ed.), *Handbook of Child Psychology, Volume 4: Socialization, Personality, and Social Development* (pp. 1–101). New York: Wiley.

MacMillan, Ross. (2000). Adolescent Victimization and Income Deficits in Adulthood: Rethinking the Costs of Criminal Violence from a Life-Course Perspective. *Criminology, 38*, 553–588.

Marcus-Newhall, Amy, William C. Pederson, Mike Carlson, & Norman Miller. (2000). Displaced Aggression is Alive and Well: A Meta-Analytic Review. *Journal of Personality and Social Psychology, 78*, 670–689.

Margolin, Gayla, & Elana B. Gordis. (2000). The Effects of Family and Community Violence on Children. *Annual Review of Psychology, 51*, 445–479.

McCarthy, Bill, John Hagan, & Todd S. Woodward. (1999). In the Company of Women: Structure and Agency in a Revised Power-Control Theory of Gender and Delinquency. *Criminology, 37*, 761–788.

McLeod, Jane D., Candace Kruttschnitt, & Maude Dornfeld. (1994). Does Parenting Explain the Effects of Structural Conditions on Children's Antisocial Behavior? A Comparison of Blacks and Whites. *Social Forces, 73*, 575–604.

Menaghan, Elizabeth G. (1999). Social Stressors in Childhood and Adolescence. In Allan V. Horwitz & Teresa L. Scheid (Eds.), *A Handbook for the Study of Mental Health: Social Contexts, Theories, and Systems* (pp. 315–327). Cambridge, U.K.: Cambridge University Press.

Merton, Robert K. (1938). Social Structure and Anomie. *American Sociological Review, 3*, 672–682.

Mirowsky, John, & Catherine Ross. (1995). Sex Differences in Distress: Real or Artifact? *American Sociological Review, 60*, 449–468.

Morales, J. R., Crick, N. R., Werner, N. E., & H. Schellin. (2000). *Adolescents' Normative Beliefs about Aggression: A Qualitative Analysis*. Manuscript Forthcoming.

Nagin, Daniel S., Greg Pogarsky, & David P. Farrington. (1997). Adolescent Mothers and the Criminal Behavior of Their Children. *Law and Society Review, 31*, 137–162.

Nagin, Daniel, & Richard E. Tremblay. (1999). Trajectories of Boys' Physical Aggression, Opposition, and Hyperactivity on the Path to Physically Violent and Nonviolent Juvenile Delinquency. *Child Development, 70*, 1181–1196.

Osterman, Karin, Kaj Bjorkqvist, Kirsti M. J. Lagerspetz, Ari Kaukianinen, Simha F. Landau, Adam Froaczek, & Caprara Gian Vittorio. (1998). Cross-Cultural Evidence of Female Indirect Aggression. *Aggressive Behavior, 24*, 1–8.

Owens, Laurence, Rosalyn Shute, & Philip Slee. (2000). 'Guess What I Just Heard!': Indirect Aggression among Teenage Girls in Australia. *Aggressive Behavior, 26*, 67–83.

Paquette, Julie A., & Marion K. Underwood. (1999). Gender Differences in Young Adolescents' Experiences of Peer Victimization: Social and Physical Aggression. *Merrill-Palmer Quarterly, 45*, 242–266.

Parke, Ross D., & Slaby, Ronald G. (1983). The Development of Aggression. In Paul Henry Mussen (Ed.), *Handbook of Child Psychology, 4th Edition* (pp. 547–642). New York, NY: Wiley.

Patillo-McCoy, Mary. (1999). *Black Picket Fences: Privilege and Peril among the Black Middle Class*. Chicago, Illinois: The University of Chicago Press.

Pearlin, Leonard I. (1989). The Sociological Study of Stress. *Journal of Health and Social Behavior, 30*, 241–256.

Pepler, Debra J., & Farrokh Sedighdeilami. (1998). *Aggressive Girls in Canada. Working Paper W-98-30E*. Ottawa, Ontario: Applied Research Branch, Strategic Policy, Human Resources Development Canada.

Portes, Alejandro. (1998). Social Capital: Its Origins and Applications in Modern Sociology. *Annual Review of Sociology, 24*, 1–24.

Poulin, Francois, & Michel Boivin. (2000). The Role of Proactive and Reactive Aggression in the Formation and Development of Boys' Friendships. *Developmental Psychology, 36*, 233–240.

Richardson, Deborah R., & Laura R. Green. (1997). Circuitous Harm: Determinants and Consequences of Nondirect Aggression. In Robin M. Kowalski (Ed.), *Aversive Interpersonal Relationships* (pp. 171–188). New York: Plenum Press.

Richardson, Deborah R., & Laura R. Green. (1999). Social Sanction and Threat Explanations of Gender Effects on Direct and Indirect Aggression. *Aggressive Behavior, 25*, 425–434.

Ridgeway, Cecilia L., & Lynn Smith-Lovin. (1999). The Gender System and Interaction. *Annual Review of Sociology, 25*, 191–216.

Risman, Barbara J. (1998). *Gender Vertigo: American Families in Transition*. New Haven: Yale University Press.

Rosenfield, Sarah. (1999). Gender and Mental Health: Do Women Have More Psychopathology, Men More, or Both the Same (and Why)? In Allan V. Horwitz & Teresa L. Scheid (Eds.), *A Handbook for the Study of Mental Health: Social Contexts, Theories, and Systems* (pp. 348–360). Cambridge, U.K.: Cambridge University Press.

Rutter, Michael, Henri Giller, & Ann Hagell. (1998). *Antisocial Behavior by Young People*. Cambridge: Cambridge University Press.

Rys, Gail S., & George G. Bear. (1997). Relational Aggression and Peer Relations: Gender and Developmental Issues. *Merrill-Palmer Quarterly, 43*, 87–106.

Sampson, Robert J. (1992). Family Management and Child Development: Insights from Social Disorganization Theory. In Joan McCord (Ed.), *Facts, Frameworks, and Forecasts: Advances in Criminological Theory*. New Brunswick: Transaction Publishers(pp. 63–93).

Sampson, Robert J. (1997). The Embeddedness of Child and Adolescent Development: A Community-Level Perspective on Urban Violence. In Joan McCord (Ed.), *Violence and Childhood in the Inner-City* (pp. 31–77). Cambridge: Cambridge University Press.

Sampson, Robert J., & John H. Laub. [1993] (1995). *Crime in the Making: Pathways and Turning Points through Life*. Cambridge, Massachusettes: Harvard University Press.

Sampson, Robert J., & John H. Laub. (1994). Urban Poverty and the Family Context of Delinquency: A New Look at Structure and Process in a Classic Study. *Child Development, 65*, 523–540.

Serbin, Lisa A., Patricia L. Peters, Valerie J. McAffer, & Alex E. Schwartzman. (1991). Childhood Aggression and Withdrawal as Predictors of Adolescent Pregnancy, Early Parenthood, and Environmental Risk for the Next Generation. *Canadian Journal of Behavioral Science, 23*, 318–331.

Sims Blackwell, Brenda. (2000). Perceived Sanction Threats, Gender, and Crime: A Test and Elaboration of Power-Control Theory. *Criminology, 38*, 439–488.

Smith-Lovin, Lynn, & J. Miller McPherson. (1993). *You Are Who You Know: A Network Approach to Gender. In Paula England, Theory on Gender/Feminism on Theory* (pp. 223–251). New York: Aldine DeGruyter.

Sprott, Jane E., & Anthony N. Doob. (1998). *Who are the Most Violent Ten and Eleven Year Olds? An Introduction to Future Delinquency. Working Paper W-98-29E.* Ottawa, Ontario, Canada: Applied Research Branch, Human Resources Development Canada.

Stinchcombe, Arthur. (1963). Institutions of Privacy in the Determination of Police Administration Practices. *American Journal of Sociology, 69,* 150–160.

Sumrall, Shannon G., Glen E. Ray, & Pamela S. Tidwell. (2000). Evaluations of Relational Aggression as Function of Relationship Type and Conflict Setting. *Aggressive Behavior, 26,* 179–191.

Suttles, Gerald. (1968). *The Social Order of the Slum: Ethnicity and Territory in the Inner City.* Chicago: University of Chicago Press.

Taylor, Jill McLean, Carol Gilligan, & Amy M. Sullivan. (1995). *Between Voice and Silence: Women and Girls, Race and Relationship.* Cambridge, Massachusetts: Harvard University Press.

Tomada, Giovanna, & Barry H. Schneider. (1997). Relational Aggression, Gender, and Peer Acceptance: Invariance across Culture, Stability over Time, and Concordance among Informants. *Developmental Psychology, 33,* 601–609.

Tremblay, Richard E., Bernard Boulerice, Holly Foster, Elisa Romano, John Hagan, & Raymond Swisher. (2001). *Neighborhood, Family, and Individual Effects on Children's Behaviour Problems in the First Cycle of the NLSCY. Report Submitted to the Canadian Ministry of Human Resources Development Canada.* Ottawa, Ontario, Canada.

Tremblay, Richard E. (1991). Aggression, Prosocial Behavior, and Gender: Three Magic Words But No Magic Wand. In Debra J. Pepler & Kenneth H. Rubin (Eds.), *The Development and Treatment of Childhood Aggression* (pp. 71–78). New Jersey: Lawrence Erlbaum Associates.

Tremblay, Richard E. (1999). When Children's Social Development Fails In Daniel P. Keating & Clyde Hertzman (Eds.), *Developmental Health and the Wealth of Nations: Social, Biological, and Educational Dynamics* (pp. 55–71). New York: The Guilford Press.

Tremblay, Richard E., Bernard Boulerice, Philip W. Harden, Pierre McDuff, Daniel Perusse, Robert O. Pihl, & Mark Zoccolillo. (1996). *Do Children Become More Aggressive as They Approach Adolescence? In Human Resources Development Canada and Statistics Canada, Growing Up in Canada: National Longitudinal Survey of Children and Youth. No. 1* (pp. 127–137). Ottawa, Ontario: Statistics Canada.

Wade, Terrance J., David J. Pevalin, & Augustine Brannigan. (1999). The Clustering of Severe Behavioural, Health and Educational Deficits in Canadian Children: Preliminary Evidence from the National Longitudinal Survey of Children and Youth. *Canadian Journal of Public Health, 90,* 253–259.

Walker, Samantha, Deborah S. Richardson, & Laura R. Green. (2000). Aggression among Older Adults: The Relationship of Interaction Networks and Gender Role to Direct and Indirect Aggression. *Aggressive Behavior, 26,* 145–154.

Wellman, Barry, & Stephen D. Berkowitz. (1988). *Social Structures: A Network Approach.* Cambridge, UK: Cambridge University Press.

Werner, Nicole E., & Nicki R. Crick. (1999). Relational Aggression and Social-Psychological Adjustment in a College Sample. *Journal of Abnormal Psychology, 108,* 615–623.

Wilson, William Julius. (1987). *The Truly Disadvantaged: The Inner City, The Underclass, and Public Policy.* Chicago, IL: University of Chicago Press.

Xie, Hongling, Dylan J. Swift, Beverley D. Cairns, & Robert B. Cairns. (2000). *Aggressive Behaviors in Social Interaction: A Narrative Analysis in Interpersonal Conflicts. Paper presented at the Society for Research in Adolescence.* Chicago, Illinois.

PART II-3-2

EVOLUTIONARY AND SOCIAL BIOLOGICAL APPROACHES

CHAPTER II-3-2.1

Evolutionary Psychology of Lethal Interpersonal Violence

Martin Daly and Margo Wilson

I. INTRODUCTION

The evolutionary psychological approach to the study of human violence is a quest to understand and predict who is likely to use violence against whom, and under what circumstances, in the light of a very general theoretical understanding of the evolutionary processes that gave form to the human psyche and the behavior that it produces. Such an approach requires a dispassionate perspective in the sense that we cannot prejudge the violence in which we are interested as pathology. It may often be so, in which case an appropriate remedial response might be therapeutic, but violence may often be better understood as the adaptive output of a healthy psyche functioning normally, in which case an appropriate remedial response must address the social and material circumstances conducive to the violence.

The very distastefulness of violence often obstructs objective analysis by inspiring value judgments that masquerade as theories and explanations. Readiness to resort to violence, for example, is regularly interpreted as "primitive" or "immature." However, there is no empirical support for the notion that violence is especially characteristic of "primitive" entities and is reduced or absent in more "advanced" forms, whether these be cultures, species, or anything else. Thus, the "primitive" label is really just a facile disparagement. Similarly, the characterization of violent action as "immature" will not bear scrutiny either. In human beings, as in most familiar creatures, violence is predominantly a recourse of fully adult individuals, not juveniles, and there is no evidence that violent people or other creatures are the products of some sort of developmental arrest.

The manifest inadequacy of such pseudo-explanations has led many scientists to shy away from general theories and to study single influences in isolation. Why do people commit violent acts? Because violent people were themselves abused in childhood. Be-

W. Heitmeyer and J. Hagan (eds.), *International Handbook of Violence Research*, 569–588.
© 2003 Kluwer Academic Publishers. Printed in the Netherlands.

cause of envy and resentment engendered by social inequities. Because the penalties are not severe enough. Because of brain tumors, hormone imbalances, and alcohol-induced psychoses. Because of the violence on television. All these answers are plausible and lead to testable hypotheses. Each addresses one small part of what we want to know when we ask "Why does violence occur?" However, there is a need for a more encompassing perspective that will account for violent acts and the specific influences of these and other factors within the framework of *a well-founded general theory of human nature*. We believe that the only viable candidate for such a theory is a Darwinian one.

II.   THEORETICAL APPROACH

1.   The Adaptationist Paradigm

Unfortunately, the phrase "human nature" has a rather negative, "bestial" connotation, and that connotation is especially likely to be invoked and even exacerbated in the present context. Textbooks of psychology commonly refer to "biology," evolution, and "human nature" primarily or solely with reference to aggression and violence. But when we and other evolutionary psychologists invoke this term, we mean it to encompass prosocial as well as antisocial adaptations, as well as basic constructs of cognition, perception, and so forth. In other words, "human nature" refers to the shared aspects (those that are neither local nor idiosyncratic) of humankind. Our reason for using the term here is to highlight the fact that all normal human beings share a very large "toolkit" of cognitive, motivational, and emotional equipment, which assumed its contemporary forms over evolutionary time because of its utility. The concept of human nature gains specific meaning only by implicit or explicit comparison to alternative natures, whether those of real animals with alternative adaptive specializations or natures that are only imagined. This essentialist construct does not imply an absence of variation among individuals within a species, but it does raise questions about the sources of species differences and the functional interrelatedness of each species' peculiar set of attributes.

If there is a general theory that has the conceptual tools to explain and predict hitherto unknown aspects of human nature (or elephant nature or mosquito nature), it is surely Darwin's theory of evolution by natural selection. Darwin proposed that random, potentially heritable, variants constantly arise within populations, and that by an ensuing process of nonrandom differential survival and proliferation, some of these novelties persist while their alternatives perish. The cumulative consequence is that organisms become complexly constructed with attributes that work together to suit their purposes. The approach that begins with a presumption that complex structures are "well designed" to achieve the organism's purposes, and that we can therefore "reverse engineer" a newly discovered organ in order to discover its utility and to predict hitherto unobserved aspects of how it functions, has come to be called "adaptationism."

The adaptationist stance avoids being trivial or tautological (i.e., avoids saying nothing more than that which is adaptive survives and that which survives is adaptive) in two ways. The first is by inspiring specific testable hypotheses concerning the match between a putative adaptation's design specifications and the functional demands of a problem posed by the creature's environment. If an adaptationist paleontologist finds a fossil jaw full of molars, for example, she may infer that grindable foods, rather than meat or plankton, dominated the diet of the extinct creature, but the matter doesn't end there. This interpretation warrants further expectations about the articulation of the teeth, the muscle attachments of the jaw, the plants in the local habitat, the design of the intestine, and, in the human case, the cultural artifacts of food production, all of which are subject to tests that might force a revision of the original interpretation. In this process of hypothesis testing, many other aspects of the organism and its environment are discovered.

The second way in which the adaptationist approach avoids triviality is by being *selectionist* as well. Adaptive function cannot be imputed, willy-nilly, to anything one happens to like or admire. Every functional component of human nature or the nature of any other organism assumed its modern form because it contributed to ancestral "fitness," that is, to the relative replicative success of alleles conducive to its development. Attributes that allow individuals to reproduce at higher rates than their same-sex, same-species rivals proliferate and become universal aspects of each species' nature. Attributes that contribute to happiness, homeostasis, ecosystem stability, beauty, or the common weal, do *not* proliferate and become universal aspects of any species' nature *unless* they also happen to promote their own fitness relative to alternative attributes.

There is every reason to suppose that psychological attributes are just as amenable to this analytical adaptationist approach as morphological attributes like teeth. It may not be obvious what the purpose of some psychological structure or process might be, but scientific progress in understanding has generally followed from assuming that the entity under consideration accomplishes something for its possessor. If it does not, then the entity in question has been wrongly described (e.g., Freud's fantastic construct of *thanatos*), or is a functionless by-product of an adaptation (e.g., male nipples), or is a pathology, that is, a failure of adaptive functioning (e.g., a cancer).

What an adaptationist and selectionist approach suggests is that behavior and the mental processes subserving it have been designed to expend the organism's very life in the pursuit of genetic posterity. However, genetic posterity is not a psychological goal. Rather, the organism's immediate goals are end states such as a full belly, safety from predators, warmth, self-esteem, happiness, and respect. Genetic posterity has been the consequence by which the mechanisms serving these goals and end states have been shaped over evolutionary time. It is a widespread misapprehension that the evolutionary approach, with its emphasis on the proliferation of those genes that are conducive to the development of adaptations, is excessively "deterministic." This accusation is naive, for if "determinism" is indeed a problem, then it is equally a problem in all scientific approaches from biochemistry to sociology. All scientists are committed to the belief that the phenomena they study have knowable causes, and strive to reduce the amount of unexplained variance. But although determinism is not what separates evolutionary psychology from other social sciences, there are genuine disagreements. Those who derive explicit inspiration from Darwinism usually expect the evolved mechanisms of the human mind to be numerous and specialized, while most social theorists seem to believe that the complexity of human thought and action can be accounted for by a relatively small number of processes or mechanisms, such as "learning," that are somehow both sophisticated and extremely general in their domains of action or purposes. Other evolutionary psychologists (e.g., Tooby & Cosmides, 1992; Pinker, 1997) have argued in detail that this view is inadequate to account for the diversity, specificity and complexity of human (and nonhuman) minds, and we will not rehearse those arguments here. Suffice to say that the proposition that the elements of human nature *must* include a mental tool kit that is at least as complex and specialized as our biochemical and anatomical equipment is reinforced almost daily by discoveries in the fields of artificial intelligence and neuroscience.

Adaptationist hypotheses are primarily claims about the functional organization of a putative adaptation with respect to its competence and efficiency in serving its hypothesized purposes. The prototype of adaptationist understanding is the analysis of the functional complexity of the vertebrate eye, the components of which play clear and distinct roles in the business of seeing, while the diversity of design features among species reflects the differential requirements for visual processing of particular significant things in particular ecological conditions. What adaptationist hypotheses are *not* is hypotheses about the existence of "genes for" the phenomenon of interest, since to say that a trait has such genetic determination is to say that it has variants in different individuals as a result of their different genotypes. Such genetic (heritable) variability is decidedly not a hallmark of adaptation, since Darwinian selection tends generally to eliminate heritable variation, and the genetic architecture underlying the ontogeny of adaptations is usually species-typical (i.e., universal across individuals). Thus, heritable variation ("genetic determination") is usually best interpreted as *prima facie* evidence that the attribute under consideration is not an adaptation, and is irrelevant to proper functioning. The eye can again be used to illustrate the point. Whereas the dimensions of an eye, its pigment chemistry, and so forth are all constrained to remain within narrow bounds if the eye is to work properly, the color of the iris is functionally irrelevant, and it is precisely *because* this variability is *not* an adaptation that it is able to remain highly heritable in populations with genes "for" eye color. We mention all this because many authors have mistakenly supposed that an evolutionary adaptationist hypothesis predicts that there will be substantial heritability of the trait in question (perhaps because the argument invokes genes "for" the putative adaptation). Sometimes, adaptationist hypotheses are even indignantly dismissed on the grounds that relevant genes have not been identified. This objection is predicated on a misunderstanding of adaptationism.

Darwin's solution to the problem of explaining the diversity of life forms transformed biology, which is (according to one dictionary) "the science of life and life processes" (Morris, 1976). This definition highlights the fact that the social sciences are, inescapably, branches of biology, and we quote it in a spirit not of interdisciplinary imperialism, but of interdisciplinary synthesis. The domains and discoveries of the social sciences can and will be integrated with insights from the more mechanistic disciplines that are sometimes referred to as "behavioral biology," and we believe that the integration can best be achieved under the umbrella of a functional understanding of "mind design." Consider the following facts: Circulating blood levels of the male gonadal hormone testosterone have a variety of subtle effects on information processing and behavior, both by virtue of action in the central nervous system itself and by virtue of other peripheral effects, but testosterone levels are themselves affected by social experience and these effects are themselves affected by culturally specific considerations. A man's perception that he has won in some sort of competition, for example, can lead to a rapid elevation of plasma testosterone even if the competition is as arbitrary as a coin toss (McCaul, Gladue, & Joppa, 1992) or as cerebral as a chess game (Mazur, Booth, & Dabbs, 1992); in another experimental study, an insult that engendered a surge of testosterone in men who had been raised in the "honor" culture of the southern United States, where retaliatory aggression is admired, had no such influence in men raised in the North, where it is not (Nisbett & Cohen, 1996). These kinds of findings indicate that psychophysiological adaptations may often be best characterized in terms of contingent responsiveness not only to immediate circumstances or stimuli, but also to the cumulative consequences of experience, including the assimilation and internalization of local cultural norms. Clearly, this contingent responsiveness, both developmental and situational, is subtle and functional, and there is no alternative to the conclusion that it represents adaptations, which evolved to promote the actors' fitness in a complex, variable, social world.

2.   An Adaptationist Perspective on Interpersonal Violence

Social science theories about violence have been overwhelmingly (and appropriately) framed in sociological terms. In a sense, these approaches stand in relation to psychology as psychology does to evolutionary biology. Sociological theories always entail assumptions or postulates about human desires, developmental susceptibilities, social inferences, and so forth. In other words, they rest on implicit models of human psychology, which must be made explicit if their consistency with what psychological science has discovered is to be evaluated. Similarly, psychological theories always entail implicit models of the functional organization of the brain/mind, and psychologists have entered and lingered in many a cul-de-sac because they did not make these models explicit and consider whether they could be reconciled with Darwinian understandings of the selective process that creates all such functional organization (Daly & Wilson, 1997).

A particularly common presumption in social (and some psychological) theories is that the functional significance of the behavior of individuals resides in the pursuit of collective goals. An evolutionary perspective suggests that this presumption needs scrutiny. Darwinian selection does not, in general, produce creatures with attributes tailored to promote the common weal. How could it, when selection itself is overwhelmingly a matter of the differential survival and reproduction of variants within a local population or a species? Individual organisms and their constituent parts have evolved to do many specific things, but collectivities above the level of the individual organism are not, in general, specifically organized to accomplish anything in particular (Williams, 1966). Some uniquely human organizations, such as political parties and clubs, are specifically formed to advance collective goals, and are conspicuous exceptions to this generalization. But most human collectivities, such as a class or subcultures or one gender or "the patriarchy" or "society" are not exceptions, and it is a mistake to imagine either that individuals act on behalf of such entities or that such large and amorphous social entities can be said to have desires or preferences or pathologies. The metaphorical attribution of these individual-level attributes to group-level entities whose unity of purpose does not approach that of individual organisms is ubiquitous, but it virtually guarantees that their causal dynamics will be misrepresented. When one speaks of "society's" influence or wishes or intentions, for example, one obscures the complexity of social processes and the ubiquity of conflicts of interest. This is not to say that groups *qua* groups have no properties worth talking about. But group-level properties are emergent and distinct from those of their constituent individuals. More specifically, group-level properties emerge from interactions among individuals with distinct and partially conflicting purposes. A society or polity or occupational group or class does not have preferences or intentions or pathologies. It has institutions, balances of power, a greater or lesser degree of consensus on each issue, and a certain distribution of wealth, among other things.

Our own research on violence has mainly focused on homicide, testing hypotheses about the social and circumstantial factors that might be expected to exacerbate or mitigate the conflicts characteristic of certain relationships and hence to elevate or reduce the risk of murder. The relevant evolutionary psychological theories, which we will illustrate below, concern the prototypical attributes of certain relationships (marital partners, parent-offspring, unrelated same-sex acquaintances, etc.), and the responses of prototypical men and women to their immediate and chronic social and material situations. We argue that certain patterns in the incidence of violence are predictable consequences of psychological processes which have been designed by the evolutionary process of Darwinian selection to make individuals effective competitors and effective nepotists, and that this perspective sheds light on the roles of certain demographic and situational variables that criminologists already consider important, as well as pointing to the likely relevance of some previously neglected risk factors. The tests reside in demographic risk patterns. For example, lethal violence between unrelated men varies as a function of the protagonists' marital and employment status, life expectancy, and economic prospects, in ways that bespeak modulation of competitiveness and risk proneness (e.g., Daly & Wilson, 1988a, 1990, 1993, 1997; Daly et al., 2001; Wilson & Daly, 1985, 1997).

Homicides are drastic resolutions of severe interpersonal conflicts, and any theory of the nature of human conflict ought to shed some light on who is likely to kill whom, why, and under what circumstances. Although relatively rare and extreme in comparison to nonlethal violence, homicides are exceptional materials for testing hypotheses about interpersonal conflict. They almost certainly have less reporting bias than the records of any lesser manifestation of conflict, and because homicides are taken so seriously, the information reported by police and government agencies is usually accurate. In taking an adaptationist (evolutionary psychological) approach, we need not (and do not) assume that homicide is itself the adaptation. It may or may not be the case that actual killing was a regular component of the selective events that shaped the human passions underlying homicide cases, but in either case, adaptation is more appropriately sought at a more psychological level. Suppose, for example, that selection has favored those sexually jealous men who so effectively intimidated their rivals and bullied their wives as to guarantee their paternity of their putative offspring. We might therefore expect to find that male sexual jealousy is a prevalent motive in interpersonal violence, including homicide, which is true (e.g., Bresse, 1989; Polk, 1994; Guttmacher, 1955; Chimbos, 1978, 1993; Dobash & Dobash, 1979, 1998; Daly & Wilson, 1988a; Daly, Wilson & Weghorst, 1982; Wilson & Daly, 1993a, 1993b, 1998a, 1998b; Crawford & Gartner, 1992), and we might go on to predict certain variations in the intensity of jealousy, and hence in rates of such homicides, as a function of circumstances, societal differences, and demographic variables (Wilson & Daly, 1993a, 1996; Daly & Wilson, 2001). This sort of analysis does not presuppose that sexual jealousy *homicides* enhance their perpetrators' fitness or ever did so. It is instead quite likely that killing is the dysfunctional tail of a distribution of responses, that is, a counterproductive overreaction. But what the analysis *does* presuppose in this case is that some lesser manifestation of the same motives—sexual jealousy with an attendant sincere threat of violence perhaps — did indeed promote the reproductive success of our male ancestors, and that jealousy has evolved to be circumstantially contingent in ways that once enhanced its effectiveness in promoting the jealous parties' fitness (Wilson & Daly, 1992).

III.   EMPIRICAL RESULTS

1.   Economic Inequity and Violence

"Competition" refers to a conflict of interests in which one party's possession or use of a mutually desired resource precludes another party's possession or use of the same (Daly & Wilson, 1988a; Enquist & Leimar, 1990; Enquist et al., 1990; Colegrave, 1994; Clutton-Brock & Parker, 1995; Machalek, 1995; Cohen & Machalek, 1988; Vila, 1994). Robbery homicides are unequivocal instances, as are many "sexual triangle" homicides. More subtle examples are the "face" and "status" disputes that constitute a very large proportion (perhaps the majority) of all U.S. homicides; the social resources contested in these cases are limited means to the end of more tangible resources (Wilson & Daly, 1985). Not all conflicts are competitive, however. If a woman spurns one suitor for another, for example, then she and the spurnee have a conflict of interests, but they are not competitors, whereas the male rivals are. In general, competition is predominantly a same-sex affair because same-sex individuals are usually more similar in the resources they desire than opposite-sex individuals.

When rewards are inequitably distributed and those at the bottom of the resource distribution feel they have little to lose by engaging in reckless or dangerous behavior, escalated tactics of social competition, including violent tactics, become attractive. When the perceived perquisites of competitive success are smaller, and even those at the bottom have something to lose, such tactics lose their appeal. If inequity and the perception thereof indeed provoke escalated tactics of social competition and hence homicide, one might expect a positive correlation between indices of income inequality and homicide rates. This has been documented for comparisons among nations (Krahn, Hartnagel, & Gartrell, 1986; Hsieh & Pugh, 1993) and within a nation such as the United States. Kennedy, Kawachi and Prothrow-Stich (1996) found that the Gini index of income inequity was significantly correlated with many components of mortality across the 50 United States in 1990, but with none more highly than homicide. Blau and Blau (1982) found that income inequality accounted for more of the variance in homicide rates among 125 U.S. cities than other measures including percent below the poverty line. Wilson and Daly (1997) analyzed data at a still finer level, comparing across 77 Chicago neighborhoods, and found a bivariate correlation of $r = .75$ between an income inequality measure and the homicide rate.

Despite this evidence, the proposition that inequity *per se* is relevant has remained somewhat controversial, largely because of the colinearity among predictors. In an early study of income inequality's effects on property crime, Jacobs (1981:14) asserted that regardless of whether one is analyzing across nations, states, or cities, the correlation between measures of inequality and measures of average prosperity is "always negative, which implies that the poorer the area, the more one can expect unequal income distributions." In the 50-state U.S. data set analyzed by Kennedy et al. (1996), for example, the correlation between Gini and median household income was $r = -.57$ ($p < .001$). Noting that this tendency for low average income and high income inequality to go hand in hand challenges the conclusion that inequity itself is critical, Daly, Wilson and Vasdev (2000) sought a suitable test case in which average income and income inequality were positively associated, and found such a case in comparisons among Canadian provinces. If inequity is the more consequential predictor of homicide rates, then variations in homicide rates between provinces should be correlated with inequity and not with poverty (Daly, Wilson,

& Vasdev, 2000). Income inequality as indexed by the Gini coefficient is a strong and significant predictor of provincial homicide rates ($r = .85$, $p < .01$) and remains so when the impact of median household income is statistically removed (partial $r = .82$, $p < .01$). Median household income is positively related to the homicide rate ($r = .39$), but not significantly so ($p = .27$), and the association is negligible when the impact of Gini is statistically controlled (partial $r = -.09$, $p = .81$). Figure II-3-2-1.1 shows the relationship between homicide rates and Gini coefficient for the 50 United States and the 10 provinces of Canada.

2.   Discounting the Future

Psychologists, economists, and criminologists have found that young adults, the poor, and criminal offenders all tend to discount the future relatively steeply (Gottfredson & Hirschi, 1990; Green, Fry, & Myerson, 1994; Lawrance, 1991; Loewenstein & Elster, 1992; Wilson & Herrnstein, 1985). Such tendencies have been called "impulsivity" and "short time horizons," or, more pejoratively, impatience, myopia, lack of self-control, and incapacity to delay gratification. Behind the use of such terms lies a presumption that steep discounting is dysfunctional and that the appropriate weighting of present rewards against future investments is independent of life stage and socioeconomic circumstance.

There is an alternative view: adjustment of discount rates in relation to age and other variables predicting future life expectancy (e.g., Roitberg et al., 1992; Basolo, 1998; Candolin, 1999) is just what we should expect of an evolved psyche functioning normally. Steep discounting may be a "rational" response to information indicative of uncertain or low probability of surviving to reap delayed benefits, for example, and "reckless" risk taking can be optimal when the expected profits from safer courses of action are negligible.

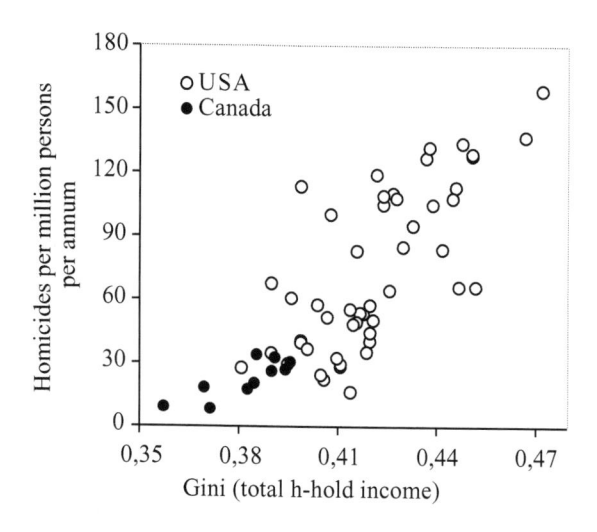

FIGURE II-3-2-1.1. **Homicide rates in the 50 United States (1990) and the 10 Canadian provinces (averaged for 1988-1992), as a function of the Gini coefficient of income inequality computed on the basis of 1990 pre-tax gross household incomes.** (See Daly et al., 2001.)

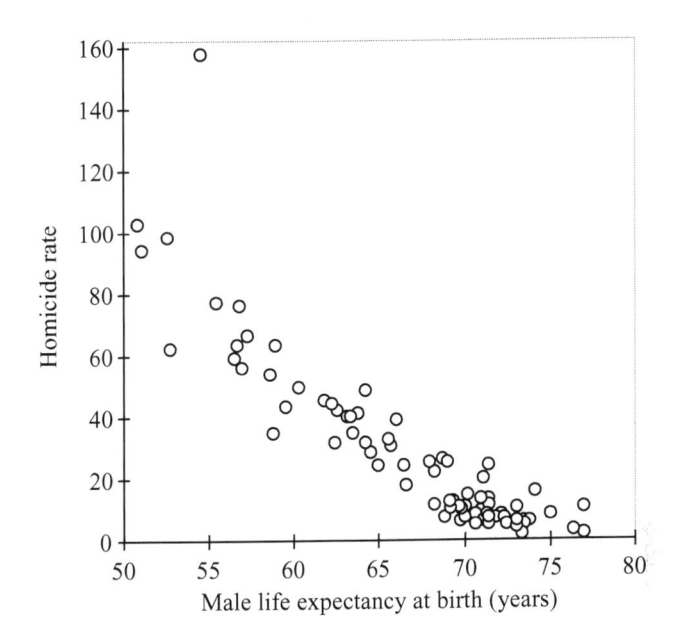

FIGURE II-3-2-1.2. Neighborhood-specific homicide rates (per 100,000 persons per annum) in relation to male life expectancy at birth (with effects of homicide mortality removed) for the 77 community areas of Chicago for the period 1988-1993. (See Wilson & Daly, 1997.)

Criminal violence can be considered an outcome of steep future discounting and escalation of risk in social competition. This is especially true of homicide in urban America, where a large majority of cases involve status or resource competition among unrelated men, and even marital homicides result from sexual proprietariness in the shadow of male–male competition. This line of reasoning suggests that criminal violence will vary in relation to local indicators of life expectancy, hence our hypothesis that homicide rates will vary as a function of local life expectancy.

The city of Chicago, U.S.A., is divided into 77 community areas or neighborhoods of some stability and distinctiveness. Information about births, deaths, causes of mortality, economic conditions, and other standard demographic measures are available for these 77 neighborhoods. For each neighborhood, we computed male life expectancy at birth, with homicide as a cause of death excluded, to test our hypothesis that homicide rates would vary with life expectancy. In Chicago, life expectancy for males at birth ranged from 54.3 years to 77.4 years, and homicide rates ranged from 1.3 to 156 per 100,000 per annum. Life expectancy and homicide rate are highly correlated (Fig. II-3-2-1.2; $r = -.88$, $p <$ .0001), confirming our hypothesis. Life expectancy reflects not only affluence, but such additional considerations as local pathogen loads, health care, and risk of violent death, and it may thus provide a more encompassing quality of life index than economic measures alone.

More than just providing a useful epidemiological index, however, we propose that an "expectation" of future life span may be psychologically salient in its own right, although it need not be a conscious, articulatable expectation. How could such a statistical abstraction as life expectancy be a cause of anything? One possibility is that the human psyche produces what is in effect a semi-statistical apprehension of the distribution of local life spans, based on the fates of salient others. If a young man's grandfathers were both dead before he was born, for example, and more than a couple of his primary school classmates are already dead too, discounting the future could be a normal, adaptive reaction. Moreover, if much of this mortality appears to represent "bad luck," incurred more or less independently of the decedents' choices of action, then becoming more risk accepting in the pursuit of immediate advantage would also make sense. Ethnographies of the U.S. urban poor contain many articulate statements about the perceived risk of early death, the unpredictability of future resources, and the futility of long-term planning (Hagedorn, 1988; Jankowski, 1992; Waldman, 1993; W. J. Wilson, 1987).

3.   Kinship Mitigates Conflict

According to current understandings of the evolution of social motives and behavior, the basic appetites, aversions, emotions, and cognitive processes characteristic of any species have been shaped by natural selection to produce social action that is effectively nepotistic: action that promotes the persistence of the actor's genetic elements in future generations by contributing to the survival and reproduction of the actor's genetic relatives (Hamilton, 1964). It follows that the basic psychological processes underlying solidarity and conflict in any social species should include processes that typically function to engender discriminative behavior in relation to cues of genetic relatedness (Alexander, 1979, 1987). In light of the ubiquity of nepotistic solidarity in the animal kingdom—people included—intrafamilial conflict and violence in the human animal would seem, at first glance, to demand explanation.

      Many commentators have suggested that a substantial proportion of violent conflicts involve relatives and close friends as an almost inescapable consequence of their high frequency and intensity of interactions (Goode, 1969). This invocation of "opportunity" is true as far as it goes, but it begs the question of whether all familial relationships are equally at risk. We controlled for opportunity by assessing the incidence of violence between members of the same household, using information on the living arrangements of the population at large to specify the universe of potential victim-of-fender pairs, and found that unrelated persons and marital partners in the same house were at greater risk than parent and child or other related dyads (Fig. II-3-2-1.3; Daly & Wilson, 1982a).

      The substance and intensity of conflicts are relationship-specific because particular social relationships—parent and child, spouses, unrelated friends, sexual rivals, and so forth—differ in their particular sources of potential and actual concordances and discrepancies in desired states of affairs. Failures of reciprocation are common sources of conflict in virtually all relationships, for example, but not in the parent-child relationship which is uniquely characterized by an unbegrudged one-way flow of resources. Instead, parent–offspring conflicts tend to revolve around an issue peculiar to that relationship, namely the location of parental resources among offspring (Trivers, 1974). This insight predicts and explains much about the peculiar epidemiology of infanticide and other kinds of parentally perpetrated violence (Daly and Wilson, 1988a, 1988b, 1994, 1995; Hrdy, 1999; Temrin, and Buchmayer, & Enquist, 2000). Other relationships have their characteristic conflicts too. When men kill their brothers, the usual issue of contention is the partitioning of familial resources, whereas when they kill their brothers-in-law, other issues, especially the

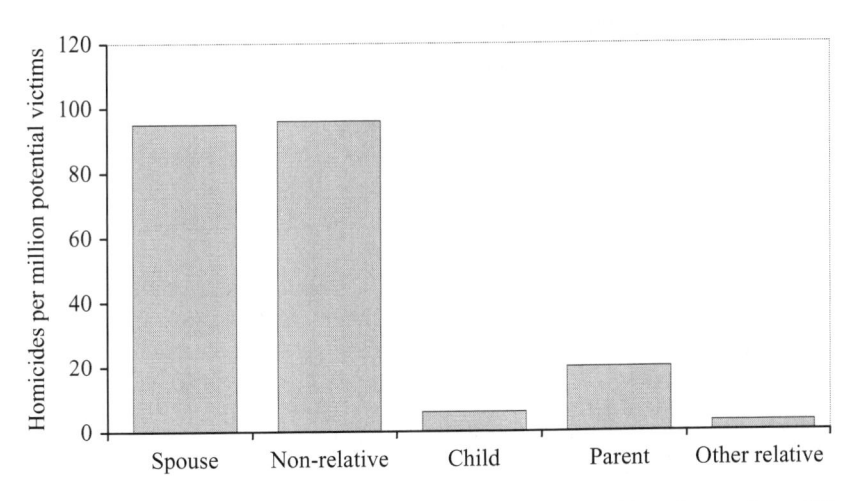

FIGURE II-3-2-1.3. Homicide rates by relationship category of victim to killer for members of the same household, Detroit (1972). (See Daly & Wilson, 1982a, 1988a, 1988b.)

mistreatment of the person's sister by her husband, predominate (Daly & Wilson, 1988a; Daly, Wilson, Salmon, Hiraiwa-Hasegawa, & Hasegawa, 2001).

Psychologists and sociologists typically locate social relationships, including familial relationships, along a continuum of intimacy, leaving out of consideration the distinctions among kin relations and distinctions by sex. If kinship and gender are taken into consideration, genealogical relationship categories are inescapable. The challenges that have faced human mothers, for example, are different from those confronting fathers or offspring or siblings or more distant relatives. Long before Trivers (1974) laid bare the logic of parent–offspring conflict, it was apparent to all who looked that the maternal relationship was special (Hrdy, 1999). Throughout human history, most women have devoted the majority of their waking hours to foraging for, educating, guarding, and otherwise nurturing their children. Hence, it is especially puzzling when mothers commit the seemingly maladaptive act of infanticide. Such events are rare, but they do remind us that parent–offspring conflict is endemic to any sexually reproducing species and the optimal allocation of effort from the mother's point of view may be different from the offspring's point of view (Trivers, 1974; Golla, Hofer, & East, 1999). It follows that the psychological processes modulating parental commitment to a particular offspring are expected to be determined in part by available predictors of that child's statistically expectable contribution to the parent's genetic posterity in past environments. In Richard Alexander's (1979: 109) words:

> Selection should refine parental altruism as if in response to three hypothetical cost-benefit questions: (1) What is the relationship of the putative offspring to its parents? (Is the juvenile really my own offspring?) (2) What is the need of the offspring? (More properly, what is its ability to translate parental assistance into reproduction?) (3) What alternative uses might a parent make of the resources it can invest in the offspring?

If infanticide is treated as a kind of "reverse assay" of parental solicitude, then infanticide does reflect valuation and discriminative solicitude according to these three general propositions. Children are at greatest risk of being killed (1) by unrelated persons *in loco parentis* (Fig. II-3-2-1.4; Daly & Wilson, 1988a, 1988b, 1996, 1998; Temrin,

Buchmayer, & Enquist, 2000), (2) when offspring need would not convert parental assistance into survivorship and reproduction, as in the case of moribund or gravely deformed infants (Daly & Wilson, 1984; Hausfater & Hrdy, 1984), (3) when parental resources would promise better returns if channeled elsewhere or in the future as in the case when present maternal incapacity cannot cope with the demands of child-rearing because of poor health, famine, abandonment by the father, or absence of other social supports (Daly & Wilson, 1984) as well as age of the mother (Daly & Wilson, 1988a, 1988b; Bugos & McCarthy, 1984).

Fatherhood has some obvious parallels with motherhood, but also some crucial differences. In particular, the chronic possibility that men unwittingly invest in another man's child means that men's paternal affection may be modulated in accordance with cues of paternity (Davies, 1992; Daly & Wilson, 1982b; Regalski & Gaulin, 1993). Suspicions or compelling evidence of nonpaternity are expected to elevate the risk of paternal abandonment and violence, and while there is abundant support for divestment and abandonment (e.g., M. Wilson, 1987), the evidence of revelations of nonpaternity elevating the risk of infanticide is merely anecdotal (Daly & Wilson, 1984, 1988a). Instead, the link between revelations of nonpaternity or suspicions of nonpaternity and men's violence against wives is much stronger (Daly & Wilson, 1988a). Even men who marry a woman with children, knowing that those children are not theirs and there's no issue of betrayal, are more likely to assault or kill her than if her children were also his (Fig. II-3-2-1.5; Daly, Singh, & Wilson, 1993; Daly, Wiseman, & Wilson, 1997; Brewer & Paulsen, 1999).

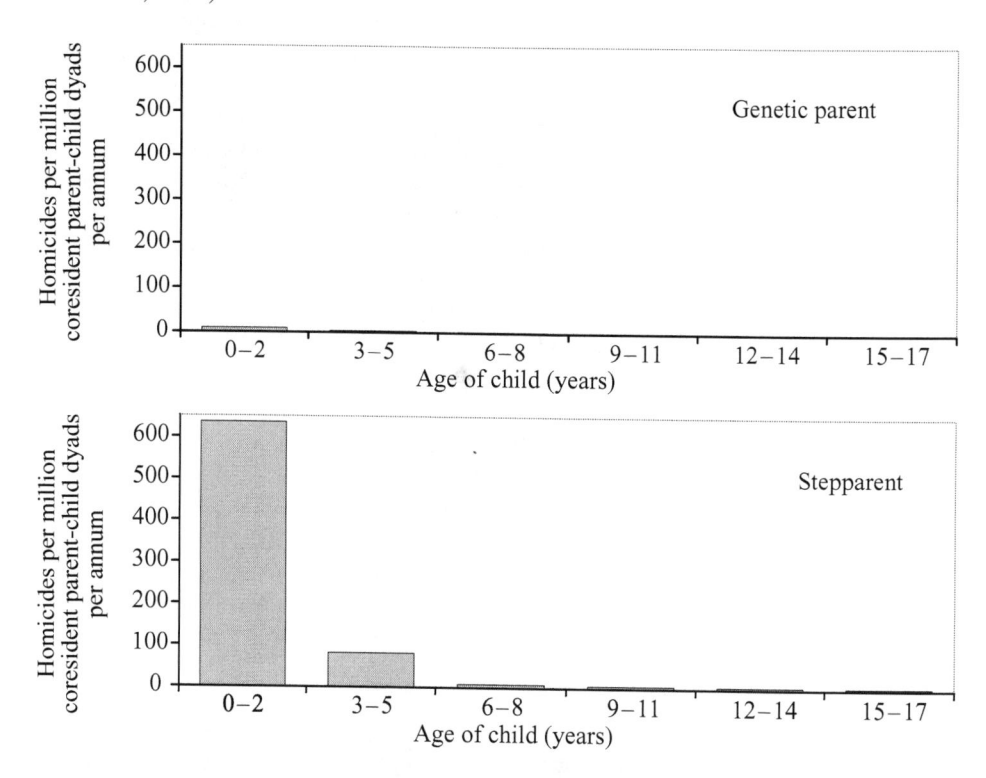

FIGURE II-3-2-1.4. Age-specific rates of child being killed by a genetic parent (upper panel) or by a stepparent (lower panel) in Canada (1974-1990). (See Daly & Wilson, 1988a, 1988b, 1996.)

Although mates are not typically close genetic relatives, kinship is often conceived of as encompassing this relationship, too. There is a certain logic to this conflation of genealogical and mating relationships: In both cases, the two parties have a commonality of interest grounded in the fact that the genetic posterity of both is promoted by the reproductive success of their common kin. There is an important difference between mateship and genetic kinship, however: The former can be more readily and irredeemably betrayed. Whatever failures of reciprocity and other provocations may strain blood-kin relations, shared interests in the welfare of common relatives have provided a countervailing force selecting for kin-specific readiness to forgive and reconcile. Marital solidarity can be abolished if one or both parties engage in extrapair mating effort. Moreover, if a husband is cuckolded and unwittingly invests his parental efforts in a rival's young, then the very acts that promote the wife's genetic posterity are positively damaging to the husband's. These considerations would seem to account for the fact that suspected or actual infidelity is a uniquely potent source of severe marital conflict and violence (Daly & Wilson, 1988a, 2000; Wilson & Daly, 1993a, 1996, 1998a, 1998b; Wilson, Daly & Scheib, 1997). Moreover, since competition for mates is more intense for males than for females, men are more likely to use coercive control and violence

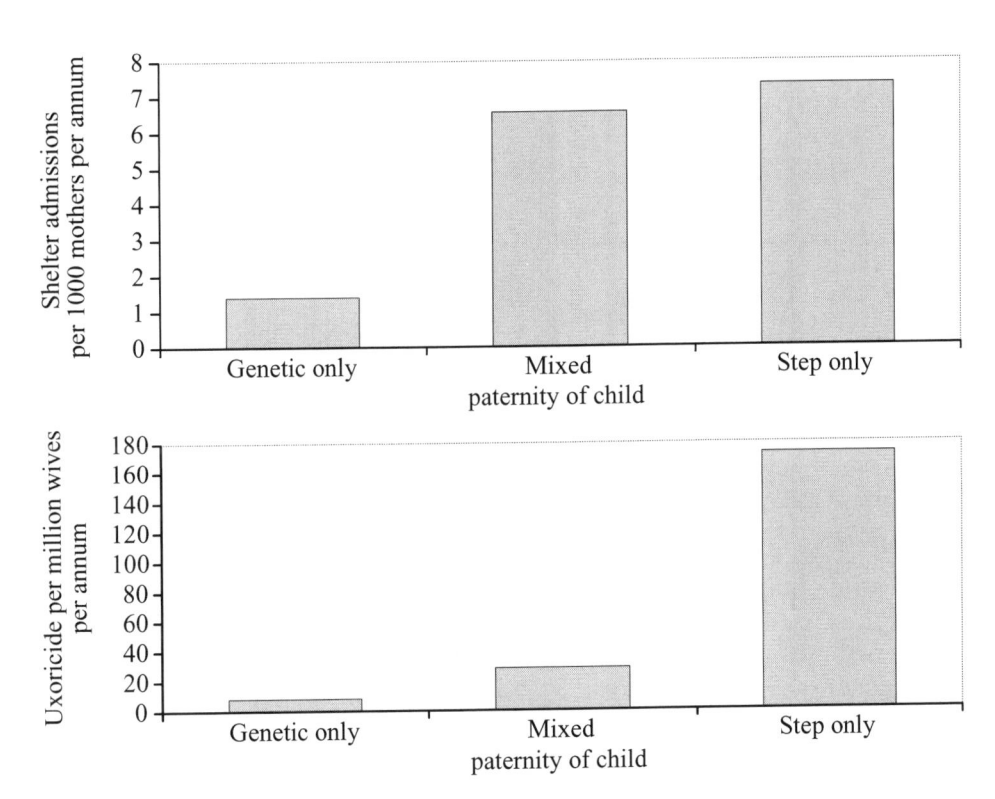

FIGURE II-3-2-1.5. Violence against wives in relation to paternity of her children, Hamilton, Canada. *Upper panel*: Comparison of rates of admission to a shelter for battered women, for women who had children according to whether her children had been sired by the present perpetrator husband or a previous partner. *Lower panel*: Comparison of uxoricide rates for wives who had children according to whether her children had been sired by the killer husband or previous husband. (See Daly, Singh, & Wilson, 1993; Daly, Wiseman, & Wilson, 1997.)

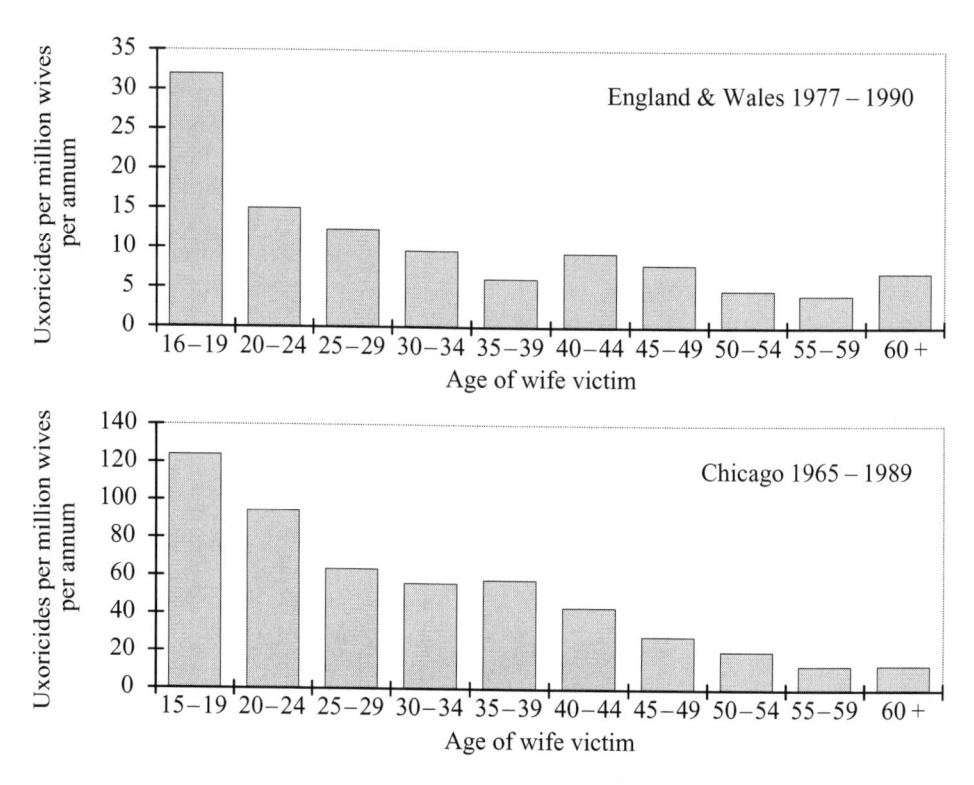

FIGURE II-3-2-1.6. **Comparision of uxoricide rates, according to age of wife victim, for England and Wales (upper Panel) and Chicago, USA (lower panel) in registered marriages.** (See Wilson and Daly 1993b.)

when wives terminate unsatisfactory relationships (Wilson & Daly, 1993b). The greater intensity of competition among men derives not only from the risk of nonpaternity but also because men more than women have a higher ceiling on potential number of off-spring and men are more variable in the number of women they monopolize in a life-time. Those demographic predictors of the probability of a woman pursuing alternative sexual and marital partnerships are expected to be associated with variable risk of vio-lent victimization by sexually proprietary husbands (Wilson & Daly, 1993a). Such pre-dictors include age of the woman (Fig. II-3-2-1.6) and type of marital relation union (Table II-3-2-1.1; Wilson & Daly, 2001).

TABLE II-3-2-1.1. **Rates of violence against wives by coresiding partners according to the type of marital union**

	Registered union	Common law union
Uxoricide	7.2	55.1
Nonlethal assault in past year	2.0	9.0

Data from Wilson, Daly and Wright 1993; Wilson, Johnson and Daly 1995. Uxoricide rates are expressed per million couples per annum, and nonfatal assault rates are expressed per hundred couples per annum.

4.   Why Violence?

In modern nations in which the state has usurped the legitimate use of violence, we can easily lose sight of the general utility of a credible threat of violence, but in nonstate societies, such a threat was (and may still be) essential if one's rivals were to be deterred from violating one's interests. And a credible threat of violence must be a genuine threat, which can occasionally be exercised. Violent capability can be an essential component of the reputation needed to acquire and maintain status and power (e.g., Chagnon, 1988, 1992; Nisbett & Cohen, 1996).

Everywhere and throughout history men have been more likely than women to use physical violence, be it fistfights or homicides, warfare or the slaughter of nonhuman animals (Murdock, 1967; Daly & Wilson, 1988a, 1990; Keely, 1995; Wrangham & Peterson, 1997; Archer, 1993). Moreover, men appear to have the morphological, physiological, and psychological means to be effective users of violence (e.g., Daly & Wilson, 1988a, 1990). The objects of male violence are usually unrelated males, but wives are frequent victims, too. And if men have evolved the ability to exploit violence to compete with other men, it is hardly surprising that they should sometimes use that ability in conflicts with women. Killing a wife is unlikely to serve the man's interests for many reasons including the fact that his children would be deprived of a mother and that wives can be hard to replace. But credible threats of violence can be a way of achieving coercive control; a way of punishing and deterring any activities perceived as not in the interests of the offender. Our premise in the case of violence against wives is that it is an outcome of self-interested male motives directed at constraining wives' autonomy by "encouraging" them to prioritize their husbands' wants rather than their own. Unfortunately, we cannot address the issue of how effective such coercion really is (or was, in premodern social environments) because there is virtually no systematic empirical evidence bearing on this issue.

The coercive use of nonlethal violence is a potentially costly way of getting others to pursue one's preferred agendas. Rather than making its victims wish to comply, violence inspires them to defy its perpetrators when the opportunity arises. Severe assaults can lead to severe self-defensive measures and to revenge by the victims or their relatives. It follows that violence is often the recourse of desperate people lacking the capacity to dispense positive incentives.

IV.   CONCLUDING REMARKS

Criminal violence is sometimes—perhaps often—aptly characterized as pathological: as a result of alcohol-induced psychoses, delusions, organic defects, and so forth (e.g., Raine, 1993; Raine et al., 2000; Aarsland et al., 1996; Giancola & Zeichner, 1995). But the concept of "pathology" demands scrutiny. Although violence is abhorrent and is often loosely referred to as a sort of sickness or dysfunction, the argument that violence is in itself pathological cannot be sustained (Monahan & Splane, 1980; Cohen & Machalek, 1994). Pathologies are failures—due to mishap, senescent decline, or subversion by biotic agents with antagonistic interests—of anatomical, physiological, and psychological parts and processes, reducing their effectiveness in achieving the adaptive functions for which they evolved (Williams & Nesse, 1991; Nesse & Williams, 1994). Violence cannot be dismissed as a mere maladaptive byproduct of such failures, because people and other animals possess psychological and physiological machinery that is evidently designed for the production and regulation of violence.

The evidence for functional design in the controls of violence is diverse. In the first place, its elicitors are typically threats to survival and reproductive prospects, and its effects are typically to counter those threats. Animals (including people) react violently to usurpation of essential resources by rivals, and they direct their violence against those rivals (Archer, 1988; Huntingford & Turner, 1987). Behavioral ecologists have analyzed the cost-benefit structure of confrontational violence in terms of the conditional determinants of the expected consequences of fight versus flight, and of escalation, and have assessed whether animals actually exhibit contingent responsiveness to available cues of the probable costs and benefits of alternative actions (e.g., Pruett-Jones & Pruett-Jones, 1994; Brick, 1998; Chase, Costanza & Dugatin, 1994; Turner, 1994; Kvarnemo, Forsgren & Magnhagen, 1995). These analyses leave little doubt that violent interactions are regulated with sensitivity to probable consequences (e.g., Clutton-Brock & Parker, 1995; Andersson, 1980; Enquist & Leimar, 1990; Enquist et al., 1990; Oliveira, McGregor & Latruffe, 1998).

In addition to contextual appropriateness, the motivational states of readiness for violence (angry arousal, rage) entail postures appropriate for attack and defense, and complex psychophysiological mobilization for effective agonistic action. There are morphological structures that function only or primarily as intraspecific weapons, and they are often sexually differentiated and characteristic of delimited life stages. There is neural machinery dedicated to aggression and this, too, is often sexually differentiated. Moreover, the sexual differentiation of physical aggression is itself variable across species, and the magnitude of sex differences in both overt weaponry and in intrasexual aggressive behavior is systematically related to the breeding system (Daly & Wilson, 1983). All of these facts testify to the potency of Darwinian selection in shaping the anatomy and psychology of intrasexual aggression.

The idea that human violence is merely pathological has perhaps been reinforced by the modern conviction that it is a product of disadvantaged backgrounds and environments (W. J. Wilson, 1987). But this association is by no means universal. In nonstate societies, violent capability and action were prevalent among the most successful men, too, and contributed to their success (see, e.g., Chagnon, 1988, 1992, 1996; Betzig, 1986). In modern state societies, the welfare of most people no longer depends on their personal violent capability or that of their allies, and violent action is likely to reflect psychological pathology. However, we suggest that a disproportionate number of violent offenders are drawn from those who lack access to the opportunities and to the protective state services available to more fortunate citizens, and who therefore find themselves in "self-help" circumstances much like those experienced by most of our human ancestors. It is not at all clear that violence in such circumstances is usefully deemed pathological, and even in those cases where there is a defect, there remains a functional organization to violence's contingent controls.

ACKNOWLEDGMENTS

Our homicide research has been supported by the Social Sciences and Humanities Research Council of Canada, the Harry Frank Guggenheim Foundation, the Natural Sciences and Engineering Research Council of Canada, and the John D. and Catherine T. MacArthur Foundation.

REFERENCES

Aarsland, Dag, Jeffrey L. Cummings, Gersev Yenner, & Bruce Miller. (1996). Relationship of Aggressive Behavior to Other Neuropsychiatric Symptoms in Patients with Alzheimer's Disease. *American Journal of Psychiatry*, *153*, 243–247.

Alexander, Richard D. (1979). *Darwinism and Human Affairs*. Seattle: University of Washington Press.

Alexander, Richard D. (1987). *The Biology of Moral Systems*. Hawthorne: Aldine.

Andersson, Malte. (1980). Why Are There so Many Threat Displays? *Journal of Theoretical Biology*, *86*, 773–781.

Archer, John. (1988). *The Behavioural Biology of Aggression*. New York: Cambridge.

Archer, John. (1993). *Male Violence*. London: Routledge, Chapman & Hall.

Basolo, Alexandra L. (1998). Shift in Investment Between Sexually Selected Traits: Tarnishing of the Silver Spoon. *Animal Behaviour*, *55*, 665–671.

Betzig, Laura L. (1986). *Despotism and Differential Reproduction: A Darwinian View of History*. Hawthorne: Aldine.

Blau, Judith, & Peter Blau. (1982). The Cost of Inequality. *American Sociological Review*, *47*, 114–129.

Bresse, Susan K. (1989). Crimes of Passion: The Campaign Against Wife Killing in Brazil, 1910–1940. *Journal of Social History*, *22*, 653–666.

Brewer, Victoria E. & Derek J. Paulsen. (1999). A Comparison of U.S. and Canadian Findings on Uxoricide Risk for Women with Children Sired by Previous Partners. *Homicide Studies*, *3*, 317–332.

Brick, Olle. (1998). Fighting Behaviour, Vigilance and Predation Risk in the Cichlid Fish Nannacara Anomala. *Animal Behaviour*, *56*, 309–317.

Bugos, Paul E., & Loraine M. McCarthy. (1984). Ayoreo Infanticide: a Case Study. In Glenn Hausfater & Sarah B. Hrdy (Eds.), *Infanticide: Comparative and Evolutionary Perspectives* (pp. 503–520). New York: Aldine Press.

Candolin, Ulrika. (1999). The Relationship Between Signal Quality and Physical Condition: Is Sexual Signalling Honest in the Three-spined Stickleback? *Animal Behaviour*, *58*, 1261–1267.

Chagnon, Napoleon A. (1988). Life Histories, Blood Revenge, and Warfare in a Tribal Population. *Science*, *239*, 985–992.

Chagnon, Napoleon A. (1992). *Yanomamo: The Last Days of Eden*. New York: Harcourt Brace Jovanovich.

Chagnon, Napoleon A. (1996). Chronic Problems in Understanding Tribal Violence and Warfare. In Michael Rutter (Ed.), *Genetics of Criminal and Antisocial Behaviour. CIBA Foundation Symposium 194* (pp. 202–236). Chichester: John Wiley & Sons.

Chase, Ivan D., Bartolomeo Costanza, & Lee A. Dugatkin. (1994). Aggressive Interactions and Inter-contest Interval: How Long Do Winners Keep Winning? *Animal Behaviour*, *48*, 393–400.

Chimbos, Peter D. (1978). *Marital Violence: A Study of Interspouse Homicide*. San Francisco: R & E Research Associates.

Chimbos, Peter D. (1993). A Study of Patterns in Criminal Homicides in Greece. *International Journal of Comparative Sociology*, *34*, 260–271.

Clutton-Brock, Timothy H., & Geoffrey A. Parker. (1995). Punishment in Animal Societies. *Nature*, *373*, 209–216.

Cohen, Lawrence E., & Richard Machalek. (1988). A General Theory of Expropriative Crime: An Evolutionary Ecological Approach. *American Journal of Sociology*, *94*, 465–501.

Cohen, Lawrence E., & Richard Machalek. (1994). The Normalcy of Crime. From Durkheim to Evolutionary Ecology. *Rationality and Society*, *6*, 286–308.

Colegrave, N. (1994). Game Theory Models of Competition in Closed Systems: Asymmetries in Fighting and Competitive Ability. *Oikos*, *71*, 499–505.

Crawford, Maria, & Rosemary Gartner. (1992). *Woman Killing: Intimate Femicide in Ontario 1974–1990*. Toronto: The Women We Honour Action Committee.

Daly, Martin, & Margo I. Wilson. (1982a). Homicide and Kinship. *American Anthropologist*, *84*, 372–378.

Daly, Martin, & Margo I. Wilson. (1982b). Whom Are Newborn Babies Said to Resemble? *Ethology & Sociobiology*, *3*, 69–78.

Daly, Martin, & Margo I. Wilson. (1983). *Sex, Evolution and Behavior: Adaptations for Reproduction. 2nd Edition*. Boston: Willard Grant Press.

Daly, Martin, & Margo I. Wilson. (1984). A Sociobiological Analysis of Human Infanticide. In Glenn Hausfater, & Sarah B. Hrdy (Eds.), *Infanticide: Comparative and Evolutionary Perspectives* (pp. 487–502). New York: Aldine Press.

Daly, Martin, & Margo I. Wilson. (1988a). *Homicide*. Hawthorne: Aldine de Gruyter.

Daly, Martin, & Margo Wilson. (1988b). Evolutionary Social Psychology and Family Homicide. *Science, 242*, 519–524.

Daly, Martin, & Margo I. Wilson. (1990). Killing the Competition. *Human Nature, 1*, 83–109.

Daly, Martin, & Margo Wilson. (1993). Evolutionary Psychology of Male Violence. In John Archer (Ed.), *Male Violence* (pp. 253–288). London: Routledge, Chapman & Hall.

Daly, Martin, & Margo Wilson. (1994). Some Differential Attributes of Lethal Assaults on Small Children by Stepfathers Versus Genetic Fathers. *Ethology and Sociobiology, 15*, 207–217.

Daly, Martin, & Margo Wilson. (1995). Discriminative Parental Solicitude and the Relevance of Evolutionary Models to the Analysis of Motivational Systems. In Michael S. Gazzaniga (Ed.), *The Cognitive Neurosciences* (pp. 1269–1286). Cambridge: MIT.

Daly, Martin, & Margo Wilson. (1996). Violence Against Stepchildren. *Current Directions in Psychological Science, 5*, 77–81.

Daly, Martin, & Margo I. Wilson. (1997). Crime and Conflict: Homicide in Evolutionary Psychological Perspective. *Crime & Justice, 22*, 251–300.

Daly, Martin, & Margo Wilson. (1998). *The Truth about Cinderella*. London: Weidenfeld & Nicolson Publishers.

Daly, Martin, & Margo Wilson. (2000). The Evolutionary Psychology of Marriage and Divorce. In Linda Waite (Ed.), *Ties that Bind: Perspectives on Marriage and Cohabitation* (pp. 91–110). Hawthorne: Aldine de Gruyter.

Daly, Martin, & Margo Wilson. (2001). Family Violence: An Evolutionary Psychological Perspective. *Virginia Journal of Social Policy and Law, 8*, 77–121.

Daly, Martin, Lisa S. Singh, & Margo Wilson. (1993). Children Fathered by Previous Partners: A Risk Factor for Violence Against Women. *Canadian Journal of Public Health, 84*, 209–210.

Daly, Martin, Margo Wilson, Catherine Salmon, Mariko Hiraiwa-Hasegawa, and Toshikazu Hasegawa. (2001). Siblicide and Seniority. *Homocide Studies, 5*(1), 30–45.

Daly, Martin, Margo Wilson, & S. Vasdev. (2000). Income Inequality and Homicide Rates in Canada. *Canadian Journal of Criminology, 43*, 219–236.

Daly, Martin, Margo I. Wilson, & Suzanne J. Weghorst. (1982). Male Sexual Jealousy. *Ethology & Sociobiology, 3*, 11–27.

Daly, Martin, Karen A. Wiseman, & Margo Wilson. (1997). Women with Children Sired by Previous Partners Incur Excess Risk of Uxoricide. *Homicide Studies, 1*, 61–71.

Davies, Nicholas B. (1992). *Dunnock Behaviour and Social Evolution*. Oxford: Oxford University Press.

Dobash, Rebecca Emerson, & Russell P. Dobash. (1979). *Violence Against Wives*. New York: Free Press.

Dobash, Rebecca Emerson, & Russell P. Dobash. (1998). Violent Men and Violent Contexts. In Rebecca Emerson Dobash & Russell P. Dobash (Eds.), *Rethinking Violence Against Women* (pp. 141–168). Thousand Oaks: Sage.

Enquist, Magnus, & Olof Leimar. (1990). The Evolution of Fatal Fighting. *Animal Behaviour, 39*, 1–9.

Enquist, Magnus, Olof Leimar, Tomas Ljungberg, Ylva Mallner, & Nils Segerdahl. (1990). A Test of the Sequential Assessment Game: Fighting in the Cichlid Fish Nannacara Anomala. *Animal Behaviour, 40*, 1–14.

Giancola, Peter R., & Amos Zeichner. (1995). An Investigation of Gender Differences in Alcohol-related Aggression. *Journal of Studies in Alcohol, 56*, 573–579.

Gottfredson, Michael R., & Travis Hirschi. (1990). *A General Theory of Crime*. Stanford: Stanford University Press.

Golla, Waltraud, Heribert Hofer, & Marion L. East. (1999). Within-Litter Sibling Aggression in Spotted Hyaenas—Effect of Maternal Nursing, Sex and Age. *Animal Behaviour, 8*, 715–726.

Goode, William J. (1969). Violence Among Intimates. In Donald J. Mulvihill, & Melvin M. Tumin (Eds.), *Crimes of Violence. Vol. 13* (pp. 941–977). Washington: U.S. Government Printing Office.

Green, Leonard, Astrid F. Fry, & Joel Myerson. (1994). Discounting of Delayed Rewards: A Life-Span Comparison. *Psychological Science, 5*, 33–36.

Guttmacher, Manfred S. (1955). Criminal Responsibility in Certain Homicide Cases Involving Family Members. In Paul H. Hoch & Joseph Zubin (Eds.), *Psychiatry and the Law* (pp. 73–96). New York: Grune & Stratton.

Hagedorn, John D. (1988). *People and Folks*. Chicago: Lake View Press.

Hamilton, William D. (1964). The Genetical Evolution of Social Behaviour I and II. *Journal of Theoretical Biology, 7*, 1–52.

Hausfater, Glenn, & Sarah B. Hrdy. (1984). *Infanticide: Comparative and Evolutionary Perspectives*. New York: Aldine Press.

Hrdy, Sarah B. (1999). *Mother Nature. A History of Mothers, Infants, and Natural Selection*. New York: Pantheon Books.

Hsieh, Ching-Chi, & M. D. Pugh. (1993). Poverty, Income Inequality and Violent Crime: A Meta-analysis of Recent Aggregate Data Studies. *Criminal Justice Review, 18*, 182–202.

Huntingford, Felicity, & Angela K. Turner. (1987). *Animal Conflict*. London: Chapman & Hall.

Jacobs, David. (1981). Inequality and Economic Crime. *Sociology and Social Research, 66*, 12–28.

Jankowski, Martin S. (1992). *Islands in the Street*. Berkeley: University of California Press.

Keely, Lawrence. (1995). *War Before Civilization*. Oxford: Oxford University Press.

Kennedy, Bruce P., Ichiro Kawachi, & Deborah Prothrow-Stich. (1996). Income Distribution and Mortality: Cross Sectional Ecological Study of the Robin Hood Index in the United States. *British Medical Journal, 312*, 1004–1007.

Krahn, Harvey, Timothy F. Hartnagel, & John W. Gartrell. (1986). Income Inequality and Homicide Rates: Cross-National Data and Criminological Theories. *Criminology, 24*, 269–95.

Kvarnemo, Charlotta, Elisabeth Forsgren, & Carin Magnhagen. (1995). Effects of Sex Ration on Intra- and Inter-Sexual Behaviour in Sand Gobies. *Animal Behaviour, 50*, 1455–1461.

Lawrance, Emily C. (1991). Poverty and the Rate of Time Preference: Evidence from Panel Data. *Journal of Political Economy, 99*, 54–77.

Loewenstein, George, & Jon Elster. (1992). *Choice over Time*. New York: Russell Sage.

Machalek, Richard. (1995). Basic Dimensions and Forms of Social Exploitation: A Comparative Analysis. *Advances in Human Ecology, 4*, 35–68.

Mazur, Allan, Alan Booth, & James M. Dabbs, Jr. (1992). Testosterone and Chess Competition. *Social Psychology Quarterly, 55*, 70–77.

McCaul, Kevin D., Brion A. Gladue, & Margaret Joppa. (1992). Winning, Losing, Mood, and Testosterone. *Hormones and Behavior, 26*, 486–504.

Monahan, John, & Stephanie Splane. (1980). Psychological Approaches to Criminal Behavior. In Egon Bittner & Sheldon S. Messinger (Eds.), *Criminology Review Yearbook, Vol. 2* (pp. 17–47). Beverly Hills: Sage.

Morris, William. (1976). *The American Heritage Dictionary of the English Language*. Boston: Houghton Mifflin.

Murdock, George P. (1967). *Ethnographic Atlas*. Pittsburgh: University of Pittsburgh Press.

Nesse, Randolph M., & George C. Williams. (1994). *Why We Get Sick*. New York: Random House.

Nisbett, Richard E., & Dov Cohen. (1996). *Culture of Honor: The Psychology of Violence in the South*. Boulder: Westview Press.

Oliveira, Rui F., Peter K. McGregor, & Claire Latruffe. (1998). Know Thine Enemy: Fighting Fish Gather Information from Observing Conspecific Interactions. *Proceedings of the Royal Society, London, Series B, 265*, 1045–1049.

Pinker, Steven. (1997). *How the Mind Works*. New York: Norton.

Polk, Kenneth. (1994). *When Men Kill: Scenarios of Masculine Violence*. Cambridge: Cambridge University Press.

Pruett-Jones, Stephen, & Melinda Pruett-Jones. (1994). Sexual Competition and Courtship Disruptions: Why Do Male Bowerbirds Destroy Each Other's Bowers? *Animal Behaviour, 47*, 607–620.

Raine, Adrian. (1993). *The Psychopathology of Crime and Criminal Behavior as a Clinical Disorder*. San Diego: Academic Press.

Raine, Adrian, Todd Lencz, Susan Bihrle, Lori LaCasse, & Patrick Colletti. (2000). Reduced Prefrontal Gray Matter Volume and Reduced Autonomic Activity in Antisocial Personality Disorder. *Archives of General Psychiatry, 57*, 119–27.

Regalski, Jeanne M., Steven J. C. Gaulin. (1993). Whom Are Mexican Infants Said to Resemble? Monitoring and Fostering Paternal Confidence in the Yucatan. *Ethology & Sociobiology, 14*, 97–113.

Roitberg, Bernhard D., Marc Mangel, Robert G. Lalonde, Carol A. Roitberg, Jacques J. M. van Alphen, & Louise Vet. (1992). Seasonal Dynamic Shifts in Patch Exploitation by Parasitic Wasps. *Behavioral Ecology, 3*, 156–165.

Temrin, Hans, Susan Buchmayer, & Magnus Enquist. (2000). Step-Parents and Infanticide: New Data Contradict Evolutionary Predictions. *Proceedings of the Royal Society of London, 267*(1446), 943–945.

Tooby, John, & Leda Cosmides. (1992). The Psychological Foundations of Culture. In Jerome H. Barkow, Leda Cosmides & John Tooby (Eds.), *The Adapted Mind* (pp. 19–136). New York: Oxford University Press.

Trivers, Robert L. (1974). Parent–Offspring Conflict. *American Zoologist, 14*, 249–264.

Turner, George F. (1994). The Fighting Tactics of Male Mouthbrooding Cichlids: The Effects of Size and Residency. *Animal Behaviour, 47*, 655–662.

Vila, Bryan. (1994). A General Paradigm for Understanding Criminal Behavior: Extending Evolutionary Ecological Theory. *Criminology, 32,* 311–359.

Waldman, Linda. (1993). *My Neighborhood: The Words and Pictures of Inner-City Children.* Chicago: Hyde Park Foundation.

Williams, George C. (1966). *Adaptation and Natural Selection.* Princeton: Princeton University Press.

Williams, George C., & Randolph M. Nesse. (1991). The Dawn of Darwinian Medicine. *The Quarterly Review of Biology, 66,* 1–22.

Wilson, James Q., & Richard J. Herrnstein. (1985). *Crime and Human Nature.* New York: Simon and Schuster.

Wilson, Margo. (1987). Impacts of the Uncertainty of Paternity on Family Law. *University of Toronto Law Review, 45,* 216–242.

Wilson, Margo I. & Martin Daly. (1985). Competitiveness, Risk-Taking and Violence: The Young Male Syndrome. *Ethology and Sociobiology, 6,* 59–73.

Wilson, Margo I., & Martin Daly. (1992). The Man Who Mistook His Wife for a Chattel. In Jerome H. Barkow, Leda Cosmides & John Tooby (Eds.), *The Adapted Mind* (pp. 289–322). New York: Oxford University Press.

Wilson, Margo I., & Martin Daly. (1993a). An Evolutionary Psychological Perspective on Male Sexual Proprietariness and Violence Against Wives. *Violence and Victims, 8,* 271–294.

Wilson, Margo I., & Martin Daly. (1993b). Spousal Homicide Risk and Estrangement. *Violence and Victims, 8,* 3–16.

Wilson, Margo, & Martin Daly. (1996). Male Sexual Proprietariness and Violence Against Wives. *Current Directions in Psychological Science, 5,* 2–7.

Wilson, Margo, & Martin Daly. (1997). Life Expectancy, Economic Inequality, Homicide, and Reproductive Timing in Chicago Neighbourhoods. *British Medical Journal, 314,* 1271–1274.

Wilson, Margo, & Martin Daly. (1998a). Sexual Rivalry and Sexual Conflict: Recurring Themes in Fatal Conflicts. *Theoretical Criminology, 2,* 291–310.

Wilson, Margo, & Martin Daly. (1998b). Lethal and Nonlethal Violence Against Wives and the Evolutionary Psychology of Male Sexual Proprietariness. In Russell P. Dobash & Rebecca Emerson Dobash (Eds.), *Violence Against Women: International and Cross-Disciplinary Perspectives* (pp. 199–230). Thousand Oaks: Sage Publications.

Wilson, Margo, & Martin Daly. (2001). The Evolutionary Psychology of Couple Conflict in Registered Versus de Facto Marital Unions. In Alan Booth, Ann C. Crouter & Mari Clements (Eds.), *Couples in Conflict.* Hillsdale: Lawrence Erlbaum

Wilson, Margo, Martin Daly, & Joanna E. Scheib. (1997). Femicide: An Evolutionary Psychological Perspective. In Patricia A. Gowaty (Ed.), *Feminism and Evolutionary Biology* (pp. 431–465). New York: Chapman-Hall.

Wilson, William J. (1987). *The Truly Disadvantaged: The Inner City, the Underclass, and Public Policy.* Chicago: University of Chicago Press.

Wrangham, Richard, & Dale Peterson. (1997). *Demonic Males: Apes and the Origins of Human Violence.* New York: Houghton Mifflin.

The Nature–Nurture Problem in Violence

LAURA BAKER

I. INTRODUCTION

1. The Approach

In recent years we have witnessed, through the media, several American middle-class, white school children from apparently good families open gunfire on their teachers, class-mates, and parents, killing and seriously wounding them in astounding numbers (see Males, 1999). In at least two different cases, the young killers did not fit the stereotypical mold of underprivileged, neglected and unsupervised individuals. In the Columbine High School shooting (April 1999) in which twelve students and one teacher were killed, the White teenage assailants, Dylan Klebold and Eric Harris, were from middle-class suburban homes. In Springfield, Oregon (May 1998), 15 year old Kipland Kinkel's parents were school teachers described as model parents, trying to do everything in their power to steer their young son away from his obsession with firearms. What may have begun as rebellious adolescent behavior turned into a shooting spree in which Kip shot nine of his classmates and killed his own parents.

These cases brought back into the limelight several long-standing questions about the roots of human aggression and violence. Is antisocial behavior primarily a product of our experiences—learning and socialization? Or are certain individuals "born bad"? What are the contributions of parents to antisocial outcomes in their offspring? Do they serve as the primary source of socialization, or do they merely pass on genetic predispositions to their children? How do peers influence delinquent behavior? Are they role models or other agents of socialization, or do individuals genetically predisposed to violence seek out similar peers and hence empower one another? All of these questions concern the nature–nurture problem in human violence.

W. Heitmeyer and J. Hagan (eds.), *International Handbook of Violence Research*, 589–607.

The familial nature of violence has been demonstrated in numerous studies. Children whose parents abuse them are more likely to be arrested for violent offenses than are non-abused children (Males, 1999). Increased levels of aggression are also found in children with histories of abuse (most often at the hands of their parents), even after controlling for socioeconomic factors (Dodge, Bates, & Petit, 1990). However, it is not clear from these studies whether violent tendencies are transmitted through environmental or genetic pathways. Parents raising their own children are genetically related to their children, while at the same time serve as role models and agents of socialization. As such, it is impossible to disentangle the roles of heredity and environmental effects in these studies of intact families. Other "genetically informative" designs, such as twin and adoption studies, are required to understand how nature and nurture may influence violence and aggression.

Behavioral genetic studies therefore provide one obvious way to evaluate the effects of nature and nurture in human violence. Indeed, numerous behavioral genetic studies spanning several countries have investigated the roles of both genetics (nature) and environment (nurture) in various forms of human antisocial behavior, including aggression and violence. These studies include a variety of definitions of antisocial behavior, including official and self-report measures of lawbreaking (criminal) behaviors, as well as more broadly defined trait aggression as rated by self, teachers, or parents. As reviewed below, there is clear evidence for the effects of *both* nature and nurture, although these effects vary over age groups and definitions of antisocial behavior. Most important, however, is the finding that genetic and environmental influences appear to interact in non-additive ways in producing antisocial outcomes. It is likely that the combination of particular nature and nurture factors are most crucial in determining an individual's propensity towards aggression and violence.

Some researchers may prefer to define the effects of nature and nurture more broadly than in terms of genes and environment. There is a vast amount of research, in fact, into biological and social bases of human violence and aggression (for reviews, see Baker, 1999 and McCord, 1999). Hormones, neurotransmitters, autonomic nervous system and brain function have been studied in relation to antisocial outcomes, along with social factors such as parental supervision and involvement, and peer characteristics. Much of this research, however, does not consider how heredity or experiences may mediate these risk factors and their relationship to violence. It is important to keep in mind that each of the social and biological variables themselves may be a product of both environmental and genetic factors. Poor parenting, for example, may be a genetically influenced trait—perhaps another form of antisocial behavior itself—which may be passed on to offspring, thereby providing them with increased genetic risk for violent or other antisocial outcomes. Conversely, biological risk factors are not necessarily entirely influenced by genetic variations. Low resting heart rate and skin conductance—both predictors of aggressive and criminal behavior—are only partially heritable, and frontal-lobe dysfunction—another indicator of antisocial behavior in adults and children—may stem from environmental causes, such as birth traumas, accidents, or illnesses (Raine, 1993). Very little research to date has investigated how genetic and environmental factors may mediate the pathways between these biological and social risk factors and antisocial outcomes, such as violence.

A behavioral genetic perspective, then, provides one of the most straightforward ways of evaluating the nature–nurture problem in human aggression and violence. An overview of behavioral genetic methods is provided here, followed by a review of studies investigating the roles of heredity and environment in antisocial behavior. Subsequently, a discussion of the most important findings and their implications for our understanding of violence, per se, is provided, along with suggestions for future research in this important area.

2. Behavioral Genetics: Methods for Disentangling Nature and Nurture

A primary objective in behavioral genetic research is to understand how genetic and environmental factors produce individual differences (i.e., variation) in psychological traits or behavioral tendencies (see Plomin, DeFries, McClearn, & Rutter, 1997; Rowe, 1994). The relative impact of (latent) genetic factors in observed ("phenotypic") trait variation is estimated by heritability (h^2), which is the ratio of genotypic to phenotypic variability. If one could measure individual genotypes (e.g., by counting the number of alleles relevant to a particular phenotype that are inherited by each person), then the squared correlation between measured genotypes (G) and phenotypes (P) would represent the heritability of that phenotype, or the proportion of phenotypic variation explained by genetic variation (r^2_{GP}). In practice, however, individual genotypes are latent variables that cannot be measured as such, so estimates of (h^2) are obtained through various correlations between relatives (e.g., identical twins separated at birth), as specified by Fisher (1918).

The relative impact of environmental influences on trait variation is indicated by environmentality (e^2), which is the ratio of environmental to phenotypic variability. Again, if one could identify and measure all relevant environmental experiences (E) for each individual, then e^2 would represent the squared correlation between environmental and phenotypic variables (r^2_{EP}). Since we do not know, *a priori*, what constitutes an environmental factor for any given phenotype, we must infer environmental effects indirectly through correlations between relatives.

Behavioral geneticists routinely distinguish between two types of environmental influences: (a) "shared" or common effects, which are shared by relatives (e^2_S); and (b) "non-shared" or unique effects, which are specific to individuals living in the same family. The relative importances of these effects are often denoted as e^2_S and e^2_{NS}, respectively. Shared environmental effects generally operate to make family members similar to one another, while non-shared environmental factors conversely make family members different from one another. Resemblance among genetically unrelated, adopted relatives provide one of the more direct methods for estimating shared environmental effects, although their effects may also be obtained by subtraction, through comparison of relatives of varying degrees of genetic relatedness (e.g., identical and fraternal twins raised together).

Another important distinction is also made between different mechanisms of gene action, which depend on the extent to which interactions occur between alleles at a given locus (i.e., genetic dominance and recessiveness) or between alleles at different loci (genetic epistasis). Such within- and between-loci allelic interactions will increase the genetic variation in non-additive (interactive) ways (d^2). There may also be variation due to additive genetic effects (a^2), which may operate with or without the presence of genetic dominance and epistasis. For most behavioral characteristics, heritable effects have been primarily of the additive variety, although not all studies have enough information to distinguish additive and non-additive genetic effects. Parent–offspring resemblance is affected only by additive genetic variance, while both additive and non-additive genetic variance affect twin and other sibling resemblance. Thus, if genetic dominance or epistatic effects are important to a given characteristic, greater sibling than parent-offspring resemblance is expected (Falconer & Mackay, 1996:152–155). This distinction will become especially important when comparing parent–offspring and twin studies of violence.

Two resulting forms of heritability are based on these different genetic mechanisms. Narrow-sense heritability refers to the variance explained only by the additive effects of genes ($h^2_N = a^2$). Broad-sense heritability includes both additive and non-additive genetic effects ($h^2_B = a^2 + d^2$). It is possible to estimate both forms of heritability in some studies, particularly those that include many different kinships. In practice, large samples are required to distinguish non-additive genetic effects from other mechanisms, including assortative mating (i.e., similarity of mating partners) and shared environment.

Studies of intact (nuclear) families are often used as a first step in establishing familial resemblance for psychological traits or behavioral tendencies in humans. Lack of familiality (i.e., neither parent–offspring, nor sibling, nor twin resemblance) would indicate that neither heredity nor shared environment is important to the characteristic under study. Once familial resemblance is established, twin and adoption studies are required to separate genetic from shared family environmental effects.

Twin studies may include either twin pairs raised together or separated at birth. In the study of aggression, violence, and other forms of antisocial behavior, there are virtually no studies of separated twins. In contrast, there have been many studies of antisocial behavior in twins reared together, which require that both monozygotic (MZ) and dizygotic (DZ) pairs must be included. MZ twins result from the separation of a single fertilized egg into two separate but genetically identical individuals. Separate fertilization of two different eggs by two different sperm results in DZ twins, who share about 50 percent of their genes, on average. (DZ twins are comparable to non-twin siblings in their average genetic similarity.)

One important assumption required in studies of twins reared together, however, is that co-twins' environments are correlated to about the same degree for MZ and DZ pairs. Although there is good evidence for the validity of this "equal environments assumption" in studies of cognitive ability (Matheny, Wilson, & Dolan, 1976) and personality (Plomin, Willerman, & Loehlin, 1976), there are good reasons to believe it may be inaccurate in studies of antisocial behavior (see Carey, 1992). Peer influences, for example, are thought to play a far more important role in socialization than parents in many behavioral domains, including antisocial behavior (see Harris, 1998). To the extent that peer influences reflect environmental variations, any greater sharing of friends and social experiences between MZ than DZ twins, would represent differential environmental similarity—a violation of the equal environments assumption. This in turn could explain any increased MZ twin similarity in behavior, rather than genetic factors. It is of particular importance to interpret results from twin studies across varying developmental periods during which environments are shared to different degrees (e.g., children living together at home, vs. adults who have lived away from each other for many years), and to compare these results to those from adoption studies.

The adoption design is, in fact, the most powerful method for disentangling the effects of heredity and environment in human behavior. Studies of adopted children may include their biological relatives, their adoptive relatives, or both. Evidence for genetic influence is indicated by greater resemblance between biologically related individuals reared in separate, uncorrelated environments. Any similarities between genetically unrelated individuals living together (e.g., adopted child and adoptive parents and/or siblings) are taken to imply environmental influence. Estimates of heritability and environmentality may be biased to the extent that children may be placed into the hands of adopting parents who are similar to the child's birth parents. Such matching procedures (termed *selective placement* in adoption studies) may inflate the adopted child's resemblance to both biological and adoptive relatives. It is important to understand, however, that it is only selective placement for characteristics related to those under study that may lead to biased heritability and environmentality for the trait being studied. That is, placing children into homes in which biological and adoptive parents are matched for physical characteristics or religious background will not affect resemblance among relatives for IQ or personality, unless these matching characteristics themselves are related to IQ or personality. Selective placement for socioeconomic status (SES), on the other hand, could inflate parent/child resemblance for antisocial behavior, due to the relationship that is known to exist between SES and antisocial outcomes (Van Dusen et al., 1983).

Nature and nurture effects are quantified in behavioral genetic analyses through these various variance components (see Fig. II-3-2-2.1 for a summary). Total phenotypic variation is typically presumed to constitute a linear combination of heritable (including additive, a^2, and non-additive, d^2) effects and environmental effects (both shared and not shared by family members—e^2_s and e^2_{NS}). It is advantageous to consider the degree of measurement error in the characteristic being studied (u^2) in order to adjust genetic and environmental effects accordingly, although studies do not consistently do this. Other more complex models may include additional variance components due, for example, to statistical interactions or correlations between genetic and environmental influences. Adoption studies are particularly helpful in detecting both genotype X environment (GxE) interactions and genotype-environment (GE) correlations. In general, the more types of kinship available in a given study, the more information is available about these various components and the power to detect them.

A review of twin, adoption, and family studies of antisocial behavior, including aggression and violence, is provided here. These studies include a wide range of definitions of antisocial behavior, from trait aggression to lawbreaking (criminal) behavior to psychiatric diagnoses (e.g., for conduct and oppositional defiant disorders in children and antisocial personality in adults). Studies also vary considerably in methods of assessing antisocial behavior, including self-report, parental and teacher ratings, structured interviews, laboratory observations, and official records from courts, police files, and schools. The extent to which findings of genetic and environmental influence in antisocial behavior vary by definitions and methods of assessment, as well as by gender and age of subjects are considered in this review.

Before reviewing behavioral genetic research on antisocial behavior, however, a few caveats are in order. First, it is important to understand that a given heritability estimate makes a statement about *individual differences* (i.e., variance) in quantitative traits or

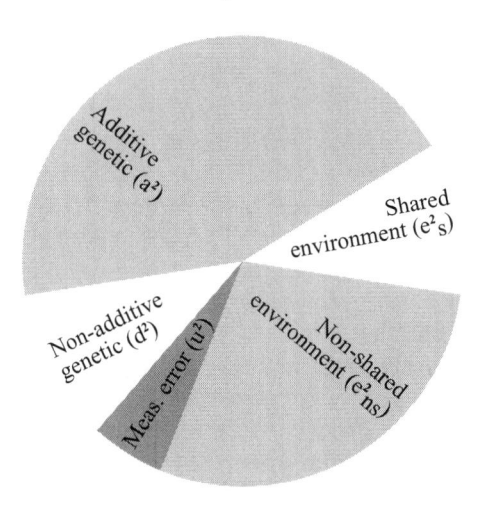

FIGURE II-3-2-2.1. Components of genetic and environmental variance.

dimensions, not *individual behaviors*. We do not generally say that one person's aggressive behavior is due to their genes or to their experiences. Rather, heritability implies that the differences among many individuals' behavioral tendencies are due to unspecified genetic differences among them. Second, behavioral genetic research does not identify genes for crime or violence. Instead, studies of criminal offending generally refer to the concept of liability, an unobserved, latent variable that is related to risk—the higher an individual's liability, the greater the probability that the individual will engage in certain behaviors, such as violent offending. Studies of criminal offending thus refer to the heritability of liability towards violent behavior (not heritability of violence). Finally, most behavioral genetic analyses of liability towards particular disorders consider the underlying causes of liability to be multifactorial, such that many genes and many environmental factors are presumed to be involved. It is highly unlikely that there is a "gene for violence," but rather a host of genetic loci that contribute, especially in combination with environmental factors, to an individual's risk for engaging in antisocial behavior, including violence.

II. BEHAVIORAL GENETIC STUDIES OF AGGRESSION AND ANTISOCIAL BEHAVIOR

There are several excellent reviews of research into the genetic and environmental basis of antisocial behavior and aggression (e.g., Cloninger & Gottesman, 1987; Venables & Raine, 1987; Mednick & Kandel, 1988; Raine & Venables, 1989; Plomin, Nitz, & Rowe, 1990; Rutter et al., 1990; DiLalla & Gottesman, 1991; Mason & Frick, 1994; Raine, 1993; Carey, 1994; Carey & Goldman, 1997). These reviews summarize twin, family, and adoption studies of various forms of antisocial behavior, including criminal arrests and convictions, symptoms of antisocial personality and conduct disorders, and trait aggression. Each of these reviews argues indisputably that genetic predispositions underlie antisocial behavior. The genetic influence, however, depends on several factors, including age and gender of subjects as well as type of antisocial behavior being studied. The major findings from these studies are reviewed here, with a comparison of patterns of results in areas of criminal offending, psychiatric symptoms, and more general trait aggression.

1. Criminal Behavior

Some of the most convincing evidence for the roles of genetic and environmental effects in antisocial behavior derives from twin and adoption studies of criminal offending. There have been several large-scale studies spanning several countries, including three in Scandinavia (Sweden, Denmark, and Norway), as well as the United States. Most of these studies rely on official records (both convictions and arrests) obtained through court and police files, although more recent studies are beginning to use self-report methods of criminal offending.

Based on a review of studies of adult twins conducted between 1931 and 1977, monozygotic (MZ) twin concordance (i.e., the proportion of pairs in which both twins were antisocial) was generally greater than dizygotic (DZ) twin concordance. Pooling across studies totaling over 600 pairs of twins, 50.6 percent of MZ pairs are concordant for antisocial behavior, compared to 23.4 percent in DZ twins (Cloninger & Gottesman, 1987). Based on the largest twin study to date of registered criminal behavior—Christiansen's study of over 10,000 Danish male and female twins—heritability of liability towards criminal offending was estimated as .54. Thus, over half of the variation in liability towards crime may be explained by individual differences in genetic predispositions.

Genetic effects for adult criminal offending have also been shown to be consistent across the two sexes. Both male and female Danish twins showed higher MZ concordance than DZ for all types of crimes (Christiansen, 1968, 1974, 1977; Cloninger et al., 1978; Gottesman et al., 1983; Cloninger & Gottesman, 1987), despite different base rates in registered crime for two sexes. The twin correlation for liability towards criminality in male–female pairs, however, is lower than for same-sex DZ twins, which suggests either sex-limited genetic effects (i.e., different genes involved in males and females) or sex-limited environmental effects (i.e., different common-environmental factors involved in males and females).

Unlike studies of adult criminal behavior, twin studies of juvenile delinquency tend to show less genetic influence. Based on Cloninger and Gottesman's (1987) review, twin concordance for juvenile offending was 82.0 percent for MZ pairs and 72.2 percent for DZ pairs. This pattern of high and nearly equal concordances for genetically identical and nonidentical twins suggests a strong effect of shared environment between the twins, and only modest heritability, if any. It should be noted, however, that juvenile criminal behavior has been studied less frequently and less rigorously in sampling and measurement procedures than adults (see Christiansen, 1977 for a review). Most early studies of juvenile delinquency have relied on official records, which may be less reliable than for adults, due to greater variations in reporting, record keeping, and leniency for children in the legal justice system. In contrast to early studies of official juvenile records, more recent studies of teenage twins have suggested significant heritability for self-reported antisocial behaviors, including lawbreaking (Rowe, 1983, 1985, 1986). In order to resolve the effects of genetic and environmental factors in juvenile delinquency, further studies are needed which combine multiple methods of assessing lawbreaking behaviors (e.g., self-report, parent-report, and school records).

Carey (1992, 1994) has emphasized the general difficulty in interpreting results from twin studies of any age, because of different base rates for MZ (highest) and DZ (same sex higher than opposite sex) twins in both sexes. This pattern suggests an "imitation" or collusion effect that would increase variance (and hence prevalence) in more genetically related pairs as a function of the magnitude of imitation and heritability (Carey, 1986). In fact, concordant MZ twins tend to collude more often in the same criminal act than DZ pairs. The increased co-offending amongst MZ twins calls into question the equal environments assumption required in studies of twins raised together. It is important, therefore, to examine adoption studies of criminal behavior, which are generally considered the most powerful method for disentangling the effects of heredity and environment.

Adoption studies have, in fact, consistently demonstrated that adult criminal behavior is under at least partial genetic influence. In major studies of adopted children and their parents—conducted in Denmark (see Hutchings, 1972), Sweden (see Cloninger et al., 1982), and the United States (see Crowe, 1972; Cadoret, 1978)—biological offspring of criminals showed a greater than average tendency towards criminal behavior, even when the offspring are raised by noncriminal adoptive parents (see Baker, 1986; Baker et al., 1989; Bohman et al., 1982; Cadoret, 1978; Cadoret, Cain, & Crowe, 1983; Cadoret et al., 1985; Cloninger, Reich, & Guze, 1975; Crowe, 1974; Hutchings & Mednick, 1975; Mednick, Gabrielli, & Hutchings, 1984, 1987; Schulsinger, 1972; Sigvardsson et al., 1982). In contrast, criminal convictions in the adoptive parents have considerably less overall effect, if any, on the children's risk of being convicted in these studies.

Most importantly, however, both the Scandinavian and US adoption studies reported a significant Gene x Environment (G x E) interaction, such that environmental effects (indicated by increased conviction rates in children of convicted adoptive parents) *were* found, but only (or especially) in combination with increased genetic risks (i.e., convicted biological parents). That is, the highest rate of criminal offending was found in all three of these major adoption studies, amongst adoptees whose adoptive *and* biological fathers had criminal records.

This striking and consistent pattern of results is illustrated in Figs. II-3-2-2.2–4, based on conviction rates for property crimes in the Danish and Swedish adoption studies (see respectively, Fig. II-3-2-2.2, adapted from Mednick, Gabrielli, & Hutchings, 1984; and Fig. II-3-2-2.3, adapted from Cloninger & Gottesman, 1987) and average number of lawbreaking behaviors in the Iowa adoption study (see Fig. II-3-2-2.4, adapted from Cadoret, Cain, & Crowe, 1983). As shown, genetic predispositions (indicated by biological parent antisocial behavior) present the greatest risk to the adopted offspring in the presence of adverse environmental conditions (indicated by adoptive parent antisocial behavior). Viewed conversely, negative environmental factors stemming from being raised by antisocial parents may exert their greatest effects on individuals who are genetically predisposed towards antisocial behavior. This finding in particular has profound implications for our understanding the role of parents and other environmental aspects in producing aggressive and other antisocial outcomes of children.

Similar to twin studies of adult criminal behavior, adoption studies generally indicate similar estimates of heritability for liability towards crime in males (h^2 = .32) and females (h^2 = .26) (Baker et al., 1989). An important sex difference has been found, however, in the relative genetic risks provided to their offspring by mothers vs. fathers. In particular, conviction rates are highest amongst offspring of convicted mothers compared to convicted fathers. This indicates that genetic predisposition to criminality must be more severe in order for a woman to become criminal than for a man. Thus, women who do eventually fall into the justice system may possess a more extreme genetic liability, which in turn will be passed on to their offspring. Prenatal effects might, of course, explain the different risk rates as a function of sex of parent. However, the greater conviction rates in parents of convicted daughters compared to sons have also been reported in both the Danish (Baker et al., 1989) and Swedish (Cloninger & Gottesman, 1987) adoption studies.

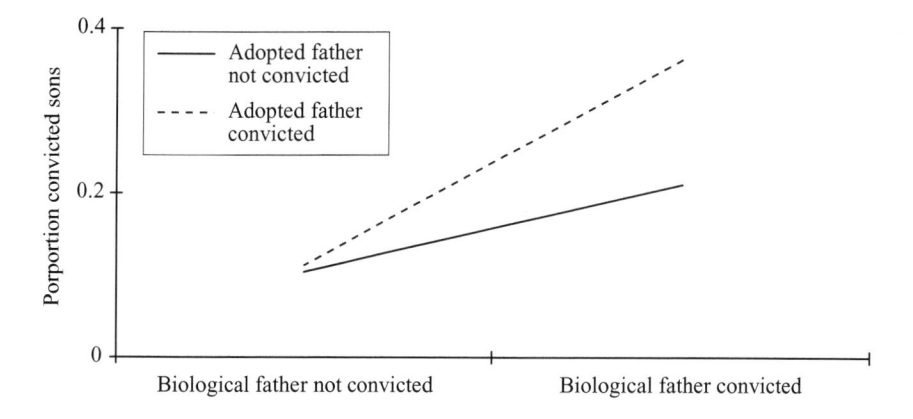

FIGURE II-3-2-2.2. **Property crime convictions in Danish adopted sons and their fathers.** *Source*: Mednick et al., 1984.

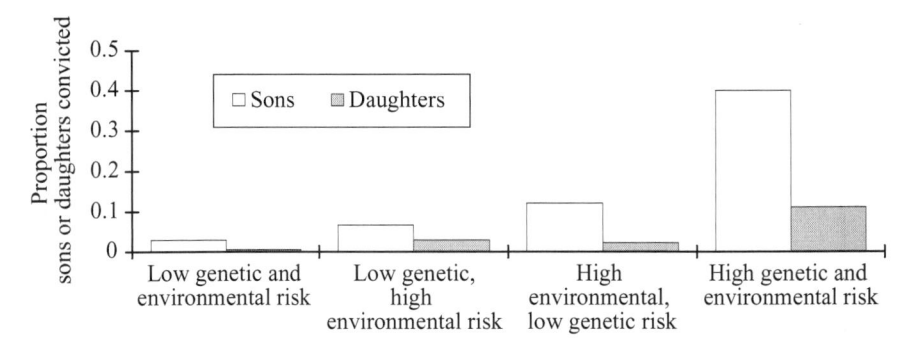

FIGURE II-3-2-2.3. Petty crime convictions in adopted sons and daughters in Sweden. *Source*: Cloninger & Gottesman, 1987.

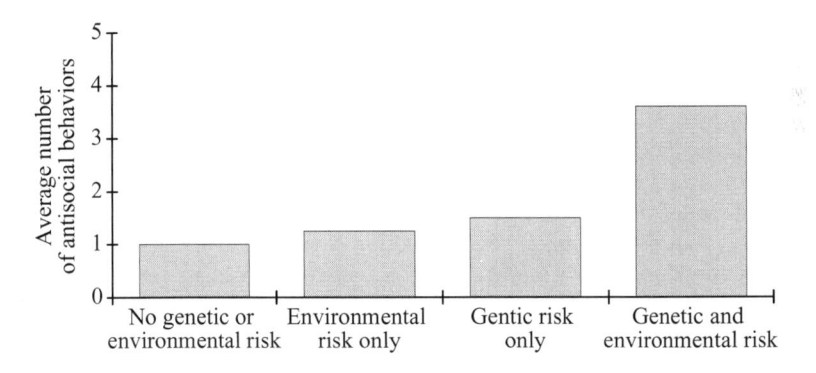

FIGURE II-3-2-2.4. Average number of antisocial behaviors in adopted sons and daughters in Iowa. *Source*: Cain & Crowe, 1983.

Taken together, evidence from both twin and adoption studies support the idea that nature, via genetic mechanisms, does play an important role in criminal behavior. Heritability estimates from adoption studies do tend to be somewhat lower than in twin studies, however. This may suggest the importance of non-additive genetic influences, which will serve to increase twin, but not biological parent–offspring resemblance. Additive genetic effects are suggested by the significant genetic influence demonstrated in the multi-generation adoption design, although additional non-additive genetic effects may also operate to increase DZ and MZ twin resemblance.

Most twin and adoption studies of criminal behavior are based on nonviolent crimes— that is, petty crimes against property, such as theft. Three studies, however, have examined separately the roles of heredity and environment in violent criminal offending, per se—the Swedish and Danish adoption studies, and the Danish twin study. All three studies are consistent in suggesting that the relative importance of genetic factors does appear to differ for violent crimes (including rape, robbery, and assault) and nonviolent crimes. However, the studies are inconsistent in whether or not they report a genetic influence in violent offending (see Carey, 1994 and Davis et al., 1999 for reviews).

A genetic influence for liability towards crimes against persons has been suggested only in the Danish twin study. Twin concordances for violent criminal offending were 41.7

percent for MZ and 20.5 percent for DZ male pairs. Correlations of liability between co-twins were also significantly different for MZ (r = .77) and DZ (r = .52) pairs, suggesting a heritability of about 50 percent for liability towards violent offending, compared to h^2 of about 78 percent for property offending. Moreover, there was no significant cross correlation between property crime in one twin with crimes against person in co-twin in MZ pairs, indicating distinct genetic and environmental etiologies for violent and nonviolent crimes (Cloninger & Gottesman, 1987).

Different underlying mechanisms for violent and nonviolent criminal offending were also apparent in the two adoption studies that distinguished between these two types of crimes. In contrast to the Danish twin study, however, no significant genetic influence in violent offending was found in either the Swedish or Danish adoption studies. An illustration of the markedly different genetic effects for violent and nonviolent (i.e., property) offending is shown in Fig. II-3-2-2.5 (adapted from Mednick, Gabrielli, & Hutchings, 1984). As shown, the number of convictions in the biological fathers is strongly and linearly related to adopted sons' conviction rates for property but not violent crimes. It is particularly surprising that there is no genetic effect for violent criminal offending, given the dramatic increase in the sons' criminality as a function of severity of property offending (indicated by recidivism or greater number of convictions) in the biological fathers. It might be expected that violent offending would reflect the more severe genetic predisposition of all. Instead, these results reiterate that different etiologies altogether may be involved in violent and nonviolent forms of antisocial behavior.

Violent crimes are also more often related to alcohol use than are nonviolent (property) crimes. For example, the Swedish adoption study reported that crimes associated with alcohol abuse are often committed against persons, whereas crime in the absence of alcohol abuse is nearly always committed against property only. In addition, paternal violence in the Swedish study significantly increased sons' alcohol abuse, but not their criminality (Bohman et al., 1982). Thus, violent criminal offending in the parents may indicate a risk for other adverse psychological outcomes, rather than liability towards violent behavior.

2. Psychiatric Disorders Related to Antisocial Behavior

There are three mental disorders for which antisocial behavior and aggression are key factors in their diagnosis, according to the Diagnostic and Statistical Manual for Mental Disorders, Fourth Edition (DSM-IV, 1994). Antisocial Personality Disorder (APD) in adults may involve aggressive, impulsive, reckless, and irresponsible behavior, with difficulty maintaining jobs and personal relationships, and a failure to conform to social norms (e.g., lawbreaking). In children, externalizing problems such as aggression towards people and animals, destruction of property, deceitfulness, or theft, and other serious violations of rules (e.g., truancy or running away from home), are symptomatic of Conduct Disorder (CD). Also, a persistent pattern of negativistic, hostile, and defiant behavior in children is characteristic of Oppositional Defiant Disorder (ODD). These disorders are typically diagnosed through structured interviews, although questionnaire methods are sometimes used to obtain self-reported symptoms.

Effects of heredity and environment in these psychiatric disorders have been investigated in both twin and adoption studies. Significant genetic influences have been consistently reported for APD symptoms and/or diagnoses in twin samples from the US (Grove et al., 1990; Carey, 1993; Lyons et al., 1993, Lyons, 1996), while shared family environ-

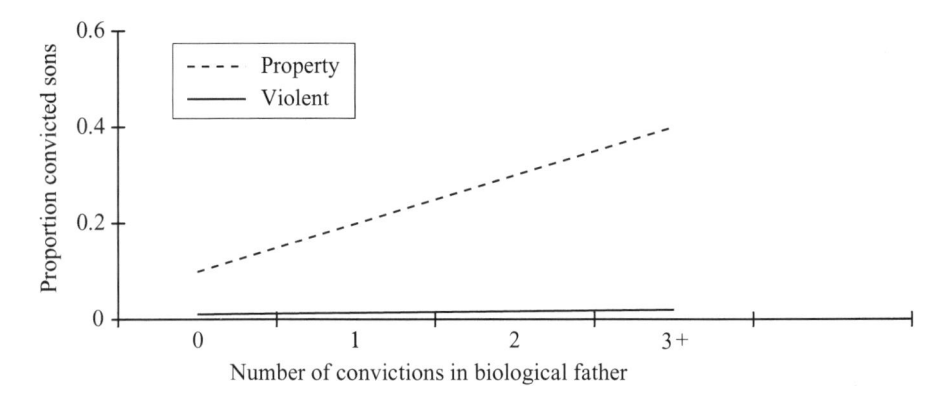

<small>Figure II-3-2-2.5. **Property and violent criminal offending in the Danish Adoption Study.** *Source*: Mednick, Gabrielli, & Hutchings, 1984.</small>

mental effects are less important, if at all, across studies. Adoption studies in the US have also found significant genetic effects for APD symptom counts (Cadoret et al., 1986; Cadoret et al., 1995). These results are in complete accord with twin and adoption studies of adult criminal offending, based on official records.

Significant genetic influences in symptoms of CD in children and teenagers have also been reported in twin (Eaves et al., 1993) and adoption studies conducted in the US (Cadoret, Cain, & Crowe, 1983; Cadoret et al., 1995). In addition, shared environmental effects were of particular importance for childhood behavioral problems across these studies. The adoption studies by Cadoret and colleagues illustrated this especially, such that CD symptoms appeared most frequently for children whose adoptive parents are divorced or show a history of psychiatric problems themselves.

A comparison of the genetic and environmental etiologies of antisocial psychiatric disorders in children and adults provides a similar pattern to that found in studies of official records of criminal offending, as reviewed previously in this chapter. Based on retrospective reports in a large sample of male twins from the Vietnam Era Twin Registry, Lyons et al. (1995) found significant genetic influences for 8 out of 10 adult symptoms of APD, but only for 5 out of 12 juvenile symptoms of CD. Shared environmental effects were also important for juvenile symptoms, and far more so than for adult symptoms. Heritability for overall liability towards APD was considerably higher ($h^2 = .43$) than for liability towards CD ($h^2 = .07$), while the converse was true for shared environmental effects ($c^2 = .05$ for APD and $c^2 = .31$ for CD).

The pattern of results for psychiatric diagnoses pertaining to antisocial behavior is consistent with those found for juvenile and adult criminal offending: Genetic influences appear far more important during adulthood, while shared environmental effects are more important during childhood and adolescence.

3. Trait Aggression

What may be considered the normal range of aggressive behavior has also been studied in behavioral genetic designs, using a variety of self-report, parental-report, and observational methods. Measures of normal-varying trait aggression may include assessments of the frequency and degree of anger responses (e.g., temper tantrums, verbal insults, throwing objects), physical fighting, teasing and bullying behaviors, and more subtle forms of manipulating or injuring others for one's own benefit (e.g., cutting in line, spreading rumors and gossip). For children, parent and teacher ratings are typically used, although a few studies have recorded observations in the laboratory (Plomin, Foch, & Rowe, 1981) or home (Ghodsian-Carpey, & Baker, 1987). Studies of adults rely almost exclusively on self-report methods using questionnaires.

Developmental differences in genetic and environmental effects appear for measures of trait aggression, similar to what has been suggested in studies of criminal behavior. For childhood aggression, there is no consistent pattern of results found for environmental and genetic factors. This is in stark contrast to results from behavioral genetics studies of other normal-varying childhood traits, such as personality and cognitive abilities, where genetic factors are invariably found across samples and designs. While some studies find clear evidence of genetic influence in childhood aggression (e.g., Ghodsian-Carpey & Baker, 1987), others do not (e.g., Plomin et al., 1981). This may, in part, be due to the wide variation in definitions and methods used for measuring aggressive behavior. In fact, as Plomin, Nitz and Rowe (1990) point out in a review, no two behavioral genetics studies have used the same measure of aggression.

Compared to children, studies of adult aggressive behavior tend to show genetic effects more consistently. Several recent twin studies of self-reported aggressive tendencies all show greater MZ than DZ resemblance (Rushton et al., 1986; Tellegen et al., 1988; Coccaro et al., 1997). Moreover, twin correlations appear similar for twins reared together and apart, suggesting little or no effect of shared environment in measures of adult trait aggression (Coccaro et al., 1993).

There may also be differential patterns of both environmental and genetic influences for different kinds of aggression and hostility. Different subscales of the Buss-Durkee Hostility Inventory (Direct Assault, Indirect Assault, Irritability, and Verbal Assault) have shown varying estimates of heritability, with contributions of additive and non-additive genetic factors being markedly different across these subscales (Coccaro et al., 1997). Ghodsian-Carpey and Baker (1987) also found evidence for varying estimates of environmental and genetic influences in different forms of childhood aggression, such as verbal and physical forms.

Sex differences in genetic and environmental etiologies of trait aggression have not been systematically studied as yet. It remains to be seen whether heritable and nonheritable influences in aggressive behavior differ in type or magnitude for males and females.

III. SUMMARY OF MAJOR FINDINGS FOR ANTISOCIAL BEHAVIOR AND IMPLICATIONS FOR UNDERSTANDING VIOLENCE

Human antisocial behavior and aggression are clearly the products of both nature and nurture. Genetic influences have been clearly demonstrated in a wide range of antisocial behaviors, including criminal offending, psychiatric diagnoses, and more broadly defined measures of trait aggression. Yet, heritability estimates are far less than unity, indicating the joint importance of nonheritable, environmental factors. Most importantly, there is no simple model that accounts for all forms of antisocial behavior. The magnitude and nature of genetic effects depend on a variety of factors, including age and sex, as well as the way in which antisocial behavior is defined and measured. Environmental factors themselves also appear to modify the degree of genetic influence in antisocial behavior. The major findings of twin and adoption studies of antisocial behavior are summarized here, with particular attention to violence.

1. Developmental Effects

The relative importance of genetic effects in liability towards criminal offending appears to vary over developmental periods, with generally smaller heritabilities for child than adult misbehavior, and larger effects of shared family environment (including between co-twins) during childhood. A strikingly similar pattern of increasing genetic influence and decreasing shared environmental influence is also found for psychiatric disorders related to aggression, including conduct disorder and antisocial personality disorder. The same trend may be suggested for normal-varying aggressive behavior, since genetic effects are more consistently found in studies of adults than in children.

Are there developmental effects in violence, per se? Although this may be one of the most important questions to be addressed, there is insufficient information to answer it at this point. Among the few behavioral genetic studies that have examined genetic and environmental factors in juvenile delinquency (i.e., lawbreaking behaviors) (see Cloninger & Gottesman, 1987; Rowe, 1985) or trait aggression (see Plomin et al., 1990), virtually none have addressed questions concerning specific etiologies of *violent* criminal behavior or *physical* aggression in children or adolescents. It remains to be seen what the developmental course of nature and nurture effects in violence may be.

It may also be important to distinguish between developmental subtypes of antisocial individuals themselves, in order to understand fully the genetic and environmental underpinnings of antisocial behavior, including violence. As Moffitt (1993) has suggested, developmentally stable ("life-course persistent") offenders may be more affected by biological (including genetic) predispositions than transitory (e.g., "adolescence-limited") offenders. This would explain the considerable influence of shared environmental effects (which most likely include peer influences) during childhood and adolescence compared to adulthood. Longitudinal, prospective studies of twins or adoptees are required to evaluate Moffitt's hypotheses about developmentally distinct subtypes with different nature and nurture underpinnings for antisocial behavior.

2. Sex Differences

The greater incidence of antisocial behavior in males is a well-established finding, which transcends race and culture, socioeconomic levels, age groups, and definitions of antisocial behavior itself. Human males display more aggressive behavior than females within the first three years of life, have higher incidences of conduct disorder during childhood, and engage more frequently in criminal behavior from adolescence through adulthood (see Daly and Wilson, in this volume). Sex differences are somewhat reduced for self-report measures, although the rate of offending in males is still at least twofold that of females (Hindelang et al., 1979). According to Criminal Justice Statistics, males of all races account for 85 percent of teenage and adult arrests and 90 percent of children's arrests for serious *violent* crimes during 1977–1997 (see Males, 1999).

In spite of the fact that males are far more likely than females to engage in antisocial, aggressive, and criminal behavior, there are no apparent differences in the *relative importance* of genetic factors (i.e., heritability) in explaining individual differences in antisocial behavior. Heritability of liability towards nonviolent criminality appears equivalent for men and women, both in studies of twins (Cloninger & Gottesman, 1987) and adoptees (Baker et al., 1989). However, *average* genetic predispositions do appear greater for criminal women compared to criminal men. This is evidenced in the finding that first-degree relatives of criminal women are at far greater risk than first-degree relatives of criminal men (Sigvardsson et al., 1982; Baker et al., 1989). Thus, although genetic factors account for comparable proportions of individual differences in criminality in both sexes, the genetic predisposition must generally be far greater for a woman to become a criminal than for a man.

Are there differences in how nature and nurture affect violent behavior, specifically, in men and women? Despite the well-documented sex difference in the base rates of violence and aggression, relatively little research has been done to investigate the different etiologies that may exist in males and females. Due, in part, to the rarity with which women engage in and become convicted of violent crimes, the majority of behavior genetic studies investigating violence have been conducted on men. The low base rates of violence in women makes it particularly difficult to study genetic and environmental effects, since large samples are generally required to do so.

3. GxE Interactions

One of the most important findings to emerge from behavioral genetic studies of antisocial behavior is that the *combination* of genetic and environmental effects is of critical importance in determining aggressive and other antisocial outcomes. In fact, the domain of antisocial behavior is one of the few, if not the only, in which genotype by environment (GxE) interactions are consistently found (see Figs. II-3-2-2.2–4).

The highly replicated GxE interaction has important implications for understanding and treating antisocial individuals, or those at risk for becoming so. First, environmental interventions may be more successful for some individuals than others. In particular, results from the three major adoption studies of criminal behavior (in which family environment effects appear strongest for those with highest genetic risk) suggest that individuals genetically predisposed towards antisocial behavior may benefit most from improved environments. Uncoupling adverse environments from genetic risks could substantially reduce criminal offending and other aggressive behaviors, including violence.

4. Violent Behavior

Amongst the plethora of twin and adoption studies of antisocial behavior, relatively few have specifically investigated violent behaviors, per se. Violence may be included in a broader definition of aggression or antisocial behavior, and may not be analyzed separately. Based on the few studies that have reported separate analyses of violent and nonviolent criminal offending, different genetic and environmental etiologies have been suggested for the two (Mednick et al., 1984). Heritability is greatest for nonviolent criminal behavior, and lower or possibly negligible for violent acts (see Fig. II-3-2-2.5).

Several reasons for the lack of genetic influence in violent criminal offending could be considered. First, the majority of studies have relied on official records (especially convictions). Convictions represent only a fraction of actual crimes actually committed, specifically those for which the perpetrator is caught and received due process in a court of law. Criminal convictions, then, may be an unrepresentative and unreliable source for measuring violence. Alternative sampling procedures (e.g., through clinics or community samples), combined with self-report methods of assessing interpersonal violence, will be especially important in future studies aimed at understanding the possible genetic bases in this area.

Second, non-additive genetic effects may be the primary source of heritable variation in violent criminal offending. This would explain the mixed results in twin and adoption studies, where no parent offspring resemblance was found in the Danish and Swedish adoption studies, yet Danish twins were significantly concordant (and more so for MZ pairs). Consistent with this idea is the study by Coccaro et al. (1993, 1997), which suggested substantial non-additive genetic variance in a several dimensions of aggression.

Third, there may be a strong heritability for predispositions towards violence, but environmental factors may substantially moderate these effects. In fact, impulsive aggression has been suggested as one of the more heritable forms of trait aggression (Coccaro et al., 1993). Given the highly replicated GxE interaction found in nonviolent offending and conduct disorders, it seems likely that such effects may also be important for violence. Favorable environmental circumstances may substantially enable an individual to overcome negative genetic predispositions.

Overall, genetic influences have not been adequately studied (e.g., across cultures, countries, birth cohorts, or research designs) to accept the idea that violent behavior is *not* heritable. Moreover, this line of inquiry has necessarily been restricted to studies of males, due to the rarity with which women are convicted of violent offenses. More behavioral genetic research of violence in both men and women is clearly warranted.

IV. IMPLICATIONS AND FUTURE DIRECTIONS

The recent cases of shootings by American middle-class schoolboys are consistent in many ways with research into the nature and nurture of violence. They illustrate, for example, the limited importance of parental factors in predicting violence. The parents in these cases appeared exemplary in many ways (middle-class, employed, law-abiding individuals who provided educational and other opportunities for success in their children), yet their sons still took violent courses of action. The lack of parental deviance is not surprising in these cases, in fact, given the noted absence of adoptive *or* biological parent–offspring resemblance for violent criminal offending in the Scandinavian adoption studies. Criminal violence in the parents does not appear to be an important predictor of violent behavior in children.

This does not rule out the possibility of biologically based neurological deficits in these children, however, which might have stemmed from genetic or environmental sources. Although detailed reliable information on the psychological status or family backgrounds in these cases is limited, there are reports that one perpetrator (Eric Harris in the Columbine High School shooting) had been prescribed an antidepressant drug (CNN April 29, 1999). Harris' prescription was for Luvox, one of a class of drugs called selective serotonin reuptake inhibitors (SSRI). SSRIs work by enhancing the brain's ability to use serotonin, a neurotransmitter released in the brain that has been shown to regulate impulsive behavior. Harris' prescription might be indicative of a serotonin deficiency, which has been shown to be related to one of the more heritable forms of impulsive, irritable, and aggressive behavior (Coccaro et al., 1989, 1993, 1994, 1997). It is also noteworthy that Coccaro's twin studies have suggested primarily non-additive genetic influences (i.e., due to dominance or recessiveness, or interaction between genetic loci) in this aggressive subtype, which would predict a lack of parent–offspring resemblance for this behavior pattern.

Important environmental effects cannot be ruled out in these cases, however. Peer influences (including conflicts with and rejection by subgroups) have been suggested in each of these cases. These are consistent with the substantial effects of shared environment (which would most likely include peer influences) suggested in twin studies of juvenile delinquency. One obvious environmental consideration in the case of Klebold and Harris is their mutual influence on each other. They may have represented a pair of individuals, each with enhanced liabilities towards general antisocial behavior or violence (stemming from genetic or environmental sources)—not unlike like "two peas in a pod," such as twins, with highly similar genetic predispositions towards violence. Similar to the twin imitation effect discussed by Carey (1992), it may have been the combination of two or more deviant youths interacting and encouraging each other, which led to more extreme behavior than either would engage in alone. In short, both nature and nurture, most likely in combination, are likely to have been forces underlying each of these children's extreme behaviors.

We may only speculate, of course, about the role of heredity and environment in individual cases such as these. Nonetheless, behavioral genetic research can help guide these speculations, based on what is known about genetic and environmental underpinnings of antisocial behavior and aggression.

As a final reminder, it is important to understand that genes do not code directly for crime and violence. It is unlikely that a "gene for violence" will ever be discovered, because of the fact that genes do not code directly for specific behaviors, as discussed earlier. Although specific genes may be discovered which contribute to *liability towards violent offending*, it is unlikely that such genes will explain a large proportion of variance in this liability. This is due to (a) the heterogeneity in definitions of aggression and violence, (b) the heterogeneity in etiologies of various forms of aggression and violence, and (c) the multifactorial nature of the genetic and environmental influences for various forms of aggression and violence. Needless to say, a great deal more research is required to clarify the nature–nurture problem in human violence.

REFERENCES

Baker, Laura A. (1986). Estimating Genetic Correlations Among Discontinuous Phenotypes: An Analysis of Criminal Convictions and Psychiatric Hospital Diagnoses in Danish Adoptees. *Behavior Genetics, 16,* 127–142.

Baker, Laura A. (1999). Biological Theories. In Ronald Gottesman & Richard M. Brown (Eds.), *Violence in America: An Encyclopedia, Vol. 1: A–F* (pp. 306–311). New York: Charles Scribner's Sons.

Baker, Laura A., Wendy A. Mack, Terrie E. Moffitt, & Sarnoff A. Mednick. (1989). Sex Differences in Property Crime in a Danish Adoption Cohort. *Behavior Genetics, 19,* 355–370.

Bohman, Michael, C. Robert Cloninger, Soeren Sigvardsson, & Ann-Liis Von Knorring. (1982). Predisposition to Petty Criminality in Swedish Adoptees: I. Genetic and Environmental Heterogeneity. *Archives of General Psychiatry, 39,* 1233–1241.

Cadoret, Remi J. (1978). Psychopathology in Adopted-away Offspring of Biologic Parents with Antisocial Behavior. *Archives of General Psychiatry, 35,* 176–184.

Cadoret, Remi J., Colleen A. Cain, & Raymond R. Crowe. (1983). Evidence for a Gene-environment Interaction in the Development of Adolescent Antisocial Behavior. *Behavior Genetics*, *13*, 301–310.

Cadoret, Remi J., Thomas W. O'Gorman, Ed Troughton, & Ellen Heywood. (1985). Alcoholism and antisocial personality: Interrelationships, genetic and environmental factors. *Archives of General Psychiatry*, *42*, 161–167.

Cadoret, Remi J., Ed Troughton, Thomas W. O'Gorman, & Ellen Heywood. (1986). An Adoption Study of Genetic and Environmental Factors in Drug Abuse. *Archive of General Psychiatry*, *43*, 1131–1136.

Cadoret, Remi J., William R. Yates, Ed Troughton, George Woodworth, & Mark Stewart. (1995). Genetic x Environmental Interaction in the Genesis of Aggressivity and Conduct Disorders. *Archives of General Psychiatry*, *52*(11), 916–924.

Carey, Gregory. (1986). A General Multivariate Approach to Linear Modeling in Human Genetics. *American Journal of Human Genetics*, *39*, 775–786.

Carey, Gregory. (1992). Twin Imitation for Antisocial Behavior: Implications for Genetic and Family Environment Research. *Journal of Abnormal Psychology*, *101*, 18–25.

Carey, Gregory. (1993). Multivariate Genetic Relationships among Drug Abuse, Alcohol Abuse, and Antisocial Personality. *Psychiatric Genetics*, *3*, 141.

Carey, Gregory. (1994). Genetics and Violence. In Albert J. Reiss, Klaus A. Miczek & Jeffrey A. Roth (Eds), *Understanding and Preventing Violence. Vol. 2. Biobehavioral Influences on Violence* (pp. 21–58). Washington: National Academy Press.

Carey, Gregory, & David Goldman. (1997). The Genetics of Antisocial Behavior. In David M. Stoff, James Breiling & Jack Maser (Eds.), *Handbook of Antisocial Behavior* (pp. 243–254). New York: John Wiley & Sons, Inc.

Christiansen, Karl O. (1968). Threshold of Tolerance in Various Population Groups Illustrated by Results from Danish Criminological Twin Study. In Anthony Vivian Smith de Reuck & Ruth Porter (Eds.), *Ciba Foundation Symposium on the Mentally Abnormal Offender* (pp. 107–116). London: J. & A. Churchill Ltd.

Christiansen, Karl O. (1974). Seriousness of Criminality and Concordance among Danish Twins. In Roger Hood (Ed.), *Crime, Criminology, and Public Policy* (pp. 63–77). London: Heinemann.

Christiansen, Karl O. (1977). A Review of Studies of Criminality among Twins. In Sarnoff A. Mednick & Karl O. Christiansen (Eds.), *Biosocial Bases of Criminal Behavior* (pp. 45–88). New York: Gardner.

Cloninger, C. Robert; Soeren Sigvardsson, Michael Bohman, & Anne-Liis Von Knorring. (1982). Predisposition to Petty Criminality in Swedish Adoptees: II. Cross-fostering Analysis of Gene-environment Interaction. *Archives of General Psychiatry*, *39*, 1242–1247.

Cloninger, C. Robert, Karl O. Christiansen, Theodore Reich, & Irving I. Gottesman. (1978). Implications of Sex Differences in the Prevalences of Antisocial Personality, Alcoholism, and Criminality for Familial Transmission. *Archives of General Psychiatry*, *35*, 941–951.

Cloninger, C. Robert, & Irving I. Gottesman. (1987). Genetic and Environmental Factors in Antisocial Behavior Disorders. In Sarnoff A. Mednick & Terrie E. Moffitt (Eds.), *Proceedings of Conference on Biosocial Bases of Antisocial Behavior* (pp. 92–109). Cambridge: Cambridge University Press.

Cloninger, C. Robert, Theodore Reich, & Samuel B. Guze. (1975). The Multifactorial Model of Disease Transmission: II. Sex Differences in the Familial Transmission of Sociopathy (Antisocial Personality). *British Journal of Psychiatry*, *127*, 11–22.

Coccaro, Emil F., Larry J. Siever, Howard M. Klar, Gail Maurer, Karen Cochrane, Thomas B. Cooper, Richard C. Mohs, & Kenneth L. Davis. (1989). Serotonergic Studies in Patients with Affective and Personality Disorders. *Archives of General Psychiatry*, *46*, 587–599.

Coccaro, Emil F., Cynthia S. Bergeman, & Gerald E. McClearn. (1993). Heritability of Irritable Impulsiveness: A Study of Twins Reared Together and Apart. *Psychiatry Research*, *48*, 229–242.

Coccaro, Emil F., Jeremy M. Silverman, & Howard M. Klar. (1994). Familial Correlates of Reduced Central Serotonergic System Function in Patients with Personality Disorders. *Archives of General Psychiatry*, *51*, 318–324.

Coccaro, Emil F., Cynthia S. Bergeman, Richard J. Kavoussi, & Alesha D. Seroczynski. (1997). Heritability of Aggression and Irritability: A Twin Study of the Buss-Durkee Aggression Scales in Adult Male Subjects. *Biological Psychiatry*, *41*, 273–284.

Crowe, Raymond R. (1972). The Adopted Offspring of Women Criminal Offenders: A Study of Their Arrest Records. *Archives of General Psychiatry*, *27*, 600–603.

Crowe, Raymond R. (1974). An Adoption Study of Antisocial Personality. *Archives of General Psychiatry*, *31*, 785–791.

Davis, Chayna, Carol A. Van Hulle, Collen M. Coffey, & Gregory Carey. (1999). Genetics: Twins, Families and Adoptions. In Ronald Gottesman & Richard Maxwell Brown (Eds.), *Violence in America: An Encyclopedia, Vol. 2: G–Q* (pp. 25–28). New York: Charles Scribner's Sons.

DiLalla, Lisabeth F., & Irving I. Gottesman. (1991). Does Violence Beget Violence? Wisdom's Untold Tale. *Psychological Bulletin, 109*(1), 125–129.

Dodge, Kenneth A., John E. Bates, & Gregory S. Petit. (1990). Mechanisms in the Cycle of Violence. *Science, 250*, 1678–1683.

DSM-VI. (1994). *Diagnostic and Statistical Manual for Mental Disorders. 4th Edition.* Washington: American Psychiatric Association.

Eaves, Lindon J., Judy L. Silberg, John K. Hewitt, Michael Rutter, Joanne M. Meyer, Michael C. Neale, & Andrew Pickles. (1993). Analyzing Twin Resemblance in Multi-symptom Data: Genetic Applications of a Latent Class Model for Symptoms of Conduct Disorder in Juvenile Boys. *Behavior Genetics, 23*, 5–19.

Falconer, Douglas S., & Trudy F. C. Mackay. (1996). *Introduction to Quantitative Genetics. 4th Edition.* Essex: Longman Ltd.

Fisher, Ronald A. (1918). The Covariation Between Relatives on the Supposition of Mendelian Inheritance. *Transactions of the Royal Society of Edinburgh, 52*, 399–433.

Ghodsian-Carpey, Jilla, & Laura A. Baker. (1987). Genetic and Environmental Influences on Aggression in 4- to 7-year Old Twins. *Aggressive Behavior, 13*, 173–186.

Gottesman, Irving I., Gregory Carey, & Daniel R. Hanson. (1983). Pearls and Perils in Epigenetic Psychopathology. In Samuel B. Guze, Felton Earls & James E. Barrett (Eds.), *Childhood Psychopathology and Development* (pp. 287–300). New York: Raven Press.

Grove, William M., Elke D. Eckert, Leonard L. Heston, Thomas J. Bouchard, Jr., Nancy Segal, & David T. Lykken. (1990). Heritability of Substance Abuse and Antisocial Behavior: A Study of Monozygotic Twins Raised Apart. *Biological Psychiatry, 27*, 293–304.

Harris, Judith. R. (1998). *The Nurture Assumption: Why Children Turn Out the Way They Do.* New York: Free Press.

Hindelang, Michael J., Travis Hirschi, & Joseph Weiss. (1979). Correlates of Delinquency: The Illusion of Discrepancy between Self-report and Official Measure. *American Sociological Review, 44*, 995–1014.

Hutchings, Barry. (1972). *Environmental and Genetic Factors in Psychopathology and Criminality.* Unpublished M. Phil. Thesis, University of London.

Hutchings, Barry, & Sarnoff A. Mednick. (1975). Registered Criminality in the Adoptive and Biological Parents of Registered Male Criminal Adoptees. In Ronald R. Fieve, David Rosenthal & Henry Brill (Eds.), *Genetic Research in Psychiatry* (pp. 105–116). Baltimore: Johns Hopkins University Press.

Lyons, Michael J., Lindon J. Eaves, Ming T. Tsuang, Seth A. Eisen, Jack Goldberg, & William R. True. (1993). Differential Heritability of Adult and Juvenile Antisocial Traits. *Psychiatric Genetics, 3*, 117.

Lyons, Michael J., William R. True, Seth A. Eisen, Jack Goldberg, Joanne M. Meyer, Stephen V. Faraone, Lindon J. Eaves, & Ming T. Tsuang. (1995). Differential Heritability of Adult and Juvenile Antisocial Traits. *Archives of General Psychiatry, 52*, 906–915.

Lyons, Michael J. (1996). A Twin Study of Self-reported Criminal Behavior. In Gregory R. Bock & Jaime A. Goode (Eds.), *Genetics of Criminal and Antisocial Behavior, Ciba Foundation Symposium, 194* (pp. 61–69). Chichester: Wiley.

Males, Mike A. (1999). Children. In Ronald Gottesman & Richard Maxwell Brown (Eds.), *Violence in America: An Encyclopedia, Vol. 1: A–F* (pp. 228–232). New York: Charles Scribner's Sons.

Mason, Dehryl A., & Paul J. Frick. (1994). The Heritability of Antisocial Behavior: A Meta-analysis of Twin and Adoption Studies. *Journal of Psychology and Behavioral Assessment, 16*, 301–323.

Matheny, Adam P., Ronald S. Wilson, & Anne B. Dolan. (1976). Relations Between Twins' Similarity of Appearance and Behavioral Similarity: Testing an Assumption. *Behavior Genetics, 6*(3), 343–351.

McCord, Joan. (1999). Intergenerational Transmission of Violence. In Ronald Gottesman & Richard M. Brown (Eds.), *Violence in America: An Encyclopedia, Vol. 2: G–Q* (pp. 174–177). New York: Charles Scribner's Sons.

Mednick, Sarnoff A., William F. Gabrielli, Jr., & Barry Hutchings. (1984). Genetic Influences in Criminal Convictions: Evidence from an Adoption Cohort. *Science, 224*, 891–894.

Mednick, Sarnoff A., William F. Gabrielli, Jr., & Barry Hutchings. (1987). Genetic Factors in the Etiology of Criminal Behavior. In Sarnoff A. Mednick, Terrie E. Moffitt & Susan A. Stack (Eds.), *The Causes of Crime: New Biological Approaches* (pp. 74–91). New York: Cambridge University Press.

Mednick, Sarnoff A., & Elizabeth Kandel. (1988). Genetic and Perinatal Factors in Violence. In Terrie E. Moffitt, Sarnoff A. Mednick (Eds.), *Biological Contributions to Crime Causation. NATO Advanced*

Science Institutes Series D: Behavioral and Social Sciences, No. 40 (pp. 121–131). Dordrecht: Martinus Nijhoff Publishing.

Moffitt, Terrie E. (1993). Adolescent-limited and Life-course-persistent Antisocial Behavior: A Developmental Taxonomy. *Psychological Review, 100*, 674–701.

Plomin, Robert, John C. DeFries, Gerald E. McClearn, & Michael Rutter. (1997). *Behavioral Genetics. 3rd Edition.* New York: W.H. Freeman.

Plomin, Robert, Terryl T. Foch, & David C. Rowe. (1981). Bobo Clown Aggression in Childhood: Environment, Not Genes. *Journal of Research in Personality, 15*, 331–342.

Plomin, Robert, Kathrine Nitz, & David C. Rowe. (1990). Behavioral Genetics and Aggressive Behavior in Childhood. In Michael Lewis & Suzanne Melanie Miller (Eds.), *Handbook of Developmental Psychopathology: Perspectives in Developmental Psychology* (pp. 119–133). New York: Plenum Press.

Plomin, Robert, Lee Willerman, & John C. Loehlin. (1976). Resemblance in Appearance and the Equal Environments Assumption in Twin Studies of Personality Traits. *Behavior Genetics, 6*, 1, 43–52.

Raine, Adrian. (1993). *The Psychopathology of Crime: Criminal Behavior as a Clinical Disorder.* San Diego: Academic Press.

Raine, Adrian, & Peter H. Venables. (1989). Antisocial Behaviour: Evolution, Genetics, Neuropsychology, and Psychophysiology. In Anthony Gale & Michael W. Eysenck (Eds.), *Handbook of Individual Differences: Biological Perspectives* (pp. 287–321). Chichester: Wiley.

Rowe, David C. (1983). Biometrical Genetic Models of Self-reported Delinquent Behavior: A Twin Study. *Behavior Genetics, 13*, 473–489.

Rowe, David C. (1985). Sibling Interaction and Self-reported Delinquent Behavior: A Study of 265 Twin Pairs. *Criminology, 23*, 223–240.

Rowe, David C. (1986). Genetic and Environmental Components of Antisocial Behavior: A Study of 265 Twin Pairs. *Criminology, 24*, 513–532.

Rowe, David C. (1994). *The Limits of Family Influence. Genes, Experience, and Behavior.* New York: Guilford Press.

Rushton, J. Phillipe, David W. Fulker, Michael C. Neale, David K. B. Nias, & Hans J. Eysenck. (1986). Altruism and Aggression: The Heritability of Individual Differences. *Journal of Personality and Social Psychology, 50*, 1192–1198.

Rutter, Michael, Patrick Bolton, Richard Harrington, Ann le Couteur, Hope McDonald & Emily Simonoff. (1990). Genetic Factors in Child Psychiatric Disorders: I. A Review of Research Strategies. *Journal of Child Psychology and Psychiatry and Allied Disciplines, 31*, 1, 3–37.

Schulsinger, Fini. (1972). Psychopathy: Heredity and Environment. *International Journal of Mental Health, 1*, 190–206.

Sigvardsson, Soeren, C. Robert Cloninger, Michael Bohman, & Ann-Liis Von Knorring. (1982). Predisposition to Petty Criminality in Swedish Adoptees: III. Sex Differences and Validation of the Male Typology. *Archives of General Psychiatry, 39*, 1248–1253.

Tellegen, Auke, David T. Lykken, Thomas J. Bouchard, Kimberly Wilcox, Nancy Segal, & Stephen Rich. (1988). Personality Similarity in Twins Reared Apart and Together. *Journal of Personality and Social Psychology, 54*, 1031–1039.

Van Dusen, Kathy T., Sarnoff A. Mednick, William Gabrielli, Jr., & Barry Hutchings. (1983). Social Class and Crime in an Adoption Cohort. *The Journal of Criminal Law and Criminology, 74*, 249–269.

Venables, Peter, & Adrian Raine. (1987). Biological Theory. In Barry J. McGurk, David M. Thornton & Mark Williams (Eds.), *Applying Psychology to Imprisonment: Theory and Practice* (pp. 3–27). London: Her Majesty's Stationery Office Books.

PART II-3-3

VIOLENT INDIVIDUALS

Sociological Approaches to Individual Violence and Their Empirical Evaluation

Günter Albrecht

I. INTRODUCTION

A description of selected sociological approaches to explaining violent crime must first begin by defining the limits of the project. It should be noted, *firstly*, that we are dealing with explanations of criminal violence, and thus the many and diverse forms of violence which criminal law does not consider to be *crimes* are excluded. Since these boundaries are defined by the respective national legal systems and historically have been subject to considerable change, the definition of the topic can never be totally precise. *Secondly*, the notion of violence reveals a narrow fixation on *physical* violence, particularly in contexts of criminal law, and given long-term changes in everyday conceptions of violence, the criminal law perspective increasingly loses step with the real "violence problems." *Thirdly*, we focus on *individual* violent crime, which on the one hand makes sense because genocides obviously require a different explanation to purse-snatching, but on the other hand this is questionable because the purely *legal* classification of a crime as the act of an *individual* cannot rule out that complex *group processes and group relations* contributed significantly to the event. Police crime statistics for Germany and many other countries reveal that the vast majority of crimes of violence are committed by one offender acting alone, and this trend has increased over the last 20 years. But this does not at all imply that the explanation of individual violent crime is thus also an explanation of violent crime in its totality. *Fourthly*, systematic distinctions *between* various forms of individual violent crime are impossible to make—not only for reasons of space here, but also because, on the one hand, many theories do not differentiate in this way, and on the other hand because the

W. Heitmeyer and J. Hagan (eds.), *International Handbook of Violence Research*, 611–656.

research literature based on official crime statistics or self-report data is unwilling or unable to make further specifications, for methodological and statistical reasons. The recent debates on the issue of specialization or versatility in the course of criminal careers (see Klein, 1984; Rojek & Erickson, 1982; Wolfgang, Figlio, & Sellin, 1972; Brownfield, 1996) suggest that specialization is rather uncommon and that the issue of inadequate specification of the dependent variable is thus less problematic. On the other hand studies show that, at least with analyses looking at the ecology of crime, predictors of individual violent crime can differ greatly depending on the type of offense, so the summary talk of individual violent crime could be an unjustified generalization (see Albrecht, 2001b).

Due to limited space we will not give a description here of the quantitative development of violent crime in its historical and international-comparative perspective. Even very cautious descriptions at pains to make subtle distinctions (see Pfeiffer, 1998 on youths and adolescents in Europe) cannot refrain from making debatable points of emphasis when interpreting their findings if they want concrete results to emerge from their data (see Albrecht, 2001a). See also the individual contributions in this volume (Eisner) and the cautious expositions in Short (1997:1–36).

A description of feminist approaches is not given here for the same reason—despite the now flourishing field of feminist criminology (for Anglo-American literature, see Carlen, 1994; Chesney-Lind, 1997; Chesney-Lind & Shelden, 1998; Daly & Maher, 1998; Messerschmidt, 1997; Simpson, 1989; Smart, 1995a, 1995b; Walklate, 1995; for research in German, see among others Franke, 2000; Kersten, 1997; Leder, 1997)—but we will refer to this wherever gender has proved relevant in research.

Although the theory of moral consciousness and moral motivation has been very well developed in the last few years, especially by Nunner-Winkler (1996, 1999; see commentary by Albrecht, 2002; for a concrete application to violent crime, see among others Guerra et al., 1994), and although it has delivered important corrections for some central sociological approaches, such as rational choice theory and the general theory of crime, and is of fundamental importance in particular for legal socialization, we have to refrain from discussion here because there is inadequate space to deal with the significant area of criminal psychology (see Lösel, 1983, 1995; Lösel & Bender, 2001). Instead, we move straight to the *sociological* approaches.

II.   EXPLICATORY APPROACHES AND THEIR EMPIRICAL EVALUATION

1.   "Classical" Sociological Etiological Approaches

1.1. DIFFERENTIAL ASSOCIATION THEORY.   Sutherland's hypotheses (1939, 1968), which are partly contradictory and partly redundant (see Opp, 1974), are based on the idea that deviant and criminal behavior (and thus also violent crime) is *learned* behavior like any other. Violent criminal behavior is learned in interaction with others in a communication process, especially in intimate personal groups. This learning includes both the techniques for carrying out the criminal act and also a specific set of motives, rationalizations and attitudes. The specific set of motives is determined by the individual learning to define particular norms—and thus also laws—in a positive or negative way. Violent crime results when the positive attitudes to the use of criminal violence outweigh those that reject it. Whether a positive or a negative attitude dominates, is a question of *differential contacts,* i.e., the net effect of contacts to various other relevant people who each exhibit their own specific attitudes to violence. This outcome is in turn a function of the person's microsocial and socio-structural integration in or belonging to particular cultural milieus which can exhibit a wide range of different attitudes to violence and have different standards regarding its use. Sutherland explains the frequency of criminal behavior as a direct consequence of these *differential* contacts, but does not account for the social distribution of the situational definitions which rate criminality positively, nor does he explain the development of the differential associations themselves. His arguments are more psychological than sociological, and indeed the modern variant of this theory elaborated in the spirit of modern learning theory is called "social learning theory and deviant behavior" (see Burgess & Akers, 1966; Akers et al., 1979; Akers, 1985; see Bandura's social learning theory 1971, 1977).

Sutherland's further specification of differential contacts according to their *frequency, duration, priority* and *intensity* makes it seem plausible that the early childhood experience of violence in the family is of extraordinary significance (see among others Pfeiffer et al., 1998)—it is an experience which lasts into adolescence, is repeated on a daily basis, and is associated in particular with people to whom there is an intensive personal relationship (here, e.g., the parents). Sutherland's assumption that above all *personal* group experiences are relevant for the learning of violent crime, and not relatively impersonal means of communication, is at odds with searching for the effects of the mass media's presentation of violence (see the contribution by Lukesch in this volume), but fits the observation that the demonstrated effects are moderated by the processes in the small groups where the recipients consume programs of this kind (see in general Bandura, 1971, 1977; see Tedeschi in this volume).

The adequacy of this approach has been empirically proved in practice many times (see the extensive list in Akers, 1998:110–117). This statement must be qualified, however, since most of the studies did not specifically include *crimes of violence*; in most cases they were simply subsumed under the overall delinquency rate. It also turns out that variables from other theories (such as the labeling approach and subculture theory) are included in these studies, with the result that the original theory has basically not been tested at all (see, e.g., Akers et al., 1979 and the critiques by Stafford & Ekland-Olson, 1982; Strickland, 1982).

The question has been posed as to whether delinquency results from differential association or, inversely, whether this is a consequence of delinquent behavior (see Hirschi, 1969); the answer is that both are true (see also Elliott and Menard [no year] on corresponding temporal development patterns; Esbensen & Huizinga, 1993). It is provable beyond doubt that self-enhancement occurs through the peer group (Thornberry et al., 1994; Thornberry, Krohn, & Lizotte, 1995). It remains unresolved which of the variants detailed above can claim to have the strongest effects (see Matsueda & Anderson, 1998 vs. Alarid, Burton, & Cullen, 2000, similarly Esbensen & Deschenes, 1998). Whereas Sutherland assumed that belonging to a delinquent group affected the delinquency of individuals via their perception of others' *attitudes* to deviant behavior, Warr and Stafford (1991) showed that this effect is minor compared to the effect of others' actual *behavior*. The role of attitudes or situational definitions was thus not central, but rather a matter of other mechanisms of social learning, e.g., imitation or substitute reinforcements. It should be noted that deviant behavioral patterns are closely related to the *routine activities* of young people's groups (see Osgood et al., 1996). The role of the gender variable for differential associations still requires more detailed research, since Giordano and Rockwell (2000) come to the result—diverging from earlier studies—that they are more significant for women than for men.

It is most significant that social learning theory not only considers the *social* processes which lead to an intensification of deviant behavior but also takes account of *nonsocial* reinforcements, and not only the consumption of drugs. Recent research has shown that in some cases exercising violence is experienced as rewarding, satisfying or thrilling in itself, independent of its occasional instrumental value (see Wood et al., 1997). This not only offers a better explanation of violent excesses, but also raises questions as to the applicability of rational choice theory. For example, the actor receives emotional satisfaction unimaginable *before* the offense, so this expectation cannot have been significant for his or her original behavior. On the other hand, the euphorizing effect of the first experience of violence can raise the probability of further violence, which in turn suggests at least partial applicability of the rational choice theory; its variant which advances the theory of deterrence, however, ignores the subjective expectation of benefit almost completely. Aside from that, a consideration of these findings could lead research into violence back toward an approach that does not prematurely restrict its object of inquiry (see Nedelmann, 1997:62).

The theory of differential association is becoming increasingly attractive because it is at pains to better reintegrate *socio-structural* factors (Akers, 1998). This is particularly important because the development of delinquent groups clearly bears some relation to developments *in society as a whole*, both in quantitative and qualitative terms. Furthermore, it should be noted that groups of youths and the networks that spring up around them can be very diverse, and not least for this reason they have most varied repercussions on the behavior of the youths involved (see Kühnel & Matuschek, 1995).

1.2. STRAIN THEORY

1.2.1. Anomie Theory.   Anomie theory, which was developed at the same time as differential association theory by Robert K. Merton (1938, 1957, 1964), endeavored to trace the social distribution of deviant behaviors back to socio-structural conditions (the best introductions in German are Bohle (1975) and Lamnek (1977); Clinard (1964) and Adler and Laufer (1995) offer an overview of the Anglo-American debate). Merton proceeds on the observation that in particular societies culture and social structure are not geared to each other perfectly but can be partly dissociated. If a society emphasizes particular central cultural values so categorically that they are internalized strongly by all members of society in the process of socialization, and if the structure of the socialization process does not guarantee that the ways and means considered legitimate for achieving those goals are internalized by individuals with the same intensity, a very precarious situation arises, particularly when there is an unequal distribution of the opportunities of achieving the common values and goals by legal means. In this situation of "strain," which is reflected at the societal level as anomie, individuals or particular social groups have specific forms of adaptation at their disposal. Of these, "innovation" is the form which maintains the common goals and values but replaces the means hitherto considered legitimate for achieving these goals with other "innovative" solutions. Other forms of adaptation are characterized by individuals abandoning the common goals but holding on to the means considered legitimate for achieving these goals (ritualism); or by distancing themselves from both the goals and the means (withdrawal), or by actively trying to replace both the goals and the means considered legitimate with other goals and means (rebellion). The unlawful use of violence can clearly be attributed above all to rebellion, but also to innovation. *Individual* violent crime, however, would seem to be more typical of innovation than of rebellion, since rebellion exhibits a certain affinity to *collective* behavior. Merton pointed to the different rates of deviant behavior in various social groups and believed he could show that clear links really did exist between the dissociation of cultural and social structure, on the one hand, which can be described as a state of *anomie*, and the distribution of deviant behavior, on the other.

This macro-sociological theory of deviant behavior, which at first glance seems quite convincing, reveals several major deficiencies (but see also Merton, 1964), which appear when one inquires whether it can be correct to assume that in highly differentiated societies all social subgroups share the central goals and values of society and internalize them to the same degree. Indeed, there were always indications that the highest goals and values could vary both qualitatively and quantitatively between individual subgroups, and thus one of the basic assumptions of anomie theory may turn out to be unrealistic (see Bohle, 1975:78–125; Bohle et al., 1997:44ff). But even the most recent studies report that the "American dream" (see Messner & Rosenfeld, 1997), the dream of great material wealth and the belief or perceived obligation that one can and must do all in one's power to make it real, is even more deeply internalized among Blacks in the USA than among Whites—contrary to the common assumption. But there is an alternative interpretation of the role of this obligation to the American dream, as suggested by *control theory* (which will be considered below). This interpretation claims that the internalization of central social values (in this case the striving for success and material wealth) is a *bond* to society which *reduces* the probability of deviant behavior. It has not been possible to prove such an effect for either Whites or Blacks, but one effect has been proved that tallies with anomie theory: the stronger the American dream and the lesser the possibilities of realizing this dream, the greater the probability of criminal behavior. This effect, too, only occurs among Whites, not among Blacks, which shows clearly that the theory has overlooked at least one important variable (see Cernkovich, Giordano, & Rudolph, 2000). In particular, it would seem appropriate to distinguish between aspirations and expectations in order to be able to make precise statements (see Albrecht, 1997:509ff).

Merton's assumed a negative correlation between social class and frequency of crime could not be substantiated despite a large number of studies, and doubts thus arose at an early stage as to Merton's conception (see the findings in Clinard, 1964). Regarding the connection between class and crime, Tittle (1983) and many other theories of crime have shown immanent inconsistencies. The relationship between class and frequency of crime seems impossible to prove, be it *globally* (Tittle, Villemez, & Smith, 1978), or when one takes account of the specifications of this relationship suggested by the theories (see Tittle & Meier, 1990). A different result was arrived at by Brownfield (1986), whose study found a close connection between belonging to the so-called "disreputable poor" and participation in violent crime, a finding corroborated by Farnworth et al. (1994). This study showed that the connection is strong when the correlation is taken into account between belonging to the "underclass," on the one hand, and committing repeated serious street crimes, on the other. In Germany, too, these kinds of connections are only revealed on the basis of self-report data for very specific offenses and social subgroups. Although generally rather scant here, the connections are clearer with offenses involving bodily harm and aggression than they are with property offenses (see Albrecht & Howe, 1992; see in general Schumann et al., 1987). Recent research shows that these rather spurious correlative findings should not be interpreted prematurely. In their study on all kinds of delinquency, where the survey took particular account of *crimes of violence*, Wright et al. (1999a) demonstrated that the noncorrelation between parental socioeconomic status and juvenile delinquency did *not* mean that the parents' class was of no *causal* significance at all. Rather, parental status has both *indirect negative* and *indirect positive* causal effects on delinquency, which overall cancel themselves out. From a theoretical point of view, it would thus be wrong to ignore the parents' class as a *causal* factor, especially since control theory's criticism of strain theory is methodologically questionable (on the latter, see Bernard, 1984; in general, Albrecht, 2001b).

1.2.2. Agnew's Tradition of General Strain Theory. After years of stagnation Agnew revived debate by attempting to expand anomie theory into a general strain theory (Agnew, 1985a, 1990a, 1992, 1995; Agnew & White, 1992). He focuses not only on causal variables such as the blocking of attempts to achieve particular positive goals, but also considers elements of the causal strain variable such as the *loss* and/or disappearance of coveted objects and the real or perceived impossibility of *avoiding* particularly painful or *frustrating experiences*. These experiences include physical or psychological wounds caused by parents, teachers, etc., which children and youths often cannot avoid in any *legal* way due to their specific social situation. This new "general" strain theory, which is obviously related to the general *stress theory* that has proved fruitful in explaining health problems (see among others Lazarus & Folkman, 1984 and the very sophisticated elaboration by Brücker, 1994), has stood up to tests fairly well. Paternoster and Mazerolle (1994) thus showed the three elements of strain to have a *direct* positive link to various types of delinquency. Additionally strain has *indirect* effects in the way it loosens the bonds with others, thus undermining inhibitions toward deviance, and also furthers the integration into deviant networks (see Hirschi, 1969). Whereas Hoffmann and Su (1997) found no gender-specific effects of strain/stress on drug abuse and delinquency (including violent crime), Broidy and Agnew (1997) proceed from the research conducted to date and assume that both sexes not only experience different kinds and intensities of strains but also react to strain somewhat differently; also, various types of strain tend to trigger off crime in specific conditions. The authors trace the different reaction of the sexes back to patterns of socialization, which are still markedly gender-specific, and also to different forms of social control, which for women are significantly more repressive (see the power-control theory by Hagan et al. below).

The logical question in view of the affinity between general stress theory and strain theory as to what extent violent crime can be considered a specific, externalizing attempt at coping, and the actors' attempt to deal with the perceived stress (see Mansel & Hurrelmann, 1998; on the relationship of extrovert versus introvert coping strategies, see Mansel & Hurrelmann, 1994), and also the question as to what extent the actors really do experience subjective relief through deviant behavior, i.e., whether deviance can thus be considered effective problem-solving behavior (at least in the short term), is affirmed by the results in Brezina (1996); delinquency, including crimes of violence, does actually reduce the negative emotional consequences of strain (see Brezina, 2000).

The macro-sociological studies inspired by anomie theory generally provide acceptable explanations, which also speaks in favor of further developing anomie theory (see Albrecht & Howe, 1992; Albrecht, 1999). Agnew's attempt (1999) at reformulating strain theory shows clearly that it has potential for development and that it can explain differing crime rates at the local level (see the new assessment of anomie theory in Ortmann, 2000).

1.2.3. Opportunity Structure and Social Inequality. Long before Merton published his anomie theory, there was a theoretical tradition which aimed above all to explain the connection between deprivation, social inequality and crime. Whereas explanations focusing on *absolute poverty* were already proved empirically inadequate at an early stage, for quite some time there was evidence of connections between economic development and the development of various forms of crime (see Roesner, 1936 on the older research, Heiland, 1983 and Albrecht, 1986 on the more recent). Relationships previously considered to have been empirically validated lost clarity over time, possibly because the causal nexus that had been intact until that time was weakened or removed completely by the development of social security systems, or because the increasingly sophisticated statistical reanalysis of earlier findings showed them to have been arrived at by methodologically antiquated means. Research has thus shifted to the connection between *social inequality* and crime, with the result that absolute impoverishment turns out to be rather insignificant compared with various conceptualizations of social inequality. But very different findings emerge on the significance of social inequality depending on the particular form of operationalization (e.g., whether it is viewed as undifferentiated inequality of income distribution, intraethnic or interethnic inequality) and depending on the importance attached to specific extrinsic factors (ethnic composition, segregation, disorganization, etc.). The findings can then be further distinguished according to the type of offense: even for various crimes of violence the connections can end up being completely different (see Parker & Smith, 1979; Albrecht, 2001b and the contribution by Crutchfield in this volume). It should also be noted that the findings vary for social subgroups.

But these findings from early studies suggesting that social-structural conditions have specific effects on subgroups would appear to be at least partially skewed due to the fact that the subgroups concerned lived in specific milieus; here the variable concerned turns out so differently that the nonlinear relationship between the given variable and violent crime—hitherto largely overlooked—means that ignoring nonlinearity leads to the development of ethnic-specific predictors—or to predictors, which are actually important, being considered irrelevant (see Krivo & Peterson, 2000). This realization must lead to a new evaluation of social inequality and social disadvantage as causes of violent crime, in which the apparent relative superiority of social disorganization theory could be lost (see Peterson, Krivo, & Harris, 2000). The same applies for the results of the study by Parker and McCall (1999), which suggest that economic deprivation and local opportunity structure have a significant influence on the rates of *intra*ethnic homicides, but *inter*ethnic inequality only influences *inter*ethnic homicides committed by *Blacks* (not Whites); the authors themselves emphasize that Blacks and Whites live under very different economic and social conditions in terms of income and social isolation. The outcome of these debates is very significant, because inadequate theoretical interpretation of the social-structural parameters means that recourse is repeatedly taken to *culturalistic* interpretations with partly open, partly concealed judgmentalism (particularly regarding family structure and sexuality), although the connections can be better explained by looking at the interaction of unemployment, economic deprivation and family structure (see Sampson, 1987; Sampson & Laub, 1994; Sampson & Wilson, 1995).

The same is true of studies of the relationship between economic development and crime using new techniques of time series analysis. Connections between economic development—in the sense of upturns and crises—and violent crime can definitely be proven (see among others Brantingham & Brantingham, 1984a, 1984b, 1984c; Cook & Zarkin, 1985; Eisner, 1995; Field, 1995; Steinberg, Catalano, & Dooley, 1981; Wolpin, 1978; Zehr, 1976), but their actual form varies depending on age, sex, ethnicity, the type of offense, etc. Another factor is that these connections develop as a result of the overlap of various partly contrary effects or those with differing time lags (see Albrecht, 1986, 2001b). Analyzing the connection between changes in the unemployment rate and various forms of crime shows just how complex the issue is: unemployment, for example, turns out to have a *direct negative* effect on the crime rate since the opportunities for committing offenses decline (e.g., through reduced use of public transport where crimes of violence are often committed, and also because more people are frequently at home), but it also has a *delayed positive* effect since gradual deprivation and/or increasing frustration raise the motivation to commit criminal acts. It stands to reason that the individual effects can combine in specific ways depending on sex, age, ethnicity and other parameters, and this explains why it is impossible to make summary statements on this connection (see Cantor & Land, 1985; Land, Cantor, & Russel, 1995).

The classical study by Hovland and Sears (1940) on the connection between economic frustration and aggression based on the example of "lynch justice" in the USA has also not been left unscathed by modern research, even if it has not been entirely disproved (see among others Beck & Tolnay, 1990, 1995; Hepworth & West, 1988; Tolnay & Beck, 1992, 1994; Tolnay, Beck, & Massey, 1989; Tolnay, Deane, & Beck, 1996). However, "hate crimes" against particular subgroups, e.g., the sexual minority of homosexuals, do not depend to any great extent on economic conditions (see Green, Glaser, & Rich 1998), although Medoff (1999), after taking other factors into account, showed that hate crimes correlate negatively with increasing income and the value of time, which thus supports a rational-choice interpretation.

1.2.4. The Easterlin Hypothesis: Cohort Size as an Opportunity Barrier. The approaches of opportunity structure theory are closely connected with a socio-demographic approach which proceeds from the causal significance of age structure (see among others Greenberg 1979), but also and above all from the quantitative size of cohorts for their opportunity structures and thus also for the extent of their deviant behavior and violent crime (see among others Easterlin, 1980; Easterlin & Crimmins, 1988). In addition to a number of confirmations (see Maxim, 1985; Menard, 1992; Smith & Welch, 1981; Steffensmeier, Streifel, & Shihadeh, 1992; see Kahn & Mason, 1987 on political alienation and O'Brien, 1989; O'Brien, Stockard, & Isaacson, 1999 on the murder rate), there are also some very skeptical assessments (see among others the criticism by Levitt, 1999; and with weak results Pampel & Gartner, 1995), which could however be due to the fact that important variables—such as the change in family structure and developments specific to the ethnic group—were not sufficiently taken into account (see Savolainen, 2000). This approach does not promise any clear long-term trend in violent crime, but rather a more cyclic pattern depending on the fluctuating sizes of particular age cohorts. Against the background of the empirically well-substantiated fact that there has been a detectable long-term rise in the homicide rate since 1960 in many societies, particularly Western ones (see Eisner, 2001; Thome, 2001, 2002), the Easterlin theory can at best explain minor peaks and troughs within longer-term trends, not the "secular" development.

1.3. SUBCULTURE THEORIES. Subculture theory proceeds from the observation that in modern societies not all subgroups of society have the same cultural ideals and standards. For example, alongside a dominant value and norm system essentially shared by all members of a society, there can be particular subgroups that manifest specific modifications of the basic cultural pattern (depending on region, social class, ethnicity, etc.), and there even are cases where there is no cultural common denominator at all, only an agglomeration of various subcultures which possibly exhibit conflicting values and norms. In one case this can mean that a society which unambiguously rejects criminal violence in principle still encompasses individual subcultures that attach different values to this kind of violence or have specific additional norms and values that tolerate or even demand the use of criminal violence under particular conditions; at the other extreme there can be cases where subgroups turn particular values of the dominant society into their opposite (centracultures).

Subculture theories thus not only question the presence of a general value consensus, but also point out that precisely the differences between various partial cultures are causally relevant for crime. Miller (1968), for example, argues that the lower class culture in Western societies, which has evolved and developed over a long period of time, exhibits particular "crystallization points" (e.g., trouble, toughness, smartness, cleverness, fate, autonomy, excitement), which inevitably give rise to conflict with the prevailing bourgeois rules and laws when youths from this subculture behave according to the expectations valid within it. The youths' behavior is driven by the search for recognition status and belonging (on the role of belonging for youths in right-wing extremist groups, see Jabs, 1995; König, 1998 and Eckert & Willems, 1993, Heitmeyer & Müller, 1995). The fact that being tough and being out for excitement are crystallization points of this kind allow us to expect a preference for physical aggression and thus crimes of violence, etc.

Cohen (1955, 1968), on the other hand, provided an explanation of the typical behavior of a type of American big-city gang particularly widespread at that time, which he saw as characteristically not utilitarian, malicious and negativistic, and to an extent exceptionally violent. He attributed these features to the problematic position of youths from lower social classes in dominant middle-class society, represented in particular by the institution of school. Here youths from lower social classes—particularly those from the underclass—encounter a world whose demands they are scarcely equipped to cope with; grave handicaps such as their lifestyle, linguistic ability and poor learning preconditions virtually predetermine that they will have the notorious experiences of failure there. Even so, a section of these youths hold on to the goal of attaining status within "middle-class society," but only few are successful. Others abandon the goal of social advancement and thus avoid some of the potential frustrations. But those underclass youths who hold on to the goal of social advancement, while continuously experiencing the failure of their attempts with the means intended within the middle-class institution of school, find themselves in a situation of *collective* frustration; under particular conditions this can lead them to intentionally infringe the institutions of middle-class society, mutually and vehemently spurring themselves on in a group situation. They work off their pent-up frustration by intentionally infringing central rules of bourgeois society and its institutions. Even the thefts committed are *nonutilitarian* since they bring no material benefit; rather, they are hedonistic insofar as violating the rules of bourgeois society can be a way of "getting a kick." In particular group situations the frustration leads them to be decidedly vicious, for instance inflicting grievous bodily harm on defenseless victims (see Short & Strodtbeck, 1965; Yablonsky, 1962, 1973).

In Germany this theoretical tradition has so far not attracted much attention, probably because the structures of the welfare state alleviate the grossest hardships of the capitalist social system. Only in recent years does change seem to have set in here through the combination of unemployment, poverty, ethnic discrimination, etc.; new studies along the lines of the exemplary work by Haferkamp (1975) are urgently required in view of the new diversity of youth subcultures exhibiting specific affinities to particular forms of deviant behavior (on skinheads and xenophobic violence, see, e.g., Mischkowitz, 1994; on the subculture of Turkish youth gangs in Germany and the role of violence, Tertilt, 1996; on the rocker subculture, Cremer, 1992, on the rapper subculture, Lamnek & Schwenk, 1995; on the hooligan subculture, Heitmeyer & Peter, 1988 and on music groups and groups on the search for common ground, Bohnsack et al., 1995).

A fruitful approach is the combination of subculture theory and *life-course theory*. Hagan (1991) reports on the connections between two different forms of subcultural patterns (*"party subculture"* and *"subculture of delinquency,"* in which violent crime also plays an important role) and the consequences for later life, which are dependent on gender and the parents' class background. For young *working-class males* identification with the *delinquent* subculture has a negative effect on the passage to early adulthood. For young *middle-class males* identification with the *party* subculture has a positive net effect on the first passage to adulthood if this subculture's negative effects on achievement in school are restricted. *Female* test persons were scarcely affected. If one connects strain theory and subculture theory and poses the question as to why the higher distress which strain theory leads us to expect with delinquent youths generally cannot be demonstrated—or why youths who identify closely with a "counter-culture to school" leave school relatively early, little burdened with problems, and take on adult roles with initial success—Hagan (1997) replies that the *delinquent* subculture evidently isolates its members *temporarily* from sources of stress to which they would otherwise be exposed. However, this oppositional disposition leads to *later* educational and employment problems which interact with the subcultural character or what remains of it to cause stress factors. This "sleeper effect" does not become relevant until early adulthood when it manifests itself in the form of serious employment problems, feelings of despair, and structural disadvantage, with commensurate risks of deviance as a result. The answer to the question expressed in the controversy between Miller (1968, 1958) and Cohen (1955, 1968) as to whether subcultural forms of delinquency and criminality are complete *rejections* or *distorted reflections* of the central values of market-oriented societies tends more toward the latter: the "culture of competition" promotes hierarchical forms of self-interest which lead to the acceptance of inequality and anomic amorality and thus, in connection with this, to group-related delinquency (see Hagan et al., 1998).

The fruitfulness of subculture theory perspectives is revealed in connection with other approaches. Jacobs and Wright (1999), for example, examining the behavior of active armed robbers, demonstrated that, while structural variables explain the pressure of financial problems, the motivation to commit acts of robbery develops out of a specific "street culture" (see the explanation of "angry aggression" in Bernard, 1990 and that of the function of subculturally mediated neutralization techniques in Agnew, 1990b, 1994; Agnew & Peters, 1986, or of subcultural definitions of situation Hagan & McCarthy, 1997; Heimer, 1997; Matsueda et al., 1992).

The thesis of Wolfgang & Ferracuti (1973) that violent behavior at an individual level is in significant respects subculturally determined provided the stimulus for many subsequent studies, albeit with contradictory findings (see Hepburn, 1971 on the theory and Hartnagel, 1980 on the limited significance of the subculture of violence for violent crime). Despite the fundamental critique by Kornhauser (1978:210), much speaks in favor of further pursuing this issue (see Huff-Corzine, Corzine, & Moore, 1986, 1991). A particularly high homicide rate is interpreted as being due to a regional "subculture of violence" which not only tolerates but even demands a rigorous defense of one's own honor and also glorifies military virtues; this is seen as a relic of the necessity of self-defense from the times of the slave-owning society before the Civil War (Reed, 1972:10). According to Reed, it would seem that relevant Southern cultural traits such as particular religious preferences, religious integration, consumer habits, lifestyle (e.g., carrying weapons; see among others O'Connor & Lizotte, 1977) and socialization practices (corporal punishment) have survived in the Southern States of the USA. Hackney (1969), for example, ascertained a regional effect on the rate of homicides in the Southern States (even after controlling for the variables of urbanization, educational level, income, unemployment and age structure). He attributed this to a greater passivity toward one's environment, a lower degree of self-responsibility and a stronger inclination to employ projections in defense of one's ego (1969:923)—tendencies which historically are the result of a "siege mentality." The greater propensity to violence thus reflects the frustrations and resulting aggressions of a defeated colony. Earlier contradictory findings on a subculture of violence (see Dixon & Lizotte, 1987; Reed, 1972) would seem to stem from the difficulty of measuring the acceptance of violence, since the Southerners would not accept violence *in general*—as most statistical methods incorrectly assume—but only that which serves *to defend oneself and one's honor*, a stance which was shaped by religious factors (see Reed, 1982; Ellison, 1991). Gastil (1971), in contrast, emphasizes the continuation of cultural traditions from before the Civil War ("border society," the tradition of the duel, the cult of honor, extreme class differences, gross ethnic cleavages, the habitual carrying of arms). Since this cultural pattern is not limited to the area of the former Confederate States, but in the course of history, not least by migration, has diffused to other neighboring areas, the "regional" factor cannot be neatly covered by the notion "Confederate State." This, the author says, is the reason for contradictory empirical findings. If this "mistake" were avoided, the Southern States effect would be seen clearly even if other relevant parameters were taken into account (Gastil, 1971). This claim was refuted, however, by Loftin and Hill (1974), Smith and Parker (1980) and Parker (1989).

Just how complex the facts of the matter are can be seen in studies conducted by Messner (1983a, 1983b): these took as their basis a sample of about 200 metropolitan areas or about 340 cities in the USA around 1970, and the poverty factor was explicitly taken into account—the studies confirmed the subcultural factor. McCall, Land and Cohen (1992), in comparison, showed for the years 1960, 1970 and 1980 that, after controlling for the population structure, resource deprivation or poverty, family structure, age distribution and the rate of unemployment, the subculture of violence can only be considered relevant, if at all, for homicides and serious physical assault, not however for rape and robbery (see also Land, McCall, & Cohen, 1990). This (Southern) subculture actually seems only to approve of violence as a defense against attacks and insults. The assumption that the regional effect (interpreted as a subcultural effect) declines over time is only partially valid, and to an extent the subculture even gains in significance. But above all this confirms that the socio-structural effects are much more significant and persistent across all the various levels of aggregation and the time axis. Therefore, social and economic inequality, population structure and social control ultimately prove to be more significant dimensions than the "subculture of violence" (there were quite similar findings for an alleged "black subculture" as an explanation for violent crime; see Liqun, Adams, & Jensen, 1997; Sampson, 1987; see also Blau & Blau, 1982 and Blau & Golden, 1986).

The explanation of violent crime as a factor of the socially induced and perpetuated development of *special* cultures is contradicted by Hagan et al. (1998) who postulate that significant elements of deviant youth behavior are a consequence of "underground" (and thus "subcultural") variants of values and are central to a market society in the age of globalization with its emphasis on the struggle of "each against all." This individualist, competitive orientation leads to all behavior being seen just from the one side in its instrumental role for one's own success; it is emphasized so strongly that binding norms are annulled and ultimately an *anomic individualism* spreads; the restriction of opportunities leads to crime and also results in violent crime toward people seen as scapegoats. According to this view, the rate of violent crime should increase in the long term, since the social tendencies mentioned seem not to be short-term freak developments but part of an epochal trend. The actual development of violent crime in different parts of Germany would seem to speak against this interpretation, as would the findings by Karstedt (2001) that the degree of individualization in a society, which is seen by many authors as a direct expression of the advance of "market society," correlates negatively with its crime rate when other relevant parameters are controlled. The increase in violent crime in Europe in the last decade has been explained as the result of a new "winner-loser culture," but critical examination is still required to see whether this will stand up to scrutiny (see James, 1995; Pfeiffer, 1998).

1.4. DIFFERENTIAL OPPORTUNITY THEORY. Whereas Merton saw the "blocking of access to *legal* means of achieving common social values for particular social subgroups" as the causal variable for the explanation of anomie, and the role of access to particular *illegal* or *illegitimate* ways of achieving these goals was ignored, Cloward and Ohlin (see Cloward, 1968 or Cloward & Ohlin, 1960) emphasize that access to *illegitimate* or *illegal* ways is also socially structured. Not every actor has the chance of choosing particular illegal paths. Cloward and Ohlin elaborated the details of the social-structural and subcultural conditions which determine which illegal means are available to the actors and which concrete forms of deviant behavior are chosen. If political organizations and the world of organized crime in the local community are linked via particular ethnic colonies, youths whose chances of achieving social values by legal means are barred can now gain easy access to the world of organized crime, for example. Under other conditions (e.g., belonging to the "wrong" ethnic group) they possibly have little choice but to join particular conflict gangs; here the frustrations that have arisen are translated into aggressive gang behavior and violent crime. In yet other specific social-structural and subcultural situations, or when particular personal and/or socialization conditions exist (e.g., physical weakness/personal "cowardliness"), youths do not have access to this alternative either, and—as "double failures"—are now possibly only able to gain access to the subculture of addicts.

This synthesis of anomie theory and subculture theory can explain the delinquency phenomenon and the age-specific, social and ethnic structuring as well as the *gender-specific* form of criminal behavior much better: the specific quality and quantity of female crime is seen as a result of women's limited access to areas of deviant behavior as well—women are distinctly underrepresented in particular areas of criminal behavior (e.g., organized crime, violent crime)—whereas in other areas (e.g., minor property offenses) they have already caught up considerably in the course of the increasing convergence of the sexes (see among others Steffensmeier, 1978, 1980; Steffensmeier & Steffensmeier, 1980). In this context it should be noted that the participation of girls and young women in gangs, in the USA at least, is markedly higher than generally assumed (see among others Curry, 1998; Swart, 1995), but that the remaining differences still lead to the role of peers and their moral influence being so highly significant for the gender-specific crime rate (see Mears, Ploeger, & Warr, 1998).

It is profitable to link these issues with the *routine activity approach*, which proceeds on the assumption that the initiation and specific social and spatial distribution of crime are a function of the prevailing routine activities of offenders and victims. Offenses of this kind occur when potential offenders meet potential victims in the course of everyday activities and where the nature of the situation leaves victims little or no chance of protecting themselves or their property (see in general Felson, 1986, 1994, 2000; on violent crime, see Felson & Cohen, 1980). Despite some inconsistencies, findings to date have been encouraging (see among others Garofalo, 1987; Kennedy & Forde, 1990; Kennedy & Silverman, 1990; Miethe, Stafford, & Long, 1987; Osgood et al., 1996; Sampson & Lauritsen, 1990; Sherman, Gartin, & Buerger, 1989; Tremblay & Tremblay, 1998; van Koppen & Jansen, 1999), since at individual level, for example, the frequency of offenses partly rises in the case of youths with increasing financial resources—evidently because they can afford to cultivate a lifestyle and thus also routine activities which increase the probability of going in for criminal acts (see, e.g., Simons & Gray, 1989; Agnew, 1990a).

1.5. Social Disorganization Theory. If subculture theory points to the significance of macro-social structural features, this is also true in slightly reduced form for variants of disorganization theory. Slum disorganization theory, for example, emphasizes that settings characterized by a high level of urbanity and anonymity, high mobility and industrialization, which destroy former social structures and with them rule systems and control mechanisms which ensured a degree of conformity, fall into chaos. The individuals affected fall into a state of personal disorganization, which greatly increases the likelihood of deviant behavior and in particular crime (see Cohen, 1959). This can occur because no regulatory mechanisms are available for the new, emerging social situation, or only such that are contradictory and allow no clear behavioral regulation.

A particular variant of disorganization theory deals with the *family* which, due to rapid social change, economic crises, high mobility, spatial separation of family members, etc., can experience crisis and no longer properly fulfill its important task of socialization. This variety of disorganization theory (see in general König, 1949, 1974a, 1974b) has long played a central role, in particular with a view to the problems of the "incomplete family" (on conceptual ideas and empirical findings in general, see Johnson, 1986; Wells & Rankin, 1986), although König (1974b:114, 117) has long since pointed out potentially flawed reasoning in this line of argumentation. It would be premature, however, to write off this question entirely. Albrecht, Howe and Wolterhoff (1991), for example, showed the relatively limited relevance of various concepts of "broken home" for the frequency of self-reported criminality; but interaction effects occur between family structure and social background which are not insignificant for self-reported delinquency (in particular with particular age-groups and types of offenses, above all for crimes of violence). Furthermore, psychological studies in particular report not only that there are particular advances in maturity of children from incomplete families, but also that parental separation can result in long-term psychological damage (see the excellent overview in Hetherington & Anderson, 1988). This seems to be less connected with the incompleteness of the family per se than with the *functional* quality of family life (see the meta-analyses by Lösel, 1991 and Wells & Rankin, 1991). In particular, it can be assumed that there is a connection between manifest parental strife or even violence and later well-being (see Hanson, 1999), but also a greater inclination toward violent behavior of the children in later life. The literature often cites a connection between maltreatment suffered at the hands of the parents and juvenile delinquency, and this is interpreted on the basis of control theory, (social) learning theory and strain theory, but these interpretations only partially stand the empirical test (Brezina, 1998); by themselves they are as yet insufficient for dealing with the complex issue.

In this context the question arises as to the consequences of corporal or otherwise severe punishment in the family of origin. To avoid the methodological problems of earlier studies, Simons et al. (2000) conducted a cross-cultural study, while taking into account the early behavioral problems of the test persons and other dimensions of parental child-rearing behavior as well as testing interaction effects and nonlinear relationships. An ethnic group with an overall medium level of corporal punishment shows virtually no connection between the severity of corporal punishment and behavioral problems. A different ethnic group with a markedly higher level of corporal punishment shows no such connection if *mothers* maintained a *warm* personal relationship to the children parallel to the severe corporal punishment; otherwise the assumed connection was found. As far as this ethnic group's *paternal* child-rearing behavior is concerned, behavioral problems would appear to be influenced on the one hand by interactive effects between severity of punishment and warmth of relationship, and on the other hand, there is evidently also a *curvilinear* relationship. That is, very severe punishment and at the same time coldness from the father leads to disproportionately strong disturbances among the test persons, and beyond a particular level of severity the behavioral problems increase exponentially.

It is of interest to note that juvenile delinquency, particularly when associated with aggressive behavior, has consequences for the use of violent conflict tactics in intimate relationships in later life. Foshee, Baumann and Linder (1999), for example, found that male and female youths alike were more likely to manifest violent behavior in intimate relationships if they experienced violence between their parents. The bridge between these socialization conditions and the individual's own violence is established with the help of variables applied in social learning theory and control theory (the latter only with males; see the very similar work of Giordano et al., 1999). According to the most recent findings, the experience of severe corporal punishment in one's family of origin has implications for violent behavior in intimate partner relationships, both directly and indirectly, in the way it causes general behavioral problems and crimes of violence in youth and early adulthood, which increase the risk of violent conflict in the partnership (see Swinford et al., 2000). The cycle of violence and socialization is thus doubly secured: experiencing violence raises the probability of delinquency, and delinquency increases the probability of violence in relationships in which socialization typically occurs.

It is encouraging that in recent years social disorganization theory has returned to its *macro*-sociological origins and tried to move away from its many and diverse abortive developments (see Bursik, 1988). Clinard (1968) in particular points to the theory's failure in the way it attempted to clearly distinguish between social change and disorganization. Central dimensions are once again the high rates of mobility and migration, ethnic tensions, processes of impoverishment and ghettoization, segregation, the lack of integration in social networks, the absence of political community structures, etc., which are seen as attendant problems of massive social change through modernization that causally "mediate" the effects of this process on the extent of deviant behavior (see among others Bursik & Grasmick, 1993a, 1993b) and are also causally significant for the developmental dynamic of violent youth gangs (Bursik & Grasmick, 1995). An increase in violent crime comes about when effective informal social control and what amounts to the population's reciprocal surveillance are no longer maintained in particular city districts, and then especially groups of youths slip out of family and neighborhood control (Bellair, 2000; Kowaleski-Jones, 2000; Short, 1997). But the seemingly impressive confirmation for Great Britain (Sampson & Groves, 1989; see similar findings from the USA in Elliott et al., 1996; Bellair, 1997) should very much be seen in context. The use of sophisticated analytical strategies has revealed, firstly, that distinctions must be made between different types of disorganization which have different effects, but above all, secondly, that the social-structural parameters, contrary to theory, have a major *direct* effect on violent crime, and thirdly, that group processes seem to be of central importance (see Veysey & Messner, 1999; Esbensen & Huizinga, 1990). The great complexity of the connections between social structure, disorganization and cohesion on the one hand, and crime on the other, can be seen clearly in the fact that the effect of structurally relevant variables depends on the context in which they are subject to change (see Morenoff & Sampson, 1997; Hirschfield & Bowers, 1997; Osgood & Chambers, 2000; Jobes, 1999; Ross, Reynolds, & Geis, 2000). The attempt by Sampson and Raudenbush (1999) to reformulate the social disorganization approach as a "theory of collective effectiveness and structural limitations" should be particularly fruitful. This theory operates with the guiding notions "cohesion of the population" and "shared expectations for the active social control of public space" (see also the successful integration into other theories, particularly taking account of poverty and ethnicity, in Short, 1997).

2. Interactionist Approaches

2.1. The Labeling Approach. Whereas the theories mentioned so far were *etiological*, an extreme variant of interactionist theory (Sack, 1968) states that the etiological question is absurd. In its view the supposedly "criminal" act is only construed as such in a subsequent definition process (see Becker, 1963; Sack, 1968, 1978). An act does not possess any "objective" behavioral qualities—its significance is negotiated by the participants in a complex set of interactions, a process in which many factors are of significance: particular everyday theories, job routines, personal interests, positions of power, etc. Since the "meaning" of the incriminated act cannot be determined *before* this process of definition, the act also cannot be causally explained in the usual sense of the word. Consequently, the causal explanation is no longer the focus of attention here; rather, one asks how it is possible that particular reactions of the agencies of informal and formal social control, working with and interpreting the interpretations and definitions of the actors, can lead to a particular label being attributed—or not—to interpretable and assessable behavior which, in principle, is very varied. A position of this kind makes the use of official statistics on deviant behavior seem questionable since these figures were developed in a very complex process of the construction of reality. Only when one has shown that neither the population's models of interpretation nor its willingness to report crimes have changed in the relevant period, nor that the inclination of the police, public prosecutors and courts to conduct investigations and impose sanctions have changed, can one conclude from changes in official crime statistics that there has been a real change in the frequency of violent "criminal" acts (see Albrecht & Lamnek, 1979).

This approach is highly explosive in terms of its relation to violent crime, considering that the discoveries of experimental psychological research into aggression show that there are actually no strictly objective behavioral features which could support a definition of behavior as "aggressive," but that one and the same behavior is categorized very differently depending on the judgment of its legitimacy, political opinion, but above all—in addition to the "actual damage" done—depending on the observers' assumption of harmful intent and the existence of norm infringement (see the figures in Mummendey, 1990:296). Since in every case it is a matter of the *attribution* of motives, the objective accuracy of which cannot be established, seeing a crime of violence as an offense is also ultimately a "social construction" (see, e.g., on rape LaFree, 1989; see the unfortunately rather neglected attempt at creating a symbolic interactionist theory of violence in Athens, 1986; Felson, 1993). This "social construction" reveals its own dynamic and can easily slip from the hands of its "makers," and it can also be abused outright with strategic intent (see the very illuminating and daring expositions in Sack, 1984).

A significant achievement of this approach is the proof it furnishes that the form and content of these definition processes have their own inherent dynamic which makes it necessary to investigate the social and individual consequences of the "creation" of deviant behavior by "social reaction" in a longitudinal perspective. The specific form of this definition process means that the "deviant actor" is often affected doubly: firstly, the informal sanctions and in particular the formal ones and their often unintentional side effects are accompanied by cuts to role repertoires (Becker, 1963; see Albrecht & Karstedt-Henke, 1987), which can be of quite considerable long-term significance and irreversible. Secondly, even if they possibly remain without grave legal consequences, definition processes of this kind can influence the actor concerned in a very negative way by triggering off changes toward negative self-concept or self-esteem (see Wells & Rankin, 1983; see the overview in Albrecht & van Kampen, 1992). However, one must distinguish here whether the reactions, for example in the field of informal sanctions, come from people whose assessment of the deviant behavior is possibly positive (e.g., peers of delinquent youths), or from formal agencies of social control which stage their reaction as a "degradation ceremony"—this may stigmatize the actor so severely that a retrospective reinterpretation of the entire career occurs in which he or she is branded as an outsider. Only then, as a rule—and this is the provocative feature of this theory—does this in turn give rise to what society's reaction already presupposed: a deviant identity. Primary deviance leads to secondary deviance (see Lemert, 1967, 1975).

Surprisingly, there are few studies which have been able to prove the effects of formal and informal labeling in a methodologically watertight manner. There are many studies which support the arguments of labeling theory, most of them however with quite weak results (see among others Frey, 1983; Kaplan & Johnson, 1991; Keane, Gillis & Hagan, 1989; Klein, 1986; Ray & Downs, 1986; Wells & Rankin, 1983; see the overview in Albrecht, 2002). On the other hand, there are numerous studies which found no relevant labeling effects (see among others Smith & Paternoster, 1990; see the skeptical conclusions drawn in Gove, 1976; Hirschi, 1975). The contradictory nature of the findings, it seems, is due to the fact that the labeling effects differ according to sex, age, ethnicity, social class and the type of offense, but above all according to the type of informal and formal sanctioning. The findings of Brown et al. (1991) are particularly irritating because they show strong results which directly contradict labeling theory. At first glance the same seems to apply for the labeling of violent crime in the studies of Sherman and Berk (1984): the stronger the stigmatizing labeling, the lesser—albeit *for a short period*—the future violent crime. But with a *prolonged* catamnesis period the effect was: the stronger the stigmatization, the stronger the relapse into violent crime in the long term (see Sherman et al., 1991; Berk et al., 1992). Evidently, the effects of labeling depend on a large number of moderating variables (regarding gender, see, e.g., Harris, 1975; Heimer, 1996; Heimer & DeCoster, 1999) which we will consider below. Obviously these effects should not be overestimated, but nor should they be neglected (see among others Albrecht, 1990; Heinz, 1996).

2.2. The Theory of Differential Social Control.

Heimer and Matsueda have attempted to integrate the labeling approach with ideas from social learning theory to make a comprehensive interactionist approach, the theory of differential social control, which in view of the stagnation of the labeling approach could offer a way forward (Heimer, 1996; Heimer & Matsueda, 1994; Heimer & DeCoster, 1999; Matsueda, 1992; Matsueda & Heimer, 1987, 1997). Heimer and Matsueda proceed from the assumption that social control takes place via a process of role adoption whereby the relation to the generalized others allows the creation of a link to the comprehensive social organization and order, since role expectations and reference groups are involved most explicitly. In conjunction with processes of differential learning, as presented in the theory of differential association, role adoption leads to conformity or deviation. This new symbolic interactionist perspective, according to which delinquency results from various elements of the role adoption, proves much better in the comparative theory test (including disorganization theory, control theory, the labeling approach and differential association theory). It is above all associating with delinquent peers, adopting and interpreting reference persons' reactions to one's delinquent behavior (reflected appraisals) and developing delinquent attitudes that are of relevance here. Bartusch and Matsueda (1996) succeeded in showing the gender-specific nature of these complex relations: the assessments/social reactions of parents significantly influence the subjective perception of evaluations (reflected appraisals), which in turn are of causal relevance for future delinquency, for young people of both sexes. However, there are differences between the sexes along the lines that (1) for boys parental assessments and the perceptions of these parental reactions have markedly greater effect on later delinquency than for girls, and that (2) evidently boys are more frequently falsely accused than are girls. Without these differences there would be an almost identical delinquency rate for male and female youths—indirect proof that the theory presented does justice to the facts.

2.3. Deviant Behavior for Defending One's Self-Esteem.

A social-psychological theory of deviation has developed with the aim of complementing the debate on labeling theory, and also in competition with it. It interprets deviant behavior as an attempt to defend one's self-esteem (Kaplan, 1975, 1980, 1982). It assumes that people have a need to maintain or raise their self-esteem, and if they are unable to conform to the standards of their reference group they are faced with the problem of falling below a particular minimum level of self-respect. By committing deviant acts which find approval and recognition in the eyes of a new, deviant reference group they experience a rise in their self-esteem. This increases the danger of further crimes because they bring respect, if only in the eyes of the *new* reference group. This means, however, that inappropriate reactions to nonachievement and behavioral problems can put the actors in a situation where committing deviant, and often violent acts seems to offer the only way out. Seen from this angle, "poor self-concept" would seem to be less the consequence of criminal behavior than its cause. Whereas Kaplan and others showed that low self-esteem could actually be of causal significance (particularly for juvenile delinquency), with the relative significance of self-esteem—compared with other causal variables—being greater with members of the middle-class than with members of the underclass, it is virtually impossible to produce proof of a rise in self-esteem *after or through* delinquency (see, e.g., Albrecht & van Kampen, 1992; Rosenberg, Schooler & Schoenbach, 1989; Scheff, Retzinger & Ryan, 1989; Wells, 1989; Jang & Thornberry, 1998). Increases in self-esteem through crime only occur, if at all, with subjects that had previously had *extremely low* self-esteem. According to Jang and Thornberry (1998), these findings could result from the fact that inadequate consideration was given to the *intervening* processes; in particular, the role of delinquent peers was overlooked, and here the authors showed that *associations* with delinquent peers raised self-esteem, *not one's deviant behavior in itself.* Recent studies have shown that relative deprivation only leads to divergent reactions when it is associated with negative self-feelings (see Stiles, Liu, & Kaplan, 2000), and this raises possibilities of linking up to anomie theory.

Whereas for reasons mentioned (Schur, 1973), the "classical" interactionist position recommended the strategy of "radical non-intervention" in particular in the case of youth crime, there are good reasons for the strategy of "re-integrative shaming," which clarifies the community's moral boundaries but avoids any stigmatization that would foster new subcultures and elicit new sources of crime (see Braithwaite, 1989, 1995). Public opinion could thus contribute decisively to the reduction of violent crime by using strong symbolism to express moral condemnation of violence and by depriving potential offenders of the belief that they are acting with the express or tacit consent of their milieu.

3. Control Theories

3.1. HIRSCHI'S CONTROL THEORY. Hirschi's control theory (1969) considers that it is not criminal behavior that requires explanation, but rather conformity. It assumes that without social control people will manifest deviant behavior. Conformity can only be explained through social bonds and control mechanisms. According to this theory, the primary bond is the dimension of *attachment* which refers to people's emotional relationships to people they are close to. The stronger and more intensive the attachment, the less likely it is that criminal behavior will occur. Actors take into account that deviant behavior would endanger the emotional bond to their parents or other people they are attached to, and for this reason avoid deviant behavior. The second type of bond in Hirschi's theory consists of *commitment*, i.e., personal devotion to particular (conformist) forms of action or particular goals. When a person has invested work and effort in a particular life design, e.g., a particular occupational goal, the strong commitment to their central goals ensures that they will not let deviant behavior endanger what they have achieved. The third type of bond consists of an obligation to particular *normative* ideas which are acquired in the process of socialization and which one can only break away from, as a rule, under very specific conditions. The more deeply these normative ideas (*beliefs*) have been internalized, the less likely it is that they will be infringed upon without very good reason; the observation by Sykes and Matza (1968) that an overwhelming majority of lawbreakers positively accept the breached norm and are ashamed if the breach of norms is discovered would thus seem plausible. The fourth bond consists in social integration, the *involvement* in networks and contexts of action, that deprive the actors of the time and opportunity for criminal behavior.

In initial empirical studies, this theory of Hirschi's proved to be quite practicable (see the overview in Agnew, 1985b; LaGrange & White, 1985; Kempf, 1993), but it had to be modified in a number of respects (see among others Krohn & Massey, 1980). However, when a longitudinal perspective is applied, as is appropriate in such research, the evaluation comes up with negative results (Agnew, 1985b, 1991, 1993). Comparative tests with other theories (see among others Alarid, Burton, & Cullen, 2000; Cernkovich et al., 2000; Matsueda & Anderson, 1998) as a rule produce the result that this approach is *not* superior to rival theories and that *reciprocal* relationships exist between parental control and delinquency, not unidirectional ones as control theory claimed (see Jang & Smith, 1997).

An important point of criticism is that this theory distances itself prematurely from a social-structural consideration of the phenomenon of crime (see Pagani et al., 1999, a recent study which Hirschi unambiguously refutes in regard to violent crime). Integration of this approach into the more general theory of social networks and social support should advance theories of crime. The social development approach of Catalano and Hawkins (1996) is an interesting attempt to integrate control theory and differential association and social learning theory; the authors proceed on the assumption that youths learn social or "antisocial" behavior in dependence on a number of factors: (1) opportunities for participation in activities and interaction with others, (2) the level of integration and interactions (3), their ability to participate in these interactions and (4) the level of rewards for participating in these activities and interactions. Even though this approach can perhaps be criticized for implying connections which in reality are due rather to social-structural background variables, it proves quite useful for individual aspects, e.g., for explaining violent careers (see among others Herrenkohl et al., 2001; Huang et al., 2001).

3.2. POWER-CONTROL THEORY. Hagan's power-control theory, which attempts to explain the different prevalence of delinquent behavior for men and women, stands out positively against other theories (Hagan, 1989; Hagan, Gillis, & Simpson, 1985, 1990, 1993; Hagan, Simpson, & Gillis, 1987, 1988). Hagan assumes that in these societies the traditional family is doubly stratified, by age and by sex. In a family adults control the socialization of the next generation, with the woman fulfilling a special role for control within the family. Secondly, the theory states that patriarchal structures dominate in this type of family, with the father of the family exercising power over both his wife and his children through dominance flowing from his role as the main breadwinner. The social control over the children is exercised above all by the woman in such a way that it guarantees the reproduction of these structures. This means that initiative, power of assertion, courage, willingness to take risks and even aggression are encouraged with boys; deviant and thus problematic behaviors which possibly arise from this are tolerated or maybe even expected, at least within certain limits. With girls, on the other hand, conformity and adaptation are sanctioned positively, while deviant tendencies are kept under close surveillance and consistently sanctioned negatively. In modern Western societies it is of crucial importance for the particular type of inner-family structure whether the parents or guardians are employed, and what they do. The family is particularly *unbalanced and patriarchal* when the father works in a senior capacity and/or is self-employed, while the mother is not gainfully employed or works in a less qualified occupation. In such cases the differential socialization of the sexes mentioned above should be blatantly distinctive, and therefore the difference in the rates of delinquent behavior between both sexes should also be particularly great. The more similar the occupational standing of the parents and thus the more equal they are, the more similar the delinquency rates of both sexes should be.

Hagan performed a number of empirical tests on this draft theory, which can be criticized in several respects, but was able to confirm the basic thrust of his hypotheses (see above; see Uggen, 2000 who takes better account of the status of the youths themselves and the occupational standing of the mother; but see also Jensen, 1993, 1997; Jensen & Thompson, 1990; Singer & Levine, 1988). Recent studies show that the different risk preferences explained in this way—and thus also the different willingness to commit crimes of violence—can also be proven for adults (Grasmick et al., 1996). The findings of Liu and Kaplan (1999) also point in a similar direction in their attempt to explain the gender-specific delinquency rate as a result of different strains or rather reactions to them: male individuals feel less bound to conventional values but more strongly to delinquent peers and thus—very much along the lines of Hagan's argumentation (see above)—have decidedly more problems with authorities. It is also of decisive significance that they experience a greater degree of frustration of their goals and achievement-related expectations, which indirectly leads to delinquency via the mediation of several intervening variables which have almost identical effects on both sexes (see also Esbensen & Deschenes, 1998).

Linking the argumentations of strain theory and power-control theory could possibly allow a better explanation of the gender-specific crime rate. Matt (1999) in fact demonstrated that for young males the transitional period of adolescence is tied up with the problems of developing an appropriate construction of masculinity. In the scope of the structures mentioned, which are still more or less patriarchal, these constructs become attached to crystallization points such as honor, saving one's face, being tough, exercising violence, etc. Since it is mainly peers of the same age group who are the "mirror" for one's own behavior and are feared as particularly strict judges because of the very significant motivation of the "search for belonging," this can result in behavior that the actors themselves basically do not approve of.

3.3. Utilitarian Theory (Theory of Deterrence). The utilitarian theory of criminal behavior, also referred to as the *theory of deterrence*, is a repeat of classical social-philosophical theories. Like the general rational choice theory, it considers the probability of criminal behavior a function of cost-benefit calculations by the actors (on the bases of this theory which links back to Jeremy Bentham, see also Becker, 1968, 1986; Ehrlich, 1973, 1979; Vanberg, 1982; also Liska, 1981:89ff). Unlike rational choice theory, in the theory of deterrence the *benefit side* of criminal behavior is generally ignored; for practical political reasons attention has shifted more to the *cost* side of crime for the actor. The chance of being caught, the expected severity of sanctioning and the speed of its imposition are relevant costs that are taken into consideration. Whereas this theory initially focused on the *objective* cost factors alone (e.g., the objective probability of sanctions), later varieties of the theory have endeavored to take the *subjective* perceptions of these cost factors into account. Relationships between the independent variables and the probability of offense are particularly complex. One *cannot* assume a simple *additive* relationship between these cost factors and the probability of criminal behavior but must assume a *multiplicative* relationship. With an additive relationship the threat of very heavy punishment with a subjective risk of being caught of zero would be translated into medium probability of a criminal act being committed; with a multiplicative relationship the product tends toward zero when one of the two variables does, i.e., however harsh the punishment is, it will still not deter, since punishment is not expected at all. It should furthermore be noted that the relationship between the individual cost factors and the probability of an offense is usually *nonlinear*, in other words increasing the probability of sanction will not result in a reduction of the probability of an offense, for example, until a particular threshold value is reached (see among others Tittle & Rowe, 1974).

Furthermore, there is empirical proof that a drastic increase in the severity of punishment as a rule reduces the probability of sanction. This is presumably because the threat of particularly severe punishment means that the criminal justice system observes the procedural rules with particular care and thus (in case of doubt) prefers not to find guilty (see Liska & Messner, 1999:95ff). The theory of deterrence has been seriously undermined by proof that the correlation between severity of sanction or probability of sanction, on the one hand, and level of offenses, on the other, can be better interpreted through an *experiential* effect than through a *deterrence* effect (see among others Saltzman et al., 1982; Minor & Harry, 1982; Paternoster et al., 1983)—test persons commit fewer acts of violence or none at all not because they assess the probability and/or severity of possible sanctions as high, but because in most cases violent criminals have got away with light sanctions or none at all and thus estimate the probability and severity of sanctions as low.

A number of empirical studies have shown that the original theory of deterrence completely oversaw some important social cost factors, in particular those of an *informal* nature (e.g., shame, embarrassment, the loss of social relationships, etc.; see Meier, Burkett, & Hickamn, 1984; on the problems of violence in marriage, see Williams, 1992; Williams & Hawkins, 1989a, 1989b, 1992), whereas overestimating considerably other cost factors (e.g., formal sanctioning). Foglia (1997), for example, showed that there is not even a *bivariate* link between the perceived probability of sanction and juvenile delinquency (see also Nagin & Paternoster, 1991), and multivariate analyses have even produced the result that contacts to peers, the behavior of adult role models and the severity of expected sanctioning by parents are decisive in determining youths' behavior. The central feature is that *internalized* norms determine the effects and the significance of social sanctions. The hope of quickly lowering the rate of violent crime by drastically increasing the severity of threatened or actual sanctions is thus deceptive. When the subjective perception of the sanction is based on *internalized* norms, harsher sanctions would possibly even be counterproductive, or at least ineffective, if they are not experienced as harsher according to the criteria of the internalized norms. Violence prevention must therefore begin with these *subjective* norms which are beyond the *direct* influence of punishment, since they have developed biographically and become part of the actor's life-world.

But it is not only the effects of *expected* sanctions on deviation or conformity that are mediated by complex structures; the same occurs with the effects of *punishments* actually suffered which can differ enormously depending on the type of offender, crime, social setting, etc. Procedural justice (the perception of the criminal justice process as fair) in the context of a punishment suffered is decisive if offenders are to admit to themselves the shame that leads to deterrence effects. Punishment perceived as unjust means that no shame is admitted, and this leads to defiant pride which encourages future deviation. Both "specific," i.e., individual defiance, and the "general" defiance developed by groups result from punishments felt to be unfair and can quickly make the overall deterrence effect disappear (see Sherman, 1993). These considerations are particularly significant for the criminal violent behavior of actors who see themselves as representatives of a particular group, especially one they consider disadvantaged. For them their criminal act represents an attempt to exercise "social control" to protect their own legitimate interests (see Black, 1983, 1984) which society has unjustly denied them. In addition, the members of underprivileged ethnic minorities must realistically assume that formal institutions of social control sanction "selectively" to their disadvantage. A general, drastic increase in the severity of sanctions would thus affect this type of violent criminals in particular—be it in appearance or in reality—and tend to aggravate "collective defiance," thus eliciting new violence (see also Klein, 1995 on the "abuse" of the doctrine of deterrence).

As yet it is hard to estimate how productive this strand of theory will be. This theory evidently takes too little account of the type of criminal behavior at hand (e.g., mala in se as distinct from mala prohibita). It is plausible that the probability of cost-benefit considerations playing a role is very different depending on the type of offense (compare the offense of murder with manslaughter). Furthermore, the theory takes too little note of the concrete circumstances in which particular offenses are committed, or of the special features of particular groups of actors who structure their cost-benefit considerations in a particular way. In this respect older children and youths, for example, would seem to differ markedly from those young adults who have stable relationships with a partner.

Although there are some very positive evaluations of this approach (e.g., most of the contributions in Cornish & Clarke, 1986), recent studies come up with rather modest results (see Bailey & Hubbard, 1990; Piliavin et al., 1986; Smith & Gartin, 1989; Berk & Newton, 1985; Klepper & Nagin, 1989, however, is different). In view of the complexity and contradictory nature of his findings, Paternoster (1988, 1989) is even of the opinion that improvement can only be brought about by developing a more comprehensive theory of informal social control, which utilitarian theory does not really offer (see also Akers, 1990).

3.4. SELF-CONTROL THEORY. Gottfredson and Hirschi's general theory of crime (1990) claims that it is able to explain all forms of deviant and risky behavior as resulting from a personality trait acquired in early childhood—low self-control. "Opportunities" for deviant behavior are also relevant in this theory, but it is still unresolved whether low self-control only has causal effects in interaction with particular opportunity structures, or whether an interaction effect can be expected, in addition to the main effects of self-control and opportunity structure. Features of low self-control are impulsiveness, a preference for simple tasks (no diligence), a preference for risky behavior (search for excitement, risk), a preference for physical activity (low cognitive competence, need for movement), self-centeredness (no empathy) and finally a low frustration tolerance/irritability. These traits arise from early childhood socialization experiences where the adult carers did not sufficiently monitor the children's behavior and did not use sanctions consistently and emphatically to clarify the accepted norms. In view of the danger of tautology through definitional fallacy between low self-control and deviant behavior, and in view of the ambiguous theoretical link between self-control and opportunities, it is not surprising that empirical tests reach different assessments of the quality of this theory. In addition to skeptical or dismissive findings (see Grasmick et al., 1993), there are at least partial confirmations in Keane, Maxim and Teevan (1993), Nagin and Paternoster (1993) and Strand and Garr (1994). In Gibbs, Giever and Martin (1998), however, the explanatory power with respect to juvenile delinquency is very modest if one considers that behavioral control by parents was additionally included. A particular shortcoming here—as with most other empirical tests on this theory—is that there is no simultaneous test of *rival* approaches, so one cannot exclude the possibility that their explanatory power would turn out to be markedly greater (see, e.g., proof of the limited effects of alcohol consumption in Eifler, 1997 and the proof of relatively substantial effects of variables of differential association theory). Although a first meta-analysis

(Pratt & Cullen, 2000) essentially confirms the theory, in longitudinal analyses the effects tend toward zero; the interactive effects of self-control and opportunities, for which Gottfredson and Hirschi's study offers only insufficient theoretical interpretation, are also particularly relevant. When at the same time the variables of social learning theory are taken into consideration, the latter still have considerable explanatory power. The findings of LaGrange and Silverman (1999) for Canadian youths regarding general delinquency, property offences, crimes of violence and drug-related crime point in the same direction; however, the effects of low self-control are gender- and offense-specific. The gender variable is an important predictor even after the variable self-control has been taken into account, i.e., gender is not only of causal significance for juvenile delinquency via the variable of self-control (similarly Nakhaie, Silverman and LaGrange (2000) regarding age, ethnicity, and gender).

In attempting to bring out the points of contact with control theory and at the same time to introduce the ideas of rational choice theory, Nagin and Paternoster (1994) arrived at the hypothesis that people with a strong orientation toward the present and toward themselves (two of the partial dimensions of low self-control) are less inclined to invest in social bonds, with the result that they are less deterred from committing crimes where the deviant behavior would jeopardize these bonds, since they have such bonds less often. After taking into account the extent of people's self-control, this hypothesis was confirmed, as were the assumptions that the intention of behaving in a deviant way is a function of the incentive of deviance, and that the preventive effect of risk perception is a function of self-centeredness and living only in the present. These results therefore represent at least partial confirmation for classical control theory and self-control theory. The two theories thus have points of contact, but whereas the former focuses on proximal, current social conditions as causal factors, self-control theory reveals affinities to social selection approaches because the personality traits which develop in early childhood lead to specific choices being made from given options. In studying the relative explanatory power of a social causation model, social selection model and integrated model on a longitudinal basis, Wright et al. (1999b) found that low self-control in childhood leads to a limitation of social bonds and to deviant behavior in adulthood, a finding which partially confirms the *selection model*. The findings that juvenile delinquency and a lack of social bonds encourage crime in adults, and what is more, that the effects of self-control are largely mediated through the quality of social bonds, amount to partial confirmation of the *social causation model*. But the social causation effects still remain significant even if the previous level of people's self-control is taken into account.

3.5. CONTROL BALANCE THEORY. Most social-structural criminality theories have been unable to explain the varied forms of criminal behavior using the same approach, and in reaction to this Tittle (1995) developed his control balance theory. He assumes that people universally strive for a particular degree of autonomy. A *balanced* relationship between the control one is subjected to by others and the control one exercises over others reduces the probability that individuals will attempt to use deviant behavior to alter this control balance in a direction appropriate to their striving for autonomy. Under specific conditions, which Tittle has developed very precisely in his theory, a control *deficit* leads individuals to employ particular forms of criminal behavior in an attempt to redress this imbalance. An extreme *control surplus*, however, is not in itself fulfilling, but entices the

actor to use deviant and criminal behavior in order to stabilize this imbalance or to assure
him- or herself of its continued existence, e.g., through decadent behavior and perverse
humiliation of those subjected to control, etc. This theory is fascinating in certain respects
but contains several inconsistencies and requires critical examination (see Braithwaite,
1997; Tittle, 1997). Initial empirical tests show that it should be worthwhile to pursue this
approach (see Piquero & Hickman, 1999), and this would require clarifying its connections with general strain theory according to Agnew, general stress theory, and control
belief theory or self-efficacy theory. In particular for the situation of youths in society
today the theory of control imbalance could be fruitful. The "destructuring of adolescence" (on the connection between adolescence and individualization, see Olk, 1985;
Heitmeyer & Olk, 1990; Münchmeier, 1998) describes a situation in which each young
person individually has to structure the complex process of attempting to attain the socially mediated goal of individual autonomy, while at the same time enduring the state of
dependence caused by the increasingly lengthy period of training and/or study; the demands this places on the individual youth are constantly increasing. The feeling of being
in control is exceptionally important for successful transition to adulthood; and in addition
to important factors such as the parental education level and the cognitive competencies of
the youths, there are many and diverse youth-typical problems which are important predictors of the success of the passage to adulthood (for empirical data on the connection
between control beliefs and the propensity to violence, see Heitmeyer et al., 1995:169ff;
in general, see Lewis, Ross, & Mirowsky, 1999).

4. Life-Course Theory

An issue which has long been at the center of research is the search for clear developmental patterns in the biographies of people who appear to manifest constant deviant behavior
at an early age and commit a disproportionately high number of offenses ("career criminals," see among others Caspi et al., 1994; Farrington, 1994a, 1994b, 1995, 1998; Moffitt,
1997). This research looks for specific characteristics in the personality of individuals, be
they genetic determinants or simply formative early childhood influences which structure
the developmental corridor of the person in question to such an extent that deviant careers
are virtually preprogrammed. We will not enter into a description of such studies here (see
Lösel & Bender, 2001) for two reasons. Firstly, because only a fraction of the people who
commit criminal acts in their youth also end up having police records in adulthood and
secondly, because as a rule these life-course studies devote their attention almost exclusively to the development of these people's personality or their intimate environment (and
even then a very confusing picture emerges with a predominance of weak outcomes; see
among others Hawkins et al., 1998). From these developments the studies only draw conclusions on individual psychological processes and fail to adequately consider the extent
to which the given development may also—and perhaps above all—be a result of social
reactions to particular (discernible or only supposed) distinctive features of the test persons (on a more cautious note, see Loeber, Farrington, & Waschbusch, 1998; Loeber &
Stouthamer-Loeber, 1998).

Instead, we will limit ourselves to such longitudinal studies that do not exclude the
second interpretation from the outset, but view criminal careers in their complex entirety.
Sampson and Laub (1990), for example, proceeded from the assumption that, although
"antisocial behavior" in childhood in many ways contributes to the probability of prob-

lematic behavior in youth and adulthood, it is social bonds (in the sense of Hirschi's control theory) in youth and adulthood that determine the development of crime in these phases. On the basis of the Glueck's data, it appears that employment career stability and a strong marital bond decisively influence crime in adulthood. In the course of people's lives there is thus both stability *and* change, and informal social control determines the extent of criminal behavior, not a genetic disposition and/or one acquired in early childhood. On the basis of the same data, Laub and Sampson (1993) show that both incremental and abrupt changes occur in the social bonds of adolescents and adults which are significant for the committing of criminal acts. It would thus be wrong to see crime in youth and adulthood as being *determined* by problematic childhood developments. Woodward, Fergusson and Bilsky (2000), on the other hand, observe a close relationship between childhood aggression and parental dysfunction, on the one hand, and later violent crime or being affected by violence (up to 18 years after the event), on the other. In Kokko and Pulkkinen (2000) the relationships between childhood aggressiveness and social conformity, in particular employment career disruptions, disappear almost entirely in adulthood if the parents had a style of upbringing which fostered child-oriented and pro-social behavior and counteracted such deviance. Whereas in the studies mentioned above, Laub and Sampson proceeded from the assumption that the development of crime was determined by changes in a person's *overall social relationships* in the course of their life (e.g., in terms of marriage, employment, military service, etc.), Warr (1998) countered that these transitions in the course of one's life achieve their effects by changing the relationships to *delinquent peers*. Elliott (1994) also interprets the seemingly close relationship between childhood aggression and later violent crime very much in this vein. The stability of aggressive violent crime in the course one's life is based more on a stability in the type and quality of social relationships and close personal bonds than in any underlying individual predisposition. Simons et al. (1998) arrive at a very similar result on this point: although there is a bivariate relationship between "antisocial" behavior in childhood and behavioral problems in adolescence, this relationship is seen to lose significance when the effects of parental social control, school and peers are taken into account. An improvement in relations to one's parents, greater commitment to school, and a restriction of relationships to delinquent peers can neutralize the problematic starting conditions in the course of a young person's further development. The relationship between childhood and adolescent delinquency thus reflects a complex developmental process and not the unfolding of a latently antisocial trait.

III. SHORTCOMINGS, DESIDERATA AND PERSPECTIVES OF THE THEORIES

1. Shortcomings and Desiderata

Progress in explaining individual violent crime will only be possible if the sociological approaches take due account of the fact that we are dealing with *violent crime*. Several theories meet this condition, but most of them ignore the problem totally, while others again (e.g., the general theory of crime) almost make a point of not taking any account of it because they lay claim to being a "general theory." But it is still an unresolved question how to explain why some actors "decide" on particular forms of crime,; because even if a specialization of multiple offenders is relatively rare, it is still unresolved why an actor in a particular situation manifested one form of crime and not another. There is also an urgent need for theories which take account of the fact that violent crime represents only one of very many behavioral strategies (e.g., in addition to psychological illnesses, physical illnesses, drug addiction, suicide, etc.) by means of which actors cope with difficult social conditions, between which there can also be complex, reciprocal causal relationships (e.g., between drug addiction and robbery). General stress theory has shown that both the perception and assessment of difficult conditions and events and also the availability of coping strategies are dependent on people's personal and social resources and thus also on microsocial and macrosocial structures; it has also shown that behavior or rather the choice between behavioral alternatives can be explained by these conditions and events. But stress theory has narrowed its view to health-related modes of behavior, while Agnew's strain theory, on the other hand, ignores the noncriminal possibilities of dealing with stress, or rather it conceives of the theory in such a way that it only explains those cases in which noncriminal coping seems not to be possible. Progress could be made if both strands of theory were integrated or if they additionally included ideas of control balance theory. Similarly, seemingly incompatible approaches such as interactionist theory and rational choice theory, could upon closer examination be used and integrated as elements of a more general theory; such a theory would define the question of subjective benefit and subjective costs, while also considering both formal and informal social control as functions of the self-image and self-esteem or the expected consequences for these. The same is true of the relationship of rational choice theory, general theory of crime and social learning theory of criminal behavior, whereby the latter, as the more general model, could be formulated in such a way that the others can be derived from it (see Akers, 1991).

2. Perspectives: Individualization Theory and Heitmeyer's Disintegration Approach

A further desideratum of prime importance would be to reestablish the link between the theories of deviant behavior and considerations of society as a whole, as individualization theory does to some extent. Whereas classical modernization theory has provided the basis for many analyses of deviant behavior and specific social problems (see Albrecht, 1999:6–13), of all the ideas of "reflexive modernization" theory only the "individualization theorem" has to date been applied to help explain violent crime. According to this theorem, the welfare state which develops over time in the course of modernization leads to an enormous rise in the standard of living, without however doing away with existing social and economic inequality. The population's level of education and qualifications is raised, there is an increase in vertical, horizontal, and also geographical mobility. This development leads to the increasing disintegration of the bonds to one's family of origin, to the parents' class or strata, to a specific social milieu, etc. Individuals can free themselves from established behavioral patterns and habits of thought: social stratification occurs "regardless of social strata and class" (see Beck, 1983).

However, this "liberation" also causes the *loss of collective feelings and models of interpretation*, undermining the preconditions for collective action. Individuals can no longer interpret the risks of modern societies as *collective fate* and deal with them accordingly: life's problems, which are caused *socially* as they always have been, are now interpretable only as experiences of personal failure which one is responsible for oneself and has to cope with *individually*. This has far-reaching consequences for coping psychologically with problematical situations. Attributing causal responsibility to particular circumstances, fate, powerful others, etc., a mechanism that can stabilize people's self-esteem and identity, is now no longer possible; the actor is ultimately alone and made to rely on him- or herself. The extent to which actors in this situation resort to attributing successes and failures to internal factors, e.g., one's own abilities and/or efforts, or conversely to external factors, be they stable or variable, depends not only on objective class or strata situations, but is also dependent on other conditions, for example personality traits, involvement in social networks, situational circumstances and their interaction. Since the type of causal attribution of success or failure or the anticipated results of actions would appear to be of central significance for triggering off various forms of conformity in reaction to a frustration of envisaged goals, it is understandable why attempted explanations such as anomie theory can hardly be confirmed in their current form. But this does not mean that they cannot be further developed along promising lines (see among others Ortmann, 2000).

Heitmeyer in particular proceeds from the assumption that the "negative individualization" inherent to the modernization process conjures up the danger of *social disintegration* which can consist in *social disorganization* and *disorientation* (e.g., Heitmeyer, 1994; Heitmeyer et al., 1995:56ff). *Disorganization* is understood as the *structural* dimension of the profound undermining of relationships between social institutions and life contexts, from which isolated and anonymized lifestyles can arise, including even the renouncement of central social institutions or exclusion from participation in them. *Disorientation* refers to the *cultural* or *personal* dimension which is involved when the pluralization of lifestyles and people's realities leads to actors' "cognitive irritation" regarding "shared common values and norms" or the interpretation of borders when norms are breached. Different developments can give rise to complex patterns with both dimensions of disintegration: when actors, who continue to belong to particular social groups and organizations, begin to emotionally reject their norms and values, this gives rise to "individual emotional disintegration;" when access to social positions and belonging to desired groups is barred—identification with the given values and goals presumed—this results in "disintegration through exclusion."

In addition to the criticisms of disorganization theory that have been listed above, there is also the objection that this approach has to date not been able to identify *explicitly in advance* which actors must be exposed to *which* form of disorganization under *which* conditions and with *which* intensity for them to react with a particular degree of disorientation. This criticism is noted in addition to the shortcoming shared with almost all sociological theories of not being able to explain which actors react to which form of disorientation with which *specific forms of behavior or psychological processes*.

Recent studies link disintegration theory and *anomie theory*, but they define anomie theory more broadly by considering social differentiation not only at the level of concrete *conditions for realization* of needs and desires but also understand "the constitution of needs and goals as well as their cultural standardization as specific characteristics of various functional areas of society or groups of the population" (Bohle et al., 1997:56). These authors take the consequences of the modernization process at *macro-sociological level* as their point of departure. In marked contrast to traditional modernization theory (see Albrecht, 1999), they see these consequences as not just embodying an inherent tendency to anomie— as in Durkheim—because *far-reaching* changes in the structure of highly industrial societies proceed at *great speed* and are condensed into very *short spaces of time*, but they also argue that these processes are largely *undirected* even today (p. 58). Under these conditions the problematic nature of the relationship between *system integration* and *social integration*, which Lockwood (1964, 1969) presented as being central, would appear even more precarious. Although the conflicts between system integration and social integration according to Lockwood must not necessarily lead to a *collapse* of the system, the tensions between the prevailing institutional order and its material base can give rise to conflicts and *far-reaching social change*. The structural conflicts between different aggregates of the social system can be interpreted as conflicts of interest which pose a threat to the institutional system.

Integration methods at a *second* analytical level (see also Sander & Heitmeyer, 1997) determine how the structural changes and structural fractures occurring in the course of the modernization process affect the various partial systems, particularly in view of *1. the social structure, 2. aspirations, 3. values and norms, and 4. social bonds*. Of course, societies do not just impassively accept the effects of massive structural change on the various partial systems and with regard to the aspects mentioned above. Rather, in the case of massive structural change the imbalances or tensions between culture and structure are expressed as a *structural crisis*; the maladjustment of aspirations to actual conditions and excessive norm pluralization can meet to produce a *crisis of regulations*; and the dissolution or very substantial weakening of social relationships and the rupture of networks is expressed as a *crisis of cohesion*.

At the *third* level we are dealing with individuals' ways of processing experiences and their modes of behavior. Here disintegration theory asserts that violence (violent crime), right-wing extremism and ethnic or culturally motivated violence can be explained through modern societies' inadequate efforts at integration. Three social or rather community *dimensions* of integration are distinguished here (see Anhut & Heitmeyer, 2000), in which specific problematic situations have to be resolved.

- In the *social structural* dimension it is an issue of *access* to the functional systems and participation in the material and cultural wealth of the society and the accompanying *recognition of positions, status*, etc.
- The *institutional* dimension concentrates on guaranteeing the balance of conflicting interests. This demands the maintenance of fundamental principles that guarantee the moral equality of the political opponent, justice, and people's safety and integrity. Fundamentally, it is an issue of the *chances of participation* in political disputes and the issue of *moral recognition* of people and basic standards.
- The third dimension emphasizes the *personal* aspect and the community, addressing the problems of establishing emotional relationships between people for the purpose of giving life meaning and for self-realization—problems which need to be resolved. The main issue here is the development of identity as well as securing *emotional recognition* so as to avoid existential crises, a lack of orientation, etc.

Coming to terms with the three tasks mentioned is described within the disintegration approach as *individual-functional* system integration (i.e., the structural dimension), *communicative-interactive* social integration (the institutional dimension), and *cultural-expressive* social integration (the socio-emotional dimension). This approach emphasizes that objectively measurable *formal* access to functional systems, the *formal* possibility of participation in public debates or *formal* belonging (e.g., to a social milieu or a family) is insufficient in itself, but that it must be viewed together with quality, i.e., the extent to which the actors subjectively perceive their *needs of recognition* to be fulfilled, and thus positional, moral and emotional recognition are judged to be adequate.

Experiences or fears of disintegration indicate the presence of unresolved problems: status-jeopardizing precariousness in material/existential terms, destabilization of social recognition, and threats to one's identity through violations of personal safety and integrity. Not every disintegration experience or its anticipation leads to violent behavior. This is *mediated* via further processes such as individual competencies, reference-group orientation, social control, individual control belief, attributions of responsibility, and processes of comparison. Furthermore, there are possibilities of compensation; i.e., when major problems arise in one dimension, it is possible that the integrative efforts in another dimension are especially activated or made available.

At the same time it is clear that very different forms of violence can result from the disintegration problems in the three dimensions of integration.

- In modern society there is increasing compulsion to individual self-assertion. In the course of processes of social comparison people have to pursue above all status attainment and status maintenance. Where negative results of processes of comparison emerge or threats to one's livelihood arise and no other equivalent sources of recognition are available, no positional recognition occurs and there is a danger of violence (violent crime) being used for status preservation or to acquire status symbols, etc.
- When in public debate people articulate their (possibly particular) perceptions of justice and experience a disdain for their positions, opinions, etc., and if they feel this disdain is serious, this gives rise to the grave problem that people respond to the perceived denial to recognize their position with the refusal to recognize the equality of other people (above all those of other ethnic origin) and their safety and integrity. This is the case with politically motivated violence, which to extent occurs collectively, such as right-wing extremism, xenophobic violence, etc.
- In the narrow area of particular communities (e.g., families) we are dealing with experiences or fears of disintegration in the form of exclusion, loss of control, loss of dependable social relationships (also through the dissolution of families) or through the violation of emotional recognition. The forms of violence that occur here are above all those which aim to maintain identity and self-esteem, to demonstrate one's power, or to regain (self-)recognition.

In general this approach aims to connect up to positions in social theory and to developments in society. Furthermore, the concept of the three *dimensions* of the integration/disintegration process at the level of individual behavior is a diversified attempt to analyze different forms of violence in connection with experiences or fears of disintegration, centering around the jeopardizing of recognition. The explanation of violence is thus connected above all with the need for recognition. This can involve *securing the status* of individual actors, achieving *collective political ambitions* toward other groups (including other ethnic groups), *demonstrating power to stabilize identity* or *reestablishing self-esteem* in collective contexts, and can take on different forms of behavior and vary according to the social context.

This draft theory, which is under constant development (see Heitmeyer, 1994, 1996, 1997a, 1997b, 1997c, 1998; Heitmeyer & Müller, 1995; Heitmeyer et al., 1995, Heitmeyer, Müller, & Schröder, 1997), offers an orientational framework for further theoretical work. It has provided the stimulus for many complex studies dealing above all with the problem of violence. In most cases, however, the focus has been not on violence *actually committed*, but on the acceptance of violence or the propensity to violence. Criticism thus demands that inner-family socialization conditions and experiences of deprivation be given more consideration and problematizes the conceptualization of "violence." But the divergent findings which critics note are probably due in part to differences between the populations studied, the sources of data used, and also to perspective (see, e.g., the problem of interpreting the disintegrative phenomenon of aggressive and xenophobic youth subcultures; see Eckert, 1990; Willems, 1993). The fact that this draft theory would seem to somehow offer an interpretation for almost every finding gives cause for skepticism. Critical examination is still required in order to ascertain whether the theory is indeed excellent or whether its use of concepts is too elastic. Important steps have already been taken to redress the particular weak points (see among others Anhut & Heitmeyer, 2000).

It cannot yet be decided whether the thesis of a causal connection between individualization and violent crime is tenable. The fact that the first great phase of individualization since the middle of the nineteenth century went hand in hand with a long-term decline in violent crime in Western societies (see Eisner, 2001; Thome, 2001, 2002) proves that the relationship must indeed be a very complex one. Although this trend has been interrupted for several decades, the comparative international study (in cross-sectional perspective) by Karstedt (2001) concludes that there is a negative relationship between the level of individualization and violent crime. Strobl and Kühnel also show that the causal significance of these variables depends on the nature of the frames chosen by particular groups of actors—without resolving, however, what this choice actually depends on (Strobl & Kühnel, 2002; see also Kühnel & Strobl, 2001). Be that as it may, it is apparent that it is still a very long way to a theoretically consistent and empirically adequate explanation. There is much to suggest that modern societies are going through a phase of the re-ethnicization of social conflicts—possibly caused by globalization. The state, which is increasingly perceived as weak, loses its grip on what used to be the basis of the process of civilization—the monopoly of violence—which in a highly individualized society encourages re-collectivization processes that make the intergroup conflicts even more violent (see among others Jacobs & Wood, 1999; in general, see Thome, 2002).

3. Meta-Theoretical Principles for Further Research

For its further work research requires that consideration be given to what we have already learned, (1) that it is necessary to distinguish between different forms of violent crime, (2) that we can expect there to be multiple influences, (3) that we should assume causal structures that are dynamic, not static, (4) that factors that trigger criminal behavior are not necessarily identical to those that maintain it, (5) that identical results of a development can be due to different causes (equifinality), (6) that, on the other hand, identical factors can yield different results (multifinality), (7) that psychological and social factors must not be viewed in isolation, but linked together in multi-level models (8) and that actors should not be considered the passive objects of social forces, but rather the creators of conditions.

Translated by Tradukas

REFERENCES

Adler, Freda, & William S. Laufer (Eds.) (1995). *The Legacy of Anomie Theory (Advances in Criminological Theory, Vol. 6)*. New Brunswick: Transaction Publ.

Agnew, Robert. (1985a). A Revised Strain Theory of Delinquency. *Social Forces, 64*, 151–166.

Agnew, Robert. (1985b). Social Control Theory and Delinquency: A Longitudinal Test. *Criminology, 23*, 46–61.

Agnew, Robert. (1990a). Adolescent Resources and Delinquency. *Criminology, 28*, 535–565.

Agnew, Robert. (1990b). The Origins of Delinquent Events: An Examination of Offender Accounts. *Journal of Research in Crime and Delinquency, 27*, 267–294.

Agnew, Robert. (1991). A Longitudinal Test of Social Control Theory. *Journal of Research in Crime and Delinquency, 28*, 126–156.

Agnew, Robert. (1992). Foundation for a General Strain Theory of Crime and Delinquency. *Criminology, 30*, 47–87.

Agnew, Robert. (1993). Why Do They Do It? An Examination of the Intervening Mechanisms between 'Social Control' Variables and Delinquency. *Journal of Research in Crime and Delinquency, 30*, 245–266.

Agnew, Robert. (1994). The Techniques of Neutralization and Violence. *Criminology, 32*, 555–580.

Agnew, Robert. (1995). The Contribution of Social-Psychological Strain Theory to the Explanation of Crime and Delinquency. In Freda Adler & William S. Laufer (Eds.), *The Legacy of Anomie Theory* (pp. 113–137). New Brunswick, London: Transaction Publ.

Agnew, Robert. (1999). A General Strain Theory of Community Differences in Crime Areas. *Journal of Research in Crime and Delinquency, 36*, 123–155.

Agnew, Robert, & Ardith A. R. Peters. (1986). The Techniques of Neutralization. An Analysis of Predisposing and Situational Factors. *Criminal Justice and Behavior, 13*, 81–97.

Agnew, Robert, & Raskin Helen White. (1992). An Empirical Test of General Strain Theory. *Criminology, 30*, 475–499.

Akers, Ronald L. (1985). *Deviant Behavior: A Social Learning Approach. 3rd Edition*. Belmont:Wadsworth.

Akers, Ronald L. (1990). Rational Choice, Deterrence, and Social Learning Theory in Criminology: The Path Not Taken. *The Journal of Criminal Law and Criminology, 81*, 653–676.

Akers, Ronald L. (1991). Self-Control as a General Theory of Crime. Besprechung von Gottfredson u. Hirschi : A General Theory of Crime. *Journal of Quantitative Criminology, 7*, 201–211.

Akers, Ronald L. (1998). *Social Learning and Social Structure. A General Theory of Crime and Deviance*. Boston: Northeastern University Press.

Akers, Ronald L., Marvin D. Krohn, Lonn Lanza-Kaduce, & Marcia Radosevich. (1979). Social Learning and Deviant Behavior: A Specific Test of a General Theory. *American Sociological Review, 44*, 636–655.

Alarid, Leanne F., Velmer S. Burton, Jr., Francis T. Cullen. (2000). Gender and Crime Among Felony Offenders: Assessing The Generality of Social Control and Differential Association Theories. *Journal of Research in Crime and Delinquency, 37*, 171–199.

Albrecht, Günter. (1986). *Die quantitative Entwicklung der Eigentumskriminalität von 1882 bis in die Gegenwart. Bericht des gleichnamigen Lehrforschungsberichtes. Vervielfältigtes Msk.* Universitätsbibliothek Bielefeld, Bielefeld.

Albrecht, Günter. (1990). Möglichkeiten und Grenzen der Prognose 'Krimineller Karrieren'. Deutsche Vereinigung für Jugendgerichte und Jugendgerichtshilfen (Editor): *Mehrfach Auffällige—Mehrfach Betroffene. Erlebnisweisen und Reaktionsformen* (pp. 99–116). Bonn: Forum Verlag.

Albrecht, Günter. (1997). Anomie oder Hysterie—oder beides? Die bundesrepublikanische Gesellschaft und ihre Kriminalitätsentwicklung. In Wilhelm Heitmeyer (Ed.), *Was treibt die Gesellschaft auseinander?* (pp. 506–554). Frankfurt a. M.: Suhrkamp.

Albrecht, Günter. (1999). Sozialer Wandel und Kriminalität. In Hans-Jörg Albrecht & Helmut Kury (Eds.), *Kriminalität, Strafrechtsreform und Strafvollzug in Zeiten des sozialen Umbruchs, Beiträge zum Zweiten deutsch-chinesischen Kolloquium* (pp. 1–56). Freiburg: edition iuscrim.

Albrecht, Günter. (2001a). Gewaltkriminalität zwischen Mythos und Realität. In Günter Albrecht, Otto Backes & Wolfgang Kühnel (Eds.), *Gewaltkriminalität zwischen Mythos und Realität*. Frankfurt a. M.: Suhrkamp(pp. 9–67).

Albrecht, Günter. (2001b). Soziale Ungleichheit, Deprivation und Gewaltkriminalität. In Günter Albrecht, Otto Backes & Wolfgang Kühnel (Eds.), *Gewaltkriminalität zwischen Mythos und Realität* (pp. 195–235). Frankfurt a. M.: Suhrkamp.

Albrecht, Günter. (2002). Jugend, Recht und Kriminalität. In Heinz-Hermann Krüger (Ed.), *Handbuch der Jugendforschung. 3rd Edition*. Opladen: Leske & Budrich.

Albrecht, Günter, & Carl-Werner Howe. (1992). Soziale Schicht und Delinquenz. Verwischte Spuren oder falsche Fährte? *Kölner Zeitschrift für Soziologie und Sozialpsychologie, 44*, 697–730.

Albrecht, Günter, & Susanne Karstedt-Henke. (1987). Alternative Methods of Conflict-Settling and Sanctioning: Their Impact on Young Offenders. In Klaus Hurrelmann, Franz-Xaver Kaufmann & Friedrich Lösel (Eds.), *Social Intervention: Potential and Constraints* (pp. 315–332). Berlin, New York: Aldine de Gruyter.

Albrecht, Günter, Carl-Werner Howe, & Jochen Wolterhoff. (1991). Familienstruktur und Delinquenz. *Soziale Probleme, 2*, 107–156.

Albrecht, Günter, & Norbert van Kampen. (1992). *Auswirkungen der Diversion auf die Entwicklung des Selbstbildes delinquenter Jugendlicher.* Bielefeld: Universität Bielefeld, SFB 227, Prävention und Intervention im Kindes- und Jugendalter.

Albrecht, Peter Alexis, & Siegfried Lamnek. (1979). *Jugendkriminalität im Zerrbild der Statistik. Eine Analyse von Daten und Entwicklungen*. München: Juventa.

Anhut, Reimund, & Wilhelm Heitmeyer. (2000). Desintegration, Konflikt und Ethnisierung. Eine Problemanalyse und theoretische Rahmenkonzeption. In Wilhelm Heitmeyer & Reimund Anhut (Eds.), *Bedrohte Stadtgesellschaft. Soziale Desintegrationsprozesse und ethnisch-kulturelle Konfliktkonstellationen* (pp. 17–75). Weinheim und München: Juventa.

Athens, Lonnie. (1986). Types of violent persons: Towards the development of a symbolic interactionist theory of violent criminal behavior. In Norman K. Denzin (Ed.), *Studies in Symbolic Interaction. An Annual Compilation of Research, 7*, 367–389.

Bailey, Susan L. & Robert L. Hubbard. (1990). Developmental Variation in the Context of Marijuana Initiation among Adolescents. *The Journal of Health and Social Behavior, 31*, 58–70.

Bandura, Albert (Ed.) (1971). *Psychological Modeling: Conflicting Theories*. Chicago: Aldine-Atherton. [German: Bandura, Albert (Ed.) (1976). *Lernen am Modell*. Stuttgart: Klett-Cotta.]

Bandura, Albert. (1977). *Social Learning Theory*. Englewood Cliffs: Prentice-Hall. [German: Bandura, Albert. (1979). *Sozial-kognitive Lerntheorie*. Stuttgart: Klett-Cotta.]

Bartusch, Dawn J., & Ross L. Matsueda. (1996). Gender, Reflected Appraisals, and Labeling: A Cross-Group Test of an Interactionist Theory of Delinquency. *Social Forces, 75*, 145–177.

Beck, E. M., & Stewart E. Tolnay. (1990). The Killing Fields of the Deep South: The Market for Cotton and the Lynching of Blacks, 1882–1930. *American Sociological Review, 55*, 526–539.

Beck, E.M., & Stewart E. Tolnay. (1995). Violence toward African Americans in the Era of the White Lynch Mob. In Darnell F. Hawkins (Ed.), *Ethnicity, Race, and Crime. Perspectives Across Time and Place* (pp. 121–144). New York: New York University Press.

Beck, Ulrich. (1983). Jenseits von Stand und Klasse? Soziale Ungleichheiten, gesellschaftliche Individualisierungsprozesse und die Entstehung neuer sozialer Formationen und Identitäten. In Reinhard Kreckel (Ed.), *Soziale Ungleichheiten. Sonderband 4 der Sozialen Welt* (pp. 35–74). Göttingen: Schwartz.

Becker, Gary S. (1968). Crime and Punishment: An Economic Approach. *Journal of Political Economy, 76*, 169–217.

Becker, Gary S. (1986). The Economic Approach to Human Behavior. In Jon Elster (Ed.), *Rational Choice* (pp. 108–121). Oxford: Basil Blackwell.

Becker, Howard S. (1963). *Outsiders: Studies in the Sociology of Deviance*. New York: Free Press.

Bellair, Paul E. (1997). Social Interaction and Community Crime: Examining the Importance of Neighbor Networks. *Criminology, 35*, 677–703.

Bellair, Paul E. (2000). Informal Surveillance and Street Crime: A Complex Relationship. *Criminology, 38*, 137–169.

Berk, Richard A., Alec Campbell, Ruth Klap, & Bruce Western. (1992). The Deterrent Effect of Arrest in Incidents of Domestic Violence: A Bayesian Analysis of Four Field Experiments. *American Sociological Review, 57*, 698–708.

Berk, Richard A., and Phyllis J. Newton. (1985). Does Arrest Really Deter Wife Battery? An Effort to Replicate the Findings of the Minneapolis Spouse Abuse Experiment. *American Sociological Review, 50*, 253–262.

Bernard, Thomas J. (1984). Control Criticisms of Strain Theories: An Assessment of Theoretical and Empirical Adequacy. *Journal of Research in Crime and Delinquency, 21*, 353–372.

Bernard, Thomas J. (1990). Angry Aggression Among the 'Truly Disadvantaged'. *Criminology, 28*, 73–95.

Black, Donald. (1983). Crime as Social Control. *American Sociological Review, 48*, 34–45.

Black, Donald. (1984). Crime and Social Control. In Donald Black (Ed.), *Toward a General Theory of Social Control. Vol. 2: Selected Problems* (pp. 1–27). Orlando et al.: Academic Press.

Blau, Judith R., and Peter M. Blau. (1982). The Cost of Inequality: Metropolitan Structure and Violent Crime. *American Sociological Review*, *47*, 114–129.

Blau, Peter M., & Reid M. Golden. (1986). Metropolitan Structure and Criminal Violence. *The Sociological Quarterly*, *27*, 15–26.

Bohle, Hans Hartwig. (1975). *Soziale Abweichung und Erfolgschancen: Die Anomietheorie in der Diskussion.* Darmstadt-Neuwied: Luchterhand.

Bohle, Hans Hartwig, Wilhelm Heitmeyer, Wolfgang Kühnel, & Uwe Sander. (1997). Anomie in der modernen Gesellschaft: Bestandsaufnahme und Kritik eines klassischen Ansatzes soziologischer Analyse. In Wilhelm Heitmeyer (Ed.), *Was treibt die Gesellschaft auseinander?* (pp. 29–65). Frankfurt a. M.: Suhrkamp.

Bohnsack, Ralf, Peter Loos, Burkhard Schäffer, Klaus Städtler, & Bodo Wild. (1995). *Die Suche nach Gemeinsamkeit und die Gewalt der Gruppe. Hooligans, Musikgruppen und andere Jugendcliquen.* Opladen: Leske & Budrich.

Braithwaite, John. (1989). *Crime, Shame, and Reintegration.* Cambridge: Cambridge Univ. Press.

Braithwaite, John. (1995). Diversion, Reintegrative Shaming and Republican Criminology. In Günter Albrecht & Wolfgang Ludwig-Mayerhofer (Eds.), *Diversion and Informal Social Control* (pp. 141–158). Berlin, New York: Aldine de Gruyter.

Braithwaite, John. (1997). Charles Tittle's Control Balance and Criminological Theory. *Theoretical Criminology*, *1*, 77–97.

Brantingham, Paul, & Patricia Brantingham. (1984a). Temporal Analysis of Crime. In Paul Brantingham & Patricia Brantingham (Eds.), *Patterns in Crime* (pp. 93–118). New York, London: Collier-Macmillan.

Brantingham, Paul, & Patricia Brantingham. (1984b). Modern Temporal Patterns in Crime. In Paul Brantingham & Patricia Brantingham (Eds.), *Patterns in Crime* (pp. 119–160). New York, London: Collier-Macmillan.

Brantingham, Paul, & Patricia Brantingham. (1984c). Long-Term Patterns in Crime. In Paul Brantingham & Patricia Brantingham (Eds.), *Patterns in Crime* (pp. 161–210). New York, London: Collier-Macmillan.

Brezina, Timothy. (1996). Adapting To Strain: An Examination of Delinquent Coping Responses. *Criminology*, *34*, 39–60.

Brezina, Timothy. (1998). Adolescent Maltreatment and Delinquency: The Question of Intervening Processes. *Journal of Research in Crime and Delinquency*, *35*, 71–99.

Brezina, Timothy. (2000). Delinquent Problem-Solving: An Interpretative Framework For Criminological Theory and Research. *Journal of Research in Crime and Delinquency*, *37*, 3–30.

Broidy, Lisa, & Robert Agnew. (1997). Gender and Crime: A General Strain Theory Perspective. *Journal of Research in Crime and Delinquency*, *34*, 275–306.

Brown, Waln K., Timothy P. Miller, Richard L. Jenkins, & Warren A. Rhodes. (1991). The Human Costs of 'Giving the Kid Another Chance'. *International Journal of Offender Therapy and Comparative Criminology*, *35*, 296–302.

Brownfield, David. (1986). Social Class and Violent Behavior. *Criminology*, *24*, 421–438.

Brownfield, David. (1996). The Drugs and Crime Connection and Offense Specialization: A Latent Variable Approach. In John Hagan, A.R.Gillis & David Brownfield (Eds.), *Criminological Controversies. A Methodological Primer* (pp. 125–156). Boulder: Westview.

Brücker, Heiner. (1994). *Sozialer Stress, Defensives Coping und Erosion der Kontrollüberzeugung. Eine empirische Studie zu Störfaktoren des gesundheitlichen Wohlbefindens von Erwachsenen.* Münster, New York: Waxmann.

Burgess, Robert L., & Ronald L. Akers. (1966). A Differential Association-Reinforcement Theory of Criminal Behavior. *Social Problems*, *14*, 128–147.

Bursik, Robert J. (1988). Social disorganization and theories of crime and delinquency: Problems and prospects. *Criminology*, *26*, 519–552.

Bursik, Robert J., & Harold G. Grasmick. (1993a). Economic Deprivation and Neighborhood Crime Rates. *Law and Society Review*, *27*, 263–285.

Bursik, Robert J., & Harold G. Grasmick. (1993b). *Neighborhoods and Crime. The Dimensions of Effective Community Control.* New York: Lexington Books.

Bursik, Robert J., & Harold G. Grasmick. (1995). The Effect of Neighborhood Dynamics on Gang Behavior. In Malcolm W. Klein, Cheryl L. Maxson & Jody Miller (Eds.), *The Modern Gang Reader* (pp. 114–124). Los Angeles: Roxbury Publ. Press.

Cantor, David, & Kenneth C. Land. (1985). Unemployment and Crime Rates in the Post-World War II United States: A Theoretical and Empirical Analysis. *American Sociological Review*, *50*, 317–332.

Carlen, Pat. (1994). Gender, Class, Racism, and Criminal Justice: Against Global and Gender-Centric Theories, For Poststructuralist Perspectives. In George S. Bridges & Martha A. Myers (Eds.), *Inequality, Crime, and Social Control* (pp. 134–144). Boulder, San Francisco, Oxford: Westview.

Caspi, Avshalom, Phil Silva, Magda Stouthamer-Loeber, Robert Krueger, & Pamela Schmutte. (1994). Are some People Crime-Prone? Replications of the Personality-Crime Relationship across Countries, Genders, Races, and Methods. *Criminology, 32*(2), 163–195.

Catalano, Richard F., & J. David Hawkins. (1996). The Social Development Model: A Theory of Antisocial Behavior. In J. David Hawkins (Ed.), *Delinquency and Crime: Current Theories* (pp. 149–197). New York: Cambridge University Press.

Cernkovich, Stephen A., Peggy C. Giordano, & Jennifer L. Rudolph. (2000). Race, Crime and the American Dream. *Journal of Research in Crime and Delinquency, 37*, 131–170.

Chesney-Lind, Meda. (1997). *The Female Offender: Girls, Women, and Crime.* Thousand Oaks, CA.: Sage.

Chesney-Lind, Meda, & Randall G. Shelden. (1998). *Girls, Delinquency, and Juvenile Justice. 2nd Edition.* Belmont: Wadsworth.

Clinard, Marshall B. (1968). *Sociology of Deviant Behavior. 3rd Edition.* New York: Holt, Rinehart & Winston.

Clinard, Marshall B. (Ed.) (1964). *Anomie and Deviant Behavior. A Discussion and Critique.* New York and London: Free Press.

Cloward, Richard A. (1968). Illegitime Mittel, Anomie und abweichendes Verhalten. In Fritz Sack & René König (Eds.), *Kriminalsoziologie* (pp. 314–338). Frankfurt a. M.: Akademische Verlagsanstalt.

Cloward, Richard A., & Lloyd E. Ohlin. (1960). *Delinquency and Opportunity. A Theory of Delinquent Gangs.* New York: Free Press.

Cohen, Albert K. (1955). *Delinquent Boys. The Culture of the Gang.* Glencoe: Free Press [German: Cohen, Albert K. (1961). *Kriminelle Jugend. Zur Soziologie jugendlichen Bandenwesens.* Reinbek: Rowohlt.]

Cohen, Albert K. (1959). The Study of Social Disorganization and Deviant Behavior. In Robert K. Merton, Leonard Broom & Leonard S. Cottrell (Eds.), *Sociology Today. Problems and Prospects* (pp. 461–484). New York: Basic Books.

Cohen, Albert K. (1968). Zur Erforschung delinquenter Subkulturen. In Fritz Sack & René König (Eds.), *Kriminalsoziologie* (pp. 372–394). Frankfurt a. M.: Akademische Verlagsanstalt.

Cook, Philip J., & Gary A. Zarkin. (1985). Crime and the Business Cycle. *Journal of Legal Studies, XIV*, 115–128, 391–410.

Cornish, Derek B., & Richard V. Clarke (Eds.) (1986). *The Reasoning Criminal. Rational Choice Perspectives on Offending.* New York, Berlin et al.: Springer.

Cremer, Günter. (1992). *Die Subkultur der Rocker. Erscheinungsformen und Selbstdarstellung.* Pfaffenweiler: Centaurus.

Curry, G. David. (1998). Female Gang Involvement. *Journal of Research in Crime and Delinquency, 35*, 100–118.

Daly, Kathleen, & Lisa Maher. (1998). *Criminology at the Crossroads: Feminist Readings in Crime and Justice.* Oxford: Oxford University Press.

Dixon, Jo, & Alan J. Lizotte. (1987). Gun Ownership and the 'Southern Subculture of Violence'. *American Journal of Sociology, 93*, 383–405.

Easterlin, Richard A. (1980). *Birth and Fortune. The Impact of Numbers on Personal Welfare.* New York: Basic Books.

Easterlin, Richard A., & Eileen M. Crimmins. (1988). Recent Social Trends: Changes in Personal Aspirations of American Youth. *Sociology and Social Research, 72*, 217–223.

Eckert, Roland. (1990). *Aggressive Gruppen. In DVJJ (Ed.), Mehrfach Auffällige—Mehrfach Betroffene. Dokumentation des 21. Deutschen Jugendgerichtstages, 30 September–4 October 1989 in Göttingen* (pp. 190–210). Godesberg: Forum Verlag.

Eckert, Roland, & Helmut Willems. (1993). Politisch motivierte Gewalt. In Informationszentrum Sozialwissenschaften (Ed.), *Gewalt in der Gesellschaft. Eine Dokumentation zum Stand der sozialwissenschaftlichen Forschung seit (1985)* (pp. 27–55). Bonn: Informationszentrum Sozialwissenschaften.

Ehrlich, Isaac. (1973). Participation in Illegitimate Activities: A Theoretical and Empirical Investigation. *Journal of Political Economy, 81*(1), 521–565.

Ehrlich, Isaac. (1979). The Economic Approach to Crime. A Preliminary Assessment. In Sheldon L. Messinger & Egon Bittner (Eds.), *Criminology Review Yearbook* (pp. 25–60). Beverly Hills, London: Sage.

Eifler, Stefanie. (1997). *Einflußfaktoren von Alkoholkonsum. Sozialisation, Self-Control und Differentielles Lernen.* Wiesbaden: Deutscher Universitätsverlag.

Eisner, Manuel. (1995). Crime and Economy. The Effects of Economic Structures and Phases of Development On Crime. In Council of Europe/Conseil de l' Europe (Ed.), *Crime and Economy. Proceedings. Reports*

Presented to the 11th Criminological Colloquium (1994), Criminological Research. Vol. 32 (pp. 13–51). Strasbourg: Council of Europe Publication.

Eisner, Manuel. (2001a). Individuelle Gewalt und Modernisierung in Europa, 1200–2000. In Günter Albrecht, Otto Backes & Wolfgang Kühnel (Eds.), *Gewaltkriminalität zwischen Mythos und Realität* (pp. 71–97). Frankfurt a. M.: Suhrkamp.

Elliott, Delbert S. (1994). Serious Violent Offenders: Onset, Developmental Course, And Termination—The American Society Of Criminology 1993 Presidential Address. *Criminology, 32*, 1–21.

Elliott, Delbert S., William J. Wilson, David Huizinga, Robert J. Sampson, Amanda Elliott, & Bruce Rabkin. (1996). The Effects of Neighborhood Disadvantage On Adolescent Development. *Journal of Research in Crime and Delinquency, 33*, 389–426.

Elliott, Delbert S., Scott Menard. no date. *Temporal and Developmental Patterns of Delinquent Peer Group Association and Delinquent Behavior.* Washington: National Institute of Mental Health (MH27552) and the National Institute for Juvenile Justice and Delinquency Prevention, Office of Juvenile Justice and Delinquency Preventions, U.S. Department of Justice.

Ellison, Christopher. (1991). An Eye for an Eye? A Note on the Southern Subculture of Violence Thesis. *Social Forces, 69*, 1223–1240.

Esbensen, Finn-A., & David Huizinga. (1990). Community Structure and Drug Use: From a Social Disorganization Perspective. *Justice Quarterly, 7*, 691–709.

Esbensen, Finn-A., & Elizabeth Piper Deschenes. (1998). A Multisite Examination of Youth Gang Membership: Does Gender Matter? *Criminology, 36*, 799–827.

Esbensen, Finn-A., & David Huizinga. (1993). Gangs, Drugs, and Delinquency in a Survey of Urban Youth. *Criminology, 31*, 565–589.

Farnworth, Margaret, Terence P. Thornberry, Marvin D. Krohn, & Alan J. Lizotte. (1994). Measurement in the Study of Class and Delinquency: Integrating Theory and Research. *Journal of Research in Crime and Delinquency, 31*, 32–61.

Farrington, David P. (1994a). Childhood, Adolescent, and Adult Features of Violent Males. In L. Rowell Huesmann (Ed.), *Aggressive Behavior. Current Perspectives* (pp. 215–240). New York, London: Plenum.

Farrington, David P. (1994b). Human Development and Criminal Careers. In Mike Maguire, Rod Morgan & Robert Reiner (Eds.), *The Oxford Handbook of Criminology* (pp. 511–584). Oxford: Clarendon.

Farrington, David P. (1995 Stabilität und Prädiktion von aggressivem Verhalten. *Gruppendynamik, 26*, 23–40.

Farrington, David P. (1998). Predictors, Causes, and Correlates of Male Youth Violence. In Michael Tonry (Ed.), *Youth Violence. Crime and Justice. Vol. 24* (pp. 421–475). Chicago: University of Chicago Press.

Felson, Marcus. (1986). Linking Criminal Choices, Routine Activities, and Informal Control and Criminal Outcomes. In Derek B. Cornish & Ronald V. Clarke (Eds.), *The Reasoning Criminal* (pp. 121–128). New York, Berlin etc.: Springer.

Felson, Marcus. (1994). *Crime and Everyday Life. Insights and Implications for Society.* Thousand Oaks: Sage.

Felson, Marcus. (2000). The Routine Activity Approach as a General Crime Theory. In Sally S. Simpson (Ed.), *Of Crime and Criminality. The Use of Theory in Everyday Life* (pp. 205–216). Thousand Oaks: Pine Forge Press.

Felson, Marcus, & Lawrence E. Cohen. (1980). Human Ecology and Crime: A Routine Activity Approach. *Human Ecology, 8*, 389–406.

Felson, Richard B. (1993). Predatory and Dispute-related Violence: A Social Interactionist Approach. In Ronald V. Clarke & Marcus Felson (Eds.), *Routine Activity and Rational Choice* (pp. 103–125). New Brunswick, London: Transaction Publ.

Field, S. (1995). Economic Cycles and Crime in Europe. In Council of Europe/Conseil de l'Europe (Ed.), *Crime and Economy. Proceedings. Reports presented to the 11th Criminological Colloquium (1994). Criminological Research. Vol. 32* (pp. 53–72). Strasbourg: Council of Europe Publication.

Foglia, Wanda D. (1997). Perceptual Deterrence and the Mediating Effect of Internalized Norms Among Inner-City Teenagers. *Journal of Research in Crime and Delinquency, 34*, 414–442.

Foshee, Vangie A., Karl E. Baumann, & G. Fletcher Linder. (1999). Family Violence and the Perpetration of Adolescent Dating Violence: Examining Social Learning and Social Control Processes. *Journal of Marriage and the Family, 61*, 331–342.

Franke, Kirsten. (2000). *Frauen und Kriminalität. Eine kritische Analyse kriminologischer und soziologischer Theorien.* Konstanz: UVK Universitätsverlag.

Frey, Hans-Peter. (1983). *Stigma und Identität. Eine empirische Untersuchung zur Genese und Änderung krimineller Identität bei Jugendlichen.* Weinheim: Beltz.

Garofalo, James (1987): Reassessing the Lifestyle Model of Criminal Victimization. In Gottfredson, Michael R. & Travis Hirschi (Eds.), *Positive Criminology* (pp. 23–42). Newbury Park: Sage.

Gastil, Raymond. (1971). Homicide and a Regional Culture of Violence. *American Sociological Review, 36,* 412–427.

Gibbs, John J., Dennis Giever, & Jamie S. Martin. (1998). Parental Management and Self-control: An Empirical Test of Gottfredson and Hirschi's General Theory. *Journal of Research in Crime and Delinquency, 35,* 40–70.

Giordano, Peggy C., Toni J. Millhollin, Stephen A. Cernkovich, Meredith D. Pugh, & Jennifer L. Rudolph. (1999). Delinquency, Identity, and Women's Involvement in Relationship Violence. *Criminology, 37,* 17–37.

Giordano, Peggy C., Sharon M. Rockwell. (2000). Differential Association Theory and Female Crime. In Sally S. Simpson (Ed.), *Of Crime and Criminality. The Use of Theory in Everyday Life* (pp. 3–24). Thousand Oaks et al.: Pine Forge Press.

Gottfredson, Michael R., & Travis Hirschi. (1990). *A General Theory of Crime.* Stanford: Stanford University Press.

Gove, Walter R. (1976). Deviant Behavior, Social Intervention, and Labeling Theory. In Lewis A. Coser & Otto N. Larsen (Eds.), *The Uses of Controversy in Sociology* (pp. 219–227). New York, London: Free Press.

Grasmick, Harold G., John Hagan, Brenda S. Blackwell, & Bruce J. Arneklev. (1996). Risk Preferences and Patriarchy: Extending Power-Control Theory. *Social Forces, 75,* 177–199.

Grasmick, Harold G., Charles R. Tittle, Robert J. Bursik, & Bruce J. Arneklev. (1993). Testing the Core Empirical Implications of Gottfredson and Hirschi's General Theory of Crime. *Journal of Research in Crime and Delinquency, 30,* 5–29.

Green, Donald P., Jack Glaser, & Andrew Rich. (1998). From Lynching to Gay Bashing: The Elusive Connection Between Economic Conditions and Hate Crime. *Journal of Personality and Social Psychology, 75,* 82–92.

Greenberg, David F. (1979). Delinquency and the Age Structure of Society. In Sheldon L. Messinger & Egon Bittner (Eds.), *Criminology Review Yearbook* (pp. 586–620). Beverly Hills: Sage.

Guerra, Nancy G., Larry Nucci, & L. Rowell Huesmann. (1994). Moral Cognition and Childhood Aggression. In L. Rowell Huesmann (Ed.), *Aggressive Behavior. Current Perspectives* (pp. 13–33). New York, London: Plenum.

Hackney, Sheldon (Ed.) (1969). Southern Violence. *American Historical Review, 74,* 906–925.

Haferkamp, Hans. (1975). *Kriminelle Karrieren. Handlungstheorie, Teilnehmende Beobachtung und Soziologie krimineller Prozesse.* Reinbek: Rowohlt.

Hagan, John. (1989). Micro and Macro Structures of Delinquency Causation and a Power-Control Theory of Gender and Delinquency. In Steven F. Messner, Marvin D. Krohn & Allen E. Liska (Eds.), *Theoretical Integration in the Study of Deviance and Crime. Problems and Prospects* (pp. 213–227). Albany: State University of New York Press.

Hagan, John. (1991). Destiny and Drift: Subcultural Preferences, Status Attainments, and the Risks and Rewards of Youth. *American Sociological Review, 56,* 567–582.

Hagan, John. (1997). Defiance and Despair: Subcultural Linkages Between Delinquency and Despair in the Life Course. *Social Forces, 76,* 119–134.

Hagan, John, A. R. Gillis, & John Simpson. (1985). The Class Structure of Gender and Delinquency: Toward a Power-Control Theory of Common Delinquent Behavior. *American Journal of Sociology, 90,* 151–178.

Hagan, John, A. R. Gillis, & John Simpson. (1990). Clarifying and Extending Power-Control Theory. *American Journal of Sociology, 95,* 1024–1037.

Hagan, John, A. R. Gillis, & John Simpson. (1993). The Power of Control in Sociological Theories of Delinquency. In Freda Adler & William S. Laufer (Eds.), *New Directions in Criminological Theory* (pp. 381–398). New Brunswick, London: Transaction Publ.

Hagan, John, Gerd Hefler, Gabriele Classen, & Hans Merkens. (1998). Subterranean Sources of Subcultural Delinquency Beyond the American Dream. *Criminology, 36,* 309–339.

Hagan, John, & Bill McCarthy. (1997). *Mean Streets. Youth Crime and Homelessness.* Cambridge, New York et al.: Cambridge University Press.

Hagan, John, John Simpson, A. R. Gillis. (1987). Class in the Household: A Power-Control Theory of Gender and Delinquency. *American Journal of Sociology, 92,* 788–816.

Hagan, John, John Simpson, A. R. Gillis. (1988). Feminist scholarship, relational and instrumental control, and a power-control theory of gender and delinquency. *British Journal of Sociology, 39,* 301–336.

Hanson, Thomas L. (1999). Does Parental Conflict Explain Why Divorce Is Negatively Associated with Child Welfare? *Social Forces, 77,* 1283–1315.

Harris, Anthony R. (1975). Imprisonment and the Expected Value of Criminal Choice: A Specification and Test of Aspects of the Labeling Perspective. *American Sociological Review, 40*(1), 71–87.

Hartnagel, Timothy F. (1980). Subculture of Violence. Further Evidence. *Pacific Sociological Review, 23*(2), 217–242.

Hawkins, J. David, Todd I. Herrenkohl, David P. Farrington, Devon Brewer, Richard F. Catalano, & Tracy W. Harachi. (1998). A Review of Predictors of Youth Violence. In Rolf Loeber & David P. Farrington (Eds.), *Serious and violent juvenile offenders: Risk factors and successful interventions* (pp. 106–146). Thousand Oaks et al.: Sage.

Heiland, Hans-Günther. (1983). *Wohlstand und Diebstahl. Eine Makroanalyse ökonomischer, sozialer und kriminalstatistischer Indikatoren unter Anwendung der multiplen Regressionsanalyse.* Bremen: Skarabäus.

Heimer, Karen. (1996). Gender, Interaction, and Delinquency: Testing a Theory of Differential Social Control. *Social Psychology Quarterly, 59*, 39–61.

Heimer, Karen. (1997). Socioeconomic Status, Subcultural Definitions, and Violent Delinquency. *Social Forces, 75*, 799–833.

Heimer, Karen, & Stacy De Coster. (1999). The Gendering of Violent Delinquency. *Criminology, 37*, 277–317.

Heimer, Karen, & Ross L. Matsueda. (1994). Role-Taking, Role Commitment, and Delinquency: A Theory of Differential Social Control. *American Sociological Review, 59*, 365–390.

Heinz, Wolfgang. (1996). Die Wechselwirkungen zwischen Sanktionen und Rückfall bzw. Kriminalitätsentwicklung. In Bundesministerium für Justiz (Ed.), *Strafrechtliche Probleme der Gegenwart, Schriftenreihe des Bundesministeriums für Justiz 76* (pp. 1–163). Wien: Bundesministerium für Justiz.

Heitmeyer, Wilhelm. (1994). Das Desintegrations-Theorem. Ein Erklärungsansatz zu fremdenfeindlich motivierter, rechtsextremistischer Gewalt und zur Lähmung gesellschaftlicher Institutionen. In Wilhelm Heitmeyer (Ed.), *Das Gewalt-Dilemma. Gesellschaftliche Reaktionen auf Gewalt und Rechtsextremismus* (pp. 29–69). Frankfurt a. M.: Suhrkamp.

Heitmeyer, Wilhelm. (1996). Ethnisch-kulturelle Konflikte in gesellschaftlichen Desintegrationsprozessen. In Wilhelm Heitmeyer & Rainer Dollase (Eds.), *Die bedrängte Toleranz. Ethnisch-kulturelle Konflikte, religiöse Differenzen und die Gefahren politisierter Gewalt* (pp. 11–27). Frankfurt a. M.: Suhrkamp.

Heitmeyer, Wilhelm. (1997a). Gibt es eine Radikalisierung des Integrationsproblems? In Wilhelm Heitmeyer (Ed.), *Was hält die Gesellschaft zusammen?* (pp. 31–63). Frankfurt a. M.: Suhrkamp.

Heitmeyer, Wilhelm. (1997b). Einleitung: Auf dem Weg in eine desintegrierte Gesellschaft. In Wilhelm Heitmeyer (Ed.), *Was treibt die Gesellschaft auseinander?* (pp. 9–26). Frankfurt a. M.: Suhrkamp.

Heitmeyer, Wilhelm. (1997c). Gesellschaftliche Integration, Anomie und ethnisch-kulturelle Konflikte. In Wilhelm Heitmeyer (Ed.), *Was treibt die Gesellschaft auseinander?* (pp. 629–653). Frankfurt a. M.: Suhrkamp.

Heitmeyer, Wilhelm. (1998). Versagt die 'Integrationsmaschine' Stadt? Zum Problem der ethnisch-kulturellen Segregation und ihrer Konfliktfolgen. In Wilhelm Heitmeyer, Rainer Dollase & Otto Backes (Eds.), *Krise der Städte* (pp. 443–467). Frankfurt a. M.: Suhrkamp.

Heitmeyer, Wilhelm, & Jörg-Ingo Peter. (1998). *Jugendliche Fußballfans. Soziale und politische Orientierungen, Gesellungsformen, Gewalt.* Weinheim und München: Juventa.

Heitmeyer, Wilhelm, Birgit Collmann, Jutta Conrads, Ingo Matuschek, Dietmar Kraul, Wolfgang Kühnel, Renate Möller, & Matthias Ulbrich-Herrmann. (1995). *Gewalt. Schattenseiten der Individualisierung bei Jugendlichen aus unterschiedlichen Milieus.* Weinheim und München: Juventa.

Heitmeyer, Wilhelm, & Joachim Müller. (1995). *Fremdenfeindliche Gewalt junger Menschen. Biographische Hintergründe, soziale Situationskontexte und die Bedeutung strafrechtlicher Sanktionen.* Bonn: Forum Verlag.

Heitmeyer, Wilhelm, Joachim Müller, & Helmut Schröder. (1997). *Verlockender Fundamentalismus. Türkische Jugendliche in Deutschland.* Frankfurt a. M.: Suhrkamp.

Heitmeyer, Wilhelm, & Thomas Olk. (1990). Das Individualisierungs-Theorem – Bedeutung für die Vergesellschaftung von Jugendlichen. In Wilhelm Heitmeyer & Thomas Olk (Eds.), *Individualisierung von Jugend. Gesellschaftliche Prozesse, subjektive Verarbeitungsformen, jugendpolitische Konsequenzen* (pp. 11–34). Weinheim und München: Juventa.

Hepburn, John R. (1971). Subcultures, Violence, and the Subculture of Violence: An Old Rut or a New Road? *Criminology, 9*, 87–98.

Hepworth, Joseph T., & Stephen G. West. (1988). Lynching and the Economy: A Time-Series Reanalysis of Hovland and Sears (1940). *Journal of Personality and Social Psychology, 55*, 239–247.

Herrenkohl, Todd I., Bu Huang, Rick Kosterman, J. David Hawkins, Richard F. Catalano, & Brian H. Smith. (2001). A Comparison of Social Development Processes Leading to Violent Behavior in Late Adolescence For Childhood Initiators and Adolescent Initiators of Violence. *Journal of Research in Crime and Delinquency, 38*(1), 45–63.

Hetherington, E. Mavis, & Edward R. Anderson. (1988). The Effects of Divorce and Remarriage on Early Adolescents and Their Families. In Melvin D. Levine & Elisabeth R. McAnarney (Eds.), *Early Adolescent Transitions* (pp. 49–67). Lexington und Toronto.

Hirschfield, A., & K. J. Bowers. (1997). The Effect of Social Cohesion on Levels of Recorded Crime in Disadvantaged Areas. *Urban Studies, 34*(8), 1275–1295.

Hirschi, Travis. (1969). *Causes of Delinquency.* Berkeley: University of California Press.

Hirschi, Travis. (1975). Labelling Theory and Juvenile Delinquency: An Assessment of the Evidence. In Walter R. Gove (Ed.), *The Labelling of Deviance. Evaluating a Perspective* (pp. 181–204). New York.: John Wiley & Sons.

Hoffmann, John P., & S. Susan Su. (1997). The Conditional Effects of Stress on Delinquency and Drug Use: A Strain Theory Assessment of Sex Differences. *Journal of Research in Crime and Delinquency, 34*, 46–78.

Hovland, Carl Iver, & Robert R. Sears. (1940). Minor Studies of Aggression: VI. Correlation of Lynchings with Economic Indices. *Journal of Psychology, 9*, 301–310.

Huang, Bu, Helene R. White, Rick Kosterman, Richard F. Catalano, & J. David Hawkins. (2001). Developmental Associations Between Alcohol and Interpersonal Aggression During Adolescence. *Journal of Research in Crime and Delinquency, 38*(1), 64–83.

Huff-Corzine, Lin, Jay Corzine, & David C. Moore. (1986). Southern Exposure: Deciphering the South's Influence on Homicide Rates. *Social Forces, 64*, 906–924.

Huff-Corzine, Lin, Jay Corzine, & David C. Moore. (1991). Deadly Connections: Culture, Poverty, and the Direction of Lethal Violence. *Social Forces, 69*(3), 715–732.

Jabs, Klaus. (1995). Vom Sinn, in einer rechten Clique zu sein. In Wolfgang Frindte (Ed.), *Jugendlicher Rechtsextremismus und Gewalt zwischen Mythos und Wirklichkeit. Sozialpsychologische Untersuchungen* (pp. 192–211). Münster, Hamburg: LIT-Verlag.

Jacobs, Bruce A., & Richard Wright. (1999). Stick-up, Street Culture, and Offender Motivation. *Criminology, 37*, 149–173.

Jacobs, David, & Katherine Wood. (1999). Interracial Conflict and Interracial Homicide: Do Political and Economic Rivalries Explain White Killings of Blacks or Black Killings of Whites? *American Journal of Sociology, 105*(1), 157–190.

James, Oliver. (1995). *Juvenile Violence in a Winner-Loser Culture: Socio-Economic and Familial Origins of the Rise in Violence against the Person.* London: Free Association.

Jang, Sung Joon, & Carolyn A. Smith. (1997). A Test of Reciprocal Causal Relationships Among Parental Supervision, Affective Ties, and Delinquency. *Journal of Research in Crime and Delinquency, 34*, 307–336.

Jang, Sung Joon, & Terence P. Thornberry. (1998). Self-Esteem, Delinquent Peers, and Delinquency: A Test of the Self-Enhancement Thesis. *American Sociological Review, 63*, 586–598.

Jensen, Gary F. (1993). Power-Control vs. Social-Control Theories of Common Delinquency: A Comparative Analysis. In Freda Adler & William S. Laufer (Eds.), *New Directions in Criminological Theory.* New Brunswick, London: Transaction Publ.(pp. 363–380).

Jensen, Gary F. (1997). Comment. 'Setting the Record Straight': A Response to Hagan, Gillis and Simpson. In Terence P Thornberry (Ed.), *Developmental Theories of Crime and Delinquency* (pp. 343–359). New Brunswick, London: Transaction Publ.

Jensen, Gary F., & Kevin Thompson. (1990). What's Class Got to Do with It? A Further Examination of Power-Control Theory. *American Journal of Sociology, 95*, 1009–1023.

Jobes, Patrick C. (1999). Residential Stability and Crime in Small Rural Agricultural and Recreational Towns. *Sociological Perspectives, 42*(3), 499–524.

Johnson, Richard E. (1986). Family Structure and Delinquency: General Patterns and Gender Differences. *Criminology, 24*, 65–84.

Kahn, Joan R., & William M. Mason. (1987). Political Alienation, Cohort Size, and the Easterlin Hypothesis. *American Sociological Review, 52*, 155–169.

Kaplan, Howard B. (1975). *Self-Attitudes and Deviant Behavior.* Pacific Palisades: Goodyear Publication Company.

Kaplan, Howard B. (1980). *Deviant Behavior in Defense of Self.* New York: Academic Press.

Kaplan, Howard B. (1982). Deviant Behavior and Self-Enhancement in Adolescence. In Morris Rosenberg & Howard B. Kaplan (Eds.), *Social Psychology of the Self-Concept* (pp. 466–482). Arlington Heights: Harlan Davidson.

Kaplan, Howard B., & Robert J. Johnson. (1991). Negative Social Sanctions and Juvenile Delinquency: Effects of Labeling in a Model of Deviant Behavior. *Social Science Quarterly, 72*, 1, 98–122.

Karstedt, Susanne. (2001). Individualismus und Gewalt: Extreme Modernisierung und Re-Traditionalisierung der Gesellschaft? Ein interkultureller Vergleich. In Günter Albrecht, Otto Backes & Wolfgang Kühnel (Eds.), *Gewaltkriminalität zwischen Mythos und Realität* (pp. 236–255). Frankfurt a. M: Suhrkamp.

Keane, Carl, A. R. Gillis, & John Hagan. (1989). Deterrence and Amplification of Juvenile Delinquency By Police Contact. The Importance of Gender and Risk-Orientation. *British Journal of Criminology, 29*, 336–352.

Keane, Carl, Paul S. Maxim, & James J. Teevan. (1993). Drinking And Driving, Self-Control, And Gender: Testing A General Theory Of Crime. *Journal of Research in Crime and Delinquency, 30*, 30–46.

Kempf, Kimberly L. (1993). The Empirical Status of Hirschi's Control Theory. In Freda Adler & William S. Laufer (Eds.), *New Directions in Criminological Theory* (pp. 143–185). New Brunswick, London: Transaction Publ.

Kennedy, Leslie W., & Robert A. Silverman. (1990). The Elderly Victim of Homicide: An Application of the Routine Activities Approach. *The Sociological Quarterly, 31*(2), 307–319.

Kennedy, Leslie W., & David R. Forde. (1990). Risky Lifestyles and Dangerous Results: Routine Activities and Exposure to Crime. *Sociology and Social Research, 74*, 208–221.

Kersten, Joachim. (1997). *Gut und (Ge)schlecht. Männlichkeit, Kultur und Kriminalität.* Berlin: de Gruyter.

Klein, Malcolm W. (1984). Offense Specialization and Versatility among Juveniles. *British Journal of Criminology, 24*, 185–194.

Klein, Malcolm W. (1986). Labeling Theory and Delinquency Policy. An Experimental Test. *Criminal Justice and Behavior, 13*(1), 47–79.

Klein, Malcolm W. (1995). Attempting Gang Control by Suppression: The Misuse of Deterrence Principles. In Malcolm W. Klein, Cheryl L. Maxson & Jody Miller (Eds.), *The Modern Gang Reader* (pp. 304–313). Los Angeles: Roxbury Publ.

Klepper, Steven, & Daniel S. Nagin. (1989). The Deterrent Effect of Perceived Certainty and Severity of Punishment Revisited. *Criminology, 27*, 721–746.

Kokko, Katja, & Lea Pulkkinen. (2000). Aggression in Childhood and Long-Term Unemployment in Adulthood: A Cycle of Maladaptation and Some Protective Factors. *Developmental Psychology, 36*, 463–472.

König, Hans-Dieter. (1998). Die rechte Subkultur und die Motive jugendlicher Gewalttäter. Sozialpsychologische Kritik der Studien von Willems u.a. zur fremdenfeindlichen Gewalt. In Hans-Dieter König (Ed.), *Sozialpsychologie des Rechtsextremismus* (pp. 177–215). Frankfurt a. M.: Suhrkamp.

König, René. (1949). Überorganisation der Familie als Gefährdung der seelischen Gesundheit. In Maria Pfister-Ammende (Ed.), *Die Psychohygiene. Grundlagen und Ziele* (pp. 130–144). Bern: Verlag Hans Huber.

König, René. (1974a). *Materialien zur Soziologie der Familie.* Reprint. Köln: Kiepenheuer & Witsch.

König, René. (1974b). *Die Familie in der Gegenwart.* München: Verlag C. H. Beck.

Kornhauser, Ruth. (1978). *Social Sources of Delinquency: An Appraisal of Analytical Models.* Chicago: University of Chicago Press.

Kowaleski-Jones, Lori. (2000). Staying Out of Trouble: Community Resources and Problem Behavior Among High-Risk Adolescents. *Journal of Marriage and the Family, 62*, 449–464.

Krivo, Lauren J., & Ruth D. Peterson. (2000). The Structural Context of Homicide: Accounting For Racial Differences in Process. *American Sociological Review, 65*, 547–559.

Krohn, Marvin D., & James L. Massey. (1980). Social Control and Delinquent Behavior. An Examination of the Elements of the Social Bond. *Sociological Quarterly, 21*, 529–543.

Kühnel, Wolfgang, & Ingo Matuschek. (1995). *Gruppenprozesse und Devianz. Risiken jugendlicher Lebensbewältigung in großstädtischen Monostrukturen.* Weinheim und München: Juventa.

Kühnel, Wolfgang, & Rainer Strobl. (2001). Junge Aussiedler als Täter und Opfer von Gewalthandlungen. In Günter Albrecht, Otto Backes & Wolfgang Kühnel (Eds.), *Gewaltkriminalität zwischen Mythos und Realität* (pp. 325–353). Frankfurt a. M.: Suhrkamp.

LaFree, Gary. (1989). *Rape and Criminal Justice. The Social Construction of Sexual Assault.* Belmont: Wadsworth.

LaGrange, Randy L., & Helen R. White. (1985). *Age Differences in Delinquency: A Test of Theory. Criminology, 23*, 19–45.

LaGrange, Teresa C., & Robert A. Silverman. (1999). Low Self-Control and Opportunity: Testing the General Theory of Crime as an Explanation for Gender Differences in Delinquency. *Criminology, 37*, 41–72.

Lamnek, Siegfried. (1977). *Kriminalitätstheorien kritisch. Anomie und Labeling im Vergleich.* München: Wilhelm Fink.

Lamnek, Siegfried, & Otto Schwenk. (1995). *Die Marienplatz-Rapper. Zur Soziologie einer Großstadt-Gang.* Pfaffenweiler: Centaurus.

Land, Kenneth C., David Cantor, & Stephen T. Russell. (1995). Unemployment and Crime Rate Fluctuations in the Post-World War II United States. Statistical Time-Series Properties and Alternative Models. In John Hagan & Ruth D. Peterson (Eds.), *Crime and Inequality* (pp. 55–79). Stanford: Stanford University Press.

Land, Kenneth C., Patricia L. McCall, & Lawrence E. Cohen. (1990). Structural Covariates of Homicide Rates: Are There Any Invariances Across Time and Social Space? *American Journal of Sociology, 95,* 922–963.

Laub, John H., & Robert J. Sampson. (1993). Turning Points in the Life Course: Why Change Matters to the Study of Crime. *Criminology, 31,* 301–325.

Lazarus, Richard S., & Susan Folkman. (1984). *Stress, Appraisal, and Coping.* New York: Springer.

Leder, Hans-Claus. (1997). *Frauen- und Mädchenkriminalität. 3.* Aufl. Heidelberg: Lang.

Lemert, Edwin M. (1967). *Human Deviance, Social Problems and Social Control.* Englewood Cliffs: Prentice-Hall.

Lemert, Edwin M. (1975). Der Begriff der sekundären Devianz. In Klaus Lüderssen & Fritz Sack (Eds.), *Seminar Abweichendes Verhalten 1. Die selektiven Normen der Gesellschaft* (pp. 433–476). Frankfurt a. M.: Suhrkamp.

Levitt, Steven D. (1999). The Limited Role of Changing Age Structure in Explaining Aggregate Crime Rates. *Criminology, 37,* 581–597.

Lewis, Susan K., Catherine E. Ross, & John Mirowsky. (1999). Establishing a Sense of Personal Control in the Transition to Adulthood. *Social Forces, 77,* 1573–1599.

Liqun, Cao, Anthony Adams, & Vickie J. Jensen. (1997). A Test of the Black Subculture of Violence Thesis: A Research Note. *Criminology, 35,* 367–379.

Liska, Allen E., & Steven F. Messner. (1999). *Perspectives on Crime and Deviance. 3rd Edition.* Upper Saddle River: Prentice-Hall.

Liska, Allen. E. (1981). *Perspectives on Deviance.* Englewood Cliffs: Prentice-Hall.

Liu, Xiaoru, & Howard B. Kaplan. (1999). Explaining the Gender Difference in Adolescent Delinquent Behavior: A Longitudinal Test of Mediating Mechanisms. *Criminology, 37,* 195–215.

Lockwood, David. (1964). Social Integration and System Integration. In George K. Zollschan & Walter Hirsch (Eds.), *Explorations in Social Change* (pp. 244–257). New York: Houghton-Mifflin.

Lockwood, David. (1969). Soziale Integration und Systemintegration. In Wolfgang Zapf (Ed.), *Theorien des sozialen Wandels* (pp. 124–137). Köln: Kiepenheuer & Witsch.

Loftin, Colin, & Robert Hill. (1974). Regional Subculture and Homicide: An Examination of the Gastil-Hackney Thesis. *American Sociological Review, 39,* 714–724.

Loeber, Rolf, David P. Farrington, & Daniel A. Waschbusch. (1998). Serious and Violent Juvenile Offenders. In Rolf Loeber & David P. Farrington (Eds.), *Serious and Violent Juvenile Offenders: Risk Factors and Successful Interventions* (pp. 13–29). Thousand Oaks et al.: Sage.

Loeber, Rolf, & Magda Stouthamer-Loeber. (1998). Development of Juvenile Aggression and Violence. Some Common Misconceptions and Controversies. *American Psychologist, 53,* 242–259.

Lösel, Friedrich (Ed.) (1983). *Kriminalpsychologie.* Weinheim: Beltz.

Lösel, Friedrich. (1991). Meta-Analysis and Social Prevention: Evaluation and a Study on the Family-Hypothesis in Developmental Psychopathology. In Günter Albrecht & Hans-Uwe Otto (Eds.), *Social Prevention and the Social Sciences. Theoretical Controversies, Research Problems, and Evaluation Strategies* (pp. 305–332). Berlin, New York: Aldine de Gruyter.

Lösel, Friedrich. (1995). Entwicklung und Ursachen der Gewalt in unserer Gesellschaft. *Gruppendynamik, 26,* 5–22.

Lösel, Friedrich, & Doris Bender. (2001). Jugenddelinquenz. In Peter F. Schlottke, Rainer K. Silbereisen, Silvia Schneider & Gerhard W. Lauth (Eds.), *Enzyklopädie der Psychologie. Bd. 5, Störungen im Kindes- und Jugendalter.* Göttingen: Hogrefe.

Mansel, Jürgen, & Klaus Hurrelmann. (1994). Außen- und innengerichtete Formen der Problemverarbeitung Jugendlicher. Aggressivität und psychosomatische Beschwerden. *Soziale Welt, 45,* 147–179.

Mansel, Jürgen, & Klaus Hurrelmann. (1998). Aggressives und delinquentes Verhalten Jugendlicher im Zeitvergleich. Befunde der Dunkelfeldforschung aus den Jahren 1988, 1990 und 1996. *Kölner Zeitschrift für Soziologie und Sozialpsychologie, 50,* 78–109.

Matsueda, Ross L. (1992). Reflected Appraisals, Parental Labeling, and Delinquency: Specifying a Symbolic Interactionist Theory. *American Journal of Sociology, 97,* 1577–1611.

Matsueda, Ross L., & Kathleen Anderson. (1998). The Dynamics of Delinquent Peers and Delinquent Behavior. *Criminology*, *36*, 269–308.

Matsueda, Ross L., Rosemary Gartner, Irving Piliavin, & Michael Polakowski. (1992). The Prestige of Criminal and Conventional Occupations: A Subcultural Model of Criminal Activity. *American Sociological Review*, *57*, 752–770.

Matsueda, Ross L., & Karen Heimer. (1987). Race, Family Structure, and Delinquency: A Test of Differential Association and Social Control Theories. *American Sociological Review*, *52*, 826–840.

Matsueda, Ross L., & Karen Heimer. (1997). A Symbolic Interactionist Theory of Role-Transitions, Role-Commitments, and Delinquency. In Terence P. Thornberry (Ed.), *Developmental Theories of Crime and Delinquency* (pp. 163–213). New Brunswick, London: Transaction Publ.

Matt, Eduard. (1999). Jugend, Männlichkeit und Delinquenz. Junge Männer zwischen Männlichkeitsritualen und Autonomiebestrebungen. *Zeitschrift für Soziologie der Erziehung und Sozialisation*, *19*, 259–276.

Maxim, Paul S. (1985). Cohort Size and Juvenile Delinquency: A Test of the Easterlin Hypothesis. *Social Forces*, *63*, 661–681.

McCall, Patricia L., Kenneth C. Land, & Lawrence E. Cohen. (1992). Violent criminal behavior: Is there a general and continuing influence of the south? *Social Science Research*, *21*, 286–310.

Mears, Daniel P., Matthew Ploeger, & Mark Warr. (1998). Explaining the Gender Gap in Delinquency: Peer Influence and Moral Evaluations of Behavior. *Journal of Research in Crime and Delinquency*, *35*, 251–266.

Medoff, Marshall H. (1999). Allocation of Time and Hateful Behavior: A Theoretical and Positive Analysis Of Hate and Hate Crimes. *American Journal of Economics and Sociology*, *58*, 959–973.

Meier, Robert F., Steven R. Burkett, & Carol A. Hickman. (1984). Sanctions, Peers, and Deviance. Preliminary Models of Social Control Process. *Sociological Quarterly*, *25*, 67–82.

Menard, Scott. (1992). Demographic and Theoretical Variables in the Age-Period-Cohort Analysis of Illegal Behavior. *Journal of Research in Crime and Delinquency*, *29*, 178–199.

Merton, Robert K. (1938). Social Structure and Anomie. *American Sociological Review*, *3*, 672–682.

Merton, Robert K. (1957). *Social Theory and Social Structure. Revised and enlarged edition.* New York: Free Press. [German: Merton, Robert K. (1995). *Soziologische Theorie und soziale Struktur.* Berlin, New York: de Gruyter.]

Merton, Robert K. (1964). Anomie, Anomia, and Social Interaction: Contexts of Deviant Behavior. In Marshall B. Clinard (Ed.), *Anomie and Deviant Behavior. A Discussion and Critique* (pp. 213–242). New York: Free Press.

Messerschmidt, James W. (1997). *Crime As Structured Action: Gender, Race, Class, and Crime in the Making.* Thousand Oaks, London: Sage.

Messner, Steven F. (1983a Regional and Racial Effects on the Urban Homicide Rate: The Subculture of Violence Revisited. *American Journal of Sociology*, *88*, 997–1007.

Messner, Steven F. (1983b). Regional Differences in the Economic Correlates of the Urban Homicide Rate. *Criminology*, *21*, 477–488.

Messner, Steven F., & Richard Rosenfeld. (1997). *Crime and the American Dream. 2nd Edition.* Belmont et al.: Wadsworth.

Miethe, Terence D., Mark C. Stafford, & Scott J. Long. (1987). Social Differentiation in Criminal Victimization: A Test of Routine Activities/Lifestyle Theories. *American Sociological Review*, *52*, 184–194.

Miller, Walter B. (1968). Die Kultur der Unterschicht als ein Entstehungsmilieu für Bandendelinquenz. In Fritz Sack & René König (Eds.), *Kriminalsoziologie* (pp. 339–359). Frankfurt a. M.: Akademische Verlagsanstalt.

Minor, William, & Joseph Harry. (1982). Deterrent and Experiential Effects in Perceptual Deterrence Research: A Replication and Extension. *Journal of Research in Crime and Delinquency*, *19*, 190–203.

Mischkowitz, Robert. (1994). *Fremdenfeindliche Gewalt und Skinheads. Eine Literaturanalyse und Bestandsaufnahme polizeilicher Maßnahmen.* Wiesbaden: BKA.

Moffitt, Terrie E. (1997). Adolescence-Limited and Life-Course-Persistent Offending: A Complementary Pair of Developmental Theories. In Terence P. Thornberry (Ed.), *Developmental Theories of Crime and Delinquency* (pp. 11–54). New Brunswick: Transaction Publ..

Morenoff, Jeffrey D., & Robert J. Sampson. (1997). Violent Crime and the Spatial Dynamics of Neighborhood Transition: Chicago, 1970–1990. *Social Forces*, *76*, 31–64.

Mummendey, Amelie. (1990). Aggressives Verhalten. In Wolfgang Stroebe, Miles Hewstone, Jean-Paul Codol & Geoffrey M. Stephenson (Eds.), *Sozialpsychologie. Eine Einführung* (pp. 275–304). Berlin, Heidelberg et al.: Springer.

Münchmeier, Richard. (1998). 'Entstrukturierung' der Jugendphase. Zum Strukturwandel des Aufwachsens und zu den Konsequenzen für Jugendforschung und Jugendtheorie. *Aus Politik und Zeitgeschichte, 31,* 3–13.

Nagin, Daniel S., & Raymond Paternoster. (1991). The Preventive Effects of the Perceived Risk of Arrest: Testing an Expanded Conception of Deterrence. *Criminology, 29,* 561–588.

Nagin, Daniel S., & Raymond Paternoster. (1993). Enduring Individual Differences and Rational Choice Theories of Crime. *Law and Society Review, 27,* 467–496.

Nagin, Daniel S., & Raymond Paternoster. (1994). Personal Capital and Social Control: The Deterrence Implications of a Theory of Individual Differences in Criminal Offending. *Criminology, 32,* 581–606.

Nakhaie, M. Reza, Robert A. Silverman, Teresa C. LaGrange. (2000). Self-Control and Social Control: An Examination of Gender, Ethnicity, Class and Delinquency. *Canadian Journal of Sociology, 25,* 35–59.

Nedelmann, Brigitta. (1997). Gewaltsoziologie am Scheideweg. Die Auseinandersetzungen in der gegenwärtigen und Wege der künftigen Gewaltforschung. In Trutz von Trotha (Ed.), *Soziologie der Gewalt. Sonderheft 37 der Kölner Zeitschrift für Soziologie und Sozialpsychologie* (pp. 59–85). Opladen: Westdeutscher Verlag.

Nunner-Winkler, Gertrud. (1996). Moralisches Wissen – moralische Motivation – moralisches Handeln. In Michael-Sebastian Honig, Hans Rudolf Leu & Ursula Nissen (Eds.), *Kinder und Kindheit. Sozio-kulturelle Muster- sozialisationstheoretische Perspektiven* (pp. 129–156). Weinheim, München: Juventa.

Nunner-Winkler, Gertrud. (1999). Sozialisationsbedingungen moralischer Motivation. In Hans Rudolf Leu & Lothar Krappmann (Eds.), *Zwischen Autonomie und Verbundenheit. Bedingungen und Formen der Behauptung von Subjektivität* (pp. 299–329). Frankfurt a. M.: Suhrkamp.

O'Brien, Robert M. (1989). Relative Cohort Size and Age-Specific Crime Rates: An Age-Period-Relative-Cohort-Size-Model. *Criminology, 27,* 57–78.

O'Brien, Robert M., Jean Stockard, & Lynne Isaacson. (1999). The Enduring Effects of Cohort Characteristics on Age-Specific Homicide Rates, 1960–1995. *American Journal of Sociology, 104,* 1061–1095.

O'Connor, James F., & Alan Lizotte. (1977). The 'Southern Subculture of Violence' Thesis and Patterns of Gun Ownership. *Social Problems, 25,* 420–429.

Olk, Thomas. (1985). Jugend und gesellschaftliche Differenzierung – Zur Entstrukturierung der Jugendphase. In Helmut Heid & Wolfgang Klafki (Eds.), *Arbeit – Bildung – Arbeitsplatz, 19. Beiheft der Zeitschrift für Pädagogik* (pp. 290–301). Weinheim-Basel: Beltz.

Opp, Karl-Dieter. (1974). *Abweichendes Verhalten und Gesellschaftsstruktur.* Darmstadt und Neuwied: Luchterhand.

Ortmann, Rüdiger. (2000). *Abweichendes Verhalten und Anomie. Entwicklung und Veränderung abweichenden Verhaltens im Kontext der Anomietheorien von Durkheim und Merton.* Freiburg i Br.: edition iuscrim.

Osgood, D. Wayne, & Jeff M. Chambers. (2000). Social Disorganization Outside The Metropolis: An Analysis of Rural Youth Violence. *Criminology, 38,* 81–115.

Osgood, D. Wayne, Janet K. Wilson, Patrick M. O'Malley, Jerald G. Bachman, Lloyd D. Johnston. (1996). Routine Activities and Individual Deviant Behavior. *American Sociological Review, 61,* 635–655.

Pagani, Linda, Bernard Boulerice, Frank Vitaro, & Richard E. Tremblay. (1999). Effects of Poverty on Academic Failure and Delinquency in Boys: A Change and Process Model Approach. *Journal of Child Psychology and Psychiatry, 40,* 1209–1219.

Pampel, Fred C., & Rosemary Gartner. (1995). Age Structure, Socio-Political Institution, and National Homicide Rates. *European Sociological Review, 11,* 243–260.

Parker, Karen F., & Patricia McCall. (1999). Structural Conditions and Racial Homicide Patterns: A Look at the Multiple Disadvantages in Urban Areas. *Criminology, 37,* 447–477.

Parker, Robert Nash. (1989). Poverty, Subculture of Violence, and Type of Homicide. *Social Forces, 67,* 983–1007.

Parker, Robert Nash, & Dwayne M. Smith. (1979). Deterrence, Poverty, and Type of Homicide. American *Journal of Sociology, 85,* 614–624.

Paternoster, Raymond. (1988). Examining Three-Wave Deterrence Models: A Question of Temporal Order and Specification. *The Journal of Criminal Law and Criminology, 79,* 135–178.

Paternoster, Raymond. (1989). Decisions to Participate in and Desist from Four Types of Common Delinquency: Deterrence and the Rational Choice Perspective. *Law and Society Review, 23,* 7–40.

Paternoster, Raymond, & Paul Mazerolle. (1994). General Strain Theory and Delinquency: A Replication and Extension. *Journal of Research in Crime and Delinquency, 31,* 235–263.

Paternoster, Raymond, Linda E. Saltzman, Gordon P. Waldo, & Theodore Chiricos. (1983). Perceived Risk and Social Control: Do Sanctions Really Deter? *Law and Society Review 17,* 457–479.

Peterson, Ruth D., Lauren J. Krivo, & Mark A. Harris. (2000). Disadvantage and Neighborhood Violent Crime: Do Local Institutions Matter? *Journal of Research in Crime and Delinquency, 37,* 31–63.

Pfeiffer, Christian. (1998). Juvenile Crime and Violence in Europe. *Crime and Justice, A Review of Research,* *23*, 255–327.

Pfeiffer, Christian, Ingo Delzer, Dirk Enzmann, & Peter Wetzels. (1998). *Ausgrenzung, Gewalt und Kriminalität im Leben junger Menschen-Kinder und Jugendliche als Opfer und Täter. Sonderdruck zum 24. Deutschen Jugendgerichtstag vom 18–22 September 1998 in Hamburg.* Hannover: Deutsche Vereinigung für Jugendgerichte und Jugendgerichtshilfe e.V.

Piliavin, Irving, Rosemary Gartner, Craig Thornton, & Ross L. Matsueda. (1986). Crime, Deterrence, and Rational Choice. *American Sociological Review, 51*, 101–119.

Piquero, Alex R., & Matthew Hickman. (1999). An Empirical Test of Tittle's Control Balance Theory. *Criminology, 37*, 319–341.

Pratt, Travis C., & Francis T. Cullen. (2000). The Empirical Status of Gottfredson and Hirschi's General Theory of Crime: A Meta-Analysis. *Criminology,* 38(3), 931–964.

Ray, Melvin C., & William R. Downs. (1986). An Empirical Test of Labeling Theory Using Longitudinal Data. *Journal of Research in Crime and Delinquency,* 23(2), 169–194.

Reed, John Shelton. (1972). *The Enduring South: Subcultural Persistence in Mass Society.* Lexington: Lexington.

Reed, John Shelton. (1982). *One South: An Ethnic Approach to Regional Culture.* Baton Rouge: Louisiana State University Press.

Roesner, Ernst. (1936). Wirtschaftslage und Straffälligkeit. In *Handwörterbuch der Kriminologie und der anderen strafrechtlichen Hilfswissenschaften, Bd. 2, Kriminalroman—Zwangs- und Fürsorgeerziehung* (pp. 1079–1116). Berlin, Leipzig: Walter de Gruyter.

Rojek, Dean G., & Maynard L. Erickson. (1982). Delinquent Careers. A Test of the Career Escalation Model. *Criminology, 20*, 5–28.

Rosenberg, Morris, Carmi Schooler, & Carrie Schoenbach. (1989). Self-Esteem and Adolescent Problems: Modelling Reciprocal Effects. *American Sociological Review, 54*, 1004–1018.

Ross, Catherine E., John R. Reynolds, & Karlyn J. Geis. (2000). The Contingent Meaning of Neighborhood Stability For Residents' Psychological Well-Being. *American Sociological Review, 65*, 581–597.

Sack, Fritz. (1968). Neue Perspektiven in der Kriminalsoziologie. In Fritz Sack & René König (Eds.), *Kriminalsoziologie* (pp. 400–431). Frankfurt a. M.: Akademische Verlagsanstalt.

Sack, Fritz. (1978). Probleme der Kriminalsoziologie. In René König (Ed.), *Handbuch der empirischen Sozialforschung 2* (pp. 192–492). überarbeitete Aufl., Stuttgart: Enke.

Sack, Fritz. (1984). Die Reaktion von Gesellschaft, Politik und Staat auf die Studentenbewegung. In Fritz Sack & Heinz Steinert (Eds.), *Protest und Reaktion. Analysen zum Terrorismus. Bd. 4.2* (pp. 107–226). Opladen: Westdeutscher Verlag.

Saltzman, Linda E., Raymond Paternoster, Gordon P. Waldo, & Theodore G. Chiricos. (1982). Deterrent and Experiential Effects: The Problem of Causal Order in Perceptual Deterrence Research. *Journal of Research in Crime and Delinquency, 19*, 172–189.

Sampson, Robert J. (1987). Urban Black Violence: The Effect of Male Joblessness and Family Disruption. *American Journal of Sociology, 93*, 348–382.

Sampson, Robert J., & W. Byron Groves. (1989). Community Structure and Crime. Testing Social-Disorganization Theory. *American Journal of Sociology, 94*, 774–802.

Sampson, Robert J., & John H. Laub. (1990). Crime and Deviance Over the Life Course: The Salience of Adult Social Bonds. *American Sociological Review, 55*, 609–628.

Sampson, Robert J., & John H. Laub. (1994). Urban Poverty and the Family Context of Delinquency: A New Look at Structure and Process in a Classic Study. *Child Development, 65*, 523–540.

Sampson, Robert J., & Janet L. Lauritsen. (1990). Deviant Lifestyles, Proximity to Crime, and the Offender-Victim Link in Personal Violence. *Journal of Research in Crime and Delinquency,* 27(3), 110–139.

Sampson, Robert J., & Stephen W. Raudenbush. (1999). Systematic Social Observation of Public Spaces: A New Look at Disorder in Urban Neighborhoods. *American Journal of Sociology, 105*, 603–651.

Sampson, Robert J., & William Julius Wilson. (1995). Toward a Theory of Race, Crime, and Urban Inequality. In John Hagan & Ruth D. Peterson (Eds.), *Crime and Inequality* (pp. 17–54). Stanford: Stanford University Press.

Sander, Uwe, & Wilhelm Heitmeyer. (1997). Was leisten Integrationsmodi? Eine vergleichende Analyse unter konflikttheoretischen Gesichtspunkten. In Wilhelm Heitmeyer (Ed.), *Was hält die Gesellschaft zusammen?* (pp. 447–482). Frankfurt a. M.: Suhrkamp.

Savolainen, Jukka. (2000). Relative Cohort Size and Age-Specific Arrest Rates: A Conditional Interpretation of the Easterlin Effect. *Criminology, 38*, 117–136.

Scheff, Thomas J., Suzanne M. Retzinger, & Michael T. Ryan. (1989). Crime, Violence, and Self-Esteem:

Review and Proposals. In Andrew M. Mecca, Neil J. Smelser & John Vasconcellos (Eds.), *The Social Importance of Self-Esteem* (pp. 165–199). Berkeley: University of California Press.

Schumann, Karl F., Claus Berlitz, Hans-Werner Guth, & Reiner Kaulitzki. (1987). *Jugendkriminalität und die Grenzen der Generalprävention. Eine empirische Untersuchung.* Neuwied, Darmstadt: Luchterhand.

Schur, Edwin M. (1973). *Radical Nonintervention: Rethinking the Delinquency Problem.* Englewood Cliffs: Prentice-Hall.

Sherman, Lawrence W. (1993). Defiance, Deterrence, and Irrelevance: A Theory of the Criminal Sanction. *Journal of Research in Crime and Delinquency, 30,* 445–473.

Sherman, Lawrence W., & Richard A. Berk. (1984). The Specific Deterrent Effects of Arrest for Domestic Assault. *American Sociological Review, 49*(2), 261–272.

Sherman, Lawrence W., Patrick R. Gartin, & Michael E. Buerger. (1989). Hot Spots of Predatory Crime: Routine Activities and the Criminology of Place. *Criminology, 27*(1), 27–55.

Sherman, Lawrence W., Janell D. Schmidt, Dennis P. Rogan, Patrick R. Gartin, Ellen G. Cohn, Dean J. Collins, & Anthony R. Bacich. (1991). From Initial Deterrence to Longterm Escalation: Short-Custody Arrest for Poverty Ghetto Domestic Violence. *Criminology, 29,* 821–849.

Short, James F., Jr. (1997). *Poverty, Ethnicity, and Violent Crime.* Boulder: Westview Press.

Short, James F., & Fred L. Strodtbeck. (1965). *Group Process and Gang Delinquency.* Chicago: University of Chicago Press.

Simons, Ronald L., & Phyllis A. Gray. (1989). Perceived Blocked Opportunity as an Explanation of Delinquency Among Lower-Class Black Males: A Research Note. *Journal of Research in Crime and Delinquency, 26,* 90–101.

Simons, Ronald L., Christine Johnson, Rand D. Conger, & Glen Elder, Jr. (1998). A Test of Latent Trait versus Life-Course Perspectives on the Stability of Adolescent Antisocial Behavior. *Criminology, 36,* 217–243.

Simons, Ronald L., Chyi-In Wu, Kuei-Hsiu Lin, Leslie Gordon, amd Rand D. Conger. (2000). A Cross-Cultural Examination of The Link Between Corporal Punishment and Adolescent Antisocial Behavior. *Criminology, 38,* 47–79.

Simpson, Sally S. (1989). Feminist Theory, Crime, and Justice. *Criminology, 27,* 605–631.

Singer, Simon I., & Murray Levine. (1988). Power-Control Theory, Gender, and Delinquency: A Partial Replication With Additional Evidence on the Effects of Peers. *Criminology, 26,* 627–647.

Smart, Carol. (1995a). *Law, Crime and Sexuality. Essays in Feminism.* London: Sage.

Smart, Carol. (1995b). Feminist Approaches to Criminology, or Postmodern Woman Meets Atavistic Man. In Carol Smart (Ed.), *Law, Crime and Sexuality* (pp. 32–48). London: Sage.

Smith, Douglas A., & Patrick R. Gartin. (1989). Specifying Specific Deterrence: The Influence of Arrest on Future Criminal Activity. *American Sociological Review, 54,* 94–105.

Smith, Douglas, & Raymond Paternoster. (1990). Formal Processing and Future Delinquency: Deviance Amplification as Selection Artifact. *Law and Society Review, 24*(5), 1109–1131.

Smith, Dwayne M., & Robert Nash Parker. (1980). Type of Homicide and Variations in Regional Rates. *Social Forces, 59,* 136–147.

Smith, James, & Finis Welch. (1981). Not Time to be Young: The Economic Prospects for Large Cohorts in the United States. *Population and Development Review, 7,* 71–83.

Stafford, Mark C., & Sheldon Ekland-Olson. (1982). On Social Learning and Deviant Behavior. A Reappraisal of the Findings (Comment on Akers et. al., ASR, August 1979). *American Sociological Review, 47,* 167–169.

Steffensmeier, Darrell J. (1980). Sex Differences in Patterns of Adult Crime, 1965–77: A Review and Assessment. *Social Forces, 58,* 1080–1109.

Steffensmeier, Darrell J., & Hoffman Renee Steffensmeier. (1980). Trends in Female Delinquency: An Examination of Arrest, Juvenile Court, Self-Report, and Field Data. *Criminology, 18,* 62–85.

Steffensmeier, Darrell J. (1978). Crime and the Contemporary Woman: An Analysis of Changing Levels of Female Property Crime, 1960–1975. *Social Forces, 57,* 566–584.

Steffensmeier, Darrell J., Cathy Streifel, & Edward S. Shihadeh. (1992). Cohort Size and Arrest Rates Over the Life Course: The Easterlin Hypothesis Reconsidered. *American Sociological Review, 57,* 306–314.

Steinberg, Laurence D., Ralph Catalano, & David Dooley. (1981). Economic Antecedents of Child Abuse and Neglect. *Child Development, 52,* 975–985.

Stiles, Beverly L., Xiaoru Liu, & Howard B. Kaplan. (2000). Relative Deprivation and Deviant Adaptations: The Mediating Effects of Negative Self-Feelings. *Journal of Research in Crime and Delinquency, 37,* 64–90.

Strand, G. C., Jr., & M. S. Garr. (1994). Driving under the influence. In Travis Hirschi & Michael Gottfredson (Eds.), *The Generality of Deviance* (pp. 131–147). New Brunswick: Transaction Publ.

Strickland, Donald E. (1982). Social Learning and Deviant Behavior: A Specific Test of a General Theory: A Comment and Critique (Comment on Akers et. al., ASR, August (1979). *American Sociological Review*, 47, 162–167.

Strobl, Rainer, & Wolfgang Kühnel. (2002, in preparation). Stimmt die These vom Zusammenhang zwischen kollektivistischen Werten und Gewalt? Theoretische Überlegungen und empirische Analysen am Beispiel von Aussiedlerjugendlichen. In Wilhelm Heitmeyer & Hans-Georg Soeffner (Eds.), *Gewalt. Neue Entwicklungen und alte Analyseprobleme*. Frankfurt a. M.: Suhrkamp.

Sutherland, Edwin H., & Donald Cressey. (1978). *Principles of Criminology. 10th Edition*. Philadelphia: J. B. Lippincott Co.

Swart, William J. (1995). Female Gang Delinquency: A Search for 'Acceptably Deviant Behavior'. In Malcolm W. Klein, Cheryl L. Maxson & Jody Miller (Eds.), *The Modern Gang Reader* (pp. 78–82). Los Angeles: Roxbury Publ.

Swinford, Steven P., Alfred DeMaris, Stephen A. Cernkovich, & Peggy C. Giordano. (2000). Harsh Physical Discipline in Childhood and Violence in Later Romantic Involvements: The Mediating Role of Problem Behaviors. *Journal of Marriage and the Family*, 62, 508–519.

Sykes, Gresham M., & David Matza. (1968). Techniken der Neutralisierung: Eine Theorie der Delinquenz. In Fritz Sack & René König (Eds.), *Kriminalsoziologie* (pp. 360–371). Frankfurt a. M.: Akademische Verlagsanstalt.

Tertilt, Hermann. (1996). *Turkish Power Boys. Ethnographie einer Jugendbande*. Frankfurt a. M.: Suhrkamp.

Thome, Helmut. (2001). Hilft uns die Kriminalgeschichte, Kriminalität in Gegenwartsgesellschaften zu verstehen? In Günter Albrecht, Otto Backes & Wolfgang Kühnel (Eds.), *Gewaltkriminalität zwischen Mythos und Realität* (pp. 165–191). Frankfurt a. M.: Suhrkamp.

Thome, Helmut. (2002, in preparation). Theoretische Ansätze zur Erklärung langfristiger Gewaltkriminalität seit Beginn der Neuzeit. In Wilhelm Heitmeyer & Hans-Georg Soeffner (Eds.), *Gewalt. Neue Entwicklungen und alte Analyseprobleme*. Frankfurt a. M.: Suhrkamp.

Thornberry, Terence B., Marvin D. Krohn, & Alan J. Lizotte. (1995). The Role of Juvenile Gangs in Facilitating Delinquent Behavior. In Malcolm W. Klein, Cheryl L.Maxson & Jody Miller (Eds.), *The Modern Gang Reader* (pp. 174–185). Los Angeles: Roxbury Publ.

Thornberry, Terence B., Alan J. Lizotte, Marvin Krohn, Margaret Farnworth, & Sung J. Jang. (1994). Delinquent Peers, Beliefs, and Delinquent Behavior: A Longitudinal Test of Interactional Theory. *Criminology*, 32, 47–83.

Tittle, Charles R. (1983). Social Class and Criminal Behavior: A Critique of the Theoretical Foundation. *Social Forces*, 62, 334–358.

Tittle, Charles R. (1995). *Control Balance. Toward a General Theory of Deviance*. Boulder, Oxford: Westview Press.

Tittle, Charles R. (1997). Thoughts stimulated by Braithwaite's analysis of control balance theory. *Theoretical Criminology*, 1, 99–110.

Tittle, Charles R., & Robert F. Meier. (1990). Specifying the SES/Delinquency Relationship. *Criminology*, 28, 271–299.

Tittle, Charles R., & Alan R. Rowe. (1974). Certainty of Arrest and Crime Rates: A Further Test of the Deterrence Hypothesis. *Social Forces*, 52, 455–462.

Tittle, Charles R., Wayne J. Villemez, & Douglas A. Smith. (1978). The Myth of Social Class and Criminality: An Empirical Assessment of the Empirical Evidence. *American Sociological Review*, 43, 643–656.

Tolnay, Stewart E., & E. M. Beck. (1992). Racial Violence and Black Migration in the American South, 1910 to 1930. *American Sociological Review*, 57, 103–116.

Tolnay, Stewart E., & E. M. Beck. (1994). Lethal Social Control in the South: Lynchings and Executions Between 1880 and 1930. In George S. Bridges & Martha A. Myers (Eds.), *Inequality, Crime, and Social Control* (pp. 176–194). Boulder, San Francisco, Oxford: Westview.

Tolnay, Stewart E., E. M. Beck, & James L. Massey. (1989). Black Lynchings: The Power Threat Hypothesis Revisited. *Social Forces*, 67, 605–623.

Tolnay, Stewart E., Glenn Deane, & E.M. Beck. (1996). Vicarious Violence: Spatial Effects on Southern Lynchings, 1890–1919. *American Journal of Sociology*, 102, 788–815.

Tremblay, Manon, & Pierre Tremblay. (1998). Social Structure, Interaction Opportunities, and the Direction of Violent Offenses. *Journal of Research in Crime and Deliquency*, 35(3), 295–315.

Uggen, Christopher. (2000). Class, Gender, and Arrest: An Intergenerational Analysis of Workplace Power and Control. *Criminology*, 38(3), 835–862.

van Koppen, Peter J., & Robert W. J. Jansen. (1999). The Time to Rob: Variations in Time of Number of Commercial Robberies. *Journal of Research in Crime and Delinquency*, 36, 1, 7–29.

Vanberg, Viktor. (1982). *Verbrechen, Strafe und Abschreckung. Die Theorie der Generalprävention im Lichte der neueren sozialwissenschaftlichen Diskussion.* Tübingen: Mohr.

Veysey, Bonita M., & Steven F. Messner. (1999). Further Testing of Social Disorganization Theory: An Elaboration of Sampson and Grove's 'Community Structure and Crime'. *Journal of Research in Crime and Delinquency, 36,* 156–174.

Walklate, Sandra. (1995). *Gender and Crime. An Introduction.* London. Prentice-Hall etc.

Warr, Mark. (1998). Life-Course Transitions and Desistance from Crime. *Criminology, 36,* 183–216.

Warr, Mark, & Mark Stafford. (1991). The Influence of Delinquent Peers: What They Think or What They Do? *Criminology, 29,* 851–866.

Wells, L. Edward. (1989). Self-Enhancement Through Delinquency: A Conditional Test of Self-Derogation Theory. *Journal of Research in Crime and Delinquency, 26,* 226–252.

Wells, L. Edward, & Joseph H. Rankin. (1983). Self-Concept as a Mediating Factor in Delinquency. *Social Psychology Quarterly, 46,* 11–22.

Wells, L. Edward, & Joseph. H. Rankin. (1986). The Broken Homes Model of Delinquency: Analytic Issues. *Journal of Research in Crime and Delinquency, 23,* 68–93.

Wells, L. Edward, & Joseph H. Rankin. (1991). Families and Delinquency: A Meta-Analysis of the Impact of Broken Homes. *Social Problems, 38,* 71–93.

Willems, Helmut. (1993). Gewalt und Fremdenfeindlichkeit. Anmerkungen zum gegenwärtigen Gewaltdiskurs. In Hans-Uwe Otto & Roland Merten (Eds.), *Rechtsradikale Gewalt im vereinigten Deutschland. Jugend im gesellschaftlichen Umbruch* (pp. 88–108). Opladen: Leske & Budrich.

Williams, Kirk R. (1992). Social Sources of Marital Violence and Deterrence: Testing an Integrated Theory of Assaults Between Partners. *Journal of Marriage and the Family, 54,* 620–629.

Williams, Kirk R., & Richard Hawkins. (1989a). The Meaning of Arrest for Wife Assault. *Criminology, 27,* 163–181.

Williams, Kirk R., & Richard Hawkins. (1989b). Controlling Male Aggression in Intimate Relationships. *Law and Society Review, 23,* 591–612.

Williams, Kirk R., & Richard Hawkins. (1992). Wife Assault, Costs of Arrest, and the Deterrence Process. *Journal of Research in Crime and Delinquency, 29,* 292–310.

Wolfgang, Marvin E., & Franco Ferracuti. (1973). Subculture of Violence: An Integrated Conceptualization. In David O. Arnold (Ed.), *Subcultures* (pp. 135–149). Berkeley: Glendessary Press. [orig.: Wolfgang, Marvin E. & Franco Ferracuti. (1967). *The Subculture of Violence* (pp. 95–113, 164–167, 324–315). London: Travistock Publications, Inc.]

Wolfgang, Marvin, Robert M. Figlio, & Thorsten Sellin. (1972). *Delinquency in a Birth Cohort.* Chicago, London: University of Chicago Press.

Wolpin, Kenneth I. (1978). An Economic Analysis of Crime and Punishment in England and Wales, 1894–1967. *Journal of Political Economy, 86,* 815–839.

Wood, Peter B., Walter R. Gove, James A. Wilson, & John K. Cochran. (1997). Nonsocial Reinforcement and Habitual Criminal Conduct: An Extension of Learning Theory. *Criminology, 35*(2), 335–366.

Woodward, Lianne, David M. Fergusson, & Jay Bilsky. (2000). Timing of Parental Separation and Attachment to Parents in Adolescence: Results of a Prospective Study From Birth to Age 16. *Journal of Marriage and the Family, 62,* 161–174.

Wright, Bradley R. Entner, Avshalom Caspi, Terrie E. Moffitt, Richard A. Miech, & Phil A. Silva. (1999a). Reconsidering the Relationship Between SES and Delinquency: Causation But Not Correlation. *Criminology, 37,* 175–194.

Wright, Bradley R. Entner, Avshalom Caspi, Terrie E. Moffitt, & Phil A. Silva. (1999b). Low Self-Control, Social Bonds, and Crime: Social Causation, Social Selection, or Both? *Criminology, 37*(3), 479–514.

Yablonsky, Lewis. (1962). *The Violent Gang.* New York: Macmillan.

Yablonsky, Lewis. (1973). The Delinquent Gang as a Near Group. In Earl Rubington & Martin S. Weinberg (Eds.), *Deviance. The Interactionist Perspective* (pp. 245–255). New York: Macmillan.

Zehr, Howard. (1976). *Crime and the Development of Modern Society. Patterns of Criminality in Nineteenth Century Germany and France.* London: Croom Helm.

Youth Violence and Guns

ALFRED BLUMSTEIN

I. GUNS AND THE GROWTH IN YOUTH VIOLENCE

Violence covers a variety of conflicts involving two or more parties, typically involving the possibility of ending in injury or death to one of the parties. It could involve an initially symmetric dispute between two people that escalates in intensity to the point that tempers flare, fists fly, perhaps more serious weapons—a knife, a baseball bat, or a gun—appear, and the result is that one or the other disputants is injured or killed. Violence may also result from predatory action by one party seeking to control the other, either to take some property, typically money, from the other (robbery), to seek some sexual control (rape or other form of sexual assault), or to injure intentionally out of anger or retaliation.

One important feature of a violent incident is the implications that flow from the kind of weaponry involved. In particular, the presence of firearms in a dispute can profoundly change the consequences of a violent encounter. This is of particular concern in the United States, where there are an estimated 200 million firearms and 75 million handguns in a population of 280 million people. With the widespread availability of lethal weapons, it becomes especially important to develop means of keeping them out of the hands of people whom the society decides should not be trusted to possess or to carry firearms, and especially handguns, which can be more easily concealed than other firearms. Various statutes typically classify these people as convicted felons or others who have been convicted of violent offenses; people with certain mental illnesses, typically those requiring involuntary confinement in a mental institution; and underage youth.

In recent years, the problem has been most visible with the youth, particularly those groups who had not previously had ready access to firearms. This problem is of particular concern with young males, who typically lack well-developed dispute-resolution skills and who often resort to fights to settle their disputes. It is fortunate that they typically do

W. Heitmeyer and J. Hagan (eds.), *International Handbook of Violence Research*, 657–677.

not have access to firearms, because such weapons can significantly change the dynamics of the dispute. Normally, one of the combatants in a fight comes to realize that he is losing the battle and so retreats, or some third-party observer intervenes and breaks up the fight. If a firearm is present, however, these harmless consequences are largely precluded because events move too fast. The situation becomes even more severe if one of the combatants suspects the other of carrying a firearm, because he then has a powerful incentive for a preemptive strike to shoot the opponent before he can fire. Thus, as guns become more prevalent in the hands of people who are not trained or skillful in using them with restraint, they can become a major stimulus to lethal violence.

Gun violence can produce significant economic costs. These costs include the straightforward direct costs of the injuries—medical costs, time lost from work, pain and suffering—but they also include economic consequences of the violence other than the injuries. These could include the costs invested in protection, the decline in real estate values in areas of high violence, closing of industrial facilities because of concern by employees about risks of violence. These costs can even include the costs of declining quality of life as a result of fear, reluctance to use parks, or even to venture into the street at certain times and places. Cook and Ludwig (2000) have used a method of "contingent valuation" by asking a sample of people how much they would be willing to pay to get a particular reduction in gun violence. Scaling this up to all gun violence led them to estimate that people in the United States would be willing to pay as much as $100 billion to eliminate gun violence, and they take that as their estimate of the economic cost of gun violence. Regardless of whether one fully accepts that estimate or not, it certainly conveys a clear sense that American society views the total cost of gun violence as extremely high and so attributes considerable value to efforts that might be directed at reducing the level and cost of gun violence.

The period of the late 1980s saw a major growth of youth violence in the United States. This was followed by similar growth in many other countries. In the United States, for example, between 1985 and 1993, the arrest rate for homicide more than doubled for all ages under twenty. The rate tripled for 15-year-olds, with the growth rate decreasing with age. For ages of thirty and older, the rate was actually about 20 percent below the 1985 rate. Since 1993, the rates of homicide have been declining steadily. Most of the growth as well as most of the decline can be accounted for by the rise and subsequent reduction in handgun homicides.

The growth of violence by these young people impelled some observers to claim that there was emerging a new breed of "superpredator" in the generation following the post-World War II baby boom. As evidence, they pointed to the kind of violent acts that reach headlines: an 11-year-old boy shooting and killing a 13-year-old girl in Chicago, a 6-year-old boy shooting and killing a female classmate outside Flint, Michigan. The context of the "superpredator" label was a suggestion that there was a new generation of young people arriving on the scene who were undersocialized, out of control, beyond redemption, and had little regard for life or for their victims' pain and suffering. Consequently, particularly aggressive steps were needed and warranted to keep them under control. Those steps would involve severe punishment to incapacitate them or to deter them—as if the rational calculus of weighing the benefits of the crime against the pain of the punishment was part of the cognitive paradigm of a "superpredator."

This characterization of the problem raises the question of the degree to which the rise in youth violence in the late 1980s and early 1990s was attributable to the arrival of this new group of superpredators who were inherently more violent than their predecessors. Alternatively, we might seek to determine the degree to which that growth in youth violence was attributable to a particular change in the environment rather than in the mix of people. In particular, we will want to explore the extent to which handguns—and especially the semiautomatic handguns with their high firepower and large clips of ammunition—became available to people who had not previously had access to handguns and who had no experience in carrying them with restraint.

In this article, we will explore the degree to which handguns have made the difference. America is plagued by the widespread availability of guns to people who cannot be trusted to use them responsibly. The nation has a strong tradition of permissiveness with regard to guns, undoubtedly reflecting the frontier tradition of the nation's early development. That tradition is embodied in the Second Amendment (part of the Bill of Rights) of the Constitution, which states, "A well regulated Militia, being necessary to the security of a free State, the right of the people to keep and bear Arms, shall not be infringed."

That tradition and its articulation in the Constitution is vigorously defended by a large number of gun owners and by the National Rifle Association (NRA), an advocacy organization that has come to wield considerable political power by raising the specter that any attempt at gun control is the first step onto a slippery slope that will eventually lead to the confiscation of all the guns from all private owners. Raising this concern to the large number of people who do feel strongly about their guns has enabled the NRA to mobilize a powerful voting bloc to whom the threat of losing their right to their weapons seems to loom much larger than the reality.

The right to have a gun is largely unchallenged in the United States, but there have been a variety of efforts to limit the universality of that right. Young people in particular are widely regarded as having only limited rights to carry a firearm, and there has been no successful challenge to statutes at the state and federal level prohibiting young people from buying a gun. The age limit varies by state, but there is a federal prohibition against anyone under twenty-one purchasing a handgun. The individual states differ considerably, with rules in the predominantly rural states being quite loose with virtually no restraint and the states with large urban populations typically being more aggressive at maintaining control over the possession and especially the carrying of firearms, and particularly of handguns.

In this section, we examine the extent of violence as a problem in the United States and the contribution of guns to that problem. We explore various efforts to control the availability of guns to those most at risk for acting violently, and we examine the future prospects for gun control.

II. TRENDS IN U.S. HOMICIDE RATES: RECENT FOCUS ON YOUTH

The best indicator of violence in the United States is the homicide rate. Between 1950 and 1970, there was a major growth from a rate of about 5 per 100,000 population to a rate of about 8 per 100,000. Over the period from 1970 to 1995, the rate oscillated between 8 and 10 per 100,000. Since 1993, the rate has displayed a steady decline, reaching a level of 5.7 in 1999, the lowest rate since 1966, thirty-three years earlier.

It is important to disaggregate that aggregate rate into different age-groups and to examine the contribution of firearms to those trends. For much of the period before about 1985, the peak ages of homicide offending occurs between eighteen and twenty-four, and the rates at those ages had typically been rather flat, with the rates falling off rather sharply at the younger ages and more slowly at the older ages.

After 1985, there was a major shift in the rate of arrest of young people for homicide. This shift is illustrated in Figs. II-3-3-2.1a–1c, which depicts the growth in arrest rate for homicide by age from 1985 to 1993, the peak year for young people's homicide. As the

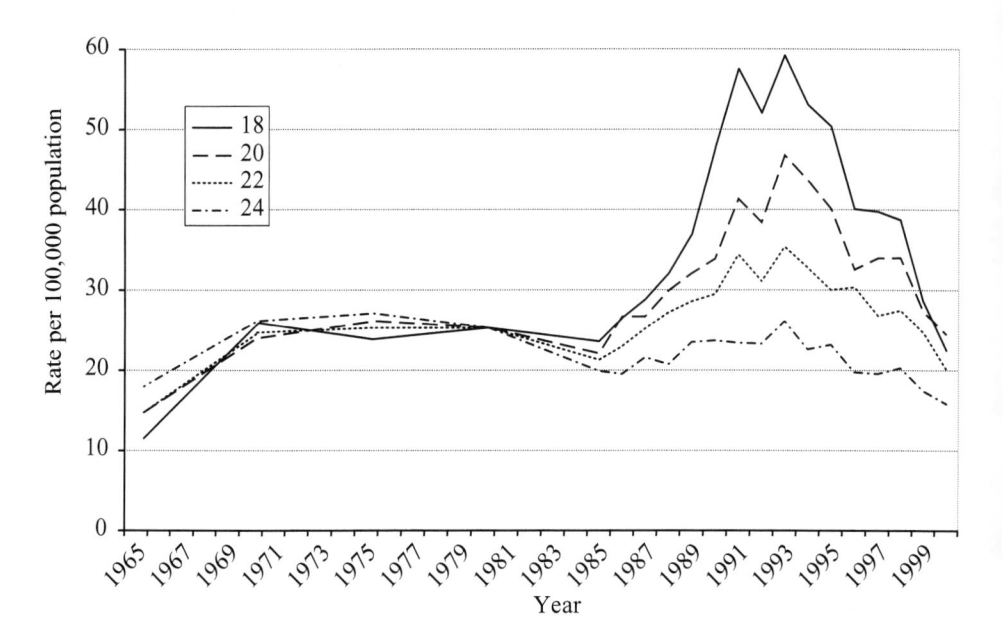

Figure II-3-3-2.1a. Trends in murder arrest rate by age (trends for the ages 18–24).

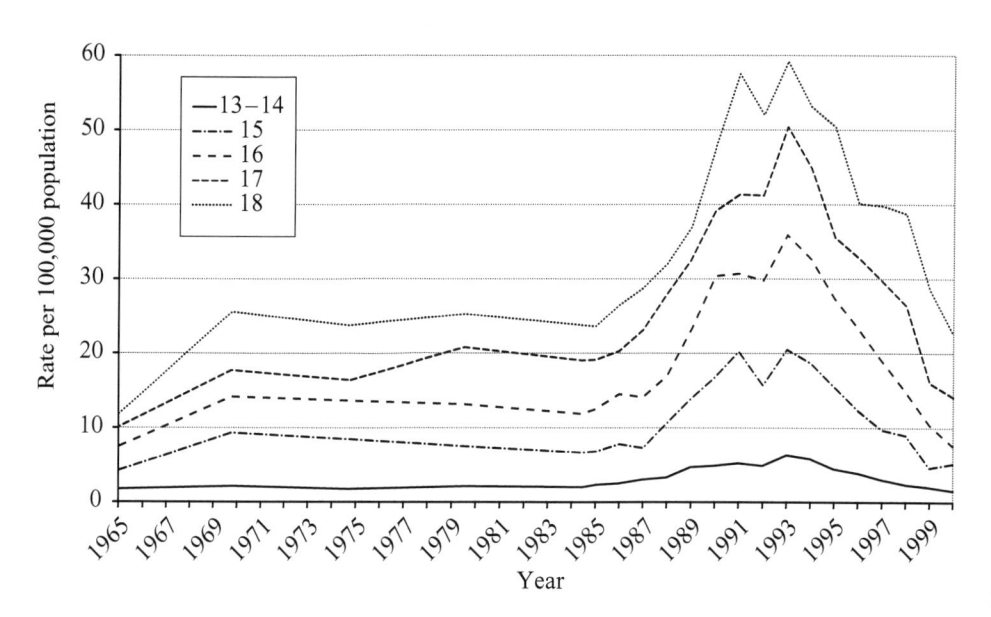

Figure II-3-3-2.1b. Trends in murder arrest rate by age (trends for the ages 13–18).

figure shows, the arrest rate of 15-year-olds more than tripled over those eight years. The growth rate declined for older ages, but was still more than double the 1985 rate for all ages under twenty. In contrast to what happened to the young people, for the ages older than thirty, there was actually a decline over that period (Fig. II-3-3-2.1c).

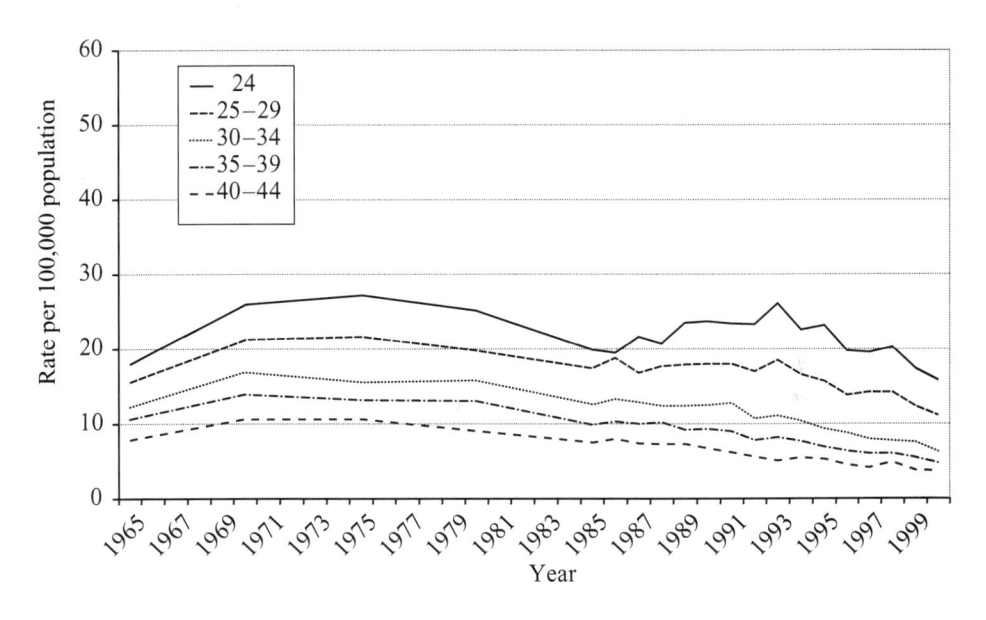

FIGURE II-3-3-2.1c. Trends in murder arrest rate by age (trends for the ages 24–44).

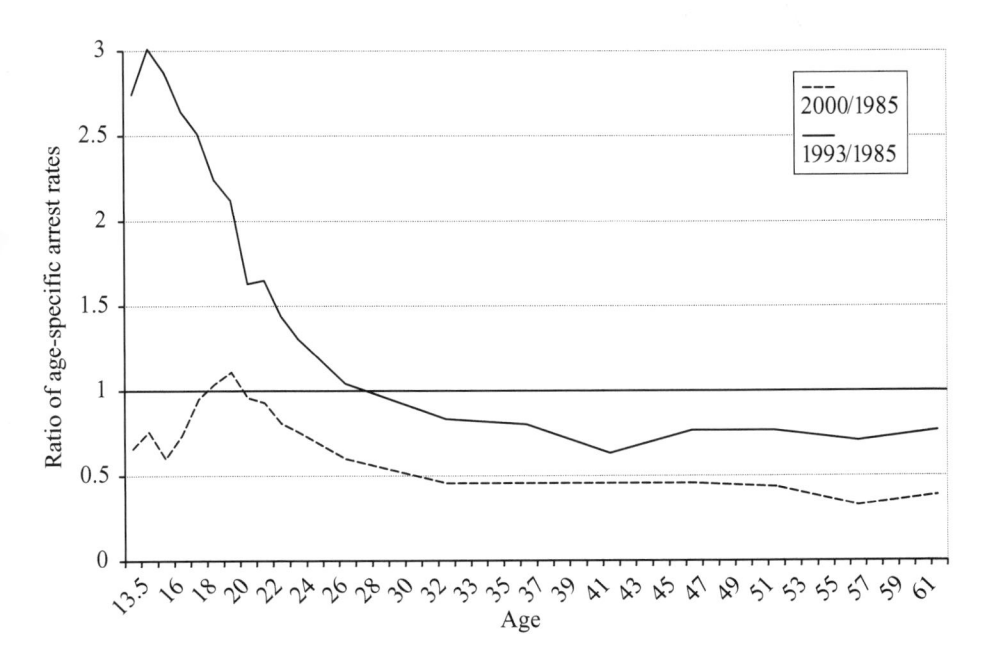

FIGURE II-3-3-2.1d. Ratios of recent age-specific rates (1993 and 2000 murder arrests re 1985).

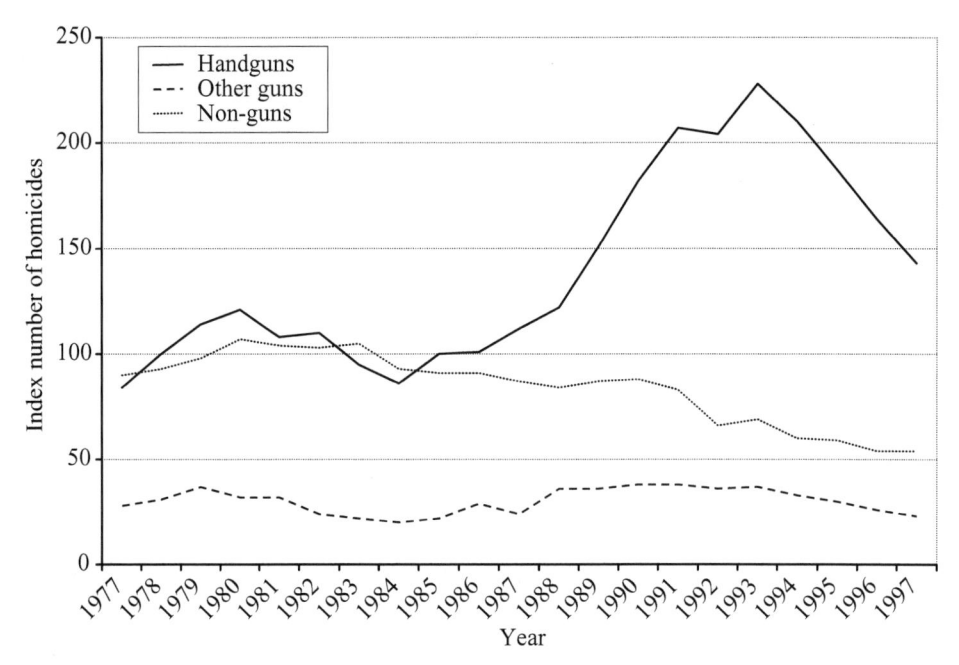

FIGURE II-3-3-2.2a. Homicide weapons by youth (18–24).

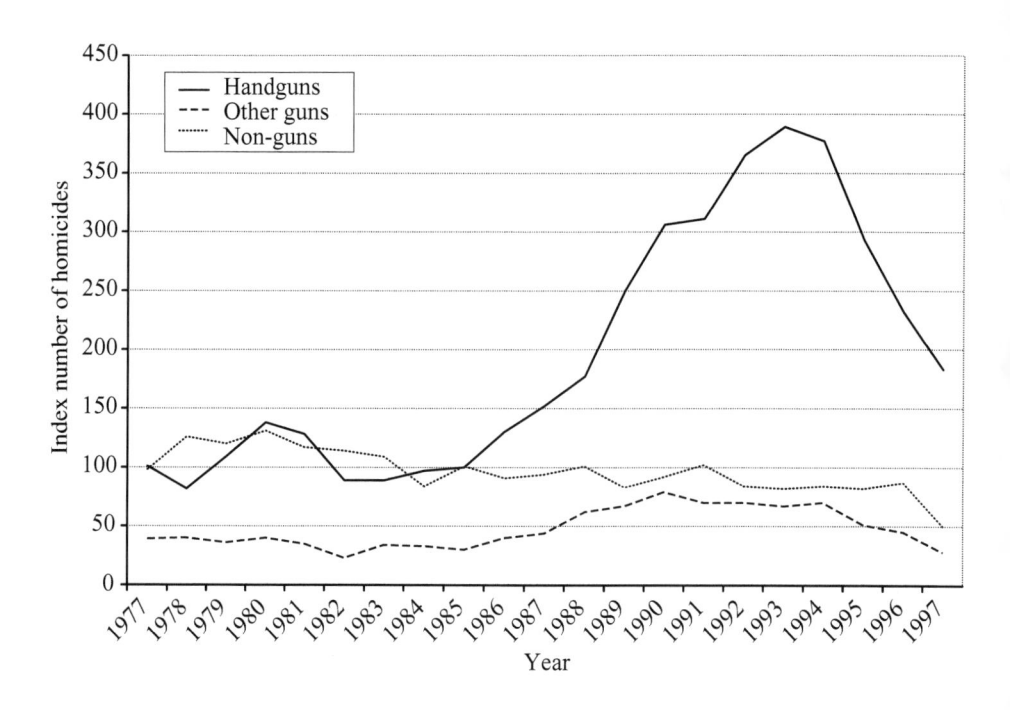

FIGURE II-3-3-2.2b. Homicide weapons by kids (under 18).

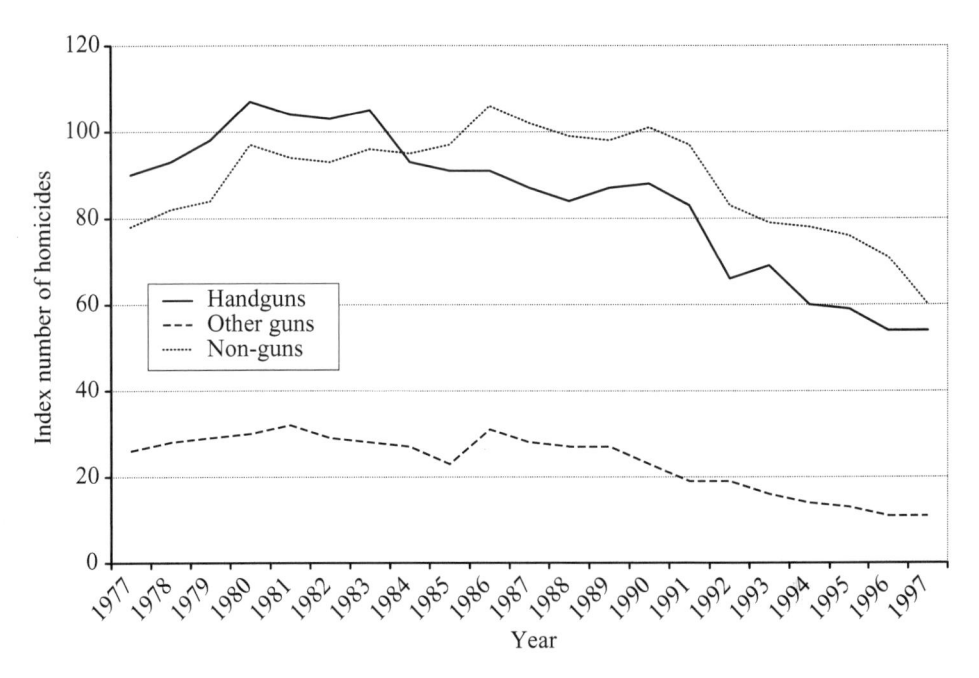

FIGURE II-3-3-2.2c. Homicide weapons by adults (25–45).

The lower graph in Fig. II-3-3-2.1d depicts the ratio of homicide arrests in 2000 compared to 1993, and shows that the events of the 1990s basically brought the young people's rate back roughly to the level that had prevailed in 1985; for the ages of fourteen to seventeen the rates are clearly below.

1. Changes in the Use of Firearms by Young People

For the young people, we know that there was a major growth after 1985 in the use of handguns in homicide. We can begin to examine that issue with Fig. II-3-3-2.2a, which displays the relative number (relative to the number of handgun homicides in 1985, which is set to an index of 100) of homicides in each year with each of three kinds of weapons: handguns, other guns, and means other than guns. This graph focuses on the weaponry used in homicides by youth between eighteen and twenty-four, using data from the Supplementary Homicide Report (SHR), an incident-level report compiled by the FBI of factors associated with individual homicide events. Before 1985, there was some oscillation, but not much of a clear trend. But between 1985 and 1993, there was an increase of over 130 percent in the homicides with handguns, with no marked change in long guns and about a 50 percent decrease in non-guns. This suggests that the handguns were partly a substitute for the non-gun weapons (e.g., knives) and partly generated new homicides that might otherwise have been merely assaults. The decline started in 1994 and, by 1997, had come down to only a 50 percent increase over 1985.

Figure II-3-3-2.2b for juveniles under eighteen almost reveals a *quadrupling* in the handgun homicides between 1985 and 1993, with an approximately doubling in the long

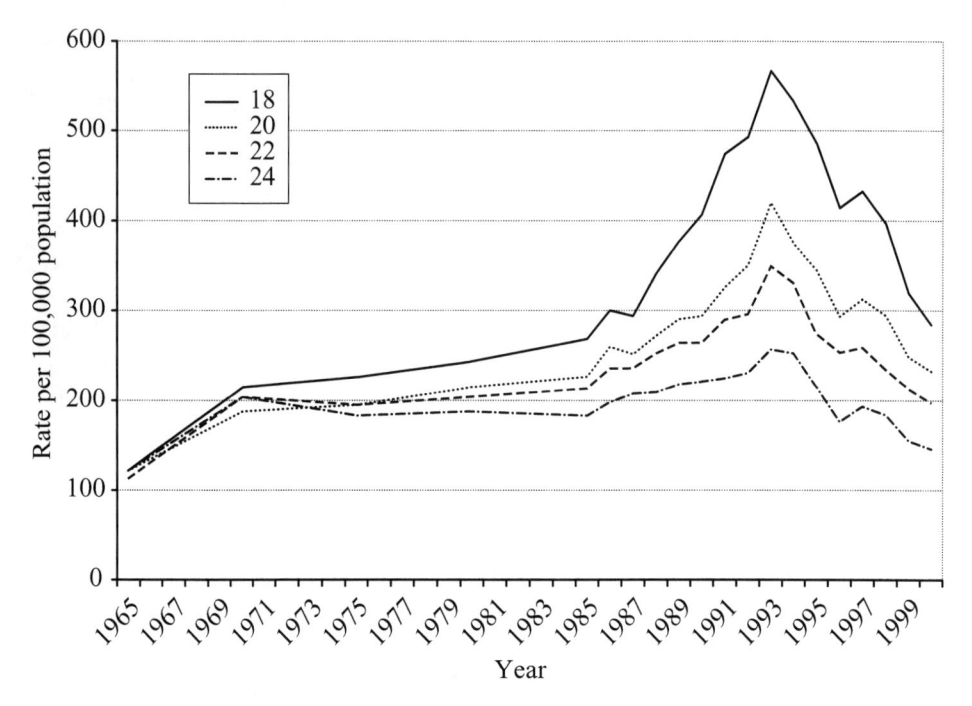

FIGURE II-3-3-2.3a. Trends: weapons arrest rate by age trends for individual ages (18–24).

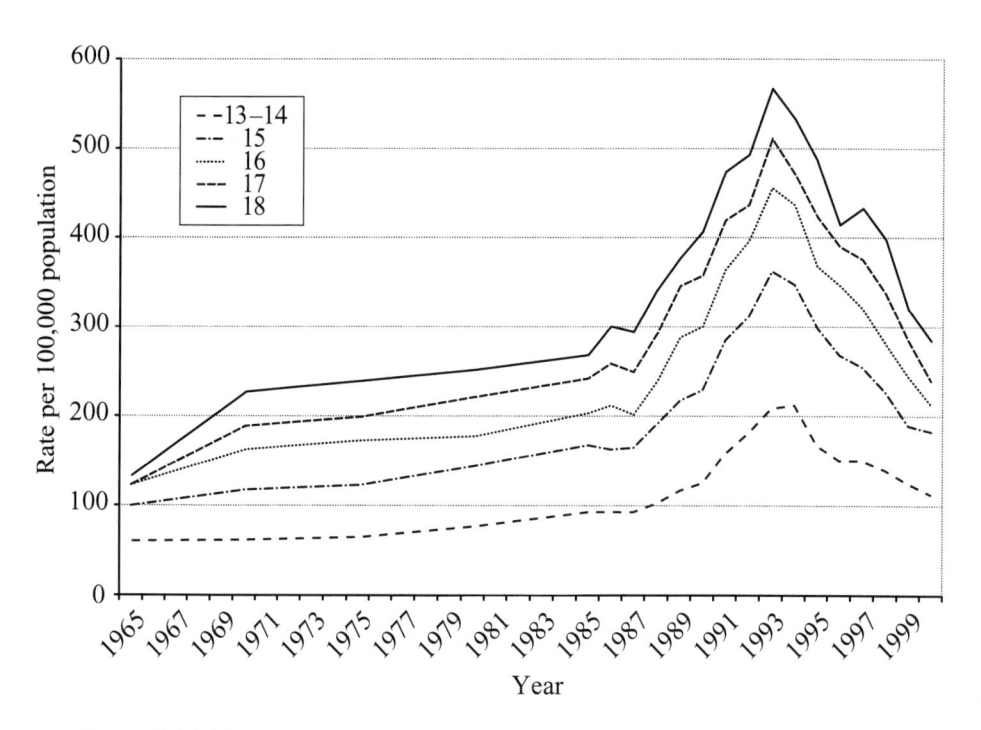

FIGURE II-3-3-2.3b. Trends: weapons arrest rate by age trends for individual ages (13–18).

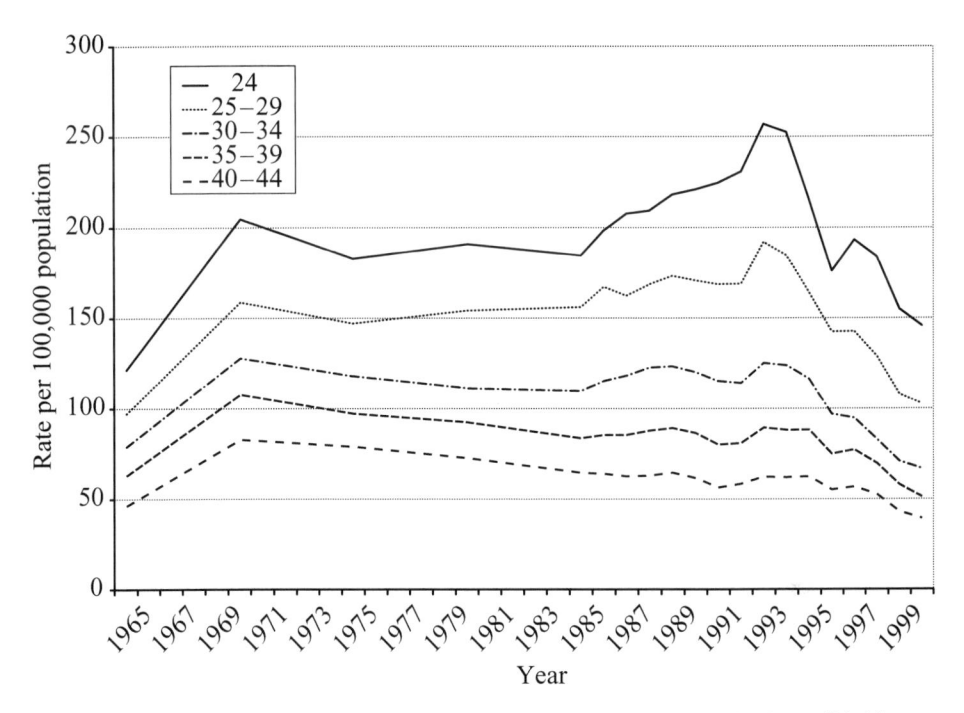

FIGURE II-3-3-2.3c. Trends: weapons arrest rate by age trends for individual ages (24–44).

gun homicides, and about a 20 percent decrease in the non-guns. After the 1993 peak, there was a sharp drop in the use of handguns in juveniles' homicides, reaching by 1997 a level that was about 80 percent over the 1985 rate.

Figure II-3-3-2.2c for twenty-five to forty-five year-old adults shows no such increase in handgun homicides, and generally shows a downward trend that accelerates after 1991 and reaches a level about 60 percent of the 1985 level in 1997.

Between 1985 and 1993, the weapons involved in settling young people's disputes changed dramatically, from fists or knives to handguns—and especially more recently to semiautomatic pistols with their much greater firepower and lethality. These weapons were coming into the hands of young people who had no prior experience in dealing with them. Older folks may well also have had more handguns during this period, but they appear to have exercised much greater restraint in their use. As a result, beginning in 1985, there was a sharp growth in the firearm homicide death rate among young people (youth and especially juveniles), but not among adults.

The decline in handgun homicides after 1993 almost mirrors the rise. Following the peak in 1993, the rate of decline was steepest for the juveniles and less steep for the youth. The adults, who displayed no peaking, nevertheless had a steady decline of almost 40 percent after 1993. These data end in 1997, two years before the age-specific homicide arrest rates reached the 1985 level, and one can anticipate that their decline continued until at least 1999.

The pattern of a rise in weapon-specific suicide death rates before 1993 was very similar to that of homicide death rates. Following a period of generally flat rates, the rate of suicide with firearms increased rather sharply after 1985, and there was no change in means other than with firearms. This shift was especially marked in suicides of African-American youth and juveniles, whose suicide rate had previously been markedly lower than that of whites (Blumstein & Cork, 1996).

These observations certainly suggest that the growth in homicide by young people was much more attributable to the weapons that found their way into their hands than to the emergence of inadequately socialized cohorts of "superpredators," as some had claimed. If the cohorts were indeed more vicious, then one would expect to see a growth in homicide with all forms of weaponry rather than only with handguns. The findings strongly suggest that teenagers fought as they always had, but that the greater lethality of handguns led to disputes that might have been resolved otherwise, but resulted in a homicide because of the lethality of their new-found weapons.

The steady decline in the handgun homicide rates after 1993 is certainly consistent with the decline in youth homicide rates shown in Figs. II-3-3-2.1a–1c. The pattern of growth and decline in handgun use is also reflected in Figs. II-3-3-2.3a–3c, which depicts the time trend in the rate of arrests for weapon possession at the various ages. The pattern here is also very similar to the age-specific homicide patterns. The weapons arrest trends show a distinct peaking in 1993, with a clear decline subsequently.

Changes in the rate of weapons arrests can result from a combination of changes in the illegal carrying of weapons and changes in police aggressiveness in pursuing illegal weapons. It is clear from Figs. II-3-3-2.3a–3b that there was considerable growth in weapon prevalence among young people during the late 1980s. It is also clear that police became more concerned about weapons, especially in the hands of young people. That combination is reflected in the rise in weapons arrests until the peak, also in 1993. There is no indication that there was any diminution in police aggressiveness in pursuing young people's guns after 1993, and so it seems likely that the decline after 1993 is due much more to a reduction in the carrying of guns than to a slackening of police efforts to capture the guns. This reduction in carrying seems to have been an important factor contributing to the decrease in homicide after 1993.

Thus, we have some clear indications through SHR data on homicide weapons and in weapons arrests that there was an important decline in the use of handguns by young people after 1993. It is difficult to sort out all the factors that contributed to that. Certainly an important contributor to that was the aggressive stop-and-frisk tactics engaged in by local police, especially in many of the cities that showed a rise in handgun violence, especially the large cities that led both the rise and the decline. Also, many cities saw community groups take an active hand in negotiating truces among gangs and seeking to establish norms that precluded the carrying of the guns.

There was also likely to have been some important federal contribution to the decline. The Brady Bill, which required a background check before anyone could buy a gun from a licensed dealer, became effective in 1994, the first year of the decline. The denial rate under the Brady Bill has been reported as about 2.5 percent of those who applied to purchase a gun (Gifford et al., 2000). The uncertainty is the degree to which these individuals simply accepted the denials or resorted to one of the many loopholes left open by the Brady Bill—purchasing a gun at a gun show, buying one from a private individual, hiring a straw purchaser to buy it, theft, or any of the other means left open to a determined illegal purchaser.

There were also approaches by the ATF (Bureau of Alcohol, Tobacco, and Firearms of the U.S. Treasury Department) intended to identify dealers and individuals disproportionately involved in the sale or purchase of "crime guns," guns associated with a crime that were captured and then traced to the original sale. To the extent that such efforts led to the deterrence of inappropriate handgun transactions, they could also have contributed to making guns harder to obtain.

All of these efforts had a mutually reinforcing effect to the extent that there was a reduction in the carrying of the handguns, either because of the threat of confiscation or because of the difficulty of acquiring one, that would lead to a reduced incentive for others to carry, and so reduce the likelihood of handgun homicides, especially among the young people for whom it was so deadly.

2. Level and Distribution of Firearm Injury and Death

The previous section highlights how the rate of homicide by young people changed dramatically in the late 1980s and 1990s because of the shifts in their use of firearms. Aside from homicide, firearms can generate considerable injury. A study by the Bureau of Justice Statistics of the U.S. Department of Justice (Zawitz & Strom, 2000) noted that 28 percent of serious nonfatal violent victimizations (not counting simple assaults) in the period from 1993 through 1997 were committed with a firearm, 4 percent were committed with a firearm and resulted in injury, and less than 1 percent resulted in gunshot wounds.

The role of handguns is particularly important here also. Where the kind of weapon in the nonfatal assaults was known, 82 percent were shot with a handgun and 18 percent with a long gun. This distribution is very similar to that in firearm homicides, where 88 percent were killed with a handgun and 12 percent with a long gun.

In this study, which examined the period from 1993 to 1997, gunshot wounds followed a declining time trend similar to that for homicide. The number of gunshot wounds from assault treated in hospital emergency rooms dropped from 64,100 in 1993 to 39,400 in 1997, a decline of 39 percent. The level of homicides committed with a firearm fell from 18,300 in 1993 to 13,300 in 1997, a decline of 27 percent.

Similar trends occurred in other than homicide firearm deaths and injuries over this same period. Firearm suicides fell by 7 percent and accidental deaths by 36 percent. Firearm injuries from suicide declined by 45 percent and unintentional firearm injuries dropped by 39 percent. This may suggest that the various efforts at gun control limiting the availability of firearms may be having some effect, but it is still too limited a period to be able to make a strong conclusion.

The relationship between homicides and injuries reflects the lethality of the firearms. Hospital emergency rooms treated 3.3 nonfatal gunshot injuries for every homicide committed with a firearm. For the accidental firearm injuries, the emergency rooms treated 11.4 nonfatal injuries for each fatality. Firearm suicides, however, are most likely to be fatal: there were only 0.3 survivors per firearm suicide.

The distribution of firearm violence over ethnic groups highlights its salience for members of minority groups. Hispanics comprise about 20 percent of the victims of nonfatal gun shot wounds from crime as well as of the overall nonfatal firearm injury. However, the majority of the victims of nonfatal and fatal gunshot wounds from crime are black, 54 percent of each group. Only 18 percent of the crime-related gunshot victims were white, but a majority of the victims of the firearm suicides or accidental injuries were white.

One of the more troublesome aspects of firearm injuries and death is the disproportionate presence of young people among the victims. Juveniles under eighteen account for 16 percent of the victims of nonfatal gunshot wounds from crime, 10 percent of firearm homicide victims, and 17 percent of the firearm homicide offenders. Extending the range to all those twenty-four or younger accounts for 54 percent of the victims of nonfatal gunshot wounds from crime, 41 percent of firearm homicide victims, and 61 percent of the firearm homicide offenders. The Youth Handgun Safety Act of 1994 strictly prohibits possession of handguns by anyone under eighteen and the Gun Control Act of 1968 prohibits any federally licensed firearm dealer from selling handguns to persons under twenty-one.

A 1997 CDC study puts this youth firearm violence rate in dramatic terms by noting that every day twelve children nineteen years old or younger in the United States are killed by gunfire. This astonishing rate of serious youth violence in the United States is not necessarily a reflection of very distinctive violent nature of juveniles, but much more a reflection of the consequences of their ready access to firearms.

3.   Role of Drug Markets in the Proliferation of Handguns

It is useful to explore what factors contributed to the sudden shifts upward and then downward in the use of handguns by young people. The most likely candidate is the arrival in U.S. cities in the mid-1980s of a new form of cocaine—crack—that had particular marketing appeal for poor people. Prior to that time, powder cocaine was available in quantities that cost hundreds of dollars, but crack could spread a given quantity of cocaine into many "rocks" which could be sold on the street for five to ten dollars, or even less.

This low price, which brought into the cocaine market many low-income people who could only buy it one "hit" at a time, greatly increased the number of transactions in those markets due to the increased number of new buyers brought in and the increased number of transactions each buyer engaged in per week. This transformed the marketing of cocaine products from predominantly surreptitious selling to more affluent consumers at a low frequency into a much higher volume of street transactions concentrated in poor communities.

With this growth in volume, compounded by the growing incarceration of the older drug sellers, the markets had to recruit a large cadre of street sellers both to meet the increased demand and as replacements for those sent off to prison. Young people were the obvious candidates. They are willing to work more cheaply than adults, partly because they were less vulnerable to the increasingly punitive adult criminal justice system that lay at the heart of the escalating "drug war" at the time. Also, they tend to be more daring and willing to take risks that more mature adults would eschew. Also, the profits available to the distributors made them most anxious to generate their labor supply however they could. The economic plight of many young urban black juveniles, many of whom saw no other comparably satisfactory route to economic sustenance at the time, made them particularly amenable to the lure of employment in the crack markets.

Participants in the crack street markets, especially those operating in inner-city areas, were particularly vulnerable to attack by street robbers who targeted their sizable assets, either the drugs or the money from the sale of the drugs. Since calling the police for protection from this threat was not available, participants in those markets, including the young people recruited into them, felt it necessary to carry guns for self-protection. Also, drug markets, like many other illegal markets, cannot have recourse to the courts for dispute resolution, and so they often have to resort to violence to settle conflicts between sellers over turf or between buyer and seller over a bad drug deal. Thus, handguns became a necessary tool of the trade in those drug markets.

Once the young people in the drug markets started carrying guns, then their friends and colleagues who go to the same school or who walk the same streets, even though not involved in the drug markets, also started to arm themselves, primarily for their own protection, but also because possession of a weapon may have become a part of status-seeking in the community. This initiated an escalating arms race: as more guns appeared in the street, any single individual had an increased incentive to arm himself. In light of the fact that young people are much more tightly networked than older people, and much more likely to imitate each other, that diffusion process could proceed very quickly. The emergence of teenage gangs in many cities at about the same time—some with their members involved in the drug markets themselves—certainly contributed to that diffusion, both within the gangs and among their neighbors.

Then, in view of the recklessness and bravado that is often characteristic of teenagers, and their low level of skill in settling disputes other than through the use of physical force, many of the fist-fights that would otherwise have taken place escalated into shootings as a result of the presence of the guns. This can be exacerbated by the problems of socialization associated with high levels of poverty, high rates of single-parent households, educational failures, and a widespread sense of economic hopelessness. By the time people reach the more mature ages beyond the early twenties, it appears that they do develop some prudence, are more cautious even if they are armed, and display greater restraint.

This hypothesized diffusion process (Blumstein, 1995) has been tested further with city-level data on juvenile arrests for drugs and homicides, taking advantage of the fact that drug markets flourished at different times in different cities, early in New York and Los Angeles, later in Washington. Daniel Cork (1999) has shown the connection between the rise in the handgun homicides and the recruitment of juveniles into the crack markets. Using an epidemic model originally used in the marketing literature, he identified in individual cities the time when juvenile arrests for drugs began to accelerate and the corresponding time when juvenile homicide arrests took off. He found most typically a one- to three-year lag between the two—homicides following the involvement in the drug markets. These results are clearly consistent with the hypothesis that the rise in juvenile homicides was attributable to the diffusion of guns from the kids recruited into drug markets to their friends and beyond. Also, his analysis of the individual cities showed that crack markets generally emerged first in the largest coastal cities, especially in New York and Los Angeles, and then diffused to the center of the nation and to smaller cities at a later time. Thus, the observed patterns of the rise of homicide by young people with handguns are highly consistent with explanations that assign central importance to the rise and decline of crack in the United States.

The presence of the drug markets in inner-city areas contributed to shifting the norms of behavior in those areas, but also because the magnitude of their presence in some communities stimulated imitation of their distinctive dispute-resolution practices in their neighborhoods, even among those who have no direct connection to the drug industry. This could include, for example, the influence of the widespread prevalence of guns among drug sellers as a stimulus to others in the community to arm themselves similarly, perhaps for self-defense, perhaps to settle their own disputes that have nothing to do with drugs, or perhaps just to gain respect.

The fall-off in the violence after 1993 is partly a reflection of the changing tastes for crack, especially in urban areas. As the recognition of its deleterious effects became widespread, the word seemed to propagate through the streets that crack was an undesirable drug, and this wisdom had a major effect on diminishing the number of new users (Johnson, Golub, & Dunlap, 2000). This contributed to a major reduction in the need for the young street sellers. Older users were still important consumers, but their demand could be served more readily and surreptitiously by individual delivery, thereby diminishing the need for the street markets. All of these changes contributed to a decline in the street markets, the recruitment of young people, and the diminished need for handguns in young people's hands following the 1993 peak. Thus, even though handguns were still in the street as this tide of crack markets turned, the presence of guns in the hands of the young people in the crack markets was no longer a driving force. This, combined with the various police and community efforts to control the guns contributed to the post-1993 de-escalation of the arms race that brought young people's gun violence back to the 1985 level by 1999.

One other important factor contributing to the decline in violence as crack demand ebbed has been the strength of the U.S. economy over the decade of the 1990s. If there were no legitimate jobs for the young people to move into, it is reasonable to anticipate that they might have turned to other criminal activity to provide economic sustenance. But the abundance of the job opportunities that extended well down into the low skill levels provided legitimate alternatives. Individuals in legitimate jobs have a strong incentive to conformity and to avoid other kinds of criminal activity, which they might more readily engage in if they were employed in illegal markets. This should provide a strong indication of the desirability of finding approaches that bring the young people into the legitimate economy through appropriate training to develop good legitimate employment opportunities.

4.   Gangs, Gang Drug Trafficking, and Policing of Gangs

The period of high crack activity was also a period of high gang activity. To some extent, this was a result of involvement of the gang as a corporate enterprise in drug selling. Gangs had some clear advantages in this role. They have ready recruits for participation, they can exploit economies of scale, they typically have some form of organization structure, and, perhaps most important, they can protect each other from the violence that is endemic to illegal markets by working together and by assuring retaliation against anyone attacking a colleague. The long-standing gangs of Los Angeles and Chicago were probably the best example of gangs that did engage in drug selling as a corporate activity of the gang. More often, however, while many gang members were involved in drug sales, they did so as individuals rather than through the corporate activity of the gang's leadership. In that way, they could gain the benefit of gang cohesion without depending on the often weak organizational structure.

In the world of drug markets, gun carrying, especially by gang members, became a necessity. They regularly encountered other illegal gun carriers and so had to carry guns to protect themselves and their turf from rival gangs. Drug dealers carry guns to protect their turf and their assets, and so many of their customers carry guns, which certainly reinforces the dealers' carrying. Also, the gang, especially those involved in drug dealing, could overcome whatever difficulties there might be in finding a supply of the guns, so that none of the members need experience those difficulties.

5.   Rampage Killers

A particular kind of youth gun violence that has understandably attracted considerable attention has been the schoolyard shootings, where one or occasionally two students—

always males—came to school with guns and killed a number of classmates or teachers. These were a class of events examined by the *New York Times* in a sample of one hundred "rampage killings" that involved a single individual who killed multiple victims not limited to his own family. Rampage killing was often part of a suicide, with a clear realization that they would either be killed in the process or kill themselves, but would exact a penalty from their "enemies" or their proxies. Unlike most offenders, rampage killers rarely left the scene of the crime, and one-third killed themselves after their crime. Many were well educated (one-third had a college degree, and so their education level was well above that of other offenders), but more than half were unemployed despite their education, so that their violent acts could be a consequence of their frustration of their underachievement, or it could be that their underemployment was a consequence of their personality problems.

They also found, not surprisingly, that most of these killers suffered from severe mental illness. Of course, only a small percentage of mentally ill people are violent and many advocates bristle at any link between mental illness and violence out of concern that it will further stigmatize an already mistreated population. Of the one hundred rampage killers, forty-seven had a history of treatment for mental health problems, sixty-three had made general threats of violence to others in advance, and in thirty-four of the cases, families and friends had tried to find help for the person, but were rebuffed by the police, school administrators, or mental health workers. A majority of the killers talked for months in advance about their murderous plans and provided explicit descriptions of who, where, or when they intended to kill.

The provisions of federal guns laws prohibit people who have been involuntary committed to mental institutions from buying a handgun. About 150,000 people a year are involuntarily committed to mental institutions by court orders in the United States, and there are currently 2.7 million people who have been involuntarily committed at some point in their lives to a mental hospital and so should be prohibited from buying a handgun. But laws in most states guard the privacy of the mentally ill, which generally prevents law enforcement agencies from having access to mental-health records. As a result, gun background checks of people with psychiatric problems rarely turn up their mental-health history.

It is also the case, however, that rampage killings increased in recent years. In the period 1976–1989, there were an average of twenty-three per year, and in 1990–1997 the average rose to thirty-four per year. There are certainly many possible explanations, but that shift certainly coincides with the increasing availability of semiautomatic handguns with larger magazines, whose greater lethality makes multiple killings in a matter of seconds much more possible than with a traditional six-shooter. Testimony to the limits of gun control in the United States is the fact that a majority of the rampage killers had obtained their guns legally. For the students in particular, they had to get the guns illegally because they were always under legal age to make the purchase. They could take the gun or guns from home, steal them from a relative or a neighbor, or recruit a straw purchaser who could buy the gun legally for them.

Despite the extremely high visibility they receive in the media when they occur, the rampage killings represent only 0.1 percent of all murders. Unfortunately, however, they are the ones that capture the public's attention and the ones that engender the greatest public fear. This is particularly the case with the various schoolyard shootings, the most notorious of which was the April 1999 massacre at Columbine High School in Littleton, Colorado, near Denver, where two boys killed fifteen people and injured twenty-three.

6. The Counterarguments: More Guns Are Better

One of the continuing debates over the role of guns in the democratic American society is the tension between those who argue that a high prevalence of guns is desirable because their prevalence deters criminals because of the risk that their victim might be armed and those who argue that a high prevalence stimulates an arms race with the greater risk of accidental shooting or preemptive shooting in an uncertain situation. The deterrence argument by the proponents of permissive gun-carrying laws is that if more people could legally carry guns in public spaces, then that would increase the chances that criminal predators would encounter well-armed potential victims. This heightened risk faced by potential attackers will in turn dissuade them from committing violent crimes.

One facet of this argument revolves around "shall issue" laws, which are laws passed by states that require local licensing agencies (usually the local sheriff) to issue a license to carry a concealed firearm to anyone who applies and meets certain minimum requirements, with the burden on the licensing authority to deny such a license. Proponents of such laws invoke the deterrence argument and opponents invoke the arms race argument.

That debate was given a technical cast with an article published in 1997 by Lott and Mustard, which, through an econometric analysis of violence rates by counties in states with "shall carry" laws compared to those with no such laws argued that the passage of "shall issue" laws reduced violent crime rates. That case was expanded a year later with a book by Lott with the provocative title, *More Guns, Less Crime*, in which he presents and interprets data to support his thesis that communities are safer when its residents are free of government restrictions on gun ownership and carrying.

Nagin and Black (1998) reanalyzed the Lott and Mustard data and challenged their conclusions, arguing that the Lott/Mustard findings were sensitive to minor changes in the specification of the model being analyzed. In particular, they showed that of ten states that adopted "shall issue" laws, one had an increase in violent crime, one had a decrease (that might be explained by other trends that were then already under way), and the other eight had no difference. In large part, that absence of a significant deterrent effect could result from the fact that passage of the law did not have a major effect on the carrying of concealed weapons nor on the awareness of the prevalence of these concealed weapons by those who consider committing a violent crime.

Another challenge to the concern about the harmful effects of guns revolves around the estimate of the frequency of acts of "defensive gun use," or the active, overt, and presumably effective use of a gun against an individual threat or potential attacker. To the extent that the frequency of such uses is high, then that would strengthen the argument of those who favor widespread availability of firearms, at least to those not in a prohibited group. Gary Kleck and Mark Gertz (1995) estimate that 2.5 million citizens use guns in self-defense each year in the United States, a rate that is almost one hundred times as large as the estimate that would be derived from the annual victimization surveys, and that exceeds the roughly one million annual number of gun crimes committed. Part of the reason for these considerable discrepancies relate to diverse interpretations of the subtle differences in the form of the question and the difficulty associated with what are inherently very low base rates of defensive gun use and their vulnerability to considerable amplification if a small number of the respondents have a stake in the answer.

III.   ATTEMPTS AT CONTROL OF GUNS

1.   Local Police

Law enforcement agencies responding to the 1998 National Youth Gang survey reported that, while gang activity continued to affect a large number of cities and counties, the number of agencies reporting active youth gangs was declining and the estimated number of gangs and gang members in the United States was also decreasing. The study concluded that more respondents perceived that their gang problem was better in 1998 than in 1997.

The 1998 survey confirmed previous findings that gang members are often involved in a variety of serious and violent crimes. Almost half of the law enforcement agencies reporting gang problems are involved in collaborative efforts with other law enforcement and criminal justice agencies to combat youth gangs and the serious and violent crimes they commit. These efforts often involve community groups. Police efforts often take the form of aggressive stop-and-frisk and intervention and prevention programs aimed at juveniles.

Some of these policing efforts to crack down on juvenile weapon carrying seem to have had dramatic impacts. In Boston, a program targeted at inhibiting gang use of guns eliminated youth gun homicides for almost two years. This project involved sending a clear message to gangs to control their level of violence or else face extremely tight police surveillance and control. It also involved collaboration with other law enforcement agencies like juvenile probation officers to be able to exploit their right to random searches, a right not generally available to police officers because of general Constitutional prohibition against police searches without probable cause.

The Kansas City Weed and Seed program demonstrated the effect of concerted efforts by police to get guns out of the hands of juveniles. Police used every encounter with youth to search for illegal weapons. In a high-risk neighborhood with a homicide rate twenty times the national average, the program reduced crime by more than 50 percent during a six-month period, without displacement to other neighborhoods.

Notable among police efforts to remove guns from juveniles are tactics, which include a mixture of aggressive stop-and-frisk in high-violence neighborhoods, introduction of programs offering a bounty to confidential informants for reports of illegal guns that lead to confiscation, and voluntary searches of homes with suspected illegal weapons. To the extent that gun carrying is reduced, the concern over self protection will also be reduced which will diminish the incentive for others to carry their own guns and contribute to the disarmament that characterized the post-1993 period.

2. Marketing Restrictions by ATF

However successful local police may be in capturing guns, their efforts can be countered by the aggressive trade in guns. The evident frustration of the efforts to control the supply of drugs, even in the face of major assaults on the supply system, has its counterpart in gun control. And the political support for the efforts to control guns is by no means comparable to the support for control of illegal drugs. In many respects, traffic in guns should be easier to control because they have serial numbers that make it much easier to trace them through both the legal and the illegal markets, at least in principle.

Because of long-standing political support for limiting the regulation of gun markets, however, there are a variety of constraints on such controls, and that has resulted in only very limited regulation of gun markets in the United States. The ATF (Bureau of Alcohol, Tobacco and Firearms of the U.S. Treasury Department) is the federal agency that licenses gun dealers and has the responsibility of enforcing laws regarding illegal traffic in firearms. They also have limited authority to impose minimum design and safety standards on domestically manufactured firearms, but no control over imported weapons. Statutory limits on the ATF, however, inhibit the ATF from being very aggressive in their controls. For example, they are limited to one inspection annually of any single licensed dealer. And perhaps most fundamentally, they have virtually no control over secondary markets like those at gun shows or by one individual to another. This makes it particularly difficult to fully enforce sales to the variety of prohibited buyers.

Manufacturers of firearms in the United States are largely exempt from regulation regarding the design and performance of their products. The Consumer Product Safety Commission, which regulates a wide variety of products ranging from pajamas to bicycles, is explicitly prohibited from establishing regulations over firearms or ammunition. Firearms are unique among consumer products in this respect. Until 1994, there were essentially no other restrictions on the design or performance of firearms manufactured in the United States. ATF has only limited authority to oversee commerce in firearms and has no jurisdiction over the design or safety of domestically produced guns.

The Brady Act was the first major recent legislative action intended to empower the federal government to take a more active role in prohibiting access to guns by people deemed as irresponsible, such a people with a previous felony conviction. The Act requires background checks of applicants desiring to purchase a gun from a licensed dealer, including pawnshop transactions that typically involve used guns. The background check is intended to identify individuals who are prohibited by the Brady Act or other legislation from purchasing or possessing firearms for many reasons including if the person is under indictment or has been convicted of a crime, is unlawfully using or addicted to a controlled substance, has been involuntarily committed to a mental institution, or is subject to a court's restraining order, a common device for regulating domestic abuse.

Over 3,000 Federal State and local agencies conduct background checks on persons who apply to purchase a firearm or for a permit that can be used to make a purchase. Each state government determines on its own the extent of involvement in the National Instant Criminal Background Check System (NICS) on all firearms. The Brady Act requires a point of contact (POC) that requests a NICS check on all handgun transfers. If the state does not maintain a local point of contact, the licensed dealers are required to contact the FBI or NICS to ensure the validity of the application and verification of the applicant. However, the minimum check required by the permanent provision of the Brady Act is the FBI's National Instant Criminal Background Check System.

From the inception of the Brady Act on March 1, 1994, to December 31, 1999, twenty-two million applications for firearm purchases have been subject to background checks, and over 500,000 of those applications have been rejected due to violations of the Federal Criminal Code. In 1999, of the eight million applications for firearms 2.4 percent were rejected. And of those rejections, about 73 percent were rejected due to a felony conviction or indictment. This is undoubtedly a result of good and accessible criminal-history records.

In contrast, only 0.5 percent of the rejections were for reasons of mental illness or disability, largely because most states have no central repository of mental-illness records that could be used to disqualify inappropriate persons from purchasing firearms. This results from the greater concern about protecting the privacy of individuals with mental illness than in protecting criminal-history records. Some states have established a repository at the state department of mental health, which can be queried just as the criminal-history repositories are queried. Then, when the inquiry comes to the mental-health repository, a simple yes–no answer is provided without revealing any of the details of the person's mental illness, but sufficient to prevent approval of the firearm purchase.

One of the problems limiting the effectiveness of the background check of firearm purchasers is straw purchasers. Straw purchases take place when the actual buyer uses another person to make a firearm purchase from a licensed dealer without disclosing that information at the time of the purchase. For example, the killers in the Columbine shooting obtained weapons through a straw purchaser because they were under the legal age to purchase weapons.

3. Crime Gun Tracing

One important approach for detecting illicit traffic in guns is through gun tracing, a program that ATF has developed to a considerable degree. When it receives a report from a police department of a confiscated crime gun with its serial number, ATF can then contact the gun manufacturer and follow the trail to the first retail purchase from a licensed dealer. Pursuing transactions beyond that initial purchase is a much more elaborate process that can be pursued in only a limited number of cases. Perhaps more informative at a strategic level is the agreement ATF has established with a number of cities to provide a trace on all the crime guns they capture. This Youth Crime Interdiction Initiative has been particularly useful for its research results. Those results have indicated that most of the crime guns captured from young users were relatively new and were purchased rather than stolen. These findings have emphasized the importance of interdicting the gun trafficking to these young users. These issues are explored more fully by Wintemute (2000) and at the twenty-seven individual cities by ATF (1999).

To try and reduce the number of violent crimes committed with handguns, ATF encourages all law enforcement agencies to submit crime guns for tracing by ATF's National Tracing Center. They analyze and categorize crimes with handguns and provide support to the investigations and arrest of illegal traffickers in firearms. The Youth Gun Crime Enforcement Act has contributed to the implementation of these efforts of tracing crime guns.

Since many crimes are committed with a gun owned by someone else, a variety of technological fixes have been proposed to limit the usability of a gun to the individual owner. Guns could be personalized by means such as a transponder in the gun that permits the gun to work only when the user is wearing a particular ring keyed to the transponder. If this were the case, then the gun's value to a thief would be appreciably reduced. If the personalization device were readily replaced, then theft would still remain an important source of guns to proscribed users. But if the device were costly to re-key or the re-keying process were only accessible through specially authorized dealers then theft of new guns properly personalized would cease to be a problem. But, of course, the personalization technology must be highly reliable in order for the original user to be able to depend on it when he needed it, and the cost must not be so high as to discourage owners from buying guns so equipped.

IV. SUMMARY

Putting guns in the hands of unruly young people who lack skill in their handling and are insensitive or uncaring about their potential for lethality to themselves and to others is a reckless activity. The problem is exacerbated by the power of contemporary handguns with their rapid fire and large magazines. Similar concerns arise about other individuals like convicted felons, domestic abusers, and the mentally deranged who can be defined by statute as comparably irresponsible if they have access to such lethal firepower. The United States has seen the consequences of some of those problems in the late 1980s and 1990s. The effects have been punctuated by the growing number of rampage killings by school children as well as mentally deranged adults. The great majority of other nations have had much more effective gun control, and so have not experienced such problems.

Surveys in the United States reveal strong public support—including substantial majorities among gun owners—for legislation to regulate firearms, to make guns safer, and to reduce the accessibility of firearms to criminals and children. There is also broad agreement that owners should be liable for injuries if a gun is not stored in a way to prevent misuse by children. The general public, as well as gun owners, support government regulation of gun design to improve safety. Even a majority of gun owners and a broader segment of the general public favor mandatory background checks in private handgun sales such as gun shows. The general public strongly supports public places such as stores and theaters being able to prohibit patrons from bringing guns on to the premises.

Nevertheless, there is a strong committed minority of gun owners who look to the NRA as their primary voice, and that community vigorously opposes any form of gun control, which they fear is the start on the "slippery slope" that will lead to confiscation of their guns. The intensity of their determination on this single issue has empowered the NRA to exercise considerable political influence, particularly in places they target, and so have been a major restraint on expanding even reasonable forms of control that would negligibly inconvenience the great majority of legitimate gun owners and purchasers, but could become more effective at keeping guns away from irresponsible people. Such possibilities include background checks at gun shows and limiting gun purchases to one gun per month to inhibit the illicit arms dealer. Until more pervasive approaches are adopted, the United States risks seeing more rampage killings and more lethal violence by youth the next time there is a major new drug market or a major downturn in the economy.

REFERENCES

ATF. February (1999). *Crime Gun Trace Analysis Reports: The Illegal Firearms Market in 27 Communities*. Washington: U.S. Department of the Treasury, Bureau of Alcohol, Tobacco and Firearms.

Blumstein, Alfred. (1995). Youth Violence, Guns and the Illicit-Drug Industry. *Journal of Criminal Law and Criminology, 86,* 10–36.

Blumstein, Alfred, & Daniel Cork. (1996). Linking Gun Availability to Youth Gun Violence. *Law and Contemporary Problems, 59,* 5–24.

Cook, Philip J., & Jens Ludwig. (2000). *Gun Violence: The Real Costs.* Oxford, New York: Oxford University Press.

Cork, Daniel. (1999). Examining Space-Time Interaction in City-Level Homicide Data: Crack Markets and the Diffusion of Guns among Youth. *Journal of Quantitative Criminology, 15*(4), 379–406

Gifford, Lee, Devon B. Adams, Gene Lauver, & Michael Bowling. (2000). *Background Checks for Firearm Transfers, 1999* (pp. 1–3). Bureau of Justice Statistics Bulletin, NCJ 180882, June 2000.

Johnson, Bruce, Andrew Golub, & Eloise Dunlap. (2000). The Rise and Decline of Hard Drugs, Drug Markets, and Violence in Inner-city New York. In Alfred Blumstein & Joel Wallman (Eds.), *The Crime Drop in America* (pp. 164–206). Cambridge, New York: Cambridge University Press.

Kleck, Gary, & Marc Gertz. (1995). Armed Resistance to Crime: The Prevalence and Nature of Self-Defense with a Gun. *Journal of Criminal Law and Criminology, 86*, 150–187.

Lott, John R., & David B. Mustard. (1997). Crime, Deterrence, and Right-to-carry Concealed Handguns. *Journal of Legal Studies, 26*(1), pp. 1–68.

Nagin, Daniel, & Daniel Black. (1998). Do 'Right to Carry' Laws Deter Violent Crime? *Journal of Legal Studies, 27*(1), 209–219.

U.S. Department of Justice, Office of Juvenile Delinquency and Delinquency Prevention. (2000). *1998 National Youth Gang Survey.* Washington: Office of Juvenile Justice and Delinquency Prevention.

Wintemute, Garen. (2000). Guns and Gun Violence. In Alfred Blumstein & Joel Wallman (Eds.), *The Crime Drop in America* (pp. 45–96). Cambridge, New York: Cambridge University Press.

Zawitz, Marianne W., & Kevin J. Strom. (2000). *Firearm Injury and Death from Crime, 1993–97.* Washington: U.S. Department of Justice, Bureau of Justice Statistics, Bulletin NCJ 182993.

Organized Crime and Violence

DICK HOBBS

I. INTRODUCTION

"And every time we got a partner that don't agree with us, we kill him" (John Gotti, in Capeci and Mustain, 1992:27).

The imposition of the will of an individual or group via the utilization of physical force or its threat can be linked in various ways to pecuniary reward, and as a consequence violence and organized crime are natural partners. Certainly in popular culture's numerous fictional renditions of organized criminal activity, violence is often presented as the primary activity of protagonists and is central to the public's insatiable fascination for the version of organized crime established by Hollywood (Warshow, 1948). Yet beyond the morality tales of gunfights and shootouts, the entrepreneurial ethic that underpins and drives modern criminal economies thrives upon variety and diversification (Bauman, 1989, 1992) by generating entrepreneurial engagements clustered around irregular trading relationships (Ruggiero, 1987; Ruggiero & South, 1997). Increasingly these engagements feature innovative networks of small flexible firms staffed by criminals whose lives are prone to chaotic, incoherent interludes (Reuter, 1983), and whose everyday language is festooned with references to violence (Schlegel, 1987).

Despite the fact that much contemporary organized crime relates to "white collar" or "enterprise crime," which apparently stands in pristine isolation from the visceral pursuits of traditional protagonists, academic research suggests a complex social field that indicates an often ambiguous relationship between social order and the brutal chaos resulting from the tension between instrumental motivation and personal action. "Where there were no rules, where cheating, lying, and stealing were accepted, even expected" (Anastasia, 1991:279).

Organized crime constitutes an ever-mutating range of complex phenomena that should be located as a point on the "spectrum of legitimacy" (Smith, 1980). As Kelly

W. Heitmeyer and J. Hagan (eds.), *International Handbook of Violence Research*, 679–699.
© 2003 Kluwer Academic Publishers. Printed in the Netherlands.

(1986) notes, the quest for a precise definition is neither possible nor desirable, certainly in such a brief review as this. However, this paper's working definition will consider forms of enterprise that, via semi-formal institutions or ever-mutating networks of career criminals, seek to make a profit through illicit activities and through the use of threats or force, and maintain a degree of immunity from law enforcement through the corruption of public officials.

In efforts to define the field, reviews of the relevant literature by Hagan (1983), Maltz (1976, 1985), and Albanese (1996) indicate that violence, or the threat of violence are major characteristics of organized crime. Indeed, regardless of the degree of maturity or sophistication enjoyed by an organized crime group, violence will always be regarded as a pragmatic resource (Gambetta, 1993:2), which is never gratuitous, but a last resort when other forms of intimidation prove inadequate (Falcone, 1993:7–9). Such a resource has proved to be highly adaptable for generations of organized criminals in the establishment of organized crime groups, the marketing of violence as a commodity, as a tool to deal with competition, and the resolution of personal disputes within the organized crime community.

II. THEORETICAL APPROACHES AND EMPIRICAL RESULTS

1. Theoretical Observations

The traditional focus for the bulk of academic work on organized crime has been Italy and the United States, and this along with the author's linguistic limitations will assure that this paper will not buck this trend. This concentration allows us to examine the evolution of ancient and modern forms of political and socioeconomic organization, and well-established intellectual traditions in both countries have created a rich vein of historical data in particular, that allow scholars to discern trajectories that are not always apparent from analysis dependant upon governmental or law enforcement sources. However, organized crime is now regarded as a problem of some magnitude in the former Soviet Union (Rawlinson, 1996; Galeotti, 1992; Handelman, 1995), in China (Wong, 1992) Southeast Asia (Sanz & Silverman, 1997) and virtually every region of the world. Further, the contemporary illegal market mirrors its legitimate counterpart in that it is typified by the dialectic between the local and the global (Giddens, 1990:64, 1991:22), and the ensuing environment, within which entrepreneurial personnel engage with the market in a variety of culturally specific forms, is extremely complex. For a growing number of scholars the subsequent threat has been labeled "transnational" (see Godson & Olson, 1993; Labrousse & Wallon, 1993; Williams, 1993; Williams & Savona, 1995; Sterling, 1994; Calvi, 1993).[1] Rogue states, weak states, and fragmented chaotic regions of contested power have all produced renditions of organized crime that are imbued with political intent, and unraveling the political from the criminal can be as pointless as attempting to distinguish between the harnessing of steam power and the onset of the industrial revolution. The point is that violence remains a central prop of these new entrepreneurs. For whether in the absence of a strong and effective state (Lee & MacDonald,

---

[1] For a discussion of some reservations concerning both the term "transnational organized crime" and the database on which it is derived see Hobbs (1998), and Naylor (1995).

1993), or as a means of challenging the state (Godson & Olson, 1993), the opportunistic nature of organized crime, as exemplified for instance by the development of criminal enterprises following the implementation of the Single European Act creating a border free market (Van Duyne, 1996; Owen & Dynes, 1990), will always value the ability to physically intimidate and obliterate.

No matter how sophisticated and market orientated organized crime becomes, and no matter to what cause its profits contribute, the cultural inheritance of traditional visceral practices remain central to the establishment, marketing, regulation, and culture of illegal markets. For the nature of the cultural collateral upon which their criminal entrepreneurship is grounded ensures that violence becomes an obligation accumulated in social networks, an obligation that can be a creative or destructive force; creating identities and reinforcing networks, or destroying temporary working arrangements. Consequently, organized crime personnel "...are obligated to respond to a perceived slight to self, or to family, with the same level of ferocity and commitment as they would to a threat to their commercial viability" (Hobbs, 1995:122).[2]

Hard Men are always vulnerable, for as they "persevere without limitation until they dominate, then they force others to confront the same choice" (Katz, 1988:100). Such confrontations can take place within public, private, familial or commercial domains and may produce outcomes which financially may be either beneficial or calamitous, but the more irrational the level of violence that is utilized, the greater the transcendence of rationality and the more valuable the reputation.[3]

The old certainties and their incumbent codes of conduct, as can be seen below in the discussion of Columbia and modern Italy, have now eroded to the point that there are now few ethical restrictions on using violence against agents of the state. Certainly, the murder of Judge Falcone and his successor are indicators of the willingness of contemporary organized crime groups to engage with state opposition to any continuation or expansion of their profitability. The move to the city and the emergence of the urban gangster with his entrepreneurial eye for market exploitation has enabled violence to be utilized purely for profit rather than some abstract notion of honor (see Richardson, 1992:70–72; Kray, 1991:137–138; Fraser, 1994:147)). This has established that violence is no longer a subordinate element in society, but a central force embedded in dominant socioeconomic structures (Arlacchi, 1986:115). The "Systems of accumulated expertise" (Giddens, 1991:3), that constitute contemporary organized crime, are malleable and not located in fixed terrain (Chaney, 1994:149), as they are manifested as local and global networks of opportunity, featuring the cultural inheritance of traditional criminogenic locales (Arlacchi, 1986:227), as well as the endless transitions of global markets.

As we will see from the following discussion, violence is an essential essence of traditional criminal organization which has successfully transmuted to the contemporary market place, and is a sufficiently flexible resource to be applied to engagements with a multiplicity of new markets, enabling the criminal firm to establish a "protected enclave" (Arlacchi, 1986:195), within and across markets.

---

[2] In April 2000, Kenneth Noye, a highly successful British criminal entrepreneur with a reported fortune of £40 million, was convicted of murder following his stabbing of a man in a road rage incident (Guardian 15/4/2000).

[3] For instance in 1960s London, two murders committed by the Kray twins, although apparently noninstrumental responses to personal affronts (Lambrianou, 1992:7–17; Pearson, 1973:201–252; Kray, 1991:95–97), served to intensify the brothers reputations and enhance their market value.

2. Empirical Analysis

a. THE ESTABLISHMENT OF AN ORGANIZED CRIME GROUP

Mafia. Studies of the genesis of the Sicilian Mafia have unpacked one of the most un-comfortable yet enduring truths concerning the nature of organized crime, namely that comprehension of the phenomena can only be attained by establishing the socioeconomic context of organized crime's parent culture, and in particular its relationship with the state.

Traditional Sicilian society was constructed around a unique set of social arrange-ments. Predominantly feudal, with absentee landlords ruling the land from afar (Blok, 1975), national systems of power emerged without usurping entrenched local systems. As a consequence the state failed to gain a monopoly over the use of force, and gaps in the social order, a theme that will be constantly returned to in this paper, were conspicuous. In the absence of a competent agent of state sanctioned violence, landowners explored an alternative method of consolidating their interests by turning to local "Men of Respect" (Catanzaro, 1992).

"What earned these men 'respect' was, first their capacity to coerce with physical violence and thus invoke fear in others" (Blok, 1975:62). We are introduced here to the notion of violence, or more specifically private violence, as a resource, a notion that will also run like a thread throughout this paper. To understand the cultural and ultimately commercial emergence of these "men of respect," we need to recognize the ideal of mas-culine personality in Sicily (Hess, 1973). Such an ideal was traditionally free from all material necessity and personified power via the exercise of violence. In such an environ-ment, "aggressiveness and violence were positively endorsed" (Arlacchi, 1986:12). Given the impotence of public authorities in Sicily, the Mafia emerged as an "expression of a need for order" (Falcone, 1993:56), which in turn was imposed by "persons who had a reputation for violence and who eschewed recourse to public authorities commanded re-spect (while) others less skilled in the realm of violence turned to them for protection" (Blok, 1975:211).

Such men commanded deference, and the emergent pattern of interdependencies that made up traditional Sicilian society relied heavily upon men skilled in the practice and threat of violence (Ruggiero, 1993:145), with careers kick started by redressing per-sonal wrongs (Blok, 1975:101), who were singled out as leaders of the community. Land-owners bereft of any effective recourse to the monopoly of violence which in orthodox terms is central to state sovereignty (Elias, 1994) turned to "Men of Respect."

The mode of violence imposed in support of the status quo was not the blunt instru-ment of an army of strangers, but was ambiguous, subtle, and most importantly in har-mony with regional culture, "an aberrant version of the traditional Sicilian way of life" (Falcone, 1993:52). The Mafia's ability and willingness to use physical force created a sys-tem of private rural policing heavily reliant upon competent image management based upon clothing style, the public display of weapons and, "…the opaque ambiguity of phrases, ges-tures and mimic signs …that set them apart from ordinary people" (Blok, 1975:61). Vio-lence functioned to keep restive peasants in submission, and created opportunities for upwardly mobile entrepreneurs of violence, and was therefore essentially conservative in its use as a mechanism of social and economic control (Falcone, 1993:62–65; Ruggiero, 1993).

The overt nature of traditional Mafia power is based upon violence, and when vio-lent reputation was established, a brokerage of power could be instituted which was both congruent with local cultural precedent and functional to the needs of a state whose ability to utilize violence was limited on the island of Sicily. In many ways the Mafia became the armed wing of the state, buttressing the dominant economic system through the use of private violence (Catanzaro, 1992). However, the hiring of men with violent reputations to protect property tells only part of the story, for in the absence of any state regulation, the locally phrased power domains that such a practice creates also become markets for extortion. Nonexistent threats to property and livestock were created, and if ignored the threat would become reality (Catanzaro, 1992:21–23; Blok, 1975:151), and noninterference pacts with other Mafiosi, created a monopoly of violence and a form of social order that could not be guaranteed by the state. By mediating between local culture and national interests as expressed through the institutional order of the nation state, the emergent entrepreneur of violence colonized the space that is urgently sought out by all organized crime groups, that interstitial space that is created by the overlapping of territory, culture, and the market.

From this monopoly of violence, and the power they wielded over the peasant population, the Mafia was also able to broker electoral support. Their management of estates enabled the extraction of profit from peasant and landowner alike and created an environment where the commercialization of traditional respect rooted in violence became a vehicle for wealth accumulation, as "Men of Respect" dominated swathes of countryside incorporating several estates. Again it is important to stress that such activity was not contrary to the mores of a society that valued violence as a resource available to all, and accepted that highly competent practitioners should be rewarded (Catanzaro, 1992:31).

In Sicily the end of feudalism did not radically alter social relationships during the nineteenth century, and land remained the primary source of power. Although it created new bourgeois landowners, peasants lost many of their traditional rights as the population expanded and competition for land was heightened. Partial and ineffective legislation by the state to make all violence illegal merely blurred further the distinction between licit and illicit violence and, "ironically enough, the public violence of the state was more likely to be considered illegitimate than the private violence of the landlords, new and old" (Catanzaro, 1992:69). While the state remained weak, unable to enforce the distinction between private and state violence, the market for violence broadened (Catanzaro, 1992:68), resulting in Mafiosi increasingly utilizing violence on their own behalf.

Mafiosi became central to a lawless class forged in violence who conspired with the remote central government to impose a system of civil administration, which included policing and criminal justice, and were dominated by the long established and recently reinforced exigencies of the local political environment. As Catanzaro expertly explains, "The conquest of autonomy on the part of the violence industry and the delegation of authority to the dominant local class constituted the preconditions for the failed affirmation of the state's monopoly of violence in Sicily—and thus the essential circumstances for the social affirmation of the Mafia" (Catanzaro, 1992:70).

Pirates.   Indeed, organized criminal violence has also been used by the state to promote its own interests and as Browning and Gerrassi (1980) have indicated both the establishment and the maintenance of British colonies was, in Elizabethan times, the prerogative of state-sponsored piracy. Unable to maintain a sufficiently powerful naval presence so far from Britain, privateers were commissioned to "attack, burn, loot, and otherwise decimate Spain's military and commercial ships" (Browning & Gerrassi, 1980:54). The fact that the privateer and his crew were paid in plunder led to a certain ambiguity regarding the use of private violence in the name of state interest, and "...pirates were highly organized, continuing, willing to use violence and, in time, absent an ideology beyond self gratification and wealth" (Kenney & Finckenauer, 1995:58).

This era of violent plunder on behalf of the state (Sherry, 1986), and the use of force to by-pass British constraints upon colonial trade (Browning & Gerrassi, 1980:ch. 4), marked a prelude to the emergence of a formal commercial culture that regarded piracy as a threat to the comportment of legitimate trade, but not before it had formed corrupt alliances with government officials (Rankin, 1969). By the second decade of the eighteenth century, orthodox patterns of trade became formalized, and America emerged as an exporting economy in its own right, leading to the withdrawal of the supporting structures, havens, and markets upon which piracy depended (Karraker, 1953). However, it is important to stress that as in the case of the Sicilian Mafia, the state's use of illegal private violence manufactured an ambiguity that was beneficial to the development of organized crime, and served to reinforce the inherent functionality of violence as a resource within arenas geographically remote from the violent monopoly of the state.

Frontier Business. The ambiguity that is apparent when the state allows organized crime to utilize violence on its behalf until it has the physical and ideological resources to gain a monopoly over the utility of violence, or at least to mount a challenge, can also be located in other arenas. Violence served a similar function amongst fledgling capitalists in nineteenth-century America, and a familiar pattern of market exploitation, violence, incorporation and institutional legitimation had succeeded in repeating itself many times over during the exploration of natural resources and subsequent establishment of the industrial and commercial empires upon which modern America was founded (Tyler, 1962:44–45). Indeed in the American West violent criminals were harnessed by the "conservative, consolidating authority of capital" (Brown, 1991:40) to exploit the absence of the rule of law to incorporate the frontier and its vast natural resources "into an America dominated by new forms of commerce, industry and finance" (Brown, 1991:56). Subsequently the fortunes of the Astors (Myers, 1937; Loth, 1938), the Vanderbilts (Andrews, 1941; Loth, 1938), the Rockefellers (Lloyd, 1963), Henry Ford (Sinclair, 1962), and other seminal figures of American capitalism were established via dubious practices and outright criminality (see Block & Chambliss, 1981; Abadinsky, 1993:59–74). As Bell points out, "The pioneers of American capitalism were not graduated from Harvard's School of Business Administration. The early settlers and founding fathers, as well as those who 'won the west' and built up cattle, mining and other fortunes, often did so by shady speculations and not an inconsiderable amount of violence" (Bell, 1953:152).

b. THE MARKETING OF VIOLENCE AS A COMMODITY

Extortion. As organized crime evolved in relation to the state, its core practices matured, and as we can see from the section above, extortion, or trust (Gambetta, 1988), becomes an increasingly vital intersectional sphere through which violence is commodified. Further, in realms where trust is fragile, violence is a valued attribute that is utilized to ensure that transactions are completed. Although the State contested the emergent urban gangster's monopoly of physical violence (Arlacchi, 1986:65), the replacement of honor, with power and conspicuous consumption as an ideal, ensured that violence remained at the core of organized crime as a means of establishing a sheltered territory. Within this territory the complex patterns of protection and extortion that had dominated the rural milieu could be replicated. As Block with characteristic insight explains, "Out of the maw of competitive capitalism and possessive individualism marched the extortionists—the entrepreneurs of violence whose function was to mediate this state of greed while they skimmed as much as they could for themselves" (Block, 1983:239).

Illegal enterprises are unable to turn to state agencies for protection (Reuter, 1983), and organized criminals emerge as entrepreneurs of trust via the threat and utility of violence. Schelling (1984), who regards the practice as central to organized crime, discusses the delicate balance between protection and extortion. For Schelling, the illegal trader must "…pay to stay in business" (Schelling, 1984:185), but the protection on offer is only against other extortionists that seek to gain a monopoly over the protection of illegal business (Buchanan, 1973). Consequently the protection is somewhat bogus, based upon a perception of the extortioner as more violent than his rivals in the securing of trust. Indeed "…one of the structural …features of protection is the toughness of the supplier, then it is part of the logic of the commodity itself to invite toughness comparisons …a Mafioso who hits harder can be expected to be a far more reliable protector. The most credible proof he can offer, in fact, consists in eliminating his competitors altogether" (Gambetta, 1988:140).

As Falcone indicates (1993:116), extortion is a highly effective vehicle for consolidating control over territory, for territorial monopoly parallels success in the protection market in a way that is not apparent in commodity markets, either legal or illegal (Behan, 1996:110–112). While the majority of commodities are traded in terms of continuous, if negotiated, quantities and prices, protection is contingent upon violence, which as Gambetta points out is a "dichotomous variable, i.e., if not you then me" (1988:141). Violence not price is the key, and the more visceral level of competence will attract the entire market within a given territory. "He who beats hardest not only does away with the beaten competitors, but advertises himself as an adequate protector" (Gambetta, 1988:140).

The establishment of the role of protector/extortionist relies upon the provider of security being more violent than his clients, and this is crucial in the case of criminal clients who may also be prone to violence. However, the establishment of extortionate relations is not confined to illegal business and particularly in those enterprises situated alongside businesses based on vice, extortion is often accepted as an informal tax. Indeed the careers of many notable organized crime figures were initially propelled by their successful involvement in extorting money from bars and clubs (Pearson, 1973). Such businesses are so closely related both territorially and culturally to pornography, prostitution, and drugs that the threat of violence and competition between entrepreneurs of violence has become a common feature of both legal and illegal enterprises in the night-time economy. Recent research in Britain (Hobbs & Hall, 2000) confirms that the use or threat of violence to extort is not restricted to illegal markets, and that the boom in the night-time economy has produced a requirement for security that cannot be supplied by the state. In this research even those establishments not linked to the drug trade but will have legitimate security concerns that are not being met by the state police find themselves leaning heavily upon the services of security firms whose primary resource is violence and intimidation, often with links to organized crime (O'Mahoney, 1997).

Labor and Management. The establishment of violence as a resource in the conflictual zone of labor and management disputes illustrates the way in which violent action creates an entrée for organized crime groups into the legitimate political economy. Conflictual relations between labor and capital created a market for violence, and organized crime groups consisting of men with well established violent reputations were perfectly placed to exploit this market (Moldea, 1978; Brooks, 1971; Neff, 1989). "As labor padrones to organize construction gangs, or as strikebreakers during the years of nascent unionism, or as general mediators between labor and industry, criminals took advantage of their reputation for violence and insinuated themselves into strategic roles within the constant of labor and management strife" (Block, 1994:51).

By controlling unions via violence, criminals held down wages and were paid off by employers (Potter & Jenkins, 1985; Block & Chambliss, 1981). Similarly, employers used organized criminals as "labor disciplinarians" (Block, 1983:195) who utilized violence to suppress efforts by workers to unionize, and their violence was bought to break strikes and protect blackleg (strikebreaking) labor (Pearce, 1976). Indeed, as these violent strikebreakers were recruited from the same working class communities as the legitimate work force, and the gangs that supplied violent labor were also involved in the corruption of politicians who in turn were allied to the police, a powerful urban coalition of organized crime, business, politicians, and police based upon violence was formed (Block, 1983:163–199).[4]

The use of violence to infiltrate unions can be regarded as functional to the smooth running of a business enterprise (Bell, 1965), but as Block and Chambliss (1979) clearly show, such a view distorts the context within which so called "labor racketeering" operates. For it was the challenge posed to business by organized labor and its ideological foundations that created the market for violence and the emergence of the subsequent alliance of the forces of capital and "those in the labor movement who employed illegal and violent means to circumvent the demands of workers" (Block & Chambliss, 1979:26). Consequently, organized crime was afforded access to the money accumulated by member's fees, and they were also able to extort employers by using intimidation over union members to threaten strikes. Further, the pension and welfare funds of union members were plundered by organized crime, providing capital for both criminal and non criminal enterprise (Block, 1991:part three; Quinney, 1975:145; Moldea, 1978:263–264; Neff, 1989).

By using violence or the threat of violence to strategically position itself between employer and employee, organized crime can dictate contract protocols and police illegal trade agreements designed to restrict competition. As Reuter et al. (1983) indicate, such activity may not involve actual violence, but "it seems reasonable to infer that the racketeers provide a credible continuing threat of violence that ensures compliance ..."(Reuter et al., 1983:11). While the reality and threat of violence remains a constant, mutations of legitimate business practice in the form of both competition and labor rigging are enabled before the circle is completed by organized crime's penetration of legal trade and commerce (Anderson, 1979; Moore, 1987; Reuter, 1987), which in turn can manufacture further illegal business opportunities which are policed by the threat of violence (Kwitny, 1979; Block & Scarpitti, 1985). Further, legitimate businesses may use organized crime connections to gain advantage in the market place (Falcone, 1993:78–81), and although actual violence exacted against legitimate businessmen is rare, "The organized crime families reputation for ruthless violence guaranteed that individuals and firms would yield to their demands" (Jacobs, 1999:118).

Such reputations constitute economic power, and enable organized crime to dominate tendering processes (Gambetta, 1993:214–220; Falcone, 1993:133–134), discourage competition, hold down wages, afford access to financial resources (Arlacchi, 1986:91–92), and imbue the criminal entrepreneur with an eternal essence of malevolent potential

---

[4] In an attempt to fight fire with fire, unions would often actively seek alliances with organized crime to resist the violence of employers, to assist in disputes with other unions, or to impose discipline within their own organization (Brill, 1978; Friedman & Schwartz, 1989; Moldea, 1978).

that informs the way that he is received in the realms of both licit and illicit enterprise. Consequently, violence can be seen to impact upon the entire "spectrum of enterprise" (Smith, 1980; Reuter, 1983), a view that underlines the role of violence in assisting us to question the prurient assumption that crime and business are distinct categories of human endeavor.[5] However, as Arlacchi notes, when two entrepreneurial criminal firms who both enjoy the competitive advantages discussed above find themselves in direct competition, coercive power can be the only deciding factor (1986:157).

Commodification. When extreme violence is commodified, its role loses the instrumental ambiguity so prevalent in extortionate relationships. Whether they operate within a criminal organization, or in a milieu composed of ad hoc groupings within an irregular economy featuring various forms of criminal activity, the ultimate commodification of violence can be found by examining the activities of individuals and groups who market murder. As we have seen above, markets are often established by violence, and commercial murder offers an ultimate form of regulation within markets that are impenetrable to normative forms of conflict resolution. Levi's study (1981) of professional killing is concerned with commercial murder, and in particular the neutralization via "re-framing" of killing as a commercial transaction. Professional killers establish a rarefied niche within the criminal labor market: by reframing the victim as a target and receiving remuneration on completion of his task, the professional murderer avoids self-stigmatization, and enhances the status of murderer to that of a supremely rational market operative. The hit man commercializes an impersonal level of violence by commodifying death, allowing us to see clearly how in illegal economies violence replaces the bureaucracy of normative capitalist market economies as it is "discharged precisely, unambiguously, continuously, and with as much speed as possible" (Weber, 1948:215).

c. CHARACTERISTICS

Rationality. However, at this juncture some caution should be shown in an overemphasis on rationality which expresses the milieu of organized crime as the flip side of legitimate business, with a structure, organization, and most importantly division of labor that are mirror images of the legitimate business world. For as Chambliss points out, "...the law enforcement system maximizes its visible effectiveness by creating and supporting a shadow government that manages the rackets" (1978:92). Further, this notion is a constant theme amongst traditional criminal justice renditions of organized crime.

Certainly, violence is a central prop in the various myths that are constructed around organized crime. For instance, in 1963 organized crime informant Joseph Valachi described a bloody feud that had erupted within America's organized criminal community in 1931. According to what has become the orthodox version of organized crime's evolution, the Castellammarese War resulted in up to sixty deaths and succeeded in bonding together previously competing crime groups to create the "new" Mafia in the form of national criminal conspiracy (Cressey, 1967; Turkus & Feder, 1951; Maas, 1968). However, despite the fact that the very existence of the Castellammarese War has since been dismissed (Block, 1978, 1983:ch 1; Inciardi et al., 1977:100), Valachi's operatic rendition of violent

---

[5] Chapter VII of Landesco's classic study of organized crime in Chicago affords a refreshingly detailed rendition of the extent to which "The gunman and gangster are, at the present time, actually in control of the destinies of over ninety necessary economic activities" (1929:167).

competition in an alien underworld (Hawkins, 1969; Block, 1978, 1983) has since matured into the foundation block of organized crime conspiracy theories and, "... the great majority of published books, articles and news items that have attempted to describe the structure of organized crime in America clearly reveal a heavy reliance on Valachi ... Not infrequently it would appear, he either withheld facts that should have been known to him or deliberately lied" (Peterson, 1983:425; cf. Potter, 1994:31–34).

The academic impact of Valachi's testimony is most clearly evident in the work of Donald Cressey, a member of the 1967 Presidential Task Force. Cressey described a formal Italian/American bureaucratic hierarchy of crime that closely resembled legitimate corporate enterprise. Cressey regarded the Castellammarese War as a defining episode for organized crime, and his evidence is heavily reliant upon Valachi's statement (Cressey, 1969:ch 3). Cressey, in making parallels with legitimate business, stressed the division of labor in organized crime groups, and emphasized the importance of violence by concentrating upon the role of the Enforcer. Cressey was extremely vague in his analysis of this role. For instance, the Enforcer is responsible for dispensing violence to members of the organized crime group, and "occasionally, non members" (1969:165). Cressey also covered all his bets by insisting that this role "is more often unoccupied than occupied ... (the member of an organized crime group) might occupy it for a few days and then never occupy it again. On the other hand he might so efficiently fulfill the rights and duties of the position that he becomes a specialist in fulfilling them" (Cressey, 1969:165). Cressey situates the Enforcer as a functionary of the group above the executioner, who carries out the Enforcers orders, and below the boss, underboss or commissioner from who he takes orders. Cressey's use of the Enforcer role, and therefore his highly influential assumptions concerning the role of violence within organized crime, serve as "evidence of the presence of complementary governmental positions, leading to our conclusion that Cosa Nostra is a government as well as a business" (Cressey, 1969:166). Further, as governments are responsible for the creation and implementation of laws, the existence of the Enforcer role further adds to the impression of a functional, if criminal equivalent of civil society, as punishments are dispensed "justly," and for the good of the organization (Cressey, 1969:166–167).

This use of violence to frame arguments concerning hierarchical bureaucracy, and totalitarian discipline, like so much journalistic, criminal justice and academic commentary on organized crime, is not backed up by empirical evidence. "Reliance on unsubstantiated accounts and the lawman's ideological preconceptions has mired the study of organized crime in the bog of conspiracy, allowing the term itself to be carelessly transformed to stand for the monolithic organization of criminals" (Block, 1978, 1994:15).[6]

Cressey's reading of organized crime, and in particular the division of labor and the function of violence as exemplified by the role of the enforcer (Block, 1994:164–167), bears close comparison with the work of Turkus and Feder (1951), the former being the Assistant District Attorney at the time of the "Murder Inc." investigation. Murder Inc. provided a model for the purely rational dispensation of violence within the organized

---

[6]Cressey's work is based largely upon myth (Morris & Hawkins, 1970; Smith, 1975). His interpretation of enforcement based evidence, and in particular of evidence emanating from the rather crude surveillance technology, assumes a high degree of efficiency (Anderson, 1979:33), that reflects all too easily the perceptions of police managers. This is despite being contradicted by the majority of empirical studies that emphasize flexibility and adaptation (Lupsha, 1981), manifold associations driven by acquisitive motives (Albini, 1971:288), interethnic cooperation (Block, 1983:ch. 2), and a nonmonopolistic, essentially fragmented market place (Reuter, 1983; Reuter & Rubinstein, 1978; Hobbs, 1997).

crime community. According to Turkus and Feder a group of New York gangsters emerged as enforcers responding to the chain of command established by a National Crime Syndicate. Apparently murder became a business, "contracts" were taken out nationwide on over eighty people as the "boys from Brooklyn" operated as staff killers on a retainer to the "organization." However, close analysis by Block (1983) paints a rather more complex picture than one inspired by the unimaginative rigors of routine commercial practice. The Murder Inc. case was based yet again upon an informant, Abe Reles, who does not talk about organization, but cooperation. Turkus and Feder are concerned with a smooth chain of command while actually Reles talks of favors, and when Reles focused upon the geographical mobility of criminals, Turkus and Feder chose to interpret this as proof of a national organization. Most importantly for the purposes of this paper however, the use of the term "contract" was taken as direct proof of murder being "real business conducted in the interests of the National Crime Syndicate and carried out by a special group of enforcers" (Block, 1978, 1994:13).

Blocks compelling analysis (1983:ch. 8) contests this naïve reading of organized crime, and succeeds in showing that the spate of killings referred to by Turkus and Feder were carried out by members of three allied crime groups who murdered as part of their extortionate activities. They were not gangland Enforcers but gangsters using violence to deal with informants or other competitive elements within the serious crime community.[7] "Murder was the only way everybody stayed in line. It was the ultimate weapon. Nobody was immune. You got out of line you got whacked" (Pileggi, 1987:128). Further, "…most of the information concerning informants was relayed …by the actual killers themselves …The executioners tended to monopolize the information process. How many personal scores were settled through deliberately false or wrong information can only be imagined" (Block, 1983:230). Indeed the culture within crime networks is essentially disorganized, dominated by paranoia and fear of both internal and external dangers, for, "… the threat of chaos is ubiquitous in the life of illicit action …" (Katz, 1988:230).[8]

The danger of presenting violence in organized crime as purely rational, regulating an alternative government (cf. Furstenburg, 1969[9]) constituted by a national syndicate, is that such a view focuses upon structure, hierarchy and above all organization itself. Consequently it ignores the specific activities and enterprises that lie at the core of what is usually meant by organized crime. Most importantly however, it encourages us to remain ignorant of the intricate social relations that make up the ever-mutating networks of serious criminality. When these webs of relationships are untangled, violence acquires distinctly personal as opposed to bureaucratic qualities.

[7] For an example of violence being used against informants who were competitors, see Pileggi (1987:129–130)

[8] For an interesting example of murders being committed against potential informants or witnesses, which also served to enhance the murderers wealth, see Pileggi's account of the aftermath of the Lufthansa robbery (1987:196–273).

[9] Furstenburg's report, part of the Staff Report presented to the National Commission on the Causes and Prevention of Violence is an extremely loose and at times careless piece of work. Furstenburg makes all the same mistakes as Cressey, but without his eloquent ability to convince. The early part of the report stresses a decline in the number of organized crime linked murders in Chicago as the century progresses. The figures are unreliable, the time scales incomparable, and the author is unable to consider "gangland" killings in the light of general trends in homicide. A vacuous case for a perceived decline in murder being linked to an increased rationality in organized crime follows, and the author follows this up with some contradictory comments about the development of La Cosa Nostra's governmental function, and more evidence-free comments regarding ethnic succession.

Competition. Within the multiplicity of illegal enterprises that constitute the real activity of what is commonly called organized crime, competition is a constant threat. Whether internally from colleagues or employees, externally from other criminal entrepreneurs or from law enforcement, the markets with which organized crime engages are rife with competitive potential, and violence is a constant feature of this competitive environment (Gambetta, 1993:40).

Prohibition. It is doubtful that any illegal market has impacted on the normative political economy like the alcohol market that emerged as a response to prohibition, which lasted from 1920 to 1933 and was a turning point in American crime.[10] This unpopular law which prohibited the manufacture, transportation, sale, and importation of intoxicating liquor generated enormous profits. It offered opportunities for a range of entrepreneurs "to establish a series of connections by which money and cunning were combined with an underpinning of violence to produce regular profit" (Lacey, 1991:53), and the meteoric rise of these "mobile marauders in the urban landscape alert to institutional weaknesses in both legitimate and illegitimate spheres" (Block, 1983:245; see also Haller, 1985:130–141), enabled the rise of individuals who were to become household names and symbols of twentieth-century American criminal entrepreneurship.

Having evolved from violent youthful street gangs, they forged powerful reputations as predatory violent adults. "Violence was natural to them. It fuelled them …It was routine. A familiar exercise. Their eagerness to attack and the fact that people were aware of their strutting brutality were the key to their power" (Pileggi, 1987:43). They live in a "… shifting, changing, bickering, competitive, murderous social world ..." (Block, 1994:13), and within such an environment violence becomes a "cultural expectation" (Wolfgang, 1959). Indeed, it "runs like a bright thread through the fabric of life" (Sykes, 1958:102). The prohibition gangsters' utility of a traditional masculine strategy such as violence within the arena of the market is, as I will later indicate, also a feature of the contemporary market place and suggests a robust perpetuation within the inherited identities of many criminal entrepreneurs.

As Daly and Wilson have indicated, "… a man's reputation depends in part upon the maintenance of a credible threat of violence" (1988:128), and organized crime personnel are "obligated to engage in combat, for their respective locations within the market place are heavily reliant upon their reputations as fighters" (Hobbs, 1995:122). This marketable threat was made very real indeed during the years before the Volstead Act was repealed, as violence was utilized as a major competitive strategy (Woodiwiss, 1993:23–25).

Landesco details 215 gangsters killed in a four-year "Beer War" in Chicago and locates the commencement of hostilities as the breakdown of a monopoly established by one crime group, a breakdown caused by a Police campaign triggered by a new political regime (Landesco, 1929:97–105). Similarly in New York a study of 242 murders committed by professional criminals during the period 1930–1949 found that the years associated with bootlegging were the most violent. Further, the occupational data on the murder victims show a high proportion with legal jobs in trades penetrated by organized crime such as transportation, and analysis of victims' illegal employment indicates that racketeering (which includes extortion) and bootlegging were exceedingly risky enterprises. Not surprisingly bootlegging as a victim category is not featured after 1933 (Block, 1983:204–215). Blocks data confirms that most (75 percent) of organized crime victims are

---

[10] For a comprehensive review of the politics of prohibition and its repeal, see Kyvig, 1979.

professional criminals, and most importantly that competition is the motive for most of the murders committed within the serious crime community.

Drugs. The vast profits generated by the drugs trade has placed a premium upon successful methodologies to deal with competitive elements. "Thus from top to bottom many drug distribution systems appear to be built, sustained, and maintained by violence or the threat of violence" (Martin & Romano, 1992:63). Violence is a feature of drug markets at both street (Williams, 1989) and wholesale levels (Thompson, 2000), and as in the case of prohibition, violence is the primary resource upon which the entire arsenal of organized crimes instrumental devices relies.

Economic competition between Columbia's Medellin and Cali cartels during the 1980s was triggered by a period of overproduction of cocaine and subsequent fall in price, and hundreds died in the bombings and shootings that followed (Lee, 1991). However, when the state and its antidrug policies were seen as the main rivals, the carnage far outstripped this. In 1989 the then dominant Medellin cartel murdered sixty-three people when it planted a bomb at the Colombian Department of Administrative Security. The Medellin cartel also murdered over thirty judges, a minister of justice, several supreme court judges, the leading candidate for the presidency, and thousands of police officers in what was a concerted effort to resist the states efforts to interfere with the cartels competitive viability (Lee, 1991). Unlike the prohibition era in the United States, in the "narcodemocracy" (Kerry, 1997) of Columbia, the extremes of violence perpetrated by the Medellin cartel were utilized to oppose and compete with legitimate government, while their counterparts in Cali were generally reluctant to use violence as a means of confronting the government (Labrousse, 1994).

d. VIOLENT PERSONAL BUSINESS. Distinguishing, as some scholars have attempted, between the various functions of violence within organized crime is an attractive method of breaking down and labeling action that is not well documented, and so vulnerable to populist clichés. Smith is one scholar who has attempted to distinguish between the different functions of violence in organized crime, by differentiating between "maintenance of internal discipline; enforcement of market conditions; and control of competition" (Smith, 1971:17). However, once actual data is made available, it is difficult to avoid the conclusion that competition holds the key. For the enacted environment of organized crime is a social as well as economic system and is grounded in a competitive ethos that dominates business and personal lives.

The notion of violence being utilized to impose internal discipline is derived largely from Cressey's theory of organized crime as an alternative government, whose strict division of labor designates an Enforcer to impose the "functional equivalent of the criminal law" (Cressey, 1969:166). However, organized crime, however we deem to define it, is not government but a business which above all else must remain competitive, and violence is used to maintain that competitiveness rather than enforce abstract laws or codes of "the fabulous underworld of bourgeois invention" (Benney, 1981 [1936]:263). The very idea of an alternative government staffed by remnants from *The Godfather* stems from "The underworld fantasy (which) is constituted by the incessant recurrence of sacred myths related to traditional strategies and iconic individuals, and functions to preserve a highly significant illusion of the perpetuation of an expert system" (Hobbs, 1997).

The entrepreneurial, flexible, and ever-mutating nature of contemporary organized crimes does not constitute a government. Even in their most visible and traditionally hierarchical and historically cohesive form (O'Brien & Kurins, 1991; Cummings & Volkman, 1992) their enacted environment is that of relatively modest cooperative enterprises operating from project to project within an enabling network of cohorts, front men and background operators (Reuter, 1983; Pileggi, 1987). Criminal enterprises do not generally indulge themselves by performing violence on behalf of abstract principles. They are essentially practical, concerned with profit and retaining commercial viability by reacting forcefully to any threat to their competitiveness.

Yet this concern with competitiveness also applies to interactions within the social system. For example in examining the nineteen murders associated with Sammy Gravano of the Gambino Crime Family, it is futile to distinguish the business from the personal. What these killings all have in common however is that the victims were perceived as posing a competitive threat either to the entrepreneurial well-being of the group, or to the overwhelming violent identity of group members. Consequently an individual could be killed because it was perceived that he was placing his personal interests above the interests of the group, or that a member was disenchanted with the group to the extent that he may prove to be direct competition (Maas, 1998). Such examples are not that dissimilar from the killing of law enforcement personnel who are a direct threat (Falcone, 1993:146–152), the murder of a colleague who has become unreliable (Pearson, 1973:212–221), the shooting of a competitor (Williams, 1989:119–120), or the killing of an individual who has made slight or insult (Pileggi, 1987:130–134). Therefore, "systemic violence" (Goldstein, 1985) is inextricable from the disordered fragmented milieu within which illegal markets are situated, "…which tends to transform impersonal market confrontations into personal antagonisms" (Arlacchi, 1986:157; see also Barnes et al., 2000:130–144; Bourgois, 1995; Thompson, 2000:43–50, 52–57).

As Block has noted, "Feuds and vendettas are endemic" (1994:33) within the serious crime community, and it is inappropriate to attribute economic rationality to all of their violent activities. Falcone points this out in his comments on the Mafia "war" of the 1980s. Although this conflict which cost hundreds of lives appears to have been a rational, and very modern dispute centering upon the apportioning of market share, Falcone's informants made it quite clear that the war was as much about ancient territorial and family feuds as it was drug trafficking (Falcone, 1993:97–98; Shawcross & Young, 1987:129–151). It is wrong therefore to disconnect and isolate personal and occupational identities, for it is a combination of both that informs the mayhem of most illegal markets. Within the enacted environment of organized crime, there are individuals who are remarkable amongst their peers for their commitment to violence, a commitment that is not bounded by legal or cultural convention, or restrained by commercial instrumentality. Commercial instrumentality can however manifest itself as a by-product of extreme violence. For the ability of professional criminals to transcend the rationality that is often afforded to violent criminal entrepreneurship[11] can, if utilized indiscriminately, compose an environment of confusion and disorder that negates the notion that organized crime is an altogether rational commercial activity that can be comprehended as a distorted reflection of normative business.

It is crucial, therefore, to comprehend the origins of organized crime personnel, and the way in which practitioners of violence are able to transform the quest for honor, outlined earlier in this paper, to a quest to establish some kind of cultural authority which in

---

[11] For a discussion of noninstrumental violence, see Katz (1988:181–185).

turn may be marketable. Within the organized crime community, violence is the familiar method by which cultural authority is established, and as Bauman indicates: "Cultural authorities turn themselves into market forces, become commodities, compete with other commodities, legitimize their value through the selling capacity they attain" (Bauman, 1992:452). The essence of their marketability rests with their willingness to embrace those confrontational options derived from a common cultural inheritance forged by a traditional schooling in rough places (Foreman, 1996:1–26), which in turn serve to propagate the very antithesis of those normative daily strategies that feature the avoidance of conflict (Hobbs, 1995:51).[12]

III.   DESIDERATA

Organized crime is a difficult subject to research contemporaneously, and organized crime personnel have little to gain from opening doors to inquisitive researchers. Yet there is a real need for academics to find ways of engaging with the organized crime community, for overreliance upon law enforcement data is an inevitably flawed methodology. The policing of organized crime is an issue that has witnessed the selective presentation of police work as organized, structured, and effective, and to this end law enforcement agencies need to confirm their assumptions and seek out criminal hierarchies that mirror the organizational hierarchies of policing (Reuter, 1986). As Chambliss points out "... the law enforcement system maximizes its visible effectiveness by creating and supporting a shadow government that manages the rackets" (1978:92). Consequently overreliance upon law enforcement sources can present day-to-day interactions between offenders as overstructured and devoid of any relationality. As a result, organized criminal violence is often presented as a purely functional resource of an enterprise that is little more than "business by other means."

What Block calls the "serious crime community" (1991) is a hidden population par excellence, and as a consequence is an ideal arena for ethnographers, particularly when the researcher possesses a biography which in some way affords them special access (Adler, 1985). Yet even for these privileged few, the field is a dangerous place. Violent action lies at the core of many of these worlds and violence may be used against ethnographers (Sanchez-Jankowski, 1991; Jacobs, 1998). Indeed, Ken Pryce, the author of a groundbreaking ethnography of Caribbean hustling culture (1979), was murdered when he turned his attentions to organized crime. Requiring researchers to enter violent environments should not be taken lightly.

However, even within the limitations of law enforcement generated data some innovation is possible. For instance studies of the weaponry available to the serious crime community, how it is used, when it is used, and the sources of supply is possible from

---

[12] This is particularly apparent when considering the early careers of prominent criminals, while they are seeking to establish themselves in organized crime, as Gravanno explains in recounting his first murder, "...this was my stepping stone in the mob ... after the hit, I would go to a disco or a club ... the owner was saying 'Hey, Sammy ... Come on in ... Sit Sammy there. Sammy what'll you have? It's on the house' ... So I wasn't waiting on lines no more. I wasn't just another tough guy on the street. I was getting a different kind of respect" (Maas, 1998:53. See also Capeci & Mustain, 1992). And indeed a different kind of business opportunity, as Gravanno went on to establish himself in a wide range of legitimate and illegitimate businesses, particularly in various aspects of the construction industry. For a discussion of organized crime's role in the construction industry see Jacobs (1999:96–115).

police and forensic sources and would generate vital data concerning some basic questions of "how," "where," "when," and "why." Further, the current interest in utilizing network analysis in organized crime studies (Sparrow, 1991) has opened up the possibility of considering the role of violence, coercion, and intimidation within less structured and formal parameters than was previously the case, and may cast some light upon activity that currently comes to light only via rumor and innuendo, bar room gossip, and highly censored media reports.

Most importantly however, the ever-mutating nature of organized crime demands that we should be constantly engaged in a process of re-evaluation of the multifunctional nature of violence in a market place that is increasingly globalized. Such a process will emphasize the multiplicity of trade-associated local systems and their indigenous forms of control, regulation and market contestation. This ongoing analysis of organized criminal violence should seek to embrace the complexity of "local contextualities" (Giddens, 1991:22), for while the essential relationality and connectedness of contemporary organized crime is necessitated by the existence of trading relationships that are indeed global (Harvey, 1989), this should not stress either a local/global-action/reaction polarity, or a spurious cultural homogeneity that prevails over difference. Local crime systems will exploit local markets which in turn will link with other related markets, and we need to examine violence as local and highly distinctive expressions of power and control, as well as a culturally specific expression of masculinity and informal dispute management. As Robertson notes, "it makes no good sense to define the global as if the global excludes the local ... defining the global in such a way suggests that the global lies beyond all localities, as having systematic properties over and beyond the attributes of units within a global system" (1995:34).

The dialectic between the local and the global indicates there are enormous variations in local crime groups, which function and prosper within the distinctiveness and viability of different localities, where the organization of criminal labor tends to mirror general trends in the organization of legitimate labor (Ruggiero, 1995). It would be of great value therefore for future research to consider the relationship between local demographic patterns, local employment and subsequent work and leisure cultures with variations in the utility of violence as both a commercial and personal tool within organized crime groups.

IV. APPROACHES TO PREVENTION

Overt violence carried out by organized crime personnel is a category of transgression that guarantees a reaction from politicians, media, and police alike. London's Kray twins were allowed to build a considerable enterprise based upon extortion until two murders were committed and the police could no longer ignore, or compromise with them (Pearson, 1973).[13]

---

[13] Crimes based on violence other than murder, although more prominent, are unlikely to inspire such decisive action amongst law enforcement agencies. One of the problems of regarding murder, or any overt act of violence, as an indicator of organized criminal activity is that, as mentioned above, intimidation or the threat of violence is the foundation of many lucrative illicit businesses. For instance, in the list of indictments obtained by the fifteen Federal Strike Force's between 1981 and 1989, only fourteen feature murder, attempted murder, or conspiracy to murder (Jacobs et al., 1994), but most of the remaining indictments feature crimes whose chances of success would be enhanced by being carried out by individuals with violent reputations e.g., loan sharking, illegal gambling, etc.

Violence is regarded as a signifier of organized criminal activity, and it usually occurs in a place called "gangland," a place that is far removed from the daily grind of normative economic life. However, reality often contradicts this view. For organized crime personnel, "There is the constant threat that the criminal justice system will suddenly wrench control of ones life" (Katz, 1988:230), and as Block's analysis of Murder Inc. clearly shows, an increase in violence can be an indicator that law enforcement is having a disruptive effect upon a serious crime network for, "When networks break down through the intervention of an outside agency ... information becomes a highly important and therefore dangerous commodity. In a volatile situation the key decision is whether to buy leniency or safety through informing ... Increased violence is among the inevitable results" (Block, 1983:235).

The state responds to a public order situation by reasserting its monopoly over the means of violence, but this is essentially a reactive fire brigade tactic in response to a public-order problem. For although the spectacular symbolic enforcement of the rough edges of criminal enterprise can have a temporary disruptive effect on criminal enterprise (Barnes et al., 2000), it can also mask the realities of contemporary enterprise crime in a cloak of visceral glamour, mopping up the usual suspects while leaving the crucial "background operators" (Mack & Kerner, 1975) well alone. By presenting violence as a typical manifestation, rather than an integral feature of organized crime, state control agents create a an impression that criminal enterprise exists on an essentially different planet from normative, regularized commerce, affording "respectable people the illusion of living in an overworld" (Benney, 1981 [1936]:194).

Violence is a highly personalized resource of organized crime, and although it seldom confronts the state head on, preferring instead a guerilla war, the state needs to maintain sufficient violent potential as a deterrent. Yet violence is a generic resource of organized crime that may well remain latent for long periods of time until it is dusted off for a period of coercive action against those that threaten either the firm or the competitive integrity of its personnel. Therefore, violence is a feature of organized crime's power, characterizing its establishment in the market place, its dominance of a section of the market, and the method by which it resolves feuds and grievances. Violence is ingrained in the very fabric of organized crime, which in turn is inherent to the multiple power relationships of contemporary society. Consequently, attempts to police organized criminal violence in isolation, is akin to trimming the fingernails of a gangrenous arm in the expectation of saving the limb.

REFERENCES

Abadinsky, Howard. (1993). *Organized Crime. 3rd Edition*. Chicago: Nelson Hall.

Adler, Patricia A. (1985). *Wheeling and Dealing*. New York: Columbia University Press.

Albanese, Jay. (1996). *Organized Crime in America. 3rd Edition*. Cincinnati: Anderson.

Albini, Joseph. (1971). *The American Mafia: Genesis of a Legend*. New York: Appleton-Century-Crofts.

Anastasia, George. (1991). *Blood and Honor: Inside the Scarfo Mob—the Mafia's Most Violent Family*. New York: Morrow.

Anderson, Annelise. (1979). *The Business of Organized Crime: A Cosa Nostra Family*. Stanford: Hoover Institute Press.

Andrews, Wayne. (1941). *The Vanderbilt Legend: The Story of the Vanderbilt Family 1794–1940*. New York: Harcourt Brace.

Arlacchi, Pino. (1986). *Mafia Business: The Mafia Ethic and the Spirit of Capitalism*. London: Verso.

Barnes, Tony, Richard Elias, & Peter Walsh. (2000). *Cocky: The Rise and Fall of Curtis Warren, Britain's Biggest Drug Baron*. Bury: Milo.

Bauman, Zygmunt. (1989). *Legislators and Interpreters: On Modernity, Postmodernity, and Intellectuals*. Cambridge: Polity.

Bauman, Zygmunt. (1992). *Intimations of Postmodernity*. London: Routledge.

Behan, Tom. (1996). *The Camorra*. London: Routledge.

Bell, David. (1953). Crime as an American Way of Life. *The Antioch Review*, *13*, 131–154.

Bell, David. (1965). *The End of Ideology: On the Exhaustion of Political Ideas in the Fifties*. London: Free Press/Collier-Macmillan.

Benney, Mark. (1981) [1936]. *Low Company: Describing the Evolution of a Burglar. Facsimile Edition*. Sussex: Caliban Books.

Block, Alan A. (1978). History and the Study of Organized Crime. *Urban Life*, *6*, 455–474.

Block, Alan A. (1983). *East Side—West Side: Organizing Crime in New York, 1930–1950*. Newark: Transaction Publishers.

Block, Alan A. (1991). *Masters of Paradise: Organized Crime and the Internal Revenue Service in the Bahamas*. New Brunswick: Transaction Publishers.

Block, Alan A. (1994). *Space, Time and Organized Crime*. New Brunswick: Transaction Publishers.

Block, Alan A., & William Chambliss. (1979). Miners, Tailors and Teamsters: Business Racketeering and Trade Unionism. *Crime and Social Justice*, *11*, 14–27.

Block, Alan A., & William Chambliss. (1981). *Organizing Crime*. New York: Elsevier.

Block, Alan A., & Frank Scarpitti. (1985). *Poisoning for Profit: The Mafia and Toxic Waste*. New York: William Morrow.

Blok, Anton. (1975). *The Mafia of a Sicilian Village, 1860–1960: A Study of Violent Peasant Entrepreneurs*. New York: Harper.

Bourgois, Philippe. (1995). *In Search of Respect: Selling Crack in El Bario*. Cambridge: Cambridge University Press.

Brill, Steven. (1978). *The Teamsters*. New York: Simon and Schuster.

Brooks, Thomas. (1971). *Toil and Trouble: A History of American Labor*. New York: Dell.

Brown, Richard M. (1991). *No Duty to Retreat: Violence and Values in American History and Society*. New York: Oxford University Press.

Browning, Frank, & John Gerassi. (1980). *The American Way of Crime*. New York: G.P. Putnam and Sons.

Buchanan, James M. (1973). A Defense of Organized Crime? In Simon Rottenberg (Ed.), *The Economics of Crime and Punishment* (pp. 119–132). Washington, D.C.: American Enterprise Institute.

Calvi, Fabrizio. (1993). *Het Europa Van de Peetvaders. De Mafia Verovert een Continent*. Leuven: Kritak Balans.

Capeci, Jerry, & Gene Mustain. (1992). *Gotti: Rise and Fall*. New York: Onyx.

Catanzaro, Raimondo. (1992). *Men of Respect: A Social History of the Sicilian Mafia*. New York: Free Press.

Chambliss, William. (1978). *On the Take: From Petty Crooks to Presidents*. Bloomington: Indiana University Press.

Chaney, David. (1994). *The Cultural Turn: Scene-Setting Essays on Contemporary Cultural History*. London: Routledge.

Cressey, Donald R. (1967). The Functions and Structure of Criminal Syndicates. In *Task Force Report: Organized Crime* (pp. 25–60). President's Commission on Law Enforcement and the Administration of Justice, Washington, D.C.: U.S. Government Printing Office.

Cressey, Donald R. (1969). *Theft of the Nation: The Structure and Operations of Organized Crime in America*. New York: Harper and Row.

Cummings, John, & Ernst Volkman. (1992). *Mobster: The Improbable Rise and Fall of John Gotti and His Gang*. London: Warner.

Daly, Martin, & Margo Wilson. (1988). *Homicide*. New York: de Gruyter.

Elias, Norbert. (1994). *The Civilizing Process*. Oxford: Basil Blackwell.

Falcone, Giovanni. (1993). *Men of Honour: The Truth About the Mafia*. London: Warner.

Foreman, Freddie. (1996). *Respect: Autobiography of Freddie Foreman, Managing Director of British Crime*. London: Century.

Fraser, Frankie. (1994). *Mad Frank: Memoirs of a Life of Crime*. London: Little Brown.

Friedman, Allen, & Ted Schwarz. (1989). *Power and Greed: Inside the Teamsters Empire of Corruption*. New York: Watts.

Furstenburg, M. (1969). *Violence in Organized Crime, Staff Report to the National Commission on the Causes and Prevention of Violence*. Washington, D.C.: U.S. Government Publishing Office.

Galeotti, Mark. (1992). Organized Crime in Moscow and Russian National Security. *Low Intensity Conflict and Law Enforcement*, *1*(3), 237–252.

Gambetta, Diego. (1988). Fragments of an Economic Theory of the Mafia. *Archives Européennes de Sociologie*, *29*, 127–145.

Gambetta, Diego. (1993). *The Sicilian Mafia: The Business of Private Protection*. Cambridge: Harvard University Press.

Giddens, Anthony. (1990). *The Consequences of Modernity*. Cambridge: Polity Press.

Giddens, Anthony. (1991). *Modernity and Self-Identity*. Cambridge: Polity Press.

Godson, Roy, & William J. Olson. (1993). *International Organized Crime: Emerging Threat to U.S. Security*. Washington, D.C.: National Strategy Information Center.

Goldstein, Paul J. (1985). The Drugs/Violence Nexus: A Tripartite Conceptual Framework. *Journal of Drug Issues*, *4*, 493–506.

Hagan, Frank E. (1983). The Organized Crime Continuum: A Further Specification of a New Conceptual Model. *Criminal Justice Review*, *8*, 52–57.

Haller, Mark H. (1985). Bootleggers as Businessmen: From City Slums to City Builders. In David Kyvig (Ed.), *Law, Alcohol, and Order: Perspectives on National Prohibition* (pp. 139–157). Westport: Greenwood.

Handelman, Stephen. (1995). *Comrade Criminal: Russia's New Mafiya*. New Haven: Yale University Press.

Harvey, David. (1989). From Managerialism to Entrepreneurialism: The Transformation in Urban Governance in Late Capitalism. *Geografiska Annaler*, *71*(1), 3–17.

Hawkins, Gordon. (1969). God and the Mafia. *The Public Interest*, *14*, 24–51.

Hess, Henner. (1973). *Mafia and Mafiosi: The Structure of Power*. Lexington: Heath.

Hobbs, Dick. (1995). *Bad Business: Professional Crime in Modern Britain*. Oxford: Oxford University Press.

Hobbs, Dick. (1997). Professional Crime: Change Continuity and the Enduring Myth of the Underworld. *Sociology*, *31*(1), 57–72.

Hobbs, Dick. (1998). The Aliens Are Not Coming: Organized Crime as a Local Problem. *International Journal of Risk, Security, and Crime Prevention*, *3*(2), 139–146.

Hobbs, Dick, & Steven Hall. (2000). *Bouncers: The Art and Economics of Intimidation. Final Report ESRC*.

Inciardi, James, Alan A. Block, & Lyle Hallowell. (1977). *Historical Approaches to Crime*. Beverly Hills: Sage.

Jacobs, Bruce. (1998). Researching Crack Dealers: Dilemmas and Contradictions. In Jeff Ferrel and Mark S. Hamm (Eds.), *Ethnography at the Edge* (pp. 160–177). Boston: Northeastern University Press.

Jacobs, James B. (1999). *Gotham Unbound: How New York Was Liberated from the Grip of Organized Crime*. New York: New York University Press.

Jacobs, James B., Christopher Panarella, & Jay Worthington. (1994). *Busting the Mob: United States v. Cosa Nostra*. New York: New York University Press.

Karraker, Cyrus H. (1953). *Piracy Was a Business*. Rindge: Richard R. Smith

Katz, Jack. (1988). *Seductions of Crime: Moral and Sensual Attractions in Doing Evil*. New York: Basic Books.

Kelly, Robert J. (1986). *Organized Crime: A Global Perspective*. Totowan: Rowman and Littlefield.

Kerry, John. (1997). *The New War: The Web of Crime that Threatens America's Security*. New York: Simon and Schuster.

Kenney, Dennis J., & James O. Finckenauer. (1995). *Organized Crime in America*. Belmont: Wadsworth.

Kray, Reginald. (1991). *Born Fighter*. London: Arrow.

Kyvig, David E. (1979). *Repealing National Prohibition*. Chicago: University of Chicago Press.

Kwitny, Jonathan. (1979). *Vicious Circles: The Mafia in the Marketplace*. New York: Norton.

Labrousse, Alain. (1994). Géopolitique de la drogue: Les contradictions des politiques de 'guerre a la drogue'. *Futuribles*, *185*, 9–22.

Labrousse, Allain, & Allain Wallon (Eds.) (1993). *La planète des drogues*. Paris: Seuil.

Lacey, Robert. (1991). *Little Man: Meyer Lansky and the Gangster Life*. New York: Little Brown.

Lambrianou, Tony. (1992). *Inside the Firm: The Untold Story of the Kray's Reign of Terror*. London: Pan.

Landesco, John. (1929). *Organized Crime in Chicago*. Chicago: University of Chicago Press. [2nd Edition 1968]

Lee, Rensselaer W. (1991). Colombia's Cocaine Syndicates. *Crime Law and Social Change*, *16*, 3–39.

Lee, Rensselaer W., & Scott B. MacDonald. (1993). Drugs in the East. *Foreign Policy*, *90*, 89–107.

Levi, Ken. (1981). Becoming a Hit Man: Neutralization in a Very Deviant Career. *Urban Life*, *10*, 47–63.

Lloyd, Henry D. (1963). *Wealth Against Commonwealth* (Thomas C. Cochran (Ed.)). Englewood Cliffs: Prentice-Hall.

Loth, David G. (1938). *Public Plunder: A History of Graft in America*. New York: Carrick and Evans.

Lupsha, Peter A. (1981). Individual Choice, Material Culture, and Organized Crime. *Criminology*, *19*, 3–24.

Maas, Peter. (1968). *The Valachi Papers*. New York: G. B. Putnam's Sons.

Maas, Peter. (1998). *Underboss: Sammy the Bull Gravano's Story of Life in Mafia.* New York: Harper Collins.

Mack, John A., & Hans-Jürgen Kerner. (1975). *The Crime Industry.* Lexington: Lexington Books.

Maltz, Michael D. (1976). On Defining 'Organized Crime'. *Crime and Delinquency, 22,* 338–346.

Maltz, Michael D. (1985). Toward Defining Organized Crime. In Herbert E. Alexander and Gerald E. Caiden (Eds.), *The Politics and Economics of Organized Crime* (pp. 21–35). Lexington: Lexington Books.

Martin, John M., & Anne T. Romano. (1992). *Multinational Crime: Terrorism, Espionage, Drug & Arms Trafficking.* Newbury Park: Sage.

Moldea, Dan E. (1978). *The Hoffa Wars: Teamsters, Rebels, Politicians, and the Mob.* New York: Paddington Press.

Morris, Norval, & Gordon Hawkins. (1970). *The Honest Politician's Guide to Crime Control.* Chicago: University of Chicago Press.

Moore, Mark. (1987). Organized Crime as a Business Enterprise. In Herbert Edelhertz (Ed.), *Major Issues in Organized Crime Control* (pp. 51–64). Washington, D.C.: Government Printing Office.

Myers, Gustavus. (1937). *History of the Great American Fortunes.* New York: Modern Library.

Naylor, Robin T. (1995). From Cold War to Crime War. *Transnational Organized Crime, 1*(4), 37–56.

Neff, James. (1989). *Mobbed Up: Jackie Presser's High-Wire Life in the Teamsters, the Mafia, and the FBI.* New York: Atlantic Monthly Press.

O'Brien, Joseph F., & Andris Kurins. (1991). *Boss of Bosses: The Fall of the Godfather, the FBI and Paul Castellano.* New York: Simon and Schuster.

O'Mahoney, Bernard. (1997). *So This Is Ecstasy?* Edinburgh: Mainstream Publishing.

Owen, Richard, & Michael Dynes. (1990). *The Times Guide to 1992: Britain in a Europe Without Frontiers: A Comprehensive Handbook.* London: London Times.

Pearce, Frank. (1976). *Crimes of the Powerful: Marxism, Crimes and Deviance.* London: Pluto.

Pearson, John. (1973). *The Profession of Violence: The Rise and Fall of the Kray Twins.* St. Albans: Panther.

Peterson, Virgil W. (1983). *The Mob: 200 Years of Organized Crime in New York.* Ottawa: Green Hill Publishers.

Pileggi, Nicholas. (1987). *Wiseguy: Life in a Mafia Family.* London: Corgi.

Potter, Gary W. (1994). *Criminal Organizations: Vice, Racketeering and Politics in an American City.* Prospect Heights: Waveland Press.

Potter, Gary W., & Philip Jenkins. (1985). *The City and the Syndicate: Organizing Crime in Philadelphia.* Lexington: Ginn Press.

Pryce, Ken. (1979). *Endless Pressure: A Study of West Indian Lifestyles in Britain.* Harmondsworth: Penguin.

Quinney, Richard. (1975). *Criminology: Analysis and Critique of Crime in America.* Boston: Little, Brown.

Rankin, Hugh F. (1969). *The Golden Age of Piracy.* New York: Holt, Rinehart and Winston.

Rawlinson, Peter. (1996). Russian Organized Crime: A Brief History. *Transnational Organized Crime, 2*(2/3), 28–52.

Reuter, Peter. (1983). *Disorganized Crime: The Economics of the Visible Hand.* Cambridge: MIT Press.

Reuter, Peter. (1986). *Methodological and Institutional Problems in Organized Crime Research.* Paper Prepared for the Conference on Critical Issues in Organized Crime Control. Washington, D.C.: The Rand Corporation.

Reuter, Peter. (1987). *Racketeering in Legitimate Industries: A Study in the Economics of Intimidation.* Santa Monica: Rand Corporation

Reuter, Peter, & Jonathan B. Rubinstein. (1978). Fact, Fancy, and Organized Crime. *The Public Interest, 53,* 45–67.

Reuter, Peter, Jonathan B. Rubinstein, & Simon Wynn. (1983). *Racketeering in Legitimate Industries.* Washington, D.C.: U.S. Government Printing Office.

Richardson, Charles. (1992). *My Manor.* London: Pan.

Robertson, Roland. (1995). Glocalization: Time—Space and Homogeneity—Heterogeneity. In Mike Featherstone, Scott Lash and Robert Robertson (Eds.), *Global Modernities* (pp. 25–44). London: Sage.

Ruggiero, Vincenzo. (1987). Turin Today: Premodern Society or Postmodern Bazaar? *Capital and Class, 31,* 25–28.

Ruggiero, Vincenzo. (1993). Brixton, London: A Drug Culture without a Drug Economy? *International Journal of Drug Policy, 4/2,* 83–90.

Ruggiero, Vincenzo. (1995). Drug Economics: A Fordist Model of Criminal Capital. *Capital and Class, 55,* 131–150.

Ruggiero, Vincenzo, & Nigel South. (1997). The Late Modern City as a Bazaar: Drug Markets, Illegal Enterprise and the 'Barricades'. *British Journal of Sociology, 48,* 54–70.

Sanchez-Jankowski, Martin S. (1991). *Islands in the Street: Gangs and American Urban Society*. Berkeley: University of California Press.

Sanz, Ken, & Ira Silverman. (1997). The Evolution and Future Direction of Southeast Asian Criminal Organization. In Patrick J. Ryan and George E. Rush (Eds.), *Understanding Organized Crime in Global Perspective: A Reader* (pp. 220–226). Thousand Oaks: Sage.

Schlegel, Kip. (1987). Violence in Organized Crime: A Content Analysis of the De Cavalcante and De Carlo Transcripts. In Timothy S. Bynum (Ed.), *Organized Crime in America: Concepts and Controversies* (pp. 55–70). New York: Criminal Justice Press.

Schelling, Thomas C. (1984). *Choice and Consequences*. Cambridge: Harvard University Press.

Shawcross, Tim, & Martin Young. (1987). *Men of Honour: The Confessions of Tammaso Buscetta*. London: Collins.

Sherry, Frank. (1986). *Raiders and Rebels: The Golden Age of Piracy*. New York: Hearst Marine Books.

Sinclair, Andrew. (1962). *Prohibition: The Era of Excess*. Boston: Little, Brown.

Smith, Dwight C. (1971). Some Things that May Be More Important to Understand about Organized Crime than Cosa Nostra. *University of Florida Law Review, 24*, 1–30.

Smith, Dwight C. (1975). *The Mafia Mystique*. New York: Basic Books.

Smith, Dwight C. (1980). Paragons, Pariahs, and Pirates: A Spectrum-Based Theory of Enterprise. *Crime and Delinquency, 26*, 358–386.

Sparrow, Malcolm K. (1991). The Application of Network Analysis to Criminal Intelligence. An Assessment of the Prospects. *Social Networks, 13*, 251–274.

Sterling, Claire. (1994). *Crime without Frontiers: The Worldwide Expansion of Organized Crime and the Pax Mafiosa*. London: Little, Brown.

Sykes, Gresham M. (1958). *The Society of Captives: A Study of a Maximum Security Prison*. Princeton: Princeton University Press.

Thompson, Tony. (2000). *Bloggs 19*. London: Warner.

Tyler, Gus (Ed.) (1962). *Organized Crime in America: A Book of Readings*. Ann Arbor: University of Michigan Press.

Turkus, Burton B., & Sid Feder. (1951). *Murder, Inc.: The Story of the Syndicate*. New York: Farrar, Straus and Young.

Van Duyne, & Petrus C. (1996). *Organized Crime in Europe*. Commack: Nova Science Publishers.

Warshow, Robert. (1948). The Gangster as Tragic Hero. *The Partisan Review, 15*, 240–244.

Weber, Max. (1948). *From Max Weber: Essays in Sociology* (Hans Gerth & Charles Wright Mills (Eds.)). London: Routledge.

Williams, Terry. (1989). *The Cocaine Kids: The Inside Story of a Teenage Drug Ring*. Reading: Addison-Wesley.

Williams, Phil. (1993). Transnational Criminal Organisations and National Security. *Survival, 36*, 96–113.

Williams, Phil, & Ernesto U. Savona (Eds.) (1995). The United Nations and Transnational Organized Crime. *Transnational Organized Crime, 1*(3). London: Cass.

Wong, Kar-Yiu. (1992). Inflation, Corruption and Income Distribution: The Recent Price Reform in China. *Journal of Macroeconomics, 14*(1), 105–123.

Wolfgang, Marvin E. (1959). *Patterns in Criminal Homicide*. Philadelphia: University of Pennsylvania Press.

Woodiwiss, Michael. (1993). Crimes Global Reach. In Frank Pearce and Michael Woodiwiss (Eds.), *Global Crime Connections: Dynamics and Control* (pp. 1–31). London: Macmillan.

Understanding Cross-National Variation in Criminal Violence

STEVEN MESSNER

I. INTRODUCTION

Cross-national inquiry can make several distinctive contributions to the understanding of criminal violence. One, it permits an assessment of variability in levels and patterns of violent crime. In his classic discussion of the "normality of crime," Durkheim (1964:66) argues that crime is "closely connected with the conditions of all social life," leading him to conclude that a society without crime is inconceivable. The same may very well hold true for violent crime in contemporary nations. Coercive action has intrinsic utility for obtaining compliance from others (see Tedeschi & Felson, 1994), and thus a certain degree of violence may be an inevitably feature of complex forms of social organization. Nevertheless, cross-national research elucidates the range of possibilities for minimizing levels of criminal violence.

Two, cross-national inquiry is indispensable for establishing the generality of theories of violence and the need for any requisite scope conditions. As Lilly, Cullen, and Ball (1989:11) observe, "social context plays a critical role in nourishing certain ways of theorizing about crime." The substantive content of theories of criminal violence, therefore, reflects to a large degree what "makes sense" to criminologists given the specific environments with which they are familiar. Therefore, notwithstanding claims to generality (e.g., Gottfredson & Hirschi, 1990), the causal processes depicted in criminological theories may in fact be limited in scope to a restricted set of sociocultural situations. The application of theories of violence beyond the confines of a single nation provides an opportunity to distinguish between causal processes that are truly general and those that are conditioned or moderated by the larger national context (Weiner & Ruback, 1995).

Three, cross-national inquiry permits an assessment of the role of macrosociological

W. Heitmeyer and J. Hagan (eds.), *International Handbook of Violence Research*, 701–716.

factors in the explanation of criminal violence. Criminological research, especially in the United States, is most commonly conducted at the individual level of analysis. This kind of research is directed toward answering the question: "What is it about individuals that explains their behavior?" (Short, 1985:53). While such inquiry is without question valuable in criminology, it is also important to consider how basic features of social organization such as demographic structures, institutional arrangements, and broad cultural orientations help explain violent crime. These kinds of variables are by their very nature properties of large-scale aggregates rather than individual persons. Moreover, to discover the causal significance of such macrolevel properties, it is necessary to observe variation. Neopolitan (1997a:xi) has made this point quite succinctly: "Trying to explain a nation's crime problem by studying only that nation is like trying to explain crime at the individual level by studying just one person."

To render the topic manageable and to avoid overlap with other contributions to the Handbook, the present chapter focuses on "criminal violence." Not all violence is criminalized, and the criminalization process itself is a topic worthy of comparative study. As a practical matter, however, much of the data for multinational inquiry derives from data collection systems that are oriented toward the criminal law (Reiss & Roth, 1993:37). In addition, concerns about comparability in legal definitions and recording systems have persuaded researchers to restrict attention in multinational analyses primarily to forms of violence that are generally recognized as criminal in all contemporary countries.

This chapter is also restricted to research dealing with nation-states. As Ember and Ember (1995) explain, two general types of comparative research can be distinguished on the basis of the units of analysis: cross-national and cross-cultural. Cross-national research compares politically organized entities, whereas cross-cultural research is directed toward "societies" in the anthropological sense (i.e., populations that occupy contiguous territories and share a common language not normally understood by outsiders).

Finally, the present study focuses primarily on research that is analytical rather than descriptive, and that employs quantitative rather than qualitative techniques. The bulk of this research is oriented to testing theoretically derived hypotheses. In recent years, quantitative, theory-testing studies almost always employ multivariate statistics.

The analysis proceeds as follows. First, I review theories that relate sociocultural, economic, and demographic properties of nations to levels and patterns of violent crime. Next, the more important results to emerge from the literature are summarized. I distinguish between findings that are reasonably robust and consistent across studies from those that are more erratic. Following my review of the evidence, I comment on the most pressing needs for future work, considering both methodological and theoretical challenges. The chapter concludes with a brief discussion of approaches to prevention. The cross-national research on criminal violence has focused mainly on the effects of basic features of social organization rather than on discrete social policies. Nevertheless, the evidence has implications for the broad types of political arrangements that are likely to be more or less conducive to high rates of violent crime in the contemporary world.

II.   THEORETICAL APPROACHES

The cross-national research on criminal violence has been informed by a variety of theoretical perspectives. Specific arguments are often complex and multifaceted, which makes it difficult to summarize the theoretical approaches concisely. Nevertheless, previous reviews of the literature offer typologies of theories that delineate core themes and that overlap to a considerable degree (Neuman & Berger, 1988; LaFree, 1999; Neapolitan, 1997a). Building upon these earlier reviews, the various theoretical perspectives can be organized into two general categories reflecting the underlying strategy for theorizing.

One strategy can be labeled macrosociological theorizing. The theories of this type begin with arguments about properties of large-scale social systems and their interrelationships. These system-level properties are then related to criminal violence (and crime more generally) by means of intervening mechanisms suggested by conventional criminological theories of crime. A second strategy, in contrast, begins with theoretical explanations developed to account for crime within nations, at either the individual, group or neighborhood-level. The specified causal processes are then linked with national characteristics and the explanations of crime are essentially extrapolated to apply to national crime rates. For convenience, this approach can be referred to as "extrapolative" theorizing about cross-national variation in violent crime.

1. Macrosociological Theories

One of the most influential macrosociological theories in cross-national research on crime is modernization theory, which draws liberally on the Durkheimian tradition. Although several prominent proponents of this approach can be identified in the literature (see Eisner, 1995, for a review), Louise Shelley (1981) is usually credited with developing the most thorough formulation of the thesis. Modernization theory posits an evolutionary model. As nations modernize, social structures are fundamentally altered, and levels and patterns of criminal activity change.

The precise nature of the consequences of modernization for crime varies depending on the stage of development and the offense under consideration. At early stages of urban and industrial growth, traditional social structures are undermined in the growing cities. The concomitant social disorganization, anomie, and weak control promote increases in property crimes. At the same time the newly arriving migrants from the countryside bring with them the traditions of violence associated with rural life, which leads to increases in violent crime. At later stages of development, patterns of crime change. Property crimes continue to rise, becoming the most prominent type of criminal activity. In contrast, the growth in criminal violence subsides as rural migrants become adjusted to urban life. The nature of violent crime is also changed. Increasingly, when criminal violence occurs, it does so in the context of the commission of property crimes. In sum, modernization theory posits changes in levels of criminal violence, and the preponderance of criminal violence relative to property crimes, that can be understood with reference to more general macrosocial processes accompanying societal development.

A second influential argument relevant to the effects of large-scale social change and criminal violence draws upon Elias's (1978) thesis of the civilizing process. According to this view, societal development entails important changes at both the micro- and macrolevel (Eisner, 1995; Heiland & Shelley, 1991). At the microlevel, personality structures are transformed. Customs and manners are refined, and action is increasingly guided by internalized self-control.

Two developments at the macrolevel complement these microlevel processes. The institutionalization of capitalist economies renders interpersonal violence largely dysfunctional because such violence undermines the mutual trust upon which markets are based.

In addition, the modern nation-state begins to monopolize power, thereby creating a relatively stable framework for social interaction (Neapolitan, 1997a:71). The clear implication of civilization thesis is that levels of criminal violence should decrease as nations become more "civilized."

A third macrosociological approach to the explanation of cross-national variation in violent crime is dependency/world systems theory. This perspective is concerned primarily with crime in the lesser developed nations. Different variants of the theory have been proposed (Chen, 1992), but the core claim is that criminogenic conditions within lesser developed nations arise from the subordinate and dependent position of these nations within the larger world economy. Economic dependency, reflected in conditions such as transnational corporate penetration and trade imbalances, promote distorted economic and political development. Extreme poverty, inequality, and political oppression characterize such development. High levels of criminal violence can be understood as a response to the "frustration and misdirected anger created by deprivation and demoralizing living conditions" (Neapolitan, 1997a:76). In sum, the distinctive claim associated with dependency theory is that the national conditions that serve as the proximate causes of violent crime must be understood within the context of an inherently exploitive international division of labor.

Finally, recent scholarship has directed attention to processes of globalization and the emergence of postmodern societies. A common theme in much of this literature is that the expansion of markets and the accompanying triumph of capitalism have unleashed a host of criminogenic forces. These include the spread of rampant individualism (Currie, 1991), the decline of social reforms that previously mitigated the more deleterious consequences of capitalist society (Teeple, 1995), and an expansion in the opportunities for organized criminal activities at a transnational level, activities which are often accompanied by violence (Castells, 1997; Mittelman, 1996). While some systematic efforts to link globalization with crime are beginning to appear (Findlay, 1999; Messner & Rosenfeld, 2000), a coherent body of criminological theorizing about these processes has yet to emerge.

2. Extrapolative Theoretical Arguments

Much of the cross-national research on violence does not involve the kind of macrosociological theorizing just described. Instead, researchers often begin with premises about the mechanisms that have been related to crime in conventional criminological theories, and then national characteristics are identified that are suggestive of the operation of these mechanisms. With this approach to theorizing virtually any theoretical perspective on crime that has been developed to explain crime within nations can be extrapolated to explain variation in crime across nations (Neapolitan, 1997a:67).

In practice, virtually all of the major sociological theories of crime have been applied in the cross-national literature on criminal violence. This has resulted in a diverse array of hypotheses encompassing a wide range of specific independent variables. In her research on homicide rates across eighteen advanced nations, Gartner (1990) proposes a useful framework for organizing the hypothesized determinants of national crime rates. She observes that traditional and more recent explanations of violent crime emphasize some combination of motivations, controls, and/or opportunities for victimization. Applying the extrapolative mode of theorizing, national characteristics can be expected to affect levels of criminal violence to the extent that they raise motivations, lower controls, and/or increase opportunities (Gartner, 1990:94).

Gartner proposes that such national characteristics can be grouped into four general types: the material context, the integrative context, the demographic context, and the cultural context. The material context refers to conditions that entail economic deprivation and stress. Variables commonly used to represent the material context include levels of poverty and income inequality, and the extensiveness of governmental efforts to alleviate economic stress through welfare policies. The integrative context refers to the strength and depth of social ties that serve to control violent behavior. Common indicators of the integrative context include measures of family structure and racial/ethnic heterogeneity. The demographic context refers to features of population structure. Age distributions, population size and growth, and the sex ratio are major components of the demographic context. The last context—the cultural context—has received the least amount of attention in the research literature because of the difficulty of devising measures of culture. In a few studies, however, researchers have called attention to the potentially important role of general value orientations (Adler, 1983; Huang, 1995; Karstedt, 1999; Messner, 1982; Smith & Kwong Wong, 1989),[1] religious values (Groves, McCleary, & Newman, 1985), and values supportive of legitimate violence (Archer & Gartner, 1984; Gartner, 1990).

In sum, a diverse array of theoretical arguments appears in the cross-national literature on criminal violence. Hypotheses are sometimes informed by theories about large-scale social changes and the consequences of these changes for violent crime. Much research also entails an attempt to derive predictions about the relationship between national characteristics and rates of criminal violence by extrapolating from conventional criminological theories, often formulated originally at a microlevel of analysis. In practice, both strategies of theorizing focus attention on a common set of explanatory variables encompassing salient features of the economic, demographic, social, and cultural contexts of nations.

III.   EMPIRICAL RESULTS

Cross-national research on crime was very limited prior to around 1970, but since that time, studies have accumulated steadily. The vast bulk of the contemporary work deals with homicide. Researchers generally agree that the comparability of definitions and the quality of official data are greater for homicide than for other offenses. Most of the quantitative studies of homicide share a basic analytic design. The effects on homicide rates of theoretically strategic national characteristics are assessed in multiple regression equations. In the discussion that follows, I first review the cross-national literature on homicide and then conclude with a few remarks about the results of recent research using unofficial data sources (self-reports, victimization surveys) to analyze nonlethal forms of personal crime.

1.   Cross-National Studies of Homicide

Comprehensive reviews of the cross-national research on homicide are available in the literature. Neuman and Berger (1988) summarize the results of the work up through the mid 1980s (see also LaFree & Kick, 1986); LaFree (1999) and Neapolitan (1997a) update

[1] The studies by Huang, Karstedt, Messner, & Smith and Kwong Wong draw upon Durkheim's theory of societal development and the consequences of development for the emergence of "moral individualism." Accordingly, these analyses might be viewed as further examples of macrosociological theorizing.

this earlier review to encompass research conducted in the late 1980s through the mid 1990s (see also Gartner, 1995). Rather than detailing the results of all the studies represented in these previous analyses, I focus on general patterns and the substantive conclusions that can be drawn from these findings. I devote special attention to the research on the effect of income inequality on homicide rates. As explained below, a positive relationship between income inequality and homicide rates is one of the most robust findings to emerge in the literature.

a. THE MATERIAL/ECONOMIC CONTEXT.   Most cross-national studies of homicide include some measure of the level of economic development. Common indicators are Gross National (or Domestic) Product per capita, prevalence of modern media of communications (telephones, radios, newspapers), energy consumption, the sectoral distribution of employment (e.g., agricultural vs. industrial), and composite indexes of such indicators. The results reported in the research are not entirely consistent, but the general picture is one of null effects on homicide rates, or possibly weak negative effects, for measures of economic development.

Numerous studies have also focused on the effects of a related concept—economic deprivation. In these analyses researchers typically distinguish between "absolute deprivation" and "relative deprivation." Indicators of absolute deprivation sometimes include the same measures as those used to represent economic development (e.g., GNP/capita). Infant mortality and unemployment rates have also been examined as indicators of absolute deprivation. Similar to the results reported for economic development, indicators of absolute economic deprivation fail to exhibit consistent associations with national homicide rates in multivariate models.

There is much more impressive support for the hypothesis that homicide rates vary with the degree of "relative deprivation" as reflected in levels of income inequality. To illustrate this, Table II-3-3-4.1 summarizes a large number of cross-national studies of income inequality and homicide rates published in English since the mid 1970s. The table identifies the authors, the measure of inequality used, the observed effect of inequality, and the homicide data source.[2] The pattern is quite striking. While there are a few exceptions, income inequality exhibits significant, positive effects on homicide rates in the vast majority of cross-national studies. This relationship is observed across different measures of income inequality (e.g., the Gini coefficient, quintile shares) and different homicide data sources.

All of the studies in Table II-3-3-4.1 except for that by Fajnzylber, Lederman and Loyaza (1998) are based on cross-sectional assessments of the effect of income inequality on homicide. In contrast, Fajnzylber et al. (1998) estimate both cross-sectional and dynamic models using pooled, cross-sectional time-series data. Their results indicate that the widely observed cross-sectional relationship between income inequality and homicide rates is replicated in longitudinal analyses: increases in the level of income inequality are associated with increased homicide rates within nations, net of other national characteristics.

A few studies have also examined the potential role of governmental efforts to mitigate the criminogenic consequences of economic deprivation through the provision of

---

[2] Interpol data refer to the *International Crime Statistics*; WHO data refer to *World Health Statistics Annual*; the UN data come from the *World Crime Surveys*; the Comparative Crime Data File was compiled by Archer and Gartner (1984).

TABLE II-3-3-4.1. Cross-national research on income inequality and homicide

Study	Income inequality measures	Observed effect	Homicide data source*
McDonald (1976)	Inter-sectoral Lorenz	0	Interpol
Krohn (1976)	Gini	+	Interpol
Braithwaite (1979)	Ordinal ranking	+	WHO
Braithwaite & Braithwaite (1980)	Inter-sectoral Gini	+	Interpol
Messner (1980)	Gini	+	Interpol
Messner (1982)	Gini	+	Interpol
Hansmann & Quigley (1982)	Gini	+	UNO
Kick & LaFree (1985)	Gini	+	CCDF
Groves et al. (1985)	Gini	–	UNO
Messner (1985)	Gini	+	Interpol
Avison & Loring (1986)	Gini	+	WHO
LaFree & Kick (1986)	Gini	+	CCDF
Krahn et al. (1986)	Gini	+	Interpol
Fiala & LaFree (1988)	quintile shares, quintile ratios	0	WHO (children)
Messner (1989)	Gini	+	Interpol
Gartner (1990)	Gini	+ (adults, 0 children)	WHO
Unnithan & Whitt (1992)	Kuznets	+, curvilinear	WHO
Neapolitan (1994)	dezile- & quintile shares	+	WHO, UNO, Interpol
Neapolitan (1996)	dezile- & quintile shares	+	Interpol, WHO, UNO
Messner & Rosenfeld (1997)	Gini	0	WHO
Neapolitan (1997b)	dezile- & quintile shares	0	Interpol
Fajnzylber et al. (1998)	1. Gini 2. quintil shares	1. + 2. +	UNO
Karstedt (1999)	Gini	+	CCDF

* Interpol = International Criminal Police Organization; WHO = World Health Organization;
   UN = United Nations; CCDF = Comparative Crime Data File

various social security and welfare benefits. Although the evidence is rather sparse, the general pattern of findings is consistent. More generous and expansive social welfare policies are associated with lower homicide rates. These effects have been observed for child homicides as well as total homicides; they have also been reported in both cross-sectional and longitudinal analyses (Fiala & LaFree, 1988; Gartner, 1990; Messner & Rosenfeld, 1997).

b. THE DEMOGRAPHIC CONTEXT. Most multivariate studies of cross-national variation in homicide rates include some measures of population structure and distribution.
Researchers drawing on modernization theory commonly examine the effects of urbanism/
urbanization, often measured as the relative size of the population residing in urban areas.
The results are mixed. The bulk of studies report nonsignificant relationships in multivariate
models, although several analyses find modest but significant negative relationships.

For the most part, other demographic factors have not emerged as robust predictors.
Population size and density typically exhibit weak or null effects. Similarly, measures of
age structure (e.g., the proportion of the population in "high risk" age-brackets) and sex
ratio are generally not related to homicide rates. These results are surprising given the
strong associations between criminal violence and age and sex at the individual level. The
one demographic factor that has emerged as a significant predictor with a fair degree of
regularity is population growth. Several studies report that rapid population growth is
associated with high homicide rates (Braithwaite, 1979; Krahn, Hartnagel, & Gartrell,
1986; LaFree, & Kick, 1986; McDonald, 1976; Messner, 1982).

There is also scant but suggestive evidence that demographic factors may interact with
other national characteristics to affect homicide rates. One study (Krahn et al., 1986) reports
an interaction effect between population density and income inequality. The positive impact
of income inequality on homicide rates is higher in the more densely populated nations.
Another (Pampel & Gartner, 1995) finds that demographic structure interacts with the degree of "collectivism" in society. Increases in the relative size of the young population tend
to elevate homicide rates under conditions of weak collectivism. A strong degree of collectivism, in contrast, mitigates the effects on homicide rates of relatively large cohorts.

c. THE INTEGRATIVE AND CULTURAL CONTEXTS. As noted above, various criminological theories emphasize the importance of social integration and cultural values in the
explanation of levels of criminal violence. Unfortunately, direct indicators of these constructs are largely unavailable for cross-national research. Researchers have thus been
forced to use measures that are at best indirect proxies.

One common way of operationalizing social integration is with measures of racial/
ethnic, linguistic, and/or religious heterogeneity. Such heterogeneity is generally interpreted as a potential source of value conflict and as an impediment to social cohesion.
While some studies find the expected positive effects of indicators of heterogeneity on
homicide rates, null effects are often observed as well. The general consensus is that conventional indicators of heterogeneity are at best only weakly related to homicide rates.
Similar to some of the results noted above for demographic variables, however, there is
some evidence to suggest that heterogeneity may interact with economic inequality to
affect homicide rates. Specifically, economic disadvantage that is rooted in group characteristics has been related to high homicide rates (Avison and Loring, 1986; Messner, 1989).

A few cross-national studies have examined the relationship between divorce rates
and homicide. Divorce is often viewed as both a consequence and a cause of weak integration. Once again, the evidence is mixed, with some studies reporting appreciable positive
effects and others null effects.

With respect to the potential impact of the cultural context, the research is also quite
limited. A few studies have reported positive associations between battle deaths and homicide rates, and between the use of capital punishment and homicide rates (Archer & Gartner,
1984; Gartner, 1990; Landau & Pfeffermann, 1988). These findings are consistent with

the claim that cultural support for the legitimate use of violence is likely to "spill over" and increase the use of illegitimate forms of violence. Similarly, a limited body of evidence relates gun availability with lethal violence (Killias, 1992; Walker, 1999). Although gun availability is sometimes interpreted as an "opportunity" factor, it has also been interpreted as an indicator of cultural values conducive to violence.

Researchers have also considered the impact of individualistic values on levels of violence. Competing theoretical arguments have been offered about whether individualism is likely to promote or inhibit criminal violence (Haferkamp & Ellis, 1991; Karstedt, 1999). The difficulties associated with the measurement of values preclude definitive conclusions. Nevertheless, there is scant but suggestive evidence pointing to the importance of values of "moral individualism." This value orientation emphasizes a universalistic respect for human rights and independence from strong collectivistic ties (especially kinship and ethnic-group ties). In one of the few efforts to use direct measures of value orientations in cross-national research on criminal violence, Karstedt (1999) reports that a measure of individualism exhibits significant negative effects on homicide rates in multivariate models (see also Huang, 1995).

2. A Comment on Nonlethal Criminal Violence and "Unofficial" Data Sources

As noted earlier, the vast bulk of quantitative cross-national research on criminal violence has examined homicide rates. Indeed, some have argued that cross-national research should be restricted to homicide because differences in legal definitions and official recording practices render the official data for nonlethal offenses suspect (Neapolitan, 1997a:38). An important methodological development in recent decades has been the application of survey techniques to overcome limitations associated with the official data on nonlethal forms of criminal violence and to generate "unofficial" data for multinational samples. The most prominent and ambitious of these efforts are a self-report study of delinquent behavior among youths for a sample of twelve advanced nations (Junger-Tas, Terlow, & Kein, 1994) and a victimization survey that, as of this writing, has been implemented in fifty-five countries (van Dijk, 1999; van Dijk, Mayhew & Killias, 1991).

The use of nonofficial data in cross-national research is relatively new, and the self-report study on offending is perhaps best regarded as exploratory (Newman & Howard, 1999:17). Moreover, both of these survey techniques have their own limitations for purposes of cross-national inquiry (Neapolitan, 1997a; Travis et al., 1995). Nevertheless, a few broad generalizations can be ventured on the basis of the research based on unofficial data sources.

First, it seems clear that national homicide rates and victimization rates for nonlethal violent crimes do not necessarily exhibit strong positive correlations. A widely observed pattern, for example, is that the United States exhibits homicide rates that far surpass those in other advanced nations, while its rate of nonlethal violent crimes is not nearly as exceptional (Zimring & Hawkins, 1997). Second, comparisons of homicide rates and victimization rates for violent crimes suggest that the discrepancies between official and unofficial data sources are reduced when attention focuses on serious forms of violent crime (Lynch, 1995; van Dijk & Kangaspunta, 2000). The more serious the offense and the greater the danger for life threatening harm, the more similar the victimization data are to the homicide data. Finally, one of the few multivariate analyses of victimization data for nonlethal violent crimes based on an appreciable sample of nations yields a finding quite consistent with the homicide literature. Specifically, van Dijk (1999) reports that a measure of economic strain emerges as the strongest predictor of levels of victimization for "contact crimes" (robbery, sexual assault, assault) in a sample of forty-nine nations. This finding is in accord with the widely observed effect of the level of income inequality on homicide rates.

III.   SUMMARY OF THE EVIDENCE AND IMPLICATIONS

Given the myriad methodological difficulties associated with cross-national research on criminal violence, it is not surprising that the literature yields a somewhat cloudy picture. A few generalizations, however, appear warranted.

From a purely descriptive standpoint, the evidence demonstrates remarkable cross-national variation in levels of criminal violence, especially in the case of lethal violence. Homicide is a major social problem and a significant cause of mortality in some nations, whereas it is a highly unusual event in others. Clearly, highly variable levels of violence are compatible with complex forms of social organization.

With respect to the more prominent macrosociological theories reviewed above, the failure to observe appreciable negative effects of standard indicators of economic development on national levels of lethal violence runs counter to simple versions of modernization theory. In particular, the evidence raises questions about the interconnectedness of different dimensions of modernization and about the utility of strict evolutionary models. The consequences of economic development for levels of criminal violence evidently depend to a considerable degree on the larger historical and cultural context of a nation (see Heiland & Shelley, 1991; Shelley, 1986). The finding of weak effects of developmental measures in the cross-national literature also suggests that the theory of a civilizing process offers a better explanation of changes in criminal violence associated with the transformation of agrarian, rural communities into industrial and postindustrial nation-states than it does of variation in violence across such nation-states. Considering dependency theories, the finding of positive effects of income inequality on homicide rates is consistent with an underlying premise of the theory. However, the distinctive prediction of this approach is that deprivation within a nation reflects a dependent position in the international division of labor, and that this deprivation statistically interprets the effect of dependency on crime. Few quantitative studies actually consider these claims (for one such study, see Chen, 1992).

Despite ambiguities about the validity of dependency theory, the research does offer clear evidence indicating the importance of the material context. Not only does income inequality emerge as a significant predictor of cross-national variation in homicides rates, indicators of governmental efforts to protect the citizenry from economic hardship also yield reasonably consistent effects. In contrast, standard demographic factors are less important than might be expected in accounting for cross-national variation in criminal violence. This suggests that simply generalizing from individual-level evidence on violence (e.g., age and gender patterns) to the national level through a simple aggregation process is potentially misleading. Evidently, "contextual" effects can modify in an important way the purely "compositional" effects associated with relatively large numbers of persons with various demographic statuses (see Messner & Sampson, 1991). Finally, as noted above, only limited evidence is available concerning the role of social integration and culture. However, when indicators of the integrative and cultural context are statistically significant, they are usually in accord with the predictions of criminological theory (Gartner, 1990).

IV. DESIDERATA

The cross-national research on criminal violence has without question advanced markedly over the course of recent decades. Researchers have become increasingly sensitive to issues of data quality; advanced techniques of causal modeling have been applied in multivariate analyses; and efforts to systematize the literature through comprehensive reviews have appeared. Nevertheless, most scholars in the field concede that knowledge about the reasons for cross-national variation in criminal violence is still at a primitive stage (see, for example, Gartner, 1995). In the sections that follow, I consider some of the more important methodological and theoretical challenges that must be confronted to enhance our understanding of cross-national variation in criminal violence.

1. Methodological Challenges

The compilation of accurate, reliable, and comparable data on criminal violence continues to be a vexing problem. The efforts of the United Nations to standardize data collection and to enhance participation in coverage in its crime surveys are encouraging. Nevertheless, as Newman and Howard (1999:11) caution, it is important to recognize that the collection of international crime statistics presupposes well-developed criminal justice systems at the national level. Some nations simply lack the reporting infrastructure to provide the data requested by multinational organizations. Victimization and self-report surveys circumvent official governmental agencies, but they are expensive to conduct (especially if the samples are to be nationally representative), and execution of such surveys on a regular, ongoing basis is probably unrealistic for the foreseeable future. To a considerable extent, advancement in cross-national research on criminal violence will be dependent on progress in the development of national criminal justice systems.

There is also a dilemma surrounding priorities for data collection. Ideally, researchers desire highly detailed information for large samples of nations. Yet the two objectives of detail and sample size are in some respects incompatible. Given the limited data-collection infrastructures in many nations noted above, research on large samples will undoubtedly be limited to broad categories of offenses, such as aggregated rates of selected forms of criminal violence. Increasingly, however, comparative criminologists have cited the need to disaggregate broad legal categories to discover and explain variation in meaningful subtypes of criminal violence (Gartner, 1995; Weiner & Ruback, 1995).[3] Such disaggregated analyses are feasible only for limited numbers of nations, those with the more sophisticated recording systems. Unfortunately, what is gained in detail on criminal violence is likely to come at the expense of generality (Neapolitan, 1997a:144). Perhaps the wisest course is to encourage both kinds of efforts, recognizing the strengths but also the limitations of each.

Cross-national research on criminal violence is also hindered by limitations in the measurement of strategic independent variables. Most studies employ a fairly standard set of predictors regardless of the theoretical objectives of the research. As Neapolitan (1997a:88–89) observes, this has led to troublesome ambiguities in the literature. Diverse concepts are often operationalized by the same measure, and the same measure may be

---

[3] A good illustration of the utility of examining refined categories of criminal violence is Wilson and Daly's (1992) research on the sex ratio in spousal killings. Their analyses reveal substantively important gender differences across nations in special types of homicide that are not detectable in the total homicide rate.

interpreted as reflecting different concepts. This practice is understandable—researchers tend to select measures of those national characteristics that are readily available in accessible publications, such as those of multinational organizations. The priorities of these organizations and participating governments, however, do not necessarily coincide with those in the scholarly community. In particular, measures of cultural orientations are not well represented in standard data sources. A key challenge for the researchers is to initiate efforts to expand the scope of nationwide data collection to encompass indicators of variables relevant to criminological theories beyond the economic and demographic data that have traditionally been compiled under governmental auspices.

Another important methodological challenge for cross-national researchers is to design, implement, and assess interventions. While a body of literature based on correlational designs has accumulated steadily, comparable efforts to conduct field experiments and intervention assessments have yet to emerge on a significant scale (Weiner & Ruback, 1995:180–181). Such research has particular significance for the development of social policies to deal with the problem of violence.

2. Theoretical Challenges

There is also a pressing need for theoretical development in the field. For the most part, researchers have drawn upon criminological theory to identify potentially important independent variables, but the nature of the relationships between these variables and levels of violence has not been stated with much precision. With few exceptions researchers implicitly assume simple additive, linear relationships (see Gartner, 1995), or "impose" nonlinearities for methodological reasons (e.g., to circumvent heteroscedasticity in regression models). Theoretical rationales for nonlinear relationships warrant greater theoretical attention. Similarly, as noted in my review of the empirical literature, several studies have detected interaction effects of various national characteristics on levels of violence. These effects are typically observed in exploratory analyses and are "under-theorized." An important task for the future is to incorporate interactions more systematically into the theorizing about criminal violence. Similar arguments apply to the examination of, and theorizing about, feedback effects of violence on national structures, i.e., reciprocal causal processes (see Fajnzylber et al., 1998).

More generally, researchers should devote greater efforts to explaining the mechanisms that link independent variables and national rates of violence. At best researchers provide a theoretical rationale for anticipating an association between some national characteristics and rates of criminal violence, but alternative interpretations for the same prediction are usually possible. The precise nature of the hypothetical processes needs to be specified so that distinctive implications of different theoretical arguments can be derived. As Gartner (1995:20) points out, testing for the presence of such intervening mechanisms will probably require the implementation of multilevel research designs.

A final task worthy of concerted attention in the future is the incorporation of diffusion processes into theories of cross-national violence. There has been a growing interest in spatial analyses of violent crime in the "within-nation" literature over recent years, and sophisticated spatial econometric techniques have been developed to identify diffusion or contagion processes in multivariate models (see, for example, the special issue of *Journal of Quantitative Criminology*, December 1999). Moreover, evidence indicates pronounced differences in levels of violence across major regions of the world (Lewis, 1999), which is consistent with diffusion processes. Further theorizing about the possible diffusion of violence is particularly important given the growing recognition that issues of crime and criminal justice increasingly transcend national borders (Arlacchi, 1999).

V. APPROACHES TO PREVENTION

The cross-national work on criminal violence has been oriented mainly toward "basic" rather than "applied" research. Indeed, the primary focus has been on fundamental properties of social organization—social structure and culture—rather than on policies targeted on the problem of violence.[4] Nevertheless, an important implication for prevention can be drawn from the literature.

Without question the most striking finding to emerge from the empirical research is the importance of the material context. The relative economic well-being of the population is one of the most reliable predictors of national rates of criminal violence. Extreme economic stratification apparently provides fertile soil for the kinds of interactions and conflicts that result in criminal violence, especially economic stratification that overlaps with group differences. Moreover, the evidence indicates that governmental assistance and redistributive policies are associated with lower levels of violent crime.

These observations are consistent with the insightful commentary offered by Karl Polanyi more than half a century ago concerning the importance of political interventions in the economies of capitalist societies (Messner & Rosenfeld, 2000). Polanyi emphasized the dangers associated with total reliance on market mechanisms in the organization of economic life, a situation he referred to as the "self-regulating market." He warned that any effort to allow the market free rein would undermine the foundations of social life. The resulting social dislocations, Polanyi (1957:73) further maintained, would lead to a host of undesirable conditions, including high levels of crime.

Capitalist societies responded to the social devastation accompanying the expansion of markets by developing welfare capitalism. In Polanyi's words the welfare state "re-embeds" the economic in social relationships and thereby mitigates the economic hardships and inequalities that are the normal consequence of market economies. Recently, serious questions have been raised about the viability of the welfare state under conditions of global capitalism (Olsen, 1996; Teeple, 1995). Throughout the advanced world political support for interventionist policies appears to be crumbling.

The cross-national literature on criminal violence suggests that movements toward the dismantling of the welfare state must be considered with due regard for undesirable consequences. Some mechanism for avoiding extreme levels of economic inequality and economic marginalization would seem to be necessary to avoid high levels of violent crime in nation-states predicated upon capitalist economies. The most appropriate arrangements for such a purpose will no doubt depend upon the historical and cultural contexts of different nations. Nevertheless, to borrow a phrase from a widely cited study by Judith and Peter Blau (1982), criminal violence may be an unintended but normal "cost of inequality." Avoiding such costs will undoubtedly pose a formidable challenge in an era of global capitalism.

---

[4]Research by Fajnzylber, Lederman and Loyaza (1998) includes indicators of the size of police forces and the conviction rates for homicide in a multivariate, time-series analysis of cross-national variation in homicide rates. Their results indicate negative effects of these measures, lending support for deterrence arguments. The paucity of research in this area, however, requires caution in drawing firm conclusions.

REFERENCES

Adler, Freda. (1983). *Nations not Obsessed with Crime*. Littleton: Fred B. Rothman.

Archer, Dane, & Rosemary Gartner. (1984). *Violence and Crime in Cross-National Perspective*. New Haven: Yale University Press.

Arlacchi, Pino. (1999). Foreword. In Graeme Newman (Ed.), *Global Report on Crime and Justice* (p. iii). New York: Oxford University Press.

Avison, William R., & Pamela L. Loring. (1986). Population Diversity and Cross-National Homicide: The Effects of Inequality and Heterogeneity. *Criminology, 24*(1), 733–749.

Blau, Judith R., & Peter M. Blau. (1982). The Cost of Inequality: Metropolitan Structure and Criminal Violence. *American Sociological Review, 47*(1), 114–129.

Braithwaite, John. (1979). *Inequality, Crime, and Public Policy*. London: Routledge & Kegan Paul.

Braithwaite, John, & Valerid Braithwaite. (1980). The Effect of Income Inequality and Social Democracy on Homicide. *British Journal of Criminology, 20*(1), 45–53.

Castells, Manuel. (1997). *The Power of Identity*. Oxford: Blackwell.

Chen, Danny J. H. (1992). *Third World Crime in the World System: A Cross-National Study*. Unpublished Ph. D. Dissertation, University at Albany, State University of New York.

Currie, Elliott. (1991). Crime in the Market Society: From Bad to Worse in the Nineties. *Dissent*, Spring 1991, 254–259.

Durkheim, Emile. (1964 [1895]). *The Rules of Sociological Method*. New York: Free Press.

Eisner, Manuel. (1995). The Effects of Economic Structures and Phases of Development on Crime. *Criminological Research, 32*, 17–43.

Elias, Norbert. (1978). *The Civilizing Process: The History of Manners*. New York: Urizen Books.

Ember, Carol R., & Melvin Ember. (1995). Issues in Cross-Cultural Studies of Interpersonal Violence. In R. Barry Ruback & Neil Alan Weiner (Eds.), *Interpersonal Violent Behaviors: Social and Cultural Aspects* (pp. 25–42). New York: Springer.

Fajnzylber, Pablo, Daniel Lederman, & Norman Loayza. (1998). *Determinants of Crime Rates in Latin America and the World: An Empirical Assessment*. Washington: World Bank.

Fiala, Robert, & Gary LaFree. (1988). Cross-National Determinants of Child Homicide. *American Sociological Review, 53*(3), 432–445.

Findlay, Mark. (1999). *The Globalization of Crime: Understanding Traditional Relationships in Context*. Cambridge: Cambridge University Press.

Gartner, Rosemary. (1990). The Victims of Homicide: A Temporal and Cross-National Comparison. *American Sociological Review, 55*(1), 92–106.

Gartner, Rosemary. (1995). Methodological Issues in Cross-Cultural Large-Survey Research on Violence. In R. Barry Ruback & Neil Alan Weiner (Eds.), *Interpersonal Violent Behaviors: Social and Cultural Aspects* (pp. 7–24). New York: Springer.

Gottfredson, Michael R., & Travis Hirschi. (1990). *A General Theory of Crime*. Stanford: Stanford University Press.

Groves, W. Byron, Richard McCleary, & Graeme Newman. (1985). Religion, Modernization, and World Crime. *Comparative Social Research, 8*, 59–78.

Haferkamp, Hans, & Hyacinthe Ellis. (1991). Power, Individualism and the Sanctity of Human Life: Development of Criminality and Punishment in Four Cultures. In Hans-Gunther Heiland, Louise I. Shelley & Hisao Katoh (Eds.), *Crime and Control in Comparative Perspective* (pp. 261–279). New York: Walter de Gruyter.

Hansmann, Henry B., & John M. Quigley. (1982). Population Heterogeneity and the Sociogenesis of Homicide. *Social Forces, 61*(1), 206–224.

Heiland, Hans-Gunther, & Louise Shelley. (1991). Civilization, Modernization and the Development of Crime and Control. In Hans-Gunther Heiland, Louise Shelley & Hisao Katoh (Eds.), *Crime and Control in Comparative Perspective* (pp. 1–19). New York: Walter de Gruyter.

Huang, W. S. Wilson. (1995). A Cross-National Analysis of the Effect of Moral Individualism on Murder Rates. *International Journal of Offender Therapy and Comparative Criminology, 39*(1), 63–75.

Junger-Tas, Josine, Gert-Jan Terlouw, & Malcolm Kein (Eds.) (1994). *Delinquent Behavior of Young People in the Western World—First Results of an International Self-Report Delinquency Study*. Amsterdam: Kugler Publications.

Karstedt, Susanne. (1999). *The Moral Strength of Weak Ties: A Cross-Cultural Analysis of Individualism and Violence. Fifty-first Annual Meeting of the American Society of Criminology* (pp. 17–20). Toronto, Canada.

Krahn, Harvey, Timothy F. Hartnagel, & John W. Gartrell. (1986). Income Inequality and Homicide Rates: Cross-National Data and Criminological Theories. *Criminology, 24*(2), 269–295.

Kick, Edward L., & Gary D. LaFree. (1985). Development and the Social Context of Murder. *Comparative Social Research, 8*, 37–58.

Killias, Martin. (1992). Gun Ownership, Suicide, and Homicide: An International Perspective. In Anna Alvazzi del Frate, Ugljesa Zvekic & Jan J. M. van Dijk (Eds.), *Understanding Crime: Experiences of Crime and Crime Control* (pp. 289–302). Rome, Italy: UNICRI.

Krohn, Marvin D. (1976). Inequality, Unemployment, and Crime: A Cross-National Analysis. *Sociological Quarterly, 17*(3), 303–313.

LaFree, Gary. (1999). A Summary and Review of Cross-National Comparative Studies of Homicide. In M. Dwayne Smith & Margaret A. Zahn (Eds.), *Homicide: A Sourcebook of Social Research* (pp. 125–145). Thousand Oaks: Sage.

LaFree, Gary, & Edward L. Kick. (1986). Cross-National Effects of Developmental, Distributional, and Demographic Variables on Crime: A Review and Analysis. *International Annals of Criminology, 24*(1–2), 213–235.

Landau, Simha F., & Danny Pfeffermann. (1988). A Time Series Analysis of Violent Crime and Its Relation to Prolonged States of Warfare: The Israeli Case. *Criminology, 26*(3), 489–504.

Lewis, Chris. (1999). Police Records of Crime. In Graeme Newman (Ed.), *Global Report on Crime and Justice* (pp. 43–63). New York: Oxford University Press.

Lilly, J. Robert, Francis T. Cullen, & Richard A. Ball. (1989). *Criminological Theory: Context and Consequences*. Newbury Park: Sage.

Lynch, James. (1995). Crime in International Perspective. In James Q. Wilson & Joan Petersilia (Eds.), *Crime* (pp. 11–38). San Francisco: ICS Press.

McDonald, Lynn. (1976). *The Sociology of Law and Order*. Boulder: Westview Press.

Messner, Steven F. (1980). Income Inequality and Murder Rates: Some Cross-National Findings. *Comparative Social Research, 3*, 185–198.

Messner, Steven F. (1982). Societal Development, Social Equality, and Homicide: A Cross-National Test of a Durkheimian Model. *Social Forces, 61*(1), 225–240.

Messner, Steven F. (1985). Sex Differences in Arrest Rates for Homicide: An Application of the General Theory of Structural Strain. *Comparative Social Research, 8*, 187–201.

Messner, Steven F. (1989). Economic Discrimination and Societal Homicide Rates: Further Evidence on the Cost of Inequality. *American Sociological Review, 54*(4), 597–611.

Messner, Steven F., & Robert J. Sampson. (1991). The Sex Ratio, Family Disruption, and Rates of Violent Crime: The Paradox of Demographic Structure. *Social Forces, 69*(3), 693–713.

Messner, Steven F., & Richard Rosenfeld. (1997). Political Restraint of the Market and Levels of Criminal Homicide: A Cross-National Application of Institutional-Anomie Theory. *Social Forces, 75*(4), 1393–1416.

Messner, Steven F., & Richard Rosenfeld. (2000). Market Dominance, Crime, and Globalization. In Susanne Karstedt & Kai-D. Bussman (Eds.), *Social Dynamics of Crime and Control: New Theories for a World in Transition* (pp. 13–26). Oxford: Hart Publishing.

Mittelman, John H. (1996). How Does Globalization Really Work? In James H. Mittelman (Ed.), *Globalization: Critical Reflections* (pp. 229–241). Boulder: Lynne Rienner.

Neapolitan, Jerome L. (1994). Cross-National Variation in Homicides: The Case of Latin America. *International Criminal Justice Review, 4*, 4–22.

Neapolitan, Jerome L. (1996). Cross-National Crime Data: Some Unaddressed Problems. *Journal of Crime and Justice, 19*(1), 95–112.

Neapolitan, Jerome L. (1997a). *Cross-National Crime: A Research Review and Sourcebook*. Westport: Greenwood Press.

Neapolitan, Jerome L. (1997b). Homicides in Developing Nations: Results of Research Using a Large and Representative Sample. *International Journal of Offender Therapy and Comparative Criminology, 41*(4), 358–374.

Neuman, W. Lawrence, & Ronald J. Berger. (1988). Competing Perspectives on Cross-National Crime: An Evaluation of Theory and Evidence. *Sociological Quarterly, 29*(2), 281–313.

Newman, Graeme, & Gregory J. Howard. (1999). Introduction: Data Sources and Their Use. In Graeme Newman (Ed.), *Global Report on Crime and Justice* (pp. 1–23). New York: Oxford University Press.

Olsen, Gregg M. (1996). Re-Modeling Sweden: The Rise and Demise of the Swedish Compromise in a Global Economy. *Social Problems, 43*(1), 1–20.

Pampel, Fred C., & Rosemary Gartner. (1995). Age Structure, Socio-Political Institutions, and National Homicide Rates. *European Sociological Review, 11*(3), 243–260.

Polanyi, Karl. (1957) [1944]. *The Great Transformation: The Political and Economic Origins of Our Time.* Boston: Beacon Press.

Reiss, Albert J., Jr., & Jeffrey A. Roth (Eds.) (1993). *Understanding and Preventing Violence.* Washington: National Academy Press.

Shelley, Louise I. (1981). *Crime and Modernization: The Impact of Industrialization and Urbanization on Crime.* Carbondale: Southern Illinois University Press.

Shelley, Louise I. (1986). Crime and Modernization Reexamined. *Annales Internationales de Criminologie, 24*(1–2), 7–21.

Short, James F., Jr. (1985). The Level of Explanation Problem in Criminology. In Robert M. Meier (Ed.), *Theoretical Methods in Criminology* (pp. 51–72). Beverly Hills: Sage.

Smith, Earl, & Siu Kwong Wong. (1989). Durkheim, Individualism and Homicide Rates Re-examined. *Sociological Spectrum, 9*, 269–283.

Tedeschi, James T., & Richard B. Felson. (1994). *Violence, Aggression, and Coercive Actions.* Washington: American Psychological Association.

Teeple, Gary. (1995). *Globalization and the Decline of Social Reform.* Atlantic Highlands: Humanities Press.

Travis, Gail, David Brown, Sandra Egger, Russell Hogg, Brian O'Toole, & Julie Stubbs. (1995). The International Crime Surveys: Some Methodological Concerns. *Current Issues in Criminal Justice, 6*(3), 346–361.

Unnithan, N. Prabha, & Hugh P. Whitt. (1992). Inequality, Economic Development and Lethal Violence: A Cross-National Analysis of Suicide and Homicide. *International Journal of Comparative Sociology, 33*(3–4), 182–196.

van Dijk, Jan J. M. (1999). The Experience of Crime and Justice. In Graeme Newman (Ed.), *Global Report on Crime and Justice* (pp. 25–41). New York: Oxford University Press.

van Dijk, Jan J. M., Pat Mayhew, & Martin Killias. (1991). *Experiences of Crime across the World: Key Findings from the 1989 International Crime Survey.* The Netherlands: Kluwer Law and Taxation Publishers.

van Dijk, Jan J. M., & Kristiina Kangaspunta. (2000). Piecing Together the Cross-National Crime Puzzle. *National Institute of Justice Journal, 1*, 34–41.

Walker, John. (1999). Firearm Abuse and Regulation. In Graeme Newman (Ed.), *Global Report on Crime and Justice* (pp. 151–169). New York: Oxford University Press.

Weiner, Neil Alan, & R. Barry Ruback. (1995). Inquiry Through a Comparative Lens: Unraveling the Social and Cultural Aspects of Interpersonal Violent Behaviors. In R. Barry Ruback & Neil Alan Weiner (Eds.), *Interpersonal Violent Behaviors: Social and Cultural Aspects* (pp. 171–182). New York: Springer.

Wilson, Margo I., & Martin Daly. (1992). Who Kills Whom in Spouse Killings? On the Exceptional Sex Ratio of Spousal Killings in the United States. *Criminology, 30*(2), 189–215.

Zimring, Franklin E., & Gordon Hawkins. (1997). *Crime Is Not the Problem: Lethal Violence in America.* New York: Oxford University Press.

Subject Index

direct violence, 21, 24, 31, 32, 84, 86, 87, 198, 314, 483, 543–561, 563–565, 600, 624, 780, 883, 911, 938, 959, 973, 1105

disability, 173, 674, 722, 743, 769, 772, 829, 857, 891, 1119

discipline, 3, 9, 11, 33, 38, 41, 52–54, 116, 117, 127, 131, 135, 136, 145, 146, 150, 172, 173, 177–180, 182, 183, 185–187, 190, 191, 193, 194, 196, 200–202, 212, 262, 272, 288, 293, 294, 304, 305, 323, 324, 327, 333, 335, 370, 371, 402, 430, 463, 468, 477, 497, 498, 500, 523, 535, 572, 588, 607, 655, 686, 688, 691, 729, 730, 733, 738, 743, 744, 748, 822, 832, 860, 864, 573–875, 889, 925, 931, 949–951, 959, 960, 974, 975, 986, 989, 991, 995, 1003, 1006, 1049, 1071, 1079, 1167, 1234

discrimination, 13, 25, 84, 85, 90–92, 95, 145, 160, 189, 218, 230, 231, 234–237, 239, 241–243, 255, 299, 347, 354, 369, 431, 438, 517, 523, 619, 715, 728, 797, 801, 811, 863, 888, 896, 1105, 1141–1143, 1158, 1237

disintegration, 5, 8, 55, 278, 297, 300, 313, 355, 410, 419, 424, 425, 431, 432, 636–639, 796, 867, 868, 967, 969, 1034, 1062, 1064, 1187

disobedience, 34, 197, 234, 369–371, 376, 465, 468, 993, 995, 996, 1004, 1048, 1085, 100, 1102–1111

disorganization, 75–77, 82, 564, 617, 623–625, 627, 637, 643–645, 652, 653, 656, 703, 824, 825, 938, 943, 1141–1145, 1168–1172, 1179

displacement, 18, 23, 157, 166, 233, 259, 264, 265, 329, 352, 461, 462, 525, 649, 673, 747, 915, 979, 1201, 1213

distribution of power, 6, 21, 34, 97, 125, 130, 147, 254, 256, 297, 299, 304, 305, 309, 312, 314, 316, 342, 352–354, 357–359, 474, 625, 695, 803, 889, 945, 978, 1046, 1117

dominance, 10, 27, 105–107, 109, 172, 230, 254, 277, 283, 409, 417, 454, 490, 553, 591, 604, 629, 634, 695, 715, 802, 877, 905, 911, 927–929, 980, 983, 1031, 1229

drugs, 75–77, 81, 82, 88, 90, 112, 174, 178, 181, 182, 198, 217, 274, 277, 279, 292, 302, 333, 339, 343, 379, 491, 603, 605, 614, 616, 633, 636, 643, 645, 648, 668, 670, 673, 676, 677, 685, 691, 692, 695–699, 743, 753, 768, 769, 775, 776, 783, 813, 815, 819, 864, 869, 871, 876, 892, 900, 902, 915, 920, 940, 947, 1065, 1068, 1075, 1124, 1125, 1142, 1170, 1173, 1174, 1177, 1209, 1218, 1220, 1222, 1223, 1230

ecology, 70, 82, 370, 375, 381, 585, 587, 612, 645, 733, 859, 872, 934

education, 4, 14, 51, 54, 87, 108, 126, 143, 155, 177, 183, 198, 203, 277, 278, 334, 386, 390, 413, 418, 466, 508, 512, 534, 535, 537, 555, 565, 603, 620, 621, 624, 636, 669, 671, 720, 722, 724, 745, 747, 748, 751, 763–765, 781, 813, 815, 827, 841, 842, 855, 861, 865, 867, 870, 872, 873, 875, 876, 878,

880, 883, 884, 897, 900, 905, 907, 917, 919, 920, 933, 934, 938, 939, 941, 945, 948–951, 968, 1044, 1102, 1106, 1117, 1123, 1144, 1152, 1153, 1176, 1192, 1196, 1217, 1235

educational science, 747, 873

elite, 21, 67, 68, 122, 126, 127, 136, 148, 151, 152, 163, 173, 179, 180, 214, 229, 254, 259, 265, 268, 276, 290, 300, 316, 339, 342, 344, 373, 384, 388, 390, 395, 396, 403, 405, 407, 408, 411–414, 445–447, 961, 964, 966, 968, 973–981, 983–985, 987, 1007, 1073, 1100, 1195

emergency, 31, 104, 158, 202, 211, 213, 217, 236, 667, 719, 738, 743, 839, 895, 973, 1048–1050, 1100–1102

emotion, 149, 466, 469, 474, 477, 479, 485, 487–489, 491–493, 538, 727, 778, 820, 831, 1142, 1165–1195, 1197–1199

employment, 53, 69, 75, 77–82, 92, 100, 105, 109, 124, 125, 146, 147, 150, 151, 155, 156, 165, 174, 177, 178, 214, 269, 272, 274, 277, 278, 309, 339, 342, 345, 362, 364, 370, 413, 418, 442, 466, 561, 563, 574, 617–621, 635, 643, 649, 650, 668, 670, 671, 685–688, 690, 691, 694, 696, 704, 706, 710, 715, 721, 723, 742–744, 751, 760, 765, 788, 793, 796, 811, 851, 867, 876, 887, 888, 890–893, 897, 940, 944, 945, 948, 950, 978, 980, 983, 1031, 1117, 1119, 1123, 1141, 1168, 1170–1173, 1182, 1183, 1185

enemy image, 362, 431, 531, 792, 1189, 1191

enmity, 264, 401, 402, 408, 411, 422, 426, 431, 904

environmental factors, 507, 558, 590–596, 600, 601, 603–606, 728, 851, 854, 868, 929, 1169

equality, 25, 34, 103, 124, 126, 133, 251, 329, 359, 381, 384, 556, 638, 639, 715, 789, 856, 888, 1106, 1107

escalation, 4, 9–11, 21, 31, 32, 49, 68, 126, 196, 233, 239, 241, 244, 248, 253–256, 258–260, 269, 270, 272, 276, 287, 289, 290, 294, 297, 300–302, 306, 333, 345, 360–362, 365, 366, 370, 376–379, 384, 388–391, 396, 397, 404, 407, 408, 411, 412, 414, 415, 417, 427, 428, 431, 432, 449, 466, 467, 474, 496, 500, 501, 503, 506, 508, 529, 532, 533, 575, 577, 584, 653, 654, 657, 668–670, 745, 799, 808, 812, 822, 825, 869, 879, 895, 904, 924, 931–933, 949, 1018, 1105, 1108, 1129, 1163, 1168, 1181

eschatology, 337, 941, 978, 979

ethics, 104, 127, 179, 190, 195, 200, 214, 221–223, 279, 288, 303, 324, 336, 337, 390, 517, 679, 681, 695, 768, 778, 919, 965, 974, 976, 979, 984, 985, 993, 1003, 1015, 1033, 1035, 1098, 1191, 1192, 1205, 1213, 1215

ethnic group, 84, 92, 134, 135, 139, 142, 227, 228, 235, 244, 245, 248–251, 254–257, 259, 265, 266, 277, 286, 297, 299, 302, 307, 351, 353, 354, 357–359, 361, 362, 416, 553, 618, 622, 624, 639, 667, 709, 789, 872, 1064, 1178, 1181, 1184

ethnic identity, 229, 230, 233, 238, 250, 256, 258, 265, 289, 966

SUBJECT INDEX

SUBJECT INDEX

Name Index

NAME INDEX

NAME INDEX

NAME INDEX

Polk, Kenneth 574, 741
Popitz, Heinrich 17, 20, 23, 25, 100, 248, 932
Popp, Ulrike 878, 1113
Popper, Karl R. 1204, 1211
Posen, Barry R. 232, 255
Potter, Gary W. 686, 688
Potter, Kimberly 795, 802
Poulin, Francois 502, 545
Powell, G. Bingham 961, 964
Powers, Jane L. 722, 723
Poznanski, Renée 153, 155
Pruitt, Dean G. 1181, 1182, 1189, 1194
Ptacek, James 742, 746, 747
Pulkkinen, Lea 544, 635
Putnam, Frank, W. 819, 822, 823, 827
Pye, Lucian W. 199, 959

Quanty, Michael B. 461, 486
Quigley, Brain M. 1220, 1222, 1227

Radbruch, Gustav 100, 1104
Raines, Adrian, J. 820, 824
Rajalin, Sirpa 923, 926, 929, 932
Rammstedt, Othein 1113, 1191
Ramsey, Elizabeth 501, 871
Rankin, Joseph. H. 623, 626
Rapoport, Anatol 1186, 1191
Rauchfleisch, Udo 14, 30
Rausch, Thomas 1205, 1207, 1214
Rawlings, Edna 520, 525
Rawls, John 993, 996, 1106–1108
Ray, Glen E. 502, 553
Reemtsma, Katrin 427, 791
Reichenbach, Peter 1079
Reinares, Fernando 299, 309–314, 317, 318
Reiner, Robert 211, 215, 218
Reinhard, Wolfgang 1058, 1060, 1062
Reis, Christa 1167, 1213
Reiss, Albert J., Jr. 702, 775
Reiter, Herbert 219, 380, 397
Rejali, Darius M. 193, 199, 200
Remschmidt, Helmut 519, 520, 534
Renan, Ernest 975, 976
Renzetti, Claire M. 110, 849
Retzinger, Suzanne M. 484, 628
Reuband, Karl-Heinz 1135, 1140
Reuter, Peter 679, 685–688, 692, 693
Rieseberg, Angela 523, 525
Riger, Stephanie 1137, 1143
Rind, Michael M. 1006–1008
Risman, Barbara J. 549, 552, 553
Robey, Ames 853, 854
Robinson, Richard 998, 1000, 1001
Rodley, Nigel S. 189–192, 194, 195
Roeder, Philip G. 229, 230, 238
Rogger, Hans 351, 354
Rose, Amanda J. 547, 557, 559, 560

Rösel, Jakob 255, 256, 353, 354, 358, 363
Rosenbaum, H. Jon 339, 346
Rosenfeld, Richard 83, 88, 615, 704, 707, 713, 1171
Rosenthal, Robert 1231, 1235
Rosenwald, Richard 853, 854
Ross, Catherine E. 558, 625, 634
Rothe, J. Peter 929, 932
Rothengatter, Talib 930, 933
Rousseau, Jean-Jacques 123, 940
Rousseaux, Xavier 42, 43, 45, 49, 53
Rowe, David C. 511, 594, 595, 600, 601
Ruback, R. Barry 701, 711, 712, 927
Rubin, Jeffrey Z. 1181, 1182, 1189, 1192, 1194
Rucht, Dieter 369–371, 373–375, 379, 384, 1169, 1187, 1191
Rueschemeyer, Dietrich 1057, 1059
Rufin, Jean-Christophe 302, 1062–1064
Ruggiero, Vincenzo 679, 682, 694
Rule, James R. 363, 372, 395
Runtz, Marsha 818, 823
Russell, Diana E. 741, 847
Rutter, Michael 543, 545, 549, 553, 555, 556, 591, 694, 722, 726, 865, 1118
Rys, Gail S. 544, 546, 548, 459, 551, 560

Sabo, Don 910, 911
Sacco, Vincent F. 111, 742, 760, 777
Sack, Fritz 625, 626, 1067, 1069, 1191
Saft, Elizabeth W. 723–726, 728, 729
Salmivalli, Christina 501, 502, 873
Saltzman, Linda E. 631, 740, 840, 846
Sampson, Robert J.67, 75, 77, 88–90, 543, 544, 549, 555, 556, 560, 617, 621, 623, 625, 634, 635, 710, 1168, 1171–1173
Sánchez-Jankowski 1168, 1172, 1174, 1175
Saunders, Daniel G. 742, 747, 847
Schachter, Oscar 1061, 1062, 1073
Schäfer, Mechthild 1222, 1228
Scharpf, Fritz 1060, 1068, 1072
Scheidle, Günter 1100–1102, 1104
Schelling, Thomas C. 685, 1182, 1186, 1196
Scherrer, Christian P. 247, 297
Schetter, Conrad 247, 250, 255
Scheuerman, William 1066, 1070, 1073
Scheungrab, Michael 511, 517, 526, 527
Schilling, Heinz 250, 1011
Schlag, Bernhard 929, 934
Schlee, Günther 261, 264, 270, 281
Schmid, Alex P. 191, 192, 197, 199, 200, 309, 311, 317
Schneider, Barry H. 545, 546, 548, 551, 560
Schneider, Hans Joachim 207, 524
Schönhammer, Rainer 929, 932
Schorsch, Eberhard 102, 105, 113
Schröder, Helmut 639, 966
Schröttle, Monika 104, 106
Schubarth, Wilfried 874, 879, 880

NAME INDEX

Toch, Hans H. 466, 468, 490, 742
Tolman, Richard M. 742, 744, 747
Tomada, Giovanna 545, 546, 548, 551, 560
Tonry, Michael H. 85, 91, 92, 94, 1071
Toprak, Ahmed 1117, 1120
Tornay, Serge 274, 281
Tremblay, Richard E. 505, 544, 545, 547, 549, 551, 555–557, 559
Trickett, Penelope K. 822, 823
Trotha, Trutz von 20, 248, 280, 354, 1058, 1061, 1062, 1113, 1167, 1185, 1210, 1211, 1233
Truscott, Susan 175, 176, 178
Tuchel, Johannes 1100, 1102
Turkus, Burton B. 687–689
Turner, Ralph H. 1160, 1187–1189

Uggen, Christopher 79, 80, 629
Ulbrich-Herrmann, Matthias 1219
Underwood, Marion K. 546, 547, 553, 558, 560

Van de Vate, Dwight, Jr. 991, 992, 997
van den Berghe, Pierre 229, 254
van der Kolk, Bessel A. 201, 817, 819, 820, 822, 823, 827
Van der Veer, Peter 351, 361, 1012
van Kampen, Norbert 626, 628
Vanberg, Victor 630, 1193
Vandello, Joe 11, 1117, 1120
Verba, Sidney 958, 959, 962, 963
Vigil, James D. 1172, 1173, 1175
Virdee, Satnam 790, 794
Virtanen, Timo 420, 421, 423
von Beyme, Klaus 403, 959

Wade, Francis C. 991, 994
Wadsworth, Tim 67, 78
Wagner, Bernd 406, 967
Wait, Tracey 175, 176, 178
Waldmann, Peter 24, 30–32, 249, 253, 255, 257, 270, 274, 275, 293–296, 299–305, 311, 313, 314, 351, 392, 399, 1105, 1190
Walker, Charles C. 1106, 1108
Walker, Samantha 546, 548, 549
Walker, Samuel 1066, 1067, 1069, 1070, 1073
Walklate, Sandra 612, 1145
Walter, Barbara F. 242, 243, 296, 297, 300, 304, 305
Walters, Richard H. 461, 463, 526
Wang, Lu-In 802, 812, 813
Warr, Mark 613, 623, 635, 1133, 1137, 1138, 1144, 1157, 1158
Warshow, Robert 679, 1027
Wasileski, Maryann 175, 178
Weber, Max 5, 17, 18, 31, 52, 53, 207, 209, 212, 213, 220, 248, 274, 285, 299, 325, 326, 331, 957, 974, 976, 978, 981, 982, 1044, 1045, 1055, 1057–1059, 1061, 1071, 1072, 1085, 1114
Weidner, Jens 1119, 1122

Weimann, Gabriel 532, 1156
Weinberg, Leonard 311, 313, 403, 406, 416, 428, 429, 792
Weingart, Gail 863
Weis, Joseph G. 68, 71, 840
Weis, Kurt 529, 774
Weiß, Rudolf H. 517, 524, 525, 529, 531
Weiss, Susanne 863, 878
Wells, L. Edward 623, 626, 628
Werner, Nicole E. 506, 560
Wertheimer, Jürgen 1025, 1035
Wessinger, Catherine 328, 332
Westley, William 215, 217
Wetzels, Peter 112, 412, 818, 1132, 1133, 1138, 1139
Wetzstein, Thomas A. 26, 1167, 1213
White, Helene R. 616, 628
White, Robert W. 314, 386, 391, 392
Whitlock, Francis A. 925, 927, 928
Widom, Cathy S. 463, 727, 840, 851
Wiesenthal, David L. 926, 929
Wieviorka, Michel 219, 312, 392, 406, 410, 416, 426, 863, 868, 946, 948
Wilde, Gerald J.S. 926, 933
Wilkinson, Paul 311, 312, 317, 383, 386
Willems, Helmut 362, 409, 412–416, 420, 619, 640, 788, 791, 792, 1113, 1116, 1119, 1120, 1168, 1181, 1182, 1187–1189, 1191, 1194, 1207, 1213
Williams, Christopher 773, 1230
Williams, George C. 573, 583
Williams, John 913, 914, 916, 917
Williams, Kirk 69, 71–74, 631, 852
Williamson, Jennifer 428, 786, 801
Willke, Helmut 1068, 1072
Willms, J. Douglas 545, 559
Willoweit, Dietmar 1046, 1101
Wilson, Barbara J. 514, 515
Wilson, James Q. 208, 466, 1069, 1141, 1145
Wilson, Margo 569, 573–584, 680, 739–741, 744, 747, 847, 848, 856
Wilson, Melvin N. 726–730
Wilson, Susan K. 110, 848
Wilson, William J. 67, 69, 71, 74–78, 80, 86–89, 558, 580, 617, 1173
Wimmer, Andreas 247, 248, 250, 253, 266, 354
Winslow, Donna 179, 181, 182
Winterhoff-Spurk, Peter 529, 530
Wiseman, Karen A. 580, 581
Witte, Rob 421, 424, 787, 789
Wolfe, David A. 110, 747, 821, 848
Wolfe, Jessica 174, 175
Wolff, Robert Paul 996–998
Wolfgang, Marvin E. 612, 620, 690, 760, 1124, 1169, 1170
Wolzendorff, Kurt 1098, 1099
Wright, Jack C. 502, 582

Yablonski, Lewis 1167, 1169

The Authors

I. THE FRAMEWORK OF THE HANDBOOK

1. Violence: The Difficulties of a Systematic International Review

Wilhelm Heitmeyer (Dr. Phil.) is Professor of Socialization and Director of the Institute for Interdisciplinary Research on Conflict and Violence at Bielefeld University. His research interests concentrate on violence, right-wing extremism, and ethnic-cultural conflicts. His publications include *Rechtsextremistische Orientierungen bei Jugendlichen* [Right-Wing Extremism Among Young People] (1987); *Gewalt* [Violence] (with colleagues) (1995); *Bedrohte Stadtgesellschaften* [Urban Societies Under Threat] (co-edited with Reimund Anhut) (2000).

John Hagan is John D. MacArthur Professor of Sociology and Law (Northwestern University) and Senior Research Fellow (American Bar Foundation). His principal research and teaching interests encompass crime, law and the life course. His books: *Mean Streets: Youth Crime and Homelessness* (with Bill McCarthy) (1997); Northern Passage: American Vietnam War Resisters in Canada (2001); Youth Violence and the End of Adolescence (with Holly Foster, American Sociological Review) (2001).

2. The Concept of Violence

Peter Imbusch (Dr. phil.) is *Privatdozent* at the Institute of Sociology at Philipps University in Marburg and Research Associate at the Institute for Interdisciplinary Research on Conflict and Violence at Bielefeld University. His principal teaching and research areas are in political sociology, sociological theory, conflict and violence, and social structures. Recent books: *Macht und Herrschaft* [Power and Rule] (ed.) (1998); *Friedens- und Konfliktforschung* [Peace and Conflict Studies] (co-edited with Ralf Zoll) (1999); *Zivilisation und Gewalt* [Civilization and Violence] (2002).

3. The Long-term Development of Violence: Empirical Findings and Theoretical Approaches to Interpretation

Manuel Eisner (Dr. phil.) is Reader in Sociological Criminology and deputy director of the Institute of Criminology at the University of Cambridge. His work focuses on the fields of social transformation and criminality, research into youth delinquency, environmental sociology, and cultural sociology. Recent publications include *Das Ende der zivilisierten Stadt? Die Auswirkungen von Individualisierung und urbaner Krise auf Gewaltdelinquenz* [The End of the Civilized City? The Effects of Individualization and Urban Crisis on Violent Delinquency] (1997); *Violent Crime in the Urban Community: A Comparison of Stockholm and Basel* (with Per-Olof Wikström, European Journal of Criminal Policy and Research, 1999); *Modernization, Self-Control and Lethal Violence—The Long-Term Dynamics of European Homicide Rates in Theoretical Perspective* (British Journal of Criminology, 2001).

II. RESEARCH ON VIOLENCE: AN INTERDISCIPLINARY APPROACH WITH A FOCUS ON SOCIAL SCIENCES

1. Societal Structures and Institutions: Social Conditions and State Agents

1.1 Social Structures and Inequalities

1.1.1 Poverty and Violence

Robert D. Crutchfield (Ph.D., Vanderbilt University) is Professor of Sociology and Department Chair at the University of Washington in Seattle. He is a past Vice-president of the American Society of Criminology and is currently on the Council of the American Sociological Association's Crime, Law and Deviance Section. His publications include *Labor Stratification and Violent Crime* (Social Forces, 1989) and *Ethnicity, Labor Markets and Crime* (1995). He co-authored many articles, e.g., *Racial and Ethnic Disparities in Imprisonment* (Government Report, 1986); *Work and Crime: The Effects of Labor Stratification* (Social Forces, 1997); *A Tale of Three Cities: Labor Markets and Homicide* (Sociological Focus, 1999).

Tim Wadsworth (M.A., University of Washington) is a Ph.D. Candidate in the Sociology Department at the University of Washington and a National Institute of Justice Dissertation Fellow. His current work focuses on the relationship between work and criminal behavior at both the individual and community levels. He published *Labor Markets, Delinquency and Social Control Theory: An Empirical Assessment of the Mediating Process* (2000) in Social Forces, as well as several public policy reports addressing issues of juvenile justice in Washington State.

1.1.2 Ethnic Segregation and Violence

James F. Short Jr. is Professor Emeritus of Sociology and Senior Research Associate of the Social and Economic Sciences Research Center at Washington State University. He was Director of Research (with Marvin Wolfgang) of the National Commission on the

Causes and Prevention of Violence (1968–1969), a member of the National Academy of Science, National Research Council Committee on Law and Justice, and that committee's Panel on the Understanding and Control of Violent Behavior. He served as editor of the American Sociological Review and as President of the American Sociological Association, the Pacific Sociological Society, and the American Society of Criminology. His latest book is *Poverty, Ethnicity, and Violent Crime* (1997).

1.1.3   A Comparative Examination of Gender-Perspectives on Violence

Carol Hagemann-White (Dr. phil.) is professor of educational theory and feminist studies at the University of Osnabrück. Her focal research areas are gender-based violence: intervention, prevention, and social change; women and health; socialization and the construction of gender; women, power and the politics of equality. Besides empirical research she is involved in building European research networks in these areas. Important publications are: *Socialization: feminine-masculine?* (1984); *Strategies against Violence in Gender Relations* (1992), *Male Violence and Control: Building a Comparative European Perspective* (in: Duncan and Pfau-Effinger: Gender, Economy and Culture in the EU, 2000); and *Comprehensive Report on the Health of Women in Germany* (with other authors) (2001).

1.2   Violence in and by State Institutions

1.2.1   Violence and the Rise of the State

Michael Hanagan (Ph.D., University of Michigan) is Senior Lecturer at the New School University in New York City. He is currently collaborating on a world history textbook and on a comparative study of the welfare state in England, France, and the United States. His publications include two books on labor history and numerous articles on world history, globalization, and violent social movements. He has co-edited several books, most recently *Expanding Rights, Reconfiguring States* (1999) with Charles Tilly and *Challenging Authority: The Historical Study of Contentious Politics* (1998) with Leslie Moch and Wayne Te Brake. He is a senior editor of *International Labor and Working-Class History*.

1.2.2   Holocaust

Peter Longerich (Dr. phil.) is a professor at Royal Holloway College, University of London. His main research interest are the Weimar Republic, National Socialism and Holocaust. Selected publications: *Politik der Vernichtung. Eine Gesamtdarstellung der nationalsozialistischen Judenverfolgung* [Policies of Extermination: An Overall Description of National Socialist Persecution of the Jews] (1998); *Der ungeschriebene Befehl. Hitler und der Weg zur "Endlösung"* [The Unwritten Order: Hitler and the Road to the "Final Solution"] (2001);. He co-edited the German edition of *Enzyklopädie des Holocaust* [Encyclopedia of the Holocaust] (3 volumes) with Eberhard Jäckel and Julius Schoeps.

1.2.3   Violence Within the Military

Gerhard Kümmel (Dr. phil.) is Research Associate at the German Armed Forces Institute for Social Research (SOWI). His current research projects include violent behavior of the youth and integration of women in the Bundeswehr. He has published books and articles on issues of international relations, European integration and security policy. One of the most important publications is *Transnationale Wirtschaftskooperation und der Nationalstaat. Deutsch-amerikanische Unternehmensbeziehungen in den 30er Jahren* [Trans-national Economic Cooperation and the Nation-State. German-American Corporate Relations in the 1930s.] (1996), *Zwischen Differenz und Gleichheit. Die Öffnung der Bundeswehr für Frauen* [Between Difference and Equality—The Opening of the Bundeswehr for Women] (2000, co-authored), *Warum nicht?—Die ambivalente Sicht männlicher Soldaten auf die weitere Öffnung der Bundeswehr für Frauen* [Why not?— The Ambivalent Attitudes of Male Soldiers toward the Integration of Women into the Bundeswehr] (2001, co-authored) He co-edited *European Security* (1997), *Military Sociology* (2000) and edited *The Challenging Continuity of Change and the Military* (2001).

Paul Klein (Dr. rer. soc.) is Acting Scientific Director at the German Armed Forces Institute for Social Research (SOWI) and Lecturer at the Bundeswehr University in Munich. His current research topics include military multinationalism and the force structure of the Bundeswehr. He has published numerous books and articles on military-sociological topics. His books include *Militär und Gesellschaft* [Armed Forces and Society] (co-edited with Ekkehard Lippert) (1979); *Deutsch-französische Verteidigungskooperation—Das Beispiel der Deutsch-Französischen Brigade* [German-French Defense-Cooperation—The Example of the German-French Brigade] (1990); *Mitbestimmung in den Streitkräften* [Co-Determination within the Armed Forces] (1991). He co-edited *Eine einzigartige Zusammenarbeit—Das Deutsch-Niederländische Korps* [A Unique Cooperation—The German-Dutch Corps] (1996).

1.2.4 Violence in Prisons/Torture

Ronald D. Crelinsten is Professor of Criminology at the University of Ottawa. His research interests include the media, policy-making and human rights, the relationship between insurgent and state violence, and problems of security and global governance in the post-Cold War era. He is editing a volume, with Iffet Özkut, on the consequences of torture for perpetrators, victims, and society-at-large.

1.2.5 Violence and the Police

Jean-Paul Brodeur (Ph.D., University of Paris) is a professeur titulaire at the Centre International de Criminologie Comparée (CICC) of the Université de Montréal. He was director of the CICC for eight years and the director of research of the Canadian Sentencing Commission. He is now the French editor of the Canadian Journal of Criminology and member of The Royal Society of Canada. He is the author of several books and articles on the various state coercive organizations. His three latest books are *Violence and Racial Prejudice in the Context of Peacekeeping* (1997), *How to Recognize Good Policing* (1998) and *Democracy, Law and Security: International Security Systems in Contemporary Europe (2002)* (Ed. together with Peter Gill and Dennis Töllborg).

2. Groups and Collectivities: Political and Ideological Violence

2.1 Ethnopolitical Conflict and Separatist Violence

Ted Robert Gurr (Ph.D.) is Distinguished University Professor at the University of Maryland, College Park, and is founding director of the Minorities at Risk project. In 1993–1994 Professor Gurr was president of the International Studies Association and in 1996–1997 he held the Swedish government's Olof Palme Visiting Professorship at the University of Uppsala. From 1994 to 2000 he was senior consultant to the U.S. government's State Failure Task Force. He has written or edited twenty books and monographs including *Why Men Rebel* (1970), *Peoples versus States: Minorities at Risk in the New Century* (2000) and, most recently, *Peace and Conflict 2001: A Global Survey of Armed Conflicts, Self-Determination Movements, and Democracy* (2001), with Monty G. Marshall and Deepa Khosla.

Anne Pitsch (Ph.D., University of Maryland) is the Conflict Management Coordinator for the University of Maryland-National University of Rwanda Partnership funded by USAID. She is also conducting individual and joint research on gacaca, the community-based system of justice that will adjudicate 120,000 genocide suspects in Rwanda, the return of the Rwandan diaspora, and a comparative analysis of autonomy agreements applied in different conflict situations. Prior to joining the Partnership, she was the Minorities at Risk Project Coordinator for four years.

2.2 Ethnic Violence

Andreas Wimmer (Dr.) is professor for comparative and historical sociology at the University of California Los Angeles. His current research interests relate to migration and intercultural relations, ethnic conflicts and nationalism, and cultural theory. Book publications include *Ethnologie im Widerstreit* [Ethnology in Contention] (Ed.) (1991); *Die komplexe Gesellschaft* [The Complex Society] (1995); *Transformationen* [Transformations] (1995); *Integration—Transformation* [Integration—Transformation] (Ed.) (1996); *Nation and National Identity* (Ed.) (1999); *Nationalist Exclusion and Ethnic Conflicts* (2002).

Conrad Schetter (Dr. phil.) is Research Associate at the Center for Development Research at Bonn University. His publications focus on ethnicity, ethnic conflicts, war economy and political transformation in Afghanistan, and nomadism in Iran. *Afghanistan in Geschichte und Gegenwart* [Afghanistan Past and Present] (Ed.) (1999); *Afghanistan—A Country without State?* (Ed.) (2002).

2.3 The Socio-Anthropological Interpretation of Violence

Georg Elwert (Dr.) is Professor of Social Anthropology at the Institute of Ethnology at the Free University in Berlin. His research interests focus on anthropological studies, and ethnicity and conflict. Publications include *Nationalismus und Ethnizität* [Nationalism and Ethnicity] (1989); *Switching of We-Group Identities* (1997); *Markets of Violence* (1999).

2.4   Civil War

Peter Waldmann (Dr. jur.) is Professor of Sociology at Augsburg University. His research concentrates on dictatorships and state violence, resistance, guerrilla movements and terrorism, ethnic minorities and conflicts, and civil wars, their consequences and possibilities for regulation. Important publications are *Der Peronismus 1943–1955* [Peronism, 1943–1955] (1974); *Ethnischer Radikalismus, Ursachen und Folgen gewaltsamer Minderheitenkonflikte* [Ethnic Radicalism, Causes and Effects of Violent Minority Conflicts] (1989); *Terrorismus, Provokation der Macht* [Terrorism, Provoking Power] (1998); *Der anomische Staat. Über Recht, öffentliche Sicherheit und Alltag in Lateinamerika* [The Anomic State: On Law, Public Security, and Everyday Life in Latin America] (2002).

2.5   Terrorism

Fernando Reinares is Professor of Political Science, as well as Academic Director of the degree and research program in security sciences, at King Juan Carlos University in Madrid. Member of the Standing Committee for Social Sciences, European Science Foundation. His most recent books on political violence and security policy include *Terrorismo y Antiterrorismo* [Terrorism and Antiterrorism] (1998); *Sociedades en Guerra Civil. Conflictos Violentos de Europa y América Latina* [Societies in Civil War. Violent Conflicts of Europe and Latin America] (1999); *European Democracies against Terrorism. Governmental Policies and Intergovernmental Cooperation* (2000), and *Patriotas de la Muerte. Quiénes han militado en ETA y por qué* [Patriots of Death. Who Joined ETA and Why] (2001). He also serves as Contributing Editor of the international academic journal *Studies in Conflict and Terrorism*.

2.6   Violence from Religious Groups

Jon Pahl (Ph.D., The University of Chicago) is Associate Professor of American Religious History at The Lutheran Theological Seminary at Philadelphia. He is member of the Colloquium Violence and Religion and is completing a manuscript entitled *Violence and the Scared in America*. He is the author *of Paradox Lost: Free Will and Political Liberty in American Culture, 1630–1760* (1992); *Hopes and Dreams of All: The International Walther League and Lutheran Youth in American Culture, 1893–1993* (1993); *Youth Ministry in Modern America: 1930–Present* (2000).

2.7   Vigilantism

David Kowalewski (Ph.D., University of Kansas) is Professor of Comparative and International Politics at Alfred University. He has been a Fulbright Scholar in the Philippines and Kenya. His works on political violence have appeared in Journal of Conflict Resolution, Social Science Quarterly, Journal of Politics, and elsewhere. He is recently the author of *Global Establishment* (1997) and *Deep Power: The Political Ecology of Wilderness and Civilization* (2000).

2.8 Pogroms

Werner Bergmann (Dr. phil.) is a professor at the Center for Anti-Semitism Research at the Technical University in Berlin. His research focuses on the sociology and history of anti-Semitism and related fields such as xenophobia, right-wing extremism, and the theory of collective behavior, in particular social movements and collective violence. Recent publications are *Antisemitismus in öffentlichen Konflikten* [Anti-Semitism in Public Conflicts] (1997), (co-author with Rainer Erb); *Anti-Semitism in Germany. The Post-Nazi Epoch since 1945* (1997); *Geschichte des Antisemitismus* [The History of Anti-Semitism] (2002). In company with Christhard Hoffmann and Helmut Walser Smith he is the editor of *Exclusionary Violence. Anti-Semitic Riots in Modern German History, 1819–1938* (2002).

2.9 Violence and New Social Movements

Dieter Rucht (Dr. rer. pol.) is Professor of Sociology at the Social Science Research Center Berlin (WZB). His research focuses on political sociology, participation, social movements and social conflict, and protest. Publications include *Modernisierung und neue soziale Bewegungen* [Modernization and New Social Movements] (1994); *Social Movements in a Globalizing World* (co-editor with Donatella della Porta and Hanspeter Kriesi) (1999); *Jugendkulturen, Politik und Protest. Vom Widerstand zum Kommerz?* [Youth Cultures, Politics, and Protest: From Resistance to Commercialization?] (co-editor with Roland Roth, 2000); *Transnationaler politischer Protest im historischen Längsschnitt.* [Transnational Political Protest: A Historical Longitudinal Section] (2001).

2.10 Violence and the New Left

Donatella della Porta (Ph.D.) is full professor of Political Science and Director of the Department of Political Science and Sociology at the University of Florence. She has carried out research on social movements and political violence in Italy, France, Germany, Spain, and the United States, and directed a cross-national research project on the control of mass demonstrations in Europe. Among her publications are: *Policing Protest* (1998) (with Herbert Reiter); *La politica locale* [Local Politics] (1999); *Social Movements: An Introduction* (1999) (with Mario Diani); *Social Movement in a Globalizing World* (1999) (with Hanspeter Kriesi and Dieter Rucht); *Identità, riconoscimento e scambio* [Identity, Recognition and Exchange] (Ed.) (2000); *Introduzione alla scienza politica* [Introduction to Political Science] (2001); *Scienza politica* [Political Science] (2001) (with Maurizio Cotta and Leonardo Morlino); *I partiti politici* [Political Parties] (2001);.

2.11 Right-Wing Extremist Violence

Wilhelm Heitmeyer (see under Framework of the Handbook)

2.12 Large-Scale Violence as Contentious Politics

Charles Tilly, after holding teaching and research appointments at Delaware, Princeton, Harvard, MIT, Toronto, Michigan, and the New School for Social Research, he now teaches social sciences at Columbia University. Among his recent books are *Roads from Past to Future* (1997); *Work Under Capitalism* (1998) (with Chris Tilly), *Durable Inequality* (1998) and (with Doug McAdam and Sidney Tarrow) *Dynamics of Contention* (2001). He has recently completed *Stories, Identities, and Political Change* (2002) and *Collective Violence* (2003). He is currently writing *Contention and Democracy in Europe, 1650–2000.*

3. Violent Individuals: Perpetrators and Motives

3.1 Processes of Learning and Socialization

3.1.1 The Social Psychology of Aggression and Violence

James T. Tedeschi (Ph.D.) († 2001) was Professor for Social Psychology at the University of Albany, State University of New York. His work centered on power, influence and self-presentation. He published about 200 papers. Most relevant for the topic of the handbook are *Violence, Aggression, and Coercive Actions* (with Richard B. Felson) (1994) and *Social Psychology of Violence* (2000).

3.1.2 Emotions and Aggressiveness

Roy F. Baumeister (Ph.D., Princeton University) holds the E.B. Smith Professorship in the Liberal Arts at Case Western Reserve University. His research interests include self and identity, self-control, self-esteem, aggression and violence, sexuality, meaning, emotion, and human nature. He has nearly 250 scientific publications, including the books *Escaping the Self* (1991); *Losing Control: How and Why People Fail at Self-Regulations* (1994); *Evil: Inside Human Violence and Cruelty* (1997) and *The Social Dimension of Sex* (2001) as well as many articles in the scientific journals in psychology.

Brad J. Bushman (Ph.D., University of Missouri) is Associate Professor at Iowa State University. His research interests are causes and consequences of aggression, violent media, social influence, experimental personality and meta-analysis. Some of the most important publications are: *Threatened egotism, narcissism, self-esteem, and direct and displaced aggression: Does self-love or self-hate lead to violence?* (co-author) (1998); *Catharsis, aggression, and persuasive influence: Self-fulfilling or self-defeating prophecies?* (co-author) (1999); *Is it time to pull the plug on the hostile versus instrumental aggression dichotomy?* (co-author) (2001); *Media violence and the American public: Scientific facts versus media misinformation.* (co-author) (2001).

3.1.3 Learning of Aggression in the Home and the Peer Group

Ernest V. E. Hodges (Ph.D., Florida Atlantic University) is an Assistant Professor of Psychology at St. John's University. His recent publications have focused predominantly on aggression and victimization among children and adolescents. He has also published recent articles involving attachment relationships, parenting practices, children's friendships, and academic achievement. His current research interests focus on how aggression and victimization by peers may lead to weapon carrying in schools.

Noel A. Card (B.A./B.S., Michigan State University) is an advanced doctoral student in clinical psychology at St. John's University. His research interests include aggression and victimization, attachment relationships, and enemy relationships among children and adolescents. His recent presentations have focused on the interpersonal dynamics of aggression among school children and relationships between victimization and the characteristics of children's enemies.

Jenny Isaacs (B.A., State University of New York, New Paltz) is an advanced doctoral student in clinical child psychology at St. John's University. Her research interests include aggression, victimization, and weapon carrying in schools. Her recent presentation have focused on the social-cognitions involved in children's decisions to carry weapons in school, as well as the social and personal factors that lead to these cognitions and the enactment of weapon carrying behavior.

3.1.4 Violence and the Media

Helmut Lukesch (Dr.) is Professor of Psychology at Regensburg University. His research interests are grouped primarily around the media and its influence. Important publications include *Wenn Gewalt zur Unterhaltung wird ...* [When Violence Becomes Entertainment ...] (1994); *Medien und ihre Wirkungen* [Media and Their Influence] (1997); *Medienkonsum und Medienwirkungen* [Media Consumption and Media Influence] (2001).

3.1.5 Patterns and Explanations of Direct Physical and Indirect Non-Physical Aggression in Childhood

Holly Foster (Ph.D., University of Toronto) is a Postdoctoral Fellow (National Consortium on Violence Research, Carnegie Mellon University, Pittsburgh). Her research interest include social contexts of youth violence. Her dissertation is entitled *Neighbourhood and Family Effects on Childhood Gendered Aggression* (2001) Publications (with John Hagan) are: *Making Criminal and Corporate American Less Violent: Public Norms and Structural Reforms* (2000) and *Youth Violence and the End of Adolescence* (American Sociological Review, 2001).

John Hagan (see under Framework of the Handbook)

3.2 Evolutionary and Social Biological Approaches

3.2.1 Evolutionary Psychology of Lethal Interpersonal Violence

Martin Daly (Ph.D., University of Toronto) is Professor of Psychology and Biology at McMaster University in Canada. His main areas of research are the behavioral ecology of desert rodents, human social cognition, and interpersonal violence. A former J.S. Guggenheim Fellow and past president of the *Human Behavior & Evolution Society*, he is the co-author (with Margo Wilson) of *Sex, Evolution & Behavior* (2nd ed., 1983); *Homicide* (1988) and *The Truth about Cinderella* (1998), and is presently co-editor-in-chief of the journals *Behaviour* and *Evolution & Human Behaviour*.

Margo Wilson (Ph.D., University of London) is Professor of Psychology at McMaster University in Canada. Her current research focuses on risk-taking and risk evaluation, marital conflict, and lethal and nonlethal violence. She is the co-author (with Martin Daly) of *Sex, Evolution & Behavior* (2nd ed., 1983); *Homicide* (1988) and *The Truth about Cinderella* (1998), and is co-editor-in-chief of the journal *Evolution & Human Behaviour*.

3.2.2 The Nature–Nurture Problem in Violence

Laura Baker (Ph.D., University of Colorado) is Associate Professor of Psychology at the University of Southern California. Of general interest are the development, refinement, and application of quantitative genetic models in the study of individual intellectual domains. Of particular interest are multivariate behavioral genetic models of juvenile delinquency, human aggression, and criminal behavior. She published *Agression: Definition and Measurement* (1999); *Biological Theories of Violence* (1999); *Psychological Theories of Human Aggression* (1999).

3.3 Violent Individuals

3.3.1 Sociological Approaches to Individual Violence and their Empirical Evaluation

Günter Albrecht (Dr. phil.) is a professor at the Faculty of Sociology at Bielefeld University and a member of the committee of the Institute for Interdisciplinary Research on Conflict and Violence. His work focuses on sociology of deviant behavior, especially criminology and psychiatric sociology, sociology of poverty, sociology of migration, and medical sociology. Publications include *Diversion and Informal Social Control* (co-editor) (1995); *Handbuch Soziale Probleme* [Handbook of Social Problems] (co-editor) (1999); *Gewaltkriminalität zwischen Mythos und Realität* [Violent Criminality between Myth and Reality] (co-editor, 2001).

3.3.2 Youth Violence and Guns

Alfred Blumstein is the Erik Jonsson University Professor of Urban Systems and Operations Research. He also directs the National Consortium on Violence Research (NCOVR). His research over the past twenty years has covered many aspects of criminal-justice phenomena and policy, including crime measurement, criminal careers, sentencing, deterrence and incapacitation, prison populations, demographic trends, juvenile violence, and drug-enforcement policy. The most important publications are: *Report of the National Academy of Sciences Panel on Research on Criminal Careers*; *Deterrence and Incapacitation: Estimating the Effects of Criminal Sanctions on Crime Rates* (co-author) (1978); *Criminal Careers and "Career Criminals"* (co-author) (1986); *Youth Violence, Guns, and the Illicit-Drug Industry* (1995); *The Crime Drop in America* (with Joel Wallmann) (2000).

3.3.3 Organized Crime and Violence

Dick Hobbs is Professor of Sociology at the University of Durham UK. He has published widely on policing, detective work, ethnography, working class entrepreneurship, professional and organized crime and various aspects of deviant cultures. The most important publications are: *Doing the Business* (Oxford, 1989); *Bad Business* (Oxford, 1995) and (with Simon Winlow, Stuart Lister and Philip Hadfield) *Night Moves* (Oxford 2002), a study of violence and the night-time economy. He is currently working with Geoffrey Pearson on a study of drug markets.

3.3.4 *Understanding Cross-National Variation in Criminal Violence*

Steven F. Messner (Ph.D., Princeton University) is Professor of Sociology and Chair at the University at Albany, State University of New York. His research has focused on the relationship between social organization and crime, with a particular emphasis on criminal homicide. He has also studied the spatial patterning of violent crime, crime and delinquency in China, and the situational dynamics of violence. In addition to his extensive publications in professional journals, he is co-author of *Crime and the American Dream* (1997); *Perspectives on Crime and Deviance* (1999); *Criminology: An Introduction Using Explorit* (2000, 4th ed.) and co-editor of *Theoretical Integration in the Study of Deviance and Crime* (1989) and *Crime and Social Control in a Changing China* (2001).

4. Victims of Violence: Individuals and Groups

4.1 *Violence against Children*

James Garbarino (Ph.D., Cornell University) is the Elizabeth Lee Vincent Professor of Human Development at Cornell University and co-director of the Family Life Development Center. He formerly served as president of the Erikson Institute for Advanced Study in Child Development in Chicago, IL. He has authored seventeen books including *What Children Can Tell Us* (1989); *Children in Danger: Coping with the Consequences of Community Violence* (1992); *How We Can Save Them, Raising Children in a Socially Toxic Environment* (1995) and *Lost Boys: Why Our Sons Turn Violent* (1999).

Catherine P. Bradshaw (M.Ed., University of Georgia) is a doctoral Student in the Department of Human Development at Cornell University and a Research Assistant for the Family Life Development Center. She has several years of clinical experience working with high-risk children and families referred for services by the juvenile court. Her current research focuses on the development of aggressive and violent behavior in children and adolescents. She is the co-author of *Multi-Observer Assessment of Problem Behavior in Adjudicated Youths: Patterns of Discrepancies* (2001) (with Brian Glaser, Georgia Calhoun, Jeff Bates and Robert Socherman); *Mitigating the Effects of Gun Violence on Children and Youth* (2002) (with James Garbarino and J. Vorrasi) and *Psychological Maltreatment* (2002) (with Joseph Vorrasi and Ellen deLara).

4.2 *Violence in Intimate Relationships*

Rebecca Emerson Dobash is Professor of Social Research and **Russell P. Dobash** is Professor of Criminology in the Department of Applied Social Science at the University of Manchester. They have co-authored several books, numerous government reports, and scores of scientific articles in journals and anthologies. Their books include *Violence against*

Wives (1979); *The Imprisonment of Women* (1986); *Woman Viewing Violence* (1992); *Gender and Crime* (1995); *Rethinking Violence against Women* (1998) and *Changing Violence Men* (2000).

4.3 Suicide

David Lester has Ph.D. degrees from Brandeis University (United States) in psychology and from Cambridge University (United Kingdom) in social and political science. He is a former President of the International Association for Suicide Prevention and Professor of Psychology at the Richard Stockton College of New Jersey, Pomona, NJ. His research interests are concentrated on suicide. Important publications are: *Why people kill themselves* (2000); *By their own hand: Suicides of the rich and famous* (2000); *Suicide prevention: Resources for the millennium* (ed.) (2001).

4.4 Violence against the Socially Expendable

Ezzat A. Fattah (Ph.D.) is Professor (emeritus) of Criminology at Simon Fraser University in Vancouver. His work centers on victimology. He is the author/co-author, editor/co-editor of fifteen books and over a hundred and twenty book chapters and scholarly papers published in learned journals in ten languages. Among his recent publications are: *Understanding Criminal Victimization* (1991); *The Interchangeable Roles of Victim and Victimizer* (1994); *Criminology: Past, Present and Future (1997)*;*Toward a Victim Policy Aimed at Healing not Suffering* (1997); *Victimology: Past, Present and Future* (2000).

4.5 Violence against Ethnic and Religious Minorities

Tore Bjørgo (Dr.) is a senior research fellow and social anthropologist at the Norwegian Institute of International Affairs in Oslo. His main fields of research are racist and right-wing violence, delinquent youth gangs, and political extremism and terrorism. His most recent books are *Racist and Right-Wing Violence in Scandinavia: Patterns, Perpetrators, and Response* (1997) and *Violence, Racism and Youth Gangs: Prevention and Intervention* (1999). He has also (co)authored books on political communications, and terrorism (in Norwegian), and has (co)edited the volumes *Racist Violence in Europe* (1993); *Terror from the Extreme Right (1995) and Nation and Race: The Developing Euro-American Racist Subculture* (1998).

4.6 Hate Crimes Directed at Gay, Lesbian, Bisexual and Transgendered Victims

Jack McDevitt is the Associate Dean for Graduate Studies and Research, Director of the Center for Criminal Justice Policy Research and an Assistant Professor in Northeastern University's College of Criminal Justice. His past research in the area of criminal justice has involved such issues as arbitrariness in the administration of the death penalty, and the role of mandatory sentence in gun control policy. He authored the first study of hate-motivated violence which became the basis of *Hate Crimes: The Rising Tide of Bigotry and Bloodshed* (1993) co-authored with Jack Levin. He also authored *The 1990 Hate Crime Resource Book for the FBI* and published *Victimology: A Study of Crimes Victims and Their Roles* (2002).

Jennifer Williamson serves as Deputy Director of Strategic Planning and Resource Development for Boston Police Commissioner Paul F. Evans. In this position she is responsible for fostering innovation in policing through strategic planning, resource development, program and partnership creation, intergovernmental relations, policy development, and documentation of "best practices."

4.7 Trauma and Violence in Children and Adolescents: A Developmental Perspective

Bessel A. van der Kolk (M.D., University of Chicago) is Professor of Psychiatry at Boston University, School of Medicine. His works centers on trauma and extreme stress. He published more then one hundred articles. His books includes: *PTSD: Psychological and Biological Sequelae* (Ed.) (1984); *Psychological Trauma* (1987); *Traumatic Stress: the effect of overwhelming experience on mind, body and society* (with Alexander McFarlane and Lars Weisaeth, Ed.) (1996).

Annette Streeck-Fischer (Dr. med.) a senior physician in the Department of Clinical Psychotherapy for Children and Young People at Tiefenbrunn Teaching Hospital, Göttingen. Since 1980 lecturer at the medical faculty of Göttingen University, co-editor of the journal "Praxis der Kinderpsychologie, Kinderpsychiatrie" [Practical Child Psychology, Child Psychiatry]. Publications on adolescence, right-wing extremism, violence, trauma, maltreatment, abuse.

5. Social Opportunity Structures: Institutions and Social Spaces

5.1 Violence in Social Institutions

5.1.1 Violence in the Family

Richard J. Gelles holds the Jeanne and Raymond Welsh Chair of Child Welfare and Family Violence in the School of Social Work at the University of Pennsylvania. He is the Director of the Center for the Study of Youth Policy and Co-Director of the Center for Children's Policy, Practice, and Research. His book *The Violent Home* was the first systematic empirical investigation of family violence and continues to be highly influential. He is the author or co-author of twenty-three books and more than one hundred articles and chapters on family violence. His latest books are: *The Book of David: How Preserving Families Can Cost Children's Lives* (1996) and *Intimate Violence in Families,* 3rd Edition (1997).

5.1.2 Violence in School

Gabriele Klewin holds a degree in education and was Research Associate in the "Gender Socialization and Violence in Schools" project at Bielefeld University from 1998 to 2000. Her research focuses on women's and gender studies, and violence in schools.

Klaus-Jürgen Tillmann (Dr. paed.) is Professor of School Education Theory at Bielefeld University and Academic Director of the Laborschule. His work concentrates on empirical school and socialization research, school and teaching theory, and reform developments in the secondary school system. His most important publications include *Sozialpädagogik in der Schule* [Social Paedagogics in Schools] (1976); *Sozialisationstheorien—eine Einführung* [Socialization Theories—An Introduction] (12th ed., 2002); *Was ist eine gute Schule?* [What is a Good School?] (1989); *Schülergewalt als Schulproblem* [Student Violence as a School Problem] (co-author with Günter Holtappels et al.) (1999).

Gail Weingart holds a degree in psychology and is a teacher. She studied in Berlin, Harvard, and Bielefeld and has many years of teaching experience in schools in the United States and Germany. Currently she is Research Associate at the Research Institute Laborschule at Bielefeld University, and also carries out school evaluation.

5.1.3 Work-Related Violence

Vittorio Di Martino is an international consultant specialized in health and safety at work, enterprise development and organizational well-being. He has been responsible for the programs on stress and violence at work at the European Foundation for the Improvement of Working and Living Conditions, Dublin, from 1980 to 1988 and at the International Labour Organisation, Geneva, from 1988 to 2001. He is Visiting Fellow in Employment Policies at the University of Bath and Senior Research Fellow at UMIST in Manchester, UK. His recent publications include *Work Organisation and Ergonomics,* ILO, Geneva, 1998; *Violence at Work,* ILO, Geneva, 1st ed., 1998, 2nd ed. 2000; *The High Road to Teleworking,* ILO, Geneva, 2001; *SOLVE Package—Managing Emerging Health Problems at Work—Stress, Violence, Tobacco, Alcohol, Drugs, HIV/AIDS—*ILO, 2002; *National Guidelines for the Prevention of Stress and Violence at the Workplace,* Malaysian Government, 2002.

5.1.4 Violence and Sport

Eric Dunning (Ph.D.) is currently Emeritus Professor of Sociology at the University of Leicester where he remains an Associate Lecturer. His sociological interests are in sociological theory, violence, race, class and gender, and "civilizing" and "decivilizing" processes. Some of his publications are: *Sport and Leisure in the Civilizing Process* (with Norbert Elias) (1986); *Roots of Football Hooliganism* (with John Williams and Patrick Murphy) (1988); *Sport Matters: Sociological Studies of Sport, Violence and Civilization* (1999).

5.2 Violence in the Public Space

5.2.1 Violence on the Roads

Ralf Kölbel (Dr. iur.) is Research Associate at the Friedrich Schiller University in Jena. His work focuses on legal sociology and traffic criminology, criminal law and criminal procedure. His publications include *Rücksichtslosigkeit und Gewalt im Straßenverkehr* [Recklessness and Violence on the Roads] (1997) and several articles in the scientific journals in law and legal sociology.

5.2.2 Juvenile and Urban Violence

François Dubet is Professor of Sociology at Bordeaux University and Director of Studies at the Ecole des Hautes Etudes en Sciences Sociales (EHESS/CNRS) in Paris. His research focuses on youth violence, social movements, and sociological theory. His publications include *A l'école* [At School] (with Danilo Martuccelli) (1996); *Dans quelle société vivons-nous?* [What Society Are We Living In?] (with Danilo Martuccelli) (1998); *Pourquoi changer l'école?* [Why Change School?] (1999); *L'hypocrisie scolaire. Pour un collège enfin démocratique* (with Marie Duru-Bellat) [Scholarly Hypocrisy: For a Secondary School that Is at Last Democratic] (2000); *Les inégalités multipliées* [Multiple Inequalities] (2001).

6. Violence Discourses: Ideologies and Justifications

6.1 Discourses and Ideologies

6.1.1 Political Cultural Studies and Violence

Thomas Meyer (Dr. phil.) is Professor of Politics at Dortmund University, Academic Director of the Friedrich Ebert Foundation's Academy of Political Education, and Deputy Chairman of the German Social Democratic Party's Basic Values Commission. His work focuses on political aesthetics, political communication, culture and politics, and socialism and social democracy. His publications include *Was bleibt vom Sozialismus?* [What is Left of Socialism?] (1991); *Alltagsästhetik und politische Kultur* [Everyday Aesthetics and Political Culture] (co-author with Berthold Flaig and Jörg Ueltzhöffer) (1993); *Identitätswahn. Die Politisierung des kulturellen Unterschieds* [Identity Obsession: The Politicization of Cultural Differences] (1997); *Die Inszenierung des Politischen* [The Staging of the Political] (2000); *Soziale Demokratie und Globalisierung* [Social Democracy and Globalization] (2001) and *Media Democracy* (2002).

6.1.2 The Role of Elites in Legitimizing Violence

Herfried Münkler (Dr. phil.) is Professor of Politics at the Department of Political Theory at the Humboldt University in Berlin. Since December 1992 he has been a member of the Berlin-Brandenburg Academy of Sciences. His publications include *Machiavelli. Die Begründung des politischen Denkens der Neuzeit aus der Krise der Republik Florenz* [Machiavelli: The Origins of Modern Political Thought in the Crisis of the Florence Republic] (1982); *Pipers Handbuch der politischen Ideen* [Piper's Handbook of Political Ideas] (co-edited with Iring Fetscher, 5 vols) (1985–1993); *Gewalt und Ordnung. Das Bild des Krieges im politischen Denken* [Violence and Order: The Image of War in Political Thought] (1992); *Hobbes* [Hobbes] (1992).

Marcus Llanque (Dr. rer. soc.) is Research Associate at the Humboldt University in Berlin, Institute for Social Sciences. His research focuses on the history of political ideas, republicanism, the Weimar Republic, and theory of democracy. His publications include *Demokratisches Denken im Krieg. Die deutsche Debatte im Ersten Weltkrieg* [Democratic Thought During War: The German Debate During World War One] (2000); *Massendemokratie zwischen Kaiserreich und westlicher Demokratie* [Mass Democracy Between the Kaiser's Reich and Western Democracy] (2000); *Verfassungsgebung als Ort politischer Kreativität* [Constitution-Writing as an Act of Political Creativity] (2001).

6.1.3 Violence in Contemporary Analytic Philosophy

Keith Burgess-Jackson (J.D, Ph.D., University of Arizona) is Associate Professor of Philosophy at The University of Texas at Arlington. He is the author of *Rape: A Philosophical Investigation* (1996); co-author (with Irving M. Copi) of *Informal Logic* (1996); editor of (and a multiple contributor to) *A Most Detestable Crime: New Philosophical Essays on Rape* (1999).

6.1.4 Sacrifice and Holy War: A Study of Religion and Violence

Volkhard Krech (Dr. rer. soc.) is fellow for Sociology at the Protestant Institute for Interdisciplinary Research in Heidelberg. His research focuses on empirical and theoretical sociology of religion, the history of the study of religion, and cultural sociology. His most important publications include *Georg Simmels Religionstheorie* [Georg Simmel's Theory of Religion] (1998); *Religionssoziologie* [Sociology of Religion] (1999); *Kunst und Religion im 20. Jahrhundert* [Art and Religion in the Twentieth Century] (co-edited with Richard Faber) (2001); *Wissenschaft und Religion. Studien zur Geschichte der Religionsforschung in Deutschland 1871 bis 1933* [Science and Religion: Studies on the History of the Study of Religion in Germany from 1871 to 1933] (2002).

6.1.5 Violence and the Glorification of Violence in Twentieth-Century Literature

Jürgen Nieraad (Dr. phil.) is Lecturer for German literature in the Department of German Language and Literature at the Hebrew University in Jerusalem. He has published on modern German literature, the Jewish-German Holocaust discourse, literary theory, and aesthetics, for example *Standpunktbewusstsein und Weltzusammenhang* [Standpoint Awareness and World Context] (1970); *Die Spur der Gewalt. Zur Geschichte des Schrecklichen in der Literatur und ihrer Theorie* [Trail of Violence: On the History of the Horrific in Literature and Literary Theory] (1994).

6.2 Justification Strategies

6.2.1 The State Monopoly of Force

Dieter Grimm (Dr. iur.) was a justice at the Federal Constitutional Court, and is Professor of Public Law at the Humboldt University in Berlin and Rector of the Institute for Advanced Study in Berlin. His work focuses on constitutional law, constitutional history, constitutional adjudication, and comparative politics. His most important publications include *Recht und Staat der bürgerlichen Gesellschaft* [Law and State in Bourgeois Society] (1987); *Staatsaufgaben* [State Tasks] (Ed.) (1994); *Die Verfassung und die Politik. Einsprüche in Störfällen* [Constitution and Politics: Objections in Problem Cases] (2001); *Die Zukunft der Verfassung* [The Future of the Constitution] (3rd ed. 2002).

6.2.2 The Monopoly of Legitimate Violence and Criminal Policy

Albrecht Funk (Dr. habil) is co-founder of the Institute for Civil Rights and Public Security at the Free University in Berlin and Research Associate at the EU Center at the University of Pittsburgh. His research focuses on the creation and transformation of the police and criminal justice systems in Europe and the United States, and the Europeanization of judicial and domestic policy. His most important publications are *Polizei und Rechtsstaat* [Police and the Constitutional State] (1985); *Die Polizei der Bundesrepublik* [Police in the Federal Republic of Germany] (co-author) (1985); *Polices d'Europe* [European Police Systems] (co-author) (1992).

6.2.3 Freedom to Demonstrate and the Use of Force: Criminal Law as a Threat to Basic Political Rights

Otto Backes (Dr. jur.) has been Professor of Criminal Law, Law of Criminal Procedure, and Legal Sociology at Bielefeld University since 1983. Co-founder of the Institute for Interdisciplinary Research on Conflict and Violence. His publications include *Strafrechtswissenschaft als Sozialwissenschaft* [Criminal Law Studies as Social Science] (1976); the volumes in the series *Verdeckte Gewalt* [Hidden Violence] (co-editor) (1990); *Gewaltkriminalität zwischen Mythos und Realität* [Violent Crime Between Myth and Reality] (2001); and he is co-author of several proposed alternatives to the Criminal Code, including *Politisches Strafrecht* [Political Criminal Law] (1968); *Umweltstrafrecht* [Environmental Criminal Law] (1971).

Peter Reichenbach, Assistant Judge, Research Associate in the Department of Criminal Law and Law of Criminal Procedure at Bielefeld University. Publications include *Ist die medizinisch-embryopathische Indikation bei dem Schwangerschaftsabbruch nach § 218a II StGB verfassungswidrig?* [Is the Medical Embryopathic Indication for Abortions Following Paragraph 218a II of the Criminal Code Unconstitutional?] (2000); *Der Anspruch behinderter Schülerinnen und Schüler auf Unterricht in der Regelschule* [The Rights of Disabled Students to Teaching in Normal Schools] (2001); *Irrungen, Wirrungen: Einige Anmerkungen zur Interpretation des § 177 Abs. 1 Nr. 3 StGB aus verfassungsrechtlicher Perspektive* [Aberrations and Confusion: Some Comments on Paragraph 177, Art. 1, Item 3 of the Criminal Code from the Constitutional Perspective] (2002).

6.2.4 The Right to Resist

Heiner Bielefeldt (Dr. phil.) is a lecturer at Bielefeld University, member of the Institute for Interdisciplinary Research on Conflict and Violence, and *Privatdozent* for Philosophy at Bremen University. Among other things, his work focuses on questions relating to the justification of human rights, legal rights of religious minorities (e.g., Muslim groups in Germany), social contract theories, and the philosophy of the Enlightenment. He has written and edited or co-edited ten books, including *Neuzeitliches Freiheitsrecht und politische Gerechtigkeit* [The Liberty and Political Justice] (1994); *Philosophie der Menschenrechte* [The Philosophy of Human Rights] (1998); *Kants Symbolik* [Symbolic Representation in Kant's Practical Philosophy] (German 2001, English 2002).

6.2.5 Individual Violence Justification Strategies

Siegfried Lamnek (Dr.) is Professor of Sociology at Eichstätt University. His work focuses on methodology and methods of social sciences, sociology of deviant behavior and social problems, sociology as profession, and violence in schools. His publications include *Der Sozialstaat zwischen "Markt" und "Hedonismus"?* [Welfare State between "Market" and "Hedonism"] (co-editor) (1999); *Zeit und kommunikative Rechtskultur in Europa. Verfassung, Medien, Biotechnologie und Datenschutz* [Time and Communicative Legal Culture in Europe: Constitution, Media, Biotechnology and Data Protection] (co-editor) (2000); *Theorien abweichenden Verhaltens, Leistungsmissbrauch, Steuerhinterziehung und ihre (Hinter-)Gründe* [Theories of Deviant Behavior, Abuse of Benefits, and Tax Evasion, and Their (Back)Grounds] (co-author) (2000).

7. Processes and Dynamics: Escalation and De-Escalation

7.1 Fear of Violent Crime

Klaus Boers (Dr. jur.) is Professor of Criminology and Juvenile Penal Law, Director of the Institute of Penal Sciences at the Westfälische Wilhelms-University in Münster and co-editor of the Neue Kriminalpolitik. His research focuses on attitudes to crime, victim and self-reported delinquency surveys, social transition and modernization processes, crime development and social control in the life course, and economic crime. His most important publications include *Kriminalitätsfurcht* [Fear of Crime] (1991); *Sozialer Umbruch und Kriminalität in Deutschland* [Social Transition and Crime in Germany] (Co-editor and author) (1997); *Wirtschaftskriminologie* [Economic Criminology] (2001); *Kriminalität und Kausalität* [Crime and Causality] (2002).

7.2 Public Opinion and Violence

Hans Mathias Kepplinger (Dr. phil.) is Professor of Communications at the Johannes Gutenberg-Universität Mainz, Germany. He served as director of the Institute for Journalism, Dean of the Faculty of Social Sciences. He is corresponding editor of the *European Journal of Communication*, and member of the advisory board of *Political Communication Research* and *Journal of Communication*. His recent books are *Die Demontage der Politik in der Informationsgesellschaft [The Dismantling of Politics in Information Society]* (2nd edition, 2000) and Die Kunst der Skandalierung und die Illusion der Wahrheit [The Art of Creating a Scandal and the Illusion of Truth, 2001].

7.3 Groups, Gangs and Violence

Wolfgang Kühnel (Dr. phil.) is Professor of Criminology at the University of Applied Sciences for Administration and Legal Affairs Berlin. His work focuses on juvenile crime, sociology of migration, group sociology, and research on the extreme right and violence. His latest book (co-authored with Rainer Strobl) is *Dazugehörig und ausgegrenzt. Analysen zu Integrationschancen junger Aussiedler* [Belonging and Excluded: Analyses on Integration Chances of Young Ethnic German Immigrants] (2000) and he is co-editor (with Günter Albrecht and Otto Backes) of *Gewaltkriminalität zwischen Mythos und Realität* [Violent Crime between Myth and Reality] (2001).

7.4 Escalation and De-Escalation of Social Conflicts: The Road to Violence

Roland Eckert (Dr. phil.) is Professor of Sociology at Trier University. His research focuses on youth and politics, new media, violence, and conflict and conflict resolution. His publications include *Wiederkehr des "Volksgeistes"? Ethnizität, Konflikt und politische Bewältigung*. [The Return of the "National Spirit"? Ethnicity, Conflict and Political Management] (Ed.) (1998); *Neue Quellen des Rechtsextremismus* [New Sources of Right-Wing Extremism] (1999 *"Ich will halt anders sein wie die anderen"—Abgrenzung, Gewalt und Kreativität bei Gruppen Jugendlicher* ["I Just Want to be Different from the Others": Exclusion, Violence, and Creativity in Groups of Young People] (co-author with Christa Reis/Thomas Wetzstein) (2000).

Helmut Willems (Dr. phil.) is Privatdozent for Sociology at the University of Trier, a committee member of the Social Science Research and Training Working Group at Trier University and a freelance project developer and consultant. His research focuses on youth sociology, violence and criminality, political sociology, democracy theory, protest and social movements, xenophobia and research into right-wing extremism, and evaluation research. His books include *Konfliktintervention: Perspektivenübernahmen in gesellschaftlichen Auseinandersetzungen* [Conflict Intervention: Adopting Perspectives in Social Conflicts] (1992); *Fremdenfeindliche Gewalt: Einstellungen, Täter, Konflikteskalationen* [Xenophobic Violence: Attitudes, Perpetrators, Conflict Escalations] (1993); *Jugendunruhen und Protestbewegungen: Eine Studie zur Dynamik innergesellschaftlicher Konflikte in vier europäischen Ländern* [Youth Unrest and Protest Movements: A Study of the Dynamics of Conflicts within Society in Four European Countries] (1997).

III. THEORETICAL AND METHODOLOGICAL ISSUES IN RESEARCH ON VIOLENCE

1. Potentials and Limits of Qualitative Methods for Research on Violence

Andreas Böttger (Dr. phil.) is member of the board and project leader at the arpos Institute e.V. in Hannover and Associate Professor in the Department of Education at Hannover University. His work focuses on youth sociology, criminology, socialization theory, research into biography, violence and right-wing extremism, euthanasia and care for the dying, and methods of empirical research. His publications include *Die Biographie des Beschuldigten im Schwurgerichtsverfahren* [The Biography of the Accused in Jury Trials] (1992); *Gewalt und Biographie* [Violence and Biography] (1998*); "Früher war ich nicht so..." Biographien gewalttätiger Jugendlicher in China* ["I Used to Be Different ..." Biographies of Violent Adolescents in China] (co-author with Jiazhen Liang und Mirja Silkenbeumer) (2001).

Rainer Strobl (Dr. phil.) is Research Associate at the Institute for Interdisciplinary Research on Conflict and Violence at Bielefeld University. He is also a member of the managing board of the arpos Institute e.V. in Hanover. His work focuses on migration sociology, victimology, research into right-wing extremism and methods of empirical research. He is the author of *Soziale Folgen der Opfererfahrungen türkischer Minderheiten* [Social Consequences of the Victimization of Ethnic Minorities] (1998); *Dazugehörig und ausgegrenzt:*

Analysen zu Integrationschancen junger Aussiedler [Belonging and Excluded: Analyses on Young Ethnic German Immigrants' Chances of Integration] (co-authored by Wolfgang Kühnel) (2000); *Wahre Geschichten? Zur Theorie und Praxis qualitativer Interviews* [True Stories? On Theory and Practice of Qualitative Interviews] (co-edited by Andreas Böttger) (1996).

2. Strategies and Problems in Quantitative Research on Aggression and Violence

Rainer Dollase (Dr. phil.) is Professor of Psychology at Bielefeld University and Deputy Director of the Institute for Interdisciplinary Research on Conflict and Violence. His research focuses on studies on intercultural integration in school classes, change-over-time studies, risk constellations in everyday police work, and empirical studies on xenophobia and violence in schools. His publications include *Soziometrische Techniken* [Sociometric Techniques] (1976); *Entwicklung und Erziehung* [Development and Education] (1985); *Demoskopie im Konzertsaal* [Demoscopics in the Concert Hall] (1986 with Michael Rüsenberg, Hans J. Stollenwerk); *Politische Psychologie der Fremdenfeindlichkeit* [The Political Psychology of Xenophobia] (co-edited with Thomas Kliche, Helmut Moser) (1999); *Temporale Muster* [Temporal Patterns] (co-edited with Kurt Hammerich, Walter Tokarski) (2000).

Matthias Ulbrich-Herrmann (Dr. phil.) is a sociologist and a member of the Scientific Services at the University of Applied Sciences of Public Administration of North Rhine-Westphalia. He is also a member of the Institute for Interdisciplinary Research on Conflict and Violence at Bielefeld University. His research relates to youth violence, social inequality, interethnic conflict, and research methods in social science. His publications include *Lebensstile Jugendlicher und Gewalt* [Youth Lifestyles and Violence] (1998). He is also co-author of *Gewalt: Schattenseiten der Individualisierung bei Jugendlichen aus unterschiedlichen Milieus* [Violence: Drawbacks of Individualization in Young People from Different Milieus] (1995) and co-editor of *Zukunftsperspektiven Jugendlicher* [Future Perspectives for Young People] (2001).